CONTEMPORARY RHETORICAL THEORY

Contemporary Rhetorical Theory SECOND EDITION

A Reader

EDITED BY

Mark J. Porrovecchio
Celeste Michelle Condit

THE GUILFORD PRESS
New York   London

Library of Congress Cataloging-in-Publication Data

Names: Porrovecchio, Mark J., editor. | Condit, Celeste Michelle, 1956–
    editor.
Title: Contemporary rhetorical theory : a reader / edited by Mark J.
    Porrovecchio, Celeste Michelle Condit.
Description: Second Edition. | New York : The Guilford Press, [2016] |
    Includes bibliographical references and index.
Identifiers: LCCN 2015045797 | ISBN 9781462526581 (paperback)
Subjects: LCSH: Rhetoric. | BISAC: LANGUAGE ARTS & DISCIPLINES / Rhetoric. |
    LANGUAGE ARTS & DISCIPLINES / Communication Studies.
Classification: LCC P301 .C574 2016 | DDC 808.001—dc23
LC record available at *http://lccn.loc.gov/2015045797*

See pages v and vi for credits.

The following articles are reprinted from *Communication Monographs* by permission of the National Communication Association: Walter R. Fisher, "Narrative as a Human Communication Paradigm: The Case of Public Moral Argument," 51 (1984): 1–22; Raymie E. McKerrow, "Critical Rhetoric: Theory and *Praxis*," 56 (1989): 91–111; Sonya K. Foss and Cindy L. Griffin, "Beyond Persuasion: A Proposal for an Invitational Rhetoric," 62 (1995): 2–18.

The following articles are reprinted from *Critical Studies in Mass Communication* by permission of the National Communication Association: Barry Brummett, "Burke's Representative Anecdote as a Method in Media Criticism," 1 (1984): 161–76; Celeste Michelle Condit, "The Rhetorical Limits of Polysemy," 6 (1989): 103–22.

The following articles are reprinted from *Philosophy and Rhetoric* by permission of The Pennsylvania State University Press, ©1968, 1973, 1976, 1983, 1989, 1991, 2002, 2004: Lloyd F. Bitzer, "The Rhetorical Situation," 1 (1968): 1–14; Richard E. Vatz, "The Myth of the Rhetorical Situation," 6 (1973): 154–57; John Poulakos, "Toward a Sophistic Definition of Rhetoric," 16 (1983): 35–48; Barbara A. Biesecker, "Rethinking the Rhetorical Situation from within the Thematic of *Différance*," 22 (1989): 110–30; Thomas Farrell, "Practicing the Arts of Rhetoric: Tradition and Invention," 24 (1991): 183–212; Robert Asen, "Imagining in the Public Sphere," 35.4 (2002): 345–67; William D. Harpine, "What Do You *Mean*, Rhetoric Is Epistemic?" 37.4 (2004): 335–52.

The following articles are reprinted from the *Quarterly Journal of Speech* by permission of Taylor & Francis Ltd. (*www.tandfonline.com*) on behalf of the National Communication Association: Edwin Black, "The Second Persona," 56 (1970): 109–19; Karlyn Kohrs Campbell, "The Rhetoric of Women's Liberation: An Oxymoron," 59 (1973): 74–86; Thomas Farrell, "Knowledge, Consensus, and Rhetorical Theory," 62 (1976): 1–14; Michael Calvin McGee, "The 'Ideograph': A Link Between Rhetoric and Ideology," 66 (1980): 1–16; Richard A. Cherwitz and James W. Hikins, "Rhetorical Perspectivism," 69 (1983): 249–66; Celeste Michelle Condit, "Crafting Virtue: The Rhetorical Construction of Public Morality," 73 (1987): 79–87; Maurice Charland, "Constitutive Rhetoric: The Case of the *Peuple Québécois*," 73 (1987): 133–50; Carole Blair, Julie R. Brown, and Leslie A. Baxter, "Disciplining the Feminine," 84 (1994): 383–409; Robert Hariman, "Status, Marginality, and Rhetorical Theory," 72 (1995): 2–17; Michael Warner, "Publics and Counterpublics (abbreviated version)," 88.4 (2002): 413–25; Charles E. Morris III, "Pink Herring & the Fourth Persona: J. Edgar Hoover's Sex Crime Panic," 88.2 (2002): 228–44; Joshua Gunn, "Refiguring Fantasy: Imagination and Its Decline in U.S. Rhetorical Studies," 89.1 (2003): 41–59; Lin-Lee Lee, "Pure Persuasion: A Case Study of *Nüshu* or 'Women's Script' Discourses," 90.4 (2004): 403–21; Kathryn M. Olson, "An Epideictic Dimension of Symbolic Violence in Disney's *Beauty and the Beast*: Inter-Generational Lessons in Romanticizing and Tolerating Intimate Partner Violence," 99.4 (2013): 448–80.

In addition, we gratefully acknowledge permission to reprint the following articles from various sources: Michael Leff, "The Habitation of Rhetoric," in *Argument and Critical Practice: Proceedings of the Fifth SCA/AFA Conference on Argumentation*, 1–9. Ed. Joseph Wenzel. Annandale, VA: SCA, 1987. Used by permission of the National Communication Association. Michael Calvin McGee, "Text, Context, and the Fragmentation of Contemporary Culture," *Western Journal of Speech Communication* 54 (1990): 274–89. Reprinted with permission of the Western States Communication Association. Robert L. Scott, "On Viewing Rhetoric as Epistemic," *Central States Speech Journal* 18 (1967): 9–16. Used by permission of the Central States Communication Association. Dilip Parameshwar Gaonkar, "Rhetoric and Its Double: Reflections on the Rhetorical Turn in the Human Sciences," in *The Rhetorical Turn: Invention and Persuasion in the Conduct of Inquiry*, 341–66. Ed. Herbert W. Simons. Chicago: University of Chicago Press, 1990. ©1990 The University of Chicago. G. Thomas Goodnight, "The Personal, Technical, and Public Spheres of Argumentation: A Speculative Inquiry into the Art of Public Deliberation," 18 (1982): 214–27; and John M. Murphy, "Critical Rhetoric as Political Discourse," 32 (1995): 1–15. Both reproduced from *Argumentation and Advocacy* by permission of the American Forensic Association. Philip Wander,

EDITOR'S NOTE: The essays reprinted in this volume appear as they did in their original publication, except for regularization of capitalization and italicization of foreign words and phrases throughout.

Preface

The second edition of *Contemporary Rhetorical Theory: A Reader* still traces its influences back to the National Developmental Project on Rhetoric in 1970 and the subsequent publication of *The Prospects of Rhetoric* in 1971. We remain interested in the ways in which contemporary rhetorical theorists since the early 1970s have grappled with the broad range of humanistic attempts to engage communication and discourse, and how they have confronted the problems and possibilities of public persuasion, identification, and representation. At the same time, however, we have broadened and extended the book's scope in light of the changes in rhetorical theory and practice in the years since the publication of the first edition in 1999. What it means to persuade, to identify, and to represent have experienced shifts both subtle and profound in light of visual, digital, and mediated changes to the nature of rhetorical discourse.

The second edition exists, then, as a continuation of and conversation with the first edition. Some works remain patently theoretical, while others reflect the practice of theorizing through criticism. We have expanded the parameters of what we consider "contemporary" as well, including works that were written forty-plus years ago, as well as essays as recent as 2013. This edition begins as the first one did, with an introductory essay that situates contemporary rhetorical theory within a larger history of both rhetorical theory and practice. What have changed are the points of contention. The tensions between modernity and postmodernity are now being supplemented by equally relevant concerns about the impact of an increasingly digitized world; alternative approaches to rhetoric that extend beyond the traditional borders of communication studies; and the coexistence of the classical and cutting-edge in matters of contemporary rhetorical theory and practice.

The first section still poses the question "What can a 'rhetoric' be?" and offers a range of contemporary answers to that question. Subsequent sections explore key topics and issues that have occupied the attention of contemporary rhetorical theorists. At the same time, they reflect the ideas of continuation and conversation that this edition upholds: rhetoric and epistemology; the evolution of the rhetorical situation; perspectives on publics; perspectives on personae in rhetorical theory; rhetoric and the problems of political change; rhetoric and the mass media; and alternatives to the rhetorical tradition. The volume concludes with an epilogue that invites students to consider the future promise and possibilities for rhetorical theory as the field of communication studies begins its next one hundred years.

The volume is designed as an introduction for both advanced undergraduate and graduate students. Each part of the volume begins with an introductory statement designed to frame the key issues and problems addressed by the essays contained therein. These headnotes are written so as to provide concrete anchors for those students who are coming to the study of rhetorical theory for the very first time, and thus to make it easier for them to identify and engage the issues that have traditionally been the concern of rhetoricians. At the same time, the headnotes are written in an open-ended manner designed to invite more advanced students to engage the materials more creatively, with an eye toward their own inventive and critical participation in conversations regarding contemporary rhetorical theory. Each headnote concludes with a brief list of selected additional readings.

Rhetoric remains a material practice, and this volume is nothing if not a rhetorical practice guided by our collective experiences in teaching contemporary rhetorical theory to undergraduate and graduate students over the decades. We are still indebted to the students who have helped to shape and develop our understanding of what is important in introducing new generations of rhetoricians to what is surely the most exciting, practical, and productive of the liberal arts. Beyond our students, colleagues and friends encouraged and assisted the project with their advice and criticism. We cannot imagine this volume without their input. Mark thanks Robert Iltis, David and Carrie Carnevale, Gabriel Wilcoxen, Gabrijela Kišiček, and Jean H. M. Wagemans for their inspiration and support. One individual merits special recognition from both of us: John Louis Lucaites, a principal editor of the first edition, graciously provided suggestions and support in making this second edition possible. Sally Caudill, also an editor on the first edition, deserves thanks for her support for as well. C. Deborah Laughton, Katherine Sommer, Laura Patchkofsky, and the rest of the staff at The Guilford Press were essential in moving this book toward completion.

We acknowledge the (initially) anonymous reviewers who helped us to refine the final list of essays: Paul Achter, Department of Rhetoric and Communication Studies, University of Richmond; James P. Zappen, Department of Communication, Rensselaer Polytechnic Institute; G. Thomas Goodnight, Department of Communications, University of Southern California; J. David Cisneros, Department of Communications, University of Illinois, Urbana–Champaign; Debra Hawhee, Department of English, Pennsylvania State University; and Amy Vidali, Department of English, University of Colorado, Denver. We also thank the authors and publishers of the essays included in this volume for their dedication to the task of producing rhetorical theory.

Mark dedicates this book to his parents, Sam and Susan. Their unwavering love guides all his endeavors, rhetorical and otherwise.

MARK J. PORROVECCHIO
Corvallis, Oregon

CELESTE MICHELLE CONDIT
Athens, Georgia

Contents

◢ Introduction

Mark J. Porrovecchio
Celeste Michelle Condit

The ability to create a sense of community, and thus the possibility of social and political life as we know it, depends on the human capacity for communication. For thousands of years, scholars and laity alike have recognized that the complexities of human communication are linked tightly to the unique and varied forms of social interaction. Twenty-four hundred years ago, for example, Isocrates—a teacher of both Plato and Aristotle, and identified by some as perhaps the most important classical advocate of a rhetorical education—advised his students that the "art of discourse" was "that power which, of all the faculties which belong to the nature of man, is the source of most of our blessings." The reasons he gave for this became central components of what was to become known as civic humanism: "In the other powers which we possess . . . we are in no respect superior to other living creatures; nay, we are inferior to many in swiftness and in strength and in other resources; but, because there has been implanted in us the power to persuade each other and to make clear to each other whatever we desire, not only have we escaped the life of the wild beasts, but we have come together and founded cities and made laws and invented arts; and, generally speaking, there is no institution devised by man which the power of speech has not helped us establish."[1]

Given the centrality of the art of discourse to human, social, and political endeavors, it is not at all surprising that academics, preachers, politi-cians, entrepreneurs, and an almost incalculable host of others have all attended closely to the problems and possibilities of human communication. This breadth of attention to the power and art of discourse by groups and individuals with fundamentally different purposes and orientations has produced a wide range of approaches to the study of human communication. One of the most powerful of such approaches from antiquity to the present has operated under the rubric of "rhetoric" or "rhetorical studies." As we note in the introduction to Part I, the definition of "rhetoric" is itself a highly contested concept, and its meaning has varied widely, both across the ages and within any given time period. And while the advent of digital communication has ushered in new ways of communicating, the need for rhetoric continues. Moreover, in an age where humans are increasingly focused on the devices that they hold in their hands and swipe with their fingers, a reminder of the centrality that rhetoric plays in important human interactions is perhaps even timelier.

Our goal in this essay is not to provide a history of the concept of "rhetoric" from classical times to the present, although we do strongly encourage anyone interested in the discipline or study of contemporary rhetorical theory to consult its long and interesting heritage and to consider the impact that its various pasts have had upon its present study and uses.[2] Rather, our purpose here is to provide a brief introduction to the contemporary issues and concerns that have animated the work of rhetorical theorists since the late 1960s—a time of great social, political, and intellectual change. Of course, the contemporary interest in rhetorical theory cannot be completely bracketed and divorced from the interests and concerns of the larger histories of rhetoric that rhetorical theorists have crafted for themselves as a discipline. By the same token, however, it would be difficult to understand the complexities and conceptual importance of contemporary rhetorical theory if we focused primarily on the relationship between past and present. Our approach here, then, is to contextualize the interests and concerns of contemporary rhetorical theorists *both* historically and conceptually as they have manifested themselves over the past fifty-some years. To that end, we begin by offering a brief survey of some of the key conceptual assumptions made by contemporary rhetorical theorists that derive from an understanding of the theory and practice of rhetoric in classical antiquity. Following that, we consider how these assumptions have been contextualized and made problematic in the work of contemporary American rhetorical theorists.

Contemporary Rhetorical Theory's Link to the Past

The earliest theorists of rhetoric are typically identified in the Western, liberal-democratic tradition as residing in ancient Greece and Rome; not so coincidentally, they are equally identified with the creation of democratic and republican forms of government. In this classical tradition, the focus on rhetoric typically emphasized the *public, persuasive*, and *contextual* characteristics of human discourse in situations governed by the problems of *contingency*.

Contingent situations occur when decisions have to be made and acted upon, but decision makers are forced to rely upon probabilities rather than certainties. Examples of such situations typically include deliberating on what the best course for future action might be, or deciding guilt or innocence where the evidence is purely circumstantial. In either situation one must rely upon judgments derived from the probability or likelihood of "truth," rather than on certain knowledge. Even when there is an eyewitness to an alleged crime, we cannot know for *certain* what the witness saw. Some witnesses might actually lie about what they saw, while the testimony of other witnesses might be tainted—inadvertently or not—by prejudice or point of view. This is one of the reasons why our contemporary judicial system places so much importance on the cross-examination of witnesses. Judgments about guilt or innocence are always about past actions, but determinations of how one ought to act in consequence of such judgments—the goals of deliberative assemblies like the legislature—are no less problematic in their reliance upon probability as a guide to belief and action. Short of consulting a crystal ball, we can never know for *certain* what the best future course of action might be, for it has yet to happen and it is impossible to take into account the multiple events that might intervene between making the decision and enacting it. The best we can do is to make reasoned decisions based on our knowledge of the past and the likelihood of future possibilities.

The emphasis on *public* discourse focused attention on communicative acts that affected the entire community and were typically performed before the law courts, the legislative assemblies, and occasional celebratory gatherings of the citizenry-at-large. Public discourse was thus distinguished from technical discourse addressed to specialized or elite audiences (e.g., the discourses of astronomy or medicine) and private discourse addressed to more personal audiences that did not directly affect the social and political community-at-large (e.g., family communication, master–slave interactions). The ability to contribute to public policy debates and to affect the direction and life of the community through public discourse was taken by classical teachers of rhetoric as an essential attribute of the educated citizen and thus very highly valued.

Quite naturally, given the classical commitments to democratic and republican forms of governance, public discourse was valorized because of its capacity for *persuasion*—that is, its ability to affect belief and behavior through the power of symbolic interaction. One entailment of this commitment was the belief that the ways in which something was expressed and engaged in public discourse had an important, determining effect on meaning and behavior. This point of view stood in contrast to the position of many philosophers (and later scientists) who treated discourse as a neutral conduit for representing an otherwise objective independent "truth." From the more philosophical point of view, discourse could function to clarify or confuse meaning, to make objective and predetermined "truths" appear more or less attractive, but it could not actually affect the truth of the thing being described or discussed. Rhetoricians vehemently disputed this point of view, arguing instead that particularly in the context of social and political affairs, the manner and form of discourse was integral to the "truth" of the thing being described and played a central role in shaping and motivating collective identity and action. So, for example, rhetoricians believed that the particular words and narratives used to characterize the Athenian "people" as "courageous" and "peace-loving" in a ceremonial funeral oration were not merely neutral descriptors of these particular qualities, but central to the act of defining what it meant to be "Athenian." And in a similar fashion, they believed that the particular "reasons" that a speaker expressed for why Athens ought to go to war with Sparta were central to their effectiveness in motivating those who thought of themselves as "Athenians" to sacrifice their lives and property for their city-state. Public discourse was thus understood as potentially (perhaps even inherently) persuasive, and hence central to life in a democratic or republican polity.

Finally, the classical rhetorical perspective treated the relationship between language and meaning as *contextual*. This is to say that the meaning of a particular linguistic usage (e.g., tropes, figures of speech, narratives, examples) derived from the particular experiences and understanding of a particular audience addressed by a particular speaker at a specific moment in time. The metaphor "I have a dream" took on a very special meaning when uttered by the Reverend Martin Luther King, Jr., in the presence of 250,000 black and white American citizens sitting literally in the shadow of the Lincoln Memorial in the early 1960s and demanding that the U.S. Congress pass civil rights legislation.

This is not to suggest that linguistic meaning is variable in all directions at all time, for language usages are also rooted in broader historical and cultural contexts. What we do mean to suggest, however, is that the capacity for meaning in any linguistic usage is almost always subject to change and adaptation. Take, for example, the evolution—over a relatively short period of time—of the Black Lives Matter campaign. A loosely organized movement addressing the problems of structural racism, the campaign got its start in the wake of George Zimmerman's shooting Trayvon Martin to death in 2013. In only two years, it had grown into both a national platform with which to challenge presidential candidates and an international concern

for marginalized voices in places like Canada and Ghana. Black Lives Matters gains resonance from the historical work done by Martin Luther King, Jr., even as it hugs the contours of contemporary, and complex, discussions relating to instances of police brutality in black communities. A rhetorical perspective on the relationship between language and meaning thus stands in stark contrast to more philosophical and scientific perspectives, which presume either that the meaning of linguistic usages is permanent and universal, or that it is essentially ahistorical, fundamentally unaffected by the particular communicative contexts in which it is employed.

The classical focus on discourse as *contingent, public, persuasive*, and *contextual* has clearly influenced the ways in which contemporary rhetoricians have treated the role and significance of public communication. Of most importance has been the focus of attention on texts that address the public-at-large, rather than on private correspondences or philosophical treatises addressed to elite, intellectual audiences. The rationale here is that whatever the private goals motivating individuals to act might be, it is usually only once a public or the citizenry is persuaded to endorse and act upon communally shared goals that history moves forward (or backward) in significant ways. The methods of transmission may vary—the pamphlet and the newspaper are being supplanted by the digital archive and database; the letter to the editor is being replaced by the Tweet and the podcast—even as the focus on *publicness* remains. Whereas someone uninterested in rhetoric might prefer to study the private letters of Winston Churchill in order to understand how his leadership helped England to stave off the threat of fascism posed by Adolf Hitler, a rhetorician would be inclined to focus on important speeches, such as Churchill's "War Situation I." While the media at large may focus on how Tweets helped to spread the righteous indignation of the Arab Spring across the Middle East and North Africa, the rhetorician would be interested in how this relatively new form of communicating influenced the action of public agents acting on the ground and in support of toppling autocratic dictators. The influence of classical rhetoric's emphasis on the public dimension of communication interaction has thus clearly been evidenced in contemporary rhetoricians' choices of artifacts to study.

The classical rhetorical emphasis on context and persuasiveness also yields a different set of questions for contemporary rhetoricians. A social scientific or philosophical view of Churchill's speech would more than likely condemn Churchill as a fuzzy-headed optimist who juggled literary tropes and figures and drastically misrepresented the world. The rhetorician, however, mindful of the power that specific metaphors have in addressing specific audiences, would likely conclude that Churchill was mindful of addressing a British audience hoping for the eventual involvement of the United States. The social scientific or philosophical approach to the use of Twitter during the Arab Spring would likely focus on quantifying the amount of data used to send Tweets or raise questions about the content's relationship to theories of nonviolence. While these are important questions, they largely ignore the increasingly important role that social media play—that is, their role in publicly declaring as concerns a set of conditions lived by people who have been marginalized and cut off from the use of rhetoric in other media to transform and empower.

The point we want to emphasize here is that classical rhetoricians brought a distinctive set of assumptions to the study of communication that underscored the ways in which advocates—typically public speakers or orators—actively sought to exert influence on a specific audience by strategically deploying language in the interest of an immediate and particular goal. These assumptions, however, were not uncontested, and over the centuries would prove to be precarious. To begin with, the trajectory of Western thought from Plato's Academy through the seventeenth- and eighteenth-century Enlightenment of reason and well into the scientific modernism of the past century spawned an intellectual predisposition for theories of knowledge in which the values of universality and objectivity were privileged over those of particularity, situatedness, and subjectivity or intersubjectivity. Rhetoric, with its commitment to the later cluster of values, has a minimal role to play in such a world.

Ironically enough, however, even as rhetoric was being held up to contempt in the intellectual world of the Enlightenment and its modernist aftermath, its presence and significance in the everyday world were increasingly pronounced, particularly in Western Europe and the United States, where the rapid growth of the public sphere came to play an increasingly prominent role in commerce and political decision making. The rapidity of that growth continues unabated. The rising influence of countries like China, India, and Brazil, and the reemergence of Russia as a contro-

versial player in political and economic matters, reinforce the need to attend to broader historical trends while attending to the particularities of culture, time, and place. In an age where the physical distance between interlocutors has been in large part reduced to the issue of access to data, where phone lines have been replaced by gigabytes, and where the concerns of the public—writ large and made increasingly global—are displayed in searchable form on increasingly sophisticated screens, the assumption that elite tastemakers control opinions is more and more contested by those once assumed to be outsiders.

We do not mean to suggest that the study of rhetoric in the post-Enlightenment and modernist eras disappeared altogether (or that it is a uniquely Western phenomenon), but only that its significance was relegated to the margins of serious Western intellectual thought. Indeed, it was not infrequently referred to as the "Harlot of the Arts." In this context, rhetorical theorists managed to preserve some academic status for their study by conceding to a secondary or derivative role, allowing rhetoric to be cast in the role of "supplement" or "handmaiden" to more authentic modes of inquiry. The primary concession here was that rhetoric existed apart from the categories of "truth" and "knowledge," whose proper intellectual domains were science and philosophy. Once one properly discovered "truth" or "knowledge," rhetoricians might help to "dress it up" so as to communicate it more effectively to a larger, more common audience; but, importantly, it was believed that rhetoric played *no* role in the actual process of discovering such "truth" or "knowledge."

At the same time that rhetoric was seen as a useful supplement to the work of science and philosophy, it was also deprecated for its role in the realm of "public debate," where "truth" and "knowledge" were allegedly subordinated to the self-interested ideology of political actors. Since public rhetoric was always oriented toward the particular, and thus generated no universal or timeless truths, its study was typically of marginal interest to serious scholars, who preferred to devote their efforts to the exploration and explanation of the putative, universal beauties of art or the enduring truths of science and philosophy. Of course there were notable exceptions, but they were relatively few and far between, and on the whole the study of rhetoric in the Enlightenment and modernist eras was generally subordinated to the study of science and philosophy.

The classical assumptions about the nature and function of rhetoric that we detail above continue to be important to those who study communication from a rhetorical perspective. However, their significance has been modified by the subsequent history of rhetoric and the distinctive dialogue that has taken place in the recent past. Our primary purpose in this volume is to introduce the most recent, significant discussions and debates about contemporary rhetorical theory as they function to extend, problematize, and move beyond these assumptions. Before we proceed, however, it is important that we qualify our particular understanding of the phrase "contemporary rhetorical theory."

To identify that which is contemporary is never a simple task. The word itself usually distinguishes those things that are "current" or "marked by characteristics of the present period."[3] In the present context, we use it to refer to the problems of rhetorical theory currently being discussed by scholars; however, we do not mean to include everyone who is presently writing about rhetorical theory in our definition. In the twentieth century, the study of rhetorical theory has generally operated within the domain of scholars in the discipline of communication studies (sometimes referred to as "speech" or "speech communication"). In recent years, however, there has been an explosion of interest in the study of rhetoric, and an increasing number of scholars from disciplines such as English and composition, philosophy and critical/cultural studies, economics, law, political science, and social psychology currently identify themselves as "rhetoricians."[4] The work being produced by these scholars is interesting and important—particularly given the historical marginalization of rhetoric within the academy—and it is frequently cited and cross-referenced by rhetoricians operating out of communication studies. However, such work is also frequently motivated by interests and concerns generated by the home discipline with which it is affiliated. Our interest here is threefold: the community of rhetorical theorists who share an identifiable disciplinary history; the way this community has generated a distinctive set of issues and concerns, starting with the common assumption that public communication matters; and finally the way in which this community has responded to larger questions—cultural, political, philosophical, and so on—in ways that are distinct and important.

What then is "contemporary rhetorical theory" as we delineate it in this volume? It is a series of problems addressed by the community of rhetoricians operating from within the discipline of communication studies since approximately the mid-1960s. As with all communities, the community of contemporary rhetorical scholars is defined and located by the discourse that has generated it. In this case, the generative discourse is not only a particular interpretation of the classical rhetorical tradition, but also the important work of a group of scholars and teachers who effected the revival of classical rhetoric in the early part of the twentieth century as they contributed to the institutionalization of communication studies as an academic discipline. In order to grasp and engage what is distinctive about contemporary rhetorical theory as we define it here, we need an understanding of its origins within twentieth-century communication studies, as well as the initial efforts to transform its study. That task is the function of the next section of this introduction.

The Rebirth of Rhetoric in Twentieth-Century Communication Studies

What today we call "communication studies" emerged as a formal discipline of study in the United States during the early part of the twentieth century and in the specific context of Progressive-era politics. Faced with the nation's imminent transformation into a mass democratic society, forward-looking intellectuals and educators like John Dewey were concerned about the ability of the citizenry to participate effectively in this new world and thus sought to alter the public education system accordingly. "Public speaking" was seen as essential to being an effective citizen, and thus became the central focus of the new discipline. Consequently, the initial study of rhetorical theory within twentieth-century communication studies focused on the historical examination of classical and civic humanist models of persuasion and governance. Such study served a dual function. On the one hand, it bestowed scholarly legitimacy on the new discipline by demonstrating its ancient and historical roots in the writings of respected philosophers and scholars such as Plato, Isocrates, Aristotle, Cicero, Quintilian, Longinus, Saint Augustine, and others. On the other hand, and perhaps more important to the subsequent development of the new discipline, the philosophical and technical treatises concerning rhetoric that had been written from classical antiquity through the Renaissance and well into the eighteenth and nineteenth centuries served as sources of effective strategies for teaching the art of rhetoric to college students.[5]

There is little wonder, therefore, that Aristotle's definition of rhetoric as the faculty or power "of discovering in the particular case what are the available means of persuasion" was so influential in shaping the emerging discipline's perception of both the meaning of "rhetoric" as a strategic art and the meaning of "rhetorical theory" as a history of the philosophy of communication.[6] And indeed, for nearly forty years—from the 1920s through the 1960s—rhetorical theory was treated largely as an exercise in intellectual history. At the same time, the creation of new rhetorical theory was subordinated to the pedagogical goal of creating effective speakers along the lines of fairly classical models represented most fully by Quintilian's *vir bonus*, "the good man speaking well."

The Seeds of Intellectual Ferment

By the mid- to late 1960s, dissatisfaction with this approach to rhetoric began to grow. It became increasingly clear that however important the intellectual history of rhetorical theory was to our understanding of rhetoric as a discipline, the pressing need was to develop "new" rhetorical theories that would adapt our understanding of rhetoric to the changing conditions of the new era. Two independent but not unrelated phenomena were of particular importance in generating the need for such theories. The first phenomenon was the meteoric rise of television as a primary mass medium of public discourse. Television not only altered the ways in which public discourse was conducted, but it began to call increasing attention to the problem of what it might mean to be a "public," as well as to the problem of how public discourse was received and interpreted by the mass and multiple audiences that attended to it.[7] As we will see subsequently, these problems have been translated into a number of significant questions that have occupied the attention of contemporary rhetorical theorists. The second phenomenon was the emergence of significant grassroots social movements such as the civil rights movement, the student/antiwar movement, and the woman's liberation movement, all of which began to question the effectiveness of classical models of rhetoric and communication for the increasingly vocal, oppositional, and marginalized groups concerned

to infiltrate and overturn what they perceived as rigid social and political hierarchies and hegemonies.[8]

The change that came about was relatively pronounced and immediate, as such things go. Between 1967 and 1976, the fundamental focus of rhetorical theory shifted from a concern with intellectual histories and simple, classical models of rhetorical pedagogy, to an eager interest in understanding the relationships between rhetoric and social theory. The initial hints that a change was stirring appeared in two articles published early in 1967. In the first essay, "The Rhetoric of the Streets," Franklin Haiman recognized that "our society today is confronted with a wide range of activities unfamiliar to those accustomed to thinking of protest in terms of a Faneuil Hall rally or a Bughouse Square soapbox orator." Accordingly, Haiman issued an impassioned call for careful consideration of the ethical and legal standards by which we interpret and evaluate "the *contemporary* rhetoric of the streets."[9] Responding to the same spirit of the times, Robert L. Scott offered a more philosophical challenge to our understanding of the substance and sociopolitical significance of rhetoric in "On Viewing Rhetoric as Epistemic."[10] In this essay, which was the starting point of significant debates in the 1970s and 1980s on the role of rhetoric in the construction of truth, Scott argued that rhetoric is not simply a means of making the truth effective, but is quite literally a way of knowing, a means for the production of truth and knowledge in a world where certainty is rare and yet action must be taken. He thereby instigated the repudiation of the secondary status that had been assigned to rhetoric and which had been largely integrated into the assumptions of those who had refounded rhetoric in the twentieth century.

These two essays provided new perspectives on two of the major issues upon which this volume focuses: the question of what constitutes a public (Part IV), and the important and puzzling relationship of rhetoric to matters of epistemology (Part II). The following year, two additional essays by Lloyd F. Bitzer and Douglas Ehninger continued to push in the direction of examining and accounting for the broader social dimensions of rhetoric. Bitzer's "The Rhetorical Situation," one of the most often cited essays in speech communication journals in the 1970s and 1980s, argued for rhetoric's status as a practical discipline by calling attention to the ways in which discourse that is rhetorical is "called into being" as a result of the relationship among three constituent elements: "exigences," "audiences," and "constraints."[11] Exigences consisted of the events and social relationships that seemed to call for some sort of interpretation. Audiences were those persons who were positioned to respond to the events in productive ways. Constraints were those things that limited the possible ways in which a rhetor could propose a response to the event. In Bitzer's words, the rhetorical situation was defined as "a complex of persons, events, objects, and relations presenting an actual or potential exigence which can be completely or partially removed if discourse, introduced into the situation, can so constrain human decision or action as to bring about the significant modification of the exigence." By locating the essence of rhetoric in the broader social situation rather than in the intent of the speaker, Bitzer posed a third critical issue for contemporary rhetorical theorists (Part III): To what extent is rhetoric bound to its context, and what is a context anyway? In "On Systems of Rhetoric," another much-cited essay of the ensuing decades, Ehninger seconded Bitzer's position in a more macroscopic way when he argued that rhetoric was a function of its culture, and thus encouraged increased attention to the multiple forms and functions of rhetorics at different times and in different places.[12]

Similar themes were being picked up by any number of other critics and theorists writing in the period. Between 1967 and 1970, several important essays on social movements were published.[13] Collectively, they raised the fourth theoretical problem addressed in this volume (Part VI): What is the relationship between rhetoric and issues of political change? These essays also had a broader impact, shifting the attention of rhetorical studies so as to address the key problems and concerns of twentieth-century social and political theory. The implications of this work began to crystallize formally at two conferences sponsored by the National Developmental Project on Rhetoric (NDPR) in 1970 and reported in an important volume edited by Lloyd F. Bitzer and Edwin Black titled *The Prospect of Rhetoric*.[14]

In the words of the founders of the NDPR, "[Its] central objective was to outline and amplify a theory of rhetoric suitable to twentieth-century concepts and needs."[15] The debates and discussions at the Wingspread Conference in January 1970, and the National Conference on Rhetoric later in May, were spirited and often heated. In the end, however, the conferees, consisting of over forty of the leading male scholars in rhetorical studies, combined to offer recommendations on the advancement and refinement of rhetorical criticism, the scope of rhetoric and the place of rhetorical studies in higher education, and the nature of rhetorical invention.[16] It is interesting to read the specific recommendations generated in each of these areas, to get a portrait of the particular issues of the times and to see how the general culture of the 1960s affected the conception of rhetoric that was developing (and thus implicitly endorsing Ehninger's suggestion that rhetorics were functions of the particular and localized cultures in which they emerged). For our purposes, however, what is even more striking and important is the "consensus judgment" that was arrived at regarding the outline of a satisfactory contemporary theory of rhetoric. It consisted of four specific recommendations:

1. The technology of the twentieth century has created so many new channels and techniques of communication, and the problems confronting contemporary societies are so related to communicative methods and contents, that it is imperative that rhetorical studies be broadened to explore communicative procedures and practices not traditionally covered.
2. Our recognition of the scope of rhetorical theory and practice should be greatly widened.
3. At the same time, a clarified and expanded concept of reason and rational decision should be worked out.
4. Rhetorical invention should be restored to a position of centrality in theory and practice.[17]

Although these recommendations were very general, they clearly resonated with the sense that rhetoric was not merely the art of teaching public speaking, but rather that to be rhetorical was a central and substantial dimension of many facets of the human social experience. To borrow a phrase that Simons would later coin to describe the increasing interest in rhetoric within the academy as a whole, "the rhetorical turn" was about to be taken in a most thorough-going fashion; no longer, at least among rhetoricians, would rhetoric be presumed as a mere supplement or "handmaiden" to philosophy, sociology, history, or English. Instead, it would constitute its own significant perspective on the problems and possibilities of life-in-society. As such, the commitment to the production and performance of rhetorical theory, rather than simply the study of the history of rhetorical theory, became a central part of rhetorical studies.

"Rhetoric" Comes of Age (Again) in the "Post-" Era

It took several years for the full implications of the findings of the NDPR to be completely understood, for the impact was quite literally to call into question and revise the assumptions undergirding our understanding of rhetoric as a fundamental, social human phenomenon. But more than that, it also had implications for how we think about the relationships between theory, criticism, and practice. Only Barry Brummett, at the time a graduate student at the University of Minnesota, began to talk in terms of a "postmodern rhetoric."[18] However, the seeds for the contemporary debate between modernism and postmodernism were sown here. And while there have been claims in recent years that "postmodernism is dead," any attempt to suggest an alternative—"post-postmodernism," "pseudomodernism," and "metamodernism" have been offered as alternatives—have failed to gain traction in communication studies. More accurately, then, we assert that postmodernism has grown to include additional concerns (such as the importance of the visual and performative) while also integrating newer approaches (postcolonial and critical) into its canon. At the same time, the history of emergent theoretical orientations—for instance, the psychoanalytical (post-)Marxism of Slavoj Žižek—are still being written. Thus, while much has changed in the years since the first edition of this book was published, the focus on the divide between modernism and postmodernism remains relevant and instructive.

The differences between modernist and postmodernist perspectives have been the focus of significant and productive debates between and among rhetorical theorists in recent years as they have addressed the specific concerns of rhetorical study, and there is every reason to believe that such debates will continue well into the twenty-first century. You will see various facets of these debates emerge in each of the eight parts of this volume as particular problems and issues are addressed. Modernism features a commitment to scientism, and to objective, morally neutral, universal knowledge.[19] In the modern worldview, the universe is a relatively simple, stable, highly ordered place, describable in and reducible to absolute formulae that hold across contexts. Disagreement, in such a worldview, is treated as an unnecessary pathology that arises primarily from ignorance and irrationality. The solution or cure for social discord therefore lies in greater research, less passion, more rationality, and more education.

By contrast, postmodernism prefers interpretation over scientific study because it operates with the assumption that all knowledge is subjective and/or intersubjective, morally culpable, and local. In the postmodern worldview, the universe is a rapidly changing, highly complex entity. From this perspective, universally applicable formulae or "covering laws" designed for the purposes of describing and controlling the world are of minimal use, for the multiple and competing factors operating in every context override even the possibility of formulaic understanding. Each situation must be addressed in its own, and often chaotic, particularity. Disagreement is thus considered a rather "natural" result of different social, political, and ethnic groups, with different logics, interests, and values, living together and competing for limited or scarce resources. In this view, struggle, not consensus, is the defining characteristic of social life; accordingly, social discord is not a pathology to be cured, but a condition to be productively managed.

The first inklings of the tensions that would be generated by these dramatically conflicting worldviews began to emerge in a published debate in the *Quarterly Journal of Speech* in 1972 concerning critical assessments of President Richard Nixon's November 3, 1969, speech to the nation on the war in Vietnam. Forbes Hill employed a neo-Aristotelian perspective to evaluate Nixon's speech.[20] Neo-Aristotelianism was a method of rhetorical criticism heavily influenced by modernist notions of objectivity and the moral neutrality of the critic. Its primary goal was to evaluate a speech in terms of the degree to which it employed what Aristotle referred to as "the available means of persuasion" in attempting to achieve its goal. To the degree that a speech employed all of the means available to it, it was judged to be a good speech; to the degree that it failed to employ all such means, it was correspondingly a bad speech. Importantly, the critic was to maintain objective distance from the critical object, and thus there was no space in neo-Aristotelian criticism for evaluating the morality of particular choices or the ultimate outcome of the speech. According to Hill, Nixon's speech employed all of the available means of persuasion, and thus he judged it to be a good speech.

In the Forum that followed Hill's essay, Karlyn Kohrs Campbell called both the method of neo-Aristotelianism and the substance of Hill's particular conclusions into question.[21] The key point of her argument was that, appearances to the contrary, Hill's reliance upon an allegedly "objective" and "morally neutral" critical perspective was ultimately neither. More importantly, she argued, Hill actively ignored the important intellectual responsibility of situating his analysis as a morally culpable, theoretical practice.

Though many at the time concluded that Kohrs Campbell had made the more compelling argument, the truly significant, albeit implicit, claim this dispute evidenced was the clear need to (re) negotiate the relationship between critical and theoretical concerns. Modernist approaches to criticism and theory that presupposed the application of neutral and objective criteria to speeches (or other communication events) as a means of judging them would no longer suffice as a means of theorizing the rhetorical. Put differently, it was becoming increasingly clear that rhetoric was not a practice that culminated in "the amassing of objective knowledge or the generation of purely abstract theory," but was rather a "performance" that needed to be interpreted and evaluated in particular, interested, local contexts.[22] Rejecting the rigid modernist spirit of positivism and scientism in rhetorical studies proved to be relatively easy. Determining specifically what ought to replace it has been a much more difficult problem, and trying to solve that problem has been an issue that the discipline has visited over and again in the subsequent twenty-five years. Indeed, it is a problem that pervades many of the essays included in this volume.

Among the most important sets of stimuli for the search to replace the spirit of modernism in this period of ferment were the issues raised by the burgeoning woman's movement. In 1973, Kohrs Campbell published "The Rhetoric of Women's Liberation: An Oxymoron" in the *Quarterly Journal of Speech*.[23] In this essay, she argued that classical rhetorical theories failed to provide an appropriate or useful guide for the type of rhetoric that shaped women's liberation. From the perspective of classical rhetoric, she suggested, women's liberation was an oxymoron. It could not succeed because it could not appeal to audiences steeped in traditionally gendered norms; in addition, it employed alternative strategies such as small-group "consciousness raising" rather than the more traditional public platform as a means of effecting persuasion. Following Kohrs Campbell's lead, a variety of scholars have continued to explore feminist issues such as the proposed Equal Rights Amendment, abortion, and women's roles, forging new critical tools from new theoretical perspectives. These inquiries have included a questioning of both the substantive and the stylistic formulae for theory construction.[24] There is little agreement today on what constitutes a feminist rhetorical theory, but this body of theoretical work continually exerts pressure for broader perspectives to be taken upon the general theories of rhetoric that are most widely circulated, and this debt of the center to the margins has not been acknowledged very widely.[25] Kohrs Campbell's work is thus important not only because it offered an important contribution to our understanding of the relationship between rhetoric and political change (Part VI), but also because it helped to spur work on the relationship between rhetoric and traditionally marginalized groups (as considered in Part VIII).

The renewal of rhetoric as a theoretical discipline that began around 1967 culminated in scholarly work done nearly a decade later. This period of scholarly growth was important not only because it embodied the renewed emphasis on rhetorical theories as a means for understanding contemporary social and political life, but also because it encouraged increased contact and conversation with the emergence (in translation) of a growing community of continental social theorists who were beginning to focus attention on discourse and communication theory. One such example, published in 1976, was Thomas Farrell's "Knowledge, Consensus, and Rhetorical Theory" (Part II). Farrell sought to recover and reconstruct Aristotle's commitment to the combination of "[an] art of rhetoric and a generally accepted body of knowledge pertaining to matters of public concern."[26] Reading Aristotle into and through the context of American pragmatism, and drawing upon the increasingly elaborate social theory of Jürgen Habermas, Farrell developed a conception of "social knowledge" that stood in contrast to "technical knowledge." He then elaborated the functional characteristics of social knowledge, identifying it as consensual, audience-dependent, generative, and normative. Farrell underscored the need to rethink the ways in which we understand and employ the key components of the rhetorical process. He thus emphasized the importance of bringing classical rhetorical perspectives (Aristotle) into dialogue with contemporary U.S. philosophical perspectives (e.g., pragmatism), as well as continental philosophy and social theory (e.g.,

Habermas's revision of Marxist critical theory). In Farrell's own work, this expansion was reflected in a broadened definition of rhetoric as "a collaborative manner of engaging others through discourse so that contingencies may be resolved, judgments rendered, action produced."[27]

After work like this, there was simply no turning back. Rhetorical studies had become substantively theoretical in its focus. The positions and perspectives of Farrell and others, such as the influential scholar Michael Calvin McGee, would come under attack, to be sure. But such efforts were framed by the theoretical projects of the mid-1970s, the culmination of the work of the previous ten years. Whereas previously theory, criticism, and history stood as starkly different dimensions of rhetorical studies, henceforth they would become increasingly implicated in and by one another (by some accounts oppressively so).[28]

Plan of the Volume

The essays in this volume mark the course and development of rhetorical theory from 1967 to the present, though we present it less as a history (for which it would be altogether incomplete and inadequate) and more as an indication of the range of specific questions, problems, issues, and approaches that have occupied contemporary American rhetorical theorists in this period and continue to occupy them today. Indeed, in an important sense we offer the volume as an invitation to beginning scholars to become part of the community and the dialogue constituted by the essays and voices that are contained herein. The volume begins with a section titled "What Can a 'Rhetoric' Be?" and ends with a section titled "Alternatives to the Rhetorical Tradition." The opening section demonstrates that even though there are overlapping assumptions within the mainstream about what rhetoric might be, there is no univocal consensus on how we should understand it. The closing section underscores and emphasizes the interplay between those operating inside and outside the mainstream. The productive results of this interaction are obvious. Scholars are actively and productively critiquing and contesting established assumptions in ways that make rhetorical studies a vital and variable, though also very contentious, field of study and action.

The remaining six parts identify the major problems and issues that have occupied contemporary rhetorical theorists in recent years, and provide a range of voices and approaches on each one. We cannot possibly provide comprehensive coverage on each topic, so we have included a brief list of additional readings in each area. Part II addresses the rhetoric and epistemology debates. We position this section early because it represents one of the most enduring debates in the period covered here, and because the position one takes on the epistemological status of rhetoric will have much to say about the stance one takes as a rhetorical theorist.

Part III examines the continuing relevance of the rhetorical situation. Contemporary rhetorical theorists have conceded Bitzer's general claim that rhetoric and discourse are in some sense inherently and historically situated, rather than timeless and universal. This position challenges some of the bedrock assumptions underlying continental discourse theories. However, even within American rhetorical theory, there is no consensus on what we mean when we say that rhetoric is "situated." The essays included in this section indicate three different ways in which we might understand context, and a further argument that we might need to move beyond the situation in light of newer methods of discourse dissemination.

Part IV focuses on the complex and contested conceptions of "publics." Throughout much of the twentieth century, this concept was treated as an uncomplicated abstraction; rhetors addressed publics, and publics responded to rhetors. Over the past fifty years, scholars have begun to conceptualize the publics to which rhetoric is addressed in novel and diverse ways. An underlying concern is how the nature of the rhetorical address shapes—and, in some cases, transforms—public responses to political and social controversies. The essays in this section vary in their responses to this concern, ranging from considerations of form (e.g., narrative or visual) to questions of conceptualization (with frames that range from the *polis* to concerns about counterpublics).

Part V directs attention to the notion of "personae" in rhetorical theory. In many respects, this is the key issue confronting rhetorical theory, particularly in the context of continued efforts to engage the relationship among rhetorical, cultural, and critical studies. Just as rhetoricians agree that rhetoric is somehow situated, so too they agree that every rhetoric is always in some ways addressed to some audience that it seeks to influence or persuade. The points of controversy lie in where and how we identify that audience. What is its status within the rhetorical process? Who is included? Who is left out? What choices do rhetors make in addressing some and not others? What options are open to those who are addressed and those who are silenced? These issues implicate the authorization of social or public knowledge, and/ or the construction of social and political identity. The essays in this section engage these questions in contentious and provocative ways.

Part VI considers the broad relationship between rhetoric and politics. There are many ways in which such a section could be organized. We have chosen a twofold path. On the one hand, we explore the range of concerns raised when different types of social groupings—including the electoral politics of the nation-state, the organized social movement, and the identity group—are taken as the unit of analysis. On the other, we consider how a particular theoretical stance on the relationship between rhetoric and political change—Marxist, for instance—might influence our thinking. These essays provide original and telling glimpses into the varying roles of rhetoric in social change in disparate circumstances.

Part VII concerns the relationship between rhetoric and the mass media. Rhetoric, of course, was a technology invented in the fifth century B.C.E. as a means of wielding power and influence. Since that time, subsequent technological innovations from the printing press to radio to digital communications have had significant and sometimes revolutionary effects upon the ways in which the rhetorical impulse is experienced and understood. The essays included in this section address this problem in the contemporary context of the mass media: television, film, cyberspace, and beyond. They call attention both to how rhetorical theory might help us better understand the social, political, and cultural significance of these media of social interaction, and to how these media direct and influence the ways in which we might think of rhetorical theory in a mass-mediated era.

Collectively, the essays in this volume represent some of the most important contributions of contemporary rhetorical theory to the larger academic discussions concerning the social and political implications of discourse. Since the mid-1960s, the academic discussion on the importance and role of discourse has framed major intellectual currents in a wide range of traditional disciplines, from anthropology, English, and history to sociology and political science. It has also been a significant, animating factor in the more recent rise of more discrete academic areas: cultural, critical, gender, and sexuality studies. We (tentatively) address the specific contributions of rhetorical studies to this larger academic conversation, at times complementary and at others contentious, in the Epilogue. We hope that after you engage the essays in this volume, you will begin to gain a sense of what rhetorical theory has been in the contemporary period—and, more importantly, of the future contributions it might make. And in that context, it is our hope that the Epilogue may actually function as the prologue to the future studies that you will produce.

To understand ourselves and the societies we create with our words is a challenging and daunting task, but we are inexorably committed to the belief that it is the richest and most rewarding of endeavors available. We offer the essays collected in this volume both as the evidence of and as contributions to that ongoing project.

NOTES

1. Isocrates, "Antidosis," in *Isocrates*, trans. George Norlin (Cambridge, MA: Harvard University Press, 1929), vol. 2, 253–55. For an important discussion of the importance of Isocrates to the rhetorical tradition, see Takis Poulakos, *Isocrates' Rhetorical Education* (Columbia: University of South Carolina Press, 1997).

2. There are numerous and quite good surveys of the history of rhetoric. The most readily available ones still in print include Thomas Conley, *Rhetoric in the European Tradition* (Chicago: University of Chicago Press, 1994); George A. Kennedy, *Classical Rhetoric and Its Christian and Secular Tradition from Ancient to Modern Times* (Chapel Hill: University of North Carolina Press, 1980); George A. Kennedy, *A New History of Classical Rhetorics* (Princeton, NJ: Princeton University Press, 1994); and Brian Vickers, *In Defense of Rhetoric* (Oxford, UK: Clarendon Press, 1988). A very good survey that includes major excerpts from significant theoretical texts is Patricia Bizzell and Bruce Herzberg, eds., *The Rhetorical Tradition: Readings from Classical Times to the Present*, 2nd ed. (Boston: Bedford-St. Martin's, 1990). A slightly dated, but nonetheless very useful, collection of bibliographical review essays on the history of rhetoric are contained in Winifred Bryan Horner, ed., *The Present State of Scholarship in Historical and Contemporary Rhetoric* (Columbia: University of Missouri Press, 1990).

3. *Merriam-Webster's Tenth Collegiate Dictionary*, s.v. "contemporary."

4. Representative examples of such work include Michael Billig, *Ideology and Opinions: Studies in Rhetorical Psychology* (Newbury Park, CA: Sage, 1991); Donald N. McCloskey, *The Rhetoric of Economics* (Madison: University of Wisconsin Press, 1985); James Boyd

White, *Heracles' Bow: Essays on the Rhetoric and Poetics of the Law* (Madison: University of Wisconsin Press, 1985); and John S. Nelson, *Tropes of Politics: Science, Theory, Rhetoric, Action* (Madison: University of Wisconsin Press, 1998). Two useful collections of essays include John Bender and David E. Wellbery, eds., *The Ends of Rhetoric: History, Theory, Practice* (Stanford, CA: Stanford University Press, 1990); and John S. Nelson et al., eds., *The Rhetoric of the Human Sciences: Language and Argument in Scholarship and Public Affairs* (Madison: University of Wisconsin Press, 1987).

5. The full history of the development of rhetorical theory in the discipline of communication studies has yet to be written. An important initial effort that emphasizes the early years in particular is Michael Leff and Margaret Organ Procario, "Rhetorical Theory in Speech Communication," in Thomas W. Benson, ed., *Speech Communication in the Twentieth Century* (Carbondale: Southern Illinois University Press, 1985), 3–27.

6. Aristotle, *The Rhetoric of Aristotle*, 1355b26, trans. Lane Cooper (New York: Prentice-Hall, 1960), 7.

7. See Kathleen Hall Jamieson, *Eloquence in an Electronic Age: The Transformation of Political Speechmaking* (New York: Oxford University Press, 1988).

8. John W. Bowers and Donovan J. Ochs, *The Rhetoric of Agitation and Control* (Reading, MA: Addison-Wesley, 1971).

9. Franklin Haiman, "The Rhetoric of the Streets: Legal and Ethical Considerations," *Quarterly Journal of Speech* 53 (1967): 99, 114.

10. Robert L. Scott, "On Viewing Rhetoric as Epistemic," *Central States Speech Journal* 18 (1967): 9–16.

11. Lloyd F. Bitzer, "The Rhetorical Situation," *Philosophy and Rhetoric* 1 (1968): 1–14.

12. Douglas Ehninger, "On Systems of Rhetoric," *Philosophy and Rhetoric* 1 (1968): 131–44.

13. See Michael Osborn, "Archetypal Metaphor in Rhetoric: The Light–Dark Family," *Quarterly Journal of Speech* 53 (1967): 115–26; Parke G. Burgess, "The Rhetoric of Black Power: A Moral Demand?," *Quarterly Journal of Speech* 54 (1968): 122–33, and "The Rhetoric of Moral Conflict: Two Critical Dimensions," *Quarterly Journal of Speech* 56 (1970): 120–30; Robert L. Scott and Donald K. Smith, "The Rhetoric of Confrontation," *Quarterly Journal of Speech* 55 (1969): 9–16; Edwin Black, "The Second Persona," *Quarterly Journal of Speech* 56 (1970): 109–19; Walter R. Fisher, "A Motive View of Communication," *Quarterly Journal of Speech* 54 (1970): 131–39; and Herbert W. Simons, "Requirements, Problems, and Strategies: A Theory of Persuasion for Social Movements," *Quarterly Journal of Speech* 56 (1970): 1–11.

14. The conferences were organized by the National Developmental Project on Rhetoric (NDPR), and sponsored by the Speech Communication Association and the National Endowment for the Humanities. See Lloyd F. Bitzer and Edwin Black, eds., *The Prospect of Rhetoric: Report of the National Developmental Project* (Englewood Cliffs, NJ: Prentice-Hall, 1971). The essays that constituted this volume were reexamined in light of more recent developments in Mark Porrovecchio, ed., *Reengaging the Prospects of Rhetoric: Current Conversations and Contemporary Challenges* (New York: Taylor & Francis, 2010).

15. Bitzer and Black, *The Prospect of Rhetoric*, v.

16. It is important to note that among the forty-plus rhetoricians invited to the conferences, there were *no* women. This might be accounted for, in part, by the dearth of women rhetoricians publishing in this time period. The notable omission of Marie Hochmuth Nichols—who had just completed a term as the editor of the *Quarterly Journal of Speech*; who had edited the third volume of the then important *History and Criticism of Public Address*; and who had published as well an important collection of lectures on the development of a "new rhetoric," *Rhetoric and Culture* (Baton Rouge: Louisiana State University Press, 1963)—is nonetheless somewhat odd. For one account, see Gerard Hauser, review of Theresa Enos, ed., *Encyclopedia of Rhetoric and Composition*, in *Quarterly Journal of Speech* 83 (1997): 243–46. The history of these conferences has been discussed in some detail. See, e.g., Theresa Enos and Richard McNabb, eds., *Making and Unmaking the Prospects of Rhetoric* (Mahwah, NJ: Erlbaum, 1997).

17. Bitzer and Black, *The Prospect of Rhetoric*, 238–39.

18. Barry Brummett, "Some Implications of 'Process' or 'Intersubjectivity': Postmodern Rhetoric," *Philosophy and Rhetoric* 9 (1976): 21–51.

19. The tension between modernism and postmodernism, and all the attendant offshoots thereof, involves complex and often conflicting narratives. We cannot hope even to begin to unpack or resolve these issues in a few short pages. A well-established body of work focuses on the debates concerning the meaning of and relationships between the conditions of modernity and postmodernity, and the philosophical positions of modernism and postmodernism. Useful introduction to the relevant issues are found in David Lyons, *Postmodernity* (Minneapolis: University of Minnesota Press, 1994); and Christopher Butler, *Postmodernism: A Very Short Introduction* (Oxford, UK: Oxford University Press, 2002). For more complex, historically situated considerations of the relationships, one might look to David Harvey's *The Condition of Postmodernity: An Enquiry into the Origins of Social Change* (Cambridge, MA: Blackwell, 2000) or to Barry Smart, *Modern Conditions, Postmodern Controversies* (New York: Routledge, 1992). Those interested in charting the tensions and debates through what many consider to be the primary texts of modernism and postmodernism might look to Lawrence Cahoone, ed., *From Modernism to Postmodernism: An Anthology Expanded* (Malden, MA: Blackwell, 2003).

20. Forbes Hill, "Conventional Wisdom—Traditional Form—The President's Message of November 3, 1969," *Quarterly Journal of Speech* 58 (1972): 373–86.

21. Karlyn Kohrs Campbell, "'Conventional Wisdom—Traditional Form': A Rejoinder," and Forbes Hill, "A Response to Professor Campbell," *Quarterly Journal of Speech* 58 (1972): 452–60.

22. Leff and Procario, "Rhetorical Theory," 5.

23. Karlyn Kohrs Campbell, "The Rhetoric of Women's Liberation: An Oxymoron," *Quarterly Journal of Speech* 59 (1973): 74–86.

24. For a provocative example of this line of theorizing, see Jane Sutton, "The Taming of *Polos/Polis*: Rhetoric as an Achievement Without Woman," *Southern Communication Journal* 57 (1992): 97–119.

25. For a description of feminist research in rhetorical studies in this period, see Celeste Michelle Condit, "Opposites in an Oppositional Practice: Rhetorical Criticism and Feminism," in Sheryl Perlmutter Bowen and Nancy Wyatt, eds., *Transforming Visions: Feminist Critiques in Communication Studies* (Cresskill, NJ: Hampton Press, 1993), 205–30.

26. Thomas Farrell, "Knowledge, Consensus, and Rhetorical Theory," *Quarterly Journal of Speech* 62 (1976): 1. The other signal essay of this period was published a year earlier by an equally influential scholar: Michael C. McGee, "In Search of 'the People': A Rhetorical Alternative," *Quarterly Journal of Speech* 61 (1975): 235–49. McGee argued that the premiere challenge facing the discipline was to recognize the significance of rhetoric as central to the constitution of collective life, not merely a matter of teaching speeches or observing their immediate effects on audiences. His point, complementing the work of Farrell, was that rhetorical theory that took itself seriously would draw critically upon concrete instances of persuasive discourse.

27. Thomas Farrell, "From the Parthenon to the Bassinet: Along the Epistemic Trail," *Quarterly Journal of Speech* 76 (1990): 83. For the fullest development of Farrell's perspective, see his *Norms of Rhetorical Culture* (New Haven, CT: Yale University Press, 1993).

28. See James Darsey, "Must We All Be Rhetorical Theorists?: An Anti-Democratic Inquiry," *Western Journal of Speech Communication* 58 (1994): 164–81.

PART I
WHAT CAN A "RHETORIC" BE?

At least since Plato's attack on rhetoric as "mere cookery," one of the enduring questions that rhetoricians have sought to answer is this: What is "rhetoric"? The answers have been many and varied, ranging from Aristotle's "the faculty wherein one discovers the available means of persuasion in any case whatsoever," to George Campbell's focus on eloquence, or "that art or talent by which discourse is adapted to its end," to Kenneth Burke's concept of "identification," which presumes that "you persuade a man only insofar as you can talk his language by speech, gesture, tonality, order, image, attitude, idea, *identifying* your ways with his," to more recent suggestions that rhetoric is a performative, embodied, critical act. In some instances, the definitions attributed to rhetoric have made it so narrow as to include little more than style and delivery within its purview; in other instances, its meaning has been so broad as to colonize and include all other forms of discourse, ranging from logic to poetics. Indeed, the range of answers to this question is so varied, and the implications of each answer so significant for how we engage the practical, critical, and theoretical problematics of rhetoric, that it seems more productive to ask a more inclusive and proactive question: What can a "rhetoric" be? The seven essays included in Part I represent a range of answers to that question. In some cases, there are points of contact. In others, the authors ask us to rethink—in at least one case, radically so—the very notion of what rhetoric can and should be.

For over a hundred years, the most prominent definition of rhetoric has been Aristotle's. This is in large measure a result of the creation of the National Communication Association (NCA) in 1914, which was then known as the National Association of Academic Teachers of Public Speaking. With the academic standing of the NCA came the development of speech departments in the 1920s. Alongside these academic activities, social forces were at play. The influence at that time of progressivism and pragmatism upon the public education of an American citizenry included a concern for the practical applications of rhetoric. These developments dovetailed with most interpretations of Aristotle's approach to rhetoric. To wit, he conceived of rhetoric as a practical and pragmatic doctrine, and his *Ars rhetorica* was initially appropriated in speech departments as a technical handbook for training fledgling orators to be effective public speakers. In "Practicing the Arts of Rhetoric: Tradition and Invention," Thomas Farrell rereads Aristotle to suggest that rhetoric is a higher-order practice entailing "the entire process of forming, expressing, and judging public thought in real life." The implications of such a characterization are significant, for it suggests that rhetoric is an ethical practice that goes beyond simple questions of individual and utilitarian effectiveness, and is measured (Farrell's term is "redeemed") by the degree to which it achieves *phronesis*, or practical wisdom, in dealing with civic matters. Rhetoric is thus a function of prudential and communal decision making. In the second half of the essay, Farrell outlines the implications of such a reconceptualization of rhetoric for rhetorical practice, rhetorical form, and rhetorical community in contemporary rhetorical culture.

Central to Farrell's notion of a revised Aristotelianism is the sense in which rhetoric is a *praxis*, in both the classical sense of combining theory and action, and in the more contemporary, Marxist, critical-theoretical sense of "the concrete embodiment of existent social forces, understood as a mode of production." The tension between classical and contemporary conceptions of *praxis* has been central to a number of efforts to identify what a rhetoric might be—and how it might function—in contemporary times. In "The Habitation of Rhetoric," Michael Leff poses the problem in terms of rhetoric's "home," questioning whether rhetoric is an independent "art" that possesses its own "substance" or whether it belongs to a more substantial discipline or body of knowledge such as philosophy or political science. Leff locates the problem in the context of a forced and unnatural division between rhetoric as product and rhetoric as process, which has made it difficult for us to understand how action and production are integrated in any given rhetorical context. According to Leff, the problem manifests itself most fully in the separation of persuasion, argumentation, and aesthetics (style), specifically in instances where "judgments must be rendered about specific matters of communal interest." The solution, according to Leff, is to return to a Ciceronian notion of decorum that helps us to understand the ways in which rhetoric is a unified *praxis* that aligns the stylistic and argumentative features of a discourse both internally as text and externally as a social force.

John Poulakos addresses the problem of *praxis* in "Toward a Sophistic Definition of Rhetoric." The Sophists were the first rhetoricians, and arguably it was in response to their power and presence in ancient Greece—and their commitment to a most radical relativism—that Plato developed his conception of philosophy and dialectic. Drawing upon the remaining fragments of sophistic treatises, Poulakos reconstructs a conception of sophistic rhetoric as "the art which seeks to capture in opportune moments that which is appropriate and attempts to suggest that which is possible." According to Poulakos, the Sophists thought of rhetoric as a *techne* (art) that operated through *logos* (the word) to produce both *pistis* (belief or proof) and *terpsis* (aesthetic pleasure). The enactment of rhetoric thus relied upon the human desire to be different or "other," and the social capacity to identify and adapt to the temporal and formal structures of the situations being addressed through the artful use of language. From this perspective, then, rhetoric is a social *praxis* that is enacted as a function of its *kairotic* (timely), aesthetic performance.

The issue of rhetoric as performance is taken up more fully in "Text, Context, and the Fragmentation of Contemporary Culture" by Michael Calvin McGee, who borrows from an Isocratean perspective that treats rhetoric as a critical form of social surgery. McGee is particularly interested in the ways in which academic rhetoricians perform their roles as critics and theorists in what he calls the "postmodern condition." In particular, he believes that rhetorical theorists and critics have devoted far too much attention in recent years to the idealized study of singular texts and have ignored the need to produce "material rhetorics"—that is, discourses that might help the members of the polity understand how to construct powerful and compelling conceptions of collective living out of the textual fragments that constitute their contemporary culture. For McGee, then, the problem of *praxis* is not so much a hypothetical concern with unifying thought and action for a homogeneous culture or understanding rhetoric as the embodiment of text and context; rather, it is a specific social force that actively engages and manages (but never totally transcends) the tensions between thought and action, and text and context, in a fragmented, heterogeneous, multicultural society.

These sorts of tensions are addressed by Robert Hariman in "Status, Marginality, and Rhetorical Theory." Although Hariman offers a definition of rhetoric as "a mode of reflection upon the sociality of language," his primary task is not so much to answer the question of what a "rhetoric" might be as to ask what is at stake in posing the question in the first place. As such, it provides, at least conceptually, a metacommentary on several of the other essays in this section. Hariman notes that most efforts at defining rhetoric have treated it generically by distinguishing it from other forms of discourse, most notably philosophy, logic, and poetry. All such efforts at definition operate in a powerful dialectic of status and marginality, which functions to empower and constrain the meaning and force of any given discourse by "activating a pattern of thinking" that locates it in a social hierarchy of desirability and potency. For Plato, the hierarchy had dialectic at the top and rhetoric at the bottom; for the Sophists, the hierarchy was reversed. In either case, however, the dialectic constitutes relations of dominance and subordination, and of an authority that seeks to conceal itself. By treating the history of the definition of rhetoric in terms of the social functions of status and marginality, Hariman argues, we ought to be in a much better position to deconstruct (or at least to understand) the political and ontological implications of the ways in which any conception of rhetoric affects how we think of and practice rhetorical theory. More importantly, perhaps, it also calls attention to the mutability of the social meanings and relations of discourse, and to the continuing need to engage rhetorical inquiry as a means of reflecting upon "the art of reclassification." As we shall see, these sorts of questions can be addressed by also considering issues of context (where does rhetoric occur?) and function (what does rhetoric do?).

In the last twenty years, the very nature of meaning and discourse has been subject to radical shifts. The other essays in this section are written with the underlying assumption that rhetoric is conducted in traditional ways: face-to-face in public venues, or through traditional media (television, radio, books). In "Digital Rhetoric: Toward an Integrated Theory," James P. Zappen points to the fact that rhetoric is increasingly going digital. As it does, what changes? One of the striking features of digital rhetoric is that it moves beyond traditional assumptions about persuasion to embrace considerations of self-expression and collaboration. At the same time, the era of the digital native carries with it questions that have yet to be resolved. Speed and reach greatly reduce the divide between senders and receivers. They also decrease attention to formality and considerations of intent. Anonymity provides a safe space to explore alternative notions of selfhood. It also engenders trolls and bullies who engage others for nefarious purposes. Interactivity allows for collaboration on a level heretofore unseen. It also carries with it decreased privacy. Zappen doesn't posit a definitive notion of digital rhetoric—which is perhaps fitting, given that the digital environment is constantly evolving and fluid. Although traditional mediums are in no danger of vanishing, they now exist alongside other forms of transmission that influence the rhetoric being conveyed.

The rise of digital communication is not the only major difference between antiquity and the present. Since classical antiquity, the theoretical questions related to the nature and scope of rhetoric have been answered primarily, if not almost exclusively, by men. This bears a certain irony when we recall that since classical antiquity rhetoric has been characterized derogatorily in female terms as "Dame Rhetoric" and "The Harlot of the Arts." Such characterizations, even those that take in sophistic or Marxist strains of thinking, engender masculinist characteristics that remain largely unchallenged. Rhetoric is viewed as *agonistic*—a competition and/or conflict carried out through words, even when it is performative and even if it conducted with propriety in mind. Further, rhetoric leads to winners and losers, to evaluations regarding who provided the better or worse rhetoric.

Sonya K. Foss and Cindy L. Griffin propose a radical rethinking of these accepted notions. In "Beyond Persuasion: A Proposal for an Invitational Rhetoric," they ask whether persuasion should even be the goal of rhetoric. They challenge the patriarchal biases found in dominant conceptions of rhetoric. Foss and Griffin urge that they should be replaced with feminist considerations of equality, immanent value, and self-determination. Rather than change another person's mind, one would seek to understand another point of view. Instead of dominating lesser interactants, one would invite them to share in exchange of ideas. Foss and Griffin offer a rhetoric that stresses the importance of safety, value, and freedom. In so doing, they invite readers to answer the long-standing question of what "rhetoric" can be in a decidedly unique way.

ADDITIONAL READINGS

Burke, Kenneth. (1945). *The Rhetoric of Motives*. Berkeley and Los Angeles: University of California Press.

Ehninger, Douglas. (1968). "On Systems of Rhetoric." *Philosophy and Rhetoric* 1: 131–44.

Gearhart, Sally. (1979). "The Womanization of Rhetoric." *Woman's Studies International Quarterly* 2: 195–201.

Group Mu [J. Dubois, F. Edeline, J.-M. Klinkenberg, P. Minguet, F. Pire, and H. Trinon]. (1981). *A General Rhetoric*. Paul B. Burrell and Edgar M. Slotkin, trans. Baltimore: Johns Hopkins University Press. [Originally published in French in 1970.]

Jarrat, Susan C. (1991). *Rereading the Sophists: Classical Rhetoric Refigured*. Carbondale: Southern Illinois University Press.

McGee, Michael Calvin. (1982). "A Materialist's Conception of Rhetoric." In Ray E. McKerrow, ed., *Explorations in Rhetoric: Studies in Honor of Douglas Ehninger* (Glenview, IL: Scott, Foresman), 23–48.

McGuire, Michael Calvin. (1982). "The Structural Study of Speech." In Ray E. McKerrow, ed., *Explorations in Rhetoric: Studies in Honor of Douglas Ehninger* (Glenview, IL: Scott, Foresman), 1–22.

McKeon, Richard. (1971). "The Uses of Rhetoric in a Technological Age: Architectonic Productive Arts." In Lloyd F. Bitzer and Edwin F. Black, eds., *The Prospect of Rhetoric* (Englewood Cliffs, NJ: Prentice-Hall), 44–63.

Scott, Robert L. (1973). "On *Not* Defining 'Rhetoric.'" *Philosophy and Rhetoric* 6: 81–96.

Sproule, Michael. (1988). "The New Managerial Rhetoric and the Old Criticism." *Quarterly Journal of Speech* 74: 401–15.

Toward a Sophistic Definition of Rhetoric

John Poulakos

When Hegel undertook to reanimate the Sophists,[1] he established with poignant observations that the message of those itinerant teachers of culture was a natural as well as a necessary link between pre-Socratic (especially Anaxagoran) and Platonic thought.[2] Thus, he endowed their views with intellectual integrity on the one hand, and gave them a place in the history of philosophy on the other. The recent plenitude of sophistic studies shows that Hegel's work was not an instance of philosophical lightning but an origin of things to come. But whereas he and others[3] after him have placed the Sophists' views historically or topically, the meaning of their rhetorical perspective has not received adequate attention.

This essay presumes that without the Sophists our picture of the rhetoric that came out of the Greek experience is incomplete. For over two millennia we have relied almost exclusively on the Platonic and Aristotelian notions of discourse while we have treated the sophistic position as an obscure but interesting historical footnote. And despite Hegel's and others' efforts to rehabilitate the Sophists, we are still bound to the directives of Plato's system of Idealism and Aristotle's system of Development. But because rhetoric came about as an activity grounded in human experience, not in philosophical reflection, we must approach it by looking at those who *practiced* it before turning to those who *reflected* about it.

In recent years the above position has been espoused by many students and teachers of rhetoric. Thus far, however, it has led mainly to studies enabling us to better understand individual Sophists. But if Greek rhetoric is indeed a trilogy, we need to concern ourselves with its first part, which to this day remains fragmentary. To do so, we must reexamine the surviving fragments of and about the Sophists and seek to articulate on probable grounds their view of rhetoric. This essay purports to do just that. More specifically, it purports to derive a "sophistic" definition of rhetoric and to discuss some of its more important implications.[4]

Although not as rigorous systematizers of thought as Plato or Aristotle, the Sophists were the first to infuse rhetoric with life. Indebted only to the poetry of their past, not to any formal rhetorical theory, they found themselves free to experiment playfully with form and style and to fashion their words in the Greek spirit of excellence. Aware of the human limitations in the acquisition of knowledge, they sought to ground the abstract notions of their predecessors[5] in the actuality of everydayness. Conscious of people's susceptibility to each other's language, they taught eloquence whose peculiar characteristic is "to show the manifold points of view existing in a thing, and to give force to those which harmonize with what appears to me to be more useful."[6] As practitioners and teachers of rhetoric, the Sophists made Greece aware of her culture and demonstrated to the rest of the world that rhetoric is an integral part of the social life of all civilized people.[7]

The definition I wish to advance is: *Rhetoric is the art which seeks to capture in opportune moments that which is appropriate and attempts to suggest that which is possible.* Very briefly, this definition intimates that rhetoric is an artistic undertaking which concerns itself with the how, the when, and the what of expression and understands the why of purpose. Further, this definition links rhetoric to a movement originating in the sphere of actuality and striving to attain a place in that of potentiality. The following discussion focuses on key notions and terms which, if seen together, constitute a coherent and defensible position on rhetoric. The example of the Sophists suggests that the notions and terms to be investigated are rhetoric as art, style as personal expression, *kairos* (the opportune moment), *to prepon* (the appropriate), and *to dynaton* (the possible).

The Sophists conceived of rhetoric primarily as a *techné*[7]* (art) whose medium is *logos* and whose double aim is *terpsis* (aesthetic pleasure) and *pistis* (belief).[8] The evidence supporting their artistic view comes from several sources. According to Philodemus, Metrodorus seems to make it clear enough that "the rhetoric of the Sophists has the status of an Art."[9] On a more specific comment, Philostratus claims that within Antiphon's forensic speeches "lies all that is derived from the art [of rhetoric]" (87 B44a). Similarly, Suidas informs us that Thrasymachus wrote, among other things, "a rhetorical art" (85 A1). In Plato's *Protagoras* (317b), Protagoras discloses that he has been many years "in the art," while Gorgias asserts in the *Gorgias* (450b) that "the rhetorical art is about words" and boasts in the same dialogue (456b), that he often persuaded reluctant patients to submit to medical treatment "through no other art than the rhetorical." In his *Encomium to Helen* (13), Gorgias extends his conception of rhetoric by implying that if a speech is to be persuasive it must be "written with art."

Conceiving of rhetoric as art is important because on the one hand it designates the sophistic view proper[10] and on the other it helps place the controversy between Plato and the Sophists in the right light. In particular, one may argue, rhetoric as art does not admit criteria appropriate to strictly epistemological or axiological matters; nor does it call for the same considerations which

rhetoric as argument does. Thus, some of the well-known Platonic charges against rhetoric become inapplicable.[11] In distinction to *episteme*, rhetoric does not strive for cognitive certitude, the affirmation of logic, or the articulation of universals. Conditioned by the people who create it, rhetoric moves beyond the domain of logic and, satisfied with probability, lends itself to the flexibility of the contingent.[12] Because the sophistic notion of rhetoric as art is a topic too large for the purposes of this essay, the following comments will be limited to the sophistic concern for the artistic aspect of discourse, or style.

The story of the Sophists' preoccupation with style is too well known to be recounted here. Collectively, they were held in contempt for dealing with "the non-essentials" of rhetoric.[13] However, this preoccupation seems to have arisen from the realization, expressed later by Aristotle, that "the way a thing is said does affect its intelligibility."[14] Antiphon is quite explicit about the grave consequences of effective or ineffective style when he says: "it is as unfair that a bad choice of words should cause a man of good behavior to be put to death as it is that a good choice of words should lead to the acquittal of a criminal."[15] Of course, there is room to argue that stylistic emphasis in discourse, that is, emphasis of the how over the what, displays a preference indicative of misplaced values. But however small its value, style is an inescapable reality of speech, one which must be attended to necessarily. Aristotle himself, who insists on the primacy of facts and their proof,[16] acknowledges the reality and necessity of style when he writes: "It is not sufficient to know *what* one ought to say, but it is necessary also to know *how* one ought to say it."[17] So, to the extent that style is allowed to be seen primarily as an aesthetical issue, the question of its superiority or inferiority to content, essentially an axiological question, becomes secondary.

The evidence of the Sophists' excellence in style is plentiful. Protagoras, who on some matters held the same opinion with Diagoras, is said to have "used different words in order to avoid its extreme forcefulness" (80 A23). Philostratus reports in the *Lives of the Sophists* that Gorgias, who did for rhetoric as much as Aeschylus did for tragedy, "was an example of forcefulness to the Sophists and of marvels and inspiration and of giving utterance to great subjects in the grand style, and of detached phrases and transitions, through which speech becomes sweeter than itself and more pompous, and he also introduced poetical words for orna-

---

*Editors' note: Footnote no. 7 appears twice in the original.

ment and dignity" (82 A1 [2]).[18] Xenophon, after re-creating the tale of Hercules' dilemma between Virtue and Vice, tells us that Prodicus, its original author, "embellished the [above] thoughts with still more magnificent words than I [have done] just now" (84 B2 [34]). Dionysius of Halicarnassus writes that Thrasymachus was "clean-cut and subtle and formidable in inventing and expressing tersely and extraordinarily that which he wants" (85 A13). According to Philostratus, Hippias "used to enchant Greece at Olympia with varied and well-heeded speeches" (86 A2 [7]). Philostratus praises Antiphon's *On Concord* by saying that it contains "brilliant and wise maxims and narrative elevated and flowered with poetical names and diffuse exposition like the smoothness of the plain" (87 B44a). Philostratus also praises the speech of Kritias for being "sweet . . . and smooth like the west breeze" (88 A1).

As the historical record indicates, the Sophists were master rhetoricians. That their excellence in the area of style has often been construed as a liability is due partly to Plato's influence on posterity and partly to the excesses of some of their successors. But if it is agreed that what is said must be said somehow, and that the how is a matter of the speaker's choice, then style betrays the speaker's unique grasp of language and becomes the peculiar expression of his personality.[19] If this is so, the Sophists need no longer be misunderstood. As some of their artifacts reveal, they were highly accomplished linguistic craftsmen with a heightened sense of the nature of *logos*, their medium.[20]

As the suggested definition of rhetoric implies, the Sophists were interested in the problem of time in relation to speaking. At least one of them, Gorgias, asserted that situations have a way of revealing themselves to man and of eliciting responses from him. As he states in his treatise *On Non-Being or On Nature*, "the external becomes the revealer of *logos*" (82 B3 [85]). But Gorgias was not alone in asserting that situations exist in time and that speech as a situational response does also. The Sophists stressed that speech must show respect to the temporal dimension of the situation it addresses, that is, it must be timely. In other words, speech must take into account and be guided by the temporality of the situation in which it occurs.

For the most part, what compels a rhetor to speak is a sense of urgency. Under normal circumstances, that is, under circumstances in which we are composed and things are "under control," there is no pressing need to speak. But during times of

stress, we feel compelled to intervene and, with the power of the word, to attempt to end a crisis, redistribute justice, or restore order. In his *Defense of Palamedes* (32), Gorgias has the speaker say, following a lengthy statement of self-praise: "But [ordinarily] it is not for me to praise myself; but the present moment necessitated . . . that I defend myself in every way possible." Illustrating the same point, Thrasymachus, we are told, once addressed the Athenians by saying: "I wish, Athenians, that I had belonged to that time when silence sufficed for young people, since the state of affairs did not force them to make speeches and the older men were managing the city properly. But since our fortune has reserved us . . . misfortunes . . . one really has to speak" (85 B1).[21] In the former example it is urgent that the defendant reinstate his threatened reputation, while in the latter it is crucial that the citizens protest against the injurious practices of their civic leaders.

Both of the above examples imply that ideas have their place in time and unless they are given existence, unless they are voiced at the precise moment they are called upon, they miss their chance to satisfy situationally shared voids within a particular audience. Moreover, the two examples seem to restrict speaking to only those times calling for it, and to suggest that silence be the alternative at all other times. In fact, Gorgias praises the dead in his *Epitaphios* for having known when to speak (*legein*) and when to be silent (*sigan*) (B6).

Clearly, speaking involves a temporal choice. The choice is not whether to speak but whether to speak now; more precisely, it is whether now is the time to speak. When a rhetor speaks, he responds to a situation. But the fact that he speaks now, the fact that he has chosen this moment over another, reminds the listener that the situation is ephemeral, urgent, and, by implication, significant. But if the rhetor chooses to address the present, he also agrees to confront the contingent elements of the situation as they unfold. As such, he is taking on a risk, the risk that his timing might not coincide with the temporal needs of the situation. According to Philostratus, Gorgias, who held in contempt those who spoke about "things that had been said many times," devoted himself to what was timely (82 A24). Further, Gorgias "was the first to proclaim himself willing to take this risk . . . that he would trust to the opportune moment to speak on any subject" (82 A1a). That addressing the present requires courage and involves the taking of a risk is apparent in the compromise of extemporaneous speaking, the kind which literally occurs out of time. Prepared speech texts betray our insensitivity to and insecurity about all that is contingent in the act of speaking. Prepared texts have a designated time in the future and a prefabricated content. But by designating the time and by prefabricating the content of a speech, we are essentially setting the parameters of a situation to come and prepare ourselves in advance to treat it in its fixity. This compromise we make out of our apprehension regarding the indeterminate aspects of a situation to which we have no immediate access.[22] The example of several Sophists, most notably that of Gorgias and Hippias, suggests that an accomplished speaker has no need for notes or a text, rehearsal, or presituational practice.

The sophistic insistence that speaking be done with respect to time does not stem from a philosophical position regarding the nature of *logos* but from the observation that if what is said is timely, its timeliness renders it more sensible, more rightful, and ultimately more persuasive. Reportedly, Protagoras was the first to expound on "the power of the opportune moment" to give speech advantages it otherwise would not have (80 A1). In the anonymous sophistic treatise *Dissoi Logoi 2* (19), the author is quite explicit about this point. Specifically, he states that "nothing is always virtuous, nor [always] disgraceful, but taking the same things the opportune moment made disgraceful and after changing [them made them] virtuous." Clearly, the notion of *kairos* points out that speech exists in time; but more important, it constitutes a prompting toward speaking and a criterion of the value of speech.[23] In short, *kairos* dictates that what is said must be said at the right time.

In conjunction with the notion of *kairos*, the Sophists gave impetus to the related concept of *to prepon* (the appropriate) apparently prescribing that what is said must conform to both audience and occasion. Illustrating *to prepon*, Gorgias praises in his *Epitaphios* the dead for having been "well-disposed toward the appropriate," while in his *Defense of Palamedes* (28) he has the defendant admit that what he is about to say is "inappropriate to one who has not been accused but suitable to one who has been accused." In the same speech, Gorgias strongly implies that the strategy of a legal defense depends largely on the speaker's audience. Specifically, he has the defendant state that while it is useful to employ appeals to pity and entreaties and the intercession of friends when the trial takes place before a mob, before noble and wise judges one must concentrate on the explanation of the truth (33).

A complement to the notion of *kairos*, *to prepon* points out that situations have formal characteristics, and demands that speaking as a response to a situation be suitable to those very characteristics. Both notions are concerned with the rhetor's response; but while the former is interested in the when, the latter is concerned with the what of speaking. *To prepon* requires that speech must take into account and be guided by the formal structure of the situation it addresses. Like *kairos*, *to prepon* constitutes not only a guide to what must be said but also a standard of the value of speech.[24] In distinction to *kairos*, which focuses on man's sense of time, *to prepon* emphasizes his sense of propriety.

Appropriateness refers to that quality which makes an expression be correlative to the formal aspects of the situation it addresses. When appropriate, speech is perfectly compatible with the audience and the occasion it affirms and simultaneously seeks to alter. An appropriate expression reveals the rhetor's rhetorical readiness and evokes the audience's gratitude; conversely, an inappropriate expression indicates a misreading on the rhetor's part and a mismeeting between rhetor and audience. If what is spoken is the result of a misreading on the part of the rhetor, it subsequently becomes obvious to us, even to him, that "this was not the right thing to say." If silence is called for and the response is speech, we have a rhetor misspeaking to an audience not ready to listen, or not ready to listen to what he has to say, or ready to listen but not to the things he is saying. If speech is needed and silence prevails instead, we have a rhetor who has misread the situation, a frustrated audience whose needs and expectations are not met, and a situation that perpetuates itself.

Both timeliness and appropriateness are rhetorical motifs whose essence cannot be apprehended strictly cognitively and whose application cannot be learnt mechanically.[25] As George Kennedy states, "The two together constitute what may be called the artistic elements in rhetorical theory as opposed to the prescribed rules."[26] Unlike rigid scientific principles, the two are more a matter of feeling. Some of the factors contributing to one's sense of the timely and the appropriate are one's discretionary powers, the cultural norms in which he participates, his reading of the situation he wishes to address, his image of his audience, and his prediction of the potential effects of his words on his listeners. Timeliness and appropriateness are similar qualities in the sense that they render an expression more persuasive. What is said, then, must be both appropriate to time, or timely, and appropriate to the audience and the occasion. Untimely and appropriate speech cannot move an audience because it is untimely; similarly, timely and inappropriate speech cannot achieve its aims because it is inappropriate. If persuasion is to occur, both qualities must be present in the spoken word. In short, the right thing must be said at the right time; inversely, the right time becomes apparent precisely because the right thing has been spoken.

As pointed out earlier, these two qualities are vague in conceptualization and elastic in application. Their observance does not "confine reality within a dogmatic scheme but allow[s] it to rage in all its contradictions, in all its tragic intensity, in all its impartiality imposed by an intelligibility which will revive the joy of truth."[27] Because the rhetorician concerns himself with the particular and the pragmatic, his way is not that of an abstract absolutism created in the spirit of *a priori* truths; rather, it is that of a relativism of concrete rhetorical situations to which situationally derived truths are the only opportune and appropriate responses. But the rhetorician is not confined to a single movement. After he captures the appropriate and places it temporally, he moves toward the suggestion of the possible. The starting point for the articulation of the possible is the ontological assumption that the main driving forces in man's life are his desires,[28] especially the desire to be other and to be elsewhere. Another relevant assumption is that the sphere of actuality always entails a lack, the absence of that which exists only in the future; more particularly, that actuality frustrates man when he dreams of being other and binds him to where he already is when he wants to be elsewhere.

Consideration of the possible affirms in man the desire to be at another place or at another time and takes him away from the world of actuality and transports him in that of potentiality. Moreover, it intensifies in him the awareness that actuality is hostile to what he wishes and, as such, denies its existence. Finally, it refines his wishes and shows him how to apply them, what to ask, and whom to reach.[29] To be sure, man walks on earth and his feet are a constant reminder of his connection to the ground. But at the same time, he looks at the horizon about him and perceives himself "not as he is, not where he is, but precisely as he is not and where he is not." Even though he functions daily in the world of actuality, he often finds himself concerned with his situation not as it is here-and-now but as it could be there-and-then. Thus, he participates at once in two worlds each of which opposes the other. For Georges Poulet, man finds himself in "two realities which simultaneously exist at a distance and which reciprocally deny each other: the reality in which one lives and that in which one does not live, the place in which one has situated one's dream and the place where with horror one sees oneself surrendered to chance and ill luck."[30]

This is where the rhetorician steps in and helps him resolve his existential dilemma. By exploiting people's proclivity to perceive themselves in the future and their readiness to thrust themselves into unknown regions, the rhetorician tells them what they could be, brings out in them futuristic versions of themselves, and sets before them both goals and the directions which lead to those goals. All this he does by creating and presenting to them that which has the potential to be, but is not. Thus it is no paradox to say that rhetoric strives to create and labors to put forth, to propose that which is not.

The rhetorician concerns himself with the possible because he refuses to keep people in their actual situation. Granted, he must initially address them as they are and where they are. The earlier discussion about *kairos* and *to prepon* established that. But subsequently he tries to lift them from the vicissitudes of custom and habit and take them into a new place where new discoveries and new conquests can be made. Gorgias hints at this notion in the *Encomium to Helen* (5) when he states that "to tell the knowing what they know has credibility but brings no delight." Gorgias is stressing here that to speak about actualities to those who are already aware of them is nearly a purposeless act[31] whose most notable defect is that it fails to please the audience. But if by relying on actualities we fall short of our rhetorical ends, where should we turn? The *Encomium to Helen* suggests that the province of rhetoric is the possible, that which has not yet occurred to the audience. Following his own example, Gorgias argues that one of the causes of Helen's abduction is the might of *logos* (a presumably novel idea not previously entertained by those familiar with her story).

A special dimension of the possible, then, is afforded by the novel,[32] the unusual, that prior to which we have no awareness, the unprecedented. As a group, the Sophists are known to have been the first to say or do a number of things. Several fragments testify to their novel claims and practices: 80 A1 (51) and (52); 82 A1 (1), A1a, A4 (4); 84 A1O; 85 A3; 86 A2. Xenophon tells us that Hippias told Socrates once: "I always try to say something new"[33] [86 A14 (6)] clarifying at the same time that he did so on matters which admit of subjective treatment (i.e., justice) and agreeing that on such subjects as arithmetic the novel has no place. Aristotle, pointing out one of the effects of the novel on audiences, refers to Prodicus, who thought that announcing that what one is about to say has never been heard before can literally awaken a drowsy audience (*Rhetoric* 1415b). Read together, the above fragments imply, as Aristotle remarks, that people are "admirers of things which are not part of their experience" (*Rhetoric* 1404b), and are drawn to them because they raise their curiosity and carry an element of surprise. New thoughts, new insights, and new ideas always attract our attention not only because we have not encountered them before but also because they offer us new ways to perceive ourselves and the world. On the other hand, things with which we are familiar condition our responses and restrict our actions.

The possible is the opposite of the actual. A derivative of the Heracleitean perspective, evoking the possible challenges the one and advances the manifold; it rejects permanence and favors change; it privileges becoming over being. Unlike the actual, the possible is not a given which can be known or verified; it exists in the future as something incomplete and dormant, something awaiting the proper conditions to be realized. Therefore, its evocation goes hand in hand with hope and modesty; hope because the speaker always awaits his listeners' contribution, which will bring the possible to completion and realization; and modesty because what the speaker says is always potentially dismissable. By voicing the possible, the rhetor discloses his vision of a new world to his listeners and invites them to join him there by honoring his disclosure and by adopting his suggestion. Essentially, he is asking them to abandon the shelter of their prudential heaven and opt for that which exists "by favor of human imagination and effort."[34] Of course, the risk always exists that the audience may decline his invitation. But this is a risk he must face if he dares stand up and offer an alternative to the mundanity, the mediocrity, or misery of those he wishes to address.

The possible is an aspect of non-actuality claiming that, given the proper chance, it can turn into something actual. And even though it opposes the actual, it always seeks to become actualized. In and through the speech of the rhetor, the seed of the possible is planted in the ground of actuality. However, its roots do not begin to form until

the audience fails to see "why not," until they cannot find any reason to frustrate or repudiate it. Granted, the rhetor must show them why they ought to adopt his possible; the tradition of rhetoric demands that propositions be justified. At the same time, he must go one step further and ask them to find reasons, their reasons, should they be inclined to say no. Thus, Gorgias asks in the *Encomium to Helen* (12): "What cause then prevents the conclusion that Helen . . . might have come under the influence of speech?" This rhetorical question pits the actual belief (Helen is blameworthy as a woman with loose morals) against the possible belief (she is not to blame because she fell under the might of speech). The same approach is taken by Thrasymachus, who asks in *The Constitution* (B1): "Why should anyone put off speaking [what] is in his mind, if [it has fallen] to him to be injured by the present situation and he thinks he is on to something that will put an end to such things?" In this instance, the possible Thrasymachus wishes to have his listeners adopt is speaking openly and with no hesitation, something which presumably will end their pain. In both cases, the rhetor is asking the audience to discover at least one reason why the conclusion suggested should not be the case. Should they fail, they ought to adopt what he says; should they succeed, they have grounds on which to reject what he advocates. In the former case, the possible is well on its way to actuality; but even in the latter, it has served a useful function: it has provided the challenge in response to which the listeners have reexamined their actual situation. That they may decide to affirm their previously held views is not that important. What is more important is that by doing so they have moved from accepting actuality uncritically, as it is and because it is, to accepting it deliberately, because it has withstood the challenge of a possible. To use Heidegger's language, they have moved closer to the realm of authenticity.

In this essay I have argued that the history of rhetoric dictates that the Sophists' views regarding the art of discourse need wider notice and further exploration. Extracting key ideas and terms from the preserved fragments of the Sophists, I have suggested a "sophistic" definition of rhetoric founded on and consistent with the notions of rhetoric as art, style as personal expression, the timely, the appropriate, and the possible. This definition posits that man is driven primarily by his desire to be other, the wish to move from the sphere of actuality to that of possibility. Moreover, it points out that as man becomes what he is not he encounters situations to which he often responds with language. It also suggests that if man's responses are to be effective, they must take into account the temporal and formal structure of the situations he addresses. As such, they must be guided by his sense of time and propriety, and must be formulated in ways consonant with himself. Finally, this definition stresses that the whole enterprise of symbolic expression falls within the region of art.

Since the time of the Sophists, the area over which this definition extends has been covered with rigor far greater than I can muster. Therefore, I do not claim to have introduced new ideas in the field of rhetorical theory. However, the contribution of this essay is threefold: (1) it establishes that the Sophists' rhetorical practices are founded upon a coherent notion of rhetoric, (2) it articulates that notion, and (3) it reinforces the often neglected idea that some of our contemporary concepts about rhetoric originated with the Sophists.

NOTES

1. By "Sophists," I refer to those commonly recognized as the major figures of this group of teachers of rhetoric, i.e., Protagoras, Gorgias, Prodicus, Antiphon, Hippias, Critias, and Thrasymachus.

2. G. W. F. Hegel, *Lectures in the History of Philosophy*, trans. E. S. Haldane (New York: Humanities Press, 1963), pp. 352–354.

3. See Mario Untersteiner, *The Sophists*, trans. Kathleen Freeman (New York: Philosophical Library, 1954); Laszlo Versenyi, *Socratic Humanism* (New Haven, CT: Yale University Press, 1963); E. M. Cope, "On the Sophistical Rhetoric," *Journal of Classical and Sacred Philology* 2 (1855): 126–169, and 3 (1856): 34–80, 253–258. For a more detailed list, see W. K. C. Guthrie, *The Sophists* (London: Cambridge University Press, 1971), pp. 9–13.

4. When I say "sophistic" rhetoric, I do not mean to disregard the fact that in many cases the Sophists differed in their views on rhetoric. Rather, I mean to emphasize those common elements among them which permit us to regard them as a group.

5. Hegel, *Lectures*, p. 355.

6. Ibid., p. 358.

7. Regarding the meaning of the term *techné*, Guthrie remarks: "No English word produces exactly the same effect as the Greek *techné*. 'Art' suffers from its aesthetic associations, and also from the opposition between 'the arts' and the natural sciences. Those who know no Greek may be helped by the term itself: its incorporation in our 'technical' and 'technology' is not

fortuitous. It includes every branch of human or divine (cf. Plato, *Soph.* 265e) skill, or applied intelligence, as opposed to the unaided work of nature" (*The Sophists*, p. 115, n. 3).

8. For an insightful discussion on the relationship between *pistis* and *terpsis*, see Charles P. Segal, "Gorgias and the Psychology of the Logos," *Harvard Studies in Classical Philology* 66 (1962): 119ff.

9. Philodemus, *Rhetoric*, 2.49. Cited in Hermann Diels and Walther Kranz, *Die Fragmente der Vorsokratiker* (Berlin: Weidmannsche Verlagsbuchhandlung, 1952), 85 B7a. All subsequent fragments are from this source. The translation of this fragment is by Francis E. Sparshott, in Rosamond K. Sprague, ed., *The Older Sophists* (Columbia: University of South Carolina Press, 1972). Unless otherwise specified, the translations which follow are mine. I have taken fewer liberties with the texts than have other translators and have tried to remain as faithful as possible to the Greek. As a result, the reader will note, the English in several cases is awkward.

10. In the *Gorgias* 463b, Socrates refers to rhetoric as *kolakeia* (flattery) and refutes Gorgias by saying that rhetoric is not art but *empeiria* and *tribe* ("habitude" and "knack"). On the other hand, Aristotle, although he does refer to rhetoric as art (*Rhetoric*, 1402a), conceives of it primarily as a faculty (*dynamis*); see *Rhetoric*, 1355b and 1359b.

11. For Plato's criticism of rhetoric, see the *Gorgias* and the *Phaedrus*.

12. A useful discussion of the notion of contingency is provided by Robert L. Scott, "On Viewing Rhetoric as Epistemic," *Central States Speech Journal* 15 (1967): 9–17 [reprinted in this volume].

13. Aristotle, *Rhetoric*, 1354a.

14. Ibid., 1404a. This is Rhys Roberts's translation and I have included it for syntactical purposes. A more literal translation is given by E. M. Cope: "for it makes *some* difference in the clearness of an explanation whether we speak in one way or another"; see Cope, in John E. Sandys, ed., *The Rhetoric of Aristotle* (London: Cambridge University Press, 1877).

15. J. S. Morrison's translation, in *The Older Sophists*.

16. Aristotle, *Rhetoric*, 1404a.

17. Ibid., 1403b; emphasis added.

18. With the exception of minor changes, this is George Kennedy's translation in *The Older Sophists*. On a more focused comment, Suidas writes that Gorgias "was the first to give to the rhetorical genre the verbal power and art of deliberate culture and employed tropes and metaphors and allegories and hypallage and catachreses and hyperbata and doublings of words and repetitions and apostrophes and isokola" (82 A2; Kennedy's translation with minor changes).

19. Georges Gusdorf, the phenomenologist, says

that "style signifies the task given to man of becoming aware of perspective. Each of us, even the most simple of mortals, is charged with finding the expression to fit his situation. Each of us is charged with realizing himself in a language, a personal echo of the language of all which represents his contribution to the human world. The struggle for style is the struggle for consciousness (la vie spirituelle)"; see *Speaking* (*La parole*), trans. Paul Brockelman (Evanston, IL: Northwestern University Press, 1965), p. 76.

20. Bromley Smith demonstrates how this is so in his article "Gorgias: A Study of Oratorical Style," *Quarterly Journal of Speech Education* 7 (1921): 335–359.

21. Sparshott's translation, in *The Older Sophists*.

22. For a discussion of the merits of impromptu speaking, see Alcidamas's *On Those Who Write Written Speeches or On the Sophists*. Since Alcidamas was Gorgias's student, it is not unreasonable to suppose that some of his views coincide with those of other Sophists.

23. This view is expressed by Isocrates in *Against the Sophists*, 293 (13): "for it is not possible for speeches to be good if they do not partake of the opportune moments, and the appropriate and the novel." For a treatment of the moment as a criterion of the value of speech, see Gusdorf's *Speaking*, p. 85.

24. Ibid.

25. Untersteiner stresses this point in *The Sophists*, p. 198.

26. George Kennedy, *The Art of Persuasion in Greece* (Princeton, NJ: Princeton University Press, 1963), p. 67.

27. Untersteiner, *The Sophists*, p. xvi.

28. Hegel, *Lectures*, p. 358.

29. Georges Poulet, *The Interior Distance*, trans. Elliott Coleman (Ann Arbor: University of Michigan Press, 1959), p. 239.

30. Ibid., p. 240.

31. Aristotle points out that "about those things which we know or have decided there is no further use in speaking about them"; see *Rhetoric*, 1391b.

32. See note 23, above.

33. Ibid. As if he is echoing Hippias's comment, Gusdorf writes: "The great artist avoids imitating even himself. He continually undertakes the task of remaining vigilantly aware of the world of words, a task forever unfinished because the world changes and is renewed, and living man with it" (*Speaking*, p. 75).

34. Richard Weaver, *The Ethics of Rhetoric* (Chicago: Henry Regnery, 1953), p. 20.

Status, Marginality, and Rhetorical Theory

Robert Hariman

The history of rhetorical studies includes recurrent discussion of the proper demarcating of rhetoric and dialectic, rhetoric and poetic, rhetoric and logic, and similar divisions of the verbal arts. Although such comparisons are unavoidable when defining any type of discourse, they have a special significance for rhetoric. Rhetoric as a tradition of erudition has been shaped powerfully by the debates over the relative worth of its subject, and these debates have been inseparable from the activity of categorizing the several kinds of discourse.

The story of the ruling comparisons in the history of rhetoric is well known: Plato placed heavy sanctions upon rhetoric by subordinating it to dialectic; Aristotle gave rhetoric a more generous appraisal; Cicero and Quintilian reversed Plato's order; Augustine recovered rhetoric from the censure of pagan letters by other Church Fathers; Ramus removed rhetoric from the major curriculum of European letters, and so forth. What has not been done is to ask why the arts of language were compared so aggressively, and compared with such a heavy emphasis upon their relative superiority or inferiority. We do have excellent glosses on the arguments advanced to justify the specific comparisons, but we have not considered the comparisons as means to an end.

This project of demarcating the universe of discourse is particularly intense today, when there is widespread intellectual debate regarding the "end of philosophy" and the resurrection by continental writers of such antiquities as hermeneutics and the rhetoric of tropes. Calvin Schrag has underscored the significance of this situation for rhetorical studies by pointing to the "complex phenomenon of the emergence of philosophy from rhetoric and its subsequent return"[1] and calling for a "complementary deconstruction of rhetoric"[2] that would create a "shared milieu of self and social understanding."[3] I propose to continue this process of radical reflection, considering how the arts of language are determined by some of the harsher elements in their common sociality.

This essay will suggest how arguments about genres of discourse often contain, as a crucial element, an attribution of *status*. That is, the act of comparing discourses implies both manifest definitions of substance and latent attributions of status for each genre, and the disputes about categorizing discourses often are concerned more with questions of status than of substance. Status is the determination by one's associates of one's worth relative to their worth, and includes one's rank, reputation, respect, esteem, prestige, or place. The attribution of status to genre is a device for establishing the privileges—and powers—of those discourses in the verbal sciences. By focusing upon those comparisons that attribute an inferior status to rhetoric, the particular dynamic of empowering through status can be identified: as superior status is a condition of social *privilege*, so inferior status is a condition of social *marginality*, and we empower discourses by imposing a social order upon the world that relegates words, writers, and speakers to zones of centrality or marginality.

My argument is about a question of significance. It is obvious that theorists always have ranked discourses, and that they have, while ranking, praised their preferred art and faulted others, and that they have, while praising and faulting, indulged the more temperamental side of their thinking. When philosophers (say, Plato) denounce rhetoric, or when rhetoricians (say, Cicero) ridicule philosophy, they seem to be engaging in the inevitable but trivial vanity and irascibility accompanying all human endeavor.[4] They do not seem to be revealing a fundamental characteristic of their arguments or, by extension, of our intellectual tradition. We should recognize, however, that such appraisals are grounded in the division of discourses: the text has been divided, according to a dissociation of terms, into the (real) language of argument and the (apparent) language of arguing. By dismissing the status claims, we overlook the deconstructive character of the theorists' texts: for the status claim accompanying the substantive conception of genre is precisely the manner in which the theoretical text simultaneously asserts and denies its own authority. It seems, then, that there is a possibility that a process of mystification has been at work in our thinking. Linguistic theorists, and especially rhetorical theorists, think by means of a technique that they also describe as trivial. Perhaps this paradox can be corrected by recognizing how sociality is an essential constituent of linguistic power in theoretical discourse and how marginality is a conventional condition of rhetorical studies.

This essay first will present representative examples of arguments about genre that contain attributions of status, then examine the dynamic of marginality that is the source of the attributions' power, and conclude by discussing the implications of these claims for the politics of rhetorical theory and the ontology of rhetorical discourse.

Status

Rhetoric will always have to answer to Plato's questioning of its merit. Moreover, Plato's investigation of rhetoric is inseparable from his relentless attack upon the status held by the Sophists in his community. Nor can we escape this fact by distinguishing between speaker (the persons he knew as Sophists) and discourse, for each serves in his dialogues as a metonym for the other. Whatever

the sublimity of the Platonic dialogues, the definitions of rhetoric are marked by irony and sarcasm. Through his famous metaphor of cookery, for example, rhetoric is simultaneously defined and shamed.

This emphasis upon Plato's tone need not deny the important qualifications to his conception of rhetoric. Contemporary scholars have devoted extensive discussion to at least four counterpoints: Plato's concomitant suggestion of an ideal rhetoric; his incorporation of some elements of *mythos* into his philosophical system; his incorporation of irony, paradox, and outright contradiction in his dialogues; and the corresponding complexity and difficulty of the dialectic he offers as an alternative to rhetoric.[5] On the other hand, emphasis upon these fascinating considerations can obstruct reconsideration of the more obvious, though not less simple, facts of the original attack and, more importantly, its historical import. This paper approaches its subject by returning to the observation Edwin Black provided several decades ago: "Indeed, the only uniformity which crystallizes from this diversity of interpretation is the judgment that Plato disapproved of rhetoric, and was, in fact, rhetoric's most effective historical opponent."[6]

Unfortunately, Plato has too often escaped Cicero's observation that "what impressed me most deeply about Plato in that book was, that it was when making fun of orators that he himself seemed to me to be the consummate orator."[7] Cicero is raising a question of motive, and indicating that Plato's strategy is to denigrate rhetoric in order to elevate philosophy as a privileged subject. For example, in the *Gorgias* Socrates contrasts philosophy to public opinion—philosophy is always true and never capricious like the public—at once stating what each subject is and marking its value.[8] The *Phaedrus* contains explicit discussions of the inferiority of writing, reading, and rhetoric when they are compared to the superior acts of philosophical discussion, reasoning, and dialectic. By the time Socrates concludes by telling the boy resolutely that the lover of wisdom must "disdain" all manner of discourse other than that of philosophy, which is discriminated as the highest form of instruction of the soul on justice, honor, and goodness, Plato has created a philosophical discourse in part by ordering all discourse beneath his own, and he has delineated philosophy by contrasting it with the inferior social good of rhetoric.[9] In Samuel Ijsseling's summary, "One can even say that Platonic philosophy arose within the polemic against the orator and the sophist."[10]

Plato's attack on rhetoric demonstrates a powerful version of a common strategy: we determine what any of the arts of language is by stating how important it is. We define dialectic, or poetics, or dialogue, or investigative reporting by both saying what it is and where it is in some social order. This strategy is more than a restatement of Kenneth Burke's "paradox of substance," for the social placement is more than saying what something is by saying what it is not.[11] That attribution of status says that something is something because it is valued as something, and this reciprocity between individual substance and social position generates more than ambiguity and the possibility of semantic transformation; I argue below that it generates power.

Moreover, this authorizing of discourses by ranking them socially often is accomplished by demonstrating how the preferred art is *not* mere rhetoric. Although there is no necessary relation between these discourses, for any can be superior or inferior (as later examples will show), the arts of language often are defined as subjects of inquiry by being declared superior to rhetoric. The denouncing of rhetoric has become a convention of linguistic theory. As diverse scholars have suggested, this convention has predominated in the modern era—that is, at least since the Enlightenment.[12]

Immanuel Kant provides the clearest example of this strategy in his *Critique of Judgment*. The chapter "Comparison of the Respective Aesthetical Worth of the Beautiful Arts" begins by granting poetry "the first rank" and identifying the substance and function of that art: "It expands the mind by setting the Imagination at liberty; . . . It strengthens the mind by making it feel its faculty . . . of considering and judging nature as . . . a sort of schema for, the supersensible."[13] Kant then interrupts his ranking to contrast poetry with rhetoric, known as the "art of persuasion, i.e., of deceiving by a beautiful show."[14] Although Kant recognizes distinctions between better and worse forms of rhetoric and does not ban its practice altogether from the arts or civil society, his basic appraisal is thoroughly negative: rhetoric uses illusion not to liberate the understanding but to preclude judgment and deprive us of our freedom. Moreover, he concludes by declaring that "the art of availing oneself of the weaknesses of men for one's own designs (whether these be well meant or even actually good does not matter) is worthy of no *respect*."[15] Only after this contrast between poetry and rhetoric does Kant return to the task of identifying the other arts by ranking them in descending order from poetry. Thus, he has elaborated his aesthetic philosophy by simultaneously defining the arts, ranking them according to a hierarchy of social values, and denigrating rhetoric.

John Locke provides another example. Locke concludes the third chapter of his *Essay on Human Understanding*, "On Words," by discussing the "Imperfection" and "Abuse" of words and offering his "Remedies." Locke faults both of the Schoolmen's arts of language—rhetoric and dialectic—and offers his remedies as the means of restoring both civil discourse and philosophy. He begins by contrasting civil and philosophical communication, giving the latter the greater exactness, and then bemoans the false estimation granted the other arts of language. Rhetoric, known by the "artificial and figurative application of words," gives us "perfect cheats" and its general practice brings Locke to conclude that:

> I cannot but observe how little the preservation and improvement of truth and knowledge is the care and concern of mankind; since the arts of fallacy are endowed and preferred. It is evident how much men love to deceive and be deceived, since rhetoric, that powerful instrument of error and deceit, has its established professors, is publicly taught, and has always been had in great reputation.[16]

Locke's argument is a bit more complicated than Kant's, for he explicitly contests a received ranking, and places more emphasis upon the deceitfulness of the art. Locke's inverting of the received hierarchy into his rightful, vernacular society of plain words has the same effect as Kant's more pedantic rebuff: his discourse is found to be more honorable than another. In sum, both the rationalist and the empiricist follow the same pattern, for in each case an argument for a change in philosophical method is joined with an argument over status containing a condemnation of rhetoric.

Note also how such discourse contains a technique for concealing its inherent textuality. Kant and Locke (and Plato) are each demonstrating the dissociation of concepts: they restructure the received unity of all discourse into separate realms of appearance and reality, and thereby erase the assumption that rhetoric and philosophy are both arts of language.[17] This dissociation is activated by identifying rhetoric with "deceit" and "show," against the implicit artlessness of their discourse.

Moreover, the simultaneous association of appearance with patently social acts—e.g., one deceives others, shows to others—also conceals the inherent sociality of the superior discourse: it suggests that their ranking of discourses is itself not constituted by the approval of others. These writers succeed not only at incorporating into their texts signs of the "transtextual" quality of truthfulness, but also at defining their opponents as merely social—rather than philosophical—creatures, while they engage in the quintessentially social act of sneering.

At this point I should stress that rhetoric does not have to be the denigrated genre. The nature of status—of any social condition—is that it exists by attribution; no praise or blame is inevitable in establishing a hierarchy. Rhetoric was the superior art in ancient Rome and throughout the Renaissance. Occasionally it has escaped mention altogether. For example, philosophy also has been aligned against poetry. Anicius Boethius begins *The Consolation of Philosophy* with a scene from his sickbed, where he is "driven by grief to shelter in sad songs."[18] The scene is conventional: author attributing his genius to the muses, whose naming will serve as his [foreword] to the work (recall the naming of the god in *Phaedrus*). This scene is interrupted, however, by a majestic woman in ethereal garb. Her gown is hemmed with the letter Pi (for practical philosophy) at the bottom and the letter Theta (for speculative philosophy) at the top, with a ladder of steps rising from the lower to the higher letter. Again, this personification of philosophy was not strange then and remains comprehensible today. But this story takes a turn away from the conventional depictions of the harmony of the arts:

> At the sight of the Muses of Poetry at my bedside dictating words to accompany my tears, she became angry. "Who," she demanded, her piercing eyes alight with fire, "has allowed these hysterical sluts to approach this sick man's bedside? They have no medicine to ease his pains, only sweetened poisons to make them worse. These are the very women who kill the rich and fruitful harvest of Reason with the barren thorns of Passion."[19]

Again, one verbal art has been placed above another in a social hierarchy, and the substance of the art (Reason) is defined simultaneously with a depiction of its status. By portraying poetry as the discourse of sluts, Boethius epitomizes the act of ranking-by-insult. The tactic is no less an ornament than the figures of personification and metaphor in his text, but it reminds us that all this ornamentation should be read reflectively,

and that the ornaments of exclusion should be included in our understanding of philosophy and of rhetoric as much as such already privileged figures of harmony as Apollo's chariot, the Symposium, or the music of the spheres.

Ranking discourses need not only privilege philosophy. Poetics has enjoyed in the twentieth century an autonomy and legitimacy previously unknown in its history. A large part of this success stems from one document—Shelley's *Defense of Poetry*, "one of the three or four greatest critical essays in the English language."[20] Shelley's essay is a response to Thomas Love Peacock's essay on "The Four Ages of Poetry," and the exchange is, start to finish, a debate about the status of poetry. Peacock's intention is to ridicule the Romantic poets already becoming renowned in his day. He proceeds by charting a cycle of four periods: of iron, gold, silver, and brass—with the Romantics then exemplifying the last. In each case he offers a perfect identification of rank and substance: for example, poetry of the iron age has, commensurate with its place in the hierarchy of human development, the subject of heroic exploits, the rhythms of oral composition, a diction of natural and supernatural images, and the social function of awakening the community to the dawn of civilization.[21] And so each rank of poetry is described, including the modern age of brass where poetry has the substance of "harmony, which is language on the rack of Procrustes; sentiment, which is canting egotism in the mask of refined feeling; passion, which is the commotion of a weak and selfish mind; pathos, which is the whining of an unmanly spirit; and sublimity, which is the inflation of an empty head."[22] Here insult piles upon insult as the moderns are condemned for their abandonment of thought and their indulgence of ornament—in sum, found unfit for the authority of "the political palm and the critical chair."[23]

Shelley's long reply takes the high road, generally eschewing insult for a sustained call to arms for his poetics, but maintains both the received fascination with status and the technique of ranking discourses. For example:

> The fame of legislators and founders of religions, so long as their institutions last, alone seems to exceed that of poets in the restricted sense; but it can scarcely be a question, whether, if we deduct the celebrity which their flattery of the gross opinions of the vulgar usually conciliates, together with that, which belonged to them in their higher character of poets, any excess will remain.[24]

Shelley's "defense" also is an attack on the neoclassical social order which valued prose over poetry and declamation over aesthetics. (Shelley's antipathy to the rhetorical training of his day is not expressed prominently in his text but was obvious to his audience.) Rather than rebuke the rhetorical tradition directly, he devotes most of his argument to evoking hierarchies—of the faculties, the historical development of the species, our personal development, the arts, and so on—that are topped by poetic properties. Each placement—for example, "Reason is to the imagination as the instrument to the agent, as the body to the spirit, as the shadow to the substance"[25]—advances the battle for poetry's status while securing the accompanying definition of its substance. Throughout the essay this social consciousness is enhanced by frequent use of such adjectives as "highest," "loftiest," "imperial," and "majestic." Finally, Shelley brings us to the greatest hierarchy of all: "Poetry is indeed something divine."[26] This universal definition of substance begins a long elaboration of the claim in Plato's *Ion* that poetry is superior to knowledge, and ends with the assertion that "poets are the unacknowledged legislators of the world."[27] The substance of poetry—inspiration—is revealed through an argument for its status, and Shelley's genius—his status—is secured through his strategy of reversing the received hierarchy of discourses by locating the power of poetry in its unacknowledgment. We must acknowledge his triumph: poetry still is presumed by many to be an autonomous art ruled wholly by its internal laws.[28]

To summarize: the previous examples suggest how attributions of status are a characteristic of arguments about discourse, and also how rhetoric—or the techniques of ornamentation typically consigned to rhetoric—often are assigned an inferior status in regard to another discourse. But why would Plato or Kant go to such trouble—why labor to debunk the subject one is not inspired to study and magnify? What is it about their inquiry—and not their individual motives, which will remain opaque to us—that draws them to this act of censure? What is it about the act of censure that contributes to their inquiry?

Marginality

Status is a concomitant of socializing. Attributing status is a social act, perhaps the quintessential social act, for status cannot exist without the cooperation of other people and can exist then without any material support, consequence, or correlative. One's status is everything—people will kill for it—and nothing—other people may never acknowledge it. Status may be compared to the theatrical scrim: a cloth that can appear solid or translucent depending on how it is illuminated. Thus, in accepting that sociality is the foundation of thinking, one must accept this reversibility as a condition of one's thought. Perhaps Plato's attack upon rhetoric was an attack upon this limitation of sociality upon the powers of the mind: rhetoric was the metonym for sociality, and the status of the Sophists the surest sign of the nature of rhetoric. "At the outset Plato denied what was for Sophism the very foundation of man's humanness, his impulse to associate with his fellows within the social institution of the *polis*. He claimed that social intercourse necessarily destroys the philosophic act. Hence, solitude became a precondition for thought as he would have it understood."[29] Yet, as Cicero observed, Plato succeeds at having thought understood to be a transcendental rather than a social act because he appropriates the very qualities of thinking he advises against.

In other words, sociality is a contested characteristic of our intellectual tradition. We are social thinkers and we suppress this fact. My claim that theoretical discourse often includes as a crucial element attributions of status obviously is a reassertion of the primacy of the social qualities of our thinking. But what is the value of again stating that philosophy is not what Plato wanted it to be? The answer is that by deconstructing his case, we can uncover and study anew those varieties of thought that he suppressed.

To better understand why ranking is so powerful, we need a model of social thinking that is active in the arguments over the status of discourses. Every society distinguishes itself not only against the surrounding welter of people, places, and things, but by discriminating more and less acceptable or coherent behaviors within its experience. Any society, that is, conceives itself as having a center, a periphery, and a beyond. And the conception of the periphery—or margin—of the society is essential to the conception of the center. Social marginality is the zone of what is recognizable as pertaining to one's identity, but is undesirable. The margin of the society contains what one is but should not be, and the disciplining of the individual to avoid the margin is the means by which one is socialized. As Emile Durkheim and others have observed, marginal behavior is an essential part of society, something that cannot be eliminated without undermining a community's morality and cohesiveness.[30]

Attribution of status activates our sensitivity to social marginality. "High" status identifies a "central" substance and "low" status identifies a "marginal" substance. The differences between a physician and a quack, or a social drinker and a drunk, or a lady and a whore, or a Brahmin and an untouchable are differences between social centrality and social marginality. In each case the marginal character is necessary for the proper identification of the central character, the images of each contain reciprocal attributions of status and identity, and these operations themselves require social validation. These dynamics are epitomized in the insult, "an act, remark, or gesture which expresses a severely negative opinion of a person or group."[31] Insult is a subversion of one's status and it works by identifying one with the signs of marginality. Plato's describing rhetoric as cookery places it in the margin of his aristocracy, and Boethius' marking the Muses of poetry as sluts places them in the margin of his civil society. And the difference between the "harlot of the arts" and her sisters is the difference between marginality and authority. In every case the insult reveals the expectations of the social order, often with more economy and force than any positive declaration. In fact, by locating marginal behavior by insult, the social order receives implicit justification: it is superior to what is scorned. This is precisely the strategy in Saint Jerome's dream of being called before the throne of heaven to hear himself denounced as a "Ciceronianus."[32] Thus, "insult is one means by which social stratification systems are both constituted and maintained."[33] And so it also is one means by which we constitute and maintain those social stratification systems that are known as theories.

Arguments about status, then, do more than "ornament" definitions of substance: the attribution of status activates a pattern of thinking. This pattern of thinking is profoundly social: it is the marking of symbols according to their centrality or marginality to the society of the thinker. And this marking gives the symbols their power within the society. For every society constitutes itself by emphasizing and deemphasizing—sanctioning and censuring—the various human potencies. Those symbols marked as central to a society draw upon those powers amplified by the society's economy, institutions, and so on. Those marked as marginal are denied those powers, but they also acquire access to those potencies suppressed by the society. That is why the argument over status is important to the arguers: they are competing for the powers of argument, the powers that they then can transfer to their own thinking. Stated otherwise, the function of placing a discourse in the condition of social marginality is to determine the conditions for power (and powerlessness) in the other, non-marginal genres of discourse. As Mary Douglas observed in her study of pollution symbolism, "granted that disorder spoils pattern; it also provides the materials of pattern. . . . its potential for patterning is indefinite. . . . It symbolizes both danger and power."[34]

The dependence of the theorist upon this pattern of thinking follows not from the accident of being socially conditioned, but from the theorist's task of discriminating and amplifying the powers of the mind. This process of selective use requires subordination of those potencies not selected. So the powers of mind are authorized by their assertion over other powers. Thus, Kant consigns to marginality the powers of appearance in order to create transcendental facts; Locke suppresses the power of social inheritance in order to create representational meanings; Boethius suppresses the power of Passion in order to create a redeeming Reason; and Shelley displaces the power of declamation in order to authorize the imagination.

Moreover, the discourse marked as marginal then acquires those powers suppressed within the society, and consequently becomes less comprehensible. Marginal discourse must be seen as essentially confused, inarticulate, flawed. This attribution of inchoateness serves the society in two ways: it is used to discipline speaking, to keep speech within the margins, and it remains a continual source of symbolic renewal, a resource for creating new hierarchies. So marginality can be understood as the internal dynamic of social thinking used to generate verbal power, and as a limitation upon the words given social sanction, and as a condition of being for those words placed in the margin. This last observation provides my point of departure for discussion of both the politics of rhetorical theory and the ontology of rhetorical discourse.

The Politics of Rhetorical Theory

The first implication of my argument, that status arguments create conditions of marginality that determine our understanding, is that theoretical discourse is political discourse—that is, it inevitably establishes relations of dominance and subordination. It is political not only because it is determined by the "extra-literary" or "material" conditions of its production, but also because it produces conditions of empowerment which also become conditions of knowing. If substance and status were wholly separate properties of genre, then questions of ranking, and of the anxieties and altercations of ranking, might be questions of circumstance and incident alone. The interdependence of status and substance provides a denominator for knowledge and power, however. Shelley's ranking of discourses is a *sine qua non* of his concept of the imagination and his assertion of its imperial role in the invention of discourse, and his ranking continues to dominate the division of powers between rhetoric and poetics. Plato's depicting rhetoric as dishonorable separated truth and textuality in Western culture, and his authority remains unassailable as long as his technique remains concealed.

The next implication is that theoretical discourse can be analyzed as a restatement of comprehensive conditions of authority and marginality. This claim is more than a restatement of Kenneth Burke's observation that any selection of reality is a deflection of reality, for the condition of marginality changes that which is deflected.[35] To empower discourse one must do what always is done to create power through discourse—consign someone to marginality—and this mutual defining of self and other as esteemed and marginal is a process of transformation: each individual is made into a social character. Consigning a type of discourse to marginality involves more than a subsequent inattention to the discourse: it necessitates an alternation, a change in the substance of the discourse. And given the shared sociality of the different genres, this change is matched by a change in the privileged discourse. Although the specific character given to any genre will depend upon the social nuances of its placement, the attribution of marginality is likely to follow a general disposition to identify the marginal with the incomplete, confused, or inchoate. Thus, we should avoid seeing Plato and Kant assigning the same marginality to rhetoric—just as we would avoid claiming that they adhere to an identical idealism—but we should ask if they each assign rhetoric mutually incongruous properties, such as being both capricious and confining. They do, and they can do so because rhetoric's marginal placement transforms it from a comprehensible practice to the condition of disorientation that must be corrected by the authorized practice of philosophy.

The fact that theories of discourse are in part arguments over the conditions of authority and marginality carries particular significance for rhetorical theory. Obviously, rhetoric often has been conceived as a marginal form of discourse, and this placement conditions the rationale for a rhetorical theory: if rhetorical discourse is marginal, either there is no need for a rhetorical theory, or there is need only for a rhetorical theory designed to monitor and restrain rhetorical discourse. The dispute over the extent of Plato's objection to rhetoric can be allayed if we consider that he was writing *Phaedrus* as a program for restraining the dangerous impulses of marginality.[36] Consider the image of Apollo reining in the dark horse alongside the white horse as they pull his chariot across the heavens. The horse has the sure marks of marginality, for he is flawed: "[he] is crooked of frame, a massive jumble of a creature, with thick short neck, snub nose, black skin, and grey eyes; hot-blooded, consorting with wantonness and vainglory; shaggy of ear, deaf, and hard to control with whip and goad."[37] Plato tells us that rhetoric cannot be banished entirely and can give us the power to approach the truth, but only if yoked to a superior form and properly controlled. Despite his case for an ideal rhetoric, Plato's definition of actual rhetoric unmistakably places it in the condition of being marginal in respect to another discourse.

But the first possibility remains the most debilitating: rhetorical theory is written under a particular burden—the inherited sentence that it should not be written at all. Stated otherwise, rhetorical theory is aggressively deconstructive, subverting its authority to adjudicate discourses by emphasizing its reliance upon philosophically unacceptable discourse. This interdiction of the tendency of rhetoric to account for itself has specific consequences. Although rhetoric cannot escape its history as the discourse conventionally used to establish the margin for authorizing other discourses, the history of rhetoric can be better understood as characterized by this tension between marginality and authority. The primary implication of my thesis for rhetorical theory is that this tradition of erudition can be analyzed as a continuing reaction to the use of rhetoric as a margin by other theorists of language. Because all theories of discourse are in part prolonged arguments for the status of their subjects, and since rhetoric often is used conventionally in those arguments as the inferior discourse, rhetorical theorists usually assume the special burden of arguing that rhetoric is *not* the inferior art. Rhetorical theory begins in the zone of the philosophically unacceptable, as an asylum. This burden is one reason why so many rhetorical theories are labeled a New Rhetoric.[38] Whereas other humanists would be happy to see their work as cumulative, the rhetorician is burdened with a commitment to a perpetual revolution. Thus Paul de Man can discover that "the aporia between performative and constative language is merely a version of the aporia between trope and persuasion that both generates and paralyzes rhetoric and thus gives it the appearance of a history."[39] Stated otherwise, rhetorical theory is grounded in the contradiction of elaborating a condition of self-doubt.

It should not be surprising that many of the "innovations" in rhetorical theory are denials of the use of rhetoric as the margin for the philosophical subject. Aristotle obviously is the most significant example here: his opening declaration that "rhetoric is the counterpart of dialectic" is a patent argument about the status of rhetoric and specifically designed to dismantle the Platonic hierarchy of discourses which obstructed an appreciative investigation of rhetoric.[40] Kenneth Burke's *A Rhetoric of Motives* not only appropriates Aristotle's appraisal of rhetorical inquiry, it also ponders mightily the "spirit of hierarchy" he finds suffusing rhetorical discourse. As he has summarized his *Rhetoric*: "It concerns the relations that characterize a ladder of Mr. Bigs and Mr. Littles, all along the line, up and down, with the 'magic' of these."[41] Much of the work done by contemporary scholars on the relationship between philosophy and rhetoric also has been directed to contest their received hierarchy of discourses (and specifically the hierarchy and logic of theoretical reduction developed by the analytical and positivist philosophers in this century).[42] Richard Weaver's work consistently was directed to rehabilitate the status of the orator to that of the nineteenth-century figure who had "a peculiar sense of stature. He always talked like a big man."[43]

Perhaps the most obvious contemporary example of a theory offering a strategy for escaping the peculiar burden of rhetorical studies is Robert L. Scott's conception of "rhetoric as epistemic." Scott begins by addressing the inferior status of rhetoric: "Professing rhetoric seems always eventually to lead to embarrassment. . . . At best good men

grant rhetoric a slight role but grudgingly."[44] His argument then works both to change our discrimination of the rhetorical subject from a skill to a way of knowing and to elevate the status of the subject. Notice also how Scott's essay moves from his urging that we read rhetoric as a way of knowing to his provision of the concepts of toleration, will, and responsibility as the means of knowing rhetorically. He has shifted from epistemology to an ethic—what he believes is the proper attitude for interlocutors to have if they are to come to know by communicating. Here Scott exemplifies another motive informing the struggle to overcome the received condemnation of rhetoric: his ethic is a *perfecting* of the condition of sociality that is the ground of rhetoric. Even marginal discourse follows the logic of elaboration Burke identified as the motive for perfection, and we find any rhetorical theorist will be disposed, even in appreciating the marginality of rhetoric, to elaborate it into versions of itself ever more formally satisfying, such that eventually Burke's irony would be confirmed by articulating a version of the marginal condition too elegant to still carry the perspective and powers of the margin.[45]

Scott's essay demonstrates that although this "rehabilitative" project is laudable, it does merit a caution.[46] Generally, we attempt to elevate ourselves by imitating our "superiors"; doing too much of that rarely is wise. In the case of rhetoric, the pursuit of such high-status commodities as "philosophy" or "hermeneutics" may result in losing the opportunity to explore the margins of our time. As rhetoric is marginal, it also is a reservoir of power—a zone of those potencies suppressed in our society. What philosophers label error is also knowable as desire or will or Eros or Thanatos or the ineradicable conflicts of the political unconscious and so on. This may be Stanley Deetz's intention when he claims that the function of rhetoric can be "intrinsic to the perception formation process, not in a positive manner, but through a denial, an affronting, of the forces of perceptual domination."[47] The rhetorical theorist inherits a tradition of study that contains ineradicable aporias, failed practices, and practices that were prevented from being valorized as traditions, and the excavation of these marginal discourses can never be a mere filling in of the record, for any change in their status will alter the authority of the dominant discourses. The convention of placing rhetoric in the margin should be read as a challenge, though not the challenge to secure respectability.

The Ontology of Rhetorical Discourse

Paolo Valesio observes that "in rhetoric more than in any other of the language sciences the metalanguage is closely interwoven with the ambiguities and conflicting connotations of the object language."[48] The reliance upon status claims is one example of how these languages partake of each other: whether a speaker claiming expert authority or a theorist dismissing another's work as partisan, rhetor and rhetorician follow a continuous pattern of ranking to activate the dynamics of marginality. At this point the politics of interpretation merges with questions about the ontology of the verbal world. I shall conclude by considering how reflecting upon the political character of rhetorical theory may lead to a better understanding of rhetorical discourse.

The division central to the conflict between philosophy and rhetoric has been that between *episteme* and *doxa*, knowledge and opinion. The relevant ontological question is, "What is the nature of *doxa*?" One answer suggested by the reciprocity of substance and status in theoretical discourse is that status is a constituent of *doxa*. More specifically, *doxa* can be understood better by identifying how it is a complex of the relations of regard, ranking, and concealment.

To the Greeks *doxa* meant not only opinion ("what seems to be the case to the person spoken of") but also reputation ("what seems to others to be the case with the person spoken of"), as well as expectation and fame. Martin Heidegger seizes upon this usage to explicate *doxa*:

> *Doxa* means aspect, regard [*Ansehen*], namely the regard in which one stands. If the regard, in keeping with what emerges in it, is a distinguished one, *doxa* means fame and glory. . . . For the Greeks glory was not something additional which one might or might not obtain; it was the mode of the highest being.[49]

Heidegger's insight exemplifies what some scholars call the "intersubjective" reality of rhetoric: that is, something that is not explained fully by the distinctions between subject and object or between fact and value.[50] The regard in which one is held is a property of (that is, changeable by) both the community and the individual, and it is both a description of one's being and one's worth. In other words, regard epitomizes the reciprocity of substance and status in the verbal world. One is what one is said to be. Although we find some

speech forms, such as encomia and insults, assuming the greater burden of invoking regard, the perseverance of this motive in even our "higher" discourses, such as those discourses about discourses we label theories, suggests that regard is a part of the sociality of discourse, and therefore a means of emphasizing the patterns of social thinking.

Regard is one product of the act of ranking, as when we say, "She is held in the highest regard." The ranking of genres so prevalent in statements about the arts and sciences suggests that ranking may be an important metonym of verbal reality. If *doxa* involves an act of regard, then it can be understood as something that is meaningful in part because ranked. This provisional conceptualization accounts for the ontological ambiguity of *doxa*: on the one hand, an opinion is an assertion that something is what it is valued to be (that is, an opinion is inextricably both descriptive and normative), yet, on the other hand, anything ranked seems to possess a being prior to being ranked—there is a separation between its existence and its position—because that thing can also be present in alternative rankings. So *doxa* can exemplify the indivisibility of being and appearance, as well as their separation. This ambiguity raises the dilemma of grounding inquiry in opinion: opinion appears to be groundless yet essential for full presentation of the *logos*, the speaking being. The provisional solution seems to be to argue for the best order of discourses, which if nothing else reproduces the structure of the object of the inquiry. (Perhaps this is why rhetorical studies have traditionally been largely a continuing reproduction of typologies.)

The ambiguities inherent in regard and ranking can be managed through addition of a third concept: concealment. No one is known in one's entirety; *doxa* consists in the means by which one is known at all. Obviously, if one were known in one's exact identity—that is, only as a complex of particulars—then no ranking would be possible. Ranking occurs through a process of selecting and deflecting, revealing and concealing, our attention to the nature of a thing. Our opinion of another requires concealing as well as revealing some of what we know, and we are known through our own acts of concealment as well as disclosure. This conception of understanding as a process of concealing and revealing is paradoxical at first glance, just as is the idea that one's regard, one's radiance in the eyes of others, is the manifestation of an act of concealment.

Doxa is created by acts of concealment, and so a complete conceptualization of *doxa* must include the idea that regard is in part achieved by the concealments of rank. This interpretation repositions *doxa*: it is no longer contrasted with *episteme*, but rather with *aletheia*, truth (literally "unhiddenness"). This is not a relation of opposites, however: *doxa* and *aletheia* are different stages in the production of meaning. This dynamic of concealment and unconcealment—of authorizing and marginalizing—is the means by which we determine what we believe, what we know, and what we believe to be true. And the identification of a discourse as the manifestation of *doxa* means that it cannot be wholly laid bare, known in its entirety, without ceasing to exist. The unconcealing of the discourse does not show us what it contains—rather, it transforms it into another type of discourse (such as *aletheia*). Concealment is an act of metamorphosis, and one not comprehensible (or valuable) without awareness of its operation within the activity of ranking. Consider the analogy of our clothing: clothes create meaning by concealment, for they cover the body to disclose its intention, and in covering identify the individual in respect to the social body. They reveal only by suggestion, yet when they are removed, the "interior" or "hidden" meaning disappears, and a person's identity can be reconstructed only by reference to the "external" society.[51] So it is with *doxa*: although we can know the truth by bringing things out of unconcealment, complete disclosure would exhaust our means of knowing at all.

This reconsideration of *doxa* as the mask of meaning gives it a limitless correspondence with *episteme* but also restricts its engagement with *aletheia*. Consider the case of the status claims attending theories of discourse. They are expressions of *doxa*, assertions of regard achieved through the concealments of rank. They attend claims of *episteme* and demonstrate not only the structure but also a function of *doxa*: being a reservoir of potential meanings for epistemic claims. Yet they cannot alone suffice for the experience of truth, for they are acts of concealment that activate all the anxieties of displacement. According to one model of verbal authority, an opinion is the weak approximation of a truth; according to my understanding of the sociality common to rhetorical theory and practice, an opinion is a truth that has been changed as a necessary part of the process of determining regard, and with that, inventing values and guiding conduct. In other words, the "social knowledge" that grounds rhetorical practice and implies "certain notions of preferable public behavior" is constituted by the dynamics of regard, ranking, and concealment.[52] Rhetorical inquiry is both an account and an example of *doxa*, and this participation in the structure of *doxa* limits the inquiry's relation to truth—it necessarily is antecedent or attendant to the experience of truth. However, if rhetorical theory is grounded in opinions about rhetorical discourse, those opinions are truths concealed according to received attributions of authority and marginality. This relation between *doxa* and *aletheia* is not quite the conventional doctrine that rhetoric can only make the truth effective, however, for once the truth is construed in terms of the conditions of authority and marginality it loses its presumption of being the authentic end of thought.

Conclusion

This reconsideration of the rhetorical subject carries additional implications for rhetorical theory. First, the conception of *doxa* as reflecting status (and the determination of the role of status in discourse theory) suggests a contribution to the "philosophical" task of systematic ontology. A status-sensitive rhetorical theory could help create a language for the description of being in both an analytical and a constitutive manner. The analytical function of rhetoric has been summarized best by Valesio: "Rhetoric is the key to ontology because it is the most concrete and precise tool that can be used in order to show that every positive ontology is an ideological construction."[53] In other words, rhetorical analysis could situate the ontological claims within a social history of discourse and a dialectic of authority and marginality. The constitutive contribution would be to reformulate the concepts of being within the activities of the *logos* as understood through the concept of *doxa*. Heidegger provides the pertinent example of this project, as summarized by Hans-Georg Gadamer: "When he says that the truth of being is the *un*truth, that is, the concealment of being in 'error', then the decisive change in the concept of 'essence' which follows from the destruction of the Greek tradition of metaphysics can no longer be ignored. For Heidegger leaves behind him both the traditional concept of essence and that of the ground of essence."[54] Whatever the particular ontology developed, the use of status as a model of being would impel both a departure from transcendental thinking and an emphasis upon the process of being constituted by the perceptions of the other.

The final implication of focusing upon status is that this emphasis recommends a particular attitude toward the evaluation of theories in the humanities. Acceptance of the inevitability of status also must include acceptance of its mutability. Although ranking is embedded in the discourse of the humanities, no one order should be seen as foundational. This claim should be taken as a restatement, although not a doctrine, of epistemological relativism. More importantly, it offers specific direction for the task of evaluation. First, we must take seriously the question of how to begin a rhetorical theory. Second, we should accept that any rhetorical theory should begin at least with a consideration of the historical and current inhibitions of its subject. That is, one should begin by locating the subject (and its rationale) within a topography of authority. For example, any theory today would have to consider how rhetoric is understood as both an antique literary language and a suspect public practice. Third, the exploration of status should culminate in the articulation of heuristic standards rather than in the endorsement of ethical charges. This distinction does not intend to escape the reproduction of status within one's argument, only to avoid the lesser version of ranking known as moralizing. Thus, rather than concluding that rhetoric is civilizing but poetry liberating, or rhetoric authentic and philosophy alienated, and so on, we should consider how any ranking is a power move even as it serves a specific intellectual purpose.

To conclude, I have argued for an understanding of the rhetorical tradition as one burdened with justifying its subject and its inquiry within a dialectic of authority and marginality. My argument has first identified how status claims typify all arguments about the classification of discourses, then analyzed those status claims in terms of a particular conception of sociality that stresses the use of marginality in the constituting of meanings, and then elaborated several implications for the politics of rhetorical theory and the ontology of rhetorical discourse. I have not attempted to develop a method for escaping this dialectic, however; that would be a mystification. Rhetorical inquiry is better appreciated as an opportunity for engagement with, rather than escape from, the problems of authority and marginality and the methods of concealment and revelation. Rather than resist marginality, we can define rhetoric as a mode of reflection upon the sociality of language.

Rather than endorse authority, we can engage in the art of reclassification.

NOTES

1. Calvin O. Schrag, "Rhetoric Resituated at the End of Philosophy," *Quarterly Journal of Speech* 71 (1985): 167.

2. Ibid., p. 168.

3. Ibid., p. 170.

4. Plato rarely misses an opportunity for the attack. Illustrative examples are the comparison with cookery in the *Gorgias* 464–465 and the description of "a hunt after young men of wealth and rank" in the *Sophist* 223; see Edith Hamilton and Huntington Cairns, eds., *Plato: The Collected Dialogues*, Bollingen Series 71 (Princeton, NJ: Princeton University Press, 1961). Cicero replies in *De oratore* 3.15.58 by depicting philosophy as a diversion for idle minds, similar to gambling; see E. W. Sutton and H. Rackham, trans., *De oratore*, Loeb Classical Library (Cambridge, MA: Harvard University Press, 1942).

5. The first two qualifications are reviewed in Edwin Black, "Plato's View of Rhetoric," *Quarterly Journal of Speech* 44 (1958), reprinted in Lionel Crocker and Paul A. Carmack, eds., *Readings in Rhetoric* (Springfield, IL: Charles C. Thomas, 1965), pp. 68–88; the second also is stressed in Ernesto Grassi, *Rhetoric as Philosophy: The Humanist Tradition* (University Park: Pennsylvania State University Press, 1980), p. 28; the third is emphasized by Paolo Valesio, *Novantiqua* (Bloomington: Indiana University Press, 1980), p. 88; the fourth is featured by James Boyd White, *When Words Lose Their Meaning: Constitutions and Reconstitutions of Language, Character, and Community* (Chicago: University of Chicago Press, 1984), pp. 93–113.

6. Black, "Plato's View," p. 68.

7. *De oratore* 1.11.47.

8. *Gorgias* 481c–482c.

9. *Phaedrus* 277e–278.

10. Samuel Ijsseling, *Rhetoric and Philosophy in Conflict* (The Hague, The Netherlands: Martinus Nijhoff, 1976), p. 14.

11. Kenneth Burke, *A Grammar of Motives* (1945; rpt., Berkeley and Los Angeles: University of California Press, 1969), pp. 21–23.

12. See C. Perelman and L. Olbrechts-Tyteca, *The New Rhetoric: A Treatise on Argumentation*, trans. John Wilkinson and Purcell Weaver (South Bend, IN: University of Notre Dame Press, 1969); Ijsseling, *Rhetoric and Philosophy*; Grassi, *Rhetoric as Philosophy*; Valesio, *Novantiqua*; Michel Foucault, *The Order of Things: An Archaeology of the Human Sciences* (1970; rpt., New York: Vintage, 1973); Richard Rorty, *Philosophy and the Mirror of Nature* (Princeton, NJ: Princeton University

Press, 1979); Alasdair MacIntyre, *After Virtue: A Study in Moral Theory* (South Bend, IN: University of Notre Dame Press, 1981); and Gerald Bruns, *Inventions: Writing, Textuality, and Understanding in Literary History* (New Haven, CT: Yale University Press, 1982).

13. Immanuel Kant, *Critique of Judgement*, 2d ed., trans. J. H. Bernard (London: Macmillan, 1931), p. 215.

14. Ibid.

15. Ibid., p. 217.

16. John Locke, *An Essay Concerning Human Understanding*, ed. Alexander Campbell Fraser (Oxford, UK: Clarendon Press, 1894), vol. 2, p. 146. Both Kant and Locke also deal with rhetoric in more subtlety, distinguishing between better and worse rhetorics. Locke parses clearness and figuration, Kant divides eloquence and oratory, but these qualifications continue and strengthen the larger ranking of the arts. The selections from Kant and Locke also are discussed by Grassi, in *Rhetoric as Philosophy*, pp. 18–19. Locke also is quoted by Nietzsche to document the continuing disrepute of rhetoric; see Carole Blair, "Nietzsche's Lecture Notes on Rhetoric: A Translation," *Philosophy and Rhetoric* 16 (1983): 127, note.

17. Perelman and Olbrechts, *The New Rhetoric*, pp. 411–459. Dissociation includes the construction of a hierarchy of terms (p. 416) that produces an equation of "reality and value" for the privileged term (p. 417). In other words, substance and status are invented reciprocally. See also the analysis of *Phaedrus* (p. 421) and the discussion of how dissociation is used to attack rhetoric (pp. 450–459). The authors provide an excellent statement of how this attack is a motive in the invention of philosophy: "But we must not overlook that everything that promotes perception of a device—the mechanical, farfetched, abstract, codified, and formal aspects of a speech—will prompt the search for a reality that is dissociated from it" (p. 453).

18. Anicius Boethius, *The Consolation of Philosophy*, trans. V. E. Watts (New York: Penguin, 1969), p. 35.

19. Boethius, *Consolation*, p. 36.

20. Gay Wilson Allen and Harry Hayden Clark, *Literary Criticism: Pope to Croce* (1941; rpt., Detroit, MI: Wayne State University Press, 1962), p. 296.

21. H. F. B. Brett-Smith, ed., *Peacock's "Four Ages of Poetry," Shelley's "Defense of Poetry," Browning's "Essay on Shelley"* (Boston: Houghton, Mifflin, 1921), pp. 4–6.

22. Peacock, "Four Ages," in Brett-Smith, ed., p. 18.

23. Ibid., p. 19.

24. Percy Bysshe Shelley, *A Defense of Poetry*, in *The Harvard Classics*, ed. Charles W. Elliot (New York: P. F. Collier and Son, 1937), vol. 27, p. 333.

25. Ibid., p. 329.

26. Ibid., p. 354.

27. Ibid., p. 359.

28. See William K. Wimsatt Jr. and Cleanth Brooks, *Literary Criticism: A Short History* (New York: Knopf, 1959), pp. 422–423: "When he [Shelley] talks about poetry getting at the motives for good, . . . the words are . . . part of an appeal for a vastly creative and autonomous power. There is no appeal to any other authority. . . . The honor conferred upon poetic imagination, though nebulous, is the highest possible." Wimsatt and Brooks strive throughout their book to promote the autonomy of poetry. For another important extension of Shelley's influence, see Cleanth Brooks and Robert Penn Warren, *Understanding Poetry*, 3d ed. (New York: Holt, Rinehart and Winston, 1960). For a broader analysis of sovereign aestheticism, see Allan Megill, *Prophets of Extremity: Nietzsche, Heidegger, Foucault, Derrida* (Berkeley and Los Angeles: University of California Press, 1985).

29. Larry Rosenfield, "An Autopsy of the Rhetorical Tradition," in Lloyd F. Bitzer and Edwin Black, eds., *The Prospect of Rhetoric* (Englewood Cliffs, NJ: Prentice-Hall, 1971), p. 68.

30. Emile Durkheim, *The Rules of Sociological Method*, 8th ed., trans. Sarah A. Solovay and John H. Mueller, ed. George E. G. Catlin (Glencoe, IL: Free Press, 1938), pp. 67–75. See also Kai Erikson, *Wayward Puritans: A Study in the Sociology of Deviance* (New York: Wiley, 1966).

31. Charles P. Flynn, *Insult and Society: Patterns of Comparative Interaction* (Point Washington, WA: Kennikat Press, 1977), p. 1.

32. Jerome, Letter 23, in *Select Letters of St. Jerome*, trans. F. A. Wright, Loeb Classical Library (New York: G. P. Putnam, 1933), p. 126. The early churchmen were able strategists when discriminating their subject of Christian faith: "Cyprian, who had been a teacher of rhetoric . . . renounced profane letters completely and for the rest of his life never again quoted a pagan poet, rhetorician, or orator." The old tradition of rhetoric (representing all pagan letters) is used as the margin for the new discourse of Christian belief. The quotation is from James J. Murphy, "Saint Augustine and the Debate about a Christian Rhetoric," *Quarterly Journal of Speech* 46 (1960): 401.

33. Flynn, *Insult and Society*, p. 39.

34. Mary Douglas, *Purity and Danger: An Analysis of the Concepts of Pollution and Taboo* (1966; rpt., London: Routledge & Kegan Paul, 1969), p. 94.

35. Burke's complete statement is: "Even if any given terminology is a *reflection* of reality, by its very nature as a terminology it must be a *selection* of reality; and to this extent it must function also as a *deflection* of reality"; see *Language as Symbolic Action* (Berkeley and Los Angeles: University of California Press, 1966), p. 45.

36. For a review of this debate, see Black, "Plato's View of Rhetoric."

37. *Phaedrus* 253e.

38. Several of the many examples available are: Marie Hochmuth Nichols, "Kenneth Burke and the 'New Rhetoric,'" *Quarterly Journal of Speech* 38 (1952): 133–144; Daniel Fogarty, *Roots for a New Rhetoric* (1959; rpt., New York: Russell and Russell, 1968); Martin Steinmann Jr., *The New Rhetorics* (New York: Scribners, 1967); Perelman and Olbrechts-Tyteca, *The New Rhetoric*.

39. Paul de Man, *Allegories of Reading: Figural Language in Rousseau, Nietzsche, Rilke, and Proust* (New Haven, CT: Yale University Press, 1979), p. 131.

40. Aristotle, *Rhetoric*, trans. W. Rhys Roberts, ed. Friedrich Solmsen (New York: Random House, 1954), 1354a.

41. Kenneth Burke, *Counter-Statement* (Berkeley and Los Angeles: University of California Press, 1968), p. 218.

42. See John Lyne, "Rhetoric of Inquiry," *Quarterly Journal of Speech* 71 (1985): 65.

43. Richard Weaver, "The Spaciousness of the Old Rhetoric," *The Ethics of Rhetoric* (Chicago: Henry Regnery, 1953), p. 185. Weaver's reaction against the devaluation of rhetoric is summed up in his essay, "Language Is Sermonic," which begins: "Our age has witnessed the decline of a number of subjects that once enjoyed prestige and esteem, but no subject, I believe, has suffered more amazingly in this respect than rhetoric"; see Richard L. Johannesen, Rennart Strickland, and Ralph T. Eubanks, eds., *Language Is Sermonic* (Baton Rouge: Louisiana State University Press, 1970), p. 201.

44. Robert L. Scott, "On Viewing Rhetoric as Epistemic," *Central States Speech Journal* 18 (1967): 9 [reprinted in this volume].

45. Burke, *Language as Symbolic Action*, pp. 17–18.

46. See Ijsseling, chap. 1, "The Rehabilitation of Rhetoric," and Vasile Florescu, "Rhetoric and Its Rehabilitation in Contemporary Philosophy," *Philosophy and Rhetoric* 3 (1970): 193–224.

47. Stanley Deetz, "Negation and the Political Function of Rhetoric," *Quarterly Journal of Speech* 69 (1983): 435.

48. Valesio, *Novantiqua*, p. 3.

49. Martin Heidegger, *An Introduction to Metaphysics*, trans. Ralph Manheim (New Haven, CT: Yale University Press, 1959), pp. 102–103. For further contrast with the modern temper, see Cicero: e.g., in *Brutus*, his musing on the problems of appraising status correctly (21.83–85), or the peroration to eminence (96.331–333); *Brutus*, trans. G. L. Hendrickson, Loeb Classical Library (Cambridge, MA: Harvard University Press, 1962). See also Larry Rosenfield, "The Practical Celebration of Epideictic," in Eugene E. White, ed., *Rhetoric in Transition: Studies in the Nature and Uses of Rhetoric* (University Park: Pennsylvania State University Press, 1980), pp. 131–155. Rosenfield argues that epideictic rhetoric was conceived as restoring, through an act of revelation, the oneness of being and appearance that was lost in deliberative rhetoric. His general argument surpasses my use of regard as a mode of being, although I believe he errs in identifying *doxa* entirely with deliberative rhetoric.

50. For the intersubjective perspective, see Barry Brummett, "Some Implications of 'Process' or 'Intersubjectivity': Postmodern Rhetoric," *Philosophy and Rhetoric* 9 (1976): 21–51, and "On Rhetorical Relativism," in "The Forum," *Quarterly Journal of Speech* 68 (1982): 425–430.

51. Kenneth Burke also has attempted to penetrate the concept of concealment in his study of rhetoric. See his chapters on Bentham on "covering devices" and on Carlyle on clothes in *A Rhetoric of Motives* (1950; rpt., Berkeley and Los Angeles: University of California Press, 1969), pp. 99–100 and 119–123.

52. Thomas Farrell, "Knowledge, Consensus, and Rhetorical Theory," *Quarterly Journal of Speech* 62 (1976): 4 [reprinted in this volume]. See also the exchange between Walter M. Carlton and Farrell in *Quarterly Journal of Speech* 64 (1978): 313–334.

53. Valesio, *Novantiqua*, p. 96.

54. Hans-Georg Gadamer, *Philosophical Hermeneutics*, trans. and ed. David E. Linge (Berkeley and Los Angeles: University of California Press, 1976), p. 234.

The Habitation of Rhetoric

Michael Leff

The problem I want to engage is both funda-mental and ancient. When Cicero wrote his *De inventione*, it already had had a long history. Yet his comments on that history still retain a lively theoretical interest for students of rhetoric and argumentation. Consequently, they can serve as an appropriate text for introducing and locating the issues addressed in this paper.

As part of the standard *accessus* to the technical precepts of the art, Cicero considers the definition of rhetoric and its placement relative to other dis-ciplines. One aspect of this task is to understand the material of rhetoric, by which he means "those subjects with which the art and power of rhetoric are concerned." He then explains that "some have thought that there are more and some less of these subjects. To cite one example, Gorgias of Leontini, almost the earliest teacher of oratory, held that the orator could speak better than anyone else on all subjects. Apparently he assigned to the profession a vast—and in fact infinite—material. Aristo-tle, on the other hand, who did much to improve and adorn this art, thought that the function of the orator was concerned with three classes of subjects, the epideictic, the deliberative, and the judicial." This commentary leads immediately to a judgment: "According to my opinion, at least, the art and faculty of the orator must be thought of as concerned with this threefold material."[1] This judgment, moreover, is consistent with Cicero's earlier definition of rhetoric as a "part of political

science" (*civilis scientiae partem*).[2] That is, Cicero here assumes that the Aristotelian genres exhaust the boundaries of political discourse.

This assumption becomes more explicit in the next section of the text, where Cicero considers another aspect of the tradition. The Hellenistic rhetorician Hermagoras of Temnos divides the material of rhetoric into two types of issues, the special and the general. The former (often called the hypothesis) refers to controversies that involve specific circumstances; Cicero identifies such issues with the subjects indicated by the three Aristotelian genres. The latter (often called the thesis) refers to disputations about abstract issues unconnected with specific circumstances—such questions as "Is there any good but honor?," or "Can the senses be trusted?" Hermagoras, Cicero argues, errs in assigning such issues to rhetoric, since "everyone understands that these questions are far removed from the business of the orator."[3] The scope of rhetoric, then, is limited to the hypothesis, which, in turn, draws its materials from the conduct of civic affairs.

This position obviously arises from a schematic and over-simplified version of the tradition. In fact, Aristotle's conception of the matter is much more complicated and ambiguous than its representa-tion in *De inventione* suggests. And as Cicero real-ized in his later works, the whole issue demands careful inquiry and sophisticated reflection on the tradition rather than mere schematization.[4] Nevertheless, whatever the defects of our text, its bald simplicity has symptomatic value. The dichotomy between a "restrained rhetoric" and a "liberated rhetoric," sketched here in such consciously emphatic terms, recurs throughout the later history of rhetorical theory, normally in forms that are better disguised though no less potent. Certainly, as he embodies this dichotomy by reference to the opposition between "neo-Aristotelian" and Gorgianic (or "neo-sophistic") approaches, Cicero anticipates one of the main problems lurking just beneath the murky surface of twentieth-century rhetorical scholarship.

Before turning to these contemporary applications, however, I want to add one more note about the text. *De inventione*, consistent with most other rhetorical treatises, deals with the scope and location of the art as though these issues raised problems of strictly logical classification. But a slight adjustment of perspective might lead us to view the matter as a rhetorical operation, as an exercise in metonymy. In moving through one side of this metonymic process, the neo-Aristotelians regard rhetoric as a thing contained; it is an art domiciled within the territory of politics and domesticated by this political confinement. Moving in the opposite direction, the neo-sophists attempt to liberate rhetoric by conceiving it as a container, or, more properly, as a containing force. Unfettered by any particular subject matter, rhetoric becomes a power that ranges across the entire domain of human discourse, containing whatever matter it encounters. Since it is pure force, it is a container that constantly shifts its own configuration as it responds to circumstances, social interests, or the free play of linguistic whimsy.

In their modern incarnations, these two approaches yield results so different that their opposition seems total. Yet, viewed within a somewhat broader context, both share at least one important characteristic. While neo-Aristotelians seek to constrain the range of the rhetorical process and the neo-sophists seek to expand it, both alike center attention in process. Rhetoric is either process confined within some larger domain from which it draws substance, or it is the unbounded action of process itself. In either case, rhetoric per se is not substantive, since it is a form of action that generates or manages material without ever resting in a material embodiment. This attenuation between activity and production is obvious in respect to the neo-sophistic position, but it may seem puzzling or even paradoxical when attributed to neo-Aristotelianism, since that position is so clearly centered around the oration itself. Nevertheless, especially when the interest is dominantly critical rather than pedagogical, neo-Aristotelianism tends to bracket the oratorical text as a product with an integrity of its own. The oration simply establishes a referent for studying contexts or for locating processes which are to be gauged in terms of their extrinsic effect. The text becomes a medium or an instrument rather than a substantive product.[5] Consequently, the metonymic strategies in neo-Aristotelianism and neo-sophisticism yield diametrically opposed conceptions of the scope of rhetoric, but they both encourage a similar preoccupation with action as opposed to substance. When either of these extremes is isolated, or when the two are set in unmediated opposition, the result is to weaken or sever the connection between action and production.

Throughout most of the history of the discipline, certain forces have militated against this kind of metonymic reduction. Most obviously, there is the pedagogical tradition that links rhetorical scholarship with the teaching of composition. So long as that connection holds, the tendency of abstract definition is checked against the concrete problems involved in teaching students how to *make* discourses, and it is only in our century that rhetorical scholarship has become clearly dissociated from its pedagogical orientation. More important, however, amidst its technical clutter, the pedagogical tradition also houses a humane philosophy concerning practical discourse and its implications. This humanistic impulse traces itself in a line that moves from Isocrates to Cicero and Quintilian and from there forward to the Renaissance; its integrity consists in the effort to balance the aesthetics of production and the requirements of ethical action within the texture of practical discourse. Perhaps the key term informing this ideal is propriety, the flexible measure that unifies the elements of a discourse even as it adjusts them to the fluid ethical and political contexts in which it appears. Approached from this angle, a rhetorical discourse can be substantive, not because rhetoric commands a particular subject matter, but because the discourse commands attention as a thing made. Rhetorical discourse thus assumes an ontological solidity different in degree but not in kind from the products of the poetic art.

Humanistic rhetoric entailed a delicate balance that was always difficult to understand, let alone realize. And it always remained open to attack because of the way it blurred categories by treating them not as stable abstract entities, but as principles manifested in production and practical action. Hence, the humanistic perspective often was eclipsed by more technical conceptions of rhetoric and by more purely theoretical schemes for conceiving the placement of the arts in general. The most dramatic of these setbacks occurred during the Enlightenment, when the mainstream of philosophical thought collapsed the space needed to sustain the humanistic position. The Enlightenment liberated the aesthetic from the perturbations of all other forms of experience—set it in a zone of free and autonomous experience where it was to remain innocent of any prudential or teleological concerns. From this perspective, oratory was an inherently dubious business, since it conflated the aesthetic with matters of practical interest. More generally, Ciceronian rhetorical philosophy became a pseudo-philosophy, a jumble of category errors which undermined the necessary separation among ethical judgment, the operation of the intellect, and the impulse of the artistic spirit.[6]

One of Jacques Derrida's best known principles is that erasures always leave their traces. In this instance, however, we should remember that traces are often difficult to find and that erasures are sometimes effective in removing items from cultural awareness. That is, we need to understand current rhetorical scholarship against the background of what the Enlightenment blocked from direct perception. By the dawn of this century, oratory and composition had lost respectability within the academy, and rhetoric, in so far as it existed at all, was reduced to the mechanics of elocution or the taxonomic classification of tropes and figures. The humanistic conception of rhetoric was not simply rejected; it had been forgotten, or at best, distorted through the alien lens of Enlightenment thought. It was inconceivable that substantive art could arise from local adjustments to practical circumstance. Thus, subsequent efforts to revive rhetoric proceeded without much regard for the density of rhetorical products. The ballast that had kept pre-modern rhetoric close to the ground had been jettisoned, and the way was opened for the free action of the metonymic process.

In that twentieth-century innovation called the American Department of Speech, the history of rhetorical scholarship is, in considerable measure, the story of competing metonymic perspectives. The general direction of this conflict is reasonably clear: it is a movement from the neo-Aristotelian toward the neo-sophistic pole, from rhetoric contained to rhetoric as container. The details of this story are well known, and I want to pause here only long enough to indicate how they adhere to the pattern I have just sketched. And mindful of the contemporary interest in narrative, I will try to tell the story as a story.

Once upon a time, but not very long ago, there was a poor waif named Rhetoric. Though once the ruler of the arts, he had been banished from Europe and had found an academic home only in a new and unstable fiefdom known as the American Department of Speech. The people who lived in this fiefdom were concerned to define its boundaries so that it would not be annexed by powerful neighbors. Most of all, they feared the Duchy of English, which might try to enslave Rhetoric and commandeer his sections of the public speaking course. The great lords of English, moreover, disdained Rhetoric, since they regarded his teachings as impure and his bearing as too ordinary and insufficiently handsome. And so the leaders in the fiefdom of Speech, who were later known as the neo-Aristotelians, undertook a defense of Rhetoric which celebrated his individuality and modest respectability. They did so in words that echoed the sentiments of Cicero's *De inventione*. Rhetoric, they maintained, was confined to a particular kind of discourse, the political oration, and the rhetorical perspective was "patently single." Rhetoric cared not a whit for "permanence, nor yet . . . beauty." Instead, he was preoccupied "with effect" and taught us to regard a "speech as a communication to a specific audience."[7] As it turned out, the lords of English were concerned with their own squabbles and had no time to invade other territories. So the fiefdom of Speech survived and held its turf. But eventually it suffered from its own internal dissensions. A new generation of scholars arose and challenged the authority of the neo-Aristotelians. They complained that the older generation had committed the high crime of being atheoretical, and besides, it had neglected forms of discourse other than the oration. They broadcast these charges in all the journals of the fiefdom and gradually won adherents. Rhetoric was no longer viewed just as a modestly respectable actor in the political arena. He now seemed a great and powerful leader of the arts whose force had to be acknowledged in all the fiefdoms of the academy.

The point of this story is nicely summarized by comparing Donald Bryant's two well-known definitions of rhetoric. The first formulation appeared in 1953 and designated rhetoric as "the rationale of informative and suasory discourse." The amended version, published twenty years later, defined rhetoric "as the rationale of the informative and suasory in discourses."[8] The shift here is from a kind of discourse to a dimension in discourse, from an emphasis on certain products to an emphasis on a certain kind of activity. Though Bryant remained conservative in his attachment to public address, this rearrangement of priorities implicitly indicated a broader and more theoretical conception of rhetoric, and others have pushed this position in more radical directions. Much the same kind of progression has occurred within the area of argumentation. As Cox and Willard observe, "Historical-critical studies of particular orators, debates, or documents—long the dominant focus of argumentation scholars—have been gradually replaced by philosophical and theoretical examinations of the field's assumptions and methods." In the process, argument itself has come to be viewed as "a distinct form of human communication"[9]— that is, as a kind of activity that transcends any particular area of application. Moreover, this tendency in our discipline reflects the more general developments in the interdisciplinary revival of rhetoric. LaCapra, after surveying a number of apparently disparate forms of this revival, locates their common ground in "the idea that rhetoric is a dimension of all language use rather than a separable set of uses or a realm of discourse."[10]

Consistent with this orientation, the recent scholarship has centered around theories, models, and organizing conceptions that generally inform the process of arguing and persuading. The number of alternatives found here is striking—cognitive processing[,] constructivist psychology, narrative, ideology, cultural theory, symbolic interactionism, and the like.[11] Yet all of them are informed by a common interest in conceiving rhetoric as an activity conducted at the level of discourse. This interest implies a tension between process and product, and in the earlier phases of this development that tension manifests itself rather forcefully.

Two entries in the report of the 1970 National Developmental Project on Rhetoric illustrate my point. In his essay "Rhetorical Studies for the Modern World," Samuel Becker presents a running critique of traditional scholarship in rhetoric and public address. Becker argues that "single message encounters" are an inadequate basis for drawing conclusions about how messages influence audiences. Consequently, he concludes that "our traditional concept of the message has severely limited usefulness for understanding contempo-

rary communication. The emphasis of rhetorical studies should probably remain upon the message, but we must define message in a more fruitful way, in a way that is more descriptive of what man as receiver is exposed to, rather than what man as source creates."[12] Wayne Brockreide supports and extends this line of argument. He emphatically rejects "the idea that the most appropriate unit of rhetoric is the 'speech,' a one-shot attempt at persuasion, the idea that a rhetorical transaction is bounded by a speaker's introduction and his conclusion." In his view, Becker "argues convincingly that the speech is not an appropriate unit of analysis." Moreover, this position cannot be "assimilated as a minor modification of a traditional concept of rhetorical communication. It is revolutionary."[13]

Hence, we achieve a nearly total, a revolutionary, disjunction between the study of the rhetorical process and a serious interest in any particular rhetorical product. This sort of argument rarely appears in the more recent literature, but I suspect the reason is that the issue seems resolved. Neo-Aristotelianism is now only an historical curiosity, not a live option, and the placement of rhetoric at the abstract level of process has become a largely unconscious but well-established orthodoxy.

Yet I think that the issue calls for reconsideration. The position outlined by Brockreide and Becker has real force when applied to neo-Aristotelianism and its presupposition that rhetoric deals solely with extrinsic effect. If rhetoric concerns itself only with the way auditors process "messages," then attention to isolated "messages" has limited utility. Viewed from a broader perspective, however, the neo-Aristotelian doctrine itself appears as an aberration negatively informed by the Enlightenment's anti-rhetorical presuppositions.

In this important respect, the position described by Becker and Brockreide is not revolutionary. Rather, it reverses the focus of attention within an existing frame of reference and corrects the older position by driving its assumptions to their ultimate conclusion. The neo-Aristotelian conception of rhetoric is largely a defensive gesture which accommodates the strict dichotomy between fine and practical arts simply by yielding to its demands. Since it is a practical art, rhetoric produces nothing intrinsically interesting, and so its products offer no more than an occasion for studying a process. In another intellectual environment, it might seem apparent that the power of a practical art would emerge from a qualitative study of its products. But the burden of the Enlightenment forces attention toward purely extrinsic standards, toward the process triggered by the product. From here it takes only a small step to bracket the product altogether. Becker's term "message" captures this reduction perfectly, since, in a way wholly consistent with the neo-Aristotelian technical psychosis, it suggests a concern for what is in and what is conveyed by a discourse without much concern for the discourse itself. A message is an abstracted thing, distanced from the voice of the speaker or the hand of the writer, embedded only at the point of its impact. Ironically, the neo-Aristotelian commitment to the particular perfects itself in the abstract study of message processing.

Brockreide clearly summarizes these tendencies when he asserts that the "speech is not an appropriate unit for analysis." On its surface, this position seems curious. Presumably, a critical study of one of Lincoln's speeches, motivated by an interest in the design of the speech per se, engages an inappropriate unit for rhetorical analysis. Imagine, if you will, a poetic theorist arguing that a Shakespearean sonnet is not an appropriate unit for poetic analysis.

Perhaps, however, the analogy makes Brockreide's point seem not so curious. Even the most ardent apologist for rhetorical art must admit that rhetoric's status as a productive discipline is much less apparent than that of poetic. The basic terminology associated with the two arts aptly illustrates the difference. In one instance, we have the terms poet, poem, and poetic, which nicely distinguish the maker, the thing made, and the process of making. In the case of rhetoric, as Bryant has observed, "we are in something of a mess."[14] The term rhetor serves as analogue for poet, as does rhetoric for poetic. But we have no word that indicates a rhetorical product in the generic sense that poem designates a poetic product. Instead, we are forced to refer to some species of rhetorical artifact—an oration, an editorial, or a pamphlet.

This lexical gap is hardly an accident. On most accounts, the distinctive feature of the rhetorical art is the way that it embeds itself in and responds to specific, public circumstances. Moreover, in accepting persuasion as its goal, rhetorical discourse strives to efface its status as a constructed thing since it calls for prudential judgments rather than judgments about its own integrity as a product. As it blends into the fabric of events and actions, such discourse seems to become a form of action, an embodiment of processes immediately connected with the referent of the discourse. By

contrast, the poetic suspension of disbelief weakens this connection and focuses attention more sharply on the fabric of the discourse itself. Thus, if as McKeon has done, we group rhetoric and poetic together as practical/productive arts, they gravitate toward different margins in the category. Rhetoric emerges most clearly at the practical margin, because of its emphasis on efficient cause and on the exercise of productive powers. Poetry emerges at the productive margin, because of its emphasis on material cause and its obvious concern with the objects produced by the art "as composite wholes."[15] This contrast suggests the problematic status of rhetoric as a productive art and the difficulty involved in attaching rhetoric to distinctive products of its own making.

Consequently, the current tendency to view rhetoric as coherent only at the global level of discursive process reflects inherent problems and not just confusions associated with the recent history of the discipline. Yet current theory too often overcomes these problems simply by refusing to acknowledge their existence. Moreover, such innocence survives only through adherence to a systematic and fundamentally anti-rhetorical dichotomy between the prudential and the aesthetic. A far richer conception of rhetoric, especially with regard to its argumentative function, arises from the effort to confront the problem and grapple with the ambiguous relationships between action and production.

At this point, I hope to have shown that the placement of rhetoric is not merely an ancient topos but a persistent and fundamental issue. The problem initially surfaces in terms of categories that define rhetoric's place within the orbit of human arts and activities, but the latent territorial imagery involved here encourages a metonymic perspective. In turn, the metonymic process yields a dichotomy between rhetoric as an art contained within some substantive domain or rhetoric as a power that ranges over various domains. The epistemological implications of this division are relatively straightforward. From the contained perspective of neo-Aristotelianism, rhetoric tends to become a domestic art that arranges and communicates the materials of the domain which subsumes it. From the liberated perspective of neo-sophisticism, rhetoric tends to become a generative force actively engaged in the acquisition and formation of knowledge. Both perspectives commonly stress the nature of rhetoric as process or activity and deflect attention from its relationship to finished products. Once recognized, this bias in the metonymic process leads us to a second question about the "placement" of rhetoric. We are forced to consider not just the domain of rhetoric, but the level of its manifestation. Is the habitation of rhetoric found at the level of discourse per se or at the level of a discourse? Does rhetoric exist only as an abstract activity or does it also exist in concrete embodiments? As the terms "manifestation" and "existence" imply, these questions have an ontological rather than an epistemological bearing.

As I have just framed it, this ontological issue implies a departure from previous attempts to locate the "substance of rhetoric." In the familiar tradition that proceeds from Hoyt Hudson through Karl Wallace, substance is found in the argumentative or inventional aspect of the rhetorical process.[16] The alternative I am now suggesting defines rhetorical discourses as substantive in themselves. The substance of rhetoric, that is, does not arise from processes attached to the logical, ethical, or psychological co-ordinates of discourse; instead, it arises from the way such processes congeal within a particular rhetorical artifact. On this view, the essence of rhetoric becomes the constructed rhetorical thing-in-itself.

Yet, for reasons outlined above, even when we set Enlightenment prejudices to the side, the task of understanding polemic discourse as "substantive" raises some exceedingly difficult problems. To approach these problems, we must develop a better refined conception of how action and production interrelate in practical discourse, and to accomplish this end, we are faced with a reconception of the basic relationships among persuasion, argument, and aesthetics.

Obviously, these matters are far too complex to be resolved in this presentation, but it does seem to me that the elements needed for the reconstruction already exist in the current literature. The defect in that literature, from my perspective, is that it divides itself into two arenas—the one concerned with the linkage between persuasion and argument, and the other concerned with persuasion and aesthetics. The two remain largely unconnected with one another, and hence a full synthesis has yet to emerge. In order to illustrate this problem and to suggest a possible resolution, I now want to turn to the first study in Paul Ricoeur's important book *The Rule of Metaphor*. Despite the complexity and erudition of that study, its main argument clearly reveals the imbalance that occurs when modernist assumptions about aesthetics are corrected without reference

to recent thought concerning argumentation. At the same time, however, Ricoeur connects poetry with ontology in a way that suggests an important expansion of current thought about rhetorical argument.

In general, Ricoeur seeks to establish the ontological significance of metaphor. He does so by tracing its operation at its various levels of manifestation—the word, the sentence, and the discourse (i.e., the poem, narrative, essay, etc.). As analysis moves through each of these stages, metaphor assumes increasing potency, until, at the hermeneutic level of discourse, it becomes the prime vehicle for redescribing reality. Yet, for Ricoeur, metaphor does not come to rest at this final level, since its place, "its most intimate abode, is neither name, nor sentence, nor even discourse, but the copula of the verb to be."[17] In short, the power of metaphor consists in its capacity to align the different levels of discourse while connecting discourse itself to the contexts in which it appears. And as it effects this extraordinary negotiation, metaphor becomes the nexus between language and world that is basic to all our ontological conceptions.

His first study presents an extended analysis of this conception as it applies to Aristotle's thought. This analysis requires consideration of both the *Rhetoric* and the *Poetics*, the two loci of his theory of metaphor. On Ricoeur's account, Aristotle assigns a single operation to metaphor in both domains; it consistently works to transfer meaning. Yet it functions differently in the two arts, and the difference follows from the goals proper to each.[18] Ultimately, this distinction leads Ricoeur to affirm the ontological solidity of poetic discourse while denying a similar status to rhetorical discourse.

The goal of poetic[s] is mimesis, and all poetic discourse must find direction from this mimetic function. Thus, all elements of the poetic art cohere in service to this single, over-arching goal. Moreover, these elements—*muthos* (plot), character, *lexis* (diction), thought, spectacle, and melody—are themselves placed in a hierarchical order, since *muthos* structures the other five in respect to their poetic operation. *Muthos*, then, is the fulcrum of the poetic act; it is the principle that organizes the other aspects of the act into a coherent internal form, while it simultaneously draws the whole apparatus towards its mimetic goal. The relationship between *muthos* and mimesis is intimate, and the complex function of *muthos* holds sense and reference together within the fabric of the poetic text. The plot, in other words, retains its integrity as a linguistic product even as it sustains reference to the world that extends beyond its self-constituted limits. As it thus wavers constructively between submission to the reality of human action and the creative action of "poetry as such," *muthos* imparts an ontological density to poetic discourse.[19] The poem, like the metaphor, both is and is not "real," and yet always remains like the real.

In the case of the *Rhetoric*, Ricoeur cannot discover any analogous principle of complex structural integrity. The goal of rhetoric is persuasion, and its proper habitat is the arena of political power. Within this space, discourse is neither free to develop its own possibilities nor is it subject to the philosophical demand for truth. Hence, in Ricoeur's view, Aristotle's purpose is to domesticate or institutionalize rhetoric,[20] and he does so by devising a means whereby philosophy can "watch over rhetoric."[21] To achieve this purpose, Aristotle constructs a theory of probable reasoning which delimits the operation of rhetorical discourse and which, through the link with dialectic, places rhetoric in some contact with first philosophy. In this way, Aristotle finds a point of equilibrium between the conflicting claims of power and truth.[22]

Yet, as Ricoeur understands the matter, this equilibrium is fragile and incapable of sustaining a coherent realm of discourse. Owing to its connection with common opinion, rhetoric cannot become a purely formal discipline, and its content sprawls throughout the entire range of human affairs. Thus, the rhetorical art seems doomed by an "overburdening content" that leaves its elements scattered and uncoordinated.[23] This problem manifests itself most obviously when Ricoeur considers the rhetorical function of metaphor.

That function is difficult to apprehend, since the connection between style and argument in the *Rhetoric* is rather tenuous. Whereas, in poetry, form and meaning blend in a way similar to sculpture, the public use of speech encourages a dissociation between style and proof. Manner in oratory appears "extrinsic" and "variable." For this reason, the devices of style in rhetoric require special adaptation to the larger purposes of the art; they cannot develop according to their own impulses, but must respond to probative ends which they do not shape. Metaphor, in this context, does not generate contact between discourse and world, but is bent in the direction of "creating the right impression." This process, Ricoeur explains,

entails its own complexities, and it does involve a certain cognitive element. Metaphor and the other aspects of *lexis* enter into rhetoric as a manifestation of a kind of thought concerned not with proof alone but with proof relative to a hearer.[24] Yet Ricoeur holds that this persuasive function of metaphor exists in a state of unresolved tension with the requirements of proof, and hence rhetorical metaphor becomes something *added to* rather than *embedded within* the discursive formations of the art.

This tension reveals the divided condition of the rhetorical art as a whole and accounts for its incapacity to describe or generate discourses that preserve an independent integrity. Moreover, Ricoeur implies that this defect is inherent in rhetoric per se and not the result of Aristotle's particular construction of the art. "The lack of consistency in the link between a treatise on argumentation and a treatise on style reveals contradictions within the very project of persuasion. Set between two limits exterior to it—logic and violence—rhetoric oscillates between its two constitutive poles—proof and persuasion. When persuasion frees itself from the concern for proof, it is carried away by the desire to seduce and please; and style itself ceases to be the 'face' (figure) that expresses and reveals the body, and becomes an ornament in the cosmetic sense of the word. But this possibility was written into the origins of the rhetorical project."[25]

To sum up Ricoeur's argument, it is apparent that poetic holds an ontologically privileged status because of its capacity to connect the resources of language with our fundamental experience of life in the world. Poetic accomplishes this fusion through the mediating force of *muthos*, an element of the poetic process that simultaneously attunes the internal constituents of poetic discourse and directs them toward the final goal of mimesis. Rhetoric, however, is a divided business, since its goal—persuasion—entails the seemingly incompatible demands of objective proof and aesthetic appeal. Lacking a principle that would coordinate these elements, rhetoric fails to achieve ontological significance at the level of discourse.

The main flaw in this analysis requires little explanation before this audience. Although Ricoeur carefully distinguishes between the rhetorical and poetic functions of style, he is curiously unaware of any functional distinction between argumentation and apodeictic proof. For him, rhetorical proof is little more than formal logic *in mufti.* As a consequence, he couples a strikingly postmodern defense of metaphor and poetry with an outmoded interpretation of Aristotle's *Rhetoric*[26] and a general view of the relationship between logic and argument that slights the main developments in the scholarship over the past three decades.[27]

Nevertheless, when Ricoeur notes the tenuous connection between argument and style in Aristotle's *Rhetoric*, he certainly stands on firm ground. Moreover, the same problem persists in the recent scholarship where, as the contrast between Perelman and Group Mu indicates, the two aspects of the tradition sometimes have been severed completely from one another. Thus, I believe that Ricoeur accurately diagnoses the main obstacle to a conception of rhetorical discourse as substantive. Moreover, once we abandon his questionable distinction between proof and persuasion, his method suggests how we might resolve this problem.

Ricoeur observes that rhetorical style achieves its distinctive characteristics because of the way it is attracted to the goal of persuasion. Rhetorical *lexis*, that is, responds to the requirements of proof relative to a specific group of auditors and a specific set of public circumstances. It thus must balance the mode of expression against the occasion, the subject, and the interests of those who render judgment. In the terms of classical humanism, the point of balance is called decorum or propriety, and the flexible standard of decorum becomes the measure for assessing the rhetorical quality of expression.

Recent conceptions of argumentation exhibit a similar concern for proof in relation to specific circumstances and audiences. To cite just one example, Blair and Johnson distinguish argumentation from the logic of implication precisely because argument presupposes interlocutors, finds its end in persuasion, and develops "against the background of heterogeneity of point of view and of other arguments."[28] Conceived in this way, persuasion and proof are not antithetical, but rather persuasion is intimately and necessarily connected with one important type of proof—the proof that operates in public deliberation. Likewise, persuasion does not function in a way that is external to the subject, but as part of an adaptive mechanism vital to any reasonable understanding of public events themselves. Consequently, formal deductive logic cannot watch over or control the argumentative practice, since its abstracted principles have "little light to cast on the appropriate standards of argument."[29] Instead, these standards arise from the historically grounded context of argument and the community of interlocutors involved in the deliberative process.[30]

This flexible, socially grounded, and audience-centered conception of argumentative proof demands that arguers exercise a form of balanced judgment. In this important sense, argumentative practice seems to engage principles that are strikingly similar to the traditional notion of decorum or propriety. Yet, to my knowledge, no contemporary theorist has invoked these terms in respect to argumentation. The reason, I suspect, is that, in its contemporary usage, "decorum" has become associated exclusively with style. But this restriction is not necessary, and as Wesley Trimpi has shown, pre-modern rhetorical theory grants a much wider application for decorum—one that embraces cognitive as well as stylistic concerns.[31] The grounds for this broader conception have a strong bearing on current argumentative theory and its relation to rhetorical style in the sense that Ricoeur describes it.

Rhetorical discourse occurs in contexts where judgments must be rendered about specific matters of communal interest. Such judgments normally invoke the general principles that categorize and direct our response to public events. Yet the application of these principles is open to question, and, in their abstract state, they are insufficient to allow for an adequate decision in any given case. Moreover, these principles themselves are subject to revision in light of our concrete experience. Consequently, rhetorical judgment cannot suffer reduction to strictly formal or methodical procedures. It always engages qualitative considerations that balance the particulars of occasion and circumstance against the more general rubrics that inform our thinking.[32] This adjustment, moreover, does not simply concern the external form of a persuasive discourse, but also enters into our very mode of understanding the subjects of such discourse. In other words, both understanding and representation entail a mediation between concrete circumstances and principles of intelligibility. Moreover, whenever discourse addresses complex circumstances and heterogeneous interests, a clear separation between expressive form and argumentative content becomes virtually impossible. Our mode of representing situations and our assessment of their nature and moral significance coalesce within the structure of rhetorical judgment. And, in fact, the most skillfully constructed rhetorical discourses blend these elements so as to render them indistinguishable. This artistic skill is neither cosmetic nor deceptive. Instead, it reflects the unity of thought and expression necessary for the comprehension and direction of life in the pluralistic space of public experience.

Decorum is the term that best describes the process of mediation and balance connected with qualitative judgment. It is the principle of decorum that allows us to comprehend a situation as a whole, to locate its meaning within a context, and to translate this understanding into a discursive form that becomes an incentive to action. As it applies to the rhetorical act, decorum orders the elements of a discourse and rounds them out into a coherent product relative to the occasion. That is, it works to align the stylistic and argumentative features of the discourse within a unified structure while adjusting the whole structure to the context from which the discourse arises and to which it responds. The locus of decorum always depends upon the particular case, and so, although it directs artistic production, it is incapable of being formulated in terms of abstract, artistic precepts. It manifests itself only as embodied in particular discourses, and it governs the integrity of the discourse as a whole. Decorum, then, is a principle of action that accounts for the adaptive power of persuasive discourse, and it also establishes a flexible standard for assessing the intrinsic merit of a rhetorical product. Thus, decorum functions as the rhetorical counterpart of poetic *muthos*, for, like *muthos*, decorum mediates between internal sense and external reference in a certain kind of discursive product, and it does so in a way that maintains a consistent link with the subjects and goals proper to the domain where it operates.

Finally, referring back to the point from which this analysis began, decorum seems a peculiarly rhetorical principle because of its ambiguous placement between action and production. Decorum has no substantive stability across situations, since it represents a constantly moving process of negotiation. It is, as Trimpi says, "an activity, rather than a possession, of the consciousness."[33] Nevertheless, the achievement of decorum in a given situation establishes a point of maximum balance and stability. At the global level, decorum is pure process, but its local manifestations are products that display a powerful solidity. So also is rhetoric a universal activity that finds its habitation only in the particular. Since it is the art of the persuasive dimension in discourse, rhetoric finds no rest at the theoretical level. Its adaptive genius cannot be circumscribed by the fixed boundaries of theoretical constructions. As a form of activity, it must retain the freedom to encounter subjects, occasions, and audiences as each situation demands. Yet, within the particular situation, this adaptive process achieves productive closure; its mobile resources of argument and expression coalesce and become embodied as they grasp the matter of an actual case. Viewed at a distance, the principle of adaptation to situations becomes a nomadic process, a constantly changing program for action. Viewed within some specific situation, this principle manifests itself as a product, as a discourse possessing the density and integrity demanded by that situation.

NOTES

1. *De inventione*, 1.7, trans. H. M. Hubbell (Cambridge, MA: Harvard University Press, 1960). All subsequent quotations from *De inventione* are taken from this translation.

2. *De inv.* 1.6.

3. *De inv.* 1.8.

4. See Wesley Trimpi, *Muses of One Mind: The Literary Analysis of Experience and Its Continuity* (Princeton, NJ: Princeton University Press, 1983), pp. 247–252.

5. For a more detailed argument concerning this point, see Michael Leff, "Textual Criticism: The Legacy of G. P. Mohrmann," *Quarterly Journal of Speech* 72 (1986): 383–385.

6. Concerning these trends in Enlightenment thought, see Hans-Georg Gadamer, *Truth and Method* (New York: Crossroads, 1984), pp. 39–73.

7. The quotations above are all from Herbert A. Wichelns, "The Literary Criticism of Oratory," in Bernard L. Brock and Robert L. Scott, eds., *Methods of Rhetorical Criticism* (Detroit, MI: Wayne State University Press, 1980), p. 67.

8. Cf. Donald Bryant, "Rhetoric: Its Functions and Its Scope," *Quarterly Journal of Speech* 39 (1953): 401–424, and "Rhetoric: Its Functions and Its Scope, 'Rediviva,'" in Bryant, *Rhetorical Dimensions in Criticism* (Baton Rouge: Louisiana State University Press, 1973), pp. 3–23.

9. J. Robert Cox and Charles A. Willard, eds., "Introduction: The Field of Argument," in *Advances in Argumentation Theory and Research* (Carbondale: Southern Illinois University Press, 1982), pp. xiii–xiv.

10. Dominick LaCapra, *History and Criticism* (Ithaca, NY: Cornell University Press., 1985), p. 17.

11. Cox and Willard, "Introduction," p. xiv, enumerate some of the approaches in the literature on argumentation.

12. In Lloyd F. Bitzer and Edwin Black, eds., *The Prospect of Rhetoric: Report of the National Developmental Project* (Englewood Cliffs, NJ: Prentice-Hall, 1971), p. 31.

13. Wayne Brockreide, "Trends in the Study of Rhetoric: Toward a Blending of Criticism and Science," in Bitzer and Black, eds., *The Prospect of Rhetoric*, pp. 125–126.

14. Bryant, *Rhetorical Dimensions*, p. 3.

15. Richard McKeon, "Rhetoric and Poetic in the Philosophy of Aristotle," in Elder Olson, ed., *Aristotle's "Poetics" and English Literature: A Collection of Critical Essays* (Chicago: University of Chicago Press, 1965), pp. 207–208.

16. See, inter alia, Hoyt H. Hudson, "Can We Modernize the Study of Invention?," *Quarterly Journal of Speech* 7 (1921): 325–334, and Karl R. Wallace, "The Substance of Rhetoric: Good Reasons," *Quarterly Journal of Speech* 40 (1963): 239–249.

17. Paul Ricoeur, *The Rule of Metaphor: Multi-Disciplinary Studies of the Creation of Meaning in Language*, trans. Robert Czerny with Kathleen McLaughlin and John Costello (London: Routledge & Kegan Paul), p. 7.

18. Ibid., p. 12.

19. Ibid., p. 39.

20. Ibid., p. 10.

21. Ibid., p. 28.

22. Ibid., p. 10.

23. Ibid., p. 30.

24. Ibid., p. 31.

25. Ibid., p. 32.

26. See my review essay, "Recovering Aristotle: Rhetoric, Politics, and the Limits of Rationality," *Quarterly Journal of Speech* 71 (1985): 363, and Thomas M. Conley, "The Enthymeme in Perspective," *Quarterly Journal of Speech* 70 (1984): 168–172, and the references cited in both these papers.

27. See Cox and Willard, "Introduction," and J. Anthony Blair and Ralph H. Johnson, "Argumentation as Dialectical," *Argumentation* 1 (1987): 41–56.

28. Blair and Johnson, "Argumentation," p. 48.

29. Ibid., p. 48.

30. Ibid., pp. 51–53.

31. Trimpi, *Muses of One Mind*, pp. 87–240.

32. My argument here owes much to Ronald Beiner, *Political Judgment* (Chicago: University of Chicago Press, 1983).

33. Trimpi, *Muses of One Mind*, p. 234.

Text, Context, and the Fragmentation of Contemporary Culture

Michael Calvin McGee

In the mid-1960s, rhetoricians were led away from their study of public address by a new way of asking questions that centered on understanding the methods rather than the substance of their academic practice. The result was a limited ability to deal effectively with new cultural conditions that require different strategies for managing the relationship between a text and its context. This essay suggests that the fragmentation of our American culture has resulted in a role reversal, making *interpretation* the primary task of speakers and writers and *text construction* the primary task of audiences, readers, and critics. (Interpretation and text construction go together like reading and writing, of course, so it is important to understand from the outset that I am not suggesting that today's critics no longer need to worry about interpretation, or that today's speakers need not make speeches. "Primary task" means "the most essential" or "crucial" operation in successful reading/listening and writing/speaking.)

Criticism in Communication Studies

For the past twenty-five years or so, the field has been preoccupied with the pure act of criticism. From the beginning, in such books as Thonssen and Baird's *Speech Criticism* (1948), we have recognized that criticism is intimately connected with any analysis of discourse. We translated Greek

and Roman theories of communication into a theory of criticism, implying that rhetoricians possess performative skills which permit role-playing the part of great speakers at the moment of eloquence, or even the part of great authors at the point of writing a masterpiece of literature. Our theory of criticism treated the finished discourse as a final choice from among possible arguments and arrangements, styles and media. This way of conceiving discourse presupposes that criticism is purposive and tendentious: Great oratory ought to be celebrated for its wisdom and eloquence; bad oratory should be exposed for its bombast and eristic. The *telos* of both kinds of judgment is ultimately pedagogical, the clear faith that fledgling orators can profit from studying the successes and mistakes of more experienced speakers.

Since 1965, however, a spate of books and essays redefined criticism, making it an *object* of study rather than a *vehicle* of study. That is, we translated *how* we study into *what* we study, suggesting that our practice as critics is self-justifying. In Black's words (1978, p. 4), "criticism is what critics do." It need not "lead" to other kinds of knowledge or "go" anywhere in particular. "The critic" became portrayed as an entirely independent agent, so much in charge of his or her intellectual labor that whatever is produced under the name of "criticism" should be acceptable in principle, subject only to criteria of internal consistency and a reader's tutored preference. As Gronbeck

(1985) tells the story, our reorientation resulted in the "death" of public address, an academic practice killed when some of us decided that we were "critics" and others that we were "analysts" (cf. Hart, 1985). Whatever you think of Gronbeck's death metaphor, "public address" has clearly dissolved, being no longer a discrete object of study nor a necessary ground for critical judgment. But notice also that *rhetoric* has dissolved! Most obviously, in the sheer linguistics of the new terminology, rhetoric shifted from noun to qualifier, and in its new adjectival state, it remains occluded by focus on "criticism." It is now more important to be familiar with the theories of those who write about "criticism" from any field of the Academy than it is to understand the nature of the "rhetorical" in human life generally, in and out of the Academy. Though we all know better, we write as if *rhetoric* were uncontested, uninteresting, a subordinate term.

Where has rhetoric gone? The term "rhetorical criticism" invites us to Black's emphasis on critical practice. The term "critical rhetoric" (McKerrow, 1989) invites emphasis on rhetorical practice, "rhetoric is what rhetoricians do." With Black's accent, rhetoric is too easily submerged in philosophical and/or literary thinking.

With Accent on Criticism

From one angle, emphasis on "criticism" dissolves rhetoric into philosophy. Nearly everyone has called Plato the "Father of Philosophy," but Richard Rorty more specifically claims that Plato "invented philosophical thinking" from the materials of rhetoric, the lore of "Sophists" (1979, pp. 156–157). Plato's criticism of rhetoric emphasizes its easy acceptance of appearance and lack of concern for truth. Rhetoricians such as Isocrates did recognize a clear tension between appearance and reality, but they described it as *opposition*, not as *contradiction*. That is, when different modes of interpretation are also at odds, each claiming to be true, rhetoricians saw a *stasis*, an impasse resolved when judges imbued with *phronesis* (practical wisdom) make decisions. Plato doubted the practical wisdom of the Athenian *polis* that usually made such judgments, claiming that decisions are often polluted by the superstition and fear of uncritical minds. He wanted a more reliable, certain criterion of truth, so he invented philosophical thinking by characterizing an opposition as more than *stasis*, as *krisis*, a contradiction that results from

the imperfection of language. Words cannot capture the reality, the truth, of what they "stand for" in discourse; but some are closer to the mark than others. We must begin with the supposition that reality is hidden by appearance, truth by discourse. We search for that interpretation which most closely mirrors nature, truth for its own sake. Rhetoricians claimed that Plato made the study of *krisis*, the act of criticism, an object rather than a vehicle—discourse should "lead" somewhere beyond truth for the sake of truth, specifically to an enactment and embodiment of practical wisdom (Isocrates, 1961, pp. 329–333). For a while yet, until Rorty and his allies succeed in reshaping "mirror of nature" philosophy, there will be a place in the Platonic tradition for "the critic" whose labor goes nowhere beyond truth for the sake of truth. But this will be, as it has ever been, a place without rhetoricians, a place where rhetoric is degraded, where truth and action, theory and practice, have precious little to do with one another.

From another angle, the emphasis on "criticism" dissolves rhetoric into literary theory. As McKerrow (1989) has suggested, we might have said "critical rhetoric" instead of "rhetorical criticism," thus keeping it clear that criticism is a vehicle for doing rhetoric. When we reduced rhetoric to its adjectival state, however, we accepted the literary habit of taking the bite out of criticism by conceiving it as a kind of interpretation. Literary critics celebrate artists and worship art. "The Critic," like the high priest of antiquity, assumes the burden of making the hidden meanings of the artist/oracle manifest. Art *is presumed* to be an articulation of truth. If you can't understand the James Joyce novel, it's not because Joyce was an incompetent communicator—the fault is yours, because you haven't invested enough intellectual labor in reading it properly. When we teach performance, rhetoricians insist on bearing a burden of communication: The responsibility for any audience's failure to understand rests with the speaker or writer. Rhetoric is artful, but it is artful *as a performance*, not as an artifact. When rhetoric dissolves into literary criticism, the performative skills of the rhetorician are devalued, buried in literature's deep association with religion and the sacred text. The Bible simply presents itself, requiring interpretation because it is sacred. A clear supposition of literary criticism is that literature deserves the same regard. This is why readers are supposed to assume a burden of interpretation in the process of understanding Joyce's *Ulysses*. A muse bit Joyce and infected him with a divine madness. What he writes is not just a *message*, but a *divine message*, a revelation like the discourse of prophets. To condemn it and ignore it for its lack of clarity is vaguely sacrilegious. Rhetorical critics who valorize discourse that is "only" communicative are thus in a double-bind: If they emphasize what distinguishes them from literary critics, their mastery of *rhetoric*, they are incompetent readers of literature, because they cannot account for transcendence ("divinity") very well. If they emphasize what they have in common with literary critics, their mastery of *critical* theory and practice, they dilute their ability to deal with materiality (the everydayness of practical discourse), for they are in the position of using techniques for interpreting "divinity" on discourse distinguished by its lack of "divinity" (by the absence, or the presence in lesser degree, of "literary value").

In terms of contemporary discourse theory, the distance between rhetoric and literature, performance and artifact, is the distance between speaking and writing. Notice how important it is to those thinkers most influential on contemporary literary theory that they are dealing with *writing*. Barthes wanted to study problems of constraint and determination, so he drew a firm line of dialectical opposition between speech as "open" communication and writing as "closed anti-communication":

> All modes of writing have in common the fact of being "closed" and thus different from spoken language. writing is in no way an instrument for communication, it is not an open route through which there passes only the intention to speak. . . . Writing is a hardened language which is self-contained and is in no way meant to deliver to its own duration a mobile series of approximations. It is on the contrary meant to impose . . . the image of a speech which had a structure even before it came into existence. What makes writing the opposite of speech is that the former always *appears* symbolical, introverted, ostensibly turned towards an occult side of language, whereas the second is nothing but a flow of empty signs, the movement of which alone is significant. The whole of speech is epitomized in this expendability of words, in this froth ceaselessly swept onwards, and speech is found only where language self-evidently functions like a devouring process which swallows only the moving crest of the words. Writing, on the contrary, is always rooted in something beyond language, it develops like a seed, not like a line, it manifests an essence and holds the threat of a secret, it is an anti-communication, it is intimidating. (Barthes, 1968, p. 19–20)

Ricoeur, whose "hermeneutics of suspicion" greatly influenced the recent "interpretive turn" in literary theory (see Mitchell, 1983), specifically excludes speaking from the meaning of the term *text*, and thus from being considered in analysis of social, political, and cultural structures, until such time as it has been *inscribed*, written down, and thus ceased to be what it is in everyday life, *spoken*:

> I assume that the primary sense of the word "hermeneutics" concerns the rules required for the interpretation of the written documents of our culture. In assuming this starting point I am remaining faithful to the concept of *Auslegung* as it was stated by Wilhelm Dilthey. . . . *Auslegung* (interpretation, exegesis) implies something more specific [than understanding, comprehension]: it covers only a limited category of signs, those which are fixed by writing, including all the sorts of documents and monuments which entail a fixation similar to writing. . . . if there are specific problems which are raised by the interpretation of texts because they are texts and not spoken language, and if these problems are the ones which constitute hermeneutics as such, then the human sciences may be said to be hermeneutical (1) inasmuch as their *object* displays some of the features constitutive of a text as text, and (2) inasmuch as their *methodology* develops the same kind of procedures as those of *Auslegung* or text-interpretation. (Ricoeur, 1971, p. 529)

Derrida and the Yale school of literary theorists mark the development of writing as a decisive moment in Western civilization. "Fixing" speech in writing introduces problems of power and domination in cultural analysis, all but irretrievably disabling discourse as a vehicle or mediator of truth:

> At the precisely calculated center of the dialogue [Plato's *Phaedrus*]—the reader can count the lines—the question of *logography* is raised. ["Logography" is the "writing down" of "speech," giving up one's own "speech" to be "spoken/read" by someone else.] Phaedrus reminds Socrates that the citizens of greatest influence and dignity, the men who are the most free, feel ashamed at "speechwriting." . . . They fear the judgment of posterity, which might consider them "sophists." The logographer, in the strict sense, is a *ghost writer* who composes speeches for use by litigants, speeches which he himself does not pronounce, which he does not attend, so to speak, in person, and which produce their effects in his absence. In writing what he does not speak, what he would never say and, in truth, would probably never think, the author of the written speech is already entrenched in the posture of the sophist:

the man of non-presence and of non-truth. Writing is thus already on the scene. The incompatibility between the *written* and the *true* is clearly announced. (Derrida, 1981, p. 68; cf. Burke, 1961)

There are some striking ironies in literary theory's fascination with problems arising from the differences between speaking and writing. The *worshipful attitude* of the literary critic is preserved, but texts themselves are profaned: The truths they contain are hidden messages of secular exploitation and dominion, not the divine revelations of an oracle. Writing and truth are incompatible; yet the scholar's time and attention should be preoccupied with the interpretation of writing. Because it is set in such stark contrast over and against writing, speaking is almost a regulative ideal of discourse: It is open, embodied, enacted, capable where writing is not, in its capacity to bear communication and engender community. Yet, among influential writers, Karl Apel (1972) and Jürgen Habermas (1981) are virtually alone in their attempt to theorize speaking as the regulative ideal of discourse—and they are almost never encountered in approving ways in the work of literary theorists.

With Accent on Rhetoric

I do not entirely disapprove of new literary theory or of the turn in some circles toward the deconstruction of the history of philosophy. These trends have been inspiration to many, myself included. I believe that Barthes in particular is responsible for setting in motion a revolution in the Academy that will ultimately unify science and the humanities in a common quest for control over unimaginably complex post-industrial societies and economies. A circle of negativism (decentering, deconstructing) should be broken, however. I think it is time to stop whining about the so-called "post-modern" condition and to develop realistic strategies to cope with it as a fact of human life, perhaps in the present, certainly in the not-too-distant twenty-first century. I believe that an assertion of critical rhetoric, a reappraisal of the way we associate the terms *criticism* and *rhetoric*, might lead to such strategies.

Instead of beginning with the claim that "criticism is what critics do," we might begin conceiving our academic practice by saying that *rhetoric is what rhetoricians do*. This announces that we are concerned more with speech than with writing (in

the same sense that the difference between speech and writing is critical in contemporary discourse theory); and, therefore, that our focus is more on the performance of discourse than on the archaeology of discourse. These two implications need to be drawn out in some detail before the argument can proceed: (a) We must understand what it means to treat discourse from the first principle that it is a performance; and (b) we must understand how this first principle affects the way we describe the features of discourse.

Textual "Fragments"

With criticism as a master term, we assume that rhetoric is a form or genre of discourse presented for study as are novels, plays, or poems. The question of what constitutes "the text" is unproblematic—the discourse as it is delivered to its audience/readers is considered "finished," whole, clearly and obviously the object (target) of critical analysis. "The text" is Martin Luther King's "I Have a Dream" speech, for example, or Leni Riefenstahl's film *Triumph of the Will*, and close textual analysis will not stray far from the terms and the resources of the target discourse's world.

By contrast, with rhetoric as a master term, we begin by noticing that rhetors *make* discourses from scraps and pieces of evidence. Critical rhetoric does not *begin* with a finished text in need of interpretation; rather, texts are understood to be larger than the apparently finished discourse that presents itself as transparent. The apparently finished discourse is in fact a dense reconstruction of all the bits of other discourses from which it was made. It is fashioned from what we can call "fragments." Further, whether we conceive it in an Aristotelian sense as the art of persuasion, or in a Burkean sense as the social process of identification, rhetoric is *influential* (see Condit, 1987a, 1987b). That is, the rhetor understands that discourse anticipates its utility in the world, inviting its own critique (the interpretation and appropriation of its meaning). So "I Have a Dream" and *Triumph of the Will* are "in between" elided parts that will make them whole. They are simultaneously structures of fragments, finished texts, and fragments themselves to be accounted for in subsequent discourse, either (a) the audience/reader/critic's explanation of their power and meaning, or (b) the audience/reader/critic's rationalization for having taken their cue as an excuse for action. As a finished text, "I Have a Dream" is an arrangement of facts, allusions, and stylized expressions. As a fragment in the critic's text, the speech is only a featured part of an arrangement that includes all facts, events, texts, and stylized expressions deemed useful in explaining its influence and exposing its meaning.

Three Structural Relationships

One can get a more developed picture of a whole "text" by considering three structural relationships, between an apparently finished discourse and its sources, between an apparently finished discourse and culture, and between an apparently finished discourse and its influence.

We are most familiar with the relationship between the apparently finished discourse and its sources. Fledgling orators and writers have for centuries been taught research skills under the heading of "invention." They go to the library, locate other discourses deemed relevant to the topic of their speech or essay, and take note on index cards of "important" or "representative" "essential" passages. Foreign policy expert Henry Kissinger may have chosen 8,000 words to express in *Foreign Affairs* his opinion of U.S. policy in the Middle East. The debater, the public speaker, the journalist, the legislator, or the essayist, however, will represent that discourse in 250 words, reducing and condensing Kissinger's apparently finished text into a fragment that seems more important than the whole from which it came. This fragment is said to be "the point" Kissinger was trying to make, "the bottom line," the argument "in a nutshell." The relationship between the fragment and Kissinger's whole essay is nominalistic or semiotic: The fragment is a sign that consists of a signifier (the whole discourse it represents) and a signified (the meaning we are urged to see in the whole discourse). The relationship between the fragment and its new location—in the rhetor's discourse—is more forensic or approbative: The truncation we call "Kissinger's opinion" is clustered with other similar fragments in relation to a claim we are asked to approve. The clearest abuse of this process is "taking something out of context," allowing the requirements of an approbative structure to determine meaning by ignoring the requirements of the fragment's semiotic structure. In the best of possible arguments, the meaning of a fragment is invariant when structuration changes. That is, the advocate will so fairly represent Kissinger's opinion that the meaning of the fragment will be the

same inside a critic's essay as in Kissinger's whole argument.

Though it is frequently featured in rhetorical theories, we are less familiar with the relationship between an apparently finished discourse and *culture*. Aristotle's notion of the *enthymeme* and Cicero's use of the *epicheireme*, as well as the discussion of *doxa* among most of the Greeks, get at what we now call "culture," though in a back-handed way. Human beings, the story goes, exist in a matrix of rules, rituals, and conventions that we "take for granted" by assuming their goodness and truth and accepting the conditions they create as the "natural order of things." This conventional wisdom (*doxa*) is identical to the concept *culture* that is so prominently featured in much contemporary discourse theory. Present-day writers, however, are primarily concerned with problems of *constraint*, investigating why, how, and with what result culture silences people. In contrast, rhetoricians have usually been concerned with *empowerment*, seeking to discover how and with what consequence *doxa* can be used to authorize a redress of human grievances. *Enthymemes* and *epicheiremes* are argument forms that incorporate *doxa* in exhortations to action. Rhetors are advised to ground their arguments in *doxa*, using the taken-for-granted rules of society as the first principle (premise) of a chain of arguments. Further, advocates are urged not to "insult the intelligence" of audiences by directly proving what can safely be taken for granted—*doxa* is silent, and it should be kept silent, unless it becomes itself the source of grievance. When *doxa* is the source of grievance, rhetoricians in both the Platonic and Isocratean schools envision a kind of "social surgery" where new cultural imperatives are substituted for old taken-for-granted conventions. The exhortations of Socrates in Plato's *Apology* and of Isocrates in orations on pan-Hellenism are clear examples, respectively, of inconsequential and influential "surgery" on Greek culture.

Since all apparently finished discourses presuppose taken-for-granted cultural imperatives, all of culture is implicated in every instance of discourse. In principle, even the most basic cultural imperative (that the discourse is in one language as opposed to another—Russian, for example, and not French) is implicated in an apparently finished discourse and is thus part of "the text." In practice, however, only a finite and discrete set of cultural imperatives, discoverable by application of a simple test, need to be treated as implicatives within a specific discourse. The test has to do with the effects of unmasking cultural imperatives, giving voice to the silences of *doxa*: If recognition and statement of a rule, ritual, or convention is necessary to understand any fragment of the discourse, or if such recognition and statement would motivate an audience/reader/critic to resist the claims of the discourse, we can infer that the discourse derives its rhetorical power more from the *silence* of the cultural imperative than from the imperative itself. Whether we supply elided premises of *enthymemes* and *epicheiremes* or keep them silenced should make no difference in interpreting or acting upon apparently finished discourses. If missing premises do make a difference, they must be clearly articulated, thus becoming part of "the text."

Considering the relationship between an apparently finished discourse and its influence calls attention to the fundamental interconnectedness of all discourse. Writing makes no sense unless there are readers. The response of an interlocutor ("feedback") is an essential component of any communicative event. Every bit of discourse, in other words, invites its own critique. It is in this sense, perhaps, that Kenneth Burke keeps reminding us that we are all critics. In the most radical sense of this claim, as "everyday critics," we make a series of "snap judgments" in response to discourse. The first is a judgment of *salience*: The discourse is silenced, dismissed and forgotten, if it seems uninteresting or irrelevant; but if it matters, the discourse will be remembered, structured into our experience. If the discourse is memorable, it will at the very least affect our *attitudes*: Even if we disapprove and disagree with what the discourse seems to be saying, it will influence what we think by altering a motive state (increasing anger, for example, or decreasing anxieties hitchhiking in descriptions of the world) and providing an example of someone else's foolishness. The discourse may also affect our *beliefs*, in dimensions of intensity and *substance*: With regard to intensity, the discourse could strengthen or weaken our confidence in what we think we know about the world, or our commitment to the truth of facts we have in the past taken on faith. With regard to substance, the discourse could simply add to our store of knowledge, or, with more complicated consequence, it could cause us to discard prior facts as erroneous and to accept new facts as truth. The fourth snap judgment of everyday critics has to do with the translation of our beliefs into *action*: At the very least, we decide to engage in a speech act when we verbalize our motive-ridden beliefs in response to a discourse judged to be salient. At the

most, we intervene in the world, physically interposing ourselves upon a problematic condition in an attempt to make the world conform to our will.

Professional critics (whether they be critics of art, society, literature, or any other thing) differ from everyday critics in that *they are always trying to make the world conform to their will*. Their criticism is on its face that sort of action which intervenes in the world. Put another way, professional critics are all rhetorical critics, in either of the two dominant contemporary senses of "rhetoric": In Aristotelian terms, professional criticism functions to persuade readers to make the same judgments of salience, attitude, belief, and action the critic made. In Burkean terms, professional criticism promotes identification with the critic, suggesting that critics give voice to communal judgments of salience, attitude, belief, and action, stating a collective will to which the world should conform. The everyday critic *may* create discourse in response to discourse; but the professional critic *always* creates formal discourse in response to discourse. (The object of criticism is always either discourse or discourse analogue, in the sense that it is treated as meaningful and in need of interpretation.) Professional critics must thus be sensitive to rhetoric in two dimensions: With regard to the object of criticism, they will be perceived as respondents and interpreters responsible for providing in a formal way the missing fragments of the object of criticism, its influence. With regard to their own formal writing, they will function as advocates or adversaries of "the text" who invent, arrange, style, remember, and deliver arguments in favor of particular judgments of salience, attitude, belief, and action (see Brockriede, 1972, 1974).

The Terms "Text" and "Context"

In calling attention to three structural relationships that make an issue out of deciding what a "text" is, I have done no more than change the way we have traditionally described the problematics of rhetorical criticism. In the past we separated "text" from "context" and discussed the sources, presuppositions, and effects of discourse as parts of "context." The result of such conceptual separation, I suggest, has been confusion about the root nature of discourse. Unfortunately, an unkind way of articulating the problem is also the clearest: Separate consideration of text and context makes question-begging too easy and attractive. "Context" can be reduced to any of its parts. If you can't chase down the fragments from which an argument was constructed (if you can't find the prosecution's case in the trial of Socrates, for example), you use the discursive equivalent of the theory of spontaneous generation and treat the argument as *ex nihilo* philosophy and/or literature, words without history, or words with only an "intellectual" or "literary" history. If you can account for the sources of discourse, but have difficulty understanding the cultural milieu in which it was socially and politically significant, you reduce the communicative event to a simple stimulus–response mechanism wherein discourse is said to have discrete and independent effects on history. (This results in such odd critical judgments as Nichols [1972] holding Lincoln to account for failing to stop the Civil War with his "First Inaugural Address.") If you understand the cultural milieu, but discover the difficulty of showing how one bit of discourse contributes to an overdetermined cultural condition, you can ignore the problem of influence altogether by celebrating the artistry (eloquence) of the rhetor who combined sources into an insightful, well-said commentary on his or her life and times. The Chicago School has even given us the conceptual wherewithal to ignore all three parts of context by performing "close textual analysis" on presumptively self-contained discourses.

My way of stating the case (using the concept "fragment" to collapse "context" into "text") emphasizes an important truth about discourse: *Discourse ceases to be what it is whenever parts of it are taken "out of context."* Failing to account for "context," or reducing "context" to one or two of its parts, means quite simply that one is no longer dealing with discourse as it appears in the world. The belief that the formation of words we call King's "I Have a Dream" oration can be construed as sufficient unto themselves is sheer fantasy. Put another way, the elements of "context" are so important to the "text" that one cannot discover, or even discuss, the *meaning* of "text" without reference to them. This is not to say that scholarship focused on parts of "the text" (as I describe it) is impossible or nonsensical. Each of the "question-begging" strategies I have discussed (and several others not enumerated here) could be reframed in a sensible and productive way. Even the Chicago School strategy of ignoring "context" altogether can be redeemed by consistently, rigorously acknowledging the "incompleteness" of the analysis. Make it clear that King's speech is a *fragment*. Look for the particular locutions that implicate its sources. Show where cultural conventions are presupposed. Locate the places where "I Have a Dream" is trying to create, or is seeking, its audience. Show where and how the speech anticipates its own "everyday" critique. Frequently the best evidence you have of the missing parts of a text are there in front of you as implications of the fragment you are looking at. Certainly, every fragment is a map of the structures that will make it complete, and in that sense focus on a part can be a speculative, "incomplete" study of the whole.

The Fragmentation of Culture

I believe that problematizing the concept "text" is generally productive, even in dealing with deeply historical fragments such as *Magna Carta* or Burke's "Speech on Conciliation with the Colonies." If the human condition had not changed so radically in the past seventy years, I could therefore be content to leave this argument with a pluralistic claim, that I have posed one of several plausible ways to account for the relationship between text and context. This announces that I would be pleased to see others follow up the suggestions made here, but that I see no *necessity* in them, nothing that makes choosing my way of thinking better than the traditional disjunction of text and context. Radical change has occurred, however, and our new condition makes it necessary to insist on the concept "fragment" and to suggest that alternatives embrace error. This point can come clear in a line of reasoning that begins by asking what features of discourse inclined critics to treat "text" as self-evident.

In the not-too-distant past, all discourses were what some social theorists call "totalizations" (see, e.g., Mannheim, 1972). That is, all structures of a text were homogeneous. Education was restricted to a scant minority, and as a result the content of an education was so homogeneous that an orator could utter two or three lines in Latin, identified only with the words "as Tully said," in complete confidence that any reader/audience/critic would be able to identify the source of the words—and even recite the next several lines from Cicero's *De oratore*! Except for everyday conversation, all discourse within a particular language community was produced from the same resources. Further, all discourse found its influence on the same small class of people who comprised the political nation. And it was the same small class that received the benefits of a homogenized education. There was little cultural diversity, no question that there was in every state a well-defined dominant race, dominant class, dominant gender, dominant history, and dominant ethnicity. The silent, taken-for-granted creed of all true-blue Americans (Frenchmen, Englishmen, etc.) could have been articulated by any one of them who had been conditioned by the education system and admitted as a member in good standing of the political nation, even those who fancied themselves revolutionaries.

Discourse practices reflected the presumed homogeneity of Western cultures. Rhetors invested a great deal of effort to insure that their discourses appeared to be "harmonious," whole, ending with allusion to their beginning. The same air of formality that dictated proper dress at public occasions and in restaurants also dictated proper discourse practices. Public argument was also formal argument modeled after the courtroom. The dice were loaded in favor of existing circumstances, so that advocates of change were forced to assume a "burden of proof" and to meet the stiff requirements of the prima facie case. Regardless of whom they silenced, what they ignored, or weakness in their argument, advocates tried mightily to write or speak as if they had an "airtight case" that accounted for all possible interpretations of evidence and all conceivable courses of action that appeared to follow from the truths the evidence appeared to support. Ethical public figures, those who refused to "stoop to demagoguery," addressed everyone in their target audiences as if the meanest laborer, the most ignorant rounder among them, had all the skills of reason and wisdom of an appellate judge, a Member of Parliament, or a U.S. senator. Adaptations to ignorance, apathy, and vulgarity were fundamentally linguistic rather than logical, the choice of a smaller vocabulary instead of truncations of what was supposed to be the rational process. This commitment to the rationality of *homo sapiens* led to the cultural imperative that we all should take our time in making deliberate judgments. The wise judgment was precisely the deliberate judgment that carefully weighed evidence and balanced alternatives with the skill of a juggler.

I believe that a persuasive history of the twentieth century could be written with the motif that presumed homogeneity has been replaced by the presumption of cultural heterogeneity. If I were telling the story, I would likely begin with the agitation that led to the passage of the 19th Amendment, the women's suffrage movement. I would point to the "psychologizing" of literally every social–political institution. Clarence Darrow invented the plea of insanity. A parole system evolved based on our presumed capacity to psychologically rehabilitate criminals. Dr. Spock inspired American families to rear children with less emphasis on the formalities and requirements of public life and more emphasis on the psychological contentment of the child. Mainstream religions put less emphasis on Christian doctrine and their role as moral watchdogs than on their community service functions ("good works"), frequently transforming the cleric into a combination social worker and therapist. The Supreme Court legitimized ethnicity in several decisions related to *Brown vs. The Board of Education* which argue, in main part, that America's traditional "melting-pot" rhetoric causes psychological harm to minorities who cannot find themselves in WASP-ish cultural depictions of the ideal society. Politicians, both in campaigns and in executing the duties of office, increasingly consult their audiences as if they were fundamentally irrational, *homo cognito* rather than *homo sapiens*. The "bottom line" of politics these days is the instantaneous public opinion poll which measures popular *reaction* to current conditions rather than the *considered, deliberate judgment* of "We, the People." John Dewey inspired a revolution in education based on our capacity to condition all citizens to the psychology of democracy. People have grown less interested in the *content* than in the *process* of a public education, suggesting that what people know is less important than the process of learning (see Cheney, 1988b). As a result, there is no longer a homogeneous body of knowledge that constitutes the common education of everyone. Students are more likely today to learn English literature by reading science fiction than by reading "the classics," and the ability to remember specific things about a particular essay or novel is no longer valorized.

We stand now in the middle (or at the end, if reactionaries have their way) of a seventy-year movement which has fractured and fragmented American culture. Contemporary discourse practices reflect this fragmentation. Indeed, changes in discourse practices have been so obviously dramatic that several theorists portray new communication technologies as *the cause* of cultural fracturing. Some take the broad view of deep intellectual history, vacillating between near-Luddite polemics that merely implicate technology in a general indictment of capitalism and science (e.g., Burke, 1945, pp. 113–117, 175–176, 214–223, 507–511) and jubilant epideictics that celebrate those fragmenting effects of new media which constitute or presage a recuperation of good things in long-lost "oral cultures" (e.g., McLuhan, 1964, and Ong, 1982). Others take a more political view, oddly enough condemning new discourse practices from both extremes of the relatively narrow spectrum of American politics. From the right, reactionaries worry about "the fate of the book" (Cheney, 1988[a]) and the alleged "closing of the American mind" (Bloom, 1987). From the left comes a voice with French accent, the voice of so-called "postmodernism," worrying about the "colonization" of the psyche (Deleuze and Guattari, 1983) and "the precession of simulacra" (Baudrillard, 1983).

Settling the cause-and-effect issue regarding the relationship between culture and discourse practices is ultimately an ineffable chicken-and-egg problem of scant interest. However we got there, the human *condition* has changed. Put whatever adjectives you want in front of the concept "condition." (I grit my teeth and shudder as I say it, but I think the term *post-modern condition* is likely to prove best.) One clear truth will not change: The public's business is now being done more often via direct mail, television spots, documentaries, mass entertainment, and "quotable quotes" on the evening news than through the more traditional media (broadsides, pamphlets, books, and public speeches). A central requirement of our new circumstance is simply finding a place to start thinking about it. Scholars are all analysts at heart, but nothing in our new environment is complete enough, finished enough, to analyze— and the fragments that present themselves to us do not stand still long enough to analyze. They fly by so quickly that by the time you grasp the problem at stake, you seem to be dealing with yesterday's news, a puzzle that solved itself by disappearing. A few years ago, for example, the Cable News Network broadcast two stories, in tandem, every thirty minutes for forty-eight hours. The first was a Romeo and Juliet tale of a tragic, dramatic teenage suicide. The second reported that a causal connection exists between news of teenage suicide and suicide attempts. By the time the network recognized the contradiction and its potential effect, it was trapped by "the public's right to know" into reporting an epidemic rash of copy-cat suicides. By the time policymakers and academics recognized that public health may require re-examination of traditional attitudes toward "free press" issues, the epidemic was over. The network had other news to confront, policymakers had no immediate cause for study or action, and academics had no opportunity for response other than adding another item to the laundry list of topics that warrant toothgnashing polemics against the insensitivity of those who run the culture industry.

I agree with Said (1983a, 1983b) that the fundamental root of frustration in such situations is our inclination to treat scraps of social problems and fragments of texts as if they were whole. In his vocabulary, the solution is to look for *formations of texts* rather than "*the* text" as a place to begin analysis. I like the term "formation," but I want to keep clear that we are dealing with fragments, not texts, and that we mean to treat a "formation" as if it were a singular text—only then can we interpret, analyze, and criticize. I would therefore state the case in two somewhat different ways:

From one angle, provided by the traditional disjunction of text and context, I would want to explore the sense in which "texts" have disappeared altogether, leaving us with nothing but *discursive fragments of context*. By this I would mean that changing cultural conditions have made it virtually impossible to construct a whole and harmonious text such as Edmund Burke's "Speech on Conciliation with the Colonies." If by "text" we mean the sort of finished discourse anticipated in consequence of an essentially homogenous culture, no texts exist today. We have instead fragments of "information" that constitute our *context*. The unity and structural integrity we used to put in our texts as they faithfully represented nature is now presumed to be *in us ourselves*.

From another angle, provided by my proposed collapse of context into text, I would want to explore the sense in which we are constantly harassed by the necessity of understanding an "invisible text" which is never quite finished but constantly in front of us. By this I would mean that changing cultural conditions have forced writers/speakers and readers/audiences to reverse their roles. At one time producers of discourse could circumscribe even the most difficult human problem in a single finished text. (With reference to the enthymeme and epicheireme, one would say that producers of discourse provided more in their texts than they presumed in their audiences.) The communication revolution, however, was accompanied by a knowledge explosion. The result is that today no single finished text could possibly comprehend all perspectives on even a single human problem, let alone the complex of problems we index in the phrase "issues of the day." The only way to "say it all" in our fractured culture is to provide readers/audiences with dense, truncated fragments that cue *them* to produce a finished discourse in their minds. In short, *text construction is now something done more by the consumers than by the producers of discourse.*

In my vocabulary, the problem calls for the skills of a rhetorician. I think we can reconcile traditional modes of analysis with the so-called post-modern condition by understanding that our first job as professional consumers of discourse is *inventing a text suitable for criticism.* I will elaborate on the subject of text construction in a subsequent essay. For now, this first step requires closure: So long as one reads historical documents ("finished" texts produced in consequence of demonstrated cultural homogeneity) it is possible to take a pluralistic attitude toward the concept "fragment." The strategy I propose can be understood as one of many alternatives in the business of managing the theoretical relationship of texts and their context. If you analyze contemporary discourse, however, "fragment" or some concept that can be made equivalent (Said's "formation," for example) is *necessary.* Only something very similar to the strategy I propose has the power to account for discourse produced in consequence of the fragmentation of culture.

REFERENCES

Apel, K. (1972). "The *A Priori* of Communication and the Foundation of the Humanities." *Man and World* 5: 3–37.

Barthes, R. (1968). *Writing Degree Zero.* Translated by Annette Lavers and Colin Smith. New York: Hill and Wang.

Baudrillard, J. (1983). *Simulations.* Translated by Paul Foss, Paul Patton, and Philip Beitchman. New York: Semiotext(e).

Black, E. (1978). *Rhetorical Criticism: A Study in Method.* 2d ed. Madison: University of Wisconsin Press.

Bloom, A. (1987). *The Closing of the American Mind.* New York: Simon & Schuster.

Brockriede, W. (1972). "Arguers as Lovers." *Philosophy and Rhetoric* 5: 1–11.

Brockriede, W. (1974). "Rhetorical Criticism as Argument." *Quarterly Journal of Speech* 60: 165–174.

Burke, K. (1945). *A Grammar of Motives.* New York: Prentice-Hall.

Burke, K. (1961). *The Rhetoric of Religion: Studies in Logology.* Boston: Beacon Press.

Cheney, L. V. (1988a). *American Memory: A Report on the Humanities in the Nation's Public Schools.* Washington, DC: National Endowment for the Humanities.

Cheney, L. V. (1988b). *Humanities in America: A Report to the President, Congress, and the American People.* Washington, DC: National Endowment for the Humanities.

Condit, C. M. (1987a). "Crafting Virtue: The Rhetorical Construction of Public Morality." *Quarterly Journal of Speech* 73: 79–97 [reprinted in this volume].

Condit, C. M. (1987b). "Democracy and Civil Rights: The Universalizing Influence of Public Argumentation." *Communication Monographs* 54: 1–18.

Derrida, J. (1981). *Dissemination.* Translated by Barbara Johnson. Chicago: University of Chicago Press.

Frye, N. (1957). *Anatomy of Criticism: Four Essays.* Princeton, NJ: Princeton University Press.

Gronbeck, B. E. (1985). "The Birth, Death, and Rebirth of Public Address." Paper presented at the annual meeting of the Speech Communication Association, Denver, CO.

Habermas, J. (1984). *The Theory of Communicative Action, Vol. 1: Reason and the Rationalization of Society.* Translated by Thomas McCarthy. Boston: Beacon Press.

Hart, R. P. (1985). "Public Address: Should It Be Disinterred?" Paper presented at the annual meeting of the Speech Communication Association, Denver, CO.

Isocrates. (1961). *Antidosis.* In *The Works of Isocrates.* Translated by George Norlin and Larue Van Hook (Cambridge, MA: Harvard University Press), pp. 181–365.

McKerrow, R. E. (1989). "Critical Rhetoric: Theory and *Praxis.*" *Communication Monographs* 56: 91–111 [reprinted in this volume].

McLuhan, M. (1964). *Understanding Media: The Extensions of Man.* New York: McGraw-Hill.

Mannheim, K. (1955). *Ideology and Utopia: An Introduction to the Sociology of Knowledge.* Rev. ed. Translated by L. Wirth and E. Shils. New York: Harvest Books.

Mitchell, W. J. T., ed. (1983). *The Politics of Interpretation.* Chicago: University of Chicago Press.

Nichols, M. H. (1972). "Lincoln's First Inaugural." In R. L. Scott and B. L. Brock, eds., *Methods of Rhetorical Criticism* (New York: Harper and Row), pp. 60–100.

Ong, W. J. (1982). *Orality and Literacy: The Technologizing of the Word.* New York: Methuen.

Ricoeur, P. (1971). "The Model of the Text: Meaningful Action Considered as a Text." *Social Research* 38: 529–562.

Rorty, R. (1979). *Philosophy and the Mirror of Nature.* Princeton, NJ: Princeton University Press.

Said, E. W. (1983a). "Opponents, Audiences, Constituencies, and Community." In W. J. T. Mitchell, ed., *The Politics of Interpretation* (Chicago: University of Chicago Press).

Said, E. W. (1983b). *The World, the Text, and the Critic.* Cambridge, MA: Harvard University Press.

Thonssen, L., and A. C. Baird. (1948). *Speech Criticism: The Development of Standards for Rhetorical Appraisal.* New York: Ronald Press.

Practicing the Arts of Rhetoric

Tradition and Invention

Thomas Farrell

Ironically mirroring the fortunes of contemporary politics, two very different senses of practice have begun to merge in our historical understanding. The first, in order of appearance, is the Aristotelian sense of *praxis*, lately articulated by Alasdair MacIntyre and a host of conservative classicists.[1] This original notion suggests a coherent mode of activity with its own internal standards of excellence. Since the cultivation and mastery of recognizable practices usually requires concentration of effort and purpose, this striving for excellence is thought to engender other worthwhile "goods" and virtues of character and civic life.[2] So, as one example, the athlete must be patient, determined, mentally "tough," and so forth. The artist must be aware of her tradition, devoted to her craft, willing to sacrifice, take risks, and so on. This original sense of *practice*, in other words, stresses its unity and coherence as a form of thoughtful action. And in an era that many have indicated as a "dark" time of self-indulgence and incoherent moral discourse,[3] the return to this sense of *practice* has promised an incremental road to recovery.

But to the classical understanding of practice must be added another, more radical understanding: that of critical theory deriving from a Marxist base.[4] This historically determinate rendering regards practice as the concrete embodiment of existent social forces, understood as a mode of production. While this latter understanding preserves the cognitive significance of the practical,

it tends to collapse the subjective region of practical choice into the existing conditions of a state of affairs.[5] A revealing recent example is the work of Anthony Giddens on structuration:

> The problem of order in social theory is how *form* occurs in social relations, or (put in another fashion) how social systems "bind" time and space. All social activity is formed in three conjoined moments of difference: temporally, structurally (in the language of semiotics, paradigmatically), and spatially; the conjunction of these express the *situated* character of social practices. The binding of time and space in social systems *always* has to be examined historically, in terms of the bounded knowledgeability of human action.[6]

On the basis of what we read in Giddens' words, there is little to disturb a classical rhetorician, except perhaps the lack of caution: "*All* social activity . . ." "The binding of time and space . . . *always* has to be examined historically." A vision of *praxis* which has banished all nuance and *modality* of indeterminacy may seem formally elegant but ethically troublesome, just as it has proved to be politically troublesome for all those who made the "wrong" choices.[7]

I noted earlier that these two senses of practice seem to have come together in our contemporary understanding. By this, I mean that the traditional understanding of *praxis* has been forced to reconsider and even revise itself in light of the less than amicable climates of modernity. At the same time, even the most sweeping forms of historicism have failed to author a definitive utopian ending for history's discordant, but insistent, voices. If these intuitions make sense, the opening of human practices to both a sense of their history *and* a sense of our human agency would invite a careful reappraisal of the rhetorical tradition. Why?

Primarily, I shall argue, it is because *rhetoric derives its materials from the real conditions of civic life, the appearances of our cultural world. At the same time, this activity makes room for disputation about the meaning, implications, direction, and value of cultural appearances.* This is another way of saying that rhetoric promises to include both of our senses of a practice. However, the discovery of such a preoccupation within rhetoric seems to raise as many issues as it resolves. For instance, it remains to be seen whether our classically grounded understandings of tradition offer a vocabulary of explanation sufficiently rich and responsive to capture the inventional possibilities for practice in contemporary life. I might note in passing that a widespread revival of Aristotelian *ethical* and *political* philosophy has thus far not been accompanied by any great interest in a renewal of the Aristotelian *rhetorical* tradition; and this is despite a much-heralded revival of interest in rhetoric.[8] A closely related issue is whether an informed appraisal of contemporary cultural settings might not disclose an environment so dark and dispirited as to be antagonistic to our classical understandings. This is, of course, our two senses of practice returning to us in more general theoretic terms.

In this essay, I outline a treatment of tradition which should emphasize how rhetorical *practice* allows reflection and invention to occur, given the sometimes diffuse and chaotic materials of civic life. While the impetus to my approach derives from an optimistic reading of Aristotelian rhetorical tradition, I should stress that the term *practice* itself is not without important normative and thus "critical" connotations. One does not have to be an Aristotelian to intuit that virtually any practice admits to a variable quality in performance. One plays the piano well or badly. And if one is "just learning," this terminology also immerses us within a family of concepts in which our aim is to get better: to reach or at least approach our "potential." These normative concerns might be expressed in quite recognizably modern ways as well. For instance, I may ask where you derive your operative notions of "well" or "badly." I may critique those examples of quality chosen as models

for emulation. I may bemoan the unequal chances many of us have to perform certain practices in the first place, and so on.

While I cannot address this matter comprehensively here, I find it difficult to avoid the assumption that discourse about *rhetorical* practice would be unintelligible without at least the pretension to rigor afforded by an acquaintance with theory. For it is theory that raises questions about the identity and vitality of rhetorical traditions, the boundaries of genre, the pertinence of conventions and proofs, the "goods" and standards of practice itself, the very *meaning* of "rhetoric" in the first place.[9] This essay, in other words, could not hope to essentialize certain distinctive qualities within the Aristotelian rhetorical tradition without employing the language of theory.

We begin with what will seem to be a paradoxical claim. I want to argue that rhetoric is a higher-order practice; *and,* I want to suggest that rhetorical practice achieves its aims in ways that allow virtually anyone to participate effectively within the practice itself.

Rereading the Rhetorical Tradition

Perhaps the most basic differentiation of activities in all of classical thought is Aristotle's own distinction between the theoretic and the productive sciences. In the productive sciences, of which ethics was one, the point was not so much to *know* virtue for its own sake, but to *become* virtuous through action.[10] Aristotle's distinction provided an important qualifier to the Platonic attempt to subsume all activities, crafts, and sciences under his own monistic philosophic vocabulary. Even within the context of the schema, however, the placement of rhetoric is still problematic. Rhetoric admits to both a theoretic quality, and to a certain form of power. And Aristotle nowhere explicitly says that the aim of rhetoric is to *be* persuasive. As near as we have been able to determine, the aim of rhetoric is to *practice* judgment (to enact *krisis*) where certain sorts of problematic materials are concerned.[11] Perhaps that is what it means to be rhetorical.

But this still leaves unsettled just what sort of practice rhetoric itself is. The modern tendency, I believe, would take rhetoric to be simply a pragmatic exertion of power through discourse, or any manner of partisanship uncovered in discourse. Either concept assumes that rhetoric only is achieving its aims when it is covering over its *true* (that is to say, "false") intent.[12] But rhetorical practice admits to a broader understanding than this. Some idea of this understanding might be suggested by Alasdair MacIntyre's useful distinction between goods that are *internal* to a practice and goods that are *external* to it. MacIntyre's specific example is that of chess. And he is able to argue, convincingly I think, that there is a recognizable difference between goods that are only casually and contingently related to quality play in chess (such as paying a child to play, or perhaps the publicity accompanying great success, for an adult), and the goods that are fundamental and integral to the mastery of this complex game ("analytic skill, strategic imagination, and competitive intensity," to use MacIntyre's language).[13]

The distinction becomes serviceable for rhetoric if we remember two things: first, that the "goods" internal to an activity are not necessarily the reason one seeks to master the practice. One does not play chess only to acquire and sophisticate these "goods." One plays chess to win. Still, with the acquisition of skill, there comes an appreciation for the well-played match, regardless of results. Second, and despite the singular focus of MacIntyre's repeated examples, the "goods" that are cultivated are not always localized within the autonomous agent alone. There is an unmistakable pedagogical sense in which improved performance by the other improves the quality of play, one's appreciation for the sport, perhaps the resolve of one's opponent. Most important, this means we should not confuse goods that are internal to a practice with virtues that are somehow interior to its practitioner alone. It is worth noting that two of MacIntyre's own interior "goods" (strategic imagination and competitive intensity) require another person in order to be practiced and thereby cultivated. They are, in other words, *relational goods*. This does not mean that they are somehow inferior to other goods; no such thing is implied by virtue of being internal to a practice. This is pivotal to rhetoric. I think we are now in a position to claim that the "goods" or qualities *internal* to rhetoric are necessarily relational.[14] Like competitiveness and strategic imagination (which mastery of rhetoric is also capable of providing), they require some *other* in order to be practiced. But beyond this, some very important civic qualities—such as civic friendship, a sense of social justice—are actively cultivated through excellence in rhetorical practice.[15] These qualities, in other words, are not merely distinctions for the autonomous agent to master; they are qualities of the body politic itself. Aristotle's original conception of rhetoric and its operation thus gives us the outline of a most intriguing form of activity, an activity admitting its own distinct goods. Truly, we have been introduced to a *practice*, that is—a coherent, creative activity admitting to certain standards of accomplishment.

But what sort of practice? It remains to be seen, for instance, whether and how this ancient art may engender "goods," "qualities," and "virtues" that are worthy of emulation. My own position, abbreviated here, is that classical rhetoric offers us a practical ideal of the appropriate; *phronesis* or practical wisdom. Rhetoric also provides us with a kind of overarching form of reasoning with *doxa*, the conventions and opinions of the civic-minded "others" around us. This is, of course, the enthymeme. And rhetoric provides a kind of location wherein all of this might occur, by carefully delimiting a certain space of civic engagement, and this we might think of as the rhetorical occasion.

Within the context of classical theory, rhetoric is an art of practice to be developed in real-life settings, where matters are in dispute and there are no fixed or final criteria for judgment.[16] It is significant that the philosopher who invented formal logic and many special disciplines saw some need for rhetoric in the first place. In his oft-cited justification for the art, Aristotle allowed that there is value in encouraging the force of the better argument to prevail, even if the matters discussed are not resolved for all time. Whether or not rhetorical practice always vindicates the force of the better argument is not nearly so important as its continual allowance for critique and improvement.[17] This means that rhetoric, like all other arts, carries with it the *possibility* of refinement.

But most important to our immediate concern, Aristotle considered rhetoric to involve practical questions that took on urgency, immediacy, and pertinence for disputants, because of the institutional time, place, and circumstances of their involvement. In other words, the questions addressed and adjudicated through rhetoric were those that could only be framed, let alone understood, within the context of a particular form of life in a culture. The formal criteria for analytic validity, like the philosophical claims to *a priori* "truth," were here less important than inference-making which invoked the presuppositions of ordinary life, and then applied them to the contingent demands of an occasion.

In earlier projects, I have emphasized the centrality of audience convictions and "habits" of thinking to the kind of practical inference which rhetoric employs to engage, animate, and complete the world of appearances. Once an audience is invoked to think along with an advocate, certain acquired background norms govern the propriety of order, emphasis, direction, subordination, and support for artistic proofs in issues of disputes.[18] By definition, these cannot be universally applicable to all cases equally, of course. Rather, they are guided by the particularity of circumstance, interest, and inclination of those who participate in the very *form* of rhetoric.

We may have happened upon an explanation of why the revival of classical philosophy has generally *not* been accompanied by a revival of Aristotelian rhetoric. For the most part, the advocates of a recovery of classicism are part of a single-minded program, where community, the *polis*, and solidarity are one and the same thing. The regrettable model for this is MacIntyre's chilling image of the "truth-bearers" huddled in the catacombs on the eve of some new dark age.[19] Yet at least as I am interpreting matters here, the whole point of the *Rhetoric* is not its monism, but its circumstantiality and eclecticism. That is what the practical ideal of *phronesis* really is all about.

But the matter that now concerns us is this whole question of *How*. How is it that *phronesis* is evoked by the *Rhetoric*? And how is this rhetorical realm of appearances really engaged by art? In a quite subtle but persistent way, the whole emphasis of the *Rhetoric* is toward the action and agency of others, as an audience in the formation of character, and the rendering of judgments. This is perhaps obvious enough in the most logocentric of Aristotle's devices—the enthymeme.[20] Here, you and I might collaborate on an inference making use of some shared normative consent. Say I observe that it is disgraceful that American-owned companies don't take more responsibility for the damage of acid rain beyond their national borders. If you agree, it is probably because you think, as do I, that their neglect has much to do with the problem, *and* that responsibility does not end at one's national or provincial borders. I don't have to say those things; yet they work as shared background conditions for forming the argument. This is a (somewhat-elliptical) enthymeme.

But I want to suggest as well that this evocation of agency is present all through the *Rhetoric*, in the markers of character, or *ethos*, in the unlikely and often unstable territory of emotion, or *pathos*, as well. Let us begin with Aristotle's ruminations about Honor:

> Honour is the token of a man's being famous for doing good. It is chiefly and most properly paid to those who have already done good; but also to the man who can do good in the future. Doing good refers either to the preservation of life and the means of life, or to wealth, or to some other of the good things which it is hard to get either always or at that particular place or time—for many gain honour for things which seem small, but the place and occasion account for it. The constituents of honour are: sacrifices; commemoration, in verse or prose; privileges; grants of land; front seats at civic celebrations; state burial; statues; public maintenance; among foreigners, obeisances and giving place; and such presents as are among various bodies of men regarded as marks of honour.[21]

For those less than sympathetic to classical rhetoric, this is the sort of passage that could confirm the worst of their stereotypes. It reads as little more than a list. But of what? It is surely an unusual way of approaching the virtue of honor. Here we have "tokens" and "marks" of honor, accounted for by the place and occasion; hence presents, and even seating position, all that persons "regard" as honor. The very mundanity here must be revealing; for this is an overview of the *appearances* of honor presented as materials for rhetoric, how honor might be recognized, presented, framed, and depicted. By whom? Let us remember that rhetoric is practical reasoning in the presence of collaborative others: in this case, those who recognize and enact the visible markers of honor for those they respect and admire. Thus, it is no exaggeration to say that their own public character is invoked and implicated by these conspicuous recognitions. Only when a sense of honor is available can honor itself be accorded. It is interesting that Aristotle moves directly from this overview in Book 1 to an examination of the various public "excellences." When he arrives at "the good," he confounds Platonists and Sophists alike by beginning with "good luck," only to include the "good in itself" as one of over forty differing and often contradictory senses of "goodness."[22] What is going on here? Again, Aristotle is overviewing for us appearances of value construed rhetorically. And far from the monolithic construals of Aristotle's many Platonic commentators, what we find instead is a sense of diversity and eclecticism. In civic life, at least, the "good" must be the outcome of timely, collaborative choice within the particularities of circumstance.

Now let us turn to the unsteady terrain of *pathos*, or emotion. Again, the conventional derogations of Aristotle need to be set aside. Gadamer finds this to be trafficking in the excitation of emotions.[23] Ricoeur views it as the most overburdening sort of pop psychology.[24] I would like to introduce a brief passage from Book 2 of the *Rhetoric*. The passage has not received much notice from rhetoricians, but I think it points in the overall direction of my position. In Chapter 8 of Book 2, Aristotle is in the process of discussing the emotion of pity. He says:

> Again, we feel pity when the danger is near ourselves. Also we pity those who are like us in age, character, disposition, social standing, or birth; for in all these cases it appears more likely that the same misfortune may befall us also. Here too we have to remember the general principle that what we fear for ourselves excites our pity when it happens to others. Further, since it is when the sufferings of others are close to us that they excite our pity (we cannot remember what disasters happened a hundred centuries hereafter, and therefore feel little pity, if any for such things).[25]

Aristotle concludes this remarkable discussion by stating:

> Most piteous of all is it when, in such times of trial, the victims are persons of noble character; whenever they are so, our pity is especially excited, because their innocence, as well as the setting of their misfortunes before our eyes, makes their misfortunes seem close to ourselves.[26]

This is one of the passages that arguably is behind the repeated references to the *Rhetoric* when Aristotle's *Poetics* attempts to explain the nature of tragic pleasure. It is also possible to sense, in the early going, that same partiality to those near and dear (in class, birth, age, character) that has received strenuous criticism from the Kantian universalist position. But who can deny that there is something much more important, even transformational, going on as well? If one lingers over this passage long enough, what emerges is a principle of *translation* among emotions. Fear for ourselves, when the matter in question does not happen to us—but rather others somehow close to us—is not fear at all but pity. While the aforementioned connection of *catharsis* is undeniable,

there are also fascinating implications for the cultivation of "civic friendship," belonging, and care that are required for a richly textured community life.[26*] For it is rhetoric that seems to remove us from the immediacy of familiar appearance so that we might formulate conditions for appreciating the needs of others. This same discussion of pity strongly implies that the cultivation of affiliative "goods" might reverse itself as well.[27] To the extent we see others as radically *unlike* ourselves, as distant in appearance, time, and place, our "pity" will recede. So, too, our ability to judge prudently the intersection of their and our interest will narrow accordingly. What may be cultivated may also, in the world of rhetorical practice, be made to disappear. Not quite a virtue, not exactly an individuated passion, pity becomes—through rhetoric—a form of proof.

Pivotal to Aristotle's understanding of rhetoric, then, is its peculiar inculcation of cognition, ethos, and emotion in the decisions and acts of collectivities. The norms and conventions for a culture thus find themselves employed as premises of recognition and also inference. The norms of social knowledge that apply to membership groups are the selfsame norms of enthymemes. As these expand or contract, they directly affect the lived reality of culture, including its extensiveness. So perhaps I can sum up this liberal textual reading by suggesting that rhetoric in the classical sense provides an important inventional capacity for the conventions, emotions, and cognitions necessary for us to affiliate in a community of civic life.

We are also on the verge of filling in an understanding of the first claim introduced earlier, that rhetoric, in its classical Aristotelian sense, is a "higher-order" practice. By this, I do not mean that rhetoric is an *elite* or fine art in some hierarchy of practices, but rather that rhetoric, in its most fully elaborated sense, helps to uncover instances of its practice in a great many of our unexamined activities; the discourse surrounding rituals of civic life: art, sports, entertainment; the more mundane practices of collecting and recollecting: diaries, scrapbooks, autobiographies, and memoirs. Each of these activities, while constituted by its own norms and conventions, may be seen to share in qualities that are undeniably rhetorical. This is because, in Allen Gross's felicitous phrase, rhetoric is not so much *something*, as *about* something.[28] And it is in this recognizably Aristotelian sense

---

*Editors' note: The footnote no. 26 appears twice in the original.

that we might think of rhetoric as a *higher-order* practice.

The more difficult question, though, is whether this practice admits any real-life practitioners. As has happened many times in the checkered history of this "art," defenders of rhetoric's "nobility" always run the risk of purifying their defendant of any meaningful content. I wish to suggest, however, that a broader picture of rhetoric as a *serial practice* or plurality of activities may help us to avoid this danger. Rhetoric is held in the lowest regard when it is identified solely with the product domain: sham enthymemes, slippery slogans, feel-good sound-bites. It is not until we think of the two-sided argument, the running controversy, the ritual that becomes a crisis: in other words, not until we admit the liminal elements of struggle, difference, and thus reflective judgment that rhetoric itself is redeemed.

Rereading Rhetorical Culture

Rhetorical Practice

This enlarged picture of rhetorical practice should offer a way of developing the second part of my claim: to show that, even in a less than 'eloquent' age, participation within rhetorical practice might cultivate recognizable relational goods. Building from the vocabulary of Aristotle's *Rhetoric*, I now outline a way of looking at contemporary rhetorical occasions, so that we might observe some features of a rhetorical practice at work. As a kind of bedrock assumption for recovering the Aristotelian tradition, we need to concede that not every sense of "culture" is equally compatible with the aims of such a project as this. Prefigured as early as the tension between *Nomos* and *Physis*, there has been a temptation to regard "culture" as *either* an entirely arbitrary assortment of symbols, conventions, and affiliations *or* as a repository of unquestioned truth as real as nature (*Physis*) itself. Each set of assumptions can lead to a kind of paralysis where rhetoric is concerned. The arbitrary assortment view can lead to vicious relativism, a less-than-benign variation on Callicles' dilemma. And the "reality" centered view reinforces either the "pre-Modern" foreclosure of alternatives or the "late Modern" sense that culture is a *second* nature, entirely analogous to the determinism of physical reality.[29]

Without suggesting that any of the above approaches are wrong, I want only to observe that they obscure our appreciation for rhetorical occa-

sions. If all assortments are relative, it would be difficult to imagine any particular configuration which might call for an "appropriate" response. And if our responses are already *over*-determined, then it is difficult to see why anyone would care much about what the nature of any particular response happens to be.

Over and against the above renderings, I want to suggest an understanding of culture as "cultivation," a durable symbolic home with valued traditions and ways of acting. From this standpoint, it becomes possible to appreciate striking differences among cultures, while appreciating that, as Michael Walzer has put it, "where one is is already a place of some value."[30] This more organic vision of culture also seems compatible with modern comprehension of rhetorical practice. For more than simply determining our prevailing patterns of response, contemporary life exposes us to a range of *propriety* where possible rhetorical audiences are concerned, to variable and disputable conceptions of social problems, definitions of the public good, even norms for the attribution of responsibility and judgment. To sense the availability of these radically different means of persuasion is to restore an important dimension of indeterminacy to public "learning."[31] Behavior may be determined, but the agency of human engagement and choice is *occasioned*.

When one is immersed within a cultural "life-world," whether it be that of an urban East Coast streetperson or that of a Japanese peasant, the rhetorical characteristics of ongoing cultural activities are likely to go unnoticed. This does not mean that they are absent or unimportant, but only that our practices themselves are taken for granted in a way that withholds our sense of their partisanship. What Gibbard has called a community of "isolation" persists to the extent that the activities of other communities have no impact upon us, even though these activities are very different from our own.[32] We are drawn into a more public awareness of rhetoric, when the different activities of others must have an impact upon our needs, priorities, and practices.

Rhetoric, in its venerable sense of an art *form*, emerges when we have recognized features of our activities as directional choices from among an array of options. With each of these cultural prototypes, rhetorical practice does afford a measure of reflection, at least to the extent that the "other" must be acknowledged as a witness to what *we*, as a collective membership group, must do. This means that rhetorical *phronesis* cannot be enacted without at least a partial intuition of what the "appropriate" *is* in each historically specific setting. And so even the most powerful imposition of rhetorical advocacy must have a reciprocal interest in the justification of its own conduct. We might even go so far as to say that public "power" is proportional to this interest.[33] Modern rhetorical *practice* is thus the performance and enactment of our sense of the appropriate with responsive interested *others*. For lack of a better term, let us call these contemporary constituencies of address *audiences*.

Rhetorical Form

Yet the very changes we have addressed in contemporary public cultures require that we employ our rhetorical vocabulary in a more expansive way. For one thing, the notion of rhetorical *form* needs to be broadened to include more than simple emergent "products" of reasoning. Like our comprehension of rhetorical tradition itself, form needs to be extended to include the whole practice of public rhetorical thinking in disputational contexts: what we might think of as *rhetorical cognition*. Our prototype for this process of inference remains the enthymeme: that abbreviated convergence of *doxa* and public conviction with the particularities of circumstance and issue. But our more expansive understanding requires that we reintroduce two characteristics of enthymematic thinking that are vital to modern rhetorical practice. First is the uncertain *referentiality* of enthymematic premises themselves. While most cultures will profess to a conception of what is good or just, honorable or honest, the individuated meanings of any such conception are entirely dependent upon the lifeworld or received traditions of the membership groups themselves. However, this need not be cause for despair. The primary function of enthymematic thinking is to bring a general value horizon together with an individuated audience understanding and a problem or object of contention. Like the practice which gives them form, then, enthymemes express an internal direction (to a membership group) and an external direction (to a larger interested constituency) at the same time. As noted earlier, social knowledge premises creatively affect the lived reality of culture, including its extensiveness. Enthymemes are, in short, *inventional*.

Second, the audience dependence of enthymematic reasoning, even in its traditional construal, gives the form a hybrid, synthetic quality of eclecticism and plurality. Here analysis is refigured by

differing senses of the public good, the culturally appropriate, even the venues for proper discussion. As an enactment of *phronesis* for the modern community, then, rhetorical cognition is best seen (in a kind of gloss on Arendt) as a quest for *meaning*, rather than truth.[34] To be more specific, the aim of rhetorical judgment is to particularize meaning by instantiating and refiguring possible categories and criteria through the world of action. It would seem, then, that a sense of rhetorical thinking might inform possible meanings of interested *others*, even as judgment must limit this meaning within a range of actual truths to what real membership groups *do*. From such a deliberately enlarged lens of vision, then, rhetorical cognition is essentially *figurative, informal, and directional reasoning that acquires force through the implied consensus of others*. It is figurative in the same sense that metaphorical and tropical discourses are figurative; in other words, through reliance upon a kind of slippage among literal sense and reference so as to capture—through indirection—some aspect of meaning that eludes exact definition. For instance, former American President Reagan frequently characterized the Contra insurgents in Nicaragua as "freedom-fighters,"[35] and even, "the moral equivalent of the Founding Fathers." Such a turn of phrase forces an inferential choice. Either the Founding Fathers were drug-dealing thugs, or the Contras must have some greater civic virtue than we thought. Rhetorical cognition is informal, for the obvious reason that analytic purity of distribution is here subordinated to the traditional aim of effective collaboration. And it is directional because, as we shall see, there are critical normative implications of rhetorical cognition for accepting authority, engaging issues, and even enriching our domain of responsibility.

The most critical point, however, is that all such convergences of generalizable normative convictions, specific circumstances, and identifiable audiences are likely to be *provisional*. Even in the world of antiquity, there could have been no such thing as an enthymeme that encompassed every aspect of a cultural setting. This is true both by virtue of the *phainomenai* which constitute rhetorical inference *and* by the elliptical quality of enthymematic form. An awareness of this in practice is rhetorical cognition in its revelatory mode, captured by the traction of unfinished rhetorical episodes. This more expansive sense of rhetorical cognition also helps to explain why rhetoric does not need to achieve the rarified horizon of eloquence in order to redeem itself as an art practice.

When we achieve that rarity, a monolithic consensus, even the least cynical among us will expect that a healthy portion of "productive ambiguity" has been at work in our discourse. And when we, much more frequently, find ourselves at odds over the causes of strife, the conduct of others, the avenues of *proper* recourse, something every bit as important is occurring. The very episodes we are unfolding are urging an encounter with other partisanships and thus a potential moment of reflection. Viewed this way, it simply misses the point to demean rhetoric as distorted or deformed discourse. For what else is an art practice, but the recognition of how rarely we realize perfection, of how much we must yet master to improve and advance our craft? This is, of course, a rhetorical question.

Rhetorical Community

The practical ideal of *phronesis* or practical wisdom has always involved an uneasy tension among form, content, and context. Ironically enough, those visions of rhetoric which paid least attention to the immediacy of circumstance ("the adjustment of ideas to people and people to ideas")[36] were usually forced to invoke the most utopian contexts to defend their craft. The distance from Socrates' "colloquium" to Aristotle's *polis* to the universal audiences of ideal speech situations may be shorter than we think.

Once more, we can identify two confounding polar approaches to the problem of context. The first option has been to insist upon an idealized "form of life" teleology, or mythic foundation as a precondition for a revitalized practice. The less obvious problem with this option is that we have no way of explaining how such hyper-realities are ever engendered, other than in the rarified horizons of myth and legend. The other option is to suggest that significant literary or rhetorical texts establish their own constitutive conditions for a community in miniature between reader and implied author. But this more optimistic approach shades over the pivotal question of how texts are selected and reflectively engaged in the first place.

Once more, I would like to explore the "excluded middle" by looking to contemporary *places*, where the normative "content" and convictions of membership groups may be identified and expressed. Our century has witnessed the emergence of a broader range of encounter settings where the ensemble of convictions, affiliations, and traditions we know as culture is introduced to a widening circle of acquaintance. These settings may be formal, informal, even conjectural and socially emergent. They are given urgency and impetus by rhetorical occasions; and within such occasions they sometimes constitute and acquire form through the critical controversies of our time. I refer to such places as instances of the local, civic, or global rhetorical *forum*.

As suggested in the work of Toulmin, Rieke, and Janik, a rhetorical "forum" is a more or less formal location, where types of reasoning and argument are practiced.[37] While the beginning made by these authors is most helpful, the very breadth of their conception makes it difficult to identify the institutional constraint of the forum within the operation of real rhetorical practice. Without unduly narrowing the idea of "forum," it may be useful to speculate further about its operation, so as to appreciate better its importance for contemporary *rhetorical* practice.

A rhetorical forum is any encounter setting sufficiently durable to serve as a recurring "gathering place" for discourse. As such, the forum provides a space for multiple expressed positions to encounter one another. And, in its most developed condition, the forum may also provide precedents and modalities for granting a hearing to positions, as well as sorting among their agendas and constituencies. This is a way of saying that a rhetorical forum provides a potential normative horizon, an avenue of mediation among discourses that might otherwise be self-confirming, incommensurable or perhaps not even heard at all.

The clearest historical antecedent for the rhetorical forum is probably found in the sense of public space which emerges in some idealist renderings of the Athenian *polis*. Here, for instance, is that Idealist Aristotelian, Hannah Arendt:

> The polis, properly speaking, is not the city-state in its physical location; it is the organization of the people as it arises out of acting and speaking together, and its true space lies between people living together no matter where they happen to be. "Wherever you go, you will be a polis": these famous words became not merely the watchword of Greek colonization, they expressed the conviction that action and speech can create a space between the participants which can find its proper location almost any time and anywhere. It is the space of appearance in the widest sense of the word, namely the space where I appear to others as others appear to me, where men [*sic*] exist not merely like other living or inanimate things but make their appearance explicitly.[38]

These words from Arendt might provide us with a helpful, albeit somewhat misleading, basis of our own understanding. Along the helpful side, Arendt reminds us that the fact of interpersonal affiliation and individuation is prior to any of its institutional embodiments. This is another way of saying that a sense of forum emerges whenever there is the potential for resistance, the third-party standpoint which might emerge at any time in any ongoing conversation. This sense of potential is critical. It is one reason why, in principle, the idea of a forum may never irreversibly be banished.

A second implication of Arendt's words is the emergence of appearances, in all of their plurality, within the web of interrelationships established through the presencing of others. It is the rhetorical forum which allows the plurality of appearances to be presented, witnessed and regarded, qualified and subverted by the perspectives of others. Yet, for all of this, I think Arendt's treatment tends to mystify and idealize the genuine presence of real live others in her rather primordial conception of classical political life. She thus lends undue weight to her own agenda of "dark times": that long-distance democracy and liberationist social movements are merely the further conformism of mass society in disguise.[39] More important, I think, than the actual physical presence of persons in each other's public space is the *conscious awareness* of each other's presence in the symbolic landscape of prospective thought and decision: the fact that other persons and constituencies make a difference and thus must be "taken into account" in our deliberations.

What is critical to the power and constraint of the forum is that two very different sorts of loci may always intersect there: first, is the cumulative weight of customary practice: convention, commonplace and *communis sensus* associated with the forum's own history; and second, the inevitably uncertain fact of otherness—not only that a sense of constituency has been made available. In principle, this is possible within any real public encounter setting. Much more important than a specific location in geographic space is that a forum have some durability and continuity over time. It needs to be accessible to those who wish to participate, recurrently so. And it needs the capacity for the projection and retrieval of messages. This creates a sense of *reflective* participation: an unavoidable supposition that one's own constituency may be tested by the interests of others who are involved, even if they are unrepresented directly by advocacy. Viewed together, these two intersecting loci

provide the tension between strict adaptation and genuine invention. This may be only another way of saying that propriety is always possessed of both an ethical and an aesthetic dimension.

We are now beginning to approach the question of how a forum interacts with rhetorical practice. The answer, which is difficult to generalize, very much depends upon how developed and historically stabilized the forum is, the breadth of its compass or scope of coverage, the genres or types of rhetorical practice involved, and the nature of the rhetorical occasion. The core of a forum may be a kind of disturbance, an issue or contested perspective. It may also be an unfolding event or an emerging public affiliation that demands a name, a language, a form of address. For instance, a live rhetorical controversy among opposition leaders to apartheid will admit to very different frames and thematic constraints upon the rhetorical practice than will—let us say—a state funeral for a fallen leader, or—for that matter—a peace conference among previously hostile groups. But however we conceptualize the meeting point of these intersecting forces, there is within the rhetorical forum a dual sense of constraint and opportunity. In the forum of institutional stability and extended duration, there is usually an accessible, or at least translatable, body of traditions, codified in charters, and made practicable by available rules, roles, and procedures. And in more volatile settings and occasions, a forum may work as a kind of "pocket" of disturbance, an "eye of the storm," or core of tension around which other disparate positions and arguments may hover. In a rough analogy to the "pocket" of modern jazz, in which wide-ranging, virtually random dissonance may and usually does begin to collect and gather itself around a central rhythmic "core," there is in every such forum a *focus* made recognizable by the emergent familiarity of departure and return. Stable or not, the critical function of the forum is to warrant, frame, and constrain the appearance, shape, and direction of rhetorical practice.

This preliminary sketch has been an attempt to show that the rhetorical forum is, like many a "social imaginary,"[40] real in its power and implication. At the point of its greatest impact, it inscribes a set of conditions for rhetoric itself to flourish. Yet, it inevitably raises certain issues itself. How are tensions among forum and practical choice to be addressed and explained? And in occasions of disturbance and controversy, how are we to find, identify, and appraise the intersecting performances of practice and forum? If we are to appreciate fully the importance of the contemporary rhetorical forum for the development of discourse practice, we need to merge our traditional senses of rhetorical *phronesis* and rhetorical cognition within this larger picture. The issues and questions we have raised may then be viewed from perspectives that are internal and external to the occasion at hand.

In what we understand as its "normalized" condition, the rhetorical forum provides loose but recognizable admission criteria as to who may speak, what may be spoken about, and how we might be held accountable for what we say and do. In a very general sense, each of these sets of constraints may be subsumed under the large category of the *appropriate*, perhaps the closest congruence we have between emancipatory reason and *phronesis*. However, a rhetorical sense of the appropriate would identify norms that are more specific than universal validity claims. In the world of *phainomenai* where rhetoric must dwell, norms for speakers, messages, and constituencies are evoked which are provisional and situation-specific. We might think of these in the following ways:

Type	Locus	Value
1. speaker-centered norm	*ethos* or perspective	norm of authority
2. message-centered norm	*stasis* or issue	norm of integrity
3. constituency-centered	*krisis* or judgment	norm of conscience[41]

As stated above, a normalized forum (say, an awards ceremony or a court of law) will admit to fairly specific constraints along all three of these continua. And yet even in these cases, there is a further characteristic worth noting about a rhetorical sense of the appropriate. Instead of presupposing the appropriate as an *a priori* validity claim in advance of speech, *rhetorical practice enacts the norms of propriety collaboratively with interested collective others*. In the rhetorical forum, rhetoric is both the animated and the animator. This is because the very conditions of propriety are continually being reindividuated and renewed with every specific case. And it is also because particularly challenging disputes about what constitutes proper authority, integrity, and responsibility can have the effect of enriching, refraining, and perhaps reinventing the boundaries of rhetorical community itself. As White has suggested of cul-

tural languages generally, this process of change and renewals is not always conspicuous, but it is surely ongoing.[42]

Authority may be considered as a variation of *ethos*, a grounded entitlement to offer a perspective on appearances based upon some claim to a constituency.[43] Even in well-structured forum contexts, the inscription of authority may be opened to propriety dispute. When newly enshrined rhetorical hero Václav Havel visited Kurt Waldheim in Austria, he was quickly denounced for having lent legitimacy to Waldheim's questionable past.[44] Havel's supporters replied by observing that Havel had visited Austria to attend the Salzburg Festival, and not to see Waldheim. His conduct, in other words, could be redeemed by a different understanding of its forum and propriety context. But once the issue is raised, this is not necessarily the end of the matter. Here, for instance, was Havel himself at Salzburg after Waldheim had introduced him:

> A person who is afraid of what is yet to come is generally also reluctant to look in the face of what has been. And a person afraid to look at his own past must fear what is to come . . . Those who falsify history do not protect the freedom of the nation but rather constitute a threat to it. The idea that a person can rewrite his autobiography is one of the traditional self-deceptions of Central Europe. Trying to do that means hurting oneself and one's fellow countrymen. When a truth is not given complete freedom, freedom is not complete.[45]

And perhaps that is why this matter of perspective is unlikely to be so easily resolved, for it is difficult to imagine eloquent and confrontational lines such as these delivered at a purely *aesthetic* occasion.

While some concerns about authority lend themselves to provisional resolution through a more proper positioning within a forum, other cases are not nearly so tidy. When the Reagan administration chose to honor German war dead at Bitburg, for instance, many questioned whether even the President of the United States possessed the breadth of perspective to authorize a redefinition for a twentieth-century marker event.[46] Yet it could be claimed that the debate about this issue was actually a positive development, rekindling an encounter with dark memory as our turbulent century draws to a close.

Integrity, as I am using the term, deals with the way issues and positions fall out and "hold up" over the course of an ongoing episode.[47] In a rhetorical sense, integrity is less an attribute specifically applicable to persons and their characters than it is an emergent, acquired trait of messages that are presented and upheld in public life. The normalized rhetorical forum's persistence in time, its durability, provides a place stable enough for the normative expectation of integrity to emerge. A forum allows the articulation of positions to "hold still" long enough to elicit some sense of *answerability*.[48] It is the openness of a rhetorical forum that brings our positions from a stance of foreclosure to a sense of *exposure*. If one's positions and messages have integrity, they will either withstand public scrutiny, or they will react, respond, and correct themselves in light of opposed positions and messages. Lacking integrity, as a great many political messages do, they will run and hide, grin and spin. There is a sense in which all serious political disputation is about integrity; for this is what allows the very *fact* of dispute to acquire meaning. For this reason, integrity may be seen as the opposite of *hypocrisy*.[49] When Senator Nancy Kassebaum voted against John Tower's confirmation as Secretary of Defense (the only Republican to do so), it was not her motives, but her statement—on the importance of women's issues—that enacted this public sense of integrity;[50] it was an issue that every other Republican Senator in the Senate chose to overlook in the interests of Party loyalty.

While not every personality or type of character easily admits to the possibility of integrity, the *norm* of integrity only becomes available to us through the unfolding of an episodic *process*. When, after nearly ten years, the Sandinistas were not overthrown, but peacefully voted out of office, it proved to be the vindication of something called the Contadora process, rather than America's covert foreign policy. How that happened is interesting. A number of Central American States—led by President Arias of Costa Rica—began the Contadora process in an attempt to find a peaceful Central American solution to the war in Nicaragua. From the beginning, the United States covertly opposed the process, even attempting to subvert and overturn it[51] at the same time as the United States officially recognized the Sandinista government *and* Congress had expressed itself as in favor of the process.[52] Despite increasingly devious American subterfuge, the process went forward, with Arias himself receiving the Nobel Peace Prize in 1988. Although almost no American newspapers mentioned the matter, I would argue that the integrity of this *public* process accomplished some-

thing a twenty-four billion dollar covert war was unable to accomplish: a peaceful transfer of power: It is, in other words, the principle of publicity and exposure that makes integrity a possibility in public life. Once a forum has been acknowledged, it becomes very difficult to ignore.

Responsibility, as conceptualized here, involves the internalization of the voice of others as an encounter with conscience. Here "conscience" may be thought of metaphorically as the state of acting as an audience and witness for what one is and does.[53] Now the propriety of such an encounter may itself be challenged. The paths and implications of action are continuous, irreversible, and ever completely foreordained. It is a curiosity of the moral claim's generality that almost any decision or act can be charged with ramifications in this area. At the same time, almost everyone would concede that not all choices and concerns are of moral significance. And for those courses of conduct which raise moral issues, there is no easy way to delimit or finalize a proper tribune of judgment.

So this third range of concerns for the practice, forms, and fora of rhetoric is a complex, and even treacherous, territory to chart. It is often the case that our intuitions direct us further than our arguments. Accordingly, I want to borrow liberally from the work of James Boyd White and suggest that the clash of moral stance need not be an end of discussion, but an inventional challenge to continuity of discourse.[54] While it is true that audiences are usually more comfortable judging their adversaries than themselves, this does not mean that reflection and rhetoric are always at odds with one another. At times, as in Lincoln's Second Inaugural, words are found to uncover themes larger than any partisan position. And even in more recent episodes, we may and do agonize over the propriety of our positions, their distance from our deeds, the boundaries for judgment and responsibility in our life and time. Occasionally, as if by a resigned process of elimination, we are reminded that our adversary is ourselves.

To illustrate some of the complexity confronting rhetorical practice as it engages the problem of conscience, we might consider two fascinating modern cases, where the practice of rhetoric occasioned a kind of moral provocation, albeit with very different results. On New Year's Day 1990, Czech playwright and dissident Václav Havel spoke as newly-elected President of his nation to a multitude of jubilant citizens.[55] Refusing to evade responsibility for decades of post-war tyranny, Havel confronted his audience directly: "If I speak about a spoiled moral atmosphere I don't refer only to our masters . . . I'm speaking about all of us. For all of us have grown used to the totalitarian system and accepted it as an immutable fact, and thereby actually helped keep it going. None of us are only its victims; we are all also responsible for it."[56] Havel's speech marked and captioned a luminous moment of public recognition; his speech has been widely acclaimed as a touchstone of eloquence.

Now consider a rather striking contrast. About two years prior to Havel's triumph, another European, Phillip Jenninger, the speaker of the West German Parliament, chose to speak publicly about the Nazi extermination policies, on the fiftieth anniversary of Krystallnacht, the date marking the burning of the Reichstag and the intensification of the anti-Jewish pogroms.[57] All evidence indicates that Jenninger's rhetorical aim was a noble one: to remind one and all of the depth and gravity of the German historical offense. But the speech apparently so shocked those assembled—diplomats, Greens, Social Democrats, Jewish survivors, Free Democrats—that many walked out.[58] Others tried to shout down passages of the speech. Reaction was so uniformly negative within Germany that Jenninger himself was forced to resign early the next morning. And so [we] have the spectacle of two distinguished national leaders, each confronting fellow citizens with evidence of willful complicity in past sins. Both are, in other words, well-intentioned attempts to articulate a sense of public responsibility. One speech is acclaimed as a masterpiece of rhetorical eloquence, while the other occasions the disgrace and embarrassment of public exile. Why? An attempt to sketch a less-than-conclusive answer to this question might still shed some light upon the mystery of conscience in the rhetorical forum.

Clearly, one can point to qualitative differences in the craft of the rhetorical agents. Havel's speech beautifully subverts the magisterial style of party encomium by speaking the sad truths hidden by decades of hyperbole.[59] It uses the mechanistic metaphor of determinism to explain the "inevitability" of his predecessor party's collapse. And in its most memorable lines: "How is it possible that so many people immediately understood what to do and that none of them needed any advice or instructions?"[60] it refigures the peaceful revolution itself as a kind of metonymy for the rebirth of the public sphere. Undeniably, then, it is an eloquent speech, if by eloquence we mean rhetoric where *a larger vision is wedded clearly to both the critical judgment and the ordinary convictions of others, all at the same time.* By any such aesthetic standard, the Jenninger speech was a disaster. In the Western press, which printed only small excerpts from the speech, the initial sense was that Jenninger had somehow conveyed the impression that he endorsed the taboo National Socialist sentiments, that he had himself given expression to anti-Semitism.[61] Later interpretations corrected this false impression, but nonetheless concluded that Jenninger had been guilty of a monumental impropriety. As the *New York Times* summed things up, "The consensus among politicians, newspapers and many Germans today was that Mr. Jenninger had seriously erred in the style and timing of his presentation."[62] Even as read in translation, problems in the technical principles of rhetoric abound. Jenninger tried to be contrite and confrontational at the same time, and all within a kind of blurred epic genre. And even as he brought his audience face-to-face with the horrors of the camps and gas chambers, he tried to establish German complicity through the astonishing choice of an ironic tone.[63] There are, in other words, a myriad of purely technical reasons why the speech had to fail.

For all the differences in craft, however, there are also critical contrasts in the way each discourse engages the difficult relationships among responsibility, conscience, and history. Havel presents the evils of the recent past from a stance of great symbolic and historical distance. He repeatedly refers to his nation's "great creative and spiritual potential,"[64] as having been squandered. His people have had "to learn not to believe in anything," as if this cuts against our very nature.[65] By framing post-war tyranny as one monstrous aberration, he is able to remain partially removed from the evil. The revolution can be regarded as a moment of return to a healthier *and a more permanent public condition.* Jenninger, on the other hand, is completely subject to an irreversible fallen condition created and foreordained by the Holocaust. He quotes Nietzsche and Dostoevsky on a world without God, the inevitability and invincibility of evil.[66] In implicating everyone in every respect, he leaves no compensatory room for reflective distance. This is a speech without hope.

Finally, it must be said that [the] weight of events themselves has exacted a different sort of toll on each of these speeches. Havel is, after all, speaking in a moment of recovery. The injuries, while staggering and permanent, may still be placed in a kind of perspective. This is why his treatment of conscience and responsibility may offer an opportunity to recognize our complicity, and thus recover—through our own acknowledg-ment's redemptive moment—the power to forgive and thus to reinvent ourselves. In Jenninger's case, the speech could not have been adequate to the unfathomable magnitude of the event. Perhaps no speech could. When Jenninger concluded that we are all, even the children, stained by the sins of the forefathers, he had lost the only conceiv-able redemptive possibility available to him. And so this failed discourse became part of a national trauma of compulsive repetition. It could do little more and nothing less.

But now, a more radical suggestion. Even though Jenninger's speech must be marked as a monumen-tal failure in conventional terms, it also managed to place the very issue of Holocaust war guilt within a larger horizon of late twentieth century constitu-encies and concerns. It is one of the first in what is likely to be an increasing series of forensic perora-tions for our millennium. If these speeches are to be honest and truthful, they can not help but be uncomfortable as well. In holding his admittedly confused, out-of-focus mirror up to a clouded taboo subject, Jenninger threw a harsh public light on painful memories. And it is interesting that as the boundaries of his controversial forum of constitu-ency broadened, so did the civic friendship of sym-pathy appear to deepen. In tens of thousands of let-ters Jenninger has received from all over the world, he says that all but forty or fifty were supportive of his intent.[67] And so, true to his spirit of atonement, Jenninger now feels that "my sacrifice in resigning from office was very much worthwhile."[68] That, of course, is not the point. It is that this dispute itself may have worked inventionally, to move us beyond pragmatics, and even personal ethics: to prompt us to reconfigure the generational bounds of moral responsibility, to place us in the uncertain horizon of a community of conscience.

Among the many examples I have alluded to throughout this essay, the case of Jenninger is the only one in which the advocate of a contested position abides by judgment in its more tradi-tional form, as if to concede error and conform to an authoritative public verdict. And as we have just seen, even this was not the end of the mat-ter. Even in cases where disputation seems to have been "resolved," what happens is more fittingly encompassed by Burke's "barnyard scramble" met-aphor. The arguments of the opposition begin to spread, even as the norms upon which they rest are clarified. Meanwhile the arguments on one's own behalf begin to splinter, falling victim to self-contradiction, and a gradual loss of ethos, and

plausibility. In the last echo of this multi-cultural *reductio*, there is usually the shrill remonstrance of faith and good intentions, and then silence. Yet in many more cases than this, and often the most interesting cases, dispute really does not resolve itself. Like the continual reinvention of rhetorical culture, it is ongoing.

Arguments and Implications

Earlier in this essay, I raised some issues about rhetorical practice that now should be addressed, along with some implications for more detailed research. Rhetoric has often been dismissed as a form of distorted communication, and one might well draw the conclusion that its most visible func-tion throughout the body of my examples has been to confirm this impression. Beyond this difficulty is the problem of how to ground claims for a rheto-ric that would move *beyond* distortion; i.e., express a reflective capacity.

These questions can at least be approached use-fully through a broadened contemporary under-standing of the rhetorical tradition. We have begun this task by refiguring the notions of *prac-tice*, rhetorical *cognition*, and the concept of the rhetorical *forum*. Part of the mastery of rhetoric as theory consists in gaining an appreciation of the possible range of variation for subject matters of civic and public interest. But if this is all we did, the mission of rhetoric would be virtually indistin-guishable from the radically reductive playground of much post-Modernism. And so rhetoric, at least as I understand it, must take another reflective turn: to ask what proofs and possible modes of conviction might best adjudicate conflicts among partisan positions in a world lacking full dialec-tical closure for practical questions. Put another way, rhetoric does not see the sudden discovery of radical variation (which the tradition has known since the younger Cicero) as proof that "the end is near," but rather as evidence that its own con-structive possibilities are far from over.

There is a specific application of this line of thought to the first reservation. Within the enlarged vantage point of rhetorical occasions, the values and norms of any single culture take on a partisan cast. So, of course, does the discourse that must articulate these values. But such a dis-cursive *process* can only be regarded as distorted in a morally deficient manner if it removes itself from any prospect for correcting and broadening the sentiments expressed. By extending our appreciation for the practical activity of rhetoric beyond the singularity of speech acts and univocal claims, it becomes possible to locate a redemptive impetus within the larger unfolding frame of its process. We might thus think of rhetoric as constantly reminding us to make room for error and comedy, for the performance of momentary pleasure: little building blocks of possibility, provisional criteria for the small victories of practical reason.

As in the world of aesthetics generally, we are reminded frequently of the inadequacy of "mere" words to capture the beauty, or perhaps the radical opposite, in a human work. Works such as Alan Resnais' *Night and Fog*, Picasso's *Guernica*, the "No Trespassing" sign from *Citizen Kane* all come to mind. It is not paradoxical, or at least it *should* not be, that these eloquent silences actually have the effect of rejuvenating discourse. Far from devaluing words and works, such willfully failed approximations may enrich and deepen our language of mood, sentiment, and expression. A language of value which is only employed technically will surely reify values. But a language of value which is *never* employed in practical settings will just as surely atrophy. Rhetoric, as I have tried to express it here, is more than the practice; it is the entire process of forming, expressing, and judging public thought in real life.

As a concluding reflection, I would suggest that a broadened vision of rhetorical practice will make little difference if we fail to extend our horizon of appreciation for the rhetorical practitioner as well. In particular, this enhanced understanding needs to include the condition of being a rhetorical audience. This is a condition in which we are called to exert our own critical capacities to a maximum extent.[69] We have to decide—quite literally—what sort of public persons we wish to be. We might be told, for instance, that because of things done in our name, in the past, there is more for us to do now. And we may also be told, and even need to hear, that there are larger affiliative responsibilities that override these past claims on our conviction and commitment. Rhetorical audiences are not known for overarching vision and long memories. Much of the time, they must feel their way through the thicket of contention and conflict. But whatever the durability of our public feelings, they only become possible when rhetoric itself is felt and heard. To make some of the conditions for such a hearing available and perhaps even contagious has been the aim of this study, and, I am tempted to say, the larger aim of rhetorical studies generally.

NOTES

1. Alasdair MacIntyre, *After Virtue: A Study in Moral Theory* (South Bend, IN: University of Notre Dame Press, 1981), pp. 175–180. MacIntyre has elaborated upon this notion in his more recent work, *Whose Justice? Which Rationality?* (South Bend, IN: University of Notre Dame Press, 1988), pp. 124–145.

2. D. S. Hutchinson, *The Virtues of Aristotle* (London: Routledge & Kegan Paul, 1986), pp. 35–87.

3. For the "dark times" hypothesis, see MacIntyre, *After Virtue*, pp. 1–23. Also see Hannah Arendt, *The Human Condition* (Chicago: University of Chicago Press, 1958), pp. 248–325; and Max Horkheimer, *Critique of Instrumental Reason* (New York: Seabury Press, 1974). An interesting communicative variation of the critique may be found in Martin Allor, "Relocating the Site of the Audience," *Critical Studies in Mass Communication* 5 (1988): 217–234. For a helpful analysis and criticism of this hypothesis, see Patrick Brantlinger, *Bread and Circuses: Theories of Mass Culture as Social Decay* (Ithaca, NY: Cornell University Press, 1983).

4. A useful introduction to the Marxist notion of *praxis* is offered by Richard Bernstein, in *Praxis and Action: Contemporary Philosophies of Human Activity* (Philadelphia: University of Pennsylvania Press, 1971), pp. 11–83. See also Henri Lefebvre, *The Sociology of Marx*, trans. Norbert Gutterman (New York: Pantheon Books, 1968), pp. 25–58.

5. A most ingenious attempt to grapple with this dilemma may be found in Raymond Williams, *Marxism and Literature* (Oxford, UK: Oxford University Press, 1977), pp. 108–120.

6. Anthony Giddens, *A Contemporary Critique of Historical Materialism: Vol. 1, Power, Property, and the State* (Berkeley and Los Angeles: University of California Press, 1981), p. 30.

7. The examples here, on either end of the political spectrum, are too numerous to mention. But one of the most poignant cases of premature "correctness" and subsequent victimage has to be that of Georg Lukács. Late in life, Lukács was still wrestling with the ethics of an overdetermined *praxis* from nearly fifty years earlier. See Georg Lukács, Hans Heinz Holz, Leo Kofler, and Wolfgang Abendroth, *Conversations with Lukács*, ed. Theo Pinkus (Cambridge, MA: MIT Press, 1975), pp. 106–109.

8. Despite a wealth of classical commentary, recent treatments of rhetorical tradition and its development have given only passing attention to Aristotle's *Rhetoric*. See, for instance, Brian Vickers, *In Defence of Rhetoric* (Oxford, UK: Clarendon Press, 1988), pp. 18–27. Also, see Thomas M. Conley, *Rhetoric in the European Tradition* (New York: Longman, 1990), pp. 13–28. It is not my intention to indict either of these fine works; I simply note the diminished attention paid to the classical tradition's most completely realized *theory* of rhetoric.

9. Thomas Farrell, "Inventing Rhetorical Culture: Some Issues of Theory and Practice," *Rhetoric Society Quarterly, 21* (1991): 17–25.

10. Aristotle, *Eudemian Ethics, Books I, II, and III,* trans. Michael Woods (Oxford, UK: Clarendon Press, 1982), 1216b.5–25, 6–7.

11. Aristotle, *Rhetoric,* trans. W. Rhys Roberts (New York: Modern Library, 1958), 1.1355b. This is Aristotle's famous defense of *Rhetoric* as essential to that which is distinctive about "man": *logos.* See also Larry Arnhart, *Aristotle on Political Reasoning: A Commentary on the Rhetoric* (DeKalb: Northern Illinois University Press, 1981), pp. 17–51.

12. This critique of rhetoric, a recognizable variation of its Kantian and even Platonic origins, is found in German critical theory. See, for instance, Jürgen Habermas, *The Theory of Communicative Action, Vol. 1: Reason and the Rationalization of Society,* trans. Thomas McCarthy (Boston: Beacon Press, 1984), pp. 286–291. Habermas's own position is a complex one, and there is reason to believe it is shifting, where the normative properties of rhetoric are concerned.

13. MacIntyre, *After Virtue,* pp. 186–189.

14. On this matter, see also Farrell, "The Tradition of Rhetoric and the Philosophy of Communication," *Communication* (1983): 151–180.

15. See Aristotle, *Rhetoric,* 2.1381a; also see Nancy Sherman, "Aristotle on Friendship and the Shared Life," *Philosophy and Phenomenological Research* (1988): 580–613.

16. Aristotle, *Rhetoric,* 1.1354a.

17. Aristotle, *Rhetoric,* 1.1355a.

18. Aristotle, *Rhetoric,* 2.1393a–403b.

19. MacIntyre, *After Virtue,* pp. 238–245.

20. Lloyd F. Bitzer, "Aristotle's Enthymeme Revisited," *Quarterly Journal of Speech* (1959): 399–408.

21. Aristotle, *Rhetoric,* 1.1361a.25–30.

22. Aristotle, *Rhetoric,* 1.136lb–3a.

23. Hans-Georg Gadamer, "Rhetoric, Hermeneutics, and the Critique of Ideology: Meta-critical Comments on Truth and Method," in Kurt Mueller-Vollmer, ed., *The Hermeneutics Reader* (New York: Continuum, 1985), p. 278.

24. Paul Ricoeur, *The Rule of Metaphor: Multidisciplinary Studies of the Creation of Meaning in Language,* trans. Robert Czerny (Toronto: University of Toronto Press, 1977), p. 30. To be fair, both Gadamer and Ricoeur attempt to recover substantial elements of the Aristotelian rhetorical tradition for their own respective projects.

25. Aristotle, *Rhetoric,* 2.1386a.15–25.

26. Aristotle, *Rhetoric,* 2.1386a–b.

27. Nancy Sherman, "Aristotle on Friendship," pp. 610–613.

28. Allen Gross, personal correspondence.

29. Eugene Rochberg-Halton, *Meaning and Modernity: Social Theory in the Pragmatic Attitude* (Chicago: University of Chicago Press, 1986), pp. 95–188.

30. Michael Walzer, "Interpretation and Social Criticism," *The Tanner Lectures on Human Values,* 8 (1968) (Salt Lake City: University of Utah Press, 1988), p. 16.

31. While there are, for instance, many variations of the "post-Modernist" position, the most radical postures seem simply to accept the pronouncements of Western technocracy at face value. Cf. Jean Baudrillard, "Consumer Society," in *Selected Writings,* ed. Mark Poster (Stanford, CA: Stanford University Press, 1988), pp. 29–56.

32. Allan Gibbard, *Wise Choices, Apt Feelings: A Theory of Normative Judgment* (Cambridge, MA: Harvard University Press, 1990), p. 236.

33. Maurizio Passerin D'Entreves, "Freedom, Plurality, Solidarity: Hannah Arendt's Theory of Action," *Philosophy and Social Criticism* 15 (1989): 326–327.

34. Hannah Arendt, in Ronald Beiner, ed., *Lectures on Kant's Political Philosophy* (Chicago: University of Chicago Press, 1982), pp. 58–64. The present essay deviates from Arendt's pronouncements by allowing for the prospect that meaning might be made to "appear" in the present through the collaborative practices of reflection. For an illuminating discussion of Arendt's problematic distinction between "meaning" and "truth," see Mark Pollock, *A Reconsideration of the Prospects for Rhetoric in Hannah Arendt's Political Philosophy* (Ph.D. diss., Northwestern University, 1989), pp. 20–37. For a most provocative attempt to synthesize practical reason with some intuitions of critical theory, see Shawn W. Rosenberg, *Reason, Ideology, and Politics* (Princeton, NJ: Princeton University Press, 1998), pp. 85–158.

35. See "Contra Manual: The Sequel," *Harper's Magazine* 272 (1986): 16–18.

36. Donald C. Bryant, "Rhetoric: Its Function and Scope," in Joseph Schwartz and John A. Rycenga, eds., *The Province of Rhetoric* (New York: Ronald Press, 1965), p. 19.

37. Stephen Toulmin, Richard Rieke, and Allan Janik, *An Introduction to Reasoning* (New York: Macmillan, 1979), pp. 14–16.

38. Arendt, *The Human Condition,* pp. 198–199.

39. Hannah Arendt, *Between Past and Future: Eight Exercises in Political Thought* (New York: Viking Press, 1965), pp. 197–227.

40. See Cornelius Castoriadis, *The Imaginary Institution of Society.* (Cambridge, MA: MIT Press, 1987), pp. 340–353, for an elaboration of this fascinating notion.

41. What I have attempted to do with this trichotomy is to take speaker-centered, message-centered, and audience- or constituency-centered approaches to the value

assumptions behind contentious practical questions. All three regions, loosely grouped under the terrain of "prudential reason," would be bracketed as validity claims according to the universal pragmatics position; and they would be presupposed as an array of received opinions or *doxa* according to the more conservative Aristotelian position. By treating them as matters of dispute admitting multiple conceptions at cross purposes, we allow for the possibility that there might be disputation about the nature of our assumptions and ends-in-view, while—at the same time—admitting the possibility that practical reason may explore and reinvent applicable criteria for reflective thought and action.

42. See James Boyd White, *When Words Lose Their Meaning: Constitutions and Reconstitutions of Language, Character, and Community* (Chicago: University of Chicago Press, 1984), pp. 290–291.

43. See Thomas Farrell, "Reason and Rhetorical Practice: The Inventional Agenda of Chaim Perelman," in James L. Golden and Joseph J. Pilotta, eds., *Practical Reasoning in Human Affairs: Studies in Honor of Chaim Perelman* (Dordrecht, The Netherlands: D. Reidel, 1987), for an elaboration of this conception of authority.

44. Following an initial editorial criticism of Havel's Salzburg visit (published in the *New York Times*, July 29, 1990), Paul Hartman wrote to the *New York Times* defending Havel (August 1, 1990). For a partial text of Havel's actual remarks, I have relied upon Václav Havel, "The Velvet Hangover," trans. Kaca Polackova Henley, *Harper's* 281 (1990): 18–21.

45. Havel, "Velvet Hangover," p. 20.

46. For a fascinating account of the Bitburg controversy, including many of the primary documents, see Geoffrey Hartman, ed., *Bitburg in Moral and Political Perspective* (Bloomington: Indiana University Press, 1986).

47. While my use of "integrity" will strike some as eccentric, the usage seems loosely consistent with what Habermas has come to call a third level of argumentative presupposition, "the rhetorical level of processes"; see Jürgen Habermas, *Moral Consciousness and Communicative Action*, trans. Christian Lenhardt and Shierry Weber Nicholsen (Cambridge, MA: MIT Press, 1990), p. 87.

48. "The individual must become answerable through and through: all of his constituent moments must not only fit next to each other in the temporal sequence of his life, but must also interpenetrate each other in the unity of guilt and answerability" (Mikhail Bakhtin, *Art and Answerability: Early Philosophical Essays by M. M. Bakhtin*, ed. M. Holquist and V. Liapunov, trans. V. Liapunov [Austin: University of Texas Press, 1990], p. 2). In our own time, we are perhaps more likely to recognize answerability through its widely praised bureaucratic opposite: "deniability."

49. Arendt, *The Human Condition*, pp. 236–246.

50. Sen. Nancy Kassebaum, *Congressional Record—Senate*, Mar. 9, 1989, S2460–2461. See also "Kassebaum Told Bush of Decision," *Washington Post*, March 10, 1989, p. A18.

51. Amazingly, a fairly detailed outline of this long-term subversive campaign surfaced in the mainstream press. See "U.S. Said to Sabotage Peace Talks for Contras," *Chicago Tribune*, May 10, 1987, p. I27. Much more detailed investigative reporting can be found by Alfonso Chardy, in the *Miami Herald*, May 10, 1987, RETLIB, take: OIZ, ver: 1.01. Special appreciation to *Tribune* international editor Judy Peres.

52. The United States Senate voted 97–1 on May 12, 1987 to endorse the Contadora peace process; see *Congressional Record*, Thurs. May 12, 1987, No. 39S3807.

53. On this elusive question of "consciences" which most persons recognize but few can explain, I am particularly indebted to Michael Hyde. See M. Hyde, "The Conscience of Rhetoric: Heidegger's Poetic Mistake" (presentation to Speech Communication Association, November 3, 1990, Chicago).

54. "The paradoxical combination of certainty and uncertainty, of clarity and silence, makes the world at once intelligible and alive with tension, both for us as readers and for the actors within it. No simple print-out of a cultural pattern, this is a world of contention and struggle in which everything can be put into question, a moral and rhetorical universe in which the actors constantly claim meanings for what is said and done and do so in competition with each other. It lives by a politics of persuasion, upon a premise of instability. In this it may be a model of all politics." The world of which James Boyd White speaks is that of Homer's *Iliad* (see White, *When Words Lose Their Meaning*, pp. 55–56).

55. See, for recent background, Thomas Omestad, "Ten-Day Wonder," *New Republic*, December 25, 1989, pp. 19–22. A fine journalistic treatment of the events in Eastern Europe, including the "Prague Fall," is now available in Timothy Garton Ash, *The Magic Lantern: The Revolution of '89 Witnessed in Warsaw, Budapest, Berlin, and Prague* (New York: Random House, 1990), esp. pp. 78–156.

56. Václav Havel, "New Year's Day Address," Jan. 1, 1990, *New York Times* translation. The complete text of this speech is available in *Vesnik*, February 1990, pp. 401, 3–5.

57. An initial account of the furor can be found in Serge Schmemann, "Blunt Bonn Speech on the Hitler Years Prompts a Walkout," special to the *New York Times*, November 11, 1988, p. 1.

58. See, for further discussion and response, Judea B. Miller, "Jewish Victims and German Indifference," *Christian Century*, December 14, 1988, pp. 1144–1145. Also see Victoria Barnett, "Jewish Victims and German Sensitivity," *Christian Century*, March 15, 1989, pp. 287–288. For a remarkable misconstrual of the speech and

the reasons for its failings, see Jeffrey Herf, "Phillip Jen-ninger and the Dangers of Speaking Clearly," *Partisan Review* (1989): 225–236.

59. Havel, *New York Times* translation.

60. Ibid.

61. Serge Schmemann, "Bonn Speaker Out after Nazi Speech," *New York Times*, p. 1.

62. Ibid.

63. Phillip Jenninger, "Speech of Commemoration," November 10, 1988. Full German text is available in *Die Zeit*, November 1988, pp. 4–6. Translation by T. Farrell and J. Stoeckler.

64. Havel, "New Year's Day Speech."

65. Ibid.

66. Jenninger, "Speech of Commemoration," p. 5.

67. Serge Schmemann, "A Very German Storm: Dust Settles and Unsettles," *New York Times*, December 14, 1988, p. A4.

68. Phillip Jenninger, quoted in Schmemann, "A Very German Storm."

69. The sense of audience reflection I have in mind is most akin to that discussed by Robert L. Scott in his seminal essay, "The Tacit Dimension and Rhetoric: What It Means to Be Persuading and Persuaded," *Pre-Text* 2(1–2) (1981): 115–124.

Beyond Persuasion

A Proposal for an Invitational Rhetoric

Sonja K. Foss
Cindy L. Griffin

Acknowledgment of the patriarchal bias that undergirds most theories of rhetoric is growing steadily in the communication discipline. As feminist scholars have begun to explicate the ways in which standard theories of rhetoric embody patriarchal perspectives, they have identified communicative modes that previously have not been recognized or theorized because they are grounded in alternative values (see, for example, Edson, 1985; Elshtain, 1982; Foss & Foss, 1991; Foss, Foss, & Trapp, 1991; Foss & Griffin, 1992; Gearhart, 1979; Griffin, 1993; Kramarae, 1989; Shepherd, 1992). Attention to non-patriarchal forms of communication, feminist scholars argue, expands the scope of rhetorical theory and enhances the discipline's ability to explain diverse communicative phenomena successfully.

One manifestation of the patriarchal bias that characterizes much of rhetorical theorizing is the definition of rhetoric as persuasion. As far back as the Western discipline of rhetoric has been explored, rhetoric has been defined as the conscious intent to change others. As Shepherd (1992) notes, in humanistic, social scientific, and critical perspectives on communication, "interaction processes have typically been characterized essentially and primarily in terms of persuasion, influence, and power" (p. 204). Every communicative encounter has been viewed "as primarily an attempt at persuasion or influence, or as a struggle over power" (p. 206). As natural as an equation of rhetoric with persuasion seems for scholars of rhetoric, this conception is only one perspective on rhetoric and one, we suggest, with a patriarchal bias. Implicit in a conception of rhetoric as persuasion is the assumption that humans are on earth to alter the "environment and to influence the social affairs" of others. Rhetorical scholars "have taken as given that it is a proper and even necessary human function to attempt to change others" (Gearhart, 1979, p. 195). The desire to effect change is so pervasive that the many ways in which humans engage in activities designed for this purpose often go unnoticed:

> We conquered trees and converted them into a house, taking pride in having accomplished a difficult task. We conquered rivers and streams and converted them into lakes, marvelling in ourselves at the improvement we made on nature. We tramped with our conquering spaceboots on the fine ancient dust of the Moon and we sent our well-rehearsed statements of triumph back for a waiting world to hear. (Gearhart, 1979, p. 196)

Embedded in efforts to change others is a desire for control and domination, for the act of changing another establishes the power of the change agent over that other. In some instances, the power of the rhetor over another is overt, as it is, for example, in laws that exert control over women's bodies, such as those concerned with abortion. In securing the adherence of women to these laws, lawmakers have power over women and their lives. But even in cases where the strategies used are less coercive, rhetors who convince others to adopt their viewpoints exert control over part of those others' lives. A student who tells another student that she ought to take a particular course, for example, controls or influences the nature of another's life, if only for a few minutes, if the other enrolls in the course or even considers enrolling in it. We suggest that a strikingly large part of many individuals' lives is spent in such efforts to change others, even when the desired changes have absolutely no impact on the lives of the change agents. Whether a friend enrolls in a particular course, for example, often is irrelevant to a student's own life.

The reward gained from successful efforts to make others change is a "rush of power" (Gearhart, 1979, p. 201)—a feeling of self-worth that comes from controlling people and situations. The value of the self for rhetors in this rhetorical system comes from the rhetor's ability to demonstrate superior knowledge, skills, and qualifications—in other words, authority—in order to dominate the perspectives and knowledge of those in their audiences. The value of the self derives not from a recognition of the uniqueness and inherent value of each living being but from gaining control over others.

The act of changing others not only establishes the power of the rhetor over others but also devalues the lives and perspectives of those others. The belief systems and behaviors others have created for living in the world are considered by rhetors to be inadequate or inappropriate and thus in need of change. The speaker's role very often "may be best described as paternalistic" (Scott, 1991, p. 205) in that the rhetor adopts a "'let me help you, let me enlighten you, let me show you the way' approach" (Gearhart, 1979, p. 195). Audience members are assumed to be naive and less expert than the rhetor if their views differ from the rhetor's own.

Rhetorical scholars have prided themselves on the eschewal of physical force and coercion and the use, in their place, of "language and metalanguage, with refined functions of the mind" (Gearhart, 1979, p. 195) to influence others and produce change. Although these discursive strategies allow more choice to the audience than do the supposedly more heavy-handed strategies of physical coercion, they still infringe on others' rights to believe as they choose and to act in ways they believe are best for them. Even discursive strategies can constitute a kind of trespassing on the personal integrity of others when they convey the rhetor's belief that audience members have inadequacies that in some way can be corrected if they adhere to the viewpoint of the rhetor. Such strategies disallow, in other words, the possibility that audience members are content with the belief systems they have developed, function happily with them, and do not perceive a need to change.

The traditional conception of rhetoric, in summary, is characterized by efforts to change others and thus to gain control over them, self-worth derived from and measured by the power exerted over others, and a devaluation of the life worlds of others. This is a rhetoric of patriarchy, reflecting its values of change, competition, and domination. But these are not the only values on which a rhetorical system can be constructed, and we would like to propose as one alternative a feminist rhetoric.

Although definitions of *feminism* vary, feminists generally are united by a set of basic principles. We have chosen to focus on three of these principles—equality, immanent value, and self-determination—to serve as the starting place for a new rhetoric. These principles are ones that explicitly challenge the positive value the patriarchy accords to changing and thus dominating others. Primary among the feminist principles on which our proposed rhetoric is based is a commitment to the creation of relationships of equality and to the elimination of the dominance and elitism that characterize most human relationships.

As Wood (1994) aptly summarizes this principle, "I don't accept oppression and domination as worthy human values, and I don't believe differences must be ranked on a continuum of good and bad. I believe there are better, more humane and enriching ways to live" (p. 4). Efforts to dominate and gain power over others cannot be used to develop relationships of equality, so feminists seek to replace the "alienation, competition, and dehumanization" that characterize relationships of domination with "intimacy, mutuality, and camaraderie" (hooks, 1984, p. 34).

Yet another principle that undergirds most feminisms is a recognition of the immanent value of all living beings. The essence of this principle is that every being is a unique and necessary part of the pattern of the universe and thus has value. Immanent value derives from the simple principle that "your life is worth something. . . . You need only be what you are" (Starhawk, 1987, pp. 115–116). Worth cannot be determined by positioning individuals on a hierarchy so they can be ranked and compared or by attending to emblems of external achievement, for worth cannot be "earned, acquired, or proven" (Starhawk, 1987, p. 21). Concomitant with a recognition of the immanent value of another individual is the eschewal of forms of communication that seek to change that individual's unique perspective to that held by the rhetor.

Self-determination is a third principle that typically comprises a feminist world view. Grounded in a respect for others, self-determination allows individuals to make their own decisions about how they wish to live their lives. Self-determination involves the recognition that audience members are the authorities on their own lives and accords respect to others' capacity and right to constitute their worlds as they choose. As Johnson (1991) explains, this principle involves a trust that others are doing the best they can at the moment and simply need "to be unconditionally accepted as the experts on their own lives" (p. 162). When others are seen as experts who are making competent decisions about their lives, efforts by a rhetor to change those decisions are seen as a violation of their life worlds and the expertise they have developed.

Our purpose in this essay is to propose a definition and explication of a rhetoric built on the principles of equality, immanent value, and self-determination rather than on the attempt to control others through persuasive strategies designed to effect change. Although we believe that persuasion is often necessary, we believe an alternative exists that may be used in instances when changing and controlling others is not the rhetor's goal; we call this rhetoric *invitational rhetoric*. In what follows, we offer a description of this rhetoric, beginning with a discussion of its definition and purpose and then describing the communicative options available to rhetors who wish to use it. We conclude our essay with two examples of invitational rhetoric and a discussion of some implications of invitational rhetoric for rhetorical theory.

Although invitational rhetoric is constructed largely from feminist theory, the literature in which its principles and various dimensions have been theorized most thoroughly, we are not suggesting that only feminists have dealt with and developed its various components or that only feminists adhere to the principles on which it is based. Some dimensions of this rhetoric have been explicated by traditional rhetorical theorists, and we have incorporated their ideas into our descrip-

tion of this rhetoric. We also do not want to suggest that the rhetoric we propose describes how all women communicate or that it is or can be used only by women. Feminism "implies an understanding of inclusion with interests beyond women" (Wood, 1993, p. 39), and its aim is not to "privilege women over men" or "to benefit solely any specific group of women" (hooks, 1984, p. 26). The rhetoric we describe is a rhetoric used at various times by some women and some men, some feminists and some non-feminists. What makes it feminist is not its use by a particular population of rhetors but rather the grounding of its assumptions in feminist principles and theories. Our goal in offering this theory is to expand the array of communicative options available to all rhetors and to provide an impetus for more focused and systematic efforts to describe and assess rhetoric in all of its manifestations.

Definition

Invitational rhetoric is an invitation to understanding as a means to create a relationship rooted in equality, immanent value, and self-determination. Invitational rhetoric constitutes an invitation to the audience to enter the rhetor's world and to see it as the rhetor does. In presenting a particular perspective, the invitational rhetor does not judge or denigrate others' perspectives but is open to and tries to appreciate and validate those perspectives, even if they differ dramatically from the rhetor's own. Ideally, audience members accept the invitation offered by the rhetor by listening to and trying to understand the rhetor's perspective and then presenting their own. When this happens, rhetor and audience alike contribute to the thinking about an issue so that everyone involved gains a greater understanding of the issue in its subtlety, richness, and complexity. Ultimately, though, the result of invitational rhetoric is not just an understanding of an issue. Because of the nonhierarchical, nonjudgmental, nonadversarial framework established for the interaction, an understanding of the participants themselves occurs, an understanding that engenders appreciation, value, and a sense of equality.

The stance taken by invitational rhetors toward their audiences obviously is different from that assumed by traditional rhetors. Invitational rhetors do not believe they have the right to claim that their experiences or perspectives are superior to those of their audience members and refuse to impose their perspectives on them. Rhetors view the choices selected by audience members as right for them at that particular time, based on their own abilities to make those decisions. Absent are efforts to dominate another because the goal is the understanding and appreciation of another's perspective rather than the denigration of it simply because it is different from the rhetor's own. The result of the invitational rhetor's stance toward the audience is a relationship of equality, respect, and appreciation.

Invitational rhetoric is characterized, then, by the openness with which rhetors are able to approach their audiences. Burke (1969) suggests that rhetors typically adjust their conduct to the external resistance they expect in the audience or situation: "We in effect modify our own assertion in reply to its assertion" (p. 237). In invitational rhetoric, in contrast, resistance is not anticipated, and rhetors do not adapt their communication to expected resistance in the audience. Instead, they identify possible impediments to the creation of understanding and seek to minimize or neutralize them so they do not remain impediments.

Change may be the result of invitational rhetoric, but change is not its purpose. When change does occur as a result of understanding, it is different from the kind of change that typifies the persuasive interactions of traditional rhetoric. In the traditional model, change is defined as a shift in the audience in the direction requested by the rhetor, who then has gained some measure of power and control over the audience. In invitational rhetoric, change occurs in the audience or rhetor or both as a result of new understanding and insights gained in the exchange of ideas. As rhetors and audience members offer their ideas on an issue, they allow diverse positions to be compared in a process of discovery and questioning that may lead to transformation for themselves and others. Participants even may choose to be transformed because they are persuaded by something someone in the interaction says, but the insight that is persuasive is offered by a rhetor not to support the superiority of a particular perspective but to contribute to the understanding by all participants of the issue and of one another.

The internal processes by which transformation occurs also are different in invitational rhetoric. In traditional rhetoric, the change process often is accompanied by feelings of inadequacy, insecurity, pain, humiliation, guilt, embarrassment, or angry submission on the part of the audience as rhetors communicate the superiority of their positions and the deficiencies of those of the audience. In invitational rhetoric, on the other hand, rhetors recognize the valuable contributions audience members can make to the rhetors' own thinking and understanding, and they do not engage in strategies that may damage or sever the connection between them and their audiences. This does not mean that invitational rhetoric always is free of pain. In invitational rhetoric, there may be a wrenching loose of ideas as assumptions and positions are questioned as a result of an interaction, a process that may be uncomfortable. But because rhetors affirm the beliefs of and communicate respect for others, the changes that are made are likely to be accompanied by an appreciation for new perspectives gained and gratitude for the assistance provided by others in thinking about an issue.

Communicative Options

The process of engaging in invitational rhetoric assumes two primary rhetorical forms. One is offering perspectives, a mode by which rhetors put forward for consideration their perspectives; the second is the creation of external conditions that allow others to present their perspectives in an atmosphere of respect and equality.

Offering Perspectives

When rhetors do not seek to impose their positions on audience members in invitational rhetoric, the presentation and function of individual perspectives differ significantly from their nature and function in traditional rhetorics. Individual perspectives are articulated in invitational rhetoric as carefully, completely, and passionately as possible to give them full expression and to invite their careful consideration by the participants in the interaction. This articulation occurs not through persuasive argument but through offering—the giving of expression to a perspective without advocating its support or seeking its acceptance. Offering involves not probing or invading but giving, a process "of wrapping around the givee, of being available to her/him without insisting; our giving is *a presence*, an *offering*, an *opening*" (Gearhart, 1982, p. 198). In offering, rhetors tell what they currently know or understand; they present their vision of the world and show how it looks and works for them.

As a rhetorical form, offering may appear to be similar to some traditional rhetorical strategies, such as the use of personal narrative as a form of support for a rhetor's position. But narrative as offering functions differently from narrative as a means of support. It is presented in offering for the purpose of articulating a viewpoint but not as a means to increase the likelihood of the audience's adherence to that viewpoint. The offering of a personal narrative is, itself, the goal; the means and the ends are the same in offering. Offering is not based on a dichotomy of cause and effect, an action done in the present to affect the future. Instead, as Johnson (1989) explains, the "'means are the ends; . . . *how* we do something is *what* we get'" (p. 35). In this mode, then, a story is not told as a means of supporting or achieving some other end but as an end in itself—simply offering the perspective the story represents.

A critical dimension of the offering of a perspective, in whatever form it takes, is a willingness to yield. Not unlike Buber's (1965) notion of the "I–Thou" relationship, the basic movement of a willingness to yield is a turning toward the other. It involves meeting another's position "in its uniqueness, letting it have its impact" (p. xiv). Tracy (1987) explains the connection between the meeting of another's uniqueness and a willingness to yield: "To attend to the other as other, the different as different, is also to understand the different *as* possible" (p. 20). When they assume such a stance, rhetors communicate a willingness to call into question the beliefs they consider most inviolate and to relax their grip on those beliefs. The process is not unlike the self-risk that Natanson (1965) describes as the risking

> of the self's world of feeling, attitude, and the total subtle range of its affective and conative sensibility. . . . [W]hen I truly risk myself in arguing I open myself to the viable possibility that the consequence of an argument may be to make me *see* something of the structure of my immediate world. (p. 15)

Scott (1976) calls this self-risk "a grave risk: the risk of the self that resides in a value structure" (p. 105). Thus, the perspective presented through offering represents an initial, tentative commitment to that perspective—one subject to revision as a result of the interaction.

A few specific examples of offering may clarify the nature of this rhetorical form. Although much rarer than we would like, offering sometimes occurs in academic settings when faculty members and/or students gather to discuss a topic of mutual interest. When they enter the interaction with a goal not of converting others to their positions but of sharing what they know, extending one another's ideas, thinking critically about all the ideas offered, and coming to an understanding of the subject and of one another, they are engaged in offering. Offering also is marked by discursive forms such as "I tried this solution when that happened to me; I thought it worked well" or "What would happen if we introduced the idea of _____ into this problem?" rather than statements with forms such as "You really ought to do _____" or "Your idea is flawed because you failed to take into account _____."

Offering may occur not only in small-group settings but also in formal presentational contexts. A rhetor who presents her ideas at an academic colloquium, for example, engages in offering when she presents her ideas as valuable yet also as tentative. She acknowledges the fact that her work is in progress; thus, she is open to the ideas of others so she can continue to revise and improve it. She builds on and extends the work of others rather than tearing their ideas apart in an effort to establish the superiority of her own. In an offering mode, she provides explanations for the sources of her ideas rather than marshalling evidence to establish their superiority. Audience members, too, may engage in offering behavior. They do so when they ask questions and make comments designed not to show the stupidity or error of the perspective presented or to establish themselves as more powerful or expert than the presenter. Instead, their questions and suggestions are aimed at learning more about the presenter's ideas, understanding them more thoroughly, nurturing them, and offering additional ways of thinking about the subject for everyone involved in the interaction.

We have tried to write this essay using such features of the offering form. We present a *proposal* for an invitational rhetoric, for example, a word we chose deliberately to suggest that what we present here is only one of many equally legitimate perspectives possible. We suggest that invitational rhetoric is a viable form of interaction in many instances but do not assert that it is the only appropriate form of rhetoric and should be used in all situations or contexts. We acknowledge the importance and usefulness of traditional theories of rhetoric even as we propose an alternative to them, and we try to build on and extend the work of other theorists—both traditional and feminist—rather than characterizing their work as inaccurate or misguided. Although we are constrained somewhat by the format of a journal article, we see this essay as in progress and plan to continue to work on our ideas; the responses of some of our colleagues and the reviewers and editor of *Communication Monographs* already have helped us clarify and improve our description of this rhetoric. We have attempted, then, to model the offering of a perspective within the perimeters allowed by a framework of scholarly discourse.

Offering also may be seen in the nonverbal realm; a perspective may be offered in the clothing individuals wear, the places in which and how they live, and in all of the symbolic choices rhetors make that reveal their perspectives. This kind of offering is illustrated by Purple Saturday, sponsored by the Women's Caucus at Speech Communication Association (SCA) conventions. On Purple Saturday, the women attending the convention (and those men who wish to show their support for women) are asked to wear purple, a color of the early women's suffrage movement, to proclaim women's solidarity and presence in SCA. When women wear purple on Saturday at the convention, they are not trying to persuade others to become feminists, to accept feminist scholarship, or to value women. Instead, they are simply offering a perspective so that those who wish to learn more about feminist scholarship or to join in the celebration of feminism may do so. Although not designed to influence others to change in particular directions, such nonverbal offerings may have that effect; some who view the wearing of purple by others at a convention may choose, for example, to explore or engage in feminist research themselves.

Another form offering may take, particularly in a hostile situation or when a dominant perspective is very different from the one held by the rhetor, is re-sourcement (Gearhart, 1982). Re-sourcement is a response made by a rhetor according to a framework, assumptions, or principles other than those suggested in the precipitating message. In using re-sourcement, the rhetor deliberately draws energy from a new source—a source other than the individual or system that provided the initial frame for the issue. It is a means, then, of communicating a perspective that is different from that of the individual who produced the message to which the rhetor is responding. Re-sourcement is not unlike Burke's (1984) notion of perspective by incongruity, but in re-sourcement, the juxtaposition of two systems or frameworks is split between rhetor and audience, with one reflected in the original message, the other in the response.

Re-sourcement involves the two processes of disengagement from the framework, system, or principles embedded in the precipitating message and the creative development of a response so that the issue is framed differently. Rorty's (1986) description of the process of generating new vocabularies points to this two-part process: "The idea is to get a vocabulary which is (at the moment) incommensurable with the old in order to draw attention away from the issues stated in the old, and thereby help people to forget them" (p. 114). In Forget's (1989) words, this kind of communication is "a swerve, a leap to the other side, which lets us . . . deploy another logic or system" (p. 136).

Although a refusal to engage in conflict or interaction under the terms proposed by a rhetor sometimes is seen as a negative, ineffective form of communication because it is interpreted as disconfirmation (e.g., Veenendall & Feinstein, 1990) or as a kind of manipulation associated with passive–aggressive behavior, it can be a positive response to a situation. It allows rhetors to continue to value themselves as well as the audience because it communicates that they are not willing to allow the audience to violate their integrity. Re-sourcement also opens up possibilities for future rhetorical choices, providing more options for rhetors than were previously available. As later options, rhetors who use re-sourcement may articulate their positions through more traditional forms of offering or standard forms of persuasion.

An example of re-sourcement is provided by Starhawk (1987) in her description of an incident that followed the blockade of the Livermore Weapons Lab in California to protest its development of nuclear weapons. She and other women were arrested and held in a school gym, and during their confinement, a woman was chased into the gym by six guards. She dove into a cluster of women, and they held on to her as the guards pulled at her legs, trying to extract her from the group. The guards were on the verge of beating the women when one woman sat down and began to chant. As the other women followed suit, the guards' actions changed in response:

> They look bewildered. Something they are unprepared for, unprepared even to name, has arisen in our moment of common action. They do not know what to do. And so, after a moment, they withdraw. . . . In that moment in the jail, the power of domination and control met something outside its

comprehension, a power rooted in another source. (p. 5)

The guards' message was framed in a context of opposition, violence, hostility, and fear; the women, in contrast, chose to respond with a message framed in terms of nonviolence and connection.

Re-sourcement in a discursive form is exemplified in a story told by Watzlawick, Weakland, and Fisch (1974) about a police officer who was

> issuing a citation for a minor traffic violation when a hostile crowd began to gather around him. By the time he had given the offender his ticket, the mood of the crowd was ugly and the sergeant was not certain he would be able to get back to the relative safety of his patrol car. It then occurred to him to announce in a loud voice: "You have just witnessed the issuance of a traffic ticket by a member of your Oakland Police Department." And while the bystanders were busy trying to fathom the deeper meaning of this all too obvious communique, he got into his cruiser and drove off. (pp. 108–109)

The initial message presented to the police officer was framed in the context of opposition and hostility; he chose, however, to respond with a message grounded in a framework of simple explanation, cooperation, and respect. Re-sourcement, as a means of offering, allowed him to diffuse the situation and to communicate his own perspective—that he was doing the job he was hired by the crowd members, as taxpayers, to do.

External Conditions

Offering can occur whether or not an audience chooses to join with a rhetor in a process of discovery and understanding. But if invitational rhetoric is to result in *mutual* understanding of perspectives, it involves not only the offering of the rhetor's perspective but the creation of an atmosphere in which audience members' perspectives also can be offered. We propose that to create such an environment, an invitational rhetoric must create three external conditions in the interaction between rhetors and audience members—safety, value, and freedom. These are states or prerequisites required if the possibility of mutual understanding is to exist.

The condition of *safety* involves the creation of a feeling of security and freedom from danger for the audience. Rhetoric contributes to a feeling of safety when it conveys to audience members that the ideas and feelings they share with the rhetor will be received with respect and care. When rhetoric establishes a safe context, the rhetor makes no attempt to hurt, degrade, or belittle audience members or their beliefs, and audience members do not fear rebuttal of or retribution for their most fundamental beliefs. Even in a volatile situation such as that described by Starhawk, when the guards were about to beat a woman seeking safe haven in a group of protesters, rhetoric that promotes a feeling of safety can be created. In this case, the women did nothing to endanger the guards or make them feel as though they would be hurt. They did not fight them physically or argue against the guards' use of force; neither did they engage in verbal abuse or ridicule the guards' training and beliefs about how to deal with prisoners.

Rhetoric that contributes to a feeling of safety also provides some means for audience members to order the world so it seems coherent and makes sense to them. When audience members feel their sense of order is threatened or challenged, they are more likely to cling to familiar ways of thinking and to be less open to understanding the perspectives of others. When a safe environment is created, then, audience members trust the rhetor and feel the rhetor is working with and not against them.

The condition of *value* is the acknowledgment that audience members have intrinsic or immanent worth. This value is what Benhabib (1992) calls "*the principle of universal moral respect*"—"the right of all beings capable of speech and action to be participants" in the conversation (p. 29). Barrett (1991) describes this condition as "respectfully, affirming others" while at the same time "one affirms oneself (p. 148).

Value is created when rhetors approach audience members as "unrepeatable individuals" and eschew "distancing, depersonalizing, or paternalistic attitudes" (Walker, 1989, pp. 22, 23). As a result, audience members feel their identities are not forced upon or chosen for them by rhetors. Rhetors do not attempt to fit audience members into any particular roles but face "the 'otherness of the other,' one might say to face their 'alterity,' their irreducible distinctness and difference from the self" (Benhabib, 1992, p. 167). Rhetors celebrate the unique and individual identities of audience members—what Benhabib (1992) describes as the actuality of my choices, namely to how I, as a finite, concrete, embodied individual, shape and fashion the circumstances of my birth and family, linguistic, cultural and gender identity into a coherent narrative that stands as my life's story. (pp. 161–162)

One way in which rhetoric may contribute to the acknowledgment and celebration of freely chosen, unique identities by audience members is through a process Gendlin (1978) calls "*absolute listening*" (p. 116), Morton (1985) describes as "hearing to speech" (p. 202), and Johnson (1987) terms "hearing into being" (p. 130). In such rhetoric, listeners do not interrupt, comfort, or insert anything of their own as others tell of their experiences. Such a stance contrasts with typical ways of listening, in which "we nearly always stop each other from getting very far inside. Our advice, reactions, encouragements, reassurances, and well-intentioned comments actually prevent people from feeling understood" (Gendlin, 1978, p. 116) and encourage them to direct their comments toward listeners' positions or orientations (Johnson, 1987). While speaking to listeners who do not insert themselves into the talk, individuals come to discover their own perspectives. Morton (1985) quotes a woman's description of her experience in the process of being heard to speech: "'You didn't smother me. You gave it [my voice] space to shape itself. You gave it time to come full circle'" (p. 205).

Value is conveyed to audience members when rhetors not only listen carefully to the perspectives of others but try to think from those perspectives. Benhabib's (1992) notion of the "'reversibility of perspectives'" (p. 145) is relevant here; it is the capacity to reverse perspectives and to reason from the standpoint of others, "making present to oneself what the perspectives of others involved are or could be" (p. 137). When value is created in a communicative situation, audience members feel rhetors see them as significant individuals and appreciate and attend to their uniqueness. They feel rhetors care about them, understand their ideas, and allow them to contribute in significant ways to the interaction.

Freedom, the power to choose or decide, is a third condition whose presence in an environment is a prerequisite for the possibility of mutual understanding. In invitational rhetoric, rhetors do not place restrictions on an interaction. Participants can bring any and all matters to the interaction for consideration; no subject matter is off limits, and all presuppositions can be challenged. The rhetor's ideas also are not privileged over those of the audience in invitational rhetoric. All the participants in the interaction are able, in Barrett's (1991) words, to "speak up, to speak out" (p. 148). Benhabib (1992) calls this "*the principle of egalitarian reciprocity*" (p. 29); within conversations, it suggests, "each has the same symmetrical rights to various speech acts, to initiate new topics, to ask for reflection about the presuppositions of the conversation, etc." (p. 29).

Freedom also is developed when a rhetor provides opportunities for others to develop and choose options from alternatives they, themselves, have created. Rather than presenting a predetermined set of options from which individuals may choose, a rhetor who wishes to facilitate freedom allows audience members to develop the options that seem appropriate to them, allowing for the richness and complexity of their unique subjective experiences. Perspectives are articulated as a means to widen options—to generate more ideas than either rhetors or audiences had initially—in contrast to traditional rhetoric, where rhetors seek to limit the options of audiences and encourage them to select the one they advocate.

Freedom of choice is made available to audiences, as well, in that, in invitational rhetoric, the audience's lack of acceptance of or adherence to the perspective articulated by the rhetor truly makes no difference to the rhetor. Some audience members will choose to try to understand the perspective of the rhetor, but others will not. Of those who do, some will choose to accept the perspective offered by the rhetor, but others will not. Either outcome—acceptance or rejection—is seen as perfectly acceptable by the invitational rhetor, who is not offended, disappointed, or angry if audience members choose not to adopt a particular perspective. Should the audience choose not to accept the vision articulated by the rhetor, the connection between the rhetor and the audience remains intact, and the audience still is valued and appreciated by the rhetor. The maintenance of the connection between rhetors and audiences is not dependent on rhetors' approval of the choices made by audience members. Rogers' (1962) notion of unconditional positive regard suggests the nature of the autonomy the rhetor accords the audience; the audience has the freedom to make choices without the possibility of losing the respect of the rhetor.

Illustrations

Invitational rhetoric offers an invitation to understanding—to enter another's world to better understand an issue and the individual who holds a particular perspective on it. Ultimately, its purpose is to provide the basis for the creation and maintenance of relationships of equality. Its primary communicative options are offering perspectives and the creation of the external conditions of safety, value, and freedom that enable audience members to present their perspectives to the rhetor. In this section, we present two examples of invitational rhetoric to clarify its primary features.

The first example is the acceptance speech given by Adrienne Rich when she was awarded the National Book Awards' prize for poetry in 1974 (Rich, Lorde, & Walker, 1974/1994). When Rich accepted the award, she read a statement that she had prepared with Alice Walker and Audre Lorde—both of whom also had been nominated for the prize. In the statement, the three women announced that they were accepting the award together: "We, Audre Lorde, Adrienne Rich, and Alice Walker, together accept this award in the name of all the women whose voices have gone and still go unheard in a patriarchal world" (p. 148).

The statement clearly articulated the women's own position: "We believe that we can enrich ourselves more in supporting and giving to each other than by competing against each other; and that poetry—if it *is* poetry—exists in a realm beyond ranking and comparison" (p. 148). They presented no arguments in favor of their belief, however, nor did they argue against the position held by representatives of the National Book Awards. Thus, they did not seek the adherence of others to their perspective but simply offered their own vision.

The speech illustrates re-sourcement as a form of offering in that the women communicated their differences with the hierarchical, competitive framework established by the National Book Awards simply by not communicating within the terms of that framework: "None of us could accept this money for herself (p. 148). They chose to respond within a different framework—one based on support and cooperation—by accepting the prize in the name of all women: "We will share this prize among us, to be used as best we can for women" (p. 148).

The three external conditions of safety, value, and freedom required for others to present their perspectives were created by the speech. The rhetors communicated safety when they suggested that they regarded the perspective of the judges as a legitimate one that they would treat with respect and care. "We appreciate the good faith of the judges for this award" (p. 148), they stated.

They accorded value in very specific ways to many individuals, both those in their immediate audience and others:

> We dedicate this occasion to the struggle for self-determination of all women, of every color, identification, or derived class: the poet, the housewife, the lesbian, the mathematician, the mother, the dishwasher, the pregnant teenager, the teacher, the grandmother, the prostitute, the philosopher, the waitress, the women who will understand what we are doing here and those who will not understand yet. (pp. 148–149)

They not only recognized these diverse and unique individuals but credited them as sources for their own work, calling them "the silent women whose voices have been denied us, the articulate women who have given us strength to do our work" (p. 149).

The brevity of the speech precluded the opportunity for the extensive development of freedom for the audience, but it is evident in that Rich, Walker, and Lorde do not specify particular options for action for women; they leave open to women whatever routes of "self-determination" (p. 148) they, themselves, choose. Nor do they suggest the kind of support women should give to each other or the particular contributions other women have made to them. Their ambiguity in these areas leaves open options for the audience and does not confine the terms of the interaction they initiated.

Feminist and animal-rights activist Sally Miller Gearhart (1993) provides a second example of invitational rhetoric in her narration of her interaction with an anti-abortion advocate. In the interaction, Gearhart used both traditional and invitational rhetoric, so her narrative provides a useful contrast between the two and the kinds of results each tends to produce. On a trip with a friend to upstate New York, Gearhart encountered a man in the Kennedy airport "railing about all these women and abortion rights." Because of her own pro-choice beliefs, Gearhart

> took him on. As a matter of fact, I took him on so loudly that we gathered a little crowd there in the Kennedy airport. I was screaming at him; I was trying to make him change. It was not successful,

and it was pretty ugly, as a matter of fact. . . . They didn't have to actually physically separate us, but it was close to that.

An hour later, as she was boarding the shuttle bus to take her to Plattsburgh, her destination, Gearhart encountered the man again: "There was only one seat on that bus, and guess who it was next to? . . . He looked at me and I looked at him as if to say, 'Oh, my God, what are we going to do?'" Rather than continue to engage the man as she had in the airport, Gearhart decided to try something different—to engage in what we suggest was invitational rhetoric: "I decided that what I would do was to try to approach this man with something different . . . and so I began asking him about his life and about the things that he did," seeking to understand his perspective and the reasons it made sense to him. "In fact," Gearhart explains, "it was even worse than I had originally thought. In fact, he was a chemist, and he had experimented on animals. He had grown up as a hunter and, of course, all that is absolutely counter to the things that I believe." But rather than attempting to convince him of the error of his ways, Gearhart continued to listen to the man, and he did the same as he shared his own perspectives and experiences with him. The invitational rhetoric in which the two engaged brought Gearhart and the man together, although neither one "had changed our original position." As the two crossed paths for the third time in the parking lot, waiting for their respective rides, they started walking toward each other. Gearhart finishes the story:

> I don't know which one of us did it first, but I guess maybe I flung open my arms and he flung open his arms and we came together in this terrific hug, both of us in tears, sobbing, crying like babies. I said, "You know, I don't know what has happened here, but my life has been totally changed after today." And he said, "My life is totally changed, too, and I don't know what's happened."

We suggest that what happened was that the two individuals had offered their perspectives and listened to and acknowledged one another's perspectives in an environment of safety, value, and freedom. Their communication thus invited understanding and brought them to a new place of awareness of and appreciation for one another. Gearhart's (1993) summary of the experience is an excellent summary of invitational rhetoric: "It's a way to disagree and at the same time not to hurt each other and to respect each other and to have, actually, something very close and tender."

We see the statement of Rich, Lorde, and Walker and Gearhart's interaction as invitational, then, in that both were rooted in the principles of equality, immanent value, and respect for others and validation of their perspectives. Rich, Lorde, and Walker offered a perspective and communicated its difference with that of the judges, but they neither sought adherence for it nor denigrated the different viewpoint of the judges. Gearhart also offered a perspective very different from that of her acquaintance and listened to one very different from her own without seeking adherence or pronouncing judgment. Each rhetor created conditions of safety, value, and freedom, contributing to an environment in which audience members were able to present their different perspectives. The result was an understanding on which relationships of equality and respect could be built.

Implications for Rhetorical Theory

The expansion of the notion of rhetoric to include invitational rhetoric has several implications for rhetorical theory. The introduction of invitational rhetoric into the scope of rhetorical theory challenges the presumption that has been granted to persuasion as the interactional goal in the rhetorical tradition. Identification and explication of a rhetoric not grounded in the intent to produce a desired change in others undermine the position of privilege accorded to efforts to influence in rhetoric. The existence of invitational rhetoric encourages the exploration of yet other rhetorics that do not involve this singular interactional goal.

A second implication is that invitational rhetoric may contribute to the efforts of communication scholars who are working to develop models for cooperative, nonadversarial, and ethical communication. Such a goal, for example, is espoused by Herrick (1992), in his discussion of the link between rhetoric and ethics, when he suggests "that a virtue approach to rhetorical ethics may provide the kind of flexible, yet directive, ethic needed" to maintain the democratic nature of a pluralistic social order (p. 147). Van Eemeren and Grootendorst (1992) also propose such a goal in their book on argumentation; their approach is designed to create an open and free exchange and responsible participation in cooperative, dialogic communication. The framework provided by invitational rhetoric may allow such theorists to achieve their laudatory missions more easily by contributing to a reconciliation of goals and means (Makau, in press). According to Herrick's and van Eemeren and Grootendorst's definitions of rhetoric as a process in which rhetors seek to secure the acceptance of their perspectives by others, rhetors tend to see their audiences as opponents and sometimes may be tempted to engage in questionable ethical practices to win their "battles" with them. Rules thus are required to contain the interaction that results from the use of such strategies. Invitational rhetoric may serve as a way to allow these scholars to develop models for interaction not characterized by the opposition and competition that make the achievement of their goal difficult.

The introduction of invitational rhetoric to the array of rhetorical forms available also serves a greater heuristic, inventive function than rhetoric previously has allowed. Traditional theories of rhetoric occur within preimposed or preconceived frameworks that are reflexive and reinforce the vocabularies and tenets of those frameworks. In rhetoric in which the rhetor seeks to impose change on others, an idea is adapted to the audience or is presented in ways that will be most persuasive to the audience; as a result, the idea stays lodged within the confines of the rhetorical system in which it was framed. Others may challenge the idea but only within the confines of the framework of the dispute already established. The inventive potential of rhetoric is restricted as the interaction converts the idea to the experience required by the framework.

Invitational rhetoric, on the other hand, aims at converting experience "to one of the many views which are indeterminately possible" (Holmberg, 1977, p. 237). As a result, much is open in invitational rhetoric that is not in traditional rhetorics—the potential of the audience to contribute to the generation of ideas is enhanced, the means used to present ideas are not those that limit the ideas to what is most persuasive for the audience, the view of the kind of environment that can be created in the interaction is expanded, and the ideas that can be considered multiply. The privileging of invention in invitational rhetoric allows for the development of interpretations, perspectives, courses of actions, and solutions to problems different from those allowed in traditional models of rhetoric. Rather than the discovery of how to make a case, invitational rhetoric employs invention to dis-

cover more cases, a process Daly (1984) describes as one of creating "an atmosphere in which further creativity may flourish. . . . [w]e become breathers/ creators of free space. We are windy, stirring the stagnant spaces with life" (p. 18).

The inclusion of an invitational rhetoric in the array of rhetorics available suggests the need to revise and expand rhetorical constructs of various kinds to take into account the nature and function of this form. Invitational rhetoric suggests, for example, that the traditional view of the audience as an opponent ought to be questioned. It challenges the traditional conception of the notion of rhetorical strategies as means to particular ends in that in invitational rhetoric, the means constitute the ends. It suggests the need for a new schema of ethics to fit interactional goals other than inducement of others to adherence to the rhetor's own beliefs.

Finally, invitational rhetoric provides a mode of communication for women and other marginalized groups to use in their efforts to transform systems of domination and oppression. At first glance, invitational rhetoric may seem to be incapable of resisting and transforming oppressive systems such as patriarchy because the most it seems able to do is to create a space in which representatives of an oppressive system understand a different—in this case, a feminist— perspective but do not adopt it. Although invitational rhetoric is not designed to create a specific change, such as the transformation of systems of oppression into ones that value and nurture individuals, it may produce such an outcome. Invitational rhetoric may resist an oppressive system simply because it models an alternative to the system by being "itself an Other way of thinking/speaking" (Daly, 1978, p. xiii)—it presents an alternative feminist vision rooted in affirmation and respect and thus shows how an alternative looks and works. Invitational rhetoric thus may transform an oppressive system precisely because it does not engage that system on its own terms, using arguments developed from the system's framework or orientation. Such arguments usually are co-opted by the dominant system (Ferguson, 1984) and provide the impetus "to strengthen, refine, and embellish the original edifice," entrenching the system further (Johnson, 1989, pp. 16–17). Invitational rhetoric, in contrast, enables rhetors to disengage from the dominance and mastery so common to a system of oppression and to create a reality of equality and mutuality in its place, allowing for options and possibilities not available within the familiar, dominant framework.

Our interest in inserting invitational rhetoric into the scope of rhetorical theory is not meant to suggest that it is an ideal for which rhetors should strive or that it should or can be used in all situations. Invitational rhetoric is one of many useful and legitimate rhetorics, including persuasion, in which rhetors will want to be skilled. With the identification of the rhetorical mode of invitational rhetoric, however, rhetors will be able to recognize situations in which they seek not to persuade others but simply to create an environment that facilitates understanding, accords value and respect to others' perspectives, and contributes to the development of relationships of equality.

A previous version of this essay was presented at the Speech Communication Association convention in Miami, Florida, in 1993. The authors wish to thank Sally Miller Gearhart, James F. Klumpp, Josina M. Makau, and Julia T. Wood for their contributions to the development of this essay.

REFERENCES

Barrett, H. (1991). *Rhetoric and civility: Human development, narcissism, and the good audience.* New York: State University of New York Press.

Benhabib, S. (1992). *Situating the self: Gender, community and postmodernism in contemporary ethics.* New York: Routledge.

Buber, M. (1965). *Between man and man* (R. G. Smith, Trans.). New York: Macmillan.

Burke, K. (1969). *A grammar of motives.* Berkeley: University of California Press.

Burke, K. (1984). *Attitudes toward history* (3rd ed.). Berkeley: University of California Press.

Daly, M. (1978). *Gyn/ecology: The metaethics of radical feminism.* Boston: Beacon.

Daly, M. (1984). *Pure lust: Elemental feminist philosophy.* Boston: Beacon.

Edson, B. A. (1985). Bias in social movement theory: A view from a female-systems perspective. *Women's Studies in Communication, 8,* 34–45.

Elshtain, J. B. (1982). Feminist discourse and its discontents: Language, power, and meaning. *Signs, 7,* 603–621.

Ferguson, K. E. (1984). *The feminist case against bureaucracy.* Philadelphia: Temple University Press.

Ferguson, M. (1980). *The aquarian conspiracy: Personal and social transformation in the 1980s.* Los Angeles: J. P. Tarcher.

Forget, P. (1989). Argument(s). In D. Michelfelder & R. Palmer (Eds.), *Dialogue and deconstruction: The Gadamer–Derrida encounter* (pp. 129–149). Albany: State University of New York Press.

Foss, K. A., & Foss, S. K. (1991). *Women speak: The eloquence of women's lives.* Prospect Heights, IL: Waveland.

Foss, S. K., Foss, K. A., & Trapp, R. (1991). *Contemporary perspectives on rhetoric* (rev. ed.). Prospect Heights, IL: Waveland.

Foss, S. K., & Griffin, C. L. (1992). A feminist perspective on rhetorical theory: Toward a clarification of boundaries. *Western Journal of Communication, 56,* 330–349.

Gearhart, S. M. (1979). The womanization of rhetoric. *Women's Studies International Quarterly, 2,* 195–201.

Gearhart, S. (1982). Womanpower: Energy resourcement. In C. Spretnak (Ed.), *The politics of women's spirituality: Essays on the rise of spiritual power within the feminist movement* (pp. 194–206). Garden City, NY: Anchor.

Gearhart, S. M. (1993, January). [Videotaped interview with Sonja K. Foss and members of the Feminist Rhetorical Theory class, Ohio State University].

Gendlin, E. T. (1978). *Focusing.* New York: Everest.

Griffin, C. L. (1993). Women as communicators: Mary Daly's hagography as rhetoric. *Communication Monographs, 60,* 158–177.

Herrick, J. A. (1992). Rhetoric, ethics, and virtue. *Communication Studies, 43,* 133–149.

Holmberg, C. (1977). Dialectical rhetoric and rhetorical rhetoric. *Philosophy and Rhetoric, 10,* 232–243.

hooks, b. (1984). *Feminist theory: From margin to center.* Boston: South End.

Johnson, S. (1987). *Going out of our minds: The metaphysics of liberation.* Freedom, CA: Crossing.

Johnson, S. (1989). *Wildfire: Igniting the she/volution.* Albuquerque, NM: Wildfire.

Johnson, S. (1991). *The ship that sailed into the living room: Sex and intimacy reconsidered.* Estancia, NM: Wildfire.

Kramarae, C. (1989). Feminist theories of communication. In E. Barnouw (Ed.), *International encyclopedia of communications* (Vol. 2, pp. 157–160). New York: Oxford University Press.

Makau, J. M. (1995). [Review of *Argumentation, communication and fallacies: A pragma-dialectical perspective*]. *Philosophy and Rhetoric, 28,* 426–430.

Morton, N. (1985). *The journey is home.* Boston: Beacon.

Natansion, M. (1965). The claims of immediacy. In M. Natanson & H. W. Johnstone, Jr. (Eds.), *Philosophy, rhetoric and argumentation* (pp. 10–19). University Park: Pennsylvania State University Press.

Rich, A., Lorde, A., & Walker, A. (1994). A statement for voices unheard: A challenge to the National Book Awards. In S. K. Foss & K. A. Foss, *Inviting transformation: Presentational speaking for a changing world* (pp. 148–149). Prospect Heights, IL: Waveland. (Speech presented 1974)

Rogers, C. R. (1962). The interpersonal relationship: The core of guidance. *Harvard Educational Review, 32,* 416–429.

Rorty, R. (1986). Beyond realism and anti-realism. In L. Nagl & R. Heinrich (Eds.), *Wo steht die Analytische Philosophie heute?* (pp. 103–115). Vienna, Austria: Oldenbourg.

Scott, R. L. (1976). Dialogue and rhetoric. In J. Blankenship & H. Stelzner (Eds.), *Rhetoric and communication: Studies in the University of Illinois tradition* (pp. 99–109). Urbana: University of Illinois Press.

Scott, R. L. (1991). The necessary pluralism of any future history of rhetoric. *Pre/Text, 12,* 195–209.

Shepherd, G. J. (1992). Communication as influence: Definitional exclusion. *Communication Studies, 43,* 203–219.

Starhawk. (1987). *Truth or dare: Encounters with power, authority, and mystery.* San Francisco: Harper and Row.

Starhawk. (1988). *Dreaming the dark: Magic, sex and politics* (rev. ed.). Boston: Beacon.

Tracy, D. (1987). *Plurality and ambiguity: Hermeneutics, religion, hope.* San Francisco: Harper and Row.

van Etmeren, F. H., & Grootendorst, R. (1992). *Argumentation, communication and fallacies: A pragmadialectical perspective.* Hillsdale, NJ: Erlbaum.

Veenendall, T. L., & Feinstein, M. C. (1990). *Let's talk about relationships.* Prospect Heights, IL: Waveland.

Walker, M. U. (1989). Moral understandings: Alternative "epistemology" for a feminist ethics. *Hypatia, 4,* 15–28.

Watzlawick, P., Weakland, J. H., & Fisch, R. (1974). *Change: Principles of problem formation and problem resolution.* New York: W. W. Norton.

Wood, J. T. (1993). Enlarging conceptual boundaries: A critique of research in interpersonal communication. In S. P. Bowen & N. Wyatt (Eds.), *Transforming visions: Feminist critiques in communication studies* (pp. 19–49). Cresskill, NJ: Hampton.

Wood, J. T. (1994). *Gendered lives: Communication, gender, and culture.* Belmont, CA: Wadsworth.

Digital Rhetoric

Toward an Integrated Theory

James P. Zappen

The concept of a digital rhetoric is at once exciting and troublesome. It is exciting because it holds promise of opening new vistas of opportunity for rhetorical studies and troublesome because it reveals the difficulties and the challenges of adapting a rhetorical tradition more than 2,000 years old to the conditions and constraints of the new digital media. Explorations of this concept show how traditional rhetorical strategies function in digital spaces and suggest how these strategies are being reconceived and reconfigured within these spaces (Fogg; Gurak, *Persuasion*; Warnick; Welch). Studies of the new digital media explore their basic characteristics, affordances, and constraints (Fagerjord; Gurak, *Cyberliteracy*; Manovich), their opportunities for creating individual identities (Johnson-Eilola; Miller; Turkle), and their potential for building social communities (Arnold, Gibbs, and Wright; Blanchard; Matei and Ball-Rokeach; Quan-Haase and Wellman). Collectively, these studies suggest how traditional rhetoric might be extended and transformed into a comprehensive theory of digital rhetoric and how such a theory might contribute to the larger body of rhetorical theory and criticism and the rhetoric of science and technology in particular.

Strategies of Self-Expression and Collaboration

Studies of digital rhetoric help to explain how traditional rhetorical strategies of persuasion function and how they are being reconfigured in digital spaces. Laura J. Gurak shows how strategies of persuasion based upon Aristotle's notions of ethos, pathos, and logos function to motivate action and belief in the online debates about Lotus MarketPlace and the Clipper Chip (*Persuasion*). In the case of Lotus MarketPlace, for example, the product—a CD-ROM database of direct-mail marketing information about American consumers—raised issues related to personal privacy, provoked strong protests via newsgroups and e-mail, and, as a consequence, was never placed on the market (19–31). According to Gurak, the protests were based upon a highly emotive and often inflammatory ethos; in contrast, Lotus' response was based upon a hard-facts corporate logos, which was both untimely and inadequate to the situation and thereby ensured the failure of the product (85–91, 93–96, 114–24). B. J. Fogg shows how the computer itself (and its associated software) functions as a persuasive technology: as a tool when, for example, it simplifies processes or customizes information; as a medium when it simulates cause-and-effect processes, environments, or objects; and as a social actor through a variety of physical, psychological, linguistic, and social cues (23–120). Fogg is particularly interested in how computers as persuasive technologies (hence captology) achieve credibility (ethos) and in the ethics of various kinds of persuasive appeals, including appeals to the emotions (pathos) (5, 121–81, 211–39).

Barbara Warnick similarly explores the uses of persuasion in digital media, especially digital texts, but she also observes the potential of these media to extend and transform traditional notions of rhetoric as persuasion. Describing attempts to attract women to the Internet and the World Wide Web in the late 1990s, for example, she notes the failure of persuasive appeals in traditional print media and in cybergrrl narratives (so-named because the "cybergrrls" were seeking to distinguish themselves from the "girls" depicted in Internet pornography), which she claims were "elitist and hierarchically motivated" (71–82). In contrast, she notes the success of Web-based alternatives to mainstream media, including e-zines, which offered a variety of forums for self-expression and new modes of interacting with others—"welcoming places where invitational discourse becomes truly inviting" (82–86). Again, describing Web-based political parody in the 2000 presidential campaign, she notes their success as persuasion, effected, however, through a heteroglossic cacophony of voices, offering opportunities for reader participation and interactivity and achieving unity of purpose not through direct appeals or explicit arguments, but through a web of reciprocal links and intertextual references (87–113). Kathleen E. Welch likewise observes the potential of digital media to transform traditional notions of persuasion when she observes characteristics of both oral and print media in the new "electric rhetoric," which she claims can be both additive and subordinate, aggregative and analytic, redundant and copious, agonistic and collaborative or participatory, situational and abstract (106, 108, 184–86). I have sought to contribute to this discussion in my epilogue to *The Rebirth of Dialogue*, where I argue that dialogue—conceived not as a mode of persuasion, but as a testing of one's own ideas, a contesting of others' ideas, and a collaborative creating of ideas—is possible in any medium: oral, print, digital (146–61). Collectively, these studies are challenging the view that associates rhetoric exclusively with persuasion, a view that has persisted for more than two millennia.

Characteristics, Affordances, Constraints

Studies of the new digital media explain some of the basic characteristics of communication in digital spaces and some of their attendant difficulties. Such basic characteristics function as both affordances and constraints and so help to explain how the new media support and enable the transformation of the old rhetoric of persuasion into a new digital rhetoric that encourages self-expression, participation, and creative collaboration. Gurak identifies some of these basic characteristics—speed, reach, anonymity, and interactivity—and explains how they function as both affordances and constraints (*Cyberliteracy* 29–46). Speed encourages an oral and casual style, but it also encourages redundant and repetitive postings (30–33). Reach permits communication among multiple participants in an array of media and thus the development of communities of interest on a global scale; however, it does not include the benefits of gatekeeping (33–37). Anonymity encourages experiments in self and gender identities, but it also problematizes notions of authorship and ownership and encourages "flaming"—the hostile expression of strong emotions (38–43). Interactivity permits closer access to other people with increased opportunities for discussion and feedback, but it also permits increased opportunities for intrusions upon personal privacy (44–46).

These characteristics accord with our everyday experiences with digital communication technologies but raise some difficulties upon closer scrutiny. Thus, Lev Manovich, for example, questions whether terms such as "digital" and "interactivity" have any real meaning. Manovich finds in the new media characteristics of numerical representation, modularity, automation, variability, and transcoding (27–48). Because new media are digitally coded assemblages of discrete components (numerically represented and modular), they enable creation of media objects at low and high levels, from the most simple photo and text manipulations to the most advanced Artificial Intelligence (AI) applications (automation) (27–36). For the same reasons, they can appear in different versions (variability) so that a media database, for example, can produce an almost infinite variety of end-user objects, which can be customized for different users, manipulated through hyperlinks, periodically updated, and scaled upon demand (33–45). Finally, new media can also be translated from one layer to another (transcoding)—from a computer layer to a cultural layer—so that the media data-base, for example, becomes a cultural form in its own right (45–48). Given these characteristics, Manovich questions the use of the term "digital," which can refer to analog-to-digital conversion, common representational code, or numerical representation, only the last having any relevance to the other characteristics (52). Similarly, he questions the use of the term "interactivity" since it states only the most basic fact about computer structures and operations and is therefore, without further qualification, simply redundant (55–56). Anders Fagerjord accepts these key characteristics as a point of departure, but he emphasizes their communicative aspect and observes the tendency of the modularized and variable components of Web media to come together in a process that he calls "rhetorical convergence" (306–13, 318). Fagerjord uses the term "rhetorical" to emphasize both the Web author's choices of topics, arguments, sequences, and words and the reader's processes of selection and semiosis—noting, however, that we have barely begun to describe and catalog these choices and these processes (307, 313). How, then, should we understand the relationship between author and reader, and how should we understand the processes by which authors and readers work together to achieve self-expression or creative collaboration?

The Formation of Identities and Communities

Studies of the new digital media also explore some of the purposes and outcomes of communication in digital spaces: not only persuasion for the purpose of moving audiences to action or belief, but also self-expression for the purpose of exploring individual and group identities and participation and creative collaboration for the purpose of building communities of shared interest. Warnick's analyses, cited above, show how the new media—"symbolic action as carried out through visual images, specialized argots, hypertext patterns"—are used to form identity and community (12, 15). Other analyses explore the processes of forming identities and communities as complex interactions, both online and offline, between ourselves and others, thus providing context and meaning for the term "interactivity." Sherry Turkle explains the processes of identity formation as interactions among multiple versions of our online selves and between these and our real selves: "As

players participate [in Multiple-User Domains, or MUDs], they become authors not only of text, but of themselves, constructing new selves through social interaction. One player says, 'You are the character, and you are not the character, both at the same time.' Another says, 'You are who you pretend to be.' MUDs provide worlds for anonymous social interaction in which one can play a role as close to or as far away from one's 'real self' as one chooses" (11–12). But these interactions between ourselves and others are not entirely of our own choosing. In some online environments, such as hypertext environments, these interactions encompass not only our selves as authors, but also our own and others' selves as readers. As Johndan Johnson-Eilola points out, "a hypertext not only invites readers to participate in making the text, but forces them to do so, requiring both readers and writers to become 'co-learners'" (145).

Such processes of identity formation through social interaction are reminiscent of the traditional rhetorical concept of ethos. As Carolyn R. Miller observes, identity formation as the creation of human character is closely associated with Aristotle's understanding of ethos as "more than our knowledge of someone's prior reputation but . . . also, importantly, a product of the ongoing performance itself, made on the fly, in the course of interaction" (269). But what is the nature of this interaction? Surely it is something more than an interaction between speaker and audience in the traditional sense but, rather, a complex negotiation between various versions of our online and our real selves, between our many representations of our selves and our listeners and readers, and, not least (as Manovich suggests), between our many selves and the computer structures and operations through which we represent these selves to others.

Similarly, the formation of communities of shared interest is an outcome of processes of interactions, both online and offline, between ourselves and others. Numerous studies have documented the close connection between online and offline communities. Anabel Quan-Haase and Barry Wellman, for example, observe a reciprocal relationship between online and offline communities and a net increase in social ties: "Rather than weakening other forms of community, those who are more active offline are more active online—and vice versa" (320). Similarly, Sorin Matei and Sandra J. Ball-Rokeach claim a "the more, the more" relationship between online and offline communities, and they also claim that this relationship holds across differences in gender, income, age, education, and ethnicity (406, 420). As a graphic illustration of this relationship, Michael Arnold, Martin R. Gibbs, and Philippa Wright offer a comment by a participant at a social gathering (with free food and alcohol) held by developers promoting new homes with intranet connectivity in a suburb of Melbourne, Australia: "Yes, an intranet is all very well, but do we still get free beer and a barbeque?" (187–88, 193).

Implications for Rhetorical Studies

Digital rhetoric is thus an amalgam of more-or-less discrete components rather than a complete and integrated theory in its own right. These discrete components nonetheless provide at least a partial outline for such a theory, which has potential to contribute to the larger body of rhetorical theory and criticism and the rhetoric of science and technology in particular. Suppose, for example, that scientific inquiry were situated within the context of digital spaces with the characteristics and potential outcomes and the strategies of self-expression, participation, and collaboration that we now associate with these spaces. What kind of rhetoric of science would we find within these spaces? What is the potential of Internet2 (http://www.internet2.edu) to foster creative collaborations, to promote the development of scientific communities, and to produce new ideas and significant research results? What is the potential of digital discussion spaces such as Slashdot (http://slashdot.org, especially the Science section) to cultivate interest, disseminate information, and encourage discussion on current issues in science and technology among both scientists and nonscientists? A theory of digital rhetoric that recognizes how the traditional rhetoric of persuasion is being transformed in digital spaces invites such questions and thus offers new opportunities for inquiry in rhetorical theory and criticism and an expanded vision of what the rhetoric of science and technology might become within the next decade and beyond.

WORKS CITED

Arnold, Michael, Martin R. Gibbs, and Philippa Wright. "Intranets and Local Community: 'Yes, an intranet is all very well, but do we still get free beer and a barbeque?'" *Communities and Technologies: Proceedings of the First International Conference on Communities and Technologies: C&T 2003*. Ed. Marleen Huysman, Etienne Wenger, and Volker Wulf. Dordrecht, The Netherlands: Kluwer, 2003. 185–204.

Blanchard, Anita. "Blogs as Virtual Communities: Identifying a Sense of Community in the *Julie/Julia Project*." *Into the Blogosphere: Rhetoric, Community, and Culture of Weblogs*. Ed. Laura Gurak, Smiljana Antonijevic, Laurie Johnson, Clancy Ratliff, and Jessica Reyman. University of Minnesota. 14 Dec. 2004 <http://blog.lib.umn.edu/blogosphere>.

Fagerjord, Anders. "Rhetorical Convergence: Studying Web Media." *Digital Media Revisited: Theoretical and Conceptual Innovation in Digital Domains*. Ed. Gunnar Liestøl, Andrew Morrison, and Terje Rasmussen. Cambridge, MA: MIT Press, 2003. 293–325.

Fogg, B. J. *Persuasive Technology: Using Computers to Change What We Think and Do*. Morgan Kaufmann Series in Interactive Technologies. San Francisco: Morgan, 2003.

Gurak, Laura J. *Cyberliteracy: Navigating the Internet with Awareness*. New Haven: Yale University Press, 2001.

_____. *Persuasion and Privacy in Cyberspace: The Online Protests over Lotus MarketPlace and the Clipper Chip*. New Haven: Yale University Press, 1997.

Johnson-Eilola, Johndan. *Nostalgic Angels: Rearticulating Hypertext Writing*. New Directions in Computers and Composition Studies. Norwood, NJ: Ablex, 1997.

Manovich, Lev. *The Language of New Media*. Leonardo. Cambridge, MA: MIT Press, 2001.

Matei, Sorin, and Sandra J. Ball-Rokeach. "Belonging in Geographic, Ethnic, and Internet Spaces." *The Internet in Everyday Life*. Ed. Barry Wellman and Caroline Haythornthwaite. Information Age Series. Malden, MA: Blackwell, 2002. 404–27.

Miller, Carolyn R. "Writing in a Culture of Simulation: Ethos Online." *The Semiotics of Writing: Transdisciplinary Perspectives on the Technology of Writing*. Ed. Patrick Coppock. Semiotic and Cognitive Studies. Turnhout, Belgium: Brepols, 2001. 253–79.

Quan-Haase, Anabel, and Barry Wellman, with James C. Witte and Keith N. Hampton. "Capitalizing on the Net: Social Contact, Civic Engagement, and Sense of Community." *The Internet in Everyday Life*. Ed. Barry Wellman and Caroline Haythornthwaite. Information Age Series. Malden, MA: Blackwell, 2002. 291–324.

Turkle, Sherry. *Life on the Screen: Identity in the Age of the Internet*. New York: Simon, 1995.

Warnick, Barbara. *Critical Literacy in a Digital Era: Technology, Rhetoric, and the Public Interest*. Mahwah, NJ: Erlbaum, 2002.

Welch, Kathleen E. *Electric Rhetoric: Classical Rhetoric, Oralism, and a New Literacy*. Digital Communication. Cambridge: MIT Press, 1999.

Zappen, James P. *The Rebirth of Dialogue: Bakhtin, Socrates, and the Rhetorical Tradition*. Albany: State University of New York Press, 2004.

PART II

RHETORIC AND EPISTEMOLOGY

The suspect status of rhetoric in Western history might well be traced to a continuing belief that rhetorical discourse is deficient in its ability to convey truth. Whether "truth" is defined as the word of God, the result of scientific experiment, or the outcome of philosophical debate, rhetoric has often been seen as self-consciously employing other methods and seeking goals other than the production of truth, such as producing conviction or motivating action. In the practical world of everyday affairs, the philosopher's suspicion represents little more than a minor irritation, for to the extent that it achieves its goals—however framed—rhetorical practices are self-validating. In the academy, however, where the search for "truth" has been valorized as one of the premiere and ultimate goals, rhetorical theorists must constantly defend their object of study. Several routes to that defense, and two criticisms, are illustrated in the essays in Part II.

The most conservative option is presented by Richard A. Cherwitz and James W. Hikins, who offer "Rhetorical Perspectivism" as a means of putting rhetoric back in harness to the truth. Cherwitz and Hikins believe that truth exists and that it is self-validating, but they restrict rhetoric to the role of a "tool" that enables human beings to approach or uncover the truth. They admit that human beings differ in their relationships to particular dimensions of reality, and therefore in their objectively different perspectives on the objects of truth. However, they maintain that such differences of position can be reconciled with a single, multidimensional object of truth. On their account, when it is operating at its best, rhetoric functions to move audiences beyond their individual and limited perspectives to a mutual understanding of a more complete, unified truth that lies below the surface of discourse.

Thomas Farrell offers a different but nevertheless traditional approach to the problem in "Knowledge, Consensus, and Rhetorical Theory." Employing an Aristotelian framework, Farrell argues that while rhetoric may be irrelevant to some kinds of truth (e.g., technical knowledge), it is the central tool for gaining a particular kind of truth (i.e., social knowledge). Since social knowledge is essential to generating social cooperation, rhetoric is valuable for the kind of truth it produces. Rhetoric is thus not a deficient purveyor of technical knowledge, but rather the only proficient supplier of the knowledge that makes social interaction possible.

Various scholars have found these two relatively traditional approaches to the problem of rhetoric and epistemology insufficiently aggressive. In 1967, Robert L. Scott rekindled the sophistic vision of rhetoric's relationship to truth, arguing that rhetoric is epistemic. In "On Viewing Rhetoric as Epistemic," Scott argues that a more productive conception of the relationship among rhetoric, knowledge, and ethics would emerge from severing ourselves from unnecessarily narrow conceptions of truth. In particular, he maintains that no deliberative argument can produce a conclusion that has the force of certainty because all such arguments rely on our past experience for their evidence or support. Short of having access to a crystal ball, we can never know if what was true in the past might continue to be true in the future. At best, Scott argues, we can only be certain of a particular claim or belief when we are actually in the presence of the thing that produces it; but of course when we are in the presence of such an object or phenomenon, no argument is needed to demonstrate its certainty. Since no argument can produce a certain conclusion, the word "truth" misleads us. Rather than seeing rhetoric as a method for conveying truths through argument, therefore, Scott suggests that we ought to see argument as a process of generating time-limited truths. In any given situation, we are always faced with conflicting (and often equally valid) obligations, interests, and values. Participating in argument allows us to choose the best actions for the particular situation, at least so long as we exercise toleration, will, and responsibility in our discussions.

According to the position framed by Scott (and extended by other scholars such as Brummett, 1976), rhetoric is the master practice responsible for the construction of all human truths. This position placed Scott and his colleagues in opposition to the dictates of modernism, which treated rhetoric as a deficient or deviant form of philosophy, science, or theology, and led to the earliest invocations of a "postmodernist" rhetoric. One consequence of this reorientation was the development of the area of study now called the "rhetoric of inquiry." Under this heading, rhetorical theorists and critics began to shift their attention away from the traditional texts of rhetorical study (e.g., public discourse focusing primarily on issues of governance). They began to focus attention on the ways in which rhetoric was involved in defining the criteria of truth and knowledge in any discourse community concerned with the problems and possibilities of human inquiry; in short, the possibility that rhetoric could function as a *hermeneutic* for a wider-ranging array of previously off-limits discourses. As such, "science" is the most obvious test case. If one could prove that science was governed by rhetoric, then, it was assumed, rhetoric's role as the master of knowledge would be secured. It was precisely the relationship between rhetoric and science that most fully occupied the interests of those working in the rhetoric of inquiry (e.g., Campbell, 1975; Condit, 1999; Gross and Keith, 1997; Lessl, 1987; Lyne and Howe, 1986; Nelson, Megill, and McCloskey, 1987; Taylor, 1991) in the last decades of the twentieth century.

Dilip Parameshwar Gaonkar's essay, "Rhetoric and Its Double: Reflections of the Rhetorical Turn in the Human Sciences," offers a critique of this development. Gaonkar suggests that an organized academic pursuit of the study of the rhetorical moves of scientific discourse is not needed. Instead, he suggests, scientists are capable of being self-reflective in times of crisis, using only the resources of ordinary language. Thus, he concludes, rhetoric may not have an appropriately epistemic function. Instead, Gaonkar maintains that rhetoric is a local practice of persuasion and trope. As the list of additional readings indicates, Gaonkar's essay opens onto many differing perspectives.

Another challenge to theoretical claims that rhetoric is epistemic is offered by William D. Harpine. Though sympathetic to the overall project, he wonders if enthusiasts have mistaken potential for progress. In "What Do You *Mean*, Rhetoric Is Epistemic?," Harpine isn't so much interested in the range that an epistemic rhetoric could cover. Rather, he is not certain that enough definitional precision has been established. To him, terms like "knowledge," "certainty," and "truth," no less "rhetoric," remain vaguely conceived. Harpine notes that Scott, as well as Cherwitz and Hikins, often offer differing explanations of what they mean when they suggest that rhetoric is generative of knowledge. One reason he posits, in reviewing the work of Brummett (1990), is that the theory was never generative of actual practice/criticism. Another is a specter that has haunted rhetoric since the foundation of departments of speech: the comparative lack of rigor and precision in speech when set against the work of philosophers. Ultimately, Harpine argues that the epistemic project simply needs more clarity; he contends that this might be achieved through dropping arguments that it can never sufficiently support, while buttressing novel ideas with more attention to the *ethical* dimensions that attracted people to the work of Scott in the first place. While the "rhetoric is epistemic" movement is not without its critics, as these final two essays amply show, it nonetheless continues to exert an influence over contemporary rhetorical theory.

ADDITIONAL READINGS

Brummett, Barry. (1976). "Some Implications of 'Process' or 'Intersubjectivity': Postmodern Rhetoric." *Philosophy and Rhetoric* 9: 21–51.

_____. (1990). "A Eulogy for Epistemic Rhetoric." *Quarterly Journal of Speech* 76: 69–72.

Bryant, Donald C. (1953). "Rhetoric: Its Functions and Its Scope." *Quarterly Journal of Speech* 39: 401–24.

Campbell, John. (1975). "The Polemical Mr. Darwin." *Quarterly Journal of Speech* 61: 375–90.

Condit, Celeste Michelle. (1999). *The Meaning of the Gene: Public Debates about Human Heredity.* Madison: University of Wisconsin Press.

Gross, Allan G., and William M. Keith, eds. (1997). *Rhetorical Hermeneutics: Invention and Interpretation in the Age of Science.* Albany: State University of New York Press.

Lessl, Thomas M. (1987). "Heresy, Orthodoxy, and the Politics of Science." *Quarterly Journal of Speech* 74: 18–34.

Lyne, John, and Henry Howe. (1986). "'Punctuated Equilibria': Rhetorical Dynamics of a Scientific Controversy." *Quarterly Journal of Speech* 72: 132–47.

Nelson, John S., Allan Megill, and Donald N. McCloskey, eds. (1987). *The Rhetoric of the Human Sciences: Language and Argument in Scholarship and Public Affairs.* Madison: University of Wisconsin Press.

Railsback, Celeste Condit. (1983). "Beyond Rhetorical Relativism: A Structural–Material Model of Truth and Objective Reality." *Quarterly Journal of Speech* 69: 351–63.

Scott, Robert L. (1976). "On Viewing Rhetoric as Epistemic: Ten Years Later." *Central States Speech Journal* 27: 258–66.

Taylor, Charles A. (1991). "Defining the Scientific Community: A Rhetorical Perspective on Demarcation." *Communication Monographs* 58: 402–20.

Thomas, Douglas. (1994). "Reflections on a Nietzschean Turn in Rhetorical Theory: Rhetoric without Epistemology?" *Quarterly Journal of Speech* 80: 71–76.

On Viewing Rhetoric as Epistemic

Robert L. Scott

Every beginning is against nature; the beginning is a leap and nature does not make leaps.
—PIERRE THEVENAZ[1]

Rhetoric is among the oldest of the arts of Western civilization. As the familiar tradition informs us, it sprung up in the fifth century B.C. during the aftermath of democratic revolts in several Greek *poleis* on the island of Sicily. But professing rhetoric seems always eventually to lead to embarrassment. In Plato's dialogue, Socrates' questions soon silence Gorgias, leaving young Polus to inquire, "Then what do you think rhetoric is?" In one way or another Socrates' answer has had a way of echoing through history.

At best good men grant rhetoric a slight role but grudgingly. A few years ago, Arthur Larson, cast in the role of rhetorician by virtue of his appointment as Director of the United States Information Agency, found himself trying to explain the importance of his mission to a Senate subcommittee. There creeps throughout the testimony the feeling that undertaking to persuade others is not quite right. Recall that Socrates remarks in responding to Polus that Gorgias has not made his profession altogether clear,[2] and consider Senator Fulbright's statement to Larson: "Well, this is a very interesting subject. I would not want to minimize the difficulty, either, by simply saying that you have not made it clear. Certainly all members of Congress have struggled with it. . . . It is a very difficult thing to sit here in peacetime and feel that it is constructive."[3]

Fulbright's remark goes to the heart of the matter. Invoking those well known arguments of Aristotle's from the opening chapter of his *Rhetoric* [will] do no good, for clearly the art of persuasion is granted sufferance only on the grounds that men are not as they ought to be. Were all men able—as some men are—to reason soundly from true premises, then rhetoric would be superfluous.

The assumption that has spanned the centuries from that dialogue in Athens to the one in Washington, DC, is that men can possess truth. If indeed one can, in the sense that "truth" is ordinarily taken, then rhetoric is of limited value. If some men can possess truth, and others understand truth, then what need the former do but present truth to the latter? Only in unusual circumstances, for example, as Fulbright's statement implies, in time of war, or for those incapable of responding to right reason, may rhetoric be sanctioned.

Accepting the notion that truth exists, may be known, and communicated leads logically to the position that there should be only two modes of discourse: a neutral presenting of data among equals and a persuasive leading of inferiors by the capable. The attitude with which this position may be espoused can vary from benevolent to cynical, but it is certainly undemocratic. Still, the contemporary rhetorician is prone to accept the assumption, to say, in effect, "My art is simply one which is useful in making the truth effective in practical affairs," scarcely conscious of the irony inherent in his statement.

It is absurd, of course, to typify in a few paragraphs the attitude that has dominated rhetoric. But inasmuch as my purpose is to set forth a different position as a starting point for rhetoric, a longer consideration would be inappropriate. My undertaking can be described as philosophizing about rhetoric. The result will not be the discovery of a fresh starting point; I merely hope to clarify through a fresh analysis a way which has always been open and sometimes chosen, but seldom in a clear, incisive manner.

Obviously I take as a sufficient meaning for "philosophy" that indicated by Maurice Natanson, who sees it as a study of beginnings, which is to say that every discipline starts with some assumptions and that it is the business of philosophy to discover those assumptions and to study their meanings.[4]

My point of departure will be drawn from the work of Stephen Toulmin. Interestingly, Toulmin's book, *The Uses of Argument*, has had a remarkably potent influence on rhetorical theory and teaching in this decade, but rhetoricians have borrowed from the third chapter of that book, "The Layout of Arguments," tending to ignore the larger concern of which that analysis is a part.

1

Plato's Socrates confronted Gorgias with a choice: "Shall we, then, assume two kinds of persuasion, the one producing belief without certainty, the other knowledge?"[5] The choice seems simple enough, but the grounds involved need examining.

The terms "certainty" and "knowledge" confront one with what has become known as epistemology. It is to a fundamental inquiry about epistemology that Stephen Toulmin directs his analysis in the book mentioned above. He argues that the question "How do I know?" is an ambiguous one. In one sense it seems to ask, "How do my senses work?" and is a physiopsychological question. As such, it requires the compilation of data which can be analyzed in an empirical fashion— *a posteriori*. This is not, however, the fashion in which epistemologists have worked. Their methods have been speculative or at least abstract and *a priori*. The goal has been to obtain some standard or standards to satisfy the question, "How can I be certain of my conclusions?"

Toulmin suggests that we can set aside the psychological aspects of the central question, "How do I know?" This is not to say that these aspects are unimportant; it simply is a maneuver to allow us to concentrate on the philosophical aspects; he sees these as logical.

The quest for certainty presents a question which is often begged simply by entering into epistemological discussion. The question may be posed, "What do you mean by *certain*?" To say, "I am certain that the sun will rise tomorrow," may be to make a common statement which will probably not elicit argument, unless one is engaged in an epistemological discussion. (The fact that this example is often used in logic textbooks is evidence supporting Toulmin's disposition to see epistemology, considered philosophically, as basically an inquiry into logic.) But to say "The sun will not rise tomorrow" does not contradict the grounds on which most people feel certain that the sun will rise. Our conclusion, based on experience, does not follow necessarily from true premises. This is to say that we are *not* certain by the standard required.

The only sort of arguments which will answer the demands of certainty made in epistemological speculation are those arguments which Toulmin calls analytic. It is questionable (although Toulmin does not put the matter in this fashion) whether or not analytic arguments should be called arguments at all since the word "argument" suggests the drawing of conclusions which are somehow fresh, new, unknown, or unaccepted otherwise. Consider Toulmin's model analytic argument:

Anne is Jack's sister;
All Jack's sisters have red hair;
So Anne has red hair.[6]

The conclusion of this argument, Toulmin says quite rightly, might better be introduced with the phrase "in other words" rather than "so" or "therefore." If the argument is to be analytic, the premise, "All Jack's sisters have red hair," can only be asserted in the presence of his sisters, including Anne.

Toulmin contrasts analytic arguments with arguments he calls substantial. He claims that analytic arguments, which have been taken to be the model to which philosophic arguments ought be held, are rare. I am inclined to believe that they are nonexistent, that is, that they can be indicated only with special sorts of notational systems which can never make existential claims. In terms of

Toulmin's example, if one is not in the presence of Anne, then the conclusion makes a claim about a present condition on the basis of past experience, i.e., all Jack's sisters *had* red hair when last we saw them. To deny the conclusion is not to contradict the truth of the premises. If one is in Anne's presence, then no argument is necessary.

The famous illustrative syllogism concerning Socrates' mortality is ambiguous. If the major premise, "All men are mortal," is taken as a statement about our past experience, then the argument is not analytic; as a matter of fact, the argument turns out to be quite like that one from which we conclude that the sun will rise tomorrow. On the other hand, if we take the premise to be one defining what we mean in part by "man," then I would have to say that we have no argument; Toulmin would say, at least, that we have no substantial argument. In the case of taking the premise to be a definition, we could define men as being purple, and our argument is as good analytically. The rejoinder, "But men are not purple," appeals to a nonanalytic criterion.

As Toulmin sees them, substantial arguments involve some sort of type shift, that is, the conclusion contains an element not present in the premises, e.g., "cause" or "other minds." The type shift Toulmin concentrates on, and one which in my opinion is crucial, is the shift in time. In substantial arguments a shift in time always occurs. If a shift in time does not occur, then one is simply reporting what is present, not arguing. That one is able to report, that is, share his perceptions with others, may be called into question if the analytic ideal is taken as the criterion for knowing.[7]

The observations thus far made lead us to believe that analytic arguments must be tenseless; they cannot exist in time.[8] The certainty demanded must arise from what has been true, is true, and shall be true, which is to say that it must be settled once and for all—immutable, changeless. Can there be substantial truths, that is, statements with content, not empty, which can be used in analytic argument? If so, then they must be stated in time and cannot be stated in time. Technically this is the conclusion of a *reductio ad absurdum*. The possibility of such truths can be rejected on formal grounds.

Although the possibility may be rejected formally, one may accept the conclusion labeled as invalid. One may not follow the reasoning or not accept the grounds. These possible responses underscore the use of the word "truth" in the foregoing paragraph. One might argue that "truth" is not coincident with the analytic ideal. It is possible but difficult to use the word without the freight of the analytic ideal. This strong tendency to associate one with the other should make us suspicious of a rhetoric which claims to be based on truth.

By "truth" one may mean some set of generally accepted social norms, experience, or even matters of faith as reference points in working out the contingencies in which men find themselves. In such cases the word might be better avoided, for in it the breath of the fanatic hangs threatening to transmute the term to one of crushing certainty. If truth is somehow both prior and substantial, then problems need not be worked out but only classified and disposed of. Unwittingly, one may commit himself to a rhetoric which tolerates only equals, that is, those who understand his "truths" and consequently the conclusions drawn from them; such a rhetoric approaches those who are not able to take its "truths" at face value as inferiors to be treated as such.

The attractiveness of the analytic ideal, ordinarily only dimly grasped but nonetheless powerfully active in the rhetoric of those who deem truth as prior and enabling, lies in the smuggling of the sense of certainty into human affairs.

2

In order to press further into the possibilities presented by rejecting prior and enabling truth as the epistemological basis for a rhetoric, I shall make several observations about the adaptations of Toulmin's concepts by contemporary rhetorical theorists. The earliest and most thorough use of his concepts has been made by Douglas Ehninger and Wayne Brockriede.[9] They have adapted Toulmin's form for "laying out" argument, holding it to be a more clear and complete pattern than the traditional syllogism, without pushing further into the philosophic issues for which Toulmin's scheme of analysis is preparatory. In this respect, Ehninger and Brockriede do not differ from others who have used Toulmin's "layout" in speech textbooks.

One might argue that these further issues are irrelevant to the interests of rhetorical theorists, although one of the purposes of this paper is to show that such a position is untenable. Furthermore, Ehninger and Brockriede take care to indicate a point of view toward debate which might be well described as a philosophical foundation for their treatment of rhetorical concepts. Although there is no evidence that their treatment owes anything to Toulmin, their description of debate as cooperative critical inquiry[10] is nonetheless congruent with some of the implications of his criticism of analytic argument as he applies it to epistemology.

When Ehninger and Brockriede describe debate as cooperative critical inquiry, they may be interpreted as taking a radical departure from the typical point of view. If debate is critical inquiry, then it is not simply an effort to make a preconceived position effective. It would be absurd for anyone who begins with the attitude that he possesses truth, in the sense in which I began this essay, to embark on any genuine enterprise of cooperative critical inquiry. Of course these statements do not mean that Ehninger and Brockriede reject investigation before speaking or the use by speakers of experience, references to social norms, or even to articles of faith. What these statements do suggest is that truth is not prior and immutable but is contingent. Insofar as we can say that there is truth in human affairs, it is in time; it can be the result of a process of interaction at a given moment. Thus rhetoric may be viewed not as a matter of giving effectiveness to truth but of creating truth.

Ehninger and Brockriede's debate-as-cooperative-critical-inquiry is one vantage point from which to see rhetoric as epistemic. This notion is most coherent when it is taken as *normative* rather than as *descriptive*. When so taken, it calls for a commitment to a standard and several matters become clear: one may be committed and, being human, fall short of the standard; further, one may make use of the attributes associated with the standard without at all being committed to it.

I have already suggested that Ehninger and Brockriede may err in not examining their philosophic position in light of the disclosures toward which Stephen Toulmin leads. I am now arguing that they err in presenting their fundamental position as *descriptive* of debate. A confusion arises from their attempt to describe the process of debate (the title of their second chapter is "The Process of Debate") as the "rationale of debate as an instrument for settling inferential questions critically."[11] As a description this statement is plainly contrary to much of our experience; we commonly use the word "debate" to refer to situations in which anything but cooperative critical inquiry is occurring. The confusion may be cleared away if we recognize that Ehninger and Brockriede's ideal is *one* of the uses of the process of debate to which men may be committed. They do argue that the process tends to assure this use, but that it *tends toward* rather

than *determines* such a use is clear. As a matter of fact, the authors modify their statements at times, e.g., "the highest tradition of debate,"[12] and are driven finally to explain that "any control, internal or external, may, of course, be circumvented, or debate may be so ineptly practiced that much of its effectiveness is lost. Such failure, however, is human and is not to be charged against debate as a method."[13] But just as the failure is not to be charged against the method neither should the success, i.e., debate at its "highest tradition," be attributed to the process itself rather than the human commitment and the energy and skill to make that commitment meaningful.

The direction of analysis, from Toulmin through Ehninger and Brockriede, leads to the conclusion that there is no possibility in matters relevant to human interaction to determine truth in any *a priori* way, that truth can arise only from cooperative critical inquiry. Men may have recourse to some universal ideas in which they are willing to affirm their faith, but these must enter into the contingencies of time and place and will not give rise to products which are certain.

3

This analysis has led toward the tragic view of life: man who desires certainty understands that be cannot be certain and, moreover, that he must act in dissonant circumstances. One of the great symbols of man, Faust, sits in his chamber at the point of suicide early in Goethe's drama. He is vastly learned in all four of the great professions, but he is certain only that he cannot be certain.[14]

Later Faust sits translating the Bible. He is working on the beginning of the Gospel according to St. John. The troublesome word is *logos*, which he renders as "word," then "mind," then "power," then "act."[15]

The word *logos* and its derivatives have long had a suggestion of divinity about them. For the ancient Greeks, it was often an expression for "universal mind"; and it retains something of this sense in Plato. Man could know because he was identified with the substance of God, that is, the universal mind. From the universal mind (*logos*), man's mind (*logos*) can reason (*logos*) to bring forth speech (*logos*). The wonderful ambiguity of *logos* retains the identity, that is, truth.

All of this may be quite right, the Greek sophist Protagoras said in effect, but I have no way of knowing that it is.[16] All I have is experiences, and my experiences, being finite, cannot reveal the infinite to me. The argument of the Greek sophist Gorgias for his famous three propositions (nothing is; if anything is, it cannot be known; if anything is and can be known, it cannot be communicated)[17] may be interpreted as an attempt to show that man can be certain of no absolute standard. We may be aware of the attributes of our experiences, but there is no way for us to recognize any attribute which is essential among experiences. (Gorgias' inquiry was into the reality of that primary attribute, *being* itself.) There may be some quality (value, norm, standard) which identifies all experiences with all others, or some with some others, but we cannot make such identifications with absolute certainty.

In human affairs, ours is a world of conflicting claims. Not only may one person contradict another, but a single person may find himself called upon to believe or act when his knowledge gives rise to directives which are dissonant. He may be caught, for example, in a conflict of duty toward his family and his country. As a father, he may reason that he ought to keep a well-paying job to provide for the material necessities of his children and by his presence help guide them during their immaturity. As a citizen, he may reason that he is obligated to lower his income and remove his presence from his home to serve in the armed forces. He may decide that his duty to country must take precedence and even that in following the demands of that duty he will in many ways serve his family, but although he is able to make such a decision, the rightness of the decision does not obviate the responsibilities generated by the rejected claim.

The illustrative example can be easily modified into other quite common sets of circumstances: a draft board considering a particular case, arguments concerning the policy of the draft, or even war as a particular or general policy. All these questions must be settled by specific men in specific circumstances. Even taking uncritically the dictates of some past solution is to take that solution in a particular circumstance.

The sophists facing their experiences found consistently not *logos* (in this context we might read "a simple explanation" or "a solitary moral imperative") but *dissoi logoi*, that is, contradictory claims.[18] From another point of view, Stephen Toulmin gives a similar suggestion: "Practice forces us to recognize that general ethical truths can aspire at best to hold good in the absence of effective counter-claims: conflicts of duty are an inescapable feature of the moral life."[19]

My argument is not that one has the choice to act on prior truth or to act to create truth. One may act assuming that the truth is fixed and that his persuasion, for example, is simply carrying out the dictates of that truth, but he will be deceiving himself. Pierre Thevenaz' statement summarizes this point of view: "The phenomenon of expression cannot be reduced to *logos*: it is both more fundamental and more general. Man acts and speaks *before he knows*. Or, better, it is *by acting* and *in action* that he is enabled *to know*."[20]

4

The attractiveness of the notion that first one must know the truth and that persuasion at its best is simply making the truth effective rests in large part on man's desire to be ethical. "How can I assure myself that my actions are good?" is the question with which he nags himself. The question is a good one. The position I have argued is not one that sets it aside but one that holds that the question cannot be answered in the abstract and that whatever principles one holds are only guides in acting consistently with moral demands.

The point of view that holds that man cannot be certain but must act in the face of uncertainty to create situational truth entails three ethical guidelines: toleration, will, and responsibility. I shall suggest why these principles follow from the point of view set forth.

If one can be certain, then one needs no commands or urgings (either from oneself or from others) to act. Failure to act can only be a sign of a momentary misunderstanding or of a flawed intellect. In either case, there is no good reason to tolerate disagreement. As a matter of fact, if one can be certain, tolerating deviations from the demands of certainty may itself be deemed evil.

On the other hand, uncertainty, taking truth as a toehold to climb into the yet-to-be-created rather than as a program to unfold regardless of the circumstances, demands toleration. It would be inconsistent with one's starting point and one's quest to act otherwise. When one's undertaking involves the belief and action of others, one spoils his own potentiality for *knowing*, by Thevenaz' criterion at least, if one fails to respect the integrity of the expression and action of others.

This demand, the *sine qua non* of a democratic state, is called by Karl Popper one of "the most important principles of humanitarian and equalitarian ethics." His phrasing of the principle is "tolerance towards all who are not intolerant and who do not propagate intolerance."[21]

If one cannot be certain, however, then one must either withdraw from the conflicts of life or find some way to act in the face of these conflicts. He must say with Gorgias, "I know the irreconcilable conflicts, and yet I act."[22] That man can so act, he knows from experience. What is true for that man does not exist prior to but in the working out of its own expression. Although this working out may not always involve attempts to communicate with others, such attempts are commonly involved, and thus we disclose again the potentiality for rhetoric to be epistemic. Inaction, failure to take on the burden of participating in the development of contingent truth, ought be considered ethical failure.

If one can act with certainty of truth, then any effects of that action can be viewed as inevitable, that is, determined by the principles for which the individual is simply the instrument; the individual acting is not responsible for the pain, for example, that his actions may bring to himself or to others. The man who views himself as the instrument of the state, or of history, or of certain truth of any sort puts himself beyond ethical demands, for he says, in effect, "It is not I who am responsible."

On the contrary, one who acts without certainty must embrace the responsibility for making his acts the best possible. He must recognize the conflicts of the circumstances that he is in, maximizing the potential good and accepting responsibility for the inevitable harm. If the person acts in circumstances in which harm is not an ever-present potential, then he is not confronted by ethical questions. Such circumstances are apt to be rare in human interaction. Looking to the future in making ethical decisions, we must be prepared to look to the past. "Certainly nothing can justify or condemn means except results," John Dewey has argued. "But we must include consequences impartially. . . . It is willful folly to fasten upon some single end or consequence [or intention] which is liked and to permit the view of that to blot from perception all other undesired and undesirable consequences."[23] To act with intentions for good consequences, but to accept the responsibilities for all the consequences in so far as they can be known is part of what being ethical must mean. "'That which was' is the name of the stone he cannot move," The Soothsayer tells Zarathustra of man. To redeem the past, man must learn "to recreate all 'it was' into 'thus I willed it.'"[24]

Perhaps a final example is necessary. Consider a story from his youth told by the Italian novelist Ignazio Silone.[25] Briefly, he and other village boys were taken to a puppet show by their parish priest. During the performance a devil-puppet suddenly turned to ask the children where a child-puppet was hiding. Rather than reporting "under the bed," the children lied. The priest was upset, for lying was contrary to the precepts he had taught them. His demands for truth were not met. "But," the children protested, "the truth is that there was the devil on one side and a child on the other. We wanted to help the child."

At best (or least) truth must be seen as dual: the demands of the precepts one adheres to and the demands of the circumstances in which one must act. The children had to act and acted to maximize the good potential in the situation. In chastising the children, as he did, the priest had to act also. He also had to make what he could of the situation as well as of his precepts. One may doubt that insisting repeatedly only that "a lie is always a lie," in the face of the children's question, "Ought we to have told the devil where the child was hiding, yes or no?" as Silone reports, the priest did make maximum the good and minimum the harm potential in the situation.

Man must consider truth not as something fixed and final but as something to be created moment by moment in the circumstances in which he finds himself and with which he must cope. Man may plot his course by fixed stars but he does not possess those stars; he only proceeds, more or less effectively, on his course. Furthermore, man has learned that his stars are fixed only in a relative sense.

In human affairs, then, rhetoric, perceived in the frame herein discussed, is a way of knowing; it is epistemic. The uncertainty of this way may seem too threatening to many. But the other way of looking at the world offers no legitimate role to rhetoric; if one would accept that way, then one may be called upon to act consistently with it.

NOTES

1. Pierre Thevenaz, "The Question of the Radical Point of Departure in Descartes and Husserl," in *What Is Phenomenology? and Other Essays*, ed. James M. Edie, and trans. James M. Edie, Charles Courtney, and Paul Brockelman (Chicago, 1962), p. 96.

2. Plato, *Gorgias*, 463.

3. *Hearing before the Subcommittee of the Committee*

on *Appropriations United States Senate, Eighty-fifth Congress, First Session on H. R. 6871, Making Appropriations for the Departments of State and Justice, the Judiciary and Related Agencies for the Fiscal Year Ending June 30, 1958*, p. 530.

4. Maurice Natanson, "Rhetoric and Philosophical Argumentation," *Quarterly Journal of Speech* 48 (1962): 28.

5. *Gorgias*, 454.

6. See Stephen Toulmin, *Uses of Argument* (Cambridge, 1958), pp. 123–130, 222–223.

7. "If a genuine claim to knowledge must be backed by an analytic argument, then there can be no authentic claim to knowledge in such fields as these. The future, the past, other minds, ethics, even material objects: about all of these we ought, strictly speaking, to admit that we *know* nothing" (Toulmin, *Uses of Argument*, p. 231).

8. Ibid., p. 235.

9. Douglas Ehninger and Wayne Brockriede, *Decision by Debate* (New York, 1963). Also see Wayne Brockriede and Douglas Ehninger, "Toulmin on Argument: An Interpretation and Application," *Quarterly Journal of Speech* 46 (1960): 44–53.

10. See Ehninger and Brockriede, *Decision by Debate*, preface and chap. 2. See also Douglas Ehninger, "Decision by Debate: A Re-Examination," *Quarterly Journal of Speech* 45 (1959): 282–287.

11. Ehninger and Brockriede, *Decision by Debate*, p. 15.

12. Ibid., p. viii.

13. Ibid., p. 17.

14. My paraphrase is intended to underscore the argument I have been making. Walter Kaufmann translates:

Called Master of Arts, and Doctor to boot,
For ten years almost I confute
And up and down, wherever it goes,
I drag my students by the nose—
And see that for all our science and art
We can know nothing. It burns my heart.
(Goethe's *Faust*, 2.360–365 [Garden City, NY, 1962]).

15. *Wort!. . . . Sinn!. . . . Kraft!. . . . Tat!* (2.1225–1237).

16. See Mario Untersteiner, *The Sophists*, trans. Kathleen Freeman (Oxford, 1954), pp. 27–28.

17. Ibid., pp. 146–156.

18. Ibid., passim.

19. Toulmin, *Uses of Argument*, p. 117.

20. Pierre Thevenaz, "What Is Phenomenology?," p. 33.

21. Karl Popper, *The Open Society and Its Enemies, Vol. 1: The Spell of Plato* (New York, 1963), p. 235.

22. Untersteiner, *The Sophist*, pp. 181–182: "If Gorgias speaks of the many virtues and not of absolute virtue, he did not deny 'the formal concept of a supreme ethical law'; rather, Gorgias' ethical concept was intended especially to overcome the rigidity of an absolute concept which historical experience also had shown to be contradictory. To make virtue possible in the active turmoil of life, Gorgias detaches it from the empyrean of an abstraction overruled by the incessant reproduction of the antitheses, and makes it relative. In the face of all idealistic dogmatism he stands for the inner turmoil of a tragic decision which gives so profound a meaning to life."

23. John Dewey, *Human Nature and Conduct* (New York, 1922), pp. 228–229.

24. Friedrich Nietzsche, *Thus Spoke Zarathustra*, Part 2, in *The Portable Nietzsche*, trans. Walter Kaufmann (New York: Viking, 1954), p. 251.

25. See Richard Crossman, ed., *The God That Failed* (New York, 1952), pp. 84–86.

Knowledge, Consensus, and Rhetorical Theory

Thomas Farrell

Long ago, Aristotle formulated a functional relationship between a fully developed art of rhetoric and a generally accepted body of knowledge pertaining to matters of public concern. In discussing the value of the rhetorical art, Aristotle urged that the speaker "frame his proofs and arguments with the help of common knowledge and accepted opinions."[1] The reason for such advice is abundantly clear; for rhetoric had application to the common subjects of deliberation, those matters to which this "common knowledge" was pertinent: "Rhetoric is applied to the recognized subjects of deliberation—things for which we have no special art or science."[2] In Aristotle's early expansive vision, then, rhetoric was the art which employed the common knowledge of a particular audience to inform and guide reasoned judgments about matters of public interest.

Aristotle has since been scolded both for the naïve idealism and the unwarranted cynicism of that original vision.[3] But both criticisms ignore the normative foundations of the rhetorical art, a foundation that is in serious need of recovery and reformulation. If such a reformulation is to prove possible, this essay maintains, it is necessary *first*, to clarify what sort of "knowledge" is pertinent to the practical art of rhetoric. A conception of *social knowledge* is defined, and elaborated here.[4] *Second*, it is necessary to explore the functional characteristics of such knowledge in relation to the art of rhetoric. *Third*, it would be valuable to derive some

normative implications for the theorist and practitioner of rhetoric from such a revitalized conception of social knowledge. While an admirable beginning to these tasks has been made in recent scholarship,[5] a tentative but more encompassing picture is offered here. This picture, whatever its eventual pattern, will emerge amid some controversy.

I. The Problem of Defining Social Knowledge

The possibility of a kind of knowledge particularly appropriate to the art of rhetoric has varied with our undemonstrated assumptions about how persons come to know and what they are capable of knowing. For Plato, the belief of the populace was but the poorest approximation of truth, a shadow of a shadow. To the extent that rhetoric was forced to depend upon such poor approximations, the poverty of rhetoric itself was sealed. By contrast, Aristotle was able to posit a body of *common knowledge* as a natural corollary to his idealizations of human nature, the potential of human reason, and the norms and procedures of public decision-making.[6] While analytic and dialectic provided foundation and structure for the facts of science and the general truths of philosophy, rhetorical method found its warrant in occasions of particular choice, its form in the enthymeme and example, and its substance in shared contingent knowledge, consisting in signs, probabilities, and examples.[7]

Ever since the prescriptive clarity of Aristotle's vision faded, the derivation and status of this common knowledge has been in question. With Bacon, new modes of scientific discovery began to claim what was previously the product of rhetorical invention. With Campbell and Hume, rhetorical principles themselves began to undergo scientistic reduction; and with Whately, the rhetorical art began its inevitable formalistic reaction.[8] With each alteration in our conception of knowledge, then, the art of rhetoric—which seems to depend upon a kind of collective knowledge—altered its status and function accordingly. If the knowledge relevant to rhetoric is to be given a contemporary redefinition, some attention must be directed toward its current philosophic context.

The early twentieth century witnessed a growth in restrictive and restricting theories of knowledge. Whether knowledge was formally, empirically, or operationally derived, "the aim," according to Jürgen Habermas, "was to exclude practical questions from discourse. They are no longer thought to be susceptible of truth."[9] An explosion of "information" with a corresponding decline in public dialogue seemed the paradoxical implication.

It is neither possible nor practical to exhaustively refute all conceptions of knowledge which once impeded the current inquiry; fortunately, it is also unnecessary. The contradictions of extreme realism, radical empiricism, and logical positivism are now clearly apparent to all but their most steadfast adherents.[10] Contemporary philosophy has now moved away from the detached derivation of criteria for knowledge and toward the more inclusive study of human activity in all its forms—even as this activity informs the process of scientific knowing itself.[11] Minds as diverse as Michael Polanyi and Thomas Kuhn have argued the necessity of a coherent and accessible universe of discourse if the normal scientific processes of reduction, prediction, and law-like explanation are to be possible. Thomas Kuhn terms consensual agreements on a structured universe of discourse "paradigms," and suggests that without such a consensual context, even the developed sciences would lose their rigor and analyticity. In asking, for instance, how scientists are "converted" to a particular paradigm, Kuhn is forced to proceed in the following manner: "What sort of answer to that question may we expect? Just because it is asked about techniques of persuasion, or about argument and counter-argument in a situation in which there can be no proof, our question is a new one, demanding a sort of study that has not previously been undertaken."[12]

Rather than eliminate the collaboration of others as a criterion for knowing, writers such as Kuhn force us to turn our attention to the kinds of cooperation which are necessary and possible in various fields of inquiry. For this much is apparent: No criterion for knowledge can be polemically proclaimed; at the very least, it must require the cooperation of others in some form. John Ziman's study of *Public Knowledge*, for instance, underscores the necessity of consensual agreement—even in the confirmation and explanation of scientific "fact": "What I have tried to show . . . is that the criteria of proof in science are public, and not private; that the allegiance of the scientist is towards the creation of a consensus. The rationale of the 'scientific attitude' is not that there is a set of angelic qualities of mind possessed by individual scientists that guarantees the validity of their every thought . . . but that scientists learn . . . to further the consensible end."[13] The analytic rigor and synthetic precision of any body of knowledge, then, would seem to vary in direct relation to *two* interdependent factors:

1. the degree of actual consensus on methods of investigation, procedures of analysis, and operations of measurement.
2. the knowers' degree of detachment from human interests related to the object of knowledge.

To the extent that either or both of these factors are absent, scientific demonstration (whether realistic, empirical, or positivistic in its root assumptions) becomes rhetorical dispute, presuming a type of knowledge which has yet to be elaborated.

Now if all knowledge must rest upon some sort of human consensus and presume some functional connection with human knowers, then it may logically be asked: What functional characterization of *knowledge* is appropriate to the art of rhetoric? In the argument that follows, I refer to a kind of knowledge which must be assumed if rhetorical discourse is to function effectively. I call this knowledge "social knowledge" and define it as follows:

Social knowledge comprises conceptions of symbolic relationships among problems, persons, interests, and actions, which imply (when accepted) certain notions of preferable public behavior.

Implicit in this definition are a number of special characteristics of social knowledge which deserve amplification. Social knowledge is a kind of general and symbolic relationship which acquires its rhetorical function when it is assumed to be shared by *knowers* in their unique capacity as audience. Whereas technical or specialized knowledge is actualized through its perceived correspondence to the external world, social knowledge is actualized through the decision and action of an audience. Because of its dependence upon some *subsequent* decision and action, social knowledge is characterized by a state of "potential" or incipience. Yet even in its incipient state, social knowledge is functionally a covert imperative for choice and action; in pragmatic parlance, it is "live" knowledge.[14] Since this analysis is predicated upon special characteristics of social knowledge as an object to be known, as well as its unique relationship to knowers, I begin by considering these.

II. The Functional Characteristics of Social Knowledge

In Jürgen Habermas' analysis of social systems, *Legitimation Crisis*, two basic environmental contexts for such systems are posited: "outer nature, or the resources of the non-human environment . . . and inner nature, or the organic substratum of the members of society. Social systems set themselves off symbolically from their social environment."[15] The boundaries between systems and environments are, of course, notoriously unstable. Nevertheless, it is possible to infer a general distinction related to the orientation a social system takes to these respective environments, and the kind of knowledge applicable to each orientation. In attempting, for instance, to control, produce, or appropriate resources of the natural and externalized environment, managers and members of a social system must presuppose a technical or specialized knowledge. This knowledge, whether localized in science, craft, or technology, will acquire its character as an object through the general patterns which are found to inhere in the natural environmental process. While reconstruction of these patterns may range from prediction, to empirical generalization, to theories constituted by law-like statements, it is the general and optimally invariant set of relationships among empirical phenomena which must preoccupy the scientist, the specialist, the social engineer. Yet much of our most ordinary and necessary social conduct

does not easily reduce to such basic formulations. Whenever members of a social system experience the need for coordinating their conduct, there is a corresponding necessity for assuming a kind of knowledge applicable to this "inner nature." And rhetoric (barring the use of force) is the primary process by which social conduct is coordinated. This process, too, must presuppose a kind of regularity.

When we say, for instance, that, *as a rule*, politicians are not to be trusted, or that, *as a rule*, people do not act against their own perceived interests, or that, *as a rule*, nations do not attack nations which are stronger than they, each utterance points to an important similarity or regularity in the ways human beings understand and act in their social world. The phrase "as a rule"[16] signifies this regularity. Uttered as idle speculation, the phrase is loosely descriptive; but as a ground for advocacy, it is transformed into a generalization of interest, culminating in a prescription for human choice and action. As a minimum condition, then, this rule-like structure of *social* knowledge assumes that persons will regularly respond to problems in similar ways and attach their own human interests to purposes in some recognizable fashion. But if that which is known is a generality inhering—*as a rule*—in matters of human choice and conduct, this same knowledge also involves a rather unique relationship to human knowers.

Conventional theories of knowledge, from Aristotle to Descartes, have made much of the "objective" detachment of knowers from the object of their knowledge. Similarly, traditional scientific method establishes an elaborate series of controls to assure that the knower's own conscious or unconscious commitments and preferences do not intervene to alter the character of what is to be scientifically "known." I have termed this knowledge "technical" or "specialized"; in any case, it is the knowledge of observation. Whenever I participate in a *rhetorical* process, however, I am depending upon much more than information, data, evidence, even the armory of persuasive tactics which still comprise our lexicons. All such conceptions of proof and strategy—*in vacuo*—still view knowledge as externalized proof or observation. And what I call "social knowledge" can be neither discovered nor verified through the detachment which observation demands. Instead, social knowledge depends upon an "acquaintance with" (to use James's phrase) or a *personal relationship* to other actors in the social world. As we decide, advocates and audiences, whether to build a dam, or raise teacher salaries, or to provide for a drug rehabilitation program, we will—of necessity—presume a kind of knowledge which depends upon our direct or indirect experience of collective "others," and which applies an interest to these others which is generalizable. Whenever we are asked to endorse or condemn a person, action, or policy, it is likely that we are also being asked to conduct ourselves as members of a human community. And with each particular decision, a reflexive act is performed—an act which gives increasing form and specificity to our relationship with others as social beings.

Now it may seem as if this conception of social knowledge has the practical effect of making everyone an authority. On some very general matters, this might be the case, but only if one were to depend upon an audience's membership in a cultural "form of life" for the purposes of further argument (as is sometimes the case, for instance, in analytic philosophy). Much more frequently, social knowledge is functionally attributed to a particular audience and applied in quite specific situations. Having considered social knowledge as both an object to be known, and as constituted by a unique kind of relationship to knowers, the nature of this "attribution" will now be explored, as well as several additional rhetorical characteristics of social knowledge: its audience dependence, its generative implications, and its normative force.

Social Knowledge as Consensus

Central to an understanding of social knowledge is the notion of consensus. Originally understood to be a range of agreement on objects of communication, consensus has been broadened by Chafee and McCleod and Thomas J. Scheff to include an awareness or understanding that agreements are held.[17] In the somewhat ideal-typical realm of communication models, consensus is considered to be both a precondition and an outcome of communication. I maintain that social knowledge rests upon a peculiar kind of consensus. That is to say, it rests upon a consensus which is attributed to an audience rather than concretely shared. This means that such knowledge does not rest upon agreement which is both fact and known to be fact. The assumption of agreement may be counterfactual. Some persons may, in fact, disagree with what is attributed. Yet it is this assumed understanding of agreement—as an hypothesis, rather than fact—which makes rhetorical argument possible. In more than an idiomatic sense,

then, social knowledge is attributed for the sake of argument. In exploring the foundations of communicative action, Habermas points to the kind of consensus which is presumed in social knowledge: "... we cannot explain the validity claim of norms without recourse to rationally motivated agreement or at least to the conviction that consensus on a recommended norm could be brought about with reasons. ... The appropriate model is rather the communication community of those affected, who as participants in a practical discourse test the validity claims of norms and, to the extent that they accept them with reasons, arrive at the conviction that in the given circumstances the proposed norms are 'right.'"[18] To further illustrate this attributive characteristic of social knowledge, it is appropriate to consider the possible varieties of consensus and the sorts of knowledge which these affirm.

Throughout the decade of the 1960s, demographers and urbanologists alike conducted extensive research on rates of growth and distribution of population in America's urban centers. Among their findings, it was agreed that a growing percentage of the urban wage-earners were leaving the inner city.[19] Now the outcome of this research may be understood as specialized or technical knowledge for the two interdependent reasons discussed above. First, it was the outcome of a mode of inquiry which treats mass behavior as a natural, externalized phenomenon—in Habermas' terms—as a phenomenon of "outer nature"; and second, this knowledge was based upon a real or fully actualized consensus as to appropriate research methods and modes of measurement. This consensus, of course, did not protect such technical knowledge from sources of error; yet even the determination and revision of error in such technical fields owes its orderly efficiency to the underlying methodological consensus held by the experts in the fields in question. By contrast, the consensus of any one segment of the national public on the significance, seriousness, or harm of the "inner-city exodus" must—even today—be attributed to that collectivity in order to employ the urban phenomenon as a reason in an argument for—let us say—governmental assistance to urban centers. Specialized or technical knowledge, then, reflects the outcome of an actual consensus on specialized modes of inquiry or procedures of research. Social knowledge must presume or attribute a consensus concerning the generalizable interests of persons in order that argument may culminate in the advocacy of choice and action.

The distinction is less exact than one might wish, of course. To the extent that our urban researchers become urban reformers (pronouncing the urban environment "desolate" and its future "grim"), they are functioning now as rhetors in that a broader consensus (concerning the limits to human acceptability of urban conditions) is being attributed to a public outside the specialized audience.[20]

Does this mean that all attributed consensus possesses the rhetorical character of social knowledge? Once again, there are complications. When I say, for instance, "Everybody knows that Los Angeles is the most polluted city in the United States," I may or may not be relying on social knowledge for rhetorical purpose. Although the assumption appears to be normative, neither the purpose nor the implications of its explicit statement are yet clear. And when the meteorologist relies upon an actual and increasingly accurate technical consensus to predict an unusually high phosphorous and ozone count in the atmosphere for a particular day, the expert in question has set forth a type of knowledge more specific than our normal understanding of social knowledge, but with clear normative implications. Some cases of attributed consensus may function in a non-rhetorical manner. And some instances of technical or specialized knowledge, when combined with further attributions (as in the case of smog alerts or earthquake predictions) may function rhetorically. What is suggested here is that the attribution of consensus is a necessary, but not a sufficient condition for social knowledge to be rhetorically impactful.

This can be demonstrated logically. If a situation is considered "rhetorical" (in Bitzer's terminology) at least two factors must be present: (1) the outcome of the situation must be indeterminate, i.e., it must always be possible for the audience to refrain from acting in the recommended manner; and (2) the exigence of a situation must be amenable to resolution by an audience's action.[21] Now if audiences and advocates alike were to operate from a fully realized consensus on all norms and "proofs" in a specific rhetorical encounter, then they would *necessarily* act and the situation would cease to be rhetorical. In other words, fully realized consensus would undermine the first constituent of rhetorical situations by rendering them determinate. Yet the above analysis presupposes that the audience was able to act. Suppose, for the sake of argument, that nothing could be done about the problem in question. In such a case, the second constituent of the rhetorical situation is missing (namely, that the exigence be amenable to resolution by the action of an audience). Even if there were a fully realized consensus on the problem of humankind's mortality, this does not undermine the necessity of attributed consensus in social knowledge. Neither the fact of death, nor its terminal character, can be altered through the choice and action of an audience. By definition, then, the knowledge which is distinctly rhetorical in function—that is, social knowledge—must be based upon a consensus which is attributed rather than fully realized.

Social Knowledge as Audience-Dependent

But more than simply being attributed to others, social knowledge is assumed to be shared by other persons in their collective capacity as audience. Even so-called "new" information, if it is to function rhetorically, must depend upon more basic assumptions of audience consensus on certain problems, interests, and actions. And it is this assumption of *audience* consensus which requires explication. As a particular advocate notes, let us say, that inner-city poverty is increasing, this advocate lays claim to a pragmatic faith in the mutuality of social interests. Now, of course, this faith cannot be empirically verified; nor will it always be well-founded. Even an audience consisting entirely of urban dwellers will exhibit, upon occasion, divided loyalties and a dishearteningly narrow conception of interest. And, no doubt, the number and intensity of potentially opposed interests will expand as the audience becomes broader and more heterogeneous. But if rhetorical argument is to operate with any effectiveness, some region of "beginning" must exist. And if it does not exist in empirical fact, then it must be presupposed. The presupposition is grounded on a formidable possibility, namely, that those who play the collective role of audience—as conscious members of an urban or even a broader social community—may become conscious that the suffering of others is pertinent to their own interests. In microcosm, this is the faith of a democracy. A conscious and civilized audience is therefore representative in more than a statistical sense, for we must assume that its collective nerve endings are alive to the interests of others within the society. The anonymous advocate, in the preceding example of inner-city poverty, does not need to assume of the audience a technical comprehension of Keynesian economics; but (s)he does presume an awareness and appreciation of certain human potentialities and skills within society and the relevance of these to the purposes of a community. In proposing a solution to the problem of inner-city poverty, the advocate presumes, at a bare minimum, some conception of poverty in relation to the social interest; without some such assumption, any real advocacy of action would be premature.

This does not mean that social knowledge is necessarily general and ambiguous. As attributed to particular audiences and referred to concrete exigencies, social knowledge can be quite specific. It may, in some cases, even center upon the character traits of certain public figures, as recent political history has shown. Yet just as this knowledge cannot be validated in each discrete individual, so it cannot be reduced to empirical operationalization. In that sense, social knowledge becomes the emergent property of a collectivity. It is an attribution which is general in scope rather than abstract in epistemic status.

But if this construct is attributed and interest-dependent, what is its epistemic status? H. N. Lee has noted that volitional and emotional factors do not serve to differentiate types of knowledge.[22] Perhaps more provocative is John Ziman's stipulation that, "Normative and moral principles cannot, by definition, be embraced in a consensus; to assert that one ought to do so and so is to admit that some people, at least, will not freely recognize the absolute necessity of not doing otherwise."[23] Ziman evades outward inconsistency by inserting "cannot" instead of "should not" in his stipulation. But this evasion renders the statement counterintuitive in application. On one level, of course, Ziman is acknowledging what has been a central position in this essay, i.e., that social knowledge is, by definition, an attributed or assumed, rather than a fully actualized consensus. Ziman's implicit denial of volitional ingredients in scientific consensus is difficult to reconcile to his own characterization of science (see note 13). But just as problematic, his inclusive use of the term "consensus" is difficult to reconcile with actual experience. Do we not—all of us—assume just such a normative consensus as we exhort our hearers on any number of important practical questions? The matter is not so easily settled. But what might be suggested is that social knowledge, just as the questions for rhetorical disputes, is probable knowledge. It is knowledge in a state of potential or indeterminance. And it is validated through the reasoned judgment and action of an audience. How is one to gain confirmation for an attribution of consensus on the financial

decay of the inner city as a community problem? If the audience acts on the problem through available procedures, (s)he will have tentative evidence. Through the reasoned action of an audience, the potential state of social knowledge is actualized. Just as the specialized consensus on modes of investigation and measurement has been validated through repeated operation, so—in a more probable sense—is social knowledge confirmed through recurrent action. The probative force of collective experience has, throughout history, been the test of democratic societies. And if rhetoric is to have application to popular decision-making, it must subject its assumptions to a similar test.

Social Knowledge as Generative

Rather than being fixed, permanent, and static, therefore, social knowledge is transitional and generative. As individual problems are encountered and, through the frustrating incrementalism of human decision-making, managed or resolved, new problems emerge; and with these, new knowledge may be attributed, based reasonably upon the collective judgments which have previously been made. Not only does social knowledge provide a context of relevance for artistic proof in collective inference making; it also establishes social precedents for future attributions of consensus in situations which have yet to be encountered.

This generative characteristic of social knowledge can be illustrated simply in the development of the traditional issues in rhetorical controversy. The four traditional issues of such controversy—conjectural, definitional, qualitative, and procedural or translative—each represent points of "rest" in the development and possible resolution of rhetorical disagreement.[24] Two or more opposing positions may—at various times—reduce their differences to a question of fact, definition, quality, or procedure: that point which, when settled, may determine the direction and eventually the outcome of controversy. Yet if this process of controversy is to operate effectively, we must presume consensus on a prior issue in order to move properly to the next. We may not, for instance, argue over the distinguishing characteristics of the financial crisis in any urban center, or the seriousness of its effects upon relevant human interests, unless we attribute to our audience or opponent a prior consensus on the presence of that crisis. And in considering each subsequent issue, the proof which will be decisive will also rest upon attributed consensus—verified through previous choice and action—for the acceptable standards of proof. Thus the ingredients of social knowledge (whether assertions of fact, definitions of character, rules of quality, or precedents of procedure) should aid each rhetorical exchange in achieving its natural "logic" of completion. When a controversy reaches a point of termination or resolution, a more fully actualized consensus is achieved which functions as a social precedent for future controversy.

Social Knowledge as Normative

The traits of social knowledge which have been considered thus far—its attributive dimension, its audience-dependence, its state of potential, and its generative implications—contribute to an understanding of the most elusive and important characteristic of social knowledge. I refer to its affective or normative impact upon decision-making.

There is an amorphous and indefinite body of knowledge that makes little or no difference to the daily conduct of our lives. We can know, for instance, that the technical ascription for water is H_2O, that Steve Garvey was the 1974 MVP in the National League, that Humphrey Bogart made four films with Lauren Bacall, and unless we happen to be chemists, baseball fans, and film fanatics, each item of knowledge is unlikely to alter our normal decision-making priorities. By contrast, consider the finding of the Citizens' Board of Inquiry, in 1968, " . . . that in the wealthiest nation in the history of the world, millions of men, women, and children are slowly starving,"[25] or the rampant starvation in Biafra and, more recently, Bangla Desh. Some knowledge *demands* that a decision be made. It forces our options, insofar as the very apprehension and comprehension of such knowledge requires that some action be taken. Even the attempt to ignore, to detach it from our lives (as a fact of "outer nature") is itself an action of sorts; it is the decision to do nothing. Knowledge which relates problems to persons, interests, and actions often implies, then, a covert imperative for choice and action.

Clearly, this covert imperative will not be a permanent or fixed property peculiar to specifiable items of information. As circumstances and social expectations gradually alter, so too will the specific knowledge which carries this curious normative force. Critics and social observers complained for some time, for instance, that the escalation of violence in America was desensitizing the American public to the mutuality of pain and suffering. Yet David Berg was able to cite one

social observer to the effect that televised publicity of wartime suffering may one day render even the just war a practical impossibility.[26] More problematic is the tendency of mass media to publicize, even create social knowledge which forces options without suggesting actional outlets for mass concern. Whether this tendency will lead to mass frustration or ambivalence to public problems is a matter for concerned speculation and research. A matter of related interest is the tendency of radical organizations to attribute consensus far in excess of its actual state. Whether this is a distinguishable trait of radical movements is not clear. What is clear is that such movements, with increasingly refined ideologies, will regard each social discrepancy as evidence of extensive covert imperatives for action. That their attributions of consensus are frequently not actualized should not be surprising.

Having considered several distinguishing rhetorical characteristics of social knowledge, it should now be apparent that rhetoric, whatever its own attributed status, is not a purely formalistic enterprise. There is something which this art is about. That "something" is a kind of knowledge which is attributed, audience-dependent, potential in state, generative, and normative in implication. And yet the functions of this knowledge reach beyond its ability to distinctly characterize the rhetorical process.

Any sophisticated social system will be confronted, throughout its existence, by serious problems which require careful deliberation and concerted action. Imagine a society in which the knowledge required to deal with such problems is absent or confined to narrow quarters. Such a system may be a collectivity of individuals; but it is far from a community of persons. The overarching function of social knowledge is to transform the society into a community. There is no way to overstate the importance of this function; philosophers from Aristotle to the present have dreamed of its possibilities. In our own time, it was John Dewey who simplified and celebrated the social function of rhetorical art:

> Symbols in turn depend upon and promote communication. The results of conjoint experience are considered and transmitted. Events cannot be passed from one to another, but meanings may be shared by means of signs. Wants and impulses are then attached to common meanings. They are thereby transformed into desires and purposes which, since they implicate a common or mutually understood meaning, present new ties, converting a conjoint activity into a community of interest

and endeavor. Thus there is generated what, meta-phorically, may be termed a general will and social consciousness.[27]

It is difficult to avoid metaphorical language when speaking of this function. The ability of rhetorical transactions gradually to generate what they can initially only assume appears to possess a rather magical ambience. But lurking in the background is a process which can be understood on more than an aesthetic level. There are at least three interdependent means by which social knowledge fulfills this significant function.

First, social knowledge helps define a "zone of relevance" in matters of human choice. Alfred Schutz defines this zone of relevance as a realm in which data, concepts, and principles pertain to operative human interests.[28] While the actual matters pertinent to our interests multiply, our contact with these matters becomes less and less direct. Schutz writes: "We are less and less deter-mined in our social situation by relationships with individual partners within our immediate or medi-ate reach, and more and more by highly anony-mous types which have no fixed place in the social cosmos. We are less and less able to choose our partners in the social world and to share our social life with them. We are, so to speak, potentially subject to everybody's remote control."[29] Social knowledge cannot, in itself, rectify an increasingly dangerous imbalance between what is and what should be known. But by establishing the outer parameters for feasible attributions of consensus, social knowledge enables both the advocate and the "informed citizen"[30] to determine what should be known and how what is known may be utilized.

Second, social knowledge is a way of imparting significance to the numerous "bits" of informa-tion which are disseminated to the mass of public citizens. Not all of this information can even be attended to, let alone successfully assimilated. That which it receives its significance due to what Edel-man calls *aesthetic* information, a larger associated body of generalized beliefs, convictions, images, contexts, and norms.[31] These are by no means the same for all. But social knowledge, when employed rhetorically, crystallizes the normative dimension of this aesthetic information, thus enabling iso-lated "bits" of information to achieve meaning and significance. Rather cryptically put, social knowl-edge gives *form* to information.

Third, social knowledge allows each social actor to confront a set of generalized assump-tions suggesting the relative priority of collective commitments held by others. To say that social knowledge provides a means of reality-testing may be somewhat extreme. What it does do is enable each conscious person to place the content, direc-tion, and intensity of personal knowledge within the context of an attributed distribution of public convictions. While this placement is no sure test of reliability in the traditionally uncertain arena of human decision-making, the ordering of per-sonalized knowledge in a more variegated public context is a necessary prelude to the validation of such knowledge. By providing pertinence, form, and context to the data of our public experiences, then, social knowledge assists in the grand trans-formation of society into community.

Retracing my procedure, it has been alleged that the rhetorical process implies, indeed *requires* a kind of knowledge appropriate to probable human decision-making. I have argued that it is *social* knowledge which provides foundation and direction to the art of rhetoric. Several rhetori-cal characteristics of this knowledge have been introduced, as well as its functional contribution to the social community. The moral implications of social knowledge are a difficult matter, complex in scope, and beyond the structure of this essay. But several directions for an analysis of this matter may be suggested here.

III. Normative Implications for Rhetorical Theory

Social knowledge, as a characteristic which is actively attributed to persons, must necessarily partake in the active dimension of the rhetorical process itself. As John Searle has suggested, certain types of linguistic utterances become *acts* when set forth in the presence of others.[32] That is, both the fact of linguistic utterance and the *presence* of others are required conditions, if the expression is to take on an active dimension—as in promise-making, or exhortation. Michael Polanyi, in pains-takingly exploring the phenomenology of such utterances, finds that many of our most common rhetorical expressions imply commitments which are by no means trivial."[33] The very basic commit-ment of respect for hearers who are party to our transactions requires, for instance, that the rhetor take seriously that consensus which is attributed to an audience. As Georges Gusdorf has noted in *Speaking,* "To respect one's word is thus to respect others as well as oneself, for it indicates what one thinks of oneself."[34] One should not forget that the rhetor speaks *on behalf of* others. That knowledge which is assumed to be held by other persons thus involves the rhetor with the complicity of *other knowers*, whose interests are now a factor for reasoned consideration.

But the commitment to others implied in the assumption of social knowledge would be purely formalistic were it not for the more concrete interdependence of the self and others. While it is the pragmatic tradition which has most carefully and clearly affirmed this interdependence, it is that most practical of arts—rhetoric—that must test this assumption in social life. Social knowledge is merely the surface tracing of a deeper identity, between the self and its conscious extension—the human community. Charles S. Peirce wrote, in 1903:

> Two things here are all-important to assure oneself of and remember. The first is that a person is not absolutely an individual. His thoughts are what he "is saying to himself," that is saying to that other self that is just coming into life in the flow of time. When one reasons, it is that critical self that one is trying to persuade; and all thought whatsoever is a sign, and is mostly of the nature of language. The next thing to remember is that man's circle of society (however widely or narrowly this phrase may be understood), is a sort of loosely compacted person, in some respects of higher rank than the person of an individual organism.[35]

Social knowledge is thus the assumption of a wider consciousness. And the corollary of such an assumption, commitment, should extend as far as consciousness itself. Both John Dewey and—more recently—his student, Richard McKeon, have defined the great community as a consequence of acting as the members of such a community.[36] Social knowledge is thus an instrument of both this action and its optimal consequence.

It is not suggested here that social knowledge is possessed of an inherent qualitative superiority to personal knowledge. Although the impulse of social knowledge is the perfectibility of personal motive, such knowledge—like the art which assumes and creates it—may be used for noble or diabolical purposes. The moral warrant afforded by the construct I have sketched is thus limited: by the parameters of situations and ultimately by the broader dialectic of history. Rhetoric may be viewed as the counterpart of this dialectic. And it is within this self-correcting context that the partiality of a culture's conviction—just as the privacy of an individual's perception will be disclosed.

NOTES

1. Aristotle, *The Rhetoric*, trans. Lane Cooper (New York: Appleton-Century-Crofts, 1932), 1355a.

2. Ibid., 1357a.

3. Underlying this sometimes amusing paradox are varying conceptions of "rationalism," "logos," "pathos," and "judgment" as assumptions or features of Aristotle's *Rhetoric*. Among the recent studies which shed light on this paradox are Edwin Black's *Rhetorical Criticism: A Study in Method* (New York: Macmillan, 1965), esp. chaps. 2 and 4; Wayne Brockriede, "Toward a Contemporary Aristotelian Theory of Rhetoric," *QJS* 52 (1966): 33–40; Douglas Ehninger, "On Rhetoric and Rhetors," *Western Speech* 31 (1967): 242–247. J. A. Hendrix, "In Defense of Neo-Aristotelian Criticism," *Western Speech* 32 (1968): 246–251; Stephen Lucas, "Notes on Aristotle's Concept of Logos," *QJS* 57 (1971): 456–458; and Forbes Hill, "The Rhetoric of Aristotle," in James J. Murphy, ed., *A Synoptic History of Classical Rhetoric* (New York: Random House, 1972), pp. 38–48. A significant step toward a resolution of the technical confusion in Aristotle's *Rhetoric* is taken by David P. Gauthier, in *Practical Reasoning* (Oxford, UK: Clarendon Press, 1963), chap. 3. The political dimension of this classical controversy emerges in a recent encounter between Forbes Hill and Karlyn Campbell, in "The Forum," *QJS* 58 (1972): 451–464.

4. The phrase "social knowledge" is used in a somewhat specialized way in this essay. While social knowledge may refer to any beliefs which are generally shared, or even beliefs and knowledge *about* society, the more restricted usage I employ is suggested in Jürgen Habermas, *Legitimation Crisis* (Toronto: Beacon, 1975); therein, social knowledge would seem to be a normative agreement, presumed by communication acts, which generalizes human interests and is applicable to practical questions. This usage is explored at greater length in the body of this essay.

5. The many diverse strands of such scholarship could not be exhausted here. Some recent examples are: Ernest G. Bormann, "Fantasy and Rhetorical Vision: The Rhetorical Criticism of Social Reality," *QJS* 58 (1972): 396–408; Thomas W. Benson and Gerard A. Hauser, "Ideals, Superlatives, and the Decline of Hypocrisy," *QJS* 59 (1973): 99–105; and Henry W. Johnstone Jr., "Rationality and Rhetoric in Philosophy," *QJS* 59 (1973): 381–390; the analysis offered in this essay owes its direction to Lloyd F. Bitzer, "The Rhetorical Situation," *Philosophy and Rhetoric* 1 (1968): 1–14 [reprinted in this volume].

6. The epistemological assumptions of Aristotle's *Rhetoric* have been subjected to careful scrutiny by scholars. While the summary offered here is attenuated, confirmation can be found in Richard McKeon, "Principles and Consequences," *Journal of Philosophy* 56 (1959): 385–401.

7. Richard McKeon, ed., "Introduction," in *The Basic Works of Aristotle* (New York: Random House, 1941), pp. xxix–xxxi.

8. Again, what is stated here is a highly abbreviated paraphrase of a complex philosophical transformation. For a careful analysis of the epistemological assumptions of George Campbell's rhetoric, see Lloyd Bitzer, ed., "Introduction," in *The Philosophy of Rhetoric*, by George Campbell (Carbondale: Southern Illinois University Press, 1963), pp. ix–xxxvii. For an analysis of Whatley's epistemological assumptions, see Douglas Ehninger, ed., "Introduction," in *The Elements of Rhetoric*, by Richard Whately (Carbondale: Southern Illinois University Press, 1963), pp. ix–xxx.

9. Habermas, *Legitimation Crisis*, p. 16.

10. Among the recent works which argue convincingly for the rejection of traditional realism, radical empiricism, and logical positivism are Richard J. Bernstein, *Praxis and Action* (Philadelphia: University of Pennsylvania Press, 1971), part 4; Jürgen Habermas, *Knowledge and Human Interests* (Boston: Beacon Press, 1971), part 2; and Michael Polanyi, *Personal Knowledge* (New York: Harper & Row, 1962). Daniel J. O'Keefe underscores Frederick Suppe's characterization of logical empiricism as "a view abandoned by most philosophers of science" in O'Keefe, "Logical Empiricism and the Study of Human Communication," *Speech Monographs* 42 (1975): 169–183. O'Keefe provides an excellent summary of the indictments which led to the abandonment of positivism.

11. See, for instance, Bernstein, *Praxis and Action*, pp. 257–269.

12. Thomas S. Kuhn, *The Structure of Scientific Revolutions*, 2d ed, (Chicago: University of Chicago Press, 1970), p. 152.

13. John Ziman, *Public Knowledge* (London: Cambridge University Press, 1968), p. 78.

14. William James first coined the term in "The Will to Believe," in *Pragmatism and Other Essays* (New York: Washington Square Press, 1963), p. 194.

15. Habermas, *Legitimation Crisis*, p. 9.

16. Stephen Toulmin employs the phrase *as a rule* as a naturalistic generalization in "Rules and Their Relevance for Understanding Human Behavior," in Theodore Mischel, ed., *Understanding Other Persons* (Oxford, UK: Blackwell, 1974), p. 190. I am extending Toulmin's initial usage in applying the phrase to human conduct and interests.

17. See Thomas J. Scheff, "Toward a Sociological Model of Consensus," *American Sociological Review* 32 (1967): 32–46, for a survey of alternative conceptions of "consensus."

18. Habermas, *Legitimation Crisis*, p. 105.

19. See esp. Philip Hauser, *Population Perspectives* (New Brunswick, NJ: Rutgers University Press, 1960), and Robert Mowitz and Deil Wright, *Profile of a Metropolis* (Detroit, MI: Wayne State University Press, 1962), for examples of this agreement. For the data base that has governed subsequent projections, see U.S. Bureau of the Census, *Statistical Abstracts of the United States, 1967* (Washington, DC: U.S. Government Printing Office, 1967), pp. 8–10.

20. Among the better examples of "rhetorical" treatments of urban population trends (i.e., treatments which presume social knowledge as a ground of advocacy) are "The Conscience of the City," *Daedalus* 97 (1968); and Jeffrey K. Hadden, Louis H. Masotti, Calvin J. Larson, eds., *Metropolis in Crisis* (Itasca, IL: F. E. Peacock, 1967).

21. Bitzer, "Rhetorical Situation," pp. 7–8.

22. H. N. Lee, *Percepts, Concepts, and Theoretic Knowledge* (Memphis, TN: Memphis State University Press, 1973), p. 136.

23. Ziman, *Public Knowledge*, p. 15.

24. See, for an illustration of this process, Wayne N. Thompson, "*Stasis* in Aristotle's Rhetoric," *QJS* 58 (1972): 134–141.

25. Citizens' Board of Inquiry, *Hunger USA* (Washington, DC: New Community Press, 1968), p. 7.

26. Robin Day is cited to that effect in David Berg, "Rhetoric, Reality, and Mass Media," *QJS* 58 (1972): 258.

27. John Dewey, *The Public and Its Problems* (1927; rpt., Chicago: Swallow Press, 1954), p. 153.

28. Alfred Schultz, "The Well-informed Citizen: An Essay in the Social Distribution of Knowledge," *Collected Papers 2* (The Hague, The Netherlands: M. Nijhoff, 1964), p. 124.

29. Ibid, p. 129.

30. An ideal type which, in Schutz's terminology, refers to the citizen who "stands between the ideal type of the expert and that of the man on the street" (p. 122).

31. Murray Edelman, *Politics as Symbolic Action* (Chicago: Markham, 1971), chap. 2.

32. John R. Searle, *Speech Acts* (Cambridge, UK: Cambridge University Press, 1970), p. 23.

33. Polanyi, esp. "Commitment," chap. 10 of *Personal Knowledge*.

34. Georges Gusdorf, *Speaking*, trans. Paul T. Brockelman (Evanston, IL: Northwestern University Press, 1965), p. 122.

35. Charles S. Peirce, "The Essentials of Pragmatism," *Philosophical Writing*, ed. Justus Buchler (New York: Dover, 1940), p. 258.

36. Richard McKeon, "Communication, Truth, and Society," *Ethics* 67 (1957): 89–99, and John Dewey, *The Public and Its Problems*.

Rhetorical Perspectivism

Richard A. Cherwitz
James W. Hikins

With characteristic foresight, Douglas Ehninger predicted that the focus of rhetorical studies in the contemporary period would become an epistemological one.[1] Indeed, since Scott's pronouncement that "rhetoric is epistemic," the literature has exhibited numerous attempts to define more precisely the role of communication in the process of coming to know.[2]

As rhetorical epistemology has developed, a number of controversies have arisen. The most notable of these concerns the nature of the "objects of knowledge" and the means by which these objects are apprehended. Some scholars posit that the objects of knowledge are the products of social/linguistic interaction. This position views reality as socially *constructed*.[3] Others contend that the objects of knowledge exist *prior to* social/linguistic interaction and are not *created*, but rather are *discovered* through discourse.[4] The former position—subtleties notwithstanding—has been variously labeled "intersubjectivity," "rhetorical subjectivism," or "rhetorical relativism;" the latter, "rhetorical objectivism," "rhetorical dialectic," or "critical rationalism."[5]

In what follows, a theory of *rhetorical perspectivism* is developed for the purposes of contributing to our understanding of the role played by rhetoric in the acquisition of knowledge, and to account for the disaffection among theorists. The first section develops the fundamental tenets of perspectivism. The second section explores the implications of

perspectivism for rhetorical epistemology, identifying a major philosophical problem common to both the intersubjectivist *and* objectivist positions. Finally, it is shown how rhetorical perspectivism better addresses this problem, underscoring important insights for rhetoric as a way of knowing.

The Philosophy of Perspective

The term "perspective" has been employed both in technical applications (such as theories of art, physics, psychology, and sociology) as well as in the vernacular. At this stage in its etymological history, the term has become a cliché.[6] Yet the term has found extensive use in philosophical epistemology. Leibniz introduced an epistemological conception of perspective in his theory of *monads*.[7] In addition to a "physical" character, each monad, according to Leibniz, also is endowed with individual consciousness from which arises human consciousness. As a result, each monad mirrors its own *perspective*, perceiving reality from a particular locus or point of view. Whitehead, again within the context of consciousness and perception, contended that one apprehends reality from a particular point in space and time, that is, from a unique perspective.[8] Combining the concepts of space and time, Whitehead advanced a theory of "perspective space" comprised of various "points of view of private space."[9] In similar ways, the theory of perspective has played an important part in the philosophies of Russell, Mead, Biser, and Ushenko.[10] However, the most systematic treatment of perspectives, employing the concept as the cornerstone of a theory of knowledge, was offered by E. B. McGilvary.

McGilvary's chief concern was to develop a defensible formulation of direct realism.[11] Thus, he held the common sense view that, when we perceive, we perceive a world that exists independently of ourselves, "out there," and when we communicate we communicate with other minds that think in large measure as we ourselves think and are located "in other persons."[12] McGilvary did not offer a demonstration for the common sense view. Rather, he followed the accepted practice of advancing direct realism as a *postulate*.

Let us offer a number of postulates as provisionally true. While technical in nature, their formulation is prerequisite to understanding *rhetoric's* inherent epistemological function. The important thing to keep in mind is that the test of any theoretical system is how such a system coheres *qua* system, both in its internal consistency as well as in its ability to account for the world that confronts us in our everyday experience.[13] The most fundamental postulates which bear on an understanding of perspectivism follow.[14]

Postulate 1: The Independence of Reality

In experience there is presented to us, directly, a world of phenomena largely independent of our attitudes, beliefs, and values. This postulate, implying a common sense philosophy somewhat akin to that advocated by Thomas Reid, is put forth solely as a beginning point to be defended in conjunction with other postulates.[15] Yet, it is not an arbitrary notion, for it is sustained by the overwhelming persistence of the belief that reality exists independent of our consciousness of it.[16] Moreover, this conviction sustains us not only as *individuals* who, in our day-to-day affairs act on the presumption that reality is in large measure independent of us, but as *rhetors* and *rhetoricians* as well. For part—indeed a vital part—of our worldview includes such concepts as *audiences*, replete with "other minds" which we inform, persuade, and entertain. What we regard as an independent reality is revealed by our behavior, if not always by our theorizing: not even the most committed subjectivist would support the thesis that reality is *purely* a mental construct by venturing into the path of an oncoming locomotive on the assumption that

mind could alter the consequences of the ensuing collision. Most of the events in human experience cannot be wished away. Likewise, McGilvary was fond of pointing out that "even the solipsist continues to have social moments when he tries to convince others of the correctness of his views, and would probably become as mad in behavior as he is in theory if the social denizens of his world were persistently to deny that they and he are what he and they seem to them and to him to be."[17]

Postulate 2: Relationality

The world is comprised of many particulars, each a member of a context of particulars, and each deriving its nature from that context. Each particular exhibits various characters which themselves emerge wholly as a function of the relations in which the particular stands to other members of its context. Simply put, entities in the universe are what they are solely because of the relationships in which they stand to other entities. As we shall see momentarily, this feature of relationality is applicable to "nonempirical" concepts (such as justice, love, and goodness), as well as to "empirical" concepts.

To understand this postulate, consider its contrary: a one-item universe, where nothing stands *in relation to* anything else. It is impossible to imagine such a universe. In experience, for example, we are confronted by tables, chairs, cats, dogs, and a saturnalia of other items. These items of experience exhibit more or less permanent characters because they are apprehended from various points of view. To illustrate, a tree may exhibit the characteristics green or brown, tall or short, rough-barked or smooth-barked, alive, dead, dormant, healthy or diseased, *depending upon the relationships between and among its various parts and the context of particulars in which it, as a whole, stands* (its relationships to the things around it). As a result, what makes the green healthy oak tree a green healthy oak and not a dead fir is the presence of some characters and the absence of others, standing in specific *relationships*, that is, the presence of those characters, "arranged" in a certain way. Similarly, Newton's laws of gravitation capture a complex set of *relationships* between "objects" with particular characters, such as mass, distance *from* one another, and velocity. In this way, the "objects" of reality are both understood and comprehended *qua* relationships.

It should be clear that relationality is advanced *not* as a description of the *nature* of the objects of the universe, but as an explanation of how those objects—be they thought of as "material," "spiritual," or whatever—come to possess the natures they have. Moreover, as argued in what follows, it is this feature of relationality which accounts not only for what is, but also for what is *thought*.

Postulate 3: Consciousness

Consciousness is a natural event which occurs when and only when an entity comes to stand in a particular relationship to other entities within a context of particulars. Consciousness is itself a character of a specific kind and is always part of a corresponding asymmetrical relation also of a specific kind. By "natural event" is meant an occurrence independent of individual attitudes, beliefs, and values. For example, while the reader may have *intended* to read these words, and while he or she may choose at any time to stop reading, nonetheless, once a particular set of relations obtains, consciousness will occur independent of what the reader "wishes." For instance, if the individual is within a certain distance of this page, under certain conditions of lighting, and assuming "normal" vision and certain "brain processes," plus the lack of any intervening set of relations (such as closed eyelids "obstructing" the view), consciousness of the words on this page will *necessarily* occur.

Of course, one might argue that a reader who "brings" certain attitudes, beliefs, or values to his or her reading may "read it" or "read *into* it" something quite different from another reader. Moreover, someone reading this paper for the first time may come away with a different "perception" than he or she would after having read it several times. The explanation for this is to be found in the difference between *consciousness of* an object (again, where "object" is to be understood as *object of thought* and not in physicalist terms) and certain notions *additional to* consciousness, such as meaning, reflection, understanding, and comprehension.

By "entity" is meant a discrete collection of characters. It is important to note that the term "entity" should not be thought of as "physical" or "mental," since what have typically been called "physical entities" and "non-physical" or "mental" entities (such as love, justice, and goodness) are not *qualitatively* distinct within the theory of perspectivism herein developed. Thus, people, inanimate objects, and values are all entities. Consciousness, then, is a *purely relational concept*, arising out of the relation in which one particular complex entity of a particular type stands to other entities.

The phrase "context of particulars" denotes all those entities and the various relationships in which they stand to one another which in any way affect or condition some other individual, specifiable entity. Thus, in this postulate, a *complete account* of the conscious state of, say, an astronomer viewing the moons of Jupiter, or a mathematician grappling with a complex equation, or an ethicist struggling to determine a proper course of action, would entail a description of all the entities and relationships among entities which have a significant bearing on the conscious event.

A conscious relation is "asymmetrical" in the sense that when an entity "A" is conscious of some other entity "B," it does not follow that "B" is necessarily conscious of "A," nor that "B" is conscious of "A's" consciousness of "B."

In summary, we have advanced three postulates: (1) there exists a world of entities in some sense independent of our attitudes, beliefs, and values—a world in which we are powerless to either will or wish away most, though certainly not all events; (2) the entities populating the world—be they trees, stones, polar bears, values, thoughts, or human beings—are what they are solely because of the relationships in which they stand to one another; and (3) consciousness is itself an occurrence arising when a particular entity, such as a human being, comes to stand in a certain relationship to another entity or entities. These entities and the conscious subject comprise a complex, interrelated array of constituents, called a "complex of particulars."

Perspectivism and Rhetorical Epistemology

One of perspectivism's most important contributions to an understanding of rhetoric's role in the process of coming to know lies in its ability to account for—and perhaps even mediate—the current debate between the rhetorical subjectivist (intersubjectivist) and rhetorical objectivist positions. As suggested at the outset, the literature in rhetorical theory reflects at least two broad categories of thought regarding the relationship between rhetoric and knowing. Some thinkers claim that reality is socially constructed through discourse; others contend that reality exists independent of and apart from discourse. This section catalogs various positions which are subsumed within these two larger categories, suggesting how the issues they raise may be addressed by perspective theory.

Subjectivism versus Objectivism

A survey of the literature in rhetorical epistemology reveals four varieties of ontological claims. Consider, for example, the claims of the subjectivists. This school, which describes itself as "intersubjectivist," abjures the possibility that there exists an "objective reality" or at minimum contends that if there is such a reality, we can never know it.[18] Therefore, so the argument continues, the notion of an objective reality is not a useful concept. We suggest that this school is more properly characterized as subjectivist because of the manner in which they develop the argument against an objective reality. Consider, for example, their reformulation of what reality is: "Reality is meaning yet meaning is something created and discovered in communication." Further, "meaning is of first importance in human affairs, and in a real sense, reality is meaning."[19] According to this analysis, all of reality is a product of meaning, literally. Moreover, the subjectivists wish to claim that this process of constructing meaning is an intersubjective process—one that is the product of a number of individual, other persons. Yet notice that other persons—or, more precisely, what we know of other persons—we know in the same sense we know trees, houses, cats, rats, or any other "external" object. This being the case, the objective existence of other persons must be regarded with the same ontological suspicion as all other things whose objective nature is called into question by the subjectivists. This is because other persons must be regarded as the product of meaning too. Now this conclusion may be warmly embraced by the subjectivists and even touted as a rationale for the preeminence of human rhetorical communication. The problem with the view, as we see it, is that it is inherently solipsistic. In the absence of any account establishing the objective existence of other subjects, intersubjectivity collapses altogether. We are left only with the contention that the reality we perceive is created through meaning. And if humans have the capacity to create reality through meaning, who is to say that this activity is not done purely subjectively, the notion of "other minds" being an elaborate conceptual illusion, just as the objective existence of trees, houses, cats, rats, and everything else is a conceptual illusion according to the subjectivists? Moreover, who is to say there is not just one mind, the mind of the thinker, everyone else merely appearing to have an intellect? In sum, intersubjectivity reduces to solipsism and hence to subjectivity, for,

if meaning determines reality, it is just as likely that the world is a product of the intrapersonal communication within a mind (subjectivity) as it is of interpersonal communication among several minds (intersubjectivity).

A less radical version of rhetorical subjectivism (mitigated subjectivism) contends that only some items of reality are the product of discourse. According to this position, the world is divided into two separate realms, a "technical" or "scientific" realm including objects somehow "external" to and "independent" of mind, and a mental or "social" realm, wherein the externality of concepts in such fields as ethics and politics (concepts such as "goodness," "justice," "virtue," and the like) is steadfastly denied.[20] The term "subjectivism" describes this school of thought for much the same reason that the term is applied to the "strict subjectivists." For despite the positing of distinct "technical" and "social" realms, the ontological status of other thinking persons in such a world remains unclear. On the one hand, these writers could be suggesting that such concepts as other persons reside in the social realm because, for example, they are "unobservable," unlike empirical, technical entities. Presumably, it is such persons who generate rhetorical discourse by "creating meaning" in much the same sense as in the case of the strict subjectivists. If this is so, any precise demarcation between what is created by subjects in the social realm and what is observed in the technical realm becomes problematic. Hence, because solipsism is again entailed, the term "subjectivism" applies. On the other hand, the "mitigated subjectivists" could locate other persons in the technical realm—a position which might render the label "subjectivist" inapropos. This, however, seems inconsistent with the spirit in which the technical/social bifurcation was advanced; placing notions like other persons into the technical category casts doubt as to whether anything falls into the social realm. Social knowledge, after all, is by implication created by persons and cannot be reduced to "empirical operationalization." It is difficult to see how social knowledge could arise as "probable knowledge . . . knowledge in a state of potential or indeterminance"[21] if it were generated by the kind of automata the "technical" alternative implies.

What are the rationales upon which these two versions of subjectivism are based? The strict subjectivists generally hold that there is no method whereby one can test the postulate that there exists an independent reality.[22] In addition, it has been argued that the positing of an independent reality is "not helpful in the pursuit of knowledge," since, for example, "science gets along very well using concepts whose 'real' existence has never been proven such as ether and phlogiston in the past and certain subatomic particles in the present."[23]

Both these arguments seem to hinge on a radical application of a kind of "verifiability criterion" not unlike that developed by the early positivists. Terms such as "test" and "proven" appear to mean "verified" in the sense that one could *measure* or visually *observe* phenomena; for the strict subjectivists, since we cannot escape the fact that our minds are inextricably involved in measuring, observing, and imputing meaning in what is measured and observed, the notion of a reality which exists "out there," independent of mind, is simply not a meaningful and, hence, not a "useful" concept.

The rationale of the mitigated subjectivists is much the same as that of the strict subjectivists. However, there is no radical application of any "verifiability criterion" to what we commonly speak of as empirical matters. These theorists postulate the existence of external objects that can be measured and observed. While denying the validity of positivism in most of their writing outside rhetorical epistemology, they nonetheless adopt what is tantamount to a positivistic approach when treating rhetoric as a way of knowing. That which is "real" and "knowable" in the ultimate sense are such things as the objects of scientific inquiry; that which is the subject of rhetoric are such things as political, moral, and religious questions—matters about which we "create" realities through discourse.[24] The former are independent of our thinking about them; the latter are a product of our mental life interacting (socially) with the mental lives of "others."

The objectivist position, as it appears in the literature in rhetorical epistemology, also evidences at least two emphases. On the one hand are those who suggest that rhetoric's function is to transmit the truths discovered by the other arts and sciences (*strict objectivism*).[25] This view is traditional in the history of rhetoric, and casts for rhetoric a "minimal epistemological role."[26] A second position within the objectivist camp (which has been called *rhetorical dialectic*) argues for the existence of independent realities in both the "empirical" and "social" realms.[27] Terms like "goodness," "justice," and the "rightness" or "wrongness" of an act are as "real" as the subjects treated within the physi-

cal sciences. Rhetoric's role is not to *create* realities about such concepts; it is rather to *discover* them and articulate relationships between or among them through the process of argumentative discourse.[28] The rationale for the objectivist position takes a number of forms, including the argument from solipsism just mentioned, and others with which the reader of this essay may be familiar.[29] Rather than assessing the arguments marshaled by both the subjectivists and objectivists, let us take their thesis statements at face value, while suggesting how perspectivism might help close the distance between the two camps.

The Implicit Problem of Dualism in Rhetorical Epistemology

To comprehend, and perhaps mitigate, the differences between the objectivist and subjectivist positions, it is necessary to understand the source of their theoretical disparities. That source is, or is much the same as, the *Cartesian dichotomy between mental entities and physical entities.* Since Descartes penned the *Meditations* in 1641, philosophy in general and epistemology in particular have been plagued by what has become known as the problem of *dualism.*[30] Simply put, if there exist mental occurrences which have their locus in a mind, and these are both quantitatively and qualitatively distinct from physical events, what is to account for the influence of one on the other? The four stances outlined above represent, in effect, four "stands" taken by rhetoricians vis-à-vis this issue.

The *strict subjectivists* circumvent the dualist problem by calling into question the existence of physical realities, emphasizing the priority of mental constructs (such as "meaning") which explain the way the world is and the way it is created or managed via discourse. One consequence of this solution, as we have seen, may be solipsism—the inability to account for or find a theoretical place for other minds, since, if the world is a mental construct, what appear to be other thinking beings may well be a construct of the thinker.

The *mitigated subjectivists*, on the other hand, squarely embrace the dualist position in their separation of mental and physical entities, without commenting on the philosophical problems which such a dualism engenders. Hence, these thinkers leave a major quandary of dualism unanswered, namely, How does one account for the influence of one realm on the other? How is it that two so qualitatively distinct worlds coexist and interact?

The *strict objectivists*, while avoiding the problem of dualism by suggesting that the only know-able objects are "physical" in nature, render impossible the conferring of epistemic status upon those ideas and beliefs which are the subject of day-to-day discourse. And, as those who have taken issue with positivism have indicated, to dismiss all non-empirical matters as meaningless and unknowable, though it may solve the dualist problem, is unacceptably counterintuitive.[31] After all, especially in the world of prudential conduct, such "nonempirical" issues are both meaningful and of crucial importance in managing our lives.

Finally, those who have taken the position of *rhetorical dialectic* have, like the mitigated subjectivists, failed to deal with the problem of reconciling the physical and mental realms which dualism has occasioned. Moreover, these scholars, in maintaining the externality of both social and scientific questions, have left themselves vulnerable to the subjectivists' complaint that questions of a contingent variety (such as moral, religious, and political issues), if they are external to mind in the same way as are empirical ones, should be similarly verifiable.

Perspectivism and Dualism

Perspectivism offers an alternative approach to the dualist enigma. By treating the constituents of the world as collections of characters which cohere *relationally* to form particulars within a context of particulars, and by treating consciousness as a phenomenon which *itself* emerges when an entity of a particular type (e.g., a human being) stands in a particular *relation* to other entities, the perspectivist dispenses with the necessity of bifurcating the world into "physical" and "mental" realms. According to our formulation, the mental/physical distinction—and the dualist problem which has arisen from it—is an unfortunate "category mistake,"[32] that is, an artificial categorization of the objects of experience. All objects of experience, including the objects of scientific inquiry, as well as such characteristics as "good," "bad," "justice," "virtue," and the like are endowed with a similar *ontological* status; they all *exist* and are all *entities* in the world of nature, deriving their separate natures according to the relationships in which they stand, both to their own characters and to the characters and complexes of characters exhibited by other entities.

The foundation of the dualist problem, then, is rooted in the familiar and ubiquitous *subject/object distinction*,[33] one which maintains an onto-logical difference between perceivers and things perceived. The existence of this bifurcation necessarily leads to the kind of epistemological differences so apparent among the four positions taken by rhetoricians. These differences are manifested in the inherent practice of thinking in terms of distinctions such as physical/mental, internal/external, contingent/apodeictic. We have, for centuries, wittingly or unwittingly, labored under the *conceptual* consequences of Cartesian dualism. In the present century, the problem has been exacerbated by the growth of science and the ensuing academic conflicts between science and the arts. In rhetoric, the tendency has been further accentuated by the elevation of Aristotle's contingent/apodeictic distinction to the status of an axiom.

The theory of perspectivism, on the other hand, is premised on the assumption that there is no *ontological* distinction among the entities populating the universe. Because everything which is is what it is by virtue of its relationship to whatever else is, the subject/object distinction is otiose. Such a conclusion is consistent with the first postulate of perspective theory, namely, that reality is independent of human attitudes, beliefs, and values. Such independence does, on the perspectivist view, obtain; however, it obtains in the sense that the *objects* of reality are collections of *relata* standing in an asymmetrical conscious relationship to human subjects that are also collections of *relata*. The ontological cement gluing all entities together, then—be they abstract entities such as justice and goodness, empirical entities such as tables, chairs, and atoms, or conscious entities such as human beings—is *the relation*. For this reason, we may still refer to perceiving entities and perceived entities without becoming ensnared in dualism, so long as we are certain to keep at the forefront of our epistemological system the realization that the perception of entities is made possible *because of relationality*.[34] But as one reader of this essay inquired: "What does it mean to enter into a relationship? Is the relationship objectively real or does *it* depend on a perspective? Do entities have existence outside relationship? Can relationships be socially determined?" These are fair questions, but space permits us only to suggest what direction a response would take.

Technically, it is impossible to enter *anew* into a relationship in the sense of entering *afresh* into the vast relational complex that is the universe. The relational determiners which, for example, prescribed the occurrence of the Beirut Massacre, were as present in the world a thousand years ago as in September, 1982. The only sense, we suggest, in which the notion of entering into a relationship can be understood is the sense in which we *become aware*, as conscious human beings, of the possibility and, in retrospect, the actuality of relationships. Relations *are*, without exaggeration, *more* than objectively real, for they themselves are the determiners of the specific items comprising reality. Hence, rather than being shaped *by* perspectives, relations form the basis *of* human perspectives. Finally, it should be seen to follow that relationships (relations) *themselves* cannot be socially determined. Thus, while a skillful rhetor might convince an audience that the assassination of John Kennedy was the result of a conspiracy, only the existence or nonexistence of individuals other than Lee Harvey Oswald standing, *in fact*, in a conspiracy relationship to the events of November 22, 1963 can make the former President's death the product of a conspiracy. At best, the rhetor can make us aware of a relationship, *possible or actual*, that we were not (or are not) conscious of prior to rhetoric. But the rhetor cannot, strictly speaking, "create" a world of both relations *and* relata in defiance of relations *actually* existing.

The doctrine of relationality underscores how perspectivism may act as a mediating influence among the four positions on rhetorical epistemology. With respect to *strict subjectivism*, relationality accounts for how it is that individuals apprehend the world in distinct and frequently conflicting ways, hence retaining a valuable portion of the strict subjectivist thesis. Because each individual stands in a unique perspective to the multiplicity of events and things in the world, such individuals' accounts of the world are often distinctive. Yet while rhetors can view the world from different perspectives, and while the propagandist may argue for combinations of relations that do not obtain (i.e., are *untrue*), this is a far cry from the strict subjectivist's contention that meaning is wholly a product of individuals or that reality is socially constructed. Thus, perspectivism seems less vulnerable to the charge of solipsism. In a world where everything is intimately *related* in strictly ontological terms, solipsistic estrangement is less likely to occur, for, as all three postulates of perspectivism taken together suggest, the solipsistic implications of strict subjectivism dissolve on the basis of relationality, direct realism, and perspective consciousness.

With regard to *mitigated subjectivism*, perspective theory would echo the belief that not all classes of items comprising reality are the same. The differences among such items stem from the fact that each and every entity within the world stands in a special and unique relationship to all else that is. Unlike the mitigated subjectivists, however, perspectivism avoids the conclusion that classes of items are *ontologically* distinct, which is the source of the dualist enigma. For the perspectivist, there is no division of the world into technical and social phenomena. In terms of the most basic explanation possible for the nature of all phenomena, it is such foundational *relations* as "difference" itself which grounds the objects of knowledge. Differentiations among *classes* of objects of knowledge may be useful for some purposes, but are not, for the perspectivist, to be made on the basis of the role of language (communication) in "creating" some classes or "assessing" others. In sum, while perspectivism recognizes one advantage of the mitigated subjectivist thesis, namely, that the objects of reality exhibit significant differences, it rejects the claim that such differences are a function of, for example, a *qualitative* mind/body-type distinction. Such a distinction is, on the perspectivist view, both artificial and improper, since all objects of reality hold equal ontological status. In this way, the dualist enigma is avoided.

In terms of *strict objectivism*, perspective theory reaffirms the claim that reality, because it is independent of us, cannot be willed into existence nor wished away. The perspectivist, though, rejects the strict objectivist's contention that the only knowable items of reality are those that are "empirical." Like the two schools of subjectivist thought, perspectivism holds that we are capable of knowing, and in fact *do* know, much about the nonempirical world of prudential affairs. As already indicated, perspectivism takes issue with the very attempt to locate qualitative ontological differences among the items comprising reality. For this reason, terms such as "empirical" and "nonempirical" are at best euphemistic, and do *not* refer to a basic ontological distinction. The doctrine of an independent reality is applicable to *all* items in the world. One can, and frequently *does*, stand in a conscious relation to "nonempirical" as well as "empirical" entities. Such a claim is less problematic, according to the perspectivist, if we keep our language and thought free of the empirical connotations which terms such as "test," "proven," and the like (mistakenly) imply. This task becomes more manageable when we remember that all phenomena are what they are because of their relationship to all else.

Finally, perspectivism offers an important extension of the *rhetorical dialectic* thesis. To begin with, the perspectivist would share the contention of the rhetorical dialectic camp that reality is largely independent of the knower's attitudes, beliefs, and values, and is capable of being known. Again, however, the perspectivist posits such a claim without introducing an empirical/nonempirical vocabulary. In this way, the perspectivist both avoids the dualist enigma and helps address the subjectivists' complaint that nonempirical items of reality, if they are independent of us in the same way as empirical items, should be similarly verifiable. For the perspectivist, the problem of verifiability is ensconced within a dualist vocabulary—the tendency to make distinctions between empirical and nonempirical objects, subjects and objects, and contingent and apodeictic knowledge. If one approaches the notion of verifiability—and for that matter the entire process of coming to know—from the standpoint of conscious relations, such distinctions become unnecessary. In short, if we think of the process of coming to know as beginning when a conscious human being becomes aware of a relation, then it is just as easy to imagine how one could have awareness of what euphemistically have been called nonempirical objects as of empirical objects, since that which permits knowledge or understanding is *the relation*.

The relational foundation of awareness can be illustrated by considering some examples of epistemic judgments which arise in day-to-day discourse. Consider:

1. 4 + 5,000,000 = 5,000,004
2. Jan followed her older, taller sister, Mary, into the room.
3. At a temperature of − 459.69 degrees Fahrenheit (absolute zero), there is an absence of molecular movement, i.e., an absence of heat.
4. Richard Nixon was a bad president.

In line with traditional thinking, one might be tempted to label statement one "mathematical," statement two "general descriptive," statement three "scientific" or "empirical," and statement four "contingent." Each statement would be taken as different in kind, perhaps involving a unique type of epistemological judgment. Adopting the point of view of the perspectivist, all four statements purport to describe various constituents of the world as collections of characters which cohere *relationally* and, on this analysis, are *not* qualitatively distinct. Thus, while the perspectivist would certainly hold that the objects comprising the

subject matter of each of the four statements are independent of the utterer's attitudes, beliefs, and values, there is no reason to introduce a subject/object vocabulary, contending that the objects in some of the statements are spatially external and, in other cases, spatially internal to mind.

The first statement, "Four added to five million equals five million and four," involves a relationship of equality. It, like other statements within pure mathematics, is a prime example of the notion of relationality, one which should be unproblematic for virtually any reader. For even the most fervent empiricist (including the strict objectivist) experiences much difficulty in explaining the "truth" of such a statement in empirical terms. The reason for this difficulty is clear: the statement treats only nonempirical concepts. It does not deal with quantities of apples or trees or tables or chairs; it deals with the *concepts* "four," "five million," "equality," and "five million and four." Nor do any of us have the slightest trouble operating with the two larger numbers in this equation, though doubtless none of us have ever *experienced* such quantities *of anything*. A consideration of similar and even more complex examples indicates that one often operates in mathematics with relations and concepts which have no instantiation in what has euphemistically (from the perspectivist's point or view) been called the "empirical world," or at least, if they are so instantiated, have never been, and likely will never be, experienced by human beings, *except in a nonempirical* sense. An individual becomes *conscious* of a mathematical equation when he or she stands in a certain relationship to that equation. The equation itself expresses a relationship among its various concepts as well as to the conscious individual, because the concepts it contains all stand in a context of particulars determined by all the interrelationships involved.

An interesting corollary of the perspectivist analysis of mathematics arises in the hypothetical case wherein all conscious entities suddenly perish from the universe (one may define perish as "to come into a state of complete and perpetual relational dissolution, so that consciousness is not possible"). In this event, the mathematical relation expressed by the first example, and all other mathematical examples, would continue to exist, since their ontological status is guaranteed so long as the mathematical relationships they express obtain. Extended to other objects of knowledge, perspectivism affirms the common sense notion that the stars and planets will continue to exist "in space" after all life is extinct on earth and no one is left to "perceive" their existence. This is because all the characters in the relational complex, save those comprising sentient earthlings, will continue to enter into relationships with each other.

In the second example, the statement "Jan followed her older, taller sister, Mary, into the room" was introduced. There are a number of easily identifiable relations which comprise this epistemic judgment, such as "older," "taller," and "followed." Other relations present that are somewhat more covert include "sisterhood." Sisterhood (which we call a "relation" in ordinary discourse) is vacuous unless treated as a relata in a world where at least two entities exist. In addition to these more or less obvious relations, terms such as "Jan" and "Mary" are relational as well, in the sense that they are terms which distinguish particular complexes of particulars from others. When one asks, "Who is Jan?," the response is likely to be, "Jan is the red-haired, short girl who is Mary's sister." Though one rarely thinks of it as such, a certain complex of particulars, Jan, is here being distinguished from among other complexes around her, including "Mary," "Paula," and "Theresa." Similar examples are ultimately analyzable into distinctions of a relational variety.

In "absolute zero," a number of relations are discernible. The numeric interval, – 459.69, as well as the scale upon which it is based, namely the Fahrenheit scale, are obvious relational concepts. The requirement that one must think in terms of "external" and "internal" (subject/object) does not appear. An understanding of statement number three (and any other) requires only the recognition that it may be analyzed wholly in relational terms. Most conspicuously absent in this epistemology is the introduction of phrases such as "internal to mind" and "external to mind." Such an account demands only recognition of: (1) independent relata; and (2) their relations. It does not require a positing either of "objects" in the physicalist sense of the term, or reified "social realities" in the subjectivist sense.

Finally, let us consider the question of Richard Nixon's presidency addressed in statement four. Unlike the strict empiricist, the perspectivist analysis of this epistemic judgment begins with the common sense assumption that the statement is as meaningful and as important as any of the others. Thus the term, "bad," like its opposite, "good," is, at minimum, a character which is part of the complex of particular characters together constituting the concept "Richard Nixon's presidency." It is questions like this one which are more tradition-

ally the domain of rhetorical discourse, though as suggested at the beginning of this section, the first three also frequently fall within the scope of rhetoric.[35] The last section of this paper focuses on these traditional rhetorical questions and explains additional implications which the perspectivist approach holds for rhetoric.

Perspectivism's Implications for Rhetoric

To this stage of the argument it has been suggested that the perspectivist views all objects of experience, broadly conceived, as having an equal ontological status. Morals, ethics, and the questions of politics are as real as trees, houses, planets, and atoms. Yet one might challenge this position on the rationale that most of the objects of the former sort (for example, the objects of astronomical inquiry, such as stars and planets) are readily observable and that the scientific questions which they occasion are not the subject of *disagreement* in the sense that, say, the question of the goodness of Richard Nixon as an American president is the subject of disagreement. After all, the argument might continue, once a scientific question has been identified, a way to *measure* or otherwise *observe* the phenomena in question is found; then, shortly, our disagreement is resolved. Yet in the case of what have been called "contingent questions," debate may continue for centuries without a resolution. How can the perspectivist account for this seeming disparity? Moreover, doesn't this feature of disagreement signal a demarcation between two realms of thought which are, epistemologically, qualitatively distinct, perhaps even serving to confirm the very Cartesian distinction which we have been attempting to dismantle?[36]

The perspectivist account of disagreement begins with the observation that there exists, especially within the more complex and advanced branches of modern science, perhaps an equivalent level of disagreement—disagreement on issues which are as difficult to verify as any question of politics or ethics. Examples range from nuclear physics, where scientists are currently grappling with disagreements that seem almost insoluble, to contemporary astronomy, where the discovery of quasars is prompting a radical reevaluation of previous conceptions of the universe.

But let us examine the fundamental tenets of perspectivism to see if they offer a clue as to both the reason for and the solution to disagreements of a "contingent" nature. Recall that the perspectivist posits a world of relationships, wherein every entity, conscious or inanimate, stands in relationship to one another. It follows that each of us will perceive the world in a different way. Moreover, as each of us confronts very complex collections of relata, the complexity of such collections will have two effects: (1) they will offer the perceiving subject multi-various characters, each one itself a relata of the relational complex; and (2) their "appearance" may alter radically as the perspective changes for each perceiver or with different perceivers.

Let us pursue the question of Richard Nixon's presidency. One could hardly find a contemporary example of a question which would generate more controversy. Was Nixon a good president? Some would answer "yes" and some would say "no." Yet both responses cannot be true, for it is both logically and conceptually impossible to entertain both answers as *knowledge* at the same time and in the same way. How, then, can we account for the existence of actual rhetorical discourse which embraces contradictory answers to the question of whether or not Richard Nixon was a good president?

It is clear that both the strict and mitigated subjectivists would answer that such a question is meaningless, since there is no "truth" or "falsity"—at least in any absolute sense—and, hence, no answer to the question apart from socially constructed attitudes, beliefs, and values. The advocate of rhetorical dialectic, on the other hand, would contend that there is an answer to this question and that it must be true or false, while the strict objectivist would contend that such a question is totally without meaning because of its "nonempirical" character. The perspectivist, however, would take a somewhat different approach. The answer to the disagreement regarding Richard Nixon's presidency lies in an understanding of each arguer's *perspective* and in the fact that they may be conscious at any one time of collections of characters or *aspects*, each of which is a relatum within the collection of particulars comprising the Nixon presidency, but which *appear* to be different because of the differing *perspectives* in which each arguer stands. On this account, the apparently contradictory judgments are really not contradictory at all, since they are *judgments about different aspects of the same object*. One arguer, for example, may frame the answer to the hypothetical question as a result of a close attention to the foreign policy aspects of the Nixon years, with an empha-

sis on such events as normalizing relations with China or negotiating arms limitation agreements. He or she may conclude "Nixon was a good president." The other arguer may focus on the disastrous effects of Watergate and conclude "Nixon was a bad president." Ultimately, we should be able to reduce the scope of our interest in the relational complex so that we are all "talking about the same thing." Then we should be able to marshal the context of particulars in which arguers stand to an object of disagreement so we are arguing on the "same plane." When this is done we can both agree on what we are disagreeing about and, perhaps, "stand inside the other's perspective." At this point, agreement should be possible.[37]

Of course, one can imagine instances where individuals engage in this argumentative process and, nonetheless, are unable to embrace, understand, or otherwise recognize an other's perspective. An example might be the racist who holds a severe prejudice against blacks. Such an individual might labor under such a prejudice purely out of ignorance, that is, ignorance that no credible studies support the notion that blacks are inherently less intelligent than whites. In an argumentative confrontation, one might enlighten the racist about the actual data. In fact, one might produce a host of research to expose the racist's error. If the evidence were overwhelming, the racist *might* be convinced that his or her former attitude toward black intelligence was, in fact, in error. Yet this person might continue to hold racist views, based on other considerations—that is, based on *other perspectives*. Or, the racist might find himself or herself unable to reconcile a new perspective with the consequences for personal behavior or interpersonal relationships among his or her peer group. In the latter case, the racist might continue to *espouse* racist views, even though the argumentative encounter had undermined the initial rationale upon which those views were grounded.

If the racist eventually abandons his or her prejudice as a result of being made aware of another perspective by the argumentative encounter, then the value of rhetorical perspectivism as a tool of inquiry becomes obvious. On the other hand, if the racist persists in his or her attitude toward blacks, perspective theory may still offer important resources for affecting potential change. First, application of the theory of rhetorical perspectivism allows us to determine whether, in fact, impasse has been reached. Perspectivism may signal, as in the case of the Nixon example, that, because we are not arguing on the same level (that is, because we are not talking about the same aspect of the problem), there are no genuine grounds for disagreement. A perspective account of such discourse, therefore, could reveal imprecision on the part of the interlocutors regarding the object of controversy, thus permitting them to redefine the issue at hand. Perspectivism, then, may make continued discussion and eventual agreement possible through the elimination of what first appeared to be an impasse.

Second, rhetorical perspectivism may allow one to move among *various* perspectives on the *same* issue. Thus, even though a racist might be correct in his or her claim that large numbers of blacks live in ghetto communities, a discussion of how those communities came into existence, covering such topics as economic segregation, the denial of educational opportunities, and the failure of white-dominated city councils to provide essential services, might offer a number of *different perspectives* concerning the *reasons* for ghetto communities. By identifying perspectives the racist may not have considered in the past, his or her attitude toward blacks may be subject to amendment.

Finally, even if additional perspectives are not identified in an argumentative exchange, and even if the isolation of particular issues does not result in continued argumentative progress, still, by identifying precisely where an impasse is occurring, we have an indication of *why* genuine argument has stagnated. Accordingly, a perspective analysis of discourse may tell us something about ourselves *qua* arguers. It may underscore those moments when our emotions, preferences, values, dogmas, and prejudices have interceded to inhibit the most rational and person-building means of inquiry.

This recognition offers us the opportunity to reduce the potential for nondiscursive forms of conflict, in a world where technology renders conflict all the more egregious. By admitting, for example, that *both* we and our potential adversaries—be they Russians, Iranians, wives, or lovers—have reached a point of impasse based on the values and myths which each uniquely holds, we can eschew charges of disingenuousness, deceit, frivolity, and truculence. Thus, while we may be required to terminate our rhetorical efforts because of such an impasse, we can at least leave the negotiating table agreeing, no, *understanding* why negotiations have broken down. By agreeing, if only about the source of disagreement, we may be able to avoid the varieties of inflammatory charges which are the progenitors of nondiscursive conflict.

Perspectivism, then, may remind us that, because we each stand in an unique perspective

to all else (thus explaining "intrinsic value differences"), we may, on occasion, be simply unable to find solutions to grave problems. Nevertheless, we may still depart from argumentative confrontations with the knowledge that, having applied perspectivism as a guide to argument, we have done all humanly possible to achieve harmony, hoping that at some future time negotiations can be reconvened and fresh perspectives pursued.[38] It should be clear from what has gone before that perspectivism offers not only the *opportunity* but, in a sense, the *responsibility* for continued efforts to solve disputes on the basis of peaceful, discursive means. This is because the theory assumes the potential for every individual to be brought to a realization of the perspective of any other and to work together to solve differences constructively. For this reason, nondiscursive forms of conflict can, and thus must, be continually set aside, and the invitation to return to the conference table continually held open. While it is doubtless true that many readers will find in such a view more "naïve" idealism than worldly "realism," we suggest there is ample evidence in the history of international diplomacy to warrant continued consideration of this position.

Conclusion

Embracing the tenets of perspectivism may allow us to retain useful and meaningful conceptions of "truth" or "knowledge," thus preserving the most important feature of objectivism. Moreover, by relieving rhetorical epistemology of the burden of the dualist enigma, perspectivism permits the introduction of a richly endowed theory of knowledge capable of extending rhetorical knowing across the entire spectrum of what there is to know, from matters previously labeled scientific to those frequently called contingent.

In addition to recasting objectivist statements of how knowledge is possible, perspectivism offers a better understanding of the nature and usefulness of theoretical constructs within subjectivist thought. For example, perspectivism makes clear the contribution of those in rhetoric who have argued for the existence of socially constructed realities. Such realities are, in effect, the perspectives which different societal groups entertain on various social phenomena. However, they do not, for the perspectivist, represent the terminus of inquiry. Rather, such social realities are to be viewed as more or less complete expositions of one perhaps limited perspective. Thus, they may be invaluable in contributing to a fuller understanding of the social phenomena under investigation; yet, for the perspectivist, a thorough understanding of a particular social phenomena can occur only when *all* relevant perspectives have been discovered, evaluated, and juxtaposed to form a more complete view of the object of inquiry. As this study suggests, it is only through an active seeking out of perspectives that such a goal may be approached. The promise of perspectivism, then, inheres in the systematic development and application, by theorist, critic, and arguer alike, of *perspective method*, a goal to which we hope this essay has contributed a modest beginning.

NOTES

1. Douglas Ehninger, "Introduction," in Douglas Ehninger, ed., *Contemporary Rhetoric: A Reader's Coursebook* (Glenview, IL: Scott, Foresman, 1972), pp. 1–14. This view may also be seen in his later works. See, e.g., Douglas Ehninger, "Science, Philosophy— And Rhetoric: A Look Toward the Future," in James L. Golden, Goodwin F. Berquist, and William E. Coleman, eds., *The Rhetoric of Western Thought* (Dubuque, IA: Kendall/Hunt, 1978), pp. 323–331.

2. Robert L. Scott, "On Viewing Rhetoric as Epistemic," *Central States Speech Journal* 18 (1967): 17 [reprinted in this volume]. A representative list of scholarship in this area includes: Robert L. Scott, "On Viewing Rhetoric as Epistemic: Ten Years Later," *Central States Speech Journal* 27 (1976): 258–266; Lloyd Bitzer, "Rhetoric and Public Knowledge," in Don Burks, ed., *Rhetoric, Philosophy, and Literature* (West Lafayette, IN: Purdue University Press, 1978), pp. 67–98; Thomas Farrell, "Knowledge, Consensus, and Rhetorical Theory," *Quarterly Journal of Speech* 64 (1976): 1–14 [reprinted in this volume]; Walter M. Carleton, "What Is Rhetorical Knowledge? A Reply to Farrell—And More," *Quarterly Journal of Speech* 64 (1978): 313–328; and Richard Cherwitz, "Rhetoric as a 'Way of Knowing': An Attenuation of the Epistemological Claims of the 'New Rhetoric,'" *Southern Speech Communication Journal* 42 (1977): 207–219. A good review of research on this topic appears in Michael C. Leff, "In Search of Ariadne's Thread: A Review of the Recent Literature on Rhetorical Theory," *Central States Speech Journal* 29 (1978): 73–91.

3. See, e.g., Barry Brummett, "Some Implications of 'Process' or 'Intersubjectivity': Postmodern Rhetoric," *Philosophy and Rhetoric* 9 (1976): 34. Although not agreeing with Brummett entirely, this position is also taken by Farrell, Scott, and Carleton. Most of this research seems to be an outgrowth of views expressed by Peter Berger and Thomas Luckmann, in their *The Social Construction of Reality* (Garden City, NY: Doubleday, 1966).

4. In particular, see C. Jack Orr, "How Shall We Say: 'Reality Is Socially Constructed through Communication?'" *Central States Speech Journal* 29 (1978): 263–274. See also Richard A. Cherwitz and James W. Hikins, "John Stuart Mill's *On Liberty*: Implications for the Epistemology of the New Rhetoric," *Quarterly Journal of Speech* 65 (1979): 12–24.

5. The term "intersubjectivity" has become commonplace in the writings of some scholars in rhetorical epistemology, most notably Brummett. Of late, however, several theorists have recognized the subjective or relative implications of intersubjectivity, preferring the terms "rhetorical subjectivism" and/or "rhetorical relativism." See, for example, Earl Croasmun and Richard Cherwitz, "Beyond Rhetorical Relativism," *Quarterly Journal of Speech* 68 (1982): 1–16. Their argument is that intersubjectivity inherently lapses back into subjectivity, despite the contention by the intersubjectivists that subjectivity is avoided. The view of "rhetorical relativism" is embraced by Scott in his 1976 essay. The distinction between "rhetorical objectivism" and "rhetorical dialectic" appears in James W. Hikins, "Plato's Rhetorical Theory: Old Perspectives on the Epistemology of the New Rhetoric," *Central States Speech Journal* 32 (1981): 160–176. "Critical rationalism" is discussed by Orr (cited in full above, note 4).

6. The earliest recorded use of the term "perspective" in English is reported as occurring in 1598. Its various uses are illustrated in, for example, *The Oxford English Dictionary*, q.v. "perspective"; Edmund Burke Feldman, *Varieties of Visual Experience* (Englewood Cliffs, NJ: Prentice-Hall, 1981), pp. 160, 215, 419, 441–444; *The Oxford New English Dictionary on Historical Principles*, q.v. "perspective"; Albert North Whitehead, *Science in the Modern World* (New York: Free Press, 1967), p. 102.

7. See Gottfried Wilhelm Von Leibniz, *The Monadology*, in *Monadology and Other Philosophical Essays*, trans. Paul Schrecker and Anne Martin Schrecker (Indianapolis, IN: Bobbs-Merrill, 1965), p. 157.

8. Whitehead, *Science in the Modern World*, p. 102.

9. Ibid., p. 102.

10. See Bertrand Russell, *The Problems of Philosophy* (London: Oxford University Press, 1959), pp. 15–16, 101ff.; George Herbert Mead, *The Philosophy of the Present*, ed. Arthur E. Murphy (Chicago: Open Court, 1932); Irwin Biser, *General Scheme for Natural Systems* (Philadelphia: Westbrook, 1932); and Andrew Ushenko, "A Theory of Perception," *Journal of Philosophy* 37 (1940): 141ff.

11. For an excellent discussion of the various formulations of philosophical realism, see Paul Edwards, ed., *The Encyclopedia of Philosophy* (New York: Macmillan/Free Press, 1962), vol, 7, pp. 77–83.

12. Evander Bradley McGilvary, *Toward a Perspective Realism* (La Salle, IL: Open Court, 1956), pp. 11, 12, 15, 16.

13. It is the basic epistemological concern of providing a proper account of how we know what we know about the world confronting us in our everyday experience that has motivated major writings in contemporary phenomenology and existentialism. See, for example, Martin Heidegger, *Being and Time*, trans. John Macquarrie and Edward Robinson (New York: Harper and Row, 1962); Edmund Husserl, *Logical Investigations*, trans. J. N. Findlay (New York: Humanities Press, 1970); and William Richardson, *Heidegger: Through Phenomenology to Thought*, vol. 13 of *Phenomenologica*, 2d ed. (The Hague, The Netherlands: Martinus Nijhoff, 1967). The reader will doubtless discover a number of parallels between this essay and the works just cited, especially in terms of the issues that are their most common progenitor. Perhaps the most significant point of departure between this study and those mentioned above involves the resolution of epistemological problems through the employment of a theory which is believed consistent with contemporary science and is treated sympathetically in a number of American and British philosophical systems, including those of Peirce and Russell, to name but two (see notes 9 and 10, above).

14. The postulates developed in this essay are, in large part, based upon the theory of perspectivism advanced by McGilvary. However, in many respects they depart from, and in some cases amplify, McGilvary's thinking.

15. See Thomas Reid, *Essays on the Intellectual Powers of Man*, in Lewis White Beck, ed., *Eighteenth-Century Philosophy* (New York: Free Press, 1966), pp. 134–150.

16. The contention that reality exists independent of consciousness is argued by McGilvary: "While in many respects we find ourselves unable to get on the same plane of meanings on which others take their stand, it is obvious that in other respects and in our unphilosophical moments we are all of us, with some unhappy exceptions, already on the same plane when we speak of 'reality.'" See McGilvary, *Toward a Perspective Realism*, p. 9.

17. Ibid., p 11.

18. In our opinion this is the position of Brummett and Carleton. In many important respects, this thesis is advocated also by Scott, "On Viewing Rhetoric as Epistemic." See also Charles W. Kneupper, "Rhetoric, Argument, and Social Reality: A Social Constructivist View," *Journal of the American Forensic Association* 16 (1980): 173–181.

19. Brummett, "Some Implications of 'Process,'" p. 29.

20. One of the more articulate expositions of this thesis appears in Thomas Farrell, "Knowledge, Consensus, and Rhetorical Theory." A reaffirmation of this position is found in Thomas Farrell, "Social Knowledge 2," *Quarterly Journal of Speech* 64 (1978): 329–334.

21. Farrell, "Knowledge, Consensus, and Rhetorical Theory," p. 9.

22. This seems to be the reasoning of Brummett, in his "Some Implications of 'Process,'" p. 27. It is interesting to note, however, that to make such a claim and argue for the concept of social realities is itself the advocacy of an independent reality. This was precisely the point made by Orr in his critique of intersubjectivity ("How Shall We Say").

23. Brummett, "Some Implications of 'Process,'" p. 27

24. See, e.g., Scott, "On Viewing Rhetoric as Epistemic," and Scott, "Ten Years Later."

25. This thesis is reminiscent of the position adopted by rhetoricians of the modern period who viewed rhetoric's role as one of "making truth effective," a notion found in François Fenelon's *Dialogues on Eloquence*. This position finds sympathetic treatment in the contemporary literature as well. See, e.g., Richard Weaver, *Language Is Sermonic* (Baton Rouge: Louisiana State University Press, 1970), pp. 11, 12, 18, 19, and 71.

26. Vincent M. Bevilacqua, "Philosophical Influences in the Development of English Rhetorical Theory: 1748–1783," *Proceedings of the Leeds Philosophical and Literary Society, Literary and Historical Section* 19(4): 192. See also Scott, "On Viewing Rhetoric as Epistemic," p. 9.

27. See Orr, "How Shall We Say."

28. See Cherwitz and Hikins, "John Stuart Mill's *On Liberty*."

29. A more thorough exploration of these arguments appears in Orr, "How Shall We Say," pp. 263–274. See also Roger Trigg, *Reason and Commitment* (Cambridge, UK: Cambridge University Press, 1973). Their implication for rhetoric is that one cannot possibly embrace the view that all reality is socially generated; to do so would render concepts such as "speaker," "audience," and even "persuasion" meaningless.

30. Rene Descartes, *Meditations on First Philosophy*, trans. Laurence J. Lafleur (Indianapolis, IN: Bobbs-Merrill, 1960). The reader should be careful not to interpret us as suggesting that "the differences between subjectivism and objectivism stem from taking Descartes seriously," as an earlier critic of this essay contended. Obviously, the subjectivist/objectivist debate has its origins in pre-Socratic philosophy. However, Descartes' contribution to the debate has been of signal importance. For one, he was the first to make epistemology the starting point of inquiry and to state the subject/object distinction in a form which caused dualism to "remain at the heart of much contemporary philosophical inquiry, the work of Gilbert Ryle and Ludwig Wittgenstein, for example, being aimed directly against what are still very powerful Cartesian conceptions." Second, Descartes' formulation of the problem of dualism underscores the priority of developing an *epistemology* before contending with questions of *ontology*. Thus, while it is true that an important issue facing rhetorical epistemology is the *meaning* of the objects of knowledge, what is,

and how one comes to know what is, are kindred questions. What one may know, how one may come to know, and what are the limits of human knowledge are questions surely conditioned by what, in fact, *is*, i.e., on the way the world is constituted. Hence, the issue of "meaning" is not only merely *part* of what any epistemology (rhetorical or otherwise) must address, but it is a question which must inevitably *be* addressed *in concert with ontological issues*, as soon as the most fundamental epistemological issues have been decided upon. To *wholly* eschew ontology on the assumption that "meaning" is a prior issue is to beg the question and point immediately toward a particular epistemological world view (subjectivism). See Bernard Williams, "Descartes, René," in Paul Edwards, ed., *The Encyclopedia of Philosophy* (New York: Macmillan, 1967), vol. 2, p. 354.

31. See *The Encyclopedia of Philosophy*, q.v. "Popper, Karl Raimund."

32. The notion of "category mistake" is treated in Gilbert Ryle, in *The Concept of Mind* (London: Hutchinson's University Library, 1949).

33. See note 30, above.

34. This view implies that a fully developed exposition of perspectivism demands discussion of a *theory of perception* and perception's relation to the communicative enterprise. Spatial limitations preclude such a discussion in this essay; however, it should be obvious that a perspective theory of perception would depart significantly from contemporary accounts, especially those advanced in physiology. Here, too, the influence of the Cartesian enigma is evident, as physiologists struggle to make sense of how *physical* phenomena (such as photons and nerve impulses) become transformed into *conscious* acts such as seeing and hearing. See, e.g. Rodney J. Hirst, *Perception and the External World* (New York: Macmillan, 1965).

35. Arguments for this position derive from a number of sources. Most conspicuous among these is the current tendency in our field to view rhetoric as playing a significant role in scientific inquiry. Representative essays in the rhetoric of science are: Mario Finocchiaro, "Logic and Rhetoric in Lavossier's Sealed Note: Toward a Rhetoric of Science," *Philosophy and Rhetoric* 10 (1977): 111–122; Michael A. Overington, "The Scientific Community as Audience: Toward a Rhetorical Analysis of Science," *Philosophy and Rhetoric* 10 (1977): 143–163; and Walter Weimer, "Science as a Rhetorical

Transaction: Toward a Nonjustificational Conception of Rhetoric," *Philosophy and Rhetoric* 10 (1977): 1–29.

36. The argument that contingent questions are qualitatively different from apodeictic ones is a distinction that cannot be maintained. The position rests primarily on the observation that contingent questions are somehow opaque to observation or measurement, in contrast to the objects of science, for instance. This does not appear to be a very probative or enlightening remark. After all, the atoms that Lucretius wrote about in his *De rerum natura* were as ephemeral in his day as "values" such as goodness or justice are to us today.

37. At this point it may seem that we have come full circle to admit that agreement is the final arbiter of truth. This is not, however, what the formulation of perspectivism suggests. Unlike the social constructivists, the contention here is not that agreement creates "truth" or "knowledge," but rather that the *independent* (in a relational sense, as *relata*) objects of reality *determine agreement* when viewed by individuals in precisely the same way, from the same "point of view."

38. The reader will undoubtedly notice a similarity between our application of perspectivist theory and the traditional concept of *status* (*stasis*). While there are many similarities, two points must be emphasized. First, the concept of stasis was designed primarily to deal with disputes that took place in courts of law (judicial stasis) and in legislative assemblies (deliberative stasis); in this way, stasis was taken almost exclusively as a method of invention for arriving at decisions. Perspectivism, on the other hand, goes beyond rhetorical discourse in such practical, *advocacy* settings. A perspective theory of rhetoric is concerned not just with arriving at legal and legislative decisions; rather, it is intended to deal with all discourse aimed at seeking truth. Unlike stasis, therefore, perspectivism applies to discovery-oriented discourse. The setting for perspectivism is one of *inquiry*, not advocacy. Second, although perspective theory has direct application to decision making situations, its primary purpose is to provide an *epistemological* foundation for concepts such as stasis. Unlike traditional stasis theory, then, perspectivism accounts on an epistemological level for many of the different approaches to a particular issue. It also explains how and why arguers may not be reaching stasis within particular categories or levels of stasis because of their unique relationships to particular aspects of the object of inquiry.

Rhetoric and Its Double

Reflections of the Rhetorical Turn in the Human Sciences

Dilip Parameshwar Gaonkar

The Flight from "Mere" Rhetoric

Rhetoric cannot escape itself. Rhetoric cannot escape its "mereness," or to use the fashionable vocabulary of our time (here I am alluding to Derridean deconstruction), it cannot escape its status as a "supplement." Yet this simple fact that there is no exit for rhetoric, nor an exit from rhetoric, escapes many friends of rhetoric. Rhetoric cannot efface itself to become its traditional counterpart, dialectic, as Perelman and Valesio would have it.[1] Nor can it recast itself, as Grassi proposes, as the seat of primordial poetic utterance, which apprehends and articulates "the first principles" on which the rational speech of philosophy, in turn, depends.[2] Nor can rhetoric be equated with a hermeneutics of suspicion, as the linguistically inclined followers of Marx, Nietzsche, and Freud would suggest.

To be sure, rhetoric stands in a historically fluctuating relationship with other disciplines, especially those formal disciples which are its neighbors. To a certain measure, its identity and its fortunes are linked to those fluctuating affiliations. For that reason, Roland Barthes tells us that "rhetoric must always be read in the structural interplay with its neighbors (Grammar, Logic, Poetics, Philosophy): it is the play of the system,

not each of its parts in itself, which is historically significant."[3] Sometimes its systemic proximity to one of the neighbors is so great and compelling that one is prone to overlook its distinctive character and its essential difference. If such a misreading of rhetoric happened but occasionally, it would be understandable.

However, when scholars repeatedly fail to distinguish rhetoric from its neighbors, and do so even in a period marked by a renewed and self-conscious interest in rhetoric, it is reasonable to suspect that something more than an accident is involved. The tenacity of this error, if error it is, should give us pause and prompt us to review this impulse (this habit of the mind) which urges us to make rhetoric into something other than itself.

What is involved in these misreadings, in my opinion, is simply a "flight from rhetoric," or to be more precise, a flight from "mere" rhetoric—that is, rhetoric conceived as a "supplement." What is so frightening, you may ask, that one should seek to flee from "mere" rhetoric in so deliberate a manner?

Once rhetoric is conceived as a "supplement," it becomes a formal, hence an empty, discipline. It is without substance, without a secure set of referents, or to put it mundanely, it has no subject matter of its own. To be sure, one can take the general and recurrent lines of arguments (topics) and certain structural/functional resources of language (tropes and figures) as the special province or the subject matter of rhetoric. But this does not resolve the difficulty. Such a view, it seems to me, while recognizing rhetoric as a mode of practical reasoning and discourse production does so precisely in terms of its formal character as a language art. Thus deprived of substance, rhetoric stands in a parasitic relationship vis-à-vis substantive disciplines such as ethics and politics. Sometimes this "parasite" becomes so deeply entangled with the affairs of an alien body, especially the "body politic," it forgets its own nature and purpose and pretends to be a substantive entity. Perhaps this is what Aristotle had in mind when he said, "It thus appears that rhetoric is an offshoot of dialectic and also of ethical studies. Ethical studies may fairly be called political: and for this reason rhetoric masquerades as political science, and the professors of it as political experts."[4] For much the same reason, Plato reached a more severe judgment and dismissed rhetoric as a counterfeit art (*Gorgias*, 464–465).

Brian Vickers, a distinguished contemporary champion of rhetoric, notes that rhetoric, having no subject matter of its own, functions a bit like a "service industry," and thereby gets into territorial disputes with other disciplines.[5] The very fact that rhetoric is without a domicile is seen as profoundly threatening to the integrity of substantive disciplines. The territorial disputes between two substantive disciplines, say, law and sociology, are far less acrimonious than when rhetoric enters the picture and attempts to transform and use the materials characteristic of either of those two disciplines. Here I am reminded of Cicero's characterization of Marc Antony as a "homeless" transgressor in the *Fourth Philippic*. According to Cicero, one could negotiate with an enemy on some "settled principle" so long as he has "a republic, a senate house, a treasury, harmonious and united citizens" which he hopes to protect and promote. But Antony, says Cicero, "is attacking your republic, but has none himself; is eager to destroy the Senate, . . . but has no public council himself; he has exhausted your treasury, and has none of his own. For how can a man be supported by the unanimity of the citizens, who has no city at all?"[6] If we substitute rhetoric for Antony, we have an apt image for the kind of danger rhetoric represents to the established disciplines. Rhetoric can spring up any time, from within or without, to pollute and possess what is not its own for the sake of temporary advantage and gratification. Thus, rhetoric is seen as a nomadic discipline that threatens the integrity of the republic of knowledge itself. Why would anyone want to admit such a discipline to the council of learning when it refuses to abide by the academic rules of property and propriety?

Such is the impulse of an empty discipline to become substantive, to become something other than itself. It is as if rhetoric were in search of its other, the substantive other, who, when found, would fill out its formal emptiness. But this other which is to provide rhetoric with a grounding, relieve it from that epistemic anxiety with which it has been burdened since Plato, will always elude us. Perhaps this is the fatal game which animates rhetoric and keeps it going.

The flight from "mere" rhetoric consists of a double movement which, in my view, regulates, shapes, and determines the self-image of rhetoric. This double movement simultaneously propels rhetoric on a vertical axis downward into its past to find itself a suitable history and on a horizontal axis sideways to situate itself within the discursive practices of special "substantive" sciences, especially the human sciences. Rhetoric moves diachronically to discover for itself an alternative historical tradition that will free it from its supplementary status, and it moves synchronically to find itself in the discursive body (textuality) of other disciplines that will confirm its "presence."

These two movements motivated by their distaste for "mere rhetoric" direct us to flee from it, especially if we are serious about this business of rehabilitating rhetoric as "the once and future queen of the human sciences."[7] They play on our disciplinary "lures" and anxieties (which are predictably many), and urge us to make rhetoric into something other than itself.

This double movement in the contemporary self-understanding of rhetoric is not necessarily fully "articulated." Nor is it an entirely "implicit" and subterranean movement which I am somehow magically bringing to light. If this movement is partially "invisible," its invisibility is not due to its obscure presence but to what Alfred Schutz calls its "taken-for-granted" character.[8]

As you may have inferred from my characterization of this double movement as a "lure," I regard it as fundamentally problematic and possibly destructive of rhetoric as a vocation. However, I am not here to reject it but to contest it. In fact, this double movement is not something which can be either accepted or rejected, for it is one of the "essentially contested" features of our discipline.[9]

The First Movement:
The Supplementary Tradition

The idea that rhetoric is no more than a "supplement" makes its initial appearance in the fabled encounter between the older sophists and the Platonic Socrates, the first site of the so-called quarrel between rhetoric and philosophy. Naturally, there are several strands to this quarrel between rhetoric and philosophy, but both historically and in our own time much of the dispute concerns the epistemic status of rhetoric.[10] The idea that rhetoric is no more than a "supplement" has its origin in the articulation of this question.

The question in its simplest form is this: Does rhetoric, the art of discovering available means of persuasion in a given case (Aristotle), have anything to do with the generation of knowledge? If not, as Socrates, Plato, and Aristotle appear to have assumed, then we may ask, as Heidegger asked of poets: *What are rhetoricians for?*

The Aristotelian compromise on this question, which sets into motion the "supplementary" tradition in rhetoric, is well known. For Aristotle, among other things, rhetoric makes knowledge more readily comprehensible and acceptable in the domain of civic discourse. That is, rhetoric cannot generate knowledge but is useful, possibly indispensable, for the transmission of knowledge discovered by philosophy and the special substantive sciences. Rhetoric, to use a term popularized by Jacques Derrida, is a supplement to knowledge, much as writing is a supplement to speech.[11]

The placing of Aristotle within the supplementary tradition is somewhat problematic. In the Aristotelian scheme, while demonstrative (apodictic) reasoning belongs to the domain of the necessary, rhetoric and dialectic operate within the domain of the contingent and the probable. Further, neither rhetoric nor dialectic "is a science that deals with the nature of any definite subject, but they are merely faculties of furnishing arguments."[12] Rhetoric, in other words, is a general art consisting not of knowledge about substantive fields but a flexible system of formal and prudential devices—topics, tropes and figures, inferential schemes, probabilities, prudential rules, and so on.[13] At the same time, however, this general art is functionally implicated in managing and transforming common opinion for persuasive ends. This functional link to common opinion, according to Leff, prevents rhetoric from becoming a purely formal discipline, and its practical applications extend to the whole field of human affairs.[14] More-

over, the functional aspect of rhetoric is particularly decisive in the civic arena when citizens have to make judgments on issues without recourse to the special sciences to guide their deliberation.[15] This unresolved tension between the formal and the functional dimensions of rhetoric threatens its identity in two distinct but contradictory ways. On the one hand, rhetoric cannot posit a substantive identity because it has no subject matter of its own; on the other hand, its functional involvement with *doxa* threatens its formal identity by what Ricoeur calls an "overburdening of content."[16] Thus, rhetoric is simultaneously empty of subject matter and overburdened with content.

It is against this background one has to negotiate the question as to whether rhetoric has an epistemic function. The centrality of "invention" in the rhetorical tradition as a whole hints at a generative rather than a purely managerial and transmissive function for rhetoric. Yet a closer examination reveals that the aim of rhetorical inquiry is quite different from that of dialectical inquiry. A distinction introduced by Kenneth Burke is particularly useful in this context. Burke, following Aristotle, recognizes that both dialectic and rhetoric begin their inquiry with a critique of common opinion in the realm of the contingent and the probable. But the two critiques have different ends. Although the dialectical critique occurs in the scenic order of truth with a view toward transcending the conflict intrinsic to opinion, the rhetorical critique occurs in the moral order of action with a view toward managing and transforming conflicting opinions in accordance with the exigencies of a given situation. Hence rhetoric, unlike dialectic, is not constitutive of general truths and propositions but of specific beliefs, attitudes, and actions.[17]

Roland Barthes arrives at a similar conclusion regarding Aristotle's treatment of the passions. What Aristotle offers in his *Rhetoric*, according to Barthes, is a "projected" psychology: a psychology as everyone imagines it—not "what is in the mind" of the public, but what the public believes others "have in mind." In Barthes' view, Aristotle's innovative treatment of the passions (in contrast to the technographers who preceded him) lies precisely in his decision to view them "in their banality" and to classify "the passions not according to what they are, but according to what they are believed to be: he does not describe them scientifically, but seeks out arguments which can be used with respect to the public's ideas about passion."[18] Rhetorical psychology is therefore quite the opposite of a reductive psychology that would try to see what is *behind* what people say and attempt to reduce anger, for instance, to something else, something hidden. For Aristotle, public opinion is the first and last datum; he has no hermeneutic notion (of decipherment): anger is what every one thinks about anger, passion is never anything but what people say it is.[19]

Rhetoric thus puts together a disparate set of materials and insights originating in common opinion and popular understanding by recourse to a flexible system of formal devices on an ad hoc basis. Despite its generality as a formal system, rhetoric is marked by a radical particularity in its practices and products. Thus, unless one is prepared to collapse the distinction between knowledge and belief, understanding and action, it seems unreasonable to invoke the authority of Aristotle to claim that rhetoric has an epistemic function.

At any rate, according to the "supplementary" tradition, the quarrel between sophistic rhetoric and Platonic philosophy, as mediated by Aristotle, was decided in favor of the latter. Rhetoric was pushed into the margins of philosophy and the special sciences, and there it was forced to function as a *supplement to knowledge*. The subsequent history of rhetoric is the history of a supplement, living in the margins of philosophy, periodically attempting to widen that margin, as in the case of Cicero and the Renaissance Humanists, or to deepen the dignity of supplementary function, as in the case of St. Augustine.[20] On the whole, however, it is not a history of violent opposition and rebellion against philosophy, but one of accommodation, adjustment, and redefinition.

This tradition of the *supplement* has led many students of rhetoric into a conceptual impasse, as illustrated by John Quincy Adams, the first holder of the Boylston Professorship of Rhetoric at Harvard. In a lecture given in 1806, he declares that rhetoric "which has exhausted the genius of Aristotle, Cicero, and Quintilian, can neither require nor admit much additional illustration. To select, combine, and apply their precepts, is the only duty left for their followers of all succeeding times, and to obtain a perfect familiarity with their instructions is to arrive at the mastery of the art."[21] The same frame of mind prompted the English scholar J. E. C. Welldon in 1886 to praise Aristotle's *Rhetoric* "as being perhaps a solitary instance of a book which not only begins a science, but completes it."[22] Such is the praise heaped on a text (an incomplete set of lecture notes to be precise) that, whatever its genius, stands profoundly divided

against itself. This is the extent to which rhetoric had been emasculated within the rubric of a "supplementary" tradition by the end of the nineteenth century.

Understandably, the revived interest in rhetoric in this century is marked by a desire to break free from such a conceptual impasse. The tale of twentieth-century rhetoric, at least in its theoretical speculations, if not in its critical practice, can be read as a revolt against the "supplementary" tradition.

The Sophistic Tradition

This escape from "mere" rhetoric takes many forms and employs many strategies. One way to escape from the conceptual impasse brought about by the "supplementary tradition" is to revive its historical opponent, the sophistic tradition. The rehabilitation of the older sophists that began in the early part of the nineteenth century under the sponsorship of Hegel in Germany and Grote in England has gained considerable momentum in this century. Their name, if not their work, is prominent in the current revival of rhetoric.[23] A return to their skeptical outlook on the "language-ridden" world of human culture is regarded as central to any serious attempt at reviving rhetoric. This revival of the sophistic tradition consists of two related sets of moves, the philosophical and the historical.

The philosophical move in restoring the sophistic tradition to its former glory requires one to decenter the epistemic question. Instead of asking whether rhetoric can generate knowledge, a more fundamental (ontological) question is pushed to the center: How is rhetoric possible?[24] This Kantian type of question refers to the ultimate grounds of rhetoric. In response to this question, two unavoidable human characteristics are offered as the ultimate grounds of rhetoric. First, to use a phrase of Kenneth Burke, humans are symbol-using (misusing) creatures. Second, to use a phrase of Hannah Arendt, life is given to humans under "the condition of plurality."[25] From these two ultimate grounds, one can derive, in turn (as de Man and Todorov do), two distinct but related concepts of rhetoric.[26] They are rhetoric as persuasion and rhetoric as trope. Although the dimension of plurality, marked by "unity in division" (Burke), imposes on humans the necessity of persuasion, the tropological dimension of language makes them susceptible to persuasion. The basic strategy here is to derive in a global fashion the inevitability of rhetoric from our social relations as they are mediated by language. This strategy clearly favors certain theories of language and social relations over others. For instance, while the theory that views language as a transparent medium for the communication of things and ideas is clearly unacceptable, the thesis that social reality, among other things, is linguistically constructed and legitimated is enthusiastically endorsed.[27] The main difficulty with this strategy, with rare exceptions, is that it operates at an extremely high level of generality and almost equates rhetoric with language use and sociability. As a result, this philosophical strategy is disconnected from the sense of rhetoric as a local phenomenon which is so central to the human experience of rhetoric as a material force.[28]

The historical move is far more intriguing. The return to the sophists requires a reconstitution of the history of rhetoric. One cannot traverse 2,500 years back to the origins of rhetoric without acknowledging the intervening steps. According to this reconstituted history, there are not one but two histories of rhetoric—a manifest history and a hidden history. And they are dominated by two different traditions—the manifest history by the "supplementary" tradition, and the hidden history by the sophistic tradition.

The manifest history begins predictably enough with the older sophists and their celebrated quarrel with the Platonic Socrates; it moves through Aristotle, Isocrates, Cicero, Quintilian, and St. Augustine in the classical world, and then through the Middle Ages and the Renaissance and the eighteenth-century neoclassical rhetoric and the Scottish School. This is the official history of Boethius, Alcuin, George of Trebizond, Agricola, Ramus, Bacon, Fenelon, Lawson, Campbell, and Blair, which finally culminates in Bishop Whately's *Elements of Rhetoric*. This is the history of rhetoric conceived as a "supplement," a history of obscure places, unfamiliar names, and forgotten texts.

The other history of rhetoric, its hidden history, also begins with the celebrated quarrel between the sophists and the Platonic Socrates, and moves indecisively alongside the manifest history until the end of the classical world; then, suddenly, it disappears, until it is *rediscovered* by Kenneth Burke. The "hidden" history places a somewhat different interpretation on the quarrel between sophistic rhetoric and Platonic philosophy. According to this version, the fabulous quarrel that held the Greek mind captive during the declining years of Periclean Enlightenment involved more than the competing claims of two skirmishing disciplines. Rather, it was a contest between two competing ways of life, the *vita activa* and the *vita contemplativa*. Their competing claims to civic attention [are] described vividly, but with a decided bias, in the Platonic dialogues, especially in the *Theaetetus* (172c–175e). Such a contest could not be settled in a single generation, even if that generation could produce so rare a phenomenon as Socrates. So it continues to engage our attention to this day in varying degrees of intensity. At any rate, for a variety of reasons, both political and intellectual, this competition for cultural hegemony ended in a defeat for the sophists, and they were promptly driven out of the cultural milieu by their philosophical detractors. Thereafter sophistry, insofar as it is a permanent opening for man, had to live an underground, subterranean existence. Later, when Aristotle made the compensatory move toward rhetoric and granted it the status of a supplement, rhetoric and sophistic became divorced. While rhetoric, in its attenuated form as a "supplement," was allowed to live in the margins of philosophy, sophistic was "repressed." Thus, rhetoric continued to function as a supplement to philosophical knowledge, where it regulated certain discursive practices and products, but it could not function as a supplement to a sophistic *Weltanschauung* marked by ethical relativity and epistemic skepticism. In this managerial placement, style retained a legitimate interest for the art, but rhetoric seems incapable of generating its own grounding as a mode of persuasion. This partly explains why the theory of invention in rhetoric became moribund, but the theory of *lexis* (*eloqutio*) was endlessly refined and elaborated.

But what is "repressed" is not erased. It must resurface in various symptomatic forms. Besides, the natural affinity between rhetoric and sophistic would continually draw the two together. Hence, there follows a series of illicit relations and subterranean connections, which constitute the "hidden" history of rhetoric. In some sense, this is the "return of the repressed." And the most distinguished chronicler of this return is none other than Kenneth Burke.

In Burke's *A Rhetoric of Motives*, this proposed reconstruction of the "hidden" history of rhetoric was brilliantly outlined, if not filled out in detail. His initial project in this book was to extend the range of rhetoric, but that extension, as he quickly realized, required an historical grounding, which forced him to depart from the manifest history.

He began "by showing how a rhetorical motive is often present where it is not usually recognized, or thought to belong":

> In part, we would but *rediscover* rhetorical elements that had become obscured when rhetoric as a term fell into disuse, and other specialized disciplines such as esthetics, anthropology, psychoanalysis, and sociology came to the fore (so that esthetics sought to outlaw rhetoric, while the other sciences we have mentioned took over, each in its own terms, the rich rhetorical elements that esthetics would ban).[29]

He continues:

> But besides this job of *reclamation*, we also seek to develop our subject beyond the traditional bounds of rhetoric. There is an intermediate area of expression that is not wholly deliberate, yet not wholly unconscious. It lies midway between aimless utterance and speech deliberately purposive.[30]

In order to analyze this rhetorical area, Burke has to shift from reliance on "persuasion" to "identification" as the key term of rhetoric:

> Particularly when we come upon such aspects of persuasion as are found in "mystification," courtship, and the "magic" of class relationships, the reader will see why the classical notion of clear persuasive intent is not an accurate fit for describing the ways in which the members of a group promote social cohesion by acting rhetorically upon themselves and one another.[31]

At this point, I am not interested in examining Burke's concept of identification, which has already received ample critical attention. What interests me is the implications of this shift from "persuasion" to "identification" for a history of rhetoric. Consider, for instance, the second part of the book, which bears the title: "Traditional Principles of Rhetoric." In the first few pages (49–84), Burke examines some classical texts by Aristotle, Cicero, Quintilian, and St. Augustine where "persuasion" is the key term. Then, on page 90, there occurs a "break," a "rupture," in the text, as Burke begins to move with "identification" as the key concept into what I would call the "hidden" history of rhetoric. Here the task of "reclamation" proper begins: Bentham's theory of fictions, Marx on "Mystification" (*The German Ideology*), Carlyle on "Mystery" (*Sartor Resartus*), Diderot on "Pantomime" (*Neveu de Rameau*), De Gourmont on "Dissociation" (*La Dissociation des Idées*), Pascal on "Directing the Intention," Administrative Rhetoric in Machiavelli, Dante's *De Vulgari Eloquentia*, and so on. After a long underground existence, the sophistic tradition in rhetoric has been rediscovered, reclaimed, and reconstituted.

Here Burke, the "reclaimer," is in his "true form." While tracking down the implications of "persuasion" in classical texts, Burke is impatient, restrained, like a tiger in a cage, summarizing the formal/topological principles laboriously catalogued by Cicero in a mere page or two, and then quickly moving on to something else, say, Longinus' *On the Sublime*. But once we come to Bentham's *Book of Fallacies*, a dazzling intellectual journey begins, a veritable *tour de force* through the corridors of the history of ideas, interweaving text upon text, in the same breath speaking of Pascal and Joyce. It is a consummate performance.

It is almost impossible not to be seduced by this other "hidden" history of rhetoric, as "reconstituted" by Burke, especially when he invites "other analysts" to join him in "the task of tracking down the ways in which the realm of sheerly worldly powers become endowed with attributes of 'secular divinity.'"[32]

Who can refuse such an invitation, especially someone about to embark on rhetoric as a vocation. If accepted, this invitation calls at one level for extending the range of rhetoric, which I find perfectly legitimate. But that extension, in turn, requires a "reinterpretation" of the history of rhetoric that is problematic, if not ill-conceived.

Such is the seductive tale of the two histories of rhetoric. There are, to be sure, many other tales about the birth, the rise, the decline, the fall, and even the "death" of rhetoric. These tales have been constructed frequently by those who are not themselves, as I am not, full-fledged historians of rhetoric. They are clearly political tales, meant to account for the troubled relationship between rhetoric and other disciplines and culture in general. They are designed so as to legitimate its claim to renewed intellectual and cultural attention. Each putative revivalist of rhetoric has to tell a tale of its glorious origins, its civilizing effects, its unjustified suppression, and its eventual demise and dispersion. So the tale I have told above on behalf of Kenneth Burke (unauthorized, to be sure) is only one among many tales circulating among the current revivalists of rhetoric. As a revivalist tale it is only partly true. And this tale, like so many of the recent tales about the history of rhetoric, is epistemologically driven. It speaks as though the quarrel between Plato and the older sophists over the epistemic status of rhetoric continually and exclusively shaped its complex history. It fails to acknowledge that from late antiquity to the High Middle Ages, Latin rhetorical instruction was largely dominated by two manuals of what George Kennedy calls "technical rhetoric": *De Inventione* and *Rhetorica ad Herrennium*.[33] It completely overlooks the third tradition in rhetoric, the tradition of civic humanism that stretches from Protagoras through Isocrates and Cicero to the Renaissance humanists, and continues to manifest itself in the activities of great orators like Edmund Burke. But these errors, repeatedly corrected by the orthodox historians like Kennedy and Vickers, continue to remain occluded from a disciplinary consciousness obsessed with abstract epistemological questions.

My reservations are quite simple. The "lure" of the hidden history has led to a denigration of the manifest history of rhetoric. One simple fact attests to this. Despite all the talk about the "Revival of Rhetoric" and the coming of the "New Rhetoric" in this century, we have yet to produce a definitive history of rhetoric. As an intellectual enterprise, rhetoric cannot continue to be viable without an adequate understanding of its own history, even if that history is an uninspiring one, which I don't think it is. If there is one thing we can learn from Jacques Derrida, it is that the history of a supplement may be more interesting than the history of that which is in need of a supplement.

The Second Movement: The Rhetoric of Inquiry

The second horizontal movement that propels rhetoric to constantly reconfirm its "presence" in the discourse of other disciplines is fashionably characterized these days as the "rhetorical turn" in the human sciences, or as the Iowa School prefers to call it the "rhetoric of inquiry."

In this paper I am not primarily concerned, as the Iowa School avowedly is, with the discovery of rhetoric by the practitioners of human sciences and the consequences of that discovery for the discursive practices of their disciplines. What interests me at this moment is the impact of that discovery on the self-understanding of rhetoric itself. To be sure, I recognize that rhetoric and the human sciences interpenetrate one another in innumerable ways, and the evolving dialectic between the two has a long history. What I seek to problematize here is but a single aspect of that dialectic.

The "rhetorical turn" refers to the growing recognition of rhetoric in contemporary thought, especially among the special substantive sciences. It means that the special sciences are becoming increasingly rhetorically self-conscious. They are beginning to recognize that their discursive practices, both internal and external, contain an unavoidable rhetorical component. *Internal* here refers to those discursive practices that are internal to a specific scientific language community; external refers to the discursive practices of that scientific language community in respect to its dealings with other scientific (or nonscientific) language communities and the society in general. While the external dimension is sometimes noted, the work of the Iowa School clearly emphasizes the internal dimension.

The existing body of literature pertaining to the internal dimension of the rhetorical turn in contemporary thought can be further divided into two groups: the explicit rhetorical turn and the implicit rhetorical turn. By explicit rhetorical turn, I refer to those works that explicitly recognize the relevance of rhetoric for contemporary thought and where rhetoric is used as a critical and interpretive method. The works of the following scholars, including those generally identified as the new rhetoricians (Chaim Perelman, Kenneth Burke, Richard McKeon, I. A. Richards, and Richard Weaver), may be placed in this category: Wayne Booth, Paul de Man, Walter J. Ong, Ernesto Grassi, Paolo Valesio, Northrop Frye, Tzvetan Todorov, Harold Bloom, Hugh Dalziel Duncan.

Clearly, however, those authors are not equally enthusiastic about rhetoric. While some of them have written several books on rhetoric, others confine their observations on rhetoric to a mere essay or two. While some of them view rhetoric as a general theory of discourse (hence a metadiscipline), others simply admit the importance of rhetoric for the human sciences and employ it as a critical instrument in their analyses of literary and social texts; and there are those who simply scatter the word *rhetoric* carelessly through their texts. For instance, there is a renewed interest in rhetoric among the literary critics. But the nature and intensity of interest varies significantly. Thus, while Wayne Booth, operating from a distinctly humanistic perspective, concentrates on the argumentative dimension of literature, especially novels, Paul de Man, operating from a deconstructionist perspective, stresses the figural dimensions of literary language.[34] Other critics, like Frye, Todorov, Mailloux, and Bloom, have paid varying degrees of attention to rhetoric, but as opposed to Booth and de Man, we could not properly entitle them "rhetorical critics."

Finally, and perhaps most important, there are also texts that evince signs of an implicit rhetorical turn. These are texts whose authors, while relatively unaware of the rhetorical lexicon, seem to be groping for a vocabulary that could adequately characterize the tropological and suasory aspects of the discursive practices that remain occluded from disciplinary consciousness.

The list of authors and their texts that evince signs of such an implicit rhetorical turn is truly formidable: Thomas Kuhn's *The Structure of Scientific Revolutions*, Paul Feyerabend's *Against Method*, Stephen Toulmin's *The Uses of Argument*, Lacan's *Ecrits*, Gadamer's *Truth and Method*, Foucault's *Archeology of Knowledge*, and Habermas's *Legitimation Crisis*, to name a few. These are the master texts of our time, and they are, we are told, bristling with rhetorical insights, even though they often are not consciously recognized.

Furthermore, on some accounts, whole "schools of thought" reveal a decisively rhetorical orientation. Here one might list the sociology of knowledge tradition (from Scheler to Berger and Luckmann), the symbolic interactionists, the dramatistic movement in anthropology and sociology (Geertz, Turner, and Goffman), and various philosophical positions that stress the role of language and language action (e.g., the "later" Wittgenstein and the "early" Heidegger, Austin, Searle, and other speech-act theorists). The contemporary intellectual landscape is, thus, replete with signs of an implicit rhetorical turn. With a bit of diligence and, of course, with requisite faith, anyone could read those signs and celebrate what they portend.

The *locus classicus* of this implicit rhetorical turn in contemporary thought is Kuhn's *The Structure of Scientific Revolutions*.[35] The reasons for the choice of this text are quite obvious. *First*, it examines the discursive practices of the hard sciences, such as physics and chemistry. Second, it brings to light the rhetorical aspect of discursive practices internal to the scientific language community. Third, Kuhn makes these profound observations without the slightest awareness of the rhetorical lexicon. Fourth, though unconscious of rhetoric, he makes a fairly radical claim for the primacy of rhetoric when he asserts that "paradigm shifts" in any scientific community are more like religious conversions than carefully considered and well-reasoned shifts in scientific practices. Fifth, he calls for a reexamination of the history of science from a sociological perspective. He rejects the textbook version of the history of science as an idealization which assumes that the growth of knowledge is a purely logical-rational enterprise.

These aspects of Kuhn's work have made him into the very embodiment of the rhetorical turn. If the discourse of the physicists cannot detach itself from rhetoric, how can the chatter of lesser mortals, such as historians and sociologists, hope to emancipate itself from rhetoric?

In short, it appears that there is more to the "rhetorical turn" than the mundane explicit turn. Just as there are two histories of rhetoric, the manifest and the hidden, there are two rhetorical turns, the explicit and the implicit. The lure of the implicit rhetorical turn is infinitely greater than the reality of the explicit rhetorical turn. Although the explicit rhetorical turn is a result of practical necessity—a literary critic like Booth, for example, is unable to make sense of novelistic prose without recourse to a rhetorical vocabulary and rhetorical sensibilities—the implicit rhetorical turn is a largely theoretical and epistemological enterprise. If the explicit rhetorical turn is only a decade or two old, the implicit rhetorical turn is of more ancient vintage. Its roots can be traced all the way back to that celebrated quarrel between Platonic Socrates and the older sophists. If Kenneth Burke is the chronicler of the hidden history of rhetoric, Professors Nelson and Megill have undertaken to chronicle the story of the implicit rhetorical turn. Nelson and Megill, along with Donald McCloskey, are the leading figures in the Iowa School, which has done much to place claims of the rhetorical turn before the scholarly community.

The Nelson and Megill Myth

In a recent essay, Nelson and Megill set out to furnish the "rhetoric of inquiry" with what they call an "animating myth."[36] They write:

> Rather, we sketch the development of the field so far, focusing on how early contributors have regarded rhetoric and inquiry. This is not the history of rhetoric, science, or philosophy widely familiar to scholars of communication. It is instead an animating myth of the new field.[37]

They are, however, certain that "what begins as myth ends as history." A myth of this sort requires a set of precursors who were but dimly aware of what they were doing, that is, preparing the way for the progressive dismantling of a logic of inquiry which is to be replaced by a rhetoric of inquiry.

Nelson and Megill do, indeed, give us a myth, a good one at that. It is reminiscent of Protagoras's reply in Plato's dialogue of that name when

Socrates asks him to identify what he does. Protagoras admits to being "a sophist and an educator" (317b). But he claims to practice an ancient art and not something new and fashionable as people assume. According to Protagoras, since sophistry seems to arouse, however unjustifiably, suspicion among people, those who practiced it before did not admit to being sophists. They adopted suitable disguises and worked under the cover of some other profession. Homer, Hesiod, and Simonides claimed to be poets, Orpheus and Musaeus claimed to be musicians, and Herodicus of Selymbria claimed to be a physician. In fact, however, they were all sophists (316d–e). But that strategy of concealment did not work. They were discovered for what they were, and their attempt to disguise their art excited even greater mistrust. So Protagoras freely admits to being a sophist and welcomes any opportunity to explain and defend his art, for only through constant public exposure can sophistry hope to overcome the undeserved fear and suspicion with which it is presently regarded.

However, the myth which Nelson and Megill want to weave for us cannot be a simple Protagorean tale of exposing one's timorous and somewhat inept precursors. For them, rhetoric, and by implication the rhetoric of inquiry, is a ubiquitous and unavoidable component in human belief and behavior. Since rhetoric always already exists, it cannot be simply discovered and enunciated. It has to be rediscovered and reconstituted. For that reason, it must be first repressed and made to disappear. If someone is going to be credited with recovering and recuperating rhetoric, then someone must be charged with its prior repression and dispersion.

The story of the progressive repression of the rhetoric of inquiry begins, predictably enough, in the seventeenth century with the birth of modern philosophy—with Descartes' quest for "clear and distinct ideas." In the quest for certainty, the "empiricist" Locke and the "idealist" Kant follow the "rationalist" Descartes. They embrace mathematics as the ideal model of conviction and "dream of dispelling disagreement through demonstration." Thus, rhetoric comes to be repressed. The repression is carried out through a series of dichotomies: truth vs. opinion, object vs. subject, conviction vs. persuasion, all of which valorize the logic of inquiry over rhetoric. This repression also had political implications. According to Nelson and Megill,

> Plato denigrated opinion and rhetoric so as to celebrate truth and order at a time of Greek conflict

and Athenian decline. Similarly, Aristotle subordinated rhythms to logos and rhetoric to dialectic. In an era when radical disagreements racked the peace of Europe, Descartes wrote off rhetoric in favor of mathematical reason and Hobbes enslaved language to the sovereign. Later, Kant sought perpetual peace through pure and practical reason.[38]

The sole voice of dissent on behalf of rhetoric in the late seventeenth and early eighteenth century was Vico, who opposed Cartesianism with the same sort of vigor with which Isocrates had once opposed Platonism. According to Nelson and Megill, effective opposition to the hegemonic rule of modern philosophy over scholarly inquiry did not occur until the late nineteenth century, and it is Nietzsche who emerges as the leading *persona*: "One implicitly rhetorical challenge to the sovereignty that modern philosophy claims over scholarship actually begins with Nietzsche's assault on the subject/object dichotomy."[39] As the opposition gathered speed and momentum in the twentieth century, the privileged set of dichotomies was challenged, undermined, and dissolved. The quest for certainty was questioned. The fear of disagreement abated. The mathematic model of conviction began to yield to the discursive model of persuasion. Modern epistemology came to be seen as a source of, rather than a shield against, the philosophical anxiety about "skepticism, solipsism, and nihilism." This challenge to "the Cartesian foundations and Kantian principles of modern philosophy" followed from a series of internal discursive crises and tensions in philosophy and science. Nelson and Megill identify three such crises (but do not discuss them): the philosophical attack on foundationalism, the philosophical reconstruction of science, and, the rhetorical conception of epistemology. And they enumerate a list of twentieth-century thinkers (a now familiar litany from Dewey and Heidegger through MacIntyre and Rorty) who recognize and grapple with these crises and thus, unwittingly, open the way to a rhetoric of inquiry.

All this intellectual ferment, Nelson and Megill conclude, leads to Iowa City in the 1980s, where the logic of inquiry is officially transformed into a rhetoric. This transformation yields a good many benefits: We will escape from the clutches of "Western rationalism and its paradox of authoritarian liberation." As we begin to pay more attention to the actual reasoning that goes on in scholarly inquiry, we will learn to "recognize that rhetoric is reasonable and reason is rhetorical." As we begin to notice that scholarship is also a mode of communication addressed to an audience, we will learn to "insist that rhetoric is contextual and context is rhetorical."

Such, then, is the history of the implicit rhetorical turn. (Note that, of the writers cited in this history, only Perelman, Burke, Booth, and White make systematic use of a rhetorical lexicon in their studies.) Nelson and Megill are, indeed, worthy successors to Kenneth Burke. They do for the implicit rhetorical turn what Burke has done for the hidden history of rhetoric.

The Lure of the Implicit Rhetorical Turn

Once again, in my opinion, the lure of the implicit rhetorical turn will gradually overwhelm, if it has not done so already, the promise of the explicit rhetorical turn. The implicit rhetorical turn will have the same sort of psychological hold over our disciplinary imagination as the hidden history of rhetoric has had since the publication of Burke's *A Rhetoric of Motives*.

The reason for this is quite simple. The study of the explicit rhetorical turn is, in the long run, a tedious affair, which is only occasionally redeemed by critical excellence and achievement, while the pursuit of the implicit rhetorical turn is a boldly constitutive, well-nigh archeological, venture, which "lures" us to discover "traces" of rhetoric virtually everywhere. The explicit rhetorical turn suffers from sheer obviousness. Once it is recognized, as it ought to be, that the discourse of the human sciences contains an unavoidable rhetorical component, the task of analysis consists in making explicit the functioning of that component in the production and the reception of discourses. There are some brilliant instances of such critical analysis. In an excellent essay, Hexter unpacks the rhetoric of history in terms of the historian's habitual and distinctive use of quotations, footnotes, and statistics in writing history, and he shows how the rhetoric of history differs from the rhetoric of natural sciences.[40] The type of rhetorical analysis of historiography that Hexter offers is unlikely to unsettle the self-understanding of rhetoric. For Hexter has merely shown how the discourse of history cannot productively emulate the rhetoric of natural sciences; and his explication of rhetorical elements in historiography is analogous to the explication of "manifest" rhetoric in any discursive practice. The model for unpacking the argumentative strategies and the play of stylistic devices is much the same in history as in oratory.

In contrast, the implicit rhetorical turn is engaged in a far more grandiose project. It is, in essence, a philosophical enterprise, or to be more precise, it is a critique of Western metaphysics that begins with Nietzsche and continues in the work of Heidegger and his deconstructive followers. It is preoccupied with the theme of the end of philosophy (modernism, or the end of modernism), and sees in rhetoric an alternative to the foundationalist epistemology. The implicit rhetorical turn is thus largely a product of an internal crisis in philosophy. Here rhetoric becomes entangled in the schemes of those who are attempting to articulate a counter-tradition in philosophy. And the story of rhetoric's initial suppression and the subsequent recuperation is read, in the Nelson and Megill version, in terms of an objectivist/subjectivist dichotomy that has fractured Western consciousness since the beginning of philosophical reflection. Nelson and Megill are quite correct in asserting that an objectivist epistemology is generally damaging to the fortunes of rhetoric, while a subjectivist/relativist epistemology is more encouraging to its growth. But this observation is so broad as to be banal and not easily translatable into concepts for use. Moreover, such an enlarged epistemological perspective makes the idea of rhetoric so thoroughly elastic as to incorporate anyone averse to objectivism and foundationalism. In short, while the explicit rhetorical turn is local in its application, the implicit rhetorical turn is global in its aspirations.

Thus, it is hardly surprising that Nelson and Megill's prospectus for the "rhetoric of inquiry" should end, not with a whimper, but with a bang:

> Our world is a creature and a texture of rhetorics: of founding stories and sales talks, anecdotes and statistics, images and rhythms; of tales told in nursery, pledges of allegiance or revenge, symbols of success and failure, archetypes of action and character. Ours is a world of persuasive definitions, expressive explanations, and institutional narratives. It is replete with figures of truth, models of reality, tropes of argument, and metaphors of experience. In our world, scholarship is rhetorical.[41]

This is, alas, the fate of rhetoric. Like Blanche DuBois in Tennessee Williams's *A Streetcar Named Desire*, we, the rhetoricians, have always relied on "the kindness of strangers," but too much kindness could kill us. We are either dismissed out of hand, excommunicated, cast out from the realm of light and truth, or we are given the whole world all to ourselves and asked to preside over "the conversation of mankind."[42]

Such is Nelson and Megill's myth for the new field. But the myth calls for some finer interpretation. How important is this story of repression and the subsequent regeneration of rhetoric of inquiry in the development of modern philosophy from Descartes to Derrida? Even Nelson and Megill will not venture to place it on the center stage. There are, to be sure, some negative comments about rhetoric in Descartes, Locke, and Kant. On the whole, however, they and their philosophical followers simply ignored rhetoric. If their work had the effect of repressing a rhetoric of inquiry, which I admit that it did, it was a latent outcome rather than a manifest intent. It would be preposterous to imagine that Kant set out to write the three critiques in order to repress rhetoric or to obviate a rhetoric of inquiry. The motivation for his labor came from different sources. Similarly, the dismantling of the modernist dogma in this century by Heidegger, Dewey, Wittgenstein, and others was not motivated by a manifest desire to make space for a rhetoric of inquiry. (I am not trying to suggest here that the suffocation of the rhetoric of inquiry under the modernist dogma was not genuine and severe simply because it was latent. Perhaps, it was more insidious because of its latency.)

Nelson and Megill will probably disagree with me on this point. For them the repression and the subsequent regeneration of the rhetoric of inquiry in modern philosophy is a critical thread. For me, it is a sideshow. The fact that it is a sideshow does not make me apologetic about the place of rhetoric in the life of the mind. The fact that it is a sideshow is in keeping with the nature and function of rhetoric.[43]

In the long and enduring quarrel between rhetoric and philosophy, the latter has not always set out to undermine the former.[44] Rhetoric has often been trampled on accidentally in philosophy's quest for certainty or whatever else it is bent on pursuing at any given time. Historically, philosophers have not evinced a profound concern with rhetoric. There is a sort of narcissistic streak in philosophy, an overdetermination of its own self-sufficiency and autonomy, which keeps it from seriously entertaining the competing claims of rhetoric.

There was only one philosopher, in my opinion, who set out earnestly to repress rhetoric; and when he couldn't, he sought to and pretty much succeeded in emasculating it. That was Plato. There was only one orator/rhetorician who seriously attempted to reconcile the competing claims of rhetoric and philosophy and pretty much succeeded in uniting the competing claims of eloquence and wisdom in his own person. That was

Cicero. We might add other names to either column in this list, but, even by a liberal standard, the list would not be long.

This brings me to the main point. Academically rhetoric has never been able to determine its own fortune. It lies embedded in the cultural practices of the time. It is always already there as a supplement, as an insert. Extract it from that to which it is a supplement or from that within which it is embedded, and it evaporates. It is present, to borrow a phrase from Lacan, only in "the discourse of the other." Ironically, the art of eloquence has no voice of its own within the academy. Pure persuasion is possible, as Kenneth Burke tells us, only in the furthest regions of religion and poetry where one hesitates, as in *Finnegans Wake*, between sound and sense.

The fortunes of rhetoric, more than any other discipline, turn on the roll of cultural dice. Rhetoric has good days and bad days, mostly bad days. This is one of the good days. If there is a myth about rhetoric, it is that of an outsider whose day of reckoning is deferred, time and again.

This is my counter-myth for an old discipline which constantly seeks to escape itself. If you had to choose between the two myths, I suspect Nelson and Megill would carry the day, despite my carping . . . At least, that is what my myth requires me to believe. After all, this is one of the good days for rhetoric.

Conclusion

Finally, what is the significance of the rhetorical turn in the self-understanding of rhetoric? At the sociological level, the rhetorical turn implies a renewed disciplinary legitimacy for rhetoric as an intellectual enterprise. If rhetoric is an unavoidable component in discourses as diverse as theoretical physics, economics, literary criticism, and psychoanalysis, then the story of rhetoric is a tale well worth telling. However, this would also suggest that the "legitimacy" of a formal discipline, such as rhetoric, is relative to its measurable "presence" in the substantive disciplines. This could be problematic, because, if rhetoric requires a constant "reconfirmation" of its "presence" in the discourse of other disciplines, it would suggest that rhetoric is a supplement to those discourses rather than constitutive of them. To put it differently, one could argue that rhetoric is parasitic vis-à-vis the special discourses rather than productive of them in the way that a "rule" is productive of a series of rule-governed actions, or that the "deep structure" of a natural language is said to be productive of its "surface structure." I believe (and this is a provisional statement) that an adequate understanding of the rhetoric of the human sciences is possible only when we have an adequate grasp of the logic of supplementarity within which rhetoric is habitually caught.

At another level, the rhetorical turn sets up an expectation that there would be a renaissance in rhetoric in the near future—that rhetoric would regain its lost glory as "the queen of the human sciences" in our time, and that it would preside over other disciplines as the metascience of culture in the Isocratean sense. The anticipation of a rhetorical turn could, thus, revive and set in motion the dormant foundational aspirations characteristic of formal, hence empty, disciplines like rhetoric, dialectic, and hermeneutics. That is, one has to travel but a short psychological distance to make that fatal move from anticipating a rhetorical turn in contemporary thought to proclaiming rhetoric as the foundational discipline (obviously, in its capacity as the general theory of discourse) for the human sciences.

Before we become intoxicated with such visions of grandeur, we have to ascertain exactly what role, if any, rhetoric as an academic discipline has played in bringing about this rhetorical turn, other than recognizing and celebrating its alleged arrival. As I indicated earlier, Kuhn's *The Structure of Scientific Revolutions*, which is treated as the *locus classicus* of the rhetorical turn, is entirely innocent of rhetoric as a discipline. This innocence or ignorance of rhetoric is not uncommon among the writers and the texts cited earlier as participating in the implicit rhetorical turn.

Even among those who write self-consciously about rhetoric and its presence, and whose texts were cited earlier as constituting the explicit rhetorical turn, few are conscious of rhetoric as an academic discipline. As for the majority, if they acknowledge their debt to rhetoric, it is usually to some classical texts, especially to Aristotle's *Rhetoric*; among the moderns, it is invariably Kenneth Burke and occasionally Perelman, and rarely I. A. Richards. For these writers, contemporary rhetoric simply means the idiosyncratic works of Kenneth Burke. This is best exemplified in the work of sociologist Hugh Dalziel Duncan, who has systematically, albeit mechanically, sought to reinterpret social theory from a decidedly rhetorical perspective, but the rhetorical perspective here simply means a Burkian perspective.[45] For other American writers like Geertz, Goffman, and Hayden White, who are clearly conscious of rhetoric, Burke provides the only link between classical rhetoric and its contemporary possibilities. The continental writers like Lacan, Derrida, Ricoeur, Genette, and Gadamer, whose texts bristle with rhetorical concepts and terms, are either entirely unaware of Burke's work or only marginally aware of it.

But on the whole, it is clear that rhetoricians have played but a limited role in bringing about this rhetorical turn. What concerns me here is not the sociological embarrassment resulting from the fact that we who celebrate this "rhetorical turn" in contemporary thought have contributed so little to its making. What does concern me is the fact that people like Kuhn and Toulmin were driven to make certain observations, which we characterize as marking a rhetorical turn in their respective thinking, by the internal logic (both synchronic and diachronic) of their own special discourses. They became, as it were, infected with a "rhetorical consciousness" by immersing themselves in their own special discourses and by tracing the discursive implications of their own distinctive theory and practice. It was not as if they were struggling for a vocabulary, absent in the ordinary language, that could articulate their "break" from the traditional discourse. The "break," or the "rupture," in the traditional discursive practices with which their names are associated neither occurred nor came to be articulated as a result of their sudden acquaintance with the rhetorical lexicon. Kuhn was not awakened from his dogmatic slumber after reading Aristotle or Burke, as Kant allegedly was after reading Hume.

To be sure, one could argue that it would have been easier for Kuhn to articulate his rhetorical insights had he been acquainted with the rhetorical tradition. This could serve as an argument for a greater dissemination of rhetorical lore in our culture, especially in the academy. But one could just as easily argue that in some situations a familiarity with the rhetorical lexicon could be a hindrance. Perhaps people like Kuhn do not really need a stylized rhetorical lexicon to recognize rhetoric; and their rhetorical insights are possibly richer, less labored, and more firmly grounded precisely because they are the insights of someone driven by the compulsions of a special discourse in search of a special knowledge, the knowledge of the world, so to speak. The ordinary language which, as Cicero reminds us, is the language of rhetoric, is sufficiently versatile to meet the needs of a Kuhn or a Toulmin. If we follow this logic, then, it would appear that an institutionalized presence of rhetoric is neither necessary nor sufficient for the rhetorical turn.

Furthermore, it may be interesting to note that these fabled rhetorical turns occur in times of crisis. Clearly, Kuhn's theory about paradigm shifts, Habermas's thesis regarding the legitimation crisis in the modern welfare state, and Derrida's method of reading as a textual "deconstruction" refer to and have their origin in specific crisis situations, be they in scientific theory, social theory, or literary theory. Perhaps it is during the discursive crises that a scientific language community becomes "rhetorically conscious." Further, we could argue that every special discourse and every scientific language community periodically goes through "rhetorical stages." And sometimes the general culture itself, passing through a general crisis, becomes rhetorically self-conscious. But with the passing of that crisis, the rhetorical consciousness once again erodes. That is, the emergence of a rhetorical consciousness is directly related to a crisis within a special discourse. That relation can be formulated as follows: A crisis, discursive or otherwise, makes rhetoric visible; that is, a crisis brings to the fore the incipient rhetorical consciousness. The sheer possibility of a rhetorical consciousness, the possibility that rhetoric is a permanent though unrealized opening for man, does not by itself induce a crisis, but it is something always waiting to be exploited when the crisis comes. In short, rhetoric is the medium and not the ground of discursive and cultural crises.

NOTES

1. Chaim Perelman and L. Olbrechts-Tyteca, *The New Rhetoric: A Treatise on Argumentation,* trans. John Wilkinson and Purcell Weaver (South Bend, IN: University of Notre Dame Press, 1969); Paolo Valesio, *Novantiqua: Rhetoric as Contemporary Theory* (Bloomington: Indiana University Press, 1980). For a tendency to subordinate rhetoric to dialectic, see Maurice Natanson, "The Limits of Rhetoric," *Quarterly Journal of Speech 41* (1955): 133–139; and Richard Weaver, "The Phaedrus and the Nature of Rhetoric," in his *The Ethics of Rhetoric* (Chicago: Henry Regnery, 1953), pp. 3–26.

2. Ernesto Grassi, *Rhetoric as Philosophy: The Humanistic Tradition* (University Park: Pennsylvania State University Press, 1980).

3. Roland Barthes, "The Old Rhetoric: An Aìde-Memoire," in his *The Semiotic Challenge,* trans. Richard Howard (New York: Hill and Wang, 1988), p. 46.

4. Aristotle, *The Art of Rhetoric,* ed. and trans. Lane Cooper (New York: Appleton-Century-Croft, 1932), p. 9.

5. Brian Vickers, "Territorial Disputes: Philosophy versus Rhetoric," in Brian Vickers, ed., *Rhetoric Revalued* (Binghamton, NY: Medieval and Renaissance Texts and Studies, 1982), p. 248.

6. Cicero, "Fourth Philippic," in Lewis Copeland and Lawrence W. Lamm, eds., *The World's Great Speeches,* 3rd ed. (New York: Dover, 1973), p. 48.

7. This phrase *alte und neue Konigin der Wissenschaften* comes from Walter Jens, *Von Deutscher Rede* (Munich: Piper, 1969), and is cited by Chaim Perelman, in *The Realm of Rhetoric,* trans. William Kluback (South Bend, IN: University of Notre Dame Press, 1982), p. 162.

8. Alfred Schutz, *The Phenomenology of the Social World,* trans. George Walsh and Frederick Lehnert (Evanston, IL: Northwestern University Press, 1967). Also see his *Collected Papers, Vol. 1: The Problems of Social Reality,* ed. Maurice Natanson (The Hague, The Netherlands: Martinus Nijhoff, 1971).

9. For a discussion of "essentially contested concepts," see W. B. Gallie, *Philosophy and the Historical Understanding* (New York: Schocken, 1964), pp. 157–191.

10. For an excellent critical survey of the literature on this question in the speech communication journals, see Michael Leff, "In Search of Ariadne's Thread: A Review of the Recent Literature on Rhetorical Theory," *Central State Speech Journal 29* (1978): 65–91.

11. Jacques Derrida, *Of Grammatology,* trans. Gayatri Chakravorty Spivak (Baltimore: Johns Hopkins University Press, 1976). Also see "Plato's Pharmacy," in Derrida, *Dissemination,* trans. Barbara Johnson (Chicago: University of Chicago Press, 1981), pp. 61–171.

12. Aristotle, *The "Art" of Rhetoric,* trans. John Henry Freese, Loeb Classical Library (Cambridge, MA: Harvard University Press, 1926), 1856a, p. 19

13. Lloyd Bitzer, "Political Rhetoric," in Dan Nimmo and Keith Sanders, eds., *Handbook of Political Communication* (Beverly Hills, CA: Sage, 1981), pp. 225–248.

14. Michael Leff, "The Habitation of Rhetoric," in Joseph Wenzel et al., eds., *Argument and Critical Practices: Proceedings of the Fifth SCA/AFA Conference on Argumentation* (Annandale, VA: SCA, 1987), p. 5 [reprinted in this volume].

15. Bitzer, "Political Rhetoric," p. 231.

16. Paul Ricoeur, *The Rule of Metaphor: Multidisciplinary Studies in the Creation of Meaning in Language,* trans. Robert Czerny with Kathleen McLaughlin and John Costello (Toronto: University of Toronto Press, 1976), p. 30.

17. Kenneth Burke, *A Rhetoric of Motives* (Berkeley and Los Angeles: University of California Press, 1969, 1950), pp. 54–55.

18. Barthes, "The Old Rhetoric," p. 73.

19. Ibid., p. 75.

20. Cicero, *De oratore*, 2 vols., trans. E. W. Sutton, Loeb Classical Library (Cambridge, MA: Harvard University Press, 1942); Saint Augustine, *On Christian Doctrine*, trans. D. W. Robertson Jr. (New York: Bobbs-Merrill, 1958). In Cicero's *De oratore*, there are a number of references to rhetoric (the art or theory of oratory) as a supplement to inborn talent and correct practice based on imitation of suitable models. Cicero, while exalting the powers of the orator in a variety of ways, repeatedly observes that the art of oratory cannot produce the orator by itself without assistance from nature, which supplies talent, and practice, which deepens and perfects talent. The art itself, according to Cicero, plays but a minor role, and what is there to understand of the art can be obtained easily and quickly. Augustine is more explicit about the status of rhetoric as a supplement. In the fourth book of *De doctrina christiana*, rhetoric is clearly drawn into the orbit of hermeneutics as a supplement to elucidate what interpretation has uncovered of the sacred texts.

21. Cited in George A. Kennedy, *Classical Rhetoric and Its Christian and Secular Tradition from Ancient to Modern Times* (Chapel Hill: University of North Carolina Press, 1980), p. 240.

22. Cited by Lane Cooper, trans. and ed., in *The Rhetoric of Aristotle* (New York: Appleton-Century-Croft, 1932), p. xii.

23. For a general overview on the sophists in the light of the current revival of scholarly interest in them, see W. K. C. Guthrie, *The Sophists* (New York: Cambridge University Press, 1971), and G. B. Kerferd, *The Sophistic Movement* (New York: Cambridge University Press, 1981).

24. For an early attempt to articulate the ontological basis of rhetoric, see Karlyn K. Campbell, "The Ontological Foundation of Rhetorical Theory," *Philosophy and Rhetoric 3* (1970): 97–108.

25. Hannah Arendt, *The Human Condition* (New York: Anchor, 1958), p. 10.

26. Paul de Man, *Allegories of Reading* (New Haven, CT: Yale University Press, 1979), pp. 103–131; Tzvetan Todorov, *Theories of the Symbol*, trans. Catherine Porter (Ithaca, NY: Cornell University Press, 1982), pp. 60–110.

27. For the most influential account of the "reality construction" thesis, see Peter L. Berger and Thomas Luckmann, *The Social Construction of Reality: A Treatise in the Sociology of Knowledge* (New York: Anchor Books, 1967).

28. For an account of rhetoric as a "material force," see Michael Calvin McGee, "A Materialist's Conception of Rhetoric," in R. E. McKerrow, ed., *Explorations in Rhetoric: Studies in Honor of Douglas Ehninger* (Glenville, IL: Scott, Foresman, 1982), pp. 23–49.

29. Burke, *A Rhetoric of Motives*, p. xiii.

30. Ibid.

31. Ibid., p. xiv.

32. Kenneth Burke, *A Grammar of Motives and A Rhetoric of Motives* (New York: Meridian Books, 1962), p. 523.

33. Kennedy, *Classical Rhetoric*, pp. 86–107.

34. Wayne C. Booth, *The Rhetoric of Fiction* (Chicago: University of Chicago Press, 1983); Paul de Man, *The Rhetoric of Romanticism* (New York: Columbia University Press, 1984).

35. Thomas S. Kuhn, *The Structure of Scientific Revolutions* (Chicago: University of Chicago Press, 1970).

36. John S. Nelson and Allan Megill, "Rhetoric of Inquiry: Projects and Prospects," *Quarterly Journal of Speech 72* (1986): 20–37. McCloskey appears to share the views of Nelson and Megill on the prospects of a rhetoric of inquiry. This same essay, with minor modifications, appears as the introductory essay in the volume of papers from the Iowa conference held on March 28–31, 1984. See John S. Nelson, Allan Megill, and Donald N. McCloskey, eds., *The Rhetoric of the Human Sciences: Language and Argument in Scholarship and Public Affairs* (Madison: University of Wisconsin Press, 1987), pp. 3–18.

37. Nelson and Megill, "Rhetoric of Inquiry," p. 20.

38. Ibid., pp. 22–23.

39. Ibid., p. 24.

40. J. H. Hexter, "The Rhetoric of History," *History and Theory 6* (1967): 1–14. For an expanded version of the same essay, see the chapter by the same title in his *Doing History* (Bloomington: Indiana University Press, 1971), pp. 15–76.

41. Nelson and Megill, "Rhetoric of Inquiry," p. 36.

42. This popular phrase among the proponents of the rhetorical turn was originally coined by Michael Oakeshott in "Poetry as a Voice in the Conversation of Mankind," in his *Experience and Its Modes* (1933), and reprinted in his *Rationalism in Politics* (New York: Methuen, 1962), pp. 197–247.

43. On the "marginality" of rhetoric in the disciplinary contest for "status," see Robert Hariman, "Status, Marginality, and Rhetorical Theory," *Quarterly Journal of Speech 72* (1986): 38–52 [reprinted in this volume].

44. The literature on the quarrel between philosophy and rhetoric is quite extensive. For both an historically and conceptually informed general view of the quarrel, see Brian Vickers, *In Defense of Rhetoric* (Oxford, UK: Clarendon Press, 1988), especially chaps. 2 and 3, pp. 83–213.

45. Hugh Dalziel Duncan, *Communication and Social Order* (New York: Oxford University Press, 1968).

What Do You *Mean*, Rhetoric Is Epistemic?

William D. Harpine

In 1967, Robert L. Scott (1967) advocated that "rhetoric is epistemic." This concept has enriched the work of rhetorical theorists and critics. Scott's essay is founded in a concept of argumentative justification in rhetoric, viewed as an alternative to analytic logic. Other writers, including Brummett (1976), Railsback (1983), and Cherwitz and Hikins (1986), have offered variations on Scott's theme. The thesis that rhetoric is epistemic has been controversial, however, and from the tone of the debate one may draw two conclusions: many rhetorical theorists feel that Scott was on to something important, and the thesis as it has been developed is flawed. Much of the dispute centers on what the thesis means. These discussions have not yet adequately clarified that issue.

The philosopher's most fundamental obligation is to define terms with care. It is in precisely this respect that the rhetoric-is-epistemic theorists have fallen short. Some of the key terms in this literature include *rhetoric, knowledge, certainty*, and *truth*. In too many cases, the writers on rhetorical epistemology have not defined their key terms at all. In other cases, their definitions are inadequate or inconsistent. This essay undertakes to sort out the most important definitional problems, which center on the rhetoric-is-epistemic theorists' habit of equivocating about the meanings of "rhetoric" and "certainty." The result makes it possible to *endorse the validity of Scott's essentially ethical conclusions*, while *dismissing a number of unnecessary complexities* in the arguments made by rhetoric-as-epistemic theorists. Finally, a few alternatives that might lead to more robust foundations for the rhetoric-as-epistemic thesis are suggested.

In 1978, after reviewing four distinct interpretations of the claim that rhetoric is epistemic, Leff concluded that clarification of what that claim means "deserves more disciplined treatment than it has received in the recent literature" (1978, 77). The same could still be said. After some thirty years of active research and speculation on the topic, one now sees fewer publications specifically advocating that rhetoric is epistemic. The distinguished rhetorical theorist Barry Brummett (1990) has declared the thesis deceased (69–72).

All the same, textbook authors treat the thesis as a given, despite their tendency to interpret it in wildly different ways. Foss, for example, puts forward a view that "in the field of communication, the idea that rhetoric creates reality is known as the notion that rhetoric is epistemic, which simply means that rhetoric creates knowledge; *epistemology* is the study of the origin and nature of knowledge" (1989, 122; emphasis in the original). This version of the thesis, claiming that rhetoric actually "creates reality," might be more ontological than it is epistemic.[1] Herrick takes a dialectical view that through rhetorical interaction, people come to accept some ideas as true and to reject others as false. Thus, rhetoric's epistemic function in society can be seen in some ways to be a result of its benefit of testing ideas. Herrick continues that "once an idea has been tested thoroughly by a group, community, and society, it becomes part of what these groups take to be knowledge." Herrick contrasts this with the rejected view that "knowledge is all objective in nature and comes to us by way of direct experience or education" (1997, 22). Both Herrick and Foss offer interesting theses, and both attribute their views to Scott, but their views are obviously very different. There can be no surer evidence of the failure to use terms precisely.

Brummett (1990) attributes the demise of rhetoric-is-epistemic research to the failure of critics to employ the idea in rhetorical criticism. Brummett might be right to the extent that much of the rhetoric-is-epistemic literature is indeed exceptionally abstract. Specific discussions might clarify some issues. Nonetheless, some notable rhetorical critics have indeed employed a concept that rhetoric is epistemic (e.g., Scott and Klumpp 1984; Sullivan 1992). The issues remain unclear. Furthermore, rhetorical criticism per se cannot clarify the meanings of theoretical terms. More likely, one sees less and less published research about the thesis that rhetoric is epistemic precisely because the thesis has not been laid out clearly enough.

On the one hand, rhetorical theorists sometimes lose patience with what they perceive to be the overly technical arguments of philosophers. On the other hand, much of what follows might strike a philosopher as rather straightforward, boilerplate philosophy. In that context, my only excuses for offering this essay are these: first, in claiming that rhetoric is epistemic, rhetoricians have walked onto Plato's playground and must expect to play by Plato's rules (that Athenian always was a stickler for definitions), and, second, if the rhetoric-is-epistemic thesis in its present forms succumbs easily to boilerplate philosophy, that cannot be a good sign.

This essay focuses on the positions laid out by Scott and by Cherwitz and Hikins, for these have been by far the most influential versions of the viewpoint. Scott deserves credit for introducing the thesis that rhetoric [is] epistemic.[2] Scott proposed what was in 1967 a new, radical way to understand rhetoric. It is in the nature of the first exposition of a new idea that the details may await clarification. Cherwitz and Hikins's work deserves attention not because they do an unusually poor job of offering definitions, but because they have done by far the most thorough job of doing so. Their view differs from Scott's in important ways, but the definitional issues that they confront are very similar.

Certainty

Scott's argument on viewing rhetoric as epistemic works from a perceived relationship between certainty and knowledge (1967). This raises a host of definitional questions. First, what is certainty? Second, what is the definitional relationship between knowledge and certainty? Most of what Scott has to say, indeed, the heart of his argument, trades on an equivocation between two meanings of "certainty." Furthermore, he seems to assume, without argument, that certainty is part of the traditional definition of knowledge. Let us take up the first issue first.

"Certainty" can be objective or subjective in its meaning (Wittgenstein 1969).[3] One might say, "It is certain that a Republican will be president in the year 2025." This is a claim for objective certainty. One might instead state that "I feel certain that a Republican will be president in 2025," which refers more to my state of mind than it does to who will actually be president. The first statement entails that a Republican will be president in 2025; the second does not. I am not making any claim about what things, if any, are objectively certain; I am just explaining two meanings that the word *certainty* has in everyday use.

It is easy to think of circumstances under which one can have either kind of certainty without the other. To illustrate: perhaps, a mathematical formula is certainly true (in the objective sense), even though no mathematician as of yet has completed a proof and knows that it is certain. It is also possible to feel completely certain about something without its being true, or even plausible. I have myself felt completely certain about matters on which events eventually proved me wrong. As Wittgenstein hints, "One always forgets the expression 'I thought I knew'" (1969, 5e).

Scott does not define "certainty," nor does he choose between these two meanings. Instead, he seems to slide from a subjective sense of certainty to an objective sense of certainty. For example, during his key argument, Scott states that "the question may be posed, 'What do you mean by *certain*?' To say, 'I am certain that the sun will rise tomorrow,' may be to make a common statement which will probably not elicit argument, unless one is engaged in an epistemological discussion." This represents a subjective sense of "certainty," that is, that certainty is a state of mind. A few sentences later, however, Scott asserts that "the only sorts of arguments which will answer the demands of certainty made in epistemological speculation are those arguments which Toulmin calls analytic" (1967, 11). This clearly implies objective certainty, one for which ironclad (i.e., analytic) proof is supposedly adduced. The conclusion of the present essay suggests that *subjective*, not *objective*, certainty is central to Scott's theory. Nonetheless, Scott's argument is fundamentally against objective certainty. Scott's argument against the concept of certainty immediately short-circuits because it is founded on this equivocation.

In a later essay, Scott writes, "When reason leads to certainties, people no longer have a reason to reason with one another, for surely those who lack certainty, lack reason" (2000, 109). This argument implies that people who believe that they have a right to be certain will treat others wrongly. Nonetheless, reason of extraordinary quality would, in principle, seem to lead to objective certainty, which is something else. So, Scott's real argument (freed from an ambiguous concept of certainty) should be something like, "People who have such confidence in their ability to reason that they cannot see the possibility of being in error, will no longer perceive a need to reason with one another . . ." This is a worthwhile point, to which this essay will return.

Furthermore, Scott's essay leads us to the critical question of defining knowledge. Is certainty, whether subjective or objective, part of his definition of knowledge? Is certainty essential to knowledge? Does Scott believe that traditional theories of knowledge require a concept of certainty, which can be evaded only by viewing rhetoric as epistemic?

Ayer states that the conditions "for knowing that something is the case are first that what one is said to know be true, secondly that one be sure of it, and thirdly that one should have the right to be sure" (1957, 35). Therefore, for Ayer, one must feel subjectively certain that something is true for one to know it. However, Alston (1989b) has argued convincingly that this kind of thinking represents a level confusion fallacy, in that for one to know something does not logically require that one is sure of it: for example, to say "Pat knows that *p* is true" means one thing, and "Pat knows that she or he knows that *p* is true" means something else. It is conceivable that I could know something without knowing that I know it, in which case I have knowledge, but might have no subjective sense of certainty (Alston 1989b). Fewer post-World War II philosophers, including the analytic philosophers against whom Scott's essay appears to be directed, seem to believe that certainty in either sense is

a defining condition of knowledge. In any case, there has been quite a lively debate on the question, and Scott assumes with little argument that epistemologists require that knowledge be certain in some sense or other.

Cherwitz and Hikins distinguish more carefully between the two meanings of "certainty," but as their study progresses they, too, equivocate between the two.[4] Like Scott, they seem to assume that some form of certainty, or near-certainty, is necessary for the traditional accounts of knowledge. However, they confuse the issue to the detriment of their position: "we need next to deal with *how* one can become certain that he or she has attained knowledge on an issue. . . . We set the ultimate, human standard for certainty at the fullest humanly possible level of confidence in beliefs." This plainly states that *subjective* certainty is a necessary condition for knowledge. Yet, a page later, one finds them talking about certainty as if it is based on justification: "Although we cannot say with certainty what precise level of justification *any* proposition must have, we are confident that in such cases [as in certain of their examples] the requisite level *has* been reached, and the propositions stand as *knowledge*" (Cherwitz and Hikins 1986, 155–56; emphasis in the original). Thus, they slide without an argument from a claim about *feeling* certain to one about being *justified* in being certain. This is a straightforward equivocation between the two meanings of certainty.

This is unfortunate for their theory, since viewing rhetoric as epistemic seemingly implies that there is a justificatory quality of some kind in rhetorical processes. Any argument for that claim short-circuits when it is founded on using a key term in more than one sense. It is, obviously, much easier to show that rhetoric can increase our feeling that we are certain (which, I think, Cherwitz and Hikins demonstrate throughout their book) than it is to show that it justifies our beliefs.

Rhetoric

Well, of course, all rhetorical theories are about rhetoric, so one takes the meaning of the word *rhetoric* for granted. Furthermore, rhetoricians have long shown a fondness for poetic definitions, like defining rhetoric as "the *rationale of informative and suasory discourse*" (Bryant 1953, 404; emphasis in the original). If we want to be clear, however, we need a more precise definition.

The root of *rhetoric* is "*rh?-*," which in Greek signifies "speech" (Aristotle 1991, 36n34). To the ancient Greeks, rhetoric was public speaking. Socrates asked Gorgias to define what his art was, and Gorgias defined it first as the ability to convince one's listeners in the law courts and public assemblies, and then quickly agreed with Socrates that rhetoric is persuasion (Plato 1961a, 452e–53a). Over the centuries, and most particularly under the inspiration of Kenneth Burke, the study of rhetoric has come to include all persuasive communication, including written and nonverbal communication. According to Campbell, for example, "rhetoric is the study of what is persuasive" (1996, 8). An essay of which Scott is a co-author implies a similar point, claiming that "the point made by Scott's and Farrell's writings is that the practice of rhetoric is epistemic (i.e., knowledge-producing) because we must be persuaded of our beliefs" (Schiappa, Gross, McKerrow, and Scott 2002, 114).

When theorists say that rhetoric is epistemic, do they mean that *persuasion* has an epistemic quality? Do they mean to distinguish communication that is persuasive, or will they allow any communication to count as rhetoric? How broad, or how narrow, a conception of rhetoric is necessary in order to make sense of the claim that rhetoric is epistemic?

Many rhetoric-is-epistemic theorists operate with a very broad definition of rhetoric. This is troublesome. It might be hard to establish a significant epistemic role for set-piece persuasive speeches, but much easier to establish an epistemic role for rhetoric if rhetoric is conceived more largely. Scott (1973) suggests that any definition of rhetoric will be inadequate. Scott (2000, 109) offers the definition that "rhetoric is the possibility of bringing reason together with passion so that in action humans may civilize themselves." This is interesting, although it fits into the category of poetic definitions. Cherwitz and Hikins, noting the importance of avoiding ambiguity, define rhetoric as "*description of reality through language*" (1986, 67; emphasis in the original). This expansive definition facilitates their argument that rhetoric is epistemic, for some epistemic function can surely be found for describing reality through language. As long as they work with this definition, they do not need to establish that persuasive communication is epistemic, for example, which would be a more difficult task.[5] Railsback's approach to seeing rhetoric as epistemic also works with a very broad conception of rhetoric: "Rhetoric thus mediates the relationship between language and external material conditions." She implies both persuasive and non-persuasive aspects for rhetoric (1983, 361).

However, the broader the definition of rhetoric, the less interesting the claim that rhetoric is epistemic becomes, as Farrell (1990) suggests. If I could provide evidence that public speaking is fundamentally epistemic, this would be controversial, even implausible, but interesting. To claim that persuasive communication is epistemic would be nearly as interesting, and, if there is anything worthwhile to the claim that rhetoric is epistemic, this would, in my opinion, be the definition of rhetoric to use. If, however, one claims that rhetoric includes all language use, then all one has to prove to establish that rhetoric is epistemic is that language has an epistemic function. This could still be controversial (one question that ought to come up is whether a small child who lacks language also lacks the ability to know), yet it is an inherently less interesting claim. If one can by definition substitute the term "language use" for "rhetoric," if all that a rhetoric-as-epistemic theorist means is that language use has an epistemic function, it is difficult to understand what the big fuss is about. The claim is too nearly obvious, too mundane, to justify so much study of the topic. To say that rhetoric means "describing reality through language" is still a very broad definition of rhetoric. (It is also a technical use of the word *rhetoric*, one not well supported by everyday use of the term by educated, reflective nonspecialists. Many uses of language to describe reality do not strike me as especially rhetorical; e.g., the rhetorical aspects of "Your telephone is ringing," "There are dandelions in my lawn," or "Yow, I hit my thumb" seem to me to be relatively unimportant.) In order for the claim that rhetoric is epistemic to be clear, one would hope for a definition that is specific enough to yield a discussion that makes worthwhile claims.

The Gettier Problem

Rhetoric-is-epistemic theories seem to assume that knowledge must be justified belief, and that the justification can, should, or must be rhetorical. Cherwitz and Hikins, for example, define knowledge as requiring "(1) truth, (2) belief, and (3) justification." They cite, among others, a statement of Butchvarov that "equates knowledge with 'true belief based on sufficient evidence'" (Cherwitz and Hikins 1986, 21).[6]

Other rhetoric-is-epistemic theorists are not so careful to define knowledge, but they often seem to operate with an implied conception that knowledge is justified true belief. A basic idea behind viewing rhetoric as epistemic is to argue that justification has a rhetorical element. Scott, for example, repeatedly discusses issues of justification. Similarly, Railsback states that "consensus must be used as our primary indicator of the most true characterizations of the time." She continues that "consensus arises from the processes of inquiry and persuasion, and serves as the basis for future inquiry" (1983, 363). If justification is not a defining quality of knowledge, that entire approach never gets started.

Lurking behind this is a problem posed in one of the most influential short essays ever published in a philosophy journal, Edmund Gettier's (1963) "Is Justified True Belief Knowledge?" A by-product of Gettier's argument is to question the assumptions behind many of the familiar conceptions of rhetoric as epistemic. The traditional definitions of knowledge typically take the form that a person X knows something *p*, if X believes *p*, if *p* is true, and if X is sufficiently justified in believing *p*. Plato seems to say something like this in *Theaetetus* (1961b, 201c–d). Ayer's definition quoted above also falls into this category. Since rhetoric-is-epistemic theorists are exploring the relationship between knowledge and rhetorical justification, their theories tend to be steeped in a similar conception of knowledge. Gettier argues that the traditional definitions fail because they do not constitute sufficient conditions for knowing something. Because of Gettier's argument, the conceptual relationship between knowledge and justification seems to be extremely problematic.

Gettier assumes, first, that it is possible to be justified in believing something that is not true. Second, Gettier assumes that if one is justified in believing one proposition, and then deduces a second proposition from the first, that one is justified in believing the second proposition (1963, 121). There seems to be no reason that rhetoricians should object to either of these assumptions.

Consider the following Gettier-type example. A political speaker sees that an election's results have been posted, and that the election officials have declared that candidate Jill Smith has received 2,220 votes, and that candidate Harry Early has received only 889 votes. The election officials have always been reliable in the past. The speaker concludes that Smith is the winner and, indeed, so announces in a speech. Unfortunately, unknown to the speaker, the election officials had, by mistake, counted the ballots from a different jurisdiction entirely. (If a jurisdiction uses the punch-card ballots that are popular in the United States as of this writing, which contain little written information, such a slip-up could happen.) When the right ballots are obtained a few days later, it turns out that Smith received 2,001 votes, and that Early received 720 votes. The speaker's belief that Smith won the election was true. It was also justified. Nonetheless, the speaker did not know that Smith was the winner. Only by chance was the speaker's belief true. Because of problems such as this, Gettier concludes that a belief can be true and justified, and yet not be knowledge.

Gettier's article has inspired a prodigious literature. At first glance, it seems that it should be easy to add a fourth condition of knowledge to the traditional definition that would rule out such accidental cases of justified true belief. Unfortunately, to this date, no such fourth condition has earned general acceptance. All of the proposed fourth conditions (one of which is mentioned by Cherwitz and Hikins; see below) have been refuted, usually rather easily, by various counterexamples.

A second solution to the Gettier problem is to require that knowledge be based entirely on true premises. For example, Armstrong (1973) states that the evidence for saying that one knows something must itself be something that is known. This solves the Gettier problem, but at the expense of ruling out most of our claims to knowledge. As Lehrer has pointed out, this very rigid condition would rule out much of what we would like to say we know (1965; see also Audi 1998). An example of this might be the following: a lawyer argues that her client, Mr. Jenkins, is innocent of murder. Her client has an excellent alibi, and the client's fingerprints do not match those of the murderer. She so pleads to a jury. She and the jury both conclude that Mr. Jenkins is innocent. Mr. Jenkins actually is completely innocent; however, his alibi later turns out to have been based on mistaken identity. Nonetheless, the fingerprints still provide excellent proof of his innocence. I would like to be able to say that the lawyer and jury know that Mr. Jenkins is innocent, but if I require that knowledge be based entirely on true premises, I cannot. Any attempt to make knowledge as strict as that seems unsettling, since requiring that all of the premises for a knowledge claim must be true rules out so much. One cannot easily imagine conducting a debate about a public policy issue, for example, if one is held to so unrealistically high a standard for one's knowledge claims. Furthermore, such an approach would defeat one of Scott's original purposes, which was to free knowledge from unreasonable standards.

A third solution to the Gettier problem, proposed by Butchvarov (1970), is to require that all justification for knowledge be ironclad, to eliminate all possibility of mistake. However, surely no rhetorical theorist would wish to define knowledge in such rigorous terms that very few beliefs can qualify as knowledge. Butchvarov, whom Cherwitz and Hikins (1986) repeatedly cite, admits that insisting on "impossibility of mistake as the criterion of knowledge," as he does, leads to the "conclusion that most of what is ordinarily called knowledge in everyday life as well as in the sciences, is not knowledge" (Butchvarov 1970, 59).

Gettier's objection vitiates Cherwitz and Hikins's theory, since they explicitly trade on the definition of knowledge as justified true belief. Referring to Gettier's argument, Cherwitz and Hikins cite Lehrer's repair as preserving "the three criteria largely intact" (1986, 21). This seems doubtful. Lehrer's definition of knowledge in the cited reference is as follows: "in addition to having a completely justified true belief that P, the following fourth condition must be satisfied when a man knows that P: for any false statement F, X would be able to completely justify his belief that P even if he were to suppose, for the sake of argument, that F is false" (Lehrer 1970, 127). It is difficult to grasp how this complex repair retains "the three criteria largely intact."

Furthermore, Lehrer's fourth condition succumbs to arguments of the "barn county" family, which deal with beliefs that are founded on a pattern of deception (Goldman 1976, 772–73). Suppose that I go to the bank, where I have done business for years, to check on the balance of my savings account. The bank and the tellers have always been flawlessly accurate. Today, however, the teller is planning an embezzlement scheme and is lying to her customers about their balances to further her criminal plan. My own account contains only $45.98, not enough for her to bother embezzling, so she tells me, alone among all of her customers, the truth. Based on her statement, I truly believe that my account has $45.98, and my belief is justified, but I do not know that my balance is $45.98 because this is true only by accident. Yet, my belief rests on no false statements and therefore satisfies Lehrer's tests. Therefore, even Lehrer's complex repair does not salvage the conception of knowledge as justified true belief.

Early in their study, Cherwitz and Hikins argue that justification must be both "relevant" and "sufficient" (1986, 28–30). Near the end of their study, however, they argue that the justification must be based on "sufficient evidence to guarantee that knowledge has been attained with the fullest humanly possible certainty" (155). This is not enough to counter Gettier's problem, since the "fullest humanly possible certainty" does not eliminate the chance of error. If they intend to require ironclad ("sufficient") justification to lie behind a belief in order for it to count as knowledge, then they would encounter the objections to that thesis discussed above. Actually, in either case, they come close enough that their definition restricts the realm of human knowledge considerably. Cherwitz and Hikins's definition is thus not strong enough to avoid the Gettier problem, but it is, unfortunately, strong enough to rule out many of our everyday claims to knowledge.

Interestingly, Railsback claims to perceive a trend in the rhetoric-is-epistemic literature to move away "from the philosophical definition of knowledge as 'justified true belief' to a formulation which indicates that truth itself is 'warranted assertability'" (1983, 362). She cites to this effect an essay by McKerrow, which she holds to be compatible with her own view, based on the "bounded network theory of language" (Railsback 1983, 362n10). In the cited essay, McKerrow proposes that an argument is valid "if, and only if, it serves as a pragmatic justification for the adoption of a belief" (1977, 135). Now, on Railsback's account, the Gettier problem (or worse) would be hard to avoid, since McKerrow clearly states that warranted assertability does not require ironclad justification. Indeed, McKerrow distinguishes that "arguments *justify* rather than *verify* their claims" (134; emphasis in the original). Since "verify" by definition means to confirm that something is true, there is clearly something here other than a claim that rhetoric is epistemic.

Although McKerrow discusses "rhetorical validity" as justification, he does not claim in the 1977 essay that a rhetorically valid argument produces either knowledge or truth. Thus, McKerrow does not try to define *knowledge* rhetorically; he is instead defining *validity*. He carefully avoids any claim that rhetorical arguments entail truth, and thus avoids the Gettier problem entirely. Such a decoupling of justification from truth and knowledge may in fact be the most practical solution to the Gettier problem. This essay's conclusion returns to such a theme.

Clarifying the Definitions

It is not clear that the thesis that rhetoric is epistemic is dead, although it most certainly has not been adequately formulated. Fixing the definitions can lead to a great deal of progress.

First, for the reasons above, rhetoric must be defined narrowly enough to produce an interesting discussion. One of the oldest and most common definitions of rhetoric is "the art of persuasion." Such a definition can lead to an interesting discussion. Defining rhetoric more broadly simply legislates an epistemic role for rhetoric by fiat; such an approach lacks interest. The question of significance to rhetorical theory is whether persuasion has an epistemic role, and that is the question that theorists should investigate.

Second, the discussion should dispense with the issue of certainty. The current philosophical literature presents no reason that *subjective* certainty is a necessary component of knowledge. Furthermore, rhetoricians in a line reaching long before Scott's time have never shown any inclination to require objective certainty. Rhetoricians obviously do not want to maintain that rhetoric is a source of knowledge, and then claim that the matters about which people engage in rhetoric are unknowable. The current philosophical literature has not taken a strong stance in favor of requiring knowledge to be either objectively or subjectively certain, so the issue may (through no fault of Scott's, who wrote in 1967) have become a red herring.

Two Ideas for a Rhetorical Epistemology

It might be useful to sketch out a few different routes that rhetorical theorists could choose while defining terms carefully.

There may be no need to examine the epistemological question at all. Scott's insight may be, for the most part, ethical and personal. Nonetheless, many rhetorical theorists find the idea that rhetoric is epistemic intriguing. Furthermore, it is difficult to sympathize with Brummett's pronouncement that the thesis that rhetoric is epistemic is dead. This essay will briefly suggest two avenues that rhetorical theorists could follow. Either of these approaches would make it possible to discuss how rhetoric is epistemic without encountering the Gettier problem or relying on unclear conceptions of certainty.

One route that rhetoric-as-epistemic theorists could take is to adopt Alston's (1989a) view that, in the normal course of life, our beliefs are justified if formed by our normal doxastic (i.e., belief-producing) practices. Alston does not imply an analytic connection between knowledge and justification. He simply argues that there is a presumption in favor of the normal ways in which we come to learn and believe things. Alston has a sense of community in mind, as he does not claim that any one individual's doxastic practices are necessarily reasonable. Rather, his point is that there is a presumption in favor of accepted doxastic practices.

Alston's view is amenable to what rhetoric-is-epistemic theorists have in mind. Indeed, there is an obvious relationship between Alston's suggestion and Scott's (1976) stress on the epistemic function of communities. Furthermore, a good case might be made that rhetoric is part of our normal doxastic practice. In addition, given that rhetoricians since the time of Aristotle have held that rhetoric typically establishes claims that are probable, not *necessarily* true, Alston's position should intrigue rhetoricians. For example, Cyphert's (2001) view that rhetoric-as-epistemic practices are culturally variable and community-based could be further developed with reference to Alston's argument.

Alston's line of reasoning is not strictly speaking *epistemic*, for he is not claiming that our doxastic practices always produce *knowledge*. However, if our normal doxastic practices are worth anything, it is good to form our beliefs in accordance with them. Following Alston's lead, rhetorical theorists would explicate how rhetoric is part of our doxastic practice, but they would sever this explanation from the definitions of knowledge and certainty. This would greatly simplify our thinking about these issues. McKerrow's (1977) argument, discussed above, already seems to be moving in a similar direction.

A second avenue worthy of consideration by rhetorical theorists is the causal theory of knowing. This theory maintains, in essence, that I know that p if my belief that p was formed as the result of a reliable causal process. Goldman (1988) develops a causal theory of knowing. Herrick (1997) seems to imply a causal idea of rhetoric as epistemic. This, for starters, divests epistemology of the concept of justification, and thus avoids the Gettier problem. Many epistemologists over the years have, in any case, argued that it is possible to know something even if one cannot offer a justification for it. That is, it is one thing to know that p, but something else entirely to be able to justify a belief that p. A cocker spaniel might know that it is time for a walk, but be unable to offer any justification.

A causal theory eliminates this awkward bump. One might think at first that this leaves little room for a rhetorician. For example, the idea behind McKerrow's notion of warranted assertability is to offer justification for one's claims. Nonetheless, presenting or receiving persuasive discourse might be a way of coming to know things, and so this theory does make it possible for rhetoric to be epistemic. Rhetoric-as-epistemic theorists would have plenty of room to discuss the reliability of the various argumentative and suasory devices that rhetoricians employ and to discuss when rhetoric does and does not reliably contribute to knowledge. A causal theory might yield interesting conclusions about value-laden, tradition-bound epideictic rhetoric, for example. What causes us to have beliefs about value issues? Are whatever processes that produce value-laden beliefs reliable? A causal theory seems to be incompatible with, for example, McKerrow's theory, but could yield interesting insights in other directions.

Railsback explains rhetoric as a means of creating knowledge. Her theory is probably as much ontological as it is epistemic: "Rhetoric is thus a creator of what is known by humankind, both technical and social knowledge" (1983, 363). Creation is a causal process, however, and discussing causal process issues in-depth might fill out theories of the category that she describes.

Epistemology, Ethics, or Both?

Looking toward a more precise understanding of what it means to say that rhetoric is epistemic, one other question arises. Can rhetoricians accomplish their purposes without analyzing and disputing concepts of knowledge, truth, and certainty at all? One might not call such an approach epistemic, but it might address the important problems that Scott raises. Much of the appeal of Scott's essays, one suspects, is due to the fundamentally ethical stance that he advocates for rhetorical discourse. Scott intends his essay to be a refutation of "the assumption . . . that men can possess truth" (1967, 10). However, why does he make such a contention? His primary purpose was never to solve abstruse epistemological problems. Instead, Scott testifies that "uncertainty demands toleration" (10). He continues that: "one who acts without certainty must embrace the responsibility for making his acts the best possible" (16–17). Indeed, in

a later essay, Scott points out the "basically ethical thrust" of his earlier article (1976, 159). Scott states that "I do not value the label 'epistemic' highly. Let it pass" (1990, 302). He argues for tolerance and pluralism, and against dogmatism. He is probably right. He pleads that a rhetorical epistemology will achieve these ends. Maybe so.

One suspects, indeed, that "knowledge" is not really at issue in a fundamental way in any of Scott's papers. Nor is objective certainty, which would be nice to have if it turns out to be possible for us ignorant travelers to the grave to get it on rare occasions. Scott's real purpose is to complain against *subjective* certainty.[7] He argues that people falsely claim certainty when they are not entitled to do so. He points out, correctly, that people are rarely, if ever, entitled to claim exclusive, immutable knowledge of truth. He recognizes the contingent, value-laden quality of rhetorical discourse. He celebrates this as a good thing to have in our uncertain universe. Scott states: "Many of our human failings in becoming and remaining civilized grow out of the false consciousness of certainty" (2000, 109). This hits the nail right on the head, and no objection can be raised to this fundamental claim.

Thus, once one cuts through the terminological problems, equivocations, and red herrings that have troubled this literature over the years, one realizes that Scott indeed is, and has been, onto something. The general feeling of rhetoricians that Scott's theory is important is fully justified. The mistake is to think that it is necessary to quarrel with the concepts of knowledge, truth, or objective certainty in order to achieve such ethical ends. Scott's claim could best be established by presenting evidence of the fallibility of the human mind. That people need to engage in rhetoric despite being fallible might lead us to suspect that rhetoric is doxastic, but there is no need.as far as the ethical argument goes.to establish that it is epistemic.

Aristotle wrote that rhetoric is the counterpart or contrary of dialectic (1991, 1354a; see 28n2). Rhetoric and dialectic do not contradict; rhetoric advocates and dialectic investigates. Dialectic, however, is in part a communicative process, a matter of give-and-take. Cicero felt that Plato's dialogues left nothing proven for sure; Plato's disputants argued both sides of the issue (Sloane 1997). Sloane discusses the practice of rhetoricians—and dialecticians too, of course—of arguing both sides of an issue. "If dialectic's function is to find a probable truth through formal validity," Sloane summarizes, "the function of rhetoric is to discern the available means of persuading people." In both, Sloane continues, "the ends are achieved by indifferently setting up equally probable arguments pro and con" (288). This does not make rhetoric an alternative to epistemology, but its counterpart, more or less in Aristotle's sense. People interact to come to mutual or opposite understandings of truth as best they can. Thus, rhetoric may help us to understand how people examine their subjective uncertainty, and Scott's approach could be vindicated.

However, scholars may wish to continue to investigate rhetoric as epistemic, and their investigations may bring considerable insights into rhetoric and epistemology alike. This inquiry must, however, define terms more carefully and consistently. To explore the relationship between rhetoric and knowledge, an analysis along one of the lines of inquiry suggested in this essay will be, one hopes, more precise and less, well, mystical, than many of those that have been circulating in the literature. Alternatively, an ethical focus could develop Scott's issues without bringing up the issue of objective certainty. It would be a mistake to accept the rhetoric-as-epistemic literature in its present form, but might be an even worse mistake to abandon Scott's insights entirely.

NOTES

1. Brinton notes the importance of the distinction between epistemology and ontology. He clarifies that "insofar as rhetoric-as-epistemic represents a serious break with traditional rhetorical theory, its claim that rhetoric is a way of knowing must be understood as grounded in a view that rhetoric is in some significant way a creator of what is known" (1982, 158).

2. Various writers feel that traces of this view can be found as far back as Aristotle, a controversial point that can await discussion at some other occasion. See, e.g., Leff (1978, 79).

3. This is not the same distinction that Brinton makes "between objective truth and subjective truth" in William James's psychology, although there are obvious analogies (1982, 165–66).

4. Cherwitz and Hikins distinguish between certainty as "*rational judgment*" and certainty as "a *dogmatic state*" (1986, 35; emphasis in the original). To his credit, Cherwitz has commented on the "lack of clarification and definition" in theories that rhetoric is epistemic (1984, 198–235).

5. Schiappa points out that a broad definition "does

not necessarily make the term meaningless or useless" (2001, 268). This is true, but does not save the rhetoric-is-epistemic theorists, who must explain why a claim that translates to "language use is epistemic" is not mundane.

6. The citation is to Butchvarov (1970, 25). On my reading of this passage, Butchvarov does discuss the traditional definition that knowledge is justified true belief, but for the purpose of refuting it in its usual form. Butchvarov states that the traditional account of knowledge is not "mistaken," but continues that "it is hopelessly inadequate" (1970, 26). Butchvarov also agrees that Gettier has identified "another paradoxical consequence of this conception of knowledge" (58n27).

7. To give Scott his due, his argument would have weight against Ayer's definition of knowledge, cited above.

WORKS CITED

Alston, William P. 1989a. "A 'Doxastic Practice' Approach to Epistemology." In *Knowledge and Skepticism*, ed. Marjorie Clay and Keith Lehrer, 1–29. Boulder, CO: Westview Press.

———. 1989b. *Epistemic Justification: Essays in the Theory of Knowledge*. Ithaca: Cornell UP.

Aristotle. 1991. *On Rhetoric: A Theory of Civic Discourse*. Trans. George A. Kennedy. New York: Oxford University Press.

Armstrong, D. M. 1973. *Belief, Truth and Knowledge*. Cambridge, UK: Cambridge University Press.

Audi, Robert. 1998. *Epistemology: A Contemporary Introduction to the Theory of Knowledge*. Routledge Contemporary Introductions to Philosophy, ed. Paul K. Moser. London: Routledge.

Ayer, A. J. 1957. *The Problem of Knowledge*. Harmondsworth, Middlesex, UK: Penguin.

Brinton, Alan. 1982. "William James and the Epistemic View of Rhetoric." *Quarterly Journal of Speech* 68:158–69.

Brummett, Barry. 1976. "Some Implications of 'Process' or 'Intersubjectivity': Postmodern Rhetoric." *Philosophy and Rhetoric* 9:21–51.

———. 1990. "A Eulogy for Epistemic Rhetoric." *Quarterly Journal of Speech* 76:69–72.

Bryant, Donald C. 1953. "Rhetoric: Its Functions and Its Scope." *Quarterly Journal of Speech* 39:401–24.

Butchvarov, Panayot. 1970. *The Concept of Knowledge*. Evanston, IL: Northwestern University Press.

Campbell, Karlyn Kohrs. 1996. *The Rhetorical Act*. 2nd ed. Belmont, CA: Wadsworth.

Cherwitz, Richard A. 1984. "Rhetoric as Epistemic: A Conversation with Richard A. Cherwitz." Charles W. Kneupper, interviewer. *Pre/Text* 5:198–235.

Cherwitz, Richard A., and James A. Hikins. 1986. *Communication and Knowledge: An Investigation in Rhe-*

torical Epistemology. Columbia: University of South Carolina Press.

Cyphert, Dale. 2001. "Ideology, Knowledge and Text: Pulling at the Knot in Ariadne's Thread." *Quarterly Journal of Speech* 87:378–95.

Farrell, Thomas B. 1990. "From the Parthenon to the Bassinet: Death and Rebirth along the Epistemic Trail." *Quarterly Journal of Speech* 76:78–84.

Foss, Sonja K. 1989. *Rhetorical Criticism: Exploration and Practice*. 2nd ed. Prospect Heights, IL: Waveland Press.

Gettier, Edmund. 1963. "Is Justified True Belief Knowledge?" *Analysis* 23:121–23.

Goldman, Alvin I. 1976. "Discrimination and Perceptual Knowledge." *Journal of Philosophy* 73:771–91.

Goldman, Alan H. 1988. *Empirical Knowledge*. Berkeley: University of California Press.

Herrick, James A. 1997. *The History and Theory of Rhetoric: An Introduction*. Scottsdale, AZ: Gorsuch Scarisbrick.

Leff, Michael C. 1978. "In Search of Ariadne's Thread: A Review of the Recent Literature on Rhetorical Theory." *Central States Speech Journal* 29:74–91.

Lehrer, Keith. 1965. "Knowledge, Truth, and Evidence." *Analysis* 25:168–75.

_____. 1970. "The Fourth Condition of Knowledge: A Defense." *Review of Metaphysics* 24:122–28.

McKerrow, Ray E. 1977. "Rhetorical Validity: An Analysis of Three Perspectives on the Justification of Rhetorical Argument." *Journal of the American Forensic Association* 13:133–41.

Plato. 1961a. *Gorgias*. In *The Collected Dialogues of Plato Including the Letters*, trans. W. D. Woodhead, ed. Edith Hamilton and Huntington Cairns, Bollingen Series 71, 229–307. Princeton, NJ: Princeton University Press.

_____. 1961b. *Theaetetus*. In *The Collected Dialogues of Plato Including the Letters*, trans. F. M. Cornford, ed. Edith Hamilton and Huntington Cairns, Bollingen Series 71, 845–919. Princeton, NJ: Princeton University Press.

Railsback, Celeste Condit. 1983. "Beyond Rhetorical Relativism: A Structural-Material Model of Truth and Objective Reality." *Quarterly Journal of Speech* 69:351–63.

Schiappa, Edward. 2001. "Second Thoughts on the Critiques of Big Rhetoric." *Philosophy and Rhetoric* 34:260–74.

Schiappa, Edward, Alan G. Gross, Raymie E. McKerrow, and Robert L. Scott. 2002. "Rhetorical Studies as Reeducation or Redescription?: A Response to Cherwitz and Hikins." *Quarterly Journal of Speech* 88:112–20.

Scott, Robert L. 1967. "On Viewing Rhetoric as Epistemic." *Central States Speech Journal* 18:9–17 [reprinted in this volume].

_____. 1973. "On *Not* Defining Rhetoric." *Philosophy and Rhetoric* 6:81–96.

_____. 1976. "On Viewing Rhetoric as Epistemic: Ten Years Later." *Central States Speech Journal* 27:258–66.

_____. 1990. "Epistemic Rhetoric and Criticism: Where Barry Brummett Goes Wrong." *Quarterly Journal of Speech* 76:300–303.

_____. 2000. "Between Silence and Certainty: A Codicil to 'Dialectical Tensions of Speaking and Silence.'" *Quarterly Journal of Speech* 86:108–10.

Scott, Robert L., and James F. Klumpp. 1984. "A Dear Searcher into Comparisons: The Rhetoric of Ellen Goodman." *Quarterly Journal of Speech* 70:69–79.

Sloane, Thomas O. 1997. *On the Contrary: The Protocol of Traditional Rhetoric*. Washington, DC: Catholic University of America Press.

Sullivan, Dale L. 1992. "*Kairos* and the Rhetoric of Belief." *Quarterly Journal of Speech* 78:317–32.

Wittgenstein, Ludwig. 1969. *On Certainty*. Trans. Denis Paul and G. E. M. Anscombe. Ed. E. E. M. Anscombe and G. H. von Wright. New York: J. and J. Harper Editions.

PART III
THE EVOLUTION
OF THE RHETORICAL SITUATION

Rhetorical discourse is frequently distinguished from philosophical, scientific, and artistic discourses because it is judged according to criteria of particularity, contingency, and propriety, no less than how effective it is in achieving its ends. Whereas philosophical and scientific discourses typically seek universal, transcendent knowledge or truth, rhetorical discourse seeks timely and fitting action. Whereas great art is judged for its "timeless" quality, great rhetoric is seen as that which aptly responds to a particular moment in historical time. Put simply, while other forms of discourse have generally been treated as if they aspired to a universalized context, or indeed to pure and contextless meaning, rhetoric has generally been understood in terms of its linkages to local moments and the exigencies of political pragmatism. In contrast to philosophy, science, and art, then, rhetoric is a discourse that addresses pressing needs in particular situations.

Although rhetoric has long been defined by its pragmatic purpose and context, this is not to say that the nature of the rhetorical situation is either self-evident or obvious. Rhetorical theory in the late twentieth century occupied itself in substantial measure with filling out the theoretical implications and dimensions of the historical bindings of rhetorical discourse. Lloyd F. Bitzer initiated a significant phase of this analysis in 1968 in the inaugural issue of the then-new journal *Philosophy and Rhetoric*. In this essay, titled "The Rhetorical Situation," Bitzer outlined the working assumptions that had guided the practice of rhetorical critics in the first half of the twentieth century. According to Bitzer, human relations operated in the context of rhetorical situations governed by "exigences"—that is, social, political, economic, and ethical urgencies that invited discursive responses. Rhetoric occurred when a speaker responded to the perception of exigence by addressing an audience that could be persuaded to make changes that would modify the urgency.

Bitzer's analysis of the rhetorical situation derived from his philosophical and epistemological commitments to realism. From this perspective, an exigence is an objective occurrence that demands particular forms of response. The rhetor who neglects to address the factors demanded by an exigent situation thus fails (at least potentially) to produce an adequate rhetorical response. So, for example, on the occasion of a eulogy for a prominent politician, Bitzer would argue that the rhetorical situation would call for the speaker to praise the important virtues and accomplishments of the deceased. If the speaker delivering the eulogy chose to ignore such conventional expectations and to focus explicitly upon the deceased's moral shortcomings and failures, Bitzer would judge that he or she had failed to respond appropriately to the exigency that called forth the speech.

Almost immediately, Richard E. Vatz and others (Consigny, 1974; Patton, 1979) challenged Bitzer's realism and its implications for how we understand the importance of a rhetorical situation. In an essay titled "The Myth of the Rhetorical Situation," Vatz maintained that exigences are not the products of objective events, but rather are matters of perception and interpretation. Hence, to say that exigences call forth rhetoric is to put the cart before the horse; rather, Vatz argued, we would be better served if we understood the sense in which rhetoric creates the perception of exigence. Bitzer had used as a prime example the way in which the assassination of President John F. Kennedy constituted a rhetorical situation that demanded the speaking of a eulogy as a fitting response. Vatz called this example into question, arguing that the particular situation it described—at least as Bitzer characterized it—might be too ritualistic and conventional to serve as a paradigm case for fully understanding the complexities of the relationship between "rhetoric" and "situation." Less conventionalized examples, he suggested, might lead to a richer understanding of how situations themselves are rhetorically constructed.

Whereas Vatz challenged Bitzer's notion that the exigence dictated the appropriate response, and thus maintained a controlling force over the speaker, Barbara A. Biesecker argued that we need to reconsider the very nature of the two concepts "situation" and "speaker." Biesecker suggested that Vatz's formulation was correct as far as it went, but in the end it simply reversed the relationship that Bitzer had described. Instead of viewing context as the controlling factor in a rhetorical situation, it granted some sense of overarching control to the speaker. According to Biesecker, this merely replaced a realist conception of "context" as objective with a realist conception of the "rhetor" or "speaker" as an autonomous, self-directed agent who consciously constructs exigences according to a carefully planned set of interests. From this perspective, she argued, the members of the audience were similar to rhetors in their autonomy and willfulness, albeit more passive. In "Rethinking the Rhetorical Situation from within the Thematic of *Différance*," Biesecker offered a new tool for disrupting such overly simple understandings of rhetors and their audiences. This tool is called "deconstruction," and it derives from the French theorist Jacques Derrida. Deconstruction urges us to see that the identities of audiences and speakers are themselves constructed in the process of the rhetorical transaction. Rhetoric is not, therefore, a simple linear process by which one individual attempts to influence others, but a complex interactive process whereby persons and collectivities articulate their shifting identities to each other within changing historical circumstances.

More recently, even the notion of "situation" as a contextual marker has been questioned. While the concept of exigence still retains a useful place in discussing numerous rhetorical acts, other examples of rhetoric point toward larger, less stable, and more fluid practices. In "Unframing Models of Public Distribution: From Rhetorical Situation to Rhetorical Ecologies," Jenny Edbauer draws from recent developments in the theorizing of publics (addressed in more detail in Part IV). Noting that developments in the theory of a rhetorical situation point away from rigid sender–receiver models and toward more open-ended conceptions, Edbauer argues for a wholesale reevaluation of the contexts where rhetoric occurs. Drawing from scholar Louise Weatherbee Phelps, she urges that rhetorical acts exist beyond discrete boundaries. Whereas "situation" suggests fixed localities, "network" points toward fluid interactions. For Edbauer, rhetoric is not a thing contained within situations; rather, it is a thing distributed, modified, and adjusted according to the needs of practitioners and their lived experience. Using the "Keep Austin Weird" campaign as her artifact, Edbauer points out how the initial campaign served to usher in other rhetorical acts that appropriated and transformed elements to serve different needs. In short, she argues that the term "ecologies" better explains the flow of rhetoric than "situations," focusing our attention on how rhetoric moves beyond sometimes arbitrary borders.

The notion of the rhetorical situation has thus maintained an important place in theorizing contemporary rhetoric. At the same time, the elemental components remain open to critique and, as Edbauer suggests, to revision. Bitzer offers up a realist position where exigences are observable facts to be acted upon. Vatz points toward the creative nature of the rhetorical act, to the choice to make certain things (and not others) salient. Biesecker adjusts focus on the power of rhetoric to influence the audience's sense of identity and positionality. Edbauer goes even further, urging that certain acts of rhetoric go farther than any of the previous theorists suggested. Traditional models of rhetoric remain valuable, and certain rhetorical acts remain localized. But contemporary methods of transmission will continue to test the boundaries of rhetoric and the range of its impact.

ADDITIONAL READINGS

Bitzer, Lloyd F. (1980). "Functional Communication: A Situational Perspective." In E. White, ed., *Rhetoric in Transition: Studies in the Nature and Uses of Rhetoric* (State College: Pennsylvania State University Press), 21–38.

Consigny, Scott. (1974). "Rhetoric and Its Situations." *Philosophy and Rhetoric* 7: 172–182.

Garret, Mary, and Xiaosui Xiao. (1993). "The Rhetorical Situation Revisited." *Rhetoric Society Quarterly* 23: 30–40.

McGee, Michael C. (1977). "The Fall of Wellington: A Case Study of the Relationship Between Theory, Practice, and Rhetoric in History." *Quarterly Journal of Speech* 63: 28–42.

Miller, Carolyn R. (1984). "Genre as Social Action." *Quarterly Journal of Speech* 70: 151–67.

Patton, John. (1979). "Causation and Creativity in Rhetorical Situations: Distinctions and Implications." *Quarterly Journal of Speech* 65: 36–55.

Smith, Craig R., and Scott Lybarger. (1996). "Bitzer's Model Reconstructed." *Communication Quarterly* 44: 197–213.

Tompkins, Phillip K., John H. Patton, and Lloyd Bitzer [Discussants]. (1980). "The Forum." *Quarterly Journal of Speech* 66: 85–95.

The Rhetorical Situation

Lloyd F. Bitzer

If someone says, That is a dangerous situation, his words suggest the presence of events, persons, or objects which threaten him, someone else, or something of value. If someone remarks, I find myself in an embarrassing situation, again the statement implies certain situational characteristics. If someone remarks that he found himself in an ethical situation, we understand that he probably either contemplated or made some choice of action from a sense of duty or obligation or with a view to the Good. In other words, there are circumstances of this or that kind of structure which are recognized as ethical, dangerous, or embarrassing. What characteristics, then, are implied when one refers to "the rhetorical situation"—the context in which speakers or writers create discourse? Perhaps this question is puzzling because "situation" is not a standard term in the vocabulary of rhetorical theory. "Audience" is standard; so also are "speaker," "subject," "occasion," and "speech." If I were to ask, "What is a rhetorical audience?" or "What is a rhetorical subject?," the reader would catch the meaning of my question.

When I ask, What is a rhetorical situation?, I want to know the nature of those contexts in which speakers or writers create rhetorical discourse: How should they be described? What are their characteristics? Why and how do they result in the creation of rhetoric? By analogy, a theorist of science might well ask, What are the characteristics of situations which inspire scientific thought? A philosopher might ask, What is

the nature of the situation in which a philosopher "does philosophy"? And a theorist of poetry might ask, How shall we describe the context in which poetry comes into existence?

The presence of rhetorical discourse obviously indicates the presence of a rhetorical situation. The Declaration of Independence, Lincoln's Gettysburg Address, Churchill's Address on Dunkirk, John F. Kennedy's Inaugural Address—each is a clear instance of rhetoric and each indicates the presence of a situation. While the existence of a rhetorical address is a reliable sign of the existence of a situation, it does not follow that a situation exists only when the discourse exists. Each reader probably can recall a specific time and place when there was opportunity to speak on some urgent matter, and after the opportunity was gone he created in private thought the speech he should have uttered earlier in the situation. It is clear that situations are not always accompanied by discourse. Nor should we assume that a rhetorical address gives existence to the situation; on the contrary, it is the situation which calls the discourse into existence. Clement Attlee once said that Winston Churchill went around looking for "finest hours." The point to observe is that Churchill found them—the crisis situations—and spoke in response to them.

No major theorist has treated rhetorical situation thoroughly as a distinct subject in rhetorical theory; many ignore it. Those rhetoricians who discuss situation do so indirectly—as does Aristotle, for example, who is led to consider situation when be treats types of discourse. None, to my knowledge, has asked the nature of rhetorical situation. Instead, rhetoricians have asked: What is the process by which the orator creates and presents discourse? What is the nature of rhetorical discourse? What sorts of interaction occur between speaker, audience, subject, and occasion? Typically the questions which trigger theories of rhetoric focus upon the orator's method or upon the discourse itself, rather than upon the situation which invites the orator's application of his method and the creation of discourse. Thus rhetoricians distinguish among and characterize the types of speeches (forensic, deliberative, epideictic); they treat issues, types of proof, lines of argument, strategies of ethical and emotional persuasion, the parts of a discourse and the functions of these parts, qualities of styles, figures of speech. They cover approximately the same materials, the formal aspects of rhetorical method and discourse, whether focusing upon method, product, or process; while conceptions of situation are implicit in some theories of rhetoric, none explicitly treat the formal aspects of situation.

I hope that enough has been said to show that the question What is a rhetorical situation? is not an idle one. I propose in what follows to set forth part of a theory of situation. This essay, therefore, should be understood as an attempt to revive the notion of rhetorical situation, to provide at least the outline of an adequate conception of it, and to establish it as a controlling and fundamental concern of rhetorical theory.

I

It seems clear that rhetoric is situational. In saying this, I do not mean merely that understanding a speech hinges upon understanding the context of meaning in which the speech is located. Virtually no utterance is fully intelligible unless meaning-context and utterance are understood; this is true of rhetorical and non-rhetorical discourse. Meaning-context is a general condition of human communication and is not synonymous with rhetorical situation. Nor do I mean merely that rhetoric occurs in a setting which involves interaction of speaker, audience, subject, and communicative purpose. This is too general, since many types of utterances—philosophical, scientific, poetic, and rhetorical—occur in such settings. Nor would I equate rhetorical situation with persuasive situation, which exists whenever an audience can be changed in belief or action by means of speech. Every audience at any moment is capable of being changed in some way by speech; persuasive situation is altogether general.

Finally, I do not mean that a rhetorical discourse must be embedded in historic context in the sense that a living tree must be rooted in soil. A tree does not obtain its character-as-tree from the soil, but rhetorical discourse, I shall argue, does obtain its character-as-rhetorical from the situation which generates it. Rhetorical works belong to the class of things which obtain their character from the circumstances of the historic context in which they occur. A rhetorical work is analogous to a moral action rather than to a tree. An act is moral because it is an act performed in a situation of a certain kind; similarly, a work is rhetorical because it is a response to a situation of a certain kind.

In order to clarify rhetoric-as-essentially-related-to-situation, we should acknowledge a viewpoint that is commonplace but fundamental: a work of rhetoric is pragmatic; it comes into existence for the sake of something beyond itself; it functions ultimately to produce action or change in the world; it performs some task. In short, rhetoric is a mode of altering reality, not by the direct application of energy to objects, but by the creation of discourse which changes reality through the mediation of thought and action. The rhetor alters reality by bringing into existence a discourse of such a character that the audience, in thought and action, is so engaged that it becomes mediator of change. In this sense rhetoric is always persuasive.

To say that rhetorical discourse comes into being in order to effect change is altogether general. We need to understand that a particular discourse comes into existence because of some specific condition or situation which invites utterance. Bronislaw Malinowski refers to just this sort of situation in his discussion of primitive language, which he finds to be essentially pragmatic and "embedded in situation." He describes a party of fishermen in the Trobriand Islands whose functional speech occurs in a "context of situation."

> The canoes glide slowly and noiselessly, punted by men especially good at this task and always used for it. Other experts who know the bottom of the lagoon . . . are on the look-out for fish. . . . Customary signs, or sounds or words are uttered. Sometimes a sentence full of technical references to the channels or patches on the lagoon has to

be spoken; sometimes . . . a conventional cry is uttered. . . . Again, a word of command is passed here and there, a technical expression or explanation which serves to harmonize their behavior towards other men. . . . An animated scene, full of movement, follows, and now that the fish are in their power the fishermen speak loudly, and give vent to their feelings. Short, telling exclamations fly about, which might be rendered by such words as: "Pull in," "Let go," "Shift further," "Lift the net."

In this whole scene, "each utterance is essentially bound up with the context of situation and with the aim of the pursuit. . . . The structure of all this linguistic material is inextricably mixed up with, and dependent upon, the course of the activity in which the utterances are embedded." Later the observer remarks: "In its primitive uses, language functions as a link in concerted human activity, as a piece of human behaviour. It is a mode of action and not an instrument of reflection."[1]

These statements about primitive language and the "context of situation" provide for us a preliminary model of rhetorical situation. Let us regard rhetorical situation as a natural context of persons, events, objects, relations, and an exigence which strongly invites utterance; this invited utterance participates naturally in the situation, is in many instances necessary to the completion of situational activity, and by means of its participation with situation obtains its meaning and its rhetorical character. In Malinowski's example, the situation is the fishing expedition consisting of objects, persons, events, and relations—and the ruling exigence, the success of the hunt. The situation dictates the sorts of observations to be made; it dictates the significant physical and verbal responses; and, we must admit, it constrains the words which are uttered in the same sense that it constrains the physical acts of paddling the canoes and throwing the nets. The verbal responses to the demands imposed by this situation are clearly as functional and necessary as the physical responses.

Traditional theories of rhetoric have dealt, of course, not with the sorts of primitive utterances described by Malinowski—"stop here," "throw the nets," "move closer"—but with larger units of speech which come more readily under the guidance of artistic principle and method. The difference between oratory and primitive utterance, however, is not a difference in function; the clear instances of rhetorical discourse and the fishermen's utterances are similarly functional and similarly situational. Observing both the traditions of

the expedition and the facts before him, the leader of the fishermen finds himself obliged to speak at a given moment—to command, to supply information, to praise or blame—to respond appropriately to the situation. Clear instances of artistic rhetoric exhibit the same character: Cicero's speeches against Catiline were called forth by a specific union of persons, events, objects, and relations, and by an exigence which amounted to an imperative stimulus; the speeches in the Senate rotunda three days after the assassination of the President of the United States were actually required by the situation. So controlling is situation that we should consider it the very ground of rhetorical activity, whether that activity is primitive and productive of a simple utterance or artistic and productive of the Gettysburg Address.

Hence, to say that rhetoric is situational means: (1) rhetorical discourse comes into existence as a response to situation, in the same sense that an answer comes into existence in response to a question, or a solution in response to a problem; (2) a speech is given *rhetorical* significance by the situation, just as a unit of discourse is given significance *as* answer or *as* solution by the question or problem; (3) a rhetorical situation must exist as a necessary condition of rhetorical discourse, just as a question must exist as a necessary condition of an answer; (4) many questions go unanswered and many problems remain unsolved—similarly, many rhetorical situations mature and decay without giving birth to rhetorical utterance; (5) a situation is rhetorical insofar as it needs and invites discourse capable of participating with situation and thereby altering its reality; (6) discourse is rhetorical insofar as it functions (or seeks to function) as a fitting response to a situation which needs and invites it. (7) Finally, the situation controls the rhetorical response in the same sense that the question controls the answer and the problem controls the solution. Not the rhetor and not persuasive intent, but the situation is the source and ground of rhetorical activity—and, I should add, of rhetorical criticism.

II

Let us now amplify the nature of situation by providing a formal definition and examining constituents. Rhetorical situation may be defined as a complex of persons, events, objects, and relations presenting an actual or potential exigence which can be completely or partially removed if discourse, introduced into the situation, can so constrain human decision or action as to bring about the significant modification of the exigence. Prior to the creation and presentation of discourse, there are three constituents of any rhetorical situation: the first is the *exigence*; the second and third are elements of the complex, namely, the *audience* to be constrained in decision and action, and the *constraints* which influence the rhetor and can be brought to bear upon the audience.

Any *exigence* is an imperfection marked by urgency; it is a defect, an obstacle, something waiting to be done, a thing which is other than it should be. In almost any sort of context, there will be numerous exigences, but not all are elements of a rhetorical situation—not all are rhetorical exigences. An exigence which cannot be modified is not rhetorical; thus, whatever comes about of necessity and cannot be changed—death, winter, and some natural disasters, for instance—are exigences to be sure, but they are not rhetorical. Further, an exigence which can be modified only by means other than discourse is not rhetorical; thus, an exigence is not rhetorical when its modification requires merely one's own action or the application of a tool, but neither requires nor invites the assistance of discourse. An exigence is rhetorical when it is capable of positive modification and when positive modification requires discourse or can be assisted by discourse. For example, suppose that a man's acts are injurious to others and that the quality of his acts can be changed only if discourse is addressed to him; the exigence—his injurious acts—is then unmistakably rhetorical. The pollution of our air is also a rhetorical exigence because its positive modification—reduction of pollution—strongly invites the assistance of discourse producing public awareness, indignation, and action of the right kind. Frequently rhetors encounter exigences which defy easy classification because of the absence of information enabling precise analysis and certain judgment they may or may not be rhetorical. An attorney whose client has been convicted may strongly believe that a higher court would reject his appeal to have the verdict overturned, but because the matter is uncertain—because the exigence *might* be rhetorical—he elects to appeal. In this and similar instances of indeterminate exigences the rhetor's decision to speak is based mainly upon the urgency of the exigence and the probability that the exigence is rhetorical.

In any rhetorical situation there will be at least one controlling exigence which functions as the organizing principle: it specifies the audience to be addressed and the change to be effected. The exigence may or may not be perceived clearly by the rhetor or other persons in the situation; it may be strong or weak depending upon the clarity of their perception and the degree of their interest in it; it may be real or unreal depending on the facts of the case; it may be important or trivial; it may be such that discourse can completely remove it, or it may persist in spite of repeated modifications; it may be completely familiar—one of a type of exigences occurring frequently in our experience—or it may be totally new, unique. When it is perceived and when it is strong and important, then it constrains the thought and action of the perceiver who may respond rhetorically if he is in a position to do so.

The second constituent is the *audience*. Since rhetorical discourse produces change by influencing the decision and action of persons who function as mediators of change, it follows that rhetoric always requires an audience—even in those cases when a person engages himself or ideal mind as audience. It is clear also that a rhetorical audience must be distinguished from a body of mere hearers or readers: properly speaking, a rhetorical audience consists only of those persons who are capable of being influenced by discourse and of being mediators of change.

Neither scientific nor poetic discourse requires an audience in the same sense. Indeed, neither requires an audience in order to produce its end; the scientist can produce a discourse expressive or generative of knowledge without engaging another mind, and the poet's creative purpose is accomplished when the work is composed. It is true, of course, that scientists and poets present their works to audiences, but their audiences are not necessarily rhetorical. The scientific audience consists of persons capable of receiving knowledge, and the poetic audience, of persons capable of participating in aesthetic experiences induced by the poetry. But the rhetorical audience must be capable of serving as mediator of the change which the discourse functions to produce.

Besides exigence and audience, every rhetorical situation contains a set of *constraints* made up of persons, events, objects, and relations which are parts of the situation because they have the power to constrain decision and action needed to modify the exigence. Standard sources of constraint include beliefs, attitudes, documents, facts, traditions, images, interests, motives, and the like; and when the orator enters the situation, his discourse not only harnesses constraints given by situation but provides additional important constraints—

for example, his personal character, his logical proofs, and his style. There are two main classes of constraints: (1) those originated or managed by the rhetor and his method (Aristotle called these "artistic proofs"), and (2) those other constraints, in the situation, which may be operative (Aristotle's "inartistic proofs"). Both classes must be divided so as to separate those constraints that are proper from those that are improper.

These three constituents—exigence, audience, constraints—comprise everything relevant in a rhetorical situation. When the orator, invited by situation, enters it and creates and presents discourse, then both he and his speech are additional constituents.

III

I have broadly sketched a conception of rhetorical situation and discussed constituents. The following are general characteristics or features.

1. Rhetorical discourse is called into existence by situation; the situation which the rhetor perceives amounts to an invitation to create and present discourse. The clearest instances of rhetorical speaking and writing are strongly invited—often required. The situation generated by the assassination of President Kennedy was so highly structured and compelling that one could predict with near certainty the types and themes of forthcoming discourse. With the first reports of the assassination, there immediately developed a most urgent need for information; in response, reporters created hundreds of messages. Later as the situation altered, other exigences arose: the fantastic events in Dallas had to be explained; it was necessary to eulogize the dead President; the public needed to be assured that the transfer of government to new hands would be orderly. These messages were not idle performances. The historic situation was so compelling and clear that the responses were created almost out of necessity. The responses—news reports, explanations, eulogies—participated with the situation and positively modified the several exigences. Surely the power of situation is evident when one can predict that such discourse will be uttered. How else explain the phenomenon? One cannot say that the situation is the function of the speaker's intention, for in this case the speakers' intentions were determined by the situation. One cannot say that the rhetorical transaction is simply a response of the speaker to the demands or expectations of an audience, for the expectations of the audience were themselves keyed to a tragic historic fact. Also, we must recognize that there came into existence countless eulogies to John F. Kennedy that never reached a public; they were filed, entered in diaries, or created in thought.

In contrast, imagine a person spending his time writing eulogies of men and women who never existed: his speeches meet no rhetorical situations; they are summoned into existence not by real events, but by his own imagination. They may exhibit formal features which we consider rhetorical—such as ethical and emotional appeals, and stylistic patterns; conceivably one of these fictive eulogies is even persuasive to someone; yet all remain unrhetorical unless, through the oddest of circumstances, one of them by chance should fit a situation. Neither the presence of formal features in the discourse nor persuasive effect in a reader or hearer can be regarded as reliable marks of rhetorical discourse: A speech will be rhetorical when it is a response to the kind of situation which is rhetorical.

2. Although rhetorical situation invites response, it obviously does not invite just any response. Thus the second characteristic of rhetorical situation is that it invites a fitting response, a response that fits the situation. Lincoln's Gettysburg Address was a most *fitting* response to the relevant features of the historic context which invited its existence and gave it rhetorical significance. Imagine for a moment the Gettysburg Address entirely separated from its situation and existing for us independent of any rhetorical context: as a discourse that does not "fit" any rhetorical situation, it becomes either poetry or declamation, without rhetorical significance. In reality, however, the address continues to have profound rhetorical value precisely because some features of the Gettysburg situation persist; and the Gettysburg Address continues to participate with situation and to alter it.

Consider another instance. During one week of the 1964 presidential campaign, three events of national and international significance all but obscured the campaign: Khrushchev was suddenly deposed, China exploded an atomic bomb, and in England the Conservative Party was defeated by Labour. Any student of rhetoric could have given odds that President Johnson, in a major address, would speak to the significance of these events, and he did; his response to the situation generated by the events was fitting. Suppose that the President had treated not these events and their significance but the national budget, or imagine that he had reminisced about his childhood on a Texas farm. The critic of rhetoric would have said rightly, "He missed the mark; his speech did not fit; he did not speak to the pressing issues—the rhetorical situation shaped by the three crucial events of the week demanded a response, and he failed to provide the proper one."

3. If it makes sense to say that situation invites a "fitting" response, then situation must somehow prescribe the response which fits. To say that a rhetorical response fits a situation is to say that it meets the requirements established by the situation. A situation which is strong and clear dictates the purpose, theme, matter, and style of the response. Normally, the inauguration of a President of the United States demands an address which speaks to the nation's purposes, the central national and international problems, the unity of contesting parties; it demands speech style marked by dignity. What is evidenced on this occasion is the power of situation to constrain a fitting response. One might say metaphorically that every situation prescribes its fitting response; the rhetor may or may not read the prescription accurately.

4. The exigence and the complex of persons, objects, events, and relations which generate rhetorical discourse are located in reality, are objective and publicly observable historic facts in the world we experience, are therefore available for scrutiny by an observer or critic who attends to them. To say the situation is objective, publicly observable, and historic means that it is real or genuine—that our critical examination will certify its existence. Real situations are to be distinguished from sophistic ones in which, for example, a contrived exigence is asserted to be real; from spurious situations in which the existence or alleged existence of constituents is the result of error or ignorance; and from fantasy in which exigence, audience, and constraints may all be the imaginary objects of a mind at play.

The rhetorical situation as real is to be distinguished also from a fictive rhetorical situation. The speech of a character in a novel or play may be clearly required by a fictive rhetorical situation, a situation established by the story itself; but the speech is not genuinely rhetorical, even though, considered in itself, it looks exactly like a courtroom address or a senate speech. It is realistic, made so by fictive context. But the situation is not real, not grounded in history; neither the fictive situation nor the discourse generated by it is rhetorical. We should note, however, that the fictive rhetorical discourse within a play or novel may become genuinely rhetorical outside fictive context—if there is a real situation for which the discourse is a rhetorical response. Also, of course, the play or novel itself may be understood as a rhetorical response having poetic form.

5. Rhetorical situations exhibit structures which are simple or complex, and more or less organized. A situation's structure is simple when there are relatively few elements which must be made to interact; the fishing expedition is a case in point—there is a clear and easy relationship among utterances, the audiences, constraints, and exigence. Franklin D. Roosevelt's brief Declaration of War speech is another example: the message exists as a response to one clear exigence easily perceived by one major audience, and the one overpowering constraint is the necessity of war. On the other hand, the structure of a situation is complex when many elements must be made to interact: practically any presidential political campaign provides numerous complex rhetorical situations.

A situation, whether simple or complex, will be highly structured or loosely structured. It is highly structured when all of its elements are located and readied for the task to be performed. Malinowski's example, the fishing expedition, is a situation which is relatively simple and highly structured; everything is ordered to the task to be performed. The usual courtroom case is a good example of a situation which is complex and highly structured. The jury is not a random and scattered audience but a selected and concentrated one; it knows its relation to judge, law, defendant, counsels; it is instructed in what to observe and what to disregard. The judge is located and prepared; he knows exactly his relation to jury, law, counsels, defendant. The counsels know the ultimate object of their case; they know what they must prove; they know the audience and can easily reach it. This situation will be even more highly structured if the issue of the case is sharp, the evidence decisive, and the law clear. On the other hand, consider a complex but loosely structured situation: William Lloyd Garrison preaching abolition from town to town. He is actually looking for an audience and for constraints; even when he finds an audience, he does not know that it is a genuinely rhetorical audience—one able to be a mediator of change. Or consider the plight of many contemporary civil rights advocates who, failing to locate compelling constraints and rhetorical audiences, abandon rhetorical discourse in favor of physical action.

Situations may become weakened in structure due to complexity or disconnectedness. A list of causes includes these: (a) a single situation may involve numerous exigences; (b) exigences in the same situation may be incompatible; (c) two or more simultaneous rhetorical situations may compete for our attention, as in some parliamentary debates; (d) at a given moment, persons comprising the audience of situation A may also be the audience of situations B, C, and D; (e) the rhetorical audience may be scattered, uneducated regarding its duties and powers, or it may dissipate; (f) constraints may be limited in number and force, and they may be incompatible. This is enough to suggest the sorts of things which weaken the structure of situations.

6. Finally, rhetorical situations come into existence, then either mature or decay or mature and persist—conceivably some persist indefinitely. In any case, situations grow and come to maturity; they evolve to just the time when a rhetorical discourse would be most fitting. In Malinowski's example, there comes a time in the situation when the leader of the fishermen should say, "Throw the nets." In the situation generated by the assassination of the President, there was a time for giving descriptive accounts of the scene in Dallas, later a time for giving eulogies. In a political campaign, there is a time for generating an issue and a time for answering a charge. Every rhetorical situation in principle evolves to a propitious moment for the fitting rhetorical response. After this moment, most situations decay; we all have the experience of creating a rhetorical response when it is too late to make it public.

Some situations, on the other hand, persist; this is why it is possible to have a body of truly *rhetorical* literature. The Gettysburg Address, Burke's Speech to the Electors of Bristol, Socrates' Apology—these are more than historical documents, more than specimens for stylistic or logical analysis. They exist as rhetorical responses *for us* precisely because they speak to situations which persist—which are in some measure universal.

Due to either the nature of things or convention, or both, some situations recur. The court-room is the locus for several kinds of situations generating the speech of accusation, the speech of defense, the charge to the jury. From day to day, year to year, comparable situations occur, prompting comparable responses; hence rhetorical forms are born and a special vocabulary, grammar, and style are established. This is true also of the situation which invites the inaugural address of a President. The situation recurs and, because we experience situations and the rhetorical responses to them, a form of discourse is not only established but comes to have a power of its own—the tradition itself tends to function as a constraint upon any new response in the form.

IV

In the best of all possible worlds, there would be communication perhaps, but no rhetoric—since exigences would not arise. In our real world, however, rhetorical exigences abound; the world really invites change—change conceived and effected by human agents who quite properly address a mediating audience. The practical justification of rhetoric is analogous to that of scientific inquiry: the world presents objects to be known, puzzles to be resolved, complexities to be understood—hence the practical need for scientific inquiry and discourse; similarly, the world presents imperfections to be modified by means of discourse—hence the practical need for rhetorical investigation and discourse. As a discipline, scientific method is justified philosophically insofar as it provides principles, concepts, and procedures by which we come to know reality; similarly, rhetoric as a discipline is justified philosophically insofar as it provides principles, concepts, and procedures by which we effect valuable changes in reality. Thus rhetoric is distinguished from the mere craft of persuasion which, although it is a legitimate object of scientific investigation, lacks philosophical warrant as a practical discipline.

NOTE

1. "The Problem of Meaning in Primitive Languages," sections 3 and 4. This essay appears as a supplement in Ogden and Richards' *The Meaning of Meaning*.

The Myth of the Rhetorical Situation

Richard E. Vatz

In the opening lines of "The Rhetorical Situation," Lloyd Bitzer states, "if someone says, That is a dangerous situation, his words suggest the presence of events, persons or objects which threaten him, someone else or something of value. If someone remarks, I find myself in an embarrassing situation, again the statement implies certain situational characteristics."[1]

These statements do not imply "situational characteristics" at all. The statements may ostensibly describe situations, but they actually only inform us as to the phenomenological perspective of the speaker. There can be little argument that the speakers *believe* they feel fear or embarrassment. Their statements do not, however, tell us about qualities within the situation. Kenneth Burke once wrote of literary critics who attributed to others the characteristic of seeking escape: "While apparently defining a trait of the person referred to, the term hardly did more than convey the attitude of the person making the reference."[2] The same goes for the attribution of traits to a situation. It is a fitting of a scene into a category or categories found in the head of the observer. No situation can have a nature independent of the perception of its interpreter or independent of the rhetoric with which he chooses to characterize it.

In his article Bitzer states, "Rhetorical discourse is called into existence by situation"[3] and "It seems clear that rhetoric is situational."[4] This perspective on rhetoric and "situation" requires a "real-ist" philosophy of meaning. This philosophy has important and, I believe, unfortunate implications for rhetoric. In this article I plan to discuss Bitzer's view and its implications and suggest a different perspective with a different philosophy of meaning from which to view the relationship between "situations" and rhetoric.

Meaning in Bitzer's "Rhetorical Situation"

Bitzer's perspective emanates from his view of the nature of meaning. Simply stated, Bitzer takes the position that meaning resides in events. As sociologist Herbert Blumer describes this point of view,

> [it is] to regard meaning as intrinsic to the thing that has it, as being a natural part of the objective makeup of the thing. Thus, a chair is clearly a chair in itself, a cow a cow, a rebellion a rebellion, and so forth. Being inherent in the thing that has it, meaning needs merely to be disengaged by observing the objective thing that has the meaning. The meaning emanates, so to speak, from the thing, and as such there is no process involved in its formation; all that is necessary is to recognize the meaning that is there in the thing.[5]

This is Bitzer's point of view: there is an intrinsic nature in events from which rhetoric inexorably follows, or should follow. Bitzer states, "When I ask, What is a rhetorical situation, I want to know the nature of those contexts in which speakers or writers create rhetorical discourse . . . what are their characteristics and why and how do they result in the creation of rhetoric."[6] He later adds, "The situation *dictates* the sorts of observations to be made; it *dictates* the significant physical and verbal responses."[7] This view is reiterated in various forms throughout the article. Situations are discrete and discernible. They have a life of their own independent in meaning of those upon whom they impinge. They may or may not "require" responses. If they do the situation "invites" a response, indeed a "fitting response" almost as a glaring sun requires a shading of the eyes, a clear S-R response.

Bitzer's views are all quite consistent given his Platonist *Weltanschauung*. He sees a world in which "the exigence and the complex of persons, objects, events and relations which generate rhetorical discourse are located in reality, are objective and publicly observable historic facts in the world we experience, are therefore available for scrutiny by an observer or critic who attends to them. To say the situation is objective, publicly observable, and historic means that it is real or genuine—that our critical examination will certify its existence."[8] If the situation is as Bitzer states elsewhere "a natural *context* of persons, events, objects, and *relations*,"[9] it is hard to see how its "existence" can be certified.

Bitzer claims there are three constituents of the rhetorical situation prior to discourse: exigence, audience, and constraints. It is the "exigence" component which interests us most. In describing "exigence" Bitzer most clearly indicates his view of the source of meaning. He states, "Any exigence is an imperfection marked by urgency; it is a defect, an obstacle, something waiting to be done, a thing that is other than it should be."[10] Not only is a "waiting to be done" now existing in the event, but we also learn that it contains an ethical imperative supposedly independent of its interpreters. Bitzer adds that the situation is rhetorical only if something *can* be done, but apparently it is only rhetorical also if something *should* be done. Bitzer seems to imply that the "positive modification" needed for an exigence is clear. He seems to reflect what Richard Weaver called a "melioristic bias." We learn, for example, that the obvious positive modification of pollution of our air is "reduction of pollution." One wonders what the obvious "positive modification" of the military–industrial complex is.

The Myth of the Rhetorical Situation

Fortunately or unfortunately, meaning is not intrinsic in events, facts, people, or "situations," nor are facts "publicly observable." Except for those situations which directly confront our own empirical reality, we learn of facts and events through someone's communicating them to us. This involves a two-part process. First, there is a choice of events to communicate. The world is not a plot of discrete events. The world is a scene of inexhaustible events which all compete to impinge on what Kenneth Burke calls our "sliver of reality."

Bitzer argues that the nature of the context determines the rhetoric. But one never runs out of context. One never runs out of facts to describe a situation. What was the "situation" during the Vietnam conflict? What was the situation of the 1972 elections? What is any historical situation? The facts or events communicated to us are *choices*, by our sources of information. As Murray Edelman points out in *Politics as Symbolic Action*, "People can use only an infinitesimal fraction of the information reaching them. The critical question, therefore, is what accounts for the choice by political spectators and participants of what to organize into a meaningful structure and what to ignore."[11] Any rhetor is involved in this sifting and choosing, whether it be the newspaper editor choosing front-page stories versus comic-page stories or the speaker highlighting facts about a person in a eulogy.

The very choice of what facts or events are relevant is a matter of pure arbitration. Once the choice is communicated, the event is imbued with *salience*, or what Chaim Perelman calls "presence," when describing this phenomenon from the framework of argumentation. Perelman says: "By the very fact of selecting certain elements and presenting them to the audience, their importance and pertinency to the discussion are implied. Indeed such a choice endows these elements with a *presence*. . . . It is not enough indeed that a thing should exist for a person to feel its presence."[12]

The second step in communicating "situations" is the translation of the chosen information into meaning. This is an act of creativity. It is an interpretative act. It is a rhetorical act of transcendence. As Perelman states, "Interpretation can be not merely a simple choice but also a creation, an invention of significance."[13]

To the audience, events become meaningful only through their linguistic depiction. As Edelman points out, "Political events can become infused with strong affect stemming from psychic tension, from perceptions of economic, military, or other threats or opportunities, and from interactions between social and psychological responses. These political 'events,' however, are largely creations of the language used to describe them."[14] Therefore, meaning is not discovered in situations, but *created* by rhetors.

As soon as one communicates an event or situation he is using evocative language. As Richard Weaver and others have pointed out language is always value-laden. Clearly the adjectives into which a "situation" are communicated cannot be the "real situation"; they must be a translation. Surely we learn from Bentham that rhetors can arbitrarily choose eulogistic or dyslogistic coverings for the same situation: We have "leaders" or "bosses," "organizations" or "machines," and "education" or "propaganda," not according to the situation's reality, but according to the rhetor's arbitrary choice of characterization. No theory of the relationship between situations and rhetoric can neglect to take account of the initial linguistic depiction of the situation.

Implications for Rhetoric

There are critical academic and moral consequences for rhetorical study according to one's view of meaning. If you view meaning as intrinsic to situations, rhetorical study becomes parasitic to philosophy, political science, and whatever other discipline can inform us as to what the "real" situation is. If, on the other hand, you view meaning as a consequence of rhetorical creation, your paramount concern will be how and by whom symbols create the reality to which people react. In a world of inexhaustible and ambiguous events, facts, images, and symbols, the rhetorician can best account for choices of situations, the evocative symbols, and the forms and media which transmit these translations of meaning. Thus, if anything, a rhetorical basis of meaning requires a disciplinary hierarchy with rhetoric at the top.

The ethical implications for this rhetorical perspective of meaning are crucial. If one accepts Bitzer's position that "the presence of rhetorical discourse obviously indicates the presence of a rhetorical situation,"[15] then we ascribe little responsibility to the rhetor with respect to what he has chosen to give salience. On the other hand, if we view the communication of an event as a choice, interpretation, and translation, the rhetor's responsibility is of supreme concern. Thus, when there are few speeches on hunger, and when the individual crime and not the corporate crime is the dominant topic of speakers and newspaper and magazine writers, we will not assume it is due to the relative, intrinsic importance of the two or even to a reading or misreading of the "exigences." Instead, the choices will be seen as purposeful acts for discernible reasons. They are *decisions* to make salient or not to make salient these situations.

To view rhetoric as a creation of reality or salience rather than a reflector of reality clearly increases the rhetor's moral responsibility. We do not just have the academic exercise of determining whether the rhetor understood the "situation" correctly. Instead, he must assume responsibility for the salience he has *created*. The potential culpability of John F. Kennedy in the "missile crisis" is thus much greater. The journalists who choose not to investigate corruption in government or the health needs of the elderly are also potentially more culpable. In short, the rhetor is responsible for what he chooses to make salient.

Essence: Rhetoric and Situations

The essential question to be addressed is: What is the relationship between rhetoric and situations? It will not be surprising that I take the converse position of each of Bitzer's major statements regarding this relationship. For example: I would not say "rhetoric is situational,"[16] but situations are rhetorical; not "exigence strongly invites utterance,"[17] but utterance strongly invites exigence; not "the situation controls the rhetorical response,"[18] but the rhetoric controls the situational response; not "rhetorical discourse . . . does obtain its character-as-rhetorical from the situation which generates it,"[19] but situations obtain their character from the rhetoric which surrounds them or creates them.

When George Aiken suggested several years ago that the United States should declare that she had won the war in Vietnam and get out, it was a declaration of rhetorical determination of meaning. No one understands or understood the "situation" in Vietnam, because there never was a discrete situation. The meaning of the war (war?, civil war?) came from the rhetoric surrounding it. To give salience to a situation in an area roughly the size of one of our middle-size states and to translate its exigencies into patriotism-provoking language and symbolism was a rhetorical choice. There was no "reality" of the situation's being in or not being in our national interest. At least George Aiken saw that the situation was primarily rhetorical, not military or political. And since it was produced rhetorically it could be exterminated rhetorically! As Edelman states " . . . political beliefs, perceptions and expectations are overwhelmingly not based upon observation or empirical evidence available to participants, but rather upon cuings among groups of people who jointly *create* the meanings they will read into current and anticipated events. . . . The particular meanings that are consensually accepted *need not therefore be cued by the objective situation*; they are rather established by a process of mutual agreement upon significant symbols."[20]

Political crises, contrary to Bitzer's analysis of Churchill, are rarely "found," they are usually created.[21] There was a "Cuban Missile Crisis" in 1962, not because of an event or group of events, but mainly because acts of rhetorical creation took place which created a political crisis as well.[22] A President dramatically announced on nationwide television and radio that there was a grave crisis threatening the country. This was accompanied by symbolic crisis activity including troop and missile deployment, executive formation of *ad hoc* crisis committees, unavailability of high government officials, summoning of Congressional leaders, etc. Once the situation was made salient and depicted as a crisis, the situation took new form. In 1970, however, in a similar situation the prospects of a Russian nuclear submarine base off Cienfuegos was *not* a "crisis" because President Nixon chose not to employ rhetoric to create one.[23]

Bitzer refers to the controlling situation of President Kennedy's assassination. The creation of salience for certain types of events such as Presidential assassinations may be so ritualized that it is uninteresting to analyze it rhetorically. This does not mean, however, that the situation "controlled" the response. It means that the communication of the event was of such consensual symbolism that expectations were easily predictable and stable. Even Bitzer describes the reaction to the assassination as resulting from "reports" of the assassination. Again, one cannot maintain that reports of anything are indistinguishable from the thing itself. Surely Bitzer cannot believe that there was an intrinsic urgency which compelled the rotunda speeches following the killing of President Kennedy (note, that the killing of important people is communicated with the evocative term "assassination"). In fact, the killing of a President of this country at this time is not a real threat to the people in any measurable way. How smooth in fact is the transference of power. How similar the country is before and after the event. (How similar are the President and Vice-President?) *But* since rhetoric *created* fears and threat perception, the rotunda speeches were needed to communicate reassurances.

Conclusion

As Edelman states, "Language does not mirror an objective 'reality' but rather creates it by organizing meaningful perceptions abstracted from a complex, bewildering world."[24] Thus rhetoric is a *cause* not an *effect* of meaning. It is antecedent, not subsequent, to a situation's impact.

Rhetors choose or do not choose to make salient situations, facts, events, etc. This may be the *sine qua non* of rhetoric: the art of linguistically or symbolically creating salience. After salience is created, the situation must be translated into meaning. When political commentators talk about issues, they are talking about situations made salient, not something that became important because of its intrinsic predominance. Thus in 1960 Kennedy and Nixon discussed Quemoy and Matsu. A prominent or high-ethos rhetor may create his own salient situations by virtue of speaking out on them. To say the President is speaking out on a pressing issue is redundant.

It is only when the meaning is seen as the result of a creative act and not a discovery, that rhetoric will be perceived as the supreme discipline it deserves to be.

NOTES

1. Lloyd Bitzer, "The Rhetorical Situation," *Philosophy and Rhetoric* 1 (1968): 1 [reprinted in this volume].

2. Kenneth Burke, *Permanence and Change* (New York: New Republic, 1936), p. 16.

3. Bitzer, "Rhetorical Situation," p. 9.

4. Ibid., p. 3.

5. Herbert Blumer, *Symbolic Interactionism: Perspective and Method* (Englewood Cliffs, NJ: Prentice-Hall, 1969), pp. 3–4.

6. Bitzer, "Rhetorical Situation," p. 1.

7. Ibid., p. 5; my emphasis.

8. Ibid., p. 11.

9. Ibid., p. 5; my emphasis.

10. Ibid., p. 6.

11. Murray Edelman, *Politics as Symbolic Action* (Chicago: Markham, 1971), p. 33.

12. C. Perelman and L. Olbrechts-Tyteca, *The New Rhetoric*, trans. John Wilkinson and Purcell Weaver (London: University of Notre Dame Press, 1969), pp. 116–117.

13. Ibid., p.121.

14. Edelman, *Politics*, p. 65.

15. Bitzer, "Rhetorical Situation," p. 2.

16. Ibid., p. 3.

17. Ibid., p. 5.

18. Ibid., p. 6.

19. Ibid., p. 3.

20. Edelman, *Politics*, pp. 32–33.

21. For a similar view regarding presidential rhetorical "crisis creation," see Theodore Otto Windt Jr., "Genres of Presidential Public Address: Repeating the Rhetorical Past" (paper delivered at the annual meeting of the Speech Communication Association of America, December 1972).

22. Quiet diplomacy was ruled out, as were Adlai Stevenson's recommendations of a "trade" of our obsolete missiles in Turkey for Russia's in Cuba. Many of our allies who had lived in the shadow of Russia's nuclear capability could not understand why the United States would find such a situation so intolerable. Moreover, Secretary of Defense McNamara did not feel that the missiles in Cuba would present an unendurable military situation for the United States. See Elie Abel, *The Missile Crisis* (New York: J. B. Lippincott, 1966), and Theodore Sorensen, *Kennedy* (New York: Harper & Row, 1965), pp. 667–718.

23. Benjamin Welles, "Soviet's Removal of Vessel in Cuba Is Awaited by U.S.," *New York Times*, November 15, 1970, p. 1, col. 8.

24. Edelman, *Politics*, p. 66.

Rethinking the Rhetorical Situation from within the Thematic of *Différance*

Barbara A. Biesecker

Critics bring to the analysis of rhetorical events various assumptions about the nature of symbolic action. Yet almost invariably they share common presuppositions about the constituent elements of the rhetorical situation and the logic that informs the relations between them. Whether theorists and critics adhere to an "old" or a "new" rhetoric, they continue to operate under the assumption that a logic of influence structures the relations between the constituent elements in any particular rhetorical situation. Symbolic action (what has historically been a linguistic text) is almost always understood as an expression that, wittingly or unwittingly, shapes or is shaped by the constituent elements of the situation out of which and for which it is produced. This long-held conception of the rhetorical situation as an exchange of influence defines the text as an object that mediates between subjects (speaker and audience) whose identity is constituted in a terrain different from and external to the particular rhetorical situation. Hence, the rhetorical situation is thought to modify attitudes or induce action on the part of consummate individuals.

I believe a rethinking of the rhetorical situation is called for on two interrelated grounds. One, the understanding of the rhetorical text as a discourse whose meaning is constituted by its relation to either an exigence operative at a particular historical moment or a consciousness anterior to the rhetorical event commits us to a naïve notion of

influence and blinds us to the discourse's radically historical character. Two, the construal of the rhetorical situation as an event made possible by way of an exchange between consummate individuals severely limits what we can say about discourse which seeks to persuade: if any symbolic act is no more than an event that links distinct and already constituted subjects, then rhetorical discourse bumps up against the impenetrable and unalterable space of the subject, "a threshold which none of the strategic [responses] manages to cross."[1] That is to say, if we posit the audience of any rhetorical event as no more than a conglomeration of subjects whose identity is fixed prior to the rhetorical event itself, then we must also admit that those subjects have an essence that cannot be affected by the discourse. Thus, the power of rhetoric is circumscribed: it has the potency to influence an audience, to realign their allegiances, but not to form new identities. Clearly, the traditional concept of the rhetorical situation forces theorists and critics to appeal to a logic that transcends the rhetorical situation itself in order to explain the prior constitution of the subjects participating or implicated in the event. If the identities of the audience are not constituted in and by the rhetorical event, then some retreat to an essentialist theory of the subject is inevitable.[2] Ultimately, this commits us to a limited conception of the subject and, in turn, to a reductive understanding of the rhetorical situation. In this essay I want to suggest that a reexamination of symbolic action (the text) and the subject (audience) that proceeds from within Jacques Derrida's thematic of *différance* enables us to rethink the rhetorical situation as articulation. Indeed, deconstructive practice enables us to read symbolic action in general and rhetorical discourse in particular as radical possibility.[3]

Obviously this is not the first attempt to mark a productive relation between the rhetorical analysis of texts and deconstruction. A plethora of theorists and critics, both within and outside the discipline of Rhetoric, have availed themselves to deconstructive practice under the shared conviction that, more than any other theoretical or critical perspective, deconstruction takes the rhetoricity of all texts seriously.[4] Deconstructive critics decipher all events as strategic impositions: as willed and therefore provisional limitations of a potentially unlimited and indeterminate textuality. Typically, Jacques Derrida and his disciples work toward the disclosure of the tropological structure of modes of thinking which, while purporting to be mere "means of expression," affect or infect the meaning produced. Beyond its demystifying function, however, deconstruction has yet to be appropriated in a productive way by critics working in the field of Rhetoric. What still remains to be done—and what this essay seeks to offer—is a reading of the rhetorical situation from within the frame of deconstructive practice in order to specify what can be produced that is useful for the analysis of rhetorical events. This essay will proceed in the following manner: In the first section, I will take up the text as a constituent element of the rhetorical situation. Here I will delineate what I take to be the productive relation between the rhetorical analysis of discrete symbolic actions and deconstruction. By way of a close reading of Jacques Derrida's thematic of *différance* as it is performed in a number of his essays, and particularly as it is staged in *Glas*,[5] I will suggest that deconstruction is a way of reading that seeks to come to terms with the way in which the language of any given text signifies the complicated attempt to form a unity out of a division, thereby turning an originary condition of impossibility into a condition of possibility in order to posit its ostensive argument. I will argue that from within the thematic of *différance* the "rhetorical dimension" of the text signifies not only the play of the tropological figures operating on its surface level, but also the (non)originary finessing of a division that produces the meaning of the text as such. That is to say, the "rhetorical dimension" names *both* the means by which an idea or argument is expressed and the initial

formative intervention that, in centering a differential situation, makes possible the production of meaning.[6] In the second section of the essay, I will fix my glance on the audience as a constituent element of the rhetorical situation. Here I will show how a deconstruction of the subject gives rhetorical critics and theorists access to the radical possibilities entailed in rhetorical events: if, as I will argue with Derrida, we conceive audience as the effect of *différance* and not the realization of identities, then our conception of rhetorical events must allow the potential for the displacement and condensation of those provisional identities. I will recommend that we rethink the rhetorical situation as governed by a logic of articulation rather than influence. Once we take the identity of audience as an effect-structure, we become obliged to read every "fixed" identity as the provisional and practical outcome of a symbolic engagement between speaker and audience.

Situation and Speaker

Twenty years ago Lloyd Bitzer simultaneously opened his seminal essay "The Rhetorical Situation" and inaugurated the journal *Philosophy and Rhetoric* with a series of questions, all of which boil down to one: How are we to define the rhetorical text? Bitzer's answer is widely known and based upon an onto-phenomenological differentiation between instrumental and expressive utterance:

> a work of rhetoric is pragmatic; it comes into existence for the sake of something beyond itself; it functions ultimately to produce action or change in the world; it performs some task. In short, rhetoric is a mode of altering reality, not by the direct application of energy to objects, but by the creation of discourse which changes reality through the mediation of thought and action.[7]

"Rhetoric," here, is the name given to those utterances that serve as instruments for adjusting the environment in accordance to the interests of its inhabitants. Of course, absolutely central to Bitzer's definition of rhetoric is the suggestion that rhetorical discourse is a response to and is called into existence by "some specific condition or situation which invites utterance."[8] In his view rhetorical discourse is an effect structure; its presence is determined by and takes its character from the situation that engenders it. As he puts it, "Rhetorical discourse comes into existence in response to a question, a solution in response to a problem." According to Bitzer, the situation is the "necessary condition of rhetorical discourse," and as such it "controls the rhetorical response in the same sense that the question controls the answer and the problem controls the solution": "Not the rhetor and not persuasive intent, but the situation is the source and ground of rhetorical activity—and, I should add, of rhetorical criticism."[9]

In 1973 Richard E. Vatz published "The Myth of the Rhetorical Situation," a gesture which challenged the validity of Bitzer's definition of rhetoric. Vatz indicts, quite correctly, Bitzer's definition of the rhetorical text as an operation that "disengage[s] the meaning [that] resides in events," and argues, to the contrary, that "statements do not imply 'situational characteristics at all': the statements may ostensibly describe situations, but they actually only inform us as to the phenomenological perspective of the speaker."[10] Vatz brought into the discussion what Bitzer had excluded—the intervention of an intending and interpreting speaker-subject. Citing Chaim Perelman and Murray Edelman, Vatz notes both how "the very choice of what facts or events are relevant is a matter of pure arbitration [on the part of the speaker]" and how the communication of "'situations' is the translation of the chosen information into meaning."[11] Hence, for Vatz rhetorical discourse is "an act of creativity . . . an interpretative act," and not something discovered in situations.

As an alternative to conceiving rhetorical discourse as the determined outcome of a situation, Vatz calls for a reversal of the cause–effect relation between situation and discourse proposed by Bitzer. Since, as Edelman states, "Language does not mirror an objective 'reality' but rather creates it by organizing meaningful perceptions abstracted from a complex, bewildering world," rhetoric "is a cause not an effect of meaning. It is antecedent, not subsequent, to a situation's impact."[12] For Vatz, as for Edelman, rhetorical discourse is to be analyzed as an expression of a speaker's intentions and interpretations which bring rhetorical situations into being.

Several essays have since been published that take up the question of the relation between the rhetorical text and the rhetorical situation. Continuing the debate between Bitzer and Vatz, critics have defended, rejected, or modified Bitzer's and Vatz's views of rhetoric and the rhetorical situation. In all cases, however, critics still take as their founding presumption a causal relation between the constituent elements comprising the event as a whole. Either speaker or situation is posited as logically and temporally prior, one or the other is taken as origin.[13] The present discussion will not try to review this body of arguments; rather, it will attempt to turn what appears to be an impasse (does situation or speaker occupy the position of origin?) into a productive contradiction, one that makes it possible for us to rethink rhetoric in a new way. Such a task may begin with Vatz's essay which, more than any other, makes visible the contradiction that rules both sides of the debate. As already noted, Vatz's ostensive purpose is to propose an alternative to Bitzer's definition of rhetoric and the rhetorical situation. Whether or not we agree with Vatz's own proposition, we may at least see his essay as a successful counterstatement. Nevertheless, and this is the mark of the double-gesture that inhabits his own writing, even as it questions the validity of Bitzer's central proposition, Vatz's essay simultaneously confirms it. After all, Vatz's statement is a response to Bitzer's essay; Vatz reads "The Rhetorical Situation" as itself a situation with an exigence that invites a response. And yet, is not Vatz's own article an effect of arbitration on the part of a choosing individual? So, then, is Bitzer right or is Vatz right? Is situation or speaker the origin of rhetorical discourse?

It is at this juncture that a deconstructive intervention might prove productive and has, in fact, already been set into operation by Vatz. As I have shown, Vatz inverts the hierarchy between situation and speaker posited by Bitzer. What if, rather than simply choosing sides, we were to suggest with Derrida that by upsetting the hierarchy and producing an exchange of properties between situation and speaker, Vatz unwittingly uncovers and undoes the operation responsible for the hierarchization, and thus displaces both the foundational logic of his own and Bitzer's argument? If both situation and speaker can stand in for cause, "if either cause or effect can occupy the position of origin, then origin is no longer originary; it loses its metaphysical privilege."[14] How, then, are we to account for the production of rhetorical texts? What are we to read rhetoric as the sign of? To answer these questions, I turn to a discussion of *différance* and try to flesh out its implications for the theorization of the rhetorical situation.

Rethinking Speaker and Situation from within the Thematic of *Différance*

Any serious consideration of the productive interface between rhetorical analysis and Derridean deconstruction must begin by charting the onto-theoretical precepts that inform deconstructive practice. Within the parameters of the present essay, this means thinking through the concept-metaphor *différance* that plays a formidable role both morphologically and historically in the works of Derrida. Derrida's notion of *différance* is rooted in Saussure's *Cours de linguistique generale*. In one of his earliest essays Derrida remarks how, in conceiving language as a system of signs whose identity is the effect of difference and not of essence, Saussure is put in the peculiar position of having to conclude that, contrary to common sense,

> in language, there are only differences *without positive terms*. Whether we take the signified or the signifier, language has neither ideas nor sounds that existed before the linguistic system, but only conceptual and phonic differences that have issued from the system. The idea or phonic substance that a sign contains is of less importance than the other signs that surround it.[15]

For Derrida, Saussure's text proposes a notion of difference that unwittingly points to a division within as well as between distinct elements in the linguistic system: the play of difference which Saussure saw operating *between* elements and thus constituting the value of any discrete element in the linguistic system is for Derrida always already at work *within* each element. This internal difference, this interval which separates every element from that which it is not, while "by the same token, divid[ing] the present [element] in itself," is, for Derrida, what lends every element its value.[16] *Différance*, as Derrida names it, marks an originary internal division, a "fundamental" nonidentity which, he tells us in *Positions*,

> forbid[s] at any moment, or in any sense, that a simple element be *present* in and of itself, referring only to itself. Whether in the order of spoken or written discourse, no element can function as a sign without referring to another element which itself is not simply present. This interweaving results in each "element"—phoneme or grapheme—being constituted on the basis of the trace within it of the other elements of the chain or system. This interweaving, this textile, is the *text* produced only in the transformation of another text. Nothing, neither among the elements nor within the system, is anywhere ever simply present or absent. There are only, everywhere, differences and traces of traces.[17]

The sign as "trace-structure," the sign as "constituted" out of a structural principle of original nonidentity or radical alterity, is precisely that which Derrida elsewhere names the "graphematic structure."[18]

In a way that will soon become evident, Derrida's *différance* effects a link between deconstruction and the analysis of rhetorical texts by supplying rhetorical critics with a mechanism that enables them to specify more adequately the rhetoricity of a text. For now, it is important to note that the thematic of *différance* is operative throughout Derrida's early as well as late essays. In fact, we could even decide to decipher most of his essays as variations on this theme. For example, we might read Derrida's essay entitled "Différance" in *Speech and Phenomena and Other Essays on Husserl's Theory of Signs* as something like the logic of *différance* or the questioning of the arche; we might decipher his earlier essay on Rousseau in *Of Grammatology* as the attempt to rename *différance* as "the graphic of the supplement"; we might describe "Signature Event Context" and "Limited Inc." in terms of a reinscription of *différance* as iteration or radical citationality. We might even go so far as to suggest that in every case Derrida's essays re-mark the trace of "the systematic play of differences, of the traces of differences, of the *spacing* by means of which elements are related to each other" in any given text.[19] In short, we could take the entire lot of Derrida's essays as an assemblage seeking to play and sometimes even perform the *différance* that structures all texts but which is always covered over in the writing.[20]

But what about this *différance*? Why should rhetorical critics struggle with this complicated internal division that is said to inhabit all writing, structure all speech, and scandalize all texts? What is so critical about this seemingly critical difference? In his essay "Différance" Derrida provides a possible answer: "*Différance* is what makes the movement of signification possible."[21] The play of *différance*, as Derrida puts it, is "the possibility of conceptuality, of the conceptual system and process in general":

> What we note as *différance* will thus be the movement of play that "produces" (and not by something that is simply an activity) these differences, these effects of difference. This does not mean that the *différance* which produces differences is before them in a simple and in itself unmodified and indifferent present. *Différance* is the nonfull, nonsimple "origin"; it is the structured and differing origin of differences.[22]

To repeat, *différance* makes signification possible. Only to the extent that we are able to differ, as in spatial distinction or relation to an other, and to defer, as in temporalizing or delay, are we able to produce anything. "*Différance*" is, as Derrida puts it, "the formation of form."[23] Here we do well to look a bit closer at an essay in which Derrida provides an extensive structural description of *différance* and then proceeds to discuss at even greater length its enabling power. In "Linguistics and Grammatology" he says,

[*Différance*] does not depend on any sensible plentitude, audible or visible, phonic or graphic. It is, on the contrary, the *condition of such a plentitude*. Although it does not exist, although it is never a being-present outside of all plentitude, its possibility is by rights anterior to all that one calls sign . . . concept or operation, motor or sensory. This *différance* is therefore not more sensible than intelligible and it *permits the articulation of signs* among themselves within the same abstract order . . . or between two orders of expression. *It permits the articulation of speech and writing*—in the colloquial sense—as it founds the metaphysical opposition between the sensible and the intelligible, then between signifier and signified, expression and content, etc.[24]

Derrida's *différance* is, as Gayatri Chakravorty Spivak points out, the name for "the lack at the origin that is the condition of thought and experience"; all writing in the narrow sense, like all speech, marks the play of this productive nonidentity.[25] *Différance*, Derrida writes, is the structural condition which makes it possible for us to perform any act.

For a concrete example of the enabling power of *différance* we can turn briefly to Derrida's *Glas*. In this work Derrida binds Hegel to Genet, Genet to Hegel. In so doing, he constructs two columns of discourse which make reading or decipherment a problem. How are we to read this two-pronged, two-pegged text? As I have already suggested, we can decide to decipher this text as the dramatization of *différance*. Indeed, it seems to me that no other work by Derrida more proficiently stages the play of *différance* than *Glas*. The very typographic form of the text ("if one decides to concentrate on one column the eye is drawn by the other"[26]) as well as the writing on both sides ("how the seeming exposition in the Hegel section seems upheld yet undone by the unruly Genet column"[27]) dramatizes the structural power of *différance* by performing it graphically. Briefly said, in *Glas* Derrida transposes the logic of *différance* into the graphic of *différance*: it is the white, what we usually take to be empty, space between the Hegel column and the Genet column that gives rise to the text.

The space between the (in)dependent columns marks a differencing zone that, as Derrida puts it in "The Double Session," "through the re-marking of its semantic void, it in fact begins to signify. Its semantic void *signifies*, but it signifies spacing and articulation; it has as its meaning the possibility of syntax; it orders the play of meaning."[28]

Glas performs the vantage point from which it becomes possible to see in a very vivid and concrete way how the value of a symbolic act, like the value of any element in a system, is a function of its place in an economy of *différance*. It is in the middle or the suspense of the two previously unjoined texts that meaning can be said to have been made. In fact we might go so far as to suggest that the blithe proposition in *Glas* is: everything deliberately and unavoidably happens in its crease, in its fold. It is in the structural space between the Hegel column and the Genet column that Derrida's text would play out its "meanings." Again, the space between the two (in)dependent texts deliberately and unavoidably stages the incision, the cut, the introduction of a differencing zone, a structure of *différance* that in being divided makes meaning possible. *Différance* is deliberately performed as the fold, where the border between inside (Hegel or Genet) and outside (Genet or Hegel) becomes undecidable as the text slips erratically from one column to the other. In short, the enabling power of *différance* is expressed or demonstrated in *Glas* as the asymmetrical (non)engagement of Hegel and Genet: "each page is folded dissymmetrically down the middle, for Hegel and Genet can never be identical. The equation is never balanced, reading and writing never coincide, and the page is never quite folded *up*."[29]

In shuttling us between the Hegel and Genet columns, Derrida's *Glas* involves us in the "active" movement of *différance*. Typographically dramatizing the economy of *différance*, he engages us in the work of a decipherment which produces the suggestion that all activity is made possible only by finessing a divided origin, a *différance*.

Such finessing, Derrida points out, in what might be taken as a metacritical comment in *Glas*, is hardly without interest:

Before attempting an active interpretation, verily a critical displacement (supposing that is rigorously possible), we must yet patiently decipher this difficult and obscure text. However preliminary, such a deciphering cannot be neutral, neuter, or passive. It violently intervenes, at least in a minimal form.[30]

The reader as well as the writer, and in the case of *Glas*, the philosopher as well as the poet, generates a discourse whose "meaning" is already, and thoroughly, constituted by a tissue of differences.[31] That meaning emerges as nothing more than a tissue of differences, however, should not be taken as a disabling discovery. In fact, Derrida points out that it is in deciphering difference as *différance* that we begin to read, and it is in transforming this condition of impossibility into a condition of possibility that we are enabled to speak and write—intervene.

Returning to the central question raised in this section of the essay, we can ask once again: How can Derrida's decision to read all texts as the trace of an inaugurating *différance* help rhetorical theorists and critics account for the production of rhetorical texts? As I mentioned at the start, deconstruction allows us to take seriously the *rhetoricity* of discursive practices. What does this mean in terms of the discussion on *différance* and what implications can it have for the practice of contemporary rhetorical criticism that takes the text as one of the constituent elements of the rhetorical situation?

Derridean deconstruction begins by considering the way in which all texts are inhabited by an internally divided nonoriginary "origin" called *différance*. The divisiveness of that "originating" moment is, so to speak, covered over or, as I put it earlier, finessed into a unity by the writing and the speaking. In fact, the finessing of the nonidentical into an identity is, as was noted above, precisely the activity that makes signification happen.

At this point, it might be emphasized that the provisional imposition of something like a unified origin is both a necessary and an interested gesture. It is necessary since the articulation of anything requires the temporary displacement of plurality, the provisional limitation of a potentially unlimited and indeterminate textuality (i.e., historical, discursive field). It is interested since, as I have shown, *différance* underwrites all discursive practices and thus exposes all beginning points, all primordial axioms, and all founding principles as constructions—impositions, traces of a will to knowledge.[32] In "Linguistics and Grammatology" Derrida describes the necessary and interested gesture this way:

> If words and concepts receive meaning only in sequences of differences, one can justify one's language, and one's choice of terms, only within a topic [an orientation in space] and an historical

strategy. The justification can therefore never be absolute and definitive. It corresponds to a condition of forces and translates an historical calculation.[33]

All symbolic action marks an intervention and an imposition—a deferral of and differencing between the historically produced discursive field—whose own authority is historically produced and, thus, provisional. As Derrida put it elsewhere, "If the word 'history' did not carry with it the theme of a final repression of *différance*, we could say that differences alone could be 'historical' through and through and from the start."[34]

The transitory character of one's choice of foundational terms is precisely that which any text cannot admit if it is going to make anything like "truth" appear; however, the text's own provisionality is also that which the language of the text repeatedly performs, despite all efforts to conceal it. We are continually reminded that although our own desire for unity and order compels us to "balance the equation that is the text's system," the textuality of the text itself "exposes the grammatological structure of the text," and reveals "that its 'origin' and its 'end' are given over to language in general."[35] Because the text is always and already given over to language in general, there is invariably a moment in the text "which harbors the unbalancing of the equation, the sleight of hand at the limit of a text which cannot be dismissed simply as a contradiction."[36] This textual knot or inadvertent "sleight of hand" marks the rhetoricity of the text and, in so doing, enables us to locate the unwitting and interested gesture that finessed *différance* in such a way that the writing could proceed. In every case the rhetoric of the text marks the intervention of *différance* onto the scene of writing. Moreover, the rhetoricity of the text also sustains the trace of the unwitting and interested gesture that, in rewriting the "originary" division as an identity, effected the text. Thus rhetoric can neither be taken as mere ornamentation for nor accessory to the "essential" argument or proposition of a text. While *différance* constitutes the structural "condition" for signification, rhetoric is the name for both the finessing of *différance* that inaugurates a text *and* the figurality of the text that puts us on its track.

The deconstructive displacement of questions of origin into questions of process frees rhetorical theorists and critics from reading rhetorical discourses and their "founding principles" as either the determined outcome of an objectively identifiable and discrete situation or an interpreting and intending subject. In fact, it implicates them in a much more complicated and unwieldy project: it obliges them to read rhetorical discourses as "the interweaving of different texts (literally 'web'-s) in an act of criticism that refuses to think of 'influence' or 'interrelationship' as *simple* historical phenomena."[37] That is to say, neither the text's immediate rhetorical situation nor its author can be taken as simple origin or generative agent since both are underwritten by a series of historically produced displacements. The implications this has for rhetorical theory and criticism will be made evident after we examine the rhetorical situation from the side of reception rather than production. Thus, the next section will suggest how we might begin to rewrite the rhetorical situation from within the thematic of *différance* by taking up the relation between the text and the audience.

Text and Audience

So far I have tried to show that Derrida's *différance* provides us with a critical edge for rethinking the relation between a rhetorical text and its speaker or situation. A deconstruction of those relations obliges us to question both the speaker's and the situation's presumed authority over the production of discourse. But where does that leave us? I would like to suggest that if we supplement our deconstructive reading of rhetorical discourse by a reading of audience that proceeds from within the thematic of *différance*, it becomes possible for us to rethink the logic of the rhetorical situation as articulation.

I begin the discussion on text and audience with the observation that whenever rhetorical theorists and critics contemplate the rhetorical situation, they do so with some notion of audience in mind. Indeed, at least in the twentieth century a preoccupation with audience has often served as *the* distinguishing characteristic of critical practice in our discipline. Yet, even in essays explicitly seeking to develop a theory of the rhetorical situation (with audience invariably identified as one of its constituent elements), the concept of audience itself receives little critical attention: in most cases, audience is simply named, identified as the target of discursive practice, and then dropped. For the most part, theorists do not approach audience as a problematic category. Lloyd Bitzer exemplifies this general complacency best when he remarks,

What characteristics, then, are implied when one refers to "the rhetorical situation"—the context in which speakers or writers create rhetorical discourse? Perhaps this question is puzzling because "situation" is not a standard term in the vocabulary of rhetorical theory. "Audience" is standard; so also are "speaker," "subject," "occasion," and "speech." If I were to ask, "What is a rhetorical audience?" or "What is a rhetorical subject?"—the reader would catch the meaning of my question.[38]

Indeed, one is expected to catch the meaning of Bitzer's question "What is a rhetorical audience?" because one is trained, at least in terms of the theoretical/critical lexicon, to think of audience as a self-evident, if not altogether banal, category. Based on what has been said about it, theorists and critics seem to agree on the nature and function of audience. Surveying the history of the concept as it has been used in the theorization and analysis of rhetorical events, Thomas Benson remarks: the term "audience" signifies for theorists and critics the presence of a body "*influencing* the design of and being *influenced* by a symbolic action."[39] In other words, as a collective animated by an identifiable and shared predisposition, audience implicitly figures into discussions about the rhetorical situation as a constraint upon rhetorical discourse. As a recipient of rhetorical messages, audience also figures forth as a confederate body susceptible to persuasion and, ultimately, "capable of serving as mediators of the change which the discourse functions to produce."[40]

There can be no doubt that the dominant concept of audience as a collectivity that both influences and is influenced by discourse is based on the traditional humanistic conception of the subject. As Michael C. McGee puts it, rhetorical theorists and critics "presuppose a 'people' or an 'audience'" that is "either (a) an objective, literal extension of 'person,' or (b) a 'mob' of individuals whose significance is their gullibility and failure to respond to 'logical' argument."[41] In both cases they hold firmly to a conception of the human being that presumes an essence at the core of the individual that is coherent, stable, and which makes the human being what it *is*. Across the board, the subject, and by extension the audience, is conceived as a consciousness, an "I" which thinks, perceives, and feels, an "I" whose self-presence or consciousness to itself is the source of meaning. For example, even though they disagree with each other on the generative ground of rhetorical discourse, both Bitzer and Vatz presume the presence of an audience that finds, in any rhetorical situation, its ontological and epistemological foundation in the notion of a sovereign, rational subject. In Bitzer's words, an audience signifies "only . . . those persons who are capable of being influenced by discourse and of being mediators of change."[42] Implied in this statement is the suggestion that rational persons respond appropriately to reasonable propositions—a suggestion Vatz's argument presupposes. What must be noted here is that theorists as diverse as Bitzer and Vatz predicate their views of audience on the common presumption that fixed essences encounter variable circumstances. Given this conceptualization of the audience, Benson is justified to define the rhetorical situation as a complex governed by the logic of influence. In the next section of the essay, I intend to problematize the feasibility of the notion of audience modeled after the sovereign subject and, by way of conclusion, offer a theorization of the rhetorical situation that provides us with an alternative to the logic of influence.

Rethinking Text and Audience from within the Thematic of *Différance*

In several of his works, Derrida challenges the presumed integrity of the phenomenological subject, the subject of the humanistic tradition that, as I have shown, plays a formidable role in our understanding of the rhetorical situation. He launches a deconstruction of the centered subject by attempting to think presence, including the subject as a consciousness present to itself, as "starting from/in relation to time as difference, differing, and deferral."[43] In short, Derrida takes seriously the possibility that the subject, like writing and speech, is constituted by *différance*.

Before fleshing out the various implications the deconstruction of the humanistic subject has for traditional notions of audience and situation, we must examine more closely Derrida's elaborate argument, one that enables him to forge the polemic suggestion that the centered subject is an effect-structure and not an ontological *a priori*. Derrida's deconstruction of the humanistic subject turns in great part on the effacement of the subject/structure binary that allows humanists like Husserl and Freud[44] to posit a self-present I, "a fixed origin" that itself "escape[s] structurality" in such a way as to limit "the play of structure."[45] Perry Anderson puts it this way:

What Derrida had seen, acutely, was that the supposition of any stable structure had always

depended on the silent postulation of a center that was not entirely "subject" to it: in other words, of a *subject* distinct *from* it. His decisive move was to liquidate the last vestige of such autonomy.[46]

As Anderson intimates, Derrida deconstructs the subject by showing us how the identity of any subject, what I earlier called the core of the human being, like the value of any element in any system is structured by *différance*. This forces us to think of subjectivity not as an essence but as an effect of the subject's place in an economy of differences. For example, in his essay "Semiology and Grammatology" Derrida writes that,

Nothing—no present and in-*different* being—thus precedes *différance* and spacing. There is no subject who is agent, author, and master of *différance*, who eventually and empirically would be overtaken by *différance*. Subjectivity—like objectivity—is an effect of *différance*, an effect inscribed in a system of *différance*.[47]

In this essay, Derrida recommends that we think the subject not as a stable presence constituted and operating outside the play of *différance*, but instead as a production or effect-structure of *différance*.

If the identity of the subject is to be taken as the effect of *différance* and not of essence, then it is marked, like any sign or any object, by an internal difference that prevents it from being present in and of itself. As Derrida puts it,

This is why the *a* of *différance* also recalls that spacing is temporization, the detour and postponement by means of which intuition, perception, consummation—in a word, the relationship to the present, the reference to a present reality, to a *being*—are always *deferred*. Deferred by virtue of the very principle of difference which holds that an element functions and signifies, takes on or conveys meaning, only by referring to another past or future element in an economy of traces.[48]

By way of the operation of *différance*, Derrida underscores the radically historical character of the subject. Against an irreducible humanist essence of subjectivity, Derrida advances a subjectivity which, structured by *différance* and thus always differing from itself, is forever in process, indefinite, controvertible. In fact,

"absolute subjectivity" would . . . have to be crossed out as soon as we conceive the present on the basis of *différance*, and not the reverse. The concept of *subjectivity* belongs *a priori and in general* to the order of the *constituted*. . . . There is no constituting subjectivity. The very concept of constitution must be deconstructed.[49]

Like any other object, the subject is a historical construct precisely because its "unique" and always provisional identity depends upon its operations within a system of differences and the larger movement of *différance*: the subject is neither present nor "above all present to itself before *différance*." Like speech and writing, "the subject is constituted only in being divided from itself, in becoming space, in temporizing, in deferral."[50] Rather than marking a place of identity, the subject designates a noncoincidence, "a complex and differential product"[51] continuously open to change.

Rewriting the Logic of the Rhetorical Situation as Articulation

What implications might the deconstruction of the subject have for our definition of the audience and, thus, for the rhetorical situation? Simply put, the deconstruction of the subject opens up possibilities for the field of Rhetoric by enabling us to read the rhetorical situation as an event structured not by a logic of influence but by a logic of articulation. If the subject is shifting and unstable (constituted in and by the play of *différance*), then the rhetorical event may be seen as an incident that produces and reproduces the identities of subjects and constructs and reconstructs linkages between them. From the vantage of the de-centered subject, the rhetorical event can not signify the consolidation of already constituted identities whose operations and relations are determined *a priori* by a logic that operates quite apart from real historical circumstances. Rather it marks the articulation of provisional identities and the construction of contingent relations that obtain between them. From within the thematic of *différance* we would see the rhetorical situation neither as an event that merely induces audiences to act one way or another nor as an incident that, in representing the interests of a particular collectivity, merely wrestles the probable within the realm of the actualizable. Rather, we would see the rhetorical situation as an event that makes possible the production of identities and social relations. That is to say, if rhetorical events are analyzed from within the thematic of *différance*, it becomes possible to read discursive practices neither as rhetorics directed to preconstituted and known audiences nor as rhetorics "in search of" objectively identifiable but yet undis-

covered audiences. *Différance* obliges us to read rhetorical discourses as processes entailing the discursive production of audiences, and enables us to decipher rhetorical events as sites that make visible the historically articulated emergence of the category "audience."

Such perspective, of course, implicates us in a larger, radically historical project that works against essentializing and universalizing claims. If rhetorical discourses (which are themselves played by *différance*) are deciphered as practices that perform the situated displacement and condensation of identities and audiences, then our tendency to gloss over differences and find refuge in a common existential or ontological condition will be checked. I believe, however, that the gift of deconstruction is that it obliges us to resist universalizing gestures, enabling us to open up a space wherein it becomes possible for us to discern the considerable heterogeneity of the social sphere and the formidable role that rhetoric plays in articulating this heterogeneity. Significantly enough, a reading of the rhetorical situation that presumes a text whose meaning is the effect of *différance* and a subject whose identity is produced and reproduced in discursive practices, resituates the rhetorical situation on a trajectory of becoming rather than Being. Finally, then, the deconstruction of the rhetorical situation and its constituent elements has taken us to a point where we are able to rethink rhetoric as radical possibility.

This essay has attempted to provide an answer to the following question: How, if at all, can the insights of deconstruction assist in the explanation and understanding of rhetorical events? Speaking generally now, the appropriation of deconstruction by rhetorical theorists and critics can bring intelligibility to the rhetorical event by enabling them to read rhetoric as a divided sign: as the name for both the unwitting and interested gesture that structures any symbolic action *and* the figurality that puts us on its track. Derridean deconstruction does not merely help rhetorical critics analyze texts; in addition, it promotes a rigorous reevaluation and rebuilding of the concept-metaphor "rhetorical situation" that drives and delimits much contemporary critical practice in this field.

This call for the appropriation of deconstructive insights deserves a final word. My attempt to use deconstructive insights as a means through which the rhetorical situation can be rethought was not meant to suggest that traditional rhetorical theories and critical practices are indefensible or that they should be replaced by Derridean deconstruction. I take deconstructive practice as one possible way to reinvigorate the field, not as the first step towards a renunciation of it. In short, I believe it is possible to open up the field of Rhetoric by using deconstruction not as a transcendental signifier that will lead the way to truth, but as a *bricoleur's* or tinker's tool—a "positive lever"[52]—that produces rather than protects the exorbitant possibilities of rhetoric.

NOTES

1. Ernesto Laclau and Chantal Mouffe, *Hegemony and Socialist Strategy: Towards a Radical Democratic Politics*, trans. Winston Moore and Paul Cammack (Great Britain: Thetford, 1985), p. 76.

2. This is precisely the kind of move that traditional theorists and critics have had to make in analyses of the rhetorical situation. For example, see: Lloyd Bitzer, "The Rhetorical Situation," *Philosophy and Rhetoric* 1 (1968): 1–14 [reprinted in this volume]; Richard Larson, "Lloyd Bitzer's 'Rhetorical Situation' and the Classification of Discourse," *Philosophy and Rhetoric* 3 (1970): 165–168; K. E. Wilkerson, "On Evaluating Theories of Rhetoric," *Philosophy and Rhetoric* 3 (1970): 82–96; Ralph Pomeroy, "Fitness of Response in Bitzer's Concept of Rhetorical Discourse," *Georgia Speech Communication Journal* 4 (1972): 42–71; Richard Vatz, "The Myth of the Rhetorical Situation," *Philosophy and Rhetoric* 6 (1973): 154–161 [reprinted in this volume]; Scott Consigny, "Rhetoric and Its Situations," *Philosophy and Rhetoric* 7 (1974): 175–186; and Alan Brinton, "Situation in the Theory of Rhetoric," *Philosophy and Rhetoric* 14 (1981): 234–248.

3. Political theorists have already begun to appropriate deconstruction for the purposes of social critique. For instance, in their most recent book, *Hegemony and Socialist Strategy: Towards a Radical Democratic Politics*, Ernesto Laclau and Chantal Mouffe consciously struggle to open up a powerful Marxist tradition which they believe no longer helps us to think social struggles in their historical specificity. They point out how from a strict Marxist perspective "diverse subject positions are reduced to manifestations of a single position; the plurality of differences is either reduced or rejected as contingent; the sense of present is revealed through its location in an *a priori* succession of stages" (p. 21). Dissatisfied with the reductionism they see as inherent in orthodox Marxism, Laclau and Mouffe recommend a post-Marxist perspective which takes as its point of departure the indeterminacy of the identity of social agents. Such a view, of course, refuses the suggestion that economically based class relations determine political relations: there "is no necessary or logical relation between social agents and productive relations." While my own discussion is informed by the work of Laclau and Mouffe, it should be noted that they do not deal explicitly with the role of rhetoric in the constitution of hegemonic groups or formations.

4. While it is not possible here to offer a comprehensive list of essays and books addressing the interface between rhetoric and deconstruction, the texts cited below (in addition to the articles cited above) are particularly useful: Jonathan Arac et al., *The Yale Critics: Deconstruction in America* (Minneapolis: University of Minnesota Press, 1984)—this volume includes essays emphasizing the early work of de Man, Hartman, Miller, and Bloom; Bloom et al., *Deconstruction and Criticism* (New York: Seabury Press, 1979)—contributors to this volume include Harold Bloom ("The Breaking of Form"), Paul de Man ("Shelley Disfigured"), Jacques Derrida ("Living On: Border Lines"), Geoffrey H. Hartman ("Words, Wish, Worth: Wordsworth"), and J. Hillis Miller ("The Critic as Host"); Jonathan Culler, *On Deconstruction: Theory and Criticism after Structuralism* (Ithaca, NY: Cornell University Press, 1982); Paul de Man, *Allegories of Reading: Figural Language in Rousseau, Nietzsche, Rilke, and Proust* (New Haven, CT: Yale University Press, 1979), and "The Epistemology of Metaphor," *Critical Inquiry* 5 (1978): 13–30; Denis Donoghue, *Ferocious Alphabets* (Boston: Little, Brown, 1981); Rodolphe Gasche, "Deconstruction as Criticism," *Glyph* 6 (1979): 177–216; Barbara Johnson, *The Critical Difference: Essays in the Contemporary Rhetoric of Reading* (Baltimore: Johns Hopkins University Press, 1980); J. Hillis Miller, "Narrative and History," *ELH* 41 (1974): 455–473; and Richard Rorty, *Philosophy and the Mirror of Nature* (Princeton, NJ: Princeton University Press, 1980).

5. Jacques Derrida, *Glas*, trans. John P. Leavey Jr. and Richard Rand (Lincoln: University of Nebraska Press, 1986).

6. Here I would like to set my own argument in counterdistinction to the approach taken by recent theorists advocating a "rhetoric as epistemic" position who, quite correctly, mark the way in which any discursive gesture is contaminated by the patterns of the perceiving subject. However, I wish to move the argument forward one more step by suggesting that the structure of the binary oppositions that engender "subjectivism" itself can be questioned by grammatological reading. As one deconstructivist put it, "The solution is not merely to say 'I shall not objectify.' It is rather to recognize at once that there is no other language but that of 'objectification' and that any distinction between 'subjectivication' and 'objectification' is as provisional as the use of any set of hierarchized oppositions" (Gayatri Chakravorty Spivak, "Translator's Preface," in *Of Grammatology* [Baltimore: Johns Hopkins University Press, 1974], p. lix). As will become evident over the course of this essay, it is imperative that we refuse to take the subject as a "given," as something that interprets. To the contrary, the subject must be thought as process, as becoming.

7. Bitzer, "Rhetorical Situation," pp. 3–4.

8. Ibid., p. 4.

9. Ibid., pp. 5–6.

10. Vatz, "Myth of the Rhetorical," p. 154.

11. Ibid., p. 157.

12. Cited in Vatz, "Myth of the Rhetorical," p. 160.

13. See essays on the rhetorical situation cited in note 2, above.

14. Jonathan Culler, On Deconstruction, p. 88.

15. Ferdinand de Saussure, Course in General Linguistics, trans. Wade Baskin (New York: Philosophical Library, 1959), p. 120.

16. Jacques Derrida, "Différance," in Speech and Phenomena and Other Essays on Husserl's Theory of Signs, trans. David B. Allison (Evanston, IL: Northwestern University Press, 1973), p. 143.

17. Jacques Derrida, "Semiology and Grammatology," in Positions, trans. Alan Bass (Chicago: University of Chicago Press, 1981), p. 26.

18. See Jacques Derrida, "Of Grammatology as a Positive Science," in Of Grammatology, pp. 74–93.

19. Derrida, "Semiology and Grammatology," p. 27.

20. On pages 131–132 of his essay "Différance," Derrida describes his own texts as an "assemblage." He says, "I insist on the word 'assemblage' here for two reasons: on the one hand, it is not a matter of describing a history, of recounting the steps, text by text, context by context, each time showing which scheme has been able to impose this graphic disorder, although this could have been done as well; rather, we are concerned with the general system of all these schemata. On the other hand, the word 'assemblage' seems more apt for suggesting that the kind of bringing-together proposed here has the structure of an interlacing, a weaving, or a web, which would allow the different threads and different lines of sense or force to separate again, as well as being ready to bind others together." In the attempt to mark the same sort of subtle operations, I reiterate Derrida's word choice.

21. Derrida, "Différance," p. 142.

22. Ibid., p. 141.

23. Derrida, "Linguistics and Grammatology," in Of Grammatology, p. 63.

24. Ibid., pp. 62–63; emphasis added.

25. Spivak, "Translator's Preface," p. xvii.

26. Gayatri Chakravorty Spivak, "Glas-Piece: A Compte Rendu," Diacritics (1977): 26.

27. Ibid., p. 26.

28. Jacques Derrida, "The Double Session," in Dissemination, trans. Barbara Johnson (Chicago: University of Chicago Press, 1981), p. 222.

29. Spivak, "Glas-Piece," p. 26.

30. Derrida, Glas, p. 5a.

31. Derrida, "Semiology and Grammatology," p. 33.

32. We should, of course, be reminded here that even though différance is more "primordial" than the substance or presence of each element in a structure, it can never be present. It also participates in the radical alterity that makes anything like "identity" possible. See Derrida, "Différance," esp. pp. 140–143.

33. Derrida, "Linguistics and Grammatology," p. 70.

34. Derrida, "Différance," p. 141.

35. Spivak, "Translator's Preface," p. xlix.

36. Ibid., p. xlix.

37. Ibid., p. lxxxiv.

38. Bitzer, "Rhetorical Situation," p. 1.

39. Thomas Benson, "The Senses of Rhetoric: A Topical System for Critics," Central States Speech Journal 29 (1978): 249.

40. Bitzer, "Rhetorical Situation," p. 8.

41. Michael Calvin McGee, "In Search of 'the People': A Rhetorical Alternative," Quarterly Journal of Speech 61 (1975): 238.

42. Bitzer, "Rhetorical Situation," p. 6.

43. Cited in Culler, On Deconstruction, p. 95.

44. See Jacques Derrida, "Freud and the Scene of Writing," in Writing and Difference, trans. Alan Bass (Chicago: University of Chicago Press, 1978), pp. 196–231.

45. Jacques Derrida, "Structure, Sign, and Play in the Discourse of the Human Sciences," in Writing and Difference, pp. 278–279.

46. Perry Anderson, In the Tracks of Historical Materialism (Chicago: University of Chicago Press, 1983), p. 54.

47. Derrida, "Semiology and Grammatology," p. 28.

48. Ibid., pp. 28–29.

49. Jacques Derrida, "The Voice That Keeps Silent," in Speech and Phenomena, pp. 84–85n.

50. Derrida, "Semiology and Grammatology," p. 29.

51. Culler, On Deconstruction, p. 162.

52. As Spivak puts it in her "Preface" to The Grammatology, "The bricoleur makes do with things that were meant perhaps for other ends" (p. xix).

Unframing Models of Public Distribution

From Rhetorical Situation to Rhetorical Ecologies

Jenny Edbauer

[P]laces . . . are best thought of not so much as enduring sites but as moments of encounter, not so much as 'presents', fixed in space and time, but as variable events; twists and fluxes of interrelation. Even when the intent is to hold places still and motionless, caught in a cat's cradle of networks that are out to quell unpredictability, success is rare, and then only for a while. Grand porticos and columns framing imperial triumphs become theme parks. Areas of wealth and influence become slums.
—Ash Amin and Nigel Thrift

Elemental Frameworks

In his multifaceted description of what constitutes a public, Michael Warner explains why certain notions of "public communication" have done us such a disservice. He writes:

> No single text can create a public. Nor can a single voice, a single genre, or even a single medium. All are insufficient . . . , since a public is understood to be an ongoing space of encounter for discourse. It is not texts themselves that create publics, but the concatenation of texts through time. . . . Between the discourse that comes before and the discourse that comes after, one must postulate some kind of link. And the link has a social character; it is not mere consecutiveness in time, but a context of interaction. (62)

Warner tells us that this is why the overly simplified models of communication—often represented through the triangulated terms *sender, receiver, text*—are nothing short of a conceptual paradox. He continues, "A public seems to be self-organized by discourse, but in fact requires preexisting forms and channels of circulation" (75). Herein lies the paradox: sender–receiver models of public communication tend to identify a kind of homeostatic relationship, which simultaneously abstracts the operation of social links and circulation. The triangle of sender, receiver, text misses the concatenations that come to constitute Warner's version of a public.

Of course, oversimplified sender–receiver models of public communication have been productively complicated by theories like Lloyd Bitzer's notion of the rhetorical situation, which theorized the contextual dimensions of rhetoric. As Bitzer explains, "When I ask, What is a rhetorical situation?, I want to know the nature of those contexts in which speakers or writers create rhetorical discourse . . ." ("Rhetorical" 382). This starting point places the question of rhetoric—and the defining characteristic of *rhetoricalness*—squarely within the scene of a situational context. In his explicit definition, Bitzer writes that a rhetorical situation is "a natural context of persons, events, objects, relations, and an exigence which strongly invites utterances. . . ." (385). As many commentators of Bitzer have pointed out, his definition locates exigencies in the external conditions of material and social circumstances. Bitzer himself tells us that exigencies are "located in reality, are objective and publicly observable historic facts in the world we experience, are therefore available for scrutiny by an observer or critic who *attends to them*" ("Rhetorical" 390; emphasis mine). In Bitzer's schema, rhetoricians answer an invitation to solve a problem through discourse, which is then rendered as rhetorical discourse. Richard Vatz's infamous critique against Bitzer's "realism" challenges the notion that exigencies exist in any autonomous sense. Whereas Bitzer suggests that the rhetor *discovers* exigencies that already exist, Vatz argues that exigencies are *created* for audiences through the rhetor's work.

In yet another critique of Bitzer, Craig Smith and Scott Lybarger argue that rhetorical situation involves a plurality of exigencies and complex relations between the audience and a rhetorician's interest. In this way, Smith and Lybarger revise Bitzer's relatively autonomous notion of exigence by making it more interactive with other elements of the situation. They offer an example of this reconceptualized situation in their analysis of two 1989 speeches from President George Bush concerning the "war on drugs." Using a modified version of Bitzer's model, Smith and Lybarger identify three main elements of Bush's speeches: exigences, audiences, and constraints. At the time of these speeches, they write, polls reported that the public felt drug abuse was a serious problem. Media reports "helped increase the interest in the problem by providing direct knowledge of it. Bush took advantage of an attitude that the press reinforced" (203). Accordingly, this public concern constrained Bush's choices of which public exigences to address in his official attention. At the same time, of course, Bush's articulation of "the drug crisis" helped to reinforce this exigence *as a* rhetorical problem that must be addressed. Smith and Lybarger emphasize the mutuality of exigence from the positions of rhetorician and audience, reflecting how both elements help to create the sense of problem. This is a careful modification of Bitzer's model in that the authors link the articulation of exigence(s) to multiple agents and constraints.

In short, Bitzer's theories, as well as the critiques and modifications like those above, have generated a body of scholarship that stretches our own notions of "rhetorical publicness" into a *contextual* framework that permanently troubles sender–receiver models. Returning to Warner for just a moment, however, we might still ask whether notions of rhetorical situation adequately account for the "constitutive circulation" of rhetoric in the social field. Do theories of rhetorical situation allow us to theorize how "concatenation of texts through time" help to create publics? Barbara Biesecker's critique of these models suggests that perhaps the answer is *no*. According to Biesecker, the problem with many takes on rhetorical situation is their tendency to conceptualize rhetoric within a scene of already-formed, already-discrete individuals. For Biesecker, this problem can be seen in the way these models often treat "audience" as a rather unproblematic and obvious site. The trouble, she writes, is that:

> if we posit the audience of any rhetorical event as no more than a conglomeration of subjects whose identity is fixed prior to the rhetorical event itself, then . . . the power of rhetoric is circumscribed: it has the potency to influence an audience, to realign their allegiances, but not to form new identities. (111)

Here we arrive at an un(der)explored line of inquiry into one of rhetoric's most familiar and most revered theoretical-pedagogical paradigms. Biesecker's critique points to the way in which various models of rhetorical situation tend to describe rhetoric as a totality of discrete elements: audience, rhetor, exigence, constraints, and text. In other words, despite their differences, these various takes on rhetorical situation tend to be rooted in the views of rhetorics as *elemental conglomerations*.

Louise Weatherbee Phelps proposes a similar critique in her argument that many theories of discourse (and, by extension, we could also say of rhetoric) represent discourse as "a set of discrete components (units and correlated functions) based on variations and elaborations of the traditional communication triangle" (60). Rhetoric and discourse thus become conceptualized as a collection of elements—often called by such names as speaker–audience–message, ethos–pathos–logos, or rhetor–audience–constraints–exigence. Although such element-based theories of discourse have important explanatory power, continues Phelps, there is also great power in describing

> how an element (e.g., the writer as "ethos") *is discriminated from a flux* and perceived as invariant, stable, and autonomous. . . . Natural and traditional categories acquire greater depth and scope when we . . . temporalize them, interpret them as metaphors, expand their range of variation,

multiply their interpretants, pursue their logic to the limit, or treat them in historical institutional terms. (60; emphasis mine)

Rather than seeing rhetoric as the totality of its discrete elements, Phelps' critique seeks to recontextualize those elements in a wider sphere of active, historical, and lived processes. That is, the elements of a rhetorical situation can be re-read against the historical fluxes in which they move. While the incarnations of rhetorical situation create complex frameworks for understanding a rhetoric's operation in a particular social scene, therefore, both Biesecker and Phelps interrogate the effects of building a model around a "conglomeration" of distinct elements in relation to one another.

The weakness of "conglomeration" models is tacitly exposed in Smith and Lybarger's analysis of Bush's "war on drugs" speeches, for instance. When Smith and Lybarger discuss the exigences involved in the "war on drugs," they point to audience perceptions, Bush's speeches, media images, and the various constraints of all participants. They emphasize the important role that perception plays, since "each auditor will have a perception of the rhetor *and* the message in addition to a perception of the issues, [which means that] rhetorical communication is always in a state of flux that requires the critic to move beyond the strict realism of Bitzer" (200). The exigence is more like a complex of various audience/speaker perceptions and institutional or material constraints. Indeed, because "exigencies are everywhere shot through with perceptions" (197), there can be no pure exigence that does not involve various mixes of felt interests. Their analysis thus suggests a problem of location; the exigence does not exist per se, but is instead an amalgamation of processes and encounters: concerns about safe neighborhoods, media images, encounters of everyday life in certain places, concerns about re-election, articulations of problems and the circulation of those articulations, and so forth. The exigence is not properly located in any element of the model. Instead, what we dub *exigence* is more like a shorthand way of describing a series of events. The rhetorical situation is part of what we might call, borrowing from Phelps, an ongoing social flux. Situation bleeds into the concatenation of public interaction. Public interactions bleed into wider social processes. *The elements of rhetorical situation simply bleed.*

In order to rethink rhetorical publicness as a context of interaction, therefore, this article proposes an augmentation to our popular conceptual frameworks of rhetorical situation. Rather than primarily speaking of rhetoric through the terministic lens of conglomerated elements, I look towards a framework of *affective ecologies* that recontextualizes rhetorics in their temporal, historical, and lived fluxes. In what follows, I want to propose a revised strategy for theorizing public rhetorics (and rhetoric's publicness) as a circulating ecology of effects, enactments, and events by shifting the lines of focus from *rhetorical situation* to *rhetorical ecologies*. Like Biesecker, Phelps, and Warner, I want to add the dimensions of history and movement (back) into our visions/versions of rhetoric's public situations, reclaiming rhetoric from artificially *elementary* frameworks. While one framework does not undermine the other, I argue that this ecological model allows us to more fully theorize rhetoric as a public(s) creation.

Situs, Situation, and the Idea of Place

We might begin this conceptual augmentation by exploring some etymological tropes that remain buried within our popular theories. Consider the following: tracking the Latin roots of "situation" brings us to the key words *situare* and *situs*, both of which resonate with our definitions for location, site, and place. The Latin word *situs* is closely tied to the originary position of objects. (Significantly, this term still has currency in legal vocabulary as reference to the places in which a crime or accident occurs, or the location of property.) By definition, then, *situs* implies a bordered, fixed space-location. Consequently, the concept of "rhetorical situation" is appropriately named insofar as the models of rhetorical situation describe the scene of rhetorical action as "located" around the exigence that generates a response. We thus find a connection between certain models of rhetorical situation and a sense of *place*. But the public existence of *situs* is complicated. As Steven Shaviro points out in *Connected*, the social does not reside in fixed sites, but rather in a networked space of flows and connections. "The predominant form of human interaction . . . is *networking*," he writes (131). Moreover, this "networked life" is a matter of actual, historically-shaped forces of flows themselves. Shaviro explains:

[T]he network is not a disembodied information pattern nor a system of frictionless pathways over which any message whatsoever can be neutrally conveyed. Rather, the force of all messages, *as they accrete over time*, determines the very shape of the network. The meaning of a message cannot be isolated from its mode of propagation, from the way it harasses me, attacks me, or parasitically invades me. (24; emphasis mine)

Temporarily bracketing the rather ominous perspective that Shaviro brings to this sense of connection, we find that networks involve a different kind of habitation in the social field. To say that we are connected is another way of saying that we are never outside the networked interconnection of forces, energies, rhetorics, moods, and experiences. In other words, our practical consciousness is never outside the prior and ongoing structures of feeling that shape the social field.

At the same time, life-as-network also means that the social field is not comprised of discrete *sites* but from events that are shifting and moving, grafted onto and connected with other events. According to Shaviro, "The space [of networks] can be exhilarating, disorienting, or oppressive, but in any case it is quite different from the space of places" (131). Our sense of place tends to remain rooted in an imaginary that describes communities as a collection of discrete elements, like houses, families, yards, streets, and neighborhoods. Nevertheless, Shaviro explains that place should be characterized less in terms of this sense of community (discrete elements taken together), and more in the interactions *between* those elements—their encounters in the crease[s] and folds:

> What's crucial about the space of places is rather something other than "community": the fact that, in large urban agglomerations, networking is less important than . . . *contact:* the serendipitous encounters between strangers. . . . These sorts of encounters happen in the pedestrian-friendly spaces of older large cities. . . . The space of places is less that of nostalgically idealized traditional communities than that of turbulent urban modernity. (132–133)

In this way, place becomes decoupled from the notion of *situs*, or fixed (series of) locations, and linked instead to the in-between en/action of events and encounters. Place becomes a space of contacts, which are always changing and never discrete. The contact between two people on a busy city street is never simply a matter of those two bodies; rather, the two bodies carry with them the traces of effects from whole fields of culture and social histories. This is what it means to say

that the social field is networked, connected, rather than a matter of place, sites, and home.

The notion of place has also recently become much more complicated in the theoretical frameworks of both cultural geographers and rhetoricians. In *Geographies of Writing*, for example, Nedra Reynolds argues that it is important "to understand geographies as embodied, and how the process of social construction of space occurs at the level of the body, not just at the level of the city or street or nation" (143). What we normally take as "sites" are not only comprised in a *situs* or fixed location. Reynolds explains that these "sites" are made up of affective encounters, experiences, and moods that cohere around material spaces. This is why sites are not just seen, but (perhaps even more so) they are felt (147). She gives the example of certain students with whom she worked during her study in Great Britain. When questioned about their city, the students had no trouble at all identifying the "bad" and "good" parts of town. Although these "good/bad" sites may even have fairly solid boundary markers (*east of the freeway, downtown, southside of town*), we might argue that these sites are not only comprised *as such* through their location or collection of elements. Instead, they obtain their descriptions as good/bad sites from the affective and embodied experiences that circulate: feelings of fear or comfort, for instance.

Even in those spaces that are more obvious examples of bordered sites, we find it increasingly difficult to speak in terms of fixed place. Take the example of cities, which cultural geographers Ash Amin and Nigel Thrift thoroughly rework in *Cities: Reimagining the Urban*. According to Amin and Thrift:

> [C]ontemporary cities are certainly not systems with their own internal coherence. The city's boundaries have become far too permeable and stretched, both geographically and socially, for it to be theorized as a whole. The city has no completeness, no centre, no fixed parts. Instead, *it is an amalgam of often disjointed processes and social heterogeneity, a place of near and far connections, a concatenation of rhythms.* . . . (8; emphasis mine)

The city itself is less a *situs*, say Amin and Thrift, than a certain way of processing. In fact, it may be more appropriate to rethink "city" less as a noun (implying a *situs*) and more of a verb, as in *to city*. We *do city*, rather than exist *in the city*. Amin and Thrift argue that cities are more about movements and processes than the elements that materially construct their borders. They explain, "We

certainly take circulation to be a central characteristic of the city. . . . [C]ities exist as a means
of movement, as means to engineer *encounters*
through collection, transport, and collation. They
produce, thereby, a complex pattern of traces,
a threadwork of intensities . . ." (81). Amin and
Thrift thus move away from the site-model framework of urban spaces, which renders the city as a
kind of "container" for the unique elements that
the city envelops.

The site-model would imagine, for example, that
Austin is a container for the local elements within
a given space, much as New York is a container for
another set of local elements. Talking about those
two different cities merely involves talking about
the different elements held by the same (kind of)
container called "city." New York might thus be
described as containing more diverse population
elements than Austin; or perhaps Austin could
be described as a container for more conservative
political elements. Yet Amin and Thrift suggest
that the city-as-container does not adequately
describe the city as an *amalgam of processes,* or as a
circulation of encounters and actions. Rather than
relying upon the container metaphor, therefore,
they offer up an ecological metaphor in order to
read the city:

> [I]t is only by moving beyond the slower times of
> the city's built fabric—which seem to form a con-
> tainer—to the constant to and fro of the move-
> ments which sustain that fabric that we can begin
> to understand what a city is. . . . The city becomes
> a kind of weather system, a rapidly varying distri-
> bution of intensities. (83)

Though cities are indeed *sites* (or can even be
described in terms of borders, boundaries, and
containers), Amin and Thrift suggest that these
sites (the *situs*) are sustained by the amalgam of
processes, which can be described in ecological
terms of varying intensities of encounters and
interactions—much like a weather system.

From Situs to Distribution

What does this discussion of cities and sites have
the do with the rhetorical situation? For one thing,
we find in the early models of rhetorical situation a
notion of rhetoric as *taking place,* as if the rhetorical situation is one in which we can visit through a
mapping of various elements: the relevant persons,
events, objects, exigence, and utterances. But this
place-based perspective becomes troubled when

[we] attend to the ecological models that cultural
theorists (such as Shaviro, Reynolds, and Amin
and Thrift) have developed alongside site-specific
models of social processes. In *The Wealth of Reality: An Ecology of Composition,* Margaret Syverson
performs one such alternative framework by arguing that writing is a radically *distributed* act, rather
than an isolated act of creation among individual
elements. According to Syverson:

> [T]he knowledge involved in "writing" . . . depends
> on activities and communications shared in inter-
> actions not only among people but also interac-
> tions between people and various structures in
> the environment, from physical landmarks to
> technological instruments to graphical represen-
> tations. . . . Our theories of composition have been
> somewhat atomistic, focusing on individual writ-
> ers, individual texts, isolated acts, processes, or
> artifacts. (8)

Syverson argues that rhetoric and composition
"has posited a triangle of writer, text, and audience," which "has tended to single out the writer,
the text, or the audience as the focus of analysis"
(23). This isolated view fails to highlight what
Syverson calls the emergent ecological process
of writing. Rather than focusing on the familiar
"triangle" that places various elements into a static
relation with the other elements, Syverson maintains that "we can speak of the distribution of . . .
[text composing] across physical, social, psychological, spatial, and temporal dimensions. . . . [T]he
social dimensions of composition are distributed,
embodied, emergent, and enactive" (23). Syverson's ecological approach places the "scene" of
writing into a field that is distributed and socially
situated. Writing is thus more than a matter of
discrete elements (audience, a writer, text, tools,
ideas) in static relation to one another (a writer
types her ideas into a computer for an audience
who reads the text). Rather, writing is distributed
across a range of processes and encounters: the
event of using a keyboard, the encounter of a writing body within a space of dis/comfort, the events
of writing in an apathetic/energetic/distant/close
group. A vocabulary of "distribution" points to
how those elements are enacted and lived, how
they are put into use, and what change comes from
the in-processes-ness itself.[1]

Much like Syverson has done in her own work,
we can tune to a model of public rhetoric that
sets its sights across a wider social field of distribution. Such attunement is important if we want
to account for rhetoric's (public) operation in the

social field. That is, if we are to explore how rhetoric circulates in a "practical consciousness of a present kind, in a living and interrelating continuity," as Raymond Williams puts it (132), we need a model that allows us to discuss such movement. Rather than imagining the rhetorical situation in a relatively closed system, this distributed or ecological focus might begin to imagine the situation within an open network. Returning to Amin and Thrift's notion of a city as a weather system, or an agglomeration of processes, we recall how we saw that "city" might better be conceptualized in terms of a verb—as in *to city*—as opposed to a noun. This grammatical oddity parallels the ways we speak in terms of *rhetoric* as a verb: we *do rhetoric*, rather than (just) finding ourselves *in a rhetoric*. By extension, we might also say that rhetorical situation is better conceptualized as a mixture of processes and encounters; it should become a verb, rather than a fixed noun or *situs*. This kind of foregrounding within an affective field offers the possibility of a vocabulary that reveals a wider context for public rhetorics.

To borrow another conceptual metaphor, we are speaking about the ways in which rhetorical processes operate within a viral economy. The intensity, force, and circulatory range of a rhetoric are always expanding through the mutations and new exposures attached to that given rhetoric, much like a virus. An ecological, or *affective*, rhetorical model is one that reads rhetoric both as a process of distributed emergence and as an ongoing circulation process. Deleuze and Guattari give us one example of such an affective rhetoric in their introduction to *A Thousand Plateaus*, where they write about the *becoming* of evolutionary processes that happen between two or more species. Rather than a hierarchical transmission of genetic information, evolution involves a kind of sharing and an emergence that happens in the in-between of species. This is what Remy Ghauvin describes as an *"aparallel evolution* of two beings that have absolutely nothing to do with each other" (quoted in Deleuze and Guattari, 10). For example, write Deleuze and Guattari:

> [Consider] Benveniste and Todaro's current research on a type G virus, with its double connection to baboon DNA and the DNA of certain kinds of domestic cats. . . . [T]here is an *aparallel evolution* . . . [between] the baboon and the cat; it is obvious that they are not models or copies of each other (a becoming-baboon of the cat does not mean that the cat "plays" baboon). . . . [Transfers of genetic material by viruses of through other

procedures, fusions of cells originating in different species, have results analogous to those of "the abominable couplings dear to antiquity and the Middle Ages." Transversal communication between different lines scramble the genealogical trees. (10–11)

The image of a viral/genetic connection between baboon and cat (two beings that, in Ghauvin's words, have absolutely nothing to do with each other) suggests a new kind of model for thinking of rhetoric's "transversal communication" and travel in the world. A given rhetoric is not *contained* by the elements that comprise its rhetorical situation (exigence, rhetor, audience, constraints). Rather, a rhetoric emerges already infected by the viral intensities that are circulating in the social field. Moreover, this same rhetoric will go on to evolve in *aparallel* ways: between two "species" that have absolutely nothing to do with each other. What is shared between them is *not* the situation, but certain contagions and energy. This does not mean the shared rhetoric reproduces copies or models of "original" situations (any more than the shared G virus turns a cat into a baboon). Instead, the same rhetoric might manage to infect and connect various processes, events, and bodies.

Situations Unbound: City Problems

In order to explore what this shifted emphasis on rhetorical ecologies might look like in our scholarship, I would like to take an example of a public rhetoric from my adopted Texas hometown, Austin. When I first moved to Austin in 1992, the economy was less than ideal. While Austin is a place of state government affairs and bureaucracy, the city economy was far from being competitive with larger Texas cities like Dallas or Houston. Few graduates from the University of Texas remained in Austin for the jobs; you stayed because you loved Austin.[2] But this all changed in the mid- to late-1990s, when the technology boom brought new infrastructure into the city. Thanks to an onslaught of dot com startup companies in the area, as well as bigger companies like Dell Computers, Austin quickly became a major player in the technology sector. The city earned the nickname "Silicon Hills," which echoed its close connection with the technologically saturated areas known as "Silicon Valley" and "Silicon Alley." Almost overnight, Austin became a major player in the financial and technological sector.

As a result of this growth, Austin experienced significant changes to its entire economy. Not only did the city's population explode, but real estate prices and median income also began to climb. According to a 2002 city council white paper on Austin economic development:

> Local economic growth in Austin has been extraordinary in recent years. A combination of corporate relocations and expansions, rapid population growth, extensive investment in technology and Internet-related start-ups, and the meteoric rise of Dell helped make Austin among the five fastest growing metropolitan areas in the United States over the last decade. Since 1990, per capita personal income has risen from $18,092 to $32,039 (during 2000), more than 280,000 jobs have been created, and the average price of a home sold has grown from $87,600 to a current estimate of $199,500, a gain of almost 130 percent. ("Austin's Economic Future")

Because of the growth in income levels and a more professional population, many large chain stores began to view Austin as a viable market for retail outlets like Home Depot, Barnes and Noble, Starbucks, Target, Borders, and other "big box" franchises. Locally owned businesses in Austin quickly began to feel the sting of increased rents in those areas that had previously been affordable. Higher costs of operation forced many smaller local businesses to either move outside of their long-established sites in central Austin or close down business completely. Sound Exchange, a popular local record store in the heart of central Austin (commonly referred to as "the Drag"), is one example of a business that was forced to shut down its operation due to higher rent. Whereas Sound Exchange's rent had previously been $2800 throughout the 1990s, the new lease in 2003 climbed to $4369 per month (Gross). After serving as one of the most unique independent record stores in Austin since 1977, Sound Exchange finally closed its doors in January 2003. The business was quickly replaced by Baja Fresh Mexican Grill, a national fast food chain.

In Austin, the experience of Sound Exchange is hardly unusual. As journalist Lacey Tauber writes in a story for the Austin Independent Media Center about local businesses along the Drag:

> On the south end, Captain Quackenbush's (aka Quack's) coffee house moved out more than two years ago to Hyde Park. The smell of incense no longer wafts down the street from the A-frame of Good Gawd, what used to be a filled-to-overflowing vintage and costume shop, now relocated to South Lamar. Banzai Japanese and sushi restaurant and its smiling Buddha mural are nowhere to be found. In their place sits the new home of Diesel clothing company, a branch of a major corporation that can set shoppers back more than $130 for a pair of jeans. . . . Continuing up the Drag, more corporate faces appear. A long-vacant area is now home to Chipotle Mexican Grill, a business that is partially owned by the McDonalds corporation. Where the old Texas Textbooks once stood, Tyler's shoe and beach shop . . . displays a giant Nike logo. ("Is Austin Slowly Losing its Character?")

By the time I began teaching first-year writing at The University of Texas in 2001, the Drag's main businesses consisted of The Gap, Chipotle Mexican Grill, Diesel, Urban Outfitters, Barnes and Noble, and Tower Records. In less than a decade, the Drag lost several independent bookstores, music stores, coffee shops, and other small businesses. It was difficult not to sense the palpable transformation that was moving throughout the city.

In 2002, two local businesses, BookPeople Bookstore and Waterloo Records, decided to take a stand against the city's plan to give tax-breaks for a large Borders Bookstore to open up directly across from the two shops. According to Steve Bercu, the owner of BookPeople:

> I was talking with the owner of Waterloo Records about our struggle to stop the City of Austin from providing incentives for a developer who planned to put a chain bookstore across the street from our stores. I suggested that we get some bumper stickers that said "Keep Austin Weird," put both our logos on them, and then give them away at our stores. We decided that we should buy 5,000 stickers and see what our customers thought. (Bercu)

These 5,000 stickers were so popular that the stores immediately ordered another 10,000 and then 25,000 stickers. Almost a year later, nearly 60,000 stickers had been distributed. Soon enough, other Austin businesses joined the call to weirdness. Local businesses began to sell t-shirts that featured their individual logos on front and the same "Keep Austin Weird" logo on the back.

The phrase "Keep Austin Weird" quickly passed into the city's cultural circulation, taking on the importance of a quasi-civic duty. One pledge pitch for a local public radio station told listeners, "You too can work towards keeping Austin weird by pledging to keep KOOP Radio 91.7FM on-the-air." In certain parts of Austin, it is nearly impossible

to go for very long without finding some display of the slogan on a t-shirt, bumper sticker, tote bag, mug, or a local business's billboard vowing to "keep it weird." Ironically enough, the injunction to "Keep Austin Weird" has even erupted at the level of city politics. In a 2002 white paper on Austin's economic development, the city council formally acknowledged the reality of "weird Austin" and its effect on the life of the city itself:

> [Q]uality of life, an umbrella term that loosely covers variables such as recreational and cultural amenities, overall cost of living, diversity of local residents, and a sense of place . . . is an increasingly important asset. This is especially the case in Austin, where there is a strong sense that the above factors combine in a unique and special way. ("Austin's Economic Future")

The white paper footnotes that this "strong sense" of uniqueness is "[e]ncapsulated in the popular bumper sticker 'Keep Austin Weird'" ("Austin's Economic Future"). With this public incorporation of the slogan, the city council legitimated the rather intangible weirdness as a very real element of Austin's everyday existence.

At this point, one familiar question seems appropriate: *What is the rhetorical situation here?* Using Bitzer's model of rhetorical situation to read Austin's "weird rhetoric," we might describe the "big box" influx as (in the eyes of many Austinites) an exigence, or an imperfection marked by urgency. Certain rhetorical bodies involved in this scene, like BookPeople and Waterloo, chose to make the exigence salient by evoking it specifically as a problem to a number of audiences— Austin residents, city government, etc. There were also a number of constraints upon anti-big boxers, including a reluctance to be seen as undermining free and fair competition. While this is only one possible (and quite truncated) reading of this scene's rhetorical situation, we can already begin

to see how this model can be useful for reading the complex relation of elements within public scenes.

But, at the same time, we can also bracket these analytical terms in order to bring something else into focus: the lived, in-process operations of this rhetoric. Here we're simply shifting field and ground of the same scene. Because the rhetoric of "weirdness" is distributed through ecologies that expand beyond audience/rhetor/exigence, we begin to see more about its public operation by bracketing these terms for a moment. Consider the ways in which this rhetoric has circulated in the social field. The original rhetoric has been expanded in the course of new calls, which adopt the phrase and transform it to fit other purposes. The University of Texas Liberal Arts' college gives away shirts that are very similar to the "weird" shirts, though they feature the slogan "Keep Austin Liberal Arts" in place of the earlier motto.

Likewise, the Austin Public Library circulated many popular bumper stickers that also kept the same "weird" font, but instead featuring the words, "Keep Austin Reading." Similarly, new businesses that emerged as replacements of older local busi-

nesses have begun to adopt the "Keep Austin Weird" slogan as advertisement. Older businesses, too, have started using the phrase as a way of promoting themselves in local publications. Even the corporate giant Cingular Wireless has created an advertisement in local publications that prominently features the phrase "Keepin' Austin Weird" beside their corporate logo. The obvious irony in Cingular's use of this phrase relates to the "weird" slogan's origination in a movement against big business and non-local corporate interests in Austin. These various rhetorics overlap through a kind of *shared contagion,* though the calls for local business support, the promotion of Liberal Arts, and the encouragement of literacy are hardly overlapping in terms of their *exigencies* or even their *audiences.* At the same time, of course, the "weird rhetoric" receives an increased circulation through these kinds of affective transmission.

In fact, even the increasingly popular counter-slogans manage to illustrate a kind of distributed ecological spread of this rhetoric. Appearing on t-shirts and bumper stickers throughout Austin, there is the "Make Austin Normal" campaign, which was the brainchild of a University of Texas business student who wanted to make a point of (and a profit from) what he sees as the ironic popularity of the "Keep Austin Weird" slogan. Of course, the "Make Austin Normal" campaign

is hardly unique. While walking along the one of the main city streets of central Austin one spring day, I stumbled across a piece of white paper pasted on the side of a newspaper stand. In all block letters, the words read: "Keep Austin fucking normal. Conform. It's just easier." Upon seeing a picture of this homemade sign, my friend laughingly commented, "Doesn't this person realize just how *weird* this sign is?" While my friend meant this comment in jest, it addresses another aspect of what I call "rhetorical ecologies." Not only do these counter-rhetorics directly respond to and resist the original exigence, they also expand the lived experience of the original rhetorics by *adding* to them—even while changing and expanding their shape. The anti-weird rhetorics of Austin add to the "weird rhetoric" ecology through a practice of mixture and encounters of extended proximity.

Distribution, concatenation, encounter. This public scene forces us into a rather fluid framework of exchanges—a fluidity that bleeds the elements of rhetorical situation. Indeed, the (neo)Bitzerian models cannot account for the amalgamations and transformations—the *viral spread*—of this rhetoric within its wider ecology. When we temporarily bracket the discrete elements of rhetor, audience, and exigence in the "Keep Austin Weird" movement, we attune to the *processes* that both comprise and extend the rhetorics. Indeed, the

rhetorical process itself plays out between the sites of these elements: the call is currently circulating on shirts and cars, it is mocked and pushed against, and it is distributed across purposes and institutional spaces. It circulates in a wide ecology of rhetorics. To play off Shaviro's words, the force of "messages," as they accrete over time, determine the shape of public rhetorics.

A New Model: Distributed Rhetorical Ecologies

Although the standard models of rhetorical situation can tell us much about the elements that are involved in a particular situation, these same models can also mask the fluidity of rhetoric. Rhetorical situations involve the amalgamation and mixture of many different events and happenings that are not properly segmented into audience, text, or rhetorician. We must therefore consider whether our popular models reflect the fullness of rhetoric's operation in public. Rhetorical ecologies are co-ordinating processes, moving across the same social field and within shared structures of feeling. The original call of Austin's "weird" rhetoric, for example, has been affected by the actions, events, and encounters that form "small events loosely joined"[3] as a kind of rhetorical-event neighborhood. Even when a multi-national corporation like Cingular coopts the phrase, placing it within a completely antithetical context from its origin, we find that Cingular's rhetoric *adds* to the (original) rhetoric of "weirdness" in Austin. They mark two different situations, of course—complete with different exigence, audience, rhetors, and constraints. But Cingular's rhetoric co-ordinates within the same neighborhood as the anti-corporate rhetoric. Thus, in the course of this evolution, the "weird

rhetoric" receives what we might call an extended half-life in its range of circulation and visibility, as well as a changed shape, force, and intensity. Like a neighborhood, the amalgamation of events can both extend the street's visibility (or impact) and its very contours.

Consequently, though rhetorical situation models are undeniably helpful for thinking of rhetoric's contextual character, they fall somewhat short when accounting for the amalgamations and transformations—the spread—of a given rhetoric within its wider ecology. Rather than replacing the rhetorical situation models that we have found so useful, however, an ecological augmentation adopts a view toward the processes and events that extend beyond the limited boundaries of elements. One potential value of such a shifted focus is the way we view counter-rhetorics, issues of cooptation, and strategies of rhetorical production and circulation. Moreover, we can begin to recognize the way rhetorics are held together trans-situationally, as well as the effects of trans-situationality on rhetorical circulation. As urban scholar Helen Liggett writes, "presentations of situation [can be] understood as somewhat open-ended processes involving relays and connections that are both theoretical and practical" (2). In other words, we begin to see that public rhetorics do not only exist in the elements of their situations, but also in the radius of their neighboring events.

By shifting the ground and field in this manner, we add the dimension of movement back into our discussions of rhetoric. Brian Massumi illuminates the dilemma of movement's absence in our theories: "When positioning of any kind comes a determining first [in our theories], movement comes a problematic second Movement is entirely subordinated to the positions it connects. . . . The very notion of movement as qualitative transformation is [therefore] lacking" (3). We hear echoes of Biesecker's critique here that rhetorical situation too often imagines an audience as a "conglomeration of subjects whose identity is fixed prior to the rhetorical event itself," which circumscribes the power of rhetoric as movement. Massumi's hope is that

movement, sensation, and qualities of experience couched in matter in its most literal sense (and sensing) might be culturally theoretically thinkable, without falling into either . . . naive realism or . . . subjectivism and without contradicting the very real insights of poststructuralist cultural theory concerning the coextensiveness of culture with the field of experience and of power with culture. (4)

Our rhetorical theories can thus acknowledge the affective channels of rhetorical communication and operation by "testifying" to them. Such testimonies would invent new concepts and deploy them in order to theorize how publics are also created through affective channels.

Producing Rhetorical Pedagogies

One implication of conceiving rhetorics in ecological or event-full terms relates to rhetoric and composition pedagogies. More specifically, I argue that this augmented framework can emerge at the level of *production*. In her discussion of classrooms as (potentially) protopublic bodies, Rosa Eberly argues that rhetoric is a process, not a substance that inheres in the collection of traits within a given text. Instead, she continues, "Rhetoric is thus *not only understood but practiced* as the powerful architectonic productive art that it is" (293). Emphasizing production should not mean falling into the trap of "real vs. artificial" writing situations, but instead should stress the ways in which rhetorical productions are inseparable from lived encounters of public life. Richard Marback calls this inseparability a "material theory of rhetoric," which "would articulate the impact of material and representational practices on each other" (87). The kinds of pedagogies I would like to pursue attune to this *mutuality* of material practice, embodied experience, and discursive representation that operate in public spaces every day. By way of concluding my discussion, I want to briefly highlight one way that this ecological publicness can inform our pedagogical *practices* in order to place greater emphasis on production in the classroom.

Whereas research is often considered by students (and even some teachers) as a process *leading to* public production and circulation (a means to an end, so to speak), we can look to the logics of a generative research method that takes the circulation of effects *as an aim*. Some of the most compelling "live" examples of generative research are city blogs, or weblogs (often written by individuals) that track the life of a place through images, text, comments, and links to relevant stories and sites. Take the example of G. Schindler's photoblog, which documents the life of Austin and its urban spaces through images. The blog writer, or "blogger," tracks the city in what we might recognize as a kind of local-research-in-the-wild. Schindler is a stalker of sorts, documenting local places without any other *telos* beyond the documentation itself. His images are unframed by extra commentary or descriptions, allowing the reader to simply drift through the city in a kind of *derive*. Through his images of signs, storefronts, abandoned couches, and handmade lost pet flyers, Schindler captures the (extraordinary details of life in the city. Instead of attempting to give readers the "true" version of Austin, he documents his own encounters with/in the city.

Call it generative research. These encounters can be tracked among (student) users as an example of how representations of place—like Austin—are constructed discursively, visually, affectively, and link-fully. Moreover, because this kind of documentation is public, often open to comments and citation in other blogs and websites, the "research" grows in social waves. The networked nature of blogs puts research into a circulation that becomes linked, put to other uses, transformed. In fact, without such citation and use by others, a blog is as good as dead. After a bit of caveat-ing, we might even dub it an act of "open source" research, exposing the myth of research as a personal process that only *later* leads to a public

Images from Schindler's photoblog

text. The photoblog's logic turns documentation into a kind of social production in itself.

Rather than thinking *only* in terms of audience, purpose, clarity, and information, therefore, the logic of the photoblog focuses on the *effects* and *concatenations* of our local ecologies. Bringing this logic into the realm of our own rhetorical pedagogy, we are reminded that rhetorically-grounded education can mean something more than learning how to decode elements, analyze texts, and thinking *about* public circulations of rhetoric. It can also engage processes and encounters. Not "*learning* by doing," but "*thinking* by doing." Or, better yet, *thinking/doing*—with a razor thin slash mark barely keeping the two terms from bleeding into each other. This is a rethinking of the "in order to later" model, where students learn methods, skills, and research *in order to later* produce at other sites (other sites in the university or workplace, for example). This one-way flow can be radically revised in everyday settings, where rhetorical ecologies are already spatially, affectively, and conceptually in practice. As Eberly puts it, "[r]hetoric matters because rhetoric—*which demands engagement with the living*—is the process through which texts are not only produced but also understood to matter" (296; emphasis mine). This "mattering" is not fully explained only by a text's elemental properties, but also in the sense of *material effects and processes*. When we approach a rhetoric that does indeed engage with the living, hooking into the processes that are already in play, then we find ourselves theorizing rhetorical publicness. We find ourselves engaging a public rhetoric whose power is not circumscribed or delimited. We encounter rhetoric.

I would like to thank Diane Davis, Jeff Rice, and Gollin Brooke for their feedback on earlier drafts of this article.

NOTES

1. Perhaps we can rephrase this notion of distribution in terms of music: the lived experience of listening to a song cannot be framed only in terms of its constituent parts; the experience also includes the distributed processes of *hearing*—and, in my apartment with the bass turned up, even *feeling* the song.

2. Jokes used to circulate about Austin being the only city in the United States where the 7-11 employees also happened to have PhDs.

3. Here I purposefully play off David Weinberger's *Small Pieces Loosely Joined*, which makes a similar kind of argument about networking and social ecologies.

WORKS CITED

Amin, Ash and N. Thrift. *Cities: Reimagining the Urban.* Cambridge, UK: Polity, 2002.

Bercu, Steve. "Letter to the Editor: Keep Everywhere Weird." *Publishers Weekly.* Dec 5, 2003. <http://print.google.com/print/doc?articleid=f3ypx1QKhYE>

Biesecker, Barbara A. "Rethinking the Rhetorical Situation from Within the Thematic of *Différance.*" *Philosophy and Rhetoric* 22.2 (1989): 110–30 [reprinted in this volume].

Bitzer, Lloyd F. "The Rhetorical Situation." *Philosophy and Rhetoric* 1.1 (1968): 1–14 [reprinted in this volume].

City of Austin. "Austin's Economic Future" November 20, 2002. <http://www.ci.austin.tx.us/redevelopment/whitepaperl.htm>.

Deleuze, Gilles, and F. Guattari. *A Thousand Plateaus: Capitalism and Schizophrenia.* Minneapolis: University of Minnesota Press, 1987.

Eberly, Rosa A. "Rhetoric and the Anti-Logos Doughball: Teaching Deliberating Bodies the Practices of Participatory Democracy." *Rhetoric & Public Affairs* 5.2 (2002): 287–300.

Gross, Joe. "Say Goodbye to Sound Exchange." *Austin-American Statesman* 9 January 2003: 11–12.

Liggett, Helen. *Urban Encounters.* Minneapolis: University of Minnesota Press, 2003.

Marback, Richard. "Detroit and the Closed Fist: Toward a Theory of Material Rhetoric." *Rhetoric Review* 17.1 (1998): 74–91.

Massumi, Brian. *Parables for the Virtual: Movement, Affect, Sensation.* Durham, NC: Duke University Press, 2002.

Phelps, Louise W. *Composition as a Human Science.* New York: Oxford University Press, 1988.

Reynolds, Nedra. *Geographies of Writing: Inhabiting Places and Encountering Difference.* Carbondale: Southern Illinois University Press, 2004.

Schindler, G. <http://www.gschindler.com/blog.htm>.

Shaviro, Steven. *Connected, or, What It Means to Live in the Network Society.* Minneapolis: University of Minnesota Press, 2003.

Smith, Craig R., and Scott Lybarger. "Bitzer's Model Reconstructed." *Communication Quarterly* 44.2 (1996): 197–213.

Syverson, M. A. *The Wealth of Reality: An Ecology of Composition.* Carbondale: Southern Illinois University Press, 1999.

Tauber, Lacey. "Is Austin Slowly Losing its Character?" *Austin Independent Media Center.* 04 Dec 2002. <http://austin.indymedia.org/newswire/display/9888/index.php>.

Vatz, Richard. "The Myth of the Rhetorical Situation." *Philosophy and Rhetoric* 6 (1973): 154–161 [reprinted in this volume].

Warner, Michael. "Publics and Counterpublics." *Public Culture* 14.1 (2002): 49–71.

Williams, Raymond. *Marxism and Literature.* Oxford, UK: Oxford University Press, 1977.

PART IV

PERSPECTIVES ON PUBLICS

Rhetoric's primary domain has generally been the field of the "probable"—which is to say, those social and civic places (in physical space as well as cyberspace) where reasoned judgments and policies are desirable, but where there is no necessary or certain knowledge from which to draw in making such decisions. Traditionally, we have thought of the law courts and legislative assemblies as two of the primary sites of the rhetorical. More and more often, though, these decisions are being made in virtual spaces where access to information has greatly increased, even if the processing of that information remains complicated. In each case, however, the ability to make decisions is contingent. From the U.S. Supreme Court to Change.org, decision making (Should gay marriage be legalized? How should we prevent bullying online?) is based on inferences and probabilities rather than on rock-solid knowledge of an immutable truth.

After all, how can one truly "know" that someone premeditated a killing and was of sound mind? Or how can one truly "know" if going to war in a particular situation represents the "public good"? Yet such judgments must be made, and in many instances they must be made in ways that draw upon and implicate the moral bearings and considerations of the public or community being enacted and/or addressed. Should we legalize abortion? What is the federal government's role in the health care of its citizenry? Who stands to gain or lose in the debate over Net neutrality? And so on. Instead of being presented as a rigid logic or form of scientific demonstration, then, rhetoric has typically been cast as an art of practical reason that functions to negotiate the course of communal belief and action where disagreement and chaos would otherwise reign.

The role of rhetoric as practical reason in public decision making, or "deliberative democracy," has long been complicated by a number of factors, including most prominently the nature of its particular form and its force in effecting public morality. Some argue, as does G. Thomas Goodnight in "The Personal, Technical, and Public Spheres of Argumentation: A Speculative Inquiry into the Art of Public Deliberation," that the quality of public deliberation has atrophied as arguments drawn from the private and technical spheres, which operate through very different forms of invention and subject matter selection, have invaded, and perhaps even appropriated, the public sphere. The effect has been to undermine and impoverish the quality of deliberation as a means of determining social knowledge and the public good. In the conclusion to his essay, Goodnight offers an impassioned appeal to refashion our sense of deliberative argument by examining the forums and modes of argument in public controversies.

One of the most elaborate responses to the role of rhetoric in public moral decision making in recent times has been the attempt to rethink the very form of public argument as narrative. In "Narrative as a Human Communication Paradigm: The Case of Public Moral Argument," Walter R. Fisher urges us to reconceptualize human communication, and by extension public moral argument, as the function of a "narrative paradigm." According to Fisher, humans are storytelling animals, and therefore the "reason" of public moral deliberation or argumentation is better understood (and perhaps more fulsomely enacted) in and through the narratives they tell, rather than through the more-or-less rigid logics prescribed by the "rational world paradigm" of the eighteenth-century Enlightenment.

An alternate approach to the problem of public moral decision making is contained in Celeste Michelle Condit's "Crafting Virtue: The Rhetorical Construction of Public Morality." According to Condit, models of public moral action that reduce public decision making to "narratives" and "conversations" reify the rhetorical process in terms of private discourse forms that ignore and undermine the ways in which collectivities actually constitute a sense of public morality. So, for example, she argues that in conversations (a privileged form of private interaction), all is lost if one interlocutor fails to understand the meaning of the other; in the public forum, however, advocates don't have to understand or even persuade one another so much as they have to achieve a consensus of opinion and judgment among a larger public audience. Rhetoric, she maintains, is best understood as a "craft" that draws upon and manages prevailing public vocabularies—which include ideographs, common *topoi*, cultural myths and metaphors, narratives, and the like—as they embody and enable the collective sense of public moral good. This embodiment, which bears the mark of the community's history and experience, establishes a kind of localized objectivity that produces what others have called a "rhetorical culture." And it is in that rhetorical culture, according to Condit, that we find the capacity to "live the moment, through the legacies of the past, with just an eye to the fact that we are crafting the future as well."

Others would seek to refashion the contours of what best constitutes a given public. Carolyn R. Miller argues that the *polis* offers a productive framework for rethinking the spaces where communal debates and discussions occur. In "The *Polis* as Rhetorical Community," she argues that the contemporary concerns about *community* are implied in historical discussions of the *polis*, or city-state. In both instances, there is a tension between the many and the few, the individual and the group. These tensions exist to be resolved and thus implicate the need for rhetoric. And, while there are distinct and explicit individuals engaged as audiences in rhetorical decision making, there is also the need to conceptualize a community as "a horizon of possibilities" and "not primarily an empirical social structure." Thus, in a contingent world, the community is the potential for disparate desires to be addressed and resolved through rhetoric.

By contrast, Robert Hariman and John Louis Lucaites argue for the power of the visual to forge public identities. In "Public Identity and Collective Memory in U.S. Iconic Photography: The Image of 'Accidental Napalm,'" the authors argue that the visual is equal to the discursive in terms of forming the identities of individuals, of strangers, who are framed as publics and communities in their engagement of specific images. Images have the ability to transform public opinions and shape discourse related to contemporary events. At the same time, the image resists the stability that critics of visual rhetoric would demand (a representation of the thing *as is*). As such, the image as rhetorical is always open to recirculation and reconstitution. It is not tethered to the situation; rather, the image shifts and moves to suit the demands of strangers-as-publics who share in engaging the same.

In "Publics and Counterpublics (abbreviated version)," Michael Warner turns his attention to those who are doubly coded as strangers: those who gather anonymously to create, share, and protect alternative identities, while also existing at a distance from the dominant public streams of discourse. Recognizing that the concept of publics is operationally flexible—by turns, a social *totality* and a concrete *audience*—Warner points toward a third meaning, one where strangers come together "only in relation to texts and their circulation." Within this connective system of meaning, counterpublics both resist and challenge dominant discursive forms. In the process, Warner argues, counterpublics face the tension of transforming publics, maintaining their own distinct oppositional characteristics, or being subsumed within the larger matrices that stand in opposition to them.

The essays here represent only some of the most recent and provocative efforts to understand the relationships between publics and rhetoric. However one evaluates the particular choices made by these scholars, it should be clear that the problem of constituting an effective deliberative democracy, particularly in an increasingly multicultural and multimediated society, will require sustained attention—not only to the range of ways in which rhetoric constitutes and is implicated in the process of public decision making, but also how newer methods, models, and mediums are integrated into the selfsame pursuit.

ADDITIONAL READINGS

DeLuca, Kevin M., and Jennifer Peeples. (2002). "From Public Sphere to Public Screen: Democracy, Activism, and the Violence of Seattle." *Critical Studies in Media Communication* 19: 125–51.

Ehninger, Douglas. (1970). "Argument as Method: Its Nature, Its Limitations, and Its Uses." *Communication Monographs* 37: 101–10.

Farrell, Thomas B., and G. Thomas Goodnight. (1981). "Accidental Rhetoric: The Root Metaphors of Three Mile Island." *Communication Monographs* 48: 271–300.

Frentz, Thomas. (1985). "Rhetorical Conversation, Time and Moral Action." *Quarterly Journal of Speech* 71: 1–18.

Jonsen, Albert R., and Stephen Toulmin. (1988). *The Abuse of Casuistry: A History of Moral Reasoning.* Berkeley and Los Angeles: University of California Press.

Klumpp, James F., and Thomas A. Hollihan. (1989). "Rhetorical Criticism as Moral Action." *Quarterly Journal of Speech* 75: 84–96.

McGee, Michael Calvin. (1984). "Secular Humanism: A Radical Reading of 'Culture Industry' Production." *Critical Studies in Mass Communication* 1: 1–33.

Peters. J. (1999). *Speaking into the Air: A History of the Idea of Communication.* Chicago: University of Chicago Press.

Porrovecchio, Mark J. (2007). "Lost in the WTO Shuffle: Publics, Counterpublics, and the Individual." *Western Journal of Communication* 71.3: 235–56.

Sloop, John M., and James P. McDaniel, eds. (1998). *Judgement Calls: Rhetoric, Politics and Indeterminacy.* Boulder, CO: Westview Press.

Wander, Philip. (1983). "The Ideological Turn in Modern Criticism." *Central States Speech Journal* 34: 1–18.

The Personal, Technical, and Public Spheres of Argument

A Speculative Inquiry into the Art of Public Deliberation

G. Thomas Goodnight

Deliberative arguments in the public sphere necessarily pertain to the domain of probable knowledge—that kind of knowledge which, although uncertain, is more reliable than untested opinion or guesswork.[1] Public deliberation is inevitably probable because the future is invariably more and less than expected. The full worth of a policy is always yet to be seen. Argumentation offers a momentary pause in the flow of events, an opportunity to look down the present road as well as paths untaken. As deliberation raises expectations that are feared or hoped for, public argument is a way to share in the construction of the future.

To debate the public good or public policy presupposes that arguers and audiences have a sense of before and after, of that which leads to debate and that which may extend beyond it. To encounter controversy over the course of future events is always to raise the question, where will our deliberations lead? If public argument can yield no more than a probable answer to questions of preferable conduct, it can offer no less than an alternative to decisions based on authority or blind chance.

My purpose here is to consider the status of deliberative rhetoric. My guiding assumptions are that rhetoric is an art, a human enterprise engaging individual choice and common activity, and that deliberative rhetoric is a form of argumentation through which citizens test and create social knowledge in order to uncover, assess, and resolve shared problems.[2] As any art may fall into periods of disuse and decline, so it is possible for the deliberative arts to atrophy. Barring anarchic conditions, though, when one way of fashioning a future is foregone, another takes its place. Distinguishing deliberative argument from the social practices which have replaced it is difficult. Many forms of social persuasion are festooned with the trappings of deliberation, even while they are designed to succeed by means inimical to knowledgeable choice and active participation. The increasing variety of forums, formats, styles, and institutional practices—each claiming to embody the public will or to represent the public voice—demands careful attention. If such practices continue to evolve uncritiqued, deliberative argument may become a lost art.

I hope to elaborate this claim by proving three propositions. First, argumentative endeavors characteristically involve, *inter alia*, the creative resolution and the resolute creation of uncertainty. Second, particular arguments emerge in concert with or in opposition to ongoing activity in the personal, technical, and public spheres. Third, argument practices arising from the personal and technical spheres presently substitute the semblance of deliberative discourse for actual deliberation, thereby diminishing public life. Each claim involves a progressively greater degree of speculation. Hopefully, by attending to the creative enterprises of argument, and by examining the inherent tensions among the variety of alternative groundings, the present status of deliberative rhetoric can be uncovered and critiqued.

Uncertainty and the Grounding of Disagreement

Whatever else characterizes an argument, to be recognizable as such, a statement, a work of art, even an inchoate feeling must partake in the creative resolution and the resolute creation of uncertainty. Some say the argumentative impulse, the quest to advance or dispense with the "incomprehensible, illogical and uncertain," arises from the human capacity for symbolization. Language itself imparts an ought which is forever broken and formed anew.[3] Others maintain that this impulse arises from a primitive feeling of dread, an unquenchable desire for completeness.[4] Of the ultimate source of uncertainty, I am not sure; but, my sentiments are in line with de Gourmont: "All activity has uncertainty for its principle."[5]

To say that all argument arises in uncertainty is not to say that all arguments are immediately controversial. O'Keefe performed a valuable service in directing attention toward ordinary encounters in life where words are exchanged instead of blows, and in pointing out that while these disputes are different from "products" produced in less personal contexts, they are nonetheless significant varieties of argument.[6] But I contend that even self-evident reasoning, the highest form of argument by some standards, while not immediately inviting clash, is argumentative as well. To the medieval world, for example, the stars were luminescences, intelligences placed in the heavens by God. That they represented the eternal in the world was made self-evident by the fact that they neither disappeared nor varied from their orbits. When a super nova appeared in 1572, as Lewis reports, what had been self-evident became the focus of controversy which ultimately contributed to the collapse of a world view.[7] Not all disconfirmations of the "obviously true" are so dramatic. Nor do all occur in this way. But since arguments involve more than simple sensory perception, being made with some ingenuity, even those propositions which seem to be well instantiated within a cultural perspective persist only against a background of uncertainty.

The recognition that some human endeavors are commonly joined by uncertainty does not lead to any particular theory of argumentation. Indeed, such a recognition is a bit subversive of the traditional task of theorists who, since the breakdown of the Medieval Synthesis, have labored mightily to construct methods, procedures, explanations, and even whole philosophies of argument. Scholars, seeking to establish that argument itself is grounded in particular theories of logic, psychology, sociology, or linguistics (or some combination), have sought to discover some underlying capacity of human existence which governs and gives meaning to the process of argument making. The work continues apace. Uncertainty persists. Until such a time when all the creative enterprises are reduced to a single underlying certainty, it may be useful to add to the repertoire of study the investigation of the manifold ways in which individuals and communities attempt to create and reduce the unknown. The study of why uncertainties appear, what they mean, how they are banished only to be reformed, and what practices shape the course of future events is important, for knowledge of argument's varieties may illuminate the values, character, and blindspots of an era, society, or person.

Members of "societies" and "historical cultures" participate in vast, and not altogether coherent, superstructures which invite them to channel doubts through prevailing discourse practices. In the democratic tradition, we can categorize these channels as the personal, the technical, and the public spheres. "Sphere" denotes branches of activity—the grounds upon which arguments are built and the authorities to which arguers appeal. Differences among the three spheres are plausibly illustrated if we consider the differences between the standards for arguments among friends versus those for judgments of academic arguments versus those for judging political disputes. Permitting a breadth between personal, professional, and public life is characteristically American. The independence of the spheres is protected by a variety of laws protecting privacy and discouraging government intervention in private affairs.

The standards for deciding which events fit into which spheres are sometimes ambiguous and shifting. Burke's notion of identification, however, lends precision to our thinking about this.[8] One form is invoked when a person tries to show "consubstantiality" with another. Another form is invoked through partisan appeals—partisanship being a characteristic of the public. The third form is invoked through a person's identification with his work in a special occupation—the essential ingredient of technical argument. These alternative modes of identification make the personal, technical, and public groundings of arguments possible.

The term "sphere" is not altogether a felicitous one because of its eighteenth- and nineteenth-century connotations of discrete, unchanging arenas where the virtuous play out life according to prevailing custom. One use of spheres as a grounding for rhetorical argument was to justify discrimination against females. Some anti-suffrage speakers justified discrimination on the basis that God had suited women to rule the home and men the professions. Their arguments were grounded in what appeared to be a natural order.[9] Yet from the changing activities of personal and public life, it should be evident that the spheres of argument are not entirely constant over time, and are subject to revision by argument.

Though it may seem historically inevitable that all groundings of argument change as lifestyles are reconfigured, as methods for discovering knowledge become modified, and as the institutions of governance change. But to reduce the spheres of argument themselves to ephemeral contexts or mere points of view is mistaken because all arguers face a similar problem in dealing with uncertainty.[10] An arguer can accept the sanctioned, widely used bundle of rules, claims, procedures, and evidence to wage a dispute. Or the arguer can inveigh against any or all of these "customs" in order to bring forth a new variety of understanding. In the first case, the common grounds for arguing are accepted, and argument is used to establish knowledge about a previously undetermined phenomenon. In the second, argument is employed as a way of reshaping its own grounds. In classical logic this choice was expressed in the contrast between inductive and deductive logic. In the variety of argument endeavors, this tension is expressed by attempts to expand one sphere of argument at the expense of another.

Distinctions among the Spheres of Argument, and an Explanation of How the Groundings of Argument Change

Scholars seek a single explanation of the varieties of argumentative endeavors. Earlier in this century, an attempt was made to ground argument in restricted notions of reasons; variations on the basic forms were imperfections awaiting correction.[11] Contemporary theorists, recognizing that not all arguing is comprised of rigorous adherence to stipulated forms, have turned to psychology and sociology to provide explanatory principles in describing the variety of processes. Cognitive psychologists maintain, roughly speaking, that individuals must make sense of the world through whatever apparatus they can employ; thus, since all argument must be conceived and perceived by individuals, the study of mental processes is preeminent.[12] In contrast, other theorists maintain that humans develop through language into an universe of symbols which shapes and is shaped by intersubjective forms of understanding; hence, since individuals can only be known through social expressions, the study of language is preeminent.[13] Others split the difference by developing theories of interaction among individuals and society.[14] These arguments about arguments are useful in extending our concepts about what any particular disagreement may *mean*. But, if the study of argument *per se* is unhinged from particular epistemological commitments, then the creative tension among alternative groundings of disagreement can be uncovered. From a critic's perspective, argument may be approached as a way of coming to understand the transformations of human activity through the variety of practices employed in making argument.

Studying the current practices of the personal, technical, and public spheres is a useful way to uncover prevailing expressions of the human conditions (the views of the world implicit in particular practices of making argument), and perhaps to discover avenues for criticism. A relatively complete investigation of these practices is the subject of a much longer treatise. However, I would like to present an illustration to demonstrate some of the divergent aspects of practice.

Begin with an example made classic by Willard, strangers arguing in a bar at the airport.[15] This is a relatively private affair. Unless an ethnomethodologist is present, it probably will not be preserved. The statements of the arguers are ephemeral. Since no preparation is required, the subject matter and range of claims are decided by the disputants. Evidence is discovered within memory or adduced by pointing to whatever is at hand. The rules emerge from the strangers' general experience at discussion, fair judgment, strategic guile, and so forth. The time limits imposed on the dispute probably have no intrinsic significance to the disagreement. The plane will take off. An interlocutor will leave. Others may join in and continue the discussion. Those formerly involved in the dispute may replay the disagreement, embroidering it in the retelling. But the chance encounter is at an end.

Suppose that the conversation is preserved, however, and that the arguments are abstracted from their original grounding to serve as examples in supporting claims about a theory of argument. Consider Professor Willard's own arguments about the argument. In his transformation of assertions, grimaces, glances, and self-reports from the original dispute into examples which illustrate observations about the nature of argument, the concrete particularity of the original dispute is lost. But what is to be gained is the advance of a special kind of understanding among members of a professional community of which Willard is a part, the community of argumentation scholars. In creating his statement, Willard narrows the range of subject matter to that of the interests of the requisite community. He brings together a considerable degree of expertise with the formal expectations of scholarly argument (footnotes, titles, organization, documentation, and so forth). The technical arguments are judged by referees as worthy of preservation. Once the research is published, the community addressed may join into the dispute. Of course, Willard and his critics may engage in *ad hominem* attacks, vestigial products of the private sphere, but what engages the community—and continues to do so long after the disputants turn to other battles— is the advance of a special kind of knowledge.

Now if the illustration can be extended just one more step, suppose that the disagreement within the technical field grows so vehement that there arises two groups in unalterable opposition: Willard followers and Willard opponents. Then neither informal disagreement nor theoretical contention is sufficient to contain the arguments involved. The dispute becomes a matter of public debate. Both groups may take to the public forums governing the technical community's business, each contesting for leadership and control of scarce resources. If one side or the other is dissatisfied with the verdict, then the boundaries of the special community are in jeopardy, as disgruntled advocates appeal to a more general public. Willard may be taken to court and tried by his peers, or he may attempt to have legislation passed that would outlaw what he and his followers believe to be harmful teachings. Once the public sphere is entered, the private and technical dimensions of

the disagreement become relevant only insofar as they are made congruent with the practices of public forums.

If a public forum is appropriately designed as a sphere of argument to handle disagreements transcending private and technical disputes, then the demands for proof and the forms of reasoning will not be as informal or fluid as those expressed in a personal disagreement. Yet, since the public must encompass its sub-sets, the forms of reason would be more common than the specialized demands of a particular professional community. Moreover, whereas the public forum inevitably limits participation to representative spokespersons (unlike a chance discussion), an appropriately designed public forum would provide a tradition of argument such that its speakers would employ common language, values, and reasoning so that the disagreement could be settled to the satisfaction of all concerned. Most characteristically, though, the interests of the public realm—whether represented in an appropriate way or not—extend the stakes of argument beyond private needs and the needs of special communities to the interests of the entire community.

The illustration need not be pursued further. The major point to be made is that the ways of making arguments are various. The notions of private, technical, and public spheres are useful in describing the manners in which disagreements can be created and extended in making argument. Some disagreements are created in such a way as to require only the most informal demands for evidence, proof sequences, claim establishment, and language use. These may typify arguments in the personal sphere where the subject matter and consequences of the dispute are up to the participants involved. Other disagreements are created in such a way as to narrow the range of permissible subject matter while requiring more specialized forms of reasoning. These typify the technical sphere where more limited rules of evidence, presentation, and judgment are stipulated in order to identify arguers of the field and facilitate the pursuit of their interests. Transcending the personal and technical spheres is the public, a domain which, while not reducible to the argument practice of any group of social customs or professional communities, nevertheless may be influenced by them. But the public realm is discrete insofar as it provides forums with customs, traditions, and requirements for arguers in the recognition that the consequences of dispute extend beyond the personal and technical spheres.

The preceding illustration is intended to be a starting point in examining the differences among argumentative practices. It is not intended to be the foundation of a taxonomical scheme which approaches the study of argumentation by the classification of statements, situations, and customs within established contexts. In the world of arguers, any particular argumentative artifact *can be taken* to be grounded in any one of the spheres or a combinatory relationship. But the question confronting those who would create ways of raising uncertainty or settling it (and this includes argumentation theorists and critics as well) is the direction in which the dispute is to be developed.

Some critics of argument attempt to provide the links between one sphere and another. Thus, neo-Aristotelian scholars attempted to explain the relation between the private life of orators and their public successes.[16] Others, perhaps musing over the creative possibilities of providing a "perspective by incongruity," rip arguments from generally accepted grounding by idiosyncratically extending the argument by analogy. Hauser and his colleagues, for example, attempted to construe Nixon's Cambodia address as comparable to a potlatch ceremony, a ritual practiced among certain tribes of North American Indians.[17] These informed criticisms *reflect* the ongoing attempts of arguers themselves to reform the grounding of disagreement.

To demonstrate how grounds of argument may be altered, I would like to draw upon several historical examples. In each case, what had been accorded as an appropriate way of arguing for a given sphere was shifted to a new grounding; different kinds of disagreement were created. The first example shows how matters of private dispute can take on a public character. The second demonstrates how matters of public judgment can become subjected to the technical domain. The final illustration involves the cooptation of the technical by the public.

In nineteenth-century America, the poor were generally considered to be poor because of personal character flaws. As explained by adherents of the Gospel of Wealth, poverty was a sign of God's disfavor. The poor were poor because they were lazy, spendthrift, or simply engaged in pursuits that did not deserve reward. Arguments made to the poor and about the poor were grounded in the private sphere; poverty was essentially an issue between a man and his Maker.[18] Thus harder work, more saving, and greater self-reliance were encouraged so that all could share in a prosperous abundance

provided by God. Help was cajoled from the rich only as a gesture of Christian charity. With the advent of the Progressive movement, however, the grounding of arguments about poverty gradually shifted from the private to the public sphere. Converting the doctrines of Darwin and his social proponents to a recognition that the environment shaped people and the environment could be altered, Progressives gradually transformed the issue of poverty to a public concern, one that was a shared rather than an individual responsibility.[19] Even though attempts to return the issue of poverty to the private sphere sometimes arose, the Progressives were successful in placing the issue on the public docket.

The public question of the treatment of the "environment" offers another example of the transformation of argument grounding. Extending from the early part of the twentieth century were various public movements to protect the heritage of all Americans from the pursuit of private interests by preserving part of pristine America. The vanishing wilderness was the common concern of artists, preachers, naturalists, indeed any citizens who wished to see nature's works preserved.[20] While these movements were successful in restricting some exploitative practices and protecting some of the wilderness, it was not until the public environmentalist movement of the 1970s that the grounds of appeal became more restricted. Rachel Carson's *Silent Spring*, a work combining lyric style and limited scientific fact, projected a future world where the growing poisonous by-products of industry permeated the cellular structure of all living individuals.[21] So strong was the public concern that a relatively new technical community blossomed, ecologists. Yet, with the competing demands for energy, a private interest made public in terms of job loss, the ecologists could not take the environmental protection principle to its ultimate extent. Rather, state-of-the-art practice becomes a tentative balancing between projections of competing demands of energy and ecology. These complicated equations are the only answer to a public movement that finds itself making opposing demands.[22]

The realm of public argument can give rise to the ascendancy of technological fields, but public interest may also circumscribe the practice of technical argument. Certainly one of the most outrageous "perspectives by incongruity" of all times was the forlorn attempt by Nazi partisans to create by act of national will a purely German science. Less obviously, national governments influence the conduct of argument communities by providing resources for equipment, training, and information transmittal. These inducements made in the "public" interest may influence the selection of subjects, techniques, and results that are made by theoretically apolitical communities of inquirers. The degree to which present defense efforts induce scientists away from other possible avenues of research is well-known. What the configuration of technical argument communities might be if they were not so subordinated to the limits placed by the public interest is an open question.

In each example, the transformation of grounding is evident. Poverty could be the matter of private disagreement so long as the issue was not grounded in questions of public interest and responsibility. The environment was a public issue; but as the implications of public interest demanded trade-offs that could be made only by technical judgments, ecology was given over largely to the technical sphere. Finally, whereas scientists at least in theory should be able to create communities of inquirers without regard to the demands of the public, public leaders nevertheless provide parameters for scientific argument. Although these examples illustrate how some disputes become transformed, it can be demonstrated that some theories of argument attempt to create an organizing perspective where a single sphere grounds all argument practice.

One example of an attempt to harness the varieties of reason under the aegis of a single sphere is that of Toulmin in *Human Understanding*.[23] In this work, it may be recalled, Toulmin seeks to explain the evolutionary development of fields. In the grand synthesis, the most highly developed forms of reason are mirrored in, but not perfectly reproduced by, developing other disciplines. At the crown sits physics. The court is made up of "compact disciplines"; the hinterlands are ruled by the "diffuse disciplines"; the colonies, by "would-be disciplines"; and political and ethical argument are found only in the wilds of the "undisciplinable." The advance of reason is equated with single-mindedness of purpose. Society supports these communities of reasoners, presumably because it benefits from the technological applications of discoveries. Such a hierarchical explanation of the uses of reason, I submit, is a technical view *par excellence*.[24] The rules and procedures of the forums guarantee critique; individual allegiances and commitments make little difference in the long run, and the relationship of the disciplines to the public is guaranteed to be felicitous.

If Toulmin's notion of fields is to be accepted as the governing method by which arguments are to be recognized, constructed, and evaluated, then what becomes of the personal and public spheres of argument? One of the contributions of Willard's critique of Toulmin is that he points out the personal dimensions to any argument which cannot be accounted for within a strict technical view.[25] It may be added that it is uncertain whether the personal inclinations, stubbornness, and curiosity of men and women attracted to scientific endeavors influence the ways in which problems come to be known and accepted as resolved as much as the independent methods to which they ascribe. The relation between Toulmin's view of argument and the public sphere is also open to question. Is it the case that a scientist's work is without intrinsic political significance? Opponents of eugenics and proponents of creationism would certainly not agree with the claim that scientific communities are propelled only by a curiosity more intense than [that of] lay folk. Is it the case that public reasoning itself can be improved by specialization and compactness? This question will receive more detailed analysis in the latter portion of the essay. For now, though, it is important to note that a theory of argument that would ground reason giving in the technical sphere is in opposition to requirements of personal and public life.

The Status of Deliberative Argument

What sphere of argument seems to be prevalent at this time? This is an important question because changes in the grounds of reason cannot be viewed as unequivocal advances. Susanne Langer reminds us that "each new advance is bought with the life of an older certainty."[26] My belief is that the public sphere is being steadily eroded by the elevation of the personal and technical groundings of argument. The decline is not entirely a new phenomenon because it is rooted in the dilemmas of twentieth-century American life.

Writing in the late 1920s, Charles Beard, a great Progressive historian, saw that America had changed. Whereas his country in the eighteenth century was characterized by "congeries of provincial societies," modern technology introduced greater specialization, interdependence, and complexity. These changing conditions challenged the loose-knit governmental structure of an earlier era. Psychology did offer new opportunities to serve the common good, especially through public health programs, but it also carried with it new problems. He observed, "Technology brings new perils in its train: falling aircraft, the pollution of streams, and dangerous explosives. It makes possible new forms of law violation: safe blowing, machine-gun banditry, wiretapping, and submarine smuggling."[27] Beyond the capacity of government to deal with new social responsibilities, the historian noted an even more fundamental issue.

Beard believed that the nature of government was being inexorably transformed to "an economic and technical business on a large scale." As "the operations of public administration become increasingly technical in nature," the governors turn increasingly to specialized knowledge provided by "chemistry, physics, and higher mathematics."[28] What startled Beard were the implications of this transformation for democratic self-government. If it is the case that specialization is necessary to make knowledgeable decisions, then what value is the participation of common citizens? Entertaining the notion that the United States might best be ruled by a technically trained elite, he concluded that even though such a group might be better acquainted with a range of facts, "it would be more likely to fall to pieces from violent differences than to attain permanent unity through a reciprocal exchange of decisions." His reason: "[T]ranscending the peculiar questions of each specialty are the interrelations of all the specialties; and the kind of knowledge or intelligence necessary to deal with these interrelations is not guaranteed by proficiency in any one sphere."[29]

Since Beard's time, the bill of particulars has changed. Presently, concerns that trouble the administration of government include unanticipated missile launchings, ozone depletion, and atomic power incidents. New technology makes possible plutonium theft, computer crime, and airplane hijacking. But the essential issue persists. Certainly technical knowledge has burgeoned over the past fifty years, but it is not certain that the general knowledge which Beard thought necessary to govern a Republic has become any more refined.

The reasons for this doubt are many. Even as politicians have come to rely upon pollsters and mass-communication strategists to formulate sophisticated rhetorics, audiences seem to disappear into socially fragmented groups. Denial of the public sphere is accompanied by celebration of personal lifestyle, producing what one critic has called the "me generation,"[30] and another, "the culture of narcissism."[31] As arguments grounded in personal experience (disclosed by averaging opinion) seem to have greatest currency, political speakers present not options but personalities, perpetuating government policy by substituting debate for an aura of false intimacy. Thus is privatism celebrated and the discourse continued.

Meanwhile, issues of significant public consequence, what should present live possibilities for argumentation and public choice, disappear into the government technocracy or private hands. As forms of decisionmaking proliferate, questions of public significance themselves become increasingly difficult to recognize, much less address, because of the intricate rules, procedures, and terminologies of the specialized forums. These complications of argument hardly invite the public to share actively the knowledge necessary for wise and timely decisions. Given the increasing tendency of political rhetoricians to produce strings of "ideographs," untrammeled by warrants or inferences, and given the tendency of government to proceed by relying upon the dictates of instrumental reason, the realm of public knowledge, identified by Dewey and later addressed by Bitzer, may be disappearing.[32]

Of course, what once constituted public argument is not entirely gone. Some of its semblance remains.[33] The mass media continue to present the drama of politics, but some vital elements of a deliberative rhetoric are carefully excised. At this juncture, I would like to reconstruct a series of "news reports," aired on some major networks during the spring and summer of 1981. Actually, the stories were not "news" at all, but projected happenings should the Reagan forces find success in making budget reductions. Each "spot" was presented on a day when the Reagan adherents had made some headway in passing their version of reform.

Typically, a female reporter comes on camera saying that she is in some small town in the hinterlands of the United States. An issue is identified, usually the reduction of funds for domestic policy or the termination of a federal program. Residents are interviewed. Some are led to say that, yes, there is no fraud or corruption, and the money has been well spent by hard-working souls. When asked what could be done if the funds were to be terminated, to a person, the interviewees responded with a rueful grin, "I just don't know. There is nowhere else to go." Since my political sentiments are somewhat in line with the implied argument of the narrative, I first mistook the reports for a reinvigorated form of public critique.

But, on one evening just after the Reagan administration had won a particularly key vote in the Congressional budget battles, an especially gripping narrative was broadcast.

The media found a woman's prison in Florida, where, in what appeared to be something like a summer cottage, female prisoners were incarcerated but allowed to stay with their newly born offspring. As the camera zooms in, the reporter says that a movement is afoot in the Florida legislature to shut down the program which would permit mother and child to remain together. The scene abruptly shifts to two wizened legislators, speaking in deep southern accents. One says in effect, "We need to save the taxpayer every dime we can." The other rejoins: "These women deserve to be punished." Back to the cottage. The female reporter asks the mother/inmate with babe in arms: "What will you do if they pass the cut?" The woman becomes terrified, and clutching the child, tearfully cries: "I don't know. He is all I have. Don't let them take my baby away."

The story was so startling that I began to wonder what could be done for this person, but upon reflection I found that there was not enough information to even begin acting. Later, as I came to think about the entire series of stories as arguments, I discovered that while the reports superficially appeared to be a form of political propaganda—which although one-sided, invites public participation at least through influencing attitudes—actually, they were a different species altogether. The reports always presented the individual as a victim of social forces. Decision-making bodies, apparently bereft of human emotion and lacking common sense, were to make decisions based upon inscrutable principles. Like viewing the winds of a rising hurricane, the signs of power politics were to be seen as a kind of natural disaster, sweeping up the deserving and undeserving alike. The reports were crafted in such a way that no intelligent assessment could be made concerning the issues involved. One had no idea of the reasons for the cuts, the credibility of the sources, the representativeness of the examples, etc. But even beyond these characteristic inadequacies, the stories simply did not invite action. These were reports of human tragedies in the making, and, like witnessing other calamities of fate, the participation invited was that of watching the drama play out.

The paradox of expanding communication technology and the decline of the public sphere is not unique to our own time. Dewey puzzled over the simultaneous appearance of new devices (the telephone, motion picture, and radio) and the disappearance of the public.[34] Another communication revolution is taking place, with the advance of improvements in broadcasting techniques, satellite transmission, and computer processing. Instead of expanding public forums, these devices seem to be geared to producing either refined information or compelling fantasy. That the media could be employed to extend knowledgeable public argument but do not suggests the decline of deliberative practice. Mass communications by and large seem to be committed to technical modes of invention. These artfully capture the drama of public debate even while systematically stripping public argument of consequences beyond the captured attention given to the media itself. And the media's own patterns of argument create a view of life where the trivial and mundane eternally interchange with the tragic and spectacular by the hour. What could be a way of sharing in the creation of a future is supplanted by a perpetual swirl of exciting stimuli. Thus is deliberation replaced by consumption.

While Beard did not project a comfortable solution to the problems of meshing technical and public argument, he did formulate a significant challenge:

> [G]overnment carries into our technological age a cultural heritage from the ancient agricultural order and yet finds its environment and functions revolutionized by science and machinery. It must now command expertness in all fields of technology and at the same time its work calls for a super-competence able to deal with the interrelations of the various departments. It must also reflect the hopes and energies, the dreams and consummation, of the human intelligence in its most enormous movements. Constantly it faces large questions of choice which cannot be solved by the scientific method alone—questions involving intuitive insight, ethical judgment, and valuation as of old. Science and machinery do not displace cultural considerations. They complicate these aspects of life; they set new conditions for social evolution but they do not make an absolute break in history as destiny and opportunity. The problem before us, therefore, is that of combining the noblest philosophy with the most efficient use of all instrumentalities of the modern age—a challenge to human powers on a higher level of creative purpose. Its long contemplation lights up great ranges of sympathies and ideas, giving many deeds that appear commonplace a strange and significant evaluation.[35]

Beard's summary of the dilemmas of *The Republic in the Machine Age* points to a critical enterprise for argumentation theorists. If the public sphere is to be revitalized, then those practices which replace deliberative rhetoric by substituting alternative modes of invention and restricting subject matter need to be uncovered and critiqued. In pointing out alternatives to present practice, the theorist of argument could contribute significantly to the perfection of public forms and forums of argument. If this task is undertaken, then deliberative argument may no longer be a lost art.

NOTES

1. For a discussion of the relation between knowledge, rhetoric, and the public, see Lloyd F. Bitzer, "Rhetoric and Public Knowledge," in Don M. Burks, ed., *Rhetoric, Philosophy, and Literature: An Exploration* (West Lafayette, IN: Purdue University Press, 1978), pp. 57–58. My own assumptions are that the public argument is a viable mode of arguing to the extent that (1) the future is not seen as completely determined; (2) discourse is viewed as capable of presenting and evaluating alternatives for acting or restraining action; (3) individual judgment and action are relevant to the options at hand; (4) the process adheres to freedom of inquiry and expression, with the longer term goal of establishing a true consensus; and (5) a community of common interests can be discovered and articulated through discourse. See G. Thomas Goodnight, "The Liberal and the Conservative Presumptions: On Political Philosophy and the Foundations of Public Argument," in Jack Rhodes and Sara Newell, eds., *Proceedings of the [First] Summer Conference on Argumentation* (Annandale, VA: Speech Communication Association, 1980), p. 308.

2. Thomas Farrell, "Knowledge, Consensus, and Rhetorical Theory," *Quarterly Journal of Speech* 62 (1976): 1–14 [reprinted in this volume]. This essay maintains Farrell's distinctions between social and technical knowledge. Although [Walter M.] Carleton's observation that the lines between social and technical knowledge are sometimes ambiguous is correct, the reply is nonresponsive to a basic problematic uncovered by Farrell. The arguer must rely either upon an actual consensus such as that which characterizes a technical field with exact specifications for argument or the arguer must project consensus from his or her own personal experience or estimation of the social milieu. See Carleton, "What Is Rhetorical Knowledge? A Response to Farrell—and More," *Quarterly Journal of Speech* 64 (1968): 313–328. That some aspects of social knowledge become subjected to technical transformation and that the implications of some fields must be resolved by social knowledge indicates merely that arguers are able to reshape the grounds upon which arguments occur.

3. Charles W. Kneupper, "Paradigms and Problems: Alternative Constructivist/Interactionist Implications for Argumentation Theory," *Journal of the American Forensic Association* 15 (1979): 223.

4. Charles A. Willard, "On the Utility of Descriptive Diagrams for the Analysis and Criticism of Arguments," *Communication Monographs* 43 (1976): 316; Charles A. Willard, "A Reformulation of the Concept of Argument: The Constructivist/Interactionist Foundations of a Sociology of Argument," *Journal of the American Forensic Association* 14 (1978): 126.

5. Remy de Gourmont, *Remy de Gourmont: Selections from All His Works*, ed. Richard Aldington (New York: Covici-Friede, 1929), p. 472.

6. Daniel J. O'Keefe, "Two Concepts of Argument," *Journal of the American Forensic Association* 11 (1978): 121–128.

7. C. S. Lewis, *The Discarded Image: An Introduction to Medieval and Renaissance Literature* (Cambridge, UK: Cambridge University Press, 1974), pp. 92–198.

8. Kenneth Burke, *The Rhetoric of Motives* (New York: Prentice-Hall, 1952), pp. 20–29. Burke establishes three major modes of identification: consubstantiality, "in being identified with B, A is 'substantially one' with a person other than himself"; partisanship, "the ways in which individuals are at odds with one another, or become identified with groups more or less at odds with one another"; and "autonomous" identification [quotation marks Burke's], "the autonomous activity's place in this wider context [a larger unit of action in which a specialized activity takes place], a place where the agent may be unconcerned." Although these modes of identification aid us to understand the groundings of each argument sphere, arguers typically import one kind of argument to serve another's function. Thus, the politician can appeal to consubstantiality in order to masque partisan interests. A partisan movement can grow by having its participants uncover consubstantial interests, as the consciousness raising techniques of the woman's liberation movement were used to increase awareness of a shared identity. Moreover, disputes over what kinds of activities are autonomous occur as responsibility and authority are contested.

9. Joseph Emerson Brown, "Against the Woman's Suffrage Amendment," in Ernest J. Wrage and Barnet Baskerville, eds., *American Forum: Speeches on Historic Issues, 1788–1900* (Seattle: University of Washington Press, 1960), pp. 333–342.

10. It may be tempting to replace the concept of argument spheres with a more popular term like "social context." Most arguments are social productions. Those that are preserved and seem recurrent enough to be labeled as providing a custom or role may be subjected to sociological mapping. See, e.g., Bruce E. Gronbeck, "Sociocultural Notions of Argument Fields: A Primer," in George Ziegelmueller and Jack Rhodes, eds., *Dimensions of Argument: Proceedings of the Second Summer*

Conference on Argumentation (Annandale, VA: Speech Communication Association, 1981), pp. 1–21. Such mappings may be useful to arguers, who sometimes must project social expectations in order to frame a useful statement. But to view social characterizations as determinative is but to reify the perspectives of a sociologist who may see argument as independent of any particular arguer. So long as one can speak ironically, cross-up and recross expectations, and transvalue social norms, social context—no matter how delicately construed or thoroughly proscribed—cannot be said to be determinative.

11. William Kneale and Martha Kneale, *The Development of Logic* (Oxford, UK: Oxford University Press, 1962), pp. 628–651.

12. See, e.g., Dale Hample, "A Cognitive View of Argument," *Journal of the American Forensic Association* 16 (1980): 151–159.

13. Ray E. McKerrow, "Argumentation Communities: A Quest for Distinctions," in *Proceedings of the [First] Summer Conference on Argumentation*, pp. 214–228; Brant R. Burleson, "On the Analysis and Criticism of Arguments: Some Theoretical and Methodological Considerations," *Journal of the American Forensic Association* 15 (1979): 137–148.

14. For an attempt to bridge the gap, see Earl Croasmun and Richard A. Cherwitz, "Beyond Rhetorical Relativism," *Quarterly Journal of Speech* 68 (1982): 1–16. In the view of these authors, "reality" somehow "impinges" on individuals thereby supplying the prerequisite veridicality to guide the arguer's judgment. While the extramental universe need not be denied as a phenomen[on] which sometimes thwarts the best-laid theories of arguers, it is difficult to rid arguers of dialectical maneuvers which not only alter the grounds upon which world views are constructed but also present problems that cannot be resolved in a purely positivistic manner.

15. Charles Arthur Willard, "Some Speculations About Evidence," in *Proceedings of the [First] Summer Conference on Argumentation*, pp. 267–268.

16. The changing trends of rhetorical criticism mark the different ways in which the relation between or among spheres of argument can be viewed. Neo-Aristotelian critics often attempted to explain public success by exploring the private training, talents, and inclinations of the orator. Symbolic interactionist criticism often focuses on the public significance of private symbol systems, as movement studies demonstrate how the public sphere is reformed through opposition. Fantasy theme analysis charts the personal responses to public statement through its attempt to uncover social dramas.

17. Richard B. Gregg and Gerard A. Hauser, "Richard Nixon's April 30, 1970, Address on Cambodia: The 'Ceremony' of Confrontation," *Communication Monographs* 40 (1973): 167–181. By taking Nixon's address away from its most obvious grounding, namely, the tradition of presidential war rhetoric, the rhetorical critics performed the critical function through poetic extension. In this manner, the grounds of argument are extended to the point that the speech itself is made to seem arbitrary. But why compare Nixon's address to a potlatch ceremony? Why not a potato harvest, a pair of cufflinks, or any other random item? Any critic, through analogical extension, can ignore the processes through which the argument is made by a person or institution and supplant his or her private identification. Unless something is made known about the relation between argument and practical grounds, or at least live alternatives, a criticism of an argument may tell us more about the critic than the argument.

18. See, e.g., Moses Rischin, ed., *The American Gospel of Success* (Chicago: Quadrangle Books, 1968), pp. 3–91.

19. Richard Hofstadter, *The Age of Reform: From Bryan to F.D.R.* (New York: Vintage Books, 1955), pp. 174–214.

20. Roderick Nash, *Wilderness and the American Mind* (New Haven, CT: Yale University Press, 1967), pp. 141–160.

21. Rachel Carson, *Silent Spring* (Boston: Houghton Mifflin, 1962).

22. Thomas B. Farrell and G. Thomas Goodnight, "Accidental Rhetoric: The Root Metaphors of Three Mile Island," *Communication Monographs* 48 (1981): 271–300.

23. Stephen Toulmin, *Human Understanding: The Collective Use and Evolution of Concepts* (Princeton, NJ: Princeton University Press, 1972), pp. 364–411. There is a variety of views extending and supplementing Toulmin's. See Ray E. McKerrow, "On Fields and Rational Enterprises: A Reply to Willard," in *Proceedings of the [First] Summer Conference on Argumentation*, pp. 401–413; Charles Arthur Willard, "Argument Fields and Theories of Logical Types," *Journal of the American Forensic Association* 17 (1981): 129–145; see also essays in this issue. Whether fields are differentiated by subject matter, logical type, language use, sociological character, or purpose is a matter of some disagreement. Perhaps one of the major characteristics of a field is the effort to define the boundaries of a specialized community of argument users. Given the tendency of those involved in rational enterprises to see the world through their specialty (Burke's notion of "occupation psychosis"), it would be surprising if a single notion of field could be acceptable.

24. The rubric of argument fields, in my estimation, is not a satisfactory umbrella for covering the grounding of all arguments. If it is claimed that anytime an arguer takes a perspective there is a field, then one term has been merely substituted for another. Alternatively, to claim that all arguments are grounded in fields, enterprises characterized by some degree of specialization and compactness, contravenes an essential distinction among groundings. Personal argument is created in a

durational time dimension, as Willard and Farrell have pointed out. Points at issue can be dropped, appear again years later, be returned to, or [be] entirely forgotten. From an external perspective, the private dispute may seem to be serendipitous, even while the interlocutors pursue the matter in its own time. The establishment of a field more or less objectifies time insofar as common procedures, schedules, measurements, and argument/decision/action sequences are set up by common agreement. Herein the personal dimension may seem to be not strictly relevant or even counterproductive, except in special cases. A time of public debate may lead to the enactment of a future which increases or decreases individual and/or field autonomy as an outcome of what are figured to be pressing exigencies. Within a democracy at least, public time is not reducible to the rhythms of any individual (unlike a pure dictatorship) or the objectifications of technicians (unlike a purely positivistic state).

25. Charles A. Willard, "On the Utility of Descriptive Diagrams," pp. 308–312.

26. Susanne Langer, *Philosophy in a New Key: A Study in the Symbolism of Reason, Rite, and Art* (Cambridge, MA: Harvard University Press, 1978), p. 294.

27. Charles A. Beard and William Beard, *The American Leviathan: The Republic in the Machine Age* (New York: Macmillan, 1930), p. 7.

28. Ibid., pp. 3–19.

29. Ibid. pp. 10–16.

30. Richard Sennett, *The Fall of Public Man: On the Social Psychology of Capitalism* (New York: Knopf, 1978), pp. 313–338.

31. Christopher Lasch, *The Culture of Narcissism: American Life in an Age of Diminishing Expectations* (New York: Norton, 1978), pp. 31–70.

32. John Dewey, *The Public and Its Problems* (Chicago: Swallow Press, 1927).

33. Although all rhetoric uses language, and although all language may be viewed as "incipient action" as it excites attitudes, distinctions should be made between those forms of discourse designed to keep us watching, while the symbols continue to dance, and those forms which invite the knowledgeable conjoining of motion and action to construct a future. If distinctions are not drawn between the aesthetic and deliberative uses of argument, then the public sphere may be coopted by default, given over to those who control the means of producing elaborate symbolic events. How can untimely, irrelevant and even fatuous "public communication" be critiqued, if all rhetoric is fantasy?

34. Dewey, *The Public and Its Problems*.

35. Beard and Beard, *American Leviathan*.

Narration as a Human Communication Paradigm

The Case of Public Moral Argument

Walter R. Fisher

The corrective of the scientific rationalization would seem necessarily to be a rationale of art—not, however, a performer's art, not a specialist's art for some to produce and many to observe, but an art in its widest aspects, an art of living.
—KENNETH BURKE

When I wrote "Toward a Logic of Good Reasons" (Fisher, 1978), I was unaware that I was moving toward an alternative paradigm for human communication. Indications of it are to be found in the assumption that "*Humans as rhetorical beings are as much valuing as they are reasoning animals*" (p. 376) and in the conception of good reasons as "*those elements that provide warrants for accepting or adhering to the advice fostered by any form of communication that can be considered rhetorical*" (p. 378). While the assumption does not seriously disturb the view of rhetoric as practical reasoning, the conception implies a stance that goes beyond this theory. The logic of good reasons maintains that reasoning need not be bound to argumentative prose or be expressed in clear-cut inferential or implicative structures: Reasoning may be discovered in all sorts of symbolic action—nondiscursive as well as discursive.

That this is the case was demonstrated in an exploration of argument in *Death of a Salesman* and *The Great Gatsby* (Fisher and Filloy, 1982). The authors concluded that these works provide good reasons to distrust the materialist myth of the American Dream (Fisher, 1973, p. 161), for

what it requires to live by it and for what it does not necessarily deliver even if one lives by it "successfully." This finding confirms Gerald Graff's thesis that a theory or practice of literature that denies reference to the world, that denies that literature has cognitive as well as aesthetic significance, is a *Literature Against Itself* (Graff, 1979). In other words, "some dramatic and literary works do, in fact, argue" (Fisher and Filloy, 1982, p. 343).

The paradigm I was moving toward did not become entirely clear until I examined the current nuclear controversy, where the traditional view of rationality did not serve well, and I read Alasdair MacIntyre's *After Virtue: A Study in Moral Theory* (1981). What impressed me most about the book was the observation that "man is in his actions and practice, as well as in his fictions, essentially a story-telling animal" (p. 201). Given this view, "enacted dramatic narrative" (p. 200) is the "basic and essential genre for the characterization of human actions" (p. 194). These ideas are the foundation of the paradigm I am proposing—the narrative paradigm. Thus, when I use the term "narration," I do not mean a fictive composition whose propositions may be true or false and have no necessary relationship to the message of that composition. By "narration," I refer to a theory of symbolic actions—words and/or deeds—that have sequence and meaning for those who live, create, or interpret them. The narrative perspective, therefore, has relevance to real as well as fictive worlds, to stories of living and to stories of the imagination.

The narrative paradigm, then, can be considered a dialectical synthesis of two traditional strands in the history of rhetoric: the argumentative, persuasive theme and the literary, aesthetic theme. As will be seen, the narrative paradigm insists that human communication should be viewed as historical as well as situational, as stories competing with other stories constituted by good reasons, as being rational when they satisfy the demands of narrative probability and narrative fidelity, and as inevitably moral inducements. The narrative paradigm challenges the notions that human communication—if it is to be considered rhetorical—must be an argumentative form, that reason is to be attributed only to discourse marked by clearly identifiable modes of inference and/or implication, and that the norms for evaluation of rhetorical communication must be rational standards taken essentially from informal or formal logic. The narrative paradigm does not deny reason and rationality; it reconstitutes them, making them amenable to all forms of human communication.

Before going further, I should clarify the sense in which I use the term "paradigm." By paradigm, I refer to a representation designed to formalize the structure of a component of experience and to direct understanding and inquiry into the nature and functions of that experience—in this instance, the experience of human communication. Masterman designates this form of paradigm "metaphysical" or as a "metaparadigm"(1970, p. 65; see also Kuhn, 1974). Since the narrative paradigm does not entail a particular method of investigation, I have not used a designation that might be suggested: "narratism." The narrative perspective, however, does have a critical connection with "dramatism," which will be discussed later.

Consistent with Wayne Brockriede's concept of perspectivism (1982), I shall not maintain that the narrative paradigm is the only legitimate, useful way to appreciate human communication or that it will necessarily supplant the traditional rational paradigm of human decision-making and action. As already indicated, I will propose the narrative paradigm as an alternative view. I do not even

claim that it is entirely "new." W. Lance Bennett has published a book with Martha S. Feldman, *Reconstructing Reality in the Courtroom* (1981), and two essays that directly bear on the present enterprise, one concerning political communication (Bennett, 1975) and one on legal communication (Bennett, 1978; see also Farrell, 1983; Gallie, 1964; Hawes, 1978; Mink, 1978; Schrag, 1984; Scott, 1978; and Simons, 1978). Except for these studies, I know of no other attempt to suggest narration as a paradigm. There is, of course, a tradition in rhetorical theory and pedagogy that focuses on narration as an element in discourse and as a genre in and of itself (e.g., Ochs and Burritt, 1973). In addition, there is an increasing number of investigations involving storytelling (e.g., Kirkwood, 1983). Here again, narration is conceived as a mode, not a paradigm, of communication.

The context for what is to follow would not be complete without recognition of the work done by theologians and those interested in religious discourse. The most recent works in this tradition include Goldberg (1982) and Hauerwas (1981). It is worth pausing with these studies, as they foreshadow several of the themes to be developed later. Goldberg claims that:

> a theologian, regardless of the propositional statements he or she may have to make about a community's convictions, must consciously strive to keep those statements in intimate contact with the narratives which give rise to those convictions, within which they gain their sense and meaning, and *from which they have been abstracted.* (p. 35)

The same can be said for those who would understand ordinary experience. The ground for determining meaning, validity, reason, rationality, and truth must be a narrative context: history, culture, biography, and character. Goldberg also argues:

> Neither "the facts" nor our "experience" come to us in discrete and disconnected packets which simply await the appropriate moral principle to be applied. Rather, they stand in need of some narrative which can bind the facts of our experience together into a coherent pattern and it is thus in virtue of that narrative that our abstracted rules, principles, and notions gain their full intelligibility. (p. 242)

Again, the statement is relevant to more than the moral life; it is germane to social and political life as well. He observes, as I would, that "what counts as meeting the various conditions of justification will vary from story to story" (p. 246). I will suggest a foundation for such justifications in the discussion of narrative rationality.

With some modifications, I would endorse two of Hauerwas' (1981) ten theses. First, he claims that "the social significance of the Gospel requires recognition of the narrative structure of Christian convictions for the life of the church" (p. 9). I would say: The meaning and significance of life in all of its social dimensions require the recognition of its narrative structure. Second, Hauerwas asserts that "every social ethic involves a narrative, whether it is conceived with the formulation of basic principles of social organization and/or concrete alternatives" (p. 9; see also Alter, 1981; and Scult, 1983). The only change that I would make here is to delete the word "social." Any ethic, whether social, political, legal or otherwise, involves narrative.

Finally, mention should be made of the work on narration by such scholars as Derrida (1980), Kermode (1980), and Ricoeur (1980). Especially relevant to this project are essays by White (1980; see also White, 1978), Turner (1980), and Danto (1982; see also Nelson, 1980; Todorov, 1977).

Purpose

If I can establish that narration deserves to be accepted as a paradigm, it will vie with the reigning paradigm, which I will refer to as the rational world paradigm. In truth, however, the narrative paradigm, like other paradigms in the human sciences, does not so much deny what has gone before as it subsumes it.

The rational world paradigm will be seen as one way to tell the story of how persons reason together in certain settings. For now, it is enough that the narrative paradigm be contemplated as worthy of coexisting with the rational world paradigm.

I shall begin by characterizing and contrasting the two paradigms. I shall then examine the controversy over nuclear warfare, a public moral argument, noting particular problems with the rational world paradigm and indicating how the narrative paradigm provides a way of possibly resolving them. Following this discussion, I shall reconsider the narrative paradigm and conclude with several implications for further inquiry. Needless to say, this essay does not constitute a finished statement. It offers a conceptual frame which, I am fully aware, requires much greater development for it to be considered compelling. At this point, as I have suggested, it is sufficient that it receive serious attention. From such attention, a fuller, more persuasive statement should emerge.

The Rational World Paradigm

This paradigm is very familiar, having been in existence since Aristotle's *Organon* became foundational to Western thought. Regardless of its historic forms, the rational world paradigm presupposes that: (1) humans are essentially rational beings; (2) the paradigmatic mode of human decision-making and communication is argument—clear-cut inferential (implicative) structures; (3) the conduct of argument is ruled by the dictates of situations—legal, scientific, legislative, public, and so on; (4) rationality is determined by subject matter knowledge, argumentative ability, and skill in employing the rules of advocacy in given fields; and (5) the world is a set of logical puzzles which can be resolved through appropriate analysis and application of reason conceived as an argumentative construct. In short, argument as product and process is *the* means of being human, the agency of all that humans can know and realize in achieving their *telos*. The philosophical ground of the rational world paradigm is epistemology. Its linguistic materials are self-evident propositions, demonstrations, and proofs, the verbal expressions of certain and probable knowing.

The actualization of the rational world paradigm, it should be noted, depends on a form of society that permits, if not requires, participation of qualified persons in public decision-making. It further demands a citizenry that shares a common language, general adherence to the values of the state, information relevant to the questions that confront the community to be arbitrated by argument, and an understanding of argumentative issues and the various forms of reasoning and their appropriate assessment. In other words, there must exist something that can be called public or social knowledge and there must be a "public" for argument to be the kind of force envisioned for it (Bitzer, 1978; Farrell, 1976). Because the rational world paradigm has these requirements and because *being rational* (being competent in argument) *must be learned*, an historic mission of education in the West has been to generate a consciousness of national community and to instruct citizens in at least the rudiments of logic and rhetoric (Hollis, 1977, pp. 165–166; Toulmin, 1970, p. 4).

Needless to say, the rational world paradigm, which is by and large a heritage of the classical period, has not been untouched by "modernism." The impact of modernism has been recounted and reacted to by many writers (Barrett, 1979; Booth, 1974; Gadamer, 1981, 1982; Lonergan, 1958; MacIntyre, 1981; Rorty, 1979; Schrag, 1980; Sennett, 1978; Toulmin, 1972, 1982; Voegelin, 1952, 1975). The line of thought that has done most to subvert the rational world paradigm is, along with existentialism, naturalism. One of its schools starts with physics and mathematics and makes the logical structure of scientific knowledge fundamental; the other school, involving biology, psychology, and the social sciences, adapts this structure and conception of knowledge to the human sciences. According to John Herman Randall Jr.:

> The major practical issue still left between the two types of naturalism concerns the treatment of values. The philosophies starting from physics tend to exclude questions of value from the field of science and the scope of scientific method. They either leave them to traditional non-scientific treatment, handing them over, with Russell, to the poet and mystic; or else with the logical empiricists they dismiss the whole matter as "meaningless," maintaining with Ayer, that any judgment of value is an expression of mere personal feeling. The philosophies of human experience—all the heirs of Hegel, from dialectical materialism to Dewey—subject them to the same scientific methods of criticism and testing as other beliefs; and thus offer the hope of using all we have learned of scientific procedure to erect at last a science of values comparable to the science that was the glory of Greek thought. (1976, p. 651)

It is clear: With the first type of naturalism, there can be neither public or social knowledge nor rational public or social argument, for both are permeated by values. As Habermas notes, "The relationship of theory to practice can now only assert itself as the purposive rational application of techniques assured by empirical science" (1967, p. 254; Heiddegger, 1972, pp. 58–59).

With the second type of naturalism, one can hope with Randall that it produces the work he sees possible in it. But the fact is that no science of values has appeared or seems likely to do so; further, Dewey (1927) himself noted the eclipse of the "public" and doubted its reemergence. His hope was the development of "communities." Interestingly, fifty-five years later, MacIntyre concludes *After Virtue* with the observation: "What matters at this state is the construction of local forms of community within which civility and the intellectual and moral life can be sustained" (1981, p. 245).

The effects of naturalism have been to restrict the rational world paradigm to specialized studies and to relegate everyday argument to an irrational exercise. The reaction to this state of affairs has been an historic effort to recover the rational world paradigm for human decision-making and communication by: (1) reconstituting the conception of knowledge (e.g., Bitzer, 1978; Farrell, 1976; Habermas, 1973; Lyric, 1982; McGee and Martin, 1983; Polanyi, 1958; Ziman, 1968); (2) reconceptualizing the public—in terms of rational enterprises, fields, and/or communities (e.g., McKerrow, 1980a, 1980b; Toulmin, 1958, 1972; Toulmin, Rieke, and Janik, 1979; Willard, 1982; see also the first nineteen essays in Ziegelmueller and Rhodes, 1981); (3) formulating a logic appropriate for practical reasoning (e.g., Fisher, 1978; Perelman and Olbrechts-Tyteca, 1969; Toulmin, 1958; Wenzel, 1977); and (4) reconceiving the conceptions of validity, reason, and rationality (e.g., Apel, 1979; Ehninger, 1968; Farrell, 1977; Fisher, 1980; Gottlieb, 1968; Johnstone, 1978; McKerrow, 1977, 1982). Many of the studies cited here intimate, if not specifically state, proposals for reconstructing the concept of argument itself. Writers explicitly working on this task include Brockriede (1975, 1977), Burleson (1981), Jacobs and Jackson (1981), McKerrow (1981), O'Keefe (1977, 1982), Wenzel (1980), and Willard (1978).

The motive underlying these various studies, and the movement of which they are an energizing force, is, as I have suggested, to repair the rational world paradigm so that it once again will serve everyday argument. One may well applaud the motive and the movement and yet ask two questions: (1) Has the reformation been successful? (2) Is there a more beneficial way to conceive and to articulate the structures of everyday argument? It is too early to answer the first question with finality but one cannot deny that much useful work has been done, especially in establishing at least the semblance of rationality for fields of argument. I shall maintain, however, that similar progress has not been made in the arena where argument is most general and is most obviously concerned with values, public moral argument, as the examination of the nuclear controversy will show later.

This failure suggests to me that the problem in restoring rationality to everyday argument may be the assumption that the reaffirmation of the rational world paradigm is the only solution. The position I am taking that another paradigm, the narrative paradigm, may offer a better solution, one that will provide substance not only for public moral argument, but also all other forms of argument, for human communication in general. My answer to the second question, then, is: "Yes, I think so." Adoption of the narrative paradigm, I hasten to repeat, does not mean rejection of all the good work that has been done; it means a rethinking of it and investigating new moves that can be made to enrich our understanding of communicative interaction. Representative of the good work that has already been done on public argument are essays by Cox (1981), Goodnight (1980), Hynes, Jr. (1980), Lucaites (1981), Pryor (1981), Sillars and Ganer (1982), and Zarefsky (1981).

The Narrative Paradigm

Many different root metaphors have been put forth to represent the essential nature of human beings: *homo faber, homo economous, homo politicos, homo sociologicus,* "psychological man," "ecclesiastical man," *homo sapiens,* and, of course, "rational man." I now propose *homo narrans* to be added to the list.

Preliminary to an attempt to delineate the presuppositions that structure the narrative paradigm, I should indicate how the *homo narrans* metaphor relates to those that have preceded it. First, each of the root metaphors may be held to be the master metaphor, thereby standing as the ground, while the others are manifest as figures. In the terminology of the narrative perspective, the master metaphor sets the plot of human experience and the others the subplots. When any of the other metaphors are asserted as the master metaphor, narration is as it is considered now: a type of human interaction-activity, an art, a genre, or mode of expression.

Second, when narration is taken as the master metaphor, it subsumes the others. The other metaphors are then considered conceptions that inform various ways of *recounting or accounting for* human choice and action. Recounting takes the forms of history, biography, or autobiography. Accounting for takes the forms of theoretical explanation or argument. Recounting and accounting for can be also expressed in poetic forms: drama, poetry, novel, and so on. Recounting and accounting for are, in addition, the bases for all advisory discourse. Regardless of the form they may assume, recounting and accounting for are stories we tell ourselves and each other to establish a meaning-

ful life-world. The character of narrator(s), the conflicts, the resolutions, and the style will vary, but each mode of recounting and accounting for is but a way of relating a "truth" about the human condition.

Third, the *homo narrans* metaphor is an incorporation and extension of Burke's definition of "man" as the "symbol-using (symbol-making, symbol-misusing) animal" (Burke, 1968, p. 16; Cassirer, 1944, p. 26; see also Langer, 1953, pp. 264ff.). The idea of human beings as storytellers indicates the general form of all symbol composition; it holds that symbols are created and communicated ultimately as stories meant to give order to human experience and to induce others to dwell in them to establish ways of living in common, in communities in which there is sanction for the story that constitutes one's life. And one's life is, as suggested by Burke, a story that participates in the stories of those who have lived, who live now, and who will live in the future. He asks: "Where does the drama get its materials?" I would modify the question to read: "Where do our narratives get their materials?" And I would accept his answer:

> From the "unending conversation" that is going on in history when we are born. Imagine that you enter a parlor. You come late. When you arrive, others have long preceded you, and they are engaged in a heated discussion, a discussion too heated for them to pause and tell you exactly what it is about. In fact, the discussion had already begun long before any of them got there, so that no one present is qualified to retrace for you all the steps that had gone before. You listen for awhile, until you decide that you have caught the tenor of the argument; then you put in your oar. Someone answers; you answer him; another comes to your defense; another aligns himself against you, to either the embarrassment or gratification of your opponent, depending upon the quality of your ally's assistance. However, the discussion is interminable. The hour grows late, you must depart. And you do depart, with the discussion still vigorously in process. (Burke, 1957, pp. 94–97; for a discussion of the nature of conversation as narration, see MacIntyre, 1981; Campbell and Stewart, 1981)

As Heidegger observes, "We are a conversation . . . conversation and its unity support our existence" (Heidegger, 1949, p. 278; Gadamer, 1982, pp. 330ff.; Rorty, 1979, pp. 315ff.).

To clarify further the narrative paradigm, I should specify how it is related to Bormann's (1972) concepts of "fantasy themes" and "rhetorical visions," and to the Frentz and Farrell (1976) language action paradigm. Fantasy, Bormann holds, is a technical term, meaning "the creative and imaginative interpretation of events that fulfills a psychological or rhetorical need" (1983, p. 434). Fantasy themes arise "in group interaction out of a recollection of something that happened to the group in the past or a dream of what a group might do in the *future*" (1972, p. 397). When woven together, they become composite dramas, which Bormann calls "rhetorical visions" (1972, p. 398). From the narrative view, each of these concepts translates into dramatic stories constituting the fabric of social reality for those who compose them. They are, thus, "rhetorical fictions," constructions of fact and faith having persuasive force, rather than fantasies (Fisher, 1980b). Nevertheless, without getting into the problem of how group-generated stories become public stories, I would note that Bormann (1973) and others have demonstrated that "rhetorical visions" do exist (e.g., Bantz, 1975; Kidd, 1975; Rarick, Duncan, Lee, and Porter, 1977.) I take this demonstration as partial evidence for the validity of the narrative paradigm. (For further empirical evidence, see Bennett, 1978; Campbell, 1984.)

With minor adaptation, I find no incompatibility between the narrative paradigm and the language action paradigm. Indeed, language action is meaningful only in terms of narrative form (Ricoeur, 1976). What Frentz and Farrell (1976) designate as "form of life" and "encounters"—implicit matters of knowledge, aesthetic expectations, institutional constraints, and propriety rules—can be considered the forces that determine the structure of narratives in given interpersonal environments. What they call an "episode," a "rule-conforming sequence of symbolic acts generated by two or more actors who are collectively oriented toward emergent goals," can be thought of as the process by which one or more authors generate a short story or chapter—deciding on plot, the nature of characters, resolutions, and their meaning and import for them and others (p. 336).

I do not want to leave the impression that the narrative paradigm merely accommodates the constructs of Bormann, Frentz and Farrell. Their work enriches the narrative paradigm. I shall rely specifically on the language action paradigm in what follows.

The presuppositions that structure the narrative paradigm are: (1) humans are essentially storytellers; (2) the paradigmatic mode of human decision-making and communication is "good reasons" which vary in form among communication situations, genres, and media; (3) the production and practice of good reasons is ruled by matters of history, biography, culture, and character along with the kinds of forces identified in the Frentz and Farrell language act; (4) rationality is determined by the nature of persons as narrative beings—their inherent awareness of *narrative probability*, what constitutes a coherent story, and their constant habit of testing *narrative fidelity*, whether the stories they experience ring true with the stories they know to be true in their lives (narrative probability and narrative fidelity, it will be noted, are analogous to the concepts of dramatic probability and verisimilitude; as MacIntyre (1981, p. 200) observes, "The difference between imaginary characters and real ones is not in the narrative form of what they do; it is in the degree of their authorship of that form and of their own deeds"); and (5) the world is a set of stories which must be chosen among to live the good life in a process of continual recreation. In short, good reasons are the stuff of stories, the means by which humans realize their nature as reasoning-valuing animals. The philosophical ground of the narrative paradigm is ontology. The materials of the narrative paradigm are symbols, signs of consubstantiation, and good reasons, the communicative expressions of social reality.

The actualization of the narrative paradigm does not require a given form of society. Where the rational world paradigm is an ever-present part of our consciousness because we have been educated into it, the narrative impulse is part of our very being because we acquire narrativity in the natural process of socialization (Goody and Watt, 1962–1963; Krashen, 1982). That narrative, whether written or oral, is a feature of human nature and that it crosses time and culture is attested by historian White: "Far from being one code among many that a culture may utilize for endowing experience with meaning, narrative is a metacode, a human universal on the basis of which transcultural messages about the shared reality can be transmitted . . . the absence of narrative capacity or a refusal of narrative indicates an absence or refusal of meaning itself" (1980, p. 6); by anthropologist Turner: "If we regard narrative ethically, as the supreme instrument for building 'values' and 'goals,' in Dilthey's sense of these terms, which motivate human conduct into situational structures of 'meaning,' then we must concede it to be a universal cultural activity, embedded in the very center of the social drama, itself another cross-cultural and transtemporal unit in social process" (1980, p. 167); and by linguist-folklorist Dell Hymes: "The narrative use of language is not a property of subordinate cultures, whether folk, or working class, or the like, but a universal function" (1980, p. 132; see also Barthes, 1977; Ong, 1982).

Gregory Bateson goes so far as to claim that "if I am at all fundamentally right in what I am saying, then *thinking in terms of stories* must be shared by all mind or minds, whether ours or those of redwood forests and sea anemones" (1979, p. 14). And Burke observes that "We assume a time when our primal ancestors became able to go from SENSATIONS to WORDS. (When they could duplicate the experience of tasting an orange by saying 'the taste of an orange,' that was WHEN STORY CAME INTO THE WORLD)" (1983, p. 1).

In theme, if not in every detail, narrative, then, is meaningful for persons in particular and in general, across communities as well as cultures, across time and place. Narratives enable us to understand the actions of others "because we all live out narratives in our lives and because we understand our own lives in terms of narratives" (MacIntyre, 1981, p. 197).

Rationality from this perspective involves, as I have proposed, the principles of narrative probability and narrative fidelity. These principles contrast with but do not contradict the constituents of rationality I have outlined earlier (Fisher, 1978, 1980). They are, in fact, subsumed by the narrative paradigm. The earlier notion was attuned to the rational world paradigm and essentially held that rationality was a matter of argumentative competence: knowledge of issues, modes of reasoning, appropriate tests, and rules of advocacy in given fields. As such, rationality was something to be learned, depended on deliberation, and required a high degree of self-consciousness. Narrative rationality does not make these demands. It is a capacity we all share. It depends on our minds being as Booth (1974, pp. 114–137) represents them in *Modem Dogma and the Rhetoric of Assent*, a key point of which is: "Not only do human beings successfully infer other beings' states of mind from symbolic clues; we know that they characteristically, in all societies, build each other's minds. This is obvious knowledge—all the more genuine for being obvious" (p. 114). The operative principle of narrative rationality is identification rather than deliberation (Burke, 1955, pp. 20–46).

Narrative rationality differs from traditional rationality in another significant way. Narrative rationality is not an account of the "laws of thought" and it is not normative in the sense that one must reason according to prescribed rules of calculation or inference making. Traditional rationality posits the way people think when they reason truly or with certainty. MacIntyre notes, "To call an argument fallacious is always at once to describe and to evaluate it" (1978, p. 258). It is, therefore, a normative construct. Narrative rationality is, on the other hand, descriptive, as it offers an account, an understanding, of any instance of human choice and action, including science (Gadamer, 1982; Heidegger, 1972; Holton, 1973; Ramsey, 1969). At the same time, it is a basis for critique, because it implies a *praxis*, an ideal democratic society (McGee, Scult, and Kientz, 1983). Traditional rationality implies some sort of hierarchial system, a community in which some persons are qualified to judge and to lead and some other persons are to follow.

For the sake of clarity, I should note that, while the narrative paradigm provides a radical democratic ground for social-political critique, it does not deny the legitimacy (the inevitability) of hierarchy. History records no community, uncivilized or civilized, without key story-makers/story-tellers, whether sanctioned by God, a "gift," heritage, power, intelligence, or election. It insists, however, that the "people" do judge the stories that are told for and about them and that they have a rational capacity to make such judgments. It holds, along with Aristotle (1954, bk. 1, ch. 1, 1355^a 20) that the "people" have a natural tendency to prefer the true and the just. Neither does the narrative paradigm deny that the "people" can be wrong. But, then, so can elites, especially when a decision is social or political. And neither does the theory deny the existence and desirability of genius in individuals or the "people" to formulate and to adopt new stories that better account for their lives or the mystery of life itself. The sort of hierarchy condemned by the narrative *praxis* is the sort that is marked by the will to power, the kind of system in which elites struggle to dominate and to use the people for their own ends or that makes the people blind subjects of technology.

Narrative rationality, then, is inimical to elitist politics, whether fascist, communist, or even democratic—if traditional rationality is the prevailing societal view. And this seems to be the case with American democracy, as subsequent examination of the nuclear controversy will show. The prevalent position is that voters are rational if they know enough about public issues; are cognizant of argumentative procedures, forms, and functions; and weigh carefully all the arguments they hear and read in a systematic, deliberative process. Contrary to this notion is that of V. O. Key Jr. In a classic study of presidential voting between 1936 and 1960, he concluded that "voters are not fools," which is what they must be considered if measured by traditional rationality. His data led him to conclude that the American electorate is not "straitjacketed by social determinants or moved by subconscious urges triggered by devilishly skillful propagandists." They are moved by their perceptions and appraisals of "central and relevant questions of public policy, of governmental performance, and of executive personality" (1966, pp. 7–8). These perceptions and appraisals of political discourse and action become stories, narratives that must stand the tests of probability and fidelity. And these stories are no less valuable than the stories constructed by persons who are rational in the traditional way. There is no evidence to support the claim that "experts" know better than anyone else who should be elected president.

Obviously, as I will note later, some stories are better than others, more coherent, more "true" to the way people and the world are—in fact and in value. In other words, some stories are better in satisfying the criteria of the logic of good reasons, which is attentive to reason and values. Persons may even choose not to participate in the making of public narrative if they feel that they are meaningless spectators rather than co-authors. But, all persons have the capacity to be rational in the narrative paradigm. And, by and large, persons are that—at least in the fashioning of their daily lives. Persons do not have the capacity to be equally rational in the rational world paradigm. Because persons have the capacity of narrative rationality, it is reasonable to have juries of lay persons and popular elections, as Bennett (1978; Bennett and Feldman, 1981) has well demonstrated. I want to stress, however, that narrative rationality does not negate traditional rationality. It holds that traditional rationality is only relevant in specialized fields and even in those arenas narrative rationality is meaningful and useful.

Certain other features of the narrative paradigm should be noted before moving to the case of public moral argument. First, the paradigm is a ground for resolving the dualisms of modernism: fact–value, intellect–imagination, reason–emotion, and so on. Stories are the enactment of the whole mind in concert with itself. Second, narratives are moral constructs. As White asserts: "Where, in any account of reality, narrativity is present, we can be sure that morality or a moral impulse is present too" (1980, p. 26; Benjamin, 1969). Third, the narrative paradigm is consonant with the notion of reason proposed by Schrag:

"Reason, as the performance of vision and insight, commemoration and foresight, occasions the recognition of a process of meaning-formation that gathers within it the logic of technical reason and the *logos* of myth" (1980, p. 126). The appropriateness and validity of this view of reason for the narrative paradigm [are] supported by Angel Medina (1979). In a statement that reiterates several of the points I have made, he writes:

> It is necessary to define our reason primarily as biographical, that is, above all narrative and then symbolic. Human reason is narrative because it extends from its inception and in every one of its acts toward the foreshadowing of its total course. It is symbolic in that the major aim in the formation of this totality is its own self-presentation within the dialogue of consciousness. The meaning of my whole life is communicative; it emerges, as such, for the benefit of another consciousness when I attempt to present myself totally to it. Reciprocally, the meaning of another life becomes a totality only when received fully within my life. (p. 30)

And, fourth, as I will attempt to show, the narrative paradigm offers ways of resolving the problems of public moral argument.

The Case: Public Moral Argument

It should be apparent by now that I think that MacIntyre's (1981) *After Virtue* is a remarkable work. Equally remarkable, in its own way, is Jonathan Schell's (1982) *The Fate of the Earth*. Schell's book is exemplary of contemporary moral argument intended to persuade a general audience, the "public." His concluding argument is:

> Either we will sink into the final coma and end it all or, as I trust and believe, we will awaken to the truth of our peril, a truth as great as life itself, and, like a person who has swallowed a lethal poison but shakes off his stupor at the last moment and vomits the poison up, we will break through the layers of denials, put aside our faint-hearted excuses, and rise up to cleanse the earth of nuclear weapons. (p. 231)

The validity of Schell's argument is not the question here. Our concern is its reception, which reveals the limits, perhaps the impossibility, of persuasive moral argument in our time, given the rational world paradigm.

Critical response to *The Fate of the Earth* is of two sorts. The first is celebratory. Reviewers in this group are obviously in sympathy with the book's moral thrust, its depiction of the results of nuclear war, and its call for action—for life instead of death—but not with every detail of its argument. Although reviewers in this group include distinguished figures from a variety of professions—journalists Walter Cronkite, James Reston, and James Kilpatrick; historians Harrison Salisbury, John Hersey, and Henry Steele Commager; and politicians Barry Commoner, W. Averell Harriman, and Walter Mondale—none is a current member of the federal administration or the defense establishment. Each of them bears witness to an attitude—opposition to nuclear annihilation—but none testifies to the technical merits of Schell's representation of "deterrence theory," his inferences about its meaning in regard to strategy and tactics, or his conclusions about national sovereignty. They, like Schell, are not "experts" in the field in which the argument is made. They, like Schell, are active in the realm of rhetorical knowledge, in the sphere of social-political policy and behavior (Bitzer, 1978; Farrell, 1976).

Reviewers in the second group, on the other hand, are purveyors of ideological, bureaucratic, or technical arguments. Such arguments may overlap, be used by the same arguer, but each is distinguished by a particular privileged position: political "truth," administrative sanction, or subject matter expertise. The thrust of the ideological argument is that one violates ultimate "facts," is fundamentally wrong-headed; the bureaucratic argument stresses feasibility in regard to administrative approval; and the technical argument alleges ignorance of the "facts," that opponents are "unrealistic," meaning they do not have a firm grasp on reality. These are, of course, the lines of refutation or subversion. Their opposites would be constructive arguments of affirmation or reaffirmation.

The subversive pattern of ideological, bureaucratic, and technical arguments is evident in the following attacks on Schell's reasoning. McCracken (1982) labels Schell an "alarmist" and concludes: "The danger is that Mr. Schell's followers may triumph and bring about a freeze that by making present inequities permanent will prove destabilizing in the short run and in the long run productive of both redness and deadness" (p. 905). Focusing on the lynch-pin arguments of *The Fate of the Earth* (Schell's interpretation of deterrence theory and his suggested solution of abolishing national sovereignty), Hausknecht (1982) first cites Alexander Haig and then observes that "it is not hard to imagine Ronald Reagan saying, 'Okay, so it may be the end of the species, but we can't let

the bastards get away with it.'" In regard to Schell's solution, he concludes that "successful political action demands significant but realizable goals" (p. 284). The same charge is leveled by Pierre (1982), who approves the moral force of Schell's position but then charges that "Schell provides no realistic alternative to our nuclear policy based on the concept of deterrence. His argument—that knowledge that nuclear weapons can extinguish mankind must be the new deterrent in a disarmed world—is very weak" (p. 1188).

The strategy of these reviews is clear: reaffirmation of the moral concern, subversion of the reasoning. The tactics are also obvious: juxtapose Schell's reasoning with what is right-headed, what is approved by the administration, or what is "realistic." Insofar as there is merit in these "arguments," it lies not in the way they foreclose dialogue but in their narrative probability and narrative fidelity. Yet this is not their intended appeal or effect. The effects are to discredit Schell as an arguer and to dismiss his argument as unfounded. Public moral argument is thus overwhelmed by privileged argument. Put another way, it is submerged by ideological and bureaucratic arguments that insist on rival moralities and technical argument which denudes it of morality altogether, making the dispute one for "experts" alone to consider (see Farrell and Goodnight, 1981).

The question that arises at this point is: What happens when "experts" argue about moral issues in public? Before considering this question, however, it is essential to sketch the general characteristics of "public moral argument."

Public moral argument is to be distinguished from reasoned discourse in interpersonal interactions and arguments occurring in specialized communities, such as theological disputes, academic debates, and arguments before the Supreme Court. The features differentiating *public* moral argument from such encounters are: (1) it is publicized, made available for consumption and persuasion of the polity at large; and (2) it is aimed at what Aristotle called "untrained thinkers," or, to be effective, it should be (1954, bk. 1, ch. 2, 1357[a] 10). Most important *public* moral argument is a form of controversy that inherently crosses fields. It is not contained in the way that legal, scientific, or theological arguments are, by subject matter, particular conceptions of argumentative competence, and well recognized rules of advocacy. Because this is so and because its realm is public-social knowledge, *public* moral argument naturally invites participation by field experts and is dominated by the rational superiority of their arguments. *Public* moral argument, which is oriented toward what ought to be, is undermined by the "truth" that prevails at the moment. The presence of "experts" in *public* moral arguments makes it difficult, if not impossible, for the public of "untrained thinkers" to win an argument or even judge them well—given, again, the rational world paradigm.

Public *moral* argument is moral in the sense that it is founded on ultimate questions—of life and death, of how persons should be defined and treated, of preferred patterns of living. Gusfield (1976) designates such questions "status issues." Their resolution, he writes, indicates "the group, culture, or style of life to which the government and society are publicly committed" (p. 173). In addition to nuclear warfare, desegregation would be included in the category as well as abortion and school prayer.

Public moral *argument* refers to clear cut inferential structures, in the rational world paradigm, and to "good reasons," in the narrative paradigm. Public moral *argument* may also refer to public controversies—disputes and debates—about moral issues. The nuclear warfare controversy is an obvious case in point, but so are the others mentioned above. One could add disputes over pornography, the ERA, and crime and punishment. This characterization of public moral *argument* is attentive to argument as product and as process (Wenzel, 1980).

The problem posed by the presence of experts in public moral argument is illustrated by the dispute between Hans Bethe and Edward Teller over the 1982 nuclear freeze proposition in California. Their positions were published in the *Los Angeles Times* (1982, October 17, Part 4, pp. 1–2), so they were public. They obviously concerned a moral issue and they were reasoned statements. Both persons are credible. Which one is to be believed and followed? Who in the general public could contend with them? Teller answers the second question in unequivocal terms: "The American public is ignorant, even of the general ideas on which they [nuclear weapons] are based" (p. 2). Here is revealed the fate of non-experts who would argue about nuclear warfare. Only experts can argue with experts and their arguments—while public—cannot be rationally questioned. As Perelman (1979) notes, rationality in and of itself forecloses discussion and debate. In the audience of experts, the public is left with no compelling reason, from the perspective of the rational world paradigm, to believe one over the other. One is not a judge but a spectator who must choose between actors. From the narrative paradigm view, the

experts are storytellers and the audience is not a group of observers but are active participants in the meaning-formation of the stories.

It may be asked at this point: How is it that freeze referendums were approved in eight out of nine states and in twenty-eight cities and counties in 1982? One answer is "fear," the "most intelligent feeling of our time" (Wieseltier, 1983, p. 7). Another answer is "distrust," distrust of those responsible for the development, deployment, and use of nuclear weapons. This answer is, I believe, more accurate. It does not deny the existence of fear. It insists on the "rationality" of those who voted for and against the referendum. Those who opposed the referendum did so because of a basic distrust of Soviet leaders and a fundamental trust of our own. What I am saying is that there are good reasons for trust and distrust, that the response of voters was rational, given the narrative paradigm. The good reasons that are expressed in public moral argument relate to issues not accounted for in the rational world paradigm. These issues include the motivations and values of the characters involved in the ongoing narrative of nuclear warfare, the way in which they conceive and behave in respect to the conflict, and the narrative probability and narrative fidelity of the particular stories they tell, which may well take the form of "reasoned argument." Experts and lay persons meet on common ground, given the narrative paradigm. As Toulmin observes, "A scientist off duty is as much an 'ordinary' man as a tinker or a bus-conductor off duty" (1982, p. 81).

From the narrative perspective, the proper role of the expert in public moral argument is that of a counselor, which is, as Benjamin (1969) notes, the true function of the storyteller. His or her contribution to public dialogue is to impart knowledge, like a teacher, or wisdom, like a sage. It is not to pronounce a story that ends all storytelling. The expert assumes the role of public counselor whenever she or he crosses the boundary of technical knowledge into the territory of life as it ought to be lived. Once this invasion is made, the public, which then includes the expert, has its own criteria for determining whose story is most coherent and reliable as a guide to belief and action. The expert, in other words, then becomes subject to the demands of narrative rationality. Technical communities have their own conceptions and criteria for judging the rationality of communication. But, as Holton (1973) has demonstrated, the work even of scientists is inspired by stories; hence, their discourse can be interpreted usefully from the narrative perspective. Holton writes tellingly of the "nascent moment" in science, the impulse to do science in a particular or in a new way, and how science is informed by "themes"—thematic concepts, methods, and hypotheses inherited from Parmenides, Heraclitus, Pythagoras, Thales, and others (pp. 28–29; see also Ong, 1982, p. 140).

Viewed from the perspective of the rational world paradigm, Schell's case, his argument and its reception, evokes despair. If one looks to MacIntyre's *After Virtue* for relief, one will be disappointed and disheartened further, for he provides the historical and philosophical reasons for the fate of *The Fate of the Earth* and similar arguments. His own argument is that "we still, in spite of the efforts of three centuries of moral philosophy and one of sociology, lack any coherent, rationally defensible statement of a liberal individualist point of view" (1981, p. 241). He offers some hope with the idea that "the Aristotelian tradition can be restated in a way that restores intelligibility and rationality to our moral and social attitudes and commitments." He observes, however, "the new dark ages" are "already upon us." The "barbarians are not waiting beyond the frontiers; they have already been governing us for quite some time. And it is our lack of consciousness of this that constitutes part of our predicament. We are waiting not for Godot, but for another—doubtless very different—St. Benedict" (p. 245).

The reasons for this state of affairs are: (1) the rejection of a teleological view of human nature and the classical conception of reason as embodied in Aristotelian logic and rhetoric; (2) the separation of morality from theological, legal, and aesthetic concerns; and (3) the evolution of the individualistic sense of self and the rise of emotivism. The consequence of these movements is a situation in which ethical arguments in public are rendered ineffectual because of "conceptual incommensurability."

A case in point is protest—where advocates of reform argue from a position of "rights" and those who oppose them reason from the stance of "utility." MacIntyre observes:

> The facts of incommensurability ensure that protestors can never win an *argument*; the indignant self-righteousness of protestors arises because the facts of incommensurability ensure equally that the protestors can never lose an argument either. Hence, the *utterance* of protest is characteristically addressed to those who already *share* the protestors' premises. . . . This is not to say that protest cannot be effective; it is to say that protest cannot be *rationally* effective. (p. 69)

Thus, when arguers appealing to justice and equality contend with adversaries who base their case on success, survival, and liberty, they talk past each other.

From the perspective of the narrative paradigm, the dynamic of this situation is that rival stories are being told. Any story, any form of rhetorical communication, not only says something about the world, it also implies an audience, persons who conceive of themselves in very specific ways. If a story denies a person's self-conception, it does not matter what it says about the world. In the instance of protest, the rival factions' stories deny each other in respect to self-conceptions and the world. The only way to bridge this gap, if it can be bridged through discourse, is by telling stories that do not negate the self-conceptions people hold of themselves.

It may be germane to note at this point that narrative as a *mode of discourse* is more universal and probably more efficacious than argument for nontechnical forms of communication (Fisher, 1982, p. 304). There are several reasons why this should be true. First, narration comes closer to capturing the experience of the world, simultaneously appealing to the various senses, to reason and emotion, to intellect and imagination, and to fact and value. It does not presume intellectual contact only. Second, one does not have to be taught narrative probability and narrative fidelity; one culturally acquires them through a universal faculty and experience. Obviously, one can, through education, become sophisticated in one's understanding and application of these principles. But, as Gadamer observes, "I am convinced of the fact that there are no people who do not 'think' sometime and somewhere. That means there is no one who does not form general views about life and death, about freedom and living together, about the good and about happiness" (1981, p. 58; see also Ogden, 1977, p. 114; Lonergan, 1958, xiv–xv, xxii–xxx). In other words, people are reflective and from such reflection they make the stories of their lives and have the basis for judging narratives for and about them. On the other hand, appreciation of argument requires not only reflection, but also specialized knowledge of issues, reasoning, rules of rationality, and so on. Third, narration works by suggestion and identification; argument operates by inferential moves and deliberation. Both forms, however, are modes of expressing good reasons—given the narrative paradigm—so the differences between them are structural rather than substantive.

Summary and Conclusions

This essay began as a study of public moral argument—the nuclear controversy. It was undertaken with the rational world paradigm well in mind. The results of my analysis were disturbing not only in what I found to be the inevitable subversion of *The Fate of the Earth* and similar such arguments, but also in that the rational world paradigm was at least partly responsible for that fate. Then came MacIntyre's (1981) *After Virtue*. Reflection set in and the narrative paradigm came out of it. I was concerned with the concept of technical reason and the way it rendered the public unreasonable; with the idea of rationality being a matter of argumentative competence in specialized fields, leaving the public and its discourse irrational; with the apparent impossibility of bridging the gaps between experts and the public and between segments of the public; and with the necessity to learn what was supposed to be of the essence of persons—rationality—so that one class of citizens can always be superior to another.

Although I do not mean to maintain that the narrative paradigm resolves these problems out of existence, I do think that it provides a basis for reconsideration of them. Before that, I am aware, the narrative paradigm itself needs further scrutiny. I know that I do not need to tell critics how to do their work—the examination of my representation of the rational world paradigm, the presuppositions of the narrative paradigm and its relationship to other constructs, my concept of public moral argument, and the analysis of the specific case. I welcome the "stories" the critics will tell.

In closing, I should like to make two additional comments. First, I think that the concepts of public and social knowledge should be reconceived in light of the narrative paradigm. The effect would be to give shape to these ideas as identifiable entities in the discourse of the citizenry, to give public knowledge a form of being. To consider that public-social knowledge is to be found in the stories that we tell one another would enable us to observe not only our differences, but also our commonalities, and in such observation we might be able to reform the notion of the "public."

Second, and closely related to the discovery of our communal identity, is the matter of what makes one story better than another. Two features come to mind: formal and substantive. Formal features are attributes of narrative probability: the consistency of characters and actions, the accommodation of auditors, and so on. In epistemological terms, the question would be whether a narrative satisfied the demands of a coherence theory of truth. The most compelling, persuasive stories are mythic in form (Campbell, 1973; Cassirer, 1944, 1979, p. 246; Eliade, 1963). Substantive features relate to narrative fidelity. Bormann has proposed two concepts pertinent to the problem of narrative fidelity: "corroboration" (1978) and "social convergence" (1983, p. 436). These concepts concern how people come to adhere to particular stories. They do not solve the problem of narrative fidelity because both suggest that narratives are valid by virtue of consensus and provide no criteria by which one can establish that one narrative is more sound than another. While there is work to be done on the problem, I think the logic of good reasons is the most viable scheme presently available by which narratives can be tested. Its application requires an examination of reasoning and "inspection of facts, values, self, and society" (Fisher, 1978, p. 382). In epistemological terms, narrative fidelity is a matter of truth according to the doctrine of correspondence. Though the most engaging stories are mythic, the most helpful and uplifting stories are moral. As John Gardner wrote, "Moral action is action that affirms life" (1978, p. 23).

One may get the impression that the conception of rationality I have presented leads to a denial of logic. It does, but only as logic is conceived so that persons are considered irrational beings. With Heidegger (1973, p. 170), I would assert that "to think counter to logic does not mean to stick up for the illogical, but only means to think the *logos*, and its essence as it appeared in the early days of thought; i.e. to make an effort first of all to prepare such an act of reflecting (*Nachdenka*)." In an earlier essay, I attempted to make such an effort by showing the relationship of the logic of good reasons to Aristotle's concept of "practical wisdom" (Fisher, 1980, pp. 127–128).

Application of narrative rationality to specific stories may further clarify its nature and value. From the perspective of narrative rationality, Hitler's *Mein Kampf* must be judged a bad story. Although it has formal coherence in its structure, as McGuire (1977) demonstrated, it denies the identity of significant persons and demeans others. It also lacks fidelity to the truths humanity shares in regard to reason, justice, veracity, and peaceful ways to resolve social-political differences. On the other hand, one may cite the cosmological myths of Lao-tse, Buddha, Zoroaster, Christ, and Mohammed which satisfy both narrative probability and narrative fidelity for those cultures for whom they were intended—and many others across time and place. Far from denying the humanity of persons, they elevate it to the profoundest moral and metaphysical level the world has known. One could also cite such works as *The Iliad* and *The Odyssey*; the tragedies of Aeschylus, Sophocles, Euripides; Virgil's *Aeneid*; Dante's *Commedia*; the plays of Shakespeare; and the novels of Tolstoy, Melville, Thomas Mann, and James Joyce. One could point to the lives of Jesus, Socrates, Lincoln, and Gandhi. Regarding political discourse, one could mention many of the speeches and writings of Adlai Stevenson and Winston Churchill. While these classic manifestations of religious, social, cultural, and political life have been celebrated by persons committed to traditional rationality, it has been because they have not restricted themselves to "logic" but have recognized and responded to the values fostered by them, by their reaffirmation of the human spirit as the transcendent ground of existence.

For a more detailed illustration of how narrative probability and fidelity can be usefully applied, I offer this brief analysis of *The Epic of Gilgamesh*, "the finest surviving epic poem from any period until the appearance of Homer's *Iliad*: and it is immeasurably older" (Sandars, 1982, p. 7). It is, in fact, 1,500 years older.

The story, in sum, is as follows: Gilgamesh, the King of Urak, two-thirds god and one-third man, is possessed of a perfect body, unbounded courage, and extraordinary strength. He is a hero, a tragic hero, the "first tragic hero of whom anything is known" (Sandars, 1982, p. 7). His youth is spent in pursuit of fame as the means of immortality.

He is restless, with no one to match his appetites and physical feats. His people ask the gods to create a companion for him, which they do in Enkidu. Enkidu is Gilgamesh's counterpart in strength, energy, and exuberance for life. After a wrestling match, they become inseparable, brothers in every way but birth. Gilgamesh learns what it means to love.

Because Enkidu begins to lose his physical prowess—he had been an inhabitant of the wilds and ran with animals—Gilgamesh proposes that they pursue and slay Huwawa, a terrible monster. At first, Enkidu is reluctant but is chided into joining the quest. The monster is met, subdued, and, because of an insult, is slain by Enkidu.

When they return to Urak, the goddess Ishtar proposes to Gilgamesh. He not only refuses her, but he and Enkidu heap scorn upon her. She goes to her father, Anu, and asks him to have the bull of heaven kill Gilgamesh. But Gilgamesh and Enkidu kill the bull instead. It appears at this point that the "brothers" cannot be defeated by man, monsters, or the gods.

It turns out, however, that in killing Huwawa, Gilgamesh and Enkidu incurred the wrath of Enlil, guardian of the forest in which the monster lived. Enlil demands the death of Gilgamesh, but the sun god intervenes and Enkidu is doomed and dies.

With Enkidu's death, the world of Gilgamesh is shattered. He has not only lost his loving companion, he must now directly confront the fact of death. Up to this point, he has lived as a willful child, acting as though the meaning of life is a matter of dominating it.

At first, Gilgamesh refuses to accept Enkidu's death as real. He becomes obsessed with death and starts a quest to learn the secret of immortality. His journey is tortured and long. He finally arrives, after incredible hardships, at the island of Utanapishtim and asks him how one gains eternal life. Utanapishtim suggests that he try not to sleep for six days and seven nights. But he soon falls asleep, for seven days, a form of living death. He is awakened and realizes there is no escape from death. He resigns himself to his fate, the fate of all humankind, and returns home. On his return he learns to value the wall he has built around the city: immortality is, he apparently concludes, to be found in the monuments that one leaves behind.

The story provides good reasons to accept not only this truth, but others as well: Life is fullest when one loves and is loved; death is real; and maturity is achieved by accepting the reality of death. We learn these truths by dwelling in the characters in the story, by observing the outcomes of the several conflicts that arise throughout it, by seeing the unity of characters and their actions, and by comparing the truths to the truths we know to be true from our own lives. In other words, the story exhibits narrative probability and fidelity across time and culture (Jacobsen, 1976).

Finally, I do not mean to maintain that "knowledge of agents" is superior to "knowledge of objects." With Toulmin, I would hold that "A decent respect for each kind of knowledge is surely compatible with conceding the legitimate claims of the other" (1982, p. 244). With knowledge of agents, we can hope to find that which is *reliable or trustworthy*; with knowledge of objects, we can hope to discover that which has the quality of *veracity*. The world requires both kinds of knowledge.

Karl Wallace was right: "One could do worse than characterize rhetoric as the art of finding and effectively presenting good reasons" (1963, p. 248). MacIntyre is also right:

> The unity of human life is the unity of a narrative quest. Quests sometimes fail, are frustrated, abandoned or dissipated into distractions; and human lives may in all these ways also fail. But the criteria for success or failure in a human life as a whole are the criteria of success or failure in a narrated or to-be-narrated quest. (1981, p. 203)

And that quest is "for the good life" for all persons.

REFERENCES

Alter, R. (1981). *The Art of Biblical Narrative*. New York: Basic Books.

Apel, K. O. (1979). "Types of Rationality Today: The Continuum of Reason between Science and Ethics." In T. F. Geraets, ed., *Rationality Today* (Ottawa, ON, Canada: University of Ottawa Press), pp. 309–339.

Aristotle. (1954). *Rhetoric*. Translated by W. R. Roberts. New York: Modern Library.

Baier, A. (1983). "Secular Faith." In S. Hauerwas and A. MacIntyre, eds., *Revisions: Changing Perspectives on Moral Philosophy* (South Bend, IN: University of Notre Dame Press), pp. 203–221.

Bantz, C. R. (1975). "Television News: Reality and Research." *Western Journal of Speech Communication* 39: 123–130.

Barrett, W. (1979). *The Illusion of Technique: A Search for Meaning in a Technological Civilization*. Garden City, NY: Anchor Press/Doubleday.

Barthes, R. (1977). "Introduction to the Structural Analysis of Narratives." In S. Heath, ed., *Image-Music-Text* (New York: Hill and Wang), pp. 79–124.

Bateson, G. (1979). *Mind and Nature: A Necessary Unity*. Toronto: Bantam Books.

Benjamin, W. (1969). "The Storyteller." In H. Arendt, ed., *Illuminations* (New York: Schocken Books), pp. 83–109.

Bennett, L. W. (1975). "Political Scenarios and the Nature of Politics." *Philosophy and Rhetoric* 8: 23–42.

Bennett, L. W. (1978). "Storytelling and Criminal Trials: A Model of Social Judgment." *Quarterly Journal of Speech* 64: 1–22.

Bennett, L. W., and M. S. Feldman. (1981). *Reconstructing Reality in the Courtroom: Justice and Judgment in American Culture*. New Brunswick, NJ: Rutgers University Press.

Bitzer, L. F. (1978). "Rhetoric and Public Knowledge." In D. Burks, ed., *Rhetoric, Philosophy and Literature: An Exploration* (West Lafayette, IN: Purdue University Press), pp. 67–93.

Booth, W. C. (1974). *Modern Dogma and the Rhetoric of Assent*. South Bend, IN: University of Notre Dame Press.

Bormann, E. G. (1972). "Fantasy and Rhetorical Vision: The Rhetorical Criticism of Social Reality." *Quarterly Journal of Speech* 59: 143–159.

Bormann, E. G. (1973). "The Eagleton Affair: A Fantasy Theme Analysis." *Quarterly Journal of Speech* 59: 143–159.

Bormann, E. G. (1979). "The Tentative and the Certain in Rhetoric: The Role of Corroboration on the Rigidity or Flexibility of Rhetorical Visions." Paper presented at the annual meeting of the Central States Speech Association, Minneapolis.

Bormann, E. G. (1983). "Fantasy Theme Analysis." In J. L. Golden, G. F. Berquist, and W. E. Coleman, eds., *The Rhetoric of Western Thought*, 3rd ed. (Dubuque, IA: Kendall/Hunt), pp. 430–449.

Brockriede, W. (1975). "Where Is Argument?" *Journal of the American Forensics Association* 11: 179.

Brockriede, W. (1977). "Characteristics of Arguments and Arguing." *Journal of the American Forensics Association* 13: 129–132.

Brockriede, W. (1982). "Arguing about Human Understanding." *Communication Monographs* 49: 137–147.

Burke, K. (1955). *A Rhetoric of Motives*. New York: George Braziller.

Burke, K. (1957). *The Philosophy of Literary Form*. Rev. ed. New York: Vintage Books.

Burke, K. (1968). "Definition of Man." In *Language and Symbolic Action: Essays on Life, Literature, and Method* (Berkeley and Los Angeles: University of California Press), pp. 3–24.

Burke, K. (1983). "Lecture Outlines. Logology: An Overall View." Personal correspondence.

Burleson, B. R. (1981). "Characteristics of Argument." In G. Ziegelmueller and J. Rhodes, eds., *Dimensions of Argument: Proceedings of the Second Conference an Argumentation* (Annandale, VA: Speech Communication Association), pp. 955–979.

Campbell, J. (1973). *Myths to Live By*. New York: Bantam Books.

Campbell, J. A. (1984). "On the Rhetoric of History: Epochal Discourse and Discovery of the Universal Audience." Unpublished paper, Department of Speech Communication, University of Washington.

Campbell, J. A., and J. R. Stewart. (1981). "Rhetoric, Philosophy, and Conversation." Paper presented at the annual meeting of the Western Speech Communication Association, San Jose, CA.

Cassirer, E. (1944). *An Essay on Man: An Introduction to a Philosophy of Human Culture*. New Haven, CT: Yale University Press.

Cassirer, E. (1979). "The Technique of Our Modern Political Myths." In D. P. Verent, ed., *Symbol, Myth, and Culture: Essays and Lectures of Ernst Cassirer* (New Haven, CT: Yale University Press), pp. 242–267.

Cox, J. R. (1981). "Investigating Policy Argument as a Field." In G. Ziegelmueller and J. Rhodes, eds.,

Dimensions of Argument: Proceedings of the Second Conference on Argumentation (Annandale, VA: Speech Communication Association), pp. 126–142.

Danto, A. C. (1982). "Narration and Knowledge." *Philosophy and Literature* 6: 17–32.

Derrida, J. (1980). "The Law of Genre." *Critical Inquiry* 7: 55–81.

Dewey, J. (1927). *The Public and Its Problems*. Chicago: Swallow Press.

Dijk, T. A. (1976). "Philosophy of Action and Theory of Narrative." *Poetics* 5: 287–388.

Ehninger, D. (1968). "Validity as Moral Obligation." *Southern Speech Journal* 33: 215–222.

Eliade, M. (1963). *Myth and Reality*. New York: Harper Colophon Books.

Farrell, T. B. (1976). "Knowledge, Consensus, and Rhetorical Theory." *Quarterly Journal of Speech* 62: 1–14 [reprinted in this volume].

Farrell, T. B. (1977). "Validity and Rationality: The Rhetorical Constituents of Argumentative Form." *Journal of American Forensics Association* 13: 142–149.

Farrell, T. B. (1983). "The Tradition of Rhetoric and the Philosophy of Communication." *Communication* 7: 151–180.

Farrell, T. B., and G. T. Goodnight. (1981). "Accidental Rhetoric: The Root Metaphor of Three Mile Island." *Communication Monographs* 48: 271–300.

Fisher, W. R. (1973). "Reaffirmation and Subversion of the American Dream." *Quarterly Journal of Speech* 9: 160–169.

Fisher, W. R. (1978). "Toward a Logic of Good Reasons." *Quarterly Journal of Speech* 64: 376–384.

Fisher, W. R. (1980). "Rationality and the Logic of Good Reasons." *Philosophy and Rhetoric* 13: 121–130.

Fisher, W. R. (1982). "Romantic Democracy, Ronald Reagan, and Presidential Heroes." *Western Journal of Speech Communication* 46: 299–310.

Fisher, W. R., and R. D. Burns. (1964). *Armament and Disarmament: The Continuing Dispute*. Belmont, CA: Wadsworth.

Fisher, W. R., and R. A. Filloy. (1982). "Argument in Drama and Literature: An Exploration." In J. R. Cox and C. A. Wilard, eds., *Advances in Argumentation Theory and Research* (Carbondale: Southern Illinois University Press), pp. 343–362.

Frentz, T. S., and T. B. Farrell. (1976). "Language-Action: A Paradigm for Communication." *Quarterly Journal of Speech* 62: 333–349.

Gadamer, H. G. (1980). *Dialogue and Dialectic: Eight Hermeneutical Essays on Plato*. Translated by P. Christofer Smith. New Haven, CT: Yale University Press.

Gadamer, H. G. (1981). *Reason in the Age of Science*. Cambridge, MA: MIT Press.

Gadamer, H. G. (1982). *Truth and Method*. New York: Crossword.

Gallie, W. B. (1964). *Philosophy and Historical Understanding*. New York: Schocken Books.

Gardner, J. (1978). *On Moral Fiction*. New York: Basic Books.

Goldberg, M. (1982). *Theology and Narrative*. Nashville, TN: Parthenon Press.

Goodnight, G. T. (1980). "The Liberal and the Conservative Presumptions: On Political Philosophy and the Foundation of Public Argument." In J. Rhodes and S. Newell, eds., *Proceedings of the Summer Conference on Argumentation* (Falls Church, VA: Speech Communication Association), pp. 304–337.

Goody, J., and I. Watt. (1962–1963). "The Consequences of Literacy." *Comparative Studies in Society and History* 5: 304–326, 332–345.

Gottlieb, G. (1968). *The Logic of Choice: An Investigation of the Concepts of Rule and Rationality*. New York: Macmillan.

Graff, G. (1979). *Literature Against Itself: Literacy Ideas in Society*. Chicago: University of Chicago Press.

Gusfield, J. R. (1976). *Symbolic Crusade: Status Politics and the American Temperance Movement*. Urbana: University of Illinois Press.

Habermas, J. (1967). *Theory and Practice: The History of a Concept*. South Bend, IN: University of Notre Dame Press.

Habermas, J. (1973). *Knowledge and Social Interests*. Boston: Beacon Press.

Hauerwas, S. (1981). *A Community of Character: Towards a Constructive Christian Ethic*. South Bend, IN: University of Notre Dame Press.

Hausknecht, M. (1982). "Waiting for the End? Prospects for Nuclear Destruction." *Dissent* 29: 282–284.

Hawes, L. C. (1978). "The Reflexivity of Communication Research." *Western Journal of Speech Communication* 42: 12–20.

Heidegger, M. (1949). *Existence and Being*. Chicago: Henry Regnery.

Heidegger, M. (1972). *On Time and Being*. Translated by J. Stanbaugh. New York: Harper and Row.

Heidegger, M. (1973). "Letter on Humanism." In R. Zaner and D. Ihde, eds., *Phenomenology and Existentialism* (New York: Capricorn Books/G. P. Putnam's Sons), pp. 147–181.

Hollis, M. (1977). *Models of Man: Philosophical Thoughts and Social Action*. Cambridge: Cambridge University Press.

Holton, G. (1973). *Thematic Origins of Modern Science*. Cambridge, MA: Harvard University Press.

Hymes, D. (1980). "A Narrative View of the World." In D. Hymes, *Language in Education: Ethnolinguistic Essays* (Washington, DC: Center for Applied Linguistics), pp. 129–138.

Hynes, T. J., Jr. (1980). "Liberal and Conservative Presumptions in Public Argument: A Critique." In J. Rhodes and S. Newell, eds., *Proceedings of the Summer Conference on Argumentation* (Falls Church, VA: Speech Communication Association), pp. 338–347.

Jacobs, S., and S. Jackson. (1981). "Argument as a Natural Category: The Routine Grounds for Arguing in

Conversation." *Western Journal of Speech Communication* 45: 118–132.

Jacobsen, T. (1976). *The Treasurer of Darkness: A History of Mesopotamian Religion.* New Haven, CT: Yale University Press.

Johnstone, H. W., Jr. (1978). *Validity and Rhetoric in Philosophical Argument.* University Park, PA: Dialogue Press of Man and World.

Kernmode, F. (1980). "Secrets and Narrative Sequence." *Critical Inquiry* 7: 83–101.

Key, V. O. (1966). *The Responsible Electorate: Rationality in Presidential Voting, 1936–1960.* New York: Vintage Books.

Kidd, V. (1975). "Happily Ever After and Other Relationship Styles: Advice on Interpersonal Relations in Popular Magazines, 1951–1973." *Quarterly Journal of Speech* 61: 31–39.

Kirkwood, W. G. (1983). "Storytelling and Self-Confrontation: Parables as Communication Strategies." *Quarterly Journal of Speech* 69: 58–74.

Krashen, S. D. (1982). *Principles and Practice in Second Language Acquisition.* Oxford, UK: Pergamon Press.

Kuhn, T. S. (1974). "Second Thoughts on Paradigms." In F. Suppe, ed., *The Structure of Scientific Theories* (Urbana: University of Illinois Press), pp. 459–482.

Langer, S. K. (1953). *Feeling and Form: A Theory of Art.* New York: Charles Scribner's Sons.

Lonergan, B. J. F., SJ. (1958). *Insight: A Study of Human Understanding.* New York: Harper and Row.

Lucaites, J. L. (1981). "Rhetoric and the Problem of Legitimacy." In G. Ziegelmueller and J. Rhodes, eds., *Dimensions of Argument: Proceedings of the Second Conference on Argumentation* (Annandale, VA: Speech Communication Association).

Lyne, J. (1982). "Discourse, Knowledge, and Social Process: Some Changing Equations." *Quarterly Journal of Speech* 68: 201–214.

MacIntyre, A. (1978). "Rationality and the Explanation of Action." In A. MacIntyre, *Against the Self-Image of the Art: Essays on Ideology and Philosophy* (South Bend, IN: University of Notre Dame Press), pp. 244–259.

MacIntyre, A. (1981). *After Virtue: A Study in Moral Theory.* South Bend, IN: University of Notre Dame Press.

Masterman, M. (1970). "The Nature of a Paradigm." In I. Lakatos and A. Musgrave, eds., *Criticism and the Growth of Knowledge* (London: Cambridge University Press), pp. 59–89.

McCracken, S. (1982, July 23). "The Peace of the Grave." *National Review,* pp. 904–905.

McGee, M. C., and M. A. Martin. (1983). "Public Knowledge and Ideological Argumentation." *Communication Monographs* 50: 47–65.

McGee, M. C., A. Scult, [and] K. Kuntz. (1983). "Genesis 1–3 as Sacred Text: An Inquiry into the Relationship of Rhetoric and Power." Unpublished paper, Department of Communication, University of Iowa.

McGuire, M. (1977). "Mythic Rhetoric in *Mein Kampf*: A Structural Critique." *Quarterly Journal of Speech* 68: 1–13.

McKerrow, R. E. (1977). "Rhetorical Validity: An Analysis of Three Perspectives on the Justification of Rhetorical Argument." *Journal of the American Forensics Association* 13: 133–141.

McKerrow, R. E. (1980a). "Argument Communities: A Quest for Distinctions." In J. Rhodes and S. Newell, eds., *Proceedings of the Summer Conference on Argumentation* (Falls Church, VA: Speech Communication Association), pp. 214–227.

McKerrow, R. E. (1980b). "On Fields and Rational Enterprises: A Reply to Willard." In J. Rhodes and S. Newell, eds., *Proceedings of the Summer Conference on Argumentation* (Falls Church, VA: Speech Communication Association), pp. 401–411.

McKerrow, R. E. (1981). "Senses of Argument: Uses and Limitations of the Concept." In G. Ziegelmueller and J. Rhodes, eds., *Dimensions of Argument: Proceedings of the Second Conference on Argumentation* (Annandale, VA: Speech Communication Association), pp. 990–986.

McKerrow, R. E. (1982). "Rationality and Reasonableness in a Theory of Argument." In J. R. Cox and C. A. Willard, eds., *Advances in Argumentation Theory and Research* (Carbondale: Southern Illinois University Press), pp. 105–122.

Medina, A. (1979). *Reflection, Time, and the Novel: Toward a Communicative Theory of Literature.* London: Routledge & Kegan Paul.

Mink, L. O. (1978). "Narrative Form as a Cognitive Instrument." In R. H. Canary, ed., *The Writing of History* (Madison: University of Wisconsin Press), pp. 129–149.

Nelson, J. S. (1980). "Tropal History and the Social Sciences: Reflections on Struever's Remarks." *History and Theory* 19: 80–101.

Ochs, D. J., and R. J. Burritt. (1973). "Perceptual Theory: Narrative Suasion of Lysias." In C. J. Stewart, D. J. Ochs, and G. P. Mahrmann, eds., *Explorations in Rhetorical Criticism* (University Park: Pennsylvania State University Press), pp. 51–74.

Ogden, S. M. (1977). "Myth and Truth." In S. M. Ogden, *The Reality of God* (San Francisco: Harper and Row), pp. 99–129.

O'Keefe, D. J. (1977). "Two Concepts of Argument." *Journal of the American Forensic Association* 13: 121–128.

O'Keefe, D. J. (1982). "The Concepts of Argument and Arguing." In J. R. Cox and C. A. Willard, eds., *Advances in Argumentation Theory and Research* (Carbondale: Southern Illinois University Press), pp. 3–23.

Ong, W. (1982). *Orality and Literacy: The Technologizing of the Word.* London: Methuen.

Perelman, C. (1979). "The Rational and the Reasonable." In *The New Rhetoric and the Humanities: Essays* on *Rhetoric and Its Applications* (Boston: D. Reidel), pp. 117–123.

Perelman, C., and L. Olbrechts-Tyteca. (1969). *The New Rhetoric: A Treatise on Argument.* Translated by J. Wilkinson and P. Weaver. South Bend, IN: University of Notre Dame Press.

Pierre, A. J. (1982). [Review of *The Fate of the Earth*, by Jonathan Schell]. *Foreign Affairs* 60: 1188.

Polanyi, M. (1958). *Personal Knowledge: Towards a Postcritical Philosophy.* Chicago: University of Chicago Press.

Pryor, B. (1981). "Saving the Public through Rational Discourse." In G. Ziegelmueller and J. Rhodes, eds., *Dimensions of Argument: Proceedings of the Second Conference on Argumentation* (Annandale, VA: Speech Communication Association), pp. 848–864.

Ramsey, I. T. (1969). "Religion and Science: A Philosopher's Approach." In D. M. High, ed., *New Essays on Religious Language* (New York: Oxford University Press), pp. 36–53.

Randall, J. H., Jr. (1976). *The Making of the Modern Mind.* New York: Columbia University Press.

Rarick, D. L., M. B. Duncan, and L. W. Porter. (1977). "The Carter Persona: An Empirical Analysis of the Rhetorical Visions of Campaign '76." *Quarterly Journal of Speech* 63: 258–273.

Ricoeur, P. (1976). *Interpretation Theory: Discourse and the Surplus of Meaning.* Fort Worth: Texas Christian University Press.

Ricoeur, P. (1980). "Narrative Time." *Critical Inquiry* 7: 169–190.

Rorty, R. (1979). *Philosophy and the Mirror of Nature.* Princeton, NJ: Princeton University Press.

Sandars, N. K. (1982). *The Epic of Gilgamesh.* New York: Penguin Books.

Schell, J. (1982). *The Fate of the Earth.* New York: Avon Books.

Schrag, C. O. (1980). *Radical Reflection and the Origins of the Human Sciences.* West Lafayette, IN: Purdue University Press.

Schrag, C. O. (1984). "Rhetoric, Hermeneutics, and Communication." Unpublished manuscript, Department of Philosophy, Purdue University.

Scott, R. L. (1978). "Evidence in Communication: We Are Such Stuff." *Western Journal of Speech Communication* 42: 29–36.

Scutt, A. (1983). "The Rhetorical Character of the Old Testament and Its Interpretation." Paper presented at the annual meeting of the International Society for the History of Rhetoric, Florence, Italy.

Sennett, R. (1978). *The Fall of Public Man: On the Social Psychology of Capitalism.* New York: Vintage Books.

Sillars, M. O., and P. Ganer. (1982). "Values and Beliefs: A Systematic Basis for Argumentation." In J. R. Cox and C. A. Willard, eds., *Advances in Argumentation Theory and Research* (Carbondale: Southern Illinois University Press), pp. 184–201.

Simons, H. D. (1978). "In Praise of Muddleheaded

Ancedotalism." *Western Journal of Speech Communication* 42: 21–28.

Todorov, T. (1977). *The Poetics of Prose.* Translated by R. Howard. Ithaca, NY: Cornell University Press.

Toulmin, S. E. (1958). *The Uses of Argument.* Cambridge, UK: Cambridge University Press.

Toulmin, S. E. (1970). "Reasons and Causes." In R. Borger and F. Cioffi, eds., *Explanation in the Behavioral Sciences* (Cambridge, UK: Cambridge University Press), pp. 1–41.

Toulmin, S. E. (1972). *Human Understanding.* Princeton, NJ: Princeton University Press.

Toulmin, S. E. (1982). *The Return to Cosmology: Postmodern Science and the Theology of Nature.* Berkeley and Los Angeles: University of California Press.

Toulmin, S. E., R. Rieke, and A. Janik. (1979). *Introduction to Reasoning.* New York: Macmillan.

Turner, V. (1980). "Social Dramas and Stories about Them." *Critical Inquiry* 7: 141–168.

Voegelin, E. (1952). *The New Science of Poetics.* Chicago: University of Chicago Press.

Voegelin, E. (1975). *From Enlightenment to Revolution.* Durham, NC: Duke University Press.

Wallace, K. (1963). "The Substance of Rhetoric: Good Reasons." *Quarterly Journal of Speech* 49: 239–249.

Wenzel, J. W. (1977). "Toward a Rationale for Value-Centered Argument." *Journal of the American Forensics Association* 13: 150–158.

Wenzel, J. W. (1980). "Perspectives on Argument." In J. Rhodes and S. Newell, eds., *Proceedings of the Summer Conference on Argumentation* (Falls Church, VA: Speech Communication Association), pp. 112–133.

White, H. (1978). *Metahistory: Tropics of History.* Baltimore: Johns Hopkins University Press.

White, H. (1980). "The Value of Narrativity in the Representation of Reality." *Critical Inquiry* 7: 5–27.

Wieseltier, L. (1983, January 10 and 17). "The Great Nuclear Debate." *New Republic*, pp. 7–38.

Willard, C. A. (1978). "A Reformulation of the Concept of Argument: The Constructivist/Interactionist Foundations of a Sociology of Argument." *Journal of the American Forensics Association* 14: 121–140.

Willard, C. A. (1982). "Argument Fields." In J. R. Cox and C. A. Willard, eds., *Advances in Argumentation Theory and Research* (Carbondale: Southern Illinois University Press), pp. 24–77.

Zarefsky, D. (1981). "Reasonableness in Public Policy Argument: Fields as Institutions." In G. Ziegelmueller and J. Rhodes, eds., *Dimensions of Argument: Proceedings of the Second Conference on Argumentation* (Annandale, VA: Speech Communication Association), pp. 99–100.

Ziegelmueller, G., and J. Rhodes. (1981). *Dimensions of Argument: Proceedings of the Second Conference on Argumentation.* Annandale, VA: Speech Communication Association.

Ziman, J. (1968). *Public Knowledge.* London: Cambridge University Press.

Crafting Virtue

The Rhetorical Construction of Public Morality

Celeste Michelle Condit

Throughout its history, rhetorical theory has bristled with disputes about the relationship between morality and rhetoric. In the founding years, Plato, Aristotle, Isocrates, and others focused some of their most determined attention on the moral status of rhetoric in the community.[1] In our own century, several refounding studies in the renaissance of rhetoric concentrated on the ethical choices faced by individual rhetors.[2] More recently, as interest in the social functions of rhetoric has become recentralized, the issue of rhetoric's impact on public morality has gained the spotlight.[3]

Recent theorists, however, have tended to derogate public moral discourse and have resorted to privatized models of morality. In a social community where no one may "impose their religious views on others," and where religion is taken as the sole or primary source of morality, privatization of morality may provide an appealing retreat. Nonetheless, I will suggest that it is possible and preferable to maintain a theory that recognizes collective discourse as the source of an active public morality. This essay will trace the errant root metaphors that nourish the "privatization" of morality, defend a theory of public morality, and provide an empirical study of race relations in America to illustrate and support that theory.

The Privatization of Morality

The case for the "privatization of morality" has been constructed through recent works by Walter Fisher, Thomas Farrell, and Thomas Frentz, all of whom draw heavily on Alasdair MacIntyre.[4] Frentz's statement of the position is the most explicit, but the perspective rests on three shared assumptions: a pessimistic view of public morality, a "conversational" model of moral discourse, and the promotion of individual moral growth rather than collective moral argument.

The pessimistic strand in these works is most striking. In Fisher's view, for example, contemporary public moral argument is in such a desperate state that there is perhaps an "impossibility, of persuasive moral argument in our time, given the rational world paradigm."[5] Fisher is so concerned as to demand an entirely new metaparadigm of thought. His despair is echoed by Farrell, who, in an insightful defense of the rhetorical tradition, nonetheless labels the human position as "tragic," refers to "the barbarism of our times," and laments that "rhetoric no longer mimes an ordered world."[6] Frentz completes the triadic chorus, bemoaning the contemporary preoccupation with vocation and lack of appreciation for Aristotelian virtues such as "family."[7] He argues that "modern rhetorical advocates have lost their sense of individual moral coherence and a teleologically grounded moral tradition" and that "rhetoric, as Aristotle envisioned it, is often inadequate for confronting the moral dilemmas of modern societies."[8] Pessimism about public morality thus provides a central motivation for the move to privatized morality.

The reliance upon a "conversational" model of discourse is also a common element among the privatized moral theories, as it is in a wide range of academic fields today.[9] In MacIntyre and Fisher, the conversational metaphor is not consciously recognized, but it is explicitly used.[10] Fisher, for example, suggests the conversational metaphor is incomplete, but claims to incorporate it.[11] More importantly, although he begins by locating the "problem" of morality in the public realm, Fisher eventually falls back on the two-party "conversation" between Plato's "Callicles" and "Socrates" for illustration. In this private conversation, the moral issue shifts to a consideration of how individuals ought to live their lives, rather than how a collectivity comes to "act morally." Fisher's conclusions about the Platonic dialogue feature, for example, the suggestion that "persons have found these [Calliclean] values *relevant* to their material lives, *consequential* in determining their survival and well-being."[12] Thus, although Fisher, like MacIntyre, begins with a concern about collective action, he is diverted by a model that returns the focus to the private realm.

It is Frentz, however, who pushes the conversational model most directly. He labels his perspective "rhetorical conversation" and focuses his critique on a movie about a dinner conversation. Frentz presents as paradigmatic *My Dinner with Andre*, the filmic account of a conversation between two effete male intellectuals who, while feasting at an expensive French restaurant, stumble by the admission that they are "bored, spoiled children who've been lying in the bathtub all day, playing with their plastic duck."[13] Frentz lauds, as an example of moral development, the journey of self-discovery that these two well-fed and self-indulgent American males go through. No doubt, for these two individuals, the social interaction provided by an enlightened conversation produces improved individual virtue. Their discovery, however, lacks breadth and depth. For example, according to Frentz's portrayal, Wally learns that he should be content to live with his family and his newspaper and his comfortable way of life. This is far from a significant answer to the moral

quandaries with which Fisher, MacIntyre, and (by bequeathal) Frentz begin—collective international problems such as nuclear war, resource allocation, and abortion.

The source of the deficiencies in this conversational model can be unearthed by returning to the original presentation of the perspective by Alasdair MacIntyre. In *After Virtue*, MacIntyre describes the positions held by competing groups on issues such as nuclear weapons, abortion, and resource distribution. Essentially he sets up a "conversation" between advocates of critical social issues, portraying the goal of this encounter as that of an academic conversation—the two parties ought to convince each other. He finds, however, that the differences between the views of the parties are so great that persuasion seems impossible. The hope of moral resolution is therefore suspended. MacIntyre's response is to insist that everyone return to a uniform set of individual moral precepts—evolving from the Aristotelian virtues—even if that means a retreat from the public realm to "local" communities of like-minded individuals.

Frentz follows MacIntyre's path closely. He sees "rhetorical conversation" as functioning in the same manner—the two parties are supposed to learn from or persuade each other. Given the impossibility of this in a world where shared ideals (or a hegemonic moral order) have broken down, Frentz also seeks an escapist solution: he turns to ambiguous "gods" and "ingenious" leaders to prod individuals toward morally enlightening conversations.[14]

Both MacIntyre's and Frentz's escape from the collective are necessitated by the conversational model around which their arguments are molded. In a conversation the outcomes of concern are the beliefs and actions of the conversational partners—the advocates themselves. If the speakers cannot be made to understand one another or learn from each other, all is lost. Fortunately, however, this is not generally the manner in which public discourse functions. Public advocates rarely convince each other, but given a rhetorical model, they do not have to do so. Competing rhetors persuade third parties—audiences—and create a "public consensus" that does not require the approval of every individual on every point—although it requires a general minimal satisfaction.[15] This course of affairs is evident, for example, in the "public consensus" on the abortion issue which, as reflected both in the Supreme Court decision and in public opinion polls, is neither that of the Pro-choice nor Pro-life view.[16] Rather, values, facts, and interests of both groups have been combined.

The abortion controversy is no historical exception. The same ongoing process of resolutions occurred for the battle over slavery, on which Americans held views which were as hostile and polar as in modern controversies. In the concluding section of this essay, I will argue that the discursive process is also evident in the controversy over Civil Rights.

Therefore, because it leads us to expect the wrong kind of results in the wrong places, a conversational model feeds pessimism, despair over the public realm, and the wrenching alternative of private morality in an immoral social world. If it can be constructed, a model that explains how public advocacy crafts a viable collective morality will lead us rather to understand the possibility of slow, painful, moral resolutions in the public realm.

The Operation of Rhetoric in Morality

Pragmatically, the assertion that public morality is constructed, implemented, and improved through public argument requires the establishment of three subordinate claims. First, it requires that we believe that morality can be *humanly* generated. Second, the claim demands that such a morality be *both* situational *and* objective; otherwise no standards for "improvement" are available or there is no solidity to that morality. Finally, the claim presumes the denial of pessimism about humanity—suggesting that in particular conditions, we are capable of, though not necessarily destined to, "doing good."

Humanity

The suggestion that morality is humanly grounded has long generated strong resistance. Frentz's attack is fresh, but representative. He claims that any humanly created morality is both capricious and limited, and hence is "relativist."[17] Frentz requires, therefore, that morality be based in some other agency that is in some way external to humanity. He seems to label this agency ambiguously as "the gods."[18] Frentz arrives at this conclusion by means of the assumption that a "collective will," as a composite entity, is no more than a group of divided individual wills (which he deprecates as mere "individual desires").[19] Specifically, Frentz opposes a moral theory that rests on "col-

lective wills of the group or community in which moral action takes place," because, he suggests, "as long as the ultimate good *for humanity* is something which can be exclusively defined, changed, and acted upon *by humanity* the moral philosophy which results will turn out to be another form of an emotivist moral system."[20]

Frentz's position rests upon a fallacy of composition and division. Frentz and others before him falsely assume that a "collective will," because its components are individual desires, can be *no more than* a bundle of individual desires, and similarly that a collective will cannot transcend the interests of the collectivity. Neither is the case. It is precisely the practice of public rhetoric that converts individual desires into something more— something carrying *moral* import, which can anchor the will of the community.

This transformation of desires is possible because *public* rhetoric requires that an individual speak a public language that includes linguistic *commitments* shared by all who are constituents of a community. This language, as Michael McGee has described it, includes the unique linguistic elements, "ideographs," which constitute social narratives for public action.[21] Collective language also includes shared social "myths" and "characterizations."[22] Such sociopolitical language units are different in quality from the same terms in private usage. The "liberty" sought by a sailor on shore leave is morally empty, whereas the "liberty" of a class of people in South Africa is a morally dense concept. Similar differences exist between isolated personal "narratives" and broad social myths.

Social discourse units carry moral import beyond individual interest, in part, then, because they indicate *shared* commitments and prescribe what each person as a member of a collectivity is *obligated* to do within the collectivity. More fundamentally, these terms are moral because the public arena, by its very nature, requires the use of terms that match the essential requirements of morality—the sacrifice of self interests for larger goods. Public argument centers on those greater goods because the contest between competing interest groups leads each group to attempt to identify their interests with larger goods. Unlike the participants of private conversations, the "public" does not endorse enactment of social policies for apparently selfish interests. Only when a policy can be presented as bearing greater goods will it be endorsed. Moreover the "goods" themselves are created and defined within these contests, because agonistic attempts to apply general concepts of "goodness" to particular issues require the definition, challenge, and transformation of "general goods" themselves. There is, thus, a "duality of communication"; moral terms in communication are "both medium and outcome."[23] All this is true even where "special interests" govern a vote; the public rationale for an action must always be expressible in the form of general goods.[24] Thus, even where discourse is ideologically distorted, the moral element (although limited or overridden) is necessarily engendered by the process of public argument.

Through particular applications, public discourse thus creates and requires the general or universal element that constitutes the core of morality. Consequently, general principles do not preexist particular moral quandaries but are produced from them. Because the general "goods" have a history of many competing particular applications, they transcend the particular situation. These generalized moral terms will even transcend the interests of the community itself, as will be indicated shortly. First, however, we must consider the reasons why Frentz and others tend to deny "objective" status to anything that is not "external" to humanity.

The problem resides in the mis-evaluation of "human desires." Frentz, for example, appears to be agreeing with MacIntyre in claiming that *because* "moral premises in modern times take root in individual desires, then no common moral grounds (except desires—which are indefinitely variable) bond reasons together and no collectively deliberated moral decisions can be expected as a matter of course."[25] The statement assumes that individual desires are somehow immoral or amoral and definitely unworthy. Their "infinite variability" feeds their unworthiness because of the presumption that only unitary and permanent things may hold "real" value.

It is possible, however, to view individual desires—for food, peace, security, and love—in a radically different light. While desires take varied forms, their basic sources are finite in their variability and widely shared. Moreover, these basic forms provide the substrate of morality. Such desires alone are not "moral"—they must be transformed by public discourse to craft a moral code—but they are nonetheless the *substance* of morality.

The strongest proof of the centrality of basic needs and desires to morality is the fact that the needs and desires of others are the foundation of the morality expressed in the general moral concept of the categorical imperative, the pervasive

Christian version of which is "Do unto others as you would have them do unto you." Other moral precepts—"Thou shalt not kill" or even "Be kind"—are based similarly on the nature of human needs and desires and the human ability, radicalized and reinforced by public rhetoric, to generalize those needs to other humans and potentially to other beings. The ability to take the perspective of the other is a basic requisite of morality, and the contents of perspective-taking are human needs, desires, values, and ideas. Consequently, the presence of individual desire and even emotion do not disqualify a code from moral status, but rather indicate the possibility of moral valuation.

Why then do Frentz, MacIntyre, and others exert so much effort to disparage individual desire? The answer, it seems, is that the many grave and evident wrongs committed on the basis of human desire lead us naturally to seek some outside, limiting force. However, it is specifically *individual desires*, or the desires of *particular* interest groups marshalled against the desires of others, that are problematic. We should not confuse these particularized interests with the underlying human capacity for desire nor with the moral force collectively forged from those basic human desires. The moral outrage of a Nazi Reich was the product of the limited desires of a narrow interest group, enforced by the brutish power of the SS. Hitler's oratory was never awe-inspiring to the Jews. In that case and similar cases it was not the basic commodity of human desire, but the limitation of the universality of the *audience* for the public moral rhetoric (a limiting of the collectivization of desire) that was at fault.

Here, a rhetorical morality must meet the challenge of ideology. To the extent that dominant elites control the means of communication and the public vocabulary, they can represent *singular* partisan interests as universal or moral ones. They can thereby evade the modifications, compromises, and larger goods wrought through agonistic competition between values and interests. Dominant elites thus hijack the moral potential for partisan ends.

Although it is probably true that the pattern of public discourse in history is more "distorted" or ideological than it is moral, two responses can be offered here. First, a history of distortion does not deny the potential for future emancipation. Second, I would also crawl out on an unpopular limb to suggest that the history of Western Civilization can be read as a patchy struggle to decrease the control of public communication by elites, and a consequent increase in collective moral breadth and depth in some areas at some times.[26] The rise of a sociopolitical philosophy advocating equality in communication as a base for morality (most notably described by Jürgen Habermas) may be a good sign of the coming-to-maturity of this particular moral code.[27] Although Habermas's criteria indisputably remain as ideals, they nonetheless point out and describe the ongoing process of a battle for greater inclusiveness, and they force us to consider a definitional set that would declare ideological discourse to be that which is relatively more partial, exclusionary, and partisan, as opposed to moral discourse, which in the public realm can be identified in part as more inclusive and open. A fuller story of the relationship between ideology and public morality will need to be told elsewhere, but I suspect it will unify our understanding of *partisan* desire and *general* good.

Objectivity

Public rhetoric can therefore be viewed as a process in which basic human desires are transformed into shared moral codes. However, to make this theory palatable for those of us who believe that morality is not simply a matter of human whim (and hence is not *solely* equivalent to ideology), we can defend the potential for "objectivity" or "solidity" in such a moral code. To do so requires that we understand "objectivity" in a somewhat different manner than may be customary. Specifically, the "objectivity" borne by a moral code is an inductive and locally derived objectivity rather than a "principled" morality imposed by the dictates of external, universal commands invariantly applied. Such an "objectivity" exerts the compelling force sought by Frentz (and many of us), because it is not fully under the control of personal or even cultural "taste." Instead, the source of the compelling, restraining, or demanding power it exercises rests in complex sets of factors in particular situations.

In order to clarify the inductive character of morality, it is useful to distinguish among arenas or types of "moral discourse." I suggest that corresponding to a hypothetical idealist realm, to the collective arena, and to individual reflection there are, respectively, "principles," "rights," and "oughts."

Moral "principles" have their greatest substantiality in the discourse arenas of religion, theology, and philosophy. As inductive ideals, however, they provide crucial reference points for all arenas. Such principles are general statements of those moral actions and beliefs that are felt to be required of every human person. Ultimately, even the professional theologians, ministers, and philosophers do not agree on any such principles, precisely. Nonetheless, the *attempt* to locate such principles is grounded in an important facet of morality—the boundary conditions of human morality.

Although relativists, structuralists, and semiologists of many stripes have argued forcefully against simple theories of objectivism that postulate one-to-one correspondences between an "objective reality" and "truth," their cases do not impugn the postulation of objective boundary conditions that impinge upon human morality. Once we accept some kind of "reality" as a probable and useful concept, we can locate universal conditions such as the existence of language, sexuality, and mortality, which have moral consequences. The fact that cultures generally have some form of proscriptions against things such as killing humans, lying in cooperative communication situations, and random sexual liaisons provides an indication of these universal boundary conditions. That is, although there is no universal proscription of *particular* types of killing, lying, and promiscuity, there are signs of these boundary conditions in the fact that these behaviors present *moral problematics* for all societies. Each culture creates careful (if differing) rules and sanctions surrounding such activities. Moreover, the general trend of these proscriptions, though not universally consistent, is similar in direction. Therefore, the widespread existence of some form of proscriptions surrounding certain behaviors does not indicate (as philosophers, theologians, and religious figures seeking unity or hegemony have maintained) a "universal" moral code, but it does signal the existence of very broad universal boundary conditions that constrain human coexistence and communication and thereby constrain, without fully determining, the construction of moral codes.

As an example, we may consider the fact that, as Ricoeur puts it, "man is not radically alien to man, because he offers signs of his own existence."[28] As a consequence, there is a forceful potential for people to feel an empathy that compels recognition of killing as horrible. On a grander scale, the costs of war always exert a restraint on the possibilities of declaring war. These restraints may be overridden by a variety of factors, but their existence and force [are] always indicated by cultural devices for carefully controlling and compensating for them. Moral principles, therefore, are simply attempts to sum up the underlying force implied by the existence of crucial boundary conditions on human life. In practice, such attempts always fail, because there is no direct translation from the multiplicitous set of objective boundary conditions to their "moral meaning." Cultures and languages must *substantialize* morality and so few societies believe in or practice the absolute "Thou shalt not kill." It is at the level of rights that moral discourse becomes concrete.

"Rights" are the moral prescriptions of sociopolitical units. In small homogeneous communities they take on the character of customs or rituals, and thus "rights–customs" form a continuum, but the social character of morality at this level is the same at both poles. Rights (and the negative form, restrictions) are general social formulations of moral boundaries. Rights and restrictions may be influenced by "principles" that are carried as salient components of the public vocabulary, but they are influenced by other elements as well. Thus, rather than the principle "Thou shalt not kill," in our society we have "first degree murder" and "involuntary manslaughter," along with "justified homicide," "just wars," and other socially sanctioned categories of human life taking. These rights and restrictions are induced from a complex set of shared experiences, a collective history that includes moral codes, incidents of killing, values, other rights, and a variety of other objective factors that constrain killing. Although it is the social code that creates meaning and therefore formulates concrete "rights," the social definition process is influenced by objective conditions derived both from the general boundary conditions noted above and from specific material factors in a particular society's situation. (Urbanization, for example, may have caused formalization of moral prescriptions against drinking because close quarters made previous drinking practices more problematic.[29])

It is a special strength of this inductive theory that it ties morality to objective forces, while leaving room for contingency—thereby allowing both variety and error. Sometimes a society may have moral prescriptions requiring its members to "do what they ought not do." Especially where participation in the public dialogue is limited, the gravitational pull of moral imperatives serving the general interest may be overridden by power conditions and particular clusters of competing objective conditions (for example, South African apartheid or the Indian custom of burning wives on their husband's funeral pyres, while grounded in sound local economics, present such cases).

Nonetheless, there are also many areas in which vastly varying social customs are perfectly defensible (as with other characteristics of most burial customs or puberty rites, for example). The recognition that there are both defensible and condemnable cultural variations is an important advance in moral theory and is necessary to avoid the twin perils of "utter relativism" and "imperialist objectivism." The adjudication between tolerance and reprobation for particular cultural practices is always an ongoing matter for public advocacy, within and without the culture.[30]

Situationalism does not, therefore, represent the application of "modifications" to universal principles so that those principles are "relativized," turning us all loose to make exceptions for ourselves at will. Rather, any principle is merely a shorthand summary for the complex and objectively compelling moral imperatives that arise from the specific conditions of moral situations, including the broad, shared boundaries of the human condition. To say therefore, that a culture's moral code arises inductively and includes its own history is not to say that it is capricious and relative. No culture freely chooses its history, but rather it faces many restraints. The cultural realm of moral "rights" is therefore objective, constrained, and yet not determined, in all cases, to "be right."

The realm of the individual "ought" is created, in part, by this gap. Because governments can be wrong, individuals and the religious institutions within which they gather in our time have a separate moral obligation that may require them to act against the social prescriptions. Moreover, because cultures can be wrong, they may choose not to prescribe all behaviors (even if they could). Individuals thus have the option to choose to violate cultural prescriptions (accepting social penalties) or, they may feel they have a moral obligation (that they "ought") to do more than is required by the society. Thus, a woman who believes she has a moral right to abortion may choose not to have one because she believes it is morally *better* not to do so.

The general, societal, and individual realms are therefore quite interdependent. Individuals will attempt to enact what they think everyone "ought" to do as cultural rights and restrictions. Battles between the individual and social realm will be augmented by arguments about what is really a "universal principle" and what merely a social or individual preference. It is the interactive dynamic of these three realms that provides us a wealth of moral protections (even if also creating a great deal of confusion about morality).

With this multiplicity of layers we can now see how the construction of human morality extends, not only beyond the interests of an individual, but also beyond the interests of specific human collectivities, or even humanity as a whole.

There are moral situations in which a collectivity recognizes that "its interests" compete with other interests and are in some moral sense outweighed by larger interests surrounding it. This may result from the boundary conditions discussed above or from the substantiality and logic of the moral code itself. Once universal terms, narratives, and characterizations are created and supported, they carry a force separate from the wishes of the collectivity. Great labor is required to restrain or reshape such commitments. Additionally, a code does not simply and univocally reflect the wishes of its creators, even at the instant of its creation—the rhetorical process and moral codes adhere to their own logic. For example, it is doubtful that when the American Catholic Bishops promoted the "sanctity of human life" as a moral warrant for banning abortion, they intended to reverse their stand on the death penalty, but that is what the public commitment to "life" pressured them to do. In this way, a "collective will," through public discourse, creates something outside its own will. Although the collectivity always retains power to modify the code, it cannot exert unlimited control. As long as the discourse process is relatively open, the nature of the code itself, as well as the broad biological, psychological, and social limitations upon human beings, exerts an important external moral force.

Consequently, in response to Frentz and other opponents of grounding morality in humanity itself, I offer the rhetorical production of moral codes. Such codes are generated by human collectives, yet they also formulate objective restraints on humanity. This model allows us to take one last bold step to suggest that there can be improvement of the public moral code.

Against Pessimism

Optimism about human morality has been, in most places and times, hard to come by. Saturated with the petty lies of politicians and the grand larcenies of corporate plunderers, we find it difficult to defend moral optimism as anything other than a charming naïveté. I have already indicated the importance of this pessimism for the "privatization of public morality" and have suggested some grounds, in the form of examples of collec-

tive American actions, for resisting such blanket despair. The demise of direct human slavery, a decreased tolerance of starvation in "developed" countries, as well as the declining acceptance of infanticide provide other examples of moral improvements made by human collectives. Further, a similar argument can be made with regard to the character of public arguments themselves. If we look, for example, at the arguments in the Civil Rights controversy, it seems difficult to maintain that "modern rhetorical advocates have lost their sense of individual moral coherence and a teleologically grounded moral tradition."[31] If we compare the Civil Rights activists' religiously and traditionally grounded plea for "life" or "freedom" with the claims of an Athenian orator urging war for booty, a feeling of moral progress might even seem to be warranted (and even our current public "warrants for war" may be marginally better than in the past).[32]

While individual human beings may or may not differ radically in their moral qualities from times past, it is possible to concede that, in two thousand years, human societies have made at least a few laudable advances in a few particular areas. All of this is not to say that we have *universally* improved ourselves, or that we have, overall, "progressed." It would be easy enough to cite a list of our continued and new moral transgressions. Nor do the patchy improvements in moral conditions authorize us to expect that moral improvement is a necessary and inevitable process of "progress" that will continue.

Our stance, therefore, cannot be joyously optimistic; we can only deny the necessity of pessimism. There is no structural, biological, or social necessity for moral impoverishment, nor for moral improvement. It is neither true that "everything will turn out all right in the end," nor that "everything" will necessarily end soon in a nuclear explosion. Instead, we simply can say that some portions of the moral code and collective behavior can be improved by particular human actions. Human morality is contingent; optimists and pessimists alike lack firm grounds, because human beings must daily and locally, as well as by the century and continent, actively craft human morality.

A quick survey of the public discourse relating Black and White Americans can illustrate this process of open crafting. I present the example of race relations in direct contrast to the foundational example offered by Frentz. Frentz examined an aesthetic object, a movie, the agents of which were two self-indulgent Americans seeking satisfaction in self-understanding. If our understanding of morality is bound by such models, I think our rhetorical theory will be impoverished by the lack of long-term perspective, of public participation, and of action. To add these dimensions, I offer a view of Americans, locked in bitter contest, speaking in public across decades, to enact a better way of life.

"Justice" for Afro-Americans

The historical relationships between Black Americans and White Americans confronts us with two conflicting moral "intuitions." On one side, there is the sense of contemporary White academics that equality between Anglo-Americans and Afro-Americans is and always has been "just." The concept or relation seems worthy of universality. On the other side, there is the disturbing and compelling fact that millions of morally sane and responsible individuals did not believe this for many years.

The typical response to this quandary has been to deny the morality of supporters of slavery and discrimination. We have tended to suggest that, by using psychological defense mechanisms such as "rationalization," otherwise good individuals were able to delude themselves or be deluded into ignoring an ever-present truth. Or, we have occasionally suggested that they knew all along that this moral truth was "self-evident" but they let their human greed interfere with their moral impulses.[33] As a result, we have tended to portray the movement towards equal rights as "inevitable," a historical necessity motivated by the American Conscience.[34] Good people had to triumph over evil.

None of these moves is sufficient. The best evidence we have indicates that there were caring and moral individuals who sincerely believed that slavery, and later, discrimination, were morally defensible institutions.[35] Moreover, to suggest the "inevitability" of the change may be comforting, but it glosses deceptively the uncertainty and struggle that was necessary to enact the moral code. We need, then, a different account.

Looking at the rhetoric produced in the situation gives us a means to understand this moral problem in historical perspective. Simply put, when racial slavery was instituted, Anglo-Americans had not yet crafted a public moral code that included Afro-Americans in the demands of "equal justice." It is

taking hundreds of years to modify that original relationship.

Two elements have been central to the development and evolution of justice for Afro-Americans. As I have suggested, one component of morality is the human need for resources—food, clothing, and material for "the pursuit of happiness." By recognizing these needs, human beings recognize that there is something about which to be just. In addition, however, in order for perspective-taking to occur, we must feel that the "other" is in some fundamental ways the "same" as us—experiencing similar needs and wants. The story of "civil rights" in America is the tale of a gradual amelioration of resource shortages and increasing identification of Whites with Blacks. These elements together, through the operation of public discourse, produced an improved (because more universalized) moral code. The resource situation, especially the resource of labor, is testified to by various historians.[36] The rhetorical process of "identification" can be sketched by a brief glance at the chief contents of the public rhetoric between 1840 and 1960.[37]

The need for rhetorical effort to build "identification" was generated by the nature of the early contact period, when Whites tensely characterized Blacks as both "similar" and radically "different." Early descriptions of Africans by Europeans indirectly recognized a basic similarity by identifying Blacks as persons (or, in the locution of the time, "men"). However, the sixteenth- and seventeenth-century travelers, traders, and chroniclers emphasized the exoticness of the people and places, downplaying the similarities. There were indeed many dramatic differences of dress, religion, eating habits, and kinship relations.[38]

These differences in the practices of daily life were morally problematic because the Western world had not yet elaborated a moral code capable of universality that transcended them. The first impediment to such a code was the lack of familiarity with the concept of "human racial difference." There was not even any clear scientific concept of "species" or "family," and the ambivalence between "human *race*" and ethnically differentiated "race" was symptomatic of the confusion.[39]

This ambiguity allowed "race" to be rapidly shaped by existing dominant social principles. The social code of the day was rife with hierarchy and "order." Monarchies survive on inequity and inferiority, and these principles were only gradually giving way to a concept of justice that included political "equality" and religious tolerance. Without a clear description of humanity in the code, and with a strong practice of coding hierarchy, the differences between Africans and Europeans were apt to be interpreted as "inferiorities," and in the most extreme cases Africans were classed as "bestial."[40]

The dominant moral codes of the day solidified and exacerbated this differentiation. The Christian Bible was the indisputable moral authority and it explicitly allowed one to enslave "strangers," but not those who were of "one's own." It said in part that "you may buy male and female slaves from among the nations that are round about you. You may also buy from among the strangers who sojourn with you . . . but over your brethren the people of Israel you shall not rule."[41]

Finally, the initial sense of difference and the acceptance of economic, political, and social inequality were amplified and reified by the economic need for labor and the subsequent patterns of slavery, which haphazardly developed. Such an economic relationship not only gave further motive to the intensification of "difference," it also led to a physical and cultural separation that prevented recognition of "similarity."

Upon these conditions—economic need, an underdeveloped code of "equality," and an ambivalent linguistic code that allowed Afro-Americans to be classed as "different" and hence outside the normal laws and bounds of "justice"—racial slavery was formed and flourished. The institution was increasingly challenged as (1) Blacks and Whites came into prolonged contact in social situations that decreased Black cultural differences such as dress, dating habits, and language, and (2) the control of "justice" was placed in the hands of those who endorsed "equality" and had direct contact with the increasingly "similar" Blacks (that is, in the North, after the American Revolution). Gradually, the operative weight of the new American code of justice began to exert force towards including Blacks.

The abolitionists' arguments were clearly based on this increasing awareness of similarity. One of the most repeated and vivid strands of abolitionist discourse was the insistence on the fundamental humanity of Blacks.[42] William Lloyd Garrison testified that his own conversion to abolitionism was based on his effort at imagining himself as a Black man, and he provides one of the most forceful statements of similarity. Responding to Henry Clay's assertion of general White supremacy, Garrison declared, "I deny the postulate that God has made, by any irreversible decree, or any inherent qualities, one portion of the human race superior to another."[43] Once Blacks were included in this manner with Whites, the dictates of the newly crafted American "justice," proclaiming all men equal, mandated that Africans could not be enslaved by other human beings.[44]

The centrality of the issue of "identification" is equally clear in the opposing proslavery rhetoric, which focused a large portion of its effort on "difference," in the form of the rhetoric of "White supremacy."[45] Albert Taylor Bledsoe was employing normal usage when he referred to the Africans as the "inferior race," and insisted that

> Slavery is not the mother, but the daughter, of ignorance, and degradation. It is, indeed, the legitimate offspring of that intellectual and moral debasement which, for so many thousand years has been accumulating and growing upon the African race.[46]

The second major strand of proslavery rhetoric similarly emphasized "difference," but this time as a general principle. Bledsoe and others denied "equality" as a viable moral obligation.[47] James A. Sloan, for example, insisted that "a system of complete equality does not seem to be in accordance with the providence of God, or with the Bible."[48]

Neither of these arguments from difference [was] ultimately successful in the national arena. From the pre-Revolutionary War period until just before the Civil War, the "antislavery impulse" spread in breadth and intensity (albeit unevenly). Gradually, the "South" was driven to *cut off public discussion* in the Congress and in the public presses. As Frederick Douglass predicted, "Slavery cannot bear discussion."[49] Latent material conditions could not be made explicit without challenging the vocabulary of public values or the conditions themselves.

Eventually, however, change was produced through rhetorical effort, adequate time to disseminate the new code, and bullets to force the acquiescence of those who would not allow persuasion. By 1865 a revolutionary moral code excluding the "rightness" of racial slavery had been publicly enacted. As a result of economic shifts, but also as a result of and through the medium of public discourse, a broader, more universal moral code had come to be accepted. "Justice" no longer could include human racial slavery, and the claims of other forms of "equality" among human beings had been expanded and strengthened.

The moral code nonetheless faced further evolution. The end of slavery came with a formal, militarily enforced recognition of the humanity of Blacks. Even many abolitionists who recognized this humanity, however, had never fully erased from their minds a sense of "difference" that implied inferiority of some sort. The merely formal sense of equality during the postwar era was translated into a very limited political equality, which was increasingly circumscribed by social and economic "difference" and "separation" in a mutually augmenting spiral. This state of affairs was legally codified in 1896 by the Supreme Court in *Plessy v. Ferguson*.[50] The Court's ruling that the races could remain "separate but equal" was a basically unstable compromise, however. "Separate" at the time clearly meant "unequal," and the continuance of separation meant a continuance of "difference." The lack of a sense of "identity" clashed with the basis of a justice premised on equality.

As a consequence of these conditions, the "post-Reconstruction rhetoric" of both Blacks and Whites consisted primarily of efforts to identify the Negroes more closely with Whites. Not a merely formal membership in the human race, but "essential similarity" was projected. Both extremes of Black rhetors worked toward the same ends. Booker T. Washington, the ultramoderate, sought to teach Blacks the "important lessons of cleanliness, promptness, system, honesty, and progressiveness" in order that each Black could contribute "his share" and smooth "the pathway for this and succeeding generations."[51] More radical men such as Marcus Garvey and W. E. B. DuBois were to develop "Black pride" in their humanity, emphasizing the worthiness of the best members of their race.[52]

Between 1940 and 1960 the White press amplified this refrain, gradually recharacterizing all Blacks as similar to Whites even in the realm of the day to day. The redefinition began during World War II with descriptions of Black workers and soldiers as "loyal," "heroic," "brave," "pleasant," "accustomed to hard work," as well as "spic and span" and "friendly."[53] After the war, the more liberal elements of the press incorporated Blacks into narratives that testified to their essentially positive nature—allowing White audiences to come to know and like Black characters, and to perceive them as *like* themselves.

Gradually, the narratives went further, suggesting that it was unjust to treat these "people like us" in nonsimilar ways. Tales of worthy "Negroes" being disallowed reward solely because of their Blackness began to arouse the emotional sympathy we call a "sense of injustice." The concept of "race" gradually was reduced to the less potent identifier, "skin color"—an item devoid of the general baggage of "race" and linguistically less capable of carrying it.

This rhetorical effort primarily reached the liberal, northern, elite, but this group was crucial. They controlled much of the public discourse and legal processes, a factor evident in the Supreme Court ruling in *Brown v. Board of Education*, which held that "separate" could not be "equal" because it inherently bred a sense of inferiority (a clear form of "difference").[54]

This rhetoric of identification also encouraged Blacks to demand "justice." Ultimately, Martin Luther King Jr. could draw on the strengthened sense of identification and, on a national platform, call forth the ultimate dream of identity that "little black boys and black girls will be able to join hands with little white boys and white girls as sisters and brothers."[55] By the late sixties, even in the South, an adequate *public* presumption had been built to identify Blacks and Whites and include Blacks in the code of justice.[56] "Massive Resistance" never materialized in large part because the similarity of Blacks and the justice of their inclusion [were] nominally accepted by an adequate number of active social agents. Although even today that expanded code is not universally shared within the United States, North or South, nor outside of our states (especially in private), it has strong and wide support among the politically active, and it meets public resistance only when it tends to encroach on other senses of "justice" (as in "affirmative action programs" felt to be unjust to others.)[57]

Across two hundred years or more, therefore, new rhetorical structures of great importance have been created. Blacks and Whites are now publicly identified, not only as human, but also as essentially similar. Moreover, a strong moral code that demands human equality has gained currency. The original Anglo-American moral code of "justice" has thus evolved into a broader "American" code that belongs to and includes persons of all descents and skin colors.

Viewing the Civil Rights controversy as a situational process of the crafting of morality through rhetoric thus allows us to understand the change in the moral code through American history. White slave owners were not necessarily deceiving themselves or allowing crass self-interests to overrule their moral impulses. Rather, because Afro-Americans had been coded as "different," and because the dominant moral code of the day featured hierarchy, there was no moral code that included Blacks in White "justice." A sense of compassion and a morality of "care" may have often dictated *humane* treatment, but that was different from treatment as "brothers." The inclusion of Blacks in White conceptions of justice (or better, the construction of shared White/ Black justice) was a *new* moral code that had to be crafted through time and rhetorical effort. We "understand" now that the Black person and the White person objectively deserve equal treatment, but we had to craft the moral code and the conditions that allowed this moral understanding to be widely available to a working plurality of citizens. Moreover, individual rhetors, both Whites like Garrison and Lydia Maria Child and Blacks like Douglass, Washington, and DuBois had to empathize, to sacrifice, to speak and write, in order to work out and spread that code.

The temptation remains to say that, nonetheless, the moral relationship or principle was there all along—simply "unrealized." With the new code, we simply "recognized" a transcendent "truth." More softly, we might say that once even a few radicals discovered the "truth" of Black/White identity, it took "a century long lag of public morals" for the rest of the population to catch up.[58]

Either of these moves obscures the fundamental nature and complexity of morality as a public process. Generally, Blacks and Whites now publicly perceive each other as fundamentally similar and agree that we should treat each other similarly. However, until the two sets of peoples came into extensive contact with each other, no moral relationship could exist. The process of constructing a moral definition of the relationship necessarily took time and discourse, and although the process might be characterized as one of "recognizing" potent objective boundary conditions, it was nonetheless an active, historically concrete process of constructing a new code. Therefore, although it may be psychologically comforting to argue that we should *always* have had that recognition, to do so is not only futile, it deprives humanity of further moral growth.

We must view morality as an open process of crafting in order to continue the process of crafting. Our broader history shows this crafting. The statement penned by Thomas Jefferson that "all men are created equal [but Negroes aren't fully men?]" as an *official document* was a radical assertion of new material from the English public moral code. The post-Civil War rewriting of that code to state that "all men are created equal" was a further rewriting and expansion of the morality. Similarly, our current efforts to once again rewrite the code to state that "all persons are created equal" may result in another step.

Our moral capacity as a people can grow, and increasing "universality" has been one aspect of that growth. If, however, we reify the current best principles, we put ourselves exactly in the position of the Southern slaveholders in 1850—we preserve an old moral order at the cost of a newer, broader one. If, for example, we maintain that the use of the Bible as an authority worked for Black rhetors in the past so we should not challenge its use for the future, or if we hold that "all persons are created equal" is a universal principle, always existent, but simply misunderstood or misapplied at times, then we stunt our ability to craft an even grander moral code as we turn the corner. The current code may be used, as such codes historically have been used, to prevent the development of a better code. To say that America has always relied on the Judeo-Christian tradition is not only to distort history by reifying that tradition, it is also not to say that she should or must be so limited in the future. To hazard a guess at an example, we can note that our current public moral code justifies the "cycle of poverty" in terms of a rhetoric of "equal opportunity," where equal opportunity counts only technical numbers of resources, not the kinds of resources necessary to make individuals capable of equality of opportunity. Blind and rigid defense of that code forestalls the development of a moral code that may someday express clearly our now vague sentiment that "because all persons are not born equal in their social and natural situation, we must shape our society to insure that they are able to develop all of their natural potential."

The "Craft" of Morality

I have tried to suggest that "morality" is constructed by collectivities through their public discourse in a process of reflexive reproduction that utilizes the capacity of discourse simultaneously to create, extend, and apply moral concepts. I have gone further, to suggest that this process is bounded by an inductive, historical objectivity. I have also tried to illustrate what this might mean for our understanding of the collective moral controversies in our past and present. I do not expect this account to be universally persuasive, but I hope I have increased the plausibility of such a perspective. There remains the issue, however, of why such an account ought to be chosen over, for example, a conversational theory, a religious explanation, or a pessimistic dismissal of all morality. The usual tests of the "explanatory power" of a theory will eventually apply here, but given the nature of the subject, another kind of test is relevant as well.

Baldly stated, for moral reasons, the best metaphor for the rhetorical construction of morality is neither MacIntyre's individual intellectual quest nor Frentz's private conversation, but the simple, collective "craft."

MacIntyre's "quest" metaphor contains two major faults. First, the requirement that all members of communities share all the same individual values and virtues is unlikely given the multiplicity of levels and dimensions of moral practices. Moreover, it is probably undesirable as well. Uniformity in morality has too often been bought at the price of oppression. MacIntyre's alternative—to ignore the public realm and form small "survival" groups for moral practice—is a retreat from responsibility that, I have suggested, is unjustified by contemporary conditions, if those conditions are compared to human history rather than to some imaginary ideal or golden age.

Second, MacIntyre concludes that the virtues and the good "are those which will enable us to understand what more and what else the good life for man is."[59] To promote, in this way, the intellectuals' pet standard of "understanding" as the central *activity* of moral practice misguidedly urges all human beings to spend their lives doing what academics do only as a matter of profession—thinking about morality rather than actively crafting it in the world. That seems to threaten moral impoverishment, rather than offering collective growth.

Frentz's "rhetorical conversation" is more constructive for the building of private virtue through local social interactions, but it too does not help us to act morally in the public realm, nor to understand collective morality. Understanding the "craft" of morality-building as including all forms of rhetoric—conversation, debate, discussion, and harangue—would seem to allow us to go farther. Like all crafts, the rhetorical construction of morality partakes of the workshop. Individual workers may produce individual creations, but the large practice of the collectivity is mostly anonymous. The rare individual may nonetheless

radically revise the social practice through particular action, insight, or merit; even in routine, each social practice is dependent on individuals. Thus, the collective and the individual interact to produce morality. The "duality of communication" dictates that it is through the arguments of individuals about enactment of particular moral rulings that the collective moral code is built. Additionally, the rhetor constructing morality, like any craftsperson, is limited by objectives, situations, and the available materials.

Lastly, as with all crafts, the rhetorical construction of morality fulfills the human urge for goodness, creativity, and perfection.[60] We have too often viewed morality as we might a great art, where a painfully transcendent beauty outside normal day-to-day experience is the high ideal. With such a model, only "the gods" can offer us morality, for indeed the bounds of the human condition are too great. But morality is not an art. It is not free to take beauty and run unbound with it. Morality must partake of beauty, and truth, and power in the conditions of the world.

In spite of these limits, a craft can, nonetheless, fulfill the human urge for unity, continuity, and teleology—an urge for good and perfection. It cannot give us "transcendence" in stepping outside of daily meaning, but it can give us a perfecting of action through meaning. Carefully monitored water systems, well-designed transportation, and accessible communication media are as important to human life as the statue of *David*, the Taj Mahal, and the *Enterprise*. When we fail to recognize the value of human craft, we sadly deplete the quality of human life. And so it is with the craft of morality. Art gives us greater beauty. Philosophy gives us grander truths. Science gives us greater power. But without rhetoric to produce and maintain morality, human life would be more seriously diminished.

Ultimately, then, to recognize morality as a collective craft is also to call ourselves to account for our participation in the ebb and flow of human morality. As Thomas Farrell would seem to indicate, the rhetorical practices of the collective are "tenuous"[61]; rhetoric indeed may be used more frequently for evil and partisan gain than for the general good. It is, however, that very contingency that makes our individual participation in the collective so crucial, infusing each of our moves with broad meaning.

Together, then, people have built the good, not with an architectural blueprint, but with a traditional knowledge of the way the tribe has built in the past and through daily assessment of the probabilities involved in a local outcome. Proceeding day by day, we do not live the moments of the present as though they sucked in the past and future at once in some dizzying, transcendent manner. Rather, the moral craft requires us to live the moment, through the legacies of the past, with just an eye to the fact that we are crafting the future as well.

NOTES

1. For example, Plato in the *Phaedrus, Republic,* and *Laws*; Aristotle in the *Rhetoric, Politics,* and *Ethics*; Isocrates in *Nicocles or the Cyprians*; Cicero in *De officii, De oratore,* and *De finibus*; Quintilian in the *Institutes.*

2. As in B. J. Diggs, "Persuasion and Ethics," *Quarterly Journal of Speech* 50 (1964): 359–373; Franklyn Haiman, "A Re-examination of the Ethics of Persuasion," *Central States Speech Journal* 3 (1952): 4–9; Edward Rogge, "Evaluating the Ethics of a Speaker in Democracy," *Quarterly Journal of Speech* 45 (1959): 419–425; Thomas R. Nilsen, *Ethics of Speech Communication* (Indianapolis, IN: Bobbs-Merrill, 1966); Richard Weaver, *The Ethics of Rhetoric* (South Bend, IN: Gateway Editions, 1953).

3. Walter R. Fisher, "Narration as a Human Communication Paradigm: The Case of Public Moral Argument," *Communication Monographs* 51 (1984:) 1–22 [reprinted in this volume]; Thomas S. Frentz, "Rhetorical Conversation, Time, and Moral Action," *Quarterly Journal of Speech* 71 (1985): 1–18; Michael Calvin McGee, "Secular Humanism: A Radical Reading of 'Culture Industry' Production," *Critical Studies in Mass Communication* 1 (1984): 1–33; Philip Wander, "The Ideological Turn in Modern Criticism," *Central States Speech Journal* 34 (1983): 1–18; Martha Solomon, "Robert Schuller: The American Dream in a Crystal Cathedral," *Central States Speech Journal* 34 (1983): 172–186; Steven Goldwig and George Cheney, "The U.S. Catholic Bishops on Nuclear Arms: Corporate Advocacy, Role Redefinition, and Rhetorical Adaptation," *Central States Speech Journal* 35 (1984): 8–23.

4. Fisher, "Narration"; Frentz, "Rhetorical Conversation"; Walter R. Fisher, "The Narrative Paradigm: An Elaboration," *Communication Monographs* 52 (1985): 347–367; Thomas B. Farrell, "Rhetorical Resemblance: Paradoxes of a Practical Art," *Quarterly Journal of Speech* 72 (1986): 1–19; Alasdair MacIntyre, *After Virtue: A Study In Moral Theory* (South Bend, IN: University of Notre Dame Press, 1981).

5. Fisher, "Narration," p. 1.

6. Farrell, "Rhetorical Resemblance," pp. 16, 2, 15.

7. Frentz, "Rhetorical Conversation," pp. 11, 13.

8. Ibid., p. 4.

9. E.g., Richard Rorty, *Philosophy and the Mirror of Nature* (Princeton, NJ: Princeton University Press, 1979); and Richard J. Bernstein, *Beyond Objectivism and Relativism: Science, Hermeneutics, and Praxis* (Philadelphia: University of Pennsylvania Press, 1983).

10. Farrell ("Rhetorical Resemblance") does not employ the conversational metaphor. Instead, ironically I think, he resorts to the metaphor of "form," as he attacks the aestheticians.

11. Fisher, "An Elaboration," p. 353.

12. Ibid., p. 363.

13. Frentz quotes the movie; "Rhetorical Conversation," p. 12.

14. Ibid., pp. 15–16.

15. The limits are reached at the level where legitimacy of the governing unit is itself challenged. See John Louis Lucaites, "Rhetoric and the Problem of Legitimacy," *Dimensions of Argument: Proceedings of the Second Summer Conference on Argumentation* (Annandale, VA: Speech Communication Association. 1981), pp. 799–811.

16. Celeste Condit Railsback, "The Contemporary American Abortion Controversy: Stages in the Argument," *Quarterly Journal of Speech* 70 (1984): 410–423.

17. Frentz, "Rhetorical Conversation," pp. 1–3, 5, 14.

18. Ibid., p. 16.

19. Ibid., p. 14.

20. Ibid., p. 14.

21. Michael Calvin McGee, "The 'Ideograph': A Link Between Rhetoric and Ideology," *Quarterly Journal of Speech* 66 (1980): 1–16 [reprinted in this volume].

22. The role of "characterizations" and "public myths" is very similar to that of ideographs, although each of these works at different levels. For explanations and illustrations, see Celeste Michelle Condit, "Democracy and Civil Rights: The Universalizing Influence of Public Argumentation," *Communication Monographs* [54: 1–18].

23. Anthony Giddens, *Central Problems in Social Theory: Action, Structure and Contradiction in Social Analysis* (Berkeley and Los Angeles: University of California Press, 1979), p. 5.

24. Michael Calvin McGee, "The Rhetorical Process in Eighteenth Century England," in Walter R. Fisher, ed., *Rhetoric: A Tradition in Transition* (East Lansing: Michigan State University Press, 1974), pp. 99–121.

25. Frentz, "Rhetorical Conversation," p. 13.

26. An example is presented below, but another might be read, against the author's intentions, perhaps, in Raymond Williams, *The Long Revolution* (Westport, CT: Greenwood Press, 1975), or in Stuart Hall, "The State in Question," in G. McLennan, D. Held, and S. Hall, eds., *The Idea of the Modern State* (Milton Keynes, UK: Open University Press, 1984), pp. 1–28.

27. See Jürgen Habermas, *Communication and the Evolution of Society*, trans. Thomas McCarthy (1976; rpt., Boston: Beacon Press, 1979).

28. Paul Ricoeur, *Hermeneutics and the Human Sciences*, ed. and trans. John B. Thompson (Cambridge, UK: Cambridge University Press, 1981), p. 49.

29. For an elucidation of situational objectivism in morality, see Renford Bambrough, *Moral Skepticism and Moral Knowledge* (Atlantic Highlands, NJ: Humanities Press, 1979). For a further elaboration of the epistemological foundations of such localistic thought, see Ludwig Wittgenstein, *Philosophical Investigations*, trans. G. E. M. Anscombe (Oxford, UK: Basil Blackwell, 1963), and Jean-François Lyotard, *The Postmodern Condition: A Report on Knowledge*, trans. Geoff Bennington and Brian Massumi (Minneapolis: University of Minnesota Press; 1984).

30. This is where I part company with Stephen Toulmin's *An Examination of the Place of Reason in Ethics* (Cambridge, UK: Cambridge University Press, 1950). He would limit such discussion to the members of a culture only.

31. Frentz, "Rhetorical Conversation," p. 4.

32. For example, see Demosthenes, "The First Philippic," in W. Robert Connor, ed., *Greek Orations* (Ann Arbor: University of Michigan Press, 1966), or the speeches of Cleon and Diodotus to the Athenian *Ecclesia*, in Thucydides, *The Peloponnesian War*, trans. E. Crawley (New York: Random House, 1951), 3.37–48. Although these two may be juxtaposed as examples of ideal and material justifications, both offer pecuniary interests as the underlying goal.

33. William Lloyd Garrison launched this attack in a forceful, early version in "William Lloyd Garrison Abandons Colonization (1830)" in John L. Thomas, ed., *Slavery Attacked: The Abolitionist Crusade* (Englewood Cliffs, NJ: Prentice- Hall, 1965), reprinted from "Henry Clay's Colonization Address," *Genius of Universal Emancipation*, February 12, 1830. Later, materialist versions tend to describe how the belief or argument that Blacks were inferior developed only after the economic interests of the slaveholders were threatened. They covertly insert the vocabulary that implies the beliefs were nongenuine. George Frederickson, for example, says the arguments began their "career as a rationale" and were a "defensive ideological consciousness." He says the southerners were "putting out propaganda" and "seeking to put to rest their own nagging fears." See "Slavery and Race: The Southern Dilemma," in Allen Weinstein and Frank Otto Gatell, eds., *American Negro Slavery*, 2d ed. (New York: Oxford University Press, 1973), esp. pp. 227–233. Similarly, Stanley M. Elkins, *Slavery: A Problem in American Institutional and Intellectual Life*, 2d ed. (1959, 1968; rpt., Chicago: University of Chicago Press, 1971), e.g., pp. 208–212.

34. Probably the most influential of such works is that by Gunnar Myrdal, with Richard Sterner and Arnold Rose, *An American Dilemma: The Negro Problem and Modern Democracy* (1944; rpt., New York: Harper and Row, 1962), pp. 24, 215.

35. Albert Taylor Bledsoe, for example, specifically objects to the abolitionists' assumption that they have moral right on their side and says that "the institution of slavery, as it exists among us in the South, is founded in political justice, is in accordance with the will of God and the designs of his providence, and is conducive to the highest, purest, best interests of mankind" (Bledsoe, *An Essay on Liberty and Slavery* [Philadelphia: J. B. Lippincott, 1856], p. 8). See also John Bell Robinson, *Pictures of Slavery and Anti-Slavery* (Philadelphia, 1863), "Introduction"; and John Henry Hopkins, *A Scriptural, Ecclesiastical, and Historical View of Slavery, from the Days of the Patriarch Abraham, to the Nineteenth Century* (New York: W. I. Pooley and Co., n.d.).

36. For instance, George M. Fredrickson, *White Supremacy: A Comparative Study in American and South African History* (New York: Oxford University Press, 1982), p. 55, or Winthrop D. Jordan, *White over Black: American Attitudes toward the Negro, 1550–1812* (Chapel Hill: University of North Carolina Press, 1968), esp. pp. 91, 320–331, 47–48.

37. These conclusions are based on the study of three separate sets of discourse. For the abolitionist period it includes an incomplete sampling of pro-slavery and abolitionist pamphlets from 1820–1860, especially during the period 1850–1860, supplemented by secondary histories of the period, of which the most helpful is William Sumner Jenkins, *Pro Slavery Thought in the Old South* (Gloucester, MA: Peter Smith, 1960). The Black rhetoric was surveyed through readings of the speeches and writings of major figures, especially Frederick Douglass, Booker T. Washington, William E. B. Dubois, Marcus Garvey, Malcolm X, and Martin Luther King Jr. The most intensive research segment was the focus on the White magazine press 1940–1960. A 10 percent structured random sample of all articles concerning "Negroes" listed in the *Reader's Guide to Periodical Literature* forms the basis of the conclusions given here.

38. Jordan, *White over Black*, pp. 3–98.

39. Ibid., pp. 216–239.

40. Ibid., pp. 29–32.

41. Lev. 25: 39–47, *The New Oxford Annotated Bible*, rev. standard ed. (New York: Oxford University Press). There was great dispute about the meanings of various biblical texts on slavery during the abolitionist period, but it seems clear that, whether or not the Bible sanctioned racial slavery in America, it explicitly sanctioned some form of slavery in the past. (Especially, but not solely, in the Old Testament.)

42. The other major strands of argument included a restatement and insistence on the principle of the Declaration of Independence that "All men are created equal" (the biblical version of which was "do unto others

as you would have them do unto you") and a recounting of the horrors of slavery. See, e.g., Rev. William H. Boole, *Antidote to Rev. H. J. Van Dyke's Pro-Slavery Discourse* (New York: Edmund Jones and Co., 1861); Frederick Douglass, assorted speeches collected in *The Life and Writings of Frederick Douglass*, 2 vols., ed. Philip S. Foner (New York: International Publishers, 1950), and works of Theodore Weld and others collected in various anthologies including John L. Thomas, ed., *Slavery Attacked: The Abolitionist Crusade* (Englewood Cliffs, NJ: Prentice-Hall, 1965), and Louis Ruchames, ed., *The Abolitionists: A Collection of Their Writings* (New York: G. P. Putnam's Sons, 1963).

43. William Lloyd Garrison, "Henry Clay's Colonization Address," in Thomas, ed., *Slavery Attacked*, p. 7.

44. Some emancipationists were colonizationists, and they generally presumed both that the Negro was inferior and that slavery was bad, but this argument, held even by Abraham Lincoln, was not the rationale eventually incorporated into the public documents and consensus. The material humanity (in numbers and form) of the Blacks prevented that rhetoric's success.

45. See, e.g., Bledsoe, *An Essay on Liberty*; Robinson, *Pictures of Slavery*, pp. 51, 67, 139, 241; Hopkins, *A Scriptural . . . View of Slavery*, p. 11; and Henry Field James, *Abolitionism Unveiled* (Cincinnati, OH: E. Morgan and Sons, 1856), pp. 17, 114, 123–125, 131.

46. Bledsoe, *An Essay on Liberty*, pp. 288, 54.

47. James, *Abolitionism Unveiled*, pp. 201–204; Robinson, *Pictures of Slavery*, pp. 227–228; Hopkins, *A Scriptural . . . View of Slavery*, pp. 18–21, 27.

48. James A. Sloan, *The Great Question Answered; or, Is Slavery a Sin in Itself* (Memphis, TN: Hutton, Galloway and Co., 1857), p. 48.

49. Douglass, in Foner, ed., *Life and Writings*, vol 2, p. 252.

50. See *Plessy v. Ferguson*, 163 U.S. 537, 16 S.Ct. 1128, 41 L. Ed. 256 (1896).

51. Booker T. Washington, "First Annual Address as President: National Negro Business League, August 14, 1900," in *Selected Speeches of Booker T. Washington*, ed. Ernest Davidson Washington (Garden City, NY: Doubleday, Doran and Co., 1932), p. 90, and other speeches.

52. Marcus Garvey, "Speech Delivered on Emancipation Day at Liberty Hall, New York City, January 1, 1922," in *Philosophy and Opinions of Marcus Garvey*, ed. Amy Jacques-Garvey (New York: Arno Press/New York

Times, 1968), pp. 79–81. W. E. B. DuBois, "On Segregation," in *A W. E. B. DuBois Reader*, ed. Andrew G. Paschal (New York: Collier Books, 1971), p. 143.

53. The description of the discourse in the White press is drawn from Condit, "Democracy and Civil Rights."

54. See *Brown v. Board of Education* 73 S.Ct. 2; 74 S.Ct. 347; 75 S.Ct. 753, 346 U.S. 483, and 349 U.S. 294 (1954, 1955). The importance of the gradual spread of a rhetoric and its relative dominance among elite power groups is particularly evident here. Harlan's dissent in *Plessy v. Ferguson* was very much similar to the decision in *Brown v. Board of Education*, but the majority in *Plessy* referred continually to the existing "customs," North and South, which legitimized "separation."

55. Martin Luther King Jr., "I Have a Dream," in Wil A. Linkugel, R. R. Allen, and Richard L. Johannesen, eds., *Contemporary American Speeches*, 5th ed. (Dubuque, IA: Kendall Hunt, 1982), p. 369.

56. This controversial claim requires two distinctions and evidence. The first distinction is that of "public" vs. "private." That which remained acceptable in local and private contexts became unacceptable in national and public contexts. Second, a numerical majority is not necessary for such changes to take effect. All that is required is a working coalition of powerful social actors and complacency by the majority. Third, the evidence is available in polls of the period. For example, one of the closest measures of acceptability and identity is the willingness to live near members of another race. The opinion polls indicate that the desirability of Black neighbors to Whites was first and more radically altered in the South in the 1950s and 1960s, and later in the North. See George H. Gallup, *The Gallup Poll: Public Opinion, 1935–1971* (New York: Random House, 1972), pp. 1572–1573, 1824, 1941.

57. This theme, that "affirmative action" is limited to those cases where it does not result in "reverse discrimination" against the rights of other individuals, is clearly articulated in *Regents of University of California v. Bakke* 438 U.S. 265 (1978).

58. Myrdal, *An American Dilemma*, p. 24.

59. MacIntyre, *Against Virtue*, p. 204.

60. Kenneth Burke, "Definition of Man," in *Language as Symbolic Action: Essays on Life, Literature, and Method* (Berkeley and Los Angeles: University of California Press, 1966), pp. 3–24.

61. Farrell, "Rhetorical Resemblance," p. 17.

The *Polis* as Rhetorical Community

Carolyn R. Miller

Rhetoric has become a prominent feature of contemporary thought, with critics willing—and eager—to discuss the rhetoric of history, of economics, of anthropology, of fiction, even of mathematics. This work has revitalized the conceptual framework and vocabulary of classical rhetoric and adapted it to a variety of current problems and conditions. At the same time, probably as part of this same general movement, the social context of language has become a major interest in a variety of disciplines—in literary study it is called the interpretive community, in sociolinguistics the speech community, in science studies the disciplinary matrix, in composition the discourse community, in argumentation the argument field or forum. "Community" has become a persuasive critical term. It is striking, however, that this particular term has no clear connection with classical rhetoric; although most contemporary concepts have long histories, in the canon of ancient rhetoric there is no cognate term for community.

"Audience" is the closest cognate, and indeed this term has long been central to rhetorical thinking. But there are important distinctions between audience and community,[1] distinctions that are outlined most conveniently by Perelman and Olbrechts-Tyteca in *The New Rhetoric*. They define audience, in fairly traditional terms, as "the ensemble of those whom the speaker wishes to influence by his [or her] argumentation."[2] But they also insist that argumentation presupposes some "intellectual contact": "For argumentation to exist, an effective community of minds must be realized at a given moment" (p. 14); the conditions for such a community are a common language, common rules for its use, and norms of social life (p. 15). A community, then, defines a horizon of possibilities for any given audience that realizes it; community includes the rhetor as well as the audience, and it includes prior specific audiences and any number of potential audiences, as well as what it is they have in common—experiences, beliefs, stories, and other ways of using language—that allows for intellectual (as well as emotional) contact. Community is a term that includes the past and future as well as the present.[3]

What I want to claim here is that although it does not show itself to us in ancient rhetoric, "community" is a *hidden* term there, an unarticulated presupposition that was at once so fundamental that it did not seem to require explication and so troublesome that it became a primary point of contention. But in order to see it, we must reread for their politics the works that are generally considered in rhetorical studies and read beyond those works to others that are usually left to the political theorists. My hypothesis is that the *polis*, the city-state as community, stands behind Greek rhetorics, and that the disagreements about rhetoric among Plato, the sophists, and Aristotle are bound up with their differing views of and desires for the *polis*.

Although, as I suggested above, community has become central in a variety of inquiries, it is not a trouble-free concept even today. Critics characterize it as an antiliberal and conformist notion, even a fascist one—that is, contrary to the Western achievement of individual liberty, the concept of rights, the primacy of reason. Privileging the communal over the individual is said to lead to the dictatorship of the crowd, to demagoguery, to oppression of difference.[4] Another general criticism is that too much emphasis on the power of community makes it difficult to account satisfactorily for change. As Stanley Fish describes the responses to his work on interpretive communities, "from the right comes the complaint that an interpretive community, unconstrained by any responsibility to a determinate text, can simply declare a change without consulting anything but its own desires; . . . [from the left comes the complaint that an interpretive community, enclosed in the armor of its own totalizing assumptions, is impervious to change and acts only to perpetuate itself and its interests."[5] Both accusations, he says, are based on the belief that an interpretive community is monolithic. Other critics complain that "community" may simply be a vague and sentimental response to the problems of twentieth-century capitalist liberalism.[6]

But in spite of these difficulties, the idea of community is insurgent. The political theorist Michael Walzer characterizes its insurgency as a critique of liberalism, a critique that sometimes focuses on liberal theory and assumptions about the "self" and sometimes on the practices and ways of life that liberalism has created for us.[7] "Communitarianism," as the political theorists have come to call this critique, challenges in both epistemological and ethical terms the primacy, even the possibility, of liberalism's autonomous moral agent, the "presocial" or "unencumbered self that judges and chooses; it also deplores the mobile, isolated, alienated lives we lead.[8] Liberalism invites such critique periodically, as Walzer points out, because it subverts itself by denying the possibility that even liberal beliefs could constitute a communal tradition.

The ancient Greeks conducted a similar debate about the problem of relations between the individual and the community. The essence of Greek tragedy, for one major example, is the conflict between the individual and the social order. The political thought of Protagoras, Thucydides, and Democritus, as Cynthia Farrar reads it, is a general effort at "dynamic reconciliation of man's particularity and autonomy with the requirements of communal life."[9] In more general philosophical terms the Greeks identified this issue as the problem of "the one and the many," a problem that had been posed originally by Parmenides: "If One, how many?" Pre-Socratic inquiry into the nature of being strongly favored the order and stability of monism. The problem, the "Eleatic dilemma," as W. K. C. Guthrie calls it, was then to account for the diversity and change in the world of experience.[10] The extreme monistic formulation of Parmenides led to the "rejection of the world men actually experience" (Farrar, p. 40) and to the sharp disjunctions between being and becoming, continuity and change, and reality and appearance that characterize much of Greek thought. The philosophical formulation, however, was apparently never applied explicitly to the political problem of unity and plurality within the *polis*.[11]

Although ultimately monism proved a more powerful perspective in Greek philosophy, there were serious pluralists, too, as Eric Havelock has argued in *The Liberal Temper in Greek Politics*. He identifies monism with the idealism of Plato and Aristotle and their intellectual predecessors (Parmenides and others) and pluralism with a group of pre-Socratic philosophers he characterizes as "anthropologists" and their successors the sophists.[12] Since history is written by winners, the record of pluralist thinking has been overpowered by that of Platonic idealism, and Havelock sees this effort to resurrect this other Greek tradition as an "act of historical justice" (pp. 18–19). As his title indicates, Havelock identifies the thinking of the pluralists as "liberal," not for its influence on modern political liberalism, however, which has been formulated within the framework of Platonic idealism (an enduring constraint he calls the "law of classic control" [p. 12]), but for its utter contrast with the authoritarianism of later idealist political theory, beginning with Plato. In his characterization, Greek liberalism consisted in the belief in the capacities of the common man (but probably not woman) and in a basic empirical and historicist approach to morality and society (p. 20); it was egalitarian, pragmatic, and situational (p. 34). In contrast to modern liberalism, which is based upon a post-Platonic notion of the autonomous individual, Greek liberalism, according to Havelock, was fundamentally communal.

While I am claiming that in ancient rhetorics the role of community is obscured, it does appear in other texts, most strategically in stories about the origins of civilization. In explaining the genesis of the *polis*, the Greeks indicate—or betray—their various beliefs about the role of rhetoric in forming communities and the role of community in shaping rhetoric. One of the most eloquent and explicit of these stories is the familiar one of Isocrates, who says:

> We are in no respect superior to other living creatures; nay, we are inferior to many in swiftness and in strength and in other resources; but, Because there has been implanted in us the power to persuade each other and to make clear to each other whatever we desire, not only have we escaped the life of wild beasts, but we have come together and founded cities and made laws and invented arts; and, generally speaking, there is no institution devised by man which the power of speech has not helped us to establish. For thus it is which has laid down laws concerning things just and unjust, and things honorable and base; and if it were not for these ordinances we should not be able to live with one another. (*Antidosis* 253–55)[13]

In this account, the human faculty of persuasive speech is given as an essential precondition for the formation of communities and the development of civilized society; it is distinctively a *political* faculty. Isocrates gives us his own version of human history, consonant with his belief in participatory democracy and in the moral dynamics of public speaking: "[P]eople can become better and worthier if they conceive an ambition to speak well, if they become possessed of the desire to be able to persuade their hearers, and, finally, if they set their hearts on seizing their advantage" (*Antidosis* 275).[14] But there were many versions of the story of civilization in fifth- and fourth-century Greece: the Greeks were apparently fascinated by speculation about the sources of their own culture.[15] In what follows, I will use these stories to explore the views of rhetorical community in sophistic thinking, in Plato, and in Aristotle. The differences among these stories can reveal the place of community in Greek rhetorical theories and help us understand our own conceptual difficulties concerning community.

The *polis* of primary reference in these accounts is Athens, of course, but Athens is to be taken not as a singularity but as the paragon of a type.[16] Historically, according to Eric Voegelin, the *polis* was a territorial and political unit with sources in the Mycenaean fortified citadels and a tribal culture for which blood-relationships were primary. Through a series of deliberate and systematic political reforms in the sixth century B.C.E. (those of Solon and Cleisthenes), making membership a

matter not primarily of family relationship but of residence, the Athenian *polis* transcended its tribal origins.[17] At the same time, the socio-economic basis of society was diversifying, with the increasing importance of trade and craft; laboring classes became more important than the remnant tribal aristocracy; and the *polis* became their locus of power, as the tribe and *oikos* had been for the aristocracy of landowners.[18] Jean-Pierre Vernant's elegant depiction of the simultaneous developments of Greek social organization and thinking shows a progressive movement away from the unity personified by a chieftain-king to the pluralism of an open, egalitarian *polis*: "The emphasis was no longer on a single person who dominated social life, but on a multiplicity of functions that opposed each other and thus called for a reciprocal apportionment and delimitation" (p. 43).

In his discussion of the *polis*, H. D. F. Kitto notes that it means "the people" as much as it means "the state."[19] He characterizes it not just as a state but as "a community," whose "affairs are the affairs of all" (p. 71), echoing the line from Pericles' "Funeral Oration": "We [Athenians] alone regard the man who takes no part in public affairs, not as one who minds his own business, but as good for nothing."[20] Kitto goes on to give us the received idealization of Athens:

> The 'polis' every Greek knew; there it was, complete, before his eyes. He could see the fields which gave it its sustenance—or did not, if the crops failed; he could see how agriculture, trade and industry dovetailed into one another; he knew the frontiers, where they were strong and where weak. . . . The entire life of the polis, and the relation between its parts, were . . . [easy] to grasp, Because of the small scale of things. Therefore to say 'It is everyone's duty to help the polis' was not to express a fine sentiment but to speak the plainest and most common sense. Public affairs had an immediacy and a concreteness that they cannot possibly have for us. (p. 73)

Although the *polis* as a form of political organization spread throughout the Aegean, where there were some 200 city-states, and the Mediterranean, where there were as many as 2300,[21] Voegelin points out that it lasted barely two centuries as an effective political form, from the time of Solon to the conquest of Athens by Macedonia (p. 120). This period was a time of great factionalism and war, within Athens, between Athens and other *poleis*, and with Persia and Macedonia. This period was also a time of increasing democratization; indeed. Wood and Wood claim that in Greece generally, "'politicization' and 'democratization' appear to have gone hand in hand" (p. 14).

Most commentators see the *polis* as a distinctive political achievement, a "radical break" with previous modes of social organization, as Wood and Wood put it (p. 26). Kitto describes its significance broadly, as providing "the focus of a man's moral, intellectual, aesthetic, social and practical life, developing and enriching these in a way in which no form of society had done before or has done since" (p. 11). Vernant is more specific, calling "the advent of the *polis* . . . a decisive event in the history of Greek thought" (p. 49); he points specifically to the "preeminence of speech over all other instruments of power" (p. 49) and the consequent "full exposure given to the most important aspects of social life" that in turn led to further democratization "in an ever widening circle" (p. 51). The state became a *res publica*, where social life took the form of *agon*, competition, in a public space, the *agora*: "[O]nce the city was centered on the public square, it was already a *polis* in every sense of the word" (p. 48). Others draw our attention more specifically to the distinctive nature of participatory citizenship that the *polis* made possible. For Wood and Wood, "It is this principle of citizenship, which submerges the qualitative differences among men in a common civic identity, and the identity of state and citizen-body that are the most obviously unique characteristics of the polis" (p. 26). Similarly, Farrar notes that the Athenians "came to regard . . . citizenship as an opportunity for more than acquiescence: for real participation. The significant political distinction no longer corresponded to the social divide between noble and commoner, nor even between free man and slave, but was defined in purely political terms: citizen versus non-citizen" (p. 22).[22]

It was in this new climate of politicized social relations that both rhetoric and politics were conceptualized, and it was the sophists who began this process. The sophists are usually credited with the invention of political theory, an invention necessary to the development of the open, participatory *polis:* they were educators for a new political world of citizen participation.[23] Although credit for the invention of rhetorical theory usually goes to Plato or Aristotle, the sophists were the first teachers of rhetoric and probably began the process of conceptualization for rhetoric, also.[24] But to say this is probably to over-clarify. The sophists taught politics *while* teaching rhetoric, and vice versa; there were not two subjects but one, civic virtue.[25] Aris-

totle was only one of many to note the irony of the sophistic position, complaining that although the sophists profess to teach politics, "not one of them practices it"[26] but of course, being itinerants, non-citizens, they were not qualified to participate in Athenian politics. Their participation took indirect forms: teaching, logography, and occasionally the devising of a constitution for a new colony.

We have, through Plato, a sophistic version of the story of civilization, that of Protagoras, who Voegelin claims made probably the "most noteworthy" contributions to the art of politics (p. 272).[27] Although it is too long to quote in full here, in summary the story emphasizes that when humans were created, they received, in lieu of natural weapons and protection, the gifts of fire and skill in the arts to keep themselves alive and that these skills were unequally distributed, so that some are expert in one art and some in another; nevertheless, Protagoras says,

by the art which they possessed, men soon discovered articulate speech and names, and invented houses and clothes and shoes and bedding and got food from the earth. Thus provided for, they lived at first in scattered groups; there were no cities. Consequently they were devoured by wild beasts, since they were in every respect the weaker, and their technical skill, though a sufficient aid to their nurture, did not extend to making war on the beasts, for they had not the art of politics, of which the art of war is a part. They sought therefore to save themselves by coming together and founding fortified cities, but when they gathered in communities they injured one another for want of political skill, and so scattered again and continued to be devoured. Zeus therefore, fearing the total destruction of our race, sent Hermes to impart to men the qualities of respect for others [*aidos*] and a sense of justice [*dike*], so as to bring order into our cities and create a bond of friendship and union.[28]

These last gifts, however, were distributed to everyone, for Zeus said, "Let all have their share. There could never be cities if only a few shared in these virtues" (322d).

In this story, the faculty of speech predates the formation of communities but is not explicitly given as a condition for social life. However, the role of rhetoric may be inferred from the whole story, which Kerferd calls "the first . . . theoretical basis for participatory democracy" (p. 144).[29] Participation here can only be rhetorical; it takes place through debate and deliberation. Through speech the virtues of justice and respect are tested, enacted, and developed, and through speech the community itself is created and recreated. Protagoras does emphasize that "in a debate involving skill in building, or in any other craft, the Athenians, like other men, believe that few are capable of giving advice . . . but when the subject of their counsel involves political wisdom, which must always follow the path of justice and moderation, they listen to every man's opinion, for they think that everyone must share in this kind of virtue; otherwise the state could not exist" (322e–323a; cf. also 323c and 324d).

What Protagoras and other sophists taught was conceived of as a general art of citizenship. As Protagoras puts it to Socrates, he teaches a student "the proper care of his personal affairs, so that he may best manage his own household, and also of the state's affairs, so as to become a real power in the city, both as speaker and man of action" (318e), a curriculum that Socrates identifies as "the art of politics [which] make[s] men good citizens" (319a). Protagoras assumes that civic virtue is teachable and that the capacity for it is universal—that anyone could learn or improve. To Socrates' objection that the qualities of justice and respect cannot be taught, Protagoras replies that no one would be punished for lack of them if people thought they could not be developed and improved (323e). He also argues that such education is an integral part of child rearing, schooling, and a city's laws and punishments. He concludes, "all are teachers of virtue to the best of their ability, and so you [Socrates] think that no one is" (327e). As Wood and Wood summarize this point, "the *polis* itself is the teacher of virtue through its laws and customs, its *nomoi*, and its citizens" (p. 135). Protagoras admits that as a teacher he can really only accelerate or focus a process that is already underway (328b); as Farrar emphasizes, what Protagoras teaches is "continuous with socialization," not only in form but also in content: "[W]hat Protagoras teaches is not a skill divorced from a consideration of human needs and ends, but rather a way of analyzing and promoting them." However, the training offered by the sophist is both more extensive and more self-conscious than normal socialization, and Farrar concludes that "the reflection he provokes is not only compatible with, but even essential to, the vitality of democratic interaction" (p. 87). Protagoras' teaching makes rhetoric and politics inseparable dimensions of each other: the democratic city requires rhetoric for its self-constituting operation, and rhetoric must take place within and concern the affairs of the city.

Three major Protagorean doctrines are relevant.[30] The first, that humanity is "the measure" of everything, is a fairly well attested statement that Kerferd suggests can "take us directly to the heart of the whole of the fifth-century sophistic movement" (pp. 85–86). It may well invoke a relativist epistemology, as many suggest; more to the point here is its invocation of localized bases of judgment and its sanctioning of diversity in perspective. Both Schiappa and Farrar argue that Protagoras may well have been responding to Parmenidean monistic absolutism, Farrar maintaining that his "point was . . . to claim that truth and knowledge are grounded in human experience and relative to human concerns" (p. 48). The second doctrine, that on any matter there are opposing arguments, is clearly consistent with the search for truth and judgment through discussion and the exercise of citizenship in an open forum. A more extreme interpretation (based on obscure Heraclean ontology), that on any matter two contrary arguments can both be true (Schiappa, pp. 90–100), at least has the virtue of emphasizing that truth is neither simple nor obvious. Finally, the related doctrine that the worse argument can be made to appear the better, the doctrine that perhaps more than any other gave the term "sophist" the tonality it has today, was attributed to Protagoras by Aristotle (*Rhetoric* II.24.1402a). From the naturalistic perspective of the sophist, however, the doctrine in no way invites the opprobrium it has received: rather than inviting deception and manipulation, it suggests the possibility of change.[31] If humans are the measure, our understanding of the relative strength of alternative arguments will depend upon who we are and how an argument has been presented to us. In its simplest form, of course, the "humanity-measure" doctrine leads to solipsism, but both Kerferd (pp. 90–92) and Farrar (pp. 48–51) argue that the doctrine can more fairly be seen as a serious attempt to base discussion on the plurality of experience. It is an easy step from that point to the rhetorical politics of the democratic *polis*.

Although sophistic thinking was not primarily interested in history, it relied on the empirical-historical perspective of the earlier "anthropologists" to conceptualize human affairs and to explore questions involving ethics, politics, and rhetoric. As itinerants, the sophists lived out the anthropological perspective, noting the variety of practices and values in the places they visited and thus coming to appreciate the power of what they called *nomos*-convention or community customs (Guthrie, p. 16; Kerferd, p. 112) and the role of education in creating cultural differences. *Nomos* was opposed in Greek thought of the time to *physis*, nature, or in Kerferd's rendering, "the way things are" (p. 111). Together, *physis* and *nomos* combine the polarities of nature/nurture and description/prescription. But the sophistic interest in *nomos* does not solve the problem of community, for although in its descriptive function *nomos* explains cultural difference, in its prescriptive, regulatory function, *nomos* requires conformity. So while Kerferd reads Protagoras' story of civilization as "a fundamental defense of *nomos* in relation to *physis*, in that *nomos* is a necessary condition for the maintenance of human societies" (p. 126), we can also read it as a defense of plurality over conformity, in that many types of people and skills are necessary within the community and many voices are to be heard in maintaining it.

Plato's opposition to the sophists can be understood in these same terms—his preference for unity and for natural, unchanging standards over plurality and variable, human standards.[32] In the *Republic*, he asks whether "we know of any greater evil for a state than the thing that distracts it and makes it many instead of one, or a greater good than that which binds it together and makes it one?" (V.462b)[33] In the *Statesman*, he substitutes for laws (*nomoi*) developed within and agreed to by the community the superior "scientific" judgment of the ruler (which would be knowledge of *physis*); in other words, he advocates "ruling without laws," as the young Socrates puts it (293e).[34] In the *Laws*, he says that the "wisest rule" of government is to make life "to the very uttermost, an unbroken consort, society, and community of all with all" (XII.942c).[35] Plato's authoritarian politics and his antipathy to rhetoric are well known; all I can do here is review their relationship, but in doing so I will focus on Plato's versions of the story of civilization. It is interesting that although Plato tells many stories about both the history of politics and the history of language, the two concerns do not often appear together in the same story. In the *Phaedrus*, for example, we have a myth about the invention of writing, in which the terms of discussion are individual, not social—will it aid or destroy memory? Does it offer wisdom or the semblance of wisdom? The *Cratylus* includes an apolitical discussion of the origins of words, which engages issues of semantics and etymology but not of virtue or community.

In his overtly political writings Plato gives us several parallel versions of the story of civilization.

The *Republic* shows Socrates and his companions speculating about the origins of the city, in order to understand the origin of justice and injustice within it (II.369a). The city they imagine begins with basic human needs (369c) and becomes more complex and differentiated until it seems "complete" (371e), but it remains peaceful, self-regulating, even idyllic, with every person living modestly and contentedly:

> Will they not make bread and wine and garments and shoes? And they will build themselves houses and carry on their work in summer for the most part unclad and unshod and in winter clothed and shod sufficiently. And for their nourishment they will provide meal from their barley and flour from their wheat, and kneading and cooking these they will serve noble cakes and loaves on some arrangement of reeds or clean leaves. And, reclined on rustic beds strewed with bryony and myrtle, they will feast with their children, drinking of their wine thereto, garlanded and singing hymns to the gods in pleasant fellowship, not begetting offspring beyond their means lest they fall into poverty or war. (372b)

But Glaucon breaks into Socrates' reverie, reminding the group that men are greedy and contentious by nature: they will want relishes for this feast, and couches. Socrates picks up the theme, adding "myrrh and incense and girls and cakes—all sorts of them" (373a). Their city becomes the infamous "city of pigs" (372d), requiring greater territory, trade in luxuries, and inevitably, war.

A similar story is told in the *Laws* about the origin of the state, through the imagined destruction of an ancient civilization and the ways in which it could be reconstituted. At a certain stage of redevelopment, people are happy, for their needs are met but conflict and war do not exist:

> Thus, they were not extremely poor . . . and so were not set at variance by the stress of penury; rich they could never become in the absence of gold and silver. . . . Now, a society in which neither riches nor poverty is a member regularly produces sterling characters, as it has no place for violence and wrong, nor yet for rivalry and envy. Thus they were good men. . . . Then I take it we may say that the many generations of men who led such a life were bound, by comparison with the age before the Deluge or with our own, to be rude and ignorant in the various arts, particularly in those of warfare, as practiced today by land or water, and again within the city, under the names of litigation and party faction, with their manifold artful contrivances for the infliction of mutual injury

and wrong by word and by deed; they were simpler and manlier, and by consequence more self-controlled and more righteous generally. (III.679)

Plato tells stories quite different from those of Protagoras and Isocrates; these are stories of decline, rather than of progress.[36] The satisfaction of needs in a rural, subsistence economy is inevitably replaced by the feeding of desires in a more developed civilization. The city is a place of corruption, temptation, and injustice; it does not foster civic virtue. In a *polis* like this, strong government is necessary to maintain order and to provide whatever justice there will be, since it cannot come from the virtue of citizens. Thus, the art of rhetoric has no place in the development of the Platonic *polis*; it is, rather, like the other arts, a consequence of the degradation of the *polis*, a degradation that Plato seemed to think inevitable.

The *Statesman* contains the only overt mention of the faculty of speech in these stories. In this dialogue, Plato describes life in two distinct cosmic eras, the current "Age of Zeus" and the preceding "Age of Cronos." In the Age of Cronos, the universe rotated in reverse; men were "born from the earth," grew younger not older, and were governed in flocks by "heavenly daemons" acting as shepherds (271b–d):

> When God was shepherd there were no political constitutions and no taking of wives and begetting of children. For all men rose up anew into Life out of the earth. . . . [T]hey had fruits without stint from trees and bushes; these needed no cultivation but sprang up of themselves out of the ground without man's toil. For the most part they disported themselves in the open needing neither clothing nor couch, for the seasons were blended evenly so as to work them no hurt, and the grass which sprang up out of the earth in abundance made a soft bed for them. (272a–b)

These "nurselings of Cronos" had a heightened faculty of speech and were even able to "converse with the animals as well as with one another" (272b). Plato is unable to tell us how they used this ability, but he makes it clear that the only wise and necessary use would have been the accumulation of knowledge through philosophical discussion with the various "tribes of creatures" (272c).

After this era comes to its destined end, the rotation of the universe reverses, there is a period of cataclysmic readjustment, procreation and aging occur as we understand them, and the Age of Zeus develops:

Bereft of the guardian care of the daemon who had governed and reared us up, we had become weak and helpless, and we began to be ravaged by wild beasts—for the many evil-natured beasts had by now turned savage. Men lacked all tools and all crafts in the early years. The earth no longer supplied their food spontaneously and they did not yet know how to win it for themselves; in the absence of necessity they had never been made to learn this. For all these reasons they were in direst straits. It was to meet this need that the gifts of the gods famous in ancient stories were given, along with such teaching and instruction as was indispensable. Fire was the gift of Prometheus, the secrets of the crafts were made known by Hephaestus and his partner in craftsmanship, and seeds and plants were made known by other gods. From these gifts everything has come which has furnished human life since the divine guardianship of men ceased—in the way our story has just described—and men had to manage their lives and fend for themselves in the same way as the whole universe was forced to do. (274b–d)

Nothing is said about the faculty of speech in the Age of Zeus, but we can assume a kind of post-Babel inability to understand other creatures. The dialogue goes on to explore the nature of the "statesman" or ruler, who has "responsible charge" or "sovereign rule" over a community, much like the daemon shepherd during better times. By omission, the faculties and abilities of the members of the community are irrelevant; in their degraded and desperate condition, ordinary people have only to "fend for themselves" and to be ruled.[37]

Plato is haunted by the problem of community, of how unity can come from plurality; the three major political works consider not only the origin and history of the *polis*-community but also (and more centrally) the ideal nature of such a community and the practical means by which the ideal community can be constructed, or at least approximated. In the earlier *Gorgias* rhetoric is an important part of this same general inquiry. Rhetoric is investigated as a phenomenon of the *polis*, as a felt power within the political community. But because there is no Protagoras present to make a good case for rhetoric as a universal and civic power (Gorgias' own claim that rhetoric is concerned with justice is not well defended),[38] the case for rhetoric is put in terms of specialized personal power, a strategy that allows Plato to press the comparison between rhetoric and other skilled crafts harder than he does in the *Protagoras*. The result, as Edwin Black has shown, is that Plato is able to separate rhetoric from political skill, making them two distinct specialties, as distinct from each other as weaving and pottery.[39] Thus, rhetoric becomes a neutral *techne*, dissociated from justice and virtue, capable of either good or evil: it must seek elsewhere for content as well as for moral purpose, and it loses its claim to be the master art of the *polis*, a role that clearly belongs to the separate art of statesmanship.

The second general step in Plato's thinking about the relationship between rhetoric and politics is to subordinate rhetoric to politics by constructing a hierarchy of arts and occupations, a hierarchy that, as Wood and Wood emphasize, conflates moral quality with social position (pp. 148–49). The dual hierarchy is illustrated vividly in the *Phaedrus*, when Socrates ranks souls according to how much divine knowledge each has: from the philosopher, to the warrior or ruler, through the man of business or trade, the athlete, prophet, poet, farmer, demagogue, and tyrant (248d–e). Wood and Wood note that the basic division of labor in Plato's state is between those who must work for a living and those who live off the labor of others. These latter are fit to rule for two reasons: they have the leisure for the proper education, and they are not corrupted by their intimate involvement with the material world (p. 149). The pursuit of wisdom occupies the top of the social/moral hierarchy, with the art of ruling tied as closely to it as is feasible; all other arts must serve the needs of the state and be informed by them.

Plato helped to turn rhetoric into an instrumental *techne* because its neutrality would then require its subordination to a higher art, dialectic, for instruction about the good. For Plato, the locus of virtue is in the realm of pure ideas, not, as it is for Protagoras and for sophists generally, in the history, traditions, and beliefs of the community itself. Thus, virtue, justice, and the good are not qualities to be developed and negotiated within a community but absolutes to be applied, administered, and coerced. As Wood and Wood put it, for Plato "the political art concerns *rule* rather than citizenship" (p. 175). In his recent book, Brian Vickers has argued that Plato repeatedly links persuasion and compulsion as the means of control a state has over its citizens[40]; thus, for example in the *Republic*, Socrates claims that the aim of the law should be "to produce [happiness] in the city as a whole, harmonizing and adapting the citizens to one another by persuasion and compulsion" (VII.519e). In the Platonic *polis* only the rulers have access to the art of rhetoric, which becomes thereby the art of propaganda; rhetoric must serve a transcendent, dialectical truth that enforces social unity, a unity to which individuals are irrelevant and democracy is damaging.

Aristotle's treatment of rhetoric and politics engages the issues raised by Protagoras and Plato and endeavors to resolve them by close analysis. Since he prefers direct observation to narrative speculation, his version of the story of civilization, which appears in the *Politics*, lacks the charm of many other versions. Arguing that the *polis* "belongs to the class of objects which exist by nature" (I.ii.1253a), he looks "at the natural growth of things from the beginning" (1252a), finding a natural cause for each stage in the development of civilization: the "*natural* urge" to reproduce leads to pair-bonding; the "satisfaction of daily needs" leads to the formation of the household, the *oikos*; the "satisfaction of something *more* than daily needs" (1252b) leads to the village; and the preservation of self-sufficiency and the possibility of "the *good* life" lead to the formation of the *polis*.[41] The *polis* is an evolutionary achievement that "is the end of those others," the natural and inevitable fulfillment of human nature:

> Obviously [he says], man is a political animal in a sense in which a bee is not, or any other gregarious animal. Nature, as we say, does nothing without some purpose; and she has endowed man alone among the animals with the power of speech. Speech . . . serves to indicate what is useful and what is harmful, and so also what is just and what is unjust. . . . It is the sharing of a common view in *these* matters that makes a household and a state. (*Politics* I.ii.1253a)

This is essentially the same argument that Isocrates made some twenty years earlier (without the teleology), an argument that reorients Protagoras' story by making the role of speech explicit. Later in the *Politics*, in his discussion of the ideal *polis*, Aristotle provides a list of "those things [both parts and functions] without which there can be no [city]-states": these are food, skills, arms, money, religion, and "most essential of all, a method of arriving at decisions about matters of expedience and justice" (VII.viii.1328a). Here it is clear that it is not the mere faculty of speech that makes community life possible but the specifically rhetorical dimension of speech-deliberation about human actions, about "things that seem to be capable of admitting two possibilities," as he put it in the *Rhetoric* (I.ii.1357a).[42] Because Aristotle treats the good and the just as matters of opinion, about which we argue and reason, his *polis* requires rhetoric, in contrast to Plato's, which forbids it because there is no need for deliberation in a community tyrannized by the truth. And this requirement shows us that Aristotle manages a role for both *physis* and *nomos*: the *polis* exists by nature as a form of association, but the specific qualities of any given *polis* are clearly matters of convention. For Aristotle, the essence of a community is the sharing of a common view, developed in and by the community; what is shared is thus localized and changeable. Plato's impulse, of course, opposes this; what is shared should be universal and thus does not require a community.

Several features of the *polis* as Aristotle conceives it have further implications for rhetoric. One is that since the *polis* should ideally be self-sufficient, it must also be pluralistic. He criticizes Plato's *Republic* on this point:

> Certainly there must be some unity in a state, as in a household, but not an absolutely total unity. There comes a point where the state, if it does not cease to be a state altogether, will certainly come close to that and be a worse one; it is as if one were to reduce concord to unison or rhythm to a single beat. (*Politics* II.v.1263b)[43]

Thus, although the primary feature of the community is the fact of association, that fact does not erase all difference; association, *koinonia* (common-ness), can be the primary social force without requiring or creating total conformity. In the spirit of the sophists, Aristotle notes that "a state is a plurality, which must depend on education to bring about its common unity" (II.v.1263b). His characterization of the arts of discourse, both dialectic and rhetoric, as the only arts "concerned with opposites" is also consistent with sophistic thinking about the plurality of experience and reasoning (*Rhetoric* I.i.1354a).

Another feature of the ideal Aristotelian *polis* is that it is participatory. This means that it cannot be too large, for "in order to give decisions on matters of justice and . . . merit, it is necessary that the citizens should know each other and know what kind of people they are" (*Politics* VII.iv.1326b).[44] Aristotle shows some impatience with definitions of the citizen that rely on parentage or residence and prefers a definition based on participation: "What effectively distinguishes the citizen proper from all others is this participation in giving judgement and in holding office" (III.i.1275a). He also notes that this definition works best in a democ-

racy (1275b) and that the nature of citizenship will differ in different city-states. The whole purpose of association is to achieve "the best life possible," which requires "an active exercise of virtue and a complete employment of it" (VII.viii.1328a)—that is, engagement in the activities and issues and with the people in the community.[45]

Finally in Aristotle's account, the community is generative of the specific shape and materials of discourse. One indication of this is that in the *Rhetoric*, we find repeated connections with politics. Rhetoric, Aristotle says early on, is an "offshoot" both of dialectic *and* of ethics, which itself is a part of politics. That is why, he says, rhetoric "dresses itself up in the form of politics" (I.ii.1356a). He is referring here to the tendency of the sophists to treat rhetoric and politics as identical and to prepare young men for citizenship by teaching public speaking. But his own treatise does not escape this tendency, deliberative oratory giving him the most obvious problem. He introduces it by reminding us (perhaps remembering Plato's arguments about the separation of the arts) that discussions of rhetoric should not "obscure its nature" by representing it as knowledge of a factual domain. "Nevertheless," he goes on, "let us now say what it is worthwhile to analyze, while leaving the full examination to political science." He then discusses the "important subjects" about which men deliberate: "finances, war and peace, national defense, imports and exports, and the framing of laws" (I.iv.1359b), adding a kind of apology—"But these subjects belong to politics, not to rhetoric" (I.iv.1360a). He ends the discussion of deliberative rhetoric by referring to his own *Politics* where more detail on the forms of government may be found (I.viii.1366a).

Many other aspects of Aristotle's conceptual apparatus for rhetoric show the imprint of community on discourse. The three genres, for example, deliberative, judicial, and epideictic rhetoric, clearly represent functions of the state: the *polis* provides exigences, forums for addressing those exigences, and topical resources by which those exigences can be mitigated (to adopt Lloyd Bitzer's vocabulary). His discussion of proof, especially comments about probability, the enthymeme, and pathos, also show sensitivity to the locatedness of rhetoric. He says, for example, "the persuasive is persuasive to someone," but also, "rhetoric [does not] theorize about each opinion—what may seem so to Socrates or Hippias—but about what seems true to people of a certain sort" (I.ii.1356b). Another particularly telling example is his repetition of the observation attributed to Socrates (from *Menexenus* 235d) that "it is not difficult to praise Athenians in Athens, but among the Spartans [is another matter]" (III.xiv.1415b; cf. also I.ix.1367b). This maxim can suggest not only a cynical pandering to the audience but also the sophistic-anthropological notion that the community, whether of Athenians or Spartans, must and should shape its own standards of praise, standards that may be incompatible with those of other communities.

So far I have emphasized the sophistic aspects of Aristotle's thinking, the ways he justifies participation and diversity. But Aristotle was Plato's student, and his political thought owes at least as much to the aristocratic tradition that Plato attempted to impose on the anti-aristocratic *polis*.[46] Aristotle participates in this project by rationalizing the hierarchical dimensions of Athenian democracy, a democracy that was selective and exclusionary, in which the disparity between citizens and residents was great—slaves, women, and metics (resident aliens, such as the sophists) being disenfranchised.[47] In Aristotle's discussion, the large numbers of non-citizens serve as the essential preconditions for the democratic *polis* by performing the commercial, mechanical, and menial labor necessary to support the economy and releasing citizens for political activity. Even among citizens there were class distinctions. The sixth-century Solonian reforms had created four political classes based on property, but the operative distinction among citizens seems to have been between those who had to work for a living and those who did not, the *penetes* and the *plousioi*.[48] In his consideration of citizens, Aristotle reflects Platonic attitudes toward labor and reproduces Plato's conflation of moral quality and social position. At one point, for example, he notes that the citizens of a democracy can be divided into the "people" (*demos*), who engage in agriculture, trade, craft, commerce, and the like, and the "notables" (*gnorimoi*), who are distinguished by wealth, birth, education, and virtue (*Politics* IV.iv.1291b). At another point, he asks whether those engaged in mechanical labor, the "banausics," ought really to be considered citizens. He answers,

> the best state will not make the mechanic a citizen. But even if he is to be a citizen, then at any rate what we have called the virtue of a citizen cannot be ascribed to everyone, nor yet to free men alone, but simply to those who are in fact relieved of necessary tasks . . . for it is quite impossible, while living the life of mechanic or hireling,

to occupy oneself as virtue demands. (III.v.1277b–1278a)[49]

Aristotle's synthesis of sophism and Platonism shows rhetoric to be shaped by the community, but does not allow the community to be shaped by discourse: the community's structure is given, determined by reference to an external standard. Whatever diversity is achievable, within or between communities, is constrained by an *a priori*, Platonic virtue that dictates social structure and moral value.

The *polis* should not represent for us the perfect rhetorical community, a golden-age model of ideal relations between the individual and the communal. That model is not available in the work of Plato and Aristotle. What they give us is not descriptions but their own idealizations, reactions to political change. Havelock calls them both "propagandists" (p. 101) and charges them both with living in a "political vacuum" (p. 381). Wood and Wood maintain that the Western political tradition has accepted as historical fact a "counter-historical redefinition of the polis" that "makes its very principles appear as its corruption" (p. 119). In fact, they assert,

> The important tiling is to understand the degree to which the class interest and class-consciousness of the lower classes, whose ethic is often held responsible for the destruction of the glories of Athens, were in fact responsible for their creation, and to be a bit cautious about the aristocratic cliches that have become so much a part of classical scholarship. The view that the nature of the polis is reflected in the ideas of Plato and Aristotle can perhaps be classed among these aristocratic cliches. (p. 73)[50]

As it was for Plato and Aristotle, and probably for the sophists, the *polis* has been for us not so much a geo-demographic entity as an ideological projection, a conception necessitated by the desire to discuss rhetorical and political relations.

The nature of this conceptual *polis* was in dispute in Greece. To the aristocratic thinkers, the *polis* was most useful if conceptualized teleologically, as the place where disruptive historical change would stop, where a final structure of just relations could come about. To the sophistic evolutionary thinkers, as Havelock notes, the *polis* was useful as a historical phase, an effective but not ideal form of society that would give way to others, possibly to Pan-Hellenic internationalism (pp. 32,

99, 228; of course, the political advantage to the sophists of an expanding notion of community should not be overlooked). The related dispute, about the nature of virtue, is central to the aristocratic rejection both of the sophists and of the newly important laboring classes. The traditional explanations for the rejection of the sophists are (according to Voegelin) that they were resented because they were "foreigners" (p. 269) or (according to Guthrie) that they should not have charged fees for instruction or claimed to be able to teach virtue, which "for the right people" should be a natural accomplishment (pp. 38–40). But a more persuasive reason for the vehemence of the aristocratic reaction is offered by Kerferd. What so provoked, he says, was "that the sophists sell wisdom *to all comers* without discrimination" (p. 25). Their instruction was intended to enable *anyone,* without regard for family, class, or occupation, to learn to become an active, effective, perhaps powerful citizen-leader; Protagoras, remember, claimed that from him a pupil could learn "to become a real power in the city, both as speaker and man of action" (*Protagoras* 318e). As Kerferd notes, "If *arete . . .* can be taught, then social mobility is . . . possible" (p. 37), and the teleological security of the *polis* as a social structure can no longer be maintained.[51] The threat of social mobility also explains the deep offense of the sophistic claim that the worse argument can appear the better: given the congruence of virtue and social class, the worse argument just *is* that of *hoi polloi.*

The sophists have traditionally been portrayed as individualists, glorifying the individual at the expense of the community, convinced that might is right, drunk with the power of the orator. Callicles in the *Gorgias* and Thrasymachus in the *Republic* are sometimes taken as portrayals of the amoral self-promotion and self-aggrandizement that sophism is assumed to involve.[52] Black's description of the Gorgian view of rhetoric adopts this perspective: he calls its claims pretentious, its formulation flaccid, and its practice that of "easy virtue" (p. 374). George Kennedy's characterization of sophistic rhetoric as emphasizing the role of the speaker and as given to "empty verbosity and self-indulgence" is consistent with the traditional view, although he does acknowledge that "most sophists have believed that the orator should be a good man" and that "their most consistent theme" has included "celebration of enlightened government."[53] What is un-sophistic about these ways of understanding the sophists is the assumption that the individual is essentially in conflict with the community; this is a modern "liberal" understanding of political relations. A "post"-modern understanding, which can inform our current understanding of the sophists, might rather emphasize the extent to which individuals are constructed by communities, by *nomoi,* and the ways in which communities are constructed by individuals and their conflicts.[54] We might suspect that some analytic distance is necessary for seeing these relationships, distance granted the sophists by their status as metics, distance granted us by post-modern disaffection. Perhaps outsiders best understand the nature of community.

The *polis* was attractive to both the aristocratic thinkers and to the sophists, although for very different reasons. But for both it was important less as a fact of life than as a set of possibilities, possibilities of hierarchy and control for the aristocratic thinkers, possibilities of participation and diversity for the sophists. The *polis* is attractive to us, too: it fascinates because it seems to offer what modern liberalism considers a paradox—a *liberal* community. Wood and Wood note that "the rise of the autonomous individual was correlative to the rise of the civic community" (p. 25), a contention that suggests that liberal individualism and communalism require each other (and that sophism made Platonism possible). Havelock, however, insists that Greek liberalism was not individualist; it was pre-individualist, rather than anti-individualist, because "Platonism had not yet invented" the requisite universalized view of human nature (p. 17). If Havelock is right, then our modernist conviction that the individual and the community are necessarily opposed is a contingent one, possibly a corrigible one. Contemporary social constructionism begins to provide such a correction: individual and community are seen to exist in dynamic interaction, each constructing each other; neither the community nor the individual can be an impenetrable isolate. If this is so, then community cannot be impervious to change: it is inherently dynamic. And because of those mutually constitutive relationships, community must be both pluralist and normative, another combination that modem liberalism has understood as paradoxical.

Greek conceptions of community operate decisively in the background of Greek rhetorics. Even though the formal conceptualizations of rhetoric do not call attention to the *polis* as such, it functions silently as the presupposed locus of the issues that are at stake: virtue, persuasion, and power.[55] It is also the case, I believe, that rhetoric operates in the background of political thought. We see this operation highlighted in the stories about how the distinctively Greek form of community came to be. Here, Greek thinkers reveal their presumptions about the power and uses of persuasion and the nature of decision-making within social groups. For us, the *polis* provides a concrete model of the relationship between rhetoric and politics at the site of their simultaneous birth. It can serve as a precursor concept to our rediscovered need for community in rhetorical thinking.

In understanding the *polis* as a specifically *rhetorical* community, it is helpful to see it not as primarily an empirical social structure (however imperfect) but as the framework for an event: as the continuing opportunity—the forum—for debate, discussion, dialogue, dispute. Both Ober and Vernant emphasize this relationship between rhetoric and politics as the crucial distinguishing feature of the *polis*. For Ober, what requires explaining is neither the birth nor the demise of democracy but its stability over the course of two hundred years, especially given the social inequalities between rich and poor and the lack of an established bureaucracy (pp. 18–19). In his view, what made the *polis* possible under these conditions was rhetoric, "the mediating and integrative power of communication between citizens . . . in a language whose vocabulary consisted of symbols developed and deployed in public arenas" (p. 35). For Vernant, it is the construction of a "new social space" (p. 125) that permits both the social and philosophical achievements of the Greeks. Thus social space, embodied in the *agora,* is both political and rhetorical; it is "common, public, egalitarian, and symmetrical, . . . intended for confrontation, debate, and argument" (p. 126). Confrontation is equalizing; Vernant cites Hesiod on this point, noting that for the Greeks "competition can take place only among peers" (p. 47). A functioning political-rhetorical community is thus necessarily both cooperative and competitive, egalitarian and agonistic.

The *polis* is a rhetorical community, then, because it is most centrally a site of contention. Certainly it was a site disputed by the sophists and the aristocrats. More generally it is the site of political debate between citizens, a locus of self-defining communal action. Because there are many citizens, there are differences; because there is one *polis*, they must confront those differences. But the polis is a rhetorical community in another sense, too. As we have seen, the *polis* is an important ideological construction both for the Greeks and for their modern interpreters. We can thus understand the *polis* as a discursive projection, a set of assumptions implicit in any argument; it is the community invoked, represented, presupposed, or developed in rhetorical discourse.[56] As a rhetorical projection the *polis* can contain our differences. At the center of the *polis*, in the *agora*, are these contradictions: the simultaneous existence of one and many, the cooperative nature of competition, the inclusion of the outsider. In such a space rhetoric is always necessary, for there will always be an opposing argument.

For helpful comments at various points in the development of this essay, I wish to thank Michael Carter, Richard Enos, Susan Jarratt, Clifford Vaida, and, especially, Dan Miller.

NOTES

1. See the discussions in Martin Nystrand, "Rhetoric's 'Audience' and Linguistics' 'Speech Community': Implications for Understanding Writing, Reading, and Text," *What Writers Know: The Language, Process, and Structure of Written Discourse,* ed. Martin Nystrand (New York: Academic Press, 1982), pp. 1–28; Lloyd Bitzer, "Rhetoric and Public Knowledge," *Rhetoric, Philosophy, and Literature: An Exploration,* ed. Don M. Burks (West Lafayette, IN: Purdue University Press, 1978), pp. 67–93; and Gerard Hauser and Carole Blair, "Rhetorical Antecedents to the Public," *Pre/Text* 3 (1982): 139–67. "The public" comes closer than "audience" to what is generally meant by "community."

2. *The New Rhetoric: A Treatise on Argumentation,* trans. John Wilkinson and Purcell Weaver (Notre Dame: University of Notre Dame Press, 1969), p. 19. Further references will be incorporated in the text.

3. Robert N. Bellah *et al., Habits of the Heart: Individualism and Commitment in American Life* (Berkeley: University of California Press, 1985), for example, suggest that a community that plays any significant role in the life of individual people serves both as a community of memory and a community of hope (pp. 152–53).

4. For a discussion of these problems specifically in terms of political theory, see Stephen Hohnes, "The Community Trap," *The New Republic* 20 (28 Nov. 1988): 24–28; and Iris Marion Young, *Justice and the Politics of Difference* (Princeton, NJ: Princeton University Press, 1990). For application to encounters between students and pedagogical authority see Patricia Bizzell, "Arguing about Literacy," *College English* 50 (1988): 141–53; Marilyn M. Cooper, "Why Are We Talking About Discourse Communities?" *Writing as Social Action* (Portsmouth, NH: Boynton/Cook, 1989), pp. 202–20; and Joseph Harris, "The Idea of Community in the Study of Writing," *College Composition and Communication* 40 (1989): 11–22.

5. "Change," *South Atlantic Quarterly* 86 (1987): 424.

6. For example, see Holmes, "The Community Trap": "Antiliberals invest this word with redemptive significance. When we hear it, all our critical faculties are meant to fall asleep" (p. 25). Michael Walzer notes that "Communitarianism is . . . the . . . articulation of . . . feelings [of sadness and discontent]. It reflects a sense of loss" ("The Communitarian Critique of Liberalism," *Political Theory* 18 [1990]: 12). See also the widely quoted observation by Raymond Williams that community is a "warmly persuasive word" that "seems never to be used unfavourably" (*Keywords: A Vocabulary of Culture and Society* [New York: Oxford, 1976], p. 66).

7. Walzer points specifically to Alasdair MacIntyre's *After Virtue: A Study in Moral Theory* (Notre Dame, IN: University of Notre Dame Press, 1981) as a critique of the first sort and to *Habits of the Heart* as a critique of the second sort.

8. "Unencumbered self" is Michael Sandel's term; see his "The Procedural Republic and the Unencumbered Self," *Political Theory* 12 (1984): 81–96. Major works in this debate as it has been conducted by political theorists include John Rawls, *A Theory of Justice* (Oxford, UK: Oxford University Press, 1971); Sandel, *Liberalism and the Limits of Justice* (New York: Cambridge University Press, 1983); Walzer, *Spheres of Justice* (New York: Basic Books, 1983); and Will Kymlicka, *Liberalism, Community, and Culture* (Oxford, UK: Clarendon, 1989). The discussion has not been purely academic, appearing recently on newspaper editorial pages and in debates about government social policies. Communitarianism shows signs of becoming a social movement, promoted by such publications as Amitai Etzioni's *The Spirit of Community* (New York: Crown, 1993).

9. *The Origins of Democratic Thinking: The Invention of Politics in Classical Athens* (Cambridge, UK: Cambridge University Press, 1988), p. 2. Further references will be incorporated in the text.

10. *The Sophists* (Cambridge, UK: Cambridge University Press, 1971; orig. pub. in 1969 as part I, vol. III of *A History of Greek Philosophy*), p. 47; further references will be incorporated in the text. See also the entries under *hen, on, plethos,* and *trias* in F. E. Peters, *Greek Philosophical Terms: A Historical Lexicon* (New York: New York University Press, 1967).

11. Jean-Pierre Vernant, *The Origins of Greek Thought* (Ithaca, NY: Cornell University Press, 1982; orig. pub. Paris: Presses Universitaires de France, 1962), p. 45 n. 10. Further references will be incorporated in the text.

12. *The Liberal Temper in Greek Politics* (London: Jonathan Cape, 1957); further references will be incorporated in the text. He identifies the "anthropologists" as Anaximander, Xenophanes, Anaxagoras, Archelaus, and Democritus.

13. Trans. George Norlin (New York: G. P. Putnam's Sons, 1929).

14. The degree of surprise that we feel about this connection between moral improvement and seizing advantage is a measure of just how different modern liberalism may be from Greek liberalism.

15. According to G. B. Kerferd, there were three distinct types of these stories, now known as the Theory of Decline, the Cyclical Theory, and the Theory of Progress (*The Sophistic Movement* [Cambridge, UK: Cambridge University Press, 1981], p. 125; further references will be incorporated in the text). There was, he says, "a very active debate on such matters in the second half of the fifth century B.C." (p. 141). Guthrie includes an appendix of such passages on human progress, by Aeschylus, Sophocles, Euripides, Diodorus, Moschion, Critias, Sisyphus, and a passage from Isocrates' *Panegyricus,* which celebrates Athens rather than the faculty of speech (*The Sophists,* pp. 79–84). The passage by Sophocles is the only one to mention both speech and cities.

16. As Raymond Plant points out in his survey of the variety of ways "community" has been used in social and political theory, our understanding of the *polis* as a model of community is largely due to German philosophers and writers in the nineteenth century ("Community: Concept, Conception, and Ideology," *Politics and Society* 8 [1978]: 79–107).

17. *Order and History,* vol. 2: *The World of the Polis* (Baton Rouge: Louisiana State University Press, 1957), pp. 114–15; further references will be incorporated in the text. See also Ellen Meiksins Wood and Neal Wood, *Class Ideology and Ancient Political Theory: Socrates, Plato, and Aristotle in Social Context* (Oxford, UK: Basil Blackwell, 1978), pp. 15–20, with further references incorporated in the text, and Farrar, *Origins,* pp. 16–21.

18. Wood and Wood, *Class Ideology,* pp. 41–58.

19. *The Greeks* (Harmondsworth, Middlesex: Penguin, 1951), p. 75; further references will be incorporated in the text. See also George Henry Liddell and Robert Scott, *Greek–English Lexicon,* 9th (new) ed. (Oxford, UK: Clarendon Press, 1940), *polis* III.

20. Thucydides, *History of the Peloponnesian War,* trans. Charles Forster Smith (Cambridge, MA: Harvard University Press, 1919), II.x1.2.

21. Jürgen Gebhardt, "The Origins of Politics in Ancient Hellas: Old Interpretations and New Perspectives," *Sophia and Praxis: The Boundaries of Politics* (Chatham, NJ: Chatham House, 1984), p. 8. Kitto places the dates of most colonization as about 750–550 (*The Greeks,* p. 81).

22. On this point there has been a fair amount of recent scholarship. One book, for example, attempts to answer the question why citizenship in Athens was "considered 'worthy and sacred,' argued about, jealously guarded, and carefully maintained" in the classical period (Philip Brook Manville, *The Origin of Citizenship in Ancient Athens* (Princeton, NJ: Princeton University Press, 1990], p. 4). See also Christian Meier, *The Greek Discovery of Politics,* trans. David McLintock (Cam-

bridge, MA: Harvard University Press, 1990); and R. K. Sinclair, *Democracy and Participation in Athens* (Cambridge, UK: Cambridge University Press, 1988).

23. Wood and Wood, *Class Ideology*, p. 89; Voegelin, *Order and History*, p. 271; Havelock, *The Liberal Temper*, pp. 156, 230.

24. Kerferd, *The Sophistic Movement*, p. 82. Guthrie says "all the leading Sophists were deeply concerned with [rhetoric] . . . both as active practitioners and as teachers, systematizers and writers of rhetorical handbooks" (*The Sophists, p.* 176). Gorgias is thought to have written a treatise on rhetoric, which does not survive (Kerferd, *The Sophistic Movement*, p. 45); see also Mario Untersteiner, *The Sophists,* trans. Kathleen Freeman (Oxford, UK: Basil Blackwell, 1954), p. 96.

25. Havelock makes this point in a negative way, calling the sophistic interest in rhetoric "ancillary to a bigger thing" (*The Liberal Temper,* p. 230). He emphasizes the sophists' central concern with the processes of opinion formation and collective decision making, with "a sense of social and political responsibility" (p. 230), but seems unwilling to identify these with rhetoric. He does note at one point, however, that "political judgment, indeed, is hardly distinguishable from communication" (p. 193).

26. *Nicomachean Ethics*, X.1180a (trans. J. A. K. Thompson, rev. Hugh Tredennick [New York: Penguin, 1976]).

27. Most scholars believe that Plato represents Protagoras fairly (Guthrie, *The Sophists,* pp. 265–66; Kerferd, *The Sophistic Movement*, p. 125; Untersteiner, *The Sophists*, p. 72 n. 24; Voegelin, *Order and History*, p. 272). See also Edward Schiappa's summary of this consensus (*Protagoras and Logos: A Study in Greek Philosophy and Rhetoric* [Columbia: University of South Carolina Press, 1991], pp. 146–48; further references will be incorporated in the text). Guthrie assumes that Plato's rendition "substantially reproduces" Protagoras' lost work titled "On the Original State of Man" (*The Sophists*, pp. 63–64). Havelock is careful to note ways in which Plato may be misrepresenting Protagoras by relying on "a series of Socratic classifications" (*The Liberal Temper*, p. 91), although he agrees that the story contains "much that carries the stamp of genuine anthropology" (p. 92). He reads Plato's account against other evidence about Protagoreanism (pp. 165–66).

28. I am using the translation by Guthrie, in *Plato: The Collected Dialogues*, ed. Edith Hamilton and Huntington Cairns (Princeton, NJ: Princeton University Press, 1961), 322a–c.

29. See also Farrar: "Protagoras was . . . the first democratic political theorist in the history of the world" (*Origins,* p. 77); Havelock: "Here is a reasoned defense of democratic process as it obtained in the mother of all democracies" (*The Liberal Temper,* p. 170); and Donald Kagan, who calls the speech "the most subtle and sophisticated statement of democratic political theory of classical antiquity" (*The Great Dialogue: History of*

Greek Political Thought from Homer to Polybius [New York: Free Press, 1965], p. 81).

30. See "Protagoras" A-1, 13, 14, 16, 19, 20, 21, *The Older Sophists,* ed. Rosamund Kent Sprague (Columbia: University of South Carolina Press, 1972). Schiappa discusses each of these doctrines in detail, considering the varieties of translations and interpretations that are possible. He also considers the nature of Protagorean "relativism," finding it more complex and well grounded than Plato's accounts of it allow for (*Protagoras and Logos,* pp. 126–30). In several places, he suggests that Protagorean thinking is consistent with or an extension of that of Heraclitus.

31. Schiappa emphasizes that there are two distinct interpretations of this doctrine, based on changing meanings of the two key terms: the moralistic "better" and "worse" are late meanings that he believes were unlikely in Protagoras' time, while earlier uses imply a comparison of strength—e.g., "stronger" and "weaker" (ibid., pp. 103–7).

32. Guthrie calls Plato an advocate of *nomos* because he represents Socrates in the *Crito* as willingly subjecting himself to the laws of Athens (*The Sophists,* p. 141), but Wood and Wood note that Plato attacked the concept "vigorously" in the *Statesman* (*Class Ideology*, pp. 178–79).

33. Trans. Paul Shorey, *Plato: The Collected Dialogues.*

34. Trans. J. B. Skemp, *Plato: The Collected Dialogues.*

35. Trans. A. E. Taylor, *Plato: The Collected Dialogues.*

36. In the *Republic* (VIII 545–546) Plato gives a similar account of the inevitable decline of forms of government from democracy, through oligarchy, democracy, and inevitably to tyranny. Havelock's chapter on Plato's histories is called "History as Regress."

37. Both Havelock (*The Liberal Temper*, p. 43) and Wood and Wood (*Class Ideology*, p. 175) read the story in the *Statesman* as a direct contrast to the one in *Protagoras*. Here, the effect is primarily to degrade the various arts and trades by which ordinary men made their livings; this enables Plato to establish ruling as a separate special art in which those busied with inferior arts need have and can have no part.

38. James L. Kastely's recent rhetorical reading of *Gorgias* emphasizes the strategic quality of the incomplete account: "Plato wrote the dialogue to offer us Socrates to refute. . . . The dialogue hopes to engage its readers by giving an incomplete account of rhetoric" ("In Defense of Plato's *Gorgias,*" *PMLA* 106 [1991]: 107).

39. "Plato's View of Rhetoric," *Quarterly Journal of Speech* 44 (1958): 361–74; further references will be incorporated in the text. See also Wood and Wood's discussion of Plato's "argument from the arts," *Class Ideology*, pp. 129–34. I should make it dear that Black claims that Plato's attack in the *Gorgias* applies only to

"a particular practice of rhetoric" ("Plato's View," p. 366) and not to rhetoric in general.

40. *In Defense of Rhetoric* (Oxford, UK: Clarendon Press, 1988), pp. 141–47.

41. Trans. T. A. Sinclair, rev. Trevor J. Saunders (New York: Viking Penguin, 1981).

42. Trans. George A. Kennedy, *On Rhetoric: A Theory of Civic Discourse* (New York: Oxford University Press, 1991).

43. He also says that "Plurality of numbers is natural in a state; and the farther it moves away from plurality towards unity, the less a state it becomes and the more a household, and the household in turn an individual. . . . So even if it were possible to make such a unification, it ought not be done; it will destroy the state" (II.ii.1261a).

44. Josiah Ober notes that Aristotle must be talking about an ideal *polis*, not about Athens, since with some 20–40,000 citizens, Athens was too large for the citizens to know each other; he also cites Thucydides on this point (*Mass and Elite in Democratic Athens: Rhetoric, Ideology, and the Power of the People* [Princeton, NJ: Princeton University Press, 1989], pp. 32–33; further references will be incorporated in the text).

45. Hannah Arendt's interpretation of the relationship that Aristotle posits between the *polis* and the exercise of virtue (*arete*) is that community Life both affords increased opportunities for individuals to distinguish themselves by their achievements (through exercising their *arete*) and also ensures that they will win fame and immortality from those achievements (*The Human Condition* [Chicago: University of Chicago Press, 1958], p. 197). This rationale for the *polis* seems rooted in the older aristocratic culture rather than in the more egalitarian *ethos* that the *polis* itself helped create. See Vernant on the change in attitude toward individual *arete* that marked a "decisive turning point in the history of the *polis*" (*Origins*, p. 64).

46. Wood and Wood: "To put it briefly, the revolutionary nature of Plato's political thought lies in his attempt to 'aristocratize' the polis, or 'politicize' aristocracy—that is, to synthesize what were in their very essence antithetical forces in the history of Athens, the *aristocratic* principle and the *political* principle" (*Class Ideology*, p. 120; see also pp. 154–60).

47. H.-I. Marrou refers in passing to the Greek *polis* as "that men's club" (*A History of Education in Antiquity*, trans. George Lamb [1956; Madison: University of Wisconsin Press, 1982], p. 28). Ober uses the following population figures for Attica during the fourth century: 30,000 citizens, 10,000 adult male metics, 40–80,000 slaves, and a total population of 150–250,000 (*Mass and Elite*, p. 7 n. 8); these figures make citizens 10–20% of the total.

48. Wood and Wood, *Class Ideology*, pp. 44, 52; Ober, *Mass and Elite*, p. 195. According to Ober, the leisure class was probably quite small, somewhere between 1200 and 2000 citizens (ibid., p. 29), or 5–10% of citizens.

49. Also, "in the state with the finest constitution, which possesses men who are just absolutely and not relatively to the assumed situation, the citizens must not have a mechanical or commercial life. Such a life is not noble, and it militates against virtue. Nor must those who are to be citizens be agricultural workers, for they must have leisure to develop their virtue, and for the activities of a citizen" (*Politics* VII.ix.1328b).

50. Similarly, Guthrie suggests that "there is some justice in recent claims [about] the academic habit of relying too heavily on Plato and Aristotle as representative of the Greek mind" (*The Sophists*, p. 18), although his reference is not specifically to these political issues.

51. Wood and Wood claim that the "historical meaning" of the *polis* is "as a principle of association expressing the power and the right of the rising classes to challenge aristocratic supremacy" (*Class Ideology*, p. 124).

52. For example, Ernest C. Barker, *Greek Political Theory: Plato and His Predecessors* (London: Methuen, 1951; orig. pub. 1918), pp. 54, 71.

53. *Classical Rhetoric and Its Christian and Secular Tradition from Ancient to Modern Times* (Chapel Hill: University of North Carolina Press, 1980), p. 40.

54. I have explored the resources in current political and rhetorical thought of such a postmodern understanding in "Rhetoric and Community: The Problem of the One and the Many" (*Defining the New Rhetorics*, ed. Theresa Enos and Stuart C. Brown [Newbury Park, CA: Sage, 1993], pp. 79–94).

55. Kastely also makes this point in his discussion of *Gorgias*: "For pragmatic discourse, the polis is given and, in its obviousness, is not subject to examination" ("In Defense," p. 104). Another clue that the role of community went unrecognized lies in the unsatisfactory conceptualization of epideictic rhetoric, which we now see as fundamentally a project of community building.

56. For similar conceptions of community, see Ronald Beiner, *Political Judgment* (Chicago: University of Chicago Press, 1983): "political judgment entails an implied responsibility for the assumption of what may be termed a shared way of life" (p. 138) as well as Perelman and Olbrechts-Tyteca's notion of a "community of minds," quoted earlier. These conceptions are compatible with Anthony Giddens's notion that social structure is a "virtual order," meaning that such structure exists "only in its instantiations in . . . practices and as memory traces orienting the conduct of knowledgeable human agents" (*The Constitution of Society: Outline of the Theory of Structuration* [Berkeley: University of California Press, 1984], p. 17).

Publics and Counterpublics (abbreviated version)

Michael Warner

This essay has a public. If you are reading (or hearing) this, you are part of its public. So first let me say: welcome. Of course, you might stop reading (or leave the room), and someone else might start (or enter). Would the public of this essay therefore be different? Would it ever be possible to know anything about the public to which, I hope, you still belong? What is a public? It is a curiously obscure question, considering that few things have been more important in the development of modernity. Publics have become an essential fact of the social landscape, yet it would tax our understanding to say exactly what they are.

Several senses of the noun *public* tend to be intermixed in usage. People do not always distinguish even between *the* public and *a* public, although in other contexts the difference can matter a great deal. *The* public is a kind of social totality. Its most common sense is that of the people in general. A public can also be a second thing: a concrete audience, a crowd witnessing itself in visible space, as with a theatrical public. Such a public also has a sense of totality, bounded by the event or by the shared physical space. A performer on stage knows where her public is, how big it is, where its boundaries are, and what the time of its common existence is. A crowd at a sports event, a concert, or a riot might be a bit blurrier around the edges, but still knows itself by knowing where and when it is assembled in common visibility and common action.

I will return to both of these senses, but what I mainly want to clarify in this essay is a third sense: the kind of public that comes into being only in relation to texts and their circulation—like the public of this essay. (Nice to have you with us, still.)

The distinctions among these three senses are not always sharp, and are not simply the difference between oral and written contexts. When an essay is read aloud as a lecture at a university, for example, the concrete audience of hearers understands itself as standing in for a more indefinite audience of readers. And often, when a form of discourse is not addressing an institutional or subcultural audience like a profession, its audience can understand itself not just as *a* public but as *the* public. In such cases, different senses of audience and circulation are in play at once. They suggest that it is worth understanding the distinctions better, if only because the transpositions among them can have important social effects.

1) A public is self-organized.

A public is a space of discourse organized by nothing other than discourse itself. It is autotelic; it exists only as the end for which books are published, shows broadcast, websites posted, speeches delivered, opinions produced. It exists *by virtue of being addressed.*

A kind of chicken-and-egg circularity confronts us in the idea of a public. Could anyone speak publicly without addressing a public? But how can this public exist before being addressed? What would a public be if no one were addressing it? Can a public really exist apart from the rhetoric through which it is imagined? If you were to put down this essay and turn on the television, would the public be different? How can the existence of a public depend, from one point of view, on the rhetorical address, and, from another point of view, on the real context of reception?

These questions cannot be resolved on one side or the other. The circularity is essential to the phenomenon. A public might be real and efficacious, but its reality lies in just this reflexivity by which an addressable object is conjured into being in order to enable the very discourse that gives it existence.

A public in this sense is as much notional as empirical. It is also partial, since there could be an infinite number of publics within the social totality. This sense of the term is completely modern; it is the only kind of public for which there is no other term. Neither crowd nor audience nor people nor group will capture the same sense. The difference shows us that the idea of a public, unlike a concrete audience or the public of any polity, is text-based—even though publics are increasingly organized around visual or audio texts. Without the idea of texts that can be picked up at different times and in different places by otherwise unrelated people, we would not imagine a public as an entity that embraces all the users of that text, whoever they might be. Often the texts themselves are not even recognized as texts—as for example with visual advertising or the chattering of a DJ—but the publics they bring into being are still discursive in the same way.

The strangeness of this kind of public is often hidden from view because the assumptions of the bourgeois public sphere allow us to think of a discourse public as a people, and therefore as a really existing set of potentially numerable humans. A public, in practice, appears as *the* public. It is easy to be misled by this appearance. Even in the blurred usage of the public sphere, a public is never just a congeries of people, never just the sum of persons who happen to exist. It must first of all have some way of organizing itself as a body, and of being addressed in discourse. And not just any way of defining the totality will do. It must be organized by something other than the state.

Here we see how the autotelic circularity of the discourse public is not just a puzzle for analysis, but also the crucial factor in the social importance of the form. A public organizes itself independently of state institutions, law, formal frameworks of citizenship, or preexisting institutions such as the church. If it were not possible to think of the public as organized independently of the state or other frameworks, the public could not be sovereign with respect to the state. So the modern sense of the public as the social totality in fact derives much of its character from the way we understand the partial publics of discourse, like the public of this essay, as self-organized. The way *the public* functions in the public sphere (as the people) is only possible because it is really *a* public of discourse. It is self-creating and self-organized, and herein lies its power, as well as its elusive strangeness.

In the kind of modern society that the idea of publics has enabled, the self-organization of discourse publics has immense resonance from the point of view of individuals. Speaking, writing, and thinking involve us—actively and immediately—in a public, and thus in the being of the sovereign. Imagine how powerless people would feel if their commonality and participation were simply defined by pre-given frameworks, by institutions and law, as in other social contexts it is defined through kinship. What would the world look like if all ways of being public were more like applying for a driver's license or subscribing to a professional group—if, that is, formally organized mediations replaced the self-organized public as the image of belonging and common activity? Such is the image of totalitarianism: non-kin society organized by bureaucracy and law. Everyone's position, function, and capacity for action [are] specified for her by administration. The powerlessness of the person in such a world haunts modern capitalism as well. Our lives are minutely administered and recorded, to a degree unprecedented in history; we navigate a world of corporate agents that do not respond or act as people do. Our personal capacities, such as credit, turn out on reflection to be expressions of corporate agency. Without a faith—justified or not—in self-organized publics, organically linked to our activity in their very existence, capable of being addressed, and capable of action, we would be nothing but the peasants of capital—which of course we might be, and some of us more than others.

In the idea of a public, political confidence is committed to a strange and uncertain destination. Sometimes it can seem too strange. Often one cannot imagine addressing a public capable of comprehension or action. This is especially true for people in minor or marginal positions, or people distributed across political systems. The result can be a kind of political depressiveness, a blockage in activity and optimism, a disintegration of politics toward isolation, frustration, anomie, forgetfulness. This possibility, never far out of the picture, reveals by contrast how much ordinary belonging requires confidence in a public. Confidence in the possibility of a public is not simply the professional habit of the powerful, of the pundits and wonks and reaction-shot secondary celebrities who try to perform our publicness for us; the same confidence remains vital for people whose place in public media is one of consuming, witnessing, griping, or gossiping rather than one of full participation, or fame. Whether faith is justified or partly ideological, a public can only produce a sense of belonging and activity if it is self-organized through discourse rather than through an external framework. This is why any distortion or blockage in access to a public can be so grave, leading people to feel powerless and frustrated. Externally organized frameworks of activity, such as voting, are and are perceived to be a poor substitute.

Yet perhaps just because it does seem so important to belong to a public, or to be able to know something about the public to which one belongs, such substitutes have been produced in abundance. People have tried hard to find, or make, some external way of identifying the public, of resolving its circularity into either chicken or egg. The idea that the public might be as changeable, and as unknowable, as the public of this essay (are you still with me?) seems to weaken the very political optimism that the accessibility of the public allows.

Pollsters and some social scientists think that their method is a way to define a public as a group that could be studied empirically, independently from its own discourse about itself. Early in the history of research in communication theory and public relations, it was recognized that such research was going to be difficult, since multiple publics exist and one can belong to many different publics simultaneously. Public opinion researchers have a long history of unsatisfying debate about this problem in method. What determines whether one belongs to a public or not? Space and physical presence do not make much difference; a public is understood to be different from a crowd, an audience, or any other group that requires copresence. Personal identity does not in itself make one part of a public. Publics differ from nations, races, professions, or any other groups that, though not requiring copresence, saturate identity. Belonging to a public seems to require at least minimal participation, even if it is patient or notional, rather than a permanent state of being. Merely paying attention can be enough to make you a member. How then could a public be quantified?[1]

Some have tried to define a public in terms of a common interest, speaking for example of a foreign-policy public, or a sports public. But this way of speaking only pretends to escape the conundrum of the self-creating public. It is like explaining the popularity of films or novels as a response to market demand; the claim is circular, because market "demand" is inferred from the popularity of the works themselves. The idea of a common interest, like that of a market demand, appears to identify the social base of public discourse, but the base is in fact projected from the public discourse itself, rather than external to it.

Of all the contrivances designed to escape this circularity, the most powerful by far has been the invention of polling. Polling, together with related forms of market research, tries to tell us what the interests, desires, and demands of a public are, without simply inferring them from public discourse. It is an elaborate apparatus designed to characterize a public as social fact independent of any discursive address or circulation. As Pierre Bourdieu pointed out, however, this method proceeds by denying the constitutive role of polling itself as a mediating form.[2] Habermas and others have stressed that the device now systematically distorts the public sphere, producing something that passes as public opinion when in fact it results from a form that has none of the open-endedness, reflexive framing, or accessibility of public discourse. I would add that it lacks the embodied creativity and world-making of publicness. Publics have to be understood as mediated by cultural forms, even though some of those forms, such as polling, work by denying their own constitutive role as cultural forms. Publics do not exist apart from the discourse that addresses them.

Are they therefore internal to discourse? Literary studies often [have] understood a public as a rhetorical addressee, implied within texts. But the term is generally understood to name something about the text's worldliness, its actual destination, which may or may not resemble its addressee. Benjamin Franklin's autobiography, to take a famous example, remained addressed to his son even after Franklin severed relations with that son and decided to publish the text; the public of the autobiography was crucially nonidentical with its addressee. Of course one can distinguish in such a case between the nominal addressee and the implied addressee, but it is equally possible to distinguish between an implied addressee of rhetoric and a targeted public of circulation. That these are not identical is what allows people to shape the public by addressing it in a certain way. It also allows people to fail, if a rhetorical addressee is not picked up as the reflection of a public.

The sense that a public is a worldly constraint on speech, and not just a free creation of speech, gives plausibility to the opposite approach of the social sciences. The self-organized nature of the public does not mean that it is always spontaneous or organically expressive of individuals' wishes. Although the premise of self-organizing discourse is necessary to the peculiar cultural artifact that we call a public, it is contradicted both by material limits—means of production and distribution, the physical textual objects, social conditions of access—and by internal ones, including the need to presuppose forms of intelligibility already in place, as well as the social closure entailed by any selection of genre, idiolect, style, address, and so on. I will return to these constraints of circulation. For the moment I want to emphasize that they are made to seem arbitrary because of the performativity of public address and the self-organization implied by the idea of a public.

Another way of saying the same thing is that any empirical extension of the public will seem arbitrarily limited because the addressee of public discourse is always yet to be realized. In some contexts of speech and writing, both the rhetorical addressee and the public have a fairly clear empirical referent: in correspondence and most e-mail, in the reports and memos that are passed up and down bureaucracies, in love notes and valentines and dear john letters, the object of address is understood to be an identifiable person or office. Even if that addressee is already a generalized role—for example, a personnel committee, or Congress, or a church congregation—it is definite, known, nameable, and numerable. The interaction is framed by a social relationship.

But for another class of writing contexts—including literary criticism, journalism, "theory," advertising, fiction, drama, most poetry—the available addressees are essentially imaginary, which is not to say unreal: the people, scholarship, the republic of letters, posterity, the younger generation, the nation, the left, the movement, the world, the vanguard, the enlightened few, right-thinking people everywhere, public opinion, the brotherhood of all believers, humanity, my fellow queers. These are all publics. They are in principle open-ended. They exist by virtue of their address.

2) A public is a relation among strangers.

Other kinds of writing—writing that has a definite addressee who can be known in advance—can, of course, go astray. Writing to a public incorporates that tendency of writing or speech as a condition of possibility. It cannot in the same way go astray, because reaching strangers is its primary orientation. In modernity this understanding of the public is best illustrated by uses of print or electronic media, but it can also be extended to scenes of audible speech, if that speech is oriented to indefinite strangers, once the crucial background horizon of "public opinion" and its social imaginary has been made available. We have become capable of recognizing ourselves as strangers even when we know each other. Declaiming this essay to a group of intimates, I could still be heard as addressing a public.

Once this kind of public is in place as a social imaginary, I might add, stranger sociability inevitably takes on a different character. In modern society, a stranger is not as marvelously exotic as the wandering outsider would have been to an ancient, medieval, or early modern town. In that earlier social order, or in contemporary analogues, a stranger is mysterious, a disturbing presence requiring resolution.[3] In the context of a public, however, strangers can be treated as already belonging to our world. More: they *must* be. We are routinely oriented to them in common life. They are a normal feature of the social. Strangers in the ancient sense—foreign, alien, misplaced—might of course be placed to a degree by Christendom, the *ummah*, a guild, or an army—affiliations one might share with strangers, making them a bit less strange. Strangers placed by means of these affiliations are on a path to commonality. Publics orient us to strangers in a different way. They are no longer merely people-whom-one-does-not-yet-know; rather, an environment of strangerhood is the necessary premise of some of our most prized ways of being. Where otherwise strangers need to be on a path to commonality, in modern forms strangerhood is the necessary medium of commonality. The modern social imaginary does not make sense without strangers. A nation or public or market in which everyone could be known personally would be no nation or public or market at all. This constitutive and normative environment of strangerhood is more, too, than an objectively describable *gesellschaft*; it requires our constant imagining.

3) The address of public speech is both personal and impersonal.

Public speech can have great urgency and intimate import. Yet we know that it was addressed not exactly to us, but to the stranger we were until the moment we happened to be addressed by it. (I am thinking here of any genre addressed to a public, including novels and lyrics as well as criticism, other nonfictional prose, and almost all genres of radio, television, film, and web discourse.) To inhabit public discourse is to perform this transition continually, and to some extent it remains present to consciousness. Public speech must be taken in two ways: as addressed to us and as addressed to strangers. The benefit in this practice is that it gives a general social relevance to private thought and life. Our subjectivity is understood as having resonance with others, and immediately so. But this is only true to the extent that the trace of our strangerhood remains present in our understanding of ourselves as the addressee.

This necessary element of impersonality in public address is one of the things missed from view in the Althusserian notion of interpellation, at least as it is currently understood. Althusser's famous example is speech addressed to a stranger: a policeman says, "Hey, you!" In the moment of recognizing oneself as the person addressed, the moment of turning around, one is interpellated as the subject of state discourse.[4] Althusser's analysis had the virtue of showing the importance of imaginary identification, and locating it not in the coercive or punitive force of the state but in the subjective practice of understanding. When the model of interpellation is extracted from such examples to account for public culture generally, the analysis will be skewed because the case Althusser gives is not an example of public discourse. A policeman who says, "Hey, you!" will be understood to be addressing a particular person, not a public. When one turns around, it is partly to see whether one is that person. If not, one goes on. If so, then all

the others who might be standing on the street are bystanders, not addressees. With public speech, by contrast, we might recognize ourselves as addressees, but it is equally important that we remember that the speech was addressed to indefinite others, that in singling us out it does *so* not on the basis of our concrete identity, but by virtue of our participation in the discourse alone, and therefore in common with strangers. It isn't just that we are addressed in public as certain kinds of persons, or that we might not want to identify as that person (though this is also often enough the case, as when the public is addressed as heterosexual, or white, or sports-minded, or American). We have not been misidentified, exactly. It seems more to the point to say that publics are different from persons, that the address of public rhetoric is never going to be the same as address to actual persons, and that our partial nonidentity with the object of address in public speech seems to be part of what it means to regard something as public speech.

The appeal to strangers in the circulating forms of public address thus helps us to distinguish public discourse from forms that address particular persons in their singularity. It remains less clear how a public could be translated into an image of *the* public, a social entity. Who is the public? Does it include my neighbors? The doorman in my building? My students? The people who show up in the gay bars and clubs? The bodega owners down the street from me? Someone who calls me on the phone, or sends me an e-mail? You? We encounter people in such disparate contexts that the idea of a body to which they all belong, and in which they could be addressed in speech, seems to have something wishful about it. To address a public we don't go around saying the same thing to all these people. We say it in a venue of indefinite address, and hope that people will find themselves in it. The difference can be a source of frustration, but it is also a direct implication of the self-organization of the public as a body of strangers united through the circulation of their discourse, without which public address would have none of its special importance to modernity.

4) A public is constituted through mere attention.

Most social classes and groups are understood to encompass their members all the time, no matter what. A nation, for example, includes its members whether they are awake or asleep, sober or drunk, sane or deranged, alert or comatose. Because a public exists only by virtue of address, it must predicate some degree of attention, however notional, of its members.

The cognitive quality of that attention is less important than the mere fact of active uptake. Attention is the principal sorting category by which members and nonmembers are discriminated. If you are reading this, or hearing it or seeing it or present for it, you are part of this public. You might be multi-tasking at the computer; the television might be on while you are vacuuming the carpet; or you might have wandered into hearing range of the speaker's podium in a convention hall only because it was on your way to the bathroom. No matter: by coming into range you fulfill the only entry condition demanded by a public. It is even possible for us to understand someone sleeping through a ballet performance as a member of that ballet's public, because most contemporary ballet performances are organized as voluntary events, open to anyone willing to attend or, in most cases, to pay to attend. The act of attention involved in showing up is enough to create an addressable public. Some kind of active uptake, however somnolent, is indispensable.

The existence of a public is contingent on its members' activity, however notional or compromised, and not on its members' categorical classification, objectively determined position in social structure, or material existence. In the self-understanding that makes them work, publics thus resemble the model of voluntary association that is so important to civil society. Since the early modern period more and more institutions have come to conform to this model. The old idea of an established national church, for example, allowed the church to address itself to parish members literate or illiterate, virtuous or vicious, competent or idiotic. Increasingly, churches in a multidenominational world must think of themselves instead as contingent on their members; they welcome newcomers, keep membership rolls, and solicit attention. Some doctrinal emphases, like that on faith or conversion, make it possible for churches to orient themselves to that active uptake on which they are increasingly dependent.

Still, one can join a church and then stop going. In some cases one can even be born into one. Publics, by contrast, lacking any institutional being, commence with the moment of attention, must continually predicate renewed attention, and cease to exist when attention is no longer predicated. They are virtual entities, not voluntary associations. Because their threshold of belonging is an active uptake, however, they can be understood within the conceptual framework of civil society; i.e., as having a free, voluntary, and active membership. Wherever a liberal conception of personality obtains, the moment of uptake that constitutes a public can be seen as an expression of volition on the part of its members. And this fact has enormous consequences. It allows us to understand publics as scenes of self-activity, of historical rather than timeless belonging, and of active participation rather than ascriptive belonging. Under the right conditions, it even allows us to attribute agency to a public, even though that public has no institutional being or concrete manifestation.

Public discourse craves attention like a child. Texts clamor at us. Images solicit our gaze. Look here! Listen! Hey! In doing so they by no means render us passive. Quite the contrary. The modern system of publics creates a demanding social phenomenology. Our willingness to process a passing appeal determines which publics we belong to, and performs their extension. The experience of social reality in modernity feels quite unlike that of societies organized by kinship, hereditary status, local affiliation, mediated political access, parochial nativity, or ritual. In those settings, one's place in the common order is what it is regardless of one's inner thoughts, however intense their affective charge might sometimes be. The appellative energy of publics puts a different burden on us: it makes us believe our consciousness to be decisive. The direction of our glance can constitute our social world.

The themes I've discussed so far—the self-organization of publics through discourse, their orientation to strangers, the resulting ambiguity of personal and impersonal address, membership by mere attention—can be clarified if we remember their common assumption, which goes a long way toward explaining the historical development of the other four:

5) A public is the social space created by the reflexive circulation of discourse.

This dimension is easy to forget if we think only about a speech event involving speaker and addressee. In that localized exchange, circulation may seem irrelevant, extraneous. That is one reason why sender/receiver or author/reader models of public communication are so misleading. No single text can create a public. Nor can a single voice, a single genre, even a single medium. All are insufficient to create the kind of reflexivity that we call a public, since a public is understood to be an ongoing space of encounter for discourse. Texts themselves do not create publics, but the concatenation of texts through time. Only when a previously existing discourse can be supposed, and when a responding discourse can be postulated, can a text address a public.

Between the discourse that comes before and the discourse that comes after one must postulate some kind of link. And the link has a social character; it is not mere consecutiveness in time, but a context of interaction. The usual way of imagining the interactive character of public discourse is through metaphors of conversation, answering, talking back, deliberating. The interactive social relation of a public, in other words, is perceived as though it were a dyadic speaker/hearer or author/reader relation. Argument and polemic, as manifestly dialogic genres, continue to have a privileged role in the self-understanding of publics. Indeed, it is remarkable how little work in even the most sophisticated forms of theory has been able to disentangle public discourse from its self-understanding as conversation.[5] In addressing a public, however, even texts of the most rigorously argumentative and dialogic genres also address onlookers, not just parties to argument. They try to characterize the field of possible interplay. When appearing in a public field, genres of argument and polemic must accommodate themselves to the special conditions of public address; the agonistic interlocutor is coupled with passive interlocutors, known enemies with indifferent strangers, parties present to a dialogue situation with parties whose textual location might be in other genres or scenes of circulation entirely. The meaning of any utterance depends on what is known and anticipated from all these different quarters. In public argument or polemic, the principal act is that of projecting the field of argument itself—its genres, its range of circulation, its stakes, its idiom, its repertoire of agencies. Any position is reflexive, not only asserting itself but characterizing its relation to other positions up to limits which are the imagined scene of circulation. The interactive relation postulated in public discourse, in other words, goes far beyond the scale of conversation or discussion, to encompass a multigeneric lifeworld organized not just by a relational axis of utterance and response but by potentially infinite axes of citation and characterization.

6) Publics act historically according to the temporality of their circulation.

The punctual time of circulation is crucial to the sense that discussion is currently unfolding in a sphere of activity. It is not timeless, like meditation; nor is it without issue, like speculative philosophy. Not all circulation happens at the same rate, of course, and this accounts for the dramatic differences among publics in their relation to possible scenes of activity. A public can only act in the temporality of the circulation that gives it existence. The more punctual and abbreviated the circulation, and the more discourse indexes the punctuality of its own circulation, the closer a public stands to politics. At longer rhythms or more continuous flows, action becomes harder to imagine. This is the fate of academic publics, a fact little understood when academics claim by intention or proclamation to be doing politics. In modernity, politics takes much of its character from the temporality of the headline, not the archive.

Publics have an ongoing life: one doesn't publish to them once for all (as one does, say, to a scholarly archive). It is the way texts circulate, and become the basis for further representations, that convinces us that publics have activity and duration. A text, to have a public, must continue to circulate through time, and because this can only be confirmed through an intertextual environment of citation and implication, all publics are intertextual, even intergeneric. This is often missed from view because the activity and duration of publics is commonly stylized as conversation or decision making. I have already suggested that these are misleading ideologizations. Now we can see why they are durable illusions: because they confer agency on publics. There is no moment at which the conversation stops and a decision ensues, outside of elections, and those are given only by legal frameworks, not by publics themselves. Yet the ideologization is crucial to the sense that publics act in secular time. To sustain this sense, public discourse indexes itself temporally with respect to moments of publication and a common calendar of circulation.

One way that the internet and other new media may be profoundly changing the public sphere, by the way, is through the change they imply in temporality. Highly mediated and highly capitalized forms of circulation are increasingly organized as continuous ("24/7 instant access") rather than punctual.[6] At the time of this writing, web discourse has very little of the citational field that would allow us to speak of it as discourse unfolding through time. Once a website is up, it can be hard to tell how recently it was posted or revised, or how long it will continue to be posted. Most sites are not archived. For the most part they are not centrally indexed. The reflexive apparatus of web discourse consists mostly of hypertext links and search engines, and these are not punctual. So although there are exceptions, including the migration of some print serials to electronic format and the successful use of the web by some social movements, it remains unclear to what extent the changing technology will be assimilable to the temporal framework of public discourse.[7] If the change of infrastructure continues at this pace, and if modes of apprehension change accordingly, the absence of punctual rhythms may make it very difficult to connect localized acts of reading to the modes of agency in the social imaginary of modernity. It may even be necessary to abandon "circulation" as an analytic category. But here I merely offer this topic for speculation.

7) A public is poetic world making.

In a public, indefinite address and self-organized discourse disclose a lived world whose arbitrary closure both enables that discourse and is contradicted by it. Public discourse, in the nature of its address, abandons the security of its positive, given audience. It promises to address anybody. It commits itself in principle to the possible participation of any stranger. It therefore puts at risk the concrete world that is its given condition of possibility. This is its fruitful perversity. Public discourse postulates a circulatory field of estrangement which it must then struggle to capture as an addressable entity. No form with such a structure could be very stable. The projective character of public discourse, in which each characterization of the circulatory path becomes material for new estrangements and recharacterizations, is an engine for (not necessarily progressive) social mutation.

Public discourse, in other words, is poetic. By this I mean not just that it is self-organizing, a kind of entity created by its own discourse, nor even that this space of circulation is taken to be a social entity, but that in order for this to happen all discourse or performance addressed to a public must characterize the world in which it attempts to circulate, and it must attempt to realize that world through address.[8] There is no speech or performance addressed to a public that does not try to specify in advance, in countless highly condensed ways, the lifeworld of its circulation: not just through its discursive claims—of the kind that can be said to be oriented to understanding—but through the pragmatics of its speech genres, idioms, stylistic markers, address, temporality, mise en scène, citational field, interlocutory protocols, lexicon, and so on. Its circulatory fate is the realization of that world. Public discourse says not only, "Let a public exist," but "Let it have this character, speak this way, see the world in this way." It then goes out in search of confirmation that such a public exists, with greater or lesser success—success being further attempts to cite, circulate, and realize the world understanding it articulates. Run it up the flagpole and see who salutes. Put on a show and see who shows up.

This performative dimension of public discourse, however, is routinely misrecognized. Public speech lies under the necessity of addressing its public as already existing real persons. It cannot work by frankly declaring its subjunctive-creative project. Its success depends on the recognition of participants and their further circulatory activity, and people do not commonly recognize themselves as virtual projections. They recognize themselves only as being already the persons they are addressed as being, and as already belonging to the world that is condensed in their discourse.

The poetic function of public discourse is misrecognized for a second reason as well, noted above in another context: in the dominant tradition of the public sphere, address to a public is ideologized as rational-critical dialogue. The circulation of public discourse is consistently imagined, both in folk theory and in sophisticated political philosophy, as dialogue or discussion among already copresent interlocutors. The prevailing image is something like parliamentary forensics. I have already noted that this folk theory enables the constitutive circularity of publics to disappear from consciousness, because publics are thought to be real persons in dyadic author/reader interactions, rather than multigeneric circulation. I have also noted that the same ideologization enables the idea that publics can have volitional agency: they exist so as to deliberate and then decide. Here the point is that the perception of public discourse as conversation obscures the importance of the poetic functions of both language and corporeal expressivity in giving a particular shape to publics. The public is thought to exist empirically, and to require persuasion rather than poesis. Public circulation is understood as rational discussion writ large.

This constitutive misrecognition of publics relies on a particular language ideology. Discourse is understood to be propositionally summarizable; the poetic or textual qualities of any utterance are disregarded in favor of sense. Acts of reading, too, are understood to be replicable and uniform.[9] So are opinions, which is why private reading seems to be directly connected to the sovereign power of public opinion. Just as sense can be propositionally summarized, opinions can be held, transferred, restated indefinitely. (The essential role played by this kind of transposition in the modern social imaginary might help to explain why modern philosophy has been obsessed with referential semantics and fixity.) Other aspects of discourse, including affect and expressivity, are not thought to be fungible in the same way. Doubtless the development of such a language ideology helped to enable the confidence in the stranger sociability of public circulation. Strangers are less strange if you can trust them to read as you read, or if the sense of what they say can be fully abstracted from the way they say it.

I also suspect that the development of the social imaginary of publics, as a relation among strangers projected from private readings of circulating texts, has exerted for the past three centuries a powerful gravity on the conception of the human, elevating what are understood to be the faculties of the private reader as the essential (rational-critical) faculties of man. If you know and are intimately associated with strangers to whom you are directly related only through the means of reading, opining, arguing, and witnessing, then it might seem natural that other faculties recede from salience at the highest levels of social belonging. The modern hierarchy of faculties and its imagination of the social are mutually implying. The critical discourse of the public corresponds as sovereign to the superintending power of the state. So the dimensions of language singled out in the ideology of rational-critical discussion acquire prestige and power. Publics more overtly oriented in their self-understandings to the poetic-expressive dimensions of language, including artistic publics and many counterpublics, lack the power to transpose themselves to the generality of the state. Along the entire chain of equations in the public sphere from local acts of reading or scenes of speech to a general horizon of public opinion and its critical opposition to state power, the pragmatics of public discourse must be systematically blocked from view.

The unity of *the* public depends on the stylization of the reading act as transparent and replicable; it depends on an arbitrary social closure (through language, idiolect, genre, medium, and address) to contain its potentially infinite extension; it depends on institutionalized forms of power to realize the agency attributed to the public; and it depends on a hierarchy of faculties that allows some activities to count as public or general, while others are thought to be merely personal, private, or particular. Some publics, for these reasons, are more likely than others to stand in for *the* public, to frame their address as the universal discussion of the people.

But what of the publics that make no attempt to present themselves this way? Their members are understood to be not merely a subset of the public, but constituted through a conflictual relation to the dominant public. They are structured by different dispositions or protocols from those that obtain elsewhere in the culture, making different assumptions about what can be said or what goes without saying. In the sense of the term that I am here advocating, such publics are counterpublics, and in a stronger sense than simply comprising subalterns with a reform program. A counterpublic maintains at some level, conscious or not, an awareness of its subordinate status. The cultural horizon against which it marks itself off is not just a general or wider public but a dominant one. And the conflict extends not just to ideas or policy questions, but to the speech genres and modes of address that constitute the public, or to the hierarchy among media. The discourse that constitutes it is not merely a different or alternative idiom, but one that in other contexts would be regarded with hostility, or with a sense of indecorousness.

Like all publics, a counterpublic comes into being through an address to indefinite strangers. (This is one significant difference between the notion of a counterpublic and the notion of a community or group.) But counterpublic discourse also addresses those strangers as being not just anybody. They are socially marked by their participation in this kind of discourse; ordinary people are presumed not to want to be mistaken for the kind of person that would participate in this kind of talk, or to be present in this kind of scene. Addressing indefinite strangers, in a magazine or a sermon, has a peculiar meaning when you know in advance that most people will be unwilling to read a gay magazine or go to a black church. In some contexts, the code-switching of bilingualism might do similar work of keeping the counterpublic horizon salient—just as the linguistic fragmentation of many postcolonial settings creates resistance to the idea of a sutured space of circulation.

Within a gay or queer counterpublic, for example, no one is in the closet: the presumptive heterosexuality that constitutes the closet for individuals in ordinary speech is suspended. But this circulatory space, freed from heteronormative speech protocols, is itself marked by that very suspension: speech that addresses any participant as queer will circulate up to a point, at which it is certain to meet intense resistance. It might therefore circulate in special, protected venues, in limited publications. The individual struggle with stigma is transposed, as it were, to the conflict between modes of publicness. The expansive nature of public address will seek to keep moving that frontier for a queer public, to seek more and more places to circulate where people will recognize themselves in its address, but no one is likely to be unaware of the risk and conflict involved.

In some cases, such as fundamentalism or certain kinds of youth culture, participants are not subalterns for any reason other than their participation in the counterpublic discourse. In others, a socially stigmatized identity might be predicated, but in such cases a public of subalterns is only a counterpublic when its participants are addressed in a counterpublic way—as, for example, African Americans willing to speak in what is regarded as a racially marked idiom. The subordinate status of a counterpublic does not simply reflect identities formed elsewhere; participation in such a public is one of the ways by which its members' identities are formed and transformed. A hierarchy or stigma is the assumed background of practice. One enters at one's own risk.

Counterpublic discourse is far more than the expression of subaltern culture, and far more than what some Foucauldians like to call "reverse discourse." Fundamentally mediated by public forms, counterpublics incorporate the personal/impersonal address and expansive estrangement of public speech as the condition of their common world. Perhaps nothing demonstrates the fundamental importance of discursive publics in the modern social imaginary more than this—that even the counterpublics that challenge modernity's social hierarchy of faculties do so by projecting the space of discursive circulation among strangers as a social entity, and in doing so fashion their own subjectivities around the requirements of public circulation and stranger sociability.[10]

NOTES

1. An instructive review of the methodological problems can be found in *Communications and Public Opinion: A Public Opinion Quarterly Reader,* ed. Robert O. Carlson (New York: Praeger, 1975); see especially Floyd D. Allport, "Toward a Science of Public Opinion," 11–26; and Harwood Childs, "By Public Opinion I Mean—", 28–37.

2. The critique of polling appears in a number of contexts in Bourdieu's work; see especially "Opinion Polls: A 'Science' without a Scientist," in Pierre Bourdieu, *In Other Words: Essays Towards a Reflexive Sociology,* trans. Matthew Adamson (Stanford: Stanford University Press, 1990), 168–76.

3. This ancient exotic is the kind of stranger that Georg Simmel has in mind in his much-cited 1908 essay "The Stranger," in Georg Simmel, *On Individuality and Social Forms* (Chicago: University of Chicago Press, 1971). Simmel fails to distinguish between the stranger as represented by the trader or the Wandering Jew and the stranger whose presence in modernity is unremarkable, even necessary to the nature of modern polities. One of the defining elements of modernity, in my view, is normative stranger sociability, of a kind that seems to arise only when the social imaginary is defined not by kinship (as in nonstate societies), nor by place (as in state societies until modernity) but by discourse.

4. Louis Althusser, "Ideology and Ideological State Apparatuses," in *Lenin and Philosophy and Other Essays* (New York: Monthly Review Press, 1971), 127–86.

5. For an example of a promising and rich analysis marred by this misapprehension, see Nina Eliasoph, *Avoiding Politics: How Americans Produce Apathy in Everyday Life* (Cambridge, UK: Cambridge University Press, 1998). Eliasoph's stated but unexamined ideal is that of a continuity of *discussion* from small-scale interaction to the highest organizing levels of politics.

6. Eyal Amiran discusses the temporality of electronic media, in a way that differs substantially from mine, in his "Electronic Time and the Serials Revolution," *Yale Journal of Criticism* 10 (1997): 445–454.

7. It is difficult to assess this change not simply because the effects of change in the medium have yet to become visible, but because the infrastructure of the medium is itself changing. On this the best account I know is Lawrence Lessig, *Code and Other Laws of Cyberspace* (New York: Basic Books, 1999). Lessig's book, although focused on the legal regulation of cyberspace, also raises important topics for the more general discussion of new media and their social implications.

8. Even if the address is indirect. The most insightful study I know of the tight relation between a public form and a mode of life is an example of indirect implication of a reception context by a form that refuses to address it outright: I am thinking of D. A. Miller's *Place*

for Us: An Essay on the Broadway Musical (Cambridge, MA: Harvard University Press, 2000).

9. In all the literature on the history of reading, the development of this ideology remains an understudied phenomenon. Adrian Johns makes a significant contribution in *The Nature of the Book: Print and Knowledge in the Making* (Chicago: University of Chicago Press, 1998), especially pp. 380–443. Johns's study suggests that the idea of reading as a private act with replicable meaning for strangers dispersed through space emerged in the very period that gave rise to publics in the modern form analyzed here; support for this conjecture can also be found in Kevin Sharpe, *Reading Revolutions: The Politics of Reading in Early Modern England* (New Haven, CT: Yale University Press, 2000); Guglielmo Cavallo and Roger Chartier, eds., *A History of Reading in the West* (Amherst: Univ. of Massachusetts Press, 1999); and James Raven, Helen Small, and Naomi Tadmore, eds., *The Practice and Representation of Reading in England* (Cambridge, MA: Cambridge University Press, 1996).

10. For an interesting limit case, see Charles Hirschkind, "Civic Virtue within Egypt's Islamic Counter-Public," *Cultural Anthropology* 16.1 (2001). Hirschkind analyzes complex modes of commentary and circulation in contemporary Egypt; what remains unclear is the degree to which this emergent and reactive discourse culture can still be called a public.

Public Identity and Collective Memory in U.S. Iconic Photography

The Image of "Accidental Napalm"

Robert Hariman
John Louis Lucaites

The growing scholarly attention to visual culture has special significance for those who study mass media, which now are using ever more sophisticated technologies of visual imaging. For the most part, however, the analysis of visual media has been guided by a hermeneutics of suspicion (Jay, 1993; Postman, 1985; Peters, 1997). From this perspective, it is unlikely that a visual practice could ever be equal or superior to discursive media for enacting public reason or democratic deliberation, or that the constitution of identity through the continual reproduction of conventional images could be emancipatory. Indeed, this skepticism imbues the two most important theoretical perspectives on the relationship between discourse and society: ideology critique and the theory of the public sphere.

Although Jürgen Habermas's account of the rise and fall of an ideal public culture has many critics, few have challenged his assumption that deliberative rationality is subverted by visual display. For Habermas, the verdict is clear: when the public assumed its specific form, "it was the bourgeois reading public . . . rooted in the world of letters" (1989, p. 85), and the subsequent disintegration of that culture was accomplished in part through the rise of the electronic mass media and its displacement of public debate by political spectacles. That said, there is also a strategy of reformulation,

employed most recently in the pages of this journal by Kevin DeLuca and Jennifer Peeples (2002), which grants the necessity of a public sphere and considers how such a culture could work if it were freed of the constraints of this or that assumption in the classical model. Thus, DeLuca and Peeples argue that in a televisual public sphere, corporate image making is balanced at times by a subaltern staging of image events which demonstrate "[c]ritique through spectacle, not critique versus spectacle" (2002, p. 134; see also DeLuca, 1999).

We want to go a step further to suggest that the public sphere depends on visual rhetorics to maintain not only its play of deliberative "voices," but also its more fundamental constitution of public identity. Because the public is a discursively organized body of strangers constituted solely by the acts of being addressed and paying attention (Warner, 2002, pp. 65–124), it can only acquire self-awareness and historical agency if individual auditors "see themselves" in the collective representations that are the materials of public culture. Visual practices in the public media play an important role at precisely this point. The daily stream of photojournalistic images, while merely supplemental to the task of reporting the news, defines the public through an act of common spectatorship. When the event shown is itself a part of national life, the public seems to see itself, and to see itself in terms of a particular conception of civic identity.

No one basis for identification can dominate, however, or the public devolves into a specific social group that necessarily excludes others and therefore would no longer be a public. As Habermas notes, "The public sphere of civil society stood or fell with the principle of universal access. A public sphere from which specific groups could be excluded was less than merely incomplete; it was not a public sphere at all" (Habermas, 1989, p. 85). The strategic value of Habermas's grounding of the public in reading is thus apparent, as the positive content of *who* is reading *what* remains tacit. Picture-viewing is another form of tacit experience that can be used to connect people: all *seem* to see the same thing, yet the full meaning of the image remains unarticulated. Most important, visual images also are particularly well suited to constituting the "stranger relationality" that is endemic to the distinctive norms of public address (Warner, 2002, pp. 74–76). The public must include strangers; it "addresses people who are identified primarily through their participation in discourse and who therefore cannot be known in advance" (Warner, 2002, p. 74). Basic principles of the Habermasian public sphere—public use of reason, the bracketing of status, topical openness, and in-principle inclusiveness—have a fundamental orientation toward interaction with strangers. One need not follow any of these norms to interact with, persuade, be persuaded by, and otherwise live amiably among those one knows; families, for example, typically require these norms to be checked at the door. If photojournalistic images can maintain a vital relationship among strangers, they will provide an essential resource for constituting a mass media audience as a public.

Even if one grants that public deliberation can be mediated visually, the question remains of the extent to which visual practices are subject to ideological control. The belief that a photograph is a clear window on reality is itself an example of the natural attitude of ideology; by contrast, it becomes important to show how a photographic image fails to achieve a transparent representation of its perceptual object. As Victor Burgin notes, all representation is structured, for at "the very moment of their being perceived, objects are *placed* within an intelligible system of relationships. . . . They take their position, that is to say, within an *ideology*" (Burgin, 1992a, pp. 45–46, emphasis in original). Photography, it seems, is no exception. "Photographs are texts inscribed in terms of what we may call 'photographic discourse,'" (Burgin, 1992b, p. 144, emphasis in original) and photographic realism is the outcome of an "elaborate constitutive process" (Tagg, 1992, p. 111). From there it's all downhill: once thought to be windows to the real, photographic images become the ideal medium for naturalizing a repressive structure of signs. And there is no doubt that they can function that way, as both prized shots and millions of banal, anonymous images reproduce normative conceptions of gender, race, class, and other forms of social identity.

This critique relies on a pervasive structuralism—and an accompanying logocentricism—that begs the question before us. There is a reading strategy available for working beyond such structural models, however, which is to emphasize the interaction of the several layers of signification that comprise photographic practices. Roland Barthes, despite his strong use of semiotics, acknowledged that the photographic image does have some degree of representational autonomy, and his critical studies focused on the ability of the image to puncture conventional beliefs (1981). Umberto Eco resolved this tension between the individual image and the social repertoire of interpretive codes by recognizing the ways in which every image operates in the context of "successive transcriptions" (1992, p. 3). Such transcriptions negotiate both the general shift between visual and verbal semiotics, and the more specific shifts in meaning that occur as the viewer is cued to specific narratives or interpretive terms by different patterns in and extending beyond the composition. The question, then, is not the autonomy of the visual or the dominance of the system of signs, but how interpretation necessarily moves across different strata of representation, each of which is incomplete yet partially closed off from the others. The full implication of this idea is stated by W. J. T. Mitchell: "The interaction of pictures and text is constitutive of representation as such: All media are mixed media, and all representations are heterogeneous; there are no 'purely' visual or verbal arts, though the impulse to purify media is one of the central utopian gestures of modernism" (1994, p. 5). Following the textual metaphor embedded in most critical discourse about visual practices, this correction applies not only to captions and other verbal materials that frame an image, but to all of the codes of the social text as well. No one code controls all signs, and any sign can shift across multiple codes.

To take this idea a step further, we need to recognize the sense in which visual images are complex and unstable articulations, particularly as they circulate across topics, media, and texts, and thus are open to successive reconstitution by and on behalf of varied political interests, including a public interest. The photographic image coordinates a number of different patterns of identification from within the social life of the audience, each of which would suffice to direct audience response, and which together provide a public audience with sufficient means for comprehending potentially unmanageable events. Because the camera records the decor of everyday life, the photographic image is capable of directing attention across a field of gestures, interaction rituals, social types, political styles, artistic motifs, cultural norms, and other signs as they intersect in any event. As a result, photographs are capable of aesthetic mediations of political identity that include but also exceed ideological control.

The ambiguous potentiality of photojournalism is particularly evident with those images that become iconic (Goldberg, 1991, pp. 135–62; Hariman and Lucaites, 2001, 2002). On the one hand, these images are moments of visual eloquence that acquire exceptional importance within public life. They are believed to provide definitive representations of political crises and to motivate public action on behalf of democratic values. On the other hand, they are created and kept in circulation by media elites (Perlmutter, 1998), they are used in conjunction with the grand narratives of official history, and they are nothing if not conventional. Most important, perhaps, is the fact that this tension between the performative embodiment of a public interest and the ideological reconstitution of that interest is played out in the process by which collective memory is created through the extended circulation and appropriation of images over time. Even though iconic images usually are recognized as such immediately, and even if they are capable of doing the heavy lifting required to change public opinion and motivate action on behalf of a public interest, their meaning and effects are likely to be established slowly, shift with changes in context and use, and be fully evident only in a history of both official and vernacular appropriations.

The iconic photograph of an injured girl running from a napalm attack provides a complex construction of viewer response that was uniquely suited to the conditions of representation in the Vietnam era, while it also embodies conventions of liberal individualism such as personal autonomy and human rights that have become increasingly

dominant within U.S. public culture since then. This ongoing mediation of public life can be explicated both by examining how the photograph's artistry shapes moral judgment and by tracking subsequent narrative reconstructions and visual appropriations of the image in the public media. In what follows, we show how this photograph managed a rhetorical culture of moral and aesthetic fragmentation to construct public judgment of the war, and how it embodies a continuing tension within public memory between a liberal-individualist narrative of denial and compensation and a mode of democratic dissent that involves both historical accountability and continuing trauma. In turn, we believe, this tension reflects and reproduces essential features of the public itself, a social relationship that, because it has to be among strangers, is ever in need of images.

Civilians in Pain

The naked little girl is running down a road in Vietnam toward the camera, screaming from the napalm burns on her back and arm. Other Vietnamese children are moving in front of and behind her, and one boy's face is a mask of terror, but the naked girl is the focal point of the picture. Stripped of her clothes, her arms held out from her sides, she looks almost as if she has been flayed alive. Behind her walk soldiers, somewhat casually. Behind them, the roiling dark smoke from the napalm drop consumes the background of the scene.

The photo (Figure 1) was taken by AP photographer Nick Ut on June 8, 1972, released after an editorial debate about whether to print a photo involving nudity, and published all over the world the next day. It then appeared in *Newsweek* ("Pacification's Deadly Price," 1972) and *Life* ("Beat of Life," 1972) and subsequently received the Pulitzer Prize. Today it is regarded as "a defining photographic icon; it remains a symbol of the horror of war in general, and of the war in Vietnam in particular" (Buell, 1999, p. 102; see also Goldberg, 1991, pp. 241–245). Amid many other exceptional photographs and a long stream of video coverage, the photo has come to be regarded as one of the most famous photographs of the Vietnam War and among the most widely recognized images in American photojournalism (Kinney, 2000, p. 187; Sturken, 1997, pp. 89–94). Its stature is believed to reflect its influence on public attitudes toward the war, an influence achieved by confronting U.S.

FIGURE 1
(Reprinted by permission of AP/Worldwide)

citizens with the immorality of their actions (Sturken, 1997, p. 90; for a more skeptical perspective see Perlmutter, 1998, p. 9).

These claims are true enough, but they don't explain much. By 1972 there had been many, many press reports and a number of striking photos that would suffice as evidence for any claim that the U.S. was fighting an immoral war. Indeed, by 1972 the public had seen burned skin hanging in shreds from Vietnamese babies, a bound Vietnamese prisoner of war being shot in cold blood, and similar pictures of the horror of war (see, e.g., Buell, 1999, pp. 62–67, 78–81; Griffiths, 1971; and Faas and Page, 1997). The photograph could not have been effective solely because of its news value, nor does it appear to be especially horrific. In addition, the captioning and other information about the causes of the event and its aftermath would seem to limit its documentary value. The story is one of "accidental napalm" (as the photo was captioned in some reports, e.g., "Accidental Napalm Attack," 1972, 1A; see also Lester, 1991, pp. 51–52); the strike was by South Vietnamese forces (not U.S. troops); the girl was immediately tended to and taken to a hospital. As an indictment, there isn't much that would stand out after

cross-examination. And why would a still image come to dominate collective memory of what is now called the first television war, a war the public experienced via kinetic images of firefights, strafing runs, and helicopters landing and taking off in swirls of dust and action (Franklin, 1994; Hallin, 1986; Sturken, 1997, p. 89)?

An image of suffering can be highly persuasive, but not because of either the realism ascribed to the photo or its relationship to a single set of moral precepts (Burgin, 1996; Griffin, 1999; Tagg, 1988). A logic of public moral response has to be constructed, it has to be one that is adapted to the deep problems in the public culture at the time, and it has to be consistent with the strengths and weakness of the medium of articulation. This iconic photo was capable of activating public conscience at the time because it provided an embodied transcription of important features of moral life, including pain, fragmentation, modal relationships among strangers, betrayal and trauma. These features are strengthened by photographic representation, particularly as they reinforce one another, and their embodiment in a single image demonstrates how photojournalism can do important work within public discourse, work that may not be done as well in verbal texts adhering to the norms of discursive rationality.

The little girl is naked, running right toward you, looking right at you, crying out. The burns themselves are not visible, and it is her pain—more precisely, her communicating the pain she feels—that is the central feature of the picture. Pain is the primary fact of her experience, just as she is the central figure in the composition. As she runs away from the cause of her burns, she also projects the pain forward, toward the viewer, and it is amplified further by the boy in front of her (his face resembles Edvard Munch's famous drawing of "The Scream"). This direct address defines her relationship to the viewer: she faces the lens, which activates the demanding reciprocity of direct, face-to-face interaction, and she is aligned with the frontal angle of the viewer's perspective, which "says, as it were: 'what you see here is part of our world, something we are involved with'" (Kress and van Leeuwen, 1996, pp. 121–130, 143). The photograph projects her pain into our world.

This confrontation of the viewer cuts deeper still. Her pain, like all great pain, disrupts and breaks up the social world's pattern of assurances. Just as she has stripped off her clothes to escape the burning napalm, she tears the conventions of social life. Thus, her pain is further amplified because she violates the news media's norms of propriety. Public representation is always constituted by norms of decorum; without them, the public itself no longer exists (see Hariman, 1995). Yet war by its nature is a violation of civility, normalcy, civic order. Thus, a visual record of war will have to negotiate an internal tension between propriety and transgression (on photojournalistic norms governing the portrayal of bodily harm see Moeller, 1989; Robins, 1996; and Taylor, 1998). So it is that lesser forms of transgression can play an important role in the representation of war. The non-prurient nudity of the napalm photo doesn't just slip past the censor's rule, for the seeming transgression of her nakedness reveals another, deeper form of concealment. The image shows what is hidden by what is being said in print—the damaged bodies behind the U.S. military's daily "body counts," "free fire zones," and other euphemisms. The photo violates one set of norms in order to activate another; propriety is set aside for a moral purpose.

Girls should not be shown stripped bare in public; civilians should not be bombed. Likewise, U.S. soldiers (and many viewers mistakenly assume the soldiers are U.S. troops) are supposed to be handing out candy to the children in occupied lands, and the United States is supposed to be fighting just wars for noble causes. Just as the photograph violates one form of propriety to represent a greater form of misconduct, that breach of public decorum also disrupts larger frameworks for the moral justification of violence. Like the explosion still reverberating in the background, the photograph is a rupture, a tearing open of established narratives of justified military action, moral constraint, and national purpose. It is a picture that shouldn't be shown of an event that shouldn't have happened, and it projects a leveling of social structure and chaotic dispersion of social energies. The picture creates a searing eventfulness that breaks away from any official narrative justifying the war.

The photograph appeared during a period when the public was recognizing that their government was waging war without purpose, without legitimacy, without end. The illusion of strategic control had been shattered by the 1968 Tet offensive, all pretense of consensus had been killed in the 1970 shootings at Kent State, and by 1972 even those prolonging the war were relying on a rhetoric of disengagement. To those living amidst the public controversy about the war, it seemed as if the war made no sense and U.S. society was coming apart at the seams.

This sense of fragmentation was amplified by the media practices defining the Vietnam War. Day after day the public saw a jumble of scenes—bombings, firefights, helicopter evacuations, patrols moving out, villages being searched, troops wading across rivers—that could seemingly be rearranged in any order. If there was any organizational principle to this flow of images, it was that of collage: a seemingly shapeless accumulation of images that contained moments of strong association, or of irony, or of unexpected allure, but that lacked any governing idea. This continual stream of images reflecting a war without clear battle lines dovetailed perfectly with the government's lack of either a plausible rationale or coherent strategy. In addition, the reproduction of the details of everyday décor and ordinary behavior underscored the general substitution of scene for purpose. Try as the proponents of the war in Vietnam might to resurrect the idea of a theater of war with clear battle lines and victories, all on behalf of a justifiable political objective, such ideas were at odds not only with the nature of that war, but also, and perhaps more important for their persuasive objectives, with the visual media that were shaping public knowledge of the war.

In short, what was a sorry truth about the war became a dominant feature of its coverage. The daily visual record of activities was likely to make the war seem to have no purpose. Although this media environment was primarily televisual, it reinforced the most significant effect that photography can have on the understanding of war. As Alan Trachtenberg has observed of Civil War photography, the "portrayal of war as an event in real space and time," rather than "the mythic or fictional time of a theater," was accompanied "by a loss of clarity about both the overall form of battles and the unfolding war as such and the political meaning of events" (1989, pp. 74–75). In other words, the photographic medium is inherently paratactic: because photographic images operate meaningfully without a connecting syntax (Barthes, 1977, pp. 37–46), these images denote only fragments of any coordinated action. They give specific events a singular significance, but they leave larger articulations of purpose outside the frame.

The accidental napalm photograph is a model fragment. Featuring anonymous figures in a featureless scene that could be occurring anywhere in Vietnam, lacking any strategic orientation or collective symbol, confounding any official rhetoric of the war's purpose or of our commitment to the Vietnamese people, devoid of any element of heroism, and clearly recording an unintended consequence, it would not seem to qualify as an event at all. But it does qualify, because the photo's fragmentation carries with it a shift in the basic definition of an event. An event is no longer an action that comes at a dramatic moment in a sequence of purposive actions; instead, it is an experiential moment having heightened intensity independent of any larger plot.

The photo's embodiment of an aesthetic of fragmentation not only captured the character of a purposeless war, it also provided a means for resolving the moral predicament the war presented to the American public. How can any idea of right conduct be established within a condition of political and representational incoherence? It is within this context that the girl's nakedness acquires additional meaning. As Michael Walzer observes, even hardened soldiers are averse to killing an out of uniform—unmarked—enemy (1977, pp. 138–143). Simple vulnerability, particularly as it is symbolized by nakedness, puts us in an elemental moral situation. More to the point, nakedness in war foregrounds the moral relationships that still bind strangers to one another. The uniformed soldier has an identity; the naked body has been stripped of conventional patterns of recognition, deference, and dismissal. Like the parable of the Good Samaritan, which featured a naked man discovered along a road, the girl's naked vulnerability is a call to obligation, and, as in the parable, one that has occurred unexpectedly. In the words of John Caputo, "Obligation happens" (1993, p. 6). Obligation can appear out of nowhere, without regard to one's social position, directly encumbering one in ways that are decidedly inconvenient and, worse, that may disrupt deep assumptions regarding how one's life is patterned and what the future should hold. Thus, the photo abruptly calls the viewer to a moral awareness that cannot be limited to roles, contracts, or laws; neither is it buffered by distance. A fragmented world is still a world of moral demands, only now they may be most pressing when least expected, and the demand itself can shatter conventional wisdom.

This identification with the stranger has both a modern face and the structure of classical tragedy. The girl's nakedness provides a performative embodiment of the modern conception of universal humanity. She could be a poster child for the Universal Declaration of Human Rights (and as an adult she has both served as a good will ambassador for the United Nations and founded an international organization to aid children harmed by war). The dramatic charge of the photo comes from its evocation of pity and terror: we see a pathetic sight—the child crying in pain—and as we enter into her experience we feel both pity for her (or compassion toward her) and the looming sense of terror that lies behind her injuries. The terror (or fear or horror) that tragedy evokes comes not from the physical injury itself but from the social rupture behind it, which is why Aristotle noted that the most effective tragedies involved harms done off stage and within the family (Poetics, 1453b). The picture reproduces this design. First, despite its patently visual nature, the napalm attack is already over and the girl's burns are not visible—most are on her back, and the photograph's low resolution minimizes the others. Second, she is a child—a member of a family—and familial relationships are either modeled (between the children) or broken (between parents and children, as the biological parents are absent and the other adults are indifferent soldiers). The pity for the child is compounded by this sense of social breakdown—again, the horror of war is the destruction of social order and of meaning itself. Her pain activates the terror of tragedy, which comes from the realization that humans can be abandoned to a world no longer capable of sympathy, a world of beasts and gods, of destructive powers and impersonal forces, of pain without end.

This tragic structure is filled out by the relationships between the children and the soldiers. The crucial fact is that the soldiers are walking along slowly, almost nonchalantly, as if this were an everyday experience. Their attitude of business as usual contrasts vividly with the girl's sudden, unexpected, excessive experience of pain and terror. The message is clear: what seems, from looking at the girl, to be a rare experience sure to evoke a compassionate response, is in fact, as evidenced by the soldiers, something that happens again and again, so much so that the adults involved (whether soldiers there or civilians in the U.S.) can become indifferent, morally diminished, capable of routinely doing awful things to other people. Precisely because the photo is operating as a mode of performance, its formal implication is that what is shown is repeated, and repeatable, behavior (Schechner, 1985, pp. 35–116; States, 1996, p. 20). The photo that will be reproduced many times is itself not the record of a unique set of circumstances, but rather a dramatic depiction of those features of the war that are recurring over and over again past the point of caring. As the girl screams and other human beings walk along devoid of sympathy, the photo depicts a world of pain that reverberates off the hard surfaces of moral indifference. This is why knowledge of the circumstantial events (such as the girl receiving treatment immediately) rightly provides no qualification to the moral force of the photograph. The knowledge that would matter would be a demonstration that this was a rare use of napalm, or that U.S. forces and their Vietnamese allies almost never harmed civilians in the war zone. But, of course, by 1972 the truth of the brutality of the war had breached the surface of national consciousness.

The photo is not about informing the public at all; rather, it offers a performance of social relationships that provide a basis for moral comprehension and response (cf., Sontag, 1973, pp. 17–19). These modal relationships in turn can exemplify morally significant actions such as self-sacrifice or betrayal. The full significance of the photo's depiction of their relationship becomes clear when one recognizes how it also reflects the dilemma of democratic accountability in modern war. On the one hand, the citizen-soldier is both agent and representative of the public; on the other hand, the public has authority for but no direct control over their troops. When those troops are projecting power far away, yet reported on daily in the national media, the situation gets even worse. It is easy for the public to find itself guilty for actions it did not sanction, and for soldiers to be blamed for events no one anticipated. Soldiers and civilians alike can feel betrayed.

The napalm photo features two betrayals. Whether American or Vietnamese, the soldiers are agents of the United States who are supposed to be protecting the girl, yet they appear content merely to herd her and the other children down the road. The soldiers are not helping, they even seem to be treating the children like prisoners of war (for guns are still drawn), and they are indifferent to the suffering before them. Thus, while a little girl seems to appeal directly to the public for help, yet it can do nothing while its representative in the picture adds insult to injury. As the girl is betrayed by the institutional figures who are supposed to protect her, so is the public betrayed by the same institution.[1]

Although the activity within the frame directs action, the fact that this is a photograph—a "static" image—means that time has been stopped. The picture holds its experience of terror and uncompleted action for all time, while having the activity within the frame eternally repeat itself (for that is what it is, performatively restored repetitive behavior). This mythic sense of eternal recurrence, and its "vertigo of time defeated" (Barthes, 1981, p. 97), corresponds perfectly to the phenomenological structure of trauma: one simultaneously feels stopped in time (or thrown outside of time, temporal movement, history, change) while constantly repeating the actions within that isolated moment (Herman, 1992; for a selected bibliography on posttraumatic stress disorder with special reference to Vietnam see "Vietnam Yesterday," 2001). The normal flow of time has been fragmented into shards of isolated events, while the traumatized subject remains trapped in the continually recurring scene, unable to break out of the ever-recurring pain. Although this phenomenological state is commonly thought to result from exposure to carnage, Jonathan Shay has pointed out how the deeper cause is a sense of betrayal (Shay, 1994, pp. 3–22). Likewise, an iconic photo that is said to capture the horror of war is not gruesome, but it does freeze the spectator in a tableau of moral failure. Betrayal short-circuits the power of institutional narratives to sublimate disturbing incidents, and the photograph perpetuates this sense of rupture. One is helpless, unable to change a thing about what happened and yet is still before one's eyes. This sense of powerlessness extends to control of the memory itself, as the image circulates through the media, recurring again and again unbidden.

Thus, the photograph came to provide symbolic representation of the U.S. public's experience of the Vietnam War. Somehow, it seems, the United States got caught in a situation not of its own making, a morally incoherent situation in which we knew we did terrible things to other people—things we still can't face and can never set right. Against processes of denial, the photograph provides at least an image of our condition: having already done the wrong thing, wanting to do the right thing, yet frozen, incapable of acting in that place at all. Nor will history oblige by allowing us to start over or restore a sense of innocence. The basic conditions of modern U.S. warfare are all there: imperial action in a distant, third world country far from the public's direct control; massive, technologically intensive firepower being used to spare our soldiers' lives at enormous rates of "collateral damage"; mass media coverage sure to confront us with our guilt while apparently providing no means for action. The moral danger of this world is captured tonally in the picture's composition of light and darkness: as the dark smoke blots out the sky and while the girl bathed in light has in fact been seared with liquid fire, the elements of the sublime are present but out of order, gone demonic. Light hurts, darkness towers over all, awe is induced by destruction, terror is not sublimated to a transcendent order. The image calls a public to moral awareness, but its rhetorical power is traumatic.

The Liberal Antidote

The photograph's activation of the structure of trauma is evident as well in its subsequent history of interpretation. According to Shay, the crucial step towards healing from a traumatic experience is to construct a narrative of one's life that can contextualize the traumatic moment (1994, pp. 181–193). The narrative does more than soothe, for it addresses the crucial characteristic of trauma, which is being bracketed from any sense of temporal continuity. The traumatic moment is stopped in time, and narrative gets time moving again so that the moment may eventually recede, dissipate, or become complicated by other elements of larger stories.

This photo has produced several narratives. The most frequently told of these is the story of the relationship between the girl in the photo and the photographer (see, e.g., Buell, 1999, pp. 102–103). Both of Vietnamese ethnicity, they became lifelong friends as he helped her relocate to Canada. The story functions as a convenient displacement of responsibilities while breaking out of the traumatic moment: both Vietnamese-American and Canadian identities provide an easy surrogacy that allows a happy ending without either involving the U.S. public directly or leaving them completely-out of the story. This easy resolution validates a significant change, however, for the anonymous girl has become an individual person. She has a name (Kim Phuc), and the story is now *her* story, a unique personal history that may or may not be publicized.

A recent variant of this story is Denise Chong's *The Girl in the Picture*, which chronicles Kim Phuc's personal odyssey of recovery while trying to free herself from the publicity generated by the photo. "She felt as though the journalistic hounds would make her into a victim all over again. 'The action of those two women [journalists, one with a camera] on the sidewalk,' she lamented to Toan, 'was like a bomb falling out of the sky' " (1999, p. 6). Note how this narrative replays the performance of the iconic photograph: allied technology continues to harm an innocent Vietnamese civilian, while the public again is drawn into an act of inflicting pain it did not authorize, an act that can only be redeemed through empathic identification with her suffering. The traumatic "scars [that] war leaves on all of us" (Chong, 1999, bookjacket flap) are then ameliorated by a narrative of her life after the war.

This relationship between the physical wound and a rhetoric of healing that can displace concerns about justice is most evident in the picture of Kim with her infant child (Figure 2) taken by photographer Joe McNally in 1995 ("Portrait," 1995; Sixtieth Anniversary, 1996, p. 102; Chong, 1999, p. 191).[2] This picture may also be an attempt at something like a visual sequel to the iconic photo, and one that supplies a Hollywood ending for the story. The continuities and discontinuities between this photo and the icon establish the key differences in effect. Her nakedness is still there, but it has been carefully controlled by changes in posture and camera angle to maintain the modesty expected of a grown woman and a tranquil public culture. Her injury is still there, of course, but now the effects of the war are to be dealt with on

FIGURE 2
(Reprinted by permission of LIFE/Joe McNally)

an individual basis, and those who created them are no longer in the picture, no longer capable of being interrogated or condemned.

Perhaps the soldiers have been replaced by the scars on her skin. The display of the scars also reveals the relationship between the physical and symbolic dimensions of the two images. In the iconic photo, her physical wounds were not visible; they were communicated by her expression and the other child's cry of terror. Thus, the physical harm that was the most basic consequence and moral fault of American military actions was depicted indirectly. In the sequel, the physical harm is revealed, but given its relationship to the other features of the picture, it acquires a different significance. Now the wounds are superficial, for they appear to have no effect on the woman's internal health. Inside, she is capable of bearing a "normal," healthy baby. And what a baby it is:

unblemished, its new, smooth skin a striking contrast to her mature scars. Now the physical damage to Kim is merely the background for a tableau of regeneration. Although she is not doing that well in one sense, for she is still scarred, she obviously has achieved one of the great milestones of personal happiness by giving birth to a beautiful child. While the past is still present, it is inert—no more than ugly tissue that has no power to prevent a new beginning and personal happiness. In the United States, history lasts only one generation.

The sunny optimism of this story of war's aftermath is validated by the rest of the composition. Her beatific expression and the figural enactment of Madonna and child portraiture suggest a serenity in which traumatic memory or persistent conflict has no place. Likewise, in place of the dark smoke from the napalm blast, the background of this photo is a darkened blank wall. This gentle décor and her carefully draped clothing invoke the conventions of retail studio photography, which in turn anchor her happiness within a familiar scene of private life: the framed portrait that is displayed proudly by the child's grandparents.

All of these changes occur within a thoroughly traditional transcription of gender roles. The muted sexuality of her late girlhood has been channeled into the conventional role of motherhood. Men clearly maintain their monopoly on violence (Ehrenreich, 1997, p. 125), while a woman embodies the virtues of nurturing; Vietnam and peace itself remain feminized while war and the American military establishment retain their masculine identity. The scene defines private life as a place centered on women and children, where mothers are devoted to and fulfilled by caring for their families.

The shift from public to private virtues has been encoded by taking a second photo for public dissemination in a manner similar to taking a photo for distribution within one's family. The substitution of photos provides a double compensation: Kim has been given a beautiful child to replace her own damaged childhood, and the second image is given to the public in recompense for its past discomfort. The baby also replaces the other children in the original scene—those running down the road and those who didn't make it. The war is over, and children who could be running in terror for their small, vulnerable lives are now sleeping quietly in their mothers' arms. Moreover, where the earlier children were Kim's siblings, and so the sign of collective identity, this child is her child, her most dear possession and a sign of the proprietary relationships essential to liberal individualism. The transformation is complete: from past trauma to present joy, and from the terrors of collective history to the quiet individualism of private life.

Thus, this sequel to the iconic photo inculcates a way of seeing the original image and the history to which it bore witness. A record of immoral state action has become a history of private lives. Questions of collective responsibility—and of justice—have been displaced by questions of individual healing. The wisdom that recognizes the likelihood of war's eternal recurrence has been displaced by a narrative of personal happiness and of a new, unblemished, innocent generation.

What is important to note here is that the reinscription of the iconic photograph by the second image is neither unique nor inappropriate. Indeed, it invokes a therapeutic discourse that has become a symptomatic and powerful form of social control in liberal-democratic, capitalist societies (see Cloud, 1998; Ehrenhaus, 1993). Two dimensions of such discourse are directly relevant to the case at hand. First, as Ehrenhaus observes, the therapeutic motif "voyeuristically dwells on intimacy and poignancy while never violating the illusion of privacy" (pp. 93–94). And second, as the emphasis shifts attention from public to private trauma, it invokes a discourse of "individual and family responsibility" that contains dissent directed towards the social and political order (Cloud, 1998, p. xv; Ehrenhaus, 1993). In the second photograph, then, Kim Phuc's "private" recovery and maternity substitute for the napalm girl's "public" cry of pain; the effect is to foreclose on acts of dissent that would question state accountability.

This narrative containment of the original image is not a wholly unwarranted imposition, however, for that image draws upon conceptions of personal autonomy and human rights that are foundational in a liberal-individualist society, it features a wounded individual crying out for help, and it produces a traumatic effect. The second photo's visual reinterpretation of the war is achieved not by distorting the iconic photo but rather by extending designs in the original that were essential for its moral significance and rhetorical appeal. In short, as the second photograph imitates aesthetic elements of the iconic image, it enhances an ideological transcription that was already available within the scene. Indeed, the "second" inflection helps to define the original image, as when the icon is celebrated in an exhibition because it is "a symbol that has helped lead toward reconciliation" (Exhibit Recalls German Destruction, 2000).

So it is that this iconic photo can be both unusually striking and unavoidably ambivalent. On the one hand, a partial record of a supposedly incidental moment became a defining event of the war, one capable of negating the moral certainty and aesthetic unity of the U.S. culture that had coalesced during World War II. On the other hand, the photograph is not only a transgression, but also the enactment of another model of political identity always available within U.S. public life and ascendant amidst the prosperity and contradictions of the post-war era. Rather than simply tear down one set of ideals, it also advances the habits of another way of life.

In this liberal sensibility, actions are meaningful because they are symptomatic of internal conditions rather than because they adhere to proven models of character. The individual's experience is the primary locus of meaning, and conflict resolution may be as much psychological as political. The individual's autonomy and human rights supercede any political identity, and obligations are encountered along the road rather than due to any sense of tradition or collective enterprise. Collective action is essentially moral and humanitarian rather than defined by national interests, but it also is *ad hoc*, not directed by long-term objectives and analysis. The fundamental tension in political life is between the individual and society; once the individual is protected, other political possibilities are likely to be deferred to the more immediate engagements of private life. And when private life is synonymous with national healing, public life becomes a dead zone: a place, as we shall see, that is inhabited by ghosts and where images become specters of reanimation.

Dissent and the Haunting of Public Culture

Barthes asks, "Mad or tame? Photography can be one or the other" (1981, p. 119). The photograph of "accidental napalm" is repeatedly tamed and in a multiplicity of ways: by the banality of its circulation, by personalizing the girl in the picture, by drawing out a liberal narrative of healing, by the segue into the celebrity photo of Kim's regeneration, and more. But it also remains mad: an indelible image of terror that obsessively repeats itself, that keeps the public audience interned in the real time of fatality rather than fantasies of renewal, staring at screams that cannot be heard and haunted by ghosts that will not speak. This madness is something that need not be far from the anger fueling political dissent, and, although grounded in the image, it does not happen by itself; rather, like taming, it is something that results from continued use of the image. Thus, the history of the iconic photograph demonstrates how a visual practice can be a site of struggle.

As images become disseminated they also become resources for public argument, particularly as advocates themselves are skilled in using visual materials. A strong example of artistic accomplishment in grass-roots public discourse is provided on a web page titled "Veritatis Vietnam," designed by Ed Chilton, a Vietnam veteran[*] and anti-Vietnam War advocate (Chilton, 2000). The first image

_____
[*]Editors' note: As this book was going to press, it was brought to our attention that Chilton was not a Vietnam veteran.

we find on that web page digitally superimposes the napalm photograph over the U.S. flag and the face of Cardinal Spellman (Figure 3). The explicit intention is to excoriate Spellman for his support of the war in Vietnam. Although the verbal text following the image may seem too much of a harangue, the visual collage is hard to get out of one's mind. It achieves this effect by reproducing key features of the original photograph's rhetorical power, but now through a seemingly supernatural projection of that image into the present. The composition is haunting, and for good reason: the girl is now a ghost, a fragment of the past that will not be assimilated into the amnesia of the present.

Once again, the photograph breaks into official representations of U.S. institutional legitimacy. Once again, it is aesthetically and morally disruptive: it should not be inserted into the image of the flag, just as the naked, terrified girl should not have been on everyone's breakfast table, and it tells the audience that things that should not happen did happen. In the composite image, the photograph's role in a struggle over the meaning of the war is heightened: by intruding into images of the flag and the two crosses on the Cardinal's shoulders, the scene becomes a battle between the icons themselves. The war is brought home, as actions over there are shown in direct clash with symbols of legitimacy here, and the dominant symbols of collective organization (religion and the state) are confronted with their complicity in the war's destruction of innocent children.

As before, the napalm image is a fragmentary scene, one obviously located in the specific historical event of the war, yet not enfolded into any sense of a progressive historical narrative or sound military strategy. Indeed, the children's screams of terror tear apart the official narratives of American political and moral superiority. This attack on institutional authority is strengthened by the image of Cardinal Spellman. His position at the front of the composition parallels the position of the soldiers in the rear as they are roughly equidistant from the children. His crosses are placed as if they were military insignia (Cardinal or General, did it matter?), and his expression can be read as either implicitly predatory (the large round head, raised eyebrows, and intently focused eyes are owl-like) or morally hardened (the facial mask is uniformly controlled and blank while his mouth is pursed as if to make a dismissive remark). Once again, the public sees its representatives—now those who promoted the war along with the soldiers who fought it—acting as if they were habituated to the suffering they imposed on others.

FIGURE 3
(Reprinted by permission of Ed Chilton)

The fact that it is *once again* is no accident. As before, the image captures the trauma victim's sense of being stuck in time. In direct contrast to the narratives of compensation and healing used in the mainstream media to neutralize the iconic photograph's sense of guilt, this image reinserts the past into the present to immobilize those attempting to "move beyond" past conflicts and historical responsibility. The superimposition of images does not just compare the past with the present, it fuses them: the image of terror and guilt now is always within the flag, an ineradicable part of the United States's legacy. Likewise, the flag and institutional religion are exposed as covering devices, symbols and discourses (such as the Cardinal's public speeches on the war) that are used to hide moral truth and public guilt. Like the icon within it, the composition evokes a psychology of eternal recurrence and denial. Although this structure of feeling can be dismissed as yet another example of Vietnam syndrome, it also is another instance of the tragic dimension of war's pathos: Why will more continue to be sacrificed? Because the knowledge gained of suffering will be lost, or denied, to those who remain.

All the advocate wants to do is blast Cardinal Spellman, and he does a pretty good job of that,

at least visually. His most important accomplishment, however, is restoring the iconic photograph to its rightful place in public discourse. As any icon floats through media space across subsequent generations, and particularly as it gets rewritten into liberal narratives of individual healing, it can lose too much of the political history and emotional intensity that are essential for participation in democratic debate. By placing the icon against the symbols of the flag and the cross, this appropriation restores the conflict, hypocrisy, complicity, confusion, and intensity that [fuel] debate about the war. Above all, it restores a sense of public life. The girl is no longer a single individual, and the question is not whether she is happy today. Once again it is a picture of the victims of American military action and those who marshaled their destruction, of the public's lack of control over a war fought in its name, of the questionable moral and political legitimacy of U.S. institutions. By restoring the public context that in turn allows the iconic photo to challenge authority, the composite image demonstrates that perhaps not everything is lost after all.

This call to public conscience is evident in another remediation of the photo, this time by

FIGURE 4
(Reprinted by permission of Jeffrey Decoster)

transposing the girl into an illustration that accompanies a *Boston Globe* review of a book on the Vietnam Veterans' Movement. The story is entitled "Soldiers of Misfortune," and the visual composition (Figure 4) is a stunning depiction of the multiple layers of suffering that characterized the Vietnam War (Decoster, 2001, D3). The girl is running forward, her arms stretched out, as she always is running, but now she is passing through a sprinkler on a suburban lawn. She still is screaming, but now she is wearing a bright polka-dot bikini. Behind her smoke still billows upward, although now it comes from the chimney of a suburban house, over which a military helicopter hovers against a pastel blue sky. Beside the girl, a U.S. veteran sits in a wheelchair. It is as if he had been parked there to watch her, but his dark glasses, blank face, and slack limbs suggest some awful combination of social isolation and internal preoccupation. He and the girl form the two rear points of a triangle; at the third point equidistant between them and at the front of the picture, there is a child's plastic ball. It is red, white, and blue.

We doubt anyone could draw a more disturbing image of the war at home, or one that better confronts the liberal-individualist narrative with democratic responsibility, or one that so vividly captures the traumatic sense of continued suffering and unresolved guilt evoked by the original photograph. The girl's magical appearance in the most characteristic contemporary U.S. setting is profoundly unsettling. She won't go away, she has even turned up here. But that is only half of it: her transposition into the suburban scene doesn't just bring the war home, it erases the ethnic difference undergirding the moral indifference to Vietnamese suffering. As with any strong appropriation, the later image amplifies key features of the original design: in this case, by (re)clothing the girl the illustrator has completed the work begun by her originally being naked. While the first image made her less Vietnamese, because universally human, this image takes the next step by placing her in the United States's most familiar sense of humanity—our own culture. To spell it out even further, it becomes even easier to recognize that it was wrong to inflict pain on girls in Vietnam, because it would be just like bombing our kids while they were playing in our backyards. Perhaps this act of imagination is made easier as immigrant Vietnamese have become ever more assimilated into U.S. public culture, but the illustration makes it clear enough: she could have been one of ours.

If left there, the picture would have been a dated and heavy-handed condemnation of Vietnam veterans. The juxtaposition of the disabled veteran changes all that. Someone incapable of walking is not going to harm civilians now, and even if he did before he has paid for it. The picture's balanced positioning of the two representative figures makes it clear that both were harmed by the war, both scarred for life. They both are victims, but that victimage is no longer the liberal pathos of individuated harm and therapeutic recovery. Instead, the picture restores the iconic photograph's depiction of types—Vietnamese civilians, not Kim Phuc—and it positions the seemingly different figures (young, female, Vietnamese civilian; adult, male, U.S. soldier) in equivalent categories of continued trauma. It is the visual equivalent of President Clinton's verbal evocation of two nations united by "shared suffering" (2000).

The two figures share another similarity. The girl's emergence in the suburban scene many years after the end of the war is supernatural—a haunting of the American imagination. This return might be indicative of society's continued traumatization by the war, or it might symbolize the failure to confront historical responsibility, but it is a haunting nonetheless. The veteran has a similar nature, for he is a ghostly figure, so transparent that you can see the outline of a tricycle behind him showing through his body. The difference between them is that she is vivid and active while he barely has strength of presence, much less a capacity to act. The contrast could be (and probably is) an argument that the public has been more fixated on one set of victims than another for which it has equal or greater responsibility. But it seems more complicated than that. She shouldn't be there but is there; he should be there but is disappearing. Neither one belongs in the scene, because both are aesthetic disruptions of the Happyville template that provides the background for the picture. The key to understanding their mutual estrangement is the two small details of the smoke and the ball. The smoke is the thick, oily product of bombing taken from the original napalm drop, but now it is coming from the furnace of the house. (Why the heat is on in the summer appears to be artis-tic license.) The dirty pollution of war is also the byproduct of U.S. affluence, because both imperial power and domestic tranquility are fueled by the same dark processes. The moral buffering produced by the United States's distance and wealth, and the dirty truth that we waste lives needlessly, are shown to be deeply linked and largely hidden. The picture exposes eloquently the complicity between the good life at home and criminal behavior in the third world.

But who then is responsible? The ball provides part of the answer. Both a perfect prop within the scene and a reference to the nation-state, it is positioned to mediate the relationship between the two figures. Together the three form a closed, harmonious form. But the red, white, and blue ball is not "Old Glory." Instead, it signifies an ersatz patriotism, the broad dissemination of national symbols that characterizes mainstream popular culture. There is only the barest trace of any sense of collective responsibility, while the object typifies the easy activities of kids' games and backyard leisure, or at most the fireworks on the fourth of July. This reduction of political identity and collective responsibility to a small, soft plastic toy is what is necessary to represent its place within the suburban scene. It is there, but ironically so and easily kicked aside.

This projection of responsibility to the front of the pictorial frame follows directly from the composition of the iconic photo. Both victims are still in need of help, and both are not likely to be helped by what little sense of collective responsibility is available in the contemporary U.S. scene. As before, the picture hails the viewer. As before, the viewer is positioned aside from the state that is the agency of harm (it has harmed the girl, brought the soldiers to harm, and is not caring adequately for those soldiers today). As before, the picture can be a sweeping denunciation of moral indifference, although now the accusation is given an additional, sharper edge: the problem is not a runaway state or uninformed public, but a nation lulled to irresponsibility by its pursuit of domestic happiness. This irresponsibility includes not listening to the Vietnamese civilians and U.S. soldiers who have had direct experience of the war, but who have been silenced subsequently. As before, the picture fragments consensus through embarrassing depictions of suffering; by placing that suffering within a context of unthinking routine it both identifies a collective responsibility and locks the experience of guilt into a haunting, eternal recurrence of traumatic memory.

The Icon, the Stranger, and American Collective Memory

The multiple transcriptions and deep ambivalences of visual eloquence allow skilled advocates a rich repertoire for democratic deliberation. Iconic photographs are calls to civic action, sites of controversy, vehicles for ideological control, and sources of rhetorical invention. Although the appropriation of such icons has to be consistent with the original photograph's basic designs, and although they typically extend its strongest tendencies, they are also a source of new and at times remarkably sophisticated appeals. Most important, perhaps, they can articulate patterns of moral intelligence that run deeper than pragmatic deliberation about matters of policy and that disrupt conventional discourses of institutional legitimacy. That is not the end of the story, however.

Vietnam veteran William Adams has remarked, "What 'really' happened is now so thoroughly mixed up in my mind with what has been said about what happened that the pure experience is no longer there. . . . The Vietnam War is no longer a definite event so much as it is a collective and mobile script in which we continue to scrawl, erase, rewrite our conflicting and changing view of ourselves" (quoted in Sturken, 1997, p. 86). The situation is even more fluid for the public audience that never experienced the war directly. Amidst a "torrent" of books, movies, articles, memorials, web sites, and more, U.S. public life continues to be defined by its conduct and loss of the war in Vietnam (Perlmutter, 1998, p. 52). Explanations for this lack of closure range from the critique of the mass media's overexposure of the war, to the war's "resistance to standard narratives of technology, masculinity, and U.S. nationalism" (Sturken, 1997, p. 87). We believe that iconic photographs emerge and acquire considerable influence because of their capacity for dealing with the dual problems of overexposure and ideological rupture.

The Vietnam War has the distinction of being a rich lode of iconic photographs. Four in particular receive the widest circulation: the burning monk, the execution of a bound prisoner of war, the napalm girl, and the girl screaming over the dead student at Kent State. By explicating several relationships within this set of images, the additional functions of the napalm photograph, its genre, and photojournalism generally can be highlighted. As Marita Sturken has noted, the common features of this set of images include their depictions of horror, their challenge to ideological narratives, and

the fact that they have acquired far greater currency than any video images of the war, including identical footage of two of the events (the execution and the napalm attack). Sturken's account of this last difference is telling: the photographs highlight facial expressions, connote a sufficient sense of the past, circulate more easily, and are "emblems of rupture" demanding narration; in addition, the filmed events are actually more chaotic or horrific (1997, p. 87).

These observations are accurate, although also at odds with the general assessment that the iconic image is the best representation of the horror of war. Our close reading of the napalm photograph suggests how that idea needs to be refined. The iconic image of the Vietnam era becomes the telling representation because of its fragmentary character. It represents not so much physical harm as the loss of meaning, the futility of representation itself in a condition "when words lose their meaning" (White, 1984). A visual medium becomes the better vehicle for representing this slippage or incapacity. The image implies that another medium (words) has already proved incapable of full representation of the war, and, because the image can show but not tell, it automatically represents both the event and the gap between the event and any pattern of interpretation. The still image performs this dual sense of representation and absence most effectively: it frames the event for close, careful examination, while also providing nothing outside the frame and interrupting any sense of continuity. The result is not blankness, however, but an "optical unconscious" (Benjamin, 1980, p. 203) that can supply both exact knowledge of the morally decisive moment and the "lacerating emphasis" of fatality as it incorporates past and future alike in the eternal present of the image (Barthes, 1981, p. 96). As we have also noted, this epistemological condition is deeply resonant with the psychological structure of trauma.

There is a three-way relationship between loss of meaning, traumatic injury, and moral response that characterizes the deep lack of resolution regarding the Vietnam War, and that also is a key feature of the iconic photographs. The photos are indeed less horrific than they could be; they show little physical damage, while pictures taken seconds later in every case show more blood or burned flesh. The performative key is not physical damage, however, but the expression or conspicuous absence of an expression of pain. This distinction between physical gore and pain is crucial, for several reasons (see also Robins, 1996; Taylor,

1998; Zelizer, [2004]). Bodily disruption does not automatically call for a moral response, as it always is subject to interpretation (think of surgery). Pain, however, by its very nature cuts through and destroys patterns of meaningfulness, while its expression is evidence of an internal world—the world within the body that Elaine Scarry (1985, p. 63) defines as the "interior content of war"—and so a basis for connection with others without regard to external circumstances. Moral response requires not evidence of harm, but a sympathetic connection that is most directly evoked by pain. For the same reason, justifications of violence always have to minimize the pain it produces.

The four icons of the Vietnam War exemplify the dialectic between displays of pain and indifference to pain. The napalm and Kent State photos are the most powerful registers of moral outrage precisely because they are performances of the pain experienced by an innocent victim of U.S. military action. "The image of the burned girl made Americans see the pain the war inflicted," and it also used that pain to bond the girl and the public emotionally (Kinney, 2000, p. 187). The girl at Kent State acts as a ventriloquist for the murdered body on the pavement in front of her, while also directly venting the pain experienced sympathetically (and, therefore, modeling sympathetic response to the dead and wounded as the appropriate form of citizenship in respect to that event) (Hariman and Lucaites, 2001). Each performance also is gendered, as a girl crying represents the "victimized, feminized" country of Vietnam and the peace movement at home (Sturken, 1997, p. 93).

The logic of conventional gender typing also structures the other two icons, each of which is notable for its repression of emotion. The expression of the man being shot is sometimes described as a searing expression, but not often; it could double as an expression one might see in a dentist's office. What is most significant is the executioner's lack of emotion. The photo's moral punch comes from its documentation of how the state can kill with such complete lack of regard for the pain it is causing. As with the laconic soldiers in the napalm photo, the officer's businesslike manner is a cue to the fact that this situation is routine, something that those in the picture see every day. The lack of empathy becomes the sign of immoral conduct, a sign that can't be erased by circumstantial knowledge about the soldiers involved. The burning monk follows a similar logic that operates in the reverse direction. The salient fact in the

photo is that someone's resolve to resist the government could be so great that he would not only commit self-immolation, but be able to do so without showing pain. The Saigon government was shown to be not only illegitimate, but so powerless that it could not conquer the body as it burned. Male suppression of pain thus becomes the vector for projecting a power that can be used either to extend or resist state control, while female expression of pain becomes the vehicle for public response to the abuse of power by the state that, unlike the male acts, can be imitated by anyone who is looking at the picture.

One conclusion to be drawn at this point is that the iconic images from the Vietnam War—along with the subsequent images of Kim Phuc that are used to put the war to rest—also create a fragmented regendering of the public sphere. The public is feminized in a manner that has both positive and negative consequences. On one hand, set against a masculine monopoly on violence and state action that is increasingly irrational, the feminized public reinstates the essential features of the classical model. In addition, this gendering corrects for various faults in that model, not least its inattention to emotion, norms of reciprocity and care, divisions between public and private life, and the need for openness in actual practice. On the other hand, such gendering hardens a number of dangerous alignments among power, violence, and masculinity, and against discourse, deliberation, and social reciprocity. Worse yet, as women only cry out and scream while remaining helpless, public speech becomes hysterical and without agency, and as their meaning is transferred to the visual medium that is featuring a woman's body, the public becomes subject to the male gaze while being reduced to the politics of spectacle. Such logics produce both more war and further constriction of public culture.

These transcriptions of gender are as important as they are obvious, but they are not the only means by which iconic photos can embody essential features of the public sphere. Michael Warner (2002) has identified, among others, two features of public culture that are especially pertinent to the case at hand: "the public is a social space created by the reflexive circulation of discourse" (p. 90), and it is a "relation among strangers" (p. 74). The still photo acquires greater mnemonic capacity due to its ease of wide and continuous circulation. Even in digital environments, video clips are more time and skill intensive, whereas still photos circulate easily and also can be reproduced across posters, editorial cartoons, book covers, t-shirts, and an astonishing range of other items (e.g., see Franklin, 2000, pp. 1–24; Hariman and Lucaites, 2002). As the public is constituted in the dissemination and circulation of texts that compete for attentiveness (and verbal "uptake") within audiences, the images that circulate best have a natural tendency to become the carriers of public consciousness (Warner, 2002, p. 87). The iconic images then stand out further because their conjunction of aesthetic form and political function allows for a reflexive representation of not only the particular event, but also the conditions of public representation most crucial to understanding the event. No one text or image can do this, but those that can capture the tensions within the discursive field will be more likely to become the markers of the field.

Because a public is always, by definition, a group whose membership cannot be known in advance, public discourse is addressed to strangers. A public "might be said to be stranger-relationality in a pure form, because other ways of organizing strangers—nations, religions, races, guilds, etc.—have manifest positive content." Perhaps most important, "We've become capable of recognizing ourselves as strangers even when we know each other" (Warner, 2002, p. 74). If the public audience is to be capable of response and action, however, those within it cannot be operating in a realm of pure relationality, not least because there is no such language available. The discourses of public address must be inflected, embodied, and otherwise provide real bases for identification through aesthetic performance, and they have to do this in a manner that also maintains the reflexive openness of public identity. Warner's own language seems to be a description of the iconic photograph:

> The development of forms that mediate the intimate theater of stranger relationality must surely be one of the most significant dimensions of modern history, though the story of this transformation in the meaning for strangers has been told only in fragments. It is hard to imagine such abstract modes of being as rights-bearing personhood, species being, and sexuality, for example, without forms that give concrete shape to the interactivity of those who have no idea with whom they interact. (2002, p. 76)

The iconic photograph is one such form for mediating stranger relationality. A relationship that is hard to imagine is in need of images, and the iconic image acquires public appeal and norma-

tive power as it provides embodied depictions of important abstractions (such as "human rights") operative within the public discourse of an historical period. In addition, the photograph becomes a condensation of public consciousness to the extent that, while it provides figural embodiment of abstractions, it also keeps the lines of response and action directed through relationships among strangers rather than specific individuals or groups. Thus, the photo of the napalmed little girl provides figural embodiment of the concepts of political innocence, human rights, third world vulnerability and victimage, mechanized destructiveness, criminal state action, and moral callousness. As it does so, it also puts the girl in the place of the stranger within the public. Her relationship with the viewer is an embodied case of stranger relationality. Set amidst characteristic features of public life (e.g., civil infrastructure, state action, press coverage) and appealing directly to the public audience (e.g., created through circulation, contrasted to the family and state in the picture, identified by no ethnic or other localized identity, not known in advance) the girl and the audience alike are anonymous, essentially strangers to each other.

Because the girl is distinguished by her pain, her strongest positive content is the internal content of the war; because the war also is conducted among strangers, it becomes a perverse form of stranger relationality. Because the girl's pain is presented directly to the viewer, she embodies the stranger we can recognize within ourselves, and so her world and ours are drawn together into a single public realm. It is at precisely this point that her Vietnamese identity is significant. As Warner notes, the stranger of modern public life is not exotic or inherently disturbing (2002, p. 75); we would add that it is different from the Other that is articulated through every form of social exclusion (i.e., all forms of nonpublic identity). One consequence is that, by coupling the two forms together, an image can bestow public identity. The girl's appeal for help would be subverted by her being perceived as one of the Other, a small, marginal figure within a minor, distant, marginalized group. Her moral force comes from being perceived as a stranger in pain, which not only activates the transcription of Biblically directed compassion, but also makes her someone who is numbered among the public and so has the right to hold the state accountable.

The iconic photograph's fragmentary framing of the girl's combination of naked expressiveness and personal anonymity also keys subsequent narratives about "the girl in the picture." As Kim Phuc becomes clothed, and then partially, modestly unclothed to reveal her scars while holding her baby, she becomes a symbol for the restoration of domestic tranquility. As she forgives those who bombed her, she becomes a symbol of political reconciliation and also a means for forgetting the obligations of political history ("Pilot Finds Forgiveness," 1997). As she becomes a celebrity promoting universal human rights, she personalizes the stranger identity that is an essential element of moral judgment in public discourse.

The other Vietnam photos offer similar mediations of public life, just as they also are subject to a range of appropriations that comprise a continuing negotiation of American political identity. Franklin's study of how the execution photo was reworked in popular films and comics to become a conservative icon provides the most dramatic example of how icons figure prominently in the continuing struggle over the meaning of the Vietnam War (2000, pp. 1–24), but all four of the images are at issue (see Hariman and Lucaites, 2001; Skow and Dionisopoulos, 1997). The napalm girl's reappearances within the mainstream public media provide a varied range of examples.[3] Such appropriations are inevitable in public discourse due to a corollary of stranger relationality: the condition of topical openness (see Habermas, 1989, p. 36). Thus, the napalm icon has been taken beyond the Vietnam War to condemn other forms of betrayal or injustice. In a cartoon protesting the Disney theme park that would have been located near the Manassas battlefield, Goofy is running down the road beside the crying girl (Toles, 1994). In a more recent cartoon protesting Nike labor practices, the girl reappears, wraith-like, as a poster on the wall of a factory in Vietnam (Danziger, 1997, A-10). As Vietnamese girls (or women) work at the assembly line, the cry of pain speaks for them, its anguish amplified further by the Nike slogan at the top of the poster: Just Do It. Their only choice is to keep working at "starvation wages," while U.S. mechanization operated by Vietnamese proxies continues to harm the Vietnamese people. The photo can operate as a rhetorical figure within the picture and as a linking device that activates historical memory and obligation (Vietnam then and now; U.S. immorality then and now; public indifference then and now) to motivate public intervention. The device works because the cartoonist has drawn on essential features of the icon in order to recreate its original effect of activating moral judg-

ment within a supposedly amoral scene (war then and the free-market economy now). The transfer of moral response is possible because Vietnam continues to be feminized while the girl has been restored to her original anonymity and pain. These devices combine to constitute a public culture known to itself by the continued circulation of iconic images.

As appropriations of the napalm photo accumulate, and as the photo slides back and forth along a continuum from public anonymity to personal celebrity, an additional dimension of public culture emerges. Stranger relationality is constituted in a field of visual representation defined by the presence of celebrities and ghosts. Both are exceptional forms of individual presence, known through their circulation, and simultaneously familiar and strange. (Icons have the same features as well.) No reader of this essay is likely to have ever met Kim Phuc in person, much less spent any time with her, but most will have known who she is. Like any icon, the celebrity is self-constitutive of public culture: created by dissemination and evidence of a broad field of attention. So it is that celebrity developed in conjunction with the ascendancy of the mass media, and the category has been a commonplace in photojournalism at least since Life magazine in the 1940s. The celebrity is the widely recognized stranger, that is, a stranger whose image is in wide circulation. More to the point, celebrity is a compensatory mechanism within the media to mask its strangeness. The celebrity image dresses the impersonal process of circulation in signs of private, personal expressiveness. Thus, the redefinition of the napalm girl as Kim Phuc accomplishes a powerful shift in public consciousness. The direct engagement with the stranger on the road is attenuated into a much more familiar world of everyday sociality where one lives among specific individuals who have more or less intimate relationships with one another.

The circulation of images doesn't stop there, however. Despite the many iterations of Kim Phuc and her message of forgiveness, her past life as the napalm girl won't go away. That image of trauma continues to appear, ghost-like, in tableaus of the American flag, suburban lawns, economic expansion, and so forth. A ghost is an afterimage, a specter that should disappear but refuses to go away, and whose very presence troubles the modern present and its logic of linear time. Photojournalism disseminates images, mechanically reproducing them by the millions and spreading them without control over their destination or use. Dissemination always has been accompanied by mythologies of haunting, including photography's early association with spirit worlds, and death remains a preoccupation in photography theory (Barthes, 1981; Peters, 1999). Ghosts are, like signs, bodies without material agency, and re-animation is itself a metaphor for the circulation and uptake constituting public culture. The ghost also embodies stranger relationality, an unbidden presence who functions as a witness to other relationships and who makes the familiar strange. More significantly, ghosts also are a reminder of unfinished business. Thus, the ghost of the napalm girl triggers another strong shift in public consciousness: the familiar social world becomes unsettled, the ghostly figure presents a call for justice, for redress, and time begins flowing backward. This powerful undertow can pull one into a world of signs, swirling images, and the eternal recurrence of traumatic memory, but it can also provide an escape from the amnesia of the present. A sense of strangeness is necessary for reflection on the limits of one's moral awareness, not least as that is produced by the mass media, and it also may be necessary for deliberation.

The celebrity is one extreme of the field of stranger relationality, and its covering device; the ghost is the other extreme, and perhaps an essential means for re-animating public consciousness amidst other forms of social reality. Both the celebrity and the ghost exemplify essential features of the modern stranger: they are within but not fully of the social group, they are in intermediate positions between the viewer and larger sources of power, they are related to the viewer abstractly rather than through more organic ties, and they are at once both far and near (Simmel, 1950). This last characteristic is especially important, as it is perfectly coordinate with the phenomenology of photographic experience: the content of the photograph is always both far and near, whether a distant scene brought into one's reading space, or a loved one placed within an impersonal medium of paper and ink. This may be why emotional response is so crucial to whether a photograph is appealing. The emotional identification temporarily overcomes any sense of artificiality or awkwardness that comes from seeing the image as an image. Likewise, in a world lived among strangers, emotional resonance becomes an important measure of connection. So it is that both incarnations of the napalm girl succeed, as both the celebrity Kim Phuc and the traumatized little girl on the road activate strong emotional responses. More generally, this iconic image, like all iconic images, marks out a particular kind of public culture. In

this culture, a strong form of stranger relationality underwrites heightened moral awareness, rational-critical deliberation about state action, and continued accountability. Even so, historical events are constituted as moments of emotional intensity rather than as decisive actions, and there may remain a permanent lack of connection between moral sentiment and any specific model of action. Neither ghosts nor celebrities do much other than circulate and watch the rest of the world. That, of course, is essentially what publics do, but they are valued because of the belief in a sense of agency. The test of that belief may lie in how the public image can influence political cognition and collective memory.

A common feature of deliberation and memory is a sense of time. We will close by considering how the iconic photo can delay or stop time. The traumatic structure of the napalm photo freezes an action that is happening quickly and would be quickly forgotten. This strong temporal delay is the visual equivalent of the extended duration of verbal deliberation, and it is a contribution to restoring meaningfulness. In addition, extended attention to the image in the present can activate a stronger connection between past and future, and one that is directed by the image and not just by larger narratives: one can see the past moment still recorded in the photograph beheld in the present, while the image projects a future which also has been fulfilled in time before the present and may be still unfolding. The iconic photo can operate in a postliterate society as a democratic moment, one that slows down the public audience to ponder both what has been lost in the rush of visual images and what is still unrealized in what has been seen. As Paul Virilio and Sylvere Lotringer have observed, "Democracy, consultation, the basis of politics, requires time," while the fundamental dynamic of modern society is the acceleration of all modes of exchange (1983, p. 28). This acceleration is driven by the combination of technological development and logistical mobilization that occurred as the economy was oriented toward a permanent condition of military preparedness. It has produced a war culture that permeates modern life while disabling democratic practices. Visual media are highly complicit in this process of social reorganization. The cinema is Virilo and Lotringer's primary example, although video and digital technologies have become the primary media and employ stronger techniques for both fragmenting and accelerating representation (Der Derian, 1992, 2000; Gray, 1997).

In respect to the mediation of public life, we might say that the problem is not the presence of a political spectacle, but the kinetic quality of that spectacle. Amidst this torrent of sights and sounds, the iconic photograph can induce a consciousness that is almost a form of slow motion. As Lester has remarked of iconic images, "Interestingly, moving films shown to television audiences were made at the same time . . . but it is the powerful stillness of the frozen, decisive moment that lives in the consciousness of all who have seen the photographs. The pictures are testaments to the power and the sanctity of the still, visual image" (1991, p. 120). This is a common sentiment in the print media (see, e.g., Eicher, 2001), but it should not be seen as mere special pleading. "The electronic image flickers and is gone. Not so with the frozen moment. It remains. It can haunt. It can hurt and hurt again. It can also leave an indelible message about the betterment of society, the end of war, the elimination of hunger, the alleviation of human misery" (Mallette, 1978, 120).

If a still photo can slow down the viewer, it might nurture a more reflective, more deliberative mentality. That deliberative moment is not a pure space, however, but one already inflected by the photo's embodiment of public discourse and its performance of public identity as stranger relationality. Photojournalism provides such resources on a daily basis that are necessary for maintaining public life, while the iconic photo then becomes a condensation of events and public culture alike that has the artistic richness necessary for continued circulation. The icon is a *lieu de mémoire*: a site where collective memory crystallizes once organic sociality has been swept away amidst the "acceleration of history" produced by modern civilization (Nora, 1989, p. 7). "Simple and ambiguous, natural and artificial, at once immediately available in concrete sensual experience and susceptible to the most abstract elaboration," iconic photographs operate in a dialectic of loss and recovery, official codification and vernacular disruption, verbal context and visual immediacy (Nora, 1989, p. 18). "In this sense the *lieu de mémoire* is double: a site of excess closed upon itself, concentrated in its own name, but also forever open to the full range of its possible significations" (Nora, 1989, p. 24). The photo of the napalm girl is not a figure of nostalgia amidst modernity's inevitable sense of alienation, however, but rather a symbolic form suited to the stranger relationality that constitutes, extends, and empowers public life. Thus, it provides the means through which moral capability can be retained by a public that has no common place, social structure, or agency. Both as a singular composition and as a figure in circulation, the icon provides a rhetorical structure for remembering and judging what otherwise would be consigned to the past.

The image of the little girl running from her pain became a moment when the Vietnam War crystallized in U.S. public consciousness. The photo could become such a "flashbulb memory" of the era not only because it represented the moral error at the heart of the U.S. war effort, but also because it embodied a process of cultural fragmentation that was accelerated by the war and its coverage. The features of that composition then became a template for remaking the public world through its continued circulation in the public media. Or worlds: the audience can choose one world where resilient individuals get on with their lives, where history has the inert presence of a scar, and moral response to others culminates in personal reconciliation. Or the audience can choose another world in which the past haunts the present as a traumatic memory, one that continues to demand public accountability for those who would betray the public by harming fellow strangers exposed to the relentless operations of imperial power. So it is that a democratic public will work out its capacity for thought and action in a discursive field where striking images can shape both moral judgment and collective memory.

An early version of this essay was presented at the Workshop on Visual Rhetoric, Iowa City, IA, August 4, 2000.

NOTES

1. On the other side, some soldiers feel as though they have been betrayed by the picture (Timberlake, 1997). Their argument is strengthened when one sees how the photograph typically has been cropped: left out are soldiers whose stance suggests that all could be in danger and a photographer who is at least as professionally preoccupied as the soldiers on the road. The last omission is the most significant: it erases any sense of journalistic complicity in the war, while it also reduces the photo's reflexivity. We are to reflect on the war, but not on how it is photographed. Another photo that was taken a few moments later as the kids ran past a gaggle of video cameramen and still photographers is even more damning in this regard (Leuhusen, 2000).

2. Another, almost identical photo is also in circulation. Taken by Anne Bayin, it, too, looks over Kim's bare, scar[r]ed shoulder as she holds her smooth-skinned

baby. As reported in a "Ms. Moment" sidebar, the photograph "is part of a nationwide exhibit entitled 'Moments of Intimacy, Laughter, and Kinship.'" Its placement in Ms. magazine is equally clear: "If there is a picture that captures the madness of war, it is the one of nine-year-old Kim Phuc running naked, burned by the napalm that U.S. troops dropped on her Vietnamese village on June 8, 1972. And if there is a picture that captures the power of hope and the joys of renewal, it is the one above . . ." ("From Hell to Hope," 2001).

3. The photo's prominent place in public memory of the Vietnam War is likely to continue. It is continually reproduced in volumes on famous and noteworthy photographs (e.g., Buell, 1999, pp. 102–103; Goldberg, 1991, p. 244; Robin, 1999, p. 59; Stepan, 2000, pp. 134–135) and it is one of two photos (the other is the execution shot) on the war in an award winning historical text for "young people" (Harkin, 2001, p. 132). Additionally, it continues to be used to join private recollection and public memory in short stories (Lam, 1998, pp. 111–121) and poetry (Durazzi, 2001a, 2001b; Vo, 2001). Other appropriations appear in Milos Forman's *The People vs. Larry Flynt* (1996) and Jon Haddock's *Screenshots* (Haddock, 2000). The photo also is used as a means for photojournalistic contextualization across the political spectrum. For example, it has been paired by an Israeli newspaper with the photo of a Palestinian father and son in the midst of a gunfight, in order to highlight the "excessive" emotional impact of the latter photo (Burger, 2000, p. 2b). More appreciatively, it was the one photograph selected for a commemorative art exhibit at the Guernica Culture House in Guernica, Spain to commemorate the 63rd anniversary of the German bombing of that town during the Spanish Civil War (Exhibit Recalls German Destruction, 2000). In addition, we are indebted to Nancy Miller for bringing to our attention a number of important appropriations of the napalm image by contemporary artists; her work on artistic remediation of the image as a form of personal testimony is an important complement to our analysis ([Miller, 2004]).

REFERENCES

Accidental napalm attack. (1972, June 9). *New York Times*, pp. 1A, 9.

Aristotle. (1973). The poetics (W. H. Fyfe, Trans.). In *Aristotle: Volume 23. Loeb Classical Library*. Cambridge, MA: Harvard University Press.

Barthes, R. (1977). The rhetoric of the image (Stephen Heath, Trans.). In *Image-Music-Text* (pp. 32–52). New York: Hill and Wang.

Barthes, R. (1981). *Camera lucida: Reflections on photography* (R. Howard, Trans.). New York: Noonday Press.

The beat of life. (1972, June 23). *Life*, 72, pp. 4–5.

Benjamin, W. (1980). A short history of photography. In A. Trachtenberg (Ed.), *Classic essays on photography* (199–216). New Haven, CT: Leete's Island Books. (Original work published 1931)

Buell, H. (1999). *Moments: The Pulitzer prize photographs, a visual chronicle of our times*. New York: Black Dog and Leventhal.

Burger, J. (2000, October 5). The influence of fear in the eyes of the child. *Ha'aretz*, p. 2B.

Burgin, V. (1992a). Photographic practice and art theory. In V. Burgin (Ed.), *Thinking photography* (pp. 39–84). London: Macmillan.

Burgin, V. (1992b). Looking at photographs. In V. Burgin (Ed.), *Thinking photography* (pp. 142–153). London: Macmillan.

Burgin, V. (1996). *In/Different spaces: Place and memory in visual culture*. Berkeley: University of California Press.

Caputo, J. (1993). *Against ethics: Contributions to a poetics of obligation with constant reference to deconstruction*. Bloomington: Indiana University Press.

Chilton, E. (2000). Veritatis Vietnam, dormant website currently unavailable. Accessed January 15, 2000.

Chong, D. (1999). *The girl in the picture: The story of Kim Phuc, the photograph, and the Vietnam war*. New York: Viking.

Clinton, W. J. (2000, November 17). Remarks at Vietnam national university in Hanoi, Vietnam, *Weekly compilation of presidential documents*, Vol. 46, no. 36. Washington, DC: Government Printing Office.

Cloud, D. (1998). *Control and consolation in American culture and politics: Rhetorics of therapy*. Thousand Oaks, CA: Sage.

Danziger, J. (1997, April 5). *The Press Enterprise*, p. A10.

Decoster, J. (2001, May 20). Soldiers of misfortune. *Boston Globe*, p. D3.

DeLuca, K. M. (1999). *Image politics: The new rhetoric of environmental activism*. New York: Guilford Press.

DeLuca, K. M. & Peeples, J. (2002). From public sphere to public screen: Democracy, activism, and the violence of Seattle. *Critical Studies in Media Communication*, 19, 125–151.

Der Derian, J. (1992). *Antidiplomacy: Spies, terror, speed, and war*. Oxford: Blackwell.

Der Derian, J. (April 3, 2000). War games: The Pentagon wants what Hollywood's got. *The Nation*, pp. 41–43.

Durazzi, A. (2001a, January 22). Phan Thi Kim Phuc at the Vietnam memorial, Veterans Day, 1996. Retrieved February 21, 2002 from http://www.deimel.org/poetry/vietnam.htm.

Durazzi, A. (2001b, July 2). Kim Phuc, found poem, veterans day, 1996. Word's Worth Poetry Readings, Seattle City Council. Retrieved February 21, 2002 from http://www.ci.seattle.wa.us/council/licata/p 0007a ad/htm.

Eco, U. (1992). The currency of the photograph. In V. Burgin (Ed.), *Thinking photography* (pp. 32–39). London: Macmillan.

Ehrenhaus, P. (1993). Cultural narratives and the therapeutic motif: The political containment of Vietnam veterans. In D. Mumby (Ed.), *Narrative and social control: Critical perspectives* (pp. 77–96). Newbury Park, CA: Sage.

Ehrenrich, B. (1997). *Blood rites: Origins and history of the passions of war.* New York: Henry Holt.

Eicher, D. (2001, September 23). Images: Despite the barrage of video footage, it's still photos that haunt us. Retrieved February 23, 2002 from www.denverpost.com/stories/0,1002,1078%1007E153737,153700.html.

Exhibit recalls German destruction of Spanish town of Guernica. (2000, April 25). Retrieved February 21, 2002 from http://www.cnn.com/2000/Style/arts/2004/2025/guernica.anniversary.ap/.

Faas, H. & Page, T. (Eds.). (1997). *Requiem: By the photographers who died in Vietnam and Indochina.* New York: Random House.

Franklin, H. B. (1994). From realism to virtual reality: Images of America's war. In S. Jeffords & L. Rabinovitz (Eds.), *Seeing through the media: The Persian Gulf war* (pp. 25–44). New Brunswick, NJ: Rutgers University Press.

Franklin, H. B. (2000). *Vietnam & other American fantasies.* Amherst: University of Massachusetts Press.

From hell to hope. (October/November 2001). *Ms.,* p. 20.

Goldberg, V. (1991). *The power of photography: How photographs changed our lives.* New York: Abbeville.

Gray, C. H. (1997). *Post-modern war: The new politics of conflict.* New York: Guilford Press.

Griffin, M. (1999). The great war photographs: Constructing myths of history photojournalism. In B. Brennan & H. Hardt (Eds.), *Picturing the past: Media, history, and photography* (pp. 122–157). Urbana: University of Illinois Press.

Griffiths, P. J. (1971). *Vietnam Inc.* New York: Macmillan.

Habermas, J. (1989). *The structural transformation of the public sphere: An inquiry into a category of bourgeois society* (T. Burger, Trans.). Cambridge, MA: MIT Press.

Haddock, J. (2000). Children fleeing, Screenshot Series. Retrieved July 18, 2002 from http://www.whitelead.com/jrh/screenshots/children fleeing.jpg.

Hallin, D. C. (1986). *The "uncensored war": The media and Vietnam.* New York: Oxford University Press.

Hariman, R. (1995). *Political style: The artistry of power.* Chicago: University of Chicago.

Hariman, R. & Lucaites, J. L. (2001). Dissent and emotional management in a liberal-democratic society: The Kent State iconic photograph. *Rhetoric Society Quarterly, 31,* 5–32.

Hariman, R. & Lucaites, J. L. (2002). Performing civic identity: The iconic photograph of the flag raising on Iwo Jima. *Quarterly Journal of Speech, 88,* 363–392.

Harkin, J. (Ed.). (2001). *All of the people, 1945–1998* (Vol. 10). New York: Oxford University.

Herman, J. L. (1992). *Trauma and recovery: The aftermath of violence from domestic abuse to political terror.* New York: Basic Books.

Jay, M. (1993). *Downcast eyes: The denigration of vision in twentieth-century French thought.* Berkeley: University of California Press.

Kinney, K. (2000). *Friendly fire, American images of the Vietnam war.* New York: Oxford University Press.

Kress, G. & van Leeuwen, T. (1996). *Reading images: The grammar of visual design.* New York: Routledge.

Lam, A. (1998). Show and tell. In B. Tran, M. T. D. Truong & L. T. Khoi (Eds.), *Watermark: Vietnamese-American poetry and prose* (pp. 111–121). New York: Asian American Writer's Workshop.

Lester, P. (1991). *Photojournalism: An ethical approach.* Hillsdale, NJ: Erlbaum.

Leuhusen, P. (2000). "Under fire" at *The Vietnam war website.* Retrieved March 12, 2001 from http://www.vietnampix.com/fire9a2.htm.

Mallette, M. F. (1978, March). Should these news pictures have been printed? *Popular Photography, 83,* 120.

Miller, N. ([2004]). The girl in the photograph: The Vietnam War and the making of national memory. [*JAC: A Journal of Rhetoric, Culture, and Politics,* 24, 261–290.] (Also presented as the Addison Locke Roach Memorial Lecture, Bloomington, Indiana, October 24, 2002.)

Mitchell, W. J. T. (1994). *Picture theory.* Chicago: University of Chicago.

Moeller, S. D. (1989). *Shooting war: Photography and the American experience of combat.* New York: Basic Books.

Nora, P. (1989). Between memory and history. *Representations,* 26, 7–25.

Pacification's deadly price. (1972, June 19). *Newsweek,* 79, p. 42.

The people vs. Larry Flynt. (1996). M. Forman (Dir.). United States: Columbia Pictures.

Perlmutter, D. D. (1998). *Photojournalism and foreign policy: Icons of outrage in international crises.* Westport, CT: Praeger.

Peters, J. (1997). Beauty's veils: The ambivalent iconoclasm of Kierkegaard and Benjamin. In D. Andrew (Ed.), *The image in dispute: Art and cinema in the age of photography* (pp. 9–32). Austin, TX: University of Texas Press.

Peters. J. (1999). *Speaking into the air: A history of the idea of communication.* Chicago: University of Chicago.

Pilot finds forgiveness—24 years after attack. (1997, April 13). *Indianapolis Star and News,* pp. 1, 2.

Portrait of Kim Phuc, the "napalm girl," 23 years later. (1995), at the *Life* magazine website. Retrieved September 15, 2002 from http://www.lifemag.com/Life/pictday/wppa04.html.

Postman, N. (1985). *Amusing ourselves to death: Public discourse in the age of show business.* New York: Penguin.

Robin, M.-M. (Ed.). (1999). *The photos of the century: 100 historic moments*. Koln: Evergreen.

Robins, K. (1996). *Into the image: Culture and politics in the field of vision*. New York: Routledge.

Scarry, E. (1985). *The body in pain*. New York: Oxford University Press.

Schechner, R. (1985). *Between theater and anthropology*. Philadelphia: University of Pennsylvania Press.

Shay, J. (1994). *Achilles in Vietnam: Combat trauma and the undoing of character*. New York: Simon and Schuster Touchstone.

Simmel, G. (1950). The stranger. In K. Wolff (Ed. and Trans.), *The sociology of Georg Simmel*. New York: Free Press.

Sixtieth anniversary of *Life*. (1996, May). *Life, 18*, p. 102.

Skow, L., & Dionisopoulos, G. (1997). A struggle to contextualize photographic images: American print media and the "burning monk." *Communication Quarterly, 45*, 393–409.

Sontag, S. (1973). *On photography*. New York: Dell.

States, B. (1996). Performance as metaphor. *Theatre Journal, 48*, 1–26.

Stepan, P. (Ed.). (2000). *Photos that changed the world: The 20th century*. Munich: Prestel.

Sturken, M. (1997). *Tangled memories: The Vietnam War, the AIDS epidemic, and the politics of remembering*. Berkeley: University of California Press.

Tagg, J. (1988). *The burden of representation: Essays on photographies and histories*. Amherst: University of Massachusetts Press.

Tagg, J. (1992). The currency of the photograph. In V. Burgin (Ed.), *Thinking photography* (pp. 110–141). London: Macmillan.

Taylor, J. (1998). *Body horror: Photojournalism, catastrophe, and war*. New York: New York University.

Timberlake, R. (1997, November). The myth of the girl in the photo. Retrieved August 18, 2001 from http://www.vietquoc.com/jul24–98.htm.

Toles, T. (1994, September 2). *The Buffalo News*.

Trachtenberg, A. (1989). *Reading American photographs*. New York: Hill and Wang.

Vietnam yesterday and today: Post-traumatic stress disorder (PTSD) a selected bibliography. (2001, January 22). Retrieved November 21, 2002 from http://servercc.oakton.edu/_wittman/ptsd.htm.

Virilio, P. & Lotringer, S. (1983). *Pure war* (M. Polizzotti, Trans.). New York: Semiotext(e).

Vo, L. D. (2001, December 14). The Girl in the photograph. Retrieved July 18, 2002 from http://grunt.space.swri.edu/lvopoems.htm.

Walzer, M. (1977). Just and unjust wars. New York: Basic Books.

Warner, M. (2002). *Publics and counterpublics*. New York: Zone Books.

White, J. B. (1984). *When words lose their meaning: Constitutions and reconstitutions of language, character, and community*. Chicago: University of Chicago.

Zelizer, B. ([2004]). The voice of the visual in memory. In K. R. Phillips (Ed.), *Framing public memory* [(pp. 157–186)]. Tuscaloosa: University of Alabama Press.

PART V

THE PERSISTENCE OF PERSONA(E) IN RHETORICAL THEORY

Rhetorical discourse is *addressed* to particular audiences. To speak rhetorically is neither to articulate abstract truths in a universal void nor to practice a purely aestheticized self-expression through language. Rather, to address an audience is to create a message that accounts for the character of a specific group of people who are imagined as the receivers of that message. To unravel what it means to address an audience, however, is a more difficult task than it might at first seem.

The paradigm case for rhetoric in the early part of the twentieth century was the political oration, a speech presented by a speaker to an audience understood as "the public." From this perspective, the public was an extension of the Enlightenment conception of "the individual" as a rational actor—the difference being that when cast as a decision-making body, the public represented an aggregation or community of rational individuals who operated on the basis of what some thinkers have called "public knowledge." In this context, "public knowledge" refers to a stable and relatively homogeneous body of facts, values, and opinions constituting the community's "objective" knowledge (e.g., Bitzer, 1978).

Such a notion is complicated by the myriad ways in which people address each other, rhetorically or otherwise, in contemporary settings. The evolution in the use of multimediated methods of communication—the pager, the beeper, the computer, the tablet, the cell phone, and so on—has given rise to forms of presentation that resist an objective label. Online, people often present themselves in ways that they would scarcely recognize in face-to-face interactions. The assumption of an anonymous posture in online postings perforce establishes another layer that separates senders and receivers of rhetorical messages. Even so, these changes rub against people's assumptions that they can know the other persons to whom they speak when they are addressing these others online. The concept of "catfishing," where people purposely develop a fabricated identity online in order to humiliate respondents, goes far beyond seemingly more quaint scams that were conducted in print, or even via email only a decade or so ago. But the point stands: who we are, who we present ourselves to be, and who we judge others to be have all undergone radical change in the era of the Internet. That said, the "I" or "You" that is being constructed is fundamentally a rhetorical device meant to draw rhetors and their audiences closer together or push them farther apart.

Hence the continued importance of "persona" and "personae." The foundational text in contemporary rhetorical theory was created by Edwin Black. In an essay titled "The Second Persona," Black posits that each instance of rhetoric constructs an implied author: the first persona. The rhetor assumes a stance that is predicated on those the rhetor wishes to address. In so doing, the rhetor also constructs an implied auditor: the second persona. So, for example, a speech reveals not only what the rhetor wants his or her audience to know or believe as a consequence of the particular topic of the speech, but it also implies who the ideal auditor for the message would be. According to Black, the character of this implied auditor is made evident in recurring stylistic tokens, such as the repetition of key metaphors. Identifying and analyzing the implications of these recurring elements allows the critic to isolate the moral character of the implied audience, and thus obligates him or her to offer a moral judgment of the rhetor's vision.

Philip Wander extends Black's insight in an essay titled "The Third Persona: An Ideological Turn in Rhetorical Theory." In this essay, Wander calls attention to the fact that just as a rhetorical discourse implies an ideal auditor, so too it excludes potential audience members from inclusion within its boundaries. According to Wander, those who are silenced by being "written out" of the public discourse represent a rhetoric's "third persona." If a primary function of public discourse is to constitute the identity of "the people" and their interests, then Wander's argument suggests the importance of analyzing and evaluating the ways in which certain groups or interests are excluded from consideration by virtue of the stylistic construction of the audience. Only by understanding who gets to be included in "the people" and whose identity and interests are excluded can we fully and fairly evaluate the potential effects and moral import of any public discourse.

There exist, however, audiences who are known only through their own silence. In "The Null Persona: Race and the Rhetoric of Silence in the Uprising of '34," Dana L. Cloud argues that certain audiences implicate themselves by their choice not to speak; these audiences constitute the null persona. Placed into a position where speaking would incur sanctions, she urges that systemic and extradiscursive forces sometimes make not engaging the strategically appropriate choice. The artifacts that Cloud examines are the transcripts of black textile workers who were involved in the industry-wide textile strikes of 1934 in the U.S. South. Mill towns enforced a hierarchical caste system where some mill workers were more equal than others and some mill workers, particularly black workers, were less so. Rather than be full participants in the strikes, black workers recognized that taking part in the strikes carried with it threats of violence. The null persona is thus an examination of powerful, often subtle issues of oppression relating to class, sex, and race. It also challenges traditional assumptions that participation is a voluntary act open to all.

There are also audiences that are implicated in the construction of first personas—ones that avoid calling out those whose rhetoric belies the truth of their personhood. In "Pink Herring & the Fourth Persona: J. Edgar Hoover's Sex Crime Panic," Charles E. Morris III identifies the complicated interaction between rhetors who craft rhetoric to obscure and audiences who allow it to pass unchallenged. Morris argues that some rhetors construct rhetoric allowing them to "pass" in situations where full disclosure would carry with it threats. Furthermore, these rhetors construct rhetoric—a "pink herring"—that deflects attention from what they wish not to disclose. In doing this, the rhetor confronts the fourth persona: an invisible audience not only aware of the rhetorical techniques being used, but also party to the "pass" and subject to the danger of the pink herring the rhetor constructed. In choosing to let the "pass" continue, the members of the fourth persona protect themselves and collude with the rhetor. Morris looks at how, in the 1930s, J. Edgar Hoover constructed the threat of the "sexual deviate" to deflect attention away from questions about his own masculinity. The fourth persona thus extends the previous conceptions of personae, arguing that rhetoric can both silence and speak to an audience that chooses to remain silent.

The rhetorical study of personae continues to demonstrate the complicated relationship between who we are and who we wish to be seen as, between the people we speak to and the audiences we hope to engage or construct. It also makes clear the complicated relationship between the members of an audience and rhetoric designed to attract and repel them. Even in an age marked by multimediated forms of communication, rhetor and audience alike remain constructions that complicate the lived experiences of actual interlocutors.

ADDITIONAL READINGS

Bitzer, Lloyd. (1978). "Rhetoric and Public Knowledge." In Don M. Burks, ed., *Rhetoric, Philosophy, and Literature: An Exploration* (West Lafayette, IN: Purdue University Press), 67–94.

_____ (1987). "Rhetorical Public Communication." *Critical Studies in Mass Communication* 4: 425–28.

Brummett, Barry, and Margaret Carlisle Duncan. (1990). "Theorizing without Totalizing: Specularity and Televised Sports." *Quarterly Journal of Speech* 76: 227–46.

Campbell, Karlyn Kohrs. (1973). "The Rhetoric of Women's Liberation: An Oxymoron." *Quarterly Journal of Speech* 59: 74–86.

Cohen, Jodi R. (1991). "The 'Relevance' of Cultural Identity in Audiences' Interpretations of Mass Media." *Critical Studies in Mass Communication* 8: 442–54.

Condit, Celeste M. (2013). "Pathos in Criticism: Edwin Black's Communism-as-Cancer Metaphor." *Quarterly Journal of Speech* 99: 1–26.

Hauser, Gerard. (1998). "Vernacular Dialogue and the Rhetoricality of Public Opinion." *Communication Monographs* 65: 83–107.

Lucaites, John Louis. (1997). "Visualizing 'the People': Individualism and Collectivism in *Let Us Now Praise Famous Men*." *Quarterly Journal of Speech* 83: 269–88.

McGee, Michael Calvin. (1975). "In Search of 'the People': A Rhetorical Alternative." *Quarterly Journal of Speech* 61: 235–49.

McGee, Michael Calvin, and Martha Martin. (1983). "Public Knowledge and Ideological Argument." *Communication Monographs* 50: 47–65.

The Second Persona

Edwin Black

The moral evaluation of rhetorical discourse is a subject that receives and merits attention. It is not necessary to dwell on why rhetorical critics tend to evade moral judgments in their criticism, or on why the whole subject has the forbiddingly suspicious quality of a half-hidden scandal. Suffice it to note that the motives for doubting the enterprise are not frivolous ones. Most of us understand that the moral judgment of a text is a portentous act in the process of criticism, and that the terminal character of such a judgment works to close critical discussion rather than open or encourage it.

Moral judgments, however balanced, however elaborately qualified, are nonetheless categorical. Once rendered, they shape decisively one's relationship to the object judged. They compel, as forcefully as the mind can be compelled, a manner of apprehending an object. Moral judgments coerce one's perceptions of things. It is perhaps for these reasons that critics are on the whole diffident about pronouncing moral appraisals of the discourses they criticize. They prefer keeping their options open; they prefer allowing free play to their own perceptual instruments; they prefer investigating to issuing dicta. These are preferences that strongly commend themselves, for they are no less than the scruples of liberal scholarship.

Nevertheless, there is something acutely unsatisfying about criticism that stops short of appraisal. It is not so much that we crave magistracy as that we require order, and the judicial phase of criticism is a way of bringing order to our history.

History is a long, long time. Its raw material is an awesome garbage heap of facts, and even the man who aspires to be nothing more than a simple chronicler still must make decisions about perspective. It is through moral judgments that we sort out our past, that we coax the networks and the continuities out of what has come before, that we disclose the precursive patterns that may in turn present themselves to us as potentialities, and thus extend our very freedom. Even so limited a quest as conceiving a history of public address requires the sort of ordering and apportioning that must inevitably be infected with moral values. The hand that would shape a "usable past" can grasp only fragments of the world, and the principles by which it makes its selections are bound to have moral significance.

The technical difficulty of making moral judgments of rhetorical discourses is that we are accustomed to thinking of discourses as objects, and we are not equipped to render moral judgments of objects. Ever since Prometheus taught us hubris, we in the West have regarded objects as our own instruments, latent or actual, and we have insisted that an instrument is a perfectly neutral thing, that it is solely the use to which the instrument is put that can enlist our moral interest. And it was, of course, the ubiquitous Aristotle who firmly placed rhetoric into the instrumental category.[1] Thanks in part to that influence, we are to this day disposed to regard discourses as objects, and to evaluate them, if at all, according to what is done with them. If the demagogue inflames his audience to rancor, or the prophet exalts their consciousness, in either case we allow ourselves a judgment, but the judgment is of consequences, real or supposed. We do not appraise the discourse in itself except in a technical or prudential way. Our moral judgments are reserved for men and their deeds, and appropriately the literature of moral philosophy is bent toward those subjects. My purpose here is by no means to challenge this arrangement. Instead, I propose exploring the hypothesis that if students of communication could more proficiently explicate the saliently human dimensions of a discourse—if we could, in a sense, discover for a complex linguistic formulation a corresponding form of character—we should then be able to subsume that discourse under a moral order and thus satisfy our obligation to history.

This aspiration may seem excessively grand until we remember that we have been at least playing about its fringes for a long time in criticism. The persistent and recurrently fashionable interest among rhetorical and literary critics in the relationship between a text and its author is a specific expression of the sort of general interest embodied in the hypothesis. Despite our disputes over whether the Intentional Fallacy is really a fallacy, despite our perplexities over the uses of psychoanalysis in criticism and the evidentiary problems they present, despite even the difficulties posed the critic by the phenomenon of ghost writing, where the very identity of the author may be elusive, we still are inclined to recognize, as our predecessors have for many centuries, that language has a symptomatic function. Discourses contain tokens of their authors. Discourses are, directly or in a transmuted form, the external signs of internal states. In short, we accept it as true that a discourse implies an author, and we mean by that more than the tautology that an act entails an agent. We mean, more specifically, that certain features of a linguistic act entail certain characteristics of the language user.

The classic formulation of this position is, of course, in the *Rhetoric* and the *Poetics*. There we find the claim developed that a speech or set of speeches, constituting either the literal discourse of a public man or the lines associated with a role in a play, reveal two dimensions of character: the moral and the intellectual. It is common knowledge that the discussion of moral character—*ethos*—in the *Rhetoric* is for many reasons an intriguing account, that the discussion of intellectual character—*dianoia*—which appears mainly

in the *Poetics* is cryptic and evidently incomplete in the form in which we have it, and that there are ample textual hints that we are to take ethos and dianoia as distinguishable but complementary constituents of the same thing. They are aspects of the psyche. In a play their tokens suggest to the audience the psyche of a character. In a speech they suggest the speaker.

It is also common knowledge that today we are not inclined to talk about the discursive symptoms of character in quite the way men did in Aristotle's time. We are more skeptical about the veracity of the representation; we are more conscious that there may be a disparity between the man and his image; we have, in a sense, less trust. Wayne Booth, among others, has illuminated the distinction between the real author of a work and the author implied by the work, noting that there may be few similarities between the two, and this distinction better comports than does the classical account with our modern sense of how discourses work.[2] We have learned to keep continuously before us the possibility, and in some cases the probability, that the author implied by the discourse is an artificial creation: a persona, but not necessarily a person. A fine illustration of this kind of sensibility appears in a report on the 1968 Republican convention by Gore Vidal:

> Ronald Reagan is a well-preserved not young man. Close-to, the painted face is webbed with delicate lines while the dyed hair, eyebrows, and the eyelashes contrast oddly with the sagging muscle beneath the as yet unlifted chin, soft earnest of wattle soon-to-be. The effect, in repose, suggests the work of a skillful embalmer. Animated, the face is quite attractive and at a distance youthful, particularly engaging is the crooked smile full of large porcelain-capped teeth. The eyes are the only interesting feature: small, narrow, apparently dark, they glitter in the hot light.[3]

Note that last twist of the knife: the eyes are "*apparently* dark." Not even the windows of the soul can quite be trusted, thanks to optometry.

The Vidal description is more nearly a kind of journalism than a kind of criticism, but its thrust is clearly illustrative of the distinction we have become accustomed to making—the distinction between the man and the image, between reality and illusion. And we have to acknowledge that in an age when 70 percent of the population of this country lives in a preprocessed environment, when our main connection with a larger world consists of shadows on a pane of glass, when our politics seems at times a public nightmare privately dreamed, we have, to say the least, some adjustments to make in the ancient doctrine of ethical proof. But however revised, we know that the concept amounts to something, that the implied author of a discourse is a persona that figures importantly in rhetorical transactions.

What equally well solicits our attention is that there is a second persona also implied by a discourse, and that persona is its implied auditor. This notion is not a novel one, but its uses to criticism deserve more attention.

In the classical theories of rhetoric the implied auditor—this second persona—is but cursorily treated. We are told that he is sometimes sitting in judgment of the past, sometimes of the present, and sometimes of the future, depending on whether the discourse is forensic, epideictic, or deliberative.[4] We are informed too that a discourse may imply an elderly auditor or a youthful one.[5] More recently we have learned that the second persona may be favorably or unfavorably disposed toward the thesis of the discourse, or he may have a neutral attitude toward it.[6]

These typologies have been presented as a way of classifying real audiences. They are what has been yielded when theorists focused on the relationship between a discourse and some specific group responding to it. And we, of course, convert these typologies to another use when we think of them as applying to implied auditors. That application does not focus on a relationship between a discourse and an actual auditor. It focuses instead on the discourse alone, and extracts from it the audience it implies. The commonest manifestation of this orientation is that we adopt when we examine a discourse and say of it, for example, "This is designed for a hostile audience." We would be claiming nothing about those who attended the discourse. Indeed, perhaps our statement concerns a closet speech, known to no one except ourselves as critics and its author. But we are able nonetheless to observe the sort of audience that would be appropriate to it. We would have derived from the discourse a hypothetical construct that is the implied auditor.

One more observation must be made about these traditional audience typologies before we leave them. It is that one must be struck by their poverty. No doubt they are leads into sometimes useful observations, but even after one has noted of a discourse that it implies an auditor who is old, uncommitted, and sitting in judgment of the past, one has left to say—well, everything.

Especially must we note what is important in characterizing personae. It is not age or temperament or even discrete attitude. It is ideology—ideology in the sense that Marx used the term: the network of interconnected convictions that functions in a man epistemically and that shapes his identity by determining how he views the world.

Quite clearly we have had raging in the West at least since the Reformation a febrile combat of ideologies, each tending to generate its own idiom of discourse, each tending to have decisive effects on the psychological character of its adherents. While in ages past men living in the tribal warmth of the *polis* had the essential nature of the world determined for them in their communal heritage of mythopoesis, and they were able then to assess the probity of utterance by reference to its mimetic relationship to the stable reality that undergirded their consciousness, there is now but the rending of change and the clamor of competing fictions. The elegant trope of Heraclitus has become the delirium of politics. Thus is philosophy democratized.

It is this perspective on ideology that may inform our attention to the auditor implied by the discourse. It seems a useful methodological assumption to hold that rhetorical discourses, either singly or cumulatively in a persuasive movement, will imply an auditor, and that in most cases the implication will be sufficiently suggestive as to enable the critic to link this implied auditor to an ideology. The best evidence in the discourse for this implication will be the substantive claims that are made, but the most likely evidence available will be in the form of stylistic tokens. For example, if the thesis of a discourse is that the communists have infiltrated the Supreme Court and the universities, its ideological bent would be obvious. However even if a discourse made neutral and innocuous claims, but contained the term "bleeding hearts" to refer to proponents of welfare legislation, one would be justified in suspecting that a general attitude—more, a whole set of general attitudes—were being summoned, for the term is only used tendentiously and it can no more blend with a noncommittal context than a spirochete can be domesticated.

The expectation that a verbal token of ideology can be taken as implying an auditor who shares that ideology is something more than a hypothesis about a relationship. It rather should be viewed as expressing a vector of influence. These sometimes modest tokens indeed tend to fulfill themselves in that way. Actual auditors look to the discourse they are attending for cues that tell them how they are to view the world, even beyond the expressed concerns, the overt propositional sense, of the discourse. Let the rhetor, for example, who is talking about school integration use a pejorative term to refer to black people, and the auditor is confronted with more than a decision about school integration. He is confronted with a plexus of attitudes that may not at all be discussed in the discourse or even implied in any way other than the use of the single term. The discourse will exert on him the pull of an ideology. It will move, unless he rejects it, to structure his experience on many subjects besides school integration. And more, if the auditor himself begins using the pejorative term, it will be a fallible sign that he has adopted not just a position on school integration, but an ideology.

Each one of us, after all, defines himself by what he believes and does. Few of us are born to grow into an identity that was incipiently structured before our births. That was, centuries ago, the way with men, but it certainly is not with us. The quest for identity is the modern pilgrimage. And we look to one another for hints as to whom we should become. Perhaps these reflections do not apply to everyone, but they do apply to the persuasible, and that makes them germane to rhetoric.

The critic can see in the auditor implied by a discourse a model of what the rhetor would have his real auditor become. What the critic can find projected by the discourse is the image of a man, and though that man may never find actual embodiment, it is still a man that the image is of. This condition makes moral judgment possible, and it is at this point in the process of criticism that it can illuminatingly be rendered. We know how to make appraisals of men. We know how to evaluate potentialities of character. We are compelled to do so for ourselves constantly. And this sort of judgment, when fully ramified, constitutes a definitive act of judicial criticism.

A Paradigm

Since a scruple of rationality mandates that claims be warranted, and since the most convincing sanction of a critical position is its efficacy, we turn now to a test. That test will be an essay in the original sense of the word: a trial, an attempt, an exploration. The subject of the essay is a small but recurrent characteristic of discourses associated with the Radical Right in contemporary Ameri-

can politics. That characteristic is the metaphor, "the cancer of communism."

The phrase, "the cancer of communism," is a familiar one. Indeed, it may be so familiar as to approach the condition of a dead metaphor, a cliché. What is less familiar is that this metaphor seems to have become the exclusive property of spokesmen for the Radical Right. Although speakers and writers who clearly are unsympathetic to the Right do sometimes use "cancer" as the vehicle of metaphors, the whole communism-as-cancer metaphor simply is not present in "liberal" or Leftist discourses.[7] Yet it seems to crop up constantly among Rightists—Rightists who sometimes have little else in common besides a political position and the metaphor itself. Perhaps the best source of illustration of the metaphor is the Holy Writ of the John Birch Society, *The Blue Book* by Robert Welch. More than most of his compatriots, Welch really relishes the metaphor. He does not simply sprinkle his pages with it, as for example does Billy James Hargis. Welch amplifies the figure; he expands it; he returns to it again and again. For example: "Every thinking and informed man senses that, even as cunning, as ruthless, and as determined as are the activists whom we call Communists with a capital 'C,' the conspiracy could never have reached its present extensiveness, and the gangsters at the head of it could never have reached their present power, unless there were tremendous weaknesses to make the advance of such a disease so rapid and its ravages so disastrous."[8] And again: "An individual human being may die of any number of causes. But if he escapes the fortuitous diseases, does not meet with any fatal accident, does not starve to death, does not have his heart give out, but lives in normal health to his three score years and ten and then keeps on living—if he escapes or survives everything else and keeps on doing so, he will eventually succumb to the degenerative disease of cancer. For death must come, and cancer is merely death coming by stages, instead of all at once. And exactly the same thing seems to be true of those organic aggregations of human beings, which we called cultures or civilizations."[9] And again: "Collectivism destroys the value to the organism of the individual cells—that is, the individual human beings—without replacing them with new ones with new strength. The Roman Empire of the West, for instance, started dying from the cancer of collectivism from the time Diocletian imposed on it his New Deal."[10] And again: "Until now, there is a tremendous question whether, even if we did not have the Communist conspirators deliberately helping to spread the virus for their own purposes, we could recover from just the natural demagogue-fed spread of that virus when it is already so far advanced."[11] And again: "We have got to stop the Communists, for many reasons. One reason is to keep them from agitating our cancerous tissues, reimplanting the virus, and working to spread it, so that we never have a chance of recovery."[12] And finally: "Push the Communists back, get out of the bed of a Europe that is dying with this cancer of collectivism, and breathe our own healthy air of opportunity, enterprise, and freedom; then the cancer we already have, even though it is of considerable growth, can be cut out."[13]

There are other examples to be taken from Welch's book, but we have a sample sufficient for our biopsy. Welch, of course, is an extreme case even for the Radical Right. He cultivates the metaphor with the fixity of a true connoisseur. But though the metaphor is not present in the discourses of all Rightists, it seems almost never to appear in the discourses of non-Rightists. It is the idiomatic token of an ideology, the fallible sign of a frame of reference, and it is what we essay to explore.

This metaphor is not the only idiomatic token of American right-wing ideology. There is, to name another, the inventory of perished civilizations that crops up in discourses that are right of center. It is a *topos* that goes a long way back into our history, and that has evidently been associated with a Rightist orientation for more than a century. Perry Miller, writing of the political conservatism of nineteenth-century revivalism, notes of a sermon delivered in 1841 that it "called the roll . . . of the great kingdoms which had perished—Chaldea, Egypt, Greece, Rome—but gave America the chance, unique in history, of escaping the treadmill to oblivion if it would only adhere to the conserving Christianity. In the same year, George Cheever, yielding himself to what had in literature and painting become . . . a strangely popular theme in the midst of American progress, told how he had stood beneath the walls of the Colosseum, of the Parthenon, of Karnak, and 'read the proofs of God's veracity in the vestiges at once of such stupendous glory and such a stupendous overthrow.'"[14] Miller goes on to observe, "William Williams delivered in 1843 a discourse entitled 'The Conservative Principle,' and Charles White one in 1852 more specifically named 'The Conser-

vative Element in Christianity.' These are merely examples of hundreds in the same vein all calling attention to how previous empires had perished because they had relied entirely upon the intellect, upon 'Political Economy,' and upon 'false liberalism.'"[15]

That *topos* is with us yet, and it is almost as much a recurrent feature of Rightist discourse as the communism-as-cancer figure. Both the *topos* and the metaphor are examples of an idiomatic token of ideology.

Regarding the communism-as-cancer metaphor, it could make considerable difference to critical analysis whether a preoccupation with or morbid fear of cancer had any psychopathological significance, whether such a fear had been identified by psychiatrists as a symptom of sufficient frequency as to have been systematically investigated and associated with any particular psychological condition. If that were the case—if psychiatry had a "line" of any kind on this symptom—such clinical information could be applicable in some way to those people who are affected by the communism-as-cancer metaphor. Moreover, if an obsessive fear of cancer were the symptom of an acknowledged and recognizable psychological condition, the tendency of Rightist discourse to cultivate this fear may work to induce in its auditors some form of that psychological condition. Such would be the enticing prospects of a marriage between science and criticism, but unfortunately both psychiatry and clinical psychology are frigid inamoratas, for the literature of neither recognizes such a symptom. It remains, then, for the critic alone to make what sense he can of the metaphor:

1. Cancer is a kind of horrible pregnancy. It is not an invasion of the body by alien organisms, which is itself a metaphor of war, and therefore suitable to the purposes of the Radical Right. Nor is it the malfunction of one of the body's organs—a mechanical metaphor. The actual affliction may, of course, be related to either or both of these; that is, some kinds of cancer may in fact be produced by a virus (invasion), or they may be the result of the body's failure to produce cancer-rejecting chemicals (malfunction), but these are only the hypotheses of some medical researchers, and not associated with the popular conception of cancer. Cancer is conceived as a growth of some group of the body's own cells. The cancer is a part of oneself, a sinister and homicidal extension of one's own body. And one's attitude toward one's body is

bound up with one's attitude toward cancer; more so than in the case of invasions or malfunctions, for neither of these is an extension of oneself. It is a living and unconscious malignancy that the body itself has created, in indifference to, even defiance of, the conscious will. And because one's attitude toward one's body is bound up with one's attitude toward cancer, we may suspect that a metaphor that employed cancer as its vehicle would have a particular resonance for an auditor who was ambivalent about his own body. We may suspect, in fact, that the metaphor would strike a special fire with a congeries of more generally puritanical attitudes.

2. In the popular imagination, cancer is thought to be incurable. Now this is a curious aspect of the metaphor. If the metaphor serves to convey the gravity, agony, and malignancy of communism, why would it not convey also its inexorability, and thus promote in the auditor a terror that robs him of the will to resist? That consequence would seem to be contrary to the Rightist's objectives. Why, then, is the metaphor not excessive? Some auditors possibly are affected by the metaphor or understand it in this way—that is, as a metaphor conveying not just the horror of communism but also the inevitability of its triumph. Hence, Rightists seem less inhibited by the fear of nuclear war than others. Perhaps there is associated with this metaphor not a different estimate of the probable effects of nuclear war, but rather a conviction that the body-politic is already doomed, so that its preservation—the preservation of an organism already ravaged and fast expiring—is not really important.

We must understand the *Weltansicht* with which the metaphor is associated. The world is not a place where one lives in an enclave of political well-being with a relatively remote enemy approaching. No, the enemy is here and his conquests surround one. To the Rightist, communism is not just in Russia or China or North Vietnam. It is also in the local newspaper; it is in the magazines on the newsstand; it is in television and the movies; it has permeated the government at all levels; it may even be in the house next door. We understand well enough that when the Rightist speaks of communism he refers to virtually all social welfare and civil rights legislation. What we understand less well is that when he refers to America, he refers to a polity already in the advanced stages of an inexorable disease whose suppurating sores are everywhere manifest and whose voice is a death rattle.

And what organs of this afflicted body need be spared amputation? The country is deathly ill. Its policies are cowardly; its spokesmen are treasonous; its cities are anarchical; its discipline is flaccid; its poor are arrogant; its rich are greedy; its courts are unjust; its universities are mendacious. True, there is a chance of salvation—of cure, but the chance is a slight one, and every moment diminishes it. The patient is *in extremis*. It is in this light that risks must be calculated, and in this light the prospect of nuclear war becomes thinkable. Why not chance it, after all? What alternative is there? The patient is dying; is it not time for the ultimate surgery? What is there to lose? In such a context, an unalarmed attitude toward the use of atomic weapons is not just reasonable; it is obvious.

3. The metaphor seems related to an organismic view of the state. The polity is a living creature, susceptible to disease; a creature with a will, with a consciousness of itself, with a metabolism and a personality, with a life. The polity is a great beast: a beast that first must be cured, and then must be tamed. The question arises, What is the nature of other organisms if the state itself is one? What is the individual if he is a cell in the body-politic? Contrary to what one might expect, we know that the Rightist places great emphasis on individualism, at least verbally. Recall, for example, Goldwater's often-used phrase, "the whole man," from the 1964 campaign.[16] It is true, the Rightist is suspicious of beards, of unconventional dress, of colorful styles of living. He has antipathy for deviance from a fairly narrow norm of art, politics, sex, or religion, so that his endorsement of individualism has about it the aura of a self-indulgent hypocrisy. Nonetheless, there is something of great value to him that he calls individualism, and if we would understand him, we must understand what he means by individualism. He probably acts consistent with his own use of the term.

It appears that when the Rightist refers to individualism, he is referring to the acquisition and possession of property. Individualism is the right to get and to spend without interference, and this is an important right because a man asserts himself in his possessions. What he owns is what he has to say. So conceived, individualism is perfectly compatible with an organismic conception of the polity. And moreover, the polity's own hideous possession—its tumor—is an expression of its corruption.

4. At first glance the metaphor seems to place communism in the category of natural phenom-

ena. If one does not create a cancer, then one cannot be responsible for it, and if communism is a kind of cancer, then it would seem that one cannot develop a moral attitude toward its agents. This would constitute a difficulty with the metaphor only if people behaved rationally. Fortunately for the metaphor—and unfortunately for us—there is a demonstrable pervasive and utterly irrational attitude toward cancer that saves the metaphor from difficulty. Morton Bard, a psychologist who investigated the psychological reactions of a hundred patients at Memorial Sloan-Kettering Cancer Center, found that forty-eight of them spontaneously expressed beliefs about the cause of their illness that assigned culpability either to themselves or to others or to some supernatural agent.[17] His study suggests, in other words, that an extraordinarily high proportion of people who have cancer—or for our purposes it may be better to say *who become convinced* that they have cancer—are disposed to blame the cancer on a morally responsible agent. Surely it is no great leap from this study to the suspicion that an auditor who is responsive to the metaphor would likely be just the sort of person who would seek culpability. The link between responsiveness to the metaphor and the disposition to seek culpability lies, perhaps, in religious fundamentalism. Various studies indicate that the members of Radical Right organizations tend also to be affiliated with fundamentalist religious sects.[18] Surely it is possible that a lifetime of reverent attention to sermons that seek a purpose behind the universe can end by developing a telic cast of mind, can end by inducing some people to seek purpose and plan behind everything, so that they must explain political misfortunes and illnesses alike by hypothesizing conspiracies.

5. Cancer is probably the most terrifying affliction that is popularly known. So terrible is it, in fact, that medical authorities have reported difficulty in inducing people to submit to physical examinations designed to detect cancer. For many, it seems, cancer has become unthinkable—so horrifying to contemplate that one cannot even admit the possibility of having it. The concept of cancer is intimately connected with the concept of death itself. Thus, to equate communism with cancer is to take an ultimately implacable position. One would not quit the struggle against death except in two circumstances: either one acknowledged its futility and surrendered in despair, or one transmuted the death-concept into a life-concept through an act of religious faith.

Given the equation, communism = cancer = death, we may expect that those enamored of the metaphor would, in the face of really proximate "communism," tend either to despairing acts of suicide or to the fervent embrace of communism as an avenue to grace. The former, suicidal tendency is already discernible in some Rightist political programs, for example, the casual attitude toward nuclear warfare that has already been remarked in another connection. If it were possible for a communist agency to increase its pressure on the United States, we could expect to see the latter tendency increasing, with some of our most impassioned Rightists moving with equal passion to the Left. John Burnham, Elizabeth Bentley, Whitaker Chambers, and others famous from the decade of the fifties for having abandoned the Communist Party have already traveled that road in the opposite direction. The path clearly is there to be trod.

6. Finally, we may note the impressive measure of guilt that seems to be associated with the metaphor. The organism of which one is a cell is afflicted with a culpable illness. Can the whole be infected and the part entirely well?

As the Archbishop in the second part of *Henry IV* says in the midst of political upheaval:

> . . . we are all diseas'd;
> And with our surfeiting and wanton hours
> Have brought ourselves into a burning fever
> And we must bleed for it . . .

The guilt is there. Coherence demands it, and the discourse confirms it. It finds expression in all the classic patterns: the zealous righteousness, the suspiciousness, the morbidity, the feverish expiations. The condition suits the metaphor; the metaphor, the condition.[19]

What moral judgment may we make of this metaphor and of discourse that importantly contains it? The judgment seems superfluous, not because it is elusive, but because it is so clearly implied. The form of consciousness to which the metaphor is attached is not one that commends itself. It is not one that a reasonable man would freely choose, and he would not choose it because it does not compensate him with either prudential efficacy or spiritual solace for the anguished exactions it demands.

In discourse of the Radical Right, as in all rhetorical discourse, we can find enticements not simply to believe something, but to *be* something. We are solicited by the discourse to fulfill its brandishments with our very selves. And it is this dimension of rhetorical discourse that leads us finally to moral judgment, and in this specific case, to adverse judgment.

If our exploration has revealed anything, it is how exceedingly well the metaphor of communism-as-cancer fits the Rightist ideology. The two are not merely compatible; they are complementary at every curve and angle. They serve one another at a variety of levels; they meet in a seamless jointure. This relationship, if it holds for all or even many such stylistic tokens, suggests that the association between an idiom and an ideology is much more than a matter of arbitrary convention or inexplicable accident. It suggests that there are strong and multifarious links between a style and an outlook, and that the critic may, with legitimate confidence, move from the manifest evidence of style to the human personality that this evidence projects as a beckoning archetype.

NOTES

1. Aristotle, *Rhetoric,* 1355a–b.

2. Wayne C. Booth, *The Rhetoric of Fiction* (Chicago, 1961), esp. Part 2, "The Author's Voice in Fiction."

3. "The Late Show," *New York Review of Books,* September 12, 1968, p. 5.

4. Aristotle, *Rhetoric,* 1.3.

5. Aristotle, *Rhetoric* 2.12–13.

6. See, e.g., Irving L. Janis et al., *Personality and Persuasibility* (New Haven, 1959), esp. pp. 29–54.

7. Norman Mailer, for example, has lately been making "cancer" and "malignancy" the vehicles of frequent metaphors, but the tenor of these metaphors,

usually implied, seems to be something like "the dehumanization that results from technological society." It clearly is not "communism," although Soviet society is not exempt from Mailer's condemnations. One can also find occasional references to the "cancer of racism" among left-of-center spokesmen, but these references seem to be no more than occasional. Where, as in Mailer, cancer is a frequently recurring metaphorical vehicle, the analysis that follows may, with appropriate substitution of tenors, be applied. In Mailer's case, at least, it works.

8. Robert Welch, *The Blue Book of the John Birch Society* (Belmont, MA, 1961), p. 41.

9. Ibid., p. 45.

10. Ibid., p. 46.

11. Ibid., pp. 53–54.

12. Ibid., p. 55.

13. Ibid.

14. Perry Miller, *The Life of the Mind in America* (New York, 1965), pp. 70–71.

15. Ibid., p. 71.

16. For example, roughly the last third of Goldwater's speech accepting the Republican nomination in 1964 was a panegyric to individuality and nonconformity.

17. Morton Bard, "The Price of Survival for Cancer Victims," *Transaction* 3 (March–April 1966): 11.

18. See, e.g., Daniel Bell, ed., *The Radical Right* (Garden City, NY, 1964), esp. Seymour Martin Lipset, "Three Decades of the Radical Right: Coughlinites, McCarthyites, and Birchers (1962)," pp. 373–446.

19. Some illuminating comments on the component of guilt in Rightist style and ideology can be found in Richard Hofstadter, "The Paranoid Style in American Politics," in *The Paranoid Style in American Politics and Other Essays* (New York, 1967), esp. pp. 30–32.

The Third Persona

An Ideological Turn in Rhetorical Theory

Philip Wander

In the Word is involved the unity of humanity, the wholeness of the human problem, which permits nobody, and today less than ever to separate the intellectual and artistic from the political and social, and to isolate himself within the ivory tower of the "cultural" alone.
—THOMAS MANN (1937)[1]

This was what Mann wrote the Dean of the Philosophical Faculty at Bonn University on learning that his name had been struck off the list of Honorary Doctors. He had fled Germany four years earlier as the fascists came to power. The great German universities failed to provide a bulwark against the dictatorship; when they did not quietly comply, they actively endorsed the fall of the Weimar Republic and the repression of the Jews. Mann, in his response, warns against the isolating potential of the ivory tower. It is in this tension between the privileged space of the university and the public space of political activity that I should like to consider the problem of understanding the nature of criticism and to respond to objections regarding an earlier effort to get at such matters, "The Ideological Turn in Modern Criticism."[2]

American scholarship is ill-equipped to understand criticism in the way that Mann would have us look at it. This becomes evident in our efforts to appropriate European thought as a source of authority, inspiration, or new methods for our own work. We are, I think, just beginning to appreciate the extent to which European intellectual activity is shaped by and centers on Marxist themes and an assumption that one has, under certain conditions, an obligation not only to oppose the state, but also to undermine the existing order.

Those themes and that assumption grow out of an historical context radically different from ours. Over the past forty years both Germany and France have had rulers who were fascists, a power elite, in other words, who controlled the state and who secured if not full then sufficient cooperation from every other institution in society—the civil service, army, courts, churches (with significant exceptions), the great universities—for among other things the slaughter of millions of innocent men, women, and children. The upper classes and the professionals in France and Germany did not renounce their privileges during this period. We read and remember those who went into exile or those who became leaders in the resistance, but the vast majority simply adapted either through silence or through actual participation in the ceremonies marking a change in government.

The only analogue in American experience which might suggest that resistance to the state could be a patriotic duty and a moral obligation lies in Vietnam. Yet even here, the comparison falters. Those who, during the Vietnam War, poured blood on induction files had to be willing to "pay the price." No records exist of debates among French, Yugoslavian, Danish, or Italian partisans over whether they should allow themselves to be arrested for climbing over fences, demonstrating without a permit, or throwing rocks and bottles at the minions of law and order. I point this out not to suggest that more violent protest was either justified or would have been theoretically defensible during the course of Vietnam, but to suggest how pale and limited the analogue is between European and American notions of intellectual activity and political resistance.

While academic scholars and literary intellectuals in Europe, after the Second World War, assumed a critical stance in relation to the state and dominant culture, and took political commitment and activity ("*praxis*") as a matter of course, American scholars, even now, worry over the implications of an arrest for trespassing at a nuclear power plant or a research laboratory designing genocidal weapons. Our teachers before us, during what we now call the "McCarthy period," blanched at the thought of having been photographed at a cocktail party with someone who might have had an affair with a fellow traveler.

It may be that on his return to Germany after the war, Theodore Adorno was accused of being "un-German," or that Sartre at some point was accused of being "un-French," or that E. P. Thompson has been charged with being "un-English." I suspect that we would find it amusing, if we did unearth some such accusation. But when in this country during the 1950s scholars and scientists such as W. E. B. Dubois, Owen Lattimore, Robert Oppenheimer, and M. I. Finley were accused of being "un-American," it was not amusing. The extent of such activities during this period is truly remarkable. In 1955 Paul Lazarsfeld reported the results of a survey involving over two thousand interviews on 165 college campuses. More than half the respondents indicated that one colleague or another had been accused, by other faculty, citizens committees, or student informers, of having subversive sympathies.[3] The files compiled during the 1960s and 1970s by the Central Intelligence Agency, Army Intelligence, and the Federal Bureau of Investigation became, with the Freedom of Information Act, a matter of public record. It would, I believe, be naïve to think that this kind of intelligence gathering no longer occurs.

The "Ideological Turn": Criticism and Response

Echoes of the McCarthy period, amplified during the Reagan administration, may be heard in reactions to the "Ideological Turn." They are not so much reflections of belligerent Americanism as they are of apoliticism and prudential neutralism—fears about being mistaken for a "partisan" or a fanatic, of being confused by political controversy or failing to achieve a balanced view. My respondents recoil from "dogmatic materialism," "avant-garde revolutionism," and the "intense connotations" associated with "Marxian polemics." Professor McGee, with his ear to the ground, solemnly declares that he is not now nor ever has been a "Comsymp."[4] His phrasing mocks the loyalty oaths and charges made by members of the House UnAmerican Activities Committee during the 1950s.

It is true that ideological criticism may lead one into a dangerous, foreboding, and deathlike environment—in Professor Rosenfield's term, a "miasma."[5] This is because such criticism leaves the asylum offered by a world of ideas to confront the world of affairs, the sensual, material "is" of everyday life. Because it seeks to understand and enter into political struggle, ideological criticism recalls the "is" shattered over Vietnam, and similar policies in the Middle East as well as Central and South America, where CIA employees and their hired mercenaries "defend freedom" and once again presume to counter, with the exception of China, a monolithic "Communist Menace." Ideological criticism, because it insists on a historical perspective in relation to cultural artifacts and political issues, need not ignore the vast slaughter of humanity in Indonesia, Chile, and Vietnam attending American policies in those areas. Because it takes humanity and not some arbitrary segment as its focus, ideological criticism is also prepared to hear the cries of victims in Poland, Afghanistan, and the Gulag. Because it is not confined by academic barriers, ideological criticism is able to address the unprecedented buildup of genocidal weapons in the United States and the Soviet Union. Because it is not a "method" of research, but rather indicates the ground on which research, scholarship, and criticism *can* be conducted, if one chooses to do so and if conditions allow for it, ideological criticism joined with rhetorical theory is prepared to critique rhetoric legitimizing actions, policies, and silences relevant to the great issues of our time.

Clearly, Rosenfield is correct: Ideological criticism can lead one into the miasma, but it is not a miasma created by the critic. Rosenfield would have the critic transcend such realities to enjoy the fullness, the ripeness, of being. Yet, it is one thing to celebrate the manifold splendors of Being;

it is quite another to treat this experience as a pre-condition for doing criticism, to renounce delib-eration, debate, and rationality, to confine criti-cism to the epideictic and then only to the bright side (i.e., praise). The problem here is similar to that Ernst Cassirer noted in Heidegger's work in the late 1920s. Like Heidegger, Rosenfield pen-etrates beyond the sphere of life into that of per-sonal existence, which he makes exhaustive use of in a religious way. Yet he remains confined to it.[6] Rosenfield's critic may be prepared to hear the survivor's scream but not, I am afraid, the cry of the victim. Cries for help call for much more than appreciation.

Does that mean that Rosenfield is wrong, that his work is unworthy? Not at all. He is right to remind us that, in the midst of political controversy, love, gentleness, and even joy may be unwittingly sacrificed. Is one who would confront political issues automatically fixed in an attitude of outrage? Is reason in such matters barred from the poetic consciousness? Is the blinding insight of the indi-vidual to be lost on the pyre of collective struggle? These are not idle questions, nor are they irrelevant to political struggle. In light of the grim conclusion of so many seemingly noble efforts, I believe that they strike at the center of some profound theo-retical issues. In the "Ideological Turn," however, I questioned the assumption that the poetic, that Being in the way Rosenfield speaks of It, has to be or should be separated from the world of affairs.[7] I approached this, in light of the challenge laid down by the appreciative critic, at two levels: sty-listically, in relation to a politicized Heidegger, and dialectically, in relation to the Manichean universe attributed to those who confront disturbing moral, political, or historical issues. I will return to these questions in my response to Professor Megill.

From Rosenfield's "appreciative" or Transcen-dental Critic, I now turn to Professor Hill's "rhe-torical" or Professional Critic. Like Rosenfield's, Hill's critic also draws back from political contro-versy. But unlike Rosenfield, who promises bursts of insight and rapture, Hill has trouble explaining why his critic should not address the social, politi-cal, and moral issues taken up in rhetorical dis-course he, unlike Rosenfield, agrees the critic ought to be examining. In his essay on Nixon's Vietnam speech of 1969, Hill denounced those who chal-lenged Nixon's motives, facts, or the consequences of his policies on the grounds that Aristotle's trea-tise on rhetoric did not allow for such license. I suggested that only in the sequestered world of the academy would invoking Aristotle to ignore pre-

ventable human suffering be found anything other than bizarre. In his response, Hill leaves off Aris-totle in favor of maxims about scholarship. The critic who would engage in controversy, he tells us, must wait until he or she "discover[s] the truth, the whole truth, and nothing but the truth."[8]

At first glance, because of its honored place in courts of law, I was inclined to let it slide, but on closer inspection and recalling the oath admin-istered to witnesses to "tell the truth, the whole truth, and nothing but the truth," it became clear that the oath had been amended. To *tell* the whole truth as one knows it is quite different from being required to remain silent until one has *discov-ered* the whole truth. A critic with a philosophi-cal bent or a respect for what the Greeks called *hubris* might be loath to claim that he or she ever could discover or know the "whole truth" about anything. Hill does not indicate how one discovers or how one knows that he or she has discovered so vast a thing. What he does tell us is that, in its absence, critics were wrong to question Nixon's speech in 1969 about its policy implications, and that it remains wrong over a decade later because Professor Kissinger still claims that it was the Viet-namese who made us kill Vietnamese.

Even if we decided that Hill's standards were not too high or that his sensitivity to controversy did not approach the condition of a nervous disor-der, we should pause at the prospect of having our freedom to contest official rhetoric depend on our access to official documents. However much con-cerned about the fate of humanity or convinced that great moral, social, and political issues are at stake, Hill's critic must wait for those in power to throw open the archives, for until the critic knows all the secrets, motivations, and information avail-able to those in a position to make policy, he or she must stifle such concerns or relinquish the role "rhetorical critic."[9]

There are truths about the human conse-quences of government policy which may be and can be known before government documents are made available and while there is still time to change bad policy. It is not at all clear why Hill's critic should ignore them. But beyond this, in the real world of politics, even a subliminal acquain-tance with the nature and extent of government classification in this country along with the mis-information on which government officials, dur-ing the war in Vietnam, were willing to rely and the disinformation they were willing to provide, should make one skeptical about discovering even the half-truths underlying official rhetoric.[10]

What is it that leads Hill to confine rhetorical critics, to so restrict their ability to critique official rhetoric? It would appear to be fear: fear, on the one hand, of the "partisan" who threatens the ideals of scholarship—the association is of course with the "fanatics" he refers to in his article on Nixon and not to the partisans venerated in European history; fear, on the other hand, of the decline of rhetorical studies in the hands of "rhetorical partisans" who, shifting their gaze away from the canon and traditional methods of research, may be blinded by the glare of politics and deafened to the demands of truth. So great is his concern over these matters that he is unwilling to risk a distinction between engaged scholarship and uninformed and poorly reasoned harangues. He would rather, like the ancient Athenians, banish those who utter impieties or who otherwise prove troublesome. In doing so, though, he contracts criticism into little more than a technical exercise and reveals, quite inadvertently, why rhetorical criticism has, over the years, rarely been troubled by the demands of either an academic or a popular audience of people genuinely concerned about the meaning and significance of public address.

I believe in the power and utility of rhetorical theory, including Hill's contribution. This should have been obvious in the "Ideological Turn"; it should become even more apparent later in this essay. I believe that rhetorical theory offers a perspective on historical struggle that would be employed even if the "field" as we know it, responding to current calls for relevant courses, is transformed into an apprenticeship program for the corporate state. My differences with Hill pivot not on his theoretical advance but on his use of it to mark off the boundaries of criticism.

The problems with ideological criticism spelled out by Rosenfeld and Hill appear to gain support from Professor Megill's response to the "Ideological Turn."[11] Megill focused his attack on the discussion of Heidegger. He notes errors, but even if there were no errors, he believes that the approach taken precludes any real understanding of Heidegger. Critics committed to a "materialist" interpretation cannot grasp the symbolic domain. They cannot "listen" to rhetorical, literary, and philosophical texts addressing attitudes and consciousness. Except for a few political speeches, Heidegger's is an "ideal world." The personal dimension in Heidegger's work, and in much modernist and postmodernist literature, makes such texts "unpromising territory" for ideological criticism.

When the issue concerns dates, bibliographic sources, or a particular reading, Megill's comments are useful. It is another matter when he attempts theory and criticism. Theory, for Megill, does not have to do with understanding the world but with prescribing interpretive strategies and texts. There are, he believes, two approaches to interpretation: Materialism, which assumes that ideas are distorted reflections of an underlying material-economic base, and Symbolism, which stresses the transcendent and the potential of the mind. There are two kinds of texts, sociopolitical texts and highly personal texts focusing on attitudes, consciousness, and ideal worlds. Materialism and Symbolism are not mutually exclusive (Megill denounces dogmatic Materialists), yet it appears that sociopolitical and highly personal texts are mutually exclusive. What is clear, however, is Megill's insistence that Materialists (i.e., ideology critics) not be allowed to interpret certain texts.

Given Megill's view of Materialism and the fact that sociopolitical texts also may focus on attitudes, consciousness, and an ideal world, there is no basis for Materialist criticism—it does not and, in Megill's view, cannot produce understanding. The case for doing away with Materialist interpretations of all symbolist and some "sociopolitical" texts, however, stands ultimately not on the properties of the texts or the intent of the author (neither of which will withstand scrutiny), but on his narrow definition of Materialism. What Megill calls Materialism he locates in the Marxist canon. The materialism Megill thinks is representative, however, was a doctrine propounded by Stalin and promoted by party ideologues during the 1930s called "mechanical Materialism." At the heart of this doctrine is the belief that ideas are not only distorted reflections of but also in some way determined by an underlying economic base. This doctrine has been the subject of a vigorous debate among Marxist scholars for several decades. Out of this debate have emerged other conceptions of both Materialism (i.e., "historical" and "dialectical" as well as "mechanical" materialism) and ideology.[12]

Following this debate, one discovers that Marx, contrary to Megill's claim, does not use the term ideology, only in the "pejorative sense" as distorted ideas. While the pejorative sense is appropriate in certain contexts and reflects the approach taken in *The German Ideology*, Marx, in the *Contribution to the Critique of Political Philosophy* (1859), writes:

The distinction should always be made between the material transformation of the economic conditions of production and the legal, political, religious, aesthetic or philosophic—in short, ideological—forms in which men become conscious of this conflict and fight it out.[13]

One also discovers, contrary to Megill, that not all Marxists hold that ideas find their "real" meaning in the productive relations underlying the social order. The Frankfurt School of critical theorists explores the "partiality" of ideas in relation not only to party interests but also to an ideal world or Totality. Herbert Marcuse warns against thinking ignoring this second dimension, for without it it would be impossible to identify the limitations of what is.

A prominent Marxist historian, Leszek Kolakowski, summed up the debate over materialism. Historical materialism is, he argues, a valuable heuristic principle; it enjoins the "student of conflicts and movements of all kinds—political, social, intellectual, religious, and artistic—to relate his observations to material interests including those derived from the class struggle." This kind of rule, he goes on,

> does not mean that everything is "ultimately" a matter of class interest; it does not deny the independent role of tradition, ideas, or the struggle for power, the importance of geographical conditions or the framework of human existence.[14]

This understanding avoids the "sterile" debate over economic determinism. At the same time, it takes seriously Marx's principle that our spiritual and intellectual life is not self-contained and wholly independent but *also* an expression of material interests. Though grounded in Marx, this view of Materialism, notes Kolakowski, is certainly not unique to Marxism.

If Megill, with his narrow definition, sensed a relationship between Symbolism and Materialism, one might assume that the relationship would blossom with a Materialism acknowledging the force of ideas and realities beyond the workings of a socioeconomic base. But Megill fails to specify the relationship, and when it comes to concrete examples of Materialist criticism, it would seem that none exists. The criticisms he comments on do not merely contain errors; they prove "abortive." They are "failures." He points to Bronner's critique of Heidegger and is dismayed ("alas") that Sheehan's "highly damaging" rejoinder was not cited. There is an affinity here. Sheehan's refutation, like Megill's, pivots on *ad hominem* attacks and dualistic thinking:

> To judge by this article, Bronner is either an incompetent or a fraud. He is the latter if he was actually aware of the many errors he makes, the former if in fact he was not aware of them.[15]

Either–or logic (either a success or a failure, either Symbolist or Materialist, either a real or an ideal world, either political-social or personal texts), an inclination to take up sides (upholding one, damaging the other), the arguments advanced by Megill and Sheehan play off unresolvable dualities. Whatever burden an encounter with "Being" or dialectical reasoning might place on a Manichean view of the world, it is a burden Megill and Sheehan have managed to overcome.

What Megill has done with the "Ideological Turn" is to arrest a few themes and interrogate them over their Materialist tendencies. He draws back from the debate over the place of politics in criticism, refuses to talk about the need to address real issues, remains indifferent to the poetry, the song, the dialectical movement between different historical contexts, the "dance of creation," in sum, the obvious and unrelenting symbolism in the critique. Professor Francesconi is puzzled by Megill's response:

> The drastic materialist interpretation Megill attributes to Wander draws attention away from the symbolic interpretation of the translation of philosophy to the world of everyday life.[16]

I am also puzzled, especially so since the question of ideology and Materialism was addressed early on in the "Ideological Turn":

> A more catholic and, I think, surer grip on ideological analysis understands that it does not force a doctrinaire rejection of Idealism in favor of Materialism or the dismissal of Aristotle in favor of Marx or Habermas. (p. 4)

It is tempting to suggest that symbolist critics do not read, cannot "listen," etc., but it would, I think, be fairer to conclude that Megill, with his notion of Materialism and ignorance of rhetorical theory, was unable to grasp the argument either substantively or stylistically. Not only does the "Ideological Turn" fail to reflect the exclusivity attributed to it (against Symbolism or Idealism, for example), but it pursues the possibilities of inclusiveness ("coalition building" to use Gouldner's phrase) aesthetically, professionally, academically, theologically (a "catholic" grip), politically, and theoretically. The issues facing us, the real issues, are much too demanding to go it alone.

If we can agree that the critic is not and should not be prevented from talking about the implications of or the silences in the most lyrical, self-indulgent flights of spiritualism (i.e., in Heidegger, or in modernist and post-modernist literature), then the great barrier between Symbolist and Materialist falls or, more accurately, is subsumed in a larger conception of criticism. Perhaps, as ideal types, the Materialist is obliged to make errors and the Symbolist is obliged to ignore history, but we do not have to look upon criticism as a struggle between ideal types. In the everyday world of doing criticism, there is not contest.

But, while there are no sides, there are different moments. In textual analysis, for example, one selects a text; one listens to what it says; and one comments on it. It is like a conversation. What the critic says will vary. Sometimes the critic will summarize what he or she has heard and the result will be largely expository. Sometimes the critic will argue with what was said or what was left unsaid, and the result will be largely polemical. Whether expository or polemical, the choice is up to the critic, the critic as a real person who listens, speaks, studies the speaking situation; who meditates on purpose, considers the audiences, examines the issues; who does his or her best to say something worthwhile about matters of importance; and who recognizes that there are times when words are not enough.

Transcendental, Professional, and Symbolist criticism—each in turn has been examined and found wanting. Are we not in a position to say that these approaches should be discarded? Have they not been outmoded? Should we not now pursue ideological criticism? If the answer is yes, we are now in a position to consider the question of method. What methods of research does ideological criticism have to offer? This line of reasoning is precisely what Professor McGee, in his response, predicts will occur. But the legitimacy of ideological criticism as a method of research must not become the issue. This is the way of "repressive tolerance." One of the questions raised through an ideological perspective concerns method—the assumption that "method" contains within it a sense of purpose or the promise of understanding. McGee rightly argues that method is better understood as a way of organizing materials than as an instrument of discovery. When a "method" acquires epistemic status, argues McGee, criticism succumbs to the lure of methodological pluralism and its promise that somewhere, sometime, some method or combination of methods will achieve certainty (i.e., will produce knowledge and, presumably, generate understanding or wisdom).

What do we have to show for our faith in method? In rhetorical studies, in communication research, and in various other fields, the result has been work which speaks only to the professional concerns of technically trained scholars. *Techne* has become an end in itself. It is no longer related to a product. McGee's argument here, and it is an important one, is not that we have been cursed with bad criticism, or that rhetorical studies has become too specialized, or that the field has not yet matured, or that we need a more "holistic" approach. It is that what is now called "criticism" is the result of an established order willing to tolerate work which is morally, socially, and politically meaningless so long as it reproduces forms associated with technical reason. It is the product of a system which asks not why is this subject important, what does it add to human knowledge, or what is its emancipatory potential, but committed to technocratic solutions, what is the "text" or object of research, what have other researchers said about it, and, above all, what method or methods are going to be employed?

McGee is quite right—ideological criticism is not a method or a professional stance. But, I would argue contrary to McGee that it is much more than a perspective. It entertains possibilities for action, and the actions it considers may go beyond actions sanctioned in the academy, namely the production of texts. This becomes apparent when we take up issues meaningful in our everyday lives—the impact, for example, of the established order, through various institutional arrangements, on how we think and talk about the victims of official violence.

But such analysis, as I conceive of it, requires a reformulation of rhetorical theory. It is, therefore, time to leave off "he said this, but I wrote this, and she failed to grasp this" format which threatens to become little more than a contest, a Heart of America Tournament for postdoctorates. My own reflections prior to the publication of the "Ideological Turn," and most certainly my encounter with a body of challenging and insightful criticism related to it—and I should here express how much I appreciate the efforts of my respondents to come to grips with the partial truths of that work—have led me to explore issues lying somewhere between theory and criticism. The remainder of my response, therefore, will consist of two meditations: (1) Ideology and dogmatism; and (2) Idealism and Materialism.

Ideology and Dogmatism

We should let ourselves be guided by what is common to all. Yet, although the Logos is common to all, most men live as if each of them had a private intelligence of his own.
—HERACLITUS[17]

Partisanship, orthodox Marxism, dogmatism—these terms, in the context of American scholarship, point to concerns about narrowed sensibilities or party discipline in contrast to freethinking and well-rounded academic humanism. The fear is that intense commitment will result not only in a loss of intellectual independence, but will also render one intolerant, unable to give other than perverse readings of those with whom one does not agree. The underlying ideal is disinterested scholarship and balanced views. In my concern with "partial" or party interests in a particular world view or "ideology," there is implicitly affirmed a whole, a total world view, or Totality ever present but never fully realized. It is here that we can, I think, get beyond the clash. The Totality does not require a revelation or even a gloss of Hegelianism. It may be posited in the face of the reality of change; in the limits of language where, even if one knew the truth whole, it could not be contained in words, and if contained could never be heard but only interpreted in light of the limits of the other; in myriad perspectives seducing one away from solipsistic isolation to engage in dialogue where question invites answer invites question into an infinite progress; or in the sheer impossibility of announcing the Totality without inventing a mode of expression beyond the ordinary—in a word, "poetry."

In an era of scientism and calculations of cost-efficiency, the Totality lies under a shroud of positivism, unbelief, and the absence of financial support. To speak of It is grounds for arrest on charges of mysticism or, worse, mystification. But while I do not presume to bring news of the cosmos, I believe that, as a theoretical construct, the Totality plays an important, even practical, role in ideological criticism. It enables such criticism to move beyond even the most persuasive bit of dogma, truth, fact, philosophy, common sense, or party line. The same principle obtains in the ancient argument between rhetoric and philosophy. The Totality or, as Perelman would have it, the "Universal Audience" moderates all claims: "The discourse of the philosopher and his [or her] conception of the universal audience is not the discourse of a god—of a universal, and eternal truth—but that of a man [or woman], inevitably conditioned by the understandings, the aspirations, and the problems of his [or her] milieu, hence the inevitable pluralism in philosophy, where incontestable truth does not exist."[18]

The Totality is that which laughs at efforts to trick up existence to look like eternity. Perelman, along with the Frankfurt School (he specifically refers to Habermas), links the Totality to democratic political theory and the assumption that no one, no party, no institution holds the truth whole. McGee alludes to this when discussing Gouldner's realm of critical discourse. In a recent essay, he explores the problem of citing God as an authority in argument.[19] God's word does not invite rebuttal; it terminates debate—a conclusion as obvious to the unbeliever as to a believer. With regard to Marxism, an important element in Critical Theory, it is the Totality which stands above and beyond attempts to use "Marxism" to legitimize party or government policy. Similarly with regard to capitalism, there is a reminder that claims made on behalf of the "Free World" also have their limits. In heaven we can set aside the need to work for worthwhile change. Change occurs in the world of affairs. The question is, To what extent can we work to make change progressive? To be progressive, change must progress toward something. That something, oriented around traditional humanist notions of human potential, is grounded in the emancipation of human potential.[20] Human potential may be blunted by the existing order; it may be effaced in a one-dimensional society where "ought" collapses into "is" and potential is equated with trend or trajectory. It also may be lost in a society lacking the means for its realization. When this is the case, humanism—whether Marxist, neo-Marxist, liberal, conservative, or academic—is obliged to consider the social, political, and economic conditions necessary for human emancipation.[21] But if history is seen as a mechanism automatically heading in some direction, an aggregate of accidental moments and meaningless events, or a past wholly detached from the present and the future, then action becomes irrelevant. History, however, as Vico understood it—a succession of presents with people whose lived present includes the possibility of constructing a future—gives meaning to concepts such as "progress," "action . . . potential," and the effort to "make history."

Bringing what is into the light of could be and ought to be, ideological criticism makes sense in an historical context—the struggle to create the future—only if a space exists where people can deliberate and act to bring about change. In democratic political theory, this is called the "public space." Without a public space, criticism lapses into eulogy or falls silent. Criticism rooted in democratic political theory, therefore, works to create and sustain a space wherein people or "publics" can reason through the possibilities for collective action. Within each party or faction, there must be room for debate; between various parties, room to negotiate; between individuals and between parties, room for deliberation. There is a pragmatic reason for this: only through coalition building can a public space become an agency for progress.[22] A critic, working within this tradition, therefore, keeps his or her own party's world view open not merely out of respect for free thinking, but also out of a practical need to join together party interests and partial truths into larger ideological configurations or, in Gouldner's term, an ideological "umbrella" under which a coalition might find a way to articulate what common interest makes possible.

Politics of this sort disappears in historical accounts interested not in the meaning but in the significance of actions and events. The meaning of an action, event, or text lies in what it means for those who participate in it. The significance lies in what it holds for an observer. To be sure, an event does not become an "event" unless someone takes an interest in it. The action making up an event and indicated through the text becomes a unit of analysis because someone after the fact finds it important. This is the meaning of "significance." Finding an event important, however, does not create it. This remains true even though calling it an "event" provides a form through which to assemble what interests us now. If the critic denies that an action, event, or text meant something to those who produced it, or that it cannot be understood or appreciated now, then all action, including the critical act, threatens to become meaningless.

There are two problems here: one is how people know what they are doing is meaningful; the other is how someone, after the fact, can determine what the meaning was for the actors. The first problem faces the critic as forcefully as it faces the historical subject. The second problem may be resolved by claiming that the critic possesses either unique sensibilities or powerful methods of investigation enabling him or her to penetrate the mask, identify the symptom, or get at a deeper structure

eluding the actors. This claim does not necessarily deny that what the critic is studying was meaningful to the participants, and, however grandiose the claim to knowledge, neither sensibility nor method can, by itself, decide from among a number of acts, events, or texts which one merits observation. Whatever it meant to the participants and however compelling the critic's insights, the question of significance takes the critic beyond self-pride and pride of method to engage in the same kind of reflection as other historical actors.

The critic may escape the labyrinth of the meaning of significance and the significance of meaning by becoming a systematic observer whose only task is to report accurately his or her findings. But this flight into technical reason, and the fascinating things it does to critical choice, flutters back to the ground when actions, events, and texts are not treated as givens, mere things divorced from human purpose, but as things lying on a state where efforts to create the future enacted in the here-and-now of real people may be likened to the critic's effort, through research, meditation, and writing, to create something in the here-and-now.

But what have we done to the critic, by introducing this person into the world of contingency facing other historical actors—an everyday world of shadows and fragrances, unspoken fears and the delights of the human voice? What are we now to make of this once familiar figure, the "critic"? The "critic," on the surface, is only a fiction—a noun, a role, a convention of academic and literary writing. The term "critic" encourages the writer to rise above the whims of subjectivity. The "critic" is less personal than "I," more formal than "we," and, aligned with "one," clearly an invitation to universalize. Like the "scholar," "researcher," "scientist," "philosopher," or "intellectual," the "critic" is another name for Ideal Observer.

But what of the Totality in the face of the more interesting Critic and the more personable Ideal Observer? What are the limits of the Critic or Ideal Observer in light of the Totality? Ideally speaking, none, for the Critic and the Ideal Observer are but other names for the Totality. Practically speaking, however, the Ideal Observer does not act, while in the world of affairs the act of "observation," especially systematic observation, is highly rewarded. And the Critic, when brought to earth in professional publications, takes on the guise of Omniscient Professional.[23] In the world of affairs, the Critic personifies the ideology of a particular profession at a certain time and place; hence the myriad qualifiers preceding the Critic such as "social," "literary," "rhetorical," "media," "film," etc.

I should like to explore the tension between Critic and "critic" in rhetorical studies, taking the humbling concept of the Totality into the *inner sanctum* of the field, rhetorical theory. In order to do this, I shall return to an issue raised during the course of the debate over the "Ideological Turn," the rules by which texts and events not mentioned in the text may be linked.

Idealism and Materialism

Rhetorical speech . . . is a "dialogue," that is, that which breaks out with vehemence in the urgency of the particular human situation and "here" and "now" begins to form a specifically human order in the confrontation with other human beings. And because the material belonging to language consists in the interpretation of the meaning of sensory appearances—for the main thing is to order and form these—it is laden with figurative expressions, colors, sounds, smells, tangibles.

—Ernesto Grassi[24]

Where is the link between "Being" and the Great War, or between Heidegger on art and the rise of Fascism? How can we move between the "text" and historical events to which the text does not refer? What sanction does this movement have outside partisan interest or personal whim? The question becomes more manageable if we ask: Where does the critic get permission to link events in the material world with the ideas in a speech when the speaker does not refer to or may even deny the relevance of such things in the speech?

In everyday life, the link between materialism and idealism is fairly obvious. Those who do not appreciate the practical are said to be "too idealistic," and those who can see only the almighty dollar are called "too materialistic." If we take this everyday observation into history and philosophy, we can explore one possibility for making a link between word and object, text and thing, speech and events—the audience and the part it can play in the absence of reference or inference through implication and connotation. Survey research in communication studies begins with a simple proposition, and I believe it applies here: The "meaning" of a speech will vary with the audience. It is useful, therefore, in debates over meaning to distinguish between the audience or audiences for whom the speech had meaning at the moment

of utterance, and the audience or audiences for whom it holds significance later on. This distinction may shed some light on what for Megill is a peremptory objection regarding an interpretation of Heidegger. "Alas," he writes,

> one gets no sense that Wander has bothered to ask himself why *Being and Time* is a philosophically significant work. Instead, in lurid language, he reminds us of the "shrieking iron and flame" of the First World War, the "blood red poppies of Flanders' fields," the "vast wasteland littered with rotting corpses."[25]

If the relevant audience for the lectures that became *Being and Time* is an audience of contemporary professional philosophers, those for whom "philosophically significant" takes on special meaning, then the "meaning" of *Being and Time* will be confined to disputes over interpretation, the precise point at which the celebrated "turn" occurred, and other questions presupposing that the whole of the Heideggerian canon is before us to be explicated. Megill is quite right. For this audience the context in which Being was or is talked about will not include dreaded events or lurid details.

But let us begin with the assumption that the audience for whom Heidegger's Being—the "Being" he articulated—took on meaning in Germany when the lectures were being presented was an audience well aware of the awesome disaster Megill serializes as the "First World War"; that this audience had experienced, was experiencing, and knew people who were experiencing, as Jung wrote at the time, the threat of insanity brought on by the collapse of what is and the fragile hope and sense of purpose anchored in existing institutional arrangements; and that this audience would, on the whole, not have found the details of the Great War "lurid," but instead common knowledge, the sort of shared experience a speaker may call upon to flesh out an argument or breathe life into a figure of speech.

For this audience, for people confronting hopelessness, the meaning of "Being" can hardly be confined—and would not have been confined for so popular a lecturer— to the responses of professional philosophers. Those who were or who might have been seeking positions in philosophy in the universities at the time—students like Marcuse, Sartre, Arendt, and Grassi—have proven less likely, over the course of their careers, to limit the context and associations to what Megill in both his response and his essay on Heidegger indicates is appropriate.

The link between Heidegger and art, specifically between his Frankfurt Lectures in 1936 and recollections of starvation and the triumph of the National Socialists in Germany at that time, is of particular interest. This link calls for an augmentation of the concept of audience in rhetorical theory to include audiences not present, audiences rejected or negated through the speech and/or the speaking situation. This audience I shall call the Third Persona. In order to approach this concept, however, we need to locate it in relation to actual audiences and in relation to a First and Second Persona.

Communication researchers using descriptive methods identify real or actual audiences—people who in fact heard, or read, or saw the speech (program, advertisement, play, etc.). Hill's contribution has been to identify the audience or audiences aimed at through the speech. There is the audience in fact reached, including both those the speaker-sender wished to reach (the "primary" audience) and those who are reached inadvertently ("secondary" audiences). The actual audience, however, does not reveal the audience or persona commended through the speech. It is one thing to say the speaker reached X and Y; it is another to say what the speaker was, on the basis of what was said, suggesting what X or Y become.

In a conscious break with Aristotelian tradition, Professor Black notes the absence of any treatment of the audience the message or "discourse," by virtue of the language employed, would create.[26] Black sets aside the question of the impact on real audiences as well as the intent of the speaker to dwell on the implications for the auditor confronted with the language of his or her community. Language, in this view, becomes a refuge for being, a medium in which it exists as a possibility for being in the world. The persona frozen in language and commended through discourse, because it gives human shape to things and because it may entail significant behavior, becomes the proper subject, in Black's view, for moral judgment. In this way Black resurrects the individual as actor and, even as the ethos of the speaker is set aside, preserves the notion of moral evaluation even in a world in which the center does not hold.

The Second Persona—being commended through discourse—is meaningful in a society made up of competing groups and rival ideologies. It enables one to look into the heart of various bodies of belief or world views and describe the

being in the world it commends. Beyond rejection and ridicule, the Second Persona exists as a fact and an invitation. It may be an invitation turned down; it may even be an offensive invitation; but it is an invitation which can be heard and responded to here and now. It becomes morally important, when one realizes that it is, beyond being, an invitation to act.

In the text conceived as speech or "discourse" involving exchange (in contrast to "sending" and "receiving" or "speaking" and "listening"), there is implied a speaker and a speaker's intent. This is the "I," or the First Persona. There is also implied, through certain features of the discourse entailing specific characteristics, roles, actions, or ways of seeing things for one who can use the language, a "you" or a Second Persona.

But, just as the discourse may be understood to affirm certain characteristics, it may also be understood to imply other characteristics, roles, actions, or ways of seeing things to be avoided. What is negated through the Second Persona forms the silhouette of a Third Persona—the "it" that is not present, that is objectified in a way that "you" and "I" are not. This being not present may, depending on how it is fashioned, become quite alien, a being equated with disease, a "cancer" called upon to disfigure an individual or a group; or an animal subordinated through furtive glance or beady eye; or an organism, as a people might be transformed, through a biological metaphor, into "parasites." The potentiality of language to commend being carries with it the potential to spell out being unacceptable, undesirable, insignificant.

The Third Persona, therefore, refers to being negated. But "being negated" includes not only being alienated through language—the "it" that is the summation of all that you and I are told to avoid becoming—but also being negated in history, a being whose presence, though relevant to what is said, is negated through silence. The moral significance of being negated through what is and is not said reveals itself in all its anguish and confusion in context, in the world of affairs wherein certain individuals and groups are, through law, tradition, or prejudice, denied rights accorded to being commended or, measured against an ideal, to human beings. The objectification of certain individuals and groups discloses itself through what is and is not said about them and through actual conditions affecting their ability to speak for themselves. Operating through existing social, political, and economic arrangements, negation extends beyond the "text" to include the ability to produce texts, to engage in discourse, to be heard in the public space.

Establishing links between what is said and audiences denied access to public space brings rhetorical theory back to earth. Was what Heidegger said in his lectures on art in Frankfurt on November 17, 24, and December 4, 1936, irrelevant to those suffering under Fascism? Might they not and should they not have interpreted what was said in ways quite different from what professional philosophers, intellectual historians, or rhetorical critics propose half a century after the moment of utterance?

Regarding the lectures, it can be argued that Heidegger did not intend to address the politically oppressed. Certainly this cannot be shown to be his primary audience. No mention of Jews, Communists, or labor organizers, for example, appears in the text. There is no evidence in the Heideggerian canon of such concern. I shall return to the limits of textual analysis and the political "intent" of these lectures, but for now the question is, Was what Heidegger said about art in his lectures relevant to this group?

If we accept that audiences at the time can provide links between, for example, a reference to food and the experience of starvation, then we have begun to establish a connection between Heidegger's imagining a woman trudging through a field and allusions to bread, childbirth, death, and events not mentioned in the text. The peasant woman's shoes, "pervaded by uncomplaining worry as to the certainty of bread, the wordless joy of having once more withstood want, the trembling before the impending childbed and shivering at the surrounding menace of death,"[27] would, less than a generation after the Great War, have touched on lived experience as well as stories heard while growing up.

The link is even clearer with an audience unable to assemble to hear the lectures, an audience composed of those persecuted by an all-powerful fascist state. For this audience, the uncertainty of bread, joy of withstanding want, trembling before the impending childbed, and the surrounding menace of death would have resonated not only with the past, but also with a problematic present.

Less than three years before the Frankfurt lectures, all non-Aryans and anyone else who opposed the dictatorship had been removed from government jobs and from teaching. The "People's Court" had been in operation for over two years trying cases of treason (broadly defined) in secret, with appeal only to the Fuhrer. A national boycott against Jewish businesses and professions had been in effect for over three years; the Nuremberg Laws, denying citizenship to Jews and forbidding intermarriage, had been in effect for a year. Labor unions had been crushed, their political parties outlawed.

For this audience, reflections on peasant life (a major theme in Nazi propaganda), paintings, a failure to address pressing issues, and a stoic or "quietistic" response would have, in a political context, and, given this context, should have taken on meaning quite different from what Heidegger intended and from the response of his primary or actual audience.

In Megill's view this is all beside the point. He does not envision a link. He worries about "overmaterializing" Heidegger's text and points to the Frankfurt lectures—he wants to call them an "essay"—as a prime example of where ideological criticism fails:

> It is odd that Wander should choose to make these connections when he completely ignores the explicit topic of the essay, namely the ontological significance of the work of art. Perhaps Wander believes that Heidegger's discussion of that topic is beneath consideration.

There is, he states, "nothing in the essay that points to the war and its aftermath."[28]

Now while I agree with Megill that the world Heidegger wants to embrace is not the extant world as "Wander understands it," the extant world Heidegger urges his audience to transcend points to war and its aftermath in a variety of ways. One textual link concerns the "things" Heidegger likens to works of art:

> Works of art are familiar to everyone. . . . If we consider the works in their untouched actuality and do not deceive ourselves, the result is that the works are as naturally present as things. The picture hangs on the wall like a rifle or a hat. A painting, e.g., the one by Van Gogh that represents a pair of peasant shoes, travels from one exhibition to another. Works of art are shipped like coal from the Ruhr and logs from the Black Forest. During the First World War Holderlin's hymns were packed in the soldier's knapsack together with cleaning gear. Beethoven's quartets lie in storerooms of the publishing house like potatoes in a cellar.[29]

Note that there is a reference to the Great War in the text, though Megill's caution about the lectures being altered for publication years later is also supported by the fact that the reference is to a war occurring before a "second" World War.

But even if there were no reference, the "things" picked out were familiar, had common associations for the audience listening to the lectures. As things naturally present—coal, logs, and potatoes—they merely exist; but they also may be thought of as symbols of security. For the primary and, in all probability, for the actual audience, such things could be transcended, and the insecurities associated with an earlier period including not only the Great War, when such things were scarce, but also the Great Depression, when they were often not affordable, could be set aside. Why? Because of the prosperity enjoyed under the National Socialists. Coal was once more coming from the Ruhr; winter did not have to be so cold. Logs were once again coming from the Black Forest; homes could be built and heated. Potatoes once more could be laid up in the cellar; no need to fear an empty stomach. When such things no longer present a problem, they become "naturally present."

From the point of view of the audience which could not assemble and could not protest, and which was being negated in and through every channel of communication, however, the suggestion that rifles be treated as commonplace and the military be associated with hymns and cleaning gear might have and, given the situation in 1936, should have struck a different note. With the imposition of police power, the abolition of free speech and assembly, a rapid buildup of the armed forces, and the omnipresent voice of the Fuhrer over newly installed radios, this audience might have found the things indicated by Heidegger more disturbing than natural. "Airplanes and radio sets," he went on, only, seven months after the reintroduction of conscription in Germany, "are nowadays among the things closest to us, but when we have in mind the last things we think of something altogether different." For the fearful and the oppressed, these "last things" might have been marked with dread, anger, or resignation: "Death and judgment—these are the last things."[30]

But consider Heidegger's method for approaching the "naturally present"—taking the familiar and making it unfamiliar by reattaching it to work and, through work with what is (i.e., equipment), to a problematic future. The peasant shoes in Van Gogh's painting become, through the critical narrative, equipment for work. They are productive of something. What kind of life are they associated with? What sort of future does this life bring

into being? What is the value in and quality of this effort? What are the fears attending or underlying the use of this equipment? These are questions addressed to what is beneath the surface of the thing—the work of art—revealed through the object imbedded in the process of living.

Francesconi puts the question in this way: "Wouldn't a complete 'releasement toward things' acknowledge our social being, our nature as beings of purpose in social involvement? Wouldn't such an analysis realize that a technological tool has an impact upon the social organization in which it operates?" (p. 52). What occurs if this type of analysis is applied to other things specified by Heidegger, and if we make comparisons between equipment and the future instead of focusing on the differences between art and non-art? Coal, logs, potatoes, radios, and airplanes, if only through government propaganda, blend symbols of security and symbols of progress and power into an overarching sense of national prosperity, pride, and potential under National Socialism. In this way "prosperity" also may become a thing whose essence must be penetrated if one is to rise above what is "naturally present." Prosperity is the product not only of work but also, in the case of "national" prosperity, of decisions made by government.

As a thing, then, "national prosperity" is associated not only with a particular government, with decisions made by those in power over the collection of taxes, distribution of funds, future projects and policies, etc. The problem with a term like "prosperity" is that it gathers in too much and, at the same time, not enough. "National Prosperity" depends, in the modern world, on abstractions such as employment statistics and productivity indexes (during 1933–1937 unemployment in Germany dropped from 6.4 to 1.8 million and productivity almost doubled). Such abstractions, however, barely touch on what is experienced in everyday life or the future being fashioned out of economic decisions made by governments summed up under terms like "economic security," "productivity," or "national prosperity."

A similar problem occurs with things treated as "objects," except that when things become objects-of-perception they may reclaim some small portion of a world of fragrances and shadows. In both cases, the entities—abstractions and objects—are detached from the lives of those who experience them over time and in light of their importance in a world of purpose and action. With objects such as coal, logs, potatoes, radios, and airplanes, and with abstractions such as national prosperity, they too, like a work of art, may become things unnoticed, part of our second nature. Disturbing their "natural presence" invites inquiry into their origin, their function in a human world, and the future they are intended to or are likely to provide.

Alongside a pair of shoes, Heidegger places other things which also hint at scenes of desolation. Grasping this requires us to penetrate our knowledge of concentration camps and World War II to reach a point from which to survey a future which, while not holding these specific events, held such grave possibilities that it had become dangerous to talk about them. It also requires us to grasp the ideological nature of our historical explanations for what occurred in Germany, specifically our understanding the causes of the economic boom following the takeover in 1933.

Traditional explanations for this boom center on Keynesianism and demand management. Recent research, however, according to V. R. Berghan, emphasizes the relationship between national prosperity and arms expenditure. The Four Year Plan, begun in 1936, writes Berghan,

fixed both the ultimate object of all this hectic rearmament activity, namely a war in four years' time, and pointed to the inexorability of national bankruptcy unless the military expenditure of the 1930s was recouped in such a war. It was clear that the debts which the government had incurred when ordering weapons and increasing the size of the armed forces would one day have to be paid.[31]

The wars such expenditures pointed to were not "world wars"—this is where thinking may become blocked by subsequent events. The National Socialists were not advocating a "Second World War." There was a need for a strong defense, for a well-armed Germany, for protecting a sphere of influence, for warding off one menace or another, for protecting Germans in other countries.

But however enormous increases in defense spending were officially explained, there were people in Germany in late 1936 who recognized the potential for war and knew its horrors. For this audience, the things associated with economic security, national prosperity, military power—coal, logs, potatoes, radios, airplanes, a desolate landscape, the "shivering menace of death," and the last things, "death and judgment"—would have seemed less arbitrary or merely illustrative. This audience would not have been reluctant to look beneath the surface of the lecture because of the reputation of the speaker. Here again our thinking

may be blocked. For us Heidegger's membership in the Party and his speeches favoring the Fuhrer in 1933 predominate; for an audience attending the lectures in 1936, the speaker was a famous philosopher who had left the Party, resigned his administrative post, was being attacked by party ideologues, and, strangely enough, had taken up the topic of "art" on a public platform.

I say "strangely enough" because for us talk about art is harmless, the sort of thing found in museum brochures or journals of aesthetics. It was not innocuous in the context in which Heidegger spoke. The difference between what "art" referred to then and what it refers to now, along with the conditions under which talk about "art" is monitored and the penalties that can be inflicted, is so great that the meaning of Heidegger's lectures is all but lost to us.

Politically sensitive is one way of characterizing the topic, the "origin of art." The government extended its control over art as far as it could. The Reich Chamber of Culture covered literature, music, films, radio, theater, fine arts, and the press. Membership in the Chamber was compulsory in every artistic profession. Denial of membership meant that one could not, in a public sense, be an "artist." The financing of art fell under government jurisdiction. Unauthorized art could be destroyed. All forms of expression were subject to censorship.

Politically dangerous is another way of characterizing efforts to talk about art under such conditions. On November 27, 1936, one week before Heidegger's third lecture, Dr. Goebbels, head of the Ministry of Propaganda and Enlightenment, announced:

Because this year had not brought an improvement in art criticism, I forbid once and for all the continuance of art criticism in its present form, effective as of today. From now on, the reporting of art will take the place of art criticism which has set itself up as a judge of art—a complete perversion of the concept "criticism" which dates from the time of the Jewish domination of art. The critic is to be superseded by the art editor. The reporting of art should not be concerned with values, but should confine itself to description.[32]

Whether or not there was an intentional link between Goebbels' announcement and Heidegger's lectures—whether Goebbels "meant" to silence Heidegger or his approach to interpretation—this much is evident: There was, under the National Socialists, a well-defined political context for anyone who would talk about "art."

Given the constraints on what could and could not be said and the clarity of the official position in these matters, one would expect to find a number of themes, like racial explanations for art, expounded. One would expect to find these themes, that is, if the speaker were one with the government and the Party. If the speaker were not in agreement, one would expect to find the topic treated in ways as far removed from sociopolitical realities as possible. Ontology, like irony and allegory, offers refuge for a speaker who is vulnerable to political attack. How far ontology may be conceived of as a rhetorical strategy in this instance I have no idea. So much depends on "intent," and so little is known about Heidegger's thinking on the underlying issues.

Clearly, ideological criticism must be able to step outside the barriers of intent when assessing the meaning of a body of discourse or a "text." This is true not only when the discourse is being treated as a symptom of some social or political problem, but also when the discourse, perhaps unintentionally, grapples with problems which can be shown to exist in context. Professor Corcoran's objection to a concept of ideology which fails to provide for the unintentional production of ideologically significant formations and his insistence on including structuralist and deconstructionist contributions to the concept are pertinent here. Ideology, he observes, is all the more effective for not being recognized as such.[33] I would only add that ideology, even when intentional, is sometimes possible only when those in power do not or cannot identify it as such.

With regard to Heidegger, while there is little room to argue that he was aware of the implications of his lectures for those whose existence lay outside the university, there is evidence to suggest that he was concerned about the impact of Nazi policies on those who worked within the university.[34] But whatever Heidegger's intent in these matters, when the political constraints about public address and the topic of art in particular are taken into account, certain contextual ambiguities appear which help to explain why Heidegger, during the middle 1930s, came increasingly under attack. Ambiguity attends both form and content at the close of his third lecture. After declaring that a people's historical existence is found in art, he asks: "Are we in our existence historically at the origin?" For Party leaders and government officials, this was no longer open to question. National Socialism was the answer—it was a New Order, the beginning of a Thousand Year Reich.

"Do we know, which means do we give heed," he goes on, "the essence of the origin? Or do we still," he asks amidst an official revival of classical realism, "merely make appeal to a cultivated acquaintance with the past?"

How did Heidegger answer these questions? He did not answer them directly; instead, he offered a standard for arriving at answers. It was not a standard endorsed by the Party, dictated by the government, or articulated by the Leader. Nothing was said about the racial origins of the "standard," though it did come from one of the heroes in the nationalist canon. It was a standard provided by a poet, and Heidegger raised it up before the established order as a standard to which it too could be held accountable:

> Holderlin the poet—whose work still confronts the Germans as a test to be stood—named it in saying:
>
>> Reluctantly
>> that which dwells near its origin departs.[35]

There are ambiguities in Heidegger's lectures on art which grow out of treating them rhetorically and situating them in the here and now of historical struggle. They rest on certain facts about the speaker—the fact that Heidegger left the Party and his administrative post in 1934, no longer praised the government or the Leader, in his seminars denounced official attempts to ground art in racial theories, and did not employ such theories in his lectures on art. They rest on references in the text—references to "coal," "logs," "potatoes," a "rifle," "soldiers," "radios," and "airplanes"—which, in the false security of a war economy and an official call for protecting Germany's sphere of influence, makes such things problematic, the same things which, when likened to works of art, should not be taken for granted as "things."[36] They rest also on the fact that the language of the text and the nature of the argument were shaped to some extent by a government which had assumed control over production, content, communication, and interpretation of the arts and of language itself.[37]

Finally, they rest on the existence of different audiences: a primary audience concerned about or interested in the "origin of art" in a society where such questions were given official answers; a secondary audience composed of Party ideologues and government censors whom Heidegger had to take into account and who already were denouncing him; and a tertiary audience, an audience which may or may not have been part of the speaker's awareness, existing in the silences of the text, the reality of oppression, and the unutterable experience of human suffering, an audience for whom what was said was relevant in ways that traditional approaches to interpretation may overlook.

I am not promoting a "new" interpretation of Heidegger or contributing another gloss on his lectures. Such things are rightly left up to those who study the "texts," know the languages, spend time in the archives. I stand in their debt in trying to puzzle out the issues. As for the interpretation offered, I take some solace from the poet:

What is spoken is never,
and in no language,
What is said.[38]

What interests me is the theoretical issue centered on the ways in which theory in general, rhetorical theory in particular, is shaped by the context in which it is propounded. To what extent does rhetorical theory oblige us to ignore audiences not addressed, unable to attend, and unable to respond to the "text?" To what extent do our academic assumptions or commitments prompt us to reflect on the meaning and significance of what is said in ways that ignore or, with Heidegger's lectures on art, actually conceal important silences?

Whatever the limitations of my critique, I believe that the Third Persona merits serious consideration as a contribution to rhetorical theory. It focuses on audiences negated through the "text"— the language, the speaking situation, the established order shaping both. It provides a space in rhetorical theory for those unable not only to find shelter in, but also to take part in the discourse. Through the Third Persona we may examine the rules for producing discourse (criticism) about discourse (rhetoric). The tendency for such rules to reflect, sanction, or obscure rules for the production of discourse in the public space when it comes to the negation of human beings (i.e., transforming some group, or class, or sex, or race into an "it") suggests a link between theory and the institutional framework underwriting the production of theory. This is, I think, a point where Critical Theory, Sartrean existentialism, and deconstructionism intersect. And it is the ground on which hermeneutics, in its flight from the heavens of purpose and potential, can alight on discovering that texts are produced by real people and that the process of production, interpretation, and communication may veil what is in various ways.

Summary

It takes two to maintain a silence: the one who remains silent, and the other who either doesn't ask questions or who is satisfied with unsatisfactory answers.
—MICHAEL SCHNEIDER[39]

Something fruitful, I hope, has emerged out of the exchange over the "Ideological Turn." It has forced me to reflect on and make explicit certain theoretical assumptions regarding a Third Persona. It is important to understand, however, that this concept refers not merely to groups of people with whom "you" and "I" are not to identify, who are to remain silent in public, who are not to become part of "our" audience or even be allowed to respond to what "we" say. Beyond its verbal formulation, the Third Persona draws in historical reality, so stark in the twentieth century, of peoples categorized according to race, religion, age, gender, sexual preference, and nationality, and acted upon in ways consistent with their status as non-subjects. The Third Persona directs our attention to beings beyond the claims of morality and the bonds of compassion. It does so not only in the past, but also, in an age of genocidal weapons, in a future of generations yet unborn whose claims on the present grow increasingly faint. There is, to be sure, a technical ring about the "Third Persona." Properly understood, however, it bursts the limits of technical reason to join the intellectual and the artistic with the political and social. Properly understood, it involves the unity of humanity and the wholeness of the human problem.

NOTES

1. Thomas Mann, "Letter to the Dean of the Philosophical Faculty of the University of Bonn, 1936," in *The Thomas Mann Reader*, ed. J. W. Angell (New York: Grosset and Dunlap, 1950), p. 518.

2. Philip Wander, "The Ideological Turn in Modern Criticism," *Central States Speech Journal* 34 (1983): 1–18.

3. Paul F. Lazarsfeld and Wagner Thielens Jr., *The Academic Mind* (Glencoe, IL: Free Press, 1958), p. 50. For an excellent overview of this era, see David Caute, *The Great Fear: The Anti-Communist Purge Under Truman and Eisenhower* (New York: Simon and Schuster, 1978), esp. "Purge of the 'Reducators,'" pp. 403–431.

4. Michael Calvin McGee, "Another Philippic: Notes on the Ideological Turn in Criticism," *Central States Speech Journal* 35 (1984): 43–50.

5. Lawrence W. Rosenfield, "Ideological Miasma," *Central States Speech Journal* 34 (1983): 119–121.

6. Ernst Cassirer, "'Mind' and 'Life': Heidegger," trans. John Michael Krois, *Philosophy and Rhetoric* 16 (1983): 162.

7. This question was also explored in my "The Aesthetic Dimension: A Note on Ideology, Criticism, and Reality," in David Zarefsky, Malcolm A. Sillars, and Jack Rhodes, eds., *Argument in Transition: Proceedings of the Third Summer Conference on Argumentation* (Annandale, VA: Speech Communication Association, 1983), pp. 159–169; and "The Aesthetics of Fascism," *Journal of Communication* 33 (1983): 70–78.

8. Forbes Hill, "A Turn Against Ideology: Reply to Professor Wander," *Central States Speech Journal* 34 (1983): 122.

9. The exchange between Professors Campbell and Hill illustrates the kind of debates which occur over the question of who can or cannot lay claim to academic legitimacy. Campbell presses Hill over the arbitrary definitions of the "field" he advances, his inability to tolerate different approaches, and the arbitrary manner in which he defends his views on Vietnam. (See Karlyn Kohrs Campbell, "Response to Forbes Hill," *Central States Speech Journal* 34 [1983]: 126–127.)

10. See Paul Joseph, "The Politics of 'Good' and 'Bad' Information: The National Security Bureaucracy and the Vietnam War," *Politics and Society* 7 (1977): 105–126.

11. Allan Megill, "Heidegger, Wander, and Ideology," *Central States Speech Journal* 34 (1983): 114–119. Megill's positions on Heidegger are laid out in more complete form in his *Prophets of Extremity: Nietzsche, Heidegger, Foucault, Derrida* (Berkeley and Los Angeles: University of California Press, 1985).

12. On "mechanical," "historical," and "dialectical" materialism, see Raymond Williams, *Keywords: A Vocabulary of Culture and Society* (New York: Oxford University Press, 1976), pp. 163–167.

13. Quoted in Williams, *Keywords*, p. 128.

14. Leszek Kolakowski, *Main Currents of Marxism*, trans. P. S. Falla (New York: Oxford University Press, 1978), vol. 1, p. 371. For the context surrounding the debate over materialism, see "Marxism as the Ideology of the Soviet State," in *Main Currents*, vol. 3, pp. 77–116.

15. Thomas Sheehan, "Philosophy and Propaganda: Response to Professor Bronner," *Salmagundi* 43 (1979): 174. Bronner, in his response, captures the tone. Sheehan, he writes, "employs pedantry and bellicose verbosity in order to smother contradictions, suppress controversies, and divert the reader from real issues" (Stephen Eric Bronner, "The Poverty of Scholasticism/A Pedant's Delight: A Response to Thomas Sheehan," *Salmagundi*, p. 185).

16. Robert Francesconi, "Heidegger and Ideology: Reflections of an Innocent Bystander, *Central States Speech Journal* 35 (1984): 51–53.

17. Heraclitus, "Fragments," in Philip Wheelwright, ed., *The Presocratics* (New York: Odyssey Press, 1966), p. 69.

18. Chaim Perelman, "The New Rhetoric and the Rhetoricians: Remembrances and Comments," *Quarterly Journal of Speech* 70 (1984): 193–194. On the historical struggle between philosophy and rhetoric, see Nancy S. Struever's incisive statement in *The Language of History in the Renaissance: Rhetoric and Historical Consciousness in Florentine Humanism* (Princeton, NJ: Princeton University Press, 1970), pp. 5–39.

19. See Michael Calvin McGee, "Secular Humanism: A Radical Reading of 'Culture Industry' Productions," *Critical Studies in Mass Communication* 1 (1984): 1–33.

20. Mihailo Markovic, *From Affluence to Praxis: Philosophy and Social Criticism* (Ann Arbor: University of Michigan Press, 1974). This book has a "Forward" by Eric Fromm, whose entire body of work may be seen as a critique of the established order in light of human potential.

21. See my "Introduction" to the new edition of Henri Lefebvre, *Everyday Life in the Modern World* (New York: Transaction Press, 1984).

22. See Alvin Gouldner, *The Dialectic of Ideology and Technology* (New York: Seabury Press, 1976).

23. "At the heart of the debate between the 'old' and 'new' left in France in the late 1960s and early 1970s was a re-evaluation of the role of the critic or 'intellectual.' Sartre identified the May 1968 'events' as pivotal. In the contrast between his 'A Plea for Intellectuals,' lectures delivered at Tokyo and Kyoto in September–October 1965, and 'A Friend of the People,' an interview given in October 1970, may be seen this change" (Jean-Paul Sartre, *Between Existentialism and Marxism* [New York: William Morrow and Company, 1976], pp. 228–298). Michel Foucault attacked the notion of the intellectual as spokesperson for the "universal," contrasting it with the realization that the intellectual, even while critiquing the established order, is part of it. Even while serving the function of "representing" others not able to speak, the intellectual perpetuates "silences" (see "Intellectuals and Power," a conversation with Gilles Deleuze recorded March 4, 1972, in *Michel Foucault: Language, Counter-Memory, Practice*, ed. D. F. Bouchard, trans. D. F. Bouchard and S. Simon [Ithaca, NY: Cornell University Press, 1977], pp. 205–217). For a brilliant attempt to integrate philosophy, criticism, and history, see Arthur Hirsh, *The French New Left: An Intellectual History from Sartre to Gorz* (Boston: South End Press, 1981).

24. Ernesto Grassi, *Rhetoric as Philosophy: Humanist Tradition* (University Park: Pennsylvania State University Press, 1980), p. 113.

25. Megill, "Heidegger, Wander, and Ideology," p. 115.

26. Edwin Black, "The Second Persona," *Quarterly Journal of Speech* 56 (1970): 109–119 [reprinted in this volume].

27. Martin Heidegger, *Poetry, Language, Thought*, trans. Albert Hofstadter (New York: Harper & Row, 1975), p. 34.

28. Megill, "Heidegger, Wander, and Ideology," p. 115.

29. Heidegger, *Poetry, Language, Thought*, pp. 18–19.

30. Ibid., p. 21.

31. V. R. Berghahn, *Modern Germany: Society, Economy, and Politics in the Twentieth Century* (New York: Cambridge University Press, 1982), p. 148.

32. George L. Mosse, ed., *Nazi Culture: Intellectual, Cultural, and Social Life in the Third Reich* (New York: Grosset and Dunlap, 1966), p. 162.

33. "The Widening Gyre: Another Look at Ideology in Wander and His Critics," *Central States Speech Journal* 35 (1984): 54–56. The partiality of a speech, message, formation, or world view may be explained through the "bad faith" of the speaker, the vested interests shaping the process of communication, or simply stand revealed in the structure or silences in the product. The *technique* for conducting an ideological critique must not overshadow its purpose, but Corcoran is quite right about the problems, especially in relation to mass media, of ignoring methods which rise above intent. See his "Television as Ideological Apparatus: The Power and the Pleasure," *Critical Studies in Mass Communication* 1 (1984): 131–145. For another approach to the same problem, see my "Cultural Criticism," in Dan D. Nimmo and Keith R. Sanders, eds., *Handbook of Political Communication* (Beverly Hills, CA: Sage, 1981), pp. 497–528.

34. In his recollection of the events of 1933–1934, when he served as Rector, Heidegger stresses his disillusionment over political pressures placed on the university as well as the political divisions within the university. When he turns to his Rectoral Speech of May 1933, Heidegger reveals his sensitivity to ideological concerns. Minister Wacker, after the rectoral dinner on the same day as the speech, he recalls, commented on the "private" National Socialism it contained, disagreed with the refusal of the idea of a "political science" promoted by the Party, and "above everything else" objected that the whole was not based upon the concept of race. Heidegger reflects on the political consequences of this speech at some length (Martin Heidegger, *The Rectorate 1933/4: Facts and Thoughts* [unpub. manuscript., n.d.], trans. R. P. Nicholls and Krin Zickler, University of Waterloo, August 1983).

35. Heidegger, *Poetry, Language, Thought*, p. 78. The ambiguity introduced by a sociopolitical context continues in the "Addendum" to these lectures added twenty years later in 1956. Because "Being . . . is a call to man" there is a human relation with regard to art. "The setting-into-work of truth" does not make it clear "who does the setting or in what way it occurs." This, writes Heidegger, referring to "*the relation between Being and human being*" (underlining in the original), has presented a "distressing difficulty" since *Being and Time* (*Poetry, Language, Thought*, pp. 86–87). When the state assumes control of the production, communication, and interpretation of art, and is willing to destroy both the creators of and audiences for certain kinds of art, the connection between Being and human being becomes doubly problematic.

36. Even the peasant in the "desolate" field becomes ideologically significant in context, in the contrast, for example, between Heidegger's figure and both the Party's view of the peasant and its depiction in popular culture. By 1937, according to George Mosse, some 50–75 percent of book sales were for "approved" National Socialist literature, and peasant novels were among the biggest sellers. Josef Berens-Totenohl was a popular novelist of the period. Her novel, *Der Femhof*, published in 1935 and characterized as "typical" of the peasant novel by Mosse, reveals a strong, virtuous, somewhat troubled peasant hero bent on purifying his life, protecting his manor, and lamenting a youthful affair with a dark-eyed, dark-haired, "gypsy" woman he wishes he had killed. Against a background of the official and the popular view of the peasant, Heidegger's stoical woman laboring in bleak surroundings was, more than atypical, antithetical (see Mosse, *Nazi Culture*, pp. 133–140, 168–176). Thus while a "textual" critic may note Heidegger's "quietistic" philosophy and call on the peasant in the "Origin of Art" to support the claim, the scene of desolation and the stoical peasant in the lectures constitute a rejoinder to perhaps even a prediction about the consequences of an optimistic, activist, militarist state.

37. On the attempt, through censorship, official dictionaries, and the like, by the National Socialists to control language itself, see Claus Mueller, *The Politics of Communication: A Study in the Political Sociology of Language, Socialization, and Legitimation* (New York: Oxford University Press, 1973), pp. 25–34.

38. Martin Heidegger, "The Thinker as Poet," in *Poetry, Language, Thought*, p. 11.

39. Michael Schneider, "Fathers and Sons Retrospectively: The Damaged Relationship between Two Generations," *New German Critique* 31 (1984): 5.

The Null Persona

Race and the Rhetoric of Silence in the Uprising of '34

Dana L. Cloud

My silences had not protected me. Your silence will not protect you. . . . Because the machine will try to grind you into dust, anyway, whether or not we speak.
—AUDRE LORDE[1]

Establishing links between what is said and audiences denied access to public space brings rhetorical theory back to earth.
—PHILIP WANDER[2]

Silence is audible only in relief from the sound of voices. During the month of September, 1934, hundreds of thousands of cotton mill workers across the Piedmont region of the southern United States stilled their weaving machines and raised their voices in protest. In an industry-wide strike, they held mass pickets outside mills and formed flying squadrons to spread what has come to be remembered as "the Uprising of '34."[3] Despite the scope and militancy of this strike and despite its contemporaneity with other, successful mass strikes,[4] the mill workers went down to defeat. The loss came after mill owners called in the National Guard and after President Roosevelt appointed a commission to "study" the problems of mill workers. Strikers were beaten, shot, discredited, and evicted from their homes in company-owned towns. Blacklisted, thousands never found work in mills again. To this day workers in Southern cotton mills are notoriously hard to organize, suspicious of unions and their promises, even as they continue to face many of the same problems—long hours, work hazards (dangerous machines, ubiquitous cotton dust), and low wages—as their 1930s counterparts.[5]

Lives of textile workers have been popularized in films such as *Norma Rae*[6] and more recently, in a documentary called *The Uprising of '34.*[7] This documentary, discussed in more detail below, features the voices of former mill workers involved in the 1934 strikes and is an important contribution to our memory of the hardships faced and struggles undertaken by workers during the Depression decade. The present article starts with this documentary and the interviews that comprise it, and expands its sights to include sections of the interviews not featured in the documentary. These interview records were gathered from the Southern Labor Archives in Atlanta, where the filmmakers placed their transcripts.

More specifically, this article examines the transcripts of interviews with black[8] workers Blanche Willis and E. O. Friday, who lived and worked around the mills during the Uprising of '34, for clues about the significance of race in those events. In addition, this article draws upon some material from interviews with members of two additional black families, the Nealeys and the Gardins. Although mill towns were, on the whole, white and racially homogeneous, race did matter in the cotton mills.[9] The sometimes coercive enforcement of unequal power relations created the conditions for a "rhetoric of silence" on the part of black workers. By "rhetoric of silence," I mean a discursive pattern in which speakers gesture incompletely toward what cannot be uttered in a context of oppression. Textual criticism of the interviews reveals patterns of self-interruption, indirection, diversion and refusal to speak about certain subjects. These interviews provide a case study of how textual scholars, working within a materialist frame, can discover symptoms of contextual power in the text itself and relate them to broader contextual features of social reality.

For many of the workers interviewed in the documentary, the primary lesson of the strike was to keep quiet. As I will suggest in an analysis of the transcripts, the silence about the strike is linked fundamentally to a system of combined race-, gender- and class-based oppression and exploitation, in which an ideology of paternalism, alongside the threat of racist violence, made for a muted, though debilitating, segregation. The descriptions of mill life and conditions for black workers, in addition to the detailed excerpts from workers' interviews, are taken from approximately five hundred pages of transcripts. The interviews are marked by a set of verbal cues, instances of self-censoring and strategic dodges that reveal a real and persistent fear of retaliation against any black worker involved in struggle. This fear reinforced the racial exclusion that limited the economic role of black women in the economy of mill towns to that of domestic servants. Their labor alongside the more common domestic labor of white women on their own behalf, in turn enabled whole families to be employed for long days in the mills. Racial and gendered ideologies, deploying slavery-era stereotypes and the threat of lynching, mitigated strongly against the integration of black men with white women. Thus in the broadest sense, the segregation of the mills allowed for the enhanced profitability of a segregated workforce.

Before turning to the transcripts themselves, the article lays out a materialist approach to the study of communicative silences. Such theoretical development is necessary to the project because I will argue below that the rhetoric of silence points to *extradiscursive*, material relations of power which are perceived for various reasons to be unspeakable. As James Aune points out in a recent essay, an exclusive "focus on rhetorical processes may neglect the role of violence and coercive manipulation of information in blocking and creating social change."[10]

After summarizing the tenets of a materialist perspective on race, class, and silence, the article next provides some historical background on the situation of millworkers before and during the 1934 strikes. The analysis of the transcripts follows that background, organized into sections about textual themes regarding class identity, familialism, domestic labor, racist violence, and strategic silence. The essay concludes with some recommendations for rhetorical-cultural studies of the labor movement. Following Wander's idea of a "Third Persona,"[11] I posit the concept of a "null persona" to characterize silence as a rhetorical strategy that points toward extradiscursive relations of power.

The Rhetorical Criticism of Silence: A Materialist Approach

A consideration of silence is almost by definition a materialist project, if one understands the materialist project to be a critical perspective that emphasizes the roles discourses about race and gender play in larger contexts of social and economic power. Silences in the vernacular discourse of the subordinate point to these contexts of economic exploitation, race- and gender-based oppression, and the terrain of silencing discourses such as those identified by Lester Olson and Robin Patric Clair.[12] What historical materialism adds to existing work on the rhetoric of silence is a novel emphasis on the non- or supra-discursive components of the contexts of silence, and on the attempt to explain how silence and silencing are connected to regimes of not only symbolic but also material power. As Teresa Ebert writes:

> Materialist critique is a mode of knowing that inquires into what is not said, into the silences and the suppressed or missing, in order to uncover the concealed operations of power and the socioeconomic relations connecting the myriad details and representations of our lives. It shows that apparently disconnected zones of culture are in fact materially linked through the highly differentiated, mediated, and dispersed operation of a systematic logic of exploitation. In sum, materialist critique disrupts "what is" to *explain* how social differences—specifically gender, race, sexuality, and class— have been systematically produced and continue to operate within regimes of exploitation, so that we can change them.[13]

My goal in this paper is to connect the silences in the Uprising of '34 transcripts to a systematic logic of exploitation, to describe how the racial and gender-based differences have been produced, then and now, to justify the profit system. On this view, class is a social relation—defining whether one owns the means for and controls the production of goods and services, or otherwise is forced to work for wages—not a discursively produced identity (although consciousness of class is a rhetorical product), figment of consciousness, or even a notion of rank or personal status.[14]

With this emphasis on the significance of class and on extradiscursive features of social power, my approach differs from some "materialist" scholarship prevalent in communication studies.[15] In contrast to either an idealist rhetorical materialism or a relativist post-materialism, the materialism I am advocating here is insistent upon the need for extradiscursive standards for critical judgment, optimistic about collective human agency, but also critical and cognizant of constraints posed for such agency in class society. This approach is rooted in the classical Marxist tradition which distinguishes between material reality and discursive reality, positing a dialectical relationship between them.[16]

Rhetoric is consequential in such a materialist model. Gramsci's theory of hegemony, developed in his prison writings, gives ruling-class rhetoric a great deal of credit in maintaining social order in the face of conflict and challenge.[17] And yet, as Gramsci elaborated later, persuasion is not only key to the maintenance of power but to the formation of conscious, oppositional blocs or movements that might challenge the *status quo*. The labor movement is one such bloc. Gramsci would remind us to examine not only the "negative moment" of the use of persuasion to win "consent" to oppressive power, but also the "positive moment" in which human beings use rhetoric to generate support for social change.[18]

Questions of power, hegemony, and workers' agency become even more pressing when one is discussing issues of race and racism in a labor context. Racism is a discursive phenomenon that persuasively justifies differential access to economic, political, and social power in society.[19] In addition, racism and sexism have enabled economic exploitation of all workers by dividing the workforce against itself, thwarting solidarity in labor struggles, and rhetorically supporting differential wages, benefits, housing, and other material advantages according to ideologically produced gendered and racialized differences. As Karlyn Kohrs Campbell explains in an examination of a 1904 debate about lynching, racism in the post-Reconstruction period encouraged white worker

and sharecropper identification with a wealthy elite, mystifying class antagonism in favor of racist division.[20] While racial and gendered ideological systems are not simply produced in a conspiratorial way in the direct service of profits, critics should examine the broader economic and social contexts of racial and gendered discourse to describe their systematic interrelationships. Thus racism has a significant communicative, cultural dimension. Rosemary Hennessy and Chris Ingraham define a perspective toward discourse and difference that explains the communicative dimensions of racism as generated out of economic and other sociopolitical contexts:

> The socially produced differences of race, gender, and nationality are not distinct from class, but they play a crucial role—both directly and indirectly in dividing the work force, ensuring and justifying the continued availability of cheap labor and determining that certain social groups will be profoundly exploited. . . . One of the key concepts of historical materialism is this recognition that the production of life is a systemic process, one that takes place through a system of related activities. Historically, these activities have taken the form of divisions of labor or relations of production, organizations of state and of consciousness or culture. Emancipatory change that aims to eliminate exploitation and oppression within a social system cannot take place by eradicating inequities only in one sphere of social life. . . . It must include civil rights and cultural reforms and extend to the social structures that allow wealth for the few to be accumulated at the expense of the many.[21]

In this essay I will follow Hennessy and Ingraham's understanding of materialism as a broad understanding of both structure and agency, economics and culture. Hazel Carby and Angela Davis also have described the ways in which, since slavery, race and gender have worked together systematically to justify the domestic subordination of women alongside the violent exclusion of black workers from privilege.[22] Carby and Davis argue that the practice of lynching, often warranted by mythic appeals to white women's purity, relied upon stereotypes of black men as brutal savages requiring discipline. Those interlocking sets of ideas enabled racist economic exploitation and discrimination against women in the workforce and public life to continue apace.

In the communication discipline, materialist rhetorical-ideological studies and critical organizational studies offer potential contexts within which to understand silence and social power in the American workplace.[23] In the context of such critical work a literature on the multiple dynamics of silence as they relate to differentials of power has emerged.[24] On the whole, this literature treats silence as an integral component of meaning-making, to be understood in the same way in which silence is the complement of sound in music. The meanings of silence are only determinable in context, an insight that naturally leads to the critic's examination of events, social relations, and other discourses surrounding the silence in question. In these contexts, silence can be a strategic choice. Barry Brummett defines "strategic silence" as being intentional; violating audience expectations of speech; encouraging attribution of meanings which may include mystery, uncertainty, passivity, and relinquishment; having directionality; and creating a passive persona.[25] Brummett's discussion of strategic silence is especially useful to my examination of black workers' transcripts insofar as he notes that sometimes it is strategically pragmatic to "lie low" even when under pressure to speak.[26]

Brummett examines silence on the part of Jimmy Carter during his presidency, a person in a position of power and authority. What happens when the rhetor who is silent is a member of a marginalized or subordinate social group? A number of scholars have called attention to the ways in which we must look beyond silence as a meaning-laden counterpart to voice, to focus on the ways in which oppressed and exploited people are not so much silent by choice as *silenced* out of necessity. Robin Patric Clair's work has argued that silencing can occur coercively through force or more covert discursive methods.[27]As a case in point, she examines the Treaty of New Echota, which was made by the United States with the Cherokee Nation in the 1830s. In the negotiations for that treaty, government discursive practices worked to silence Cherokee ancestral and personal narratives. Clair's more recent work has invoked Gramsci's theory of hegemony to make a similar argument in the context of sexual harassment, arguing for a feminist perspective on the power-imbued contexts of women's silences in the workplace.[28] Clair's case rests on feminist theories describing the ways in which Western culture has rendered woman as "Other," both present and absent, silent in her connection to a mute natural world.[29] In a context of male violence against women, one cannot regard silence as a voluntary choice, although it may be a survival strategy and/or a form of counterhegemonic resistance.

In this vein, Radha Hegde has criticized the understanding of communicative agency as voluntaristic, characteristic of the field of communication studies.[30] In other words, she criticizes the "democratizing agenda" of the field which has been conducted almost exclusively in terms of voice, neglecting a critique of the "controlling hierarchies that exist socially and in research practices."[31] In an ethnographic study of women residents of a battered women's shelter in India, she finds that her meetings with the women "were often filled with silences that came from a wrenching desire to talk and a simultaneous inability to do so."[32] Hegde argues:

> The silence of these three women is not rooted in communication apprehension, communicative dysfunction, or stereotypical passivity. Traditional approaches that assess individual consent and compliance from the point of view of the autonomous actor miss the politically complex ways in which individuals negotiate their identities. . . . Were these women operating from a position of free rational choice?[33]

To this question, Hegde answers no, arguing that we must tie silence to the presence of patriarchal power. Similarly, Lester Olson examines Audre Lorde's call to give voice to the unspoken, asking "what underlying cultural conditions encourage or discourage speaking in public forums? What sociological facts, for example, account for speech and silence?"[34] The emphasis in Lorde, as in Olson's account of her speech, is on how one must transcend silence to achieve connection with diverse others in progress toward human liberation. Although Olson foregrounds cultural or discursive conditions (even arguing that physical violence is a symbolic practice) as constraints on speech, he also notes that silence "is sometimes a product of oppression, a survival skill in dealing with domination and violence, at other times a chosen form of liberation, and yet on other occasions the exercise of a fundamental human right, as in the right to remain silent."[35] Olson encounters the limits of rhetoric "at the point where words fail us [in the] silence imposed by child abuse, by grief, by incest, rape and other forms of physical assault."[36] One can extend these lessons regarding the supra- or extra-rhetorical determinants of silence to an account of racialized silences in the presence of regimes of racial exclusion and exploitative labor relations.

The work of literary theorist Henry Louis Gates Jr. is most useful in this regard. In *The Signifying Monkey*, Gates identifies a theory of criticism inscribed with the black vernacular tradition. "Signifyin(g)" refers to a series of discursive strategies employed by African-Americans, emerging from the situation of enslavement and oppression; it is the figure of the double-voiced, characterized by a play of voices in narration, the use of indirection, pastiche (or echoing other sources), parody, humor, and introduction of the unexpected.[37] As the analysis of the transcripts will demonstrate, the black workers in Southern textile mills *signify* through not only what they choose to say, but also what they choose not to. The creative strategies Gates identifies—especially humor and indirection—are at work in the interviews, both signaling meanings outside of what is actually said and protecting the men, who continue to fear retaliation even into 1995.

To date, work on textile workers and on the Uprising of '34 has focused on the workers' culture, either minimizing the question of race or attributing systematic racist exclusion to the tight-knit enclaves formed by white workers.[38] The present analysis of the Uprising of '34 transcripts will suggest that the racial exclusion of the mills was influential in the lives of all workers but not necessarily inherent in their culture or consciousness. In order to answer the question about race in the Uprising of '34, one must look beyond discourses to fill in their gaps.

Documenting the Uprising and Its Vernacular Legacy

Rhetoricians should regard oral histories of the words and experiences of rank-and-file workers as rhetorical texts that reveal patterns of influence, strategy, and vernacular agency on the part of workers. The words of ordinary workers are rhetorical interventions into labor struggles and political issues in the present day, and it is the responsibility of rhetorical scholars and labor historians to bring these narratives to light and to try to understand their strategic importance.[39] Jacqueline Dowd-Hall et al. write:

> We knew that memory does not provide a direct window on the past, but we had learned from experience to trust the interpretive authority of ordinary people. We also assumed the moral and intellectual value of listening to those who lacked access to power and, thus, the means of influencing historical debate.[40]

My work, likewise, stems from a position of solidarity with that moral, intellectual, and political commitment to the interpretive authority of ordi-

nary people, or what has been called "the study of vernacular discourse."[41] As Gerard Hauser writes, "To revive a rich sense of discourse as the basis for public opinion, the theory of public opinion itself must be informative of how rhetorically engaged actors deliberate over social, political and cultural issues. *Such a rehabilitation must widen the discursive arena to include vernacular exchanges, in addition to those of institutional actors.*"[42]

The film *Uprising of '34* captures some of this vernacular legacy, taking viewers through the events of the strike, from the failures of New Deal labor legislation to ameliorate conditions in the mills, the special national meeting called by the United Textile Workers of America in August of 1934 to discuss the possibility of a strike, to the strike itself, which began on Labor Day and lasted three weeks—until the National Guard was called out in Georgia, North Carolina, and South Carolina to put down the unrest.[43] The film opens with poignant images of mill interiors, accompanied by workers' voice-overs describing mill jobs as, on the one hand "pretty good," but on the other hand marked by high pressure and paternalistic surveillance.[44]

Beginning in 1929, textile workers began to protest; the industry was shaken with strikes in Elizabethton, Tennessee; Marion, South Carolina; Gastonia, North Carolina; and other locations.[45] Each of these strikes was met with brutal force on the part of employers, police, and federal troops. In addition to staging walkouts and organizing strikes, workers wrote the Roosevelt administration in the early 1930s about these concerns. The New Deal was having little effect on work conditions, despite the 1933 National Industrial Recovery Act's (NIRA's) provisions for worker self-organization and collective bargaining. The first major board of the National Recovery Administration (formed under the NIRA) was the Cotton Textiles National Industrial Relations Board, or the Bruere Board, charged with establishing a code for labor in the mills. But the Code Authority, placed under control of mill owners, did nothing to enforce the code's requirements regarding wages, work hours, stretch-out, or child labor.[46]

Furthermore, labor historian Philip Foner calls our attention to the very real exclusion of black workers from the provisions of the NIRA.[47] Members of the Nealey family describe in their transcript how, during the New Deal, black workers served in cleaning and other menial jobs, exempt from the provisions of the New Deal. An uncle of the interviewees had worked in the mills and had written General Hugh Johnson, who headed the NRA, for relief:

> I read in the newspapers that cleaners are not considered in the code of the Mills. General Johnson you know in the south, especially in South Carolina 95 percent of the cotton mills labor is white. . . . General Johnson the kind of wage that is paid to colored people, fifty cents, seventy-five cents a day. Domestic help, porters, janitors, make five and six dollars a week. Cooks and chauffeurs, maids, women, one-fifty to two dollars a week. . . . the colored man have to pay the same for a leading product as a mill employee. . . . it cost him as much to live as anybody else in the mill but the Negro cannot work in the mills. . . . A Negro couldn't look out the same window as a white.

The Nealey family members recall that this uncle who had the courage to write Hugh Johnson was "carried out by the Ku Klux Klan one night."

Members of the Gardin family also describe what it was like to be a black worker around the mills:

> My father he worked down here in Spencer's Mountain, right down here—below here. And he worked in the Opening Room. And he was—the place was out in just a big old open building with the big doors open and in the wintertime it would be so cold in there his fingers would almost freeze, you know just trying to stay warm and all. But it was just—that was about the only job that a black person had that was inside. The rest of the jobs were on the outside. Garbage disposal, trucking cotton. Unloading the cars. They'd have to go up the ramp and unload the freight car and take the truck on down to the mill where you'd unload them. You know it had to be winter and summer, you know hot and cold. Blacks weren't allowed inside, not even to sweep.

Gardin family transcripts contain a section in which family members read a 1934 letter by a black worker to Hugh Johnson. The letter reads:

> Dear Sir, I am writing you this letter to let you know just how we poor Negroes are being treated here at Manville Jenkins Company, Loray Mills. There are some work out there eight hours, some ten, eleven, twelve hours a day, make only twenty cents per hour, and our boss man, T. A. Gershman, tell us—your mill code law don't cover us Negroes for twelve dollars a week. It is just for white people. Will you please, sir look after this and do something for us poor Negroes? . . . I have five in my family and I can't buy food enough to last me from one payday to another. At the price of food, I can't have dry bread. Please do something for us, or we will starve.

While the black workers received not even the nominal protection of New Deal legislation, white workers suffered as well under lax enforcement of the textile code.[48] The United Textile Workers, under the leadership of Francis Gorman, led the strike against mill conditions, shutting down more than half of the mills across the South. Force and hunger drove many workers back to work, bolstered by Roosevelt's appointment of the Winant Board to study the problem of stretch-out. By most labor historians' accounts, the UTW's agreement to end the strike on October 3 was a devastating surrender. Strikers were blacklisted and work conditions remained unchanged.

For some labor historians, the vital culture unique to mill towns served as a source of compensatory hope and agency for the workers in the face of continuing safety hazards, low wages, and long work hours. Rural isolation of life in company towns meant that workers were close-knit and proud of their traditions. Mill owners have suggested that the towns were good for workers, and that workers lived like a well-cared-for family under the paternalistic gaze of mill owners. The familial metaphor is significant; rhetorically, it encourages cross-class identification between workers and their employers who profited from the low-wage work at long hours performed by workers. Thus the metaphor has a "domesticating" rhetorical effect. In addition, the invocation of a "mill family" suggests a kind of plantation mentality in which race was a significant factor.[49] It is in this context that we should understand the role that race and racism played in the mill towns. While some scholars attribute the segregation and white dominance of these towns to the insular culture of white mill workers, I am suggesting that in a broad sense, racism enabled the domestication of mill workers and thus served employers', not workers', interests. A close reading of the transcripts reveals that it was not white workers' culture or consciousness that prohibited racial solidarity in the mills, but rather a regime of paternalism and force that kept the races separate and unequal and the plants profitable from day to day.

"It's a Hush Thing": Black Mill Workers on the Margins

So far it has been argued that a materialist perspective on race, class, gender, and culture can help us to understand the structured silences and incomplete voicing of workers on the margins. From this perspective, the conditions described above are significant to this analysis because they constitute, in large part, the meanings of silence in this case.[50] We cannot take the absence of vocalization on a particular subject to indicate ignorance or limited consciousness of the issues any more than we can equate the presence of voice with emancipation. The silences of the millworkers take on significant meanings that a critic might not notice without a materialist frame emphasizing the material conditions of the men interviewed. The silences in the interviews point us to spaces and relations outside of themselves, located in the social conditions constraining voice.

Methodologically, the following close reading of the transcripts was guided by both Gates's theory of Signifyin(g) and Lynn Mikel Brown and Carol Gilligan's description of the ways in which, in interviews with girls, the researchers "listened for movement within the interview session, for stops and starts, for silences and struggles. . . . We listened for girls' sense of themselves—the way they spoke of themselves, the presence and absence of an 'I' in their stories of relational conflicts."[51] These feminist scholars suggest that the listener attend to "the symbolic nature not only of what is said but also of what is *not* said. We know that women, in particular, often speak in indirect discourse, in voices deeply encoded, deliberately or unwittingly opaque."[52] Although any analogy between the status of women and the status of black workers is imperfect, the dynamics of voice, silence, and power may be similar across the two oppressed groups. Like many women and girls today, black Americans have been continually in a situation of unequal hierarchical power relations that necessitate great strategic care in giving voice to grievances of racism and exploitation. Following these listening guidelines, my examination of transcripts of worker interviews looked for the sense of human agency and speaking persona in the voices of the workers; it also notes places where the interviews point to the not-said, in indirect, opaque, and self-silencing modes.

The analysis reveals four themes about race, class, unions, and the agency of black workers. First, black workers saw their oppression as linked to the economic exploitation of mill workers in general. They wanted to join the union in solidarity with white workers, and the white union organizers were not opposed to their joining. Second, the interviews clarify the role of black workers in the "mill family" as domestic workers and other fringe workers who, though marginalized, were integral to mill town life. The ideological con-struction of mill towns and their constituents as a corporate family is the third theme the analysis will address. Finally, and most profoundly, the narratives are marked by the thematics of fear of racist violence against black workers who participated in agitation. As Larry Blakeny, a black worker who appears in the documentary, said about the strike, "It's a hush thing. Keep quiet. Let's don't pull our skeletons out of the closet." The purpose of the following sections is to describe each of these patterns in some detail and to suggest how they may be related to the rhetorical criticism of silence.

Class Consciousness and Solidarity

The transcripts, alongside other accounts of mill life in the 1930s, show that racism, though an influential barrier to interracial organizing, was not inherent in the consciousness of workers, white or black. The documentary addresses the fact that black workers were organized into unions, usually in separate locals from white workers. Yet Dowd-Hall et al. cite instances in which white workers consciously invited black workers to participate in the textile unions. For example, a white mill hand named Clarence Swink actually wrote a letter to the NRA's Hugh Johnson on behalf of black workers, who, he wrote, "are getting the worst of it."[53] In a similar instance, a white worker named Eula McGill advocated organizing black workers into her UTW local at Selma Manufacturing. Her supervisor, looking to perpetuate division, laughed and said, "Hey, you going to call her sister?" McGill replied, "Sure, I'm going to call her sister. I work with her, don't I?"[54] Likewise, a worker named Ella Mae Wiggins self-consciously attempted to cross the race divide that the Depression intensified: Wiggins told interviewers that she wanted black workers to see that "she was poor and humble like themselves."[55]

These examples demonstrate a sense that, at least among some of the more militant workers (and Eula McGill was a leader during the Uprising), racial antagonism and difference were put aside in a common class-based consciousness, born of working alongside and sharing the experiences of another person. Likewise, black workers saw their specifically racial oppression as remediable through the economic strategies of the unions. For example, a black worker named Blanche Willis described in her interview with the filmmakers how unions were badly needed in both the past and the present at the Fieldcrest Cannon mills, where Blanche's daughter Kay works today. Blanche and

Kay describe "unfair treatment" of black workers, suggesting the union as the answer, connecting racial grievances to an economic strategy for change: union organization and strikes. These observations are resonant with a study performed by Rhonda Zingraff and Michael Schulman of class consciousness of textile workers across race. They conclude that "whites manifest less class conflict consciousness than blacks" and that all groups become more class conscious regardless of race if exploitation and job insecurity are heightened."[56] Labor scholars Larry Griffin and Robert Korstad have suggested that labor studies should "advance or adapt conceptualizations of how class meshes with other social categories," and regard race and gender-based grievances as therefore fused with and compounded by class dissatisfaction.[57]

This fusion is evident in the testimony of E. O. Friday, who had worked at the Modena Cotton Mill in Gastonia, North Carolina during the 1930s. Friday explicitly endorsed unions even though he was excluded from joining them. He said to the interviewer, "I think they did the right thing. You see, if they [white unionized workers] moved up, then we would move up. See, eventually, we would move up." Friday also indicates that there was cross-racial identification among black and white workers during the Depression. He says, "Well, some of the whites had it hard too. If they didn't have connection with the bossman, they had it about as hard as we did." Friday also notes that his family allowed striking white workers to fish from their property and gather vegetables from their garden. Interestingly, Friday comments often in his interview that his and other black workers' marginal status in plants left them better off in terms of work conditions. The few black workers in peripheral jobs were not subject to the strategies of shop floor speed up, stretch-out, and constant managerial discipline that white workers faced. In addition, black workers inhabited a double-edged paternalistic relationship with mill owners, who often hired the black hands directly and employed them under their nominal protection from white violence.

These statements provide evidence that, contrary to cultural explanations of racial division, white and black workers in the mills of the 1930s shared common consciousness of their status as workers. In addition, black workers saw unions as a place to organize against economic injustice and against specifically racial oppression. Why, then, were there no black workers in the forefront of the Uprising of '34? What system of constraint existed

to mitigate against turning awareness of common cause into solidarity in action? Another piece of the answer comes from an understanding of the role of black women in the 1930s mill economy.

Domesticating Mill Towns: Gendered Contradictions

White women played a key role as workers in textile mills, coming as they did from rural homesteads and farms on which all family members toiled equally. Women's presence in the mills was also necessary to their families' survival; one worker per family could not earn enough to make ends meet.[58] How, then, did the "mill family" as a system and the individual families of workers perform the labor of social reproduction (child rearing, housekeeping, cooking, laundry, and so forth)? As Lindsey German explains, domestic labor is necessary to the broader economy insofar as it makes possible the socialization, upkeep, and regeneration of laborers. Women mill workers faced a double burden when social responsibility was privatized.[59] Dowd-Hall et al. contains many testimonials of the exhaustion of women who worked 14 hours in the mill and then cared for their families almost single-handedly.[60]

In the mill towns, black women augmented this labor as domestic servants in the homes of white mill workers. A Gardin family member (whose name does not appear in the transcript) recalls that "My sisters and my mother did washings for the—and ironings for the white people that was on the village. We would go down, walk a mile down to their houses and pick up their laundry and carry them (sic) home on our backs." Another Gardin sibling adds:

> Well after we grew up, and to cook and all that, then we would walk down and maybe stay for the whole week cleaning and tending to the white ladies' kids. . . . But most of them, after you could take your black hands and you could stir it in their dough, and you could take your black body and lay in the bed with the child and protect them. But you couldn't come in their front door.

For black women, the mill community was not a site of voice and agency as it was for white women. Blanche Willis comments:

> That was our occupation at the time. We weren't— there weren't any black women in the mill at that time. They did not hire black women in the mill. So we worked in homes and took care of the

children—cooked and washed and took care of the whole house. . . . I have worked and stayed the eight hours and took care of the children and did all the work and then come when they got off at three o'clock, I came back home until the next morning. And then I would go back on my job and continue my works, take care of the home, just as a housewife. You could call it just as a housewife, 'cause we did the housewife's job.

Willis's remarks show that it was the general role of black women in mill towns to care for the children of white workers, sometimes in the homes of workers, and sometimes at sites nearer to the plant. Although, as Dowd-Hall et al. note, very few white women mill workers could afford domestic help, E. O. Friday also vividly recalls his mother hanging frozen laundry in the dead of winter for white families. Brewer cites the textile industry as an important case in which black women's domestic work is "matched by the pervasive peripherization of Black men from manufacturing work and the labor force. . . . [This] exemplifies a division of waged labor built on racial norms and values as well as material arrangements embedded in a gendered division of labor."[61]

It is important to point out that the white mill workers' employment of black domestic workers is not the same phenomenon as the employment of domestic servants by elite urban or other non-wage-laboring women. While one could argue that domestic servants wholly relieve elite women of the burdens of labor, the working class women of mill towns did not hire black women in order to indulge in leisure. Rather, the employment of black women in the homes of white mill families allowed for the mill owners to super-exploit entire families while ensuring that there was a system— albeit a private one for which the owners bore no responsibility— in place to care for workers' domestic needs. White workers were only able to pay black domestics a small amount, fifty cents or a dollar per day. But the mill workers themselves were only earning between ten and twelve dollars a week. Thus in the mill towns, the complex interaction of race and gender-based discrimination and exclusion enabled a broader privatization of social responsibility without constraining employers' use of families as laborers. The industrial economy has increasingly required the labor of women both in the paid workforce and in the home. The presence of black domestic workers functioned to resolve the tension between those two roles for the white women, enabling them not only to work in

the mills but also to take part in union activities and protest.

"Like a Family": The Ideology of Workplace Paternalism

Indeed, it helps if we understand the mill town system in terms of the mill bosses' own metaphors. Repeatedly in the documentary and in the literature on mill towns, mill owners are quoted as exonerating themselves for exploiting workers on the basis of a familial metaphor. They construct an image of owners as benevolent fathers watching over, protecting, and bettering the lives of employees, who are figured as children and expected to be as docile. Workers themselves adopted the language of familial connection, but not only to describe their relationship to bosses. Dowd-Hall et al. provide extensive oral historical evidence that workers saw their links to each other in terms of a family; these usages of the familial metaphor suggest a class solidarity or kinship rhetorically distinct from cooperation with employer paternalism. The integrated structure of mill villages allowed workers to adapt their rural heritage to a new, industrial context. And while company villages gave manufacturers access to entire mill families, social control in the villages was never complete. The centralization and integration of mill villages also meant that "customs of incorporation created in each locality a broad network of obligation, responsibility, and concern. In times of need family relations might be extended to include the village as a whole."[62] Thus a kinship metaphor was a source of class solidarity and affective connection among workers.[63]

On the other hand, the familial rhetoric had a domesticating, conservative edge that cut against workers' interests. The present-day mill owner and son of a 1930s Gastonia, North Carolina mill boss comments in the documentary that mill towns were "a family type of environment that workers liked." Later he describes mill cottages, store, and utilities as benefits for workers despite the complete control of mill owners of every facet of mill town life: "It [access to housing, utilities, etc.] was a big plus for a family." Another relative of a mill owner describes how the management philosophy in the 1930s was hands-on, a philosophy of "management by personal appearance." He comments, "We were one big family in the mill village . . . But whoever was in charge had to be in charge." The linkage of benevolence and social control evident in this statement makes for a set of double-edged consequences for workers who adopt the language of familial rather than class based solidarity (which would pit workers against owners rather than encouraging cross-class identification and acquiescence to social control).

Thus, mill owners used the kinship metaphor to encourage self-reliance on the part of the workers so that owners would bear less social and economic responsibility. Wages were so low that many workers suffered from malnutrition, yet owners encouraged mutual aid among workers rather than raise wages.[64] Elsewhere I have argued that the privatization of social responsibility is the primary impetus of familialist rhetorics.[65] Such discourses deflect public attention away from power relations and inequalities, and from the possibility of structural redress of grievances over wages, racism, poverty, and so forth. An overemphasis on the independence of mill workers also risks minimizing the very real and intense level of social control in the mill villages, in which unruly workers could be evicted or denied medical care. The churches routinely preached pro-management and anti-union lessons. For black workers, constructed along the stereotype of "house slaves" in the mill village family model, the price of conceding to the familial metaphor was very high—a black worker challenged the authority of the paternal boss only under threat of death.

A final drawback of the familial metaphor for mill town life is that it encouraged affective rather than political identification. This means that during times of conflict or crisis, people are bound by emotional obligations that might prevent critique or controversy. During the Uprising, mill villages were emotionally riven by conflict within and across families. The familial metaphor can thus engender a kind of silence or inaction if speaking out might mean breaking with people constructed as "kin." The remarks of Edna McNeil, an anti-union manager from the East Newman mills, noted that "They never did organize us. I was always close to my people. They were family to me." This comment reveals how the family metaphor can replace, quite deliberately, a sense of class consciousness to the detriment of pro-worker organization.

In the mill village "family," women's double burden and black women's domestic labor became integral to the locating of social responsibility with the workers themselves rather than their employers. Indeed, for the system to work, the black workers had to remain peripheral. If black men and women were offered employment openly in the mills, the domestic labor on which mill town life depended would evaporate. Further, a broader social regime of racial exclusion that worked in other industries to divide work forces, lower wages, and replace striking workers would have been profoundly challenged by such integration. For this reason, racial exclusion and segregation were maintained under threat of force. Larry Blakeny, a black worker who appears in the documentary, describes living in "the man's" house: "He really had you under control. If you did anything he didn't like, he could put you out of the house, take your job, where are you going to go?"

Racist Violence and the Rhetoric of Silence

When the filmmakers asked members of the Gardin family to comment on photographs of thousands of white strikers during the Uprising of 1934, the Gardins, who are black, noted that although the white workers were in almost the same position as black workers, their position as agents was less constrained: "They had the choice to—they could speak." A woman interrupts, "I think it had a lot to do with slavery, slavery. They could speak where we couldn't speak." The paternal protection of mill owners came at a price: never speaking out against the mill. Another black worker, from the Nealey family, lived in the house of the mill owner, Sam Love, rather than in the mill village. The filmmaker comments that "the pattern we found was that the few blacks who did get work in the mills kind of belonged to . . ." and a Nealey member interjects with "the owner." Gardin family members recall relatives living in houses close to "Mr. Patterson's house. The big house. We thought that was the finest house in the world." Clearly, black workers around mill towns relied upon the mill owners as they would have a plantation owner before the end of slavery.

The transcripts of E. O. Friday's interview with the filmmakers are extremely poignant in this regard, indicating a set of slavery-era social relations adapted to industrial life. Throughout the interview, Friday demonstrates what rhetoricians might label "strategic ignorance"—though he clearly knows about the strike, the unions, and the need to protest work conditions, he fears to align himself in the documentary with labor's cause. His remarks suggest that he is, even in the contemporary moment of the film's making in 1994–95, afraid of retribution against a black man who would speak out in the South. Friday comments:

We got along with [the bosses] real good up there at the Modena Mill. Because the man that owned the mill—my dad rented ground from him. And he's done a lot of work for him. And they know not to bother my dad cause he would run them off. Cause see, in other words, back in those days they said that's my nigger. You don't bother my nigger. . . . And if you—they say if you a good nigger they going to help you. But if you a bad nigger they going to put the Ku Klux Klan on you. Yeah. So I was raised up in a church and I was good all the time (laughs).

From this passage one can see how the social relations of slavery and then of sharecropping influenced the place of black workers in mill towns. So long as black workers are conceived of as property of mill owners, they are under the owners' protection.

The pauses and self-interruptions reveal a certain caution and self-silencing on Friday's part. Friday's joke about being good and his laughter suggest that his obedience and propriety be read as ironic and self-conscious, the products of coercion and threatened violence rather than authentic identification with the mill owners' regime. The semi-proprietary status of black workers meant that the "good black"–"bad black" dichotomy, invented during slavery to discipline slaves by equating goodness with unquestioning obedience was still at work justifying Klan violence against disobedient black servants.

The reason this insight is so important is that too often textual scholars take what is on the page or in the speech as evidence for what is in a person's consciousness or culture. In other words, critical rhetoricians sometimes risk mistaking the persuasive for what is true,[66] assuming there is no material reality outside of and referenced (even incompletely) in rhetorical texts. While Friday expresses allegiance to the paternalistic mill system, he does so in an ironic way that indicates that there is a truth—a hard reality—constraining his discourse from outside the text. Thus a corrective to the conflation of persuasion and truth can be found in the concept, introduced in communication studies by Herb Simons in 1972, of *coercive persuasion*:

Coercive persuasion applies to any situation in which at least one party sees himself in genuine conflict with another, has some coercive power over the other, and finds it expedient to establish, persuasively, any or all of the following: (1) his relative capacity to use coercive force, (2) his relative willingness to use coercive force, (3) the relative legitimacy of his coercive force, (4) the relative desirability of his objectives.[67]

Clearly, symbol use is instrumental in representing one's capacity, willingness, and legitimacy in using coercive force. Yet it is the material potentiality of coercive force itself that backs up such representations and makes them persuasive. Simons adapted the concept of coercive persuasion from a study of brainwashing of American POWs by Chinese Communists in the 1950s, which concluded that we cannot understand the success of the brainwashing without understanding that the prisoners "were subjected to unusually intense and prolonged persuasion in a situation from which they could not escape; that is, they were coerced into allowing themselves to be persuaded."[68] The situation for black workers during the 1930s was similar in their subjection to a situation from which they could not escape. The appearance of acceptance or even internalization of racist ideologies and exclusion became a matter of survival.

Friday's interview is rife with remarks indicating fear of the Klan. Amazingly, whenever he is asked what he knew about the union or black involvement in protest at the mills, he invokes the KKK. This strategy is a classic example of Gates's description of indirection and the introduction of the unexpected as strategies for conveying meaning without risking one's neck. For example, in one section of the transcript he responds to a question about the Uprising, "Only thing we would—would have trouble with, is the Klansmen. The Klansmen was pretty bad back in them days. They'd catch you out at night, certain time of night, they'd beat you. Yeah. I'd never be going nowhere at night. We'd never go nowhere." Repetition, self-interruption, and the use of the word "yeah" for emphasis lend weight to the sense of fearfulness in this passage. When the filmmakers show him a letter to the NRA signed by 14 black mill workers protesting their work conditions, he becomes very anxious: "That—that's a good letter, but, there, but I wonder what happened to them fourteen people, down in Georgia. I know they lost their jobs, but, they—they lost more than that. Because, see anytime you try to stick your neck out for your own race, they gonna get you, just like Martin Luther King." The fear expressed in this passage is notable in two ways. First, it is oblique; rather than openly indicting racist violence, Friday hints, "they lost more than that." The implication is that Friday fears for their lives, but is still, in 1994, afraid to even say so. Second, the comments are politicized. Friday says, "Anytime you try to stick your neck out for your own race, they gonna get you, just like Martin Luther King." In other words, he is conscious that his own political agency in speech was curtailed by the possibility of retaliatory violence. He is conscious that there is a need to "stick one's neck out" for his race. Consciousness and speech in this instance do not match, because of extradiscursive forces preventing the transformation of heightened social consciousness into political speech.

When asked if he wondered why he could not work inside the mill, he said, "Well, I—I knew too—what the problems were but I never did say anything about it because you might lose your job back then. You know back then you know you couldn't—you'd just have to be quiet and go along with the flow." Here he is not yet talking about racist violence, but the frequent gaps in his narrative, marked by dashes and self-interruptions and repeated phrases, all suggest significant self-censoring. This is especially evident in the last two sentences of the passage where he can't even say what it is black workers could not do, even though he "knew, too." Ominously, he silences himself, saying, "you'd just have to be quiet."

Repeatedly in the transcripts of interviews not included in the film, the documentarists press E. O. Friday to discuss the union protests. Repeatedly, Friday insists that he was ignorant of the union's activity. "No, I tell you, I know that, I mean, *I didn't know what was going on*. In fact, I didn't know what was going on. But—wasn't none of the blacks. They [wouldn't be doing] it nowhere, they wouldn't be doing it. 'Cause they was outnumbered you know. The Klansmen was in that, the union, too. So you better not mess with that. We understood that. *We knew what was going on*" (emphasis added). The dramatic shift in this statement between not knowing and knowing is significant and double-voiced in Gates's sense. Clearly, Friday knew about his work conditions, about the union (which he discusses earlier in the interview, wondering why the union excluded the black workers), and about the strike. But what he also knew, and clearly still feels in the context of the interview itself, is fear of retribution for challenging the racist social relations of the mills. This passage again reflects a certain strategic muteness on Friday's part, a knowing what it is one is not supposed to know about, a knowing one's place.

The documentarists similarly encourage a number of black workers to discuss their specific oppression in the mills. In one segment of the film, inter-viewer George Stoney asks a worker named Bruce Graham who worked outside at Eagle Yarn in Belmont, North Carolina, "Do you wonder why there were no blacks at the machines?" Graham replies, "I don't know, do you know?" He is laughing as he repeats, "I don't wonder why, do you?" Then Stoney responds, "I have a pretty good idea. They were saving the jobs for the white men." Graham concludes, "That's what I thought. *I was letting you say it first*" (emphasis added). In this example of what Gates refers to as pastiche, or the saying of something (in this case, something dangerous) by echoing someone else's utterance, it is clear that Graham did know about racial discrimination in the mills. In fact, Graham had written a signed letter to the NRA in 1934 protesting work conditions for black workers; he had been working overtime, and was paid less than 30 cents an hour for operating three machines at once. But his remarks suggest that he knows the dangers of admitting to certain kinds of knowledge. His laughter as he says, "I don't wonder" suggests that his not wondering is a witting, strategic choice. He is "lying low" as a means of survival. To my ear it is chilling to recognize the degree to which awareness of threat of racist retribution censors these workers even in the present, to the point where they are afraid to wonder out loud about their own long-past experience.

Similarly, the Nealey family, when shown a letter written by their courageous uncle Alirod Nealey to Hugh Johnson of the NRA, had never heard a thing about black men struggling in the 1930s to better their conditions. Nealey had written that Roosevelt had promised "something for the forgotten man. And that is the Negro in the South." Isaac Nealey explains his ignorance of the letter by invoking the silences that marked their experience: "What really happened back then was whenever the people did things they wouldn't let their younger people know about it. They kept it to themselves. That is why we don't know more about this letter than we do."

Susan Gal, a feminist scholar, has argued that while silence can represent a kind of powerlessness that comes with the absence of voice, it can also be a strategic defense and even protest against dominant signification practices and regimes of power.[69] Gal cites research on gender and language to show that differences in power produce differences in ways of talking, including strategies of silence, humor, fragmentation, deliberate inarticulateness, and indirectness on the part of the less powerful in an interaction. Although her work is based on gendered power differences, she notes that low-status men often use the same defensive strategies; and clearly the strategies she describes parallel in large part those identified by Gates. E. O. Friday, Blanche Willis, Larry Blakeny, and the other black workers whose voices are heard in the documentary and in the transcripts clearly demonstrate the same strategic silence, use of humor (as in Bruce Graham's interview described above), fragmented reporting of experience (as in self-interruption and subject changes), and indirectness (e.g., waiting for the interviewer to spell out dangerous lessons) that Gal notes among women's interaction with men. While the strategic muteness of these men in 1934 appears to be a kind of self-defense, I hesitate to herald such survival strategies as resistance. The regimes of domestication and racial violence at work meant that across the South and across the nation, enforced segregation mitigated against labor solidarity in many different struggles.

The violence Friday feared was a specifically racialized kind of violence. Yet it is connected to the broader social relations of exploitation and coercive force that broke the strike. Dowd-Hall et al. note that white women working in the mills also felt fear and faced retribution when speaking out, and in the end it was white workers who were victims of massacres at the hands of police, private thugs, and the National Guard. Just as we cannot attribute the failure of interracialism in this instance to culture or consciousness, we cannot attribute the defeat of the strikers to rhetorical inefficacy or cultural incompetence. The limits of the labor movement have as much to do with the constraint of repressive force as with discursive savvy, progressive consciousness, or rhetorical strategy.

Race and gender mattered profoundly in mill towns to the profitability of the mills and to the ongoing functioning of everyday life. The ways in which stereotypes of "good" domesticated black servants contributed to the exploitation of labor and conditions which led up to the strike are indirect and complex, yet audible in these transcripts of black workers' voices. That there was no interracial life in common in mill towns, not to mention the absence of interracial solidarity in unions, is not a matter of Southern cultural exceptionalism, as if racism were endemic to workers' character and culture and thus irredeemable. The combination of slavery-era social norms articulated to the profit system meant that inter-racialism was an impossibility, because segregation was imposed and maintained from outside the workers' culture in the service of textile mill owners' profits.

The Silences of Rhetorical Criticism and the Rhetorical Criticism of Silence

Thus we cannot take E. O. Friday's silences on the question of solidarity with the strikes as evidence of his lack of class consciousness or unwillingness to see his oppression as fundamentally economic in nature. To the contrary, he is less silent than *silenced*, suggesting a self-censorship born of necessity rather than lack of knowledge, sense of common cause, or desire for change. Labor historian Michael Honey has noted that under a system of coercive constraint it often appears to be impossible to unite workers.[70] Yet, in many instances of labor agitation, even in the South, there have been vibrant interracial struggles. The workers' ability to challenge joint economic exploitation depended upon also challenging racism and segregation. [71] While Southern workers did participate in barring black workers from the mills and other workplaces and reinforcing segregation, the story is not a monolithic one.[72]

Today we are seeing the beginning of a resurgence of the labor movement after a long period in the doldrums.[73] At the same time, racial antagonism is still a prominent feature of American society. The most recent report of the Milton Eisenhower Foundation has concluded that the economic and racial divide in the United States has become wider since the 1960s: "The rich are getting richer, the poor are getting poorer, and minorities are suffering disproportionately."[74] While the national jobless rate is below five percent, unemployment rates for urban black workers have topped 30 percent in the last few years. The child poverty rate in America is four times the western European average, while the incarceration rate of black men in the United States is quadruple that of South Africa under apartheid.[75]

Such statistics show that in large part, racism is a matter of disproportionately bearing a class burden.[76] Therefore, overcoming racial and gendered barriers in the labor movement is the responsibility of activists in that movement. It is incumbent upon activists to attend to the reasonable distrust and fear of those most vulnerable to economic exploitation and repressive state force. Michael Honey raises the question of connecting labor movement to civil rights: "Were unions only there to win higher wages and better working conditions? Or did unionism's agenda include larger social goals, such as ending an apartheid system that had helped to lock generations of southern workers into economic squalor and political incompetence?"[77] Today, the broader social goals of unions should include protecting and organizing not only black workers but also immigrant workers whose positions in the contemporary economy parallel the marginal yet necessary place of black mill workers in the 1930s.

The commonplace argument that white workers benefit from racial privilege, or, in other words, that racism serves their interests, has an unfortunate corollary: that racial separation is also in the best interest of black workers. However, it is clear that for labor organizers and labor historians, racial and gender-based divisions have posed some of the most recalcitrant barriers to common cause and success in the labor movement.[78] Especially in the South, organizing across such divisions has been a major challenge. Yet, as Kim Moody and Philip Foner have pointed out, progressive industrial unions in the CIO, alongside Communist-led unions like the Mine Metal and Smelter Workers, self-consciously dedicated themselves to combating racism and organizing workers for economic justice across racial lines.[79] In contemporary labor studies, the problem of racism is sometimes described as endemic to workers' culture, a matter of consciousness unconnected to the broader profit imperative or racist political motives fostered from outside of workers' communities. For example, David Roediger has argued that racism garners a kind of psychological "wage" for white workers, who feel better about themselves in racist signification systems that put them on top of a symbolic hierarchy even though they may experience exploitation, poverty, and lack of economic control alongside black workers.[80] This influential explanation obscures the ways that racism and sexism serve systemic interests and can be generated and promoted from the top of society, even if the ideas end up circulating within working-class vernacular communities. Further, such explanations imply that racism is a psychological phenomenon of consciousness motivated by psychological and symbolic needs, rather than being connected to economic power structures. The result is a "blame-the-workers" perspective that is, at its core, pessimistic about the possibility of a successful multiracial challenge to systemic, material, injustice.[81]

The idea that oppressed groups must fight their oppression separately, and that oppressions based on identity are specific and autonomous from economic relations, is sometimes referred to as identity politics.[82] This position is profoundly pessimistic and debilitating to the labor movement, in addition to being one-sided in its attention to labor history. First, it mistakes psychological gratification for real material benefits. A materialist stance would use material criteria for assessing harms and benefits. Racism in its modern form came into being as a distinct ideological justification of slavery, and thus was always linked to economic motive and to a system of economic reward and deprivation. Racism is used to deny equal wages, housing, health care, education, and other material resources to those marked as inferior in a racist ideological system. Thus racism is closely tied to the workings of capitalism; to challenge racism is to challenge the division and inequality required for exploitation to occur. Now, it makes sense that an effective fightback against an exploitative system would also take economic form and unite people with common interests across the artificial racial barriers constructed in modern society. The politics of identity retreats from this strategy in favor of isolating groups on the basis of identity and having them struggle for gains on the terrain of identity itself. In a labor struggle context, such a strategy can be disastrous, allowing employers to replace workers of one race with members of another when the groups are not acting in solidarity.

That workers have acted in solidarity across race and gender lines in the past is evidence of the potential for class-based common cause in labor movement. The reverse is also true. There are many instances in American history where the failure of white organizations to make the bridge to black workers resulted in the defeat of all workers (for example, in an 1887 sugar strike in Louisiana, broken when black workers replaced white strikers, but at much lower wages). In the 1920s and 1930s, the AFL excluded black workers as a matter of routine. But even in those racist unions, racism was shown to have ill benefited white workers. Foner notes, "The exclusion of black workers from the AFL was a serious problem in industries in which a significant number of black workers were employed. When workers in those industries struck, black workers were forced to quit or work as scabs."[83] Thus the notion that white workers benefit from racism is spurious, as it is clear that racism has been tragic for everyone struggling for a better life.

For this reason, among many others, we should not mistake silence on questions of solidarity for lack of common cause. Paying attention to what cannot be said in certain material contexts reveals that the crafting of consciousness may not be the Alpha and the Omega of social change. The silences of the transcripts are matched by silences in the field of communication studies, which has, largely, ignored the labor movement.[84] This silence represents a missed opportunity to explore the interaction between economic and symbolic power. The over-emphasis on talk or discourse as the engine of social reality sometimes causes us to overlook the extent to which symbolic consolations—such as the cultural autonomy experienced by mill workers—serve as substitute for material redress rather than as the agency of progressive social or organizational change. Thus it is imperative for scholars of social movements and of labor specifically not to mistake perceived benefits or the appearance of new subjects on the cultural stage, for real benefits ameliorating injustice. This axiom is related to another for the field of communication studies. Just as one cannot take symbolic gains on the terrain of identity and difference as a real indicator of power, one cannot always take consciousness as reality. In other words, we need to be able to account for barriers to bottom-up agency that are non-discursive and non-rhetorical in nature. Workers, like the ones involved in the 1934 mill strikes, often exhibit a split between consciousness and expression, making rhetorical discourses alone an unreliable hermeneutic source—unless we listen very carefully to the silences.

Philip Wander also argued in his article "The Third Persona" that we should attend to what is not present or spoken in discourses.[85] In that essay, Wander argued that rhetorical critics should pay attention to audiences not invoked or constructed by a rhetor as symptomatic of communities and interests excluded in dominant rhetoric. He writes:

> Just as the discourse may be understood to affirm certain characteristics, it may also be understood to imply other characteristics, roles, actions, or ways of seeing things to be avoided. What is negated through the Second Persona forms the silhouette of a Third Persona—the 'it' that is not present. . . . the Third Persona, therefore, refers to being negated . . . being negated in history, a being whose presence, though relevant to what is said, is negated through silence.[86]

Wander is extending Edwin Black's essay "The Second Persona," which argues that a rhetor (the First Persona) constructs an image or a way of being for an intended audience, calling that audience (the Second Persona) into being.[87] The process of being negated, or the formation of a silenced silhouette, can also apply to the speaker or rhetor. If the first persona is the rhetor, perhaps the phenomenon of self-silencing noted in these transcripts could be referred to the constitution of oneself in the role of "null persona." The null

persona refers to the self-negation of the speaker and the creation in the text of an oblique silhouette indicating what is not utterable. The crafting of a null persona might signal critics to examine extradiscursive constraints on a group's rhetorical agency. To paraphrase Wander, "the objectification of certain individuals and groups discloses itself through what is and is not said about [or by] them and through actual conditions affecting their ability to speak for themselves."

The "null persona," as constructed by E. O. Friday and other black workers above, does exhibit discursive markers. But those markers point directly toward extradiscursive power relations involving economic exploitation and physical coercion that we must regard as supra-symbolic in nature in order to assess their significance. In other words, the oppression "discloses itself through what is not said and through actual conditions." Wander adds that negation extends beyond text and operates through extradiscursive social, political, and economic arrangements.[88] Therefore, the structural negation of voice is as crucial to understanding workers' rhetoric as the presence of voice. To date, the emphasis of critical organizational communication research has been on giving workers a voice in decision-making, which, as Cheney notes, usually does not extend to control over wages or benefits. Further, as we have seen in the Uprising of '34 transcripts, we need to attend to the material, economic, and other repressive constraints on voice—a voice that E. O. Friday and others in his position were denied or strategically refused.[89]

This analysis of the Uprising of '34 demonstrates the significance of considerations of power, economics, and social control in the study of antiracist and labor movements. All of the black workers interviewed for the documentary, many of them second- and third-generation millworkers, report ongoing discrimination in hiring, wages, and promotion in the mills. Members of the Gardin family describe ongoing Klan threats. An approach that regards movements as primarily or exclusively discursive phenomena cannot account for this material, coercive context. Critical scholars cannot take silence as indication of the absence of something—counter-ideological consciousness in a social movement—any more than we can take social movement discourses as sufficient evidence of meaning in a movement. Racism (and sexism) are not just features of culture but are conduits of repressive economic and state power. As scholars and activists, we need to sustain attention to the role of such power in movements, while maintaining optimism about making a struggle against capitalism out of whole cloth, rather than settling for the scraps the system will allow.

This work was supported by a University of Texas Special Research Grant and a College of Communication Dean's Fellowship. Parts of this paper were presented at the Southern Labor Studies Conference in Williamsburg, Virginia, in September 1997 and at the National Communication Association Meeting in Chicago during November 1997. [The author] would like to thank Robert Woodrum at Georgia State University for his archival assistance in gathering transcripts at the Southern Labor Archives, and Robert Jensen at the University of Texas for his helpful advice on earlier drafts. Additional debts of gratitude are owed to Steven Goldzwig, the editor of this special issue, and to three anonymous reviewers whose suggestions strengthened this work.

NOTES

1. Audre Lorde, "The Transformation of Silence into Language and Action," in *Sister Outsider* (Freedom, CA: Crossing Press, 1984), 41.

2. Philip Wander, "The Third Persona: An Ideological Turn in Rhetorical Theory," *Central States Speech Journal* 35 (1984): 197–216 [reprinted in this volume].

3. Jeremy Brecher, *Strike!* 2d ed. (Boston: South End, 1997), 184–92.

4. For example, mine workers, auto workers, and rubber workers led a number of successful sit-down strikes that led to the historic recognition of CIO unions in those industries and pressured the New Deal to pass the Wagner Act explicitly granting workers the right to independent organization and collective bargaining. See Brecher, 193–235.

5. Kevin Sack, "Union Again Fails To Win Over Workers at Big Textile Plants," *New York Times*, August 15, 1997.

6. Martin Ritt, *Norma Rae* (Los Angeles, CA: Twentieth Century-Fox, 1979).

7. George Stoney, Judith Helfand, and Susanne Rostock, *The Uprising of '34* (New York: First Run/Icarus Films, 1995).

8. In order to conform to the *Rhetoric & Public Affairs* style sheet, the author has allowed the term "black" to appear in lower case lettering. However, in solidarity with an oppressed minority, the author registers her strong preference for Black to appear as a capitalized term, as it does throughout the corpus of her work as a dignifying gesture.

9. E. O. Friday, interview by George Stoney, Judith Helfand, and Susanne Rostock, 1995. Atlanta: Southern Labor Archives, Box 17, folders 1–2 of Uprising of '34 Collection; Gardin Family, interview by George Stoney, Judith Helfand, and Susanne Rostock, 1995.

Atlanta: Southern Labor Archives, Box 14, folder 9 of Uprising of '34 Collection; Louise Thornburg, interview by George Stoney, Judith Helfand, and Susanne Rostock, 1995. Atlanta: Southern Labor Archives, Box 25, folders 4, 5, 6 of Uprising of '34 Collection; Blanche Willis, interview by George Stoney, Judith Helfand, and Susanne Rostock, 1995. Atlanta: Southern Labor Archives, Box 14, folder 9 of Uprising of '34 Collection.

10. James Arnt Aune, "The Power of Hegemony and Marxist Cultural Theory," in *Rhetoric and Community: Studies in Unity and Fragmentation*, ed. J. Michael Hogan (Columbia: University of South Carolina Press, 1998), 62–74.

11. Philip Wander, "The Third Persona," 197–216.

12. Lester C. Olson, "On the Margins of Rhetoric: Audre Lorde Transforming Silence Into Language and Action," *Quarterly Journal of Speech* 83 (1997): 49–70; Robin Patric Clair, *Organizing Silence: A World of Possibilities* (Albany: State University of New York Press, 1998).

13. Teresa Ebert, *Ludic Feminism and After: Postmodernism, Desire, and Labor in Late Capitalism* (Ann Arbor: University of Michigan Press, 1996).

14. Lindsey German, "Theories of the Family," in *Materialist Feminism: A Reader in Class, Difference, and Women's Lives*, ed. Rosemary Hennessy and Chrys Ingraham (New York: Routledge, 1997), 147–61.

15. The following authors have summarized the recent variations on materialism in communication studies: Dana L. Cloud, "Materiality of Discourse as Oxymoron," *Western Journal of Communication* 58 (1994): 141–63; Sharon Crowley, "Reflections on an Argument that Won't Go Away: Or, a Turn of the Ideological Screw," *Quarterly Journal of Speech* 78 (1992): 450–65; Ronald Walter Greene, "Another Materialism," *Critical Studies in Mass Communication* 15 (1998): 21–41; David J. Sholle, "Critical Studies: From the Theory of Ideology to Power/Knowledge," *Critical Studies in Mass Communication* 5 (1988): 16–41. One version of materialism, common among rhetoricians—including Michael McGee, "The 'Ideograph': A Link Between Rhetoric and Ideology," *Quarterly Journal of Speech* 66 (1980): 1–16 [reprinted in this volume]; "Text, Context, and the Fragmentation of Contemporary Culture," *Western Journal of Communication* 54 (1990): 274–89 [reprinted in this volume]; "A Materialist's Conception of Rhetoric," in *Explorations in Rhetoric*, ed. Raymie E. McKerrow (Glenview, Ill.: Scott, Foresman, 1982), 23–48, and Celeste Condit, "Clouding the Issues: The Ideal and the Material in Human Communication," *Critical Studies in Mass Communication* 14 (1997): 197–200—is a kind of "linguistic materialism" that acknowledges that texts cannot be understood except in relation to their contexts, yet defines those contexts as themselves intertextual, rather than including economic or other extradiscursive dimensions. A somewhat different, Foucauldian approach to the question of

materiality is represented by Ronald Greene ("Another Materialism"), who criticizes materialist theories that either posit rhetoric as ruling class persuasion (ideology) or emphasize rhetoric's constitution of subjectivity. Greene argues that critics should regard power as productive of social truths rather than as ideologies that mask truth and thus require demystification. Ideology critics, on the other hand, stand by a hermeneutics of suspicion or what John Thompson calls "depth hermeneutics," which does posit an extradiscursive standard of judgment. Greene argues for "getting beyond" the logic of representation that characterizes these approaches, in favor of a Foucauldian conception of power as productive of subjects, in which regimes of truth regulate public problems by policing a population, place and/or object. Despite the break with other linguistic materialists on the question of representation, he does not break with the idealism of communication studies' emphasis on text and consciousness as the primary sites of investigation and struggle. Further, Greene's approach is relativist, in other words, it conflates the persuasive with what is "in the true," arguing that critics cannot posit an extradiscursive truth standard against which to judge even the most propagandistic or ideological discourses. Greene posits a transhistorical, abstract government or set of governing apparatuses, that "polices a population, space, and/or object by articulating an ensemble of human technologies into a functioning network of power to improve public welfare" (22). From a materialist perspective, it is extremely troubling to jettison class-based critique (or, as Greene puts it, a "bipolar model of power" (24)) in favor of a theory that posits governing apparatuses as improving the welfare of a population—without asking which population is benefiting. As Stuart Hall points out in an interview criticizing Foucauldian appropriations of the Gramscian concept of articulation, Foucault maintains a theory of power but abdicates the question of politics, because in the model of productive power, "he has no idea of the 'relations of force'" (Hall, 136). He goes on to comment that in such a model "there is no way of conceptualizing the balance of power between different regimes of truth" (Hall, 135–36). John B. Thompson, *Ideology and Modern Culture* (Stanford, CA: Stanford University Press, 1990). Stuart Hall, "On Postmodernism and Articulation," in *Stuart Hall: Critical Dialogues in Cultural Studies*, ed. David Morley and Kuan-Hsing Chen (London: Routledge, 1996), 131–50.

16. Thompson, *Ideology.*

17. Antonio Gramsci, *Selections from the Prison Notebooks*, trans. Quentin Hoare and Geoffrey Nowell Smith (1936; reprint, New York: International Publishers, 1971). See also Karlyn Kohrs Campbell, "The Power of Hegemony: Capitalism and Racism in the 'Nadir of Negro History,'" *Rhetoric and Community*, 36–61. Campbell discusses the ways in which the hegemony of overtly racist messages can mitigate against refraining issues of race and class.

18. Dennis K. Mumby, "The Problem of Hegemony: Rereading Gramsci for Organizational Communication Studies," *Western Journal of Communication* 61 (1997): 343–75; James Arnt Aune, *Rhetoric and Marxism* (Boulder, CO: Westview, 1994).

19. Colette Guillaumin, *Racism, Sexism, Power, and Ideology* (London: Routledge, 1995), 33.

20. Campbell, "The Power of Hegemony," 46–47.

21. Hennessy & Ingraham, *Materialist Feminism*, 3–4.

22. Hazel V. Carby, "On the Threshold of Woman's Era: Lynching, Empire, and Sexuality in Black Feminist Theory," *Critical Inquiry* 12 (1985): 262–77; Angela Davis, "Rape, Racism, and the Myth of the Black Male Rapist," in *Women, Race, and Class* (New York: Vintage, 1983), 172–201.

23. Aune, *Rhetoric and Marxism*; Kenneth Burke, *Permanence and Change* (1936; reprint, Berkeley: University of California Press, 1984); Crowley, "Reflections"; McGee, "'Ideograph'"; Raymie E. McKerrow, "Critical Rhetoric: Theory and Praxis," *Communication Monographs* 56 (1989): 91–111; Philip Wander, "The Ideological Turn in Modern Criticism," *Central States Speech Journal* 34 (1983): 1–18; Michael Burawoy, *Manufacturing Consent: Changes in Labor Process Under Monopoly Capitalism* (Chicago: University of Chicago Press, 1979); George Cheney, "Democracy in the Workplace: Theory and Practice from the Perspective of Communication," *Journal of Applied Communication Research* 23 (1995): 167–200; George Cheney et al., "Democracy, Participation, and Communication at Work: A Multidisciplinary Review," in *Communication Yearbook 21*, ed. Michael E. Roloff (Thousand Oaks, CA: Sage, 1997), 35–91; Stanley A. Deetz, *Democracy in an Age of Corporate Colonization* (Albany: State University of New York Press, 1992); Stanley Deetz and A. Kersten, "Critical Models of Interpretive Research," in *Communication and Organizations: An Interpretive Approach*, ed. Linda Putnam and M. E. Pacanowsky (Newbury Park, CA: Sage, 1983), 147–72; Stanley A. Deetz and Dennis K. Mumby, "Power, Discourse, and the Workplace: Reclaiming the Critical Tradition," *Communication Yearbook 13*, ed. James Anderson (Thousand Oaks, CA: Sage, 1993), 18–47; Dennis K. Mumby, *Communication and Power in Organizations: Discourse, Ideology, and Domination* (Norwood, NJ: Ablex, 1988); Dennis K. Mumby, "Ideology and the Social Construction of Meaning: A Communication Perspective," *Communication Quarterly* 37 (1989): 291–304; Dennis K. Mumby, "Critical Organizational Communication Studies: The Next 10 Years," *Communication Monographs* 60 (1993): 18–25; Mumby, "The Problem of Hegemony," 343–75.

24. Here is a partial bibliography of the literature on rhetoric and silence: Barry Brummett, "Towards a Theory of Silence as Political Strategy," *Quarterly Journal of Speech* 66 (1980): 289–303; Thomas J. Bruneau, "Communicative Silences: Forms and Functions," *Jour-*

nal of Communication 23 (1973): 17–46; Robin Patric Clair, "Organizing Silence: Silence as Voice and Voice as Silence in the Narrative Exploration of the Treaty of New Echota," Western Journal of Communication 61 (1997): 315–37; Robin Patric Clair, Organizing Silence: A World of Possibilities (Albany: State University of New York Press, 1998); Radha S. Hegde, "Narratives of Silence: Rethinking Gender, Agency, and Power from the Communication Experiences of Battered Women in South India," Communication Studies 47 (1996): 303–17; Adam Jaworski, ed., The Power of Silence: Social and Pragmatic Perspectives (Newbury Park: Sage, 1993); Adam Jaworski, ed., Silence: Interdisciplinary Perspectives (Berlin: deGruyter, 1997); J. Vernon Jenson, "Communicative Functions of Silence," ETC: A Review of General Semantics 30 (1973): 249–57; Richard L. Johannesen, "The Functions of Silence: A Plea for Communication Research," Western Speech 38 (1974): 25–35; Olson, "On the Margins": Robert L. Scott, "Rhetoric and Silence," Western Speech 36 (1972): 146–58.

25. Brummett, "Towards a Theory."

26. Brummett, "Towards a Theory," 294.

27. Clair, Organizing Silence.

28. Clair, Organizing Silence.

29. Simone de Beauvoir, The Second Sex, trans. H. M. Parshley (1949; reprint, New York: Bantam, 1961); Mary Daly, Beyond God the Father: Toward a Philosophy of Women's Liberation (Boston: Beacon, 1973); Elaine Hedges and Shelley Fisher-Fishkin, Listening to Silences: New Essays in Feminist Criticism (New York: Oxford University Press, 1994); Robin Tolmach Lakoff, Language and Woman's Place (New York: Harper and Row, 1975); Lorde, Transforming Silence; Catherine MacKinnon, Only Words (Cambridge, MA: Harvard University Press, 1993); Tillie Olsen, Silences (New York: Delta[/Seymour Lawrence], 1989); Julia Stanley Penelope, Speaking Freely (New York: Pergamon, 1990); Dale Spender, Man Made Language (London: Routledge and Kegan Paul, 1980).

30. Hegde, "Narratives," 303–317.

31. Hegde, "Narratives," 303.

32. Hegde, "Narratives," 306.

33. Hegde, "Narratives," 309.

34. Olson, "On the Margins"; Lorde, Transforming Silence.

35. Olson, "On the Margins," 64.

36. Olson, "On the Margins," 65.

37. Henry Louis Gates Jr., The Signifying Monkey (New York: Oxford, 1988), xxv, 94.

38. Jacquelyn Dowd-Hall et al., Like a Family: The Making of a Southern Cotton Mill World (Chapel Hill: University of North Carolina Press, 1987).

39. Julius G. Getman, The Betrayal of Local 14 (Ithaca, NY: Cornell University Press and ILR Press, 1998).

40. Dowd-Hall et al., Like a Family, xiv.

41. Gerard A. Hauser, "Vernacular Dialogue and the Rhetoricality of Public Opinion," Communication Monographs 65 (1998): 83–108, 90; Kent A. Ono and John M. Sloop, "The Critique of Vernacular Discourse," Communication Monographs 62 (1995): 19–46.

42. Hauser, "Vernacular Dialogue."

43. All references to the documentary are to Stoney, Helfand, and Rostock, The Uprising of '34.

44. The conditions that sparked the previously docile workers to a general strike have also been documented by journalists of the day, in union documents, and by labor historians. See Victoria Morris Byerly, Hard Times Cotton Mill Girls (Ithaca, NY: Cornell University Press and ILR Press, 1986); Sinclair Lewis, "Cheap and Contented Labor: Picture of a Southern Mill Town in 1929," United Features Syndicate, 1929; Jack Hardy, The Clothing Workers (New York: International Publishers, 1935); James A. Hodge, New Deal Labor Policy and the Southern Cotton Textile Industry, 1933–1941 (Knoxville: University of Tennessee Press, 1986); James L. Hoffman, A Study of the United Textile Workers of America in a Cotton-Mill in a Medium-Sized Southern Industrial City: Labor Revolt in Alabama, 1934. Ed.D. Thesis, University of Alabama, 1986; Myra Page, Southern Cotton Mills and Labor (New York: Workers Library 1929); United Textile Workers of America, Sixth Biennial and Thirty-Third Annual Convention Minutes (New York: August 13–18, 1934); United Textile Workers of America, A History of the United Textile Workers of America (Washington, DC: UTWA, 1950). Cotton mills produced nearly a billion dollars worth of goods per year during the 1930s (Hodge, 9). Entire families—men, women, and children—worked 12- to 14-hour days, six days a week, in cotton mills across the Piedmont region of the Southern United States. Mill owners built company towns to house the workers, so that every facet of a worker's life was dependent upon the employer, who owned not only the mill and the houses, but also the stores, the schools, the churches, and all public utilities and services. Safety was also a serious issue in the mills. In the economic crisis of the Depression, mill owners demanded increased productivity from workers to mitigate against falling profits. The resulting speed-up of machines and the necessity of each worker staffing several machines at once (a trend referred to as "stretch-out") were sources of stress and danger on the job.

45. The Gastonia Strike in 1929 at Loray Mills is perhaps the best known of this series. According to Tom Tippett [When Southern Labor Stirs (New York: Cape and Smith, 1931)], "a Communist union [the National Textile Workers] for the first time raised its head in the South, and the response was a storm of hysteria and mob violence and murder that shocked the whole country" (76). Some of the worst conditions in mill towns prevailed in Gastonia. The strikers called for a 20 dollar weekly wage, better working conditions, an end to piece

work, and the eight hour day. During the strike, local newspapers and town leaders, clergy, businessmen, and police denounced the union and went to unprecedented lengths to defeat the workers. Governor Gardner sent the state militia into the Loray village four days into the strike, ending pickets and clubbing and beating strikers in the streets. Militiamen broke up pickets and parades by force every day, but the strikers would reform and march into the clubs and rifles. Strikebreakers destroyed the union headquarters. Weakened, the strike continued until police opened fire onto strikers, who replied with gunfire, killing a police officer. Townspeople hunted and imprisoned the strikers, a number of whom were later convicted of murder and imprisoned. By the winter of 1930, there was no sign of labor organizing or activity at Loray mill; the radical union and the movement in Gastonia had been crushed. Incidentally, Ella Mae Wiggins, mentioned at some length below, played a key role as a labor songwriter and singer during the Gastonia strike. See John A. Salmond, *Gastonia, 1929: The Story of the Loray Mill Strike* (Chapel Hill: University of North Carolina Press, 1995).

46. Hodge, *New Deal*, 92.

47. Philip Foner and Ronald L. Lewis, *Black Workers: A Documentary History from Colonial Times to the Present* (Philadelphia: Temple University Press, 1989), 281.

48. For a discussion of the interrelationship of labor movement pressure and New Deal reforms, see Milton Derber and Edwin Young, *Labor and the New Deal* (Madison: University of Wisconsin Press, 1957); Michael Goldfield, "Worker Insurgency, Radical Organization, and New Deal Labor Legislation," *American Political Science Review* 83 (1989): 1257–82; Theda Skocpol and Kenneth Finegold, "Explaining New Deal Labor Policy," *American Political Science Review* 84 (1990): 1297–1304; Michael Goldfield, "Response to Skocpol and Finegold," *American Political Science Review* 84 (1990): 1304–1315; and Lisbeth Cohen, *Making a New Deal: Industrial Workers in Chicago, 1919–1939* (Cambridge, UK: Cambridge University Press, 1990).

49. Elizabeth Ann Sharpe, "History and Legacy of Mississippi Plantation Labor," in *Culture, Gender, Race, and U.S. Labor History*, ed. Ronald Kent, Sara Markham, David Roediger, and Herbert Shapiro (Westport, CT: Greenwood Press, 1993), 105–20.

50. This understanding of discrete texts as insufficient to the making and criticism of meaning differs from the argument of Michael McGee, "Text, Context, and the Fragmentation of Contemporary Culture," *Western Journal of Communication* 54 (1990): 274–89 [reprinted in this volume]. McGee argues that audiences and critics assemble meaningful wholes from fragments offered them in discourse (151). However, McGee's argument risks embracing the flaws (from a materialist perspective) of an idealist critical stance that does not account for extradiscursive power relations as integral to meaning. Instead of discovering the economic or politi-

cal interests at work in determining what may be given voice and what must be silenced, the critic is reduced to examining the swirl of fragmented voices, disconnected from systematic explanation.

51. Lyn Mikel Brown and Carol Gilligan, *Meeting at the Crossroads: Women's Psychology and Girls' Development* (Cambridge, MA: Harvard University Press, 1992), 20–21.

52. Brown and Gilligan, *Meeting at the Crossroads*, 23–24.

53. Dowd-Hall et al., *Like a Family*, 318.

54. Dowd-Hall et al., *Like a Family*, 318; similarly, Foner and Lewis (*Black Workers*) note examples of mill workers who wanted and tried to recruit black workers, even though black workers were scarce around the mills.

55. Dowd-Hall et al., *Like a Family*, 235.

56. Rhonda Zingraff and Michael D. Schulman, "Social Bases of Class Consciousness: A Study of Southern Textile Workers with a Comparison by Race," *Social Forces* 63 (1984): 98–116,113.

57. Larry J. Griffin and Robert R. Korstad, "Class as Race and Gender: Making and Breaking a Labor Union in the Jim Crow South," *Social Science History* 19 (1995): 425–54, 431, 437.

58. Thus the Uprising of 1934 is one instance of a mass strike in which women were centrally involved in union organizing and militancy. Louise Thornburg, a leader of the Uprising interviewed for the documentary, describes the Uprising as a site of women's community, agency, and voice. Similarly, Dowd-Hall et al. (*Like a Family*) hail the mill towns as places where women could break out of traditional and oppressive dominant gendered norms. As workers in the mills, white women were not expected to conform to standards of domesticity and passivity that excluded women from heavy labor in other regions.

59. German, "Theories of the Family."

60. Dowd-Hall et al., *Like a Family*.

61. Rose M. Brewer, "Theorizing Race, Class, and Gender," in *Materialist Feminism*, 238–47; 241.

62. Dowd-Hall et al., *Like a Family*, 145.

63. Karen Beckwith also notes that mineworkers used familial metaphors during the Pittston strike of 1989 in order to signal solidarity across gender and generation in the mining community. "Collective Identities of Class and Gender: Working-Class Women in the Pittston Coal Strike," *Political Psychology* 19 (1998): 147–67.

64. Dowd-Hall et al., *Like a Family*, 146–47.

65. Dana L. Cloud, "The Rhetoric of Family Values: Scapegoating, Utopia, and the Privatization of Social Responsibility," *Western Journal of Communication* 62 (1998): 387–419.

66. Ronald Walter Greene, "Another Materialism," 21–41.

67. Herbert W. Simons, "Persuasion in Social Conflicts: A Critique of Prevailing Conceptions and a Framework for Future Research," *Speech Monographs* 39 (1972): 227–47; 232.

68. Edgar H. Schein, *Coercive Persuasion* (New York: Norton, 1961), 18

69. Susan Gal, "Between Speech and Silence: The Problematics of Research on Language and Gender," in *Gender at the Crossroads of Knowledge: Feminist Anthropology in the Postmodern Era*, ed. Micaela de Leonardo (Berkeley: University of California Press, 1991), 175–203; 176.

70. Michael K. Honey, *Southern Labor and Black Civil Rights: Organizing Memphis Workers* (Urbana: University of Illinois Press, 1993).

71. Labor historians have provided a great deal of evidence in the form of specific cases of interracial unionism among miners, dockers, and other groups. For example, Joe William Trotter Jr., "Class and Racial Inequality: The Southern West Virginia Black Coal Miners' Response, 1915–32," in *Organized Labor in the Twentieth-Century South*, ed. Robert H. Zieger (Knoxville: University of Tennessee Press, 1993, 60–83) takes as a case southern West Virginia black coal miners, who organized across race lines with white miners. Although there were racial tensions, both groups saw the union as serving their interests. Trotter notes that it is not difficult to see and feel a sense of common cause when most workers of any race worked side-by-side in the hazardous conditions of the coal mine (66); see also Joe William Trotter Jr., "African-American Workers: New Directions in U.S. Labor Historiography," *Labor History* 35 (1994): 495–523; Alan Dawley and Joe William Trotter Jr., "Race and Class," *Labor History* 35 (1994): 486–94. Eric Arnesen's groundbreaking work on inter-racialism among dock workers in New Orleans at the turn-of-the-century notes, "longshore workers sustained a movement that ran counter to the dominant trend of black subordination, exclusion, and segregation in the age of Jim Crow" [*Waterfront Workers of New Orleans* (New York: Oxford University Press, 1991), ix]. Arnesen argues that such vibrant inter-racialism was enabled by strong black unions and an overall pro-union climate on the docks. Foner and Lewis (*Black Workers*) describe a victorious miners' strike in Alabama in 1908, during which (to the public's outrage), the United Mine Workers held interracial meetings and events. Also effective at achieving interracial solidarity were the left-wing led unions such as the Trade Union Education League (TUEL), which came out explicitly against Southern white terror against black workers (Foner and Lewis, 436).

72. Robert H. Zieger, *Organized Labor in the Twentieth-Century South* (Knoxville: University of Tennessee Press, 1991), 7.

73. Kim Moody, *An Injury to All* (London: Verso, 1988).

74. Milton S. Eisenhower Foundation, *The Millennium Breach* (Washington, DC: Eisenhower Foundation, 1998); as quoted in Deb Reichman, "Economic and Racial Gap Widening, Report Finds," Associated Press Newswire, March 1, 1998.

75. Reichman, "Economic and Racial, "A7.

76. For primary documents establishing this link, see Julius Jacobson, ed., *The Negro and the American Labor Movement* (New York: Anchor Books, 1968).

77. Honey, *Southern Labor*, 7.

78. Robert Asher and Charles Stephenson, eds., *Labor Divided: Race and Ethnicity in United States Labor Struggles, 1835–1960* (Albany: State University of New York Press, 1990).

79. Kim Moody, *Workers in a Lean World* (London: Verso, 1997); Foner and Lewis, *Black Workers*.

80. David Roediger, *The Wages of Whiteness: Race and the Myth of the American Working Class* (London: Verso, 1991).

81. In my view, some recent work in cultural studies also has erred in the direction of formulating racism, its consequences, and the interests of black workers and other minorities in symbolic, psychological, or exclusively textual terms. For example, Stuart Hall, guided by the hypothesis that global capitalism is disorganizing, has argued that we should work within the productive cultural space of marginality and embrace a "cultural politics of difference, of the struggles around difference, of the production of new identities, of the appearance of new subjects on the political and cultural stage" [Stuart Hall, "What is This 'Black' in Black Popular Culture?" *Black Popular Culture*, ed. Gina Dent (Seattle, WA: Bay Press, 1996), 21–36]. On the one hand, this analysis legitimates attention to cultural production as a site of struggle around race. On the other hand, it also formulates a kind of retreat from organized struggle, suggesting that we settle for symbolic gains around "new identities," "new subjects," on a cultural (rather than political or economic) stage in lieu of actual social change benefiting black Americans. This approach seems to elide the fact that African Americans and other oppressed groups suffer not only or even primarily from an identity crisis so much as they do from physical deprivation based on discrimination with regard to education, employment, wages, housing, and the justice system. Studies of the labor movement and its cultural practices around issues of race might restore dialectical balance to models of discourse, materiality, and the project of social change.

82. Stanley Aronowitz, *Politics of Identity: Class, Culture, Social Movements* (New York: Routledge, 1992).

83. Foner and Lewis, *Black Workers*, 39.

84. A survey of the Matlon index to journals in communication studies (Robert J. Matlon, *Index to Journals in Communication Studies through 1990*, Annandale, VA: Speech Communication Association, 1992) reveals that

the few published articles on labor rhetoric, scattered over six decades, fall into the following categories:

- Very old studies of internal union communication, including James P. Dee, "Written Communications in the Trade Union Local," *Journal of Communication* 9 (1959): 99–109; Dee, "Oral Communication in the Trade Union Local," *Journal of Communication* 10 (1960): 77–86; Dee, "Channels of Talk in the Union Local," *Today's Speech* 10 (April 1962): 7–8, 23; Dee, "Communication Needs of the Active Union Member," *Journal of Communication* 18 (1968): 65–72; Richard J. Jensen and Carol L. Jensen, "Labor's Appeal to the Past: The 1972 Election in the United Mine Workers," *Central States Speech Journal* 28 (1977): 173–84; Howard K. Slaughter, "How Free is Labor's Speech?" *Today's Speech* 7 (February 1959): 8–10; Charles J. Stewart, "The Internal Rhetoric of the Knights of Labor," *Communication Studies* 42 (1991): 67–82.

- Appreciative studies of labor rhetors, including Bernard J. Brommel, "Eugene V. Debs: The Agitator as Speaker," *Central States Speech Journal* 20 (1969); 202–14; David A. Carter, "The Industrial Workers of the World and the Rhetoric of Song," *Quarterly Journal of Speech* 66 (1980): 365–74; James Darsey, "The Legend of Eugene Debs: Prophetic Ethos as Radical Argument," *Quarterly Journal of Speech* 74 (1988): 434–52; David Hayworfh, "Samuel Gompers, Orator," *Quarterly Journal of Speech* 22 (1936): 578–84; Mari Boor Tonn, "Militant Motherhood: Labor's Mary Harris 'Mother' Jones," *Quarterly Journal of Speech* 82 (1996): 1–22.

- And, finally, calls for further research on labor communication, including Mark L. Knapp and James C. McCroskey, "Communication Research and the American Labor Union," *Journal of Communication* 18 (1968): 160–72. There are also occasional mentions of labor in organizational communication literature, usually from the perspective of managerial interests, with the exceptions of the critical organizational research cited earlier in this article. None of the work cited encompasses a consideration of the interrelationship between rhetorical and economic interests and strategies.

85. Wander, "The Third Persona," 197–216.

86. Wander, "The Third Persona," 209–210.

87. Edwin Black, "The Second Persona," *Quarterly Journal of Speech* 56 (1970): 109–119 [reprinted in this volume].

88. Wander, "The Third Persona," 210.

89. As in organizational communication, the rhetorical study of social movements has been, on the whole, concerned with warranting specifically rhetorical attention to those movements as distinct and exclusively discursive phenomena, as opposed to more sociological methods that emphasize economics, social structure, and power in movements. Unfortunately, even critical communication scholars sympathetic with progressive causes tend to reduce social antagonisms and struggle to matters of language. For example, McGee suggests in several essays that "social movement" is a set of meanings requiring interpretation rather than explanation in terms of concrete, objective situations (Michael McGee, "Social Movement: Phenomenon or Meaning?", *Central States Speech Journal* 31 [1980]: 233–44). Elsewhere, McGee advises scholars to "see 'movement' as an ideological state and rhetoric as constitutive or representative of that state" ("Social Movement as Meaning," *Central States Speech Journal* 34 [1983]: 77). Recent works on social movements have continued to focus nearly exclusively on symbolic, rhetorical features such as how meanings of ideographs have shifted in social movements and how social movements have emerged from and continue an Old-Testament prophetic rhetorical tradition; see Celeste Condit and John Louis Lucaites, *Crafting Equality: America's Anglo-African Word* (Chicago: University of Chicago, 1993) and James Darsey, *The Prophetic Tradition and Radical Rhetoric in America* (New York: New York University Press, 1997).

Several recent works from other fields reinforce the discursive bias. Scholars have suggested that identity-based movements of women, African-Americans, etc., marked a qualitative shift in movement strategy, away from demands for direct and immediate economic redress and toward more identity-based strategies and less tangible goals, such as "pride" or "difference." The result has been a scholarly emphasis on "new social movements," often supported as a corrective to "old" (either liberal, legislation-oriented or socialist, labor-oriented) models of organization. These arguments suggest that rather than organizing mass movements for broad political and economic reforms, activists and intellectuals should settle for new kinds of agency found in consumer culture and lifestyle politics; see Ron Eyerman and Andrew Jamison, *Social Movements: A Cognitive Approach* (University Park: Pennsylvania State University Press, 1991); Ernesto Laclau and Chantai Mouffe, *Hegemony and Socialist Strategy* (London: Verso, 1988); Louis Maheu, *Social Movements and Social Classes* (London: Sage, 1995); Alberto Melucci, "Liberation or Meaning?: Social Movements, Culture, and Democracy," *Development and Change* 23 (1995): 43–77; S. Tarrow, "Costumes of Revolt: The Symbolic Politics of Social Movements," *Sisyphus* 8 (1992): 53–71; Alain Touraine, *Critique of Modernity* (Cambridge, UK: Blackwell, 1995). Some scholars have claimed that the era of collective protest is over, replaced by strategies for personal emancipation through consumption and the elaboration of identities and lifestyles; see Jan Pakulski and Malcolm Waters, *The Death of Class* (London: Sage, 1996); Anthony Giddens, *Modernity and Self-Identity* (Stanford, CA: Stanford University Press, 1991). Clearly, however, for the black mill workers stakes have been more material in nature.

Pink Herring & the Fourth Persona

J. Edgar Hoover's Sex Crime Panic

Charles E. Morris III

Secrecy, J. Edgar Hoover discovered prior to the Cold War, could be measured in feet. "[H]e . . . walks with a mincing step, dresses fastidiously, with Eleanor blue as the favorite color for matched shades of tie, handkerchief and socks," a *Collier's* reporter revealed.[1] For Hoover, as for many Americans sobering from Prohibition's embrace of the pansy, this mischievous comment reinforced a vexing realization: the contours of masculinity had begun to blur at the same time that gender norms tightened. Presumptive silences were becoming audible, as audible as the sound of expensive shoes on a city sidewalk. To keep step with the passing crowd, one must not be caught mincing.

At the time his mincing was exposed in 1933, Hoover had for five years been in a relationship with fellow bachelor and Associate Director of the FBI Clyde Tolson. Until then, Hoover and Tolson had been spared speculation about their sexuality by the prominent cultural presence of the pansy, whose dramatic features offered a code that relieved those who fell somewhere else on the rather fluid spectrum of male homosocial desire.[2] Whatever other males might do sexually, their identity remained largely unquestioned because, given the pansy, most Americans "knew" a homosexual when they encountered one.

Prohibition's demise in the 1930s claimed with it the pansy's public sphere. As it controlled the burgeoning deviant subculture, the anti-crime movement successfully forced the pansy to the periphery of a visible social world. In chasing the most licit expression of male[3] homosexual desire into the shadows, regulators briefly unhinged homosexual meaning at a time when masculinity already suffered the debilitating effects of the Depression. What counted as homosexual and as homosocial (and heterosexual), therefore, had become unclear.

This tumultuous period, I contend, was marked by a "homosexual panic"[4] that transformed the homosexual from pansy into "menace."[5] The ensuing contest over sexual meaning entailed increased scrutiny and, correlatively, rhetorical performance. A wide range of male rhetorical behavior occurred that I interpret as "passing," the self-fashioning that constructs and preserves an ethos of gender and sexual "normalcy." Hoover's own rhetorical agency is implied by Richard Gid Power's conclusion that "Of all Hoover's secrets, the most tightly guarded were his own."[6]

In what follows I do not hazard conclusions about Hoover's secrets. Proof of Hoover's sexuality is not required to establish his public response to the homosexual panic that gripped straight and gay men alike. The question of what constituted the (homo)sexual on the homosocial continuum at the time would have been a dangerously open one for Hoover and other men. That he exhibited a style and enjoyed a relationship vulnerable to speculation tells us much about his felt exigence but nothing about his love life. The *question* of his sexuality, however, remains of central importance to the particular rhetoric I explore in this essay.

This question has proved rather troublesome and currently prohibits meaningful engagement of the relationship between Hoover's policy and sexual identity. Until recently, sexuality constituted the chief domain into which scholars feared to tread. The burden of proof too high, they acknowledged rumors of Hoover's relationship with Tolson only to omit, discredit, or diminish those scant scraps of circumstantial evidence too paltry to interpret. Because the governing assumption was that Hoover's private life, although intriguing, had no significant bearing on his federal responsibilities, such timidity seemed judicious.[7]

Anthony Summers raised the historiographical stakes with his 1993 expose that sensationalized Hoover's alleged sex life under the auspices of credible research.[8] Its allure hinged on titillating those wondering about Hoover's boudoir and satisfying longings to see him convicted of hypocrisy. Summers legitimated rumors of cross-dressing and little boys, rubber gloves, and photographs depicting the Director on his knees, despite an appalling lack of substantive evidence. His homophobic fun-house projection has been dangerously consequential in raising doubts about the historical relevance of Hoover's sexuality, inviting a wide range of reactionary apologia.

The most vocal of these apologists is Athan Theoharis, who meticulously refuted Summers's "shoddy journalism."[9] Unfortunately, Theoharis's passionate corrective also inadvertently paralyzed the issue of Hoover's sexuality. Whereas in his earlier biography Theoharis considered the possibility that Hoover was closeted, he argued here that

> Whether or not Hoover was a homosexual—and I doubt that he was—the wily and cautious FBI director would never have put himself in a position that publicly compromised his sexuality. . . . If he was a practicing homosexual, he would also have taken whatever safeguards were needed to ensure that such a dark secret would go with him to the grave.[10]

Consequently, any meaningful discussion appears foreclosed, because, as Theoharis concluded, "Hoover's leadership of the FBI can best be understood not in terms of Summers's morality play of compromised homosexuality but as a by-product of the politics of Cold War America. . . . This story of institutional politics remains to be told."[11]

My critical effort resists such foreclosures in order to argue that sexual identity was signifi-

cant to FBI policy in the years prior to Hoover's Cold War dominance. Toward that end, I explore Hoover's *pink herring*, which utilized moral panic about sex crime to alleviate his homosexual panic, thus diverting attention from his sexuality and silencing those who might question it. I interpret this as a tactic in his passing, and a peculiar response to an invisible audience I term the *fourth persona*. Having examined Hoover's pink herring in text and context, I conclude by drawing some relevant implications regarding passing as an object of rhetorical study.

The Passing Crowd

Secrecy is a necessarily rhetorical phenomenon. As Sissela Bok argues, "The word 'secrecy'. . . . denotes the methods used to conceal, such as codes or disguises or camouflage, and the practices of concealment. . . . Accordingly I shall take concealment, or hiding, to be the defining trait of secrecy."[12] A secret of dangerous difference motivates some to develop and sustain a double-consciousness in order to survive amid and sometimes to resist dominant, oppressive cultural practices. Especially when the markers of one's difference—skin, behavior, dress— can be camouflaged, "double-lives" manifest themselves publicly in skilled performances evincing the rhetorical forms of secrecy and disclosure.[13] To succeed in veiling one's identity, i.e., convincing certain audiences of an "acceptable" persona, these rhetors-with-secrets employ tactics of impersonation, deflection, and silence in the public sphere. Collectively, these elements constitute a species of secrecy and a mode of rhetorical action that I call "passing."[14]

Peter Rabinowitz offers a useful distinction between "social passing," by which one misleads others into believing he is something that he is not, and "rhetorical passing," which "is not simply a disguise, but a virtuoso tightrope performance." The rhetorical passer engages in "unnameable [*sic*] speech acts" that unfold before two audiences: "one audience that's ignorant and another that knows the truth *and remains silent about it*."[15] Similarly, Amy Robinson highlights two audiences in discussing the "triangular theater of the pass": "In such an economy of readable identity, the successful passer only disappears from view insofar as she appears (to her reader) to be the category into which she has passed. Adopting the presumptive mechanisms that read a racially and/or sexually indeterminate subject as an overdetermined legible social identity, it is the spectator who manufactures the symptoms of a successful pass." Passing requires the dupe, one to be fooled, but also the "in-group clairvoyant" who, because "it takes one to know one," collaborates by recognition and silence.[16]

Often we attend to what appears to be an exclusive audience of dupes as the centerpiece of passing's rhetorical action. Indeed, there is no gainsaying the significance of the dominant audience, whose face must be mirrored in order for dangerous difference to be successfully camouflaged. The "overdetermined legible social identity" depends on dupe participation invited by a *subversive enthymeme*: an appeal that manipulates the assumptions of heteronormativity to achieve the telos of sexual secrecy; dupes facilitate the masking performance that deceives them.

I want to emphasize, however, the paramount significance of an invisible audience for whom the pass is legible; who in turn collaborates in preserving by silence the perilous secret kept from unsuspecting dupes. Every act of passing is enacted, in other words, by means of the *fourth persona*: a collusive audience constituted by the textual wink.[17] Similar to its counterpart, the second persona,[18] the fourth persona is an implied auditor of a particular ideological bent, presumably one who is sexually marginalized, understands the dangers of homophobia, acknowledges the rationale for the closet, and possesses an intuition that renders a pass transparent. A central distinction between these two personae, however, is that passing rhetoric must imply two ideological positions simultaneously, one that mirrors the dupes and another that implies, via the wink, an ideology of difference. The fourth persona also resembles its other counterpart, the third persona, in its partial constitution by silence.[19] Instead of a silence that negates and excludes, as with the third persona, here silence functions constructively as the medium of collusive exchange. What is not said is nonetheless performative, a speech act that can be read by certain audiences, and calls those audience members into being as abettors.[20]

Most passing rhetors embrace the fourth persona as a welcome beacon of safety, solidarity, and success. The motive of others, however, may be what Rabinowitz has labeled "social passing," emanating from a desire to blend with the normative without detection *by anyone*. I have argued elsewhere,[21] however, that the closet always functions rhetorically to disclose, in some fashion, the very secrets we would at all cost keep to ourselves. As a prospective social passer comes to realize this, that clairvoyants lurk everywhere among the dupes, a rather different rhetorical situation presents itself.[22] Like one who is the only person in a room seeing an apparition, the social passer's fear of being recognized manifests itself in the paranoid style.[23] One gay man quoted in George Henry's 1955 study *All the Sexes* captures well a feeling that, while affirming for most passers, would terrify the social passer: "The eyes of the homo usually stare right through you. He looks a second or two longer than the average, and as you gaze into his eyes, if you are a homo, there is a lighteninglike [sic] magnetic response, and a thrill passes through the very heart of you."[24] In response, the social passer might resist by rendering those clairvoyants transparent so as to eliminate them and fortify an enthymematic relation with his dupes.

In Hoover's case, the homosexual panic of the 1930s rendered him vulnerable to the shifting public signifiers of gender and sexuality. Men would have felt pressure to pass the muster of heteronormativity, an exigence more pressing and frustrating because normative standards were in flux. For many gays passing during this panic, the fourth persona would have afforded a means of community in the teeth of intensified homophobia. For some others, passing probably was accompanied by a homophobic paranoia regarding the fourth persona, which, to varying degrees, contributed to the pernicious construction of the panic's bogey, the homosexual menace. Fearing clairvoyants in his midst, Hoover's pink herring can be read as a subversive enthymeme forged on the hides of those most likely to read him for dangerous difference and, thus, most in need of silencing.

A Tale of Two Panics

When Hoover met Tolson in 1928, he probably felt little anxiety about his marital status. Among his other attractions, Tolson provided the homosocial companionship Hoover cherished most when not working long hours at the FBI. Their preference for bachelorhood, far from anomalous, would have seemed normative during a decade experiencing a "cult of singleness."[25] *The New York Times Magazine,* for instance, proudly proclaimed, "For the nation's bachelors, this city is the Mecca."[26] Even if one were a *particular* sort of bachelor, his status as an unmarried man would not by itself have signified homosexuality.

During the 1930s, however, the rich bachelor subculture began to erode: "As American society struggled to emerge from the hard times . . . the bachelor life that had been so prominent in the previous half century faded beneath emphases on family solidarity and the communal effort to battle economic and foreign demons."[27] Those demons found their surest victim in masculinity. Michael Kimmel observes, "For most men the Depression was emasculating both at work and at home. Unemployed men . . . saw themselves as impotent patriarchs. And the consequences . . . were significant."[28] The disturbance of male homosociality was one significant consequence, resulting, I argue, in a homosexual panic. Although blame for the paralyzing assault on masculinity was dispersed as well among women, African Americans, and immigrants, homosexuals occupied a distinctive role in this crisis as men braced themselves against the pervasive threat of effeminacy and degeneracy.

The irony of this emerging panic is that it was intensified by the efforts employed to eradicate it. Homosocial bonds and, correlatively, dominant cultural meanings of homosexuality and heterosexuality, had been anchored in part by the pansy, an openly and flamboyantly gay fixture of the Prohibition era. The Pansy Craze, lasting roughly from 1920 until 1933, focused the cultural imagination squarely on a conception of homosexuality that had less to do with what men did sexually than how one performed one's gender and sexuality. "Today there is scarcely a school boy who doesn't know what a 'pansy' is," wrote La Forest Potter in 1933.[29] The primary marker of that knowledge, Potter asserted, was "the feminine gait of the effeminate homosexual . . . [which] is one of the most constant differences that exist between the homosexual and the heterosexual man."[30]

The pansy emerged as middle-class dominance of sociability crumbled during the 1920s, a product of working class and immigrant defiance of moral policing. Prohibition culture offered the pansy both the comforts and safety of sanctioned visibility. Although largely an urban phenomenon, the pansy's proliferation in mass media provided limited tolerance that was national in scope.[31] In return, the pansy provided succor to those who wished to control the meaning of sexuality by naming it, in keeping with Sedgwick's notion that "The importance . . . of the category 'homosexual,' . . . [is] its potential for giving whoever wields it a structuring definitional leverage over the whole range of male bonds that shape the social consti-

tution."[32] Men engaging in homosocial behavior, but who did not behave like pansies, would not be considered homosexual: "At a time when the culture . . . might have undermined conventional sources of masculine identity, the spectacle of the pansy allowed men to confirm their manliness and solidarity with other men by distinguishing themselves from pansies."[33]

The onslaught of the Depression ended the pansy's reign. Motivated by cultural instability, authorities sought to restore moral order by mobilizing against "degenerates." By 1933, the visibility of pansies was resisted with the force of law, including the Volstead Act, which legalized alcohol precisely so that social spaces could be regulated.[34] The Motion Picture Production Code, strengthened in 1934, as well as other widespread measures against "obscenity," represented similar systemic efforts to extinguish the pansy's cultural presence.[35]

Historians have argued that this period of repressive moral backlash accounts for a shift to a new definition of homosexuality. I want to explain more clearly the dynamics of that symbolic shift as sexual and gender norms tightened en route to stability. The pansy's sudden invisibility produced ambiguity and uncertainty in sexual meaning, proliferating connotation even as "the coding of a wide range of behavior as homosexual and its definition as disorderly served to establish and enforce the boundaries of the normative gender order."[36] Implied here is a cultural struggle animated by homophobic fear; in other words, a homosexual panic.

As Sedgwick explains, homosexual panic constitutes a "secularized and psychologized homophobia" that structures male gender generally, and male homosocial bonds specifically, through the threat of guilt by homosexual identification. Insofar as homosexuality's definition is "arbitrary and self-contradictory" in nature, men are left wondering and worrying whether they will be labeled as such.[37] This panic functions as a "kind of ideological pincers-movement": "no man must be able to ascertain that he is not (that his bonds are not) homosexual. In this way, a relatively small exertion of physical or legal compulsion potentially rules great reaches of behavior and filiation."[38]

During historical periods when a clear locus of homosexual meaning is lacking, or gender norms are unsettled, homosexual panic erupts, precisely because of the indeterminacy of cultural identity. In the absence of homosexual denotation, according to D. A. Miller, one witnesses a proliferation of connotation, which, while readily deniable, also tends toward an "effluvium of rumination" and "limitless mobility."[39] Miller explains, "Yet if connotation has the advantage of constructing an essentially insubstantial homosexuality, it has the corresponding inconvenience of tending to raise this ghost all over the place."[40] Accompanied as it is by paranoia, such connotation sparks a struggle for denomination that Sedgwick describes accordingly: "the ability to set prescriptive and descriptive limits to the forms of male homosocial desire—[becomes] the object of competition among those who [wish] to wield it, as well as an implement of oppression against those whose practices it at a given time proscribed."[41]

During the post-pansy panic, that competition took a variety of homophobic forms, two of which warrant elaboration. Beginning in 1935, the Committee for the Study of Sex Variants convened with the express purpose of gathering multidisciplinary perspectives on the sex variant, its term for the homosexual, in order to offer counsel to a culture dealing with this expanding "problem."[42] The Committee's charge was to distinguish the sex variant from the "normal population," a charge forged by an assumption that "heterosexuality seemed to be imperiled as a result of inordinate modern pressures and cultural taboos that gave rise to 'substitute activities,' the most common of which seemed to be homosexuality."[43] The timing, scope, and theoretical bases of the study seem in keeping with the context of homosexual panic I have described, as Jennifer Terry's account makes clear:

> The paradigm of the CSSV researchers caused them to go to great lengths to tether homosexual orientation to gender and sex inversion. This tendency revealed that the Committee was as interested in demarcating norms of masculinity and femininity as it was in comprehending the distinct qualities that pertained to sexual attractions between women or between men. By focusing on the former, researchers generally believed they were accounting for the latter. In the end, the CSSV's conclusions indicate that remedying the problem of sex role inversion was part and parcel of a larger effort to place heterosexuality (i.e., sexual adjustment) back on stronger footing. . . . The Sex Variant Study was thus as much an effort to construct and maintain hygienic heterosexuality as it was to investigate homosexuality.[44]

Despite the CSSV's benevolent posture, its findings reified the assumption that homosexuality

was a pathology in need of psychological adjustment, thus fueling rather than undermining trenchant homophobia.

At the same time, a sex crime panic gripped the nation, animating its quest to distinguish, and extinguish, the sexual deviant. This panic, which dates from the Lindbergh kidnapping case in 1932, solidified between 1935 and 1937 as the press prominently featured the cases of Albert Fish, Salvatore Ossido, Lawrence Marks, Thomas Smith, and many others.[45] The Literary Digest sounded an alarm commonplace throughout the nation: "At large . . . thousands of potential sex slayers, many of them well known to the authorities . . . walked the streets, human rattlesnakes coiled in the path of unsuspecting women and children."[46]

By the end of 1937 the panic had reached its zenith, constituted in the public discourse as a crime "wave" linked to sexual perversion.[47] Time magazine reported: "With these appalling examples of pedophilia, the lust of mature men for prepubescent children, spreading daily in the Press, it looked to laymen as if a national wave of sex crimes against children was in full surge."[48] Skeptical of the hysteria, Bertram Pollens, in his 1938 book The Sex Criminal, nonetheless concluded, "It almost seems as though sex, the 'evil urge', had suddenly broken loose from its long confinement and was on its devastating path to strike wherever it could."[49]

Pressure on law enforcement and politicians as a result of what Fredric Wertham called "almost a mass hysteria" culminated in crackdowns on any deemed to be sexually degenerate.[50] During this period, sexual psychopath laws were passed in California, Ohio, Minnesota, Michigan, and Illinois; citizens were urged to join the police in identifying potential suspects. Austin H. MacCormick, NYC Commissioner of Correction, advised: "The police . . . would make many more arrests if people were intelligent enough to report to them things that are very often common neighborhood knowledge." He concluded that the panic's solution required a clear conception of the problem: "[W]e must face the fact that the roots of the problem lie deep in some of the least known elements of human behavior. It is sex with which you are dealing—sex in its abnormalities rather than in its normal expression and in its aberrations rather than in its natural course."[51]

Chief among those aberrations was homosexuality.[52] Pollens emphasized that the problem "reaches down to the home of our best friend and next door neighbor, and . . . we may even find it lurking in a corner very close and proximate to our own hearth—the unknown skeleton in the closet."[53] The pervasive sense that those skeletons were homosexual derived from several assumptions. Terry explains:

> Much of the popular reporting about sex crimes reinforced an existing notion that homosexuals were, by definition, child molesters. This idea was abetted by the assumption that homosexuals were trapped at an arrested age in development which led them to prey upon innocent children to satisfy their perverse desires. . . . Since all homosexual acts were against the law and most were classified as "sex offenses," homosexual men were lumped together in the public imagination with violent offenders, rapists, and child molesters.[54]

For example, Potter argued, "homosexuals and abnormals are perhaps the only class of neurotics . . . who derive satisfaction in converting heterosexuals to their practices."[55] Utilizing the same assumptions, McCormick offered homosexuals as a prime example of sex criminals: "The number of people convicted of such offenses is comparatively small, but the number who commit them is very large. We have in our institutions . . . less than forty men known to be homosexuals. Anyone who knows anything about the subject knows that there are thousands of homosexuals in New York City."[56]

The cultural embodiment of homosexuality had begun to shift perceptibly from an innocuous pansy to a dangerous "menace." That the panic marked a struggle not merely to end sex crimes but also to eradicate gender and sexual ambiguity can be discerned in the hysterical tone and awkward link between homosexuality and assaults on women and children. Herein lies the answer to Henry Gerber's tortured question, found in his 1932 gay manifesto: "And why harp on the very few homosexuals who find satisfaction for their pathological craving to deal with the young boys, when the papers are at present full of details of atrocious killings of little girls by mentally deranged heterosexual men?"[57]

Hunting the Fourth Persona: Hoover's Pink Herring

In response to the post-pansy homosexual panic, J. Edgar Hoover engaged in a skillful and insidious passing performance, the centerpiece of which was his *pink herring*. By defining the "sex deviate" as the chief moral threat to the nation's children, and in positioning himself as a hunter of those deviates, Hoover's pink herring helped to fix again the meaning of homosexuality and sought to vanquish debilitating speculation regarding his sexuality. In other words, a moral panic provided the rhetorical resources that would relieve Hoover's homosexual panic.

Given his long reign and nearly impenetrable persona, Hoover's vulnerability is scarcely imaginable. During the 1930s, thanks to Courtney Ryley Cooper, Hoover achieved iconic status as the nation's "master detective," a new hero who "represented the full power of American Justice, in 'getting his man.'"[58] Keenly aware of the potential afforded by this media blitz, Hoover learned to manage the FBI's rapidly growing public image. As Richard Powers argues, "While Hoover was not responsible for the country's fascination with celebrity criminals during the depression, and while he had not played the leading role in turning the anticrime movement into a ritual of national unity, he was imaginative enough to realize that Hollywood had given him a once-in-a-lifetime chance to turn his obscure agency into a major cultural force."[59]

These were formative years, however, even if Hoover was a quick study of the art of publicity. Prior to 1933, the FBI barely registered culturally, and invested almost no energy or resources in developing its public persona. Moreover, at that time Hoover's institutional power did not include unrestricted domestic surveillance. To make matters more precarious, FDR's original choice as Attorney General, Thomas Walsh, intended to fire Hoover; Hoover was spared only by Walsh's untimely death on Inauguration Day. Even as the friendlier replacement, Homer Cummings, launched the New Deal anticrime movement, Hoover's position in the hierarchy of leadership remained uncertain. Despite his position as FBI Director, Hoover was not nearly as invincible in the mid-1930s as he would be by the end of the decade.[60]

This brief period of vulnerability coincided with the homosexual panic undermining the nation's manhood. Like other men, Hoover could not escape the homophobic fear that accompanied turbulence in gender and sexual norms. Indeed, given his own position on the continuum of homosocial bonds, and as a newly minted celebrity, he was a likely target for cultural scrutiny. Although the public never gained access to Hoover's private world, dangerous signifiers abounded: he was a bachelor who lived with his mother; he did not date; his closest friend was Clyde Tolson, another bachelor with whom he rode to and from work, ate meals, socialized, traveled on business, and vacationed.[61] *Time,* which featured Hoover on its cover in August 1935, offered the once benign but now ominous description:

> Like all leaders of enterprises which require great morale, Director Hoover can always be counted on for an effective theatrical gesture where one seems needed. like all men of action, he has a strong streak of sentimentality. . . . He is a bachelor, living with his semi-invalid mother. . . . His job gives him little time for friends, who are few and include no women.[62]

Hoover's demeanor and dress also drew attention. Ray Tucker's mischievous account in *Collier's* of his "mincing step" and preference for "Eleanor blue as the favorite color for the matched shades of tie, handkerchief and socks"[63] was not atypical. Jack Alexander, in his three-part profile in the *New Yorker,* observed, "From the day he entered the Department, certain things marked Hoover apart from scores of other young law clerks. He dressed better than most, a bit on the dandyish side."[64]

These markers are significant for the *questions* raised and the exigence those questions created for Hoover. Various factors may have contributed to increased gossip, his growing celebrity or accumulation of political enemies, to name two obvious examples; however, the context of homosexual panic goes far to explain why the subject of his sexuality and the suspicious reading of his signifiers heightened during these years. A decade earlier rumors about what these characteristics meant, which now circulated in the Bureau, nightclubs, and popular press, did not surface.[65] One agent's purported conclusion, "If he isn't queer, then he's weird," reveals a typical cultural judgment about bachelorhood, male companionship, and dress that made sense during a homosexual panic.[66] The dynamism of the panic expressed itself in the use of masculinity as a litmus test for cultural legitimacy and a weapon for character assassination. During a 1936 budget hearing, Kenneth McKellar, Chairman of the Senate Appropriations Committee and longtime critic of Hoover, attacked the Director's heroism and leadership by questioning his lack of prowess in arresting criminals.[67] A fuming Hoover surmised correctly "that his manhood had been impugned."[68]

Hoover seems to have been keenly aware for some time that his manhood was regularly evaluated and discussed. In the wake of *Collier's* insinuation, to cite the earliest instance, watchful eyes recognized public adjustments in Hoover's carriage. A *Washington Herald* gossip columnist asked if "anybody [had] noted that the Hoover stride has grown noticeably stronger and more vigorous since Tucker charged him with 'walking with mincing steps.'"[69] Moreover, Senator McKellar's assault may have inspired his high-profile participation in Alvin Karpis's arrest a month later. Curt Gentry writes, "There are those who suspected that Hoover's newly adopted 'tough cop' image was, at least in part, an attempt to counteract the rumors of his homosexuality. The publicist Lou Nichols . . . implied as much when, many years later, he told the author 'That [Karpis's capture] pretty much ended the "queer" talk.'"[70] Equally telling is the press coverage that Hoover helped shape, which often exaggerated his manliness. In *Liberty Magazine,* Frederick L. Collins, who collaborated with Hoover, observed that his "compact body, with shoulders of a light-heavyweight boxer, carries no ounce of extra weight—just a hundred and seventy pounds of live, virile masculinity."[71]

John Loughery has suggested that such efforts at bolstering the appearance of one's masculinity would have been sufficient to stave off speculation. "Many gay men who were of marrying age in the 1930s knew the terms of the social contract and counted on the timidity and willful ignorance of their peers and elders to shield them. . . . allow[ing] people to give men such as Hoover . . . the benefit of the doubt."[72] For an audience of dupes, which included most dominant audience members, the passing implied here might well have been successful.

Lurking, even haunting, however, is the fourth persona. Far from timid or willfully ignorant, the "in-group clairvoyant," one deeply intuitive regarding the tactics of passing because "it takes one to know one," looms as the ubiquitous source of anxiety for this hopeful social passer who, attempting to thwart the imagined inquisition, has already given himself away. Hoover's behavior suggests that, amid an "effluvium of rumination," garden-variety passing would not suffice; menacing clairvoyants needed to be exorcised, not ignored. Thus we witness Hoover's investment in the sex crime panic that so occupied the nation. By hunting the (homosexual) "sex deviate," Hoover might appear the model of heteronormativity, stabilizing sexual norms and his reputation while silencing his fourth persona. This was Hoover's pink herring, a vicious deflection that throws dupes off the scent of lavender by snuffing out those who nose best.

I turn now to two textual manifestations of Hoover's pink herring. Despite the public hysteria, it must have seemed odd that Hoover would declare "War on the Sex Criminal" in the September 26, 1937, issue of the *New York Herald Tribune*.[73] Prior to this moment, he had scarcely uttered a word on the sex crime wave that had surged for the better part of two years. Strangely, the sex criminal had not been among Hoover's *Thousand Public Enemies* (1935) or *Persons in Hiding* (1938), those celebrity bank robbers, forgers, and murderers that had given him national celebrity. Yet in this most recent war declaration, he pronounced the sex fiend the "most loathsome of the vast army of crime." One senses here a discrepancy between the novelty of this criminal and his unparalleled notoriety. Every public enemy in the 1930s served Hoover's ethos; this new face on the most-wanted poster could be no different.

Whereas the continuous *presence* of Dillingers, Barkers, and Barrows had been required for the G-Man persona to burn brilliantly in the public eye, *absence* would provide the only sure measure that the taint of sex (and thus sexuality) had been eliminated. To achieve this absence, Hoover needed to distinguish the sex criminal from those public enemies craved by dominant audiences. In his opening salvo Hoover sounded an alarm that hyperbolized contemporary discourse regarding the sex crime wave: "The sex fiend, most loathsome of all the vast army of crime, has become a sinister threat to the safety of American childhood and womanhood."

Playing on the audience's familiarity with his criminal knowledge, Hoover labeled the sex fiend "the most loathsome" of that ignominious group so as to polarize and isolate him while fanning mass hysteria. "From one end of the United States to the other, women and little girls have been murdered by this beast. No parent can feel secure that his children are safe from attack. The sex fiend may strike anywhere, at any time. In one large eastern city alone, an arrest for sex crime is made every six hours, on the average, night and day." The severe dissonance Hoover invited here derives from the ubiquity and magnitude of the threat. There is no haven beyond the grasp of the beast, no hour of restful slumber while the sex fiend lurks. An apt portrayal too, I surmise, of the threat Hoover imagined his fourth persona to pose.

Lest the sex criminal become a caricature, which might preserve him, Hoover revealed the true "human beast": "He isn't some fabled monster; he isn't some demon, born full-blown, that suddenly descends upon women and little girls; he isn't a 'product of our modern age,' he is a definite and serious result of the apathy and indifference in the handling of out-of-the-ordinary offenders." Hoover had identified a rather innocuous category of offenders rapidly gaining national notoriety, that he constituted as more dangerous for their lack of monstrous proportion. He implies that the "beast" had long been in the midst of his victims, allowed to fester by a public's "apathy and indifference." This account sounds remarkably like the post-Repeal pansy. As Potter warned of homosexuality: "For the very foundations of our social structure, and its sane and normal relations may be threatened by our ignorance, our neglect and our bat-blind indifference to what may, before long, become a menace to every family in the land."[74]

Further indication that Hoover targeted homosexuals without explicitly naming them is found in his proclamation that the sex criminal is an "ordinary offender [turned] into a dangerous, predatory animal, preying upon society because he has been taught he can get away with it. . . . sex fiends. . . . [who] have been repeatedly dealt with as petty offenders when, in truth, their every action was a blazing signpost to a future of torture, rape, mutilation and murder." The timing here is central to understanding his implication because 1937 was the high-water mark of the sex crime panic that had rendered this "petty offender" presumptively homosexual. Terry explains, "increased arrests for homosexual-related activities, generally classified as sex crimes, fueled the dual perceptions that homosexuality was actually increasing and that it represented something as horrific as rape, lust, murder, and sexual assaults on children."[75]

In this appeal, Hoover crafted a subversive enthymeme by fashioning himself and the sex-fiend (i.e., homosexual) in mutually exclusive terms. Already reputed as an expert criminal hunter, Hoover's dramatic account of the sex fiend implicitly bolstered his ethos of sexual normalcy; a man so dedicated to this scourge of degenerates certainly could not be one. To insure that they invested in this portrayal, Hoover challenged his dupes (by scolding them) to look for and recognize the "blazing signpost(s)" that marked the slippery slope to tragedy. Here reading is fundamental, and the FBI, embodied in Hoover, provided the model: "The Federal Bureau of Investigation inquires into every phase of an offender's past history, and, as a result, we have learned volumes as to what part parental indifference, parole abuses, political protection, and other factors have played" in the creation of the sex fiend.

Hoover's passion, however, also alerts us to the question that clairvoyants, but not dupes, would likely have asked: why are *you* so adept at reading the "blazing signpost"? Is it because it takes one to know one? They, unlike the dupes, could decode the "Jekyll and Hyde lives" described by NYC Police Commissioner Lewis Valentine: "Some of them appear to be and are most of the time normal, reasonable citizens, some holding highly responsible positions . . . you would be surprised to know what positions some of them hold."[76] If his pass were to succeed, therefore, it required both deflection (by defining the homosexual in contrast to his masculine, crime-hunting persona) and exposure (the fiend, i.e., fourth persona, must *actually* be eliminated).

In order to rout clairvoyants from the shadows, Hoover enlisted common citizens and professionals in the hunt. "The present apathy of the public toward known perverts, generally regarded as 'harmless,' should be changed to one of suspicious scrutiny." Psychiatrists were urged to dedicate themselves to the "pathological and psychological study of perversion," and, if necessary, "the surgeon must play his part in removing the sex criminal as a distinct menace." Law enforcement must do its "utmost to bring about a public confidence whereby citizens will be more prone to make complaints and follow these by prosecution." Hoover echoed a growing popular consensus that "Until such a method of conducting a civilization by having the members take in each other's moral washing can be made feasible, the sexual offender will remain in our midst, as a continually terrifying problem."[77]

One might think it counterintuitive for a man avoiding suspicion to insist on a high-profile hunt of would-be deviants; however, recall Sedgwick's notion that "the ability to set proscriptive and descriptive limits to the forms of male homosocial desire [becomes] . . . an implement of oppression against those whose practices it at a given time proscribed."[78] Hoover's effort to make the sex criminal and, thus, the homosexual visible was the means by which to control him and stabilize sexual norms. In doing so, Hoover's passing performance placed him in the spotlight but, ironically and strategically, beyond the pale of speculation.

In December 1937, Hoover reiterated his war declaration in a speech delivered before the Association of Life Insurance Presidents.[79] The speech is not significant for its innovations but for the train of Hoover's thought, the repetition that solidified his pink herring. "To those who pay you premiums on their life insurance, there is a personal realization of risk which causes them to be much more receptive to your educational programs. . . . Our efforts in education, however, while as thoroughly vital and while directed to the very same persons, who have an equally personal investment in the matter, all too often meet with apathy." Again Hoover stressed the twin themes of apathy and education, vital elements in reducing the nation's risk. That risk, Hoover emphasized, loomed larger for the apathy that abetted it. "Were it not for this widespread public indifference toward crime conditions, for a too general attitude of 'let the other fellow do it,' we should not be faced with the fact that the criminal army of America is composed of over 4,300,000 persons."

Hoover's words resembled his earlier claim that chief among that vast army was the degenerate treading an inevitable path to homicide: "there are roaming at large today some 200,000 potential murderers who during their lifetime will account for the deaths by violence of more than 300,000 persons, unless the present murder rate is reduced." Hoover's hyperbole, designed to fan panic, is familiar. So, too, is his enthymematic gesture toward that which popular discourse made plain. "It should interest you also to realize that many of these crimes are those of degeneracy, often committed by persons afflicted with diseases which only recently have been discussed in public." As I have described above, such degeneracy was naturally linked to homosexuality.

To complete the subversive enthymeme, Hoover rather deftly praised his audience for their skilled recognition of the problem: "[W]ithin the last few years you have been courageous path-finders in the distribution of information concerning the viciousness of our so-called social diseases. To my mind, crime is as malignant as any cancer, and it is as distinct a subject of health as tuberculosis." This ingratiation had everything to do with motivating his charges to join him in a particular understanding of that which was both legion and contagion, alien and yet communicable, but preventable if only they were vigilant.

Having achieved deflection, Hoover aimed to expose and eradicate his fourth persona. "The surprising increase of sex crimes within the last few years revealed an urgent necessity for corrective action by every public-minded body. . . . There should be given to the cure of degeneracy the same thought, the same eager perseverance, the same persistent investigation, that has resulted in the lessening of many other dangerous diseases." In the urgency of this anaphoric request, Hoover betrayed his need to search, find, name, and thus "cure" this "dangerous disease," a disease that was understood in gender/sexual and criminal terms, and included his menacing clairvoyants.

Before leaving my reading, I offer an epilogue which functions as *corroborative context*. Although historians are convinced that Hoover's 1937 war declaration rendered him the cultural ballast against sex crime,[80] and I am sure of his inspiration, there is little textual evidence to establish these claims. These texts lend compelling credence to such conclusions, but plausible deniability—endemic to this rhetorical mode—haunts and sabotages them, a legacy of the closet and the homophobic forces that forge it.

As corroborative context, therefore, it is significant that 1937 was the year that Hoover, having been granted greater latitude in Federal surveillance, launched a Sex Deviate Index Card File that "provided a centralized aid for identifying and retrieving all reports of alleged homosexuality."[81] Striking is the absence of evidence in this file of *heterosexual* men who molested children or assaulted women. Its obsession (over 300,000 documents by 1977, when the file was destroyed) began with what must have seemed central for eradicating sex crime: the homosexual. I would posit a further concern, namely the clairvoyants plaguing one gripped by homosexual panic.

Virtually his own institution of power by the 1940s, Hoover aggressively extended his policing of homosexuality, particularly rumors alleging his predilection for men. Any speculative comment was to be reported immediately, and in turn addressed by local agents.[82] To cite a typical example, a woman visiting her nephew (and FBI agent) in New Orleans related a second-hand story told at her bridge party in Cleveland, for which the offending gossip was severely chastised. According to her sworn statement of apology:

[Name Withheld] claimed that she never said anything about this [the story of Hoover being queer that she overheard in a Baltimore restaurant] nor had she thought anything about it until the day of this bridge party. She said during the course of the bridge party . . . some mention was made of the Director. One of the girls pointed out that the Director was a bachelor and she wondered why. To this [Name Withheld] . . . replied she understood Mr. Hoover was queer. She said . . . she thought it should not have been made and . . . she was going

to point out to each of those present [each named, with her address, in the report] that her statement was not founded on fact and that she was deeply sorry that she made it and that it should not have been made at all.[83]

Coercive measures had replaced the pink herring as the means of insuring the Director's normalcy, but his motivating impulse seems unchanged. In response to a prominent New Yorker's comment (gleaned in an FBI interrogation) that he had heard the queer rumors, Hoover ranted, "I never heard of this obvious degenerate. Only one with a depraved mind could have such thoughts."[84] His persistent fear expressed here can be crystallized in the motto of the fourth persona: it takes one to know one.

At his most pernicious, Hoover matured after World War II into an avowed and champion homophobe. He manipulated a second sex crime wave in the late 1940s to lubricate the ascendancy of McCarthyism,[85] and by 1951 had unilaterally transformed his Sex Deviate Index Card File into a full-fledged program that provided information regarding the alleged homosexuality of present and past Federal employees (and later university and law enforcement employees) for the express purpose of purging them. Curt Gentry observed: "It was axiomatic, at the time, that the main reason homosexuals should be denied government employment was their susceptibility to blackmail. FBI Director J. Edgar Hoover proved that this was true, by blackmailing them himself."[86]

Whether or not Hoover was homosexual, there is no question that he was preoccupied with those bogeys that threatened his gendered/sexual public persona. His response to this threat began as a rhetorical exercise in passing, only to evolve into a highly sophisticated system of coercion, blackmail, and persecution. One constant seems to have been Hoover's intuition regarding the two passing audiences, dupes whose complicity depended on a performance that simultaneously played to, or attempted to annihilate, clairvoyants. Early on, Hoover's passing domesticated one panic by fanning another, producing the semblance of a man thought to be unimpeachable. As Courtney Ryley Cooper described him, "he has become the voice of honesty against the crime world; for the first time, someone in high office of law enforcement has risen who is able to picture crime in such a way that the average man can understand it and do something about it—because he knows the thing which he is facing."[87] Honest and the archenemy of crime—sex crime, in this context, meaning anti-homosexual—Hoover's passing achieved the perfect deflection. Except, of course, for the fourth persona, those menaces who understood *why* "he knows the thing which he is facing."

The Perils of Passing

Passing implies peril. Its inventional impulse reverberates in one who feels jeopardized by difference, or perceived difference. It entails a precarious combination of secrecy and disclosure. Its goal, an ethos transparently normative, constitutes less an achievement than a risky venture continuously engaged. As a critical object, it always threatens to elude and ensnare its pursuer. In charting the promise of passing as an object of rhetorical study, let me briefly reflect on these perils.

As rhetorical action, passing is distinguishable from familiar rhetorical situations. Exigence is always dramatically urgent and perpetual; audience is bifurcated between the visible and invisible; trope and argument create parallel and contradictory dimensions of meaning; constraints propel instead of prohibit the unsayable; and consensus is forged largely on deceit. Passing should entice us to explore the closet's rhetoric, a sophisticated persuasive praxis manifested daily by our marginalized predecessors as they "made do" in a broader homophobic culture. To say that the closet is rhetorically significant is to make a historically situated case for the existence of a subversive art of self-fashioning in the public sphere, an art "on the make," as it were, in the presence of specific, and perilous, audiences under palpable and shifting situational constraints.

In this essay I have highlighted features of passing that call to mind Foucault's notion that:

> Silence itself—the things one declines to say, or is forbidden to name, the discretion that is required between different speakers—is less the absolute limit of discourse, the other side from which it is separated by a strict boundary, than an element that functions alongside the things said, with them and in relation to them within over-all strategies. . . . There is not one but many silences, and they are an integral part of the strategies that underlie and permeate discourses.[88]

Pink herring, of course, is a queer version of the familiar tactic of deflection that protects a silent subject avoiding exposure. The stakes in this game of hide and seek, it must be remembered, are high.

Unlike its conventional counterpart, pink herring must always deflect and signify at the same time. Obfuscation and intimation are the twin acts of every pass. Paradoxically, passing's silence must prove at once to be utterly mute while speaking incessantly.

This paradox is mandated by the presence of the *fourth persona,* a silent, savvy but discreet audience constituted as collaborator in making duplicitous utterances appear legitimate before an audience of dupes. "It is the double audience," Peter Rabinowitz writes, "and the kind of flaunting that makes it possible, that structurally distinguishes rhetorically passing texts from other complex texts that happen to have hidden meanings beneath the surface."[89] A delicate triangulation is required to invite comp

licity from a dupe who ultimately aids in constructing the passer's *subversive enthymeme* (and his own deception), all the while evoking the fourth persona as a stealth partner who quietly affirms and colludes by acknowledging the pass. For Hoover, the fourth persona proved menacing instead of comforting, confounding the dynamics of his passing, and inspiring rhetorical innovation with grave consequences for the clairvoyants in his midst.

J. Edgar Hoover was certainly no queer hero or, unfortunately, a passing phase. Simple justice, if not retribution, for his violence against gays and lesbians can be found in the irony that, for all his efforts, he could never escape the "effluvium of rumination" regarding his sexuality. The issue of his relationship with Clyde Tolson persisted throughout his life, fascinating politicians and hairdressers alike. As further penance, we here exact from Hoover lessons on passing he would never willingly have taught. We expose to critical scrutiny a decade in which he suffered the terror of homosexual panic, so as to witness him deflecting suspicion by entrapping homosexuals in a menacing denotation of his own making. He could protect his love story, if there was one, only by passing as the chief hunter of those dangerous bachelors he most resembled.

Earlier versions of this essay were presented at the Stonewall Center of the University of Massachusetts, at the "Speaking the Discourse of Difference" Symposium at the University of Washington, and at the Seventh Biennial Public Address Conference at Penn State University. The author wishes to thank numerous friends and colleagues, and the anonymous reviewers, for their generous and insightful feedback, and Scott Rose for his perpetual encouragement.

NOTES

1. Ray Tucker, "Hist! Who's That," *Collier's* (August 19, 1933), 49.

2. Male homosociality designates a continuum of non-sexual and sexual relations among men that shape broadly economic, social, and cultural dynamics. The male homosocial continuum is forged by homophobia and therefore distinguishes explicidy (disruptively) between homosexual and homosocial. It is historically contingent, and desire should be understood as an "affective or social force," or the "glue" in these powerful relations. See Eve Kosofsky Sedgwick, *Between Men: English Literature and Male Homosocial Desire* (New York: Columbia University Press, 1985).

3. Although the panic I describe likely affected lesbians as well, the effects that directly shaped exigence for Hoover specifically related to homosexual males and, therefore, constitute my explicit focus.

4. "Homosexual panic" refers to one's fear that he might be homosexual, harbor homosexual longings, or be thought homosexual by others. See Edward J. Kempf, *Psychopathology* (St. Louis, MO: Mosby, 1920), 477–515; Sedgwick, *Between Men*, 83–96; Eve Kosofsky Sedgwick, *Epistemology of the Closet* (Berkeley: University of California Press, 1990).

5. See George Chauncey, *Gay New York: Gender, Urban Culture, and the Making of the Gay Male World, 1890–1940* (New York: Basic Books, 1994); John Loughery, *The Other Side of Silence: Men's Lives and Gay Identities: A Twentieth-Century History* (New York: Henry Holt, 1998); Estelle B. Freedman, "'Uncontrolled Desires': The Response to the Sexual Psychopath, 1920–1960," in *Passion and Power: Sexuality in History,* ed. Kathy Peiss and Christina Simmons (Philadelphia: Temple University Press, 1989).

6. Richard Gid Powers, *Secrecy and Power: The Life of J. Edgar Hoover* (New York: Free Press, 1987), 2.

7. See Richard Gid Powers, *Secrecy and Power,* 172–73; Athan G. Theoharis and John Stuart Cox, *The Boss: J. Edgar Hoover and the Great American Inquisition* (Philadelphia: Temple University Press, 1988), 108; Curt Gentry, *J. Edgar Hoover: The Man and His Secrets* (New York: W. W. Norton, 1991), 190–91.

8. Anthony Summers, *Official and Confidential: The Secret Life of J. Edgar Hoover* (New York: G. P. Putnam's Sons, 1993).

9. Athan Theoharis, *J. Edgar Hoover, Sex, and Crime: An Historical Anecdote* (Chicago: Ivan R. Dee, 1995).

10. Theoharis, *J. Edgar Hoover, Sex, and Crime,* 55.

11. Theoharis, *J. Edgar Hoover, Sex, and Crime,* 80.

12. Sissela Bok, *Secrets: On the Ethics of Concealment and Revelation* (New York: Pantheon, 1982), 6.

13. See Edwin Black, "Secrecy and Disclosure as Rhetorical Forms," *Rhetorical Questions: Studies of Public Discourse* (Chicago: University of Chicago Press, 1992), 51–78.

14. For discussions of gender/sexual passing, see Sedgwick, *The Epistemology of the Closet*; Judith Butler, *Bodies That Matter: On the Discursive Limits of 'Sex'* (New York: Routledge, 1993); Elaine K. Ginsberg, ed., *Passing and the Fictions of Identity* (Durham, NC: Duke University Press, 1996); George Chauncey, *Gay New York*; Charles E. Morris III, "'The Responsibilities of the Critic': F. O. Matthiessen's Homosexual Palimpsest," *Quarterly Journal of Speech* 84 (August 1998): 261–82.

15. Peter J. Rabinowitz, "'Betraying the Sender': The Rhetoric and Ethics of Fragile Texts," *Narrative* 2 (October 1994), 202–205.

16. Amy Robinson, "It Takes One to Know One: Passing and Communities of Common Interest," *Critical Inquiry* 20 (Summer 1994), 715–724.

17. For an excellent discussion of the "homosexual wink," see James Creech, *Closet Writing/Gay Reading: The Case of Melville's Pierre* (Chicago: University of Chicago Press, 1993).

18. Edwin Black, "The Second Persona," *Quarterly Journal of Speech* 56 (1970): 109–119 [reprinted in this volume].

19. Philip Wander, "The Third Persona: An Ideological Turn in Rhetorical Theory," *Central States Speech Journal* 35 (1984): 197–216 [reprinted in this volume].

20. On silence in passing, see Rabinowitz, "'Betraying the Sender,'" 204–205; Sedgwick, *Epistmology of the Closet*, 3–4 and chapter 1.

21. Charles E. Morris III, "Contextual Twilight/Critical Liminality: J. M. Barrie's *Courage* at St Andrews, 1922," *Quarterly Journal of Speech* 82 (August 1996): 207–227.

22. Erving Goffman observes: "The presence of fellow-sufferers (or the wise) introduces a special set of contingencies in regard to passing, since the very techniques used to conceal stigmas may give the show away to someone who is familiar with the tricks of the trade, the assumption being that it takes one (or those close to him) to know one." Goffman, *Stigma: Notes on the Management of Spoiled Identity* (New York: Simon & Schuster, 1963), 85.

23. Richard Hofstadter, *The Paranoid Style in American Politics and Other Essays* (New York: Alfred A. Knopf, 1965), 3–40. Like Hofstadter, I see the paranoid style as a feeling of persecution systematized in grandiose theories of conspiracy. He distinguishes the political from the "clinical" paranoid by stressing that the latter does not see the conspiracy as directed against him. For the paranoid passer the opposite is true. I find it telling that researchers in the 1930s found an "intimate relationship between paranoidism and homoeroticism," specifically paranoia as a "defense reaction against a repressed homoerotic wish phantasy." James Page and

John Warkentin, "Masculinity and Paranoia," *Journal of Abnormal and Social Psychology* 33 (1938): 527–31.

24. George W. Henry, *All the Sexes: A Study of Masculinity and Femininity* (New York: Rinehart, 1955), 292.

25. Kevin White, *The First Sexual Revolution: The Emergence of Male Heterosexuality in Modern America* (New York: New York University Press, 1993), 169–71; Howard P. Chudacoff, *The Age of the Bachelor: Creating an American Subculture* (Princeton, NJ: Princeton University Press, 1999), 247–50.

26. "The Bachelors of New York," *New York Times Magazine*, September 9, 1928.

27. Chudacoff, *The Age of the Bachelor*, 253.

28. Michael Kimmel, *Manhood in America: A Cultural History* (New York: Free Press, 1996), 199.

29. La Forest Potter, *Strange Loves: A Study in Sexual Abnormalities* (New York: The Robert Dodsley Company, 1933), 4.

30. Potter, *Strange Loves*, 101. Chauncey more thoroughly describes the signifiers that bespoke one's status as a pansy, including "unconventional styles in personal grooming," but also carriage, demeanor, dress, and speech, all of which signaled the gender inversion or effeminacy thought to be constitutive of homosexuality. Chauncey, *Gay New York*, 54–56.

31. See James Levin, *The Gay Novel in America* (New York: Garland, 1991); Vito Russo, *The Celluloid Closet: Homosexuality in the Movies*, Revised Edition (New York: Harper and Row, 1987). On the geographic scope of the craze, see Chauncey, *Gay New York*, 320; David K. Johnson, "The Kids of Fairytown: Gay Male Culture on Chicago's Near North Side in the 1930s," in Brett Beemyn, ed., *Creating a Place for Ourselves: Lesbian, Gay, and Bisexual Community Histories* (New York: Routledge, 1997), 97–118.

32. Sedgwick, *Between Men*, 86. See also Jonathan Ned Katz, *The Invention of Heterosexuality* (New York: Dutton, 1995).

33. Chauncey, *Gay New York*, 328.

34. See Chauncey, *Gay New York*, chapter 12.

35. See Russo, *The Celluloid Closet*; Felice Flanery Lewis, *Literature, Obscenity, and Law* (Carbondale: Southern Illinois University Press, 1976).

36. Chauncey, *Gay New York*, 346.

37. Sedgwick, *Epistemology of the Closet*, 185.

38. Sedgwick, *Epistemology of the Closet*, 185; *Between Men*, 86–7.

39. D. A. Miller, "Anal Rope," in *Inside/Out: Lesbian Theories, Gay Theories*, ed. Diana Fuss (New York: Routledge, 1991), 123–29.

40. D. A. Miller, "Anal Rope," 125.

41. Sedgwick, *Between Men*, 87.

42. See Jennifer Terry, *An American Obsession: Science, Medicine, and Homosexuality in Modern Society* (Chicago: University of Chicago Press, 1999), especially chapters 6–8; and George W. Henry, *Sex Variants: A Study in Homosexual Patterns*, 2 vols. (New York: Paul B. Hoeber, 1941).

43. Terry, *An American Obsession*, 179.

44. Terry, *An American Obsession*, 214.

45. Philip Jenkins, *Moral Panic: Changing Concepts of the Child Molester in Modern America* (New Haven, CT: Yale University Press, 1998), chapters 2–4.

46. "Sex Crime Wave Alarms U.S.," *The Literary Digest* 123 (April 10, 1937), 5.

47. See "To Counsel Hurley on Sex Crime Laws," and "Views of Conferees," *New York Times* (September 5, 1937), 7; Sheldon Glueck, "Sex Crimes and the Law," *The Nation* 145 (September 25, 1937), 318–20; Charles J. Dutton, "Can We End Sex Crimes?" *The Christian Century* 51 (December 22, 1937), 1594.

48. "Pedophilia," *Time* 30 (August 23, 1937), 42–44.

49. Bertram Pollens, *The Sex Criminal* (New York: The Macaulay Company, 1938), 17.

50. Fredric Wertham, "Psychiatry and the Prevention of Sex Crime," *JAICLC* 28 (1938), 847.

51. Honorable Austin H. MacCormack, "New York's Present Problem," *Mental Hygiene* 22 (January 1938), 9–10.

52. See George W. Henry, "Psychogenic Factors in Overt Homosexuality," *The American Journal of Psychiatry* 93 (January 1937), 889–908; Special Issue, "The Challenge of Sex Offenders," *Mental Hygiene* 22 (January 1938), 1–24; George W. Henry, "Social Factors in the Case Histories of One Hundred Under-privileged Homosexuals," *Mental Hygiene* 22 (1938), 591–611; Jack Frosch, "The Sex Offender—A Psychiatric Study," *American Journal of' Orthopsychiatry* 9 (October 1939), 761–69.

53. Pollens, *The Sex Criminal*, 22–23. He notes further, "The problem of homosexuality deserves our attention not only because of the number who commit sexual crimes, but also because of the untold misery which many of them bring to their families in their feeble attempts to cast this shadow from them." Pollens, *The Sex Criminal*, 132–33.

54. Terry, *An American Obsession*, 272. Katz concurs: "Although all the reported sex crimes concerned adult males and little girls [t]he use of the same language to refer to coercive adult–child relations and homosexual relations between consenting adults confounded these behaviors in the public mind." Jonathan Ned Katz, *Gay/Lesbian Almanac: A New Documentary* (New York: Carroll & Graf, 1983), 531.

55. Potter, *Strange Loves*, 62.

56. "Crimes against Children," *The Literary Digest* 124 (October 2, 1937), 16.

57. Parisex [Henry Gerber], "In Defense of Homosexuality." In *A Homosexual Emancipation Miscellany, c. 1835–1952* (New York: Arno Press, 1975), 296.

58. Courtney Ryley Cooper, "Getting the Jump on Crime," *American Magazine* 116 (August 1933), 100. Cooper wrote several books and twenty-three articles on the FBI in *American Magazine* between 1933 and 1940, ushering Hoover into the cultural spotlight See Richard Gid Powers, *G-Men: Hoover's FBI in American Popular Culture* (Carbondale: Southern Illinois University Press, 1983).

59. Powers, *G-Men,* 113.

60. Theoharis and Cox, *The Boss,* 111–16; Gentry, *J. Edgar Hoover,* 153; Powers, *G-Men,* 33–34; *Secrecy and Power,* 180–85.

61. See Powers, *Secrecy and Power,* 169–73; Theoharis and Cox, *The Boss,* 107–08, 133–34; Gentry, *J. Edgar Hoover,* 159, 190–192; William W. Turner, *Hoover's F.B.I.* (1970; New York: Thunder's Mouth Press, 1993), 80–82.

62. "Sleuth School," *Time* 26 (August 5, 1935), 12.

63. Tucker, "Hist! Who's That," 49.

64. Jack Alexander, "Profiles: The Director-II," *The New Yorker* 13 (October 2, 1937), 21.

65. See Ralph Blumenthal, *Stork Club: America's Most Famous Nightspot and the Lost World of Cafe Society* (Boston: Little, Brown, 2000), 38–39; Gentry, *J. Edgar Hoover,* 159, 192; Turner, *Hoover's F.B.I.,* 80–81.

66. Theoharis and Cox, *The Boss,* 108.

67. See Alexander, "Profiles: The Director-II," 26; Alexander, "Profiles: The Director-Ill," *The New Yorker* 13 (October 9, 1937), 22. See also Gentry, *J. Edgar Hoover,* 182–188; Theoharis and Cox, *The Boss,* 136–37.

68. Ralph de Toledano, *J. Edgar Hoover: The Man and His Time* (New Rochelle, NY: Arlington House, 1973), 132.

69. *Washington Herald,* August 28, 1933.

70. Gentry, *J. Edgar Hoover,* 179–80.

71. Frederick L. Collins, "The Private Life of J. Edgar Hoover," *Liberty Magazine* 17 (March 16, 1940), 10. Collins argued that Hoover certainly could have married but seldom went to parties, had incredibly high standards, and cared more for the job than "domesticity." Agents in the 1950s similarly declared, "He *is* married, to the FBI." *New York Times,* October 8, 1959.

72. Loughery, *The Other Side of Silence,* 101.

73. J. Edgar Hoover, "War on the Sex Criminal," *New York Herald Tribune,* September 26, 1937. All subsequent quotations are from the text.

74. Potter, *Strange Loves,* 10–11.

75. Terry, *An American Obsession,* 189; 275–281.

76. Quoted in "Sex Crime Wave Alarms U.S.," 7.

77. "Crimes against Children," 16. See also Special Issue, "The Challenge of Sex Offenders," *Mental Hygiene* 22 (January 1938), 1–24.

78. Sedgwick, *Between Men,* 87.

79. John Edgar Hoover, "Combatting Lawlessness: America's Most Destructive Disease," *Vital Speeches of the Day* 4 (February 5, 1938), 269–72. All subsequent quotations are from the text.

80. Historians typically cite Freedman, "'Uncontrolled Desires,'" 206. See also Jack Frosch and Walter Bromberg, "The Sex Offender—A Psychiatric Study," *American Journal of Orthopsychiatry* 9 (October 1939), 761; Sheldon S. Levy, "Interaction of Institutions and Policy Groups: The Origin of Sex Crime Legislation," *The Lawyer and Law Notes* 5 (Spring 1951), 7; Terry, *American Obsession,* 271–72, 323–24; Jenkins, *Moral Panic,* 55–56.

81. Athan Theoharis, *From the Secret Files of J. Edgar Hoover* (Chicago: Ivan R. Dee, 1993), 292, 357–58.

82. Name Withheld #75 and #113 folders and John Monroe folder, Official and Confidential File of FBI Director J. Edgar Hoover; The Director folder, Official and Confidential File of FBI Assistant Director Louis Nichols.

83. Memo, June 30, 1943, Name Withheld #75 folder, Hoover O & C File.

84. Memo, June 27, 1944, Name Withheld #75 folder, Hoover O & C File.

85. For the second sex crime panic, see George Chauncey, Jr., "The Postwar Sex Crime Panic," in *True Stories from the American Past,* ed. William Graebner (New York: McGraw-Hill, 1993), 160–178.

86. Gentry, *J. Edgar Hoover,* 413.

87. Courtney Ryley Cooper, "Foreword," in J. Edgar Hoover, *Persons in Hiding* (Boston: Little, Brown, 1938), xviii.

88. Michel Foucault, *The History of Sexuality,* vol. I, *An Introduction* (New York: Pantheon, 1978), 27.

89. Rabinowitz, "'Betraying the Sender,'" 203.

PART VI
RHETORIC AND THE PROBLEMS OF POLITICAL CHANGE

Rhetoric is central to all efforts to bring about social change, as it is to the maintenance of social stability. It is appropriate, therefore, that the issue of rhetoric's role in social change processes has been a dominant concern of contemporary rhetorical theory. There are, however, many different situations in which social change processes occur, and therefore many different theoretical approaches to the relationship between rhetoric and social change. These situational differences have only increased in the age of the Internet. Traditional venues for rhetorical expression, while remaining important as much for who they include as those they exclude, are being supplemented—indeed, some would say, supplanted—by online mechanisms for political expression. The Arab Spring, for instance, saw the rise of media like Twitter. People on the ground, so to speak, generated powerful rhetorical messages that filtered back to the traditional stakeholders. At the same time, historical developments that began without the influence of digital media are now being augmented by them. The rugged course experienced by Russia as it moved from Czarism to dictatorial communism to a representative government leaning toward autocracy, for instance, is a powerful reminder of the contingencies of rhetoric and social change. Amidst all these changes, in places of conflict and online, there still exist insiders and outsiders staking claim to political ground. This claim staking remains rhetorical in nature.

The tendency to focus on prominent leaders is only one of the many precepts of classical rhetorical studies challenged by Karlyn Kohrs Campbell's essay, "The Rhetoric of Women's Liberation: An Oxymoron." Campbell's analysis of the rhetoric of the women's liberation movement in the 1960s argues that the efforts of women to speak violated such fundamental assumptions of Anglo-American public discourse that their rhetoric radically challenged both the traditional discourse and the classical modes of rhetoric. Campbell points out how the consciousness-raising group served as a model for women's liberation rhetoric. Such rhetoric occurred in fundamentally leaderless small groups that focused on raising one's consciousness and thus altering one's identity, rather than on promoting particular policies in the more traditional model of public deliberation. Such rhetoric, and its study, also seriously challenged the classical definition of rhetoric as *public* discourse. In her analysis, Campbell highlights the fact that personal and public discourse are so highly interdependent that it becomes virtually impossible to understand rhetoric as operating solely in the public sphere. Campbell's essay has thus stimulated multiple challenges to the classical assumptions of rhetorical studies of social change.

Another important essay that urges a more complex understanding of the relationship between rhetoric and social theory by looking beyond the campaign event or the organized social movement is Michael Calvin McGee's "The 'Ideograph': A Link Between Rhetoric and Ideology." According to McGee, public discourse is not simply a conveyor belt that brings "ideas" to the public; rather, it is a material entity in its own right. To characterize rhetoric or discourse as material is to recognize the substantive effect that it has on an audience at the moment of its impact. And according to McGee, that impact is a direct result of the unique and complex configurations of language—not merely the ideas supposedly "carried" by such language—employed by rhetors at particular moments in time. To this end, McGee encourages the study of the meaning and uses of "ideographs," the key terms that define the ideological contours of a community or collectivity—terms such as "liberty," "property," and "public service." According to McGee, such terms appear in public discourse primarily as a means of warranting or justifying otherwise troubling or problematic acts of collective power. On McGee's account, the key thing to know about an ideograph is that it is not an abstract, timeless ideal to which cultures universally aspire. Rather, the meaning (and effect) of an ideographic term, such as "liberty," is created by the actual discourse in a particular society. Thus the term "liberty" does not refer to an ideal that means the same thing to all people in all cultures, however distorted its universal meaning may be by different local vocabularies. Rather, as an ideograph, the meaning of "liberty" is specific to a particular rhetorical culture; as the culture changes across time, so too will the range of legitimate meanings accorded to its understanding of "liberty."

While such ideographs circumscribe the possible identities of the members of the culture, and specify what actions the collectivity can take, ideographs constitute the substance of any social group. In line with this thinking, Maurice Charland looks at how rhetoric calls an audience to take part in political change in "Constitutive Rhetoric: The Case of the *Peuple Québécois.*" Through *identification*, he argues, people are called to take part in the ongoing process of discourse, claiming membership in an audience created within rhetoric. While Charland notes that this audience is an "ideological fiction," he nonetheless urges that it persuades people to take part in the very process of rhetoric via *interpellation*. Therein, they are both persons and personae: living people dedicated to a newfound cause—in this case, the campaigns of the *Mouvement Souveraineté-Association* (MSA) and *Parti Québécois* (PQ) in the 1960s and 1970s—and theoretical constructions constituted by the rhetoric itself.

Tending to another facet of this constitutive construction, Robert Asen looks at the rhetorical functions of *imagining* in the public (and counterpublic) spheres. In "Imagining in the Public Sphere," Asen argues that political discourse always points to groups inside and outside its permeable boundaries; thus there is a need to critically investigate "the ways in which included and excluded people appear in public spheres." The processes of representation, both visual and linguistic, offer pivot points within collective imagining. While they constrain and restrict counterpublics, they also offer potential opportunities for counterpublics to assert their identities, engage larger publics, and change the nature of political discourse.

Raymie E. McKerrow's widely cited essay, "Critical Rhetoric: Theory and *Praxis*," offers yet a further exploration of the implications and suppositions of extending the study of sociopolitical rhetoric beyond the boundaries of a narrowly drawn situational framework. McKerrow articulates a critical theoretical program that is substantially different from earlier examinations of the rhetorical processes of social change. Whereas the study of political campaigns, social movements, and even ideographic forces has typically been heavily descriptive and explanatory, often narrowly restricting its offices to the consideration of the instrumental and strategic dimensions of rhetoric, McKerrow recalibrates the central goal for rhetorical studies in terms of a critical rhetoric concerned to "unmask and demystify the discourse of power" at the same time that it offers a reconstructive vision of what the society can become, if only for the moment. His essay synthesizes a range of important insights drawn from contemporary rhetorical and social theories to encourage rhetoricians to question more directly the basic terms of the societies in which they live.

Others, however, have questioned the underlying implications of the critical project. John M. Murphy, in "Critical Rhetoric as Political Discourse," argues that the end result of this approach is never-ending skepticism. This result is ideally suited to at least two trends: the postmodern moment that occurred in the waning years of the previous century, and a need to raise rhetoric's status within the corridors of the academic world. Such a break with tradition carries with it an important shift: from rhetorical criticism of discrete artifacts to critical rhetoric of doubt and flux. In Murphy's view, this transition also erodes some of the fundamental assumptions that guided approaches to political rhetoric previously—among them deliberation, consensus, and practical reason. He urges that Mikhail Bakhtin's concept of *novelization*, "a process in which previously unquestioned discourses come to interanimate one another, might better characterize our current situation than the claim of a postmodern condition." Thus Murphy urges that we deal with the complications of the past, rather than breaking with traditions that still send out trace echoes in current rhetorical (indeed, political) practices.

Many other avenues are opening up as we move further into the second decade of this century. The following list of additional readings provides a starting point for exploring some of these. Not all engage the wired world. But all engage the challenges of contemporary political discourse and can be useful in examining the rhetoric therein, regardless of the situation in which it occurs.

ADDITIONAL READINGS

Blair, Carole. (1992). "Contested Histories of Rhetoric: The Politics of Preservation, Progress, and Change." *Quarterly Journal of Speech* 78: 403–28.

Burgess, Parke G. (1968). "The Rhetoric of Black Power: A Moral Demand?" *Quarterly Journal of Speech* 44: 122–33.

Carlson, A. Cheree. (1986). "Gandhi and the Comic Frame: 'Ad Bellum Purificandum.'" *Quarterly Journal of Speech* 72: 446–55.

Charland, Maurice. (1990). "Rehabilitating Rhetoric: Confronting Blindspots in Discourse and Social Theory." *Communication* 11: 253–64.

DeLuca, Kevin Michael. (1999). *Image Politics: The New Rhetoric of Environmental Activism*. New York: Guilford Press.

Gronbeck, Bruce. (1978). "The Functions of Presidential Campaigning." *Communication Monographs* 25: 268–80.

Lucaites, John Louis. (1997). "Visualizing 'the People': Individualism vs. Collectivism in *Let Us Now Praise Famous Men*." *Quarterly Journal of Speech* 83: 269–88.

Lucas, Stephen E. (1988). "The Renaissance of American Public Address: Text and Context in Rhetorical Criticism." *Quarterly Journal of Speech* 74: 241–60.

McGee, Michael Calvin. (1980). "The Origins of 'Liberty': A Feminization of Power." *Communication Monographs* 47: 23–45.

McKerrow, Raymie E., ed. (1993). *Argument and the Postmodern Challenge. Proceedings of the Eighth Summer Argumentation Conference.* Annandale, VA: SCA/AFA.

Ono, Kent A., and John Sloop. (1992). "Commitment to *Telos*: A Sustained Critical Rhetoric." *Communication Monographs* 59: 48–60.

Zaeske, Susan. (2002). "Signatures of Citizenship: The Rhetoric of Women's Antislavery Petitions." *Quarterly Journal of Speech* 88: 147–68.

The Rhetoric of Women's Liberation

An Oxymoron

Karlyn Kohrs Campbell

Whatever the phrase "women's liberation" means, it cannot, as yet, be used to refer to a cohesive historical–political movement. No clearly defined program or set of policies unifies the small, frequently transitory groups that compose it, nor is there much evidence of organizational unity and cooperation.[1] At this point in time, it has produced only minor changes in American society,[2] although it has made the issues with which it is associated major topics of concern and controversy. As some liberation advocates admit, it is a "state of mind" rather than a movement. Its major manifestation has been rhetorical, and as such, it merits rhetorical analysis.

Because any attempt to define a rhetorical movement or genre is beset by difficulties, and because of the unusual status of women's liberation I have briefly described, I wish to state explicitly two presuppositions informing what follows. First, I reject historical and sociopsychological definitions of movements as the basis for rhetorical criticism on the grounds that they do not, in fact, isolate a genre of *rhetoric* or a distinctive body of *rhetorical acts*.[3] The criteria defining a rhetorical movement must be rhetorical; in Aristotelian terminology, such criteria might arise from the relatively distinctive use or interpretation of the canons and modes of proof. However, rather than employing any codified critical scheme, I propose to treat two general categories—substance and style. In my judgment, the rhetoric of women's liberation (or any other body of discourses) merits *separate* critical treatment if, and only if, the symbolic acts of which it is composed can be show to be distinctive on both substantive and stylistic grounds. Second, I presume that the style and substance of a genre of rhetoric are interdependent.[4] Stylistic choices are deeply influenced by subject matter and context,[5] and issues are formulated and shaped by stylistic strategies.[6] The central argument of this essay is that the rhetoric of women's liberation is a distinctive genre because it evinces unique *rhetorical* qualities that are a fusion of substantive and stylistic features.

Distinctive Substantive Features

At first glance, demands for legal, economic, and social equality for women would seem to be a reiteration, in a slightly modified form, of arguments already familiar from the protest rhetoric of students and blacks. However, on closer examination, the fact that equality is being demanded *for women* alters the rhetorical picture drastically. Feminist advocacy unearths tensions woven deep into the fabric of our society and provokes an unusually intense and profound "rhetoric of moral conflict."[7] The sex role requirements for women contradict the dominant values of American culture—self-reliance, achievement, and independence.[8] Unlike most other groups, the social status of women is defined primarily by birth, and their social position is at odds with fundamental democratic values.[9] In fact, insofar as the role of rhetor entails qualities of self-reliance, self-confidence, and independence, *its very assumption is a violation of the female role.* Consequently, feminist rhetoric is substantively unique by definition, because no matter how traditional its argumentation, how justificatory its form, how discursive its method, or how scholarly its style, it attacks the entire psychosocial reality, the most fundamental values, of the cultural context in which it occurs. As illustration, consider the apparently moderate, reformist demands by feminists for legal, economic, and social equality—demands ostensibly based on the shared value of equality. (As presented here, each of these demands is a condensed version of arguments from highly traditional discourses by contemporary liberationists.)

The demand for legal equality rises out of a conflict in values. Women are not equal to men in the sight of the law. In 1874 the Supreme Court ruled that "some citizens could be denied rights which others had," specifically, that "the 'equal protection' clause of the Fourteenth Amendment did not give women equal rights with men," and reaffirmed this decision in 1961, stating that "the Fourteenth Amendment prohibits any arbitrary class legislation, except that based on sex."[10] The legal inferiority of women is most apparent in marriage laws. The core of these laws is that spouses have reciprocal—not equal—rights and duties. The husband must maintain the wife and children, but the amount of support beyond subsistence is at his discretion. In return, the wife is legally required to do the domestic chores, provide marital companionship, and [supply] sexual consortium but has no claim for direct compensation for any of the services rendered. Fundamentally, marriage is a property relationship. In the nine community property states, the husband is considered the head of the "community," and so long as he is capable of managing it, the wife, acting alone, cannot contract debts chargeable to it. In Texas and Nevada, the husband can even dispose of the property without his wife's consent, property that includes the income of a working wife. The forty-one common law states do not recognize the economic contribution of a wife who works only in the home. She has no right to an allowance, wages, or income of any sort, nor can she claim joint ownership upon divorce. In addition, every married woman's surname is legally that of

her husband, and no court will uphold her right to go by another name.[11]

It seems to me that any audience of such argumentation confronts a moral dilemma. The listener must either admit that this is not a society based on the value of equality or make the overt assertion that women are special or inferior beings who merit discriminatory treatment.[12]

The argument for economic equality follows a similar pattern. Based on median income, it is a greater economic disadvantage to be female than to be black or poorly educated (of course, any combination of these spells economic disaster). Although half of the states have equal pay laws, dual pay scales are the rule. These cannot be justified economically because, married or single, the majority of women who work do so out of economic necessity, and some 40 percent of families with incomes below the poverty level are headed by women. Occupationally, women are proportionately more disadvantaged today than they were in 1940, and the gap between male and female income steadily increases.[13] It might seem that these data merely indicate a discrepancy between law and practice—at least the value is embodied in some laws—although separating values and behavior is somewhat problematic. However, both law and practice have made women economically unequal. For example, so long as the law, as well as common practice, gives the husband a right to the domestic services of his wife, a woman must perform the equivalent of two jobs in order to hold one outside the home.[14] Once again, the audience of such argumentation confronts a moral dilemma.

The most overt challenge to cultural values appears in the demand for social or sexual equality, that we dispense forever with the notion that "men are male *humans* whereas women are human *females*,"[15] a notion enshrined in the familiar phrase, "I now pronounce you *man* and wife." An obvious reason for abolishing such distinctions is that they lead to cultural values for men as men and women as wives. Success for men is defined as instrumental, productive labor in the outside world whereas "wives" are confined to "woman's place"—child care and domestic labor in the home.[16] As long as these concepts determine "masculinity" and "femininity," the woman who strives for the kind of success defined as the exclusive domain of the male is inhibited by norms prescribing her "role" and must pay a heavy price for her deviance. Those who have done research on achievement motivation in women conclude that: "Even when legal and educational barriers to achievement are removed, the motive to avoid success will continue to inhibit women from doing 'too well'—thereby risking the possibility of being socially rejected as 'unfeminine' or 'castrating.'"[17] And "the girl who maintains qualities of independence and active striving (achievement-orientation) necessary for intellectual mastery defies the conventions of sex appropriate behavior and must pay a price, *a price in anxiety*."[18] As long as education and socialization cause women to be "unsexed" by success whereas men are "unsexed" by failure, women cannot compete on equal terms or develop their individual potentials. No values, however, are more deeply engrained than those defining "masculinity" and "femininity." The fundamental conflict in values is evident.

Once their consequences and implications are understood, these apparently moderate, reformist demands are rightly seen as revolutionary and radical in the extreme. They threaten the institutions of marriage and the family and norms governing childrearing and male–female roles. To meet them would require major, even revolutionary, social change.[19] It should be emphasized, however, that these arguments are drawn from discourses that could not be termed confrontative, alienating, or radical in any ordinary sense. In form, style, structure, and supporting materials, they would meet the demands of the strictest Aristotelian critic. Yet they are substantively unique, inevitably radical, because they attack the fundamental values underlying this culture. The option to be moderate and reformist is simply not available to women's liberation advocates.

Distinctive Stylistic Features

As a rhetoric of intense moral conflict, it would be surprising indeed if distinctive stylistic features did not appear as strategic adaptations to a difficult rhetorical situation.[20] I propose to treat "stylistic features" rather broadly, electing to view women's liberation as a persuasive campaign. In addition to the linguistic features usually considered, the stylistic features of a persuasive campaign include, in my view, characteristic modes of rhetorical interaction, typical ways of structuring the relationships among participants in a rhetorical transaction, and emphasis on particular forms of argument, proof, and evidence. The rhetoric of women's liberation is distinctive stylistically in rejecting certain tra-

ditional concepts of the rhetorical process—as persuasion of the many by an expert or leader, as adjustment or adaptation to audience norms, and as directed toward inducing acceptance of a specific program or a commitment to group action. This rather "antirhetorical" style is chosen on substantive grounds because rhetorical transactions with these features encourage submissiveness and passivity in the audience[21]—qualities at odds with a fundamental goal of feminist advocacy: self-determination. The paradigm that highlights the distinctive stylistic features of women's liberation is "consciousness raising," a mode of interaction or a type of rhetorical transaction uniquely adapted to the rhetorical problem of feminist advocacy.

The rhetorical problem may be summarized as follows: women are divided from one another by almost all the usual sources of identification—age, education, income, ethnic origin, even geography. In addition, counter-persuasive forces are pervasive and potent—nearly all spend their lives in close proximity to and under the control of males—fathers, husbands, employers, and so on. Women also have very negative self-concepts, so negative, in fact, that it is difficult to view them as an audience, i.e., persons who see themselves as potential agents of change. When asked to select adjectives to describe themselves, they select such terms as "uncertain, anxious, nervous, hasty, careless, fearful, dull, childish, helpless, sorry, timid, clumsy, stupid, silly, and domestic . . . understanding, tender, sympathetic, pure, generous, affectionate, loving, moral, kind, grateful, and patient."[22] If a persuasive campaign directed to this audience is to be effective, it must transcend alienation to create "sisterhood," modify self-concepts to create a sense of autonomy, and speak to women in terms of private, concrete, individual experience, because women have little, if any, publicly shared experience. The substantive problem of the absence of shared values remains: when women become part of an audience for liberation rhetoric, they violate the norms governing sex appropriate behavior.

In its paradigmatic form, "consciousness raising" involves meetings of small, leaderless groups in which each person is encouraged to express her personal feelings and experience. There is no leader, rhetor, or expert. All participate and lead; all are considered expert. The goal is to make the personal political: to create awareness (through shared experiences) that what were thought to be personal deficiencies and individual problems are common and shared, a result of their position as women. The participants seek to understand and interpret their lives as women, but there is no "message," no "party line." Individuals are encouraged to dissent, to find their own truths. If action is suggested, no group commitment is made; each must decide whether, and if so which, action is suitable for her.[23] The stylistic features heightened in this kind of transaction are characteristic of the rhetoric as a whole: affirmation of the affective, of the validity of personal experience, of the necessity for self-exposure and self-criticism, of the value of dialogue, and of the goal of autonomous, individual decision making. These stylistic features are very similar to those Maurice Natanson has described as characteristic of genuine argumentation:

> What is at issue, really, in the risking of the self in genuine argument is the immediacy of the self's world of feeling, attitude, and the total subtle range of its affective and conative sensibility. . . . I open myself to the viable possibility that the consequence of an argument may be to make me see something of the structure of my immediate world . . . the personal and immediate domain of individual experience. . . .
> . . . feeling is a way of meaning as much as thinking is a way of formulating. Privacy is a means of establishing a world, and what genuine argument to persuade does is to publicize that privacy. The metaphor leads us to suggest that risking the self in argument is inviting a stranger to the interior familiarity of our home.[24]

Even a cursory reading of the numerous anthologies of women's liberation rhetoric will serve to confirm that the stylistic features I have indicated are characteristic. Particularly salient examples include Elizabeth Janeway's *Man's World; Woman's Place,* "The Demise of the Dancing Dog,"[25] "The Politics of Housework,"[26] *A Room of One's Own,*[27] and "Cutting Loose."[28] The conclusion of the last essay cited will serve as a model:

> The true dramatic conclusion of this narrative should be the dissolution of my marriage; there is a part of me which believes that you cannot fight a sexist system while acknowledging your need for the love of a man. . . . But in the end my husband and I did not divorce. . . . Instead I raged against him for many months and joined the Woman's Liberation Movement, and thought a great deal about myself, and about whether my problems were truly all women's problems, and decided that some of them were and that some of them were not. My sexual rage was the most powerful single emotion of my life, and the feminist analysis has become for me, as I think it will for most women of

my generation, as significant an intellectual tool as Marxism was for generations of radicals. But it does not answer every question. . . . I would be lying if I said that my anger had taught me how to live. But my life has changed because of it. I think I am becoming in many small ways a woman who takes no shit. I am no longer submissive, no longer seductive. . . .

> My husband and I have to some degree worked out our differences. . . . But my hatred lies within me and between us, not wholly a personal hatred, but not entirely political either. And I wonder always whether it is possible to define myself as a feminist revolutionary and still remain in any sense a wife. There are moments when I still worry that he will leave me, that he will come to need a woman less preoccupied with her own rights, and when I worry about that I also fear that no man will ever love me again, that no man could ever love a woman who is angry. And that fear is a great source of trouble to me, for it means that in certain fundamental ways I have not changed at all.

> I would like to be cold and clear and selfish, to demand satisfaction for my needs, to compel respect rather than affection. And yet there are moments, and perhaps there always will be, when I fall back upon the old cop-outs. . . . Why should I work when my husband can support me, why should I be a human being when I can get away with being a child?

> Women's liberation is finally only personal. It is hard to fight an enemy who has outposts in your head.[29]

This essay, the other works I have cited here, and the bulk of women's liberation rhetoric stand at the farthest remove from traditional models of rhetorical discourse, judged by the stylistic features I have discussed. This author, Sally Kempton, invites us into the interiority of her self, disclosing the inner dynamics of her feelings and the specific form that the problem of liberation takes in her life. In a rhetorically atypical fashion, she honors her feelings of fear, anger, hatred, and need for love and admits both her own ambivalence and the limits of her own experience as a norm for others. She is self-conscious and self-critical, cognizant of the inconsistencies in her life and of the temptation to "cop out," aware of both the psychic security and the psychic destruction inherent in the female role. She is tentatively describing and affirming the beginnings of a new identity and, in so doing, sets up a dialogue with other women in a similar position that permits the essay to perform the ego functions that Richard Gregg has described.[30] The essay asks for the participation of the reader, not only in sharing the author's life as an example of the problems of growing up female in this society, but in a general process of self-scrutiny in which each person looks at the dynamics of the problems of liberation in her own life. The goal of the work is a process, not a particular belief or policy; she explicitly states that her problems are not those of all women and that a feminist analysis is not a blueprint for living. Most importantly, however, the essay exemplifies "risking the self" in its most poignant sense. The Sally Kempton we meet in the essay has been masochistic, manipulative, an exploiter of the female role and of men, weak, murderous, vengeful and castrating, lazy and selfish. The risk involved in such brutal honesty is that she will be rejected as neurotic, bitchy, crazy, in short, as not being a "good" woman, and more importantly, as *not like us*. The risk may lead to alienation or to sisterhood. By example, she asks other women to confront themselves, recognize their own ambivalence, and face their own participation and collaboration in the roles and processes that have such devastating effects on both men and women. Although an essay, this work has all the distinctive stylistic features of the "consciousness raising" paradigm.

Although the distinctive stylistic features of women's liberation are most apparent in the small group processes of consciousness raising, they are not confined to small group interactions. The features I have listed are equally present in essays, speeches, and other discourses completely divorced from the small group setting. In addition, I would argue that although these stylistic features show certain affinities for qualities associated with psychotherapeutic interaction, they are rhetorical rather than expressive and public and political rather than private and personal. The presumption of most psychotherapy is that the origins of and solutions to one's problems are personal;[31] the feminist analysis presumes that it is the social structure and the definition of the female role that generate the problems that individual women experience in their personal lives. As a consequence, solutions must be structural, not merely personal, and analysis must move from personal experience and feeling to illuminate a common condition that all women experience and share.

Finally, women's liberation rhetoric is characterized by the use of confrontative, nonadjustive strategies designed to "violate the reality structure."[32] These strategies not only attack the psychosocial reality of the culture, but violate the norms of decorum, morality, and "femininity" of the women

addressed. Essays on frigidity and orgasm,[33] essays by prostitutes and lesbians,[34] personal accounts of promiscuity and masochism,[35] and essays attacking romantic love and urging man-hating as a necessary stage in liberation[36] "violate the reality structure" by close analysis of tabooed subjects, by treating "social outcasts" as "sisters" and credible sources, and by attacking areas of belief with great mythic power. Two specific linguistic techniques, "attack metaphors" and symbolic reversals, also seem to be characteristic. "Attack metaphors" mix matrices in order to reveal the "nonconscious ideology"[37] of sexism in language and belief, or they attempt to shock through a kind of "perspective by incongruity."[38] Some examples are: "Was Lurleen Wallace *Governess* of Alabama?" A drawing of Rodin's *Thinker* as a female. "Trust in God; She will provide."[39] "Prostitutes are the only honest women because they charge for their services, rather than submitting to a marriage contract which forces them to work for life without pay."[40] "If you think you are emancipated, you might consider the idea of tasting your menstrual blood—if it makes you sick, you've got a long way to go, baby."[41] Or this analogy:

> Suppose that a white male college student decided to room or set up a bachelor apartment with a black male friend. Surely the typical white student would not blithely assume that his black roommate was to handle all the domestic chores. Nor would his conscience allow him to do so even in the unlikely event that his roommate would say, "No, that's okay. I like doing housework. I'd be happy to do it. . . ." But change this hypothetical black roommate to a female marriage partner, and somehow the student's conscience goes to sleep.[42]

Symbolic reversals transform devil terms society has applied to women into god terms and always exploit the power and fear lurking in these terms as potential sources of strength. "The Bitch Manifesto" argues that liberated women are bitches—aggressive, confident, strong.[43] W.I.T.C.H., the Women's International Terrorist Conspiracy from Hell, says, in effect, "You think we're dangerous creatures of the devil, witches? You're right! And we're going to hex you!"[44] Some feminists have argued that the lesbian is the paradigm of the liberated female;[45] others have described an androgynous role.[46] This type of reversal has, of course, appeared in other protest rhetorics, particularly in the affirmation that "black is beautiful!" But systematic reversals of traditional female roles, given the mystique associated with concepts of wife, mother, and loving sex partner, make these reversals especially disturbing and poignant. Quite evidently, they are attempts at the radical affirmation of new identities for women.[47]

The distinctive stylistic features of women's liberation rhetoric are a result of strategic adaptation to an acute rhetorical problem. Women's liberation is characterized by rhetorical interactions that emphasize affective proofs and personal testimony, participation and dialogue, self-revelation and self-criticism, the goal of autonomous decision making through self-persuasion, and the strategic use of techniques for "violating the reality structure." I conclude that, on stylistic grounds, women's liberation is a separate genre of rhetoric.

The Interdependence of Substantive and Stylistic Features

The rhetorical acts I have treated in the preceding section, particularly as illustrated by the excerpt from an essay by Sally Kempton, may seem to be a far cry from the works cited earlier demanding legal, economic, and social equality. However, I believe that all of these rhetorical acts are integral parts of a single genre, a conclusion I shall defend by examining the interdependent character of the substantive and stylistic features of the various discourses already discussed.

Essays such as that of Sally Kempton are the necessary counterparts of works articulating demands for equality. In fact, such discourses spell out the meaning and consequences of present conditions of inequity and the implications of equality in concrete, personal, affective terms. They complete the genre and are essential to its success as a persuasive campaign. In the first section, I argued that demands for equality for women "attack the entire psychosocial reality." That phrase may conceal the fact that such an attack is an attack on the *self* and on the roles and relationships in which women, and men too, have found their identities traditionally. The effect of such an argument is described by Natanson: "When an argument hurts me, cuts me, or cleanses and liberates me it is not because a particular stratum or segment of my world view is shaken up or jarred free but because *I* am wounded or enlivened—*I* in my particularity, and that means in my existential immediacy: feelings, pride, love, and sullenness, the world of my actuality as I live it."[48] The only effective response to the sensation of being threatened existentially is a rhetorical act that treats the per-

sonal, emotional, and concrete directly and explicitly, that is dialogic and participatory, that speaks from personal experience to personal experience. Consequently, the rhetoric of women's liberation includes numerous essays discussing the personal experiences of women in many differing circumstances: black women, welfare mothers, older women, factory workers, high school girls, journalists, unwed mothers, lawyers, secretaries, and so forth. Each attempts to describe concretely the personal experience of inequality in a particular situation and/or what liberation might mean in a particular case. Rhetorically, these essays function to translate public demands into personal experience and to treat threats and fears in concrete, affective terms.

Conversely, more traditional discourses arguing for equality are an essential counterpart to these more personal statements. As a process, consciousness raising requires that the personal be transcended by moving toward the structural, that the individual be transcended by moving toward the political. The works treating legal, economic, and social inequality provide the structural analyses and empirical data that permit women to generalize from their individual experiences to the conditions of women in this society. Unless such transcendence occurs, there is no persuasive campaign, no rhetoric in any public sense, only the very limited realm of therapeutic, small group interaction.

The interrelationship between the personal and the political is central to a conception of women's liberation as a genre of rhetoric. All of the issues of women's liberation are simultaneously personal and political. Ultimately, this interrelationship rests on the caste status of women, the basis of the moral conflict this rhetoric generates and intensifies. Feminists believe that sharing personal experience is liberating, i.e., raises consciousness, because all women, whatever their differences in age, education, income, etc., share a common condition, a radical form of "consubstantiality" that is the genesis of the peculiar kind of identification they call "sisterhood." Some unusual rhetorical transactions seem to confirm this analysis. "Speakouts" on rape, abortion, and orgasm are mass meetings in which women share extremely personal and very negatively valued experiences. These events are difficult to explain without postulating a radical form of identification that permits such painful self-revelation. Similarly, "self-help clinics" in which women learn how to examine their cervixes and look at the cervixes of other women for purposes of comparison seem to require extreme identification and trust. Feminists would argue that "sisterhood is powerful" because it grows out of the recognition of pervasive, common experience of special caste status, the most radical and profound basis for cooperation and identification.

This feminist analysis also serves to explain the persuasive intent in "violating the reality structure." From this point of view, women in American society are always in a vortex of contradiction and paradox. On the one hand, they have been, for the most part, effectively socialized into traditional roles and values, as research into their achievement motivation and self-images confirms. On the other hand, "femininity" is in direct conflict with the most fundamental values of this society—a fact which makes women extremely vulnerable to attacks on the "reality structure." Hence, they argue, violations of norms may shock initially, but ultimately they will be recognized as articulating the contradictions inherent in "the female role." The violation of these norms is obvious in discourses such as that of Sally Kempton; it is merely less obvious in seemingly traditional and moderate works.

Conclusion

I conclude, then, that women's liberation is a unified, separate genre of rhetoric with distinctive substantive-stylistic features. Perhaps it is the only genuinely *radical* rhetoric on the contemporary American scene. Only the oxymoron, the figure of paradox and contradiction, can be its metaphor. Never is the paradoxical character of women's liberation more apparent than when it is compared to conventional or familiar definitions of rhetoric, analyses of rhetorical situations, and descriptions of rhetorical movements.

Traditional or familiar definitions of persuasion do not satisfactorily account for the rhetoric of women's liberation. In relation to such definitions, feminist advocacy wavers between the rhetorical and the nonrhetorical, the persuasive and the nonpersuasive. Rhetoric is usually defined as dealing with public issues, structural analyses, and social action, yet women's liberation emphasizes acts concerned with personal exigences and private, concrete experience and its goal is frequently limited to particular, autonomous action by individuals. The view that persuasion is an enthymematic adaptation to audience norms and values is confounded by rhetoric which seeks to persuade by "violating the reality structure" of those toward whom it is directed.

Nor are available analyses of rhetorical situations satisfactory when applied to the rhetoric of women's liberation. Parke Burgess' valuable and provocative discussion of certain rhetorical situations as consisting of two or more sets of conflicting moral demands[49] and Thomas Olbricht's insightful distinction between rhetorical acts occurring in the context of a shared value and those occurring in its absence[50] do not adequately explicate the situation in which feminists find themselves. And the reason is simply that the rhetoric of women's liberation appeals to *what are said to be* shared moral values, but forces recognition that those values are *not* shared, thereby creating the most intense of moral conflicts. Lloyd Bitzer's more specific analysis of the rhetorical situation as consisting of "one controlling exigence which functions as the organizing principle" (an exigence being "an imperfection marked by urgency" that "is capable of positive modification"), an audience made up "only of those persons who are capable of being influenced by discourse and of being mediators of change," and of constraints that can limit "decision and action needed to modify the exigence"[51]—this more specific analysis is also unsatisfactory. In women's liberation there are dual and conflicting exigences not solely of the public sort, and thus women's liberation rhetoric is a dialectic between discourses that deal with public, structural problems and the particularly significant statements of personal experience and feeling which extend beyond the traditional boundaries of rhetorical acts. A public exigence is, of course, present, but what is unavoidable and characteristic of this rhetoric is the accompanying and conflicting personal exigence. The concept of the audience does not account for a situation in which the audience must be *created under the special conditions* surrounding women's liberation. Lastly, the notion of constraints seems inadequate to a genre in which to act as a mediator of change, either as rhetor or audience member, is itself the most significant constraint inhibiting decision or action—a constraint that requires the violation of cultural norms and risks alienation no matter how traditional or reformist the rhetorical appeal may be.

And, similarly, nearly all descriptions of rhetorical movements prove unsatisfactory. Leland Griffin's early essay on the rhetoric of historical movements creates three important problems: he defines movements as occurring "at some time in the past"; he says members of movements "make efforts to alter their environment"; and he advises the student of rhetoric to focus on "the pattern of public discussion."[52] The first problem is that the critic is prevented from examining a contemporary movement and is forced to make sharp chronological distinctions between earlier efforts for liberation and contemporary feminist advocacy; the second problem is that once again the critic's attention is diverted from efforts to change the self, highly significant in the liberation movement, and shifted toward efforts to change the environment; and the third is a related deflection of critical concern from personal, consciousness raising processes to public discussion. Herbert Simons' view of "a leader-centered conception of persuasion in social movements" defines a movement "as an uninstitutionalized collectivity that mobilizes for action to implement a program for the reconstitution of social norms or values."[53] As I have pointed out, leader-centered theories cannot be applied profitably to the feminist movement. Further, women's liberation is not characterized by a *program* that mobilizes feminist advocates to reconstitute social norms and values. Dan Hahn and Ruth Gonchar's idea of a movement as "socially shared activities and beliefs directed toward the demand for change in some aspect of the social order"[54] is unsuitable because it overlooks the extremely important elements of the personal exigence that require change in the self. There are, however, two recent statements describing rhetorical movements that are appropriate for women's liberation. Griffin's later essay describing a dramatistic framework for the development of movements has been applied insightfully to the inception period of contemporary women's liberation.[55] What makes this description applicable is that it recognizes a variety of symbolic acts, the role of drama and conflict, and the essentially moral or value-related character of rhetorical movements.[56] Also, Robert Cathcart's formulation, again a dramatistic one, is appropriate because it emphasizes "*dialectical enjoinment in the moral arena*" and the "*dialectical tension growing out of moral conflict.*"[57]

And so I choose the oxymoron as a label, a metaphor, for the rhetoric of women's liberation. It is a genre without a rhetor, a rhetoric in search of an audience, that transforms traditional argumentation into confrontation, that "persuades" by "violating the reality structure" but that presumes a consubstantiality so radical that it permits the most intimate of identifications. It is a "movement" that eschews leadership, organizational

cohesion, and the transactions typical of mass persuasion. Finally, of course, women's liberation is baffling because there is no clear answer to the recurring question, "What do women want?" On one level, the answer is simple; they want what every person wants—dignity, respect, the right to self-determination, to develop their potentials as individuals. But on another level, there is no answer—not even in feminist rhetoric. While there are legal and legislative changes on which most feminists agree (although the hierarchy of priorities differs), whatever liberation is, it will be something different for each woman as liberty is something different for each person. What each woman shares, however, is the paradox of having "to fight an enemy who has outposts in your head."

NOTES

1. A partial list of the numerous groups involved in women's liberation and an analysis of them is available in Julie Ellis, *Revolt of the Second Sex* (New York: Lancer Books, 1970), pp. 21–81. A similar list and an analysis emphasizing disunity, leadership problems, and policy conflicts is found in Edythe Cudlipp, *Understanding Women's Liberation* (New York: Paperback Library, 1971), pp. 129–170, 214–220. As she indicates, more radical groups have expelled members for the tendency to attract personal media attention, used "counters" to prevent domination of meetings by more articulate members, and rejected programs, specific policies, and coherent group action (pp. 146–147, 166, 214–215). The most optimistic estimate of the size of the movement is made by Charlotte Bunch-Weeks, who says that there are "perhaps 100,000 women in over 400 cities" (see her "A Broom of One's Own: Notes on the Women's Liberation Program," in Joanne Cooke, Charlotte Bunch-Weeks and Robin Morgan, eds., *The New Women* [1970; rpt., Greenwich, CT: Fawcett, 1971], p. 186). Even if true, this compares unfavorably with the conservative League of Women Voters with 160,000 members (Cudlipp, *Understanding Women's Liberation*, p. 42) and the National Council of Women representing organizations with some 23 million members whose leadership has taken an extremely antiliberationist stance (see Lacey Fesburgh, "Traditional Groups Prefer to Ignore Women's Lib," *New York Times*, August 26, 1970, p. 44.)

2. Ti-Grace Atkinson said: "There is no movement. Movement means going some place, and the movement is not going anywhere. It hasn't accomplished anything." Gloria Steinem concurred: "In terms of real power—economic and political—we are still just beginning. But the consciousness, the awareness—that will never be the same." ("Women's Liberation Revisited," *Time*, March 20, 1972, pp. 30, 31.) Polls do not seem to indicate marked attitude changes among American women.

(See, e.g., *Good Housekeeping*, March 1971, pp. 34–38, and Carol Tavris, "Woman and Man," *Psychology Today*, March 1972, pp. 57–64, 82–85.)

3. An excellent critique of both historical and sociopsychological definition of movements as the basis for rhetorical criticism has been made by Robert S. Cathcart in "New Approaches to the Study of Movements: Defining Movements Rhetorically," *Western Speech* 36 (Spring 1972): 82–88.

4. A particularly apt illustration of this point of view is Richard Hofstadter's "The Paranoid Style in American Politics," in *The Paranoid Style in American Politics and Other Essays* (New York: Knopf, 1965), pp. 3–40. Similarly, the exhortative and argumentative genres developed by Edwin Black are defined in both substantive and stylistic grounds in *Rhetorical Criticism: A Study in Method* (New York: Macmillan, 1965), pp. 132–177.

5. The interrelationship of moral demands and strategic choices is argued by Parke G. Burgess in "The Rhetoric of Moral Conflict: Two Critical Dimensions," *QJS* 56 (1970): 120–130.

6. The notion that style is a token of ideology is the central concept in Edwin Black's "The Second *Persona*," *QJS* 56 (1970): 109–119 [reprinted in this volume].

7. See Burgess, "Rhetoric of Moral Conflict," and "The Rhetoric of Black Power: A Moral Demand?" *QJS* 54 (1968): 122–133.

8. See Matina S. Horner, "Femininity and Successful Achievement: A Basic Inconsistency," in Michele Hoffnung Garskof, ed., *Roles Women Play: Readings toward Women's Liberation* (Belmont, CA: Brooks/Cole, 1971), pp. 105–108.

9. "Women's role, looked at from this point of view is archaic. This is not necessarily a bad thing, but it does make woman's position rather peculiar: it is a survival. In the old world, where one was born into a class and a region and often into an occupation, the fact that one was also sex-typed simply added one more attribute to those which every child learned he or she possessed. Now to be told, in Erik Erikson's words, that one is 'never not-a-woman' comes as rather more of a shock. This is especially true for American women because of the way in which the American ethos has honored the ideas of liberty and individual choice . . . woman's traditional role in *itself* is opposed to a significant aspect of our culture. It is more than restricting, because it involves women in the kind of conflict with their surroundings that no decision and no action open to them can be trusted to resolve" (Elizabeth Janeway, *Man's World; Woman's Place: A Study in Social Mythology* [New York: William Morrow, 1971], p. 99).

10. Jo Freeman, "The Building of the Gilded Cage," *The Second Wave* 1 (1971): 33.

11. Ibid., pp. 8–9.

12. Judicial opinions upholding discriminatory legislation make this quite evident. "That woman's physical structure and the performance of maternal functions place her at a disadvantage in the struggle for subsistence is obvious. . . . The physical well-being of woman becomes an object of public interest and care in order to preserve the strength and vigor of the race. . . . Looking at it from the viewpoint of the effort to maintain an independent position in life, she is not upon an equality. . . . She is properly placed in a class by herself. . . . The reason . . . rests in the inherent difference between the two sexes and in the different functions in life which they perform" (*Muller v. Oregon*, 208 U.S. 412 [1908] at 421–23). This and similar judicial opinions are cited by Diane B. Shulder, in "Does the Law Oppress Women?," in Robin Morgan, ed., *Sisterhood Is Powerful* (New York: Vintage Books, 1970), pp. 139–157.

13. Ellis, *Revolt*, pp. 103–111. See also Caroline Bird, with Sara Welles Briller, *Born Female: The High Cost of Keeping Women Down* (1968; rpt., New York: Pocket Books, 1971), esp. pp. 61–83.

14. "The Chase Manhattan Bank estimated a U.S. woman's hours spent at housework at 99.6 per week" (Juliet Mitchell, "Women: The Longest Revolution [Excerpt]," in Deborah Babcox and Madeline Belkin, eds., *Liberation Now!* [New York: Dell, 1971], p. 250). See also Ann Crittenden Scott, "The Value of Housework," Ms., July 1972, pp. 56–59.

15. Aileen S. Kraditor, *Up from the Pedestal: Selected Writings in the History of American Feminism* (Chicago: Quadrangle Books, 1968), p. 24.

16. The concepts underlying "woman's place" serve to explain the position that women hold outside the home in the economic sphere: "Are there any principles that explain the meanderings of the sex boundaries? One is the idea that women should work inside and men outside. Another earmarks service work for women and profit-making for men. Other rules reserve work with machinery, work carrying prestige, and the top job to men. Most sex boundaries can be explained on the basis of one or the other of these three rules" (Bird and Briller, *Born Female*, p. 72).

17. Horner, "Femininity and Successful Achievement," p. 121.

18. From E. E. Maccoby, "Woman's Intellect," in S. M. Farber and R. H. L. Wilson, eds., *The Potential of Woman* (New York: McGraw-Hill, 1963), pp. 24–39; cited in Horner, "Femininity and Successful Achievement," p. 106.

19. In the economic sphere alone, such changes would be far reaching. "Equal access to jobs outside the home, while one of the pre-conditions for women's liberation, will not in itself be sufficient to give equality for women. . . . Society must begin to take responsibility for children; the economic dependence of women and children on the husband-father must be ended. The other work that goes on in the home must also be changed—communal eating places and laundries for example.

When such work is moved into the public sector, then the material basis for discrimination against women will be gone" (Margaret Bentson, "The Political Economy of Women's Liberation," in Garskof, ed., *Roles Women Play*, pp. 200–201).

20. The individual elements described here did not originate with women's liberation. Consciousness raising has its roots in the "witnessing" of American revivalism and was an important persuasive strategy in the revolution on mainland China. Both the ancient Cynics and the modern Yippies have used violations of the reality structure as persuasive techniques (see Theodore Otto Windt Jr., "The Diatribe: Last Resort for Protest," *QJS* 58 [1972]: 1–14), and this notion is central to the purposes of agit-prop theater, demonstrations, and acts of civil disobedience. Concepts of leaderless persuasion appear in Yippie documents and in the unstructured character of sensitivity groups. Finally, the idea that contradiction and alienation lead to altered consciousness and revolution has its origins in Marxian theory. It is the combination of these elements in women's liberation that is distinctive stylistically. As in a metaphor, the separate elements may be familiar; it is the fusion that is original.

21. The most explicit statement of the notion that audiences are "feminine" and rhetors or orators are "masculine" appears in the rhetorical theory of Adolf Hitler and the National Socialist Party in Germany. See Kenneth Burke, "The Rhetoric of Hitler's 'Battle,'" in *The Philosophy of Literary Form* (1941; rpt., New York: Vintage Books, 1957), p. 167.

22. Jo Freeman, "The Social Construction of the Second Sex," in Garskof, ed., *Roles Women Play*, p. 124.

23. The nature of consciousness raising is described in Susan Brownmiller, "Sisterhood Is Powerful," and in June Arnold, "Consciousness Raising," in Stookie Stambler, ed., *Women's Liberation: Blueprint for the Future* (New York: Ace Books, 1970), pp. 141–161; Charlotte Bunch-Weeks, "A Broom of One's Own," pp. 185–197; Carole Hanisch, "The Personal Is Political," Kathie Sarachild, "A Program for Feminist 'Consciousness Raising,'" Irene Peslikis, "Resistances to Consciousness," Jennifer Gardner, "False Consciousness," and Pamela Kearon, "Man-Hating," all in Shulamith Firestone and Anne Koedt, eds., *Notes from the Second Year: Women's Liberation, Major Writings of the Radical Feminists* (New York: By the Editors, 1970), pp. 76–86.

24. Maurice Natanson, "The Claims of Immediacy," in Maurice Natanson and Henry W. Johnstone Jr., eds., *Philosophy, Rhetoric, and Argumentation* (University Park: Pennsylvania State University Press, 1965), pp. 15, 16.

25. Cynthia Ozick, "The Demise of the Dancing Dog," in Cooke, Bunch-Weeks, and Morgan, eds., *The New Women*, pp. 23–42.

26. Redstockings, "The Politics of Housework," *Liberation Now?*, pp. 110–115. Note that in this, as in other cases, authorship is assigned to a group rather than an individual.

27. Virginia Woolf, *A Room of One's Own* (New York: Harbinger, 1929).

28. Sally Kempton, "Cutting Loose," *Liberation Now!*, pp. 39–55. This essay was originally published in *Esquire*, July 1970, pp. 53–57.

29. Ibid., pp. 54–55.

30. Richard B. Gregg, "The Ego-Function of the Rhetoric of Protest," *Philosophy & Rhetoric* 4 (1971): 71–91. The essay is discussed specifically on pp. 80–81.

31. Granted, there are humanistic or existential psychological theorists who argue that social or outer reality must be changed fully as often as psychic or inner reality. See, for example, Thomas S. Szasz, *The Myth of Mental Illness* (1961; rpt., New York: Dell, 1961); R. D. Laing and A. Esterson, *Sanity, Madness, and the Family* (1964; rpt., New York: Basic Books, 1971); and William H. Grier and Price M. Cobbs, *Black Rage* (New York: Basic Books, 1968). However, the vast majority of psychological approaches assumes that the social order is, at least relatively, unalterable, and that it is the personal realm that must be changed. See, for example, Sigmund Freud, *A General Introduction to Psychoanalysis*, trans. Joan Riviere (1924; rpt., New York: Washington Square Press, 1960); Wilhelm Stekel, *Technique of Analytical Psychotherapy*, trans. Eden Paul and Cedar Paul (London: William Brown, 1950); Carl A. Whitaker and Thomas P. Malone, *The Roots of Psychotherapy* (New York: Blakiston, 1953); and Carl R. Rogers, *Client-Centered Therapy* (Boston: Houghton Mifflin, 1951).

32. This phrase originates with the loose coalition of radical groups called the Female Liberation Movement (Ellis, *Revolt*, p. 55). See also Pamela Kearon, "Power as a Function of the Group," in Firestone and Koedt, eds., *Notes from the Second Year*, pp. 108–110.

33. See, e.g., Anne Koedt, "The Myth of the Vaginal Orgasm," in *Liberation Now!*, pp. 311–320; Susan Lydon, "The Politics of Orgasm," and Mary Jane Sherfey, M.D., "A Theory on Female Sexuality," in Morgan, ed., *Sisterhood Is Powerful*, pp. 197–205, 220–230.

34. See, e.g., Radicalesbians, "The Woman-Identified Woman," in *Liberation Now!*, pp. 287–293; Ellen Strong, "The Hooker;" Gene Damon, "The Least of These: The Minority Whose Screams Haven't Yet Been Heard," and Martha Shelley, "Notes of a Radical Lesbian," in Morgan, ed., *Sisterhood Is Powerful*, pp. 289–311; and Del Martin and Phyllis Lyon, "The Realities of Lesbianism," in Cooke, Bunch-Weeks, and Morgan, eds., *The New Woman*, pp. 99–109.

35. Sally Kempton's essay is perhaps the most vivid example of this type. See also Judith Ann, "The Secretarial Proletariat," and Zoe Moss, "It Hurts to Be Alive and Obsolete: The Ageing Woman," in Morgan, ed., *Sisterhood Is Powerful*, pp. 86–100, 170–175.

36. See Shulamith Firestone, "Love," and Pamela

Kearon, "Man-Hating," in Firestone and Koedt, eds., *Notes from the Second Year*, pp. 16–27, 83–86.

37. This term originates with Sandra L. Bem and Daryl J. Bem, "Training the Woman to Know Her Place: The Power of a Nonconscious Ideology," in Garskof, ed., *Roles Women Play*, pp. 84–96.

38. This phrase originates with Kenneth Burke and is the title of Part 2 of *Permanence and Change*, 2d rev. ed. (Indianapolis, IN: Bobbs-Merrill, 1965).

39. Emmeline G. Pankhurst, cited by Ellis, in *Revolt*, p. 19.

40. Ti-Grace Atkinson, cited by Charles Winick and Paul M. Kinsie, in "Prostitutes," *Psychology Today*, February 1972, p. 57.

41. Germaine Greer, *The Female Eunuch* (New York: McGraw-Hill, 1970), p. 42.

42. Bem and Bem, "Training the Woman," pp. 94–95.

43. Joreen, "The Bitch Manifesto," in Firestone and Koedt, eds., *Notes from the Second Year*, pp. 5–9.

44. "WITCH Documents," in Morgan, ed., *Sisterhood Is Powerful*, pp. 538–553.

45. See, for example, Martha Shelley, "Notes of a Radical Lesbian," in Morgan, ed., *Sisterhood Is Powerful*, pp. 306–311. Paralleling this are the negative views of some radical groups toward heterosexual love and marriage. See "The Feminists: A Political Organization to Annihilate Sex Roles," in Firestone and Koedt, eds., *Notes from the Second Year*, pp. 114–118.

46. See, for example, Carolina Bird, "On Being Born Female," *Vital Speeches of the Day*, November 15, 1968, pp. 88–91. This argument is also made negatively by denying that, as yet, there is any satisfactory basis for determining what differences, if any, there are between males and females. See, e.g., Naomi Weisstein, "Psychology Constructs the Female, or the Fantasy Life of the Male Psychologist," in Garskof, ed., *Roles Women Play*, pp. 68–83.

47. Elizabeth Janeway makes a very telling critique of many of these attempts. She argues that the roles of shrew, witch, and bitch are simply reversals of the positively valued and socially accepted roles of women. The shrew is the negative counterpart of the public role of the wife whose function is to charm and to evince honor and respect for her husband before others; the witch is the negative role of the good mother—capricious, unresponsive, and threatening; the bitch is the reversal of the private role of wife—instead of being comforting, loving, and serious, she is selfish, teasing, emasculating. The point she is making is that these are not new, creative roles, merely reversals of existing, socially defined roles (*Man's World; Woman's Place*, pp. 119–123, 126–127, 199–201).

48. Natanson, "Claims of Immediacy," pp. 15–16.

49. Parke G. Burgess, "Rhetoric of Moral Conflict."

50. Thomas H. Olbricht, "The Self as a Philosophical Ground of Rhetoric," *Pennsylvania Speech Annual* 21 (1964): 28–36.

51. Lloyd F. Bitzer, "The Rhetorical Situation," *Philosophy & Rhetoric* 1 (1968): 6–8 [reprinted in this volume].

52. Leland M. Griffin, "The Rhetoric of Historical Movements," *QJS* 38 (1952): 184–185.

53. Herbert W. Simons, "Requirements, Problems, and Strategies: A Theory of Persuasion for Social Movements," *QJS* 56 (1970): 3.

54. Dan F. Hahn and Ruth M. Gonchar, "Studying Social Movements: A Rhetorical Methodology," *Speech Teacher* 20 (1971): 44, cited from Joseph R. Gusfield, ed., *Protest, Reform, and Revolt: A Reader in Social Movements* (New York: Wiley, 1970), p. 2.

55. Brenda Robinson Hancock, "Affirmation by Negation in the Women's Liberation Movement," *QJS* 58 (1972): 264–271.

56. Leland M. Griffin, "A Dramatistic Theory of the Rhetoric of Movements," in William H. Rueckert, ed., *Critical Responses to Kenneth Burke* (Minneapolis: University of Minnesota Press, 1969), p. 456.

57. Robert S. Cathcart, "New Approaches to the Study of Movements," p. 87.

The "Ideograph"

A Link Between Rhetoric and Ideology

Michael Calvin McGee

In 1950, Kenneth Burke, apparently following Dewey, Mead, and Lippmann, announced his preference for the notion "philosophy of myth" to explain the phenomenon of "public" or "mass consciousness" rather than the then-prevalent concept "ideology."[1] As contemporary writers have pushed on toward developing this "symbolic" or "dramatistic" alternative, the concept "ideology" has atrophied. Many use the term innocently, almost as a synonym for "doctrine" or "dogma" in political organizations;[2] and others use the word in a hypostatized sense that obscures or flatly denies the fundamental connection between the concept and descriptions of mass consciousness.[3] The concept seems to have gone the way of the dodo and of the neo-Aristotelian critic: As Bormann has suggested, the very word is widely perceived as being encrusted with the "intellectual baggage" of orthodox Marxism.[4]

Objecting to the use or abuse of any technical term would, ordinarily, be a sign of excessive crabbiness. But in this instance conceptualizations of "philosophy of myth," "fantasy visions," and "political scenarios," coupled with continued eccentric and/or narrow usages of "ideology," cosmetically camouflage significant and unresolved problems. We are presented with a brute, undeniable phenomenon: Human beings in collectivity behave and think differently than human beings in isolation. The collectivity is said to "have a mind of its own" distinct from the individual qua individual.

Writers in the tradition of Marx and Mannheim explain this difference by observing that the only possibility of "mind" lies in the individual qua individual, in the human organism itself. When one appears to "think" and "behave" collectively, therefore, one has been tricked, self-deluded, or manipulated into accepting the brute existence of such fantasies as "public mind" or "public opinion" or "public philosophy." Symbolists generally want to say that this trick is a "transcendence," a voluntary agreement to believe in and to participate in a "myth." Materialists maintain that the trick is an insidious reified form of "lie," a self-perpetuating system of beliefs and interpretations foisted on all members of the community by the ruling class. Burke, with his emphasis on the individuals who are tricked, concerns himself more with the structure of "motive" than with the objective conditions that impinge on and restrict the individual's freedom to develop a political consciousness. Neo-Marxians, with their focus on tricksters and the machinery of trickery, say that the essential question posed by the fact of society is one of locating precise descriptions of the dialectical tension between a "true" and a "false" consciousness, between reality and ideology.[5]

Though some on both sides of the controversy would have it otherwise, there is no *error* in either position. Both "myth" and "ideology" presuppose fundamental falsity in the common metaphor which alleges the existence of a "social organism."

"Ideology," however, assumes that the exposure of falsity is a moral act: Though we have never experienced a "true consciousness," it is nonetheless theoretically accessible to us, and, because of such accessibility, we are morally remiss if we do not discard the false and approach the true. The falsity presupposed by "myth," on the other hand, is amoral because it is a purely poetic phenomenon, legitimized by rule of the poet's license, a "suspension of disbelief." A symbolist who speaks of "myth" is typically at great pains to argue for a value-free approach to the object of study, an approach in which one denies that "myth" is a synonym for "lie" and treats it as a falsehood of a peculiarly redemptive nature. Materialists, on the other hand, seem to use the concept "ideology" expressly to warrant normative claims regarding the exploitation of the "proletarian class" by self-serving plunderers. No error is involved in the apparently contradictory conceptions because, fundamentally, materialists and symbolists pursue two different studies: The Marxian asks how the "givens" of a human environment impinge on the development of political consciousness; the symbolist asks how the human symbol-using, reality-creating potential impinges on material reality, ordering it normatively, "mythically."

Errors arise when one conceives "myth" and "ideology" to be contraries, alternative and incompatible theoretical descriptions of the same phenomenon. The materialists' neglect of language studies and the consequent inability of Marxian theory to explain socially constructed realities is well publicized.[6] Less well described is the symbolists' neglect of the nonsymbolic environment and the consequent inability of symbolist theory to account for the impact of material phenomena on the construction of social reality.[7] I do not mean to denigrate in any way the research of scholars attempting to develop Burke's philosophy of myth; indeed, I have on occasion joined that endeavor. I do believe, however, that each of us has erred to the extent that we have conceived the rubrics of symbolism as an *alternative* rather than *supplemental* description of political consciousness. The assertion that "philosophy of myth" is an alternative to "ideology" begs the question Marx intended to pose. Marx was concerned with "power," with the capacity of an elite class to control the state's political, economic, and military establishment, to dominate the state's information systems and determine even the consciousness of large masses of people. He was politically committed to the cause of the proletariat: If a norm was preached by the upper classes, it was by virtue of that fact a baneful seduction; and if a member of the proletarian class was persuaded by such an argument, that person was possessed of an "ideology," victimized and exploited. Not surprisingly, symbolists criticize Marx for his politics, suggesting that his is a wonderfully convenient formula which mistakes commitment for "historically scientific truth." By conceiving poetic falsity, we rid ourselves of the delusion that interpretation is scientific, but we also bury the probability that the myths we study as an alternative are thrust upon us by the brute force of "power." While Marx overestimated "power" as a variable in describing political consciousness, Burke, Cassirer, Polanyi, and others do not want to discuss the capacity even of a "free" state to determine political consciousness.[8]

If we are to describe the trick-of-the-mind which deludes us into believing that we "think" with/through/for a "society" to which we "belong," we need a theoretical model which accounts for both "ideology" and "myth," a model which neither denies human capacity to control "power" through the manipulation of symbols nor begs Marx's essential questions regarding the influence of "power" on creating and maintaining political consciousness. I will argue here that such a model must begin with the concept "ideology" and proceed to link that notion directly with the interests of symbolism.

I will elaborate the following commitments and hypotheses: If a mass consciousness exists at all, it must be empirically "present," itself a thing obvious to those who participate in it, or, at least, empirically manifested in the language which communicates it. I agree with Marx that the problem of consciousness is fundamentally practical and normative, that it is concerned essentially with describing and evaluating the legitimacy of public motives. Such consciousness, I believe, is always false, not because we are programmed automatons and not because we have a propensity to structure political perceptions in poetically false "dramas" or "scenarios," but because "truth" in politics, no matter how firmly we believe, is always an illusion. The falsity of an ideology is specifically rhetorical, for the illusion of truth and falsity with regard to normative commitments is the product of persuasion.[9] Since the clearest access to persuasion (and hence to ideology) is through the discourse used to produce it, I will suggest that ideology in practice is a political language, preserved in rhetorical documents, with the capacity to dictate decision and control public belief and behavior. Further, the political language which manifests ideology seems characterized by slogans, a vocabulary of "ideographs" easily mistaken for the technical terminology of political philosophy. An analysis of ideographic usages in political rhetoric, I believe, reveals interpenetrating systems or "structures" of public motives. Such structures appear to be "diachronic" and "synchronic" patterns of political consciousness which have the capacity both to control "power" and to influence (if not determine) the shape and texture of each individual's "reality."

Hypothetical Characteristics of Ideographs

Marx's thesis suggests that an ideology determines mass belief and thus restricts the free emergence of political opinion. By this logic, the "freest" members of a community are those who belong to the "power" elite; yet the image of hooded puppeteers twisting and turning the masses at will is unconvincing, if only because the elite seems itself imprisoned by the same false consciousness communicated to the polity at large. When we consider the impact of ideology on freedom, and of power on consciousness, we must be clear that ideology is transcendent, as much an influence on the belief and behavior of the ruler as on the ruled. Nothing *necessarily* restricts persons who wield the might of the state. Roosevelts and Carters are as free to indulge personal vanity with capricious uses of power as was Idi Amin, regardless of formal "checks and balances." The polity can punish tyrants and maniacs after the fact of their lunacy or tyranny (if the polity survives it), but, in practical terms, the only way to shape or soften power at the moment of its exercise is prior persuasion. Similarly, no matter what punishment we might imagine "power" visiting upon an ordinary citizen, nothing *necessarily* determines individual behavior and belief. A citizen may be punished for eccentricity or disobedience after the fact of a crime, but, at the moment when defiance is contemplated, the only way to combat the impulse to criminal behavior is prior persuasion. I am suggesting, in other words, that social control in its essence is control over consciousness, the *a priori* influence that learned predispositions hold over human agents who play the roles of "power" and "people" in a given transaction.[10]

Because there is a lack of necessity in social control, it seems inappropriate to characterize agencies of control as "socializing" or "conditioning" media.

No individual (least of all the elite who control the power of the state) is *forced* to submit in the same way that a conditioned dog is obliged to salivate or socialized children are required to speak English. Human beings are "conditioned," not directly to belief and behavior, but to a vocabulary of concepts that function as guides, warrants, reasons, or excuses for behavior and belief. When a claim is warranted by such terms as "law," "liberty," "tyranny," or "trial by jury," in other words, it is presumed that human beings will react predictably and autonomically. So it was that a majority of Americans were surprised, not when allegedly sane young men agreed to go halfway around the world to kill for God, country, apple pie, and no other particularly good reason, but, rather, when other young men displayed good common sense by moving to Montreal instead, thereby refusing to be conspicuous in a civil war which was none of their business. The end product of the state's insistence on some degree of conformity in behavior and belief, I suggest, is a *rhetoric* of control, a system of persuasion presumed to be effective on the whole community. We make a rhetoric of war to persuade us of war's necessity, but then forget that it is a rhetoric—and regard negative popular judgments of it as unpatriotic cowardice.

It is not remarkable to conceive social control as fundamentally rhetorical. In the past, however, rhetorical scholarship has regarded the rhetoric of control as a species of argumentation and thereby assumed that the fundamental unit of analysis in such rhetoric is an integrated set-series of propositions. This is, I believe, a mistake, an unwarranted abstraction: To argue is to test an affirmation or denial of claims; argument is the means of proving the truth of grammatical units, declarative sentences, that purport to be reliable signal representations of reality. Within the vocabulary of argumentation, the term "rule of law" makes no sense until it is made the subject or predicable of a proposition. If I say "The rule of law is a primary cultural value in the United States" or "Charles I was a cruel and capricious tyrant," I have asserted a testable claim that may be criticized with logically coordinated observations. When I say simply "the rule of law," however, my utterance cannot qualify logically as a claim. Yet I am conditioned to believe that "liberty" and "property" have an obvious meaning, a behaviorally directive self-evidence. Because I am taught to set such terms apart from my usual vocabulary, words used as agencies of social control may have an intrinsic force—and, if so, I may very well distort the key terms of social conflict, commitment, and control if I think of them as parts of a proposition rather than as basic units of analysis.

Though words only (and not claims), such terms as "property," "religion," "right of privacy," "freedom of speech," "rule of law," and "liberty" are more pregnant than propositions ever could be. They are the basic structural elements, the building blocks, of ideology. Thus they may be thought of as "ideographs," for, like Chinese symbols, they signify and "contain" a unique ideological commitment; further, they presumptuously suggest that each member of a community will see as a gestalt every complex nuance in them. What "rule of law" means is the series of propositions, all of them, that could be manufactured to justify a Whig/Liberal order. Ideographs are one-term sums of an orientation, the species of "God" or "Ultimate" term that will be used to symbolize the line of argument the meanest sort of individual *would* pursue, if that individual had the dialectical skills of philosophers, as a defense of a personal stake in and commitment to the society. Nor is one permitted to question the fundamental logic of ideographs: Everyone is conditioned to think of "the rule of law" as a *logical* commitment just as one is taught to think that "186,000 miles per second" is an accurate empirical description of the speed of light even though few can work the experiments or do the mathematics to prove it.[11]

The important fact about ideographs is that they exist in real discourse functioning clearly and evidently as agents of political consciousness. They are not invented by observers; they come to be as a part of the real lives of the people whose motives they articulate. So, for example, "rule of law" is a more precise, objective motive then such observer-invented terms as "neurotic" or "paranoid style" or "*petit bourgeois.*"

Ideographs pose a methodological problem *because* of their very specificity: How do we generalize from a "rule of law" to a description of consciousness that comprehends not only "rule of law" but all other like motives as well? What do we describe with the concept "ideograph," and how do we actually go about doing the specific cultural analysis promised by conceptually linking rhetoric and ideology?

Though both come to virtually the same conclusion, the essential argument seems more careful and useful in Ortega's notion of "the etymological man" than in Burke's poetically hidden concept of "the symbol-using animal" and "logology":

Man, when he sets himself to speak, does so *because* he believes that he will be able to say

what he thinks. Now, this is an illusion. Language is not up to that. It says, more or less, a part of what we think, and raises an impenetrable obstacle to the transmission of the rest. It serves quite well for mathematical statements and proofs. . . . But in proportion as conversation treats of more important, more human, more "real" subjects than these, its vagueness, clumsiness, and confusion steadily increase. Obedient to the inveterate prejudice that "talking leads to understanding," we speak and listen in such good faith that we end by misunderstanding one another far more than we would if we remained mute and set ourselves to divine each other. Nay, more: since our thought is in large measure dependent upon our language . . . it follows that thinking is talking with oneself and hence misunderstanding oneself at the imminent risk of getting oneself into a complete quandary.[12]

All this "talk" generates a series of "usages" which unite us, since we speak the same language, but, more significantly, such "talk" *separates* us from other human beings who do not accept our meanings, our intentions.[13] So, Ortega claims, the essential demarcation of whole nations is language usage: "This gigantic architecture of usages is, precisely, society."[14] And it is through usages that a particular citizen's sociality exists:

A language, *speech*, is "what people say," it is the vast system of verbal usages established in a collectivity. The individual, the person, is from his birth submitted to the linguistic coercion that these usages represent. Hence the mother tongue is perhaps the most typical and clearest social phenomenon. With it "people" enter us, set up residence in us, making each an example of "people." Our mother tongue socializes our inmost being, and because of this fact every individual belongs, in the strongest sense of the word, to a society. He can flee from the society in which he was born and brought up, but in his flight the society inexorably accompanies him because he carries it within him. This is the true meaning that the statement "man is a social animal" can have.[15]

Ortega's reference, of course, is to language generally and not to a particular vocabulary within language. So he worked with the vocabulary of greeting to demonstrate the definitive quality of linguistic usages when conceiving "society."[16] His reasoning, however, invites specification, attention to the components of the "architecture" supposedly created by usages.

Insofar as usages both unite and separate human beings, it seems reasonable to suggest that the functions of uniting and separating would be represented by specific vocabularies, actual words or terms. With regard to political union and separation, such vocabularies would consist of ideographs. Such usages as "liberty" define a collectivity, i.e., the outer parameters of a society, because such terms either do not exist in other societies or do not have precisely similar meanings. So, in the United States, we claim a common belief in "equality," as do citizens of the Union of Soviet Socialist Republics; but "equality" is not the same word in its meaning or its usage. One can therefore precisely define the difference between the two communities, in part, by comparing the usage of definitive ideographs. We are, of course, still able to interact with the Soviets despite barriers of language and usage. The interaction is possible because of higher-order ideographs—"world peace," "detente," "spheres of influence," etc.—that permit temporary union.[17] And, in the other direction, it is also true that there are special interests within the United States separated one from the other precisely by disagreements regarding the identity, legitimacy, or definition of ideographs. So we are divided by usages into subgroups: Business and labor, Democrats and Republicans, Yankees and Southerners are *united* by the ideographs that represent the political entity "United States" and *separated* by a disagreement as to the practical meaning of such ideographs.

The concept "ideograph" is meant to be purely descriptive of an essentially social human condition. Unlike more general conceptions of "Ultimate" or "God" terms, attention is called to the social, rather than rational or ethical, functions of a particular vocabulary. This vocabulary is precisely a group of *words* and not a series of symbols representing ideas. Ortega clearly, methodically, distinguishes a usage (what we might call "social" or "material" thought) from an *idea* (what Ortega would call "pure thought"). He suggests, properly, that *language gets in the way of thinking*, separates us from "ideas" we may have which cannot be surely expressed, even to ourselves, in the usages which imprison us. So my "pure thought" about liberty, religion, and property is clouded, hindered, made irrelevant by the existence in history of the ideographs "Liberty, Religion, and Property."[18] Because these terms are definitive of the society we have inherited, they are *conditions* of the society into which each of us is born, material ideas which we must accept to "belong." They penalize us, in a sense, as much as they protect us, for they prohibit our appreciation of an alternative pattern of meaning in, for example, the Soviet Union or Brazil.

In effect, ideographs—language imperatives which hinder and perhaps make impossible "pure

thought"—are bound within the culture which they define. We can *characterize* an ideograph, say what it has meant and does mean as a usage, and some of us may be able to achieve an imaginary state of withdrawal from community long enough to speculate as to what ideographs *ought* to mean in the best of possible worlds; but the very nature of language forces us to keep the two operations separate: So, for example, the "idea" of "liberty" may be the subject of philosophical speculation, but philosophers can never be *certain* that they themselves or their readers understand a "pure" meaning unpolluted by historical, ideographic usages.[19] Should we look strictly at material notions of "liberty," on the other hand, we distort our thinking by believing that a rationalization of a particular historical meaning is "pure," the truth of the matter.[20] Ideographs can *not* be used to establish or test truth, and vice versa; the truth, in ideal metaphysical senses, is a consideration irrelevant to accurate characterizations of such ideographs as "liberty." Indeed, if examples from recent history are a guide, the attempts to infuse usages with metaphysical meanings, or to confuse ideographs with the "pure" thought of philosophy, have resulted in the "nightmares" which Polanyi, for one, deplores.[21] The significance of ideographs is in their concrete history as usages, not in their alleged idea-content.

The Analysis of Ideographs

No one has ever seen an "equality" strutting up the driveway, so, if "equality" exists at all, it has meaning through its specific applications. In other words, we establish a meaning for "equality" by using the word as a description of a certain phenomenon; it has meaning only insofar as our description is acceptable, believable. If asked to make a case for "equality," that is, to define the term, we are forced to make reference to its history by detailing the situations for which the word has been an appropriate description. Then, by comparisons over time, we establish an analog for the proposed present usage of the term. Earlier usages become precedents, touchstones for judging the propriety of the ideograph in a current circumstance. The meaning of "equality" does not rigidify because situations seeming to require its usage are never perfectly similar: As the situations vary, so the meaning of "equality" expands and contracts. The variations in meaning of "equality" are much less important, however, than the fundamental, categorical meaning, the "common denominator" of all situations for which "equality" has been the best and most descriptive term. The dynamism of "equality" is thus paramorphic, for even when the term changes its signification in particular circumstances, it retains a formal, categorical meaning, a constant reference to its history as an ideograph.

These earlier usages are vertically structured, related each to the other in a formal way, every time the society is called upon to judge whether a particular circumstance should be defined ideographically. So, for example, to protect ourselves from abuses of power, we have built into our political system an ideograph that is said to justify "impeaching" an errant leader: If the president has engaged in behaviors which can be described as "high crimes and misdemeanors," even that highest officer must be removed.

But what is meant by "high crimes and misdemeanors"? If Peter Rodino wishes to justify impeachment procedures against Richard Nixon in the Committee on the Judiciary of the House of Representatives, he must mine history for touchstones, precedents which give substance and an aura of precision to the ideograph "high crimes and misdemeanors." His search of the past concentrates on situations analogous to that which he is facing, situations involving actual or proposed "impeachment." The "rule of law" emerged as a contrary ideograph, and Rodino developed from the tension between "law" and "high crimes" an argument indicting Nixon. His proofs were historical, ranging from Magna Carta to Edmund Burke's impeachment of Warren Hastings. He was able to make the argument, therefore, only because he could organize a series of events, situationally similar, with an ideograph as the structuring principle. The structuring is "vertical" because of the element of *time*; that is, the deep meanings of "law" and "high crime" derive from knowledge of the way in which meanings have evolved over a period of time—awareness of the way an ideograph can be meaningful *now* is controlled in large part by what it meant *then*.[22]

All communities take pains to record and preserve the vertical structure of their ideographs. Formally, the body of nonstatutory "law" is little more than literature recording ideographic usages in the "common law" and "case law."[23] So, too, historical dictionaries, such as the *Oxford English Dictionary*, detail etymologies for most of the Anglo-American ideographs. And any so-called professional history provides a record in detail of the events surrounding earlier usages of ideographs—indeed, the historian's eye is most usually attracted precisely to those situations involving ideographic applications.[24] The more significant record of vertical structures, however, lies in what might be called "popular" history. Such history consists in part of novels, films, plays, even songs; but the truly influential manifestation is grammar school history, the very first contact most have with their existence and experience as a part of a community.

To learn the meanings of the ideographs "freedom" and "patriotism," for example, most of us swallowed the tale of Patrick Henry's defiant speech to the Virginia House of Burgesses: "I know not what course others may take, but as for me, give me liberty or give me death!" These specific words, of course, were concocted by the historian William Wirt and not by Governor Henry. Wirt's intention was to provide a model for "the young men of Virginia," asking them to copy Henry's virtues and avoid his vices.[25] Fabricated events and words meant little, not because Wirt was uninterested in the truth of what really happened to Henry, but rather because what he wrote about was the definition of essential ideographs. His was a task of socialization, an exercise in epideictic rhetoric, providing the youth of his age (and of our own) with general knowledge of ideographic touchstones so that they might be able to make, or comprehend, judgments of public motives and of their own civic duty.

Though such labor tires the mind simply in imagining it, there is no trick in gleaning from public documents the entire vocabulary of ideographs that define a particular collectivity. The terms do not hide in discourse, nor is their "meaning" or function within an argument obscure: we might disagree metaphysically about "equality," and we might use the term differently in practical discourse, but I believe we can nearly always discover the functional meaning of the term by measure of its grammatic and pragmatic context.[26] Yet even a complete description of vertical ideographic structures leaves little but an exhaustive lexicon understood etymologically and diachronically— and no ideally precise explanation of how ideographs function *presently*.

If we find forty rhetorical situations in which "rule of law" has been an organizing term, we are left with little but the simple chronology of the situations as a device to structure the lot: Case 1 is distinct from Case 40, and the meaning of the ideograph thus has contracted or expanded in the intervening time. But time is an irrelevant matter *in practice*. Chronological sequences are provided by analysts, and they properly reflect the concerns of theorists who try to describe what "rule of law" *may* mean, potentially, by laying out the history of what the term *has* meant. Such advocates as Rodino are not so scrupulous in research; they choose eight or nine of those forty cases to use as evidence in argument, ignore the rest, and impose a pattern of organization on the cases recommended (or forced) by the demands of a current situation. As Ortega argues with reference to language generally, key usages considered historically and diachronically are purely formal; yet in real discourse, and in public consciousness, they are *forces*:

> [A]ll that diachronism accomplishes is to reconstruct other comparative "presents" of the language as they existed in the past. All that it shows us, then, is changes; it enables us to witness one present being replaced by another, the succession of the static figures of the language, as the "film," with its motionless images, engenders the visual fiction of a movement. At best, it offers us a cinematic view of language, but not a *dynamic* understanding of how the changes were, and came to be, *made*. The changes are merely results of the making and unmaking process, they are the externality of language and there is need for an internal conception of it in which we discover not resultant *forms* but the operating *forces* themselves.[27]

In Burke's terminology, describing a vertical ideographic structure yields a culture-specific and relatively precise "grammar" of one public motive. That motive is not captured, however, without attention to its "rhetoric."

Considered rhetorically, as *forces*, ideographs seem structured horizontally, for when people actually make use of them presently, such terms as "rule of law" clash with other ideographs ("principle of confidentiality" or "national security," for example), and in the conflict come to mean with reference to synchronic confrontations. So, for example, one would not ordinarily think of an inconsistency between "rule of law" and "principle of confidentiality." Vertical analysis of the two ideographs would probably reveal a consonant relationship based on genus and species: "Confidentiality" of certain conversations is a control on the behavior of government, a control that functions to maintain a "rule of law" and prevents "tyranny" by preserving a realm of privacy for the individual.

The "Watergate" conflict between Nixon and Congress, however, illustrates how that consonant relationship can be restructured, perhaps broken, in the context of a particular controversy: Congress asked, formally and legally, for certain of Nixon's documents. He refused, thereby creating the appearance of frustrating the imperative value "rule of law." He attempted to excuse himself by matching a second ideograph, "principle of confidentiality," against normal and usual meanings of "rule of law." Before a mass television audience, Nixon argued that a President's conversations with advisers were entitled to the same privilege constitutionally accorded exchanges between priest and penitent, husband and wife, lawyer and client. No direct vertical precedent was available to support Nixon's usage. The argument asked public (and later jurisprudential) permission to expand the meaning of "confidentiality" and thereby to alter its relationship with the "rule of law," making what appeared to be an illegal act acceptable. Nixon's claims were epideictic and not deliberative or forensic; he magnified "confidentiality" by praising the ideograph as if it were a person, attempting to alter its "standing" among other ideographs, even as an individual's "standing" in the community changes through praise and blame.[28]

Synchronic structural changes in the relative standing of an ideograph are "horizontal" because of the presumed consonance of an ideology; that is, ideographs such as "rule of law" are meant to be taken together, as a working unit, with "public trust," "freedom of speech," "trial by jury," and any other slogan characteristic of the collective life. If all the ideographs used to justify a Whig/Liberal government were placed on a chart, they would form groups or clusters of words radiating from the slogans originally used to rationalize "popular sovereignty"—"religion," "liberty," and "property." Each term would be a connector, modifier, specifier, or contrary for those fundamental historical commitments, giving them a meaning and a unity easily mistaken for logic. Some terms would be enshrined in the Constitution, some in law, some merely in conventional usage; but all would be constitutive of "the people." Though new usages can enter the equation, the ideographs remain essentially unchanged. But when we engage ideological argument, when we cause ideographs to *do work* in explaining, justifying, or guiding policy in specific situations, the relationship of ideographs changes. A "rule of law," for example, is taken for granted, a simple connector between "property" and "liberty," until a constitutional crisis inclines us to make it "come first." In Burke's vocabulary, it becomes the "title" or "god-term" of all ideographs, the center-sun about which every ideograph orbits. Sometimes circumstance forces us to sense that the structure is not consonant, as when aware-ness of racism exposes contradiction between "property" and "right to life" in the context of "open-housing" legislation. Sometimes officers of state, in the process of justifying particular uses of power, manufacture seeming inconsistency, as when Nixon pitted "confidentiality" against "rule of law." And sometimes an alien force frontally assaults the structure, as when Hitler campaigned against "decadent democracies." Such instances have the potential to change the structure of ideo-graphs and hence the "present" ideology—in this sense, an ideology is dynamic and a *force*, always resilient, always keeping itself in some consonance and unity, but not always the *same* consonance and unity.[29]

In appearance, of course, characterizing ideo-logical conflicts as synchronic *structural* disloca-tions is an unwarranted abstraction: An ideologi-cal argument could result simply from multiple usages of an ideograph. Superficially, for example, one might be inclined to describe the "busing" controversy as a disagreement over the "best" meaning for "equality," one side opting for "equal-ity" defined with reference to "access" to education and the other with reference to the goal, "being educated." An ideograph, however, is always understood in its relation to another; it is defined tautologically by using other terms in its cluster. If we accept that there are three or four or however many possible meanings for "equality," each with a currency and legitimacy, we distort the nature of the ideological dispute by ignoring the fact that "equality" is made meaningful, not within the clash of multiple usages, but rather in its relation-ship with "freedom." That is, "equality" defined by "access" alters the nature of "liberty" from the relationship of "equality" and "liberty" thought to exist when "equality" is defined as "being edu-cated." One would not want to rule out the pos-sibility that ideological disagreements, however rarely, could be simply semantic; but we are more likely to err if we assume the dispute to be seman-tic than if we look for the deeper structural dislo-cation which likely produced multiple usages as a disease produces symptoms. When an ideograph is at the center of a semantic dispute, I would suggest, the multiple usages will be either metaphysical or diachronic, purely speculative or historical, and in either event devoid of the force and currency of a synchronic ideological conflict.[30]

In the terms of this argument, two recogniz-able "ideologies" exist in any specific culture at one "moment." One "ideology" is a "grammar," a historically-defined diachronic structure of ideo-graph meanings expanding and contracting from the birth of the society to its "present." Another "ideology" is a "rhetoric," a situationally-defined synchronic structure of ideograph clusters con-stantly reorganizing itself to accommodate specific circumstances while maintaining its fundamental consonance and unity. A division of this sort, of course, is but an analytic convenience for talking about two *dimensions* (vertical and horizontal) of a single phenomenon: No present ideology can be divorced from past commitments, if only because the very words used to express present dislocations have a history that establishes the category of their meaning. And no diachronic ideology can be divorced from the "here-and-now" if only because its entire *raison d'être* consists in justifying the form and direction of collective behavior. Both of these structures must be understood and described before one can claim to have constructed a theo-retically precise explanation of a society's ideology, of its repertoire of public motives.

Conclusion

One of the casualties of the current "pluralist" fad in social and political theory has been the old Marxian thesis that governing elites control the masses by creating, maintaining, and manipulat-ing a mass consciousness suited to perpetuation of the existing order.[31] Though I agree that Marx probably overestimated the influence of an elite, it is difficult *not* to see a "dominant ideology" which seems to exercise decisive influence in political life. The question, of course, turns on finding a way accurately to define and to describe a domi-nant ideology. Theorists writing in the tradition of Dewey, Burke, and Cassirer have, in my judg-ment, come close to the mark; but because they are bothered by poetic metaphors, these symbolists never conceive their work as description of a mass consciousness. Even these writers, therefore, beg Marx's inescapable question regarding the impact of "power" on the way we think. I have argued here that the concepts "rhetoric" and "ideology" may be linked without poetic metaphors, and that the linkage should produce a description and an explanation of dominant ideology, of the relation-ship between the "power" of a state and the con-sciousness of its people.

The importance of symbolist constructs is their focus on *media* of consciousness, on the discourse that articulates and propagates common beliefs.

"Rhetoric," "sociodrama," "myth," "fantasy vision," and "political scenario" are not important because of their *fiction*, their connection to poetic, but because of their *truth*, their links with the trick-of-the-mind that deludes individuals into believing that they "think" with/for/through a social organism. The truth of symbolist constructs, I have suggested, appears to lie in our claim to see a legitimate social reality in a vocabulary of complex, high-order abstractions that refer to and invoke a sense of "the people." By learning the meaning of ideographs, I have argued, everyone in society, even the "freest" of us, those who control the state, seem predisposed to structured mass responses. Such terms as "liberty," in other words, constitute by our very use of them in political discourse an ideology that governs or "dominates" our consciousness. In practice, therefore, ideology is a political language composed of sloganlike terms signifying collective commitment.

Such terms I have called "ideographs." A formal definition of "ideograph," derived from arguments made throughout this essay, would list the following characteristics: An ideograph is an ordinary-language term found in political discourse. It is a high-order abstraction representing collective commitment to a particular but equivocal and ill-defined normative goal. It warrants the use of power, excuses behavior and belief which might otherwise be perceived as eccentric or antisocial, and guides behavior and belief into channels easily recognized by a community as acceptable and laudable. Ideographs such as "slavery" and "tyranny," however, may guide behavior and belief negatively by branding unacceptable behavior. And many ideographs ("liberty," for example) have a nonideographic usage, as in the sentence, "Since I resigned my position, I am at liberty to accept your offer." Ideographs are culture-bound, though some terms are used in different signification across cultures. Each member of the community is socialized, conditioned, to the vocabulary of ideographs as a prerequisite for "belonging" to the society. A degree of tolerance is usual, but people are expected to understand ideographs within a range of usage thought to be acceptable: The society will inflict penalties on those who use ideographs in heretical ways and on those who refuse to respond appropriately to claims on their behavior warranted through the agency of ideographs.

Though ideographs such as "liberty," "religion," and "property" often appear as technical terms in social philosophy, I have argued here that the ideology of a community is established by the usage of such terms in specifically rhetorical discourse, for such usages constitute excuses for specific beliefs and behaviors made by those who executed the history of which they were a part. The ideographs used in rhetorical discourse seem structured in two ways: In isolation, each ideograph has a history, an etymology, such that current meanings of the term are linked to past usages of it diachronically. The diachronic structure of an ideograph establishes the parameters, the category, of its meaning. All ideographs taken together, I suggest, are thought at any specific "moment" to be consonant, related one to another in such a way as to produce unity of commitment in a particular historical context. Each ideograph is thus connected to all others as brain cells are linked by synapses, synchronically in one context at one specific moment.

A complete description of an ideology, I have suggested, will consist of (1) the isolation of a society's ideographs, (2) the exposure and analysis of the diachronic structure of every ideograph, and (3) characterization of synchronic relationships among all the ideographs in a particular context. Such a description, I believe, would yield a theoretical framework with which to describe interpenetrating material and symbolic environments: Insofar as we can explain the diachronic and synchronic tensions among ideographs, I suggest, we can also explain the tension between *any* "given" human environment ("objective reality") and any "projected" environments ("symbolic" or "social reality") latent in rhetorical discourse.

NOTES

1. Kenneth Burke, *A Rhetoric of Motives* (New York: Prentice-Hall, 1950), pp. 197–203; John Dewey, *The Public and Its Problems* (New York: Henry Holt, 1927); George H. Mead, *Mind, Self, and Society* (Chicago: University of Chicago Press, 1934); and Walter Lippmann, *Public Opinion* (1922; rpt., New York: Free Press, 1965). Duncan groups the American symbolists by observing that European social theorists using "ideology" were concerned with "consciousness" (questions about the *apprehension* of society), while symbolists using poetic metaphors were concerned with a "philosophy of action" (questions about the way we do or ought to *behave* in society). In rejecting the concept and theory of "ideology," Burke refused to consider the relationship between consciousness and action except as that relationship can be characterized with the agency of an *a priori* poetic metaphor, "dramatism." His thought and writing, like that of a poet, is therefore freed from truth criteria: Supposing his *form*, no "motive" outside the dramatistic terminology need be recognized or accounted for *in its par-*

ticularity. Though Burkeans are more guilty than Burke, I think even he tends to redefine motives rather than account for them, to cast self-confessions in "scenarios" rather than deal with them in specific. One might say of "dramatism" what Bacon alleged regarding the Aristotelian syllogism, that it is but a form which chases its tail, presuming in its metaphoric conception the truth of its descriptions. See Hugh Dalziel Duncan, *Symbols in Society* (New York: Oxford University Press, 1968), pp. 12–14; Richard Dewey, "The Theatrical Analogy Reconsidered," *American Sociologist* 4 (1969): 307–311; and R. S. Perinbanayagam, "The Definition of the Situation: An Analysis of the Ethnomethodological and Dramaturgical View," *Sociological Quarterly* 15 (1974): 521–541.

2. See, e.g., Arthur M. Schlesinger Jr., "Ideology and Foreign Policy: The American Experience," in George Schwab, ed., *Ideology and Foreign Policy* (New York: Cyrco, 1978), pp. 124–132; and Randall L. Bytwerk, "Rhetorical Aspects of the Nazi Meeting: 1926–1933," *Quarterly Journal of Speech* 61 (1975): 307–318.

3. See, e.g., William R. Brown, "Ideology as Communication Process," *Quarterly Journal of Speech* 64 (1978): 123–140; and Jürgen Habermas, "Technology and Science as 'Ideology,'" in *Toward a Rational Society*, trans. Jeremy J. Shapiro (1968; Boston: Beacon Press, 1970), pp. 81–122.

4. Bormann's distrust of "ideology" was expressed in the context of an evaluation of his "fantasy theme" technique at the 1978 convention of the Speech Communication Association (S.C.A.). See "Fantasy Theme Analysis: An Exploration and Assessment," S.C.A. 1978 Seminar Series, audiotape cassettes. For authoritative accounts of the various "encrustations," see George Lichtheim, "The Concept of Ideology," *History and Theory* 4 (1964–1965): 164–195; and Hans Barth, *Truth and Ideology*, 2d ed., trans. Frederic Lilge (Berkeley and Los Angeles: University of California Press, 1976).

5. See Kenneth Burke, *Permanence and Change*, 2d ed., rev. (1954; rpt., Indianapolis, IN: Bobbs-Merrill, 1965), pp. 19–36, 216–236; Karl Marx and Frederick Engels, *The German Ideology* (1847), trans. and ed. Clemens Dutt, W. Lough, and C. P. Magill, in *The Collected Works of Karl Marx and Frederick Engels*, 9 vols. (Moscow: Progress Publishers, 1975–1977), vol. 5, pp. 3–5, 23–93; Karl Mannheim, *Ideology and Utopia*, trans. Louis Wirth and Edward Shils (1929; rpt., New York: Harvest Books, 1952); and Martin Seliger, *The Marxist Conception of Ideology: A Critical Essay* (Cambridge, UK: Cambridge University Press, 1977). My purpose here is to expose the issue between symbolists (generally) and materialists (particularly Marxians). This of course results in some oversimplification: With regard to the brute problem of describing "consciousness," at least two schools of thought are not here accounted for, Freudian psychiatry and American empirical psychology. Freudians are generally connected with the symbolist position I describe here, while most of the opera-tional conceptions of American empirical psychology (especially social psychology) may fairly be associated with Marxian or neo-Marxian description. Moreover, I treat the terms "ideology" and "myth" as less ambiguous than their history as concepts would suggest. My usage of the terms, and the technical usefulness I portray, reflects my own conviction more than the sure and non-controversial meaning of either "myth" or "ideology."

6. See, e. g., Willard A. Mullins, "Truth and Ideology: Reflections on Mannheim's Paradox," *History and Theory* 18 (1979): 142–154; William H. Shaw, "'The Handmill Gives You the Feudal Lord': Marx's Technological Determinism," *History and Theory* 18 (1979): 155–176; Jean-Paul Sartre, *Critique of Dialectical Reason*, trans. Alan Sheridan-Smith (London: NLB, 1976), pp. 95–121; and Jean-Paul Sartre, *Search for a Method*, trans. Hazel E. Barnes (New York: Vintage, 1968), pp. 35–84.

7. See W. G. Runciman, "Describing," *Mind* 81 (1972): 372–388; Perinbanayagam, "Definition of the Situation"; and Herbert W. Simons, Elizabeth Mechling, and Howard N. Schreier, "Mobilizing for Collective Action From the Bottom Up: The Rhetoric of Social Movements" (unpublished manuscript, Temple University), pp. 48–59 [now in Carroll C. Arnold and John Waite Bowers, eds., *Handbook of Rhetorical and Communication Theory* (Boston: Allyn & Bacon, 1984)].

8. Adolph Hitler, this century's archetype of absolute power—as well as absolute immorality—rose to dominance and maintained himself by putting into practice symbolist theories of social process. Hitler's mere existence forces one to question symbolist theories, asking whether "sociodramas" and "rhetorics" and "myths" are things to be studied scientifically or wild imaginings conjured up from the ether, devil-tools playing upon human weakness and superstition, and therefore things to be politically eradicated. In the face of Hitler, most symbolists adopted a high moral stance of righteous wrath, concentrating on the evil of the man while underplaying the tools he used to gain and keep power. But subtly they modified their logics: Burke is most sensitive to the problem, but in the end he does little more than demonstrate the moral polemical power of dramatistic methods of criticism, becoming the "critic" of his early and later years rather than the "historian" and "theorist" of his middle years. Cassirer's reaction is more extreme, backing away from the logical implications of the symbolist epistemology he argued for before Hitler, begging the problem of power by characterizing the state itself as nothing but a "myth" to be transcended. Hitler was an inspiration to Polanyi, causing him to take up epistemology as a vehicle to discredit social philosophy generally. In the process Polanyi became an unabashed ideological chauvinist of his adopted culture. See, resp., Kenneth Burke, "The Rhetoric of Hitler's 'Battle,'" in *The Philosophy of Literary Form*, 3d ed. (Berkeley and Los Angeles: University of California Press, 1973), pp. 191–220, and cf. Kenneth

Burke, *Attitudes Toward History* (Boston: Beacon Press, 1961), pp. 92–107; Ernst Cassirer, *The Philosophy of Symbolic Forms*, trans. Ralph Manheim (New Haven, CT: Yale University Press, 1953), vol. 1, pp. 105–114; Ernst Cassirer, *The Myth of the State* (New Haven, CT: Yale University Press, 1946); Michael Polanyi, *The Logic of Liberty* (Chicago: University of Chicago Press, 1951), pp. 93–110, 138–153; and Michael Polanyi, *Personal Knowledge: Towards a Post-Critical Philosophy* (Chicago: University of Chicago Press, 1962), pp. 69–131, 203–248, 299–324.

9. I am suggesting that the topic of "falsity" is necessary whenever one's conception of consciousness transcends the mind of a single individual. This is so because the transcendent consciousness, by its very conception, is a legitimizing agency, a means to warrant moral judgments (as in Perelman) or a means to create the fiction of verification when verification is logically impossible (as in Ziman and Brown). To fail to acknowledge the undeniable falsity of *any* description of mass or group consciousness is to create the illusion that one or another series of normative claims have an independent "facticity" about them. In my view, Brown and Ziman are reckless with hypostatized "descriptions" of the consciousness of an intellectual elite, a "scientific community," which itself is in fact a creature of convention, in the specific terms of "description" a fiction of Ziman's and Brown's mind and a rhetorical vision for their readers. See Brown, "Ideology as a Communication Process"; P. Perelman and L. Olbrechts-Tyteca, *The New Rhetoric: A Treatise on Argumentation*, trans. John Wilkinson and Purcell Weaver (South Bend, IN: University of Notre Dame Press, 1969), pp. 31–35, 61–74; J. M. Ziman, *Public Knowledge: An Essay Concerning the Social Dimension of Science* (Cambridge, UK: Cambridge University Press, 1968), pp. 102–142; and contrast George Edward Moore, *Principia Ethica* (Cambridge, UK: Cambridge University Press, 1965), esp. pp. 142–180; and Bruce E. Gronbeck, "From 'Is' to 'Ought': Alternative Strategies," *Central States Speech Journal* 19 (1968): 31–39.

10. See Kenneth Burke, "A Dramatistic View of the Origins of Language and Postscripts on the Negative," in *Language as Symbolic Action* (Berkeley and Los Angeles: University of California Press, 1966), pp. 418–479, esp. pp. 453–463; Hannah Arendt, "What Is Authority?," in *Between Past and Future* (New York: Viking, 1968), pp. 91–141; Hannah Arendt, "Lying in Politics: Reflections on the Pentagon Papers," in *Crises of the Republic* (New York: Harcourt Brace Jovanovich, 1972), pp. 1–47; Jürgen Habermas, "Hannah Arendt's Communications Concept of Power," *Social Research* 44 (1977): 3–24; J. G. A. Pocock, *Politics, Language, and Time* (New York: Atheneum, 1973), pp. 17–25, 202–232; and Robert E. Goodwin, "Laying Linguistic Traps," *Political Theory* 5 (1977): 491–504.

11. See Kenneth Burke, *A Grammar of Motives* (New York: Prentice-Hall, 1945), pp. 43–46, 415–418; Burke, *Rhetoric*, pp. 275–276, 298–301; Ernst Cassirer, *Language and Myth*, trans. Susanne K. Langer (New York: Dover, 1953), pp. 62–83; Richard M. Weaver, *The Ethics of Rhetoric* (Chicago: Gateway, 1970), pp. 211–232; and Rosalind Coward and John Ellis, *Language and Materialism* (London: Routledge & Kegan Paul, 1977), pp. 61–152.

12. José Ortega y Gasset, *Man and People*, trans. Willard R. Trask (New York: Norton, 1957), p. 245.

13. Ibid., pp. 192–221, 258–272.

14. Ibid., p. 221.

15. Ibid., p. 251.

16. Ibid., pp. 176–191.

17. See Murray Edelman, *Political Language* (New York: Academic Press, 1977), pp. 43–49, 141–155; Schwab, *Ideology and Foreign Policy*, pp. 143–157; and Thomas M. Franck and Edward Weisband, *Word Politics: Verbal Strategy Among the Superpowers* (New York: Oxford University Press, 1972), pp. 3–10, 96–113, 137–169.

18. Ortega, *Man and People*, pp. 243–252. Further, contrast Ortega and Marx on the nature of "idea"; see José Ortega y Gasset, *The Modern Theme*, trans. James Cleugh (New York: Harper, 1961), pp. 11–27; and Marx and Engels, *German Ideology*, pp. 27–37. See also Coward and Ellis, *Language and Materialism*, pp. 84–92, 122–135.

19. Ortega, *Man and People*, pp. 57–71, 94–111, 139–191. Husserl's recognition of *praxis* and contradiction in his doctrine of "self-evidence" confirms Ortega's critique; see Edmund Husserl, *Ideas: General Introduction to Pure Phenomenology*, trans. W. R. Boyce Gibson (London: Collier Macmillan, 1962), pp. 353–367. See also Alfred Schutz and Thomas Luckmann's elaboration of the bases of Carneadean skepticism, in their *The Structures of the Life-World*, trans. Richard M. Zaner and H. Tristram Engelhardt Jr. (Evanston, IL: Northwestern University Press, 1973), pp. 182–229.

20. Michel Foucault, *The Archaeology of Knowledge*, trans. A. M. Sheridan Smith (New York: Pantheon, 1972), pp. 178–195; H. T. Wilson, *The American Ideology: Science, Technology, and Organization as Modes of Rationality in Advanced Industrial Societies* (London: Routledge & Kegan Paul, 1977), pp. 231–253; and Roger Poole, *Towards Deep Subjectivity* (New York: Harper & Row, 1972), pp. 78–112.

21. Michael Polanyi and Harry Prosch, *Meaning* (Chicago: University of Chicago Press, 1975), pp. 9, 22: "We have all learned to trace the collapse of freedom in the twentieth century to the writings of certain philosophers, particularly Marx, Nietzsche, and their common ancestors, Fichte and Hegel. But the story has yet to be told how we came to welcome as liberators the philosophies that were to destroy liberty. . . . We in the Anglo-American sphere have so far escaped the totalitarian nightmares of the right and left. But we are far from home safe. For we have done little, in our free intellectual endeavors to uphold thought as an inde-

pendent, self governing force." Contrast this "personal knowledge" explanation with Max Horkheimer and Theodor W. Adorno, *Dialectic of Enlightenment*, trans. John Cumming (New York: Herder and Herder, 1972), pp. 255–256; and Jacques Ellul, *Propaganda: The Formation of Men's Attitudes*, trans. Konrad Kellen and Jean Lerner (New York: Vintage, 1973), pp. 52–61, 232–257.

22. See Peter Rodino's opening remarks in "Debate on Articles of Impeachment," U.S. Congress, House of Representatives, Committee on the Judiciary, 93rd Cong., 2nd sess., 24 July 1974, pp. 1–4. The "vertical/horizontal" metaphor used here to describe the evident structure of ideographs should not be confused with Ellul's idea (*Propaganda*, pp. 79–84) of the structural effects of "propaganda." Lasky's analysis of "the English ideology" represents the "vertical" description I have in mind; see Melvin J. Lasky, *Utopia and Revolution* (Chicago: University of Chicago Press, 1976), pp. 496–575.

23. See Edward H. Levi, *An Introduction to Legal Reasoning* (Chicago: University of Chicago Press, 1948), esp. pp. 6–19, 41–74; Perelman and Tyteca, *The New Rhetoric*, pp. 70–74, 101–102, 350–357; and Duncan, *Symbols in Society*, pp. 110–23, 130–140.

24. Collingwood suggests that the content or ultimate subject matter of history should consist of explaining such recurrent usages ("ideographs") as "freedom" and "progress"; see R. G. Collingwood, *The Idea of History* (London: Oxford University Press, 1972), pp. 302–334. See also Herbert J. Muller, *The Uses of the Past* (New York: Oxford University Press, 1952), pp. 37–38.

25. See William Wirt, *Sketches of the Life and Character of Patrick Henry*, 9th ed. (Philadelphia: Thomas Cowperthwait, 1839), Dedication and pp. 417–443; Judy Hample, "The Textual and Cultural Authenticity of Patrick Henry's 'Liberty or Death' Speech," *Quarterly Journal of Speech* 63 (1977): 298–310; and Robert D. Meade, *Patrick Henry: Portrait in the Making* (New York: Lippincott, 1957), pp. 49–58.

26. At least two strategies (i.e., two theoretical mechanisms) have the capacity to yield fairly precise descriptions of functional "meaning" within situational and textual contexts: see Hans-Georg Gadamer, *Philosophical Hermeneutics*, trans. David E. Linge (Berkeley and Los Angeles: University of California Press, 1976), pp. 59–94; and Umberto Eco, *A Theory of Semiotics* (Bloomington: Indiana University Press, 1976), pp. 48–150, 276–313.

27. Ortega, *Man and People*, p. 247. Cf. Ferdinand de Saussure, *Course in General Linguistics*, trans. Wade Baskin, ed. Charles Bally and Albert Sechehaye in collaboration with Albert Riedlinger (New York: McGraw-Hill, 1966), pp. 140–190, 218–221.

28. See Richard M. Nixon, "Address to the Nation on the Watergate Investigation," in *Public Papers of the Presidents of the United States* (Washington, DC: U.S. Government Printing Office, 1975), Richard Nixon, 1973, pp. 691–698, 710–725. Lucas's analysis of "rhetoric and revolution" (though it is more "idea" than "terministically" conscious) represents the "horizontal" description I have in mind; see Stephen E. Lucas, *Portents of Rebellion: Rhetoric and Revolution in Philadelphia, 1765–76* (Philadelphia: Temple University Press, 1976).

29. See Jürgen Habermas, *Communication and the Evolution of Society*, trans. Thomas McCarthy (Boston: Beacon Press, 1979), pp. 1–68, 130–205.

30. See Foucault, *Archaeology of Knowledge*, pp. 149–165.

31. See Nicholas Abercrombie and Bryan S. Turner, "The Dominant Ideology Thesis," *British Journal of Sociology* 29 (1978): 149–170.

Constitutive Rhetoric

The Case of the *Peuple Québécois*

Maurice Charland

In the *Rhetoric of Motives*, Kenneth Burke proposes "identification" as an alternative to "persuasion" as the key term of the rhetorical process. Burke's project is a rewriting of rhetorical theory that considers rhetoric and motives in formal terms, as consequences of the nature of language and its enactment. Burke's stress on identification permits a rethinking of judgment and the working of the rhetorical effect, for he does not posit a transcendent subject as audience member, who would exist prior to and apart from the speech to be judged, but considers audience members to participate in the very discourse by which they would be "persuaded." Audiences would embody a discourse. A consequence of this theoretical move is that it permits an understanding within rhetorical theory of ideological discourse, of the discourse that presents itself as always only pointing to the given, the natural, the already agreed upon.[1] In particular, it permits us to examine how rhetoric effects what Louis Althusser identifies as the key process in the production of ideology: the constitution of the subject, where the subject is precisely he or she who simultaneously speaks and initiates action in discourse (a subject to a verb) and in the world (a speaker and social agent).[2]

As Burke recognizes, "persuasion," as rhetoric's key term, implies the existence of an agent who is free to be persuaded.[3] However, rhetorical theory's privileging of an audience's freedom to judge is problematic, for it assumes that audiences, with

their prejudices, interests, and motives, are *given* and so extra-rhetorical. Rhetorical criticism, as Grossberg points out, posits the existence of transcendental subjects whom discourse would mediate.[4] In other words, rhetorical theory usually refuses to consider the possibility that the very existence of social subjects (who would become audience members) is already a rhetorical effect. Nevertheless, much of what we as rhetorical critics consider to be a product or consequence of discourse, including social identity, religious faith, sexuality, and ideology is beyond the realm of rational or even free choice, beyond the realm of persuasion. As Burke notes, the identifications of social identity can occur "spontaneously, intuitively, even unconsciously."[5] Such identifications are rhetorical, for they are discursive effects that induce human cooperation. They are also, however, logically prior to persuasion. Indeed, humans are constituted in these characteristics; they are essential to the "nature" of a subject and form the basis for persuasive appeals. Consequently, attempts to elucidate ideological or identity-forming discourses as persuasive are trapped in a contradiction: persuasive discourse requires a subject-as-audience who is already constituted with an identity and within an ideology.

Ultimately then, theories of rhetoric as persuasion cannot account for the audiences that rhetoric addresses. However, such an account is critical to the development of a theoretical understanding of the power of discourse. If it is easier to praise Athens before Athenians than before Laecedemonians, we should ask how those in Athens come to experience themselves as Athenians. Indeed, a rhetoric to Athenians in praise of Athens would be relatively insignificant compared to a rhetoric that constitutes Athenians as such. What I propose to develop in this essay is a theory of constitutive rhetoric that would account for this process. I will elaborate this theory of constitutive rhetoric through an examination of a case where the identity of the audience is clearly problematic: the independence movement in Quebec, Canada's French-speaking province. There, supporters of Quebec's political sovereignty addressed and so attempted to call into being a *peuple québécois* that would legitimate the constitution of a sovereign Quebec state.

Central to my analysis of the constitutive rhetoric of Quebec sovereignty will be Althusser's category of the subject. Examining what Michael McGee would term Quebec's rhetoric of a "people," I will show how claims for Quebec sovereignty base themselves upon the asserted existence of a particular type of subject, the "Québécois." That subject and the collectivized "peuple québécois" are, in Althusser's language, "interpellated" as political subjects through a process of identification in rhetorical narratives that "always already" presume the constitution of subjects. From this perspective, a subject is not "persuaded" to support sovereignty. Support for sovereignty is inherent to the subject position addressed by *souverainiste* (pro-sovereignty) rhetoric because of what we will see to be a series of narrative *ideological effects*.

The Quest for Quebec Sovereignty

In 1967, the year of Canada's centennial, a new political association was formed in Quebec. This organization, the *Mouvement Souveraineté-Association* (MSA), dedicated itself to Quebec's political sovereignty as it proclaimed the existence of an essence uniting social actors in the province. In French, Quebec's majority language, the MSA declared: "Nous sommes des Québécois" ("We are *Québécois*") and called for Quebec's independence from Canada.[6] This declaration marked the entry of the term "Québécois" into the mainstream of Quebec political discourse. Until that time, members of the French-speaking society of Quebec were usually termed "Canadiens français" ("French-Canadians"). With the MSA, a national

identity for a new type of political subject was born, a subject whose existence would be presented as justification for the constitution of a new state. Thus, the MSA's declaration is an instance of constitutive rhetoric, for it calls its audience into being. Furthermore, as an instance of constitutive rhetoric, it was particularly effective, for within a decade of the creation of that *mouvement*, the term "Québécois" had gained currency even among certain supporters of the Canadian federal system, and Quebec voters had brought the MSA's successor, the *Parti Québécois* (PQ), to power.

Quebec voters gave the *Parti Québécois* control of the Quebec government on November 15, 1976. The party obtained 41.4% of the popular vote and won 71 of 110 seats in the *Assemblé nationale*, Quebec's legislature.[7] This election marked a major transformation in Canada's political life, for the PQ asserted that those in Quebec constituted a distinct *peuple* with the right and duty to political sovereignty, and was committed to leading Quebec, Canada's largest and second most populous province, out of Canada.

The PQ's major campaign promise was to hold a referendum on Quebec's political sovereignty during its first term of office. In preparation of this plebiscite, the Quebec government issued, on November 1, 1979, a formal policy statement, a "white paper," that outlined a proposed new political order in which Quebec would be a sovereign state associated economically with Canada.[8] While the Quebec–Canada economic association would include free trade, a customs union, a shared currency and central bank as negotiated, and the free movement of persons across the Quebec–Canada border, each government would have the full sovereignty of a nation-state.[9] The White Paper asserted that those in Quebec constituted a *peuple* and called upon them to support this project by voting OUI in a forthcoming referendum. Such a positive vote by the Quebec electorate would mandate their provincial government to negotiate for the envisioned new constitutional status with the federal government in Ottawa.[10]

The White Paper, as it articulated the reasons for Quebec's political independence, was a rhetorical document. It offered a variety of arguments demonstrating that *Québécois* were an oppressed *peuple* within the confines of Canada's constitution who would be better off with their own country. These arguments were presented in the context of the constitutive rhetoric of the "peuple québécois." This constitutive rhetoric took the form of a narrative account of Quebec history in which *Québécois* were identified with their fore-bears who explored New France, who suffered under the British conquest, and who struggled to erect the Quebec provincial state apparatus.

The Referendum on sovereignty-association was held May 20, 1980. Although a majority of the populace voted against the measure, over 45% of the French-speaking population assented to their provincial government's interpretation of Quebec society.[11] Those voting OUI granted the legiti-macy of the constitutional claims the White Paper asserted. Clearly, even if a majority of *Québécois* were not ready to seek sovereignty, a *malaise* pow-erful enough to dominate political debate and gov-ernment priorities existed in the province. There was a strong sense in which "Québécois" was a term antithetical to "Canadien."

The election of the *Parti Québécois* and the strength of its *souverainiste* option in the Refer-endum reveals the significance of the constitu-tive rhetoric of a "peuple québécois." While some might consider the White Paper to be a rhetorical failure because less than half of Quebec's French-speaking population opted for independence, the outcome of the Referendum reveals that its constitutive rhetoric was particularly powerful. This rhetoric, which presents those in Quebec as *Québécois* requiring and deserving their own state, constituted at least close to half of Quebec vot-ers such that they, as an audience, were not *really* Canadians.

What the debate in Quebec reveals is that the very character of a collective identity, and the nature of its boundary, of who is a member of the collectivity, were problematic. In other words, in Quebec there existed a struggle over the consti-tution of political subjects. In Quebec, the pos-sibility of an alternative *peuple* and history was entertained. Thus, the movement for sovereignty permits us to see how peoples are rhetorically con-stituted.

"Peuple" as Legitimating Principle

As Michael McGee has noted, the term "people" can rhetorically legitimate constitutions.[12] Not surprisingly then, the independence debate in Quebec, as it developed since the formation of the MSA, centered upon whether *a peuple québé-cois* exists, and more importantly, on whether that *peuple* is the kind of "people" that legitimates a sovereign state. In Quebec, competing claims were

made as to the nature of the *peuple*. Consider, for example, Claude Morin's polemical history of Quebec–Ottawa constitutional disputes from 1960 to 1972, where he distinguishes the emergent Quebec collectivity from its predecessor, French-Canada, as he identifies the perspective of the Quebec government: "Like many other peoples, Quebeckers have experienced an awakening of self-consciousness. They want to assert themselves, not as French-speaking Canadians, but as Québé-cois, citizens who, for the moment, suffer the want of a country that is their own."[13] In Morin's view, not only are those in Quebec *Québécois*, but they constitute the kind of *peuple* that warrants a sov-ereign state. Morin's observation confirms that populations can at different historical moments gain different identities that warrant different forms of collective life. Furthermore, if we consider that Morin's observation is contentious and par-tisan,[14] and that many in Quebec would contest his assessment of their collective identity, we find confirmation of McGee's further assertion that the identity of a "people," as a rhetorical construct, is not even agreed upon by those who would address it.[15] Rather, supporters and opponents of Quebec sovereignty both seek to justify their position on the basis of what they assert is a will intrinsic to their version of the *peuple's* very being. Their rhet-oric is grounded in the constitution of *Québécois* as political subjects.

The debate over sovereignty in Quebec clearly reveals the degree to which peoples are consti-tuted in discourse. Those in Quebec could be "Québécois"; they could also be "Canadiens fran-çais." The distinction is crucial, for only the former type of "people" can claim the right to a sovereign state. Indeed, the debate in Quebec permits us to see the radical implication of McGee's argu-ment, for not only is the character or identity of the "people" open to rhetorical revision, but the very *boundary* of whom the term "people" includes and excludes is rhetorically constructed: as the "peuple" is variously characterized, the persons who make up the "peuple" can change. Thus, consider the rather extreme counter-argument to Morin's claim that a *peuple québécois* exists and is gaining self-awareness, as articulated by William Shaw and Lionel Albert, two Quebec opponents of sovereignty, who conversely assert that no Que-bec *peuple* exists, that the term "Québécois" prop-erly only applies to residents of the City of Quebec, and that the term as used by Quebec nationalists constitutes a "semantic fraud":

Separatists measure the degree of their penetration of the public consciousness by the extent to which the people are willing to call themselves *Québécois*. The more they can persuade the French Canadians in Quebec to call themselves *Québécois*, the easier the task of insinuating the idea that those French Canadians who happen to live in eastern or northern Ontario or in northern New Brunswick are somehow "different" from those living in Quebec. Once that idea has been established, then the idea that Quebec's borders, which are criss-crossed daily by tens of thousands of French Canadians, could somehow be thought of, not as casual signposts along the highway, but as a full-fledged international boundary, can also be established.[16]

Shaw and Albert display a keen sensitivity to the workings of the *péquiste* rhetoric of collective identity, even if as advocates, these opponents of Quebec independence assert that a French-Canadian *peuple* "really" exists outside of rhetorical construction. What Shaw and Albert ignore, of course, is that the French-speaking *peuple* or nation that they assert exists also becomes real only through rhetoric. Indeed, the possibility of political action requires that political actors be within a "fictive" discourse. More precisely, as Althusser asserts: "there is no practice except by and in an ideology."[17] Political identity must be an ideological fiction, even though, as McGee correctly notes, this fiction becomes historically material and of consequence as persons live it.

The Rhetoric of Interpellation

As we have seen, rhetorical claims for a sovereign Quebec are predicated upon the existence of an ideological subject, the "Québécois," so constituted that sovereignty is a natural and necessary way of life. Furthermore, and hardly surprisingly, the ultimate justification for these claims is the subject's character, nature, or essence. This is so because this identity defines inherent motives and interests that a rhetoric can appeal to. The ideological "trick" of such a rhetoric is that it presents that which is most rhetorical, the existence of a *peuple*, or of a subject, as extrarhetorical. These members of the *peuple* whose supposed essence demands action do not exist in nature, but only within a discursively constituted history. Thus, this rhetoric paradoxically must constitute the identity "Québécois" as it simultaneously presumes it to be

pregiven and natural, existing outside of rhetoric and forming the basis for a rhetorical address.

We find a treatment of this constitutive phenomenon in Edwin Black's discussion of the "second persona."[18] As Michael McGuire observes, Black's process of transforming an audience occurs through *identification*, in Burke's sense.[19] However, to simply accept such an account of this process would be inadequate. It would not fully explain the significance of becoming one with a persona, of entering into and embodying it. In particular, to simply state that audiences identify with a persona explains neither (1) the ontological status of those in the audience before their identification, nor (2) the ontological status of the persona, and the nature of identifying with it. In order to clarify these ontological issues, we must consider carefully the radical edge of Burke's identificatory principle. Burke asserts that, as "symbol using" animals, our being is significantly constituted in our symbolicity. As Burke puts it, "so much of the 'we' that is separated from the nonverbal by the verbal would not even exist were it not for the verbal (or for our symbolicity in general[)]."[20] In this, Burke moves towards collapsing the distinction between the realm of the symbolic and that of human conceptual consciousness. From such a perspective, we cannot accept the 'givenness' of "audience," "person," or "subject," but must consider their very textuality, their very constitution in rhetoric as a structured articulation of signs. We must, in other words, consider the textual nature of social being.

The symbolically based critique of humanist ontology implicit in Burke has been developed in a tradition sharing much with him, that of structuralism.[21] Structuralist semiotics and narrative theory have deconstructed the concept of the unitary and transcendent subject. And, with rhetorical theory, they share an appreciation of the power of discourse, of its effects. Thus, in order to develop the radical implications of Burke's lead, it is to this tradition that I will turn.

Althusser describes the process of inscribing subjects into ideology as "interpellation":[22]

I shall then suggest that ideology "acts" or "functions" in such a way that it "recruits" subjects among the individuals (it recruits them all), or "transforms" the individuals into subjects (it transforms them all) by that very precise operation which I have called *interpellation* or hailing, and which can be imagined along the lines of the most commonplace everyday police (or other) hailing: "Hey, you there!"[23]

Interpellation occurs at the very moment one enters into a rhetorical situation, that is, as soon as an individual recognizes and acknowledges being addressed. An interpellated subject participates in the discourse that addresses him. Thus, to be interpellated is to become one of Black's personae and be a position in a discourse. In consequence, interpellation has a significance to rhetoric, for the acknowledgment of an address entails an acceptance of an imputed self-understanding which can form the basis for an appeal. Furthermore, interpellation occurs rhetorically, through the effect of the addressed discourse. Note, however, that interpellation does not occur through persuasion in the usual sense, for the very act of *addressing* is rhetorical. It is logically prior to the rhetorical *narratio*. In addition, this rhetoric of identification is ongoing, not restricted to one hailing, but usually part of a rhetoric of socialization. Thus, one must already be an interpellated subject and exist as a discursive position in order to be part of the audience of a rhetorical situation in which persuasion could occur.

The "Peuple" as Narrative Ideological Effect

Events in Quebec demonstrate that the "peuple" is a persona, existing in rhetoric, and not in some neutral history devoid of human interpretation. But note, personae are not persons; they remain in the realm of words. As McGee observes, a "people" is a fiction which comes to be when individuals accept living within a political myth.[24] This myth would be ontological, constitutive of those "seduced" by it. In Quebec, what McGee terms the myth of the "people" is articulated in the Quebec government's White Paper. This document, speaking in the name of the independence movement, as institutionalized in a party and a government, offers a narrative of Quebec history that renders demands for sovereignty intelligible and reasonable.

The White Paper's narrative of the *peuple* since the founding of New France, through the British Conquest, the development of Canada into a federated state, and the setting up of the Referendum on Quebec sovereignty is, in McGee's sense, a myth. It paradoxically both reveals the *peuple* and makes it real. This making real is part of the ontological function of narratives. Indeed, as Jameson points out, "history . . . is inaccessible to us except

in textual form, and . . . our approach to it and the Real itself necessarily passes through its prior textualization, its narrativization in the political unconscious."[25] Because the *peuple* exists as a subject in history, it is only intelligible within a narrative representation of history. In other words, this *peuple*, and the individual subject, the *Québécois*, exist as positions in a text.

Narratives "make real" coherent subjects. They constitute subjects as they present a particular textual position, such as the noun-term "peuple québécois" as the locus for action and experience. Roland Barthes well expresses this ultimate textuality of narratives when he asserts that: "Narrative does not show, does not imitate; the passion which may excite us . . . is not that of a 'vision' (in actual fact, we do not 'see' anything)."[26] In other words, narratives work through a representational *effect*. Texts are but surfaces; characters are, in a sense, but "paper beings," to use Barthes' phrase. These paper beings *seem* real through textual operations. The distinct acts and events in a narrative become linked through identification arising from the narrative form. Narratives lead us to construct and fill in coherent unified subjects out of temporally and spatially separate events. This renders the site of action and experience stable. The locus of yesterday's acts becomes that of today's. Consequently, narratives offer a world in which human agency is possible and acts can be meaningful.

All narratives, as they create the illusion of merely revealing a unified and unproblematic subjectivity, are ideological, because they occult the importance of discourse, culture, and history in giving rise to subjectivity, and because, as G. H. Mead and Freud have made clear, subjectivity is always social, constituted in language, and exists in a delicate balance of contradictory drives and impulses. Narratives suppress the fact that, in a very real sense, no person is the same as he or she was a decade ago, or last year, or indeed yesterday. In raising the ultimate "falsity" of narratives, my intention is not, however, to decry them and hold out for some unmediated consciousness. Nor am I here concerned with a philosophical critique of the subject in Western civilization. My intention is to show the degree to which collective identities forming the basis of rhetorical appeals themselves depend upon rhetoric; the "peuple québécois," and "peoples" in general, exist only through an ideological discourse that constitutes them. Furthermore, if the subject in all narratives is ideological, a "peuple" is triply so, for it does not even have a unitary body corresponding to its imputed unitary agency and consciousness. The persona or subject "peuple québécois" exists only as a series of narrative ideological effects.

In the rhetoric of Quebec sovereignty, the "Québécois" is a collective subject. It offers, in Burke's language, an "ultimate" identification permitting an overcoming or going beyond of divisive individual or class interests and concerns.[27] This identity transcends the limitations of the individual body and will. This process of constituting a collective subject is *the first ideological effect* of constitutive rhetoric. If a *peuple* exists, it is only in ideology, as McGee makes clear. That ideology arises in the very nature of narrative history. To tell the story of the *Québécois* is implicitly to assert the existence of a collective subject, the protagonist of the historical drama, who experiences, suffers, and acts. Such a narrative renders the world of events understandable with respect to a transcendental collective interest that negates individual interest. Consider the following passage from the White Paper's account of early French North America:

> Our ancestors put down their roots in American soil at the beginning of the 17th century, at the time the first English settlers were landing on the East coast of the United States. As they were clearing the land of the St. Lawrence valley, they explored the vast continent in all directions, from the Atlantic to the Rocky Mountains, and from Hudson Bay to the Gulf of Mexico. Through discovering, claiming, and occupying the land, *Québécois* came to consider themselves North-Americans.
>
> In 1760, our community was already an established society along the St. Lawrence. North American by geography, French by language, culture, and politics, this society had a soul, a way of life, traditions, that were its very own. Its struggles, its successes, and its ordeals had given it an awareness of its collective destiny, and it was with some impatience that it tolerated the colonial tie.[28]

In a radically empiricist mood, I could assert that a society *qua* society has no soul, no struggles, no successes. Clearly, history proceeds by the acts of individuals. But, of course, individuals can act in concert or as a mass, they can respond to apersonal historical forces, and we can interpret the sum total of their individual actions with respect to a collective agent. Historical narratives offer such interpretations. In the telling of the story of a *peuple*, a *peuple* comes to be. It is within the

formal structure of a narrative history that it is possible to conceive of a set of individuals as if they were but one. Thus, the "struggles" and "ordeals" of settlers, as a set of individual acts and experiences, become identified with "community," a term that here masks or negates tensions and differences between members of any society. The community of *Québécois* is the master agent of a narratized history.

In the above passage, note also how the past is presented as an extension of the present through the use of the pronoun "our" and the term "Québécois" as signifiers of both eighteenth century settlers who termed themselves "Canadiens" and those living in Quebec today. The White Paper, and histories of peoples in general, offer a "consubstantiality," to use Burke's expression, between the dead and the living. This positing of a transhistorical subject is the *second ideological effect* of constitutive rhetoric. Here, ancestry is offered as the concrete link between the French settlers of North America, those in Quebec today, and a collectivity. Time is collapsed as narrative identification occurs: today's Quebec residents constitute a *peuple* and have a right to their own state because members of their community have discovered, claimed, and occupied the land. This interpretive stance is perfectly reasonable. It is also perfectly tautological, for it is a making sense that depends upon the a priori acceptance of that which it attempts to prove the existence of, a collective agent, the *peuple québécois*, that transcends the limitations of individuality at any historical moment and transcends the death of individuals across history.

Form renders the "Québécois" a real subject within the historical narrative. The "Québécois" does not, however, become a free subject. Subjects within narratives are not free, they are *positioned* and so constrained. All narratives have power over the subjects they present. The endings of narratives are fixed before the telling. The freedom of the character in a narrative is an illusion, for narratives move inexorably toward their *telos*. The characters in a story are obviously not free. Only in Woody Allen's *The Purple Rose of Cairo* can characters abandon their script and walk off the screen. What Allen's film and Barthes' analysis of narratives so clearly illustrate is that narratives are but texts that offer the illusion of agency. The subject is constituted at the nodes of a narrative's surface. What Walter Fisher terms "narrative probability" is a formal and ideological constraint upon the subject's possibilities of being.[29] To be constituted as a subject in a narrative is to be constituted with a history, motives, and a *telos*. Thus, in the rhetoric of Quebec sovereignty, "Québécois" is not merely a descriptive term, but identifies and positions the Quebec voter with respect to his or her future.

The White Paper presents *Québécois* as agents, capable of acting freely in the world. However, the narrative's existence as a text is predicated upon *Québécois* asserting their existence as a collective subject through a politics of independence. In the White Paper on sovereignty, *Québécois* are constituted in the choice of national solidarity. As Burke observes is the case in ideological narratives, the White Paper effects an identification of the temporal sequence of its plot with the logical development of an ultimate principle.[30] In the resultant hierarchy, *Québécois* are free to choose only one course of action:

THE WILL TO SURVIVE

Sooner or later, this society would have shaken off the colonial yoke and acquired its independence, as was the case, in 1776, for the United States of America. But in 1763 the hazards of war placed it under British control. . . . Faced with this defeat, francophones spontaneously chose to be faithful. There could be no question of passing over to the winner's camp to reap the benefits that awaited them. They would adapt to the new situation, come to terms with the new masters, but above all preserve the essential of that which characterized our *peuple*: its language, its customs, its religion. At all costs, they would survive.[31]

The freedom of the protagonist of this narrative is but an illusion. This illusion of freedom is the *third ideological effect* of constitutive rhetoric. Freedom is illusory because the narrative is already spoken or written. Furthermore, because the narrative is a structure of understanding that produces totalizing interpretations,[32] the subject is constrained to *follow through*, to act so as to maintain the narrative's consistency. A narrative, once written, offers a logic of meaningful totality. *Québécois*, precisely because they are the subjects within a text, within a narrative rhetoric, must follow the logic of the narrative. They must be true to the motives through which the narrative constitutes them, and thus which presents characters as freely acting towards a predetermined and fixed ending.

The Effective Power of Constitutive Rhetoric

The ideological effects of constitutive rhetoric that I have outlined are not merely formal effects inscribed within the bracketed experience of interpreting a text. In other words, these do not only permit a disinterested understanding of a fictive world. What is significant in constitutive rhetoric is that it positions the reader towards political, social, and economic action in the material world and it is in this positioning that its ideological character becomes significant. For the purpose of analysis, this positioning of subjects as historical actors can be understood as a two-step process. First, audience members must be successfully interpellated; not all constitutive rhetorics succeed. Second, the tautological logic of constitutive rhetoric must necessitate action in the material world; constitutive rhetoric must require that its embodied subjects act freely in the social world to affirm their subject position.

Audiences are, to use Althusser's famous phrase, "always already" subjects. This is to say that if we disregard the point at which a child enters language, but restrict ourselves to "competent" speakers within a culture, we can observe that one cannot exist but as a subject within a narrative. The necessity is ontological: one must already be a subject in order to be addressed or to speak. We therefore cannot say that one is persuaded to be a subject; one is "always already" a subject. This does not imply, however, that one's subject position is fixed at the moment one enters language. Indeed, the development of new subject positions, of new constitutive rhetorics, is possible at particular historical moments. The subject is a position within a text. To be an embodied subject is to experience and act in a textualized world. However, this world is not seamless and a subject position's world view can be laced with contradictions. We can, as Burke puts it, encounter "recalcitrance."[33] In addition, as Stuart Hall observes, various contradictory subject positions can simultaneously exist within a culture:[34] we can live within many texts. These contradictions place a strain upon identification with a given subject position and render possible a subject's rearticulation. Successful new constitutive rhetorics offer new subject positions that resolve, or at least contain, experienced contradictions. They serve to overcome or define away the recalcitrance the world presents by providing the subject with new perspectives and motives.

Thus, for example, the subject position "Québécois" arises from a rearticulation of two positions, that of "Canadien français," and that of the Quebec resident and voter with a collective will ostensibly represented by the Quebec government. Because some French-Canadians live outside of Quebec and not all those in Quebec are French-speaking, the identity "Canadien français" cannot permit the articulation of a French-speaking nation-state in North America. As the White Paper never fails to remind its audience, to be "Canadien français" is to be a member of an impotent minority without a proper homeland. The White Paper, penned by the Quebec government, invokes the contradiction of being a member of a French-speaking collectivity, or *nation,* that does not have a sovereign state apparatus, for the Quebec government remains subject to Canada's Federal government in Ottawa, and French-Canadians are subjects of the Federal state, a state that can be represented as ultimately foreign.

French-Canadians in Quebec had to live the contradiction of not being exclusively subjects of the state they collectively controlled. "Québécois" resolves this contradiction at the discursive level, by identifying the populace with a territory and a francophone state, rather than with an ethnic group. Constitutive rhetorics of new subject positions can be understood, therefore, as working upon previous discourses, upon previous constitutive rhetorics. They capture alienated subjects by rearticulating existing subject positions so as to contain or resolve experienced dialectical contradictions between the world and its discourses. The process by which an audience member enters into a new subject position is therefore not one of persuasion. It is akin more to one of conversion that ultimately results in an act of recognition of the 'rightness' of a discourse and of one's identity with its reconfigured subject position.

The White Paper's constitutive rhetoric, as it articulates the meaning of being "Québécois," is not a mere fiction. It inscribes real social actors within its textualized structure of motives, and then inserts them into the world of practice. The White Paper offers a collectivized subject position that constitutes those in Quebec as members of a *peuple* which is transcendent of the limits of their biological individuality. This position thus opens the possibility for them to participate in a collective political project. The White Paper's narrative is characterized by a set of formal ideological effects that permit it to be intelligible as one

accepts and enters into the collective consciousness it articulates. The White Paper offers, therefore, a particular instance of narrative rhetoric that, in Fisher's language, "give[s] order to human experience and . . . induce[s] others to *dwell in [it]* to establish ways of living in common, in communion in which there is sanction for the story that constitutes one's life" (italics added).[35] This dwelling place is, of course, prerequisite to the power of the rhetoric of Quebec sovereignty. To be *Québécois* as configured by the White Paper is to embody in the world the narrative and the motives it ascribes to members of the *peuple.*

To enter into the White Paper's rhetorical narrative is to identify with Black's second persona. It is the process of recognizing oneself as the subject in a text. It is to exist at the nodal point of a series of identifications and to be captured in its structure and in its production of meaning. It is to be a subject which exists beyond one's body and life span. It is to have and experience the dangerous memories of British conquest and rule. It is to live towards national independence. Then, the power of the text is the power of an embodied ideology. The form of an ideological rhetoric is effective because it is within the bodies of those it constitutes as subjects. These subjects owe their existence to the discourse that articulates them. As Burke puts it: "An 'ideology' is like a god coming down to earth, where it will inhabit a place pervaded by its presence. An 'ideology' is like a spirit taking up its abode in a body: it makes that body hop around in certain ways; and that same body would have hopped around in different ways had a different ideology happened to inhabit it."[36] Thus, from the subjectivity or point of view of the embodied *souverainiste* discourse, not only would there exist "good reasons" for supporting sovereignty, but good *motives* as well, motives arising from the very essence of the *Québécois'* being. Within the White Paper's account is embedded a "logic," a way of understanding the world, that offers those in Quebec a position from which to understand and act.

Identification with a Constitutive Rhetoric

If the White Paper and historical narratives were but dead history, mere stories, their significance to ideology could easily be dismissed. However, constitutive rhetorics, as they identify, have power because they are oriented towards action. As Althusser and McGee both stress, ideology is material, existing not in the realm of ideas, but in that of *material practices*. Ideology is material because subjects enact their ideology and reconstitute their material world in its image.[37] Constitutive rhetorics are ideological not merely because they provide individuals with narratives to inhabit as subjects and motives to experience, but because they insert "narratized" subjects-as-agents into the world.

The insertion of subjects into the world is a product of both the identificatory and referential functions of the White Paper's historical narrative and its ideological effects. In particular, it is the third ideological effect, the constitution in action of a motivated subject, that orients those addressed towards particular future acts. Since narratives offer totalizing interpretations that ascribe transcendent meanings to individual acts, the maintenance of narrative consistency demands that a certain set of acts be chosen. This is amplified in the White Paper because it offers a narrative without closure. The White Paper offers an unfinished history: the *peuple québécois* has yet to obtain its independence. Thus, the *Québécois* addressed by the White Paper must bring to a close the saga begun by the subjects of the White Paper's history. In other words, while classical narratives have an ending, constitutive rhetorics leave the task of narrative closure to their constituted subjects. It is up to the *Québécois* of 1980 to conclude the story to which they are identified. The story the White Paper offers is of a besieged *peuple* that has always continued to struggle in order to survive and to assert its right to self-determination. Nevertheless, in this account, each advance is blocked by the colonial power. The story proceeds through the recounting of a series of episodes, each exhibiting the same pattern.

As we have already seen, the White Paper asserts that the new *peuple's* aspirations were blocked by British conquest. This act of conquest recurs in other guises at other moments in the *peuple's* saga. Thus, in the rhetoric of Quebec sovereignty, for example, the victims of the conquest of 1760 become the protagonists in the parliamentary wrangles of 1837. Individual subjects, the *Québécois*, and their collective subject, the *peuple*, are somehow the same, even though the actual personages, institutions, material conditions, and struggles have changed. *Québécois* as explorers become political subjects. Thus, the White Paper asserts:

The Parliament of Lower Canada, where the language was French, proposed laws and a budget that were submitted for approval to the Governor, who exercised executive power on behalf of London. The *peuple's* will was often blocked by the veto of the Governor, particularly sensitive to the interests of the English minority of Lower Canada and those of the imperial power. The consequent tension was leading, by 1830, to exasperation. The representatives drew up a set of resolutions in which they expressed their demands: control by the Assembly of taxes and spending, and the adoption of urgent social and economic measures. The Governor refused and dissolved the House. In the elections that followed, the *Patriotes*, headed by Papineau, won 77 out of 88 seats with 90% of the vote. To the same demands, the Governor responded by dissolving the House once again.[38]

The rhetorical significance of this passage is twofold. First, it typifies the text's constitution of a subject subjugated by Britain. Note how it confronts victory with power. In doing so, it highlights what can be presented as an inherent contradiction of "French-Canadian" as a subject position that interpellates French-Canadians both as French ethnic subjects and Canadian political subjects. Second, this passage, again typically, rearticulates this subject position: it articulates "Québécois" as a *political* subject battling on the terrain of parliament. In doing so, it dissolves any possible contradiction between loyalty to an (ethnic) nation and the federal state and it articulates both a site for and an object of struggle: the Quebec state apparatus and its legitimated institutions.

The White Paper offers a narrative characterized by a ideological movement towards emancipation. If the root cause of the struggle of the *peuple* is the natural impossibility of the *peuple* to exist without self-determination, control of the state machinery becomes the point of resolution of a drama that began while *Québécois* were still under the rule of the French king. The narrative offers sovereignty as the ultimate point that must be reached in order to attain narrative closure and liberate its subjects. The White Paper offers no alternative but for *Québécois* to struggle against annihilation. To offer but one example among many, the recounting of the 1837 uprising by a nationalist party known as the *Patriotes* and their speedy defeat makes clear that *Québécois* are constituted in a struggle for life itself, a struggle, furthermore, that cannot be won militarily:

After their lone victory at Saint-Denis, the *Patriotes* were crushed at Saint-Charles and Saint-

Eustache. The repression was cruel: hundreds of *Patriotes* were imprisoned and twelve were hanged; here and there, farms were ablaze.[39]

Within the context of contemporary attempts to secure Quebec's independence, the White Paper offers a condensed historical narrative of the *peuple québécois* as teleologically moving towards emancipation. The historical account of the White Paper is decidedly presentist and rhetorical, for a society of the seventeenth century is identified with a society today: the seventeenth century colonists who termed themselves "Canadiens" are termed "Québécois"; past struggles are presented as warranting action in the present. The particular issues over which nineteenth century parliamentarians battled are rendered in ideological terms that are then applied to current battles between Quebec and Canada's Federal government. Each episode in the history moves the *peuple* as subject towards the Quebec Referendum on sovereignty-association. The narrative form provides a continuity across time in which the practices of the past are increasingly identified with the present day order. Thus, the British Conquest, parliamentary wrangles, and the rebellions of 1837, find their counterpart in the "imposition" of a Canadian constitution:

> At the constitutional conferences of 1864 and 1866, the Quebec delegates and those of the other provinces were pursuing very different goals. Upper Canada in particular wanted a supraprovincial parliament, endowed with as many and as important powers as possible, that would have presided over the fates of the new country; Quebec, on the other hand, wanted to grant itself a responsible government, enjoying a large degree of autonomy, that would guarantee once and for all the existence and progress of the Quebec *peuple*— and that would have been its *real* government. The opposition between a centralized federalism and a decentralized confederation was already making itself felt. The first idea finally won out. Granted, *Québécois* acquired an autonomous responsible government, but with its autonomy limited to jurisdictions seen then as being primarily of local interest.[40]

The *peuple québécois* is presented as preceding the Canadian state. Confederation, like the Conquest, the defeat of the *Patriotes*, and the unification in 1849 of the predominantly English-speaking colony of Upper Canada with the predominantly French-speaking colony of Lower Canada disrupted the movement of the *peuple* towards the "natural" ideal of its own constitution,

responsible government, and a state. The implicit presumption that political structures should provide a means for the articulation and execution of a *peuple's* aspirations, as connoted by the term "peuple" itself, is set in opposition to this account of Canada's formation. The government in Ottawa is not a *real* government. Ottawa's power is represented as illegitimate. The *Quebec peuple* is frustrated, denied progress and its very existence. This narrative's movement towards closure is frustrated by the English presence. The emancipation of the *peuple* is blocked by the pattern of conquest and resistance *(narratio interrupta)*. The conquerors stand against narrative teleology as well as history's grand laws.

In the rhetoric of Quebec sovereignty then, the Government of Canada does not arise from the Quebec *peuple* and hence disrupts the teleological flow of history that the narrative form provides. Canada is an antagonist in this life-drama of a *peuple*. As such, Canada must be overcome so that the tensions in the mythic narrative and in history can be resolved. The "natural" principle that *peuples* attain control of their future is denied because Ottawa will preside over destiny. Within the context of the repression of the *Patriotes*, this new order does not arise from the *peuple québécois* but from external constraints. Confederation is but another manifestation of the Conquest to which, in this account, the *peuple* never assented: *Québécois* never acquiesce, but always struggle within the constraints of the possible. The change heralded by Confederation was but a small gain within the British system. Confederation is not the end of the struggle, only a new battleground. On this terrain, the *peuple* is threatened by a political reality that denies its very being.

The White Paper, having constituted *Québécois* in a struggle for survival, moves them and the narrative into the present. The current constitution that the independence movement opposes is represented as forming the basis for the continued subjugation of the *peuple*:

> The institution of the Canadian federal regime thus sanctioned, and favored as well, the hegemony of a Canada become English. It is quite natural that in such a regime the interests and aspirations of *Québécois* and Francophones in other provinces should take second place. In 1885, for example, all Quebec took the side of Louis Riel, who was fighting for the survival of francophone communities in the West. On the other hand, the federal government fought him and Louis Riel died on the scaffold.[41]

Any possibility that Confederation was advantageous for Quebec is denied. The will of the *peuple*, as instantiated in historical practice, is shown to be undermined in the federal regime. The White Paper describes various defeats of the will of the *peuple* in Confederation: Louis Riel fought for "survival" and climbed the scaffold; rights to French language education outside Quebec were denied; *Québécois* were forced to participate in British wars.[42] The accounts form a tragic tale; the francophones in Canada including the *peuple québécois* are without control of their circumstances.

The narrative concludes by identifying a threat to its very existence as a narrative. Canadian Confederation would deny that Québécois exist and so would deny the very possibility of this constitutive rhetoric and so of an audience inhabiting it. As the White Paper puts it: "The very balance of the system, as the Canadian majority wants it, requires that Quebec remain a province—or perhaps a territory—among ten others, and forbids the formal and concrete recognition of a Quebec nation."[43] This version of Quebec would require a revision of the meaning of "Québécois" such that it no longer positioned its subjects as members of both a nation and state. The "Québécois" would be but the Quebec resident, who might also be a French-Canadian defined in ethnic terms. Thus, in its concluding summary exhorting *Québécois* to vote OUI in the Referendum on sovereignty-association, the White Paper characterizes a NON vote as constituting:

> Only a brutal ending to the healthiest form of progress, one that leads an entire *peuple*, as naturally as an individual, to its maturity. We would simply fall back into line, remain in the state of oblivion kindly granted us by those outsiders who have been keeping a close eye on our progress. . . .
>
> On the contrary, we believe that we are mature enough, and big enough, and strong enough, to come to terms with our destiny. Because that is what is true.[44]

To be constituted as a *Québécois* in the terms of this narrative is to be constituted such that sovereignty is not only possible, but necessary. Without sovereignty, this constitutive rhetoric would ultimately die and those it has constituted would cease to be subjects, or at least would remain, like children, partial and stunted subjects, lacking maturity, responsibility, and autonomy. In consequence, true *Québécois* could not vote NON. Only a OUI vote would be in harmony with their being

and their collective destiny: "Indeed, the choice should be easy, for the heart as well as the mind. We need only give a little thought to how faithful we have been in the past and how strong we are at present; we must think also of those who will follow us, whose futures depend so utterly on that moment."[45]

In sum, the White Paper calls on those it has addressed to follow narrative consistency and the motives through which they are constituted as audience members. Its rhetorical effect derives from their interpellation as subjects and on their identification with a transhistorical and transindividual subject position. It is in this sense of textualizing audiences, therefore, that we can understand the process Black treats in his discussion of the second persona and McGee discusses in his study of the "people." From this perspective, we can see that audiences do not exist outside rhetoric, merely addressed by it, but live inside rhetoric. Indeed, from the moment they enter into the world of language, they are subjects; the very moment of recognition of an address constitutes an entry into a subject position to which inheres a set of motives that render a rhetorical discourse intelligible. These subject positions are bequeathed by the past, by yesterday's discourses. Furthermore, the contradictions between discourses as well as the dialectic between discourse and a changing concrete world open a space for new subject positions. Tensions in the realm of the symbolic render possible the rhetorical repositioning or rearticulation of subjects.

Conclusion

Early in this essay, I identified two problems deserving examination: the first regarding the ontological status of those addressed by discourse before their successful interpellation; the second regarding the ontological status of the persona and the process by which one is identified with it. I have treated the latter problem by introducing the concept of the subject and by showing that audiences are constituted as subjects through a process of identification with a textual position. This identification occurs through a series of ideological effects arising from the narrative structure of constitutive rhetoric. As for the first problem I posed, I have in a sense circumvented it through my analysis. Persons are subjects from the moment they acquire language and the capacity to speak and to be spoken to. As such, constitutive rhetoric is part of the discursive background of social life. It is always there, usually implicitly, and sometimes explicitly articulated. It is more than a set of commonplaces, but is the con-text, the pre-rhetoric that is necessary to any successful interpellation.

Our first subject positions are modest, linked to our name, our family, and our sex. As we enter the adult world, they become more complex, as different constitutive rhetorics reposition us with respect to such formal and informal institutions as the state, the economy, the church, and the school. Thus, though we are subjects through language, and indeed can only speak as subjects, our subjectivity and ideological commitments are not fixed at our first utterance. As Quebec public address illustrates, particular subject positions can undergo transformation: "Canadien français" can become "Québécois," an identity permitting claims for a new political order. At particular historical moments, political rhetorics can reposition or rearticulate subjects by performing ideological work upon the texts in which social actors are inscribed.

In this essay, I have suggested that Burke's privileging of the term "identification" and an understanding of rhetoric's constitutive and ontological effect, as suggested by structuralist discourse theory, have certain consequences for the theory and practice of rhetoric. A theory of constitutive rhetoric leads us to call into question the concept, usually implicit to rhetoric's humanist tradition, of an audience composed of unified and transcendent subjects. If we are left with a subject, that subject is partial and decentered. History, and indeed discourse itself, form the ground for subjectivity. Consequently, even what Fisher terms "narrative fidelity" has an ideological character, for the experiential ground to which narratives would be faithful are always already ideologically framed within the very being of the experiencing subject.[46]

Because ideology forms the ground for any rhetorical situation, a theory of ideological rhetoric must be mindful not only of arguments and ideographs, but of the very nature of the subjects that rhetoric both addresses and leads to come to be. Indeed, because the constitutive nature of rhetoric establishes the boundary of a subject's motives and experience, a truly ideological rhetoric must rework or transform subjects. A transformed ideology would require a transformed subject (not a dissolving of subjectivity). Such a transformation requires ideological and rhetorical work. This can proceed at two levels: (1) it can proceed at the level of the constitutive narrative itself, providing

stories that through the identificatory principle shift and rework the subject and its motives; (2) it can also proceed at the aesthetic level of what Williams terms the "structure of feeling" and Grossberg describes as the "affective apparatus."[47] Since, as Fisher observes, the truth of a narrative resides in its "fidelity," which is an aesthetic quality, new true narratives become possible as new modes of aesthetic experience emerge and gain social meaning. Ideological rhetorical practice is not restricted to explicitly political public address, but can include a range of aesthetic practices, including music, drama, architecture, and fashion, that elicit new modes of experience and being.

The significance of the rhetorical tradition is that it has long realized that discourse has eminently political and practical effects. In recognizing the contingency of the social, it offers the possibility of social critique and the development of *praxis*. However, in order to overcome the constraints of ideology, rhetorical theory must see through the 'givenness' of what appears to be the delimitable rhetorical situation, where the ontological status of speaker, speech, audience, topic, and occasion offer themselves as unproblematic. It must recognize that ultimately, the position one embodies as a subject is a rhetorical effect.

This essay is in part derived from [Maurice Charland's] dissertation (University of Iowa, 1983), directed by Michael Calvin McGee. Portions of an early draft of this essay were presented at the Second Summer Conference on Argumentation (1981) and were published in its proceedings.

NOTES

1. By ideology I mean a symbolic system, the discourse of which (1) is "false" in the sense that it is based on the presuppositions of some "terministic screen," (2) denies its historicity and linguisticality—pretending to but present a naturally or self-evidently meaningful world, (3) denies or transforms contradictions, and (4) legitimates and structures power relations. As such, my usage is much like the one suggested in, Anthony Giddens, *Central Problems in Social Theory: Action, Structure and Contradiction in Social Analysis* (Berkeley: University of California Press, 1979), 165–197.

2. For a discussion of discourse-based theories of the subject, see, Kaja Silverman, *The Subject of Semiotics* (New York: Oxford University Press, 1983), 43–53, 126–131.

3. Kenneth Burke, *A Rhetoric of Motives* (1950; rpt. Berkeley: University of California Press, 1969), 50.

4. Lawrence Grossberg, "Marxist Dialectics and

Rhetorical Criticism," *Quarterly Journal of Speech* 65 (1979): 249.

5. Kenneth Burke, *Language as Symbolic Action: Essays on Life, Literature, and Method* (Berkeley: University of California Press, 1966), 301.

6. Mouvement Souveraineté-Association, founding political manifesto, 1968, in *Le manuel de la parole: Manifestes québécois*, éd. Daniel Latouche and Diane Poliquin-Bourassa (Sillery, Quebec: Editions du boréal express, 1977) vol. 3, 97.

7. André Bernard and Bernard Descrôteaux, *Québec: élections 1981* (Ville LaSalle, Québec: Editions Hurtibise HMH, Limitée, 1981), 15, 23.

8. Quebec (Prov.), Conseil exécutif, *La nouvelle entente Québec-Canada: Proposition du Gouvernement du Québec pour une entente d'égal à égal: La souveraineté-association*. Quebec: 1979. This document, a soft cover book sold in bookstores, consists of a foreword, six chapters which explain the Quebec government's reasons for seeking sovereignty, and a concluding direct address by Quebec's premier, René Levesque, calling for a OUI vote in the forthcoming referendum. The significance of the document arises from its clear articulation of Quebec's rhetoric of sovereignty as it had developed for over a decade in Quebec public address, and from its institutional status, offering the official rhetoric of the government's pro-sovereignty position.

9. Quebec, *La nouvelle entente*, 62–64.

10. As adopted by the Quebec *Assemblé nationale*, 20 March 1980, the following question appeared on the ballot:

"Le Gouvernement du Québec a fait connaitre sa proposition d'en arriver, avec le reste du Canada, à une nouvelle entente fondée sur le principe de l'égalité des peuples; cette entente permettrait au Québec d'acquérir le pouvoir exclusif de faire ses lois, de percevoir ses impôts et d'établir ses relations extérieurs, ce qui est la souveraineté—et, en même temps, de maintenir avec le Canada une association économique comportant l'utilisation de la même monnaie; aucun changement de statut politique résultant de ces négociations ne sera réalisé sans l'accord de la population lors d'un autre référendum; en conséquence, accordez-vous au Gouvernement du Québec le mandat de négocier l'entente proposée entre le Québec et le Canada?

OUI   NON

The Government of Québec has made public its proposal to negotiate a new agreement with the rest of Canada, based on the equality of nations; this agreement would enable Québec to acquire the exclusive power to make its laws, levy its taxes and establish relations abroad—in other words, sovereignty—and at the same time, to maintain with Canada an economic association including a common currency; no change in political status resulting from these negotiations will be effected without approval by the people through another referendum; on these terms, do you give the Government of Québec the mandate to negotiate the proposed agreement between Quebec and Canada?

YES   NO"

Quebec (Prov.), Directeur Général des élections, *Rapport des résultats officiels du scrutin, référendum du 20 mai 1980*, 9.

11. In the May 1980 referendum on "sovereignty-association," 85.6% of eligible voters cast valid ballots. Of these, 40.4% voted OUI. See, *Rapport des résultats*, 19. Among francophones, the vote was slightly higher and is estimated at 46%. See, Jean-Claude Picard, "Le gouvernement et le Parti Québécois analysent l'échec référendaire de mardi," *Le Devoir*, Thursday, 22 May 1980.

12. Michael C. McGee, "In Search of 'The People': A Rhetorical Alternative," *Quarterly Journal of Speech* 61 (October 1975): 239.

13. Claude Morin, *Quebec versus Ottawa: The Struggle for Self-Government, 1960–1972*, trans. Richard Howard (Toronto: University of Toronto Press, 1976), 5.

14. Claude Morin's text was written as a reflection on his experience of federal–provincial relations as a high-ranking civil servant. He was also an early and active proponent of sovereignty and member of the *PQ* who became a cabinet minister in the *PQ* government.

15. McGee, 246.

16. William F. Shaw and Lionel Albert, *Partition* (Montreal: Thornhill Publishing, 1980), 143–144.

17. Louis Althusser, *Lenin and Philosophy and Other Essays*, trans. Ben Brewster (New York: Monthly Review Press, 1971), 170.

18. Edwin Black, "The Second Persona," *Quarterly Journal of Speech* 56 (April 1970): 109–119 [reprinted in this volume].

19. Michael D. McGuire, "Rhetoric, Philosophy and the *Volk*: Johann Gottlieb Fichte's *Addresses to the German Nation*," *Quarterly Journal of Speech* 62 (April 1976): 135–136.

20. Burke, *Symbolic Action*, 5.

21. Burke reveals a structuralist tendency in his discussions of the formal interplay between the elements of his "pentad," which are constitutive of motives. While Burke differs with the French structuralist tradition, particularly in holding on to the concept of "act," his denial of a foundational character for any of his pentadic terms and his sensitivity to unresolvable ambiguities do lead him, just like the French structuralists, to consider the agent's constitution in symbolic structures. See Frank Lentricchia, *Criticism and Social Change* (Chicago: University of Chicago Press, 1983), 66–83.

22. "Interpeller" is a rather commonly used French verb which designates the act of calling upon someone by name and demanding an answer. It is not surprising that Althusser, in the quote that follows, uses the example of a policeman's hailing, since a person who is

interpellé is usually under some constraint to respond. Thus, the term is used to refer to the questioning of ministers by members of parliament and to the formal address of a judge or bailiff as part of a legal act. *Petit Larousse illustré*, 1979, s. v. "interpeller," "interpellation."

23. Althusser, 174.

24. McGee, 244.

25. Fredric Jameson, *The Political Unconscious: Narrative as a Socially Symbolic Act* (Ithaca, NY: Cornell University Press, 1981), 35.

26. Roland Barthes, *Image, Music, Text*, trans. by Stephen Heath (New York: Hill & Wang, 1977), 124.

27. Burke, *Rhetoric of Motives*, 194.

28. Québec, *La nouvelle entente*, 3. The primary language of Quebec public discourse is French. As such, political life proceeds through a French "terministic screen." To be true to the political consciousness of that society, this essay is based on the analysis of the French primary texts. It is for this reason that I continue to use the terms "peuple" and "Québécois" throughout this essay. Note specifically that "peuple," the French term for "people" is a singular noun; in French, one would write "the people is." Note also that there is no adequate translation of "Québécois." The closest equivalent, "Quebecker," lacks all of the French term's nationalist connotations. While analyzed in French, cited passages are presented in English translation for the reader's convenience. My translation is in large measure based on the simultaneously published official English version of the White Paper: *Québec-Canada a New Deal: The Québec Government Proposal for a New Partnership between Equals: Sovereignty-Association* (Quebec: 1979).

29. Walter Fisher, "Narration as a Human Communication Paradigm: The Case of Public Moral Argument," *Communication Monographs* 51 (March 1984): 8 [reprinted in this volume].

30. Burke, *Rhetoric of Motives*, 197.

31. Quebec, *La nouvelle entente*, 3–4.

32. Paul Ricoeur, *Hermeneutics and the Human Sciences*, ed. and trans. John B. Thompson (New York: Cambridge University Press, 1981), 278–279.

33. Kenneth Burke, *Permanence and Change: An Anatomy of Purpose*, 2nd rev. ed. (Indianapolis, IN: Bobbs-Merrill, 1954), 255.

34. Stuart Hall, "Signification, Representation, Ideology: Althusser and the Post-Structuralist Debates," *Critical Studies in Mass Communication* 2 (June 1985): 107–113.

35. Fisher, 6.

36. Burke, *Symbolic Action*, 6.

37. McGee and Althusser adopt a similar strategy in order to assert the materiality of meaning. Althusser argues that, "Ideology . . . prescrib[es] material practices governed by a material ritual, which practices exist in the material actions of a subject in all consciousness according to his belief" (Althusser, 170). Similarly, McGee, after tracing out the relationship of myth to ideology, asserts: "Though [myths] technically represent 'false consciousness,' they nonetheless function as a means of providing social unity and collective unity. Indeed, 'the people' *are* the social and political myths they accept" (McGee, 247).

38. Quebec, *La nouvelle entente*, 5.

39. Quebec, *La nouvelle entente*, 6.

40. Quebec, *La nouvelle entente*, 7–8.

41. Quebec, *La nouvelle entente*, 11.

42. Quebec, *La nouvelle entente*, 11–12.

43. Quebec, *La nouvelle entente*, 44-45.

44. Quebec, *La nouvelle entente*, 109–110.

45. Quebec, *La nouvelle entente*, 118.

46. Fisher, 8.

47. Raymond Williams, *Marxism and Literature* (New York: Oxford University Press, 1977), 128–135; Lawrence Grossberg, "Is There Rock after Punk," *Critical Studies in Mass Communications* 3 (March 1986): 69–70.

Critical Rhetoric

Theory and *Praxis*

Raymie E. McKerrow

Since the time of Plato's attack marginalizing rhetoric by placing it at the service of truth, theorists have assumed a burden of explaining why rhetoric is "*not* an inferior art" (Hariman, 1986, p. 47). Attempts to rescue rhetoric from its subservient role have often been dependent on universal standards of reason as a means of responding to Plato's critique. While rehabilitating rhetoric in some degree, the efforts nonetheless continue to place it on the periphery, at the service of other, more fundamental standards. Habermas's (1984, 1987) "ideal speech situation," Perelman's (1969) "universal audience," and Toulmin's (1972) "impartial standpoint of rationality" all privilege reason above all else as the avenue to emancipation. In so doing, they preserve for rhetoric a subordinate role in the service of reason. If we are to escape from the trivializing influence of universalist approaches, the task is not to rehabilitate rhetoric, but to announce it in terms of a critical practice.

In response to this challenge, this essay articulates the concept of a *critical rhetoric*—a perspective on rhetoric that explores, in theoretical and practical terms, the implications of a theory that is divorced from the constraints of a Platonic conception. As theory, a critical rhetoric examines the dimensions of domination and freedom as these are exercised in a relativized world. Thus, the first part of this essay focuses on what I am terming a "critique of domination" and a "critique of free-

dom." The critique of domination has an emancipatory purpose—a *telos* toward which it aims in the process of demystifying the conditions of domination. The critique of freedom, premised on Michel Foucault's treatment of power relations, has as its *telos* the prospect of permanent criticism—a self-reflexive critique that turns back on itself even as it promotes a realignment in the forces of power that construct social relations. In practice, a critical rhetoric seeks to unmask or demystify the discourse of power. The aim is to understand the integration of power/knowledge in society—what possibilities for change the integration invites or inhibits and what intervention strategies might be considered appropriate to effect social change. The second part of the essay delineates the *principles* underlying a critical practice. While the principles are not an exhaustive account, they constitute the core ideas of an *orientation* to critique. As will be argued, the principles also recast the nature of rhetoric from one grounded on Platonic, universalist conceptions of reason to one that recaptures the sense of rhetoric as contingent, of knowledge as doxastic, and of critique as a performance. In so doing, a critical rhetoric reclaims the status (Hariman, 1986) of centrality in the analysis of a discourse of power.

Before considering the twin critiques of domination and freedom, the generic features of a "critical rhetoric" need to be set forth. These features name the enterprise and determine its overall *telos*. First, a critical rhetoric shares the same "critical spirit" that is held in common among the divergent perspectives of Horkheimer, Adorno, Habermas, and Foucault. Second, what Slack and Allor (1983) identify as the "effectivity of communication in the exercise of social power" (p. 215) refers to the manner in which discourse insinuates itself in the fabric of social power, and thereby "effects" the status of knowledge among the members of the social group. As Mosco (1983) suggests, "Critical research makes explicit the dense web connecting seemingly unrelated forces in society" (p. 239). By doing so, a critical rhetoric serves a demystifying function (West, 1988, p. 18) by demonstrating the silent and often nondeliberate ways in which rhetoric conceals as much as it reveals through its relationship with power/knowledge. As Marx (1843) put it, a critique serves as "the self-clarification of the struggles and wishes of the age" (cited in Fraser, 1985, p. 97). Third, "a critical social theory frames its research program and its conceptual framework with an eye to the aims and activities of those oppositional social movements with which it has a partisan though not uncritical identification" (Fraser, 1985, p. 97). Critique is not detached and impersonal; it has as its object something which it is "against."[1] Finally, a critical practice must have consequences. In Misgeld's (1985) view, "The ultimate test for the validity of a critical theory of society consists in the possibility of the incorporation of its insights into practically consequential interpretations of social situations" (p. 55). Whether the critique establishes a social judgment about "what to do" as a result of the analysis, it must nonetheless serve to identify the possibilities of future action available to the participants.

A Theoretical Rationale for a Critical Rhetoric

A critical rhetoric encompasses at least two complementary perspectives. The critiques of domination and freedom may not embrace all of those possible, but they allow us to establish the general thrust of critical rhetoric's analysis of discourse. A specific critique may focus on one or the other, or may select elements of both in exploring rhetoric's central role in the creation of social practices. Following the "theoretical rationale," the essay considers the principles that govern analysis within or across these perspectives.

The Critique of Domination: The Discourse of Power

The focus of a critique of domination is on the discourse of power which creates and sustains the social practices which control the dominated. It is, more particularly, a critique of ideologies, perceived as rhetorical creations. The interrelationships between these key concepts deserves closer examination.

Domination, Power, and Ideology

A traditional critique of ideology has been in terms of the domination thesis. Giddens (1979) provides a theoretical rationale for viewing power in terms of the dominant or ruling class. He distinguishes between "ideology *as referring to discourse* on the one hand, and ideology *as referring to the involvement of beliefs within 'modes of lived existence'* " (p. 183), and goes on to insist "*that the chief usefulness of the concept of ideology concerns the critique of domination*" (p. 188). This does not mean that the emphasis on discourse itself has been reduced or rejected. Instead, the emphasis has shifted from the question "is this discourse true or false?" to "how the discourse is mobilized to legitimate the sectional interests of hegemonic groups" (p. 187). The critique is directed to an analysis of discourse as it contributes to the interests of the ruling class, and as it empowers the ruled to present their interests in a forceful and compelling manner.

Domination occurs through "the construction and maintenance of a particular order of discourse . . . [and] the deployment of non-discursive affirmations and sanctions" (Therborn, 1980, p. 82). The ruling class is affirmed by recourse to *rituals* wherein its power is expressed; its role as ruler is sanctioned, in a negative sense, by the ultimate act of *excommunicating* those who fail to participate in or accede to the rituals. The social structures of discourse, taking their cue from Michel Foucault's "orders of discourse," begin with "*restrictions* on who may speak, how much may be said, what may be talked about, and on what occasion" (Therborn, 1980, p. 83). These restrictions are more than socially derived regulators of discourse; they are institutionalized rules accepted and used by the dominant class to control the discursive actions of the dominated. The ruling class does not need to resort to overt censorship of opposing ideas, as these rules effectively contain inflammatory rhetoric within socially approved bounds—bounds accepted by the people who form the community. As Hall (1988) notes:

> Ruling or dominant conceptions of the world do not directly prescribe the mental content of the illusions that supposedly fill the heads of the dominated classes. But the circle of dominant ideas *does* accumulate the symbolic power to map or classify the world for others; its classifications do acquire not only the constraining power of dominance over other modes of thought but also the inertial authority of habit and instinct. It becomes the horizon of the taken-for-granted: what the world is and how it works, for all practical purposes. (p. 44)

Within the world of the "taken-for-granted," discourse is further *shielded* by accepting only certain individuals as the authorities who can speak. The Moral Majority, for example, would typify this order of discourse by limiting the "word" to the Bible and its author, God. Their discourse is further shielded by allowing repetition by God's servants on earth, only so long as their pronouncements conform to the valid meaning of the original text. Governmental "gag orders" perform the same function, only in this case the intent is to protect interests by limiting the privilege of speech to those whose words can be counted on to be supportive of the establishment. Finally, the structuring of the discursive order involves the *delimited appropriation of discourse,* whereby its reception is restrictively situated. This is not a new category, as research on genre has already established the nature and form of "delimited" address in particular contexts (see Simons and Aghazarian, 1986).

Those who are dominated also participate in the social structure and are affected by—and affect—the orders of discourse by which their actions are moderated. Bisseret (1979) suggests that "the more the speaker is subjected to power, the more he situates himself conceptually in reference to the very place where power is concretely exercised" (p. 64). A person cannot escape from the influence of dominant actors, even though the discourse of the latter involves no overt attempt to censor or to entrap the dominated. One can participate in the "dialectic of control" (Giddens, 1979, p. 149) and thereby affect the discourse of power by which individual choice is governed. Nevertheless, the impetus to so function, and the possibility of change, is muted by the fact that the subject already is interpellated with the dominant ideology. Actions oriented toward change will tend to be conducive to power maintenance rather than to its removal.

The locus of the "dialectic of control" can be found in discourse which articulates between class and people. The dominant and the dominated both have recourse to a rhetoric which addresses the people in terms of the classes to which they belong. Domination requires a subject—and the manner of articulation will determine the mode of discourse required to address either "class" or "people." There is no necessary connection between a given ideology and a given class, either ruling or subordinate, at any moment in history (Therborn, 1980, p. 54). As Hall (1988) notes, "Ideologies may not be affixed, as organic entities, to their appropriate classes, but this does not mean that the production and transformation of ideology in society could proceed free of or outside the structuring lines of force of power and class" (p. 45). An emphasis on class does not mean that the "people" either cease to exist or fail to be of major theoretical import in the analysis of power relationships. Laclau (1977) differentiates class struggles (dominated by the relations of production) and struggles between a people and the ruling elite (when antagonism cannot be traced clearly to relations of production alone). In the latter sense,

> The "people" or "popular sectors" are not, as some conceptions suppose, rhetorical abstractions or a liberal or idealist conception smuggled into Marxist discourse. The "people" form an objective determination of the system which is different from class determination; the people are one of the poles or the dominant contradiction in a social formation, that is, a contradiction whose intelligibility depends on the ensemble of political and ideological relations of domination and not just the relations of production. If class contradiction is the dominant contradiction at the abstract level of the mode of production, the people-power bloc contradiction is dominant at the level of the social formation. (pp. 107–108)

The *people,* as is clear from the above, have no clear class content. As subjects, they are very much involved in the struggle for hegemony: "The very articulation of the subject's diverse positions is the result of a struggle for hegemony. . . . Hegemony is the very process of constructing politically the masses' subjectivity and *not* the practice of a preconstituted subject" (Laclau, 1983, p. 118). What is important here is the interaction between class and people in the articulation of a "position" as subject: To win adherence to a class position, the themes are expressed in terms of the rhetoric of the "people." To maintain power, the ruling class also must address themes in terms of a "people." Where, in Therborn's formulation, the nexus of struggle is between differentiated ideological themes or terms, here the nexus is between the ruling elite's and the class's demarcation of the people. The ideological discourse that expresses the will of the people at the same time it constitutes the people as a rhetorical force (Charland, 1987) will reflect a broader interpretation of the "interests" of both dominant and dominated. The creation of a sense of ideological unity derives from the constitution of a discourse of the people; the discourse of the people overrides that of the class in establishing an overall ideological structure. In Laclau's formulation, "*Classes cannot assert their hegemony without articulating the people in their discourse*" (1977, p. 196). Additionally, the ruling class cannot maintain its hegemony without clearly articulating its motives for support in terms of the "people."

The "people" are both real and fictive. They exist as an "objective determination" (Laclau, 1977, p. 165); one can define their presence in economic and social terms. An agent can construct a definition of "people" to whom discourse is addressed. They are fictive because they exist only inside the symbolic world in which they are called into being (McGee, 1975). They are constituted in the "field of the symbolic" (Laclau and Mouffe, 1985, p. 97) and have no meaning outside of this context. As Charland (1987) notes in his case study of the constitutive nature of rhetoric, the *peuple québécois* "do not exist in nature, but only within a discursively constituted history" (p. 137). They are called into being by discourse (McGee, 1980), and from that moment forward, are "real" to those whose lives their discourse affects—the boundaries of their membership can have "real" economic indexes and sociopolitical connections.

Critical Practice

A critique of domination can proceed from Therborn's (1980) classification of ideology types, keeping in mind that these are "class-specific *core themes* of discourses that vary enormously in concrete form and degree of elaboration" (p. 79). Therborn isolates "ego" ideologies as those core themes identifying "who we are"; these exist in conjunction with "alter" ideologies that define what we are not. In the 1950s "patriot" was a key term of the ego ideology, while "communist" was a key term of the corresponding "opposing" ideology. Within contemporary feminism, a core egocentric theme

might be "cooperation," with "competition" serving as the "alter" term. In the case of class formations, the conflict between ego and alter ideologies serves as the battleground. Both are inscribed in the social practices of the society and both serve as the impetus for maintenance and change: "From the standpoint of the constitution of class-struggle subjects, the crucial aspect of the alter-ideology is, in the case of exploiting classes, the rationale for their domination of other classes; in the case of exploited classes, it is the basis for their resistance to the exploiters" (Therborn, 1980, p. 61). In pre-Civil War days, to property owners, the perception of slaves as "property" served as a reason to keep them under control. To the slaves, the same perception served as the impetus for revolt. In this sense, it is not so much how I see myself as how I see the Other—my appropriation of an alter ideology for the Other defines the locus of our struggle. The "ego–alter" distinction, as with others Therborn delineates, serves as potential *topoi* for the unraveling of universes of discourse, as well as for locating the nexus of struggle.

A second key element in the unraveling of the discourse of power within this context is to recognize that the issue is not one of simple oppositions. If it were, societal members would be in a relatively "fixed" state, they would "relate to a given regime in a conscious, homogeneous . . . and consistent manner" (Therborn, 1980, p. 102). If this were the case, one would assume the following:

> *Either* a regime has legitimacy *or* it does not; people obey *either* because of normative consent *or* because of physical coercion; *either* the dominated class or classes have a conception of revolutionary change *or* they accept the status quo or are content with piecemeal reforms; people *act* either on the basis of true knowledge *or* on the basis of false ideas. (Therborn, 1980, p. 102)

The world of the social is not this simple. There are a variety of positions which the dominated and dominant alike can take at any given moment. Hegemony, as Laclau and Mouffe (1985) note, is "not a determinable location within the topography of the social" (p. 139). The analysis of the discourse of power thus must begin with the assumption that any articulatory practice may emerge as relevant or consequential—nothing can be "taken-for-granted" with respect to the impact of any particular discursive practice.

Finally, a critical practice must recognize that the critique of domination alone is not an exhaustive account of the potential discourses of power which govern social practices. This is not to deny the importance of a focus on domination, as there is a compelling sense in which power is negative or repressive in delimiting the potential of the human subject. It is easy to accept the force of the dominant thesis—if you were a Black American in the 1840s, or even in the 1940s, if you are a contemporary feminist, the power of the ruling group may indeed be (if not only appear to be) repressive. The discourse which flows from or expresses power functions to keep people "in their place" as that status is defined and determined by the interest of the dominant class in maintaining its social role. Nevertheless, a focus on the hierarchy of dominant/dominated may deflect attention from the existence of multiple classes, groups, or even individuals with varying degrees of power over others. For this reason, there is a need to examine the critique of power relations across a broader social spectrum.

The Critique of Freedom and the Discourse of Power

Michel Foucault, whose works concern the pervasive effects of power in daily life, articulates a broader conception of power by challenging the power–repression formula endemic to the domination thesis. In the process, he articulates a specialized form of critique that is amenable to the needs of a critical rhetoric. In his terms, "The work of profound transformation can only be done in an atmosphere which is free and always agitated by permanent criticism" (Foucault, 1982, p. 34). The search is not towards a freedom *for* something predetermined. As noted at the outset of this essay, the *telos* that marks the project is one of never-ending skepticism, hence permanent criticism. Results are never satisfying as the new social relations which emerge from a reaction to a critique are themselves simply new forms of power and hence subject to renewed skepticism. His is not the skepticism of Descartes or Hume. Attempts at transformation do not end in futility. As Rajchman (1985) observes, "Sextus Empiricus is Foucault's precursor. Foucault's philosophy does not aim for sure truths, but for the freedom of withholding judgment on philosophical dogmas" (p. 2). Skepticism is a healthy response to a society which takes universalist dogma and the "truths" it yields for granted: "To question the self-evidence of a form of experience, knowledge, or power, is to free it for our purposes, to open new possibilities for thought and action" (Rajchman, 1985, p. 4).

This approach to questions of social relations yields, for Foucault, a nontraditional historical analysis. Reacting against the "totalizing" emphasis of traditional intellectual history, Foucault is decidedly "anti-Whig" (Kent, 1986). By seeking differences rather than similarities, Foucault's analysis of history focuses on discontinuities in an attempt to discover why certain social relations occurred and not others. History teaches us that there are no certainties, there are no universalizing truths against which we can measure our progress toward some ultimate destiny (Clark and McKerrow, 1987). In consequence, the most we can do is to ever guard against "taken for granteds" that endanger our freedom—our chance to consider new possibilities for action.

Concomitantly, Foucault is not seeking a particular normative structure—critique is not about the business of moving us toward perfection (it is not transcendental in the Neo-Kantian, Habermasian sense), nor is it avowedly anarchistic (Fields [1988, p. 143] overstates the case). Rather, it is simply nonprivileging with respect to the options its analysis raises for consideration. On demonstrating the manner in which our social relations constrain us, often in ways that are virtually invisible, which occur at such a deep and remote level in our past as to be anonymous, the possibility of revolt is opened. Anarchism is freedom without a point, and once realized is content to defend its privileged position. Foucault's project privileges nothing, hence contains no such contentment.[2]

The Pervasiveness of Power

As noted earlier, the analysis of power relations need not focus solely on the question of the legitimacy of the state. As Foucault (1980a) notes, "One impoverishes power if one poses it solely in terms of legislation and constitution, in terms solely of the state and the state apparatus" (p. 158). Foucault's analysis of power, in terms of relations that are existent throughout the "social body" (1980a, p. 119), is a radical critique that eschews both analyses of state and economic power, and politically-oriented analyses that have as their motive the "demystification of ideologically distorted belief systems" (Fraser, 1981, p. 272).[3] Instead, the focus is on power as it is manifest across a variety of social practices. His contrast between two historically grounded conceptions of power offers a beginning point for our examination: "The contract–oppression schema, which is the juridical one, and the domination–repression or war–repression schema for which the pertinent opposition is not between the legitimate and illegitimate, as in the first schema, but between struggle and submission" (1980a, p. 92). Within these two versions, it is clear that the discourse of power will be qualitatively different. That is, discourse which upholds a juridical theme of power will speak in terms of rights, obligations, and of the possibility of exchanging power through the legal mediation of conflicting interests. In essence, it is a Western, democratic conception of power that is rational and orderly, and whose discursive themes are deeply imbedded in the historical consciousness of the participants. Contemporary criticism of political rhetoric "buys in" to this perception of power as a model which grounds evaluative claims.

The discourse emanating from what Foucault terms "Nietzsche's hypothesis," on the other hand, will draw on the themes of the opposition of forces in conflict, struggle, and ultimately war. The theme of oppression in the juridical perspective will occur when rights are overextended, contracts are broken, or obligations are left unfulfilled. In the case of power as "the hostile engagement of forces," the discursive theme of repression will occur both as a justification for a resort to force and as an account of the "political consequences of war" (1980a, p. 91). One could argue that critical assessments of Western "war rhetoric" are implicitly trapped by the established vision of the dominant group. They are not, as Wander (1983) would argue, essays which take an "ideological turn," as this "reflects the existence of crisis, acknowledges the influence of established interests and the reality of alternative world-views, and commends rhetorical analyses not only of the actions implied but also of the interests represented" (p. 18).

Over against these orientations toward power, Foucault presents a third perspective in his attempt to relate the "mechanisms [of power] to two points of reference, two limits; on the one hand, to the rules of right that provide a formal delimitation of power; on the other, to the effects of truth that this power produces and transmits, and which in their turn reproduce this power. Hence, we have a triangle: power, right, truth" (1980a, pp. 92–93). Of importance for our purpose is the role of discourse in this interactive network: "There are manifold relations of power which permeate, characterize and constitute the social body, and these relations of power cannot themselves be established, consolidated nor implemented without the produc-

tion, accumulation, circulation and functioning of a discourse" (1980a, p. 93). The discourse identified herein brings power into existence in social relations and gives expression to the ideology that the exercise of power in that relation represents. The sense of "power" brought into being through discourse is not conceived as a stable, continuous force:

> Discourses are not once and for all subservient to power or raised up against it, any more than silences are. We must make allowance for the concept's complex and unstable process whereby discourse can be both an instrument and an effect of power, but also a hindrance, a stumbling block, a point of resistance and a starting point for an opposing strategy. Discourse transmits and produces power; it reinforces it, but also undermines and exposes it, renders it fragile and makes it possible to thwart it. (1980b, pp. 100–101)

Discourse is the tactical dimension of the operation of power in its manifold relations at all levels of society, within and between its institutions, groups, and individuals. The task of a critical rhetoric is to undermine and expose the discourse of power in order to thwart its effects in a social relation (the task is not so dissimilar from Burke's [1961] own attempt in *Attitudes Toward History*).

In this context, an examination of the power of the state would take on a special cast: "The power of the state would be an *effet d'ensemble*, the result of an attempt to immobilize, to encode, to make permanent, and to serialize or realign or homogenize innumerable local (and necessarily unstable) confrontations. The state gives an immobilizing intelligibility to the scattered, wildly productive effects of these power generating confrontations" (Bersani, 1977, p. 3). Outside the state, the localization of power lies within an unstable and shifting environment of social relations: "There is no single underlying principle fixing—and hence constituting—the whole field of differences" between and among the social practices that could be energized by a discourse of power (Laclau and Mouffe, 1985, p. 110). Foucault's object in analyzing this dimension of power, in his *History of Sexuality*, for example, is "to define the regime of power-knowledge-pleasure that sustains the discourse on human sexuality in our part of the world" (1980b, p. 11). In this context, the analysis of power in terms of a juridical model, or in terms of a "war" model, would be too far from the mark to be helpful. As Fraser (1981) notes, "If power is instantiated in mundane social practices and relations, then efforts to dismantle or transform the regime must address those practices and relations" (p. 280). The critic must attend to the "microphysics of power" in order to understand what *sustains* social practices. Power, thus conceived, is not repressive, but productive—it is an active potentially positive force which creates social relations and sustains them through the appropriation of a discourse that "models" the relations through its expression.

Underlying Foucault's approach is the belief that power, exercised in terms of law and sovereign right, transforms, or in Therborn's terms, "naturalizes" the social relation: it becomes the norm, and discourse related to its maintenance is "normal." Challenges are therefore abnormal and irrational by definition. This stigma attached to the agents of change is present even though they might work within the confines of the "order of power." Consider, for example, Edelman's (1988) observation that "the language of the helping professions functions as a form of political action" (p. 107) within the established social structure. Challenges to the social relations normalized within the "helping professions" would be met, by those still adhering to the established order, with arguments that assert naïveté or irrationality on the part of the "naysayers." Power, in this context, is *not a possession or a content*—it is instead an integral part of social relations. The discourse of power creates and perpetuates the relations, and gives form to the ideology which it projects. Ideology, regardless of its expression, begins with these social relations as integral to its creation, continuance, and change. A thoroughgoing Foucauldian critique, however, would go beyond Edelman's (1988) analysis, conducted primarily at the level of "agents of change." Power is expressed anonymously, in nondeliberate ways, at a "deep structure" level, and may have its origins in the remoteness of our past (carried forward through a particularizing discursive formation).

To be an agent for change requires, from a Foucauldian perspective, an understanding of the reasons for the current social relations of power—and those reasons do not necessarily have to presuppose an earlier production via a named agent. The "denial" of an agent as productive of contingently derived social practices does not rule out the present role of persons as active participants in "revolt" against the present dangers. Otherwise, there is no point to positing the possibilities of freedom—and a Sartrean angst is preordained as the condition of passive acceptance of one's fate.

Power and Truth in the Critique of Freedom

Foucault's analysis of the relationship between power and truth raises the question of the role of discourse as an agent of truth. The rejection of transcendental or universalist standards against which rhetoric is evaluated, as suggested in the beginning of this essay, raises a question: "Have we abandoned the Platonic quest and embraced sophism?" The answer is "yes." The orientation is shifted from an expression of "truth" as the opposite of "false consciousness" (and away from the naïve notion that laying bare the latter would inevitably move people toward revolution on the basis of a revealed truth). Engels stated the case for a view of ideology predicated on "false consciousness": "Ideology is a process accomplished by the so-called thinker consciously, it is true, but with a false consciousness. The real forces impelling him remain unknown to him" (1893, p. 459, cited in Therborn, 1980, p. 4). This assumes, however, that (1) all ideology is necessarily false and (2) that "only scientific knowledge is 'true' or 'real' knowledge" (Therborn, 1980, p. 8). In contemporary accounts of culture, this perception has been discredited (Hall, 1988; but see Markovic, 1983). There is an advantage to dispensing with a perception of truth that is hidden behind a "cloud of unknowing" (Hall, 1988, p. 44): If ideology is not equated with false consciousness, it "is no longer treated as untextual, homogeneous, cultural mush—as a synonym for ideas in general, distorted ideas in general, *Weltanschauung*, ethos, spirit of the times, and so forth" (Mullins, 1979, p. 153). To consider ideology in terms of truth and falsity is to focus attention on its character and to typify it as product rather than as process.

Nevertheless, a consideration of "truth" is an appropriate focus of a critical rhetoric. In Foucault's (1980a) words, "The problem does not consist in drawing the line between that in a discourse which falls under the category of scientificity or truth, and that which comes under some other category, but in seeing historically how effects of truth are produced within discourses which in themselves are neither true nor false" (p. 118). By focusing on the "effects of truth," as expressed in a social relation typified by power, one approximates an Isocratean sense of "community knowledge":

The important thing here, I believe, is that truth isn't outside power, or lacking in power: Contrary to a myth whose history and functions repay further study, truth isn't the reward of free spirits, the child of protracted solitude, nor the privilege of those who have succeeded in liberating themselves. Truth is a thing of this world: It is produced by virtue of multiple forms of constraint. And it induces regular effects of power. Each society has its regime of truth, its "general politics" of truth: that is, the types of discourse which it accepts and makes function as true; the mechanisms and instances which enable one to distinguish true and false statements, the means by which each is sanctioned; the techniques and procedures accorded value in the acquisition of truth; the status of those who are charged with saying what counts as true. (Foucault, 1980a, p. 131)

The analysis of the discourse of power focuses on the "normalization" of language intended to maintain the status quo. By producing a description of "what is," unfettered by predetermined notions of what "should be," the critic is in a position to posit the possibilities of freedom. Recharacterization of the images changes the power relations and re-creates a new "normal" order. In this interaction, "truth" is that which is supplanted by a newly articulated version that is accepted as a basis for the revised social relation. Once instantiated anew in social relations, the critique continues.

The Principles of *Praxis*

Discourse lives, as it were, beyond itself, in a living impulse . . . toward the object; if we detach ourselves completely from this impulse all we have left is the naked corpse of the word, from which we can learn nothing at all about the social situation or the fate of a given word in life.
—BAKHTIN, *The Dialogic Imagination*, p. 292

Bakhtin's observation about the relation between selves and words is an appropriate grounding for the discussion of the "principles of *praxis*." This section of the essay does not seek to establish the *methodology* (in the narrow sense of formula or prescription) appropriate to a critical rhetoric. Rather, it seeks to outline the "orientation" (invoked in Burke's sense) that a critic takes toward the object of study. The "object" of a critical rhetoric, however, requires reconsideration prior to a discussion of the principles of a critical practice.

Critical Practice as Invention

Public address, as traditionally conceived, is *agent-centered*. Even the study of social movements has been dominated by this perspective. Given public address's "quasi-theological" (to borrow Cawelti's [1985] term) nature, there is the danger that the inclusion of a "critical rhetoric" perspective would merely perpetuate the traditional model of criticism. The acceptance of a critical rhetoric is premised on the reversal of the phrase "public address"—we need to reconceptualize the endeavor to focus attention on *that symbolism which addresses publics*. The term "address" conjures up the image of a preconceived message, with a beginning, a middle, and an end—a ratiocinative discourse which can be located in space and time as an isolated event, or can be placed in a "rhetorical situation" out of which it grew and to which it responds. More often than not, the products of discourse are mediated—are no longer the simple property of a speaker–audience relation. In the context of such mediated communication, Becker (1971) noted the *fragmented* nature of most of the messages impinging on any one consumer. More recently, McGee (1987) has exhorted critics to attend to "formations of texts" in their original fragmented form. What he calls for is the role of a critic as "inventor"—interpreting for the consumer the meaning of fragments collected as *text* or *address*. To approach mediated communication as rhetorical is to see it in its fragmented, unconnected, even contradictory or momentarily oppositional mode of presentation. The task is to construct addresses out of the fabric of mediated experience prior to passing judgment on what those addresses might tell us about our social world. The process one employs is thus geared to uncovering the "dense web" (Mosco, 1983, p. 239), not by means of a simple speaker–audience interaction, but also by means of a "pulling together" of disparate scraps of discourse which, when constructed as an argument, serve to illuminate otherwise hidden or taken for granted social practices.

The reversal of "public address" to "discourse which addresses publics" places the critic in the role of "inventor." As such, s/he is more than an observer of the social scene. And s/he will have as the *text* more than traditional "speaker–audience" scenarios in engaging in a critique. The movement toward communication as "mediated," including the analysis of popular culture, is one way to recover what Turner (1986) refers to as "missed opportunities" in the practice of criticism. If the reversal is not in place, there is the danger that a "public address" vision of popular culture would be constrained to think in terms of "agent" rather than symbol as the focus of attention. There also is the danger that such extension of traditional forms of analysis would simply perpetuate modernist clichés in constructing, through the myopic lenses of a predefined vision of the media as a "cultural wasteland," elitist standards of excellence. *Facts of Life* may never aspire to inclusion in the "canons of oratorical excellence," but it may have more influence on a teenager's conception of social reality than all the great speeches by long-dead great speakers. To ignore "symbols which address publics" in all their manifest forms has, as its ultimate consequence, the perpetuation of sterile forms of criticism.

Principles of a Critical Practice

In the discussion which follows, the principles of a critical *praxis*, and the alterations in rhetoric's nature they imply, encompass both the critique of domination and of freedom. Neither critique, although it may be carried out alone, is ultimately "complete" without attention to the other. It *is* the case that state power exists, is repressive, and is accessible to critique. It is *equally* the case that power is not only repressive but potentially productive, that its effects are pervasive throughout the social world, and that these effects are accessible to analysis. While a critical practice need not focus on both, the overall analysis of the impact of the discourse of power requires, at a minimum, attention to each dimension. A thoroughgoing critical rhetoric, therefore, is one whose principles provide an orientation common to both perspectives on *ideologiekritik*. More precisely, then, an *ideologiekritik* is "the production of knowledge to the ends of power and, maybe, of social change" (Lentricchia, 1983, p. 11). Whether cast as a critique of domination or of freedom, the initial task of a critical rhetoric is one of re-creation—constructing an argument that identifies the integration of power and knowledge and delineates the role of power/knowledge in structuring social practices. Reconceptualizing address as textual fragments, and assuming the orientation of a critical rhetoric, brings a critic to the discourse of power with a blank slate if there are no additional principles underwriting the perspective. While not pretending to catalog an exhaustive list, the following "principles" serve to describe, without limiting, the orientation suggested by a critical rhetoric.

Principle #1: "Ideologiekritik Is in Fact Not a Method, but a Practice" (McGee, 1984, p. 49).

McGee (1984, 1987) is correct in chastising critics for paying too much attention to methodological concerns. If reading Burke prompts any lesson, it is that creative insights are constrained by the systematicity of method. This lesson was lost on legions of academics who, by imposing a system on an unmethodological critic, created their own fiction and termed it a method.[4] Considered as practice, understanding and evaluation are one: "Understanding is impossible without evaluation. Understanding cannot be separated from evaluation: they are simultaneous and constitute a unified integral act. . . . In the act of understanding [unless one is a dogmatist and therefore impervious to change] a struggle occurs that results in mutual change and enrichment" (Bakhtin, 1986, p. 142). In this context, "description" implies evaluation by the very fact of choice with respect to what is described, as well as what is not. Burke's (1966, p. 45) dictum that a selection of reality is also a deflection and a rejection applies to the act of criticism as well as to other symbolic acts that are taken as the object of a critical perspective. This does not mean a critic functions as an anarchist. Rather, it means one operates from a "perspective" (McGee, 1984, p. 47) or an "orientation": embracing a set of principles does not commit one to prescriptivism any more than it renders the critical act directionless. An orientation is the least restrictive stage from which the critical act might be launched; it maximizes the possibilities of what will "count" as evidence for critical judgment, and allows for creativity in the assessment of the "effects of truth" upon social practices.

Principle #2: The Discourse of Power Is Material.

An ideology exists, in a material sense, in and through the language that constitutes it (McGee, 1982). As Therborn (1980) notes, "Ideology operates as discourse. . . . [It] is the medium through which men make their history as conscious actors" (pp. 15, 3). Participants are not passive bystanders, simply absorbing the ideology and having no power to alter its force or its character. Ideology is a property of the social world, but agents have the capacity to interact in that world to modify the discourse (see Mumby, 1987). They do not come to the particular ideology as a tabula rasa: They come to a system of discourse with an ideological grid already in place and participate in terms of that grid's determinative nature. This is the implication of Burke's (1966) "terministic screens" as mechanisms which control how alternate discourses are heard. As Althusser (1971) has noted, "Ideology has always-already interpellated individuals as subjects" (p. 164). This focuses our attention on the social dimension or consciousness of the collectivity that utilizes or adheres to a particular discourse. As Charland (1987) has illustrated, a traditional speaker–audience model presumes that an audience is already constituted as subject, and employs discourse in a manner to sustain present relations of domination. He succeeds in carrying the "constitution of a subject" a step backward to its initiation in a discourse—as the audience is called into being as a *peuple québécois* (p. 134). In either case, the rhetor is capable of participating in a "dialectic of control" to shape the ongoing nature of the social relation being sustained or entered into. In fact, to the extent that a person fails to enter into a dialectical relation with the ideology, that individual ceases to function as an *agent* in the social system (see Giddens, 1979, p. 149).

The materiality of discourse focuses attention on the sense of "*praxis*" utilized in a critical rhetoric. Aristotle's vision of *praxis* identified it with the goals of *phronesis* or practical wisdom (the "doing of fine and noble deeds" [Benhabib, 1986, p. 157] in the service of virtue). A critical rhetoric no longer looks at *praxis* in its ethical dimension, tying it to an ideal lifestyle. Rather, a critical rhetoric links *praxis*, both as object of study and as style, to "a mode of *transformative activity*" (Benhabib, 1986, p. 67) in which the social relations in which people participate are perceived as "real" to them even though they exist only as fictions in a rhetorically constituted universe of discourse. What is differentiated for the purposes of critical practice is not a rejection of ethical values, but a reordering of the perspective to one in which *transformation* (or at minimum, the delineation of the possibilities for transformation) is seen as the ultimate aim. Even theorizing, in this sense, is critical practice, as it lays out the preconditions for transformation within a set of social relations. The product of a critique may be seen in the Aristotelian sense of a "noble deed," but that is not its *raison d'être*.

What is constituted as "real" is not only so structured through discursive practices. What is perceived as real to the populace, in economic, social, and political terms also is created in non-discursive ways. Following Laclau and Mouffe (1985), the practice of a critical rhetoric

> rejects the distinction between discursive and non-discursive practices. It affirms: (a) that every object is constituted as an object of discourse inso-

far as no object is given outside every discursive condition of emergence; and (b) that any distinction between what are usually called linguistic and behavioural aspects of a social practice is either an incorrect distinction or ought to find its place as a differentiation within the social production of meaning which is structured under the form of discursive totalities. (p. 107)

This is not to diminish the importance of nondiscursive practices, but rather to acknowledge that the discussion of such practices takes place in terms of discursive practices. The analysis of social *praxis* must, if it is to accomplish its transformative goal, deal in concrete terms with those relations which are "real"—that do in fact constrain discourse, and do so in ways that are seldom seen without such analysis.

Principle #3: Rhetoric Constitutes Doxastic Rather Than Epistemic Knowledge.

A critical rhetoric must be grounded on a reconstitution of the concept of *doxa* (Hariman, 1986). Plato's impact on the status of rhetoric needs little elaboration—the attempts to rehabilitate rhetoric, to save it from its own "shame" are many and varied (Hariman, 1986; Nelson and Megill, 1986). In essence, that is what the "epistemic"[5] movement attempts, regardless of its claim to establish rhetoric's role in the constitution of subjects. By subsuming the constitution of subjects under the rubric of *episteme*, theorists do no more than attempt to rescue rhetoric from the oblivion to which Plato consigned it. Considerations of rhetoric as epistemic are inextricably linked to a neo-Kantian definition of what constitutes knowledge, as that will always be seen in terms of independent, universal standards of judgment (whether invoked by Perelman, Toulmin, or Habermas). In the process, the rehabilitation remains subservient to a Platonic, neo-Kantian perception of rhetoric's "true" role in society. A more positive approach is to reassert the value of rhetoric's province—*doxa*—and thereby resituate theory and practice in a context far more amenable to its continuance.

Nelson and Megill (1986), writing on the nature of the "rhetoric of inquiry," observe the history of "certitude" under which rhetoric has served:

> Plato denigrated opinion and rhetoric so as to celebrate truth and order at a time of Greek conflict and Athenian decline. Similarly, Aristotle subordinated mythos to logos and rhetoric to dialectic. In an era when radical disagreements racked

the peace of Europe, Descartes wrote off rhetoric in favor of mathematical reason and Hobbes enslaved language to the sovereign. Later, Kant sought perpetual peace through pure and practical reason. Craving certainty as a path to peace and order in our own troubled times, many of us may be tempted by similar visions. But after more than three centuries of such abstract utopias, not to mention the programs for their enforcement, we have every reason to resist their temptation and revise their anti-rhetorical premises. (p. 23)

As they demonstrate, there is a wealth of philosophical support for the rejection of such anti-rhetorics. Their own limitation, notwithstanding brief references to the social and political facets of inquiry, is that the rhetoric of inquiry ends in description.[6] In this sense, the rhetoric of inquiry, as is the case with the Habermasian project, remains locked into a mode of reason (even when viewed as rhetorical [Brown, 1987]) that aims for universalizing the standards of judgment—in this case, across the academy. A critical rhetoric ends in transformation of the conditions of domination or in the possibility of revolt as the consequence of a critique of freedom. Thus, even though the rhetoric of inquiry is premised on a positive reassertion of rhetoric's role in society, its rationale (wedded to rhetoric as epistemic) does not go far enough to embrace the practice of a critical rhetoric.

Hariman (1986) offers a reconceptualization of *doxa* that removes it from an opposition to *episteme*. *Doxa*, as he notes, includes not only the traditional characteristic of "opinion" but also "reputation" or "regard" and functions as much by concealment as by revelation: "*Doxa* is created by acts of concealment, and so a complete conceptualization of *doxa* must include the idea that regard is in part achieved by the concealments of rank. This interpretation repositions *doxa*: it is no longer contrasted with *episteme*, but rather with *aletheia*, truth (literally 'unhiddenness'). . . . This dynamic of concealment and unconcealment [truth]—of authorizing and marginalizing—is the means by which we determine what we believe, what we know, and what we believe to be true" (pp. 49–50). Doxastic knowledge functions as the grounding of a critical rhetoric.[7] Rather than focusing on questions of "truth" or "falsity," a view of rhetoric as doxastic allows the focus to shift to how the symbols come to possess power—what they "do" in society as contrasted to what they "are."

The sense of *doxa* as concealment is implied in Bourdieu's (1977, 1979) notion of *doxa* as the realm of the "undiscussed." Bourdieu (1977, 1979, 1980)

employs metaphors of capitalism in his examination of the relationships between authority to speak and the appropriation of symbols—those in authority simply have more "capital" at their disposal, as well as enjoy control of the means of distribution of symbols. They have, as a result, the interest of conserving or preserving the "state of *doxa* in which the established structure is not questioned" (Thompson, 1984, p. 49). Bringing the "undiscussed" or concealed to the forefront is an act of heterodoxical rhetoric, met, naturally enough, by an orthodox rhetoric of defense of the status quo. Central to this discussion of *doxa*, as in the case of Hariman's analysis, is the recognition of its contingent nature, as well as its implicit sense of having an inscribed status (estimate of worth) by having been appropriated as the symbolic capital of the dominant group. Those with less capital are accordingly "marginalized" until or unless their heterodoxical rhetoric can successfully supplant that of the ruling elite.

Principle #4: Naming Is the Central Symbolic Act of a Nominalist Rhetoric.

The power of language to constitute subjects implicit in "naming as an interpretive act" (in Burke's [1941, pp. 5–71] sense; see Blankenship, 1976, p. 236) suggests that it is a justifiable principle to incorporate in a critical perspective. The principle encompasses all that has been said in criticism under the rubric of "rhetorical visions," "ideographs," and "condensation symbols." As a specific example, though it is not discussed in any of these terms, consider Hall's (1985) own treatment of his personal experience as a "coloured" person in Jamaica and then as a person from Jamaica. As the contexts shift, so too do the meanings inherent in social practices legitimated by reactions to a label. The subject is "fractured" into a multiplicity of selves as the perception/label shifts. Bakhtin's (1986) observation that "nothing is absolutely dead: every meaning will have its homecoming festival" (p. 170) applies: A return to Jamaica brings with it all of the old associations that one has grown away from in another cultural milieu. In the recent Iran-Contra hearings, McFarlane legitimated a foreign country's contribution to the Contras, at a time when solicitation was expressly forbidden by Congress, as "not a solicitation per se." One can't put too fine an edge on the power or process of naming, when potentially illegal actions are justified by linguistic sleights of hand.

What is left out of the above analysis is perhaps the most crucial aspect of the process of naming. Consonant with recapturing a sense of rhetoric as doxastic rather than epistemic, a reinterpretation of rhetoric as nominalist fits well with the contingent nature of the social reality in which humans are both subject and subjected (Therborn, 1980). Rajchman (1985) observes of Foucault that "his histories are *themselves* nominalist histories. They are not histories of things, but of the terms, categories, and techniques through which certain things become at certain times the focus of a whole configuration of discussion and procedure" (p. 51). For a critical rhetoric, the significance is the parallel sense in which rhetoric itself adopts a nominalist stance. Foucault's nominalist history is directed against the totalizing and deterministic effects of an intellectual (Whiggish) history which sacrifices difference in the search for similarity. In similar fashion, a nominalist rhetoric is directed against the universalizing tendencies of a Habermasian communicative ethics or a Perelmanesque philosophical rhetoric (see Benhabib, 1986; McKerrow, 1986).

The implications of a nominalist rhetoric are evidenced in a comparison of different forms of hermeneutic analysis:

> Hermeneutic realism, for example, assumes a stability of meaning before any rhetorical acts take place. Meaning is determinate, objective, and eternally fixed because of constraints in the text itself that are independent of historically situated critical debate. In a strangely similar way, hermeneutic idealism also assumes a stability of meaning outside situated practices. Meaning is determinate, intersubjective, and temporarily fixed because of constraints provided by the communal convention in readers' and critics' minds. (Mailloux, 1985, p. 630)

Rhetorical hermeneutics, on the other hand, tries to correct the error of "presupposing the possibility of meaning outside specific historical contexts of rhetorical practices" (Mailloux, 1985, p. 630). A nominalist rhetoric shares, with Mailloux's formulation of a rhetorical hermeneutics, a sense that terms are contingently based—the reasons for their emergence are not premised on fixed, determinative models of inquiry.

Principle #5: Influence Is Not Causality.

This simple claim has profound implications for understanding the assumptive framework under-

lying the analysis of the discourse of power. As Condit (1987) argues, "To say that something 'influences' a process, or has 'force,' eschews the determinism latent in the term 'cause.' An influence or force may be overridden or supplemented by other forces. It may even require the active participation of other forces (e.g., 'human choice') to become actualized" (p. 2). Thus, given the contingency with which rhetoric historically concerns itself, to say that a symbol has influence is to claim that it impacts on others (one might term this a soft cause if one wished to retain the term).

Presence of a symbol is not actuality, but at least is potentiality. The potential for images of crime to influence the social reality of the elderly is present through the depiction of such symbolic acts on nightly crime drama. As empirical studies have shown, such acts do in fact influence the elderly's perception of the amount of actual crime in their own social community.

The claim separates a critical rhetoric from the structural causality inherent in an Althusserian critique of culture, as well as from other "pure" Marxist reductionisms of the determinist stripe. Seen in this context, the notion of "influence" rejects the twin claims that nothing is connected to anything else (culturalism) and that everything is determined by something (structuralism) (see Hall, 1985). Hall's own cultural perspective is far more amenable to this principle, as it allows for contingency in the convergence of events that would determine social practices, or social change. Noting that there is no "necessary correspondence" between an ideological expression and one's social class does not invalidate the possibility of social change. From a rhetorical perspective, what it implies is that the impetus for change has not yet been articulated—the necessary symbolic act bridging the ideology and the social position has not yet been created. This doesn't imply that it won't or can't be formulated. The following statement from Hall (1985) identifies the role of rhetoric, without so naming it: "The aim of a theoretically-informed political practice must surely be to bring about or construct the articulation between social and economic forces and those forms of politics and ideology which might lead them in practice to intervene in history in a progressive way—an articulation which has to be *constructed* through practice precisely because it is not guaranteed by how those forces are constituted in the first place" (p. 95).

If there is a lack of correspondence between

an ideology and a class position, symbols must be invented in such a way as to accommodate the "difference" that exists. In the various analyses of Hart's debacle, there is ample suggestion of the variance between cultural mores and the position of the candidate. Hart's "affair," or more recently, the travails of Jimmy Swaggart, are not morality plays. They are, much more fundamentally, failures to bridge the gap between a lived practice and a noncorresponding ideology. As Abravanel (1983) points out, the contradiction is between a moral sense of "what should be done" and "what is being done" (p 280). The contradiction is mediated, both in the life of the individual and within the public realm, by recourse to suitable myths that gloss the incompatibilities, and thereby provide a rationalization for action. The task of a critical rhetoric is to call attention to the myth, and the manner in which it mediates between contradictory impulses to action.

Principle #6: Absence Is as Important as Presence in Understanding and Evaluating Symbolic Action.

Hall's experience is again helpful; as he writes, "Positively marked terms 'signify' because of their position in relation to what is absent, unmarked, the unspoken, the unsayable. Meaning is relational within an ideological system of presences and absences" (1985, p. 109). Terms are not "unconnected"; in the formation of a text, out of fragments of what is said, the resulting "picture" needs to be checked against "what is absent" as well as what is present. Wander's analysis of media also supports the influence of the "not said," particularly as it reinforces that which is said (1981). To the extent that the following is an accurate statement about what appears on television, the negation also may be considered an accurate reflection of reality:

> Most characters on prime time conform to conventional standards of beauty—they tend to be white or near white, fine-featured, young, well proportioned, and of average height.
> NEGATION: Few characters appear on prime time who are fat. Not many have scars, limps, or protruding lips. Few adult characters are under five feet or over six feet, four inches tall. Not many characters appear to be over 65. When physically "deviant" characters do appear, they tend not to be cast as intelligent, strong, or virtuous. (pp. 518–519)

As the culture changes, and the "said" shifts in identifiable patterns, the negation can be revised.

The Iran-Contra hearings provide a very different exemplar: over and over, the concern was with what was left out, the "unsaid" in a situation. McFarlane may have said that such and such knowledge is "not known concretely" but did not say that such knowledge is known in some degree. Answers to specific questions may only be partial statements, accurate insofar as they are expressed, but certainly not the answers that would be given if other questions were asked. Inferences based on such answers more often than not play directly into the hands of those in control of both knowledge and the power that it provides.

Principle #7: Fragments Contain the Potential for Polysemic Rather Than Monosemic Interpretation.

This probably shouldn't need saying. Nevertheless, given the dominance of a modernist critique which, as a particularizing example, sees mediated communication as a corruptive influence, as promoting the declining standards of the culture, such a claim deserves renewed attention. First, to use Cawelti's (1985) term, the early "quasi-theological" cast of much media criticism is on the wane. As Grossberg (1984) and Becker (1986) suggest in their respective surveys of media criticism, there is a much stronger influence from ideological, social/cultural perspectives currently in vogue. Even so, as Fiske (1986) notes, ideological criticism has been myopic in its vision of television as a monosemic text, underwriting the dominant cultural forces at work in society. An underlying weakness of a critique which sees the viewer as ultimately passive and unable to participate in social change limits ideological criticism to that "of increasing the viewer's ability to resist the imposition of cultural meanings that may not fit one's own social identity, and in so doing to resist the homogenization of culture" (p. 399). While this has value, it is, in the main, a negative one. A polysemic critique is one which uncovers a subordinate or secondary reading which contains the seeds of subversion or rejection of authority, at the same time that the primary reading appears to confirm the power of the dominant cultural norms. As Fiske (1986) says, "Different socially located viewers will activate" the meaning of a text differently. Those who come to the experience from the domain of power may see only legitimization, while those subjected to power can "take the signifying practices and products of the dominant" and "use them for different social purposes" (p. 406).

Principle #8: Criticism Is a Performance.

This is the thrust of McGee's (1987) analysis of the critique of culture. In the sense of a critical rhetoric, it places the focus on the activity as a statement; the critic as inventor becomes arguer or advocate for an interpretation of the collected fragments. Is this to say anything more than Brockriede (1974), who long ago acknowledged that criticism is an argumentative activity? If I understand McGee's point, the emphasis goes beyond the simple assertion that any interpretation must give reasons. In McGee's (1987) words, "Rhetoricians are performers" (p. 8). The act of performing, within the context of our expertise as critics/readers of the social condition, moves the focus from criticism as method to critique as practice.

This principle also encompasses the recent advocacy of an "ideological turn" in criticism. Wander (1983) argues that "criticism takes an ideological turn when it recognizes the existence of powerful vested interests benefiting from and consistently urging politics and technology that threatens life on this planet" (p. 18). As written, however, the frame of reference for the insertion of ideological intent is unnecessarily confined to a narrow range of human experience. The function of an *ideologiekritik* is to counter the excesses of a society's own enabling actions, its "repressive tolerance" in Marcuse's terms, that underwrites the continuation of social practices that ultimately are harmful to the community (see McGee, 1984). Thus, the sense of that which is harmful may be much broader than Wander implies.

To escape the implication that what Wander desires is for academics to take to the streets as practicing revolutionaries (and that may, in fact, be what he desires) there is an important caveat. The practice of a critical rhetoric can take refuge in Foucault's (1980a) defense of his own writing as that of a *specific intellectual* (p. 126). To borrow Lentricchia's (1983) statement of the practice, a specific intellectual is "one whose radical work of transformation, whose fight against repression is carried on at the specific institutional site where he [she] finds himself [herself] and on the terms of his [her] own expertise, on the terms inherent to his [her] own functioning as an intellectual" (pp. 6–7). This also gives meaning to theorizing

as a critical practice—as a performance of a rhetor advocating a critique as a sensible reading of the discourse of power.

Summary: Theory, *Praxis,* and the Future

I have, in this essay, taken Jensen's (1987) observation, "communication media engage audiences in the construction of cultural forms" (p. 24) as a given. My purpose has been to suggest a theoretical rationale and a set of principles for the critique of domination and of freedom. As such, this essay serves as a "synthetic statement" of both forms of critique. There are many other forms of criticism, and of critiques; the conception of a critical rhetoric need not displace all other rhetorics. What it must do, however, is provide an avenue—an orientation—toward a postmodern conception of the relationship between discourse and power. In so doing, it announces a critical practice that stands on its own, without reliance on universal standards of reason. Instead, a critical rhetoric celebrates its reliance on contingency, on *doxa* as the basis for knowledge, on nominalism as the ground of language meaning as doxastic, and critique viewed as a performance. Rhetoric, in the context of these principles, emerges with *status* (Hariman, 1986) in the analysis of a discourse of power.

What then of the "future" of a critical rhetoric? If I have been marginally successful in setting forth the "image" of a critical rhetoric as theory and *praxis,* I rest my case on Blankenship and Muir's (1987) observation that such an image contains "both the vision of the future and the [instrument] for realizing it" (p. 6).

NOTES

1. As may be obvious, this is a more violent wrenching of traditional modes of rhetorical criticism than some may tolerate (e.g., Campbell, 1983; Hill, 1983).

2. It is in this sense that his project is antihumanist (see Blair and Cooper, 1987, and Fisher, 1985, to the contrary). By privileging no one subject or topic, Foucault is not antihuman, but antihumanist in the sense that he does not place humans at the center or core of our philosophical tradition. He places nothing, and especially not transcendental reason, at the center, so to claim an "antihumanism" stance is simply to affirm that "human choice and freedom" (Blair and Cooper, 1987, p. 167) will not be constrained by an *a priori* privilege.

3. In the process, Foucault suspends traditional rationalistic orientations toward truth and falsity (a tradition Marxist analysis of false consciousness embraces, though for different effects), and "brackets" questions of epistemic and normative justifications of social practices (Fraser, 1981, pp. 273–275). The suspension of criteria of justification is consonant with the absence of privilege alluded to earlier.

4. There is a similar danger in perceiving Foucault's "perspective" as a "method" (Blair and Cooper, 1987, p. 161). As Shiner (1982) argues, "If one persists in seeing Foucault as a methodologist, the phrase 'genealogy of power' which from 1972 replaces 'archaeology of knowledge' will be even more grossly misinterpreted. . . . His method is an anti-method in the sense that it seeks to free us from the illusion that an apolitical method is possible" (p. 386). There is not an apparent contradiction between a political project (any analysis of the relations of knowledge and power is inherently political) and the absence of privilege, even of a method of analysis. To privilege any one method, including genealogy or its precursor, archaeology, is to preordain the conclusion and hence restrict freedom. What Blair and Cooper (1987) see as a method is in actuality a parody—what a method might be if one were to consciously adopt it—that Foucault has no intention of following slavishly (Clark and McKerrow, 1987).

5. For representative essays, see Scott (1967, 1976), Farrell (1976, 1978), Leff (1978), and Cherwitz and Hikins (1986).

6. For representative essays, see Simons (1985), McGee (1980, 1987), Lyne (1985), Nelson and Megill (1986), Nelson, Megill, and McCloskey (1987), and Hariman (1986).

7. The orientation to knowledge grounds the critique of domination's focus on what is concealed as well as revealed in the discourse of power (thereby conferring status on the elite and marginalizing the dominated). Foucault's concern with understanding how certain "mentalities" came into being at a particular time also resonates well with this reconceptualized sense of *doxa*—certain discursive formations are granted status within social relations while others are marginalized. The aim of a Foucauldian critique is, in these terms, to set forth the conditions by which the nature of what is taken to be doxastic knowledge at any given time can be recast.

REFERENCES

Abravanel, H. (1983). "Mediatory Myths in the Service of Organizational Ideology." In L. R. Pony, P. J. Frost, G. Morgan, and T. C. Dandridge, eds., *Organizational Symbolism* (Greenwich, CT: JAI Press), pp. 273–293.

Althusser, L. (1971). *Lenin and Philosophy, and Other Essays*. Translated by B. Brewster. London: NLB.

Bakhtin, M. M. (1981). *The Dialogic Imagination*. Edited by M. Holquist. Translated by C. Emerson and M. Holquist. Austin: University of Texas Press.

Bakhtin, M. M. (1986). *Speech Genres and Other Late Essays*. Edited by C. Emerson and M. Holquist. Translated by V. McGee. Austin: University of Texas Press.

Becker, S. (1971). "Rhetorical Studies for the Contemporary World." In E. Black and L. Bitzer, eds., *The Prospect of Rhetoric* (Englewood Cliffs, NJ: Prentice-Hall), pp. 21–43.

Becker, S. (1986, November). "Rhetoric, Media, and Culture, or the Rhetorical Turn in Media Studies." Paper presented at the annual meeting of the Speech Communication Association, Chicago.

Benhabib, S. (1986). *Critique, Norm, and Utopia: A Study of the Foundations of Critical Theory*. New York: Columbia University Press.

Bersani, L. (1977). "The Subject of Power." *Diacritics* 7: 3.

Bisseret, N. (1979). *Education, Class Language, and Ideology*. London: Routledge & Kegan Paul.

Blair, C., and M. Cooper. (1987). "The Humanist Turn in Foucault's Rhetoric of Inquiry." *Quarterly Journal of Speech* 73: 151–171.

Blankenship, J. (1976). "The Search for the 1972 Democratic Nomination: A Metaphorical Perspective." In J. Blankenship and H. G. Stelzner, eds., *Rhetoric and Communication: Studies in the University of Illinois Tradition* (Urbana: University of Illinois Press), pp. 236–260.

Blankenship, J., and J. K. Muir. (1987). "On Imaging the Future: The Secular Search for 'Piety.'" *Communication Quarterly* 35: 1–12.

Bourdieu, P. (1977). *Outline of a Theory of Practice*. Translated by R. Nice. Cambridge, UK: Cambridge University Press.

Bourdieu, P. (1979). "Symbolic Power." Translated by R. Nice. *Critique of Anthropology* 4: 77–85.

Bourdieu, P. (1980). "The Production of Belief: Contribution to an Economy of Symbolic Goods." Translated by R. Nice. *Media, Culture, & Society* 2: 261–293.

Brockriede, W. (1974). "Rhetorical Criticism as Argument." *Quarterly Journal of Speech* 60: 165–174.

Brown, R. H. (1987). *Society as Text: Essays on Rhetoric, Reason, and Reality*. Chicago: University of Chicago Press.

Burke, K. (1941). *The Philosophy of Literary Form*. Baton Rouge: Louisiana State University Press.

Burke, K. (1961). *Attitudes Toward History*. Boston: Beacon Press.

Burke, K. (1966). *Language as Symbolic Action*. Berkeley and Los Angeles: University of California Press.

Campbell, K. K. (1983). "Response to Forbes Hill." *Central States Speech Journal* 34: 126–127.

Cawelti, J. G. (1985). "With the Benefit of Hindsight: Popular Cultural Criticism." *Critical Studies in Mass Communication* 2: 363–379.

Charland, M. (1987). "Constitutive Rhetoric: The Case of the *Peuple Québécois.*" *Quarterly Journal of Speech* 73: 133–150 [reprinted in this volume].

Cherwitz, R. A., and J. Hikins. (1986). *Communication and Knowledge: An Investigation in Rhetorical Knowledge.* Columbia: University of South Carolina Press.

Clark, E. C., and R. E. McKerrow. (1987). "The Historiographical Dilemma in Myrdal's American Creed: Rhetoric's Role in Rescuing a Historical Moment." *Quarterly Journal of Speech* 73: 303–316.

Condit, C. (1987). "Democracy and Civil Rights: The Universalizing Influence of Public Argumentation." *Communication Monographs* 54: 1–18.

Edelman, M. (1988). *Constructing the Political Spectacle.* Chicago: University of Chicago Press.

Engels, F. (1942). "Engels to Mehring, July 14, 1893." In *K. Marx and F. Engels: Selected Correspondence, 1846–1895,* trans. D. Torr (New York: International Publishers), vol. 29, pp. 511–512.

Farrell, T. B. (1976). "Knowledge, Consensus, and Rhetorical Theory." *Quarterly Journal of Speech* 62: 258–266 [reprinted in this volume].

Farrell, T. B. (1978). "Social Knowledge, Part 2." *Quarterly Journal of Speech* 64: 329–334.

Fields, A. B. (1988). "In Defense of Political Economy and Systemic Analysis: A Critique of Prevailing Theoretical Approaches to the New Social Movements." In C. Nelson and L. Grossberg, eds., *Marxism and the Interpretation of Culture* (Urbana: University of Illinois Press), pp. 141–156.

Fisher, W. (1985). "The Narrative Paradigm: An Elaboration." *Communication Monographs* 52: 347–367.

Fiske, J. (1986). "Television: Polysemy and Popularity." *Critical Studies in Mass Communication* 3: 391–408.

Foucault, M. (1980a). *Power/Knowledge.* Edited by C. Gordon. Translated by C. Gordon, L. Marshall, J. Mephau, and K. Soper. New York: Pantheon Books.

Foucault, M. (1980b). *The History of Sexuality,* Vol. 1. Translated by R. Hurley. New York: Vintage Books.

Foucault, M. (1982). "Is It Really Important to Think?: An Interview." Translated by T. Keenan. *Philosophical and Social Criticism* 9: 29–40.

Fraser, N. (1981). "Foucault on Modern Power: Empirical Insights and Normative Confusions." *Praxis International* 1: 272–287.

Fraser, N. (1985). "What's Critical about Critical Theory?: The Case of Habermas and Gender." *New German Critique* 35: 97–131.

Giddens, A. (1979). *Central Problems in Social Theory.* Berkeley and Los Angeles: University of California Press.

Giddens, A. (1984). *The Constitution of Society: Outline of a Theory of Structuration.* Cambridge, UK: Polity Press.

Grossberg, L. (1984). "Strategies of Marxist Cultural Interpretation." *Critical Studies in Mass Communication* 1: 391–421.

Habermas, J. (1984). *The Theory of Communicative Action, Vol. 1: Reason and Rationalization of Society.* Translated by T. McCarthy. Boston: Beacon Press.

Habermas, J. (1987). *The Philosophical Discourses of Modernity.* Translated by F. Lawrence. Cambridge, MA: MIT Press.

Hall, S. (1985). "Signification, Representation, Ideology: Althusser and the Post-Structuralist Debates." *Critical Studies in Mass Communication* 2: 91–114.

Hall, S. (1988). "The Toad in the Garden: Thatcherism among the Theorists." In C. Nelson and L. Grossberg, eds., *Marxism and the Interpretation of Culture* (Urbana: University of Illinois Press), pp. 35–57.

Hariman, R. (1986). "Status, Marginality, and Rhetorical Theory." *Quarterly Journal of Speech* 72: 38–54 [reprinted in this volume].

Hiley, D. (1984). "Foucault and the Analysis of Power." *Praxis International* 4: 192–207.

Hill, F. (1983). "A Turn against Ideology: Reply to Professor Wander." *Central States Speech Journal* 34: 121–126.

Jensen, K. B. (1987). "Qualitative Audience Research: Toward an Integrative Approach to Reception." *Critical Studies in Mass Communication* 4: 21–36.

Kent, C. A. (1986). "Michel Foucault: Doing History or Undoing It?" *Canadian Journal of History* 21: 371–396.

Laclau, E. (1977). *Politics and Ideology in Marxist Theory.* London: NLB.

Laclau, E. (1980). "Populist Rupture and Discourse." Translated by J. Grealy. *Screen Education* 34: 87–93.

Laclau, E. (1983). "'Socialism,' the 'People,' 'Democracy': The Transformation of Hegemonic Logic." *Social Text* 7: 115–119.

Laclau, E., and C. Mouffe (1985). *Hegemony and Socialist Strategy: Towards a Radical Democratic Politics.* Translated by W. Moore and P. Cammack. London: Verso.

Leff, M. (1978). "In Search of Ariadne's Thread: A Review of the Recent Literature on Rhetorical Theory." *Central States Speech Journal* 29: 73–91.

Lentricchia, F. (1983). *Criticism and Social Change.* Chicago: University of Chicago Press.

Lyne, J. (1985). "Rhetorics of Inquiry." *Quarterly Journal of Speech* 71: 65–73.

Mailloux, S. (1985). "Rhetorical Hermeneutics." *Critical Inquiry* 11: 620–641.

Markovic, M. (1983). "The Idea of Critique in Social Theory." *Praxis International* 3: 108–120.

McGee, M. C. (1975). "In Search of 'the People': A Rhetorical Alternative." *Quarterly Journal of Speech* 61: 235–249.

McGee, M. C. (1980). "The 'Ideograph:' A Link Between Rhetoric and Ideology." *Quarterly Journal of Speech* 66: 1–16 [reprinted in this volume].

McGee, M. C. (1982). "A Materialist's Conception of Rhetoric." In R. E. McKerrow, ed., *Explorations in Rhetoric* (Glenview, IL: Scott, Foresman), pp. 23–48.

McGee, M. C. (1984). "Another Philippic: Notes on the Ideological Turn in Criticism." *Central States Speech Journal* 35: 43–50.

McGee, M. C. (1987, April). "Public Address and Culture Studies." Paper presented at the annual meeting of the Central States Speech Association, St. Louis.

McKerrow, R. E. (1986). "Pragmatic Justification and Perelman's Philosophical Rhetoric." In J. Golden and J. J. Pilotta, eds., *Practical Reasoning in Human Affairs: Studies in Honor of Chaim Perelman* (Dordrecht, The Netherlands: D. Reidel), pp. 207–225.

Misgeld, D. (1985). "Critical Hermeneutics versus Neoparsonianism?" *New German Critique* 35: 55–82.

Mosco, V. (1983). "Critical Research and the Role of Labor." *Journal of Communication* 33: 237–248.

Mullins, W. A. (1979). "Truth and Ideology: Reflections on Mannheim's Paradox." *History and Theory* 18: 141–154.

Mumby, D. K. (1987). "The Political Function of Narrative in Organizations." *Communication Monographs* 54: 113–127.

Nelson, J. S., and A. Megill. (1986). "Rhetoric of Inquiry: Prospects and Projects." *Quarterly Journal of Speech* 72: 20–37.

Nelson, J. S., A. Megill, and D. N. McCloskey, eds. (1987). *The Rhetoric of the Human Sciences*. Madison: University of Wisconsin Press.

Perelman, C., and L. Olbrechts-Tyteca. (1969). *The New Rhetoric: A Treatise on Argumentation*. Translated by J. Wilkinson and P. Weaver. South Bend, IN: University of Notre Dame Press.

Rajchman, J. (1985). *Michel Foucault: The Freedom of Philosophy*. New York: Columbia University Press.

Ross, S. D. (1985). "Foucault's Radical Politics." *Praxis International* 5: 131–144.

Scott, R. L. (1967). "On Viewing Rhetoric as Epistemic." *Central States Speech Journal* 18: 9–17 [reprinted in this volume].

Scott, R. L. (1976). "On Viewing Rhetoric as Epistemic:

Ten Years Later." *Central States Speech Journal* 27: 258–266.

Shiner, L. (1982). "Reading Foucault: Anti-Method and the Genealogy of Power/Knowledge." *History and Theory* 21: 382–398.

Simons, H. (1985)."Chronicle and Critique of a Conference." *Quarterly Journal of Speech* 71: 52–64.

Simons, H., and A. A. Aghazarian, eds. (1986). *Form, Genre, and the Study of Political Discourse*. Columbia: University of South Carolina Press.

Slack, J. D., and M. Allor. (1983). "The Political and Epistemological Constituents of Critical Communication Research." *Journal of Communication* 33: 208–218.

Therborn, G. (1980). *The Ideology of Power and the Power of Ideology*. London: NLB.

Thompson, J. B. (1984). *Studies in the Theory of Ideology*. Berkeley and Los Angeles: University of California Press.

Toulmin, S. (1972). *Human Understanding*. Princeton, NJ: Princeton University Press.

Turner, K. (1986, April). "Rhetoric of, by, and for the Media: Public Address Studies in an Age of Mass Communication." Paper presented at the annual meeting of the Central States Speech Association, Cincinnati.

Wander, P. (1981). "Cultural Criticism." In D. Nimmo and K. Sanders, eds., *Handbook of Political Communication* (Beverly Hills, CA: Sage), pp. 497–528.

Wander, P. (1983). "The Ideological Turn in Modern Criticism." *Central States Speech Journal* 34: 1–18.

West, C. (1988). "Marxist Theory and the Specificity of Afro-American Oppression." In C. Nelson and L. Grossberg, eds., *Marxism and the Interpretation of Culture* (Urbana: University of Illinois Press), pp. 17–29.

Critical Rhetoric as Political Discourse

John M. Murphy

Aristotle concludes his Rhetoric with the words: "I have spoken; you have listened, you have [the facts], you judge" (p. 282). It is significant, as Beiner (1983, p. 97) notes, that Aristotle ends the Rhetoric with the concept of *krinate*, or judgment.[1] The persuasive task of the work is to legitimate the study of rhetoric. Aristotle's rationale rests on the need for citizens to make public judgments. He forwards a "more generous appraisal" (Hariman, 1986, p. 38) of rhetoric than Plato by emphasizing its role in human affairs as a *techne* and a *dynamis* (Farrell, 1993a, p. 65) designed to invent judgments for the good of the community. Warnick (1989, p. 305) observes, "rhetoric consisted of observing the available means of persuasion and considering how they could be applied so as to achieve good for the state and its citizenry through *phronesis*." *Phronesis*, in turn, is the "practical wisdom" needed to deliberate well about the needs of the community and to call forth appropriate action. Rhetoric finds its end in *phronesis* and its justification as a field of study in the necessity for a group of citizens to make appropriate judgments concerning the future of their community.

Aristotle's rationale for rhetoric has cast its shadow over American rhetorical studies (at least in speech departments) since the founding of what became the Speech Communication Association in the early twentieth century. Despite significant debates over *how* to study public speech, *whose* speech to study, and *what* counts as public speech, the justification for the practice of rhetorical studies generally found its way back to Aris-

totle's founding text and the needs of democracy. Wichelns (1925; rpt. 1993, p. 2) asserted, "Oratory is intimately associated with statecraft," and proclaimed, "the conditions of democracy *necessitate* both the making of speeches and the study of the art" [my emphasis]. So let it be said, so let it be done.

Nor did Wichelns' immediate academic descendants waver in the true faith. Bryant (1953) and Wallace (1963) affirmed the intimate link between rhetoric, criticism, and democratic choice. Medhurst has artfully summed up the dominant perspective: "To be able to articulate a point of view, defend a proposition, attack an evil, or celebrate a set of common values was seen as one of the central ways in which the people retained their freedoms and shaped their society. Training in public address was thus understood to be preparation for citizenship in a democratic Republic" (Medhurst, 1993, p. xi; see also Wander, 1983). The humanist vocation of speech communication scholars was clear. Democracy required rhetorical critics.

The reversal of that proposition plagues contemporary descendants of Wichelns: Rhetorical critics may well require democracy. If the primary critical task in the 1970's concerned the reconstruction (and proliferation) of method in the wake of *Rhetorical Criticism: A Study in Method* (Black, 1965; rpt. 1978), then the pivotal issue that has emerged of late is the precarious state of the "public sphere" (Goodnight, 1982; Cox, 1990) needed for democratic decision making, and, perhaps, for rhetorical criticism. As early as 1972, Wander and

413

Jenkins, as well as Campbell, questioned critics' taken-for-granted belief in a full and fair democracy and their academic detachment from political issues (Wander and Jenkins, 1972; Campbell, 1972). McGee's (1975; 1980; 1982) appropriation of European social theory, Goodnight's (1982; 1989) elegaic rendering of the public sphere, and Fisher's (1984) espousal of the narrative paradigm, accelerated concern over the perceived decline in public deliberation. This erosion of faith in the "possibility of public discourse itself" (Cox, 1990, p. 327), and the suspicion that the good of the state did not necessarily coincide with that of its citizenry, undermined not only traditional rhetorical criticism, but also the vocation of critic. If public deliberation does not exist, then neither can its student: the rhetorical critic.

This is Raymie E. McKerrow's position in "Critical Rhetoric: Theory and *Praxis*" (1989). Following in the footsteps of Wander, McGee, Goodnight, et al., McKerrow carries that line of argument to its ultimate conclusion and opens the door to see what might lie on the other side.[2] If we no longer have public deliberation, then what might rhetorical critics become? Critical rhetoricians. McKerrow offers his colleagues a new name and, consequently, a new "orientation" (p. 100). McKerrow seeks to revitalize his vocation in a time of corrosive doubt by using and sustaining that doubt to invent a new role for the critic.

The "*telos* that marks the project is one of never-ending skepticism, hence permanent criticism" (p. 96). The critic is a "specific intellectual," who seeks to reveal, in a "critique of domination," and a "critique of freedom," the "discourse of power." McKerrow, unlike his predecessors, does not anguish over the fate of democratic deliberation. He assumes that it can no longer exist in the manner articulated by Wichelns. Deliberation has become "symbolism which addresses publics" (p. 101); said symbolism is a discourse of "power/ knowledge." Efforts for social change produce new relations of oppression. Critical rhetoricians take on the Sisyphean task of demystifying and recharacterizing ongoing, oppressive discursive formations. Consistent with the role he advocates, McKerrow seeks, in his arena, "transformation" of the "set of social relations" named rhetorical criticism into "critical rhetoric" (p. 103).

He asks us, then, to take a "postmodern turn" in rhetorical studies. Best and Kellner (1991, pp. 5–28) note that a postmodern era has been declared for 100 years. Critical to an understanding of its character is the ambivalence inherent in the term; as Best and Kellner (p. 29) argue, the "post" can signify "an active term of negation which attempts to move beyond the modern era and its theoretical and cultural practices." But the "post" also implies "a dependence on, a continuity with, that which it follows." McKerrow (1991a, p. 75) believes that such "tension is inevitable." But the very presence of "post" signals a desire to separate the modern from what follows. Best and Kellner (1991, p. 30) agree: "The discourses of the postmodern therefore presuppose a sense of an ending, the advent of something new, and the demand that we develop new categories, theories, and methods to explore and conceptualize this *novum*, this novel social and cultural situation."

The call for critical rhetoric, I suggest, can best be characterized as rhetoric's effort to chart this "*novum*." In that sense, the rhetoric of critical rhetoric maintains a familial relation with conservative claims of an end of history or racism and with radical celebrations of a hyperreality. In each case, the symbolic charge of the discourse rests on the assertion of a rupture between past and present and a consequent need for a new orientation. In what follows, I explore the discourse of critical rhetoric as a kind of millenial appeal (e.g., Bercovitch, 1978; Brummett, 1984) that posits a new time for rhetoric and asserts the centrality of a critical rhetoric in a postmodern condition.

I examine three key differences between rhetorical criticism and critical rhetoric that mark this new era. First, following the lead of Gaonkar (1993), I focus on McKerrow's juxtaposition of reason and rhetoric. Second, I turn to the disjunction between the text and the fragment. Finally, I explore the audience in rhetorical criticism as opposed to the subject of critical rhetoric.

In each case, critical rhetoric advocates characteristically employ "dissociation" as their key rhetorical strategy (Perelman and Olbrechts-Tyteca, 1969, pp. 411–59). The apparent value of the first (modernist) term in each pair is undermined by the second (postmodernist) term, a movement which concludes with the disjunction between rhetorical criticism and critical rhetoric. In this essay, I explore and extend Hariman's observation (1991, p. 67) that a modernist style of argument, marked by impersonal, dissociative, analytical strategies, shapes McKerrow's essay.

Unlike McKerrow's rather easy response to Hariman's critique (1991a, pp. 75–76), I do not think that those of us who identify with the spirit of critical rhetoric (e.g., Murphy, 1992) should reify the oppositions created by dissociation. Form matters and the formal oppositions shaping this discourse merely reverse the terms, while replicating the dialectic, between authorizing and marginalizing theoretical practices (Hariman, 1986). Rather than arguing that "the advantage of a critical rhetoric lies in its reversal of the traditional terms" (McKerrow, 1991a, p. 76), we should encourage the languages of criticism and critique to inform each other so that, in a phrase lifted from the Reverend Jesse Jackson, we can move to "a higher ground." In pursuit of that goal, I argue that Bakhtin's (1984) concept of "novelization," a process in which previously unquestioned discourses come to interanimate one another, might better characterize our current situation than the claim of a postmodern condition.

Reason and Rhetoric

McKerrow begins his presentation of critical rhetoric with a dissociation (Perelman and Olbrechts-Tyteca, 1969, pp. 411–59). Specifically, he (1989, p. 91) employs the appearance/reality pair. Previous efforts to save rhetoric, including "Habermas's 'ideal speech situation,' Perelman's (1969) 'universal audience,' and Toulmin's 'impartial standpoint of rationality'" only appear to do so because, in reality, they "preserve for rhetoric a subordinate role in the service of reason." McKerrow establishes a series of equivalences. "Reason" is renamed "universalist approaches" which, in turn, become "the constraints of a Platonic conception" (p. 91). A new dialectical pair appears. "Critical rhetoric" emerges as the pivotal term opposing a "Platonic conception" of rhetoric. As such, critical rhetoric commands a considerable symbolic charge. Opponents to a Platonic view of rhetoric fall under the banner of critical rhetoric; others remain wedded to the "trivializing influence of universalist approaches" (p. 91).

Gaonkar (1993, p. 150) also notes this strategy: "What is remarkable about this passage is the stark opposition it posits between reason and rhetoric." He urges McKerrow to seek an alliance with those who would rehabilitate reason, but he recognizes that that may be impossible: "It is precisely this stubborn refusal of reason (rather than a critique of domination) that gives the CR project a distinctly postmodern aura" (p. 150). What remains unclear in McKerrow and Gaonkar, however, is the definition of reason. What precisely is McKerrow rejecting?

On the one hand, McKerrow endorses those in rhetorical studies and elsewhere who discard norms of universalist reason. Consistent with the "rhetoric is epistemic" project (Scott, 1967, 1976),

with Farrell's (1976, 1978, 1993a) championing of social knowledge, and with the symbolic interactionist/Burkean frame that informs much public address study (e.g., Zarefsky, 1989), McKerrow adopts an "anti-foundationalist" position. Reason cannot create universal standards for conduct nor can it provide a secure foundation for knowledge claims. McKerrow's concern over the universalist elements in Habermas's work, for instance, is shared by Farrell (1993a, pp. 188–213).

On the other hand, there is considerable evidence that McKerrow goes well beyond this position. He distrusts all consensus, foundational or not, as an infringement of individual freedom. That doubt dismisses not only universalist reason, but also reason based on community knowledge or practical wisdom. His patterns of association/dissociation support this view. In the opening, McKerrow distances Habermas, Perelman, and Toulmin from his project. Subsequently, in his discussion of *doxa* (pp. 103–105), Scott, Farrell, Leff, Nelson, Megill, Cherwitz, and Hikins are grouped together as "theorists" who "do no more than attempt to rescue rhetoric from the oblivion to which Plato consigned it. Considerations of rhetoric as epistemic are inextricably linked to a neo-Kantian definition of what constitutes knowledge, as that will always be seen in terms of independent, universal standards of judgment (whether invoked by Perelman, Toulmin, or Habermas)" (p. 104; fn. 5, p. 109). Scholars from Scott to Cherwitz are dismissed as neo-Kantians.

Surely, McKerrow understands the considerable differences between these theorists. Yet for the critical rhetoric project, these divergences matter little, as a more detailed examination of McKerrow's version of *doxa* reveals. He draws on Hariman's (1986) explanation. Hariman argues that *doxa* has generally been contrasted to *episteme*; the former rests on opinion, the latter on true knowledge. Absent a belief in "Truth," *doxa* becomes so diffuse as to lack any use. If everything is *doxa*, then nothing is *doxa*. To retrieve *doxa*, Hariman (p. 50) repositions it in terms of *aletheia*, "truth (literally 'unhiddenness'). . . . This dynamic of concealment and unconcealment—of authorizing and marginalizing—is the means by which we determine what we believe, what we know, and what we believe to be true."

As Hariman's language reveals, he retains an interest in epistemological issues as resting beside, and potentially interrogating, the claims of *doxa*. He later objects to McKerrow's dissociation of *doxa* and *episteme* by noting, "The relationship is linear, not oppositional" (1991, p. 69). The spatial metaphors infusing Hariman's (e.g., "zones of centrality and marginality," p. 39) 1986 essay testify to the relevance of epistemological discourse, and to its place in rhetoric (it has its "zone"), if only as interlocutor for doxastic reason.

McKerrow, however, dispenses with epistemology. Rather, the only social dynamic is the rhythmic alteration between concealing and revealing. The point of critical rhetoric becomes, consistent with the millenialist cast of a postmodern condition, revelation. Critical rhetoric will "reveal," "unmask," "demystify," "make explicit," and "expose," the names that are the "effects of truth." These names are the elements of *doxa*. Unlike Scott, Farrell, et al., who see the materials of community *doxa* as having emancipatory potential, McKerrow wants to work through *doxa* to *aletheia*. *Doxa* creates marginality (1989, p. 105), operates as "concealment," (p. 104), and conserves "cultural capital" for those in authority (pp. 104–105). Critical rhetoric reveals the "dense web" of *doxa* and its oppressive effects.

McKerrow sees rhetorical critics as neo-Kantians because, whatever the differences between *doxa* and *episteme*, both perform the same political task. They elide difference in pursuit of consensus and end up "appropriating" the "symbolic capital" of a community to the detriment of marginalized peoples (p. 105). Critical rhetors respond skeptically to *doxa* because, even if a critique produces emancipatory social knowledge, all social knowledge is tainted by power. Consistent with his Foucauldian leanings, McKerrow sees knowledge/power as constituted by, and constitutive of, one another (1989, pp. 97–100). Any relaxation of skepticism allows a new normal order to establish itself and oppressive practices to continue. We need to take McKerrow seriously when he says that critique should "shift to how the symbols come to possess power—what they 'do' in society as contrasted to what they 'are'" (p. 104). Whether discourses "are" grounded or not, they "do" the same thing: preserve the status quo (p. 105). *Doxa* throws a shadow as long and ominous as *episteme* because both enforce consensus and disdain marginal practices.

McKerrow, then, not only dissociates universalist reason from critical rhetoric, but also reason that could "locate the contingent good for a particular community at a particular time and place" (Charland, 1991, p. 73). McKerrow (1991, p. 77), in his reply to Charland, rejects a consensus that relies on only contingency and probability. He does so, I suspect, because consensual adoption of any "good" erodes the need for permanent skepticism. Similarly, when he responds to Sproule's

elucidation of propaganda studies as a language for ideological critique, McKerrow avers a series of dissociations ("Criticism/Critique," "Permanence/ Change," etc.) that reject Sproule and criticism as a "perpetuation of the ideals of a 'rational democracy'" (1991b, p. 250).

McKerrow dissociates from critical rhetoric all forms of reasoning that aim at consensus. The critical rhetoric project views the wisdom of a community with deep suspicion because it is the commonality of common sense, the widespread acceptance of "good reasons," and the "norms of a rhetorical culture," that oppress individuals and prevent them from asserting differences. No one argument or advocate can or should represent the diversity of a community. Rational democracy cannot be privileged because it relies on such representation. Similarly, "a ratiocinative discourse which can be located in space and time as an isolated event" and which purports to represent a community's judgment must be fragmented (1989, p. 101).

Text and Fragment

I have argued that McKerrow rejects not only the usual focus of rhetoric's distrust, universal reason, but also reason rooted in the deliberative practice of a community. The dissociation of practical reason from critical rhetoric seems to lead naturally to the second dissociation between text and fragment. As Burke (1966, p. 19) says, "A given terminology contains various implications, and there is a corresponding 'perfectionist' tendency for men [women] to attempt carrying out those implications." The dissociations in McKerrow's argument stake out a new language to cope with a new era. Like all symbolic action, that vocabulary has implicit within it a "principle of perfection." If community *doxa* and practical reason come under suspicion, then so should the articulation of consensual wisdom: the rhetorical text.

The debate over the text was fully joined in a now famous 1990 issue of the *Western Journal of Speech Communication*, but, McKerrow reveals (1989, pp. 100–101), McGee's work, in the form of convention papers, had already influenced McKerrow. McGee offers the critical rhetoric project two promising metaphors. Fragmentation, the first, provides the visual image of pieces swirling about in a maelstrom of postmodern textuality. The second, critic as inventor (McGee, 1990, p. 288; McKerrow, 1993b, p. 120), provides, especially in mainstream American culture, the image of a garage tinkerer (McKerrow, 1991a, p. 78), arranging, fitting, and playing with the fragments that fill the workshop.

In support of the fragmentation thesis, McGee (1990, pp. 284–86) develops a plausible narrative. The homogeneity of the nineteenth century has given way to a very different twentieth century culture. Various social movements, from feminism to civil rights, fractured the ruling consensus. Concomitantly, the "public's business is now being done more often via direct mail, television spots, documentaries, mass entertainment, and 'quotable quotes' on the evening news than through the more traditional media (broadsides, pamphlets, books, and public speeches)" (p. 286). As a result, "the human condition has changed" (p. 286). McKerrow (1989, p. 101) implicitly endorses this position: "More often than not, the products of discourse are mediated—are no longer the simple property of a speaker–audience relationship" [my emphasis]. To hammer home the point, McKerrow repeats the term "mediated" four times in five sentences (p. 101).

This new environment requires the critic to become the inventor. The old critical strategies will not do. Propelled by new communication technologies and freed from the constraints of a stable political vocabulary, fragments "fly by" too quickly (McGee, 1990, p. 287) for conventional analysis. They are "disparate scraps" (McKerrow, 1989, p. 101) which only have meaning as threads of the "fabric of mediated experience," as part of the "'dense web' (Mosco, 1983, p. 239)" of discourse. By viewing the world as discursively fragmented, critical inventors can attend to discourses "in their original, fragmented form" (McKerrow, 1989, p. 101); inventors tinker with the fragments in order to reconstruct "otherwise hidden or taken for granted social practices" (p. 101).

If I have read McKerrow and McGee correctly, the "fragments" do not remain "disparate scraps" for long. Critical tinkerers arrange, move, and play with the pieces in order to display the "web" of cultural practices. McKerrow's assertion (1989, p. 105) that "Naming is the central symbolic act of a nominalist rhetoric" supports this claim; reweaving the web and renaming the fragments alter social practices. McKerrow (1989, p. 100) notes that "recharacterization of the images changes the power relations and recreates a new 'normal' order."[3] That done, the process begins again.

These two metaphors perform potent dissociative functions. Putting aside the history's accuracy, the metaphors paint a persuasive contrast between past and future and a powerful rationale

for critical rhetoric. First, the account of historical change naturalizes a postmodern condition. It is here and, as McGee (1990, p. 278) asserts, the time has come to "stop whining" about it and, instead, "develop realistic strategies to cope with it as a fact of human life."[4] Second, consistent with Best and Kellner's observation that postmodernism justifies itself as the only way to cope with a new time, critical rhetoric sees itself as historically "necessary" (p. 288). Only critical rhetoric presents "realistic strategies" for a postmodern condition, gets at discourse in its "original" form, and comprehends the mediated qualities of today's fragments. In short, critical rhetoric avoids "the perpetuation of sterile forms of scholarship" (McKerrow, 1989, p. 101).

Finally, as the tone of the preceding comment indicates, the role of a critical rhetorician is decidedly superior to that of a rhetorical critic. Rhetors, unlike critics, do rhetoric. As the name change symbolizes, rhetoric is transformed from an ephemeral quality, an adjective, into a real entity, a noun: rhetorical criticism/critical rhetoric. In addition, critical rhetoricians, as McGee emphasizes (1990, pp. 274, 288) at the beginning and end of his essay, engage in "text construction" and invention rather than in interpretation. Critical rhetoricians invent texts; rhetorical critics interpret texts. The attribution of status is clear. After all, those who can, do. Those who can't, teach.

In other words, the "new wine" of postmodernism cannot be poured into the "old wineskins" of rhetorical criticism lest the "skins burst, and the wine is spilled, and the skins are destroyed; but new wine is put into fresh wineskins, and so both are preserved" (Matthew 9:17). McKerrow's "secularization" of this logological pattern (Burke, 1961; rpt. 1970) is, perhaps, the most prominent example of the millennialist cast of critical rhetoric. With the status and authority of a biblical prophet, McKerrow gives us a new time, an era in which rhetoric (the last shall be first and the first shall be last) "emerges with status" (original emphasis; p. 109). The disjunction between past and future, between rhetorical criticism and critical rhetoric, could hardly be more complete.

Together, the dissociative pairs of reason/rhetoric and text/fragment construct a formal opposition between rhetorical criticism and critical rhetoric. Consistent with the emphasis on "difference," and the desire to "reverse the traditional terms," these pairs open a gulf between the two practices and occlude the possibility of dialogue. But that is not all. The dismissal of social knowledge and the dominance of the fragment suggest yet another pair. If texts no longer articulate the consensual wisdom of a community in action, then what happens to the community?

Audience and Subject

The oxymoron of an "active subject" has been the Achilles' heel of any project, such as critical rhetoric, influenced by Foucault. Even those critics not immersed in the optimism of rhetoric (Charland, 1990, pp. 262–63) are put off by this aspect of his work. Best and Kellner (1991, p. 70) note, "On Foucault's account, power is mostly treated as an impersonal and anonymous force which is exercized apart from the actions and intentions of human subjects." Giddens (1982, p. 222) says that Foucault confuses "history without a transcendental subject and history without knowledgeable human subjects." Feminists are deeply suspicious of a "decentered" subject: "Why is it that just at the moment when so many of us who have been silenced begin to demand the right to name ourselves, to act as subjects rather than objects of history, that just then the concept of subjecthood becomes problematic?" (Hartsock, 1990, p. 162).

McKerrow (1989, p. 99) creates similar questions: "Power is expressed anonymously, in nondeliberate ways, at a 'deep structure' level and may have its origins in the remoteness of our past (carried forward through a particularizing discursive formation)." People can be "active participants in 'revolt' against the present dangers," but the means are unclear, especially when he denies agents the capacity to be "productive of contingently derived social practices" (p. 99). Consistent with his view of reason, even contingency is precluded. Well might he say, "the project leaves one wondering about the 'who' that is engaging in the performance of rhetor or critic" (1993a, p. 52).

Addressing that issue consumes "Critical Rhetoric and the Possibility of the Subject" (1993a). Acknowledging the rhetorical problem that he faces, McKerrow says that critical rhetoric "does not dismiss the subject in its entirety" (p. 51). The elision forecasts another dissociative strategy. McKerrow couples the rational and the decentered subject, a pair in which "Term II provides a criterion, a norm which allows us to distinguish those aspects of term I which are of value from those aspects which are not" (Perelman, 1982, p. 127). The materiality of the subject is valuable. The body, in a symbolic reversal of Burkean rhetorical theory, will become the grounds for a politically active subject.

McKerrow (1993a, p. 52) notes, "Before the subject is the body. That much is obvious." This assumption is key to the development of an active subject in postmodernity. McKerrow (1993a, p. 54) says, "The potentiality is present for the body, as prior to the subject, to enact political change—to address or present for revision the social practices that constrain the subject's freedom." The body, in McKerrow's analysis and in Foucault's later work, is one place that might not be colonized by reason. Or, at minimum, physical action might be the means by which one can escape the domineering influence of a discursive formation. If one physically moves out of discourse, one defies discourse.[5] McKerrow (p. 54) quotes Martin, "'the body's will to action, the concrete sense of possibility, subverts the passivity engendered by the dominance of the sign. The subject as performer confronts the culture of spectatorship.'" Burke is reversed. The physical is the realm of action; the discursive is the realm of motion.[6]

Rhetoric becomes the care of the self, the art of the body, the realm of the physical, and the subversion of the sign. Reason becomes the culture of spectatorship, the arena of dominance, the realm of the discursive, and the passivity "engendered" (!) by the sign.[7] The extent of the change that McKerrow proposes for rhetoric is symbolized by the title of the book he most often offers up as the path to political engagement: *The Care of the Self*. Whether one accepts or rejects the contours of rhetorical thought from Aristotle to the present, the difference between the sociality of that tradition and a "Care of the Self" is profound.

I am not at all sure that McKerrow's characterization of the subject will gain widespread support, even among advocates of critical rhetoric. The body, by McKerrow's own account, is positioned within a discursive formation. In these times, it is often named ("subjected") before it is born. If we grant the notion of a "deep structure," that "may have its origins in the remoteness of our past," we cannot easily accept the disjunction between the subject and the body.

McGee (1990, p. 274), for instance, eschews the language of the "subject," forthrightly aligns critics with audiences, and argues that both construct texts. This position is implicit in McKerrow's 1989 endorsement of polysemy. He argues, "Fragments contain the potential for polysemic rather than monosemic interpretation," and, quoting John Fiske (1986), speaks surprisingly (given his later determination to see the sign itself as corrupt) of subjects' ability to "'take the signifying practices and products of the dominant' and 'use them for different social purposes'" (p. 108). Ono and Sloop (1995) argue similarly when they justify a focus on the "vernacular community" as a site for critique and describe strategies which might allow such a community to engage in polysemic practices and political change.[8] To put it mildly, tensions and contradictions criss-cross these ruminations on the subject.

It is no accident that critical rhetoricians have struggled with the problem of audience. On the one hand, they feel the need to reverse the traditional terms and chart a new era. On the other hand, if they eliminate the audience, to whom do they speak? Charland (1990, p. 256) has noted, "Rhetorical analysis proceeds with 'audience' as its ground . . . rhetoric produces new social knowledge as it offers public interpretations of social experience and proceeds to make normative claims." This stance is anathema to McKerrow's determination to avoid normative claims, consensual reason, and coherent texts. If rhetoric must "reverse the traditional terms," then the theoretical commitment to audience as agent needs to change.

Yet the dismissal of the "symbol-user" comes back to haunt McKerrow. It may be that the critical rhetorician can escape the confines of a discursive formation, whether as a "specific intellectual" (McKerrow, 1989, p. 108) or as Ono and Sloop's ironist (1992). But, again, to whom do they speak if the rest of us are produced by power? The perceived nihilism of critical rhetoric results not from the stance of the critic, as Ono and Sloop (1992) seem to believe, but from the position of the audience. Polysemy may be one way out, but, even discarding serious worries about the concept (Condit, 1989), Fiske's optimism about the power of socially situated viewers is in sharp contrast to McKerrow's belief in "deep structures" and "hidden social practices" that confine the audience.

Rather, McKerrow's faith that critical rhetoricians can "unmask" and "illuminate" the "hidden" structures of knowledge coincides more clearly with millennialism than with John Fiske. Like the "elect" of Puritan discourse (Bercovitch, 1978), the critical rhetor reveals the truth of our times. But this elitism coexists uneasily with the "critical spirit" of the project and I doubt that its practitioners really think of themselves as an elect. The dissociations characteristic of the critical rhetoric argument, however, push its believers toward that stance.

It is on the issue of audience that the dissociations making up critical rhetoric flounder. Even

in a postmodern condition, rhetors (critics) must speak to others. Yet the apparent need to demarcate critical rhetoric as different from, and superior to, criticism demands a "subjected" audience. That need also infuses the disregard for the traditional ground of rhetoric, social knowledge, and its concrete manifestation, the public address text. But the very presence of these dissociations suggests that critical rhetoric cannot quite escape the old way of making arguments. The modernist style and purpose of critical rhetoric discourse haunts its declaration of a new world in which rhetoric will emerge with "status." It would be better to acknowledge frankly (and, perhaps, ironically) the dependence of the new upon the old.

Novelization

In that spirit, I begin with a recharacterization of McGee's (1990, pp. 284–86) narrative. Rather than seeing the nineteenth century as a time of totalizing discourse, we should recognize that the "Whig" consensus, held in place partly through material and political power, was given to claims of certainty and, in Bakhtin's terms, to a certain naivete (1984, p. 271). The always present centripetal forces of language held sway over the also always present centrifugal forces. The assumptions underlying public speech, detailed by McGee, enforced the naive notion that there was only one way of seeing the world, one way of engaging in public deliberation, and one kind of person who could participate in rhetorical action.

Yet, as John Angus Campbell points out (1990, pp. 355–56), that discourse had always been challenged by a wide variety of advocates. To some extent, they reinforced the status quo by attacking the consensus "in its own name" and revealing its contradictions (Gitlin, 1979, p. 265). Early woman's rights advocates, for example, framed the "Declaration of Sentiments" as a parody of the Declaration of Independence because it "expresses in the most forceful and least controversial form the radical notion that all human beings have certain fundamental rights as humans, that the function of government is to protect those rights from encroachment, and that when and if government does not perform that duty, revolutionary change is appropriate" (Campbell, 1989, p. 52). Certainly, these women affirmed the language of traditional liberal ideals.

But the presence of woman in the Declaration transformed that language. The Declaration became "internally dialogized" (Morson and Emerson, 1990, p. 299); after the Declaration of Sentiments, the phrase "all men and women are created equal" animated "all men are created equal." Even if one continued to agree with the male hegemony of the original phrase, it had lost its naivete. It had been tested and even agreement, as opposed to unquestioned acceptance, is a dialogic relation. The language of masculine liberalism now had to take "a sideward glance at other ways of speaking" (p. 304). Specific changes would be a long time in coming, and would require much effort, but the stage was set.

Novelization is a reaccentuation of naive languages, such as the masculinity of the Declaration of Independence. Bakhtin, constantly concerned with linguistic multiplicity, privileges the novel because he thinks that it best captures the multiple languages (heteroglossia) and multiple voices (polyphony) of the social world. When the novel encounters monologic genres, it refracts the spotlight of naive speech. A particular way of speaking, once unselfconsciously holding absolute authority, becomes polemical, polyphonic, or, to invoke Burke's language (1945; 1969, pp. 511–517), ironic. Burke (p. 513) says, for example, that an ironic sense of history

> would be a dialectic of characters in which, for instance, we should never expect to see 'feudalism' overthrown by 'capitalism' and 'capitalism' succeeded by some manner of national or international or non-national or neo-national or postnational socialism - but rather should note elements of all such positions (or 'voices') existing always, but attaining greater clarity of expression or imperiousness of proportion of [in?] one period than another.

Bakhtin puts it another way: the language becomes Galilean rather than Ptolemaic (1981, pp. 366–67).

Yet even in Galileo's view, the earth continued to exist. The language of the Founders, as anyone who watched Robert Bork struggle with "original intent" in his confirmation hearings can attest, affects public speech in our so-called postmodern age. Ways of speaking do not disappear; they adapt, they go underground, they return, they inflect other ways of speaking, but they do not depart at the announcement of a new age. In short, McGee's story contains another dissociation: a homogeneous nineteenth century vs. a heterogeneous twentieth century. Neither characterization is "precisely right or precisely wrong.

They are all voices, or personalities, or positions, integrally affecting one another" (Burke, 1945; 1969, p. 512). Rather than thinking of American rhetorical history in diametrically opposed terms, it might be better to chart the novelization of public speech, the gradual loss, on the part of some genres, of authority to speak for the culture, and the gradual gain, on the part of other genres, of cultural authority.

Jasinski (1995a, 1995b) and Zulick (1991, 1992) have begun to sketch the outline of a novelized rhetorical world.[9] The hub of critical work, in Jasinski's (1995a, pp. 17–19) view, becomes "performative traditions." Such traditions consist of a specific idiom, enacted by particular speakers, marked by characteristic figurative and argumentative devices, and shaped by a variety of textual practices. A multiplicity of traditions infuse the social world; speakers orchestrate the resources of traditions in acts of rhetorical invention aimed at extending, transforming, or adapting rhetorical possibilities to specific circumstances.

Zulick (1992, p. 142), for instance, traces the composition of the Book of Jeremiah, in the face of political and military disaster, as a "community's effort to redeem its own religious imagination through the dialogic invention of a prophet's life." That book, in turn, inspired the jeremiad as Puritans sought to make sense of their catastrophes and redeem their errand into the wilderness (Bormann, 1977). Inventive American revolutionaries adapted the form to their needs (Bercovitch, 1978) and the tradition has persisted well into the twentieth century as an interpretive lens for communal crisis (Murphy, 1990).[10]

I do not pretend that a focus on performative traditions offers critics a panacea for all that afflicts them, nor do I wish to claim that this orientation is necessary. Rather, I argue that a key advantage of such a view (and I am sure that there are other possibilities) is that it dissolves the dissociations permeating critical rhetoric. The performance of epistemological reason, for instance, becomes a tradition that challenges all of us, including McKerrow, every time we use the word "know" without acknowledging its heteroglossia (Cherwitz and Darwin, 1995).

Similarly, social knowledge becomes a heterogeneous mishmash of performative traditions, simultaneously opening emancipatory and oppressive opportunities. The heteroglossia of language, a term describing the multiple genres and language styles existing in the world, refracts a seemingly monologic discourse. Any "discursive formation" contains within it the potential, if not the actuality, of layered consciousnesses, a variety of voices brought into dialogue, as when the voice of woman threads her way into masculine liberal discourse. As voices assert themselves and become distinct (a Susan B. Anthony or a Sojourner Truth), a critic apprehends polyphony: recognizable "voice zones" (Bakhtin, 1984, p. 6) occupied by speakers who embody ideological positions in a performative tradition. The multiplicities of the linguistic world offer skilled advocates the chance to erode a "language of domination by working cunningly within it, using, appropriating, even speaking through its key mechanisms of repression" (Lentricchia, 1983, p. 24).

And, while he does not emphasize it, Bakhtin takes pains to apprehend languages of repression. Three points need to be made for those who have known only the theorist of the carnivalesque. First, Bakhtin recognizes the centrifugal and centripetal forces of language (Bakhtin, 1981, p. 270; Morson and Emerson, 1990, pp. 30–31). The latter wish to impose order on the former and, at times, temporarily succeed. Second, Bakhtin also notes the power of genre. For Bakhtin, genres are ways of seeing the world and they "accumulate forms of seeing and interpreting particular aspects of the world" (quoted in Morson and Emerson, 1990, p. 288). Speakers never begin from scratch; utterances require too much preliminary work for that. Rather, we speak through genres and those genres can either be liberating (as when Dostoevsky sensed the possibilities implicit in the [Menippean] satire) or constraining (as with the epic). Finally, Bakhtin understands the language of dominance because he encounters it in his own work. The historic oppression and neglect of the novel, of prosaics, by poetics is detailed and attacked in virtually his entire corpus.

The multiplicity and unity of the linguistic world allow for the coherence of a rhetorical text. Bakhtin insists that linguistic styles, "upon entering the novel, combine to form a structured artistic system, and are subordinated to the higher stylistic unity of the work as a whole, a unity that cannot be identified with any single one of the unities subordinated to it" (1981, p. 262). Conversely, as styles and voices participate in the higher unity of the work, they never lose their own integral unity nor their particular "character zones." It is precisely the orchestration of various, even unreconcilable voices, that, paradoxically, creates dialogic unity in a specific text. This is not the unity of a Hegelian dialectic nor the organic whole of a

New Critic. Rather, the styles and voices are held in tension, come into conflict, and may not ever reconcile, just as voices of the social world may not ever identify with each other.

In rhetorical terms, then, a speaker may articulate an authoritative judgment in the name of a community by allowing the voices of a community to percolate through the text. Multiplicity and diversity are not lost; rather, the audience speaks through the discourse of a skilled rhetor and acts for the social good. The voices of the rhetor and of community members are never totally reconciled but never totally at odds either. The unity of the dialogue, of the performative tradition, provides the norms for a contingent assessment of the good at that particular time and place. As Miller (1992) has argued of Martin Luther King, Jr.'s speeches, for instance, the languages of the African-American homiletic tradition, of American civil religion, and of liberal white Protestant preaching, shone through each other. In King's discourse, they remained independent, but interanimated, and lit the way toward a judgment that "Now is the time" for civil rights.

Audiences, then, act partly through texts and are, in one sense, fictive (McGee, 1975; McKerrow, 1989, p. 95). Yet that is not the whole story. Rhetorical critics and critical rhetoricians alike, for reasons that probably involve raising the status of rhetoric, have too eagerly embraced the textuality of the social world (Farrell, 1993b). If communities and audiences are solely textual, then we occupy the center of the academic world. They are not. Charland (1990, p. 256) has noted that it was Aristotle who led rhetorical theorists to conceive of the audience as a class, at least in terms of "basic demographics." Charland (p. 256) transforms that view by noting that "contemporary theorists" see the "audience as existing within a rhetorical culture, which is to say a culture in which 'good reasons' for interests and motives exist in discourse." Might I suggest that the material, physical experiences of domestic violence and rape, for instance, also constitute good reasons for women to think of themselves as a class. In the absence of a convincing articulation of those experiences, class action might never occur. But the articulation is also dependent upon a common experience (see Hall, 1988).

Cloud (1994) has commented upon the linguistic idealism of critical rhetoric, Fraser (1987) has noted the "metaphysics of textuality" in the work of Dominick LaCapra, a major influence on Jasinski (1995a), has explored this tendency in Bakhtin's writings. As I have argued elsewhere (Murphy, 1992, p. 63), a preoccupation with changes in discursive formations, public vocabularies, performative traditions, or whatever label one wishes to use, can occlude the struggles of those, such as the Freedom Riders, who put their lives at risk as they struggle for change in material circumstances: for the right to use a restroom at a bus stop. If a focus on performative traditions is not to "degenerate very easily into an intellectual study of influence," then critics should establish, but also go beyond "influence in textual action" (Jasinski, 1995a, p. 20). We should, to continue my example, explore how the performative traditions living in King's speeches shed discursive light on the burning buses outside of Anniston, Alabama and were, in turn, illuminated by the flames.

Conclusion

In this short sketch, I cannot fully develop an orientation focused on performative traditions; that can only be done by critical work. I offer this perspective, however, to support the claim that critics can cope with the multiplicity and diversity of the world without sacrificing the multiplicity and diversity of disciplinary traditions. The dissociations that characterize critical rhetoric's argumentation posit a sharp break between past and future. The disjunctions between reason and rhetoric, text and fragment, audience and subject privilege critical rhetoric over rhetorical criticism and exclude so-called "sterile forms of scholarship." In this view, the millennium has arrived; consequently, as Ono and Sloop (1995, p. 40) argue, the work of critical rhetors "is not simply a matter of adapting rhetorical criticism by focusing on vernacular cultures with the same methods we have used in the past, but rather as a result of such studies, the entire rhetorical project may be reshaped." I believe such reshaping to be neither necessary nor desirable.

Although each generation of critics may perceive a "rendezvous with destiny," we must remain aware, in the words of abolitionist and woman's rights advocate Abby Foster Kelly, that "bloody feet, sisters, have worn smooth the path by which you have come hither." The discourse that we engage has its history; the "critical spirit" that we invoke has lived before; and the work that we do can benefit from those who have come before. Faith, not skepticism, is the hard work in an era of Gingrich and Foucault. I suspect, however, that a restoration of faith in the possibility of public deliberation will be neither as arduous nor as impossible as some suggest if we can learn from, rather than dismiss, the wisdom of living communities.

A version of this paper was delivered at the 1933 convention of the Speech Communication Association.

NOTES

1. It is worth noting that Aristotle concludes the *Rhetoric* with a discussion of conclusions. The last lines, a quotation from Eratosthenes, serve as an example of a conclusion and as the conclusion to the *Rhetoric*. Aristotle is asking for the reader's judgment on the *Rhetoric* even as he enacts an appropriate strategy for a conclusion by quoting a conclusion. It is an intriguing rhetorical device and an admonition to those who believe that the *Rhetoric* does little to address issues of linguistic style and theoretical reflexivity.

2. I owe the analogy to Stuart Hall (1986, pp. 56–7).

3. In what I consider to be his strongest enactment of critical rhetoric, McKerrow's voluminous source citation in the 1989 essay can be read as a "recharacterization" of the images of rhetorical criticism in order to transform it into critical rhetoric. Gaonkar (1993, p. 151) has also noted this evidential strategy, claiming that McKerrow "generates a sort of theoretical collage in which he allows a series of propositions to recline against each other like figures in a family album." While I believe the placement of the figures is ultimately determined by the strategies of dissociation, McKerrow comes close here to demonstrating what he means by critical rhetoric. He rearranges the names to produce a new normal order.

4. Cloud (1994) and Campbell (1990) have taken particular exception to critical rhetoric's story as a narrative of material, historical change. I, too, have some serious doubts and, in the concluding section, I will present an alternative interpretation.

5. This assumption forms the basis of Miller's (1993) controversial interpretation of Foucault's life and work.

6. McKerrow seems to equivocate later in the essay: "The body is not rhetorical, but those messages that the body conveys (either eclipsed by the mind or acting on its own) can be accessed. The conditions of subjectivation can be expressed via bodily action. Where the voice is silenced, the body may be the messenger" (p. 61). The limitation on the body in the first sentence is undercut by the last sentence. If the body is the messenger, it is rhetorical. Such an interpretation jibes with McKerrow's emphasis on art, dance, etc. as emancipatory social practices.

7. The "engendered" outline of rhetoric presented in the 1993a piece is noticeable. Rhetoric should be self-centered, physical, and active, while reason is social,

discursive (talkative?), and passive. While a feminist analysis of critical rhetoric would be another paper, I believe that Hartsock's (1990) suspicions about a decentered subject have a firm foundation.

8. Unfortunately, Ono and Sloop do not help their case very much with the critique. After a long theoretical section, they proceed to reveal, in mind-numbing detail, the oppression of Japanese-American women during World War II. I am not at all clear how this critique demonstrates the emancipatory potential of the vernacular community.

9. Jasinski and Zulick, of course, may not fully agree with my interpretation of this perspective.

10. As I have argued, it also informs the laments of McGee and McKerrow over the status of rhetoric!

REFERENCES

Aristotle. (1991). *On rhetoric: A theory of civic discourse* (G. Kennedy, Trans.). New York: Oxford University Press.

Bakhtin, M. M. (1981). *The dialogic imagination* (trans. by C. Emerson and M. Holquist). M. Holquist (Ed.). Austin: University of Texas Press.

Bakhtin, M. M. (1984). *Problems of Dostoevsky's poetics* (trans. by C. Emerson and M. Holquist). M. Holquist (Ed.). Austin: University of Texas Press.

Beiner, R. (1983). *Political judgment.* Chicago: University of Chicago Press.

Bercovitch, S. (1978). *The American jeremiad.* Madison: University of Wisconsin Press.

Best, S. and Kellner, D. (1991). *Postmodern theory: Critical interrogations.* New York: Guilford Press.

Black, E. (1965; rpt. 1978). *Rhetorical criticism: A study in method.* Madison: University of Wisconsin Press.

Bormann, E. (1977). Fetching good out of evil: A rhetorical use of calamity. *Quarterly Journal of Speech,* 63, 130–139.

Brummett, B. (1984). Premillennial apocalyptic as a rhetorical genre. *Central States Speech Journal,* 35, 84–93.

Bryant, D. C. (1953). Rhetoric: Its functions and its scope. *Quarterly Journal of Speech,* 39, 401–424.

Burke, K. (1966). *Language as symbolic action.* Berkeley: University of California Press.

Burke, K. (1945; rpt. 1969). *A grammar of motives.* Berkeley: University of California Press.

Burke, K. (1961; rpt. 1970). *The rhetoric of religion: Studies in logology.* Berkeley: University of California Press.

Campbell, J. A. (1990). Between the fragment and the icon: Prospect for a rhetorical house of the middle way. *Western Journal of Speech Communication,* 54, 346–376.

Campbell, K. K. (1972). "Conventional Wisdom—Traditional Form": A rejoinder. *Quarterly Journal of Speech,* 58, 451–454.

Campbell, K. K. (1989). *Man cannot speak for her: A critical study of early feminist rhetoric,* Volume I. Westport, CT: Greenwood Press.

Charland, M. (1990). Rehabilitating rhetoric: Confronting blindspots in discourse and social theory. *Communication,* 11, 253–264.

Charland, M. (1991). Finding a horizon and *telos*: The challenge to critical rhetoric. *Quarterly Journal of Speech,* 77, 71–74.

Cherwitz, R. A. and Darwin, T. J. (1995). Why the "epistemic" in epistemic rhetoric? The paradox of rhetoric as performance. *Text and Performance Quarterly,* 15, 189–205.

Cloud, D. L. (1994). The materiality of discourse as oxymoron: A challenge to critical rhetoric. *Western Journal of Communication,* 58, 141–163.

Condit, C. M. (1989). The rhetorical limits of polysemy. *Critical Studies in Mass Communication,* 6, 103–122 [reprinted in this volume].

Cox, J. R. (1990). On "interpreting" public discourse in post-modernity. *Western Journal of Speech Communication,* 54, 317–329.

Farrell, T. B. (1976). Knowledge, consensus, and rhetorical theory. *Quarterly Journal of Speech,* 62, 1–14 [reprinted in this volume].

Farrell, T. B. (1978). Social knowledge II. *Quarterly Journal of Speech,* 64, 329–334.

Farrell, T. B. (1993a). *The norms of rhetorical culture.* New Haven, CT: Yale University Press.

Farrell, T. B. (1993b). On the disappearance of the rhetorical aura. *Western Journal of Communication,* 57, 147–158.

Fisher, W. R. (1984). Narration as a human communication paradigm: The case of public moral argument. *Communication Monographs,* 51, 1–22 [reprinted in this volume].

Fiske, J. (1986). Television: Polysemy and popularity. *Critical Studies in Mass Communication,* 3, 391–408.

Fraser, N. (1987). On the political and the symbolic: Against the metaphysics of textuality. *Enclitic,* 9, 100–114.

Gaonkar, D. P. (1993). Performing with fragments: Reflections on critical rhetoric. In R. E. McKerrow (Ed.). *Argument and the postmodern challenge* (pp. 149–155). Annandale, VA: Speech Communication Association.

Giddens, A. (1982). *Profiles and critiques in social theory.* Berkeley: University of California Press.

Gitlin, T. (1979). Prime time ideology: The hegemonic process in television entertainment. *Social Problems,* 26, 251–266.

Goodnight, G. T. (1982). The personal, technical, and public spheres of argument: A speculative inquiry into the art of public deliberation. *Journal of the American Forensic Association,* 18, 214–227 [reprinted in this volume].

Goodnight, G. T. (1989). Toward a social theory of argumentation. *Argumentation and Advocacy,* 26, 60–70.

Hall, S. (1986). On postmodernism and articulation: An interview with Stuart Hall. L. Grossberg (Ed.). *The Journal of Communication Inquiry,* 10, 45–60.

Hall, S. (1988). The toad in the garden: Thatcherism among the theorists. In C. Nelson & L. Grossberg (Eds.). *Marxism and the interpretation of culture* (pp. 35–57). Urbana: University of Illinois Press.

Hariman, R. (1986). Status, marginality, and rhetorical theory. *Quarterly Journal of Speech*, 72, 38–54 [reprinted in this volume].

Hariman, R. (1991). Critical rhetoric and postmodern theory. *Quarterly Journal of Speech*, 77, 67–70.

Hartsock, N. (1990). Foucault on power? A theory for women? In L. J. Nicholson (Ed.). *Feminism/postmodernism* (pp. 157–175). New York: Routledge.

Jasinski, J. (1995a). Instrumentalism, contextualism, and interpretation in rhetorical criticism. Paper presented at the convention of the Speech Communication Association, San Antonio, Texas.

Jasinski, J. (1995b). The forms and limits of prudence in Henry Clay's (1850) defense of the compromise measures. *Quarterly Journal of Speech*, 81[, 454–478].

Lentricchia, F. (1983). *Criticism and social change*. Chicago: University of Chicago Press.

McGee, M. C. (1975). In search of the "people": A rhetorical alternative. *Quarterly Journal of Speech*, 61, 235–249.

McGee, M. C. (1980). The "ideograph": A link between rhetoric and ideology. *Quarterly Journal of Speech*, 66, 1–16 [reprinted in this volume].

McGee, M. C. (1982). A materialist's conception of rhetoric. In R. E. McKerrow (Ed.). *Explorations in rhetoric* (pp. 23–48). Glenview, IL: Scott, Foresman.

McGee, M. C. (1990). Text, context, and the fragmentation of contemporary culture. *Western Journal of Speech Communication*, 54, 274–289 [reprinted in this volume].

McKerrow, R. E. (1989). Critical rhetoric: Theory and *praxis*. *Communication Monographs*, 56, 91–111 [reprinted in this volume].

McKerrow, R. E. (1991a). Critical rhetoric in a postmodern world. *Quarterly Journal of Speech*, 77, 75–79.

McKerrow, R. E. (1991b). Critical rhetoric and propaganda studies. In J. A. Anderson (Ed.). *Communication yearbook/14* (pp. 249–255). Newbury Park: Sage.

McKerrow, R. E. (1993a). Critical rhetoric and the possibility of the subject. In I. Angus and L. Langsdorf (Eds.). *The critical turn* (pp. 51–67). Carbondale: Southern Illinois University Press.

McKerrow, R. E. (1993b). Overcoming fatalism: Rhetoric/argument in postmodernity. In R. E. McKerrow (Ed.). *Argument and the postmodern challenge* (pp. 119–121). Annandale, VA: Speech Communication Association.

Medhurst, M. J. (1993). The academic study of public address: A tradition in transition. In M. J. Medhurst (Ed.). *Landmark essays on American public address* (pp. ix–xlii). Davis, CA: Hermagoras Press.

Miller, J. (1993). *The passion of Michel Foucault*. New York: Anchor Books.

Miller, K. D. (1992). *Voice of deliverance: The language of Martin Luther King, Jr. and its sources*. New York: Free Press.

Morson, G. S., and Emerson, C. (1990). *Mikhail Bakhtin: Creation of a prosaics*. Stanford: Stanford University Press.

Mosco, V. (1983). Critical research and the role of labor. *Journal of Communication*, 33, 237–248.

Murphy, J. M. (1990). "A time of shame and sorrow": Robert F. Kennedy and the American jeremiad. *Quarterly Journal of Speech*, 76, 401–414.

Murphy, J. M. (1992). Domesticating dissent: The Kennedys and the freedom rides. *Communication Monographs*, 59, 61–78.

Ono, K. A. and Sloop, J. M. (1992). Commitment to *telos*: A sustained critical rhetoric. *Communication Monographs*, 59, 48–60.

Ono, K. A. and Sloop, J. M. (1995). The critique of vernacular discourse. *Communication Monographs*, 62, 19–46.

Perelman, C. (1982). *The realm of rhetoric* (W. Kluback, Trans.). Notre Dame, IN: University of Notre Dame Press.

Perelman, C. and Olbrechts-Tyteca, L. (1969). *The new rhetoric: A treatise on argumentation* (J. Wilkinson and P. Weaver, Trans.). Notre Dame, IN: University of Notre Dame Press.

Scott, R. L. (1967). On viewing rhetoric as epistemic. *Central States Speech Journal*, 18, 9–17 [reprinted in this volume].

Scott, R. L. (1976). On viewing rhetoric as epistemic: Ten years later. *Central States Speech Journal*, 27, 258–266.

Wallace, K. R. (1963). The substance of rhetoric: Good reasons. *Quarterly Journal of Speech*, 49, 239–249.

Wander, P. (1983). The ideological turn in modern criticism. *Central States Speech Journal*, 34, 1–18.

Wander, P. and Jenkins, S. (1972). Rhetoric, society, and the critical response. *Quarterly Journal of Speech*, 58, 441–450.

Warnick, B. (1989). Judgment, probability, and Aristotle's *Rhetoric*. *Quarterly Journal of Speech*, 75, 299–311.

Wichelns, H. A. (1925; rpt. 1993). The literary criticism of oratory. In M. J. Medhurst (Ed.). *Landmark essays on American public address* (pp. 1–32). Davis, CA: Hermagoras Press.

Zarefsky, D. (1989). The state of the art in public address scholarship. In M. C. Left and F. Kauffeld (Eds.). *Texts in context: Critical dialogues on significant episodes in American political rhetoric* (pp. 13–28). Davis, CA: Hermagoras Press.

Zulick, M. D. (1991). Pursuing controversy: Kristeva's split subject, Bakhtin's many-tongued world. *Argumentation and Advocacy*, 28, 91–102.

Zulick, M. D. (1992). The agon of Jeremiah: On the dialogic invention of prophetic ethos. *Quarterly Journal of Speech*, 78, 125–148.

Imagining in the Public Sphere

Robert Asen

Contemporary public sphere scholarship has been motivated significantly by a concern to overcome historical and conceptual exclusions in public spheres. Recent theory and criticism [have] investigated direct and indirect exclusions. Direct exclusions expressly prevent the participation of particular individuals and groups in public discussions and debates. Prohibitions against women speaking in public, for example, have served historically to inhibit women's participation in various forums (see, e.g., Landes 1998). Indirect exclusions function tacitly through discursive norms and practices that prescribe particular ways of interacting in public forums. Indirect exclusions compel participants to conform to established modes of discourse that effectively negate the perspectives and contributions of previously directly excluded individuals and groups. Calls for "objective" and "dispassionate" debate, for instance, sometimes have restricted public agendas by portraying culturally specific forms of address as universally practiced (see, e.g., Warner 1993). Indirect exclusions may regulate discourse in various forums even when direct exclusions have been counteracted. Scholarship seeking to overcome these exclusions has proceeded on two levels. On one level, scholars have recounted the efforts of excluded persons to participate in public life despite restrictions by developing alternative modes of publicity (see, e.g., Ryan 1990; Zaeske 2002). On a second level, theorists have proposed more inclusive conceptual models of the public sphere that may overcome historical exclusions of the bourgeois public sphere

while retaining a commitment to critical publicity (see, e.g., Asen 1999; Benhabib 1996; Hauser 1999; Mouffe 2000).

Practicing democratic discourse fairly and justly depends indispensably on enabling inclusion. Proponents of deliberative democracy argue that political legitimacy arises from processes of inclusive public debate. Seyla Benhabib asserts that "legitimacy in complex societies must be thought to result from the free and unconstrained public deliberation of all about matters of common concern" (1996, 68). Others regard inclusive public discourse as crucial for the formation of affirmative individual and collective identities. Craig Calhoun faults bourgeois notions of publicity for treating "identity formation as essentially private and prior to participation in the idealized public sphere of rational-critical discourse" (1993, 274). Identity formation entails mutual recognition among members of diverse cultures, yet theorists have observed that truncated discursive processes may inhibit mutual recognition. Charles Taylor writes that practicing a politics of recognition requires an openness toward other cultures—a presumption of value tested through sustained engagement so that "what we have formerly taken for granted as the background to valuation can be situated as one possibility alongside the background of the formerly unfamiliar culture" (1994, 67). Inclusiveness is also important for individuals and groups seeking to advance self-fashioned interpretations of their interests and needs against interpretations imposed by others. Nancy Fraser explains that self-fashioning is necessary because in public debates and controversies "*who* gets to establish authoritative thick definitions of people's needs is itself a political stake" (1989, 164).

Although inclusion is indispensable, exclusion is never total. Sometimes, people force their way into public forums and agendas. For example, participation by activists in discussions of AIDS research and treatment often has been limited by researchers' assertions of expert privilege in investigating scientific matters. Valeria Fabj and Matthew J. Sobnosky (1995) detail how AIDS activists have responded by engaging in discursive acts of redefinition and translation to gain entry into previously circumscribed forums. At other times, people surreptitiously access public arenas. Prison writing is one way that those officially banished from public view nevertheless continue to participate in oppositional discourses and movements. Gerard A. Hauser (2001) considers how dissident Adam Michnik remained a vibrant voice in Polish civil society through his writings even after his imprisonment in the 1980s by an authoritarian regime. At still other times, typically excluded people may be invited to participate in public discussions. Members of the AIDS activist group ACT UP occasionally have testified in the traditional setting of the congressional committee hearing as invited witnesses. Daniel C. Brouwer (2001) maintains that politically sympathetic committee chairs facilitated ACT UP's "official" appearances before members of Congress. Whether invited or insisted, participation in wider publics by previously excluded individuals and groups runs the risk of co-optation—wider publics may attempt to recuperate dissident appeals by creating an institutionally sanctioned and politically innocuous space for the expression of opposition. Still, advocates and theorists alike regard inclusion as crucial for reasons of political legitimacy, identity formation, cultural diversity, and needs interpretation.

Exclusion also is never total because the dynamics of inclusion and exclusion operate on multiple levels. Participation in public discussions does not proceed only through voice and body; inclusions and exclusions also occur in the perceptions of others—the imagining of others. Sometimes, individual and groups "appear" in debates from which they are physically absent as images (linguistic and/or visual representations) circulate in public discourse. For instance, as members of Congress debated various welfare reform proposals throughout the 1980s and 1990s, fewer than 4 percent of the witnesses testifying before participating House

and Senate committees identified themselves as current or former welfare recipients (Asen 2002). Yet poor people were by no means absent from the debates; vivid, disabling images of current and potential public assistance recipients elicited intense scrutiny from most debate participants. In the early 1980s, policymakers told tales of deceitful "welfare queens" who lived lavishly on government benefits. Images of prodigality receded as the debates proceeded, but in their place arose images of recipients as unwed teenage mothers who engaged in promiscuous sexual activity knowing that the federal government would support their liaisons.

This essay seeks to draw critical attention to processes of imagining as important aspects of the dynamics of inclusion and exclusion in public spheres. I argue that imagining affects participants in public discussions differently, often disadvantaging socially and historically marginalized people and groups while tacitly aiding the appeals of others. I develop this argument in three sections. The first section elucidates a concept of imagining as a collective, constitutive, and active force that forms part of our shared social world. The second section unpacks connections between imagining and representation. Imagining enacts a politics of representation and deploys multiple modes—linguistic and visual—of representation. The third section amplifies the varying advantage that imagining affords to individuals and groups by linking imagining with recent scholarship in public sphere studies that has developed under the heading of "counterpublic." I maintain that critical attention to imagining may complement existing counterpublic theory and criticism, which explicitly considers questions of inclusion and exclusion and alternative publicities. The examples to which I refer to illustrate my conceptual argument address a common topic: U.S. welfare policy. This is an area of public discourse with an extensive history of marginalization of and negative imagining about its putative beneficiaries: poor people. Public debates over U.S. welfare policy offer a dramatic example of how actual processes of imagining create advantages for some and disadvantages for others.

A Conception of Imagining

In this section, I develop a preliminary concept of imagining as a constitutive social force. My discussion is preliminary because imagining as a social force draws its power from a capacity to represent people, objects, and ideas—a power that, for analytic purposes, I address subsequently. However, I do not wish to advance an ontological or phenomenological argument. My goal is not to situate imagining as an originative social process, nor do I aim to develop an account of imagining that describes objective social phenomena. Rather, my conception is a critical one. I offer my conception of imagining as a tool that may inform critical investigations of the ways in which included and excluded people appear in public spheres.[1]

Imagining may be conceived individually or collectively. As an individual concept, imagining typically has been defined as a mental faculty capable of forming images and impressions, combining disparate ideas, or perceiving phenomena. Yet the imagination in this view traditionally has been regarded as subordinate to reason. According to Wolfgang Iser, "from Aristotle through the beginnings of the modern age, imagination has been regarded as an inferior faculty" (1993, 176). Writers such as John Locke described and denounced the imagination as pleasurable, mysterious, and uncontrollable, even as they implicitly appealed to its manifold powers. Jean-Paul Sartre departed famously from a faculty view in describing the imagination as a constitutive act of consciousness. Sartre developed a relational view of the imagination as connecting consciousness to objects through mental images: "The word image can therefore only indicate the relation of consciousness to the object; in other words, it means a certain manner in which the object makes its appearance to consciousness, or, if one prefers, a certain way in which consciousness presents an object to itself" (1948, 8). While attributing a constitutive power to imagining, Sartre maintained an individual conception.

An individual conception also has appeared in ostensibly unlikely sources. In a widely cited study, Benedict Anderson examines how imagining inculcates and promotes ideas of nationhood. Anderson defines the nation as an imagined community: "It is *imagined* because the members of even the smallest nation will never know most of their fellow-members, meet them, or even hear of them, yet in the minds of each lives the image of their communion" (1991, 6). Anderson situates imagining within sociopolitical processes of nationalism, and he writes of the ways in which interactions among colonial subjects engendered notions of mutuality, yet his definition of the nation as imagined locates this community in individual cognition. The nation resides in the "minds of each" inhabitant. As constitutive of selves and nations, individual acts of imagination demand critical attention. An individual conception of the imagination offers a compelling retort to deterministic theories of human thought and perception that elevate rationality at the expense of other processes. An individual conception also may elucidate, as Anderson demonstrates with nationalism, how seemingly disparate societal developments cohere in the perspectives of particular people and attain a symbolic significance. My focus in this article, however, is on the collective dimension of imagining.

Collective imagining does not emerge through the aggregation of individual thoughts and perceptions. Rather, collective imagining takes shape through discursive engagement among interlocutors in contexts of varying structure, scope, and formality. Discourse functions in this process not as a vehicle for transmitting information and beliefs but as a constitutive force. Reducing discourse to the role of transmitter would presume that individuals enter into processes of social dialogue with their opinions already formed and ordered. Sometimes this may be the case, but people also may develop opinions only after discussing issues with others, or they may change previously held views, or they may reorder their priorities. Moreover, the "collective" modifying collective imagining suggests that social dialogue enables the formation of opinions that did not exist prior to discursive engagement. The images produced by processes of collective imagining emerge in specific moments of interaction; they cannot be ascertained in advance. Collective imagining thus retains the relational quality of the imagination explicated by Sartre, but its relation shifts. Rather than describing a relationship between objects and consciousness, collective imagining refers to those images that emerge in intersubjective relations. In this way, collective imagining indicates a public process: interlocutors engage in processes of imagining about people they regard as similar to and different from themselves, and the processes and products of the collective imagination are accessible to others.

In conceptualizing imagining as collective and constitutive, I do not wish to make this process synonymous with what some theorists have termed the "social construction of reality." Kenneth J. Gergen defines this latter perspective as holding that "what we take to be real is an outcome of social relationships" sustained through discourse

(1999, 237). Imagining may participate in constructing our shared social world, but it is not the only participant. To be sure, some theorists have ascribed an apparently all-encompassing role to the imagination. A prominent theorist in this vein is Cornelius Castoriadis, who attributes an originative role to the imagination in constituting self and society. He holds that the imagination constitutes the self as "a condition for all thought" (1987, 336). On the level of society, Castoriadis develops a notion of "social imaginary significations" to describe how imagining institutes society. He maintains that some imagined concepts—he references terms such as "citizen," "justice," "money," and others—serve a central role in structuring societies. Collective understandings of these intertwined central concepts order relationships among the persons and objects through which they are represented. Yet he does not regard this as a relationship between signs and their referents: "Central significations are not significations 'of' something—nor are they, except in a second-order sense, significations 'attached' or 'related' to something. They constitute that which, for a given society, brings into being the co-belonging of objects, acts and individuals which, in appearance, are most heterogeneous. They have no 'referent'; they institute a mode of being of things and individuals which relate to them" (364). From one vantage point, Castoriadis's notion of the instituting force of the imagination stands as a provocative statement against referential views of language. However, in locating the symbolic action of discourse exclusively in the imagination, Castoriadis presents a deterministic view of representation that undermines his commitment to overdetermined signification. Moreover, his all-encompassing conception of the imaginary secures a prominent role for imagining by sacrificing its critical purchase. So long as it stands for everything, Castoriadis's concept of imagining does not critically illuminate anything in particular.

A more modest situation appears in the theorizing of Charles Taylor, who locates the collective imagination between a realm of social habit and a realm of explicit doctrine. Both distinctions, in varying degrees, are useful. Imagining should not be equated with routine behaviors or customs even as imaginative processes sometimes may induce people to act unreflectively. Imagining also resists the systematization connoted in doctrines. As systems of belief or articulated positions and principles, doctrines suggest a propositional structure and a susceptibility to tests of propositional logic that do not characterize imagining. However, Taylor's distinction becomes problematic in implying that processes of imagining themselves may not be explicit. He describes the collective imagination as "a level of images as yet unformulated in doctrine" (1993, 219). Insofar as it restricts imagining to the background of public discourse, this description understates the power of imagining and neglects how imagining may be employed to achieve specific ends.

Collective imagining may function as a background process or it may be engaged actively. As a background process, the collective imagination constitutes a constellation of shared assumptions, values, perceptions, and beliefs for matters identified explicitly as topics of discussion. For instance, present-day beliefs regarding private enterprise as more innovative and efficient than government institutions condition debates about the future of public programs such as social security retirement benefits. Likewise, commitments to "family values" tacitly inform debates over appropriate public policy remedies for teen pregnancy (see Cloud 1998). Nancy Fraser invokes the background functioning of the collective imagination when she sets out to analyze the "political imaginary of social welfare" by considering "various taken-for-granted assumptions about people's needs and entitlements" (1993, 9). Active engagement of the collective imagination occurs in situations where advocates explicitly call upon their audiences to rethink relations to one another. At these moments, participants in public discussions explicitly reflect on the rights, responsibilities, and obligations granted, entitled, and owed to one another. Active engagement proceeds, for example, when policymakers heed the frequent calls of their colleagues to reevaluate and to reorient the demands that government agencies place on adult welfare recipients.

Processes of collective imagining may be most active in public debates and controversies. Controversy unsettles taken-for-granted values and beliefs and raises the stakes of public discourse for participants and excluded others who nevertheless may be affected by the outcomes of particular debates (Olson and Goodnight 1994). Controversial issues often are highly visible issues that rally widespread support and opposition and stir strong feelings. Contestation accompanies controversy: advocates have to advance particular images against competing constructions as they engage interlocutors in the public sphere. Understood this way, controversy resists traditional scholarly treatments that view controversy as something to be avoided because it putatively departs from or perverts formal rules of disputation or reason. Instead, as G. Thomas Goodnight contends, controversy may be seen as a practice that pushes and expands the available limits of communication. Goodnight characterizes controversy as a "site where the taken-for-granted relationships between communication and reasoning are open to change, reevaluation, and development by argumentative engagement" (1991, 5). This view of controversy broaches the fluid and unstable quality of collective imagining. Collective imagining does not proceed through fixed, teleological processes of discursive engagement; its images are not constant and eternal. Imaginings change. Controversy engenders moments especially amenable to changes in imagining by unsettling background understandings and engaging imagining as an active force.

A comparative example may serve to illustrate the conception of imagining I have developed thus far. A number of scholars have held that the bifurcation of the U.S. welfare state into social insurance and public assistance programs sustains a two-tiered, gendered structure (see, e.g., Fraser 1989; Gordon 1994; Mink 1995; Orloff 1991). Social insurance programs that tie participation to paid labor, distribute generous and geographically uniform grants, and require no further actions from recipients historically have served men and their dependents. Such programs have been celebrated in political discourse and their benefits have been characterized as "money owed." Images of elderly recipients circulate in public discourse as honored senior *citizens* to whom politicians have binding obligations. By contrast, public assistance programs such as, until its 1996 repeal, Aid to Families with Dependent Children (AFDC) historically have occupied an inferior position in the U.S. welfare state. These programs generally serve mothers with young children, tie participation to household income, disperse meager grants that vary geographically, and require the satisfaction of various corollary conditions by recipients. Public assistance programs have been vilified in political discourse and their benefits often denounced as wasteful government spending. Adult recipients of public assistance have been portrayed as clients benefiting from public charity. These contrasting images of recipients have circulated despite the operational similarities of social insurance and public assistance programs.

Although the structural inequities of social insurance and public assistance date back to the 1935 Social Security Act, the contrasting images of recipients have transformed over time. Policymakers initially portrayed adult female welfare recipients as valued and virtuous nurturers and caregivers forced by circumstances beyond their control to assume the role of breadwinner for their families. Policymakers believed Aid to Dependent Children (ADC), as AFDC was then called, would allow poor mothers to resume their important domestic responsibilities; they did not disparage ADC recipients. In its report to the president, the U.S. Committee on Economic Security, the chief architectural body of the Social Security Act, asserted that "we are strongly of the opinion that these families should be differentiated from the permanent dependents and unemployables" (1935, 6). Similarly, images of social insurance recipients have changed. When the Social Security Act was enacted, social insurance for the elderly was a smaller and decidedly less popular program than Old Age Assistance, which distributed more generous and more widespread benefits. Wishing to attract public support for its newly created social insurance program, the Social Security Board began a public relations campaign to promote social insurance as an honored entitlement for citizens (Gordon 1994, 282–83). This campaign proceeded in part by denigrating all forms of public assistance—whether or not such assistance served an elderly population (Cates 1983, 104–35).

Imagining and Representation

Imagining engages a particular power of discourse: a power of representation. In this section, I consider the relationship between imagining and representation by addressing the politics and modalities of representation. Representing is not a disinterested process, but one that implicates social judgments and relations of power. In this way, representing enacts a politics of representation. Representing does not proceed exclusively through one mode of communication, but may employ linguistic and visual symbols simultaneously and complementarily. In doing so, representing functions as a multimodal process.

To say that representation enacts a politics is to say that all representation is tendentious. When participants in public discourse describe themselves and others, they do not engage in a value-neutral and transparent process. Rather, representational processes implicate participants in (often unacknowledged) choices regarding how people should be portrayed. As Linda Hutcheon explains, these processes do not "*reflect* society as much as grant meaning and value within a particular society" (1989, 24–25). Representing does not occur outside of history and society, but works with the symbolic materials of specific cultures. In this way, representing invokes social values and beliefs as well as the interests of participants in public discourse. Representing engages relations of power and social hierarchies. Further, the politics of representation produces consequences—both for those representing and those represented. Our attitude toward and treatment of others depends crucially on how we imagine others, and representations express our collective imagination (see Dyer 1993; Scarry 1996).

The intimate connection between representations and social values, beliefs, and interests indicates that representational processes may frame public debates, identify proper objectives for collective action, and suggest appropriate remedies. One can note unobjectionably that the percentage of eligible people receiving AFDC increased nearly three-fold from the early 1960s through the early 1970s (Patterson 1994, 179). Disagreements arise, however, as soon as one offers an interpretation of this trend. Some commentators view this rise in AFDC receipt as evidence of a misguided federal policy subsidizing pathological behavior and thus encouraging family break-up and the dissolution of the work ethic among poor people. Conservative social critic Charles Murray characterizes this trend as a "generous revolution." He argues that the federal government changed the system of punishments and rewards facing poor people "to make it more profitable for the poor to behave in the short term in ways that were destructive in the long term" (1994, 9). Others see this same development as the successful outcome of efforts by community activists and poverty lawyers seeking to transform a situation in which a minority of eligible poor people participated in programs ostensibly designed for them to one in which the vast majority did. The scholar/activists Frances Fox Piven and Richard A. Cloward describe the rise in welfare roles as an act of resistance. They insist that "the great rise in relief insurgency can be understood as a rebellion by the poor against the circumstances that deprived them of both jobs and income" (1979, 265). Both interpretations offer images that link up with larger political programs. From one perspective, the poor person appears as a naïve subject led astray by arrogant government officials. From another perspective, the poor person appears as a triumphant agent holding state officials to their word.

Despite their political power (or, perhaps, as an augmentation of their political power), representations purport to be natural, universal, and essential renderings of objective phenomena. Frank Lentricchia refers to the tendency of representations to hide their constructed character as the "coercive power" of representations. He explains that representations assert "an ontological claim, used like a hammer, that some part of the whole *really does* stand in for the whole" (1983, 153). Created in particular sociopolitical contexts, representations may draw attention away from these contexts. In these cases, their persuasive power arises in important respects from their ability to appear detached from political struggles. Representing thus becomes a "cover-up" by concealing itself as "an agency of specific political power" and by obscuring "social and cultural difference and conflict" (153). Representations are at their most political when they appear to be non-political.

A fundamental tension in representation between absence and presence, between standing for something and embodying that something, bolsters this political power. Representation historically has meant both standing for something absent and making something present (see Williams 1983). Representation as absence informs theories of representative democracy whereby elected officials in parliamentary or legislative bodies speak on behalf of their constituents. Representation as presence orients theories of aesthetic realism that judge artworks by their ability to portray the elements of our physical world in a lifelike manner (Derrida 1982; Pitkin 1967). Yet each notion of representation implicates the other: standing for something absent may create a sense of presence, and making something present may overcome its absence. Employing the terms "speaking for" and "speaking about," Linda Alcoff situates this mutual implication of absence and presence in the context of participants and non-participants in public discourse. She observes that "when one is speaking for others one may be describing their situation and thus also speaking about them." Similarly, "when one is speaking about others, or simply trying to describe their situation or some aspect of it, one may also be speaking in place of them, that is, speaking for them" (1991–92, 9). As Alcoff notes, neatly separating these two senses may be possible only analytically. Absence and presence create an irreducible tension in representing: the representation is and is not the person, object, or idea represented.

This tension between absence and presence in representation critically influences collective imagining by interacting with dynamics of inclusion and exclusion in public spheres to operate on participants and excluded others. Imagining can make those present absent and those absent present. Negative circulating images may lead some people to self-censor their contributions to public debates, and negative images may prompt other participants to disregard their contributions. People affiliated with historically marginalized groups seem especially susceptible to both outcomes, since they often are subjected to negative imagining. Iris Marion Young notes that participatory norms of discourse "are powerful silencers or evaluators of speech in many actual speaking situations where culturally differentiated and socially unequal groups live together" (1996, 124; see also Young 2000, 53–55). Imagining may effectively silence and make absent some debate participants. The reverse process of making present those absent typifies the relation of poor people to welfare policy debates. Negative images of poor people as members of a dangerous "underclass," for example, have often attained an ominous presence in media and policy forums. In his popular 1982 book *The Underclass*, journalist Ken Auletta grouped long-term welfare recipients with street thugs, hustlers, drifters, mental patients, and others as comprising the underclass. Tying these figures together through a singular focus on deviance, he asserted that the "underclass usually operates outside the generally accepted boundaries of society. They are often set apart . . . by their deviant or antisocial behavior, by their bad habits, not just by their poverty" (28). The image of a fearsome underclass spurred subsequent reform efforts. In a 1987 U.S. House Education and Labor Committee hearing, Representative Harris Fawell expressed his desire for welfare reform legislation in starkly pragmatic terms: "We are scared, too. I mean the whole problem is terrible. . . . We have communities sitting by watching [their] own community go to hell, so to speak" (339). As Fawell's apprehension reveals, the "underclass" did not need to participate directly in the debates to attain a presence.

Representing may enact a politics through multiple communicative modes. Thus far I have focused on imagining as a linguistic process. When witnesses appear before congressional committees to tell stories of increased illegitimacy, unemployment, or crime among poor people, they do so principally through written and oral testimony. When editorialists, opinion columnists, and talk show hosts censure poor people for perpetuating a deleterious "underclass," they do so chiefly through the printed or spoken word. The same can be said for less formal and more prevalent forms of vernacular exchange that constitute the public sphere as a multiplicity of diverse and partially overlapping discursive venues: When suburbanites gathered at a neighborhood picnic decry the expenditure of tax dollars on "undeserving" poor people, the primary medium they employ is talk. And, when poor people join together to confront negative images about them circulating in politics, media, and middle-class society, they sometimes invent and disseminate alternative vocabularies to express their interests, identities, and needs. But imagining should not be limited to its linguistic manifestations.

Processes of collective imagining may employ both linguistic and visual modes of representation. The polysemic character of "image"—which denotes a physical likeness, optical reflection, mental representation, figure of speech, and public perception—suggests the multimodality of imagining. Visual artifacts and linguistic texts may work together to produce compelling circulating images. Along these lines, Cara A. Finnegan cautions critics against viewing visual and linguistic elements of a rhetorical artifact as self-contained and binary. She argues instead that "the goal of analyzing the imagetext [a synthetic combination of visual image and linguistic text] is not simply to compare images to texts, but rather to recognize the inherent tensions in the marriage of image and texts and investigate how those tensions make or negotiate meaning" (2000, 340; see also Mitchell 1994). Similarly, Catherine Helen Palczewski (2002) considers how public debates may proceed through the mutual invocation of visual and verbal elements.[2] In a revealing study, Martin Gilens considers how visual images have appeared in print media to project racial images of poor people. Analyzing pictures of poor people that appeared in the national newsweeklies *Time*, *Newsweek*, and *U.S. News and World Report* between the years 1950 and 1992, Gilens (1999, 122–25) reaches two troubling conclusions. First, blacks were overrepresented among pictures of poor people. They appeared in 53.4 percent of the pictures though their proportion among the poor during this period was 29.3 percent. Second, as the negative tone of the coverage of poverty increased, so too did the percentage of blacks pictured, and as the negative tone of the coverage decreased, so too did the percentage of blacks among pictures of the poor. So, for example, in the years 1972–73, as public concerns about rising welfare costs and caseloads waxed and as the optimism of the 1960s waned, the percentage of blacks pictured topped

70 percent. However, as an economic downturn developed in the 1970s and a focus on unemployment increasingly occupied magazine articles, the percentage of blacks pictured dropped to 49 percent.

In the objects investigated by Gilens, linguistic and visual elements worked together to engender processes of imagining. In the periods when the articles primarily portrayed poverty as a result of behavioral deficiencies, presaging contemporary concerns about an urban "underclass," pictures of blacks helped construct a racially coded image of poor people. Yet when the main focus of the articles shifted from behavior to environment, partially absolving poor people of blame for their economic woes, more racially diverse pictures invited connections between the subjects of the articles and the magazines' mostly white readership. Gilens's study contains two implications for considering the relationship between linguistic and visual modes of representation. First, whether linguistic, visual, or both modes of representation are functioning and, in the latter case, whether one mode predominates depends crucially on context. In certain forums in the public sphere, such as the formal site of the congressional committee hearing room and the vernacular sites of neighborhood gatherings, linguistic modes may function primarily. In other forums, such as the mass mediated site of television campaign advertising or news coverage of political demonstrations, visual modes may function primarily. And still in other forums, neither mode may predominate and instead create irresolvable tensions. Second, the point is not to assert the primacy of either mode but, in those moments when processes of imagining engage both linguistic and visual representation, to explore their interaction.

Imagining and Counterpublics

I have touched on the theme of the advantages and disadvantages afforded to participants in multiple public spheres through processes of imagining by discussing how the politics of representation engages dynamics of inclusion and exclusion to make those present absent and those absent present. In this section, I connect these dynamics to counterpublic theory and criticism. I suggest through examples some specific ways in which imagining creates varying degrees of advantage: by impugning the credibility of counterpublic agents, by concentrating historical animosities in negative images, and by creating a cumulative imaginary field that constrains the choices of successive participants.

Counterpublic theory explicitly addresses acts of inclusion and exclusion in multiple public spheres (see, e.g., Dawson 1995; Doxtader 2001; Fraser 1992; Squires 2001). As a critical term, "counterpublic" refers to those publics that form through mutual recognition of exclusions in wider publics, set themselves against exclusionary wider publics, and resolve to overcome these exclusions. Recognition of exclusion is crucial for the formation and investigation of counterpublics. Counterpublic loses its critically illuminating force if it refers to excluded people per se. Individuals do not necessarily recognize exclusions and resolve to overcome them by virtue of their location in a social order. Invoking counterpublic in this manner would reduce the term to the identity of particular participants and presume a shared set of interests among people who may not see themselves as allies. One does not participate in a counterpublic formed around issues of poverty simply through receipt of public assistance. For example, former AFDC recipient Nancy Peterson appeared before the Human Resources Subcommittee in 1996 to support the punitive tone of the debates and to endorse strict time limits and unequivocal work requirements. Evaluating reforms adopted in her home state, she judged that "the changes that Michigan has made have been positive changes. We do not need to be as soft as it has been. I am motivated. But other people are not. There needs to be a little bit of a push to motivate people to work, to get a feel of what that is like, to make them responsible" (U.S. House 1995, 58). In casting doubt on the work habits of other recipients, Peterson did not call into question disabling discursive practices, but reaffirmed larger themes informing the debates. Moreover, critical attention to recognition facilitates exploration of counterpublics constituted not only by persons excluded from wider publics, but by coalitions of people of varied social, economic, and political status dedicated to overcoming exclusions.

As explicitly articulated alternatives to wider publics that neglect the interests of their participants, counterpublics contest direct and indirect exclusions. Overcoming direct exclusions enables counterpublic agents to access previously restricted forums. Yet counterpublic agents often must continue their struggle to reconstitute these forums so that contributions from diverse participants may not only be permitted but also appreciated. Contestation draws attention to discursive norms and practices: how exclusions prevent participation by some people, how exclusions deflect attention from certain discussion topics, and how exclusions circumscribe particular ways of speaking. Invoking the absence and presence of representation, imagining may function as a discursive practice that disadvantages counterpublic agents in moments of interaction among multiple publics.

Imagining in a multiple public sphere is multidirectional. Wider publics may imagine themselves (as, for example, patriotic and hard-working Americans) and actual or potential counterpublics. Wider public imagining may spur counterpublicity. Regarding wider processes of imagining as a source of grievance, social actors may join together to resist objectionable images circulating in public discourse. For their part, counterpublic agents may imagine themselves and others. Imagining appears to function crucially for counterpublicity insofar as recognition of exclusion invokes an image of wider forums unfairly and unjustly closed off to outside participation and populated by ideologically driven and/or mean-spirited people.[3] In this imaginary realm, counterpublic agents stand as indignant social reformers seeking to uphold a greater good. Processes of imagining, then, may be inwardly and outwardly directed both for counterpublics and wider publics. My concern in this section is those interactive moments among publics and counterpublics when some counterpublic agents have gained access to wider forums but have not yet reconstituted the discursive exclusions of wider publics.

In such interactive moments, counterpublics suffer from what I call the doubly disabling tendencies of representation. Counterpublics often struggle to gain access to the very forums in which others are imagining them, often in ways objectionable to counterpublic agents. The doubly disabling tendencies of representation arise from this dynamic: Voices and bodies largely absent from public discourses may be made present through disabling images. The various goods that theorists associate with inclusive public deliberation suggest that the consequences of the doubly disabling tendencies of representation implicate issues of political legitimacy, identity formation, cultural diversity, and needs interpretation. Moreover, these consequences affect counterpublic participation even after some agents have entered particular forums. Negative imagining constitutes a symbolic hurdle that counterpublic agents—but not other participants—have to overcome.

Negative images circulating in wider forums impugn the character of counterpublic agents participating in these forums.[4] Negative images compel counterpublic agents to engage the statements of others from multiple vantage points; counterpublic agents may wish to assert their interests and identities as they see them, and yet they may need to counteract negative images representing counterpublics. Christine Pratt-Marston confronted this discursive obstacle when she testified before the U.S. House Public Assistance and Unemployment Compensation Subcommittee in 1981 to object to proposed budget cuts in AFDC and other social programs. Pratt-Marston explained to the subcommittee that low-wage labor required her to receive AFDC benefits. Yet she refused to be seen as an "AFDC recipient" in the pejorative sense of the term—as someone choosing to live comfortably on government aid while avoiding the demands of paid labor. Instead, Pratt-Marston sought to complicate simplistic representations of poor people's lives. She introduced herself to the subcommittee as a single parent, a foster parent, a taxpayer, and a disabled person. She shared with committee members the aspirations of many poor people—and the frustrations they experienced in the low-wage labor market. Connecting her own experiences to others, she explained, "when we try to become employed, we find that we cannot make it. We cannot pay for daycare, we do not have health services for our children, and we cannot pay the rent to feed our children. So we find ourselves going back on welfare" (84). As Pratt-Marston's references to daycare and medical care demonstrate, she sought to advocate a policy agenda capable of ameliorating the lives of poor people. Yet she also had to confront negative images of welfare recipients that may have raised doubts about her credibility among committee members. As Pratt-Marston explained, negative images of welfare recipients often arose from confounding and contradictory social expectations: "When I am home taking care of my four children and two foster children, I am a lazy welfare broad. And when I go across the street and take care of my neighbor's one child, I am employed. And I fail to understand the rationale of that" (84). Pratt-Marston could not ignore negative circulating images if she wished to advance positive interpretations of her identities and interests.

Competing societal expectations of child rearing and paid employment intimate another obstacle that imagining creates for counterpublic agents: negative images may invoke historical animosities and concentrate these animosities in conflicts over representation. After completing her testimony, Pratt-Marston responded to questions from various subcommittee members. Representative John Rousselot appeared especially skeptical of her claims regarding the inadequacy of AFDC and its connection to the low-wage labor market. He asked Pratt-Marston: "Now, what do you suppose the problem is in going back to work?" Without waiting for an answer, Rousselot shared his own view: "What we are really saying, then, is that they are not able to get a job to encourage them to go back to work that is [at] a level of pay that can compete with what they are getting" (U.S. House 1981, 95). His answer invoked an image of welfare recipients as comfortable individuals insufficiently motivated to seek paid employment. Pratt-Marston's reply advanced an alternative image: "I would not say it is a matter of competing with what they are getting. I would say it is a matter of a level of pay that allows them to survive and feed their children and pay their rent" (95). In her reply, Pratt-Marston imagined welfare recipients—including herself—as valiant but struggling parents desperately attempting to provide for their children. Rousselot retorted that he too wanted poor people to survive, but reiterated, "they are not able to get something in the employment field that is competitive with what they are receiving" (95). Pratt-Marston in turn highlighted welfare recipients' lack of training, which prompted a discussion of federal job training programs launched in the 1960s. Rousselot labeled these programs a failure. Pratt-Marston pointed to a lack of jobs for program participants and countered that these programs had provided social services and offered an irreplaceable supplement to poor people's incomes. Beginning with the relationship of public assistance and low-wage labor, Rousselot and Pratt-Marston proceeded to an evaluation of Great Society programs. Their differing judgments reflected divergent political outlooks that placed varying emphasis on the proper role of government as an ameliorative social force. In this way, they entered into a long-standing and wide-ranging debate, and their points of entry and critical judgment relied significantly on contrasting images of poor people.

Informing particular interactions between counterpublic agents and others, circulating images do not disappear when specific discussions conclude. Some images linger in the public imagination. These images constitute a cumulative imaginary field that constrains the choices of successive participants; they shape subsequent rhetorical situations. Calls for budget cuts in social programs in 1981 gained strength from earlier charges of waste and fraud in public assistance programs. In his unsuccessful 1976 presidential campaign, Ronald Reagan repeatedly relayed the alleged exploits of the "Chicago welfare queen." At many campaign appearances, he enraged audiences with the story of a woman in Chicago who "has 80 names, 30 addresses, 12 Social Security cards and is collecting veterans' benefits on four nonexisting deceased husbands. And she's collecting Social Security on her cards. She's got Medicaid, getting food stamps and she is collecting welfare under each of her names. Her tax-free cash income alone is over $150,000" (quoted in "Welfare Queen" 1976, 51; see also Weiler 1992, 232). By 1981, images of fraud had become so widespread that they elicited parodies from policymakers who supported public assistance programs. Pete Stark, chairperson of the Public Assistance and Unemployment Compensation Subcommittee and a longtime advocate of federal anti-poverty programs, solicited one witness's help in locating a particularly notorious welfare cheat who roamed his district. He wanted to track down "this woman, and for some reason it is a woman, who is ahead of each one of my constituents in the checkout line at a supermarket and has bought a tremendous amount of Perrier and chickens. Actually, they are never chickens; they are Cornish game hens stuffed with wild rice. A whole carton of these go into the trunk of . . . a new Cadillac." Fed up with her behavior, Stark announced a plan to stop this woman and others who may have been tempted to follow her example: "I have a bill that I am about to introduce that would make it a felony for a Cadillac salesman to accept food stamps in full or partial payment for the Cadillac" (U.S. House 1981, 74). To call attention to the cumulative force of imagining is not to ascribe a determinative force to imagining. Circulating images and other aspects of collective imagining may be only one element informing specific discursive engagements in the public sphere. And discourse may be constrained variously and to varying degrees. Still, prominent images compel an accounting from future participants. As welfare reform debates continued throughout the 1980s and 1990s, participants had to address the question of whether the non-needy had been vanquished from the welfare rolls.

Conclusion

Hoping to redeem a promise of critical publicity, contemporary public sphere scholarship has drawn critical attention to direct and indirect exclusions in multiple public spheres. I have sought to contribute to this effort by considering the interrelationship of exclusions operating on multiple levels. Specifically, I have considered how dynamics of inclusion and exclusion may be engaged at the level of the imagination. Imagining proceeds importantly in this regard as a collective process that participates in constructing a shared social world. Collective imagining draws its power as a representational process, one that enacts a politics and utilizes linguistic and visual modalities. In interactive moments between counterpublics and wider publics, collective imagining functions as a symbolic hurdle for counterpublic agents insofar as it circulates negative images that undermine their credibility and concentrates historical animosities in conflicts over representation. Moreover, prominent circulating images constitute a cumulative imaginary field that constrains the choices of successive participants.

Attention to imagining reveals that including more and more voices in multiple public spheres—a form of direct inclusion—is an indispensable but by itself insufficient reformulation of critical models of the public sphere. As with other discursive norms and practices, imagining may inform interactions even in ostensibly accessible forums. The consequences of collective imagining appear in the doubly disabling tendencies of representation that absent some people from public discourse and yet present them through disabling images. Counterpublic agents encounter these negative images as they enter previously foreclosed forums. Yet disabling tendencies of representation should not prompt a scholarly flight from imagining and its representational power. A flight of this sort would return public sphere scholarship to a reconstructed bourgeois public sphere as a singular public forum in which everyone—at least in principle—is free to participate. Existing scholarship has demonstrated that such a sphere would most likely betray its legitimating discourses at the level of direct exclusions. A flight from representation also would require a renunciation of political legitimacy, identity formation, cultural diversity, and needs interpretation as appropriate topics of public discourse, for these are social goods. More hopefully, representation ought not to be disavowed because imagining need not be disabling. Counterpublics may interact with wider publics to construct affirmative images of themselves and others that may engender discourses capable of advancing the multiple aims of discourse in the public sphere. Scholars may contribute to this process by elucidating how various forums may exclude potential participants in voice, body, and imagination.

NOTES

1. Michael Osborn has developed a notion of "rhetorical depiction" to explain how rhetors may prompt visualization in their audiences. He observes that "contemporary rhetoric seems dominated by strategic pictures, verbal or nonverbal visualizations that linger in the collective memory of audiences as representative of their subjects when rhetoric has been successful" (1986, 79). He quotes George Campbell's view of significant metaphor to describe depiction as "an allegory in miniature" (1986, 80). Though "depiction" resonates with "imagining," Osborn's invocation of allegory suggests a more directed symbolic process. Moreover, Osborn does not consider depiction as a collective process, nor does he explore the political dimension of representation.

2. See also Lake and Pickering 1998. Scholarly attention to the communicative qualities of visual images has produced a provocative, growing field of inquiry (see, e.g., Biesecker 1998; DeLuca 1999; DeLuca and Demo 2000; Lucaites 1997). Sometimes, however, statements asserting the prominence of visual modes of communication extend into the hyperbolic. For instance, although he initially describes political messages as "*complex composites of multiple discourses created in verbal, visual, and acoustic languages*" (1995, 219), Bruce Gronbeck stresses the visual as the primary mode of discourse in the contemporary public sphere. He writes: "The telespectacle, for better or worse, is the center of public politics, of the public sphere. . . . We must recognize that the conversation of the culture is centered not in the *New York Review of Books* but in the television experience" (235). Gronbeck's characterization of the contemporary public sphere is problematic on several counts. First, his remarks betray a desire to locate a center, while the public sphere may be better appreciated as a multiplicity with no primary focal point. Second, he sets up two overly restrictive options for discourse between the "telespectacle" on the one hand and detached proto-academic discussion on the other. Most discourse in the public sphere likely lies between these two poles. Third, Gronbeck privileges mass-mediated discourse over more vernacular forms of political communication. Although thousands of people appear each year on television, many millions more do not—yet they nevertheless engage in "public politics" that participates in constituting a multiple public sphere.

3. I invoke ideology here in its classical sense as the false representation of the interests of the few as the interests of the many. On the diverse and sometimes contradictory ways in which theorists have understood ideology, see Eagleton 1991.

4. This potential obstacle appears especially harmful in light of the role that character (*ethos*) plays in adjudicating tensions of dissent and consensus in a multiple public sphere. Erik Doxtader explains that "the *ethos* of an advocate marks these oppositions [expressions of dissent] with a concession: the merit of the dissident's proposal turns on whether an audience is able to see

why and how the speaker is willing to bear the risk of her own transgression" (2000, 360). Ethos functions as a constitution of the self that permits recognition of an other: "*Ethos* is a figure of accountability (a mean) that offers some insight into the relation between the improvisation of creative reasoning and the procedures of intersubjective dialogue" (360). Negative imagining precludes this assertion of responsibility insofar as it circumscribes how one may appear.

WORKS CITED

Alcoff, Linda. 1991–92. "The Problem of Speaking for Others." *Cultural Critique* 20: 5–32.

Anderson, Benedict. 1991. *Imagined Communities: Reflections on the Origin and Spread of Nationalism*, rev. ed. London: Verso.

Asen, Robert. 1999. "Toward a Normative Conception of Difference in Public Deliberation." *Argumentation and Advocacy* 35: 115–29.

_____. 2002. *Visions of Poverty: Welfare Policy and Political Imagination*. East Lansing: Michigan State University Press.

Auletta, Ken. 1982. *The Underclass*. New York: Random House.

Benhabib, Seyla. 1996. "Toward a Deliberative Model of Democratic Legitimacy." In *Democracy and Difference: Contesting the Boundaries of the Political*, ed. Seyla Benhabib. Princeton, NJ: Princeton University Press.

Biesecker, Barbara. 1998. "Rhetorical Ventriloquism: Fantasy and/as American National Identity." In *Argument in a Time of Change*, ed. James F. Klumpp. Annandale, VA: National Communication Association.

Brouwer, Daniel C. 2001. "ACT-ing UP in Congressional Hearings." In *Counterpublics and the State*, ed. Robert Asen and Daniel C. Brouwer. Albany: State University of New York Press.

Calhoun, Craig. 1993. "Civil Society and the Public Sphere." *Public Culture* 5: 267–80.

Castoriadis, Cornelius. 1987. *The Imaginary Institution of Society*. Trans. Kathleen Blamey. Cambridge: MIT Pres.

Cates, Jerry R. 1983. *Insuring Inequality: Administrative Leadership in Social Security, 1935–54*. Ann Arbor: University of Michigan Press.

Cloud, Dana L. 1998. "The Rhetoric of Family Values: Scapegoating, Utopia, and the Privatization of Social Responsibility." *Western Journal of Communication* 62: 387–419.

Dawson, Michael C. 1995. "A Black Counterpublic?: Economic Earthquakes, Racial Agenda(s), and Black Politics." In *The Black Public Sphere*, ed. Black Public Sphere Collective. Chicago: University of Chicago Press.

DeLuca, Kevin Michael. 1999. *Image Politics: The New Rhetoric of Environmental Activism*. New York: Guilford Press.

DeLuca, Kevin Michael, and Anne Teresa Demo. 2000. "Imaging Nature: Watkins, Yosemite, and the Birth of Environmentalism." *Critical Studies in Media Communication* 17: 241–61.

Derrida, Jacques. 1982. "Sending: On Representation." *Social Research* 49: 294–326.

Doxtader, Erik. 2000. "Characters in the Middle of Public Life: Consensus, Dissent, and *Ethos*." *Philosophy and Rhetoric* 33: 336–69.

_____. 2001. "In the Name of Reconciliation: The Faith and Works of Counterpublicity." In *Counterpublics and the State*, ed. Robert Asen and Daniel C. Brouwer. Albany: State University of New York Press.

Dyer, Richard. 1993. *The Matter of Images: Essays on Representation*. New York: Routledge.

Eagleton, Terry. 1991. *Ideology: An Introduction*. London: Verso.

Fabj, Valeria, and Matthew J. Sobnosky. 1995. "AIDS Activism and the Rejuvenation of the Public Sphere." *Argumentation and Advocacy* 31: 163–84.

Finnegan, Cara A. 2000. "Social Engineering, Visual Politics, and the New Deal: FSA Photography in *Survey Graphic*." *Rhetoric & Public Affairs* 3: 333–62.

Fraser, Nancy. 1989. *Unruly Practices: Power, Discourse, and Gender in Contemporary Social Theory*. Minneapolis: University of Minnesota Press.

_____. 1992. "Rethinking the Public Sphere: A Contribution to the Critique of Actually Existing Democracy." In *Habermas and the Public Sphere*, ed. Craig Calhoun. Cambridge: MIT Press.

_____. 1993. "Clintonism, Welfare, and the Antisocial Wage: The Emergence of a Neoliberal Political Imaginary." *Rethinking Marxism* 6.1: 9–23.

Gergen, Kenneth J. 1999. *An Invitation to Social Construction*. Thousand Oaks, CA: Sage.

Gilens, Martin. 1999. *Why Americans Hate Welfare: Race, Media, and the Politics of Antipoverty Policy*. Chicago: University of Chicago Press.

Goodnight, G. Thomas. 1991. "Controversy." In *Argument in Controversy*, ed. Donn W. Parson. Annandale, VA: Speech Communication Association.

Gordon, Linda. 1994. *Pitied but Not Entitled: Single Mothers and the History of Welfare*. Cambridge, MA: Harvard University Press.

Gronbeck, Bruce E. 1995. "Rhetoric, Ethics, and Telespectacles in the Post-everything Age." In *Postmodern Representations: Truth, Power, and Mimesis in the Human Sciences and Public Culture*, ed. Richard Harvey Brown. Urbana: University of Illinois Press.

Hauser, Gerard A. 1999. *Vernacular Voices: The Rhetoric of Publics and Public Spheres*. Columbia: University of South Carolina Press.

_____. 2001. "Prisoners of Conscience and the Counterpublic Sphere of Prison Writing: The Stones that Start the Avalanche." In *Counterpublics and the State*, ed. Robert Asen and Daniel C. Brouwer. Albany: State University of New York Press.

Hutcheon, Linda. 1989. "The Politics of Representation." *Signature: A Journal of Theory and Canadian Literature* 1: 23–44.

Iser, Wolfgang. 1993. *The Fictive and the Imaginary: Charting Literary Anthropology.* Baltimore: Johns Hopkins University Press.

Lake, Randall A., and Barbara A. Pickering. 1998. "Argumentation, the Visual, and the Possibility of Refutation: An Exploration." *Argumentation* 12: 79–93.

Landes, Joan B. 1998. "The Public and the Private Sphere: A Feminist Reconsideration." In *Feminism, The Public & The Private,* ed. Joan B. Landes. New York: Oxford University Press.

Lentricchia, Frank. 1983. *Criticism and Social Change.* Chicago: University of Chicago Press.

Lucaites, John Louis. 1997. "Visualizing 'the People': Individualism vs. Collectivism in *Let Us Now Praise Famous Men.*" *Quarterly Journal of Speech* 83: 269–88.

Mink, Gwendolyn. 1995. *The Wages of Motherhood: Inequality in the Welfare State, 1917– 1942.* Ithaca, NY: Cornell University Press.

Mitchell, W. J. T. 1994. *Picture Theory: Essays on Verbal and Visual Representation.* Chicago: University of Chicago Press.

Mouffe, Chantal. 2000. *The Democratic Paradox.* London: Verso.

Murray, Charles. 1994. *Losing Ground: American Social Policy, 1950–1980,* 10th Anniversary ed. New York: Basic Books.

Olson, Kathryn M., and G. Thomas Goodnight. 1994. "Entanglements of Consumption, Cruelty, Privacy, and Fashion: The Social Controversy over Fur." *Quarterly Journal of Speech* 80: 249–76.

Orloff, Ann Shola. 1991. "Gender in Early U.S. Social Policy." *Journal of Policy History* 3: 249–81.

Osborn, Michael. 1986. "Rhetorical Depiction." In *Form, Genre, and the Study of Political Discourse,* ed. Herbert W. Simons and Aram A. Aghazarian. Columbia: University of South Carolina Press.

Palczewski, Catherine Helen. 2002. "Argument in an Off Key: Playing with the Productive Limits of Argument." In *Arguing Communication & Culture,* ed. G. Thomas Goodnight. Washington, DC: National Communication Association.

Patterson, James T. 1994. *America's Struggle Against Poverty 1900–1994.* Cambridge, MA: Harvard University Press.

Pitkin, Hanna Fenichel. 1967. *The Concept of Representation.* Berkeley: University of California Press.

Piven, Frances Fox, and Richard A. Cloward. 1979. *Poor People's Movements: Why They Succeed, How They Fail.* New York: Vintage Books.

Ryan, Mary P. 1990. *Women in Public: Between Banners and Ballots, 1825–1880.* Baltimore: Johns Hopkins University Press.

Sartre, Jean-Paul. 1948. *The Psychology of Imagina-*

tion. Trans. B. Frechtman. New York: Philosophical Library.

Scarry, Elaine. 1996. "The Difficulty of Imagining Other People." In *For Love of Country: Debating the Limits of Patriotism,* ed. Martha C. Nussbaum. Boston: Beacon Press.

Squires, Catherine. 2001. "The Black Press and the State: Attracting Unwanted (?) Attention." In *Counterpublics and the State,* ed. Robert Asen and Daniel C. Brouwer. Albany: State University of New York Press.

Taylor, Charles. 1993. *Modernity and the Rise of the Public Sphere,* Tanner Lectures on Human Values, vol. 14. Salt Lake City: University of Utah Press.

———. 1994. "The Politics of Recognition." In *Multiculturalism: Examining the Politics of Recognition,* ed. Amy Gutmann. Princeton, NJ: Princeton University Press.

U.S. Committee on Economic Security. 1935. *Report to the President of the Committee on Economic Security.* Washington, DC: U.S. Government Printing Office.

U.S. House. 1981. Committee on Ways and Means. Subcommittee on Public Assistance and Unemployment Compensation. *Administration's Proposed Savings in Unemployment Compensation, Public Assistance, and Social Services Programs.* 97th Cong., 1st sess. 11 March.

———. 1987. Committee on Education and Labor. *Hearings on Welfare Reform: H.R. 30, Fair Work Opportunities Act of 1987 and H.R. 1720, Family Welfare Reform Act of 1987.* 100th Cong., 1st sess. 5 May.

———. 1995. Committee on Ways and Means. Subcommittee on Human Resources. *Welfare Reform Success Stories.* 104th Cong., 1st sess. 6 December.

Warner, Michael. 1993. "The Mass Public and the Mass Subject." In *The Phantom Public Sphere,* ed. Bruce Robbins. Minneapolis: University of Minnesota Press.

Weiler, Michael. 1992. "The Reagan Attack on Welfare." In *Reagan and Public Discourse in America,* ed. Michael Weiler and W. Barnett Pearce. Tuscaloosa: University of Alabama Press.

"'Welfare Queen' Becomes Issue in Reagan Campaign." 1976. *New York Times,* 15 February, late city edition.

Williams, Raymond. 1983. *Keywords: A Vocabulary of Culture and Society,* rev. ed. New York: Oxford University Press.

Young, Iris Marion. 1996. "Communication and the Other: Beyond Deliberative Democracy." In *Democracy and Difference: Contesting the Boundaries of the Political,* ed. Seyla Benhabib. Princeton, NJ: Princeton University Press.

———. 2000. *Inclusion and Democracy.* New York: Oxford University Press.

Zaeske, Susan. 2002. "Signatures of Citizenship: The Rhetoric of Women's Antislavery Petitions." *Quarterly Journal of Speech* 88: 147–68.

PART VII

RHETORIC AND THE MASS MEDIA

Classical rhetorical theory was formulated to account for the relationship between discourse and power in ancient Greece and Rome. Contemporary rhetorical theory has endeavored to modify the formulations of classical rhetoric to account for the changing circumstances and practices of rhetoric in our own time. The most obvious difference between the classical era and our own time is the dominance of the mass media, particularly television and film, as well as the increasing importance of online communication.

The rhetorical study of television and film requires a fairly substantial shift in some of the underlying assumptions concerning the relationship between public discourse and social and political power. The most substantial shift concerns the fact that film and television are predominantly commercial media. The primary goal of most television programming and film releases is to attract a paying audience, not to gain political support for a particular policy, party, or person. Nonetheless, wittingly or not, the content of television programs and movies almost always incorporates significant political messages. Sometimes these messages relate to specific policies currently being deliberated in the public sphere. For example, a program portraying the horrible results of an illegal abortion conveys a message about the desirability of legalizing abortion. More often, perhaps, a film or program conveys messages about more diffuse social practices or hidden threats. Thus a program on abortion probably also conveys images of appropriate gender roles, while a film such as *Ex Machina* (2015) may convey more subtle messages about the threat that advanced technology poses to individual identity.

Because the political messages in film and television are often not explicitly connected with particular policies being publicly debated, the study of the rhetorical practices embedded in such mass media involves a shift of focus. Rhetoric is thus not solely a study of governance, but is also, and significantly, a study of culture and identity. For rhetoricians, of course, culture is not an apolitical phenomenon. Nevertheless, to interpret the political through the lenses of culture and entertainment rather than through the lens of deliberative governance is to change the way in which one understands the functions and scope of rhetoric. Most significantly, such a perspective diffuses the nature of the rhetorical situation. The exigences that create the conditions for the production and dissemination of the movie *Star Wars: Revenge of the Sith* (2005), or even for more politically charged movies like *Selma* (2014), are not specifically locatable incidents, such as the assassination of a president or a military attack. Rather, they create and respond to trends that span much larger periods of time.

These sorts of trends—rapid technological change, changing perceptions of the roles that gender and race play in U.S. history, threats to security that are both national and international and conducted online and on the ground—are now being tempered, indeed transformed, by a range of relatively recent methods of transmission. The magazine and newspaper are being replaced by online versions of the same and by social aggregate sites that lure more, and more varied, consumers. Traditional tastemakers—television and film critics—find their opinions recirculated on Rotten Tomatoes and IMDb, and offset by opinion leaders (both professionals and amateurs) who exist solely online. Word of mouth is being replaced with the ease of a swipe, the speed of a text, and the impact of a Tweet. Even these forms are subject to relatively rapid shifts. Where once there was MySpace, now there is Facebook. The desktop became a laptop, which became a tablet, which became a smartphone and even a watch now linked to the Internet of Things. This transformative speed is a reason for pause. It is also a rationale for why, in each of the following essays save two, the focus remains on television and film while we wait to see how transformative these newer methods are when it comes to actual rhetorical practices relating to mass media.

It is obvious that there is an enormous range of approaches to the modes of rhetoric represented in the mass media. Barry Brummett's examination of "Burke's Representative Anecdote as a Method in Media Criticism," for example, views the contents of mass media as though they were directed at helping individuals to cope with situations in their personal lives. As such, Brummett argues that in periods when technological change has been perceived as particularly intimidating, movies have helped audiences to cope with the apparent threats to their individuality and livelihood.

Another approach to understanding the rhetoric of the mass media is offered by Celeste Michelle Condit in her essay "The Rhetorical Limits of Polysemy." This essay examines the ways in which two audience members—a pro-life activist and a pro-choice activist—respond to an episode of the television show *Cagney and Lacey* that dealt with abortion. Condit argues that the differences in interpretations offered by these readers and their respective enjoyment of the program are constrained by a variety of factors, including the content of the episode itself, the availability of other media images of abortion, the amount of labor each viewer has to perform to produce a profitable interpretation of the episode, and the exposure of each viewer to other interpretations of abortion. Her conclusion is that a rhetorical reading of the mass media needs to be situated in sociopolitical contexts with regard both to ongoing political initiatives and to the range of coverage of a topic within the mass media and alternative media as a whole.

A third approach looks at the ways the filmic form can embed, often in subtle ways, powerful rhetorical representations of what is and is not appropriate behavior. Kathryn M. Olson, in "An Epideictic Dimension of Symbolic Violence in Disney's *Beauty and the Beast*: Inter-Generational Lessons in Romanticizing and Tolerating Intimate Partner Violence," argues that the symbolic representations of violence in the film legitimate domestic versions of the same. By adjusting the narrative to cater to Disney's split demographic base of children and adults, *Beauty and the Beast* rhetorically moves beyond mere entertainment. The film engages in an epideictic display that shapes and defines appropriate behavior for the audience. Scenes of cartoon violence, particularly between the characters Beast and Belle, legitimate power relationships where certain types of violence are understood as expected, understandable, and acceptable.

There now exist challenges to mass media that extend beyond the televised and filmed frames discussed above. These are both embodied and virtual rhetorical acts. In "Pranking Rhetoric: 'Culture Jamming' as Media Activism," Christine Harold details the move from an activist culture of "jamming" to the realm of the prankster. Whereas culture jamming seeks to undermine and expose the suspect practices of multinational corporations, it also tends to engage and thus reinforce the persuasive forms it challenges. At the same time, jamming—with its focus on edginess and irony—has been coopted by those very same corporations in a bid to appeal to younger consumers. The prankster, in contrast and building off the work of Situationists, engages in *détournement*. Hijacking the raw materials used by these corporations, the prankster appropriates and affirms, rather than merely opposing and sabotaging. Harold argues that the prankster takes a cue from jazz music, rearranging extant messages—in cases like the Barbie Liberation Organization and the Biotic Baking Brigade—so as to open up a space to challenge contentious issues such as gender roles, or the lack of corporate transparency and accountability.

Foretelling the popular culture rise of "catfishing," John W. Jordan discusses the real rhetorical impact of fictional personae inhabiting the virtual world. In "A Virtual Death and a Real Dilemma: Identity, Trust, and Community in Cyberspace," he recounts the troubling case of Kaycee Nicole Swenson. Using a blog, Swenson shared her struggle with leukemia with interested online others until she succumbed to the disease in 2001. Except that she didn't. Kaycee Nicole was a fictitious creation of Debbie Swenson. Jordan argues that this hoax highlights the tensions involved in forging both identity and community in cyberspace, in navigating what is true and what is false in a virtual world of forged and faked, felt and found, Internet connections. He urges that the rhetoric involved during and after the hoax demonstrates the potential and pitfalls of forging real relationships online.

Attention to the ways in which the media of film and television change rhetoric and demand its retheorization are well established. At the same time, as the Jordan essay suggests, the analysis of the rhetorical implications of the computer and the Internet as primary communication media are ongoing. The readings below suggest the ways in which mass media engage, modify, and reshape long-held assumptions about rhetoric's role in disseminating popular messages to ever-expanding audiences.

ADDITIONAL READINGS

Aune, James Arnt. (1997). "The Work of Rhetoric in the Age of Digital Dissemination." *Quarterly Journal of Speech* 83: 230–42.

Chesebro, James W., and Dale A. Bertelsen. (1996). *Analyzing Media: Communication Technologies as Symbolic and Cognitive Systems*. New York: Guilford Press.

Cuklanz, Lisa M. (1996). *Rape on Trial: How the Mass Media Construct Legal Reform and Social Change*. Philadelphia: University of Pennsylvania Press.

Dow, Bonnie J. (1996). *Prime-Time Feminism: Television, Media Culture, and the Women's Movement since 1970*. Philadelphia: University of Pennsylvania Press.

Eyman, Douglas. (2015). *Digital Rhetoric: Theory, Method, Practice*. Ann Arbor: University of Michigan Press.

Fiske, John. (1986). "Television: Polysemy and Popularity." *Critical Studies in Mass Communication* 3: 391–408.

Frentz, Thomas S., and Janice Hocker Rushing. (1993). "Integrating Ideology and Archetype in Rhetorical Criticism, Part 2: A Case Study of *Jaws*." *Quarterly Journal of Speech* 79: 61–81.

Gurak, Laura J. (1997). *Persuasion and Privacy in Cyberspace: The Online Protests over Lotus Marketplace and the Clipper Chip*. New Haven, CT: Yale University Press.

Haynes, W. Lance. (1988). "Of That Which We Cannot Write: Some Notes on the Phenomenology of Media." *Quarterly Journal of Speech* 74: 71–101.

Hess, Aaron. (2007). "In Digital Remembrance: Vernacular Memory and the Rhetorical Construction of Web Memorials." *Media, Culture, and Society* 29.5: 812–30.

Lanham, Richard. (1993). *The Electronic Word: Democracy, Technology, and the Arts*. Chicago: University of Chicago Press.

Lucaites, John Louis, and Maurice Charland. (1989). "The Legacy of [LIBERTY]: Rhetoric, Ideology, and Aesthetics in the Postmodern Condition." *Canadian Journal of Political and Social Theory* 13: 31–48.

Ono, Kent A., and Derek T. Buescher. (2001). "Deciphering *Pocahontas*: Unpackaging the Commodification of a Native American Woman." *Critical Studies in Media Communication* 18.1: 23–43.

Rushing, Janice Hocker, and Thomas S. Frentz. (1991). "Reintegrating Ideology and Archetype in Rhetorical Criticism." *Quarterly Journal of Speech* 77: 385–406.

Wolff, Michael. (2015). *Television Is the New Television: The Unexpected Triumph of Old Media in the Digital Age*. New York: Portfolio.

Burke's Representative Anecdote as a Method in Media Criticism

Barry Brummett

Invasion of the Body Snatchers

One of Kenneth Burke's central concepts is the idea that literature is "equipment for living" (1941/1967, pp. 293–304; 1935/1965). By that he means that through types, components, or structures of literature people confront their lived situations, celebrate their triumphs and encompass their tragedies. For instance, some literary *forms* seem to be used reliably to help people adjust to agriculture lifestyles, while other forms seem better adapted to urban and industrial situations (Burke, 1935/1965, pp. 37–49, 237–246; 1937). Elsewhere Burke argues that people communicate using clusters of key terms which anchor symbolic structures of association and dissociation necessary for social life (1945/1962a). He describes the ways in which classical plot forms of tragedy and comedy are used by people to assuage guilt and repair social rifts (1937, vol. 1, pp. 41–118; 1941/1967, pp. 191–220; 1945/1962a). Writing in the Depression, Burke recommended new forms of public discourse to provide more effective symbolic equipment for a changing economy, and to replace the existing modes of discourse which had resulted in "trained incapacities" (1935/1965, pp. 7–9, 48–49). Throughout his writings runs the idea that types, components, or structures of literature *recur* as appropriate responses to recurring types of situations; that there are ways of *speaking about* war, victory, civil unrest, marital problems, etc., which will reliably equip us to live through those situations.

Thus, it becomes the task of the Burkean critic to identify the modes of discourse enjoying currency in a society and to link discourse to the real situations for which it is symbolic equipment. In this way, by examining what people are *saying*, the critic may discover what cultures are celebrating or mourning—and the critic may recommend other ways of speaking which may serve as better equipment for living. For Burke, criticism is epistemic rather than merely evaluative; it generates knowledge of the human condition.

Burke focused more on fiction and poetry than on any other form of discourse; but he draws upon a wide variety of discourses in different media, including news reports, sermons, popular songs, etc. There is nothing in his theories which [would] disqualify them for application today to all forms of mass media, including the electronic media. In fact, the major purpose of this article is to suggest one method of Burkean criticism which is a fruitful tool for analyzing mass media content. I shall also argue that the dramatic characteristics of the media make Burke's dramatistic method relevant for media criticism. To reflect this wider application, I shall substitute the term *discourse* for Burke's *literature*, and include in that term mass media content. That content is, of course, the equipment for living relied upon by millions today. That raises for the critic these epistemological and methodological questions: What aspect of media content should one look at, and how, if one wishes to discover ways in which that discourse equips people for living? What critical methods will allow the critic to take the pulse of a society, to link the discourse it uses with the situations it encounters?

The Method

The generic term for Burke's methodology is *dramatism* (1945/1962a). The Burkean studies all symbolic action as if it were a play, even if the discourse under study displays no explicit narrative or fictional characteristics. All of Burke's more specific methods flow from, and are informed by, this root metaphor of the drama.

Burke picks drama as the central metaphor for his method because of his insistence that any method should represent rather than reduce its subject matter. To *represent* something is to sum up its essence; and the *dramatic* aspects of what people do and say are the *essence* of human action (Burke, 1950/1962b, pp. 13–15). One aspect of the drama is the *plot* or *story line* that it follows. Burke argues that to treat discourse as if it were the enactment of a plot represents (and thus, *reveals*) the essence of that discourse well (1941/1967, p. 103; 1937, p. 208). And therefore, one key Burkean method stemming from his dramatistic metaphor is his insight that the content or "terminology" of whole discourses or groups of discourses will imply, or will seem to be based upon, a *representative anecdote* (Burke, 1945/1962a, pp. 59–60, 323–325, 503–507). He means for us to take "anecdote" explicitly in the dramatic sense of a story, a tale. For instance, he argues that the discourse of the psychologists of his time was based upon anecdotes containing the central claims that "humans are chemicals" or "humans are white rats" (Burke, 1945/1962a, p. 59). Burke identifies the "making of the Constitution" explicitly as an anecdote underlying his *Grammar of Motives* (1945/1962a, pp. 323–401), and he analyzes his own discourse to show why that anecdote was better than others based upon war or train terminals. He explicitly bases the first part of his *Rhetoric of Motives* (1950/1962b, p. 17) on the anecdote of Samson among the Philistines. The anecdote is a macroscopic tool in the array of Burkean methods, in contrast to the pentadic, cluster agon, or other more word-specific approaches. And we shall see that this is a method that represents well what happens in the media because the *media* are anecdotal.

What *is* a representative anecdote; what does one look for? An anecdote is a dramatic form which underlies the content, or the specific vocabulary, of discourse. Burke says (1945/1962a, p. 49) that "dramatism suggests a procedure to be followed in the development of a given calculus, or terminology. It involves the search for a 'representative anecdote,' to be used as a form in conformity with which the vocabulary is constructed." To identify an anecdote, one should ask, "If this discourse were based upon a story, an anecdote, what would the form, outline, or bare bones of that story be"?

The anecdote need not have been explicitly uttered in the discourse under analysis. Instead, the anecdote is a method used by the *critic*. The anecdote is a lens, filter, or template through which the critic studies and reconstructs the discourse. The critic *represents* the essence of discourse by viewing it as if it follows a dramatic plot. The psychologists Burke indicts for using the white rat anecdote did not explicitly say that people were white rats; but Burke reveals the essence of their claims by showing that their discourse implies that anecdote. The critic in search of an anecdote must therefore exercise his or her powers of abstraction to detect a form or pattern which is a plot, a story line, immanent within the content of the discourse and able to represent the discourse. To take an explicitly dramatic example so as to illustrate the point easily, the critic might boil down the play *Pygmalion* or the musical and film *My Fair Lady* to the essential anecdote underlying it: "A person of high economic and social status patronizes a younger person of lower status for motives that seem not entirely altruistic. The younger person is radically altered and encounters difficulties adjusting to his or her new status. A break between the two people occurs, and it is healed through the alteration of the older person as well," etc.

Because one is looking for an abstract dramatic form, one is looking for the same *story structure* to be told in different guises. The representative anecdote underlying *Pygmalion* and *My Fair Lady* underlies other discourse in other media: the play and television special *The Corn Is Green*, the television series *Diff'rent Strokes*, nonfictional documentaries on paternalism in our society, news coverage of an elder statesperson who took a younger politician into tutelage, etc. One does not look for *Pygmalion* per se, one looks for the anecdote upon which it is based. Thus, the representative anecdote is useful for studying widely used symbolic strategies in many different media, because it sifts out those discourses which offer the same formal symbolic equipment to an audience.

Sometimes the initial examination of explicitly dramatic discourse suggests the anecdote most clearly, but the critic need not start from fictional or dramatic discourse at all. Using the anecdote as a form, the critic then *displays* the discourse under examination according to the pattern of the form. Now, when a critic analyzes a thing or a discourse, the critic does not present the whole discourse but rather chooses certain aspects of it that can stand for the whole; and in doing so, one must be careful not to choose *un*representative aspects which will reduce the discourse. Burke argues that psychologists who approached humans as white rats reduced rather than represented humanity. But Burke must be careful, in finding that anecdote within the psychologists' discourse, not to become reductive in turn. This is the pitfall to be guarded against with the representative anecdote. A choice of anecdotes is representative rather than reductive if much of the discourse under analysis can be shown to embody it. If a critic is aware of the representative anecdote underlying *Pygmalion*, etc., then he or she can search across many media for messages of different sorts that can be arrayed according to the dramatic form of the anecdote.

Of course, many different representative anecdotes underlie discourses. For instance, one such anecdote is, "There is something that serves as a safe but confining haven for people. It is moving towards a goal in time or space. It is surrounded by hostile forces which attempt to invade or destroy it. The people in the haven must rely entirely on their inner resources within the haven or what comes to them by chance for survival." That anecdote underlies a number of recent discourses, including the television show *Battlestar Galactica*, the venerable *Robinson Crusoe* and *Swiss Family Robinson*, newscasts of bathysphere explorations and of spacecraft flight, documentaries about Asian and Haitian "boat people," westerns about covered wagon trains moving through Indian territory.

To identify a representative anecdote as immanent within a number of media discourses is to sum up the essence of a culture's values, concerns, and interests in regard to some real-life issues or problems. The anecdote is one component of discourse that equips for living because its dramatic form (1) allows people to express their hopes and fears in familiar (and thus manageable) patterns (Duncan, 1968, pp. 61, 64; Burke, 1941/1967, p. 109). If one fears that he or she will lose a job, seeing a television show about unemployment better equips one to live through that experience. Running throughout Burke's writings is the theme that

articulation of a situation in discourse "vicariously" helps the audience to understand and act through their own similar situations, and that such articulation suggests helpful motives for the audience to embrace in confronting their trials (1935/1965, parts 1 and 2; 1945/1962a). The dramatic form of the anecdote also, (2) naturally "invites participation" in its rhythms (Burke, 1950/1962b, p. 58), thus enabling "the mind to follow processes amenable to it" (Burke, 1931/1968, p. 143). Burke defines form as "the creation of an appetite in the mind of the auditor, and the adequate satisfying of that appetite" (1931/1968, p. 31). By posing the problem of unemployment to the unemployed, for instance, discourse activates or addresses their "appetites" or concerns. When discourse satisfactorily shows a "solution" to unemployment, following one of several narrative forms accepted in a culture, the formal *completion* of the discourse is satisfying to the audience and thus provides them with the motives, hope, and symbolic resources to face their real situations. *Stories* do not merely pose problems, they suggest ways and means to resolve the problems insofar as they follow discursively a pattern that people might follow in reality.

The critic's task is then to *link* discourse embodying the formal anecdote to an audience's problems, to show how the anecdotal form equips a culture for living in that situation. The critic follows Burke's idea that recurrent *types* of anecdotes are "good for" types of situations. Sometimes that linkage can be done by showing *who* attends to discourses enacting a particular anecdote. If it were discovered that the young and poor tend to follow discourses embodying the *Pygmalion* anecdote, for instance, then the critic might speculate that such an anecdote, whenever it is reindividuated in discourse, is used as a symbolic remedy for poverty and social immobility. At other times, it may be discovered that discourse embodying an anecdote appears more often during some periods or in response to some exigencies than others. An examination of those periods, with special attention to complaints or celebrations common to both periods, may show how the anecdote is available for use by audiences facing such trials or triumphs. This essay provides an example of that second sort of analysis.

The representative anecdote is a critical tool especially well-suited to analysis of the media, first, because of their "anecdotal" nature. Television, newspapers, film, popular magazines, etc., mediate reality to people by recasting the chaotic, disjointed world into "story exposition forms" (National Institute of Mental Health, 1982, p. 23), presenting the world to audiences in the brief, one-half-hour to two-hour dramas of newscasts, articles, sitcoms, limited series, etc. "The parallels between television and story-telling are quite obvious" (Granzberg, 1982, p. 48), so that it is more real than metaphorical to refer to "media dramas" (Duncan, 1968, pp. 33–34; Nimmo and Combs, 1983). Because the audience *expects* the world to be mediated to them dramatically, and because the media do so by calling up standard, recurrent, culturally ingrained *types* of dramas, the anecdotal form of the media fits well with Burke's notion of form as the arousing and satisfying of expectations. We expect newscasts of Presidential election results to be cast into a "horse-race" plot, for instance. Because the media are anecdotal, because audiences expect dramatic structure in media content, critical analysis of the media ought to be sensitive to form and drama. That kind of sensitivity is precisely what is engendered by the method of the representative anecdote, which is trained awareness of types of dramatic form. Because the anecdote detects the same dramatic form within different discourses across several media, it alerts critics to the essential similarity in diverse media content. The anecdote can help us to see what is *anecdotal about* the media, and what ties together some diversity in media exposure.

A second reason why the representative anecdote is particularly appropriate for media analysis is that audiences use the dramatic or anecdotal nature of the media as equipment for living. Burke's argument, noted above, that people receive from discourse the symbolic resources to cope with life is thus similar to Gerbner's "cultivation effect" thesis (Gerbner, Gross, Morgan, & Signorielli, 1980). Basing their work on Gerbner's theory, Buerkel-Rothfuss and Mayes (1981, p. 108) found that "heavy systematic exposure to any systematically distorted view of the world will result in similarly distorted viewer perceptions." In their study of daytime television serials, or soap operas, the authors found that people who watch the serials tend to have problems similar to those of soap characters. They disclaim assertion of a causal relationship (p. 114); however, Burke's concept of discourse as equipment for living suggests that viewing the dramatic and formal expression and resolution of one's real problems is psychologically satisfying, even necessary, so that perhaps people with problems are drawn to the anecdotal treatment of them. Through the dramatic form embodied in a representative anecdote, as Herzog noted for soap opera audiences, "listeners are helped to accept their fate" (Herzog, 1965, p. 55). "Help"

seems to be a function of media in general. For instance, the National Institute of Mental Health reports that "films and videotape have been used successfully to help people learn to cope with fears and phobias" (1982, p. 5), that "television leads its viewers to have television-influenced attitudes" (p. 7), and that "television does contribute to viewers' conceptions of social reality" (p. 62). The representative anecdote is a particularly *representative* tool for media analysis, then, because it resonates with the anecdotal, representative, dramatic form of the media, and because the content carried by that form is used by millions as equipment for living, a function to which the method of the anecdote is especially well attuned. The representative anecdote is therefore a method that taps what a culture *most* deeply fears and hopes, and how that culture confronts those concerns symbolically. The remainder of this essay illustrates the utility of Burke's anecdotal method in media criticism. First, I shall identify some economic and political concerns shared by the Fifties and late Seventies. Then, I shall identify a representative anecdote that has been embodied in different types of discourse and media, an anecdote that I shall call *xeroxing*. Since the anecdote emerged during periods that shared similar fears and concerns, the Fifties and late Seventies, I shall argue that discourse embodying the xeroxing anecdote served as equipment for living.

The Situation

Let me begin by showing the kind of situation in which discourse embodying the xeroxing anecdote helps people to live. A complex of concerns occurred nationally in both the Fifties and in the late Seventies. To make historical judgments about a period as near to us as the late Seventies is perilous unless it can be anchored in the analogous, and better-understood Fifties. So let us briefly examine some historians' conclusions about the Fifties and its exigencies, and let us consider how such exigencies mirror those of the late Seventies.

The Fifties were a time of change and transition "more swift and sweeping than any previous generation of Americans had known" (Goldman, 1965, p. 119). The post-war world was "a strange and unruly world" (Goldman, 1965, p. 249). Changes and fears arose in many areas: "The pressures and crises of the cold war continued undiminished. Inflation and recession posed threats to prosperity. Racial, religious, and ideological tensions added their disruptions to the normal problems of a mobile society" (Link and Catton, 1974, p. 160). The same might be said for the Seventies; let us examine technological, economic, and political instability.

Both the Fifties and late Seventies saw vast technological changes, including automation in the Fifties and, in the late Seventies, the new wave of genetic engineering and computer technology. These changes in each case presaged a new era of technology that would be unfamiliar to the average worker (Degler, 1968, p. 173). The worker in the Fifties was threatened by an "expanding revolution in technology" (Link and Catton, 1974, p. 19), as was the worker of the late Seventies. The Fifties saw the introduction of "an increasingly automated and sophisticated economic system" (Link and Catton, 1974, p. 54), as did the late Seventies at the start of the ongoing genetic and silicon chip revolution (Link and Catton, 1974, pp. 20, 54). Technological change found many workers in both periods unprepared, for "it took a heavy toll of unskilled laborers, farmhands and inexperienced young manual workers" (Leuchtenberg, 1973, p. 719). Personal inadequacy took the form of fear that one would be *replaced* by technology: "The word 'automation' struck fear in the heart of the American working man. 'The worker's greatest worry,' explained a writer, 'is that he will be cast upon the slag heap by a robot'" (Leuchtenberg, 1973, p. 719). Such fears are likely to arise in eras when technological change forces dislocation in the economy, as did the flood of inexpensive computers in the late Seventies. The Fifties and late Seventies also saw a collective anxiety about the quality of American technology in relation to the rest of the world. While the Fifties experienced the embarrassment of Sputnik (Goldman, 1965, pp. 308–310), the late Seventies experienced the embarrassment of Japanese and European advances in technology such as automotive engineering, and a fear that despite rapid change, our industry would become obsolete. Therefore, fear of foreign superiority joined with suspicion of technology. Whittaker Chambers, for instance, proclaimed "the scientific method" as the very source of Communism (Wittner, 1974, p. 123).

Economically, the Fifties was a time of instability (Goldman, 1965, p. 265), as were the late Seventies. The Fifties saw relatively high inflation (Goldman, 1965, p. 200), as did the late Seventies. The economic influence upon the social structure changed in both periods, for new respect for business shifted personal allegiance to one's corporate affiliations (Goldman, 1965, p. 264). In both the Fifties and the Seventies, one consequence of

the "incorporation" of America was the growth in power and prestige of a "business elite" allied with government (Wittner, 1974, p. 114), "a distant corporate bureaucracy" (p. 132) manipulating business beyond the control or knowledge of the average worker. Herbert Lehman wrote of the Fifties, and could have said of the late Seventies, that "the big business firms not only dominate our economy to an increasing extent; they are, in fact, beginning seriously to affect our culture, our education, and the intellectual climate of our times" (Lehman, 1969, p. 74).

The growth of big business in both eras led to a fear that the nation was becoming too careful and too conformist. The bland, careerist and consumerist orientation felt on so many campuses in the late Seventies mirrored the "near-unanimity" of concern in the Fifties that society was breeding a generation of "careful young men" (Leuchtenberg, 1973, p. 747). Henry Steele Commager declared "the new loyalty" in the Fifties to be, "above all, conformity" (Wittner, 1974, p. 122). "The typical American, social analysts complained, had become both conformist and bland" (Leuchtenberg, 1973, p. 744). "Whether the individual survives as a self-reliant, self-providing person or becomes a regimented automaton of the state" (Shanks, 1969, p. 28) was a Fifties concern echoed in such late Seventies discourse as Ronald Reagan's campaign rhetoric; we find repeatedly a fear that the individual would become "a calculating automaton cut off from the social context" (Hecksher, 1969, p. 35).

The political atmosphere of both the Fifties and late Seventies presented similar problems. Both periods followed controversial wars with Communist opponents. The Fifties saw the intensification of the cold war while the late Seventies saw the collapse of detente. The Fifties saw (and the late Seventies presaged) the election of conservative Republican Presidents, and a perceived swing of the political mood to the right (Goldman, 1965, pp. 212–213). Underlying these events was a deep sense that the nation was losing control over events at home and abroad: "America found that it could not control the world it had won fair and square. Things would've been different if it hadn't been for the Communists" (Lester, 1969, p. 20). In the Fifties, "irritation rasped through American life" (Goldman, 1965, p. 201) and "gloom was pervasive" (Link and Catton, 1974, p. 56). This sense of frustration and irritation released "a chronic American tendency to suspect that their way of life is being subverted by an internal conspiracy of evildoers" (Link and Catton, 1974, pp. 19, 56). The enemy was an alleged international Communist conspiracy that "was so powerful and so pervasive that its agents might strike anywhere, from within the country as well as from without" (Degler, 1968, p. 36). This "popular fear . . . that the nation, and particularly the federal government, swarmed with communist espionage agents" (Wittner, 1974, p. 87) amounted to a "political stampede" (p. 97). At times concern for lurking conspiracies reached the level of "hysteria" (Christie and Dinnerstein, 1976, p. 5). One never knew in the Fifties when one's neighbor may have fallen victim to that conspiracy, for "it was enough for a man to be considered a Communist because he would not say he wasn't" (Lester, 1969, p. 21). Although the Fifties were more explicitly paranoid than the late Seventies in terms of the Communist threat, the latter era nonetheless had its share of conspiracy fears, with the belief that monolithic Communism was on the march again, orchestrating terrorism at home and abroad, violating the SALT treaty, contributing to the downfall of Iran.

I have reviewed a number of fears and hopes that concerned the nation in the Fifties and late Seventies. I shall now show that some of the media content of these two periods also shows similarities. Specifically, the discourses I shall examine follow the same dramatic *form* insofar as they all seem to be following the same representative anecdote, which I shall call *xeroxing*. And these discourses engage, literally and metaphorically, those shared concerns of the Fifties and late Seventies. The discourses express the concerns and develop them dramatically through the representative anecdote. Therefore, the media contained equipment for living through technological, economic, and political change. I am not arguing that those real-life concerns never occurred at any other period, nor am I claiming that media content never followed the xeroxing anecdote in, let us say, the Sixties. Rather, I am arguing that these problems and this form of discourse occurred together, in those two eras, rather more often and more intensely than in other periods, and that therefore the discourse was available as a symbolic remedy for the problems had a troubled audience chosen to attend to it.

The Anecdote

The representative anecdote analyzed in this essay could be summed up like this: Xeroxing is the duplication and replacement of humans with

evil, inhuman copies that are difficult to detect. The act of duplication occurs in a scene of rapid change and decay. This act of duplication is carried out through technological conspiracies. The replacements themselves are marked by a poverty and uniformity of purpose, the sign of a loss of humanity.[1]

A number of discourses in different media which appeared in the Fifties and again in the late Seventies followed the form of xeroxing. Two films and a book serve as paradigm cases of that anecdote. Jack Finney's (1955/1978) book, *Invasion of the Body Snatchers*, was produced as a film in 1956 (Wanger, 1956) and remade in 1978 (Solo, 1978). A shower of spores from outer space falls on the earth (landing near a small town in Finney's book and in the 1956 film, or near San Francisco in the 1978 film). These spores produce flowering pods which, when placed near sleeping people, take on the form of those people; in the process of reproducing them, the pods destroy the original. The pods are distributed by a conspiracy of technocratic pod people in a scene of social and physical change and decay. A small group resists this threat (Doctor Miles Bennell in Finney and in the 1956 film, Health Inspector Matthew Bennell in the 1978 film; Becky Driscoll in Finney and in the 1956 film, Elizabeth in the 1978 film; and the Belicecs, Jack and Theodora, in all versions). Pods are produced *en masse*, and although the replacements look like the individual, differentiated originals, they have absolutely uniform emotions, drives, and motives.

Although the *Body Snatchers* films and book embody the xeroxing anecdote clearly, the anecdote informs much discourse about *automation* that appeared in the Fifties especially, but also in the late Seventies in response to computer technology. The anecdote underlies much late Seventies discourse about *cloning*. Cloning mass-produces uniform duplicates of living things, and some fear that it might duplicate humans. Cloning is but a part of the genetic engineering revolution that developed in the late Seventies. The structure of my analysis will follow the structure of the xeroxing anecdote as given at the start of this section. In reviewing each component of the dramatic form, I shall show how it corresponds to the situational concerns given in the previous section.

A Changing, Decaying Scene

As noted in the previous section, the social and political context of the Fifties and late Seventies was one of change and instability. Contexts put into anecdotal form become scenes, stage-settings. We find this fear of a strange world changing beyond one's control articulated in discourse grounded in the xeroxing anecdote. In xeroxing, as in the reality of both eras, change and strangeness seem universal and growing. In Finney, Earth's moon and Mars for instance, were thriving planets that were zapped by pod invasions (1955/1978, pp. 184–185). In the 1956 film, Miles and Becky witness the distribution of pods to representatives from surrounding communities. Miles pounds on the passing cars in an attempt to warn them of the danger and shouts, "It's here already. You're next." In the 1978 film, the pod threat has become global. Matthew sees pods being loaded onto oceangoing freighters, bound for distant ports.

The late Seventies and the Fifties fear of rapid change is also reflected in xeroxing. The 1956 film covers three days and three nights, and in that time the entire town goes under. The 1978 film shows just as rapid a change. "It was like the whole city had changed overnight," says Elizabeth on the morning of the second day. In nonfiction discourse about automation, one finds uncontrolled technological change articulated as a fear: "As a button-pusher on an automated machine, a man now stands outside his work and whatever control existed is finally shattered" (Karsh, 1957, p. 209). The bewildering scene of automation was "a society of such complexity that an individual with the best of motives may be powerless either to grasp or to deal with the many facets of a specific situation" (Carr, 1956, p. 667). Toffler (1970, p. 197) describes the scene of clone xeroxing as one of rapid change: "Advances in genetics have come tripping over one another at a rapid pace," so that soon "man will be able to make biological carbon copies of himself."

With a fear of change comes a sense that change means decay. Finney's city (1955/1978, p. 88) abounds with broken glass and "For Rent" signs, and prior to the pod invasion Miles remarks that "the town's dying" (p. 123). In the 1956 film, creeping decay accompanies the pod invasion; Miles notices that farmer Grimaldi's vegetable stand is littered and closed, and we discover that Grimaldi has become a pod. Scenic decay reaches its peak in the 1978 film. Matthew Bennell plies his trade among the garbage cans of the city and delights in the discovery of "rat turds" masquerading as capers in restaurants. Elizabeth notes after some research in the 1978 film that the tiny pod-flowers seem to "thrive on devastated ground."

The average worker of the Fifties and Seventies, faced with overwhelming change, felt unskilled and weak in the face of newness. And so we find xeroxing discourse articulating that fear. Nonfiction discourse of the Fifties stressed the superiority of robots over the ordinary "American worker [who] is pitifully *undereducated* and *underskilled*" (Gerbracht and Scholfield, 1957, p. 113). Automation especially threatened a "decline in unskilled jobs" (Wolfert, 1955, p. 45; Bronowski, 1958, p. 250). Writing on the issue of automation and robots, Rorvik refers to Arthur Clarke's belief that "man will ultimately be superseded by humanlike computer entities. . . . The computer being will go on to construct even greater intelligences" (1970, p. 155).[2] Human weakness and unpreparedness can pave the way for undesirable change; that concern is reflected in the *Body Snatchers* as the need to stay awake, for one becomes a pod when one sleeps. "He's got to go to sleep some time" say the pod people as they hunt for Matthew in the 1978 film. In the 1956 film, Jack Belicec warns, after he has turned into a pod, "Sooner or later you'll have to go to sleep." Miles recognizes the danger: "We can't close our eyes all night." But Becky is weak and cannot resist sleeping as she and Miles try to escape. This weakness is fatal: "A moment's sleep and the girl I loved was an inhuman enemy bent on my destruction. That moment of sleep was death to Becky's soul." Because audiences are accustomed to seeing the world mediated to them, these literal and literary media depictions of a *strange* world would conform to their private anxieties.

The Enemies

The troubled Fifties and Seventies attributed their strange world, as we have seen, to the conspiratorial machination of Communists, big business elites, and government bureaucrats. Xeroxing expresses that fear of The Enemy. And because story-telling depends upon antagonists and protagonists, because the media do well at unidimensional caricature instead of complex characterization, we find The Enemy given as monsters embodying both eras' concerns. The word "strange" or "strangers" is often used to describe these conspirators. In the 1956 film, Miles Bennell perceived that "there must be strangers in town" on the morning that pods were trucked in for secret distribution. In the 1978 film, "strange people" is a recurring remark made by the protagonists: "Geoffrey was meeting all sorts of strange people." Agents who perpetrate automation and cloning are also perceived as alien. A 1954 story, "The Father Thing," by Philip K. Dick, depicts an automated robot "bug" that duplicates a little boy's father, and the father now seeks to xerox the child. This creature's eyes contain "something alien and cold" (Dick, 1959, p. 246).

Much of the strangeness of the villainous enemies stems from their overwhelming power. Miles Bennell in the 1956 film notes that the pods are "fantastically powerful, beyond any comprehension." The title of Aute Carr's article (1956, p. 667) asks, "Automation—Substitute for God?" and foresees "the danger that this new, wonder-working technology will become the 20th century substitute for God." More recently, cloning "smacks of scientists playing God" (Randall, 1978, p. 12). The cloned replacements might even become deathless: "A person's own awareness of the world might somehow survive the death of the body—in the locus of cloned consciousness" (Rorvik, 1978, p. 21).

A fear of powerful strangers spreading change in the world is expressed dramatically as the presence of conspiracies. Xeroxing thus gives shape to the Fifties and late Seventies fear of secretive, organized forces at work. Elizabeth says in the 1978 film, "I keep seeing these people recognize each other. Something is passing between them. It's a conspiracy, I know it." Matthew's inability to persuade the police of the pod danger does not surprise Jack, who says, "Of course, it's a conspiracy." In the 1956 film, Dr. Bennell suspects that "somebody or someone wants this duplication to take place." As Miles and Becky try to escape through the haunted streets of Mill Valley, Miles "wondered if phones were being lifted in the houses we passed and if the air wasn't filled with messages about us" (Finney, 1955/1978, p. 41).

Xeroxing expresses the paranoid fear that conspiracies are both pervasive *and* invisible. In the 1956 film, when Miles returns to Mill Valley, "at first glance, everything looked the same. But it wasn't. Something evil had taken possession of the town." In Finney, "Something impossibly terrible, yet utterly real was menacing us in a way beyond our comprehension or abilities" (Finney, 1955/1978, pp. 112–113). Xeroxing in other kinds of discourse also contains conspiracies that insinuate themselves quietly into the scene. Rorvik (1970, p. 83) speculates that "when the [robot] 'takeover' comes it is likely to be a bloodless one; possibly it won't even register as a takeover in the consciousness of man. It could be argued, even, that the takeover has already taken place."

The technocrats of the Fifties and late Seventies become characters in the xeroxing anecdote. In Finney (1955/1978, p. 74) Miles's friend Mannie Kaufman, having become a pod, tries to explain strange occurrences by appealing to Bennell's scientific training: "Hell, you're a doctor, Miles; you know something about how this sort of thing works." In the 1956 film, the conspirator Kaufman appeals to Miles as a technologist: "Miles, you and I are scientific men, you can understand the wonder of what's happened." In the 1978 film, the conspirators corner the protagonists in Bennell's office, amid a vast array of scientific apparati. Articles by technocrats in the Fifties reflected a sinister optimism in automation as "dynamic and forward looking" (Sotzin, 1956, p. 151). Workers could not possibly have been cheered by the technocrats' hope that automation's "promise of future usefulness is vast" (Wolfert, 1955, p. 43).

Conspirators in xeroxing are so powerful that they control government and business, reflecting the Fifties and late Seventies concern with those two sectors. In the 1978 film, Matthew Bennell's attempt to notify the federal authorities is hopeless. As Jack Belicec says, "The FBI? The CIA? They're pods already"! In recent xeroxing an MIT professor said, "It wouldn't surprise me at all if the government had some crazy cloning scheme going on" (Johnson, 1978, p. 100). Observers of automation feared that it would lead to "a totalitarian form of government" (Bronowski, 1958, p. 250; Shull, 1959, pp. 339–340). In a 1954 story, "The Tunnel Under the World," by Frederik Pohl (1975), businessmen control an entire town that was destroyed and then copied in miniature for the purpose of advertising research. These conspirators control every experience the "townspeople" robots have. In Finney, pod people control that symbol of corporate power, the telephone company. Jack Belicec cries in despair, "They've got the phones" when an operator feigns inability to connect him with the FBI (Finney, 1955/1978, p. 111). In the 1978 film, the operator knows Matthew Bennell's name even though he has not given it to her, prompting strong suspicion that the pods have hold of AT&T. Thus, xeroxing confirms and sanctions the workers' fears that their employers are evil strangers up to no good.

Dehumanization and Uniformity

The key action of xeroxing is duplication of people. That element of the anecdote articulates the real-life fear of "replacement of human beings by machines" (Harrington, 1955, p. 177): "These new brains are going to replace workers—a lot of workers" (Bendiner, 1955, p. 15). A worker might arrive on the job to find a clanking, steaming, whirring copy of him or herself performing a job with more efficiency. In Robert Heinlein's "Waldo" (1959), for instance, the inventor Waldo's hands have been copied: "Everywhere were pairs of Waldoes, large, small, and life-sized" (p. 188).

Duplication is repugnant. In Niven's *A World Out of Time* (1976), an omniscient computer-robot offers to clone the hero to extend his life: "We can clone men. We can clone you." But the protagonist replies, "You're talking about grinding me up into chemically leeched hamburger" (p. 49). Why should it be so terrible to be replaced?

The danger of duplication articulates the real-life fear of uniformity, blandness, corporate amalgamation, and sterility, fears that haunted the Fifties and late Seventies. Those fears are expressed in xeroxing where uniformity of *appearance* signals uniformity of substance. For instance, although most experts agree that physically identical clones would be emotionally different ("The Road to Cloning," 1978, p. 26; Johnson, 1970, p. 102), laymen often assume that physical sameness indicates emotional and intellectual uniformity as well (Bylinsky, 1978, p. 108).

In the *Body Snatchers*, when the pods mature, their emotions and purposes are uniform. Sameness of feeling was forecast by physical sameness in the pods' early development. Details make people individuals, and the fetal pods have none. In the 1978 film, Jack Belicec finds that the new pod meant for him has "no detail, no character, it's unformed." In the 1956 film, Dr. Bennell noted that, physically, Jack's pod "has all the features but no character, no details, no lines." Finney (1955/1978, p. 37) echoes the same theme: "No lines, no *details*, no character."

The physical sameness of xeroxing is evident in automation if one remembers that robots or machines, being mass-produced, look very much alike. Rod Serling's "Mighty Casey" features a robot of the same name with "a face that looked as if it had been painted on. Even the voice. Dead. Spiritless" (1960, p. 7). His story "The Lonely" features an isolated criminal who is given a robot companion "made in his image" (Serling, 1960, p. 167). But the robot gives no physical sign of purpose and life: "There was no expression in the eyes. There was a deadness, a lack of vitality" (pp. 155–156).[3]

Once a person becomes a pod, all individuating purpose, all emotional difference and character [are] gone. This development is the articulation of what people feared would happen to them in factories and offices. In the 1956 *Body Snatchers* film, Wilma Lenz fears that her Uncle Ira, who has become a pod, has lost all feeling: "There's no emotion." Dan Kaufman, having turned into a pod, says that "There's no need for love," and Miles Bennell responds, "No emotion. Then you have no feelings." Finney (1955/1978, p. 184) also shows no individuating purpose in the pod agents: "There's no real joy, fear, hope or excitement in you, not any more. You live in the same kind of grayness as the filthy stuff that formed you."

Xeroxed replacements in other discourses also have no individuating emotions and thus share an internal sameness of purpose. Technocrats seek a uniform "mechanization without purpose" (Kelley, 1957, p. 558). The only value allowed replacements is "dynamic conformity" with no originality or independence (Kelley, 1957, p. 560). Dick's "The Father-Thing" (1959, p. 252) depicts a father who has been duplicated by a robot alien. He/it is "humorless and utterly without emotion." Neurosurgeon Robert White, discussing cybernetic amalgamations of humans and robots, foresees "the stage where you can turn men into robots, obedient sheep," without purposes of their own (Toffler, 1970, p. 214). Loss of individual purpose proves the replacements, in xeroxing as in the fears of the Fifties and late Seventies, are not human. Kael (1978, p. 48) sees a major theme of the *Body Snatchers* as "trying to hang on to your human individuality while those around you are contentedly turning into vegetables." Becoming uniform means losing one's humanity. "We may wake up changed to something evil and inhuman," says Becky in the 1956 film. In the 1978 film, Elizabeth's friend Geoffrey "has become less human" as a result of turning into a pod. Some commentators in the Fifties complained that "the human being and his efforts are almost entirely by-passed" by those who "rush to embrace every new non-human force" (Memoli, 1955, p. 23; Karsh, 1959, p. 383). The new, inhuman technocrat of the Fifties was described as "the Martian prototype, the new race, all brain" (Mannes, 1957, p. 39). Being xeroxed through cloning also leads to a loss of humanity. Rorvik (1970, pp. 55–56) hypothesizes that "a cloned individual might suffer a serious identity crisis, finding it difficult to distinguish himself from his donor." This enforced sameness threatens the humanity of the clone: "When you start manipulating genes at the level of cloning, you are changing our whole concept of what it is to be human" (Dobbie, 1978, p. 69). Jeremy Rifkin argues "that human cloning is an antisocial, inhuman, criminal technology. It's the assembly-line production of carbon copies of humans, and our whole value system about the uniqueness of life is based on the essential difference between individuals" (Johnson, 1978, p. 98).

We have seen xeroxing discourses *articulate* the fears and hopes of the Fifties and late Seventies, and we saw that articulation in and of itself equips people for living. The formal rhythm which completes the cycle of xeroxing is important, too, for it provides audiences with closure of one sort or another. The book and 1956 film versions of the *Body Snatchers* end happily: The FBI is called in, with promise of salvation. Dick (1959) also ends happily, with escape from "the father-thing." Such is not the case for the 1978 *Body Snatchers* film, which gives strong indications that the pod invasion is irresistible. And the townspeople in Pohl's 1954 "The Tunnel Under the World" (1975) are doomed to never-ending slavery under their industrialist captors. In each case, although the stories end differently, an answer is given to the question of "What will happen to me at the factory, office, etc.?" Thus symbolically prepared, audiences are armed to accept, reject, or attempt to change the real course of events depicted in the media.

Conclusion

A time of rapid and uncontrolled change, fear of conspirators at home and abroad, new technological developments and their corresponding social and economic changes: these are the exigencies which formed the context for some distinctive discourses in several media in the Fifties and late Seventies. Xeroxing reveals the essence of that media content as symbolic medicine which equips people for living when they face those difficulties. The anecdote is individualized in fiction and nonfiction, in print and electronic media, and in both serious and entertaining discourse. Knowing this, critics may be on the lookout for discourses in the future which embody xeroxing. The anecdote that some discourse embodies may explain why the discourse appears and how or whether it appeals to its audiences.

The task remains for critics to catalogue other representative anecdotes and to link them with the situations that they equip people to confront. Xeroxing only illustrates the central goal of this essay: to show how Burke's anecdotal method allows the critic to study mass media content as equipment for living. Other fears and hopes confront society, and people turn to mass media for the symbolic means to encompass those situations. The media are equipment for living because they recast this world, its hopes and fears, into anecdotal form, and thus an anecdotal method can help reveal that form. Burke would remind us that media content tells a story, and that critical methods which look for stories are thus appropriate tools for media analysis. To reveal the formal stories being told, and the real or symbolic ills they cure, gives media criticism the ability to move from social commentary to social knowledge.

NOTES

1. Although this anecdote bears some resemblance to the "Frankenstein" or "Doppelganger" myths, its uniqueness as a whole lies in the combination of its elements, especially the *mass* production of copies, the element of *conspiracy*, and the loss of *purpose* in copies.

2. Although Rorvik (1970) was originally printed before the late Seventies, the popularity of Rorvik (1978) caused the earlier work to be marketed again at the end of the decade. The same was true of Toffler (1970).

3. Serling's book is, of course, based on original *television* shows, broadcast during the Fifties.

REFERENCES

Bendiner, R. (1955, April 7). The age of the thinking robot, and what it will mean to us. *Reporter*, pp. 12–18.

Bronowski, J. (1958, March 22). Planning for the year 2,000. *Nation*, pp. 248–251.

Buerkel-Rothfuss, N. L., & S. Mayes. (1981). Soap opera viewing: The cultivation effect. *Journal of Communication 31*: 108–115.

Burke, K. (1937). *Attitudes toward history*. New York: New Republic.

Burke, K. (1962a). *A grammar of motives*. Berkeley and Los Angeles: University of California Press. (Original work published 1945)

Burke, K. (1962b). *A rhetoric of motives*. Berkeley and Los Angeles: University of California Press. (Original work published 1950)

Burke, K. (1965). *Permanence and change*. Rev. ed. Berkeley and Los Angeles: University of California Press. (Original work published 1935)

Burke, K. (1966). *Language as symbolic action*. Berkeley and Los Angeles: University of California Press.

Burke, K. (1967). *Philosophy of literary form*. Rev. ed.

Berkeley and Los Angeles: University of California Press. (Original work published 1941)

Burke, K. (1968). *Counter-statement.* Rev. ed. Berkeley and Los Angeles: University of California Press. (Original work published 1931)

Bylinsky, G. (1978, June 19). The cloning era is almost here. *Fortune,* pp. 100–104, 108–110.

Carr, A. L. (1956, May 30). Automation—substitute for God? *Christian Century,* pp. 666–667.

Christie, L., & L. Dinnerstein (Eds.). (1976). *America since World War II.* New York: Praeger.

Degler, C. N. (1968). *Affluence and anxiety.* Glenview, IL: Scott, Foresman.

Dick, P. K. (1959). The father-thing. In A. Boucher (Ed.), *A treasury of great science fiction* (vol. 1, pp. 245–254). Garden City, NY: Doubleday.

Dobbie, J. (1978, April 3). Cloning: Has man's reach exceeded his grasp? *Maclean's,* pp. 68–69.

Duncan, H. D. (1968). *Symbols in society.* New York: Oxford University Press.

Finney, J. (1978). *Invasion of the body snatchers.* New York: Dell. (Original work published 1955 [as *The body snatchers*])

Gerbner, G., L. Gross, M. Morgan, & N. Signorielli. (1980). The "mainstreaming" of America: violence profile no. 11. *Journal of Communication 30:* 10–29.

Gerbracht, C., & F. Scholfield. (1957, April). . . . And the problems of life related to these changes . . . *Industrial Arts and Vocational Education,* pp. 113–114.

Goldman, E. F. (1965). *The crucial decade—and after.* New York: Knopf.

Granzberg, G. (1982). Television as a storyteller: The Algonkian Indians of Central Canada. *Journal of Communication 32:* 43–52.

Harrington, M. (1955, May 20). The advance of automation. *Commonweal,* pp. 175–178.

Hecksher, A. (1969). Liberalism, conservatism, and freedom. In D. G. Baker & C. H. Sheldon (Eds.), *Postwar America: The search for identity* (pp. 34–35). Beverly Hills, CA: Glencoe Press.

Heinlein, R. (1959). Waldo. In A. Boucher (Ed.), *A treasury of great science fiction* (vol. 1, pp. 170–244). Garden City, NY: Doubleday.

Herzog, H. (1965). Motivations and gratifications of daily serial listeners. In W. Schramm (Ed.), *The process and effects of mass communication* (pp. 50–55). Urbana: University of Illinois.

Johnson, J. (1970). *As man becomes machine.* New York: Pocket Books.

Kael, P. (1978, December 25). The current cinema: Pods. *New Yorker,* pp. 48–51.

Karsh, B. (1957, October 5). Automation's brave new world. *Nation,* pp. 208–210.

Karsh, B. (1959). Work and automation. In H. Jacobson & J. Roucek (Eds.), *Automation and society.* New York: Philosophical Library.

Kelley, J. B. (1957, February 16). Man and automation. *America,* pp. 558–560.

Lehman, H. H. (1969). Big business and the plight of the individual. In D. G. Baker & C. H. Sheldon (Eds.), *Postwar America: The search for identity* (pp. 73–74). Beverly Hills, CA: Glencoe Press.

Lester, J. (1969). *Search for the new land.* New York: Dial Press.

Leuchtenberg, W. E. (1973). *The unfinished century.* Boston: Little, Brown & Co.

Link, A. S., & W. B. Catton (1974). *American epoch.* 4th ed. New York: Knopf.

Mannes, M. (1957, July 11). Channels: Lonely men and busy machines. *Reporter,* pp. 39–41.

Memoli, F. (1955, February 12). Ignorant of values. *Saturday Review,* p. 23.

National Institute of Mental Health. (1982). *Television and behavior: Ten years of scientific progress and implications for the eighties,* Vol. 1. Rockville, MD: U.S. Department of Health.

Nimmo, D., & J. E. Combs. (1983). *Mediated political realities.* New York: Longman.

Niven, L. (1976). *A world out of time.* New York: Ballantine.

Pohl, F. (1975). *The best of Frederik Pohl.* Garden City, NY: Doubleday.

Randall, J. (1978, May). The cloning controversy. *Progressive,* pp. 11–12.

Randall, J. (1978, October). The road to cloning. *Chemistry,* pp. 25–27.

Rorvik, D. (1970). *As man becomes machine.* New York: Pocket Books.

Rorvik, D. (1978). *In his image: The cloning of a man.* New York: Pocket Books.

Serling, R. (1960). *From the Twilight Zone.* Garden City, NY: Doubleday.

Shanks, C. M. (1969). Common man in an uncommon decade. In D. G. Baker & C. H. Sheldon (Eds.), *Postwar America: The search for identity* (pp. 28–29). Beverly Hills, CA: Glencoe Press.

Shull, C. W. (1959). Political aspects of automation. In H. Jacobson & J. Roucek (Eds.), *Automation and society.* New York: Philosophical Library.

Solo, R. [Producer]. (1978). *Invasion of the body snatchers* [Film]. Culver, CA: United Artists.

Sotzin, H. A. (1956, May). Automation—A blessing or a menace? *Industrial Arts and Vocational Education,* pp. 149–151.

Toffler, A. (1970). *Future shock.* New York: Random House.

Wanger, W. [Producer]. (1956). *Invasion of the body snatchers* [Film]. New York: Allied Artists.

Wittner, L. S. (1974). *Cold war America: From Hiroshima to Watergate.* New York: Praeger.

Wolfert, I. (1955, May). What's behind this word "automation"? *Reader's Digest,* pp. 43–48.

The Rhetorical Limits of Polysemy

Celeste Michelle Condit

The recent, energetic critical program focused on the receivers of mass communication emphasizes the autonomy and power of audiences to exert substantial control of the mass communication process, and hence to exercise social influence. The polysemic character of texts, these studies argue, allows receivers to construct a wide variety of decodings and thereby prevents simple domination of people by the messages they receive (Fiske, 1986; Hall, 1980; Morley, 1980; Radway, 1986).

These theoretical claims are supported by substantial evidence demonstrating the active character of audience viewing. The theoretical conclusions, however, overstate the evidence because they oversimplify the pleasures experienced by audience members. As many of the preeminent scholars in critical audience studies themselves admit, audiences are not free to make meanings at will from mass-mediated texts (Fiske, 1987c, pp. 16, 20, 44). Consequently, the pleasures audiences experience in receiving texts are necessarily complicated. In this essay I employ a multidimensional rhetorical critique of a single television text to suggest that the ability of audiences to shape their own readings, and hence their social life, is constrained by a variety of factors in any given rhetorical situation. These factors include audience members' access to oppositional codes, the ratio between the work required and pleasure produced in decoding a text, the repertoire of available texts, and the historical occasion, especially with regard to the texts' positioning of the

pleasures of dominant and marginal audiences. I conclude that mass media research should replace totalized theories of polysemy and audience power with interactive theories that assess audience reactions as part of the full communication process occurring in particular rhetorical configurations.

Critical Studies of the Audience

Audience-centered critical research argues that viewers and readers construct their own meanings from texts. Audiences do not simply receive messages; they decode texts. Members of mass audiences are therefore not mere "cultural dupes" of message producers. As John Fiske (1987c, p. 65) describes the process, viewers have the "ability to make their own socially pertinent meanings out of the semiotic resources provided by television." As a consequence, "viewers have considerable control, not only over its meanings, but over the role that it plays in their lives" (p. 74). Janice Radway (1984, p. 17) makes a similar argument about mass-produced fiction: "Because reading is an active process that is at least partially controlled by the readers themselves, opportunities exist within the mass-communication process for individuals to resist, alter, and reappropriate the materials designed elsewhere for their purchase."

Critical audience analysts position their work as a radical break with the history of critical media studies, which they depict as having emphasized

454

the power of the media to impose a dominant ideology or to control beliefs and behaviors (Fiske, 1986; Morley, 1980; Radway, 1986). The new studies indicate that disparate audiences do not decode messages in uniform ways (Katz and Liebes, 1984; Morley, 1980; Palmer, 1986), in the precise directions critics have suggested they might (Radway, 1984), or even as the messages' authors seemed to have intended (Hobson, 1982; Steiner, 1988).[1] These studies conclude that texts which link producers' intended messages and actual audiences are not univocal. Reworking structuralist insights, they emphasize that all texts are polysemic (Fiske, 1986; Newcomb, 1984), that is, capable of bearing multiple meanings because of the varying intertextual relationships they carry (esp. Bennett and Woollacott, 1987) and because of the varying constructions (or interests) of receivers.

The study of the polysemic character of texts has thus included two research schools, often not clearly distinguished. Works in the American school (Kellner, 1982; Newcomb, 1984) emphasize the variety of ideological positions contained within the mass media. In contrast, the British approach highlights the variety of decodings possible from a single text or message (e.g., Burke, Wilson, and Agardy, 1983; Morley, 1980).

Whether based in the variety of available texts or in the flexibility of decoding processes, polysemy has been taken to be a widespread or even dominant phenomenon, bearing significance for theories of social change. Rather than portraying the mass media as the channel of oppression generated through the top-down imposition of meanings, such a perspective allows for the suggestion that the pleasures of the popular media might in fact be liberating. Radway (1984, p. 184), for instance, claims that because of the pleasure women derive from romance reading, "they at least partially reclaim the patriarchal form of the romance for their own use." Fiske (1987c, p. 239) finds similar pleasures and effects are operative in television: "The pleasure and the power of making meanings, of participating in the mode of representation, of playing with the semiotic process— these are some of the most significant and empowering pleasures that television has to offer." Fiske argues that, even without the active step of circulating one's own representations, these pleasures may offer a real resistance to the dominant ideology. Escape, he indicates (p. 318) may itself be liberating, because to escape from dominant meanings is to construct one's own subjectivity, one that is an important step in more collective moves toward social change. Fiske (p. 230) concludes:

> While there is clearly a pleasure in exerting social power, the popular pleasures of the subordinate are necessarily found in resisting, evading, or offending this power. Popular pleasures are those that empower the subordinate, and they thus offer political resistance, even if only momentarily and even if only in a limited terrain.

Recent critical audience studies thus repudiate prior portrayals of television as a sinister social force in favor of a celebration of the ability of audiences, enabled by the broad referential potentiality of texts, to reconstruct television messages. Television, because it is popular, therefore becomes a force for popular resistance to dominant interests.

These audience studies and the theories they are generating offer a useful counter-balance to the flat assertion that messages produced by elites necessarily dominate social meaning-making processes. Nonetheless, the scope and character of audience power have not yet been delimited, and I believe they are as yet over-stated.[2] It is clear that there are substantial limits to the polysemic potential of texts and of decodings. If television offered a true "semiotic democracy" (Fiske, 1987c, p. 236) we would have to assume either that television—with all the distortions described by the last fifty years of quantitative and critical analysts—is in fact an accurate producer of the popular interest or that it will soon reform itself to be such. This seems either too dark a description or too optimistic a forecast. The underlying agonistic theory common to British cultural studies, postmodern theory, and American rhetorical studies seems to offer a more appropriate line of approach. We need to begin to describe the precise range of textual polysemy and the power held by the audience in its struggle with texts and message producers.

These limits ought to be found both in production and reception conditions (Meehan, 1986) and in texts. As a rhetorical critic, I will focus my attention on the latter, exploring, in a variety of ways, the communication event occasioned by the broadcast on November 11, 1985, of an episode of *Cagney and Lacey* concerning the topic of abortion. Because rhetorical criticism focuses on language usage as a means of distributing power among a particular group of agents who are uniquely situated in a communication process (e.g., McGee, 1982), this critique examines two particular audience members for the program, then the specific political codes made present in the message, and, finally, the historical occasion of the broadcast. While this case study leads to a focus on television, the implications extend to other national mass media as well.

The Polysemous *Cagney and Lacey*

My own viewing of the abortion episode leads me to describe the central plot as follows: Police detectives Cagney and Lacey help a pregnant woman (Mrs. Herrera) to enter an abortion clinic where pickets (led by Arlene Crenshaw) are blocking access. Lacey, married and pregnant, eagerly helps Mrs. Herrera, while Cagney, feeling conflicted, resists any assistance beyond that necessitated by her job. When the abortion clinic is bombed and a vagrant dies as a result, the detectives investigate and locate the bomber who, in a climatic scene, threatens to blow up herself and the detectives. She gives up when confronted with the inconsistency of killing Lacey's "pre-born" child for a Pro-life cause.[3]

Two viewers, selected from a larger project I am conducting, offer particularly interesting responses to the episode. The two were college students recruited through local-scale organizations active in the abortion controversy. They were asked to view the program and to respond, during commercial breaks and after the program ended, to my open-ended and nonjudgmental questions. These two college students and their responses are not presented because of their "typicality." I do not claim their responses are representative, but rather that they are suggestive of new questions that must be asked in order to gain an accurate picture of the relative power of encoding and decoding as social processes. The first respondent, whom I'll call "Jack," was the leader of a student Pro-life group. A twenty-one-year old male, first exposed to the abortion issue through a required essay in a Catholic all-boys high school, Jack described himself as not being a particularly successful student and as having a life goal of becoming a major league baseball umpire. "Jill," a first-year student, was the daughter of a feminist mother. Active in the student Pro-choice organization, her goal was to complete a doctorate. Neither of these two leaders of politically active groups had seen the episode previously, but both reported having heard about it and having talked about it in their organizations when the episode was broadcast. While Jill displayed more familiarity with the series, Jack showed more knowledge about the political preferences and activities of the actresses and producers and reported having read about the episode in newspapers and magazines.

At one important level, the eighteen single-spaced pages of responses provided by these two opposed activists confirm the polysemy thesis. Their replies to my questions agreed less than 10 percent of the time. For example, when asked about the fairness of the presentation, Jill replied "Yeah, I think it is fair," whereas Jack said "I think it's really grossly unfair." Jill responded to Arlene Crenshaw by saying "I don't like her. I don't respect her," whereas Jack listed her as his favorite character, noting that she was the "lone good-guy type of figure in the show." Similarly, Jill claimed that the value of "family" was "definitely portrayed as positive," whereas Jack concluded "I don't think they take a very pro-family type response." Throughout their interviews, Jill and Jack provided virtually diametrically opposed opinions of the episode.

There were, nonetheless, important elements in their responses which lead me to suggest that the term "polyvalence" characterizes these differences better than does the term "polysemy." Polyvalence occurs when audience members share understandings of the denotations of a text but disagree about the valuation of those denotations to such a degree that they produce notably different interpretations. In this case, it is not a multiplicity or instability of textual meanings but rather a difference in audience evaluations of shared denotations that best accounts for the two viewers' discrepant interpretations. Careful listening and examination of the transcripts make it clear that neither Jill or Jack misunderstood the program, and they did not decode the images and words as holding different denotations. Their plot summaries, although extremely rough, were not inconsistent. More importantly, perhaps, each advocate was able to predict what the other's response to the program would be. If we accept the premise that understanding is effectively assessed by the ability to predict another's interpretation, this is an important test that both pass. After claiming that the episode "presents both sides of the story," for example, Jill admitted that "I'm sure that a lot of Pro-life people would hate it because it ends up that they are criminals at the end." Jack shared the ability to reflect on how the text might be read by others with different values: "A lot of people . . . would say, 'Oh, it's great, it's a fair portrayal, it presents our side very well and does a good job of the other one too,' whereas the Pro-lifers would say 'It's a terrible portrayal, it's absolutely biased against our side.'" On another occasion, in talking about his preference for Arlene Crenshaw as a character, he noted "You know, obviously, coming from my point of view, I can see if I was pro-abortion, she'd be like the 'bad-guy.'"

On a number of specific counts it further becomes clear that both viewers shared a basic construction of the denotations of the text. Both described Cagney as the character "in the middle." Both cited the transformation of the lieutenant's attitudes. Both noted the poverty and minority status of Mrs. Herrera. Ultimately, there was nothing in their responses to suggest that they did not share a basic understanding of what the program was trying to convey.

This finding is consistent with other major audience studies. In Morley's (1980) published transcripts of interviews surrounding the program *Nationwide*, I detect little fundamental inconsistency in the denotations processed by the viewers; instead, it is the valuation of those denotations and the attached connotations that they draw upon which become important (see also Eco, 1979, pp. 54–56). Similarly, in Radway's (1984) contrast of the professional critics with the Smithton readers, it is not that these two sets of readings are inconsistent, but simply that the critics disvalue any patriarchal codings, whereas the Smithton women accept some of those codings as consistent with their values. The only instance in which true shifts in denotations are recorded, to my knowledge, is Katz and Liebe's (1984) study of Arab readers of *Dallas*, and in this case it requires massive cross-cultural differences and language shifts to produce such discrepant interpretations.

The emphasis on the polysemous quality of texts thus may be overdrawn. The claim perhaps needs to be scaled back to indicate that responses and interpretations are generally polyvalent, and texts themselves are occasionally or partially polysemic. It is not that texts routinely feature unstable denotation, but that instability of connotation requires viewers to judge texts from their own value systems. Different respondents similarly understand the messages that a text seeks to convey. They may, however, see the text as rhetorical—as urging positions upon them—and make their own selections among and evaluations of those persuasive messages. As I note in the conclusion, this will have profound implications for the practice of critical reading. For clarity, then, we might reserve the term "inter-textual polysemy" to refer to the existence of variety in messages on mass communication channels, the terms "internally polysemous" or "open texts" for those discourses which truly offer unstable or internally contradictory meanings, and the term "polyvalence" to describe the fact that audiences routinely evaluate texts differently, assigning different value to different portions of a text and to the text itself. Such revisions imply the need to generate a more careful account of the actual social force of popular or mass communication. Such an endeavor begins with a more detailed exploration of audience interpretations.

Audiences: Groups of Individuals

The claim that audiences have the ability to create their own empowering responses to mass-mediated texts loses little of its force when it is acknowledged that the polysemic freeplay of discourse has been overestimated. Whether deriving from decoding processes related to denotation or connotation, critical audience studies have indicated fairly clearly that viewers can construct a variety of responses to any given mass-mediated text. The central issue remains, however, to what extent do these responses constitute liberating pleasure and social empowerment? The situation of audiences as members of groups in a social process constructs some fundamental limits to these pleasures and powers which can now be explored.

The proposition that decoding a message always requires work is a fundamental postulate supporting the claim that audiences have control of the mass communication process. As Morley (1980, p. 10) puts it, "The production of a meaningful message in the TV discourse is always problematic 'work.'" The work receivers must do inserts them into a position of influence in relationship to the text. Such accounts, however, fail to note that decoding requires *differential* amounts of work for different audiences. Jack's responses to *Cagney and Lacey* consumed more than twice the space and time of Jill's replies. Jill was positioned to give a reading of the text that was dominant or only slightly negotiated (e.g., she objected to the tokenization of minorities in the program and the lack of women in the more powerful job hierarchies). Jack was required to provide a largely oppositional reading.

Not only did Jack's interpretation require more space, and visibly more effort (his nonverbal behavior was frequently tense and strained), it showed itself to be more incomplete and problematic in other ways. Frequently, Jack's responses departed from the program altogether to provide the background of a fairly extended Pro-life argument. In reacting to the abortion clinic's male physician, Jack cited the doctor's story about a twelve-year-old girl who came in to get an abortion, arguing

> . . . little does he tell them now, however, that it is easier for the younger, anywhere from a twelve- to eighteen-year-old, statistically and medically, to bear children than it is for women who are over twenty-five or thirty, only because it's like, their bodies are ripe and just developing, as opposed to either at the peak or really past that. See, they don't want to get into that; he just talks about how terrible it allegedly or supposedly is for the young women to have children. So it's the best thing to do, get them in there, you know, do the abortion, and get them out, no worries. Do they ever talk about post-abortion counseling that that doctor might do? . . . Are they willing to go so far as to say that he just does the abortion and have [sic] nothing more to do with her?

Jack thus worked very hard to oppose his own ideology to the program. At times this entailed distortions of the truth which were probably unintentional. For example, Jack's statistics are skewed. More importantly for Jack, at times he was simply unsuccessful at producing a consistent response. At several key points he was reduced to a position of virtual incoherence, and he indicated his frustration in nonverbal ways. For example, at one point he became trapped between his denial that normal Pro-life people are violent and his attempt to project how the network should portray abortion clinic bombers. He concluded:

> If I was [sic] nuts enough to bomb, I'd go about it real calmly, talk to them, and wait until they dig up some more information before I went, got overly nervous. I think they did a good job of portraying her as, well, see, she was involved in the sixties and seventies and all these demonstrations, the typical type. Why couldn't they portray, if they are going to, a bomber who is just an average everyday American? They did a good job of portraying her as an extreme fanatic. That is to say that, see, they're all like this. They're the type who did that and they'll do this again. It's rather illogical.

Jack was unable to come up with a consistent characterization of clinic bombers. He described them as "nuts" and asked that they be portrayed as "an average everyday American," displaying his difficulty in putting together a response to the text

that was persuasive (either to himself or to me). Jill did not show such strain in her interpretations.

Finally, Jill and Jack differed with regard to the chief tests they put to the text. For Jill, the recurrent test was "Is this realistic?" Accusing the text of committing errors, she argued that the portrayal of the Pro-life leaders and the bomber as women was inaccurate, but that Pro-lifers in fact generated violence, and so on. For Jack, the reality criterion emphasized motives rather than facts. His most frequent strategy was to talk about what the text omitted: the character of the fetus, the "ripeness" of young women, the poor quality of counseling the women received. For Jill, therefore, the negotiation process was simply one of relatively minor factual corrections. For Jack, the process was a matter of filling in major motivational absences in the text (see Scholle, 1988; Wander, 1984).

For Jack, in short, the work of interpreting the text and resisting its persuasive message was much more difficult than the accommodative response was for Jill. Although these differences may have been caused by factors other than their political positions (e.g., differential academic ability or familiarity with the series), they provide grounds for considering the important possibility that oppositional and negotiated readings require more work of viewers than do dominant readings. This possibility is reinforced as well by work with public speakers (Lucaites and Condit, 1986). Three factors give impact to the difference in audience work load: its silencing effects, its reduction of pleasure, and its code dependence.

The first consequence of the greater work load imposed on oppositionally situated audience groups is the tendency of such burdens to silence viewers. In its most stark form, this leads to turning off the television, a widespread phenomenon, especially among minority groups (Fiske, 1987c, p. 312; Morley, 1980, p. 135). If the particular range of television's textual polysemy excludes marginal group messages, and if oppositional reading requires comparatively oppressive quantities of work, then minority groups are indeed silenced, even as audiences, and therefore discriminated against in important ways.

Another consequence of this work load is disproportional pleasure for oppositional and dominant readers. As Fiske (1987c, p. 239) points out, it is clearly the case that viewers can take great pleasure in constructing oppositional readings simply because of the human joy in constructing representations. Nonetheless, this does not mean that the pleasures of the text are fairly distributed. Jill indicated that she enjoyed the episode of *Cagney and Lacey* very much, she found it "powerful," and her nonverbal response indicated a restful, enjoyable experience. Jack, on the other hand, clearly took some pleasure in his ability to argue against the text, but he also displayed clear signs of pain and struggle in that decoding. Jack's relative displeasure may be widely shared, given that even a popular program enlists only twenty million viewers out of a population of over two hundred and forty million, and that most of those viewers are simultaneously engaged in other activities (Meyrowitz, 1985, p. 348). The disparity is made pernicious given that the most highly sought audiences have the characteristics of more elite groups (Feur, 1984a, p. 26; Kerr, 1984, p. 68). Programs are tailored for the greater pleasure of a relative elite.

A similar disparity of pleasures in the mass publishing industry is suggested by Radway (1984, pp. 104, 165–167) when she reveals that the repressed pornography that producers of romance believe to be attractive to women may not actually be women's primary interest and that an extremely different genre of stories might bring greater pleasures to these audiences. As Fiske (1987c, p. 66) notes, to be popular enough to gain economic rewards, mass media must attract a fairly large audience. That popularity, however, is only relative to other programming the producers are willing to construct. Hence, the trade-off among what majority audience groups want, and what the producers are willing to give them as a compromise may still retain a great deal of control for producers and dominant groups.

Mass-mediated texts might be viewed, therefore, not as giving the populace what they want, but as compromises that give the relatively well-to-do more of what they want, bringing along as many economically marginal viewers as they comfortably can, within the limitations of the production teams' visions and values. If so, the differential availability of textual pleasures and the costs in pain become as important as any absolute statements about viewer abilities. It is not enough to argue that audiences can do the work to decode oppressive texts with some pleasure. We need to investigate how much more this costs them, and how much more silencing of oppositional groups this engenders. In addition, we need to understand better the various conditions that best enable oppositional decoding.

A third consequence of the differential work load required of viewing groups provides further clues to the variability of audience experiences.

Among oppositional readers of the *Cagney and Lacey* text, Jack was in a particularly empowered position. As a leader of a Pro-life group, he was experienced in producing Pro-life representations and had access to a large network of oppositional codes. This experience and access were evident throughout his interview (as in the instance here he used Pro-life rhetoric to point out "gaps" in the doctor's story). The utility of such experience and skill in helping viewers produce self-satisfying decodings is echoed throughout the audience literature. Morley (1980, p. 141) especially notes the enhanced ability of shop stewards to produce oppositional codings more successfully than do rank and file union members. Importantly, most of the content-based audience research thus far taps into audiences where group leadership exists and where audience members have access to counter-rhetorics. Radway's study (1984) relies on a group centered on Dorothy Evans, who encodes negotiated readings, giving access to a resistive code to her group members. Linda Steiner's study (1988) relies similarly on a site, *Ms.* magazine, where oppositional rhetorics are provided.

In sum, the strongest evidence about the actualization of audiences' abilities to decode messages to their own advantage comes from studies that select audiences or conditions in which we would expect the receivers to be relatively advantaged as opponents to the message producers. Moreover, in cases with the weakest access to group organization, it also seems that the oppositional interpretations are weaker. In his study of adolescent female responses to Madonna, for example, Fiske (1987a, p. 273; 1987c, p. 215) suggests that the young girls are only "struggling" to find counter-rhetorics. They experience only distinctly limited success at resistance.

The commonalities in these studies suggest two conclusions. First, there is a need for research to assess the typicality of oppositional readings. The tendency to notice successful oppositional decodings may have led scholars to overplay the degree to which this denotes typical behavior. Correctives could come from comparing audiences with different access to oppositional codes on a particular topic and from studies of the relative degrees of oppositionality in typical decodings. Only if a strong and pervasive response to dominant messages can be demonstrated can we assert that the limited repertoire of mass-mediated messages really co-exists with a semiotic democracy.

Second, these commonalities also re-establish the importance of leadership and organized group interaction. Leadership always has been largely a matter of the ability to produce rhetorics that work for the group. While being human may mean having the ability to encode and decode texts (Burke, 1966), it is not the case that all human beings are equally skilled in responding to persuasive messages with countermessages. The masses may not be cultural dupes, but they are not necessarily skilled rhetors. Here, another fragment from the abortion communication event is instructive.

In interviews of abortion activists in California, Kristin Luker (1984, p. 111) noticed an interesting phenomenon. The women who became abortion activists reported one factor that led to replacing their guilt and negative feelings about abortions with active campaigning for a right to choose. It was not the experience of abortion per se; many of them had had abortions long before the change in their attitude. It was, they said, the ability of a few articulate rhetors that had been instrumental in helping them to resist the prior, dominant views. The presentation of different codings had helped them to resist the dominant rhetorics. If popular media are only oppositional to the extent that countermedia exist to help audiences decode dominant messages, the mass media's role in social change processes may be extremely limited. In this case, Fiske (1987c, p. 326) is not wrong when he concludes that "resistive reading practices that assert the power of the subordinate in the process of representation and its subsequent pleasure pose a direct challenge to the power of capitalism to produce its subjects-in-ideology." It is simply that we do not yet know how widespread such resistive interpretative practices are, given the more substantial obstacles outlined here. In contrast, we should weigh the power that these texts give to dominant audiences.

Codes and the Public

The disproportional viewing pleasures experienced by elite groups might present only a minor social problem if turning off the television set sufficiently closed down the influence of its texts. However, even in such relative silence, the television texts continue to go about constructing hegemony in important ways. This becomes evident if we shift our perspective so that the important audience for television is no longer individual viewers (even grouped by social interest) but "the public."

The term "public" is highly contested (Bitzer, 1987; Goodnight, 1987; Hauser, 1987; McGee,

1987). By it I mean those members of a nation-state who have had their interests articulated to a large enough mass of people to allow their preferred vocabulary legitimacy as a component in the formation of law and behavior. I suggest that television's political functions are not confined to its address to the pleasures of individuals. In addition, television "makes present" particular codings in the public space (Perelman and Olbrechts-Tyteca, 1971). Once such codings gain legitimacy they can be employed in forming public law, policy, and behavior. Even if they are not universally accepted, their presence gives them presumption (the right to participate in formulations, and even the need for others to take account of them in their policy formulations). Crucially, the upscale audience courted by television advertisers is also the group most likely to constitute the politically active public (e.g., "Young Blacks Have," 1987). Hence, television, or any mass medium, can do oppressive work solely by addressing the dominant audience that also constitutes the public.

It is because television "makes present in public" a vocabulary that prefers the dominant audience's interests that the dominant audience gets the most pleasure from television and that television actively promotes its interests. The fact that other groups can counter-read this discourse, and [enjoy] doing so, does not disrupt the direct functions of governance that television serves for dominant groups. A return to the case of the broadcast of abortion practices will explain this point more thoroughly.

Prime-time television addressed the practice of abortion in clearly patterned ways. The very few, highly controversial programs concerning abortion in the sixties and early seventies occasioned sponsor withdrawal, boycotts of sponsors who did not withdraw, and extended editorial treatment by opponents of legalized abortion (Condit, 1987). Probably as a consequence of this extra-popular control mechanism, a second round of abortion programs did not really appear until the mid-eighties, more than a decade after abortion had been legalized through the actions of state legislators and the Supreme Court. For many years, television producers were dissuaded from making present the practice of abortion. When abortion re-appeared, it did so with a dominant-preferring code firmly, if cleverly, in place.

The evolution of prime-time television's treatment of abortion between the years 1984 and 1988 was such that it began to include increasingly more problematic cases of abortion, and it featured distinctive types. Nonetheless, the main clump of programs between 1984 and 1986 constructed a limited repertoire of meanings.

Different viewers, with different viewing habits, may have found themselves introduced to abortion in the mass culture in one of three ways. For viewers with traditional affiliations, those who enjoyed "family" programs, *Call to Glory, Webster, Family, Dallas,* or *Magruder and Loud* would have provided them with episodes in which prominent female characters found themselves unintentionally pregnant, decided against having an abortion, and then were relieved of the consequences of that decision through miscarriage or the discovery that they were not pregnant after all. Fans of MTM productions, and their liberal values (Feuer, 1984b), would have been introduced to abortion in a different manner. On *Cagney and Lacey, Hill Street Blues,* and *St. Elsewhere,* professionals supported the choices of transitory female characters to have abortions, and confronted the violence of the Pro-life movement. Finally, viewers might have first encountered televised abortion in a more sharply conflicted manner through *Spenser for Hire, L.A. Law,* or a second episode of *St. Elsewhere.* In these programs, central women characters made highly contested choices to undergo abortions.

Prime-time television thus introduced the public to the practice of abortion with a polysemic voice. The mass-mediated *message* itself appeared to bring different textual resources to different audiences. As has been previously argued, however, this textual polysemy had very clear limits (Condit, 1987). Regardless of whether the program was primarily "pro" or "anti," abortion was portrayed as a morally problematic act that was nonetheless the woman's choice. Although female characters decided in favor of and against abortions in a wide variety of problem situations, the abortions presented in prime time were never those of women in optimal reproductive situations. Women in caring, financially secure marriages did not abort healthy fetuses. Moreover, the practicalities of abortion were absent. There was no direct mention of the problem of payment, the pain of the operation, or the real but difficult alternatives of adoption or contraception.

As a consequence, dominant group vocabularies and practices were normalized (Condit, [1990]). Career women could get abortions and feel more comfortable with the practice, even though their role or obligation as mothers was not erased. This was both an attractive enactment of career women's own reproductive practices and a discursive instantiation of their "choices" in the public vocabulary. The power distributed through such reinforcement is immense; it is virtually the entire social glue that allows dominant groups to coordinate their efforts in a democracy, and thereby maintain power. Moreover, the reinforcement shields dominant groups from understanding the ways in which different conditions might make different practices necessary or right for others. In the face of such a public culture, it was relatively easy for the Reagan administration, in its second term, to withdraw virtually all indirect financial support of abortion *and* of family planning both in the national and international arenas.

In contrast, prime-time television neither informed the poor how to finance abortions nor told the young how to avoid needing them and why they might want to avoid such need. No constructive efforts on their behalf provided useful information or created pleasurable self-validation for these other groups of women. Hence, even if other groups were active interpreters of these programs, in order to seek legitimacy or cultural sympathy for their own practices they would have had to do double work—deconstructing the dominant code and reconstructing their own. In addition, to effect favorable policies, marginal groups also would have had to make a public argument in some other, *less pleasurable* arena, counterposing their interests and vocabulary to this now-dominant vocabulary. Finally, even if they were able to present an equally attractive argument, they would still, at best, be able to win a compromise with this already-legitimated dominant code (a position they would not have faced, absent its broadcast).

In sum, television disseminates and legitimates, in a pleasurable fashion, a political vocabulary that favors certain interests and groups over others, even if by no other means than consolidating the dominant audience by giving presence to their codes. Given the interest of advertisers in dominant economic groups, the ability of marginal groups to break this grip seems particularly unlikely. Fiske's conclusion (1987c, p. 319) that homogenization will lead to the inclusion of these other groups presumes much about the demographics of television audiences that is yet to be established. It also rests on imprecise definitions of "the popular" which do not seem to distinguish who the dominant elites are (the rich or the middle and well-to-do working class [e.g., automotive unions]?) and who the "resisting populace" might be (secretaries or the unemployed?). Further examination of that relationship will require more careful studies of the economic side of this question. If, however, maximal economic return can be purchased through appeal to dominant audiences, then the fact that programs also attract oppositional readers around the globe may be only of minimal importance. In short, the jury is still out on the "popularity" of the mass media.

A second political consequence of television's coding of abortion practices has to do with the dissemination of new information to individuals. It can be explored through a turn to the third component of rhetorical events.

Occasion: Historical Agents

Historical agents are embedded in particular occasions with specific power relationships, communicated through ideologies. Recent interpretations of ideology have begun to explore its character as information (Foucault, 1972; Lyotard, 1984; Scholle, 1988). In place of the old "ideology vs. science" equation, some analyses suggest that one of the primary ways that ideology functions is by making present or dominant certain pieces of information to certain audiences. On this account, one important function of the broadcast of the *Cagney and Lacey* abortion episode was the extent to which it gave access to new and useful information about the practice of abortion.

To make such an evaluation of the *Cagney and Lacey* episode requires an accounting of the historical situation and self-consciousness about criteria. In the mid-1980s, it was clear that the legality of abortion was a widely shared knowledge. Less widely shared was information of many kinds: about the types of women who have abortions and their reasons, about the experience of the operation, about women's control over their sexuality and fertility, and perhaps about the character of the fetus. *Cagney and Lacey* distribute information about some of these issues (especially about the wide variety of "good" women who have abortions), but not about others (the character of the operation and of the fetus).

The social impact of the program was in part a matter of the particular information it disseminated to different groups, even to groups able to decode the program through their own value structures. Jack, for example, was forced by the program's presence to confront the fact of abortion's "so-called social acceptability by too many people." Television programs distribute varying sorts of information about abortion, even to viewers who wish to change that practice and who actively and negatively decode the program.

Evaluating the impact of *Cagney and Lacey* on this learning dimension might seem to imply survey research, but that approach is unlikely to be cost-effective. Research in the "direct effects" tradition of rhetorical studies indicated the virtual impossibility of quantitatively tracking learning and persuasion impacts on large audiences (e.g., Baran & Davis, 1975). Most important, in historical studies scholars can never go back and get the kind of data that would meet the tests of quantitative-style knowledge claims. Further, academics are rarely prescient enough to know what programming is important with enough lead time to prepare for such surveys. Knowledge claims thus must be critically based.

Historically based evaluations need to take into account a more sensitive gauge than has been applied previously (and this might well be the most important moral of Radway's work on romance novels). Rather than describing a text and its readings simply as good or bad, critics need to develop judgments of better and worse. From this perspective, *Cagney and Lacey* should be evaluated on several comparative grounds. First, it should be placed as the earliest of the second wave of televisualization of abortion. Second, it should be compared to other programs and entertainment media. On this scale, the episode was far more conservative in the amount of information it provided than *St. Elsewhere*, with its far greater detail about the experience and emotions of having an abortion and inclusion of the issue of contraception. However, it is far more informative than episodes such as *Webster* or *Call to Glory*, neither of which ever directly even name abortion as "the option" nor deal with the consequences.

Such an evaluation process will lead not to a condemnation or simple praise of a program but to a calibrated understanding of the particular role it played in introducing certain limited pieces of information to different ranges of audiences at different times. Critical analysis should therefore, at least at times, be rhetorical; it should be tied to the particularity of occasions: specific audiences, with specific codes or knowledges, addressed by specific programs and episodes (McGee, 1982; Wichelns, 1972). Such an approach does not deny the wisdom of also exploring the intertextuality of programs, the stripped character of the viewing experience (Newcomb, 1984, p. 44), and the disengaged character of much viewing. It merely adds one additional vector to our understanding.

Evaluation

After considering the historical moment, the public code constructed, and the range of audience readings, we might be in a position to provide an evaluation of *Cagney and Lacey*. I wish to turn that evaluation to the key criterion on which I see Fiske, Hall, Morley, Radway, and others (but probably not Newcomb) converging, that is, the judgment of a mass communication event based on its "resistance" to the dominant ideology. This judgmental criterion rests on the assumption that academics have a duty to the society that pays their salaries to try to produce a better world. This is a duty widely accepted for the ever more technically oriented scientists, although with admittedly different procedures. In the humanities and social sciences, however, the execution of that criterion is eternally and politically controversial, and that deters us from encouraging scholars in communication studies to undertake endeavors of a sort we virtually demand from scholars in natural studies. I nonetheless support such efforts.

For many years, critics interested in bringing about positive social changes assumed that the deconstruction of the dominant ideologies contained in popular and political texts was the best contribution toward human progress. This kind of criticism gradually became too predictable to suit the tastes of an academic machine that voraciously devours "new ideas" in preference to the good execution of old ones. Furthermore, at its worst, and too frequently, such criticism merely imposed the ideology/methodology of a particular political preference upon dominant texts, threatening to produce nothing but a blanket condemnation of the status quo, rather than insight into how to improve society.

Today, with the rise of attention to audiences, such a textual approach has come under further attack. Fiske (1987c, p. 64; see also 1987b) writes, for example, that

> Textual studies of television now have to stop treating it as a closed text, that is, as one where the dominant ideology exerts considerable, if not total, influence over its ideological structure and therefore over its reader. Analysis has to pay less attention to the textual strategies of preference or closure and more to the gaps and spaces that open up to meanings not preferred by the textual structure.

In placing enormous faith in the capacity of audiences to resist, however, a similar blindness may be on its way to being produced on the other side. We can endlessly generate studies that demonstrate that clever readers can take pleasure in reconstructing texts, but this does not certify that mass communication in general functions as a force for positive social change.

The assumption that pleasure liberates is too simplistic on a myriad of counts. To begin with, note that Fiske's argument (1987c, p. 19) is based on the premise that "Pleasure results from a particular relationship between meanings and power. Pleasure for the subordinate is produced by the assertion of one's social identity in resistance to, in independence of, or in negotiation with, the structure of domination." This is a flat assertion with no support. It is based on the claim that "escape" is always escape from the dominant ideologies' subjective positioning of the marginal person (p. 317). While Fiske documents that this kind of escape can and does sometimes occur, he does not demonstrate that it is the only kind or primary kind of pleasure to be gained from a text by a subordinate. There are a wide variety of pleasures, some of them are merely temporary escape from truly painful thoughts and activities, and these do not challenge the subjective identity television programs present. The most important of these is what Kenneth Burke (1969, p. 19) has called "identification." One can fully identify with the rich patrons of *Dynasty*, enjoying the vicarious experience of opulence, without building any oppositional identity. I have reveled in such play, the pleasure coming from a temporary "giving in" rather than from resistance. My female career-oriented students generally admit relishing the Cinderella myth offered by *An Officer and a Gentleman*. Such pleasurable identification does not require that we are naïvely confusing reality and our own position (a different thesis which Fiske [1987c, pp. 44–47, 63–72] argues against forcefully and accurately). We know that we are not as rich as Krystal and will never be. Nonetheless, we can enjoy playing that we are. This kind of pleasure offers only temporary escape.

I would not willingly deny any of us such pleasures. Human life is hard, under capitalism or any other system human beings have yet devised. Radway's Smithton readers need a pleasurable escape from their oppressive husbands and demanding children. However, we should be very cautious about our portrayal of such escape as liberating. Attention to the discrepancies between critical readings of television's embedding of subjects in patriarchy and those subjects' own readings (the opening of Radway's book) should not obscure the

realization that both personal pleasure and collective domination can go on at the same time
(the conclusion of Radway's book). We need to
make a clear distinction between the personal or
"private" experience of pleasure which temporarily liberates us from the painful conditions of our
lives and the collectivized pleasures which, in the
right historical conditions, may move us toward
changing those conditions. Because of the character of the mass media, both are social pleasures,
but *collectivized* (grouped, internally organized
through communication production) action and
pleasure are essential to social change. Alterations
in subjectivity may indeed provide a first step in
that later process, but it is an extremely limited
step and it is not the case that all pleasurable readings produce such resisting subjectivities (Scholle,
1988, p. 33). Moreover, if the cost of mildly altered
subjectivities is complacence, the potential for
change may be offset. Television does not, therefore, simply offer "a set of forces for social change"
(Fiske, 1987c, p. 326); television is engaged in a set
of social forces within which actors may or may
not promote social change.

To assess the social consequences of a mass
communication event requires, consequently, that
we dispense with the totalized concept of "resistance." It is not enough to describe a program or
an interpretation of a program as oppositional. It
is essential to describe what particular things are
resisted and how that resistance occurs. In part,
this requires taking more seriously the melding of
liberal interest group theory and Marxism evident
in Fiske's work (1987c, p. 16). Fiske's explicit political theory dismantles views of politics that portray
it either as an evenhanded barter between various interest groups (the classic liberal account) or
as the dominance of a unified, all-powerful elite.
Instead, he argues (1987c, p. 16) as do I ([1990]),
that politics is a battle and barter among a wide
range of groups, each of which is differently and
unevenly empowered. Unfortunately, like most
other audience theorists, Fiske does not carry
this theory through into his analysis. Instead, he
reduces the multiplicity of differently empowered
groups to "the dominant" and "the resistant." Such
a totalized concept of resistance from a system is
at odds with a theory that posits a wide range of
groups with a wide range of investments in the
system they share. Given that perspective, for my
interpretation of *Cagney and Lacey*, I would offer
the following evaluations.

From the perspective of women like Jill, the
decisions by the production team headed by Bar-
ney Rosenzweig, which resulted in this particular
treatment of abortion on prime-time television,
were mildly progressive. Jill's interpretation needs
to be supplemented by that of other women, but
for her, the program portrayed powerful characterizations of "good" women having abortions and
reaffirmed the evaluation that abortion was not
a repudiation of familial love. Most importantly,
it affirmed that even though abortion is the morally problematic termination of the potential of a
growing creature's life, it is always the woman who
must weigh the principles and factors involved to
make the decision. This is perhaps surprisingly
mild progressive ideological work for a production team that dealt in outstanding detail with
the experience of rape and that treated the fallout
of the AIDS crisis on single adults with gingerly
directness. The program, however, was the leader
of the second wave of telecasts and took a great
deal of public criticism even for these steps. For
Jill's group, it accomplished some important ideological work.

For women in poverty and women of color the
program is more mixed. It explicitly affirmed the
choices of a particular minority woman, but it
did not deal with the ways in which poor women
might fund abortion or contraception. It did not
deal with the options provided by extended families, or with the importance of motherhood in different cultures. It offered a sugary and unrealistic
moral, "Have an abortion so you can go to school
and get off welfare," that may have appealed to
latent racism in white audiences more than assist-
ing poor women with real options. In the face of
such silences, the Republican administration could
continue its largely hidden work at pro-natalism by
dismantling funding for family planning. From the
perspective of these groups of viewers, this represents a serious short-coming of this episode.

The situation is much grimmer from Jack's perspective as a clearly marginal viewer of this text,
and in many ways a person whom I sensed to be
involved in popular culture (especially sports), but
disempowered by the dominant political economy.
I find it difficult to argue that Jack found his reading of this text, resistant and skilled as it was, to
be either a predominantly pleasurable or liberating
experience. Jack expressed the following general
response to the program's significance: "I think it's
a [sic] pretty much a devastating blow, not that it's
totally going to stop the movement, but it set us
back." For Jack, as for other relatively unempow-
ered males, especially of Pro-life positions, *Cagney
and Lacey* did not promote the social changes they

preferred. Even their resistant readings left them with the feeling of oppression by the media.

The *Cagney and Lacey* broadcast about abortion broke new ideological ground, inserting new political codes into the public culture. It was thus a progressive but not radical text that tended to oppose the interests of marginally positioned traditional males. It favored the interests of career women, but only marginally supported other groups of women.

I have, of course, stacked the deck here by probing readings that scramble the left's general presumption that marginal readers of texts are the potential source of liberation, the groups with whom we, as academics, ought to identify and praise. I have done so to heighten my point that "resistance" and the metaphor of a "dominant system" is a bad way to phrase what it is those interested in social change should praise. History creates "hegemonies," but hegemonies are not equivalent to dominant ideologies. A hegemony is a negotiation among elite and nonelite groups and therefore always contains interests of non-elite groups, though to a lesser degree. To resist the power of dominant groups may be safe, but to resist the hegemony that is constructed in negotiation with those groups is always also to resist what is partially of one's own interests. The totalizing concept of resistance should give way to historically particular acts in order to bring about specific social changes. This shift will require academics to affirm particular goals, rather than to simply critique that which is.

Conclusions

Recent reemphasis on the audience as an important component of what happens in the process of mass communicating is a useful redress of an old imbalance. We should avoid, however, totalizing the audience's abilities. The receiver's political power in mass mediated societies is dependent upon a complex balance of historically particular forces which include the relative abilities of popular groups and their access to oppositional codes, the work/pleasure ratio of the available range of the media's intertextual polysemy, the modifications programs make in the dominant code, and the degree of empowerment provided to dominant audiences.

To scholars, this balance of forces presents a series of challenges. There is a need to explore more precisely the relative decoding abilities of audiences and their access to counter-rhetorics.

There is also a need to continue to explore what texts "make present," even without regard to their "seams," through careful historically grounded studies of the particular issue contents of television programming. There is, finally, a need to explore the "occasion" of a discourse in terms other than the family viewing context (contexts emphasized in Fiske [1987c, p. 239] and Morley [1986, p. 14]). Different families and different members of families are always embedded in larger political occasions that create collective experiences across family walls. Unless we ask about the particular contents of particular sets of programs, the relationship of those contents to the stasis of the issue for viewers and for the larger society at the time of broadcast, we will not be able to assess fully television's roles in the process of social change for its various constituencies.

There are additional implications for scholars as teachers. One of the primary ways through which we can bring about positive social change is through our teaching of undergraduates for whom our arcane battles about research protocols are rightfully boring and meaningless. For our students, decoding alternatives, through painful effort, can become pleasurable resources they can use throughout life. A perspective that emphasizes the receiver's placement within a complexly balanced process suggests the need to continue to use classrooms to teach students a range of decodings for possible texts, a project that may include increasing their ideological range (the ability to see *An Officer and a Gentleman* as Cinderella, Sonny Crockett as a 1980's John Wayne, *Dallas* as the costs inherent to capitalism). It might also include familiarizing students with the history of the various issue contents of the mass media. Studies of the participation of news and entertainment programming in particular social movements and issues might be added to genre studies and analyses of private audiences (e.g., Hallin, 1986; Rushing, 1986a, 1986b).

As a whole, the effort to gain a more variegated picture of audiences is an important one. However, the tendency to isolate the audience from the communication process and then pronounce the social effects of mass communication based on the ability of some receivers to experience pleasure in producing oppositional decoding is undesirable. It simply repeats the error of message-dominated research which attempted to describe the mass media's influence solely by investigating texts (or, in the other research strands, presumed intents of sources). Audience members are neither simply resistive nor dupes. They neither find television simply pleasurable, simply an escape, nor simply obnoxious and oppressive. The audience's variability is a consequence of the fact that humans, in their inherent character as audiences, are inevitably situated in a communication *system*, of which they are a part, and hence have some influence within, but by which they are also influenced. To study the role of that communication system in the processes that change our humanity and the system itself therefore requires a multiplicity of approaches to the critical analysis of the massive media.

NOTES

1. I am aware that to locate intent in television programs is a difficult matter because of the multiplicity of inputs into such productions. However, this multiplicity does not negate the fact that messages have sources and therefore some collection of intended meanings. To abrogate the use of the term simply because intent is complex would be to ignore an important component of the communication process.

2. Radway (1984, 1986) begins such a delimitation with regard to her case study of romance readers.

3. I choose the terms "Pro-life" and "Pro-choice" because they are the names employed by the members of the respective movements to define themselves.

REFERENCES

Baran, S. J., and D. K. Davis. (1975). "The Audience of Public Television: Did Watergate Make a Difference?" *Central States Speech Journal* 26: 93–98.

Bennett, T., and J. Woollacott. (1987). *Bond and Beyond: The Political Career of a Popular Hero*. New York: Methuen.

Bitzer, L. F. (1987). "Rhetorical Public Communication." *Critical Studies in Mass Communication* 4(4): 425–428.

Burke, J., H. Wilson, and S. Agardy. (1983). A Country Practice *and the Child Audience: A Case Study*. Melbourne: Australian Broadcasting Tribunal.

Burke, K. (1966). "Definition of Man." In *Language as Symbolic Action*. Berkeley and Los Angeles: University of California Press.

Burke, K. (1969). "Identification." In *A Rhetoric of Motives*. Berkeley and Los Angeles: University of California Press.

Condit, C. (1987). "Abortion on Television: The 'System' and Ideological Production." *Journal of Communication Inquiry* 11: 47–60.

Condit, C. ([1990]). *Decoding Abortion Rhetoric: Communicating Social Change*. Urbana: University of Illinois Press.

Eco, U. (1979). "Denotation and Connotation." In *A Theory of Semiotics*, 54–56. Bloomington: Indiana University Press.

Feuer, J. (1984a). "MTM Enterprises: An Overview." In Jane Feuer, Paul Kerr, and Tise Vahimagi, eds., *MTM: "Quality Television"* (London: British Film Institute), pp. 1–31.

Feuer, J. (1984b). "The MTM Style." In Jane Feuer, Paul Kerr, and Tise Vahimagi, eds., *MTM: "Quality Television"* (London: British Film Institute), pp. 32–60.

Fiske, J. (1986). "Television: Polysemy and Popularity." *Critical Studies in Mass Communication* 3(4): 391–408.

Fiske, J. (1987a). "British Cultural Studies and Television." In R. C. Allen, ed., *Channels of Discourse* (Chapel Hill: University of North Carolina Press).

Fiske, J. (1987b). "*Cagney and Lacey*: Reading Character Structurally and Politically." *Communication* 9: 399–426.

Fiske, J. (1987c). *Television Culture*. New York: Methuen.

Foucault, M. (1972). *The Archaeology of Knowledge*. New York: Pantheon Books.

Goodnight, G. T. (1987). "Public Discourse." *Critical Studies in Mass Communication* 4(4): 428–432.

Hall, S. (1980). "Encoding/Decoding." In S. Hall, D. Hobson, A. Lowe, and P. Willis, eds., *Culture, Media, Language* (London: Hutchinson), pp. 128–138.

Hallin, D. C. (1986). *The "Uncensored War": The Media and Vietnam*. New York: Oxford University Press.

Hauser, G. A. (1987). "Features of the Public Sphere." *Critical Studies in Mass Communication* 4(4): 437–441.

Hobson, D. (1982). *Crossroads: The Drama of a Soap Opera*. London: Methuen.

Katz, E, and T. Liebes. (1984). "Once Upon a Time in *Dallas*." *Intermedia* 12(3): 28–32.

Kellner, D. (1982). "TV, Ideology, and Emancipatory Popular Culture." In H. Newcomb, ed., *Television: The Critical View*, 3rd ed. (New York: Oxford University Press), pp. 386–421.

Kerr, P. (1984). "The Making of (the) MTM (Show)." In Jane Feuer, Paul Kerr, and Tise Vahimagi, eds., *MTM: "Quality Television"* (London: British Film Institute), pp. 61–98.

Lucaites, J., and C. Condit. (1986). "Equality in the Martyred Black Vision." Paper presented at the annual meeting of the Speech Communication Association, Chicago.

Luker, K. (1984). *Abortion and the Politics of Motherhood*. Berkeley and Los Angeles: University of California Press.

Lyotard. J. F. (1984). *The Postmodern Condition: A Report on Knowledge*. Minneapolis: University of Minnesota Press.

McGee, M. (1982). "A Materialist's Conception of Rhetoric." In R. E. McKerrow, ed., *Explorations in Rhetoric* (Glencoe, IL: Scott, Foresman, and Co.), pp. 23–48.

McGee, M. C. (1987). "Power to 'The People.'" *Critical Studies in Mass Communication* 4(4): 432–437.

Meehan, E. R. (1986). "Conceptualizing Culture as Commodity: The Problem of Television." *Critical Studies in Mass Communication* 3(4): 448–457.

Meyrowitz, J. (1985). *No Sense of Place*. New York: Oxford University Press.

Morley, D. (1980). *The "Nationwide" Audience: Structure and Decoding*. London: British Film Institute.

Morley, D. (1986). *Family Television: Cultural Power and Domestic Leisure*. London: Comedia.

Newcomb, H. (1984). "On the Dialogic Aspects of Mass Communication." *Critical Studies in Mass Communication* 1: 34–50.

Palmer, P. (1986). *The Lively Audience: A Study of Children around the TV Set*. Sydney: Allen and Unwin.

Perelman, P., and L. Olbrechts-Tyteca. (1971). *The New Rhetoric: A Treatise on Argumentation*. South Bend, IN: University of Notre Dame Press.

Radway, J. (1984). *Reading the Romance: Woman, Patriarchy, and Popular Literature*. Chapel Hill: University of North Carolina Press.

Radway, J. (1986). "Identifying Ideological Seams: Mass Culture, Analytical Method, and Political Practice." *Communication* 9: 93–123.

Rushing, J. (1986a). "Mythic Evolution of 'The New Frontier' in Mass-Mediated Rhetoric." *Critical Studies in Mass Communication* 3(3): 265–296.

Rushing, J. (1986b). "Ronald Reagan's 'Star Wars' Address: Mythic Containment of Technical Reasoning." *Quarterly Journal of Speech* 72(4): 415–433.

Scholle, D. J. (1988). "Critical Studies: From the Theory of Ideology to Power/Knowledge." *Critical Studies in Mass Communication* 5(1): 16–41.

Steiner, L. (1988). "Oppositional Decoding as an Act of Resistance." *Critical Studies in Mass Communication* 5(1): 1–15.

Wander, P. (1984). "The Third Persona: An Ideological Turn in Rhetorical Theory." *Central States Speech Journal* 35(4): 197–216 [reprinted in this volume].

Wichelns, H. (1972). "The Literary Criticism of Oratory." In Robert L. Scott and Bernard L. Brock, eds., *Methods of Rhetorical Criticism: A Twentieth-Century Perspective* (New York: Harper and Row), pp. 27–60.

Young Blacks Have Higher Voting Rate than 18–24 Whites. (1987, October 7). *Champaign-Urbana News-Gazette*, p. A13.

Pranking Rhetoric

"Culture Jamming" as Media Activism

Christine Harold

Pranks aren't reactive like acts of revenge. They don't punish,
they provoke. . . . Revenge is a science, pranking is an art.
  —REVEREND AL, of the Cacophony Society pranking
    group (quoted in Branwyn, 1997, p. 277)

Illusion is a revolutionary weapon.
  —BURROUGHS (1998, p. 284)

In late 2003, *Adbusters*, the activist magazine known for its parodic "subvertisements" and scathing critiques of consumer culture, launched its most ambitious anti-branding campaign yet. Its "Blackspot" sneaker, an unassuming black canvas shoe, with a large white spot where one would expect a corporate logo, is intended to "uncool" sportswear giant Nike by offering an ethically produced alternative to the Nike swoosh. The magazine's first goal is to challenge Nike's controversial CEO by way of a full-page ad in *The New York Times* declaring:

> Phil Knight had a dream. He'd sell shoes. He'd sell dreams. He'd get rich. He'd use sweatshops if he had to. Then along came the new shoe. Plain. Simple. Cheap. Fair. Designed for only one thing. Kicking Phil's ass. The Unswoosher. (Blackspot website, 2004)

Adbusters is also encouraging its readers to help spread the "Blackspot virus" by graffiti-ing black spots on Niketown windows and displays across the U.S. and Canada. Although it remains to be seen whether the campaign will, as *Adbusters* hopes,

"set a precedent that will revolutionize capitalism" (Blackspot, 2004), to date well over 200 independent shoe stores and 4000 individuals have placed orders for the shoes, and Blackspot was featured in *The New York Times Magazine*'s special "Year in Ideas" issue as one of the "best ideas of 2003."

Adbusters is at the forefront of an insurgent political movement known loosely as "culture jamming." This movement seeks to undermine the marketing rhetoric of multinational corporations, specifically through such practices as media hoaxing, corporate sabotage, billboard "liberation," and trademark infringement. Ad parodies, popularized through magazines such as *Adbusters* and *Stay Free!* and countless websites, are by far the most prevalent of culture jamming strategies. Ad parodies attempting to serve as rhetorical x-rays, revealing the "true logic" of advertising, are a common way for so-called "subvertisers" to talk back to the multimedia spectacle of corporate marketing. An *Adbusters* parody of Calvin Klein's "heroin chic" ads of the mid-1990s, for example, features a female model hunched over a toilet, vomiting, presumably to maintain her waifish figure. The ad tells viewers that women are dissatisfied with their own bodies because "the beauty industry is the beast." In another, Joe Chemo, a cancer-ridden cartoon camel, derides the infamous Joe Camel campaign and a Tommy Hilfiger spoof depicts his customers as sheep, wanting only to "follow the flock." The Gap's infamous appropriation of the likenesses of counter-culture heroes Jack Kerouac and James Dean to sell khaki pants inspired a similar response from the adbusting community. To the Gap's claim that "Kerouac wore khakis," a group of Australian subvertisers responded with the likeness of another 20th century icon who wore khakis as well—Adolf Hitler. As such, Gap khakis were recoded as a means not to rugged individuality but genocidal totalitarianism—the conformist impulse writ large.

Ad parodies such as these might be categorized as a strategy of rhetorical sabotage, an attempt to impede the machinery of marketing. *Adbusters'* own "culture jammer's manifesto," for example, declares: "We will jam the pop-culture marketers and bring their image factory to a sudden, shuddering halt" (Lasn, 1999, p. 128). The industrial imagery here is telling. It invokes the most traditional target of sabotage—the factory. Historically, sabotage, or monkey-wrenching, has been a dominant oppositional response to industrial power. The word "sabotage," according to Merriam-Webster's dictionary (1993), emerged in Europe around 1910, at the height of the industrial revolution. Indeed, it is a term that is inextricably linked to industrial capitalism. The first definition of sabotage offered in Webster's is the "destruction of an employer's property or the hindering of manufacturing by discontented workers." Webster's explains that the word comes from "sabot," the name for the wooden shoes worn in many European countries in the 19th century. "Saboter," then, meant "to clatter with sabots" or to "botch," presumably by throwing one's wooden shoes into the machinery. "Sabotage" means literally to "clog" with one's clogs.

I suggest that while the advertising sabotage articulated by *Adbusters* is not without some rhetorical value, it does little to address the rhetoric of contemporary marketing—a mode of power that is quite happy to oblige subversive rhetoric and shocking imagery. Indeed, parody and irony are the dominant motifs of many successful mass-marketing campaigns. Through a kind of nudge-and-wink knowingness, Madison Avenue culture jammers make every effort to subvert traditional advertising tropes—selling, as cultural critic Thomas Frank (1997) has put it, edgy brands as tickets to the rhetorical "lynching" of consum-

erism. As Fredric Jameson (1991) has famously argued, the cultural logic that accompanies this era of late capitalism is defined by a codification of the eccentric modernist styles of resistance. For example, contemporary advertising is teeming with the language of revolution. But, as Jameson points out, these flagrantly rebellious styles "ostentatiously deviate from a norm which then reasserts itself, in a not necessarily unfriendly way, by a systematic mimicry of their willful eccentricities" (1991, p. 16). In other words, parody becomes one of many social codes—codes that are as available to the capitalist as they are to the artist—and, as such "finds itself without vocation" (p. 16) as a rhetoric of protest in late capitalism.

Further, I want to suggest that despite its deconstructive sensibility, parody, an example of what Mikhail Bakhtin (1984) would describe as turning the world upside down, perpetuates a commitment to rhetorical binaries—the hierarchical form it supposedly wants to upset. The frustration expressed by *Adbusters'* readers (if the magazine's often scathing letters section is any indication) implies that being told what is best for them is no more welcome coming from *Adbusters* than it is coming from advertisers. This may be, in part, because the parodic form neglects what literary theorist Jeffrey Nealon (1993, p. 30) calls the "crucial operation" of deconstruction, *reinscribing* oppositions—for example, health/sickness or authenticity/conformity— back into a larger textual field. Hence parody, as negative critique, is not up to the task of undermining the parodist's own purchase on the Truth as it maintains both a hierarchy of language and the protestor's role as revealer. Parody derides the *content* of what it sees as oppressive rhetoric, but fails to attend to its *patterns*.

In this essay, I explore the rhetorical strategies of an alternative sort of culture jammer—the prankster—who resists less through negating and opposing dominant rhetorics than by playfully and provocatively folding existing cultural forms in on themselves. The prankster performs an art of rhetorical jujitsu, in an effort to redirect the resources of commercial media toward new ends. In what follows, I first detail the theoretical frame through which I engage the political art of culture jamming including why, specifically, the prankster's ethic may offer a more compelling response than parody to contemporary cultural and economic forces. Second, in an effort to explore pranking in action I offer three contemporary case studies of radical and mainstream efforts to hijack popular media forms: the culture jamming collective ®™ark (pronounced "artmark"); the San Francisco-based Biotic Baking Brigade; and the American Legacy Foundation's INFKT Truth campaign. Finally, I conclude by suggesting that although pranking strategies do perform the Aristotelian notion of exploiting available means, for them to be fully imagined as rhetoric, rhetoric itself may have to be somewhat recalibrated in its role as a mass-mediated political art. As I will discuss, although culture jamming should not be seen as a replacement for more traditional modes of civic engagement, the playful and disruptive strategies of the prankster have much to offer social justice movements in the so-called "post-industrial" era.

Intensifying Media Forms: A Theory of Culture Jamming

The term "culture jamming" is based on the CB slang word "jamming" in which one disrupts existing transmissions. It usually implies an interruption, a sabotage, hoax, prank, banditry, or blockage of what are seen as the monolithic power structures governing cultural life. Like Umberto Eco's "semiological guerrillas" (1986, p. 135), culture jammers seek to "introduce noise into the signal" that might otherwise obliterate alternatives to it (Dery, 1993). Culture jamming is usually described as a kind of "glutting" of the system; it is an amping up of contradictory rhetorical messages in an effort to engender a qualitative change. In this sense, jamming need not be seen only as a damming, or a stopping of corporate media, as Adbusters' monkey-wrenching imagery implies. Rather, it may be more useful to consider jamming as an artful proliferation of messages, a rhetorical process of intervention and invention, which challenges the ability of corporate discourses to make meaning in predictable ways.

Many contemporary culture jammers describe themselves as political heirs to the Situationists, a group of avant-garde artists that flourished in 1950s and 1960s Europe. The Situationists were committed to detouring pre-existing political and commercial rhetorics in an effort to subvert and reclaim them. For the Situationists, led by Society of the Spectacle author Guy Debord, everyday life was being overrun by the Spectacle, a novel mode of social domination in which the industrial age's coercive manual labor was replaced by capitalism's deceitful promise of fulfillment through entertainment and consumption. Their main strategy, détournement, was an effort to "devalue the currency of the Spectacle" (Lasn, 1999, p. 108) that they claimed had kidnapped authentic life. Examples include everything from rewording conversations between popular comic strip characters, to reworking the sign on a storefront, to making subversive collages out of familiar commercial and government images. Détournement can be translated as "detour" or "diversion" but other, more subtle meanings in the French include "hijacking," "embezzlement," "corruption," and "misappropriation" (Sadler, 1999). Although many ad parodists, such as those at Adbusters, see themselves as carrying the revolutionary mantle of the Situationists, Debord and his comrades were decidedly opposed to parody as an effective rhetorical strategy, because it maintained, rather than unsettled, audiences' purchase on truth.

As I have mentioned, a major limitation of the adbuster's reliance on parody as a revelatory device is that this device has been enthusiastically embraced by marketers as well. This insistence on revealing a hidden truth also becomes a problem for other reasons. Such an insistence disallows a forceful response to what it faces because it can only *react*. It is a rhetoric that resentfully tells its audience "Things are not as they should be" without affirming possible alternatives. Saying no is itself an often satisfying alternative, but it is hardly one on which to build a lasting political movement.

The no-sayer is, in essence, yoked in a dialectic tug of war with the rhetoric it negates. Adbusters' Blackspot sneaker campaign, for example, may be more proactive than its subvertisements (Adbusters is, for example, proposing to build a "clean" factory in China should the campaign succeed), but the rhetorical message is similar. It is mobilized, first and foremost, by a desire to "kick Phil's ass." Second, then, because the no-sayer has not challenged the essential form of the binary, one can never negate adequately by its own, dialectical standards. A rhetoric that is defined by negation must always encounter more boundaries that must be overcome. More transgression is always required, which inevitably produces more cynicism and resentment. Certainly, saying no is sometimes a crucial political strategy. However, I suggest that asceticism may not be an effective intervention into the scintillating world of consumer culture; and ironically, by ardently pursuing the authentic realm "out there," one plays one's role as consumer in the fullest possible sense, endlessly chasing after something just beyond reach.

Finally—and most crucial for the discussion of pranking that follows—whereas parody may have significant impact in certain rhetorical situations, it should not be seen as a transhistorical category that is inherently subversive; primarily because capitalism itself is not a transhistorical system. It is constantly taking new shapes and producing different kinds of effects. A specific conversation between two theorists of contemporary capitalism, Michel Foucault and Gilles Deleuze, offers a productive model through which to conceptualize the political practices of culture jamming (Deleuze, 1990). Foucault and Deleuze conceived contemporary capitalism as undergoing a shift from *disciplinarity* to *control*. Under disciplinary societies, most famously theorized by Foucault, previously feudalist modes of production were brought together, organized, and confined in order to maximize efficiency and profit. Disciplinary societies operate primarily through the confinement and atomization of individuals (for example, through the familiar models of the prison, the classroom, or the factory). This was the mode of power most appropriate to a Fordist world in which assembly-line style production was the most efficient way for capital to expand. Fordism required a certain level of *standardization* to function. Workers were more or less interchangeable and labor practices were repeated with as little variation as possible. Concurrently, the advertising industry emerged to standardize the consumers who would make up the markets for these newly mass produced products.

Deleuze pursues Foucault's acknowledgement late in his career that the West is now undergoing a transformation from the disciplinarity necessary for an industrial economy to a service economy organized, in part, through the increased control of consumer desires. Control societies do not operate through the confinement and silencing of individuals but "through continuous control and communication" (1990, p. 174). That is, people are not denied access to information and knowledges but are granted ever greater access to them through the opening up of technologies and the hybridization of institutions. However, what might appear as new freedoms also enable business to increasingly modulate every aspect of life. I suggest that the proliferation of the rhetoric of consumerism, in part, marks this shift from discipline to control. Because of this emerging shift from disciplinarity (which spotlights the political rhetoric of the nation-state) to control (which increasingly relies on the visual rhetoric of the market), the opportunities for political protest have shifted as well.

At least two modes of intervention or resistance emerge out of and in response to the logics of disciplinarity and control—sabotage and appropriation. I loosely affiliate sabotage with disciplinarity and appropriation with control. However, I want to be careful, here, to complicate any neat distinction between the two. Although appropriation may be increasing in the face of greater control, both strategies continue to function in response to similar problems through deploying different tools. As Deleuze has suggested, disciplinarity does not disappear with the emergence of control. Control is an intensification, rather than a replacement, of discipline.

Media pranksters, an increasingly active type of consumer activist, prefer affirmation and appropriation to opposition and sabotage. Whereas the culture jammer as saboteur opposes commercialism through revelatory rhetoric such as parody, pranksters can be seen as comedians, as playful explorers of the commercial media landscape. In the third essay of *On the Genealogy of Morals*, Nietzsche (1989) argues that the ascetic ideal, that resentful no-saying of the first order, "has at present only *one* kind of real enemy capable of *harming* it: the comedians of this ideal—for they arouse mistrust of it" (p. 160). Unlike the ascetic, the comedian is not interested in revenge or "bringing the people to consciousness" as if she can use her comedy to expose the truth or push the limits of power until they reveal their true logic. These are the goals of the parodist, not the comedian. To reveal, one must stand in a familiar place and know just what is behind the spectacular curtain. In contrast, the comedian is something of a surfer with no firm, knowable ground on which to stand. Rather, she learns to navigate a force that is already in motion and will continue to be in motion long after she has passed. Whereas parodists attempt to change things in the name of a presupposed value, comedians diagnose a specific situation, and try something to see what responses they can provoke.

Legendary New York performance artist and media hoaxer Joey Skaggs has been provoking people for over three decades. Since 1966, Skaggs has been putting people on, using the news media's own insatiable appetite for sensational images as his canvas. Skaggs says of his work:

I had concepts that I thought would make a statement. *I was using the media as a medium*. Rather than sticking with oil paint, the media became my medium; I got involved with the phenomenon of the media and communication as my art. (Vale & Juno, p. 36, emphasis mine)

Skaggs's most famous and widely disseminated "image event" (DeLuca, 1999) was his 1976 "Cathouse for Dogs," a phony doggie brothel in a makeshift storefront where one could supposedly have one's dog sexually "serviced." To begin, Skaggs simply issued press releases and ran the following advertisement in the *Village Voice*:

CATHOUSE FOR DOGS

Featuring a savory selection of hot bitches. From pedigree (Fifi, the French Poodle) to mutts (Lady the Tramp). Handler and vet on duty. Stud and photo service available. No weirdos, please. Dogs only. By appointment. Call 254-7878.

On the face of it this silly prank hardly seems the kind of thing that would garner much reaction save from a few perverts or curious thrill-seekers. However, Skaggs's "Cathouse for Dogs" received more attention than even he imagined. Several New York television stations sent camera crews, the *Soho News* ran a piece, and the ASPCA, the Bureau of Animal Affairs and the NYPD vice squad, as well as the Mayor's office, all campaigned to put Skaggs out of business.

His greatest exposure, though, came by way of an *ABC News* interview. With little more than some footage of mating dogs and an interview with Skaggs, ABC produced a standard "wrap-around" news piece—interview–footage–interview— and aired it in a larger story about animal abuse. Skaggs's hoax quickly spread, earning him international media attention as well as a lawsuit from the ASPCA. Skaggs is careful to point out that his production was purely rhetorical:

I didn't want customers—it was never my intent to defraud or deceive people for money. Deceit—yes, fraud—no. . . . An artist is much different from a con-man. I am a con-man, but I'm a con-fidence, con-ceptual, con-artist. That's different. (Vale & Juno, 1987, p. 40)

Artistic intentions aside, that year, Skaggs was subpoenaed by the Attorney General's office for "illegally running a cathouse for dogs" (Vale & Juno, 1987, p. 40). Meanwhile, ABC's documentary piece featuring Skaggs's cathouse was nominated for an Emmy as "best news broadcast of the year" (pp. 40–41)! Facing criminal charges, Skaggs

publicly revealed his cathouse as a hoax. Facing professional humiliation, the ABC journalists never retracted their story, despite Skaggs's revelation.

Skaggs's hoax illustrates an important characteristic of the media. It functions, in his words, as something of a "telephone game" in which meaning and content mutate with each repetition:

In this day and age, with electronic telecommunications instantaneously darting around the globe and people feeding off everyone else's network of nerve endings, a misspelled word or a misplaced explanation mark can totally change what is being said. And it's almost impossible to determine where the accidental change came from. And that's on a mild level. It's even *intentionally* done. Governments are doing it, corporations are doing it. Individuals within the media itself are doing it, and people like myself are doing it to make sociopolitical commentaries [about the irresponsibility of the news media]. (Vale & Juno, 1987, pp. 40–41)

As Skaggs suggests, his strategy is not uniquely his own, the domain only of the political subversive. Rather, he observes that unpredictable differentiation is an unavoidable effect as texts are disseminated across the mediascape. Messages and images mutate as they migrate through the vast variety of media outlets, until questions of source and original intent cease to matter. As he notes, governments and corporations often sponsor disinformation campaigns, using the media to start rumors or deflect the public's attention from potential scandals. Indeed, thanks to ABC's professional constraints, Skaggs's cathouse for dogs remains on the record as historical "fact."

Skaggs's cathouse for dogs event—as well as his many others, which included a "celebrity sperm bank" and a Thanksgiving world hunger performance piece—is noteworthy because it exemplifies pranking as a strategic mode of engagement with commercial media and consumer culture in general. Skaggs's project clearly functions as a prank in its most familiar sense: a trick, a practical joke, or a mischievous act. This is a prank in the mundane sense of tying a classmate's shoelaces together under the desk, or short-sheeting a bed. A prank affords the prankster a certain "gotcha!" pleasure at having pulled one over on an unsuspecting party. But, more importantly for our purposes here, Joey Skaggs's prank—as well as the others I will discuss shortly—also illustrates two alternative senses of the word:

(1) In Middle English, to prank was to add a stylistic flourish as to one's dress: to deck, or adorn as in "to dress, or deck in a gay, bright, or showy manner; to decorate; to deck oneself *out*, dress oneself *up*."

(2) Prank can also mean a fold, or a "pleat, as in the figurative sense of 'wrinkle'" (Vale & Juno, 1987, preface, page not enumerated).

These alternative senses of prank are imperative for this discussion of culture jamming. In neither alternative is a prank an act of dialectical opposition. In the first alternative sense, as in to "deck in a showy manner," a prank is a *stylistic exaggeration*. It is a kind of *layering up* of adornment in a conspicuous way that produces some sort of qualitative change. Prank, in this sense, is an augmentation of dominant modes of communication that interrupts their conventional patterns. In the second alternative sense, a prank is a wrinkle, or a fold. Like a fold, a prank can render a qualitative change by turning and doubling a material or text. This qualitative change is produced not through the addition of novelty, but through reconfiguration of the object itself. For analytical purposes, let us continue to stretch and layer the meaning of prank to include a folding over of mass-mediated rhetoric. Dominant texts are wrinkled, they are folded, they ravel and unravel as a result of these stylistic layerings. In the case studies that follow, I will play with these alternative senses of prank—adornment and folding—in an attempt to describe the rhetorical possibilities of media pranking.

While we are playing with definitions, however, let us consider another: I propose an alternative sense of jamming itself. Ultimately, if marketing is, as Deleuze suggests, "now the instrument of social control" (1990, p. 181), then perhaps activists must better learn to play and manipulate that instrument. Rather than approach jamming as simply a monkey-wrenching or opposition to marketing rhetoric, as the activists at *Adbusters* might have it, perhaps activists might approach it as well-trained musicians do music—as a familiar field on which to improvise, interpret, and experiment.

Earlier, I discussed the etymological roots of sabotage (literally, throwing one's clogs into the machinery) in the industrial revolution. This is a response to a disciplinary model of power that ad parodists continue to practice, despite the waning of the factory as both the symbolic and material engine of the contemporary marketplace. However, in what is little more than a side note in its definition of sabotage, *Webster's* states that, in addition to referring to wooden shoes, "sabot" also denotes "a thrust transmitting carrier," or a kind of "launching tube." This second definition provides a compelling alternative sense of the concept of sabotage. As we have seen, in its monkey-wrenching version, sabotage implies destruction or the stopping and hindering of flows through the introduction of an outside element. Put simply, it is a clogging. However, in the word's second sense, as a launching tube, sabotage also implies a channeling, or a transmission of energy or resources through a conduit. This implies that resistance can also enable and direct energy flows rather than merely thwart them. With this in mind, one's rhetorical tools need not come from outside at all, as an oppositional model might insist. Further, as the invocation of tube and carrier implies, and as we have seen from the previous examples of culture jamming, sabotage is not a chaotic, shapeless, anarchic practice, but one that is restrained and shaped by the machinery from which it emerges; without the transmitting carrier, no thrust. In other words, constraints can be seen as immanent to those flows that seek to transform them.

Jamming, in this second, interpretive sense, requires both practice and knowledge of one's instrument as well as a dynamic exchange among a community of agents. Jamming, although it often implies a free-form chaos, requires knowledgeable and disciplined players to work. Recall, for example, Joey Skaggs's description of the work he put into his cathouse for dogs. He painstakingly set up an image event that would appeal to the needs of the televisual news media. He employed the strategies of a television producer in an effort to fold the medium over on itself. As Skaggs suggests, the broadcast media itself is his canvas. And Skaggs knows the contours of his canvas well:

> First there's the hook, when I do the performance; next, I document the process of miscommunication, or how the media twists the content and meaning of the message; finally, I talk about the serious issues underlying the performance piece. The media often trivialize the third stage by saying "Oh, he's a hoaxter, he has an ego problem, he wants attention, etc." (quoted in Frauenfelder & Branwyn, 1995, pp. 40–41)

Skaggs's strategies do not oppose dominant modes of power; they utilize them. As he suggests, "You're already being pranked everyday. If you think *I'm* the prankster, you are sadly mistaken" (p. 41).

To jam as a musician does is to interpret an existing text. I do not mean here, interpret as in trying to make one word correspond directly to its equivalent as one does when translating a text from one language to another, where the interpreter is obliged to make the translation as correct as possible. Rather, I mean interpret in its sense as appropriation, as when a group of jazz musicians appropriate an existing piece of music, or a set of chord progressions and, in doing so, produce a new interpretation. This interpretation does not necessarily correspond to anything outside itself. It does not fail or succeed at representing an original. However, it does contain familiar textual residues. Jamming as appropriation, in these ways, differs from jamming as sabotage.

Pranking as Rhetorical Appropriation

This section focuses on three contemporary examples of media pranking. The first two, the Barbie Liberation Organization and the Biotic Baking Brigade, typify much pranking activism: both are protean collections of activists temporarily stealing the limelight of the mainstream organizations or leaders they target. Both can easily be categorized as engaging in guerrilla media strategies in the terms described above. The third example, the American Legacy Foundation's Truth campaign, an official organization's attempt to thwart teen smoking, maintains a guerrilla aesthetic and ethic but differs from the others in terms of its scope and resources. Unlike the other examples, which operate on shoestring budgets and the media savvy of activists, the Truth campaign is well funded by court-ordered tobacco industry dollars. It is the result of a successful hybrid of traditional legal advocacy and a deployment of the comedic sensibility of the prankster.

Hacking Gender: ®™ark and the Barbie Liberation Organization

In 1989, a group of culture jammers known only as the Barbie Liberation Organization (BLO) pranked the infamously litigious Mattel Corporation through its most prized brand: Barbie. Barbie and Hasbro, Inc.'s military action figure G. I. Joe are notorious for reinforcing unrealistic, even dangerous, gender stereotypes. But, for the BLO, Mattel's Teen Talk Barbie proved to be the last straw. The doll, enhanced with a computer chip "voice box," was programmed to giggle random phrases

when a button on her back was pressed. Mattel's chosen phrases included: "Math class is tough!"; "I love shopping!"; and "Will we ever have enough clothes?" (*Culture Jammer's Encyclopedia*). In response, the Manhattan-based BLO organized a prank that continues to generate discussion on feminist and culture jamming websites. Taking advantage of the mechanical similarities between Teen Talk Barbie and her male counterpart Talking Duke G. I. Joe, the BLO purchased hundreds of each doll from local stores, took them home and switched their voice chips. At the height of the Christmas shopping season, they returned the dolls to stores so they could be resold to unknowing shoppers. When children opened their toys on Christmas morning, instead of Barbie chirping cheerful affirmations of American girlishness she growled, in the butch voice of G. I. Joe: "Eat lead, Cobra!"; "Dead men tell no lies!"; and "Vengeance is mine!" Meanwhile, Joe exclaimed: "Let's plan our dream wedding!"

The rhetorical message of the Great Barbie Hack may be somewhat obvious. The sheer dissonance created by hearing gender inappropriate voices and sentiments may have made absurd otherwise normalized gender norms. As one BLO operative put it: "Our goal is to reveal and correct the problem of gender-based stereotyping in children's toys" (quoted in Greenberg, 1994, para. 5). Another told *The New York Times*: "We are trying to make a statement about the way toys can encourage negative behavior in children, particularly given rising acts of violence and sexism" (Dery, 1994, para. 5). Political goals aside, the dolls have become something of a collector's item. As another BLO member jokingly told National Public Radio's Scott Simon, the BLO is good for business:

> Nobody wants to return [the dolls] . . . We think that our program of putting them back on the shelves [benefits] everyone: The storekeepers make money twice, we stimulate the economy, the consumer gets a better product and our message gets heard. (Dery, 1994, para. 9)

It also may have confused and upset children on Christmas morning. But not seven-year-old Zachariah Zelin who received one of the altered G. I. Joes. When asked "whether he wanted Santa to take back the feminine Joe, he responded sharply 'No way. I love him. I like everything about him'" reports one Associated Press writer (Greenberg, 1994, para. 13).

What was truly inspired about the BLO was their media savvy. Each "hacked" doll had a sticker on its back urging recipients "Call your local TV news," ensuring television journalists would have real disgruntled families to interview for their reports (*Culture Jammer's Encyclopedia*). Further, the group later utilized the new medium of the Internet to disseminate detailed instructions on how to perform such hacks, complete with pictures and diagrams, enabling others to perpetuate the practice. The BLO claims to have inspired similar hacks in Canada, France, and England. Finally, using a strategy increasingly popular with media activists, the BLO produced its own pre-packaged news pieces to be distributed to content-hungry local television stations. The video documentaries showed doll hackers at work, "post-op" Barbies and Joes, and interviews with BLO members explaining their project. The videos were sent out to television stations complete with press releases explaining what BLO had done and why.

When reporters asked the toy manufacturers for their reaction, one Hasbro, Inc., spokesman simply called the attack "ridiculous." Another was amused, but nonplussed: "This will move us to have a good laugh and go on making more G. I. Joes. Barbie dolls and G. I. Joes are part of American culture." Mattel officials downplayed the attack, saying they had received no complaints from consumers (Greenberg, 1994, para. 10).

The BLO was the first and most prominent culture jamming project funded by ®TMark, something of a culture jamming clearing house that has modeled itself after a corporation. Although its actual numbers are somewhat ambiguous, according to the group's website:

> ®TMark is a brokerage that benefits from "limited liability" just like any other corporation; using this principle, ®TMark supports the sabotage (informative alteration) of corporate products, from dolls and children's learning tools to electronic action games, by channelling funds from investors to workers for specific projects grouped into "mutual funds." (®TMark website, Frequently Asked Questions, para. 7)

®TMark exploits rather than condemns a corporate luxury that rankles many culture jammers—a corporation's ability to skirt certain legal restrictions that individuals are obliged to heed. As a private corporation, the group enables activists and investors to participate in illegal product tampering without much personal risk. As the group describes its mission: "®TMark is indeed just a corporation, and it benefits from corporate protections, but unlike other corporations, its 'bottom line' is to improve culture, rather than its own pocketbook; it seeks *cultural* profit, not financial" (®TMark website, Frequently Asked Questions, para. 8).

®TMark spokesperson Ray Thomas argues that many people still think of power in "the old terms"—that is, government power. His group seeks to make explicit the increasing power of corporations: "They are so adaptable, and they're so organic that it's hard to speak of any one corporation as the enemy. It's more the system that allows tremendous abuse" (*How to make trouble*, December 7, 1998). Rather than attempting to dismantle the corporate power system, Thomas and the other activists at ®TMark exploit it; they observe the "adaptable" and "organic" nature of corporations and approach it as fertile soil for rhetorical and political appropriation. As one Australian journalist notes, ®TMark has "cleverly aped the structures and jargons of a financial institution, even down to a smarmingly corporate-sounding promotional video" (*How to make trouble*, December 7, 1998). Opening with warnings from Abraham Lincoln about unfettered corporate power, the aforementioned video— "Bringing IT to YOU!"—offers viewers a history of the corporation and rehearses ®TMark's style of corporate sabotage. In the spirit of pranking as I want to conceive it here, ®TMark folds and augments the corporate model in a way that offers new dimensions for rhetorical invention.

Pie Crimes and Misdemeanors: The Biotic Baking Brigade

In 1998, Nobel prize-winning economist Milton Friedman (along with conservative California governor Pete Wilson, multi-millionaire Steve Forbes, and former Secretary of State under Ronald Reagan, George Schultz) was attending a conference on the benefits of privatizing public education. As Friedman was greeting well-wishers, a young man emerged from the crowd, exclaiming "Mr. Friedman, it's a good day to pie!" and heaved a coconut crème pie into the face of the famous Chicago-school economist. With that, the Biotic Baking Brigade (BBB) executed the first of what would be many successful missions: publicly delivering pies to "pompous people." Since its inception, BBB victims have included Microsoft founder Bill Gates, CEO of genetic engineering giant Monsanto Robert Shapiro, Chevron CEO Kenneth Derr, San Francisco Mayor Willie Brown, and World Trade Organization Chief, Renato Ruggiero.

When reporting the public pieing of Mayor Willie Brown (who had just mandated a city-wide sweep of the homeless), a confused San Francisco anchorman asked: "Is it funny? Is it some kind of statement? A physical assault?" (*The Pie's the Limit*, 1999). The BBB is consistently ready with pointed answers for journalists asking the inevitable question—"Why?" In the case of Milton Friedman, for example, BBB "special agent" Christian Parenti says:

> Milton Friedman is the chief architect of neo-liberal economics. [His] particular brand of economics further allows multi-national corporations to rape the land, to plunder social systems . . . to prevent any type of popular resistance to occur. So, even though Milton Friedman may seem like a strange target, like just some fuddy-duddy old geek, the man is like a purveyor of an ideological poison that is central to the kinds of policies and politics that are threatening the health of the planet and threatening the interests of common people all over the planet. (*The Pie's the Limit*, 1999)

A pie in the face of Milton Friedman becomes what rhetoricians would call a *synechdoche*; it is an easy visual shorthand for a whole host of grievances against globalization's prevailing economic ideology.

The BBB's Rahula Janowski explains the logic behind the group's choice of "weapon": "Pie is an example that you don't have to revere someone just because they're more powerful than you . . . Pie is the great equalizer. How wealthy and powerful are you with pie dripping off your face?" Janowski points out that many CEOs and other powerful people do not often put themselves in situations where they hear dissent. So the BBB seeks them out in public fora, often where the target is giving a speech in some controlled, formal environment:

> It's a message of "we know who you are and we don't agree with what you're doing." And it also puts a face on that dissent. Here's this person and they're willing to come right up and put the pie in your face. Like, "we *really* don't like what you're doing." (*The Pie's the Limit*, 1999)

Importantly, the face that gets disseminated throughout the mediascape is not that of an angry protestor, as is often the case, but the often well-known face of a captain of industry. The face of Bill Gates is a familiar image for evening news audiences; however, after being pranked by the BBB, its ability to convey authority and influence is momentarily disenabled.

Although their message is clearly one that opposes the ideologies and practices of their targets—genetic engineering, neo-liberal economics, clear cutting of the redwoods, or corporate monopolies—their tactic of choice, pie-throwing, expresses that opposition in such a way that makes it difficult for targets to respond or audiences to understand in traditional ways. As one BBB agent, Rosie Rosebud explains: "A clown, a comedian, is someone who can laugh at themselves, they can laugh at society, and their rulers" (*The Pie's the Limit*, 1999). The BBB's rhetoric, when its agents speak to reporters, is clearly oppositional in nature, but it is their comedic posture and creation of spectacular images that get them the interviews in the first place.

The BBB understands well how to get its agenda into newspapers and television broadcasts. Unlike *Adbusters*, the BBB does not remain resentfully on the outside, denied access to what DeLuca and Peeples (2002) call the "public screen" by the commercial media. Instead, they hijack events that are already orchestrated for television—public speeches, rallies, meet-and-greets, and so on. They know that the image of a famous politician or captain of industry getting a pie in the face is so striking, the image-hungry media cannot help but cover it. Bill Gates with lemon meringue dripping from his nose *will* make the five-o'clock news. Unlike its more ascetic counterparts, the BBB does not condemn the news; it makes it by cooking up tasty images for the Spectacle to consume. As San Francisco prankster Mark Pauline puts it in another context:

> The media can never deny coverage to a good spectacle. No matter how ridiculous, absurd, insane or illogical something is, if it achieves a certain identity as a spectacle, the media has to deal with it. They have no choice. They're hamstrung by their own needs, to the extent that they're like a puppet in the face of such events. (Vale & Juno, 1987, p. 14)

Again, BBB agents are always on-hand to offer journalists a quick interpretive sound bite, such as "Monsanto CEO Robert Shapiro is the Pinochet of the food world [so] he's gotten his just desserts!" But the image of the powerful being pied says more than a spoken message ever could. As Janowski explains: "The American public understands the impact of the message that is put forth by a pie. I mean, I think of the Three Stooges. Think of the Marx Brothers. It's *very, very plain* what's happening when a pie is delivered" (*The Pie's the Limit*, 1999). A pie in the face becomes a powerful rhetorical symbol that requires little explanation. Agent "Salmonberry" puts it most succinctly: "I think the history of pie-throwing shows that it's a form of visual *Esperanto*. It's a universal language. Everyone understands the pie in the face. [It's about] taking their spectacle and just spinning it around. It allows people to have a laugh at the expense of the rich and powerful and otherwise unaccountable" (*The Pie's the Limit*, 1999). The BBB, then, mobilizes two familiar but dissonant visuals—a sober public speaker and a pie in the face—and by joining them, produces a kind of political jujitsu, using the power of the broadcast media toward its own ends.

To ensure its images make the news, the BBB sends its own camera operators on missions. In some cases, as with the pieing of Chevron CEO Kenneth Derr, the news media cannot be counted on to capture the moment on video. Like the Barbie Liberation Organization, the Biotic Baking Brigade happily provides budget-strapped local news stations with ready-made video packages, complete with interviews and images. This is a strategy often used by corporate advertisers hoping to create a "buzz" around a new product. Advertisers regularly offer pre-produced marketing stunts packaged as news features (known in the PR world as "video press releases"), which local news stations can easily queue up for broadcast. Result: free content for the station and free advertising for the corporation. Media pranksters like those in the BLO or the BBB just borrow that strategy, turning the media's love of images over on itself, creating a venue for issues that the commercial media often ignore. Further, BBB agents, despite their somewhat militant politics, are always clean cut, articulate, and wear a sly smile. Hence, they are not easily dismissed as militant hippie radicals creating anarchy. They realize that they, too, must look the part for broadcast television if they are to gain access to it. As BBB agents are always sure to tell reporters, civil disobedience is "as American as apple pie."[1]

INFKT Truth: Pranking Big Tobacco

One of the most successful models of media pranking comes in the form of an institutionally sanctioned public service campaign: the American Legacy Foundation's "INFKT Truth" campaign.

Funded with more than $100 million of tobacco money per annum ("Arnold faces anti-smoking challenges," 2002) after the 1998 "master settlement" agreement between tobacco companies and 46 states, the impeccably produced television, print, radio, and web campaign distinguished by a bright orange background and the cyber-style font and graphics popular in rave and gaming culture, Truth seeks to mobilize young people against Big Tobacco. As its use of the phonetic device "INFKT" implies, the Truth campaign encourages young people to infect their peers with knowledge about how the tobacco industry markets to children.

Unlike Nancy Reagan's "Just say no" campaign that was, by most accounts, a dismal failure in the 1980s, Truth invites young people to assume a subversive posture that is far more active than just impotently saying no to tobacco. An underlying assumption of INFKT Truth is that Nike's provocation to "just do it" has proven far more compelling to young people than Reagan's message of abstinence could ever be. In an article about teen anti-smoking campaigns, one Scottish newspaper sarcastically asks: "Would you embrace a drug-free lifestyle on the advice of an emaciated former actress with concrete hair and a designer clothes habit many times more expensive than the average teenager's dope habit?" (Harris, 1996, p. 14). Whereas the "just say no" admonishment came from the First Lady, an unmistakable symbol of the establishment, the Truth campaign takes seriously young people's anti-authoritarian attitudes and positions itself with them. Rather than asking teenagers to correct their own individual behavior, Truth encourages a critical analysis of tobacco as an industry.

Before the American Legacy Foundation launched its Truth campaign in 2000, the most prominent voice against underage smoking was the tobacco industry itself, forced by a series of courtroom battles to sponsor anti-smoking public service announcements. At first blush, these tobacco-sponsored announcements seemed well-intentioned, but their rhetoric was so out of touch with the tropes of so-called "Generation Y" that they seem purposefully ineffective. Take, for example, tobacco giant Lorillard's "Tobacco is Wacko (if you're a teen)" campaign that supposedly sought to discourage kids from picking up the habit. First, let us assume that for most of today's teens and "tweens" as the market has so cleverly labeled pre-adolescents, "wacko" is probably not on the slang radar. More importantly, Lorillard neglects the fact that being "outside the box," "on the edge," "Xtreme" or, okay, even slightly "wacko" is exactly what is understood as cool for today's kids. Other advertisers pursuing the volatile teen market have known this for some time. Although even the most cursory analysis of market-produced rebellion shows that kids are encouraged to rebel symbolically in a mass produced way—by purchasing the latest "edgy" product—kids at least want to feel that they are choosing not to run with the herd when buying this or that brand of widget.

On the face of it, then, it might seem that Lorillard misses what proves effective with the youth market when it states that it is wacko (read: edgy) to smoke cigarettes. Although it hopelessly fudges the vernacular of today's teens, it perpetuates the aura that makes smoking so sexy to kids in the first place. Smoking is what distinguishes you from the pack. It is what makes you a rebel. In this light, Lorillard's choice of the outdated "wacko" is clearly not misguided at all. In fact, it is most likely that the company's court-ordered anti-smoking campaign was ineffective by design. As one anti-tobacco website puts it:

> The tobacco industry favors only measures that are known not to work well and may even be counter-productive—such as age-related restrictions, retailer schemes, exhortation from parents and teachers, and "finger wagging" messages that smoking is only for grown ups. These methods deflect attention away from the industry, are difficult to enforce, and present cigarettes as a "forbidden fruit" reserved for adults—exactly what most young people aspire to be! (*Exposing the truth*, para. 6)

Indeed, the outdated choice of "wacko" makes the "Don't Smoke" message all the more unhip, which leaves tobacco products untainted by any odor of unfashionability. In all, the tobacco industry spent a lot of money to tell kids that more than anything else its product makes you a rebel, which is precisely the message sent by every other successful youth marketer.

In contrast, the Truth campaign does not just tell kids not to smoke. In fact finger-waving messages never appear in its literature or imagery at all. Instead, Truth encourages young people to become culture jammers, or pranksters, themselves, and even provides them with the tools to do it. The Truth campaign is successful because it maximizes a truism in contemporary marketing: kids want to feel like they are "sticking it to the man" even if

"the man" provides them the tools with which to do so. One of the group's slogans makes its non-conformist posture clear: "Join Truth now! But, don't think of it as 'joining' something." Whereas the tobacco industry's pseudo-attempt to curb teen smoking continues to afford the smoker the rebellious subject position, Truth flips that equation. In the Truth campaign, the non-smoking teen is the rebel, and tobacco executives, rather than parents and teachers, represent "the man." By rehearsing a series of pranks instigated by ordinary teenagers, Truth offers kids a new mode of agency in relation to tobacco advertising. It is an agency that is born of engaged mischief and hip rebellion rather than no-saying and abstention.

For example, one series of magazine ads provides kids with an incredibly simple way to become anti-tobacco activists. In several popular teen magazines, the group took out double-page spreads featuring Truth's trademark orange background and bold white letters. One spread read, "CIGARETTE SMOKE HAS ARSENIC," and the other, "AMMONIA IS ADDED TO CIGARETTES." On the following page is a picture of bookstores, magazine stands, and grocery store checkouts with magazines opened to these Truth "billboards" (see Figure 1). The demonstrative ads urge readers to "Spread the knowledge. Infect truth." Not only does Truth provide mini billboards inside teen magazines, it shows contexts in which those billboards might be displayed. In doing so, it provides young people with a quick and easy way to protest, to feel as if they are committing a subversive act, however small and temporary.

In another magazine campaign, Truth provides stickers in the shape of blank conversation bubbles as in a comic strip. Next to the free stickers is a picture of a Marlboro Man advertisement "augmented" by one of the stickers (see Figure 2). In this case, someone has written: "When I get tired of counting cow patties, I like to count the 4,000 chemicals in cigarette smoke." The bubbles are outlined in the familiar Truth orange but are otherwise just blank slates, ready for kids to contribute their own messages to the vast sea of advertising. In short, it demonstrates an easy way for kids to hijack the advertisements that so saturate their landscape. As tobacco giant R. J. Reynolds itself is aware, the visual vocabulary of comic books appeals to kids. In a 1973 memo on how to better market its Camel cigarettes to young people, an R. J. Reynolds executive wrote "Comic strip type copy might get a much higher readership among

FIGURE 1. INFKT Truth: a simple two-page spread provides the means for a quick and easy form of media activism

FIGURE 2. The Marlboro Man is subjected to a *détournement*

younger people than any other type of copy" (*Tobacco Facts*). The company put this wisdom to use years later in its controversial Joe Camel campaign. In response, Truth launched its bubble campaign, folding Tobacco's enthusiasm for the rhetorical power of comic book imagery over on itself and, in doing so, allowing kids to participate in the construction of a new narrative.

The Truth bubble campaign borrows a common mode of *détournement* employed by the Situationists who often revised the dialogue in popular comic strips as a venue for their own subversive messages. As Situationist René Viénet (1981, p. 214) argued, "comic strips are the only truly popular literature of our century" and as such were a potentially powerful vehicle for rhetorical intervention. The Situationists hijacked existing comics, but they also borrowed the familiar dialogue bubbles that had become part of the popular vernacular as vehicles for revision in other venues. Viénet writes: "it is also possible to detourn *any* advertising billboards—particularly those in subway corridors, which form remarkable sequences—by pasting over pre-prepared placards" (p. 214). Anticipating terminology popular with contemporary culture jammers, he described the practice as "guerrilla media" warfare (p. 214). In this spirit, the Truth campaign, in effect, trains young people to practice their own brand of Situationism, by confiscating a small space from commercial advertising and using it as a site for rhetorical invention. The goal to reclaim public space from the increasing "contamination" of commercial messages is shared by many culture jammers—billboard liberators, graffiti artists, and hackers, for example—but these practices usually require a criminal act, defacing private property. The Truth bubble strategy is no different in that it is, in effect, encouraging young people to vandalize a corporation's property. But, unlike other culture jammers who readily embrace their role as cultural guerrillas, Truth's suggested hijack is noteworthy in that it comes from a government-regulated organization working with legally granted tobacco money.

The content of the Truth campaign's rhetoric is not fundamentally different from the *Adbusters* strategy of negative critique. What differentiates the two is the form of their rhetorical strategy. Unlike the magazine's Joe Camel parody, Joe Chemo, which critiques cigarette smoking and the ads that promote it, Truth unabashedly appropriates the rhetorical tropes of branding; it taps into the language of the market. Its signature color orange, its use of white asterisk pop-ups to connote

a virus spreading, and its digital font are consistent in its magazine, television, and Internet campaigns. In effect, Truth is an excellent example of good brand management. The current INFKT Truth campaign experiments with a mode of rhetoric that is not grounded in the proclamations of any individual speaking subject. It promotes a kind of word-of-mouth dissemination of arguments against the tobacco industry. As such, it capitalizes on what may be two favorite pastimes of many teens: rebellion and gossip.

Conclusion: Pranking Rhetoric in the Commercial Mediascape

The title of this essay, "pranking rhetoric," was carefully chosen. On one hand, it names a category of rhetorical action: pranking. On the other, it articulates an underlying premise of this analysis. That is, in order to consider pranking as rhetoric, rhetoric itself must be, well, pranked. And, here, I mean prank in all its forms: to trick, but also to fold, and to adorn. The practices discussed in this essay—pranks, hoaxes, *détournements*—are not explicitly persuasive, if we understand persuasion as a targeted change in meaning structures. As I have suggested, they do not necessarily rely on that "aha!" moment when an audience becomes conscious of some new insight. Also, their effectiveness does not depend on the ethos or charisma of a specific rhetor. Hence, they fall outside the expectations of what conventionally qualifies as effective rhetoric. Clear arguments do often follow pranks—as in the Biotic Baking Brigade's critique of neo-liberal economics—but those arguments are translations of pranks. They do not account for the power of the pranks themselves. One might even argue that such translations dilute the rhetorical power pranks have to confuse and provoke. In other words, attaching an explicit argument, making a prank make sense, may undermine what is unique about pranking's signifying rhetoric in the first place.

The mass-mediated pranks and hoaxes discussed here do not oppose traditional notions of rhetoric, but they do repattern them in interesting ways. Media pranksters undermine the proprietary authority of rhetoric by hijacking its sanctioned venues, as does the Biotic Baking Brigade. Hoaxes challenge rhetoric's relationship to truth (either the art's "misuse" as a tool for propaganda, or its "correct use" in revealing facts to audiences), because they produce rhetorical effects that have little to do with facts or evidence, as in Joey Skaggs's cathouse for dogs. In general, pranking has the potential to unravel rhetoric's continued reliance on individual auteurs (be they presidents or protestors) because a prank's source is often impossible to locate and, ultimately, irrelevant to its political impacts.

Traditionally, communication has largely been conceived in industrial, Fordist terms. Arguments are systematically and rationally assembled. Messages move teleologically toward an end product—persuasion. Perhaps the strategies of pranking and branding (its commercial counterpart) may have something to teach communication scholars. As North America moves into an economy driven as much by information and marketing as the production of tangible goods, it becomes all the more crucial that communication scholars attend to the battles being waged over commercialization. A basic tenet of both the marketing and prankster world is that ideas and innovations spread less like widgets coming off an assembly line than like viruses in an ecosystem (see, for the most prominent example, Rushkoff, 1996). Indeed, viruses *communicate* diseases, yet they cannot be said to possess intentions nor progress teleologically, as a factory model might imply.

Vale and Juno (1987), in *Pranks!*, their edited collection of interviews with political pranksters, acknowledge that pranking can often be funny, even trivial. However, they remind us that pranks can also pose a "direct challenge to all verbal and behavioral *routines*, and [undermine] the sovereign authority of words, language, visual images, and social conventions in general" (Vale & Juno, 1987, preface, page not enumerated). Contemporary commercial culture depends upon consumers having somewhat routinized responses to words and images; however, these responses need not be completely homogenous. Indeed, it is the protean, polysemic nature of brands that allows them to be disseminated globally, across individuals and cultures. For example, Nike's swoosh may signify "self-discipline" to one person, and "liberty" to another; and it is likely that the Nike corporation does not much care how people interpret it as long as they keep buying Nike products. This is the viral power of the brand—its ability to provoke through sheer replication of form.

Pranking—as intensification, augmentation, folding—is conceptually and practically quite different from how we often consider rhetorics of protest. Pranking is often comedic, but not in a satirical, derisive sense that prescribes a "correct"

political position. It takes the logic of branding seriously. As the famous rallying cry of Nike CEO Phil Knight—"Brands! Not products!"—illustrates, successful brands are not limited to a closed system of representation. The swoosh has the capacity to signify much more than sneakers, or even products, and that is just the way Nike wants it. Nike understands that in an age where the factory has largely been moved overseas, it is now in the business of producing something much more profitable than sportswear: its product is seductive imagery and the loyal consumers it attracts.

As I have argued throughout, pranking repatterns commercial rhetoric less by protesting a disciplinary mode of power (clogging the machinery of the image factory) than by strategically augmenting and utilizing the precious resources the contemporary media ecology affords. In doing so, pranksters, those comedians of the commercial media landscape, make manifest Michel Foucault's (1983) observation that one need not be sad to be militant. Rather than using political action to discredit a line of thought (as the parodist might have it), Foucault urges us to "use political practice as an *intensifier* of thought, and analysis as a multiplier of the forms and domains for the intervention of political action" (1983, p. xii).[2] Culture jamming multiplies the tools of intervention for contemporary media and consumer activists. It does so by embracing the viral character of communication, a quality long understood by marketers. So-called "cool hunters," for example, employ the tools of anthropologists who engage in "diffusion research" to determine how ideas spread through cultures. These marketers, like their anthropologist counterparts, have learned that people tend to adopt messages less in response to rational arguments than through exposure and example (Gladwell, 1997). Activists with a prankster ethic, such as those promoting the INFKT Truth campaign, capitalize on this capacity of ideas to multiply and disseminate like viruses. Further, although *Adbusters'* campaign to spread the Blackspot virus may still promote oppositional content, its embrace of the viral form indicates the group's advertising savvy. Tellingly, the magazine's focus on advertising parodies has waned in recent years.

It is important to note that the opportunities offered by culture jamming should not be seen as supplanting other, more traditional modes of engagement that continue to produce powerful rhetorical and political effects. Culture jamming—largely a response to consumerism and corporate power—may not be as productive in rhetorical situations that call for legal or policy interventions, for example. Further, culture jamming may be an effective strategy for engaging corporations who rely heavily on positive public relations, but may do little in the face of those which benefit from working beneath the public's radar. For these reasons, it may be most helpful to take seriously culture jamming, and pranking in particular, as important components of rhetorical hybrids, collections of tools that activists and scholars can utilize when intervening in the complex world of commercial discourse.

Finally, whereas ad parodies and satire offer up alternative interpretations of marketing rhetoric, pranks potentially upset the obligation of rhetoric to *represent* at all. Pranks intensify the polysemic quality of the signs on which marketing campaigns rely. They exacerbate the slippage in the signification process in such a way that polysemy may no longer serve the corporate author's effort to spread its ultimate message: buy! As Vale and Juno write, pranks

> attack the fundamental mechanisms of a society in which all social/verbal intercourse functions as a means toward a future *consumer exchange*, either of goods or experience. It is possible to view *every* "entertainment" experience marketed today either as an act of consumption, a prelude to an act of consumption, or both. (1987, preface, page not enumerated)

In response to the increasing rhetorical prominence of marketers, who Deleuze (1990) describes as "the arrogant breed who are our masters," pranks enact his insistence that "We've got to hijack speech. Creating has always been something different from communicating. The key thing may be to create vacuoles of noncommunication, circuit breakers, so we can elude control" (p. 175). In this sense, pranks—precisely because they border on the non-sensical—reconfigure the very structures of meaning and production on which corporate media and advertising depend. Pranking—by layering and folding the rhetorical field—addresses the *patterns* of power rather than its *contents*. It does so by taking its cue, in part, from the incredible success of commercial rhetoric to infect contemporary culture.

This article was drawn from a dissertation completed at Pennsylvania State University under the direction of Stephen H. Browne. Portions of this essay were presented at the 2003 National Communication Association convention in Miami, Florida and the 2003 Argumentation Conference in Alta, Utah. The author is especially grateful to Marco Abel, Bonnie Dow, and Ken Rufo for their helpful feedback on the arguments presented in this essay.

NOTES

1. The phrase is reminiscent of Black Panther leader Huey Newton's famous phrase: "Violence is as American as cherry pie."

2. In his preface, Foucault is interpreting the themes of Gilles Deleuze and Felix Guattari (2000).

REFERENCES

®™*ark*. Retrieved January 27, 2004, from: http://www.rtmark.com/faq.html.

Arnold faces anti-smoking challenges. (2002, January). *Adweek*, p. 1.

Bakhtin, M. M. (1984). *Rabelais and his world* (H. Iswolsky, Trans.). Bloomington: Indiana University Press.

Blackspot. Retrieved January 21, 2004, from http://www.blackspotsneaker.org/sneaker.html

Branwyn, G. (1997). *Jamming the media: A citizen's guide*. San Francisco: Chronicle Books.

Burroughs, W. S. (1998). Word virus. In J. Grauerholz & I. Silverberg (Eds.), *Electronic revolution* (pp. 294–313). New York: Grove Press.

Culture jammer's encyclopedia. Retrieved January 25, 2004, from http://www.sniggle.net/barbie.php.

Deleuze, G. (1990). *Negotiations*. New York: Columbia University Press.

Deleuze, G., & Guattari, F. (2000). *Anti-Oedipus: Capitalism and schizophrenia*. Minneapolis: University of Minnesota Press.

DeLuca, K. M. (1999). *Image politics: The new rhetoric of environmental activism*. New York: Guilford Press.

DeLuca, K., & Peeples, J. (2002, June). From public sphere to public screen: democracy, activism, and the "violence" of Seattle. *Critical Studies in Media Communication, 19*, 125–151.

Dery, M. (1993). *Culture jamming: Hacking, slashing and sniping in the empire of the signs*. Westfield, NJ: Open Pamphlet Series.

Dery, M. (1994). *Hacking Barbie's voice box: "Vengeance is mine!"* Retrieved January 25, 2004, from http://www.levity.com/markdery/barbie.html.

Eco, U. (1986). *Travels in hyperreality*. New York: Harcourt Brace Jovanovich.

Exposing the truth: Tobacco industry "anti-tobacco" youth programs. Retrieved January 21, 2004, from http://www.essentialaction.org/tobacco/aofm/0103. Published March 2001.

The ethical sneaker. (2003, December14). *The New York Times Magazine*, p. 64.

Frank, T. (1997). Why Johnny can't dissent. In T. Frank
& M. Weiland, (Eds.), *Commodify your dissent: Salvos
from* the Baffler. New York: Norton.

Frauenfelder, S., & Branwyn, K. (Eds.). (1995). *The
happy mutant handbook*. New York: Riverhead Books.

Gladwell, M. (1997, March 17). The coolhunt. *The New
Yorker*. Retrieved January 25, 2004, from http://www.
gladwell.com/1997/1997 03 17 a cool.htm.

Greenberg, B. (1994, Spring). The BLO—Barbie liberation organization—strikes. *The Unit Circle Magazine*.
Retrieved January 21, 2004, from http://www.etext.
org/Zines/UnitCircle/uc3/page10.html.

Hacking Barbie with the Barbie Liberation Organization.
Retrieved January 21, 2004 from http://www.brillo-
mag.net/No1/blo.htm.

Harris, G. (1996, January 16). Just say no to the preaching and scaremongering. *The Scotsman*, 14.

How to make trouble and influence. *The Australian
Broadcasting Corporation*. Retrieved January 21,
2004 from http://www.abc.net.au/arts/headspace/rn/
bbing/trouble/b.htm

Jameson, F. (1991). *Postmodernism: Or, the cultural logic
of late capitalism*. Durham, NC: Duke University
Press.

Lasn, K. (1999). *Culture jam: The uncooling of America*TM. New York: Eagle Brook.

Merriam-Webster's collegiate dictionary. (10th ed.).
(1993). Springfield, MA: Merriam-Webster.

Nealon, J. T. (1993). *Double reading: Postmodernism after
deconstruction*. New York: Cornell University Press.

Nietzsche, F. (1989). *On the genealogy of morals and Ecce
Homo* (W. Kaufmann, Trans.). New York: Vintage.

*The pie's the limit!: A documentary on the global pasty
uprising*. (1999). Video recording. San Francisco:
Whispered Media.

Rushkoff, D. (1996). *Media virus!* New York: Ballantine
Books.

Sadler, S. (1999). *The situationist city*. Cambridge, MA:
MIT Press.

Tobacco facts. Retrieved January 21, 2004, from http://
www.tobaccofacts.org/ozone/o2z-howtheyseeyou.
html.

Vale, V., & Juno, A. (Eds.). (1987). *Pranks!* San Francisco: RE/Search.

Viénet, R. (1981). The situationists and the new forms
of action against politics and art. In K. Knabb (Ed.),
The situationist international anthology (pp. 213–216).
Berkeley, CA: Bureau of Public Secrets.

A Virtual Death and a Real Dilemma

Identity, Trust, and Community in Cyberspace

John W. Jordan

The strange events surrounding the life and death of Kaycee Nicole Swenson captivated a multitude of Internet users for over 2½ years. Using a Web log, or "blog,"[1] Kaycee chronicled her tragic struggle with leukemia in postings that drew many supporters who added their own statements of encouragement for this all-American, teenage girl. During her illness, Kaycee's circle of online friends drew bigger and closer to her, shared their concerns, and offered her and each other sympathetic support in a virtually perfect model of virtual community. But the most compelling turn in Kaycee's story was not her battle with leukemia nor even the day she eventually succumbed to her illness and died, all of which were observed dutifully by her online cohort. The real revelation about Kaycee Nicole Swenson was that she had never been alive. She was a digital dream, a carefully constructed and maintained fictional persona affected by her "mother," Debbie Swenson, a very real person living in a small Kansas town.[2] Debbie never informed anyone or even hinted that Kaycee was fictional until after she had posted news of Kaycee's "death" to her blog, a bombshell announcement that precipitated a major crisis within their virtual community. Debbie insisted that she meant no harm, but her actions left many hurt feelings and questions about the relationships between computers, community, and communication.

Given the ever-increasing use of fear appeals in Internet rhetoric (J. W. Jordan, 2000), it is hard to say that we have not been warned about online hoaxes or that we should be particularly shocked when the Internet plays host to deception. As one Web designer avers, "The Internet did not create grifters. . . . If anything, the Net has just changed the dynamics of the game" (Powazek, 2002, pp. 147–148). Avoiding online deception is now considered a priority for Internet users, and consumer-oriented cyberfraud books insist that the medium's vulnerability to ill purposes requires users to adopt a healthy skepticism when online (Thomes, 2000, p. xiv). But warnings such as these tell only half the story of online deception. What emerges far less clearly is a sense of how Internet users respond to and deal with the aftermath of crises in their virtual communities. The Kaycee Nicole Swenson story provides an example of how one group of Internet users addressed such a crisis and the impact it had on them as individuals and as members of a virtual community. Those persons who participated in the Kaycee blog and its related Web pages, either by posting material or following Kaycee's reports on her progress, constituted a virtual community in that they were bound together by their common interest and desire to communicate with one another. The aftermath of this online community's betrayal can be used to observe the rhetorics of community and citizenship as articulated by the community members themselves during a time when their values and beliefs in virtual citizenship were rocked to their core. The Internet is not a shy medium, and Kaycee's virtual death prompted many of her blog participants to post messages about their understanding of and regard for the prospects of virtual community, identity, and trust. Theirs was a rhetorical struggle among participants who shared neither similar definitions nor visions of community, and this divergence is a large part of what makes their rhetoric compelling testimony with respect to contemporary attitudes toward trust, technology, community, and computers.

This essay critiques the Kaycee community's online debates over their attitudes toward virtual identity and online citizenship in the wake of Debbie's hoax. A critical rhetorical analysis of the ways in which community members articulated these issues engages with fundamental questions about identity, authority, and anonymity in computer mediated communication. I begin by discussing the need for critical analyses of virtual communities that examine the rhetorical work community members do in the service of online citizenship, particularly when confronted with a divisive crisis. I then review theories of online identity, rhetoric, and authority that inform a critical reading of online deception and the stakes for participants deciding how and to what extent their virtual communities should be governed. Next, I analyze the Kaycee community members' responses to these issues, presented in public Web documents ranging from posted e-mails, statements in journalistic accounts, and blogs for their rhetorical conceptualizations of the nature and function of virtual community. I conclude by discussing how this case demonstrates the importance of rhetorical communication to online community members' interactions and their ability to contend with crisis.

Observing the Aftermath of Online Deception

The lens through which I examine the Kaycee Nicole Swenson hoax is that of critical rhetorical inquiry, which provides an analytical framework for assembling the various discursive artifacts of the hoax into a "text" that can be analyzed in terms of how competing rhetorical forces engage with one another (McKerrow, 1989, p. 101). Toward this end, I employ several critical tools united by their common interest in explaining how rhetorical communication is used in generating notions of community, trust, and identity.

My primary textual pool for this analysis is comprised of the numerous statements generated by Web users in response to the Kaycee hoax. These statements are scattered across the Web in various blogs, personal Web pages, and mainstream news articles about the hoax, but they are united figuratively by their common interest in Kaycee and literally through shared hypertext links. These statements reveal not only the varied attitudes the community participants had toward the future of online community, but also how they articulated and made meaningful their attitudes through rhetorical language.

My purpose in analyzing the community members' statements is not to offer definitive pronouncements about what virtual identity is or is not. Rather, I seek to demonstrate how these participants engaged in debates over identity and what it meant in the context of their articulations of virtual community. As is common in rhetorical definitions of key concepts (Schiappa, 2003, p. 4), debates amongst the Kaycee community members argued both for particular definitions of virtual community and against the validity of others. The public statements generated from these debates constituted a rhetorical space on the Internet where "social issues collide, where political issues are struggled over and subject positions . . . are constituted" (Ono & Sloop, 2002, p. 2). The role of community was clearly important to these people, making their disharmony over these definitions compelling statements deserving critical investigation in order to understand better how virtual communities use rhetorical communication in their relational activities.

In online and offline contexts alike, the true test of a community is not how well it manages during times of harmony, but how it confronts crisis. A critical rhetorical inquiry into the discourse generated in the aftermath of the Kaycee hoax evinces the importance of rhetoric to the work Internet users do in maintaining their communities. This aspect of community is often overlooked in popular and journalistic accounts of web hoaxes.[3] These reports are informative and offer important counterstatements to the often effusive praise virtual communities receive in other venues (e.g., Connery, 1997; Rheingold, 1993), and usefully describe how "the Internet has breathed new life into the phenomenon" of hoaxing while providing tips to readers on how to avoid online scams (F. Jordan, 2001, p. B1). At the same time, the overall message generated by many of these reports too often drifts into moralistic cautioning about the "dark side" of the Internet that treats hoaxes as singular, self-contained incidents rather than as moments in a virtual community's continuum. The effect of such messages implicitly endorses anti-community biases by emphasizing the acts of deceptive individuals irrespective of community reactions. The Internet's ability to serve as a communal space where users discuss and debate their responses to hoaxes is diminished as are the possibilities for community enactment online.

News reports of the Kaycee hoax serve as a case in point. Stories documenting the hoax typically begin by describing how, "by the thousands, the virtual community embraced Kaycee Nicole Swenson. Reached out to her, protected her, comforted her, prayed for her. Loved her" (Roeper, 2001, p. 11). Then they reveal the hoax with melodramatic phrases like "Kaycee Nicole hadn't died. She never existed" (Dunne, 2001) or "the sad fact wasn't that a 19-year-old girl had died. The real tragedy was that she'd never existed at all" (Lynch, 2001). These juxtapositions become springboards for broader discussions on online privacy ("World Wide," 2001), commentaries about Debbie Swenson's mental state and/or ethics ("Girl's Illness," 2001), and ruminations over the difficulties fluid Internet identities present for safety (Carroll, 2001; Senft, 2001). This dramatic reporting style effectively gathers readers' attention but necessarily narrows the scope of the story to focus on an individual's act of deceit. A few articles provide comments from members of the Kaycee community (e.g., Hafner, 2001), mostly as evidence of the emotional devastation wrought by Debbie Swenson, but none offer sustained commentary on how the community confronted the hoax and its aftermath. A critical rhetorical analysis of the community members' own statements picks up where these accounts leave off and offers insight into what may be an even more important issue for online citizenship: how the idea of "virtual community" is reconceived and enacted by community members in the wake [of] a disastrous event.

A Recipe for Deception?: Identity, Community, and Rhetoric in Cyberspace

Hoaxes may have a history as old as communication, but some hoaxes are better suited to particular media than others. How a technology provides opportunities for ambiguity in communication significantly impacts how identity is performed via that medium and, by extension, how identity deception can be carried out. Orson Welles' famous "War of the Worlds" broadcast, for example, likely would not have had the same shocking impact had it been aired as a television program because the most convincing element of the story, radio listeners' vivid imaginations, would have been dampened by television's over-determined visual cues. Although the Internet increasingly is becoming a visual medium, many online activities still require users' imaginations to fill in gaps and gloss over inconsistencies in their interactions, particularly the communicative exchanges made between ambiguously represented cyber-identities. With respect to the present analysis, in order to understand the impact the Kaycee Nicole hoax had on its blogging community, it is important first to consider the nature and function of both identity and community in cyberspace.

Identity and Authority Online

One of the most touted beliefs about Internet communication is that the medium strips away users' offline identities and leaves them free to reconstruct a tetherless online persona. This quality of performative ambiguity is the source for much of the optimism and skepticism surrounding the idea of virtual community. One's online persona frequently is discussed in terms of a potentially liberating performance within an Internet where "you can be yourself, against a duplicitous world in which you have to conform to the expectation of others" (Coyne, 1999, p. 4). Fluid identity is often cited as a mainstay of life on the Net, "hardwired within the very form of multiple-simultaneous online chat communication" (Waskul & Douglass, 1997, p. 394; see also McRae, 1997; Rheingold, 1993; Turkle, 1995; Warschauer, 2000). In a similar vein, the Internet has been characterized as an "identity laboratory" (Wallace, 1999, p. 48), a metaphor echoed in claims that "almost the sole purpose of chatrooms and MUDs is the construction of and experimentation with the user's identity" (Bolter, 2000, p. 23). Despite the commonality of this perspective, the meaning and function of identity experimentation are not agreed upon. The potential discordance between online and offline identity raises concerns regarding the "drawbacks of malleable persona" that ask users to consider that "if we couldn't see who we were talking to, how could we trust them?" (Dean, 2000, p. 10). While some maintain that the Internet allows them to escape into a more liberating world, others worry that the escape is into a world with even more duplicity and danger than the offline world.

Much of the tension concerning trust rests on an audience's ability to distinguish between "assessment signals" and "conventional signals" in online communication contexts (J. S. Donath, 1999, p. 32). Assessment signals are difficult to fake and are therefore taken to be trustworthy signifiers of a person's "true" identity. If a woman claiming to be a bodybuilder has bulging muscles, her body serves as an assessment signal authenticating her claim. A conventional signal is much easier to forge and therefore carries lower authority. If a woman claims to be a bodybuilder but her only proof is a bumper sticker that reads, "Bodybuilder Extraordinaire," people likely will not be convinced by that signal alone because it lacks authority. The difficulty presented by computer-based community forums like blogs is that they blur the boundary between assessment and convention signals and are limited in the types and amounts of signals that they make available to users. Proving or disproving the authenticity of an online signal becomes difficult. Just because someone has "Bodybuilder" as his or her screen name does not mean that he or she is or is not a bodybuilder, and this ambiguity creates dilemmas for assessing trust and credibility in online activities.

The Web, with its graphical interface, significantly increases the richness of online expression (Kollock & Smith, 1999) but also makes deception easier by allowing a deceiver to "authenticate" his or her message with links, pictures, and other Web-friendly signals that point an audience's mind in the desired direction (J. S. Donath, 1999, p. 50). A conventional signal can be given the appearance of an assessment signal by faking the appropriate signifiers, and the malleability of signifiers in a digital environment like the Web makes it difficult to establish one signifier as more authentic than another. Debbie Swenson was able to convince others that Kaycee was authentic by forging signifiers of her identity, such as posting pictures of a teenage girl and writing her blog posts in a teenager's voice. On the few occasions when Kaycee was required to speak on the phone, Debbie delivered a performance effective enough to fool even the *New York Times*.[4] These types of evidence count in Web communication because the medium does not readily allow for the use of more authoritative assessment signals. None of these signals may have been entirely convincing in and of themselves, but taken together they achieved the desired effect and convinced numerous people that Kaycee was really a very ill, rural Kansas teen who loved basketball and computers and needed some online friends. When it comes to making decisions about authenticity online, the standard seems to be more about consistency than absolute certainty. An online persona is deemed authentic if enough of its pieces seem to fit together.

It is important to highlight the aspect of audience assessment, for virtual identity is not the strict province of an offline individual carrying out the performance. Audiences are an important and active part in any online persona's development, even an inauthentic one. Blogging veterans consider audience interaction essential to a blogger's persona, noting that "The advice 'Write for yourself,' while appropriate for a self-help course, applies poorly to the Web. . . . You skip the step of requiring an editor and publisher, but no one is willing to skip the step of requiring an audience" (Clark, 2002, p. 63). The self "emerges in the process of interaction" (Waskul & Douglass, 1997, p. 382), a product of social interaction in that there is one who performs but there must also always be someone for whom the performance is given. Even anonymous identities are social constructs in that "anonymity requires an audience of at least one person" (Marx, 1999, p. 100). From these perspectives, online identity appears as a dialogic construct in that "Internet discourse constitutes the subject as the subject fashions him or herself, [and] individuals construct their identities in relation to ongoing dialogues, not as acts of pure consciousness" (Poster, 1997, p. 211). While this dialog maybe skewed in favor of the performer, identity performance is viable only if it is convincing to another participant, "presented and negotiated in an ongoing process of communication" (Waskul & Douglass, p. 387). Audiences authenticate an identity by assessing its performance within the context of the community, making identity an issue of rhetorical expression, debate, and evaluation. It is important to recognize, however, that these processes relate more to the acceptance of an identity than to its authenticity, for it is this gap between acceptance and authenticity that enabled Debbie to bring Kaycee into existence.

Rhetoric and Virtual Community

Scholarship on the relationship between rhetoric and community is too extensive to be reviewed comprehensively. What I discuss here are the ways in which this scholarship can assist in developing critical rhetorical readings of virtual community discourse. Technological advancements ushered in during the last century have made it clear that the idea of community in general increasingly is "conceptualized not in terms of physical proximity but in terms of social networks" (Kollock & Smith, 1999, p. 17), and that "computer networking, for better and for worse, has become part of this process of producing social spaces" (Saco, 2002, p. 199). This view should not imply, however, that virtual communities are thought of simply as "community + computers." Virtual community members perceive cyberspace "not as merely a series of interconnected computers but as a tangible place—a medium and environment that cannot be explained or reduced to its technological components alone" (Waskul & Douglass, 1997, p. 378). Participants in communities see cyber*space* more in terms of cyber*places* where they "have strong interpersonal feelings of belonging, being wanted, obtaining important resources, and having a shared identity" (Wellman, 2001, p. 40). This sense of place is particularly relevant for critical rhetorical inquiries, where the dispersed and transient nature of online interaction puts a unique focus on rhetoric's use in virtual community maintenance (Stone, 1994; Wellman & Gulia, 1999).

The strength of any community, whether online [or] offline, is founded on effective rhetorical communication. As Hogan (1998) explains, "Communities are living creatures, nurtured and nourished by rhetorical discourse . . . [and] unite around common life experiences or shared visions of the future—commonalities manifested in their rhetorical discourse" (p. 292). Rhetoric, through its capacity for "adjusting ideas to people and people to ideas" (Bryant, 1953, p. 413), gives meaning to communities and the identities that inform them. As is true of both the ancient Agora and the modern online community, rhetoric "takes as its practice daily participation in civic and political life" (Ono & Sloop, 2002, p. 7). Rhetoric is used in everyday settings to "giv[e] form to the vague and disordered flow of human experience. Rhetoric gives shape to social reality and, in so doing, makes sense of it" (Herman, 1999, p. 6). Through rhetoric, communities develop and adjust to changing conditions and memberships, enabling a random group of individuals to become a relatively coherent social and political body. As they join together, participants also come to understand that "the problem of community is, in significant measure, a rhetorical problem" (Hogan, 1998, p. 295). Virtual communities use rhetoric to carve out a place for themselves and to develop their own codes of ethics, articulations of shared interests, and visions of purposeful action (Sloop & Herman, 1998).

The rhetorical and social processes that inform all communities similarly relate to online interactions, and it is here that community intersects with identity on the Internet. Virtual communities are made, not populated. Users must work together, albeit not always peacefully, to negotiate between individual desires and communal needs. In order for a virtual community to develop, participants must "engag[e] in a constant effort to structure experience together and to establish order in conventions of discourse so that shared meanings are possible" (Wynn & Katz, 1997, p. 302). Communities develop over time in response to the emerging issues generated by the articulation of shared interests, even if the aim and pursuit of those interests are contested. In this way, Internet communities are "underdetermined," meaning that they are "open to practice; they do not direct agents into clear paths; they solicit instead social construction and cultural creation" (Poster, 2001, p. 17). The collaborative ethos necessary for community growth also helps to explain why, despite calls for heightened paranoia regarding Internet frauds and predators, researchers find that many Internet users seem willing to give their fellow users the benefit of the doubt on matters of trust, even in ambiguous situations (J. S. Donath, 1999, p. 31).

Dialogic tensions between self/other and persona/community drive online community interactions and establish the trust that binds members together. They also reveal the extent of the dilemma faced by community members when they suspect one of their own of being a hoaxer. If their suspicions are confirmed, they face the potential loss of not just an individual community member, but of the foundation of the community itself. If identity is dialogic, then a hoax implicates *all* community members, even if only marginally, as it was their mutual acceptance of the fraudulent persona that allowed the hoax to succeed. This consequence may help to explain why users who take a "serious" attitude toward online identity may not appreciate those users who see it as mere "play." As Waskul and Douglass (1997) explain, "Ultimately, it makes no difference whether a person intends a genuine or nongenuine self-enactment, whether interactions are playful or serious—in the final analysis, the meaning of the enterprise is established in the expressive–impressive dimensions of communication" (p. 391). Only if everyone agrees that online interactions are just "play" can the consequences of hoaxes and pranks be considered harmless fun. If others take these interactions seriously, however, and invest their real emotions in the community, then a hoax can have devastating effects, even in those situations where the perpetrator claims his or her actions were mere jest. As the Kaycee example demonstrates, even in online environments that privilege the authority of a single entity, such as the blog author, persons who become involved in that blogging community may develop attachments that they take seriously and will seek to maintain, rationalize, and, if necessary, defend.

A Tangled Web of Blame: Marginalization, Suspicion, and Trust

Debbie Swenson's admission that Kaycee was a fictional persona had a devastating, embarrassing, and immediate effect on her blogging community.[5] Randall van der Woning (2001), the Web developer who voluntarily hosted and maintained Kaycee's Web site, immediately removed the blog from the Web upon receiving Debbie's confession, saying that he "refused to support a lie for even one second longer." Though it caused much turbulence, the removal of her blog did not immediately destroy the community that had built up around Kaycee, nor did it resolve their crisis. Conversations among community members arose in a variety of other forums spread across the Internet, where Kaycee's authenticity was debated along with issues of online citizenship, trust, and identity. One participant seemed to recognize the significance of the event in commenting, "Blogging community, welcome to your first real scandal" (tweebiscuit, MetaFilter). That the Kaycee blog participants were willing, if not perhaps eager, to debate these community issues in public forums necessitated that they engage with other community members, curious eavesdroppers, and even a few party crashers who came to witness the aftermath, the culmination of which gave their discussions a broader scope and relevance to the Internet community as a whole.

As the community members engaged with each another and outside interjectors, a wide range of emotional reactions transformed into purposeful rhetorical stances. Those members who felt betrayed by Debbie developed logics for blaming her and insisted that the Internet be regarded as a place of distrust and skepticism. Those members who believed, in the brief period between Kaycee's "death" and Debbie's confession, that Kaycee had been real took the opposing perspective and attempted to rebut the arguments put forth by the skeptics. After Debbie's confession, they reworked their optimistic rhetoric into a generalized call to preserve an attitude of trust within online communities. Others professed an ambivalent attitude toward Kaycee's (non)existence and stated that whether or not she was real was immaterial, what mattered was that Kaycee's blog had brought virtual strangers together and fostered a sense of community spirit amongst the participants. They expressed their hopes that others online would keep this in mind before placing every claim made by every member of their community under a microscope. From a critical rhetorical perspective, these stances are compelling because the participants engaged in issues of communal status and marginality in which their ethical precepts were articulated and defended. Throughout this section, I discuss how community members allocated blame to Debbie Swenson for her role in the hoax, the skepticism that emerged as a response to her actions, and some community members' attempts to reclaim "trust" as a virtue of "good" citizenship in the wake of Debbie's hoax.

Marginalizing Debbie

The "Kaycee Nicole (Swenson) FAQ" admonishes its readers to "Remember: The Web isn't evil, evil people are evil" (Geitgey, 2001). But Debbie Swenson did not immediately come to symbolize the embodiment of evil within the community. In the brief period between the announcement of Kaycee's death and Debbie's confession, many community members defended Debbie against the charges of trickery made by members who posted their doubts about Kaycee's story. But once Debbie's confession and subsequent claim that "I am the only person who is to blame" (Swenson, 2001) made the rounds of the various Kaycee-related Websites, Debbie inevitably became the focal point for much of the community's rage, and people ceased defending her. Debbie's vilification, in fact, was the sole point of agreement shared by all community members, who quickly abandoned a dialogic view of identity and agreed that all fault did indeed rest with Debbie alone. There was not as much agreement, however, about what these events meant for the future of their community or for virtual communities in general. Some pointed to Debbie as the very reason why no one could be trusted online, others attempted to portray her as an exception to the general rule of trust, and still others sought to exorcise her completely from the discussion by focusing on the communal goodwill rather than Debbie's personal motives or actions.

If the community members disagreed over what Debbie's actions meant for the future of virtual communities, those members who expressed an opinion on the matter seemed certain that Debbie's actions were entirely of her own accord and motivation. None of the posters had met Debbie in person, but many had strong opinions about what kind of person she was: "It's pretty obvious that this person is extremely troubled, needs professional help and is likely to be mentally unstable right now" (y2kira, Powazek's Forum). The presumption of Debbie's mental instability practically was prerequisite for any commentary: "For whatever reason this woman said she did it for, she must have problems" (animoler, MetaFilter). Some used their negative assessment of Debbie to highlight their detective skills by pointing out that "when you photoshop photos to fit into the delusion you've perpetrated for almost 2 years, you fall into the decidedly not sane category" (zebra_monkey, MetaFilter). Others gave their marginalizing comments a considerably nastier edge. One poster vilified Debbie by writing, "This woman is a chronic liar, nothing she says is true. . . . What a horrible person, to hurt so many just to play her little game. Those who are willing to forgive her are to be commended, but she doesn't deserve their compassion" (Stephanie Dragon, Powazek's Forum). Another poster arrived at a far less sympathetic conclusion: "If this is a hoax, the perpetrator should die alone and unloved" (sjc, MetaFilter).

A few bloggers made efforts at offsetting their negative regard for Debbie with pro-community sentiments. In outlining his reasons for removing the Kaycee blog, van der Woning (2001) stated, "I do not see the value in promoting *anything* that was published when I know the mind behind it manipulated and used people for her [Debbie's] own agenda." His parental concern for the Kaycee community was echoed by another poster who explicitly made the distinction between "good" and "bad" community members via Debbie's marginalization: "Shame on 'Debbie' and who ever else was involved, but as for the rest of you, I still love you all!" (Mike Thomas, Powazek's Forum). These posts expressed an optimistic attitude toward their fellow community members, but they also made it clear that any and all blame began and ended

with Debbie and excused the other bloggers from having any role in the affair other than unwitting victim. No one questioned that Debbie should be marginalized; the debate was over what her marginalization signaled for the future of their community.

Debbie's marginalization revealed some important rhetorical tensions between virtual community and identity. Specifically, the attention given to Debbie and her presumed motives was not entirely consistent with the aforementioned theories that posited a dialogic view of virtual identity. When it came to Debbie's subjectivity, community members rhetorically negated the dialogic view of identity as a strategy for preserving their community and their own innocence. Debbie's actions needed to be seen as intentional and selfish in order for them to be seen as cruel. In order for this scapegoating to work, Debbie needed to be seen as the sole entity responsible for Kaycee, which meant that the community as a whole could no longer see itself as having participated dialogically in Kaycee's creation. Furthermore, in contrast to previous statements about virtual communities as individual-centered "experiments," the members of this community clearly indicated that they take the idea of virtual identity very seriously and that communal participation is more than just one person's "play," even if no harm was meant. This perspective resulted in community members rewriting Kaycee's interactions as Debbie's intentional manipulation of their emotions, an action that drew a clear and distinct line between Debbie/Kaycee and her interlocutors. Community members could not simultaneously be partners in Kaycee's construction *and* victims of Debbie's hoax, and so they chose the latter position as a means of preserving their own status within the community.

Debbie's marginalization rhetorically reasserted the concept of identity as "one per person," and any breach of this concept became an abomination and a betrayal. In this revised perspective, online identity is dialogic as long as one's intentions are true; false intentions excuse the community from being implicated as collaborators. Ironically, this claim actually reaffirmed the dialogic properties of identity for the remaining community members, for Debbie's marginalization required as much community participation as any other aspect of her blog. Debbie's marginalized subjectivity as cruel hoaxer became the vessel through which the other bloggers articulated their responses, and this new role for her was created through the community's participation in her vilification. One observer was attuned to this apparent contradiction, writing that s/he was fascinated by "a wad of cyber-entities debating the existence of another cyber-entity. A gathering of ephemeral avatars, most of whom remain unattributable to an avatar-master, trying to decide whether a deceased avatar's master followed it into the netherworld. . . . I'm watching a bunch of made-up people trying to decide if another made-up person's maker-upper is dead" (Opus Dark, MetaFilter). Interestingly, no one responded directly to this thread, preferring to continue the discussion in terms of Kaycee's (in)authenticity.

Even the normal conventions of Internet communication, such as the use of ambiguous screen names, were brought into service for Debbie's marginalization. Although all posters used screen names, some of which made it impossible to speculate as to the "true" identity of the poster, their discussion of Debbie made it clear that they considered their identities authentic online personae whereas Debbie's use of "Kaycee" was inauthentic. The community's view was that identity could be playful as long as it was also honest, and the Internet could be an "identity laboratory" as long as everyone was informed and gave consent. In order for their community to function optimally, identity needed to be dialogic *and* communal, meaning it must conform to what community members saw as the "rules" for interaction. By the Kaycee community's standards, their use of screen names was permissible because the intent was in keeping with communal rules, but Debbie's use of a fictional persona violated the community ethos because it used a disingenuous performance to snare their real sympathies.

The community concluded that although Kaycee was not real, Debbie's deception was. Marginalizing Debbie did more than find someone at whom fingers could be pointed; it served as catharsis and warrant for further discussions regarding identity and trust in online communities. Debbie's marginalization became an important, but not final, chapter in the history of their online community. Attributing deceptive motives to Debbie's actions allowed the community to negate her "experiment" while keeping the idea of their community intact long enough for participants to debate their disagreeing viewpoints.[6] Those members who urged extreme skepticism used Debbie as proof that blind trust is foolish when online, while the more optimistic posters used Debbie as an example of how a virtual community could cast out a bad apple before it spoils the barrel.

Everyone Is Suspect

Soon after suspicions were raised about Kaycee's authenticity, several community members joined in a kind of online scavenger hunt for "evidence" that could settle the question. Photographs of Kaycee were scrutinized, her blog was searched for inconsistencies and errors, and skeptics began posting their suspicions to the community. But before Debbie's confession validated their efforts, these members' actions were protested against by those within the community who still believed in Kaycee's authenticity. Some were "aghast at the nature of this thread—and [I] am very depressed at the amount of venom flying about. What would it take to convince you people?" (crankyrobot, MetaFilter). Another asked incredulously, "Debbie just buried her daughter, and is expected to provide proof to a bunch of insensitive buffoons?" (EricBrooksDotCom, MetaFilter). As "proof" of Kaycee's existence, several community members described their e-mail and phone conversations with her, although each admitted that they never had physical or face-of-face contact with her (e.g., bwg, MetaFilter; Chazio, MetaFilter; halcyon, MetaFilter; IndianaSweetie, MetaFilter; kaya, MetaFilter). The basic disagreement with the skeptics' position was that their "fact finding" cheapened Kaycee's memory and threatened the community's foundation by calling into question its dearly departed centerpiece. A concerned poster summarized this sentiment by writing, "I think this thread really underlines the paranoia and distrust of people on the Internet" (bargle, Metafiler). The sole fact revealed through this inquisition, the offended grievers argued, was not Kaycee's non/existence but the insensitivity of the skeptics who questioned her existence.

Despite these protests, many within the community still favored an investigation into Kaycee's authenticity and lauded the skeptics' willingness to pose such questions. The supporters' arguments reconfigured the investigation from a specific inquiry about an individual into a political position on virtual community involvement. One member wrote, "I feel more comfortable knowing that our online peers are assertive enough to debate this openly. It's a better alternative to blindly believing or anonymously spreading rumours behind

kv, MetaFilter). Other posters con-
to sympathize with people who say
awful, or that we are awful for simply
about the situation. This is an open forum
king about someone that put themselves in the
public eye. It doesn't hurt anyone, and it shouldn't
have any affect on anyone who is 'grieving'" (justgary, MetaFilter). Somewhat ironically, the supporters of the skeptical inquiry argued that by
banding together to disprove Kaycee's existence,
they in fact were enacting the ideals of community cooperation. Such was the opinion shared
by those members who viewed the situation as an
"intense and impressive community investigation"
in which "a lot of people worked hard to uncover
the truth" (Geitgey, 2001). Several posters added
their support to those "brave enough to voice their
doubts" (mechaieh, Powazek's Forum). Another
wrote, "I'm amazed to see how much the online
community has come together over this, and just
how much investigating and reporting some people have done. It's incredible! It makes me happy"
(~y2kira, Powazek's Forum). A few posters noted
that they had little interest in Kaycee *per se,* but
found the overall discussion illuminating: "What
we have here is basically a perfectly legitimate public discussion of a purposely public life, touching on
issues of trust, privacy, and community" (kindall,
MetaFilter). Although their efforts struck at the
center of their community, the skeptics and their
supporters rhetorically reinvented their efforts as
signs of community strength.

Following Debbie's confession, the skepticism
mutated from debates over specific pieces of evidence to a general discussion of the relationship
between trust, computers, and community. Many
of the investigators were emboldened by Debbie's
admission, which they took as validation of their
efforts. Some rearticulated their vaunted technical
knowledge as a kind of transcendent Web savvy
and boasted that they had known all along that
Kaycee was a hoax, that the clues were completely
obvious, and [that] everyone else was a dupe for
not having been more suspicious. "I knew after a
couple of paragraphs it was a joke," bragged one
commentator (Molly Campbell, Netslave), and
another mocked the "stupid people [who] are
taken in by a pretty picture" (S.Jensen, Netslave).
Others applied their savvy more philosophically
and advised that "the community of the 'web' is
nothing but a collection of personalities be they
fake or real" (10931, Netslave). Some articulated
their skepticism with an aura of weary detachment: "I treat everything on the net as possible

fiction, and I don't allow myself to get emotionally involved in anything I know soley [*sic*] by
the net" (justgary, MetaFilter). Others warned,
"Don't believe ANYTHING you READ on the
Internet" (A_fool_and_their_money, Netslave),
and quipped, "The Internet: Connecting stupidity with technology" (Anonymous, Netslave). Dis-
enchanted participants claimed that the episode
"illustrated a clear danger of the Internet for many
by saying that someone 'met' Kaycee on a Web site.
You can't 'meet' anyone on the Internet. The Kaycee tale may be instructive for people who think
they know someone through cyberspace communication alone" (Imhoff, 2001, p. G6). These comments clearly sought to establish a hierarchy of
Internet intelligence: If other netizens were more
like the skeptics, then they would not have been
fooled by Debbie. By extension, they implied that
in order for a community to work everyone must
adopt the cool skepticism of these "Internet elite."

These statements illustrate how the Kaycee
hoax became a means for many bloggers to distinguish themselves within the Internet community either by demonstrating their detective skills,
boasting about their own intellectual superiority,
or relating anecdotes about other Internet cons
to show that they had "been around." For these
skeptics, "trust" was a sign of naïveté and demonstrated lack of Internet know-how. Their rhetoric
turned the tables on the members who previously
had chastised them for daring to doubt Kaycee's
authenticity. Now it was the optimistic "believers"
who were bad community members for trying to
halt the investigation and for being blind to the
realities of Internet life. One skeptic chided the
"believers" by saying, "The fact that people are
willing to blithely ignore 'truth' because they were
emotionally involved in the story is really sick"
(zebra_monkey, MetaFilter). Debbie's confession
not only validated the skeptics' efforts, but served
as confirmation that the best protection for bloggers was to be highly suspicious of others and what
they say. One commentator summed up this attitude by writing, "Let Kaycee Nicole serve a lesson
to us all: on the Net, a little paranoia goes a long
way" (Stamper, 2001).

Questioning Kaycee developed rhetorically into
a generalized policy of distrust and self-policing.
One poster commented, "I think a self-policing
community is important. It means that people
feel comfortable asking hard questions about
emotional issues. People are willing to fact-check.
People are willing to hold others accountable to
what they say" (Roe, Powazek's Forum). This atti-

tude was supported by those who asserted that "the fact that it's self-policing makes it that much more trustworthy" (Register, Powazek's Forum). It is interesting to note, however, that self-policing in this context was not discussed as an individually internalized disciplining, but as the communal "self" that would suspect, investigate, and then reject or validate the statements made by individual community members. For advocates of this approach, pervasive suspicion was simply a means for preserving what were considered to be the higher-order principles of open debate and inquiry, even if the target was someone within their own community. On her own blog site, one community member evinced this position by lambasting the "mob" of anti-investigation supporters who sent her threatening e-mail after she questioned Kaycee's authenticity. She wrote, "It wasn't enough that Kaycee supporters believed in her—they had to quash anyone who suggested, in any way, that her story might not be true. . . . Were you one of the bullies? Did you help create an atmosphere of intolerance? Do you preach about the wonder of personal expression on the web, and at the same time try to silence anyone who says something you don't agree with?" (Thomas, 2001).

The skeptical faction of Kaycee bloggers promoted suspicion as a positive, democratic aspect of virtual community in that everyone had the right to be suspicious of everyone else. Although the ideology informing this definition of a democratic community was itself highly suspect, several members of the blogging community voiced their support for a self-policing policy, both as it related to the Kaycee forum and as a general ethos for virtual community. From a rhetorical standpoint, the skeptics' approach to online community may have been persuasive because it took a complex and troubling issue and divided members into two distinct camps, provided a venue for the two sides to engage one another, and, perhaps most importantly, gave one side a chance to claim superiority over the other. At the very least, a community ethos based on skepticism provided some members with a reason to continue to participate in the Kaycee community, even if the resulting course of action amounted to little more than the pandemic scrutinizing of each others' statements. Although clearly not an utopian model of community, we cannot ignore the fact that this perspective received support within the community by participants who seemed satisfied by the debates it generated and optimistic about the outcome it promised.

(Re)Building Communities of Trust in the Shadow of Suspicion

Debbie's marginalization served as the basis for a second rhetorical articulation of virtual community that expressed almost exactly the opposite attitude toward "trust" than the one advanced by the skeptics. Debbie's actions were still vilified by these participants, but they maintained an optimistic appreciation for what they viewed as an open and inviting sense of online community. For them, the revelation of Kaycee's nonexistence came to mean that even though Debbie was a "bad" community member, her actions did not invalidate the "real" concern and emotions that had been invested in the community, nor did they need to abandon their belief in the concept of "trust." They argued that the dynamics of online community are such that the worth of the community never rests on the actions of a single member but on the overall, shared effect generated by the members as a whole. Their community remained valid as long as people came to it with good intentions. Rhetorically, Debbie remained guilty within this perspective but her marginalization led to the exoneration of all other community members, reaffirmed their commitment to "trust" as a foundational principle, and allowed them to reach out to others in their virtual community.

One way in which "community" was rearticulated according to this logic was by drawing a distinction between the "real" emotions of the community members and the fraudulent emotions of the hoaxer. Debbie's marginalized subjectivity was used to signify "evil" in order to illuminate a positive juxtaposition between the "good" and "bad" intentions that validated their trusting attitudes. "In the end," explained one blogger, "the only thing I *know* was real is the love that people gave to someone who, it turns out, was manipulating them. And that's a shame. But the great thing about love is, there's always more to give" (dmp, Powazek's Forum). Another poster also praised fellow community members by denuding Debbie's falsehoods: "This has brought the blogging community together. It has torn us apart. It has allowed us to trust, and it has torn the trust down. . . . We were betrayed, but at least we came together" (GeekMeltdown, Powazek's Forum). These posts rhetorically transformed deception into affirmations of communal trust and kinship. After summarizing the hoax, one commentator concluded that "It's important not to lose faith in everyone as the result of a few disturbed

that the vast majority of people I
.re being truthful with me" (Powa-
. 148). These statements clarified the
between the skeptics and the optimists.
.ere the skeptics understood Debbie as typical of the untrustworthiness inherent to Internet
communication, the optimists used Debbie as the
exceptional case that proved the general rule.
Trust, as defined through the optimists' rhetoric,
was an overall capacity functioning within virtual
communities and could weather the deceit of a
single malcontent.

As part of their rhetorical reappropriation of
trust as a civic virtue online, optimists embraced
the hoax and acknowledged that they had been
deceived. This approach left these bloggers vulnerable to charges of naïveté, but also enabled
them to claim that they were now wiser and that
their belief in trust was stronger because they had
endured this trial by fire. Posters insisted that
the hoax "actually renews my faith in humanity,
because a whole bunch of strangers were moved to
care" (Sharon, Powazek's Forum). This sentiment
surfaced as a theme in several posts: "I'm glad people were touched by Kaycee's story. They should
be. You can call it rank sentimentality if you like,
but it shows that people have a capacity to sympathize and to care. That should be a vital part
of our lives" (tranquileye, Metafilter). These posts
further defined trust as an essential, if occasionally abused, quality that enabled communities to
grow stronger and more assured. This stance was
effective rhetorically because it offered bloggers a
way to acknowledge their deception without having to change their behavior or admit that their
optimism was naive, which allowed them to reaf-
firm their ideology within the community. As one
long-time Kaycee blogger proclaimed, "I followed
my heart. Sometimes that requires an optomism
[sic] tax. It stings to pay it, but in the long run,
it's a bargain. . . . I'd rather be duped 100 times
than shut off my compassion" (Halcyon, Powazek's
Forum). Such optimism created a rhetorical means
for the admission of gullibility to become a badge
of honor identifying the blogger as a compassionate individual committed to the transcendent ideals of virtual community.

Not surprisingly, these statements drew fire
from the skeptics. In response to the bloggers who
belittled their optimism, pro-trust community
members challenged the assumption that wholesale suspicion was the only way to guarantee a safe
community environment and sought to reward
optimism by arguing that its benefits were worth

the risks: "I want, I *need*, to still have faith in
humanity. And I think I'm still willing to keep
that faith, despite the risks" (Noah, Powazek's
Forum). Another wrote, "I, too feel used . . . [but] I
do not regret having faith in [Kaycee]. It is always
better to have faith than to be cynical. That's how
I feel" (Redgie, Powazek's Forum). Some optimists
challenged the skeptics' ideology on the grounds
that, although flaws had been revealed in Kaycee's
story, there could be no doubt of the community
members' intentions: "The important thing to
remember is that the emotions that Kaycee's blog
evoked in people are real. And you can't take that
compassion and that generosity away from the
people who gave it; it's still there" (kristina, Powazek's Forum).

As with the skeptics, specific concerns about
the role technology played in the hoax surfaced in
the optimists' rhetoric. Some addressed the impact
of the scandal within the context of blogging
technology itself. Their comments recognized the
influence of technology on identity formation and
the omnipresent possibility for misuse, but posited
communal interests and emotional connection
as transcendent qualities that exist apart from
any particular medium: "This saga isn't going to
make me stop trusting what I read on the web, the
relationships I form here, because what enables
trust, compassion and love is the message, not the
medium. . . . I found out a friend died recently,
because her daughter called up and told me. I do
not hate the phone. I hate the fact that she died"
(Meg, Powazek's Forum). Sentiments such as this
tend to oversimplify the distinctions between
communication technologies and how people use
them to communicate, but they fit the general
tenor of the pro-trust claims in that they refocused
attention on the relationships between community members rather than the medium through
which those relationships were formed. Other
posters were even more buoyant and argued that
the emotional support demonstrated by sympathetic members of the Kaycee community proved
that the Internet was a caring place. "Everyone
allowed themselves to feel," proclaimed one sup-
porter. "They connected not just with 'Kaycee'
but with each other. For those brief moments the
idea of cold, plastic space was diminished. That
was real. That existed" (Peter, Powazek's Forum).
Others concurred that good people made for a
good medium: "The memories I'll take from this?
Friends pulling together to honor a spirit that
showed great courage, great compassion, and a
great hope for the future. Good, real people who

are trying, hard, to make a new 'medium' work" (Dominik, 2001).

Perhaps the most confrontational rebuttal advanced by the optimists was that the skeptics' investigation had missed the point of virtual community altogether: "Sure it might not be real. Does it really matter? If nothing else, the story of Kaycee's death was a moving experience for some people" (moz, MetaFilter). Another asserted, "Whether you believe Kaycee is real or not . . . , absolutely *no one* can deny that she brought a great amount of hope and inspiration to many, *many* people" (Noah, MetaFilter). One poster critiqued the skeptics by making a value comparison of the "truths" revealed through the skeptics' investigation and the "truths" that emerged through the optimists' defense: "I feel like picking apart related websites, scrutinizing post times and examining meta tags is somehow beside the point. . . . Reflecting on how this has made a huge 'community' pull together and applying that energy to other causes, even on an individual basis, could make the 'truth' beside the point" (jennaratrix, MetaFilter). Advocates of the communal trust perspective attempted to reverse the skeptics' notion of healthy suspicion by deriding its supposed benefit to the community. Those members who spent their time "picking apart" Websites in order to disprove some claim did so for selfish motives, whereas a "good" community member used trust to advance the goals of the entire community.

Through these arguments, "trust" became a rhetorical vessel used to distinguish and evaluate the types of communal activity that emerged in response to Kaycee's death and Debbie's confession. The optimists valued their idea of trust because it allowed them to argue that positive intentions were more important than negative consequences. It is important to remember, however, that this articulation of trust was predicated on Debbie's permanent exile from the Kaycee community. In other words, in order for the optimists' definitions of trust and community to come to fruition, they needed to portray Debbie as the antithesis of all these values. This approach meant that even within the most pro-trust elements of the Kaycee community, a healthy amount of distrust and suspicion circulated, albeit localized to a particular individual. When Debbie insisted that her actions were "not done for any reason other than sharing the love for life they [cancer victims] gave to those they loved," and that she "regret[ed] any pain I caused but I do not regret putting their thoughts out to be read" (Swenson, 2001), the

rhetorical foundation of the optimists' concep of virtual community necessitated that her words be read as an insincere plea for forgiveness rather than as a testament to emotional sharing, despite the striking similarity between Debbie's words and the optimists' own rhetoric. In order for trust to be vindicated, Debbie had to be absolutely and irreconcilably guilty and never allowed to claim that her misguided intentions were more important than the consequences of her deception. Her ascribed position as banished Other effectively trumped all other readings of her confession. Debbie's marginalization, despite the claims made by the skeptics and optimists, demonstrates that the distinction between the two community factions was more an issue of degree than strict separation. The skeptics advocated suspicion of all community members whereas the optimists implied that almost everyone could be trusted, but each agreed that at least one member, Debbie, had to remain "outside" in order for their community to overcome the crisis.

This apparent contradiction in the optimists' position may account for why not everyone was convinced that a presumption of trust could be salvaged simply by voicing support for it, and some in the optimists' camp took an even harder line against the skeptics and Debbie. These bloggers expressed their pleasure in seeing the community come together during the crisis, but warned about the consequences a "suspect everyone" attitude would have for the idea of virtual community and for blogs' ability to function as arenas for social support. Their argument was not only that a suspicious attitude "missed the point" of community but that a pervasive attitude of suspicion caused as much damage to the community as the hoaxer it sought to expose. Posters writing from this perspective saved their harshest words for the investigators and linked Debbie's deception with the "rabid fascination and investigation that followed" (Grohol, 2001). Debbie's actions were hurtful enough, they claimed, and scrutinizing her and others' posts only compounded the problem: "The truth is, had the online community not investigated the matter as thoroughly as they did, it is unlikely anyone would have been hurt by Kaycee's 'death.' . . . It is for the sheer sake of curiosity and uncovering the 'truth' . . . that the community brought the hurt upon itself" (Grohol, 2001). Refuting the claim that the investigative efforts brought the community together, their argument distributed the blame for the crisis between Debbie and the skeptics and implied that the investiga-

.rdless of their intent, ultimately .aging to the community than the .overed.

.s who advocated this position were con- .ed not only with this particular case but also with the ramifications of distrust for the blogging community in general. They feared that the escalating scrutiny demonstrated by the skeptics would create a slippery slope of suspicion that would needlessly undermine authentic blogs' abilities to generate social support for their members. In their estimation, the real consequence of the Kaycee Nicole Swenson saga was that too many blog readers would adopt a skeptical attitude and assume that every claim of illness and every request for sympathy were inherently spurious, and that it was more important for community members to find flaws in such stories than to listen sympathetically. The broad adoption of this attitude would in effect silence the voices of people in real pain who use the Internet to reach out to others. One concerned poster commented, "The thing that bothers me about this kind of hoax is that, will others think that I'm a phoney, too, if I should publish a blog or journal or whatever? Or will people basically believe first and question later?" (splash, Forums@Grohol.com). Describing his spouse's blog detailing her battles with breast cancer, one observer sympathized with these worries by saying, "The story of the despicable Ms. Swenson deflates me a bit. I imagine how the wonderful people who wrote to me would have felt if our story had been a hoax" (M. Donath, 2001, p. G11).

These community members rhetorically linked the concept of trust not to suspicion but, rather, to a sympathetic understanding of the Internet as an arena for coping with illness and tragedy, even if some used the technology for selfish and deceptive purposes. As one member explained, "Those of us who do put our lives online build a trust with those who read our words. Every single time one of those hoaxes . . . come[s] to light, those of us who are honest and sincere are hurt" (Sandy, MetaFilter). Although critical of the skeptics' investigative efforts and their underlying motives, these bloggers were sympathetic to those members who had been deceived. Their argument did not ask community members to abandon common sense but to remain open to the possibility that many, if not most, blogs were authentic. Ironically, this sentiment was expressed most eloquently by the investigative journalist credited with being the first to have raised doubts about Kaycee's authenticity, and who herself maintained a blog detailing her

own battles with a chronic disease. Her concern was for

> People who have journals and blogs too, and people who are all getting hate mail, and skeptic mail doubting every single world [sic] they say, examining every inch of their journal or blog, and have lost their ability to be open and honest dealing with their disease online. . . . I can't say I'm thrilled that some poor kid is deleting his mail unread because no one believes him anymore. Then again, I can't blame people for being extremely suspicious right now. . . . I'm angry at Debbie Swenson, for stealing my tongue. (Mitchell, 2001)

Although careful to sympathize with the community members who were misled by Debbie, Mitchell's comments are most sympathetic to those whom she regards as truly deserving of sympathy and for whom the Internet may be the most accessible means for communicating with others. Shifting the grounds of debate to this notion of sympathy and communal goodwill transforms the issue under contention into a matter of silencing all authentic pleas for compassion instead of exposing a single fraud.

Advocates of communities founded on trust rather than suspicion argued that theirs was the better means for securing a space for authentic voices who wished to use the Internet to share their meaningful experiences and seek companionship and comfort from others. Their position was problematic, however, because it did not address directly the concerns of members who did not want to be "duped" and were not content to file their betrayal under "live and learn." Although trust advocates convincingly enumerated the harms that unchecked skepticism could create in an online community, more practical approaches to the problems of anonymity and trust remained unaddressed. What was offered instead was akin to a Golden Rule of Virtual Community: "Trust in others as you would want to be trusted." Although noble, this approach was problematic because it hyperpersonalized community issues, such that any questioning of a participant's identity would be viewed as a personal attack against an individual. Bloggers adhering to this pro-trust approach would be placed in the difficult position of having to accept all personae as authentic or risk being labeled cold-hearted skeptics. But this all-or-none approach was undermined by the pro-trust members' own assertions that a successful community must stem from the authentic goodwill of its participants. Unfortunately, nothing beyond personal anecdotes [was] given by the optimists as a means for understanding how trust could be gauged in online community interactions. Bloggers who followed the optimists' community-through-trust arguments and personal examples were left with a better understanding of the relationship between virtual community and authenticity, but were just as likely to find themselves back at square one when the next Kaycee came along.

Summary and Implications

When the Internet was little more than a few networked computer terminals shared by a handful of computer scientists, simply having access to the network at all told users a great deal about the likely identity of the person on the other end of the modem. Now that the Internet population has grown much larger and more diverse, these initial assumptions are no longer viable. We are left pondering how it is that we can invent something as marvelous as the Internet yet continually fail to arrive at a common definition of "community." This hubristic frustration has been discussed as a kind of "technoromanticism," where "the technologies that support virtual communities . . . imply a certain self exaltation or conceit on the part of humankind, a presumption that we can have total control or omnipotence" (Coyne, 1999, p. 4). Stories like Kaycee's serve as apt examples of technoromanticism's Frankenstein-like twist and admonish us to remember that the power to create does not translate directly into the power to control. Given the immensity and diversity of the Internet, it may be more practical to abandon the dream of control and focus more on the contingent circumstances that bring users and crises together online, and explore how people can, do, and must use rhetorical language to adapt and respond to the demands of their online communities.

The Kaycee Nicole Swenson saga exemplifies several challenges facing Internet communities today and the role rhetoric plays in their development. It also reveals some pitfalls and lingering problems which netizens and communication scholars alike should continue to explore. In contrast to many popular press reports, we find that virtual communities do not always end at the act of deception but instead struggle with their problems and attempt to make sense of crises while developing and debating future courses of action. The Kaycee community took the issues of identity and community quite seriously, demonstrated

by their passionate debates over the usefulness of anonymity, the role of trust, the obligations individuals have to their virtual communities, and the consequences of their proposals for future communal relations. In acknowledging their use of rhetoric to work through their crisis, however, we should not be too quick to praise them simply for discussing these issues nor to scold them for not having reached a definite conclusion. These questions are too important and the issues too complex to expect a tidy ending. Nevertheless, it is important to recognize and seek to understand how the Kaycee community members argued toward their respective solutions.

The participants in the Kaycee community debates never resolved their arguments or formally concluded their discussions. The Kaycee community is now largely abandoned; most of the message forums are inactive and the bloggers have moved on to other sites, topics, and controversies. And yet, from a critical rhetorical standpoint, the decline of the community proves instructive. The picture that emerges from the rhetoric of the Kaycee story is one of concerned advocates in a virtual community creating and articulating a variety of complex arguments and experiencing great difficulty reaching a consensus about the meaning of an event that brought them together. The Kaycee community ultimately fell apart not because of irresolvable problems inherent to the technology or because Debbie Swenson spoiled the Internet for the other users, but because the community members were unable to make their rhetorical arguments purposeful and community oriented. Theirs were passionate rhetorics, but rhetorics without a common *telos*. Many arguments were made, but it was difficult to find the common purpose that could have led to a collaborative revisioning of their community. Agreements were short lived and generally unsympathetic to opposing views, giving only terse acknowledgment to others' feelings before quickly devolving into divisive harangues about compassion, trust, and sociotechnical savvy. The most contentious postings were those in which individual posters narcissistically held themselves out as champions of the community, either because of their advanced technological know-how or their ability to empathize with the "true" suffering of deserving bloggers. Such posturing made it difficult, if not impossible, to see the common ground that existed between the different members' stances. Polarizing rhetoric made community issues a matter of personal pride and ultimately closed off the

.ch side's stated desire to pro-
..cratic vision of virtual commu-
.. claiming that the goals the various
. pursued were meritless, but that the way
which they pursued these goals compounded
their problems and hindered their progress. The
community members may have had more success
had they recognized that identification must be
"logically prior to persuasion" (Charland, 1987,
p. 133). If members of an online community in
crisis are serious about reestablishing their common interests and repairing their communal foundation, they should seek to articulate better what
they desire an online community to be *before* they
engage in debates over why it should be that way.
Particularly in the discursive realms of cyberspace,
community pursuits can be supported only by the
pillars of shared interests.

The Kaycee Nicole Swenson story—as told
through the hoax, its aftermath, and the tensions
that arose between the skeptics and optimists—
illustrates that rhetoric is very much an active
and important part of virtual communities facing crises. Those persons who would dismiss the
prospects of online community negate the time,
energy, and effort these members put into debating
the issues confronting them and miss an opportunity to observe how community is enacted in the
everyday activities of this still new and developing social environment. Though this particular
community was unable to reach a mutually agree-
able resolution, it is encouraging to recognize
that the ways in which these bloggers debated
trust, authority, and community demonstrated an
awareness among Internet users of the seriousness
of these issues with respect to both the technology involved and the idea of online citizenship.
Internet culture, on the level of community interaction, is showing signs of maturing into a complex and dynamic communication space, "warts
and all." Communication scholars would do well
to continue to investigate how online participants
negotiate this space, their identities, and their
respective desires as they work to transform virtual
communities from playful experiments into fully-
realized social settings.

NOTES

1. A "blog" is defined as "an easily updated Web site
that works as an online daybook, consisting of links
to interesting items on the Web, spur-of-the-moment
observations and real-time reports on whatever captures
the blogger's attention" (Levy, 2002, p. 52). Blogs are
an amalgam of Web portals and personal opinions for
public consumption (Mead, 2002). Their participatory
nature and ease of use have made blogs a popular Web
attraction, with an estimated 2.4 to 2.9 million active
blogs as of June 2003 (Greenspan, 2003). In a typical
blog, one user or group is responsible for providing the
main content, but readers from anywhere on the Web
may post their own comments in blog message boards
and chat rooms, or continue a conversation across distinct blogs by linking to different threads and/or separate Web pages, thus creating a blogging community
around common themes more than a common location.
For thorough discussions of user interactivity as constitutive of online community, see Connery (1997) and
Poster (1997; 2001, pp. 171–188).

2. For comprehensive summaries of the Kaycee
Nicole Swenson saga, see Geitgey (2001), Lynch (2001),
and van der Wonig (2001).

3. Two notable exceptions are Dibble's "A Rape in
Cyberspace" (1994) and Stone's critique of "The Cross-
Dressing Psychiatrist" (1995). Both accounts discuss
community reactions to deception, but tend to focus
more on the ramifications of deception for individuals
rather than for communities as a whole.

4. The *New York Times* interviewed Kaycee for an
article on virtual communities. The *Times* published
a correction to its story after the Kaycee hoax was
revealed ("Editor's Note," 2001, p. A2).

5. The community postings discussed in the following sections are culled from several blogs, Web sites, and
message boards that shared a common interest in the
Kaycee hoax. These postings were publicly accessible
(i.e., there were no subscription charges or other membership barriers to reading and posting to these sites).
For the sake of efficiency and cohesion, my citations for
these postings consist of the screen name used by the
poster and the forum from which it came. The URLs for
these forums are:

Forums@Grohol.com: http://forums.psychcentral.
    com/showflat.php?Cat=&Number=5&page=0&
    rview=collapsed& sb=5&o=&fpart=1
Netslave: http://www.netslaves.com/messages/
    pg-message_redirect.asp?id=9905649690&to
    pic=990564969
Powazek's Forum: http://www.powazek.com/zoom/
    log/archive/00000058.shtml
MetaFilter: http://www.metafilter.com/comments.
    mefi/7819

6. From the existing information, it appears that
Debbie has not attempted to contact the groups directly
(i.e., using her identifiable screen name) following her
posted confession, although she may have made contact
and/or posted using an alternate screen name. Even so,
Debbie's participation (or lack thereof) is not requisite
to her marginalization because the community has publicly stated that she is not welcome in any capacity.

REFERENCES

Bolter, J. D. (2000). Identity. In T. Swiss (Ed.), *Unspun: Key concepts for understanding the World Wide Web* (pp. 17–29). New York: New York University Press.

Bryant, D. C. (1953). Rhetoric: Its functions and its scope. *Quarterly Journal of Speech, 39,* 401–424.

Carroll, J. (2001, June 5). The sad yet untrue story of Kaycee. *San Francisco Chronicle,* p. B10.

Charland, M. (1987). Constitutive rhetoric: The case of the *Peuple Québécois. Quarterly Journal of Speech, 73,* 133–150 [reprinted in this volume].

Clark, J. (2002). Deconstructing "You've got blog." In J. Rodzvilla (Ed.), *We've got blog: How weblogs are changing our culture* (pp. 57–68). Cambridge, MA: Perseus.

Connery, B. A. (1997). IMHO: Authority and egalitarian rhetoric in the virtual coffeehouse. In D. Porter (Ed.), *Internet culture* (pp. 161–180). New York: Routledge.

Coyne, R. (1999). *Technoromanticism: Digital narrative, holism, and the romance of the real.* Cambridge, MA: MIT Press.

Dean, J. (2000). Community. In T. Swiss (Ed.), *Unspun: Key concepts for understanding the World Wide Web* (pp. 4–16). New York: New York University Press.

Dibbell, J. (1994). A rape in cyberspace. In M. Dery (Ed.), *Flame wars: The discourse of cyberculture* (pp. 237–261). Durham, NC: Duke University Press.

Dominik, J. P. (2001, May 21). I have a confession to make. Retrieved June 8, 2002, from http://jdominik.rearviewmirror.org/2001/20010521.html.

Donath, J. S. (1999). Identity and deception in the virtual community. In M. A. Smith & P. Kollock (Eds.), *Communities in cyberspace* (pp. 29–59). New York: Routledge.

Donath, M. (2001, June 14). Real life, real emotion. *New York Times,* p. G11.

Dunne, S. (2001, May 28). The short life of Kaycee Nicole. Retrieved March 30, 2002, from http://media.guardian.co.uk/Print/0,3858,4193662,00.html.

Editor's note. (2001, May 31). *New York Times,* p. A2.

Geitgey, A. (2001). The Kaycee Nicole (Swenson) FAQ. Retrieved June 7, 2002, from http://rootnode.org/article.php?sid=26.

Girl's illness was web hoax. (2001, May 25). Retrieved March 30, 2002, from http://cjonline.com/stories/052601/kan_webhoax.shtml.

Greenspan, R. (2003, July 23). Blogging by the numbers. *Cyberatlas.* Retrieved July 23, 2003, from http://cyberatlas.internet.com/big_picture/applications/article/0,,1301_2238831,00.html.

Grohol, J. M. (2001). Deconstructing Kaycee. Retrieved June 5, 2002, from http://psychcentral.com/blogs/kaycee.htm.

Hafner, K. (2001, May 31). A beautiful life, an early death, a fraud exposed. *New York Times,* p. G1.

Herman, A. (1999). *The "better angels" of capitalism: Rhetoric, narrative, and moral identity among men of the American upper class.* Boulder, CO: Westview Press.

Hogan, J. M. (1998). Conclusion: Rhetoric and the restoration of community. In J. M. Hogan (Ed.), *Rhetoric and community: Studies in unity and fragmentation* (pp. 292–302). Columbia: University of South Carolina Press.

Imhoff, E. F. (2001, June 7). Exposing the Web's limits. *New York Times,* p. G6.

Jordan, F. (2001, October 20). Urban legends. *Loveland Daily Reporter-Herald,* p. B1.

Jordan, J. W. (2000). Where politicians fear to tread: Advertising for Internet security. *Journal of Communication Inquiry, 24,* 292–311.

Kollock, P., & Smith, M. A. (1999). Communities in cyberspace. In M. A. Smith & P. Kollock (Eds.), *Communities in cyberspace* (pp. 3–25). New York: Routledge.

Levy, S. (2002, May 20). Will blogs kill the old media? *Newsweek,* p. 52.

Lynch, D. (2001, May 30). Not dead: Beautiful cancer "victim" only in mind's eye. *ABCNews.com.* Retrieved May 31, 2001, from http://abcnews.go.com/sections/scitech/WiredWomen/wiredwomen010530.html.

Marx, G. T. (1999). What's in a name?: Some reflections on the sociology of anonymity. *The Information Society, 15,* 99–112.

McKerrow, R. (1989). Critical rhetoric: Theory and praxis. *Communication Monographs, 56,* 91–111 [reprinted in this volume].

McRae, S. (1997). Flesh made word: Sex, text and the virtual body. In D. Porter (Ed.), *Internet culture* (pp. 73–86). New York: Routledge.

Mead, R. (2002). You've got blog. In J. Rodzvilla (Ed.), *We've got blog: How weblogs are changing our culture* (pp. 47–56). Cambridge, MA: Perseus.

Medhurst, M. J. (1998). Martial decision making: MacArthur, Inchon, and the dimensions of rhetoric. In J. M. Hogan (Ed.), *Rhetoric and community: Studies in unity and fragmentation* (pp. 145–166). Columbia: University of South Carolina Press.

Mitchell, S. (2001, May 24). The Debbie effect. Retrieved June 7, 2002, from http://www.anywhere-beyond.com/2001/0501/052401.html.

Ono, K. A., & Sloop, J. M. (2002). *Shifting borders: Rhetoric, immigration, and California's proposition 187.* Philadelphia, PA: Temple University Press.

Poster, M. (1997). Cyberdemocracy: Internet and the public sphere. In D. Porter (Ed.), *Internet culture* (pp. 201–218). New York: Routledge.

Poster, M. (2001). *What's the matter with the Internet?* Minneapolis: University of Minnesota Press.

Powazek, D. M. (2002). *Design for community: The art of connecting real people in virtual places.* Indianapolis, IN: New Riders.

Rheingold, H. (1993). *The virtual community: Homesteading on the electronic frontier.* Reading, MA: Addison-Wesley.

). The sad story of Kaycee, can-
.. *Chicago Sun-Times*, p. 11.
*Cybering democracy: Public space and
.et.* Minneapolis: University of Minnesota
.s.

chiappa, E. (2003). *Defining reality: Definitions and the politics of meaning.* Carbondale: Southern Illinois University Press.

Senft, T. M. (2001, June 14). Debating reality: An online hoax is not a pox. Retrieved June 21, 2002, from http://www.nytimes.com/2001/06/14/technology/14REAL.html.

Sloop, J., & Herman, A. (1998). Negativland, out-law judgments, and the politics of cyberspace. In T. Swiss, J. Sloop, [&] A. Herman (Eds.), *Mapping the beat: Popular music and contemporary theory* (pp. 291–311). Malden, MA: Blackwell.

Stamper, C. (2001). Kaycee Nicole rests in pieces. Retrieved March 30, 2002, from http://www.net-slaves.com/comments/990564969.shtml.

Stone, A. R. (1994). Will the real body please stand up?: Boundary stories about virtual cultures. In M. Benedikt (Ed.), *Cyberspace: First steps* (pp. 81–118). Cambridge, MA: MIT Press.

Stone, A. R. (1995). *The war of desire and technology at the close of the mechanical age.* Cambridge, MA: MIT Press.

Swenson, D. (2001). Kaycee_Letter. Retrieved June 5, 2002, from http://psychcentral.com/blogs/kaycee_letter.htm.

Thomas, K. (2001, May 25). KristinThomas: 25may01. Retrieved June 5, 2002, from http://web.archive.org/web/20010627202509/http://www.sperare.com/archives/mav01/25may01.html.

Thomes, J. T. (2000). *Dotcons: Con games, fraud and deceit on the Internet.* San Jose, CA: Writers Club Press.

Turkle, S. (1995). *Life on the screen: Identity in the age of the Internet.* New York: Touchstone.

van der Woning, R. (2001). The end of the whole mess. Retrieved June 5, 2002, from http://bigwhiteguy.com/mess.shtml.

Wallace, P. (1999). *Psychology of the Internet.* Cambridge, UK: Cambridge University Press.

Warschauer, M. (2000). Language, identity, and the Internet. In B. E. Kolko, L. Nakamura, & G. B. Rodman (Eds.), *Race in cyberspace* (pp. 151–170). New York: Routledge.

Waskul, D., & Douglass, M. (1997). Cyberself: The emergence of self in on-line chat. *The Information Society, 13,* 375–397.

Wellman, B. (2001). Physical place and cyberplace: The rise of networked individualism. In L. Keeble & B. D. Loader (Eds.), *Community informatics: Shaping computer-mediated social relations* (pp. 17–42). New York: Routledge.

Wellman, B., & Guilia, M. (1999). Virtual communities as communities. In M. A. Smith & P. Kollock (Eds.), *Communities in cyberspace* (pp. 167–194). New York: Routledge.

World wide web of lies. (2001, June 20). *BBC World Service.* Retrieved June 7, 2002, from http://www.bbc.co.uk/worldservice/sci_tech/highlights/010620_deception.shtml.

Wynn, E., & Katz, J. E. (1997). Hyperbole over cyberspace: Self-presentation and social boundaries in Internet home pages and discourse. *The Information Society, 13,* 297–327.

An Epideictic Dimension of Symbolic Violence in Disney's *Beauty and the Beast*

Inter-Generational Lessons in Romanticizing and Tolerating Intimate Partner Violence

Kathryn M. Olson

Tale as old as time
True as it can be
Barely even friends
Then somebody bends unexpectedly.

Just a little change
Small to say the least
Both a little scared
Neither one prepared, beauty and the beast.[1]

So warbled Angela Lansbury as the voice of the enchanted teapot/cook Mrs. Potts in Disney's 1991 animated film *Beauty and the Beast.*[2] According to these lyrics, neither boy nor girl is "prepared" for the role of intimate in a romantic relationship. This essay begs to differ, arguing that community-approved texts such as Disney's wildly popular (e.g., re-released in Blu-ray in 2010 and 3-D in 2011) film might be an important part of viewers' "preparation" for the roles they will play when it comes to participating in or observing others' intimate relationships, epideictically providing models of and explanations for acceptable behavior. Critically reading the film's use of violence as a rhetorical strategy to give pleasure, advance the plot, and coach viewers' sympathies demonstrates how it is possible and why it is socially important to consider the film's symbolic patterns through the lens of intimate partner violence. The violent episodes shown and contextualized by supporting charac-

ters' discussions may offer or reinforce epideictic lessons for inter-generational audiences that encourage an admirable, but compliant "victim" to believe she can reform a violent mate through nurturing care as well as for excusing rough behavior as intense romantic passion. An essential part of what makes Beast sympathetic is his mortal combat with and textual invitations to compare him to Belle's more violent suitor Gaston.

Most disturbing are the ways adult characters repeatedly minimize or justify, in the presence of a child, recurring threats and violence in this couple's relationship, in spite of textual evidence that they know from past experience Beast's actual capacity for violence. I use the term "violence" to denote using words or actions to negate another's value or being. It includes blows, verbal put-downs, and insults about the self. "Symbolic violence" includes representations of violence as well as threats short of blows, physical destruction

501

) or cherished by the other,
..other through intimidation or
..c force will be used unless there is
..c. Under this view, rhetoric can consti-
..iolence, but it is neither inherently violent
..or the violation of another, as some have argued.[3]
Wayne Brockriede, Henry H. Johnstone, Jr., and
Maurice Natanson develop process-based rhetorical ethics showing how people may argue or persuade without violating the other's value, being, or
ability to respond rhetorically.[4] Wayne C. Booth
demonstrates how a similar ethical approach to
persuasion can enhance effectiveness, rejecting
the notion that ethical rhetoric is, by its nature,
ineffective.[5] Surveys show that almost half of US
adults have experienced psychological aggression
from a romantic partner and a third physical violence.[6] Yet seven in ten adults—the same number
who claim they would intervene if they recognized
partner violence in progress—say it is difficult to
tell whether a witnessed instance (including slap-
ping, hitting, threats, verbal abuse) constitutes or
warns of romantic violence.[7] Repeated instances,
even when varied, can constitute a pattern—one
that presents a stronger argument for the presence
of intimate partner violence. This essay, in offering one explanation for the contradictory statistics
on the prevalence versus recognition of intimate
partner violence, will argue that what appears to
be an innocuous story of crassness transformed by
love can be read otherwise.

The first section shows how Disney narrowed
and marketed its version as an animated representation of the romance genre, adding generous
doses of violent action to make the story sensible
and appealing across generations in light of the traditional legend elements it jettisoned. It examines
the prevailing themes in both positive and negative responses to Disney's film. The second section
argues that Disney's film, as positioned by the studio and the positive responses it garnered, invites
analysis as an instance of epideictic successfully
addressing inter-generational audiences. It examines specifically the role of the invented violence in
pleasing and teaching inter-generational audiences
and introduces the critical concept of an epideictic dimension, which may exist in texts that are
not generically epideictic. An epideictic dimension
contains patterns of rhetorical choices that reinforce conservative social positions on issues other
than the values to which the text is ostensibly dedicated or that cultivate its featured conservative
lessons in unexpected ways. Using child character

Chip as a framing device and interpretive categories from the Centers for Disease Control (CDC)
and Walker's Cycle Theory of Violence,[8] the third
section contends that Disney's rhetorical choices
create an epideictic dimension that normalizes and
romanticizes intimate partner violence for both
potential participants and bystanders. The conclusion examines the moral and rhetorical implications of this normalizing move.

Disney's Textual and Marketing Choices: Magnifying the Romance and Adding Violence

Subtracting Elements That Facilitate More Varied Epideictic Lessons in Earlier Legend Versions

While no legend is fixed, and this one has been
elastic enough to reflect variations of culture and
creativity, this story for centuries was knit together
by a central core of motifs, images, characters, and
conflicts that endured because those elements
are magnetic to each other structurally and to
people, variably but almost universally.[9] According to Beauty and the Beast legend expert Betsy
Hearne, "The story's effectiveness as a literary/
artistic whole steadies it through myriad historical
changes. In a sense, the most powerful elements
of the story shake off all reformers to assume a
singular, distinctive shape over and over again
despite vagaries of aesthetic invention and moral
intention."[10] Although Gabrielle de Villeneuve's
362-page French salon version preceded it, most
historians defer to Madame Le Prince de Beaumont's 1757 version, written as a tale for the moral
improvement of girls to reinforce the intellectual
and educational goals of a meritocracy, as authoritative.[11]

But Disney changed "the essential characters
of Belle, her father, and the Beast" and radically
altered the legend's "basic plot."[12] Disney truncated
Belle's role and character. In Beaumont's version,
"the Beast's metamorphosis is only one aspect
of a multifaceted story, and Beauty's character
development is at issue as much as the Beast's."[13]
Hearne distinguishes a narrative structure focused
on "journeys of action and maturation" as one of
the three central elements of the enduring tale.[14]
But Disney quickly short-circuited Beauty's "quest"
subplot and gradual moral development, recasting
her as a spirited, yet primarily nurturing home-
body.

Belle's quest for adventure and education will be swallowed by the romance plot. . . . To her credit, Belle is adventurous and brave, as her determination to find her father and her proposal that she take his place as a prisoner both demonstrate. . . . In spite of Belle's aspirations to educate herself, the film locates her real value in her capacity to nurture.[15]

Disney replaced Belle's usual moral development with "consumer feminism."[16]

Disney's Belle is therefore barely recognizable as a relative of the traditional fairy tale Beauty, but instantly recognizable as a feisty Disney heroine. . . . constructed to be acceptable and entertaining to both children and adults.[17]

Furthermore, Disney reduced the story to Beauty–Beast's relationship, refashioned it to fit modern romantic conventions, and drove the plot through violent action, manipulative scheming, and jealous conflict rather than nightly dinner conversations; in order to quicken the pace and add action appealing to young viewers, it invented an enchanted household staff to interact with the couple and facilitate the romance.[18] According to TV Guide, Walt Disney Studios chair Jeffrey Katzenberg found

the "problem" with the original storyline, the French court tale popularized by Madame Le Prince de Beaumont in 1757, was that "it's basically about two people who eat dinner together every night." Fine for Jean Cocteau's dark, poetic 1945 movie version, but hardly kiddie matinee fare. Hence the talking teapot, rousing song-and-dance and "Home Alone"-style slapstick.[19]

Disney focused "narrative attention on courtship as plot advancement and marriage as denouement," thus "de-emphasiz[ing] most of the earlier version's concern with virtue, further intensifying the focus on the 'romantic angle.'"[20] Given its fundamental rhetorical changes, Belle might be seen as no longer an agent instigating her father's predicament or the heroine who saves him but as an "object of desire, not the active subject" and "an observer of two guys fighting over a girl."[21] In the truncated story, violence substitutes for missing legend elements.

Although it is clear that "Beauty and the Beast" has always been in part a love story, earlier printed versions of the tale offer valuable lessons in addition to emphasizing the love relationship. Disney, on the other hand, strips the traditional fairy tale of anything but the romantic trajectory, throws in a dose of violence, and woos its audience into believing it has been educated as well as entertained.[22]

Disney eliminated or minimized complex character roles and non-violent plot devices that facilitate the romance in, as well as various epideictic lessons about moral development and meritocracy from, earlier legend versions. Gone are Belle's two treacherous sisters, who rhetorically served some of the tale's didactic messages on virtue, and her dreams' female confidante with Belle's best interests at heart.[23] Disney revised the father from a successful merchant into a hapless, infantilized inventor, relieving him of all responsibility and prompting the Belle–Beast confrontation at the castle rather than having the father, as agent, deliver a daughter.[24] The studio changed legend "details" like the Beast demanding that the father pay with his life or deliver a daughter only after the father steals a rose bush bough to fulfill Belle's gift request and after the Beast has graciously accommodated him overnight during a bad storm.[25] Disney demoted Belle from a princess (de Villeneuve's version) or a merchant's daughter learning that education and perseverance are necessary to succeed in a meritocracy (Beaumont's version) to the "working-class daughter of a village hobby-inventor" whose transformation is accomplished simply by marrying into the aristocracy.[26] Having discarded the legend's mutually magnetic plot features, Disney also changed the rose into a literal "ticking clock" or "hourglass" to nominally keep that element and rush the romance, but also to answer the plot question that is a pretext for adding violence: "Why would it tick off Beast so much?"[27] Beast's personal moral development from earlier legend versions is also compromised:

Beast, of course, learns nothing at all, really, except how to get girls. . . . In this outrageous turn around, it is Beast who is advertised to be the possessor of "beauty" and Belle must learn its nature. . . . It is Belle—robbed of her traditional [inquisitive, intellectual] Beauty—who is being instructed in how to elicit beauty [which ultimately turns to or is indicated by physical beauty] from beastliness. . . . For Disney to extract this moral requires outrageous disregard of the worst aspects of Beast—his cruelty, rages and hostage-taking.[28]

did not just "disregard" ...vior; the studio invented ...hat it would increase inter- ...ppeal, yet in the process dramatizing ...stitutes "acceptable" violence in roman- ...ationships, a pattern showing repeated viola- ...ons uncomfortably similar to a cycle of violence that many real-life victims endure unaided.

Inventing Violence as a Substitute Plot-Driver and to Engage Inter-Generational Audiences

One might contend that fairy tales are meant to be morality tales, which often include violence as a narrative means. However, the long tradition of the Beauty and the Beast legend, which Disney used to help authorize its film and promote it as an inter-generational must-see, is an exception. Historical research indicates that Beast's violence (particularly intimate partner violence) is not an inherent part of the legend, but a Disney innovation. This film's other violents and victims (e.g., Gaston, the townspeople, the castle staff) also do not appear in earlier versions—let alone drive the plot, code for audiences good and evil characters and acceptable versus unacceptable violence, and coach with whom to sympathize as they do in Disney's version. Unprecedented violent acts and scenes appeared in the film (e.g., Belle and Beast's encounter in his lair, the wolf attack) to substitute for what had been removed in order to make familiar sense of the revised, romance-focused plot and to engage inter-generational viewers. These choices are certainly Disney's right to make, as story-teller, but responsibility for their potential consequences cannot be ignored or attributed to the legend's authorizing tradition.

First, Disney invented the castle staff, their antics, and Beast's violence toward them. The staff is a pivotal narrative and pedagogical device that, given the legend elements that were discarded to broaden the film's inter-generational appeal, enables and interprets the now-central romantic angle even as it entertains young viewers. Disney gave a prominent narrative role to the enchanted housewares who indicate to viewers the reality of Beast's violence, yet coax along the romance.

Second, Disney added Beast's violence toward and in defense of Belle. "In earlier versions Beast, while monstrous, never threatens Beauty enough to make her want to leave."[29]

Disney's Beast has an angry, violent streak that is not present in Beaumont's version. Her Beast is cordial, gentle, and refined; as Beauty puts it, he has "virtue, sweetness of temper, and complaisance" (202). Disney's Beast, on the other hand, is characterized by a terrible temper, manifested through physical power, which causes him to tear apart his private chambers and frightens the castle's inhabitants. . . . That the Disney writers portray the Beast as an ignorant monster instead of as an intelligent being also substantially changes the meaning of Beauty's acceptance of him.[30]

Susan Jeffords notes that Disney's is the only version to enlighten the audience in the prologue to the existence and nature of Beast's curse and its antidote (traditionally not revealed until the conclusion), to give the antidote an expiration date to rush the plot (Beast's 21st birthday or the curse is permanent), and to ensure audience sympathies for Beast, even if he is somewhat responsible for his plight, by adding the potential collateral damage that the innocent servants will be forever bewitched, too.[31] The pivotal wolf attack that brings Belle back to the castle is also Disney's invention. Belle flees Beast only to be attacked by wolves; Beast, who is following, rescues Belle. This act defines him as a hero and facilitates the "romantic set piece" where she returns and nurses his wounds.[32] Violence uniquely defines Disney's Beast, sympathetically and relative to other key characters, and advances the romance in ways not needed when magnetic legend elements were intact.

Third, by adding the handsome, yet obnoxious alternative suitor Gaston, Disney introduced much cinematic violence and re-made the traditionally tender storyline into a romantic competition. Gaston is a major character for whom there is no precedent in earlier versions except for Avenant in Cocteau's film; over the years, the Beauty and the Beast tale sometimes included alternative suitors for Belle, but only as minor characters.[33] Gaston adds exciting violence and brutality to engage young viewers and sets up an unprecedented love triangle, in spite of Belle's disinterest in him.[34] Disney's "violation of profound elements" and its addition of "frenetic" speed and competition "have turned the folklore journey into a chase."[35]

Marketing Disney's Version as an Animated Romantic Classic for All Ages

Such rhetorical disconnections from earlier versions, both subtractions and additions, were intentional.[36] The New York Times's Janet Maslin wrote, "If this *Beauty and the Beast* is a long way from Jean Cocteau's 1947 [sic] black-and-white version, it's also a long way from the original fairy tale, which has been largely jettisoned in favor of a more timely story."[37] The studio took pains to make the animated violence and title characters' reactions to it (particularly for the climactic confrontation when Beast finds Belle in his lair) as human and emotionally powerful as possible.[38] Disney's realistic depictions of violence, rage, fear, and remorse are partly achieved by recording the characters' voices first, then having the animators draw, incorporating the real-life actors' mannerisms and emotions into the animated characters.[39] To perfect characters' movements, live-action actors were video recorded doing scenes against blank backgrounds until the director was satisfied; these were printed out frame-by-frame to provide inspiration for animators to humanize movements and make them unobtrusively life-like and "convincing" to viewers.[40] Howard Ashman, "the simplicity police," insured that anything non-essential to Disney's version was omitted and assured that "every single scene" was amped until it had a palpable umbrella of emotion.[41] Even the songs provide exposition integral to the revised plot, rather than being unrelated interludes from the action.[42] Such choices humanized the title characters' movements and emotions in a way written stories cannot, facilitating easy identification and transferability of subtle epideictic lessons to viewers, young and old.

From the beginning, Disney designed and marketed its animated film as a classic romance for all ages. At its release, *TV Guide*'s Rick Marin called the film "surprisingly sexy" and noted "Disney's double-edged marketing campaign. One of the movie posters is kid-cartoonish, the other moodily grown-up with a line that reads 'The most beautiful love story ever told.' . . . So far, the adult pitch seems to be working."[43] Disney's marketing attempts and rhetorical choices worked to make the film appealing to adults who consider themselves liberated in terms of sexual politics and hope to teach children the same. Disney "frequently point[ed] to the feminist sensibilities of Linda Woolverton, the woman writer behind the screenplay. In addition, they've aggressively marketed their new heroine as a strong, active heroine who hungers for adventure."[44] *Sight and Sound* reports,

> This is a fairy tale that's vividly aware of contemporary sexual politics; it has consciously picked out a strand in the tale's history and developed it for an audience of mothers who grew up with Betty Friedan and Gloria Steinem, who have daughters who listen to Madonna and Sinead O'Connor. Woolverton's screenplay gives us a heroine of spirit who finds romance on her own terms.[45]

Significantly, when considering the epideictic dimension, Disney's version will become "canonical" and marginalize earlier non-violent legend versions.[46] Evidence suggests it already has for many American adults, who choose this film as family, not just individual, entertainment, and explicitly celebrate it as an exemplary love story, not just a child's cartoon. For example, the American Film Institute's 2002 list of the 100 greatest love stories in 100 years of film history recognizes Disney's version as number 34, and *Premiere* magazine includes it as one of the ten films that defined the decade of the '90s.[47] Perhaps more to the point, adults outside the film industry treat Disney's *Beauty and the Beast* as a paradigmatic romantic story. For instance, a poll of *Ladies' Home Journal* readers listed it as one of "The 10 Most Romantic Movies" of all time, along with *Gone with the Wind* and *Pretty Woman*.[48] Likewise, a Popcorn review claims that the little details and classic moves in the Disney film are what "make up the TRUE date movies of all time."[49] As Hearne remarks, "the sheer sophistication and international dominance of the Disney commercial machine guarantee that a Disney version of a fairy tale or classic will be THE authorized version for millions and millions of young viewers all over the world."[50]

Critics' and Reviewers' Responses to Disney's Version

Disney's offering was rich enough to support multiple critical readings, dominant and resistant, positive and negative, though the positive ones far outnumber the negative ones. The primarily positive reactions feature four prominent themes. The first two themes are technical excellence and success at blending the classic and modern to maximize inter-generational appeal. Many admire the realistic animation and technical cinematic skill that earned the film Oscar nominations and a Golden Globe Award.[51] Roger Ebert praised the film for "penetrat[ing] directly into my strongest childhood memories, in which animation looked more real than live action features."[52] Others celebrate its proven ability to appeal across inter-generational audiences by blending the classic and the modern.

Reviewer Chris Hicks terms it "a first-class winner all the way [that] should provide sufficient entertainment value for every age."[53] The *Washington Post*'s Hal Hinson calls the film "more than a return to classic form, it's a delightfully satisfying modern fable, a near-masterpiece that draws on the sublime traditions of the past while remaining completely in sync with the sensibility of its time."[54] Even self-admitted anti-Disney critics are enthusiastic about this film's merit and intergenerational appeal. Mark R. Leeper opens his review by sharing his usual disdain for Disney films, but then raves, "*Beauty and the Beast* demonstrates that a lot more can be done in this medium. . . . Parents should go with their kids. If you don't have kids, go anyway."[55] Ten years later at the film's re-release, James Berardinelli observed:

> Walt Disney's 1991 instant classic, *Beauty and the Beast*, is not only the finest animated movie ever made, but deserves a prominent position on any list of all-time greats. . . . *Beauty and the Beast* attains a nearly-perfect mix of romance, music, invention, and animation. While many animated features claim to appeal equally to adults and children, *Beauty and the Beast* is one of the rare ones that actually achieves that lofty goal. It's a family feature that someone over the age of 18 can venture into without an accompanying child.[56]

Two other prominent positive response themes celebrate Belle as updated gender model and embrace the film's undercurrent of irrepressible romantic hopefulness. Elaine Showalter calls *Beauty and the Beast* "the first feminist Disney film, a liberated love story for the '90s."[57] Harriett Hawkins lauds Belle as "a post-feminist heroine" who is "independent, adventure-seeking, unconventional, province-hating, and hunk-despising. And also a *bookworm*."[58] Belle is hailed as a relative improvement in gender representations and lessons over previous Disney heroines, classic and recent.[59] One critic even proclaims Belle "the first liberated cartoon creation."[60]

For some, reading Belle as a progressive gender model went hand-in-hand with seeing the film's romantic hopefulness as a positive. The message that change is possible appealed to many. For instance, Susan Z. Swan's Jungian feminist reading of the film as a Gothic romance praises Disney's rhetorical choices that "appeal overtly to audiences looking for traditional romance while at the same time subverting the dominant ideology, caricaturing traditional roles, and transforming the model for accomplishing romance between women and men" into one of interdependence and equality.[61] Sharon D. Downey's deft dialectical reading uses the "gender conflict juxtaposing male and female experiences" to resist Disney's overt privileging of the male and recast the preferred reading's romantic ideal.[62] Her resistant reading extracts a more progressive model of relational fulfillment by interpreting the film as a story of male–female mutual empowerment and completion. Others reluctantly embrace the dominant reading as itself a positive message on gender and romance. *Sight and Sound*'s Marina Warner confesses,

> Liking a Disney film doesn't come easily. . . . But this version of *Beauty and the Beast* is funny, touching and lively, and communicates *romantic hopefulness* with panache and high spirits. It's a true inheritor of a long literary tradition of romance, sieved through the consciousness of 70s feminism, which asked for plucky fairy-tale heroines and got this: a Hollywood belle who prefers books to hunks [italics added].[63]

Although recognizing that Disney splits "the male into the good beast and the bad beast," this critic seems untroubled by the romantic hope that "all he ['good' Beast] needed was the love of a good woman"—even while acknowledging that "such a huge helping of female autonomy, *responsibility*, self-determination, and *the powers of salvation* add up to a *mighty charge* for one small Belle to shoulder [italics added]."[64] Such comments imply that Disney satisfied those with suspicions about its gender representations and pleased them with its hopeful romantic arc.

Negative reactions to the film also share some consistent themes, most exhibited earlier in the section on Disney's changes to the legend. Besides earlier noted objections to the overall level of violence added to Disney's version and its radical narrative alterations changing an enduring, sophisticated moral tale into a conventional modern romance and chase story, two additional themes emerge. First, many contend that the film is as "misogynist" as Disney's other animated classics and Belle is not an updated gender model, but just the usual patriarchal fare splashed with a few "liberated" codes, such as love of reading and a professed desire for adventure. Kathi Maio notes that the studio went "out of its way to neutralize" criticisms about sexual politics that it suffered for *The Little Mermaid*, yet Disney's "proof" that Belle is a model of female independence is "that she reads. . . . Her favorite book appears to be a romance about a prince and his sweetheart."[65] And Belle's quest for adventure is quickly overwhelmed by her need to nurture first her father, then the Beast, so that "those dreams take her only as far as the forbidding castle on the other side of the river, to a suitor even more terrifying than the loutish Gaston" where "Belle throws her freedom away in an act of feminine self-sacrifice that even Ariel would have thought twice about."[66] Further evidence for this negative theme is the focus on Beast's story with Belle marginalized as a plot device and object of desire. Elizabeth Dodson Gray argues,

> While Beauty gets cobilling in the story title and movie, the whole focus is really upon the Beast. The central question is, "Will Beast be delivered from his enchantment? Will he be returned to his true identity?" . . . The old macho hero may be dead, but the Beast . . . is the clear mythopoetic representation of the man who is totally preoccupied with his own salvation, who is prone to violence, and who is still very much "under the spell" of an enchantment [i.e., the institutional patriarchal system].[67]

And Belle's "lesson" is not greater self-awareness, but about how to appreciate a partner in spite of his rages and selfishness and to coax beauty from his beastliness. Highlighting this "night-and-day" departure from the traditional legend's more balanced story, Maio offers further proof in producer Don Hahn's comment that "our version is the Beast's story. It's about a guy with a very serious problem;" Maio adds "namely, his brutal temper and total selfishness."[68]

A second theme in negative reactions objects to the film's message that the "love of a good woman" can fix a flawed man and it is her duty to provide that nurturing until it succeeds. Gray notes, "The spell that is upon the Beast is broken 'by the love of a good woman,' and Beauty frees him finally to become his concealed wondrous self. . . . All this is a typical patriarchal tale about what is required of a good woman."[69] Instead of reading this as healthy romantic hopefulness against the odds,[70] these respondents find it concerning. Maio observes,

> Is [Beast] a romantic hero? He is, according to Disney, after Belle rehabilitates him through the magic of her femininity. Touched by the love of a good woman any devil will become a docile, devoted gentleman. . . . Would that it were so! But the millions of women battered by husbands and lovers each year can testify just how false—and dangerous—Disney's little fantasy is.[71]

Gray, who acknowledges that this film can be read as "a nasty replay of patriarchal scripts exploiting women into endless self-denial and self-sacrifice" or as giving "to women—and only to women—the power to 'break the enchantment' of patriarchy," rejects both positions to argue that men need to take responsibility for male violence toward women and for ending it.[72]

My reading of the film shares themes from both camps (e.g., the film engages viewers with violence; it promotes and rewards romantic hopefulness against the odds, which is double-edged; it reinforces the notion that the love of a good woman changes a beast and she is responsible to provide that nurture) as well as Maio's and Gray's concerns about the real-life stakes if this idealized romantic hopefulness is not fulfilled in viewers' lives (i.e., "Does the Beast's psychological profile in the film remind you of a violence prone wife batterer?"[73]). However, this epideictic dimension approach treats the film's violence and romance as rhetorically inseparable. Although individuals might find inspiration in Disney's film for a more progressive vision of what romance should become, the essay's next two sections make the case for its conservative, society-wide potential to excuse some violence's intersection with romance.

Inter-Generational Epideictic, Processed through Violence, and the Significance of Chip

Epideictic and Coaching Continuity in Inter-Generational Community Attitudes and Dispositions

By its ubiquity, repetitive themes, and positioning as "entertainment," popular culture can serve an epideictic function, though that is not its only function. Epideictic "has significance and importance . . . because it strengthens the disposition toward action by increasing adherence to the values it lauds."[74] Epideictic's power is not in calling for some immediate decision or response but in laying the groundwork for and intensity of a disposition to act one way over another in a range of unspecified future encounters.[75] According to Celeste Michelle Condit, epideictic serves three social functions: display/entertainment, shaping/ sharing of community, and definition/understanding; the second term in each pair identifies a function for audiences, which is the more relevant consideration when interpreting popular culture texts.[76]

The entertainment uses of Disney's film by audiences of all ages are unquestionable. American adults, who have their own experiential bases on which to draw, largely praised the film's depiction of romance and used it for family entertainment; for child viewers, with no parallel experiential bases by which to evaluate the film's depictions of romance, it might serve as an educational initiation into how what their adult caregivers treat as praiseworthy romance operates. Veronica Hefner and Barbara J. Wilson's recent study of romantic comedy films' influence on young people's beliefs about romance suggests why films might be even more powerful than more studied television genres (e.g., soap operas, reality-based shows):

> Movies offer stories that trace relationships from the beginning to the end in one packaged narrative. In contrast to the romantic relationships on television, which often take several seasons to fully develop the characters, movies are viewed in a single sitting. These presumably potent messages could boost the impact on attentive viewers.[77]

One immediately learns the consequences of characters' choices, including how they use and react to violence in romances. Although ideal romantic beliefs may be challenged by more "realistic" views also presented in romance films, such narratives' ultimate happy endings and the relative happy/unhappy fates of the characters who endorsed versus challenged romantic ideals (e.g., "love conquers all") ultimately reinforce idealized beliefs over realistic ones.[78]

When the romance genre goes animated and inter-generational, the plot and relevant belief structure must be made even more pronounced via textual devices (e.g., violence, explicit exposition from appropriate characters and in songs) so that children can enjoy and understand. On-screen violence is the simplest device to both entertain and teach. Based on their classic studies of television violence in popular fare, George Gerbner and Larry Gross argue that mediated violence reminds community members of accepted power relationships. It "is the cheapest and quickest dramatic demonstration of who can and who cannot get away with what against whom. It is an exercise in norm-setting and social typing, . . . depicting violations and enforcement of the rules of society."[79] Intentionally or not, epideictic lessons are efficiently and dramatically taught through undisputed displays of violence in a community's popular texts.

Positioned in popular entertainment, violence often performs a socially conservative function by reiterating established power and positional relationships: "As action, violence hurts, kills, and scares. The last is its most important social function because that is what maintains power and compels acquiescence to power. Therefore, it is important who scares whom and who is 'trained' to be the victim."[80] To preserve a social order, both "violent" and "victim" (and, I would add, tolerant, non-intervening bystander) roles must be learned; violence is "a dramatic demonstration of power which communicates much about social norms and relationships, about goals and means, about winners and losers, about the risks of life, and about the price for transgressions of society's rules."[81] Mediated violence thus teaches the uninitiated and reminds more experienced members whose privileges and position the community will likely back in real-life confrontations.[82] The issue is not copy-cat violence, but reinforcing dominant power positions and acquiescing to their privileges. The film's explanation and resolution may normalize concrete signs of intimate partner violence for viewers in ways that make them unremarkable, even romantic. *Beauty and the Beast* is not alone in these representational practices. But it provokes special concern because it introduces an inter-generational audience to them and explicitly instructs viewers, via the cute character Chip, in an ideology on appropriate romance, the victim's role and ability to "manage" partner violence, and bystander duties.

Second, via epideictic's shaping/sharing function, a "community renews its conception of itself and of what is good by explaining what it has previously held to be good and by working through the relationships of those past values and beliefs to new situations. . . . Definitions of community are often advanced by contrast with 'others' outside [the values] of the community" (e.g., Gaston's unacceptable violence).[83] Significantly, the values shaped may be "undisputed though not formulated."[84] As argued next, violence in *Beauty and the Beast* codes heroes and villains and creates a hierarchy of social acceptability for violence. The results coach viewers' sympathies for and acceptance of Beast and explain why Belle should stay and reform him.

Finally, with its understanding function, epideictic explains some confusing or "troubling issue in terms of the audience's key values and usual practices. Through the resultant understanding, the troubled event will be made less confusing and threatening, providing a sense of comfort for the audience."[85] Understanding symbolically tames the world by making it fit within existing beliefs and values. Via the subplot of Chip's education in love, the film addresses a troubling cultural ambiguity (i.e., socially acceptable intersections of love and violence) with rhetorical choices that can be read as explaining and quieting concerns about it.

As with education generally, the perspectives and action dispositions that epideictic coaches for audiences tend to conserve and justify present power relationships.[86] However, the nature of this conservative dynamic may differ according to the audience member. Aristotle, an early authority on the subject, suggests that epideictic operates via praise or blame to mark what a community considers honorable or disgraceful.[87] He goes on to claim that all people "individually and in common" aim at "happiness and its component parts" and so the various genres, each in its own way, facilitate that pursuit.[88] The puzzle, then, emerges from Book II, Chapter 14 in which Aristotle sharply distinguishes among the young, the old, and people in their prime and differentiates what tends to constitute "happiness" for each based on life experiences to date (e.g., for the young, the noble; for the old, the useful; for those in life's prime, the mean between noble and useful). Yet Aristotle makes no attempt to address how a particular text or genre or speaker simultaneously might address intergenerational audiences or variously serve epideictic's conservative function for those with generationally divergent experiences and views.

Instead Aristotle ignores the reality of intergenerational audiences even in his own time and simply recommends audience segmentation, with the caveat that only "like" can credibly address "like": "Wherefore, since all men are willing to listen to speeches which harmonize with their own character and to speakers who resemble them, it is easy to see what language we must employ so that both ourselves and our speeches may appear to be of such and such a character."[89] Contextually, "character" here means from the same age demographic. Given the importance of epideictic to stabilizing a community's values across generations and the observation that this function regularly occurs without audience segmentation, there is an unmet need to rhetorically analyze how epideictic's conservative dynamic—whether as a genre or a dimension of various kinds of texts—might operate differently across generations in a single text, at once teaching and reinforcing community values. This question is particularly pressing when

the subject is romance, where adults have firsthand experience but children have only what they witness and how they are taught to interpret what they witness. In *Beauty and the Beast*, problematic adult relationships are made meaningful and less threatening for inter-generational audiences, educating immature community members and reassuring adults that troubled romantic partnerships have meaning and merit the hope inspired by traditional, idealized romantic beliefs.

Ultimately, this exercise is more than a reading of a single film. It demonstrates the heuristic potential of examining texts for their epideictic dimensions. An epideictic dimension need not be the dominant or preferred reading of the text—mine certainly will not be—nor is it one that emphasizes the possibilities for change that a text might also support; it is one that shows how a text coherently, elaborately, and powerfully promotes and justifies values, beliefs, and practices that maintain status quo power relationships, even when those are not its ostensible lessons. This criticism also demonstrates versatile rhetorical processes by which inter-generational offerings might epideictically address troubling community issues and make complicated social lessons understandable and appealing to the uninitiated as well as to the experienced, who may have found that life has not lived up to the promises for happiness that abiding by the proffered social arrangement promised. Finally, it makes concrete and recognizable, in a single text designed for an intergenerational community, rhetorical processes that account for the "cultivation" effect documented by Gerbner and his colleagues. While cultivation analysis focuses on exposure to total patterns offered by television "to define the world and legitimize the social order" rather than on individual genres or programs, textual analysis of this representative anecdote of inter-generational lessons in romance (taught and supported through violence) might illustrate at a micro-level how "cultivation of shared conceptions of reality among otherwise diverse publics"[90] occurs.

Though far from the only text exhibiting acceptance of some romantic violence, *Beauty and the Beast*'s epideictic lessons might be especially potent because of the trusted source, adults' approval of children enjoying the film's many pleasures, and textual choices that make the film explicitly instructive on proper romance. This combination is reason to suspect that the film is consistent with the community's bedrock of unformulated, though undisputed values about romantic violence. A Catholic priest who teaches the children of his parish precepts of Catholicism is an epideictic educator, reckon Chaim Perelman and Lucie Olbrechts-Tyteca, though the same rhetor giving the same lesson to adults of another religious affiliation changes him into a propagandist. The key difference is that "the educator has been commissioned by a community to be the spokesman for the values it recognizes, and as such, enjoys the prestige attaching to his office."[91] Disney largely enjoys such a role in US society. Parents and babysitters trust Disney to align with and promote undisputed, if unformulated, social values and impart them to children through entertainment.[92] Over time, Disney's child viewership has gotten progressively younger and viewing venues more intimate; families approvingly watch *Beauty and the Beast* together, and two-year-olds "swarm with their caretakers to the theater, or sit propped before their electronic babysitters"[93] watching a DVD.

While children might absorb the lessons from whatever entertainment caregivers provide, Disney films in general and *Beauty and the Beast* in particular are ones that adults choose for family as well as personal entertainment. The young, as Aristotle characterized them, "know" only by virtue of social conventions and are ashamed if they violate them because as yet they have developed no other compass.[94] As Gerbner and Gross argue, fictional stories presented for entertainment via visual media "need not present credible accounts of what things are to perform the more critical function of demonstrating how things really work"[95] for the uninitiated as well as longtime community members. Chip, the teacup, is this epideictic dimension reading's central framing figure, both because he is the film's only child and so may be the character with whom immature viewers might most readily identify and because his witness and questions to adults on how to interpret what he sees provide a main conduit for expressing the film's ideology on romance. He is the character who needs/wants love explained to him, who witnesses Beast's violence and attends to adults' discussions of a troubled romance, and who supplies, at key moments, the hopeful interpretations to be learned.

The Pleasures and Epideictic Potential of Violence in *Beauty and the Beast*

Disney's plot and character departures from the legend's history, and the violence that they intro-

duce and depend on as rhetorical strategies, can bring pleasure to an intergenerational audience. As justified by the studio, the addition of violence and slapstick action (from Beast repeatedly terrifying his servants to Gaston beating up his friends and neighbors for fun as well as to signal social dominance), sometimes to rousing music (e.g., "No one fights like Gaston, no one bites like Gaston, . . . no one hits like Gaston"), appeals to viewers who might otherwise be bored with the traditional plot moved primarily through conversation.[96] These choices simplify a legend usually rich with more varied epideictic lessons and moral quests for both main characters into primarily a modern romantic plot with a love triangle. That simplification, clarified through violence, makes the story easy to follow and familiar for children, while also authorizing it for adults in the tradition of great romances where the suitor must fight to win the girl. In the world of this text, violent rhetorical choices offer viewers pleasure in at least three ways.

First, the rhetorical uses and variations on violence establish an evaluative hierarchy of actions and male characters; not all violence is equal. Gaston's gratuitous and excessive violence toward his friends and neighbors, efforts to forcibly institutionalize Maurice, and attempts to kill Beast (particularly his sneak attack after Beast mercifully spares his life) are opportunities for audiences to jeer Gaston and recognize him as the villain. In spite of his good looks and the swooning trio of beauties who fawn for his attention, Gaston's violent disrespect toward Belle personally and what she values (e.g., her books, her father) reinforces the film's rhetorical coding of him as the villain and an undesirable suitor for Belle (if not for the trio of village beauties, a question that the film's choices leaves unresolved). "Honorable" Disney-concocted uses of violence that develop the romantic plot and code Beast as the hero and superior love interest include his savage fight with the wolves to save Belle after she fled from him in terror and his violence in self-defense against Gaston and the murderous mob. Between these extremes is a range of violent acts open to greater interpretation, such as Beast terrorizing Belle's father and the castle staff and his behavior toward Belle as he "courts" her.

Second, the film's violent coding of the key male characters rhetorically coaches viewers' sympathies for Beast and against Gaston. Although both potential mates physically threaten and imprison Belle, try to cut her off permanently from her family, have ulterior motives for wooing her (i.e., breaking the spell, preserving status in the community), and never apologize to Belle, the film's choices cultivate viewers' negative reactions toward Gaston and their positive ones, perhaps by default, toward Beast in this romantic contest with Belle as the prize. By dramatic comparison, Gaston's unrepentant violence, which includes pinning Belle against a wall and destroying her valued possessions, makes Beast's symbolic violence toward her less noticeable and disturbing even for savvy adult critics. For instance, Showalter's favorable film review calls Gaston "the real beast, a sadistic, self-loving bully."[97] Another complimentary reviewer relatively favors Beast by calling Gaston "supremely macho and . . . to be macho is to be beastlike" and Beast "super-macho, but [who] knows it is a curse both literally and figuratively."[98] A third labels them "the bad beast and the good beast."[99] Gaston is "the true beast, Calvinist and unredeemed, socially deviant in his supremacist assumptions."[100] Narratively what differentiates Beast is that he is redeemable from, if unapologetic for, his violence, but the film suggests that this redemption is *Belle's* project, not his sole responsibility. This portrayal, of course, perpetuates the stereotype that a "good" woman can/should change a "bad" boy. With Disney's extreme caricature of a handsome but relatively more violent romantic competitor against whom to direct viewers' disapproval (i.e., a more obvious representation of a dangerous companion), Beast seems more sympathetic, misguided, and "amenable to instruction."[101]

Third, Belle's responses to her suitors' violence may help the film please by negotiating an acceptable position in sexual politics for many adult viewers, which may compensate for or deflect attention from Beast's partner violence. Disney uses both rhetorical and marketing choices to code Belle as someone who can take care of herself, minimizing viewers' need to worry about or sympathize with her when Beast acts violently. Disney rhetorically fashions Belle as the kind of person we want to be and want our children to become: smart, with a voracious appetite for books, learning, and adventure; strong enough to be non-conformist in spite of her neighbors' criticisms; pretty, but not vain and not herself attracted to someone based merely on looks or popularity (i.e., Gaston); loyal to her family, however ditzy and inept; self-reflexive enough to know that she wants to escape "this provincial life"; initially dismissive of being limited to the role of wife. Belle pluckily rejects the advances of her handsome, yet more, and more gratuitously, violent suitor Gaston. Based on these textual choices, Belle, like many actual victims of intimate partner violence, does not seem like the kind of individual who would get involved or stay with a potentially violent partner, so there seems no need to worry about her.

In these ways and in the absence of the non-violent magnetic elements that enabled earlier legend versions, violence helps diverse viewers "make sense" of the film's plot, characters, and sexual politics, shapes their sympathies, and gives knowledge and pleasure. The productive network of power enacted through this film's violence pleases on multiple levels and may please different generations differently, even as it educates all. Young viewers may enjoy it as action that engages them and clarifies who and what is good or bad. Older viewers might appreciate both Beast's and Gaston's violence toward Maurice as devices that efficiently propel the plot and mark for whom to root. The violence pleases as it paradoxically explains and reaffirms both romantic ideals *and* violent status quo relationship patterns that fall short of those ideals. Examining this film's coherent, yet little discussed, epideictic dimension on the socially meaningful intersection of violence and romance demonstrates how a text not ostensibly presented as socially conservative or educational fare on that topic might serve those purposes.

Normalizing and Romanticizing Practices and Patterns of Intimate Partner Violence

The prevalence of violence's intersection with intimacy in so many US adults' romantic involvements gives moral significance to reading this epideictic dimension of a film authorized by its place in the traditions of great romances, classic legends, and family entertainment. The CDC's comprehensive[102] *National Intimate Partner and Sexual Violence Survey: 2010 Summary Report* categorizes psychological aggression (short of physical blows) toward an intimate partner as expressive aggression (e.g., acting angry in a way that seems dangerous) or coercive control (e.g., isolation from family and friends; keeping track of partner's whereabouts) and indicates that experiencing frightening aggression from a partner is fairly common. Based on telephone interviews with more than 16,500 adults, nearly half of US women (48.4 percent) report experiencing at least one form of sychological aggression in an intimate relationship, with approximately 40 percent experiencing expressive aggression and 41 percent reporting coercive control; one in three women had been slapped, pushed, or shoved, while one in four had suffered more severe physical violence.[103] Almost half of men surveyed (48.8 percent) had experienced psychological aggression by an intimate partner, with 31.9 percent reporting expressive aggression and 42.5 percent experiencing coercive control.[104] Romantic violence, including psychological aggression short of blows, seems widespread and commonplace in this country.

Yet, concrete acts of intimate partner violence have somehow been rendered invisible to well-intentioned Americans, perhaps by the idealized messages of "romantic hopefulness" that popular culture provides. For example, a 2006 survey conducted by Opinion Research Corporation and RF Insights concludes that a radical public "information" or "knowledge" gap about the *patterns* or *practices* of partner abuse prevents many well-meaning Americans from recognizing and acting when they witness violent signs or acts in others' romances.[105] Stacy Morrison, editor in chief of *Redbook*, which co-sponsored the survey, observes,

> The survey confirms that Americans continue to fail to recognize both the blatant [two in five did not mention hitting, slapping, or punching] and subtle [90 percent failed to define *repeated* emotional, verbal, or sexual abuse or controlling behaviors] signs of domestic abuse. Domestic violence ranges from pushing and shoving to demeaning talk and isolation from family and friends. . . . I want people to know what it looks like and not be afraid to step in and help someone who needs it.[106]

What explains such counter-intuitive results? Certainly reluctance to get involved and doubts about whether an incident is isolated or part of a larger pattern explain some inaction. But inability to identify or see partner violence as unacceptable—which are prior to and necessary, but not sufficient, for intervention—might also be epideictically cultivated by normalizing and romanticizing its patterns and signs in a community's celebrated inter-generational texts.

Disney's family film is infused with typical signs, practices, and patterns of romantic violence played out between a sympathetic violent and a self-sufficient victim who couple quickly and young.[107] It introduces immature viewers to an ideological microcosm (or cultivation theme) of popular culture's conservative interpretation of romantic violence and shapes/shares community norms for coping with it. Disney's rhetorical choices make concrete acts of romantic violence both realistic and familiar, yet position them as not causes for concern or sympathy for the victim or as a reason to end a relationship; instead, it signals an opportunity for the lover to reform the violent with the result that the efforts end in happily-ever-after love.

Making Familiar and Romanticizing Practices of Expressive Aggression and Coercive Control

Disney's film shows Beast repeatedly engaging in *expressive aggression* and *coercive control* toward Belle, yet codes him, with the community's endorsement, as a great romantic hero. Via these choices, the film might negotiate for an inter-generational audience the potentially troubling issue of the frequency and possible progression of expressive aggression and coercive control in some romantic relationships (one's own or those of others), without endorsing any social changes. It makes romantic violence meaningful, individually fixable, and less troubling. All seems to turn out well when bystanders ignore the Gestalt of a pattern of abuse and facilitate the romance so that the couple can work through the issue themselves—with special emphasis on the victim's responsibility to foster the violent partner's change. Critically reading this epideictic dimension shows how the film might soothe and reassure adults that their troubled relationships (or ones they witness) are not exceptional, should be endured with hope, and can be turned blissful via proper victim effort; it shows how immature community members might be introduced to this ideology and coached in responses that make partner violence an unremarkable and "private" part of romantic life.

The violence that Beast enacts toward Belle in Disney's film bristles with the primary *expressive aggression* and *coercive control* behaviors characterizing real-life relationships with repeated intimate partner violence: (a) controlling behavior; quick to anger; wants to know the partner's whereabouts at all times; angry if the partner is late; (b) quick involvement in the relationship; "I've never felt loved like this by anyone!" (c) isolation; the abuser may cut the partner off from friends, family, and resources; (d) blaming others for the violent partner's feelings or angry actions; (e) breaking or striking objects when angry, which may prefigure personal violence; (f) overt threats of violence.[108]

In a display of coercive control common with intimate partner abusers, the first moves Beast makes are to exact Belle's promise never to leave him, to imprison her at home, and to separate her from her family. Belle's father Maurice begs Beast "please spare my daughter" to which Beast responds: "She's no longer your concern." As Beast sends Maurice unceremoniously and permanently on his way, Belle sobs: "You didn't even let me say good-bye. I'll never see him again. I didn't get to say good-bye." In the same scene, Beast makes his love interest swear that she will never leave him, no matter what—and the situational context in which the promise is extracted (i.e., an exchange of Maurice's life for hers) suggests that there will be severe consequences for Belle, and possibly also her father, if she breaks that vow. "BEAST: . . . you must promise to stay here forever. BELLE: You have my word." Victims in abusive romantic relationships often report that the abuser systematically cuts them off from communication with and the support of the family and friends who most care about their well-being and might threaten harm to those people to keep the victim compliant.

Beast broadens his coercive control by restricting Belle's food intake when he finds she is not only late but refusing to come to dinner as he ordered. (Earlier, "LUMIERE: [whispering in his ear] Dinner—invite her to dinner. BEAST: [Growing angry] You . . . will join me for dinner. That's not a request!") Later, "BEAST: What's taking so long? I told her to come down. Why isn't she here yet?!" When Beast learns that Belle is not coming, he bellows and charges upstairs to bang on her bedroom door, while the pleading objects trail, trying desperately to calm him.

BEAST: (Yelling) I thought I told you to come down to dinner!

BELLE: (From behind the door) I'm not hungry.

BEAST: You'll come out or I'll . . . I'll break down the door!

LUMIERE: (interrupting) Master, I could be wrong, but that may not be the best way to win the girl's affections.

COGSWORTH: (pleading) Please! Attempt to be a gentleman.

BEAST: (growing angrier) But she is being so . . . difficult!

MRS. POTTS: Gently, gently.

BEAST: (very dejected) Will you come down to dinner?

BELLE: No!

(BEAST looks at the OBJECTS, very frustrated.)

COGSWORTH: Suave. Genteel.

BEAST: (Trying to act formal, bowing at the door) It would give me great pleasure if you would join me for dinner.

COGSWORTH: Ahem, ahem, we say "please."

BEAST: (once again dejected) . . . please.

BELLE: (Mad at BEAST) No, thank you.

BEAST: (furious) You can't stay in there forever!

BELLE: (provokingly) Yes I can!

BEAST: Fine! Then go ahead and STARVE!!!! (To OBJECTS) If she doesn't eat with me, then she doesn't eat at all!

Beast retreats, slamming a door so hard that a piece of ceiling plaster falls on quivering Lumiere.

In this scene, not only does Beast physically threaten, control, and attempt to deprive his love interest of food, enlisting the help of others to do so, but also he blames his outburst on Belle "being so difficult." Then the Beast self-righteously retreats to his lair to spy on her, "knocking over and destroying things in his path. BEAST: I ask nicely, but she refuses. What a . . . what does she want me to do—beg? (Picking up the MAGIC MIRROR) Show me the girl." As the story and the coercive control progress, Beast spies on Belle without her knowledge using his magic mirror, listens in on her private conversations, and requires his surrogates to monitor her whereabouts at all times—or pay the price they know can be exacted by his violent temper. For example, when Belle leaves her room and goes down to the kitchen where some of the enchanted objects insist on feeding her, against Beast's orders, clock/butler Cogsworth comments: "Well keep it down. If the master finds out about this, it will be our necks!" The film includes other instances of Beast blaming Belle for either his angry feelings or his violent actions, such as in the scene when they talk about the blow-up that motivated Belle to run away, which Disney treated as a key encounter in filming and which is analyzed in the next subsection.

Disney Makes Familiar, Safe, and Romantic a Cycle of Violence That Keeps Victims Hopeful

Beyond familiarizing viewers with a plethora of classic behaviors of expressive aggression and coercive control in romances, Disney's rhetorical choices can be read as portraying those acts consistent with the observed pattern of Walker's Cycle

Theory of Violence. Based on interviews with victims of repeated intimate partner violence, educational psychologist Lenore Walker explains why victims in violent relationships stay. Over time, this theory "has become the most enduring explanation for why battered women stay in abusive relationships."[109] Her decades of research suggest that a predictable three-part battering cycle is common, though not inevitable. Beast's multiple demonstrations of violence toward Belle and the responses to it by both Belle and the bystanders can be read as fitting and facilitating this recognized cycle. Disney's choice to allude, via Chip's final question and Mrs. Potts's answer, that this romance turns out happily credentials an epideictic lesson that witnessing or experiencing signs or episodes of the cycle is not cause for concern. My claim is not that lesser violent acts or threats inevitably lead to violence or to more serious violence (they do not) or that copy-cat violence is the main worry or that Beast inevitably will threaten Belle with increasing severity during their marriage. We do not and cannot know the latter, and Chip's closing comment as he watches the wedding dance pointedly asks his mother for reassurance that the pair will live happily, which she gives. Rather it is that the film, including this reassurance that romantic ideals triumph, may familiarize viewers with and encourage them to overlook, excuse, or romanticize not only isolated acts but patterns of intimate partner violence that often bode ill in real-life relationships and may cultivate expectations that a happy ending will emerge, if the victim loves enough.

In what follows, the application of Cycle Theory of Violence's phases to the film is not a "textbook case" but mimics its general progression in ways that render familiar and simultaneously romanticize a similar, if not exact, pattern of blame and violent actions toward an intimate partner. In phase one, tension gradually builds, with the aggressor expressing dissatisfaction and hostility and the victim placating the partner. The victim may succeed temporarily, "which reinforces her [or his] unrealistic belief that she [or he] can control"[110] the partner's anger. Eventually, in phase two, the aggressor's angry response pattern breaks through the victim's efforts to please, and an acute battering incident (psychological or physical) occurs. For example, in an act of coercive control, Beast restricts his love interest's freedom of movement. He not only makes her promise to stay inside the castle, but declares part of that space off-limits to her. Tensions and Beast's temper build as Belle questions his proclamation.

BEAST: The castle is your home now, so you can go anywhere you wish, except the West Wing.
BELLE: (looking intrigued) What's in the West Wing?
BEAST: (stopping angrily) It's forbidden!

At first Belle complies. But when she investigates the West Wing, the film's most carefully orchestrated scene has Beast lashing out in a realistic fury that escalates to expressive aggression.

BEAST: (growing angry) Why did you come here?
BELLE: (Backing away, scared) I'm sorry.
BEAST: I warned you never to come here!
BELLE: I didn't mean any harm.
BEAST: (Angrier) Do you realize what you could have done? (Begins to thrash at the furniture)
BELLE: (Pleading, but still scared) Please, stop! No!
BEAST: (Screaming) Get out!!!! GET OUT!!!!

In his uncontrolled rage, Beast throws and breaks inanimate objects around Belle as she cringes, her back against an armoire. The instant she moves aside Beast destroys the wardrobe against which she had been cowering with a ferocious backhanded blow. He does not touch Belle, but, in a classic warning sign of abuse that approaches phase two in its severity, emotionally terrorizes her with symbolic violence so physically near that the only remaining step in escalation is bodily contact. Belle flees, and Beast goes after her, saving her from the wolf pack and setting up the film's move to phase three.

In the Cycle Theory of Violence's third "loving-contrition" phase, the aggressor

> may apologize profusely, try to assist his victim, show kindness and remorse and shower her with gifts and/or promises. The batterer himself may believe at this point that he will never allow himself to be violent again. The woman wants to believe the batterer and, early in the relationship at least, may renew her hope in his ability to change. The third phase provides the positive reinforcement for remaining in the relationship.[111]

Victims who stay convince themselves that the partner they see in the "loving-contrition" phase is the "real" person and that, if the behavior of phases one and two is fixed, they will be left with the good "essence" of the person with whom they fell in love.[112] However, in real life, if the partners (however worldly and educated) stay together and the violent does not admit a problem and seek help outside the relationship, research shows that "tension-building" behavior may become more frequent, while "loving-contrition" behavior declines.[113] Violence may not only repeat but escalate over time.[114] In adult-targeted entertainment, violent cues foreshadowing perhaps the most romanticized marital rape in cinematic history by Rhett Butler in MGM's *Gone with the Wind* fit this pattern—including the man kicking in a door to prove to the strong woman that nothing could keep him out of her bedroom. The film romanticizes his violence further by showing a blissfully satisfied Scarlett in bed the morning after her husband's attack. She acts confused by Rhett's apology and dismayed at his promise never to do it again, seriously blurring the line between violence and passion and suggesting violence's romantic appeal to this victim.

When Belle despairs and flees from the castle after the fierce confrontation in Beast's lair, she encounters a pack of menacing wolves, a Disney addition. "Loving-contrite" Beast, who has come after Belle, fights them off and is injured in the process. This event might be easily read through Walker's observations that the violent's outburst is followed by "loving-contrition," including trying to assist his victim—but might quickly circle back to expressive aggression and blaming the victim for the problems. Belle brings Beast back to the castle and is nursing his wounds when this scene occurs, with Chip and the other enchanted objects watching:

> (Fade to int of den, with BELLE pouring hot water out of MRS. POTTS. She soaks a rag in the water, then turns to BEAST, who is licking his wounds.)
>
> BELLE: Here now. Oh, don't do that. (BEAST growls at her as she tries to clean the wound with her rag.) Just . . . hold still.
>
> (She touches the rag to the wound and BEAST roars in pain. The OBJECTS, who have been watching, jump back into hiding from the outburst.)
>
> BEAST: That hurts!
>
> BELLE: (In counterpoint) If you'd hold still, it wouldn't hurt as much.
>
> BEAST: Well if you hadn't run away, this wouldn't have happened!
>
> BELLE: Well if you hadn't frightened me, I wouldn't have run away!
>
> BEAST: (Opens his mouth to respond, but has to stop and think of a good line) Well you shouldn't have been in the West Wing!
>
> BELLE: Well you should learn to control your temper!

Finally, consistent with a violent in the "loving-contrition" phase, Beast tries to patch up his troubled romance by offering extravagant gifts. As Beast discusses with his servants how to best impress Belle, the manipulative side of promises and gift giving as a means to an end in romantic relationships might be taught to Chip and young viewers through word and example.

> COGSWORTH: Well, there's the usual things—flowers, chocolates, promises you don't intend to keep . . .
>
> LUMIERE: Ahh, no no. It has to be something very special. Something that sparks her inter—wait a minute.

Given Belle's love of reading, Lumiere suggests Beast give her the library, and she is delighted. The enchanted objects watch Belle's reaction and discuss, in Chip's presence, how well the gift seems to be serving the end of keeping her in a romantic relationship with Beast. Though they will not answer Chip's direct questions about how such gift-giving "works," the tone of the discussion clearly indicates the mature bystanders' approval of romantic manipulation.

Consistent with the repeat victim role that Walker describes, Belle convinces herself that when Beast is on his "loving-contrition" phase behavior she is seeing the "real" him. For instance, as the couple feeds the birds and Belle teaches Beast to treat them gently, the film's heroine blames herself for not focusing exclusively on Beast's good side and implies that this, not his outbursts, is his "truer" self. Belle's minor teaching successes (e.g., table etiquette) helps convince her that she can and should reform Beast into a gentle, well-mannered partner, singing:

> There's something sweet
> And almost kind
> But he was mean
> And he was coarse and unrefined.
> But now he's dear
> And so unsure,
> I wonder why I didn't see it there before.
> New, and a bit alarming
> Who'd have ever thought that this could be?
> True, that he's no Prince Charming
> But there's something in him that I simply didn't see.

While this legend is ostensibly about looking past appearances to find a more genuine interior—the most double-edged of messages when Beast turns back into a handsome prince[115]—Disney's version may also teach viewers to look beyond or distrust warning signs of romantic violence.

Just as Disney's choices may quiet viewers' concerns, Belle models quieting her own doubts. Viewers witness how Belle's own childish education on love (e.g., reading popular culture romances) has normalized her expectation that princes come in disguise and their true characters are only revealed over time. In an early scene, Belle describes the book that she finds most captivating to a flock of sheep:

> Oh! Isn't this amazing!
> It's my favorite part because, you'll see!
> Here's where she meets Prince Charming
> But she won't discover that it's him 'til chapter three!

Like other intimates who stay with violent partners, fueled by the hope that they can successfully change them, Belle takes on the project of "transforming" or "restoring" Beast in hopes that she can make him regularly his true self from the "loving-contrition" phase. However, this is not a project that Belle willingly adopts at first, even though, from the moment she arrives, the bystanders press her to undertake it and break the spell that makes this Beast beastly.

Despite evidence that real-life romantic relationships characterized by repeated expressive aggression and coercive control rarely turn loving, safe, and happy, absent outside help, and Walker's research showing that escalating violence may threaten victims who stay in such relationships, this film minimizes these concerns for intergenerational audiences. We do not know whether violence returns to this couple's romance after the wedding, but we are encouraged to believe it does not—that the cycle is broken because of their love. When Belle and Beast marry, Chip asks his mother: "Are they gonna live happily ever after, mama?" "Of course, my dear. Of course," she assures him. This soothing resolution may function to excuse the foregoing violence without strong social challenge, reinforcing the acceptable existence of violence in blossoming relationships and making it an "individual" matter to be solved by love. Given the story line, the didactic message might be read as suggesting through enactment that couples who start in violent romantic relationships but stay together live happily ever after without others' intervention. While Disney certainly is not claiming this is true in every case, its arguably atypical, but reassuring take on troubled romance

might discourage vigilance and devalue seeking or giving help. It may reinforce belief in myths that have been shown to keep victims' trapped in violent relationships and feeling responsible for them (e.g., "love is blind, love conquers all, love entails both pain and ecstasy, and love is passionate"); Mrs. Potts's explicit reassurance that the troubled courtship viewers have witnessed ends happily might epideictically endorse "the notion that love can solve any problem (including violence), and that the negative aspects of courtship will remit once marriage takes place."[116] As the research stresses, such real-life romantic hopefulness is too often misplaced.

Enabling, Normalizing, and Romanticizing Intimate Partner Violence: The Castle Bystanders

As disturbing as Belle and Beast modeling the intricacies of classic roles, practices, and patterns of intimate partner violence in family entertainment is, I find the reactions and choices of the adult characters witnessing the danger signs in the presence of young Chip even more distressing. The adults' behavior and comments repeatedly might convey lessons to Chip, and so to viewers, on how to and why one should accept, enable, and romanticize a relationship that exhibits repeated signs of intimate partner violence rather than intervene or discourage it. Initially, it is important to clarify that the entire castle staff, including Chip, his behavior suggests, is well aware of Beast's temper and his capacity for violence prior to when the film's plot ensues. For instance, when Belle's father first wanders into the castle and the enchanted objects welcome him, they all pull away in fear when Beast enters. Two other examples, mentioned earlier (i.e., "it will be our necks" and the objects diving for cover when Beast roars as Belle nurses him), demonstrate the staff's acute awareness of Beast's violent tendencies. When counseling Beast on how to win over Belle, Mrs. Potts and Lumiere remind him in unison, "You must control your temper!" In spite of their knowledge, the staff prods Belle into a romantic relationship by both cultivating her blind hope in a happy ending and encouraging her to ignore her own perceptions of risk and safety instincts. They coax her to instead stay and "get along" by complying with Beast's demands. When Belle mourns being imprisoned with "I've lost my father, my dreams, everything," Mrs. Potts urges her to stay and hope for a happy ending, although she gives no good reason to do so: "Cheer up, child. It'll turn out all right in the end. You'll see." When Belle tries to avoid Beast's temper by staying in her room, Wardrobe, fearing Beast's reaction if Belle does not appear for dinner, insists. "BELLE: That's very kind of you, but I'm not going to dinner. WARDROBE: Oh, but you must!"

After Beast's explosion over Belle's dinner absence and as he spies on her with his magic mirror, Wardrobe soothingly minimizes the Beast's violent behavior to a sobbing Belle, whose instincts are telling her to protect herself. Wardrobe diminishes her experience and encourages Belle to overlook the outburst, to give Beast another chance to show his "true" self.

> WARDROBE: (in mirror pleading) Why the master's not so bad once you get to know him. Why don't you give him a chance?
>
> BELLE: (still disturbed by the attack) I don't want to get to know him. I don't want to have anything to do with him!

Again, after the even more bodily threatening outburst in Beast's lair and as Belle grabs her cloak and rushes for freedom, castle bystanders encourage her to repress the urge to flee:

> LUMIERE: Wh-Where are you going?
>
> BELLE: Promise or no promise, I can't stay here another minute!
>
> COGSWORTH: Oh no, wait, please wait!

All four adult bystanders model responses—for Chip and inter-generational viewers who might witness signs of violence in real-life romances—that minimize and enable that relationship's continuation and the possible reoccurrence of violence. They may epideictically cultivate the importance of urging a victim to stay put, to overlook or personally fix a partner's violence, and to offer the violent ever more chances—hoping love will eventually halt the violence.

A final dysfunctional lesson that these bystanders might teach or reinforce for inter-generational audiences is that the victim is "really" in control of the violent's explosions, a perspective that Jones claims animates the many scientific studies of intimate partner violence that focus primarily on victims' characteristics.[117] For example, Cogsworth blames Belle for Beast's outburst outside her bedroom when she declines his dinner "invitation." He says, without contradiction, to Mrs. Potts: "Well, if you ask me, she was just being stub-

born. After all, the master did say 'please.'" Cogsworth's statement affirms Beast's prerogative to command and coerce Belle, ignores Beast's yelling and the threats that both preceded and followed this nicety, and overlooks the fact that someone else had to prompt Beast to even utter that "please." Instead, this undisputed comment suggests to viewers that Belle, who was barricaded in her room, was in control of the situation because her absence triggered Beast's tantrum. Thus, his subsequent devolution into violence might be read as her fault. She is responsible to avoid triggering the violent's phase two outbursts and to reform them, if she finds them unacceptable. In pursuit of an inter-generational market and greater profits, Disney introduced rhetorical devices that might familiarize viewers with, desensitize them to, or coach tolerance of warning signs, practices, and patterns of intimate partner violence. The ending may reassure viewers that all eventually turns out well in a truly romantic relationship, if the participants are committed. While the film's violence, woven in sophisticated ways through these rhetorical choices, offers pleasure to different generations for different reasons, all paths offer pleasure from the violence and might lead to the conclusion that acts of romantic violence are not causes for concern or intervention but explicable, even "natural," parts of a very passionate, blossoming romance.

It is worth noting that the romantic "violent"–"victim" (and bystander) roles that Disney's film might model and justify are not limited by gender or sexuality. Given the paucity of positive romantic relationship models in popular culture for LGBTQ couples (especially in family-targeted entertainment), these early models may also be powerful in defining and explaining "passionate love" in the less publicly charted territory of same-sex relationships. Although far less comprehensively and reliably studied than heterosexual relationships, available research suggests that intimate partner violence occurs among LGBTQ romantic partners at least as often as among heterosexual couples.[118] The effects of community-approved epideictic suggesting [that] intimate partner violence enacts romantic love and passion and is the path to happily-ever-after might be especially destructive for populations in which victims already receive less support from the criminal justice and social service systems than do heterosexual victims.[119] While popular culture presenting images of romanticized violence as normal and acceptable is not the only factor in LGBTQ abuse any more than it is in heterosexual partner violence, the additional complications of LGBTQ relationships underscore the moral importance of providing a better variety of community-approved, intergenerational entertainment representing mutually respectful, non-violent romances.

Conclusion

This essay suggests an answer to the puzzle left by Aristotle on how a single text can successfully address an inter-generational audience. Epideictic texts and dimensions of texts especially need to engage and educate inter-generational audiences in order to justify and maintain through time a community's practices, norms, expectations, and power relations. Inter-generational audiences struggle with the mysterious nature and norms of romantic courtship generally, and, given statistics showing how widespread yet invisible US romantic violence is, with the common, but seemingly contradictory intersection of romance and psychological or physical aggression. Murphy explains how epideictic can craft a shared world and expectations for diverse adult audiences regarding troubling issues by providing "the backdrop of values and beliefs, heroes and villains, triumphs and tragedies against which and through which deliberative and forensic judgments are made in a ceaseless swirl of discourse."[120] This effect need not come from traditional eloquence, but can arise from offering "a clear and compelling vision of the world."[121] In this animated film, heroes, villains, and plot are simplified, and the lessons are clarified and underscored through violence, coded community-valued virtues (e.g., Belle's), the relative ends that different characters meet, and supplemental explanations from adult to child characters on how to interpret the action. Even children can grasp such a compelling vision of the world and what the text's affirming community sees as acceptable or admirable, can be primed to interpret, judge, and behave similarly in future encounters, and are encouraged to have faith in the community-approved recommendations. Shows of violence that reinforce prevalent values and beliefs, witnessed by a child character who is instructed in interpreting them by trusted adults, can effectively substitute for "like" rhetors addressing "like" audiences.

In addition to demonstrating how violence as a rhetorical device effectively but unobtrusively teaches as it pleases inter-generational audiences, this essay introduces and illustrates the value of the theoretical concept "epideictic dimension." Epideictic dimensions cut across genres as well as texts that fit no recognized genre. They are constituted by textual layers that teach and maintain a community's "common" beliefs and values to guide members' behavior beyond the immediate situation so that status quo practices and power distributions are justified and continue to operate smoothly. The notions of dominant and resistant readings do not completely cover or explain operations of this textual dimension. My reading of how *Beauty and the Beast*'s rhetorical choices collectively, yet subtly, might coach inter-generational audiences to accept and romanticize intimate partner violence is not the dominant or a preferred reading, but it is also not a resistant reading because it shows how the status quo's troubles are explained and its usual practices, patterns, and power relationships made resistant to sweeping change. Identifying the internally consistent rhetorical patterns that subtly but consistently assume, communicate, and potentially reinforce socially conservative beliefs and values, especially when that is not a text's expressed purpose, is valuable because it brings critical questions of epideictic analysis to bear on an important textual dimension that crosses deliberative, forensic, and epideictic texts ostensibly aimed at cultivating different values (e.g., "real beauty" may not be visible on the outside), as well as texts that do not fit any genre.

Dominant and resistant readings are simultaneously possible, of course, and can coexist and collaborate with analysis of a text's many epideictic dimensions. Dominant and resistant readings frequently focus on the large power relationships related to race, gender, and class; reactions to Disney's film focused largely on these aspects. However, every community's operation relies on many other beliefs and values, some equally dark, being reinforced and accepted as justified, even taken for granted. Epideictic dimension analysis focuses on how a text might cultivate such reactions, both questionable and praiseworthy. For instance, this particular reading used Chip as the framing device to show how Disney's film communicates and repeats complex lessons on the appropriate intersection of romance and violence, making it easy for even young viewers to absorb. But one could use this same approach to look for the epideictic lessons (positive and negative) foregrounded if one focuses on, say, Gaston as a framing device. In that reading, one might unexpectedly find Gaston's role indispensable to unequivocally teaching the text's ostensible moral that "beauty and virtue do not necessarily go together." After all, Belle exudes beauty and virtue throughout the story. And Beast, once he performs virtue by becoming lovable to Belle, is rewarded with the return of his princely good looks. Only Gaston, with his excessive violence and good looks (and possibly the vapid trio of village beauties who covet him), remains to drive home for young viewers the central lesson on appearance's unstable link to virtue. Thus, analyzing a text's epideictic dimensions may yield stabilizing social messages that do not call attention to themselves otherwise, as well as yet-unrecognized rhetorical means by which a text advances its explicit epideictic purposes.

Another important difference between analyzing a text's epideictic dimensions and practices of resistant readings is that the former is much easier. It takes relatively less critical work for epideictic lessons to make sense and appeal to non-specialized viewers because they jibe with the familiar status quo. Different readings of a text require different amounts of effort and knowledge brought to the reading and yield varying amounts of pleasure; resistant readings are more work and usually yield less pleasure than dominant ones.[122] My reading requires scant effort to see or absorb, compared to resistant readings of the film; one need not know the categories from Walker's theory or the CDC or have any specialized rhetorical training to absorb this film's conventional lessons on romantic violence. The text matter-of-factly presents evidence that is dramatic, repetitive, internally coherent, and so overwhelming that, with Chip's help, even a child viewer can grasp the film's undisputed, if unformulated, beliefs about what to consider "good" or "acceptable" in romantic violence. This reading requires no resistant spirit or intellectual sophistication or new behaviors by community members because it aligns readily with soothing, conservative messages consistent with the authorizing community's current approach to romance mixed with psychological and physical violence. It explains the film's appeal and epideictic potential with respect to romance for viewers of all ages and sophistication. It is a "downhill" reading whose very ease is what makes its potential impact, if left unrecognized and unaddressed, so concerning.

Consequently, this reading illustrates how a community-approved popular culture text whose value is authorized by celebrating its multiple traditions (i.e., classic legends, great romances, family entertainment, cinematic achievement) might function as an inherent barrier to progressive social change. I have argued for greater attention to the stock issue of inherency on practical social concerns (in this case, intimate partner violence).[123] Inherency is not about placing blame or finding who caused a shared problem; instead it seeks to identify what perpetuates a recognizable shared problem in spite of attempts to address it or why previous solutions have failed. Only once one recognizes how the existing system, intentionally or unintentionally and directly or indirectly, facilitate[s] the problem by its very nature can effective solutions be advanced.[124] Disney is not the only community narrator circulating conservative lessons on romanticizing partner violence, but it does tailor these messages to massive intergenerational audiences including children hungry to learn appropriate conventions. For instance, one way in which this text might subtly cultivate resistance to broad social change is by making ambiguous and potentially acceptable some romantic violence. Gaston's violence toward Belle is coded as odious, but Beast's is treated as explicable frustration that is manageable with Belle's help.

The proven strength of this particular attitudinal barrier suggests the importance of not cultivating it for inter-generational audiences initially—or at least of not letting its cultivation go unremarked upon—rather than just later trying to "cure" it in adults. Changing attitudes toward the acceptability of romantic violence, especially those fostered from childhood on, is most difficult. Research on "batterer intervention programs" demonstrates that even abusers who complete intensive re-education programs and diminish their own violent practices toward romantic partners do not change their attitudes about violence.[125] Until potential barriers to change—such as attitudes and unequal power relationships authorized and romanticized by a community's celebrated inter-generational epideictic popular texts—are critically exposed and openly discussed, structural solutions (e.g., laws, required arrests on domestic violence calls, victim shelters) are unlikely to ameliorate widespread intimate partner violence.

This research was supported in part by funds provided by the University of Wisconsin–Milwaukee. An earlier version of the essay was presented at the Symbolic Violence Conference, Texas A&M University, College Station, TX, in February 2012. The author thanks Brian Wismar for his assistance with proofreading the manuscript and Raymie McKerrow, John Jordan, Lindsay Timmerman, and the reviewers for their helpful suggestions.

OTES

1. All film quotations are from http://www.fpx.de/fp/Disney/Scripts/BeautyAndTheBeast.txt.

2. Consistent with inter-generational marketing, both Angela Lansbury and Celine Dion sang the title song in the 1991 version. For the film's 2010 Blu-ray release, *American Idol* champion Jordin Sparks recorded a new version and shot a princess-themed music video, extending the appeal to new young audiences. Tanner Stransky, "Jordin Sparks Does *Beauty and the Beast*," *Entertainment Weekly*, June 4, 2010, http://www.ew.com/ew/gallery/0,,20385926_20386375_20790029,00.html.

3. Sally Gearheart, "The Womanization of Rhetoric," *Women's Studies International Quarterly* 2 (1979): 195–201; Sonja K. Foss and Cindy L. Griffin, "Beyond Persuasion: A Proposal for an Invitational Rhetoric," *Communication Monographs* 62 (1995): 2–18 [reprinted in this volume].

4. Wayne Brockriede, "Arguers as Lovers," *Philosophy and Rhetoric* 5 (1972): 1–11; Henry W. Johnstone, Jr., "Toward an Ethics of Rhetoric," *Communication* 6 (1981): 305–14; Maurice Natanson, "The Claims of Immediacy," in *Philosophy, Rhetoric, and Argumentation*, ed. Maurice Natanson and Henry W. Johnstone, Jr. (University Park: Pennsylvania State University, 1965), 10–19.

5. Wayne C. Booth, "The Rhetorical Stance," in *Contemporary Rhetoric: A Reader's Coursebook*, ed. Douglas Ehninger (Glenview, IL: Scott, Foresman, 1972), 218–24. (Original work published 1963).

6. Michele C. Black, Kathleen C. Basile, Matthew J. Breiding, Sharon G. Smith, Mikel L. Walters, Melissa T. Merrick, Jieru Chen, and Mark R. Stevens, *The National Intimate Partner and Sexual Violence Survey: 2010 Summary Report* (Atlanta, GA: National Center for Injury Prevention and Control, Centers for Disease Control and Prevention, 2011).

7. "Despite Its Prevalence, the Patterns of Domestic Violence Are Not Understood by Many Bystanders," *PRNewswire*, September 21, 2006. Available at Michigan Poverty Law Program http://www.mplp.org/Resources/mplpresource.2006-12-21.0455588147/family3.htm.

8. Lenore E. Walker, *The Battered Woman* (New York: Harper & Row, 1979); Lenore E. A. Walker, *The Battered Woman Syndrome*, 2nd ed. (New York: Springer, 2000).

9. Betsy Hearne, *Beauty and the Beast: Visions and Revisions of an Old Tale* (Chicago: University of Chicago Press, 1989), 1.

10. Hearne, *Beauty and the Beast*, 124.

11. Allison Craven, "Beauty and the Belles: Discourses of Feminism and Femininity in Disneyland," *European Journal of Women's Studies* 9 (2002): 126, 132.

12. June Cummins, "Romancing the Plot: The Real Beast of Disney's *Beauty and the Beast*," *Children's Literature Association Quarterly* 20 (1995): 23.

13. Cummins, "Romancing the Plot," 24.

14. Hearne, *Beauty and the Beast*, 140.

15. Cummins, "Romancing the Plot," 25.

16. Craven, "Beauty and the Belles," 127.

17. Craven, "Beauty and the Belles," 130.

18. Chris Hicks, "Beauty and the Beast," Review, *Deseret News*, November 22, 1991, para. 7, http://www.desnews.com/movies/view/1,1257,154,00.html.

19. Rick Marin, "Sexy Enough for Adults, Magical for Kids," *TV Guide*, November 16–22, 1991, 15.

20. Cummins, "Romancing the Plot," 22, 26.

21. Cummins, "Romancing the Plot," 25; Betsy Hearne, "Disney Revisited, or, Jiminy Cricket, It's Musty Down Here!" *Horn Book Magazine* 73 (1997): para. 15, http://people.lis.illinois.edu/_ehearne/disney.html.

22. Cummins, "Romancing the Plot," 22, 25.

23. Cummins, "Romancing the Plot," 26; Craven, "Beauty and the Belles," 138.

24. Cummins, "Romancing the Plot," 26–27.

25. Craven, "Beauty and the Belles," 125.

26. Craven, "Beauty and the Belles," 132.

27. Bob Thomas, *Disney's Art of Animation: From Mickey Mouse to Beauty and the Beast* (New York: Hyperion, 1991), 147.

28. Craven, "Beauty and the Belles," 132–33.

29. Craven, "Beauty and the Belles," 135.

30. Cummins, "Romancing the Plot," 26.

31. Susan Jeffords, "The Curse of Masculinity: Disney's *Beauty and the Beast*," in *From Mouse to Mermaid: The Politics of Film, Gender, and Culture*, ed. Elizabeth Bell, Lynda Haas, and Laura Sells (Bloomington: Indiana University Press, 1995), 166–67.

32. Craven, "Beauty and the Belles," 135.

33. Cummins, "Romancing the Plot," 27.

34. Cummins, "Romancing the Plot," 27.

35. Hearne, "Disney Revisited," para. 20, 16.

36. Both Disney's producer and its script-writer purposely discarded earlier fairy tale, film, and television versions to "make our own," Thomas, *Disney's Art*, 140, 143.

37. Janet Maslin, "Disney's *Beauty and the Beast* Updated in Form and Content," *New York Times*, November 13, 1991.

38. David Ansen, "Just the Way Walt Made 'em: Disney's 'Beauty and the Beast' Is an Instant Classic," Review, Newsweek, November 18, 1991, 74–75, 80; Thomas, *Disney's Art*, 124–203, esp. 115, 183, 193, 198. The confrontation during the pivotal lair scene was

vocally recorded ten times, with a co-director urging voice actors to ever-greater emotional heights, Thomas, *Disney's Art*, 128.

39. Ansen, "Just the Way," 80.

40. Thomas, *Disney's Art*, 70–71, 129.

41. Thomas, *Disney's Art*, 144.

42. Katrina Ames, "A Little Saint-Saens, A Lot of Fun," *Newsweek*, November 18, 1991, 74–75; Ansen, "Just the Way;" Craven, "Beauty and the Belles," 125.

43. Marin, "Sexy Enough," 14–15.

44. Kathi Maio, "Mr. Right Is a Beast: Disney's Dangerous Fantasy," *Visions Magazine* 7 (Summer 1992): 44.

45. Marina Warner, "Beauty & the Beasts," *Sight and Sound*, 2, no. 6 (October 1992): 11.

46. Cummins, "Romancing the Plot," 23.

47. *AFI's Greatest Romance Movies—A Kiss Isn't Just a Kiss*, n.d., http://movies.about.com/library/weekly/aaafitoplista.htm; "10 Movies That Defined Our Decade," *Premiere*, October 1997, 63–80.

48. "The 10 Most Romantic Movies," *Ladies' Home Journal*, February 2002, 44.

49. "Popcorn: Beauty and the Beast," Review, n.d., para. 6, http://members.tripod.com/_Reviews/Beauty.htm.

50. Hearne, "Disney Revisited," para. 7.

51. James Berardinelli, Review, 2001, para. 6, Movie-reviews.colossuss.net/movies/b/beauty.html; Roger Ebert, "Beauty and the Beast," Review, *Chicago Sun-Times*, November 22, 1991; Ansen, "Just the Way," 80.

52. Ebert, "Beauty and the Beast."

53. Hicks, "Beauty and the Beast," para. 9.

54. Hal Hinson, "Beauty and the Beast," Review, *Washington Post*, November 22, 1991.

55. Mark R. Leeper, "*Beauty and the Beast* (1991)," Review, 1991, para. 1, 9, http://www.imdb.com/reviews/11/1182.html.

56. Berardinelli, Review, para. 1, 11.

57. Elaine Showalter, "*Beauty and the Beast*: Disney Meets Feminism in a Liberated Love Story for the '90s," *Premiere*, October 1997, 66.

58. Harriett Hawkins, "Maidens and Monsters in Modern Popular Culture: *The Silence of the Lambs* and *Beauty and the Beast*," Textual Practice 7 (1993): 263.

59. See, for example, Dawn Elizabeth England, Lara Descartes, and Melissa A. Collier-Meek, "Gender Role Portrayal and the Disney Princesses," *Sex Roles* 64 (2011): 555–67; Cynthia Erb, "Another World or the World of an Other? The Space of Romance in Recent Versions of *Beauty and the Beast*," *Cinema Journal* 34, no. 4 (1995): 50–70.

60. Unnamed critic quoted in Maio, "Mr. Right," 44.

61. Susan Z. Swan, "Gothic Drama in Disney's *Beauty and the Beast*: Subverting Traditional Romance by Transcending the Animal–Human Paradox," *Critical Studies in Mass Communication* 16 (1999): 351.

62. Sharon D. Downey, "Feminine Empowerment in Disney's *Beauty and the Beast*," *Women's Studies in Communication* 19 (1996): 192, 207.

63. Warner, "Beauty & the Beasts," 11.

64. Warner, "Beauty & the Beasts," 11.

65. Maio, "Mr. Right," 44–45. See also Cummins, "Romancing the Plot," 25.

66. Maio, "Mr. Right," 45.

67. Elizabeth Dodson Gray, "*Beauty and the Beast*: A Parable for Our Time," in *Women Respond to the Men's Movement: A Feminist Collection*, ed. Kay Leigh Hagan (San Francisco: Pandora, 1992), 160. Jeffords claims that older versions all feature Belle's story, "The Curse of Masculinity," 167.

68. Maio, "Mr. Right," 45.

69. Gray, "*Beauty and the Beast*," 160. See also Jeffords, "The Curse of Masculinity," 171.

70. See, for example, Warner, "Beauty & the Beasts," 11.

71. Maio, "Mr. Right," 45.

72. Gray, "Beauty and the Beast," 163, 165–67.

73. Gray, "Beauty and the Beast," 159.

74. Chaim Perelman and Lucie Olbrechts-Tyteca, *The New Rhetoric: A Treatise on Argumentation*, trans. John Wilkinson and Purcell Weaver (Notre Dame, IN: University of Notre Dame Press, 1969), 50.

75. Perelman and Olbrechts-Tyteca, *New Rhetoric*, 52–53.

76. Celeste Michelle Condit, "The Functions of Epideictic: The Boston Massacre Orations as Exemplar," *Communication Quarterly* 33 (1985): 288.

77. Veronica Hefner and Barbara J. Wilson, "From Love at First Sight to Soul Mate: The Influence of Romantic Ideals in Popular Films on Young People's Beliefs about Relationships," *Communication Monographs* 80 (2013): 152.

78. Hefner and Wilson, "From Love at First Sight," 160–62.

79. George Gerbner and Larry Gross, "The Violent Face of Television and Its Lessons," in *Children and the Faces of Television: Teaching, Violence, Selling*, ed. Edward L. Palmer and Aimee Dorr (New York: Academic Press, 1980), 152.

80. Gerbner and Gross, "Violent Face," 160.

81. Gerbner and Gross, "Violent Face," 156.

82. Gerbner and Gross, "Violent Face," 155.

...dit, "Functions," 289.

. Perelman and Olbrechts-Tyteca, *New Rhetoric*,

85. Condit, "Functions," 288.

86. Perelman and Olbrechts-Tyteca, *New Rhetoric*, 54.

87. Aristotle, *"Art" of Rhetoric*, trans. John Henry Freese (Cambridge, MA: Harvard University Press, 1926), I.iii.1–6.

88. Aristotle, *"Art" of Rhetoric*, I.v.1–2.

89. Aristotle, *"Art" of Rhetoric*, II.xiii.16.

90. George Gerbner, "Cultivation Analysis: An Overview," *Mass Communication & Society* 3/4 (1998): 178.

91. Perelman and Olbrechts-Tyteca, *New Rhetoric*, 52.

92. See Downey, "Feminine Empowerment," 187.

93. Hearne, "Disney Revisited," para. 18.

94. Aristotle, *"Art" of Rhetoric*, II.xiv.10–11, note b.

95. Gerbner and Gross, "Violent Face," 151.

96. Ansen, "Just the Way," 74–75; Marin, "Sexy Enough," 15; Thomas, *Disney's Art*, 149.

97. Showalter, *"Beauty and the Beast,"* 66.

98. Leeper, *"Beauty and the Beast,"* para. 3.

99. Warner, "Beauty & the Beasts," 11.

100. Warner, "Beauty & the Beasts," 11.

101. Warner, "Beauty & the Beasts," 11.

102. Ashley Hayes, "Survey: 1 in 3 Women Affected by Partner's Violent Behavior," *CNN Health*, December 15, 2011, http://www.cnn.com/2011/12/15/health/violencesurvey?iref+obinsite; Mike Stobbe, "Survey: 1 in 4 Women Attacked by Intimate Partner," *APA Top News Package*, December 14, 2011.

103. Black et al., *National Intimate Partner*, 45–47, 42–44.

104. Black et al., *National Intimate Partner*, 45–47.

105. "Despite Its Prevalence."

106. Quoted in "Despite Its Prevalence," para. 12.

107. Thomas, *Disney's Art*, 161, 182.

108. Marquette County Prosecutor's Office, Domestic Violence, n.d. http://www.co.marquette.mi.us/departments/prosecutor_s_office/domestic_violence.htm.

109. Linda G. Mills, *Violent Partners: A Breakthrough Plan for Ending the Cycle of Abuse* (New York: Basic Books, 2008), 28.

110. Walker, *Battered Woman Syndrome*, 126.

111. Walker, *Battered Woman Syndrome*, 127.

112. Walker, *Battered Woman Syndrome*, 136.

113. Walker, *Battered Woman Syndrome*, 128, 132. See also Leslie Morgan Steiner, *Crazy Love: A Memoir* (New York: St. Martin's Press, 2009), 236–42.

114. Walker, *Battered Woman Syndrome*, 136.

115. See Jonathan Romney, "Beauty and the Beast," *Sight and Sound* (October 1992): 46.

116. Sally A. Lloyd, "The Darkside of Courtship: Violence and Sexual Exploitation," *Family Relations* 40 (1991): 16.

117. Ann Jones, *Next Time, She'll Be Dead: Battering & How to Stop It* (Boston: Beacon Press, 1994), 139.

118. Claire M. Renzetti, "Violence and Abuse among Same-Sex Couples," in *Violence Between Intimate Partners: Patterns, Causes and Effects*, ed. Albert P. Cardarelli (Boston: Allyn and Bacon, 1997), esp. 70–77; Christopher W. Blackwell, "Domestic Violence in Gay, Lesbian, Bisexual, and Transgender Persons: Populations at Risk," in *The War Against Domestic Violence*, ed. Lee E. Ross (Boca Raton, FL: CRC Press, 2010), 130–31. Given society's heterosexist biases, LGBTQ partner abusers have additional weapons, such as threatening to "out" the victim, Renzetti, "Violence and Abuse," 74.

119. Renzetti, "Violence and Abuse," 88–89; Blackwell, "Domestic Violence," 133–36; Mills, *Violent Partners*, 36.

120. John M. Murphy, "'Our Mission and Our Moment': George W. Bush and September 11th," *Rhetoric & Public Affairs* 6 (2003): 610.

121. Murphy, "'Our Mission,'" 625.

122. Celeste Michelle Condit, "The Rhetorical Limits of Polysemy," *Critical Studies in Mass Communication* 6 (1989): 103–22 [reprinted in this volume].

123. Kathryn M. Olson, "The Practical Importance of Inherency Analysis for Public Advocates: Rhetorical Leadership in Framing a Supportive Social Climate for Education Reforms," *Journal of Applied Communication Research* 36 (2008): 219–41.

124. Olson, "Practical Importance," 224–25.

125. Mills, *Violent Partners*, 37.

PART VIII

ALTERNATIVES TO
THE RHETORICAL TRADITION

Historically marginalized groups—women, various ethnic minorities, people of color, members of LGBTQ communities, persons with disabilities, and so on— have long struggled in Western societies to achieve the enlightened values of universal human rights and equality. Often these struggles have been formalized and the otherwise silenced voices of these marginalized groups have been mobilized, occasionally with dramatic and perspective-shifting results (as in the U.S. Supreme Court's decision to recognize same-sex marriage in June 2015, or in South Carolina Governor Nikki Haley's decision a month later to remove the Confederate flag from the statehouse in the wake of the shootings in Charleston). Increasingly, the rhetoric of marginalized groups has gained visibility not only in public demonstrations of solidarity, but also in online forums designed to promote awareness.

Since the early 1970s, the discipline of rhetorical studies has given increased attention to such groups, focusing both on the ways in which rhetoric has been used to effect such efforts and on the implications such efforts have had for who and what we are as a "people." The incorporation of marginalized voices into the contemporary study of rhetoric has significantly challenged the historical biases represented in the canon of great works privileged by the rhetorical tradition, including both technical and philosophical treatises, as well as those texts identified as exemplars of rhetoric-in-action. The addition of such voices has also challenged the methods employed in the study of rhetoric. The majority of groups marginalized in Western society fall into one or more categories of class, gender, race (broadly construed to include the interests and concerns of both ethnic minorities and postcolonial groups), and sexual choice. The essays in this section offer an introduction to this continuing trend toward inclusion, emphasizing voices that have until recently been ignored, as well as theoretical approaches that have been underutilized. The thinking behind the choices in this section is clear: As rhetorical theory becomes more attentive to marginalized voices, so too must the range of methods and approaches expand. This approach also works in reverse: As we move beyond traditional rhetorical methodologies, we might also awaken to the potential including disparate voices—no less, objects and artifacts of the same—under the awning of rhetoric.

As we survey this movement, it is important to note that the primary route by which marginalized voices have been incorporated within the discipline of rhetorical studies has not been the avenue of philosophically oriented, theoretical work, but rather the various byways of critical and historically grounded theory. Such work typically either has incorporated the rhetorical practices of marginalized groups as instances of rhetoric worthy of criticism, or has employed the rhetorical and ideological insights of marginalized groups as a site from which to critique mainstream rhetorical practices. The more philosophical (re)theorizing of contemporary rhetorical studies from the perspective of the margins, a relatively recent event, has emerged in the wake of such historical and critical theoretical engagements. We offer four theoretically motivated essays that examine the problems and possibilities of rhetoric from three marginalized positions: class, gender, and race. We also offer one essay that goes beyond these categories, urging the inclusion of a traditionally marginalized theoretical orientation— namely, psychoanalytical theory.

James Arnt Aune's "Cultures of Discourse: Marxism and Rhetorical Theory" examines the dual repression of "rhetoric" within Marxist theory and of "Marxist" terminologies within the history and theory of public argument and debate. His argument is a provocative one that urges a revitalized conception of "traditional rhetorical theory" through a Marxist vocabulary organized around the metaphor of "modes of production" as a means of engaging the "social dislocations and class tensions" so prominent in contemporary social and political discourse. Although this approach is only speculative at this stage, Aune suggests that it might well be time to effect a critical and theoretical articulation of Marxism and rhetoric with the goal of producing "a more humane practice of public argument."

Carole Blair, Julie R. Brown, and Leslie A. Baxter's "Disciplining the Feminine" speaks directly to the ways in which the discipline of rhetorical studies may well be animated by an oppressive patriarchalism. As the case for their study, they examine a set of comments written by anonymous journal reviewers who rejected the publication of an earlier study by Blair, Brown, and Baxter that was critical of the methodological and theoretical assumptions undergirding the evaluation of female scholars in rhetorical and communication studies. The essay speaks to the problems and concerns of rhetorical theory at several important levels, but none more so than in the ways in which it appropriates Michel Foucault's theory of discipline and punishment to demonstrate and evaluate the dominance of a masculinist ideology within the "discipline" of speech communication. The essay has been highly controversial, both for its suggestion that speech communication imposes a masculinist discipline on all its scholars, and for its critique of the larger, academic practice of "blind review" of journal articles—that is, the practice of allowing the reviewers of journal articles to maintain anonymity. Although gains have been made since the essay's initial release, and although female perspectives have continued to be integrated, the specter of anonymity (and the challenges it poses) still looms over the processes of publication.

The dominant rhetorical tradition in departments of communication has typically been written from within a Westernized perspective by scholars of European ethnic origin. As global communication and transportation systems have increased interaction among world cultures, it has become increasingly evident that such rhetorical theory does not embrace sufficiently the full range of human rhetorical possibilities. Accordingly, it should be obvious that there is a major need to identify and evaluate rhetorical theories that have been developed in non-Western contexts and with attention to the implications of racial and ethnic difference. As a consequence of this recognition, there has been increasing attention to a variety of non-Western perspectives on rhetoric from Asian, Aboriginal, and Middle and Near Eastern cultural contexts. Raka Shome's "Postcolonial Interventions in the Rhetorical Canon: An 'Other' View" and Lin-Lee Lee's "Pure Persuasion: A Case Study of *Nüshu* or 'Women's Script' Discourses" represent some of the work pushing in such directions. While the former argues for a wholesale reevaluation in light of postcolonial theorizing, the latter points to how traditional sources of theoretical insight can be enriched by examining nontraditional artifacts.

Shome operates from the assumption that Western theories of rhetoric are hampered in their ability to speak to the problems of communication because they are grounded in a narrow and limited "Eurocentrism"—that is, the modernist assumption that Western European beliefs and values, particularly those that emphasize the autonomous rational individual, have universal applicability. The alternative Shome presents is "postcolonialism," a theoretical perspective that questions the role of modernist, neocolonial patterns of intellectual domination in reproducing the hegemony of "first world" nations, and thus examines more closely the ways in which dominant, Western rhetorical theories and practices serve to facilitate such reproduction. In addition, it emphasizes the "hybrid location of cultural values" and thus offers the basis for reconceptualizing the inventional practices of rhetoric as a form of "border crossing."

Lee instead focuses on a by-now-well-established contributor to rhetorical theory: Kenneth Burke. More specifically, she works to unravel the implications of what Burke called "pure persuasion," an idealized and abstract notion that he nonetheless suggested had a base in particular examples. Noting that pure persuasion "has close affinities to drama, ritual, and poetics," Lee goes on to focus on thousand-year-old Chinese *Nüshu* ("women's scripts"). These oral performances, enacted by women and the creative results of cross-cultural fertilization and domestic realities, served no traditional rhetorical function. Instead, Lee argues, *Nüshu* enacted a form of pure persuasion meant to express and validate the feelings of the women who wrote, performed, and handed them down to successive generations. Engaging the religious, dramatic, and celebratory features of Burke's complicated concept, *Nüshu* "has as its sole purpose the transformation of the symbolic world of participants" who lived in a culture where their everyday lives were circumscribed by the realities of cultural convention.

In "Refiguring Fantasy: Imagination and Its Decline in U.S. Rhetorical Studies," Joshua Gunn also looks to a well-established part of the contemporary rhetorical canon: Ernest Bormann's fantasy theme analysis. He argues that Bormann went only so far in pushing the limits of what rhetorical theory can do in terms of dealing with the imagination, urging that a truly "posthumanist" approach to rhetoric would embrace the complicated notions of the "imaginary" and the "unconscious" as found in psychoanalytical theory. This push would, if developed into an "imaginary paradigm," further displace the cherished status of "rational, deliberate argument" in rhetorical studies. In so doing, Gunn engages in a wide-ranging survey of the imagination and its relationship to work in rhetorical theory and criticism. He seeks to integrate a host of outside influences, harnessing the work of Sigmund Freud, Michel Foucault, Louis Pierre Althusser, Gilles Deleuze, and Jacques Marie Émile Lacan, among others. Gunn charts this work back to Aristotle, Francis Bacon, and Giambattista Vico. This truly historical survey poses important questions for rhetorical theory—questions to which the answers are still emerging.

The essays in this section challenge the conventions of contemporary rhetorical theory by urging that notions of class, race, sex, and even theoretical orientation cannot remain static. They point to the fact that what is and is not "contemporary" is always contested and fluid, subject as much to past conditions as to current developments. Online or in person, these essays augur a robust future for theorizing, as well as for practicing and enacting, rhetoric.

ADDITIONAL READINGS

Asante, Molefi Kete. (1993). "An Afrocentric Theory of Communication." In Molefi Kete Asante, ed., *Malcolm X as a Cultural Hero and Other Afrocentric Essays* (Trenton, NJ: Africa World Press), 171–87.

Aune, James Arnt. (1994). *Rhetoric and Marxism.* Boulder, CO: Westview Press.

Biesecker, Barbara. (1992). "Coming to Terms with Recent Attempts to Write Women into the History of Rhetoric." *Philosophy and Rhetoric* 25: 140–61.

_____. (1998). "Rhetorical Studies and the 'New' Psychoanalysis: What's the Real Problem? Or Framing the Problem of the Real." *Quarterly Journal of Speech* 84.2: 222–40.

Campbell, Karlyn Kohrs. (1989). *Man Cannot Speak for Her: A Critical Study of Early Feminist Rhetoric.* 2 vols. New York: Greenwood Press.

Dow, Bonnie J. (1995). "Feminism, Difference(s), and Rhetorical Studies." *Communication Studies* 46: 106–17.

Gaonkar, Dilip Parameshwar. (2002). "Towards New Imaginaries: An Introduction." *Public Culture* 14.1: 1–19.

Garrett, Mary M. (1993). "Pathos Reconsidered from the Perspective of Classical Chinese Rhetorics." *Quarterly Journal of Speech* 79: 19–39.

Gearhart, Sally Miller. (1979). "The Womanization of Rhetoric." *Women's Studies International Quarterly* 2: 195–201.

Green, Ronald Walter. (2004). "Rhetoric and Capitalism: Rhetorical Agency as Communicative Labor." *Philosophy and Rhetoric* 37.2: 188–206.

Kennedy, George A. (1998). *Comparative Rhetoric: An Historical and Cross-Cultural Introduction.* New York: Oxford University Press.

Lee, Wen Shu. (1998). "In the Names of Chinese Women." *Quarterly Journal of Speech* 84.3: 283–302.

McDaniel, James P. (2000). "Mortal Coiling: Peters via Emerson and Žižek on Eros and Communication." *Quarterly Journal of Speech* 86:3: 354–67.

McPhail, Mark Lawrence. (1998). "From Complicity to Coherence: Rereading the Rhetoric of Afrocentricity." *Western Journal of Communication* 62: 114–40.

Nakayama, Thomas K., and Robert L. Krizek. (1995). "Whiteness: A Strategic Rhetoric." *Quarterly Journal of Speech* 81: 291–309.

Ratcliffe, Krista. *Anglo-American Feminist Challenges to the Rhetorical Traditions: Virginia Woolf, Mary Daly, Adrienne Rich.* Carbondale: Southern Illinois University Press.

Cultures of Discourse

Marxism and Rhetorical Theory

James Arnt Aune

On November 10, 1837, soon after becoming a student at the University of Berlin, Karl Marx wrote a letter to his father. The letter described the development of Marx's two great loves: for Hegel's philosophy and for his future wife, Jenny von Westphalen. There are at least two items of interest in the letter for the student of rhetoric. First, in the introduction Marx deprecated the love poems he recently sent to Jenny: "All the poems of the first three volumes I sent to Jenny are marked by attacks on our times, diffuse and inchoate expressions of feeling, nothing natural, everything built out of moonshine, complete opposition between what is and ought to be, rhetorical reflections instead of poetic thoughts." Second, he described the writing of a twenty-four-page dialogue, "Cleanthus, or the Starting Point and Necessary Continuation of Philosophy," where in attempting to unite art and science, he was led to the acceptance of the Hegelian system. His philosophical endeavors left him in an agitated state. He sought relief by joining his landlord on a hunting expedition and, on his return, by immersing himself in what he called "positive studies." These "positive studies" included the reading of works on the law of property, criminal law, canon law, and a work on the artistic instincts of animals. He then translated parts of Aristotle's *Rhetoric* (Marx and Engels, 1975, pp. 10–21).

It is unclear from the letter or from other writings of Marx what parts of the *Rhetoric* he translated or

what effect they had on his work. Nonetheless, I choose this letter for an introduction to a discussion of Marxism and public argument because it serves as a kind of representative anecdote for the reception of rhetoric in the Marxist tradition: if mentioned at all, rhetoric is consigned to the margins of serious discourse, is rigidly separated from both art and philosophy, and is considered, at best, to be a branch of "positive studies." As Kenneth Burke writes, "The Marxist persuasion is usually advanced in the name of no-rhetoric" (Burke, 1969, p. 102), a lesson which Burke no doubt first learned when his venture into Marxist rhetorical theory, *Revolutionary Symbolism in America*, "was roundly condemned at the Communist Writer's Congress in 1935" (Burke, 1935).

The possibility that Marx knew something about the rhetorical tradition is at first sight an intriguing one, but the inevitable conclusion to be drawn from his writings is that the tradition had a negligible influence. To be sure, the historical writings, especially *The Eighteenth Brumaire of Louis Bonaparte* (Marx, 1963), display a nearly Ciceronian style, full of antitheses and copia, but the absence of classical notions of invention or audience is rather obvious. In contrast, we know that the father of capitalist political economy, Adam Smith, wrote a series of lectures on rhetoric and that two of the most important nineteenth-century rhetorical theorists, Thomas De Quincey and Richard Whately, wrote books defending

One wonders what a Marxist rhetoric ʲʳ like, then and now.[2]

On the other hand, if Marxism has been silent about the rhetorical tradition, the rhetorical tradition has been almost equally silent about Marxism, both as a historical phenomenon and as a theoretical perspective on discourse. Despite Philip Wander's (1983) immensely important work on ideological criticism and Michael Calvin McGee's (1982) ongoing project for a materialist rhetoric, serious discussion of Marxism (as opposed to a sort of eclectic American radicalism) remains limited to a few partisans of political economy or cultural studies, two research traditions notable for their inattention to rhetoric. The term "ideology" has attained quasi-canonical status in rhetorical criticism, but Marx's central focus on class struggle has been thoroughly ignored by rhetorical scholars. Students of social movements in our field virtually have ignored labor, perhaps because many of them came to political consciousness at a time when the working class was no longer in fashion among liberal academics. Perhaps the most impressive work of Marxist rhetorical theory yet produced, Lawrence Grossberg's (1979) "Marxist Dialectics and Rhetorical Criticism," uses the concept of "class" only once, and there it is in the context of a discussion of Stalinism.

At first sight, the substitution of "ideology" for "class" in left academic discourse seems to solve some problems. It eliminates the putative economic determinism of classical Marxism and opens up the possibility of explaining larger patterns of argument in a culture instead of just focusing on a single speech and its effects. The work of Celeste Condit is perhaps the best example of a productive use of the concept of ideology in the study of public argument. One could also point out that substituting "ideology" for "class" also opens up left academic discourse for the analysis of oppression based on race and gender divisions (Condit, 1987). It seems curious, however, to claim that an analysis of public discourse based on certain observations about the capitalist mode of production is incomplete or maybe even "patriarchal," when no one has examined seriously how capitalism has affected the theory and practice of rhetoric. Further, substituting "ideology" for "class struggle" as a key term runs the risk of making oppression largely a linguistic or cultural matter. The ambiguous position of academics within the class structure of advanced capitalism makes ideological criticism appealing but scarcely more

useful politically than when the Frankfurt School invented it in the 1930s.

The focus of this essay, then, is on the repression of rhetoric in Marxist theory and on the reading of the history of theories of public argument in Marxist terms. A critical "articulation" of Marxism and the rhetorical tradition is perhaps premature.[3] It may well be the case that a commitment to Marxist categories by its nature eliminates a rhetorical understanding of public argument. It may also be the case that a commitment to the rhetorical tradition necessitates that one be either a reformist or a conservative. This essay is intended to be an invitation to dialogue, not the raising of a dogmatic flag. I will proceed by: (1) outlining the communicative dilemma created by certain key silences in the classical texts of Marx and Engels, (2) creating a typology of later Marxist responses to this communicative dilemma, and (3) proposing a rereading of the history of rhetorical theory in Marxist terms.

The Two Marxisms and Marx's Rhetorical Problem

Sometimes it appears that the term "Marxist" is so ambiguous as to be useless, unless one is using it solely for propaganda purposes, as in "The Marxist regime in Nicaragua. . . ." Inasmuch as mainstream historians and social scientists accept many of Marx's once controversial doctrines, why keep using the term? Or, given the tremendous political (and moral) distance between, say, Antonio Gramsci and Joseph Stalin, is it reasonable to argue that both were "Marxists"? These objections aside, I do believe that it is possible to describe the outlines of a Marxist "paradigm," at least as an analytic method. It seems less possible to argue that there exists a specific Marxist *politics*, mainly because Marxism after Marx has realized that Marx lacked a politics (among other things). On the other hand, to suggest that Marxism is simply a method, deserving of a sort of affirmative action treatment in the contemporary university, ignores Marx's own intention, which was, quite simply, "to change the world" (Marx, 1972, p. 145).

At a rather high level of abstraction, the following assumptions are common to the many "Marxisms" (see Heilbroner, 1985): (1) "Labor" is a central, if not the central, characteristic of human beings. (2) The mode of production in a given social totality—the level of development of productive forces in addition to the type of work relations that accompany those forces—is a determining factor in establishing that totality's social "being." (3) All hitherto existing societies have been characterized by a class struggle over the control or allocation of the surplus from production. (4) The level of development of the productive forces determines, in the sense of setting boundary conditions for, the sort of class structure and class struggle in a given social system. (5) Because the productive forces tend to develop over time, "history" is generally predictable in terms of the succession of modes of production. (6) That class which controls the mode of production in a given society tends to repress, either through the threat of violence or through promoting a particular set of beliefs in the legitimacy of the existing order, radical alterations in control of the productive forces. (7) Capitalism has outlived its usefulness as a mode of production; that is, it helped develop the productive forces to their currently high level, but its chronic crises, and its wastefulness of natural resources and human talent, mean that it will pass away eventually. (8) The precise mode of capitalism's passing away will vary, depending on the political assumptions of the various schools of Marxism.

Despite the great number of Marxisms, Alvin Gouldner's (1980) division of all hitherto existing Marxisms into "Two Marxisms" is a useful category system. The first is scientific Marxism, and the second is critical Marxism. Followers of the first school would include Lenin, Althusser, and "evolutionary" social democrats such as Eduard Bernstein. These writers view Marxism as science, not critique, and their "canon within the canon" of Marx's writings is the "mature" political economy of *Capital* and not the "ideologized" anthropology of the *1844 Manuscripts*. They stress a deterministic view of ideology, devalue individual experience and action, and emphasize the law-like character of historical change. In contrast, critical Marxists "conceive of Marxism as critique rather than science, they stress the continuity of Marx with Hegel, the importance of the young Marx, the ongoing significance of the young Marx's emphasis on 'alienation,' and are more historicist" (Gouldner, 1980, p. 39). Representative critical Marxists are Gramsci, Sartre, and the Frankfurt School.

Critical Marxism sought to respond to an apparent contradiction in Marx's texts. Gouldner (1980) writes, "The problem is that if capitalism is indeed governed by lawful regularities that doom it to be supplanted by a new socialist society (when the requisite infrastructures have matured), why then stress that 'the point is to change it'? Why go to great pains to arrange capitalism's funeral if its demise is guaranteed by science? Why must persons be mobilized and exhorted to discipline themselves to behave in conformity with necessary laws by which, it would seem, they would in any event be bound?" (p. 32). In other words, Marxism has a rhetorical problem: either the classless society is inevitable and scientifically grounded with individual choice being irrelevant, *or* the classless society comes about through the persuasion of individuals and thus ceases to be grounded in scientific laws of history—laws that, as Kenneth Burke ([1950] 1969b) has pointed out, are a major source of Marxism's rhetorical power in the first place (p. 101). The source of the dilemma is Marx's own failure to create a political theory that would explain how the working class struggles and gains power in or over the state. More precisely, Marx did not explain the psychological and rhetorical prerequisites for revolution.

The Marxist tradition has tended to fill in the gap between what we might call *structure* and *struggle* in roughly four ways:

The first is *Leninism*, which is given its quintessential philosophical expression in the work of Lukács. As Lenin (1961) writes in *What Is to Be Done?*, the working class, left to its own devices, will develop at best trade union consciousness, but never revolutionary consciousness (pp. 31–32). Hence the need for a revolutionary vanguard party that anticipates a fully realized class consciousness (Lukács 1971, pp. 41–42, 51). This party can prepare for revolution and guide the masses at the time of collapse of the capitalist system. In order for the party to be ready for revolution, it must be tightly disciplined, periodically purge itself, and possess a rigidly correct theory of Marxism—concepts that can be summarized by Lenin's wonderfully Orwellian phrase, "democratic centralism." A Leninist party, of course, runs the risk of losing touch with the workers, privileging the role of intellectuals, and eventually becoming totalitarian. The Leninist model of organization also has been notably unsuccessful in advanced industrial societies.

A second alternative, which can be traced back to Rosa Luxemburg, and perhaps even further back to Bakunin, does not privilege the role of the party in fomenting revolution, but rather depends on

.neous revolution in the masses them-
.o at the time of capitalist crisis will form
..ally the councils to deal with political and
economic issues (see Albert and Hahnel, 1978).
This view is represented also by the early new
left, which called for participatory democracy.
It also has been influential in the abandonment
of what C. Wright Mills (1969) called Marxism's
"labor metaphysic" (p. 28). In Herbert Marcuse's
(1964) view, for example, the agent of revolution
will not necessarily be the industrial working class,
but those people marginalized by the status quo—
blacks, students, women, homosexuals, for example
(pp. 256–257). The danger in this version of Marxism is its tendency toward leftist adventurism or
toward what Lukács, in a moment of self-criticism,
called "revolutionary messianism." Perhaps a more
important limitation is that "new class" theorists
from Marcuse to Gouldner were unable to predict
the reversion of capitalism to more brutal ideological forms (Reaganism, Thatcherism) after the
economic crisis of the 1970s (see Gouldner, 1979,
p. 92).

Two other variants of Marxism specifically
address problems of communication. The first,
the Frankfurt School, views all mass communication in advanced industrial society as inherently
manipulative. Perhaps the most popular expression of this view is Christopher Lasch's (1977) *The
Culture of Narcissism*, although Horkheimer and
Adorno's (1972) Dialectic of Enlightenment and
Marcuse's (1964) pre-New Left *One*-Dimensional
Man remain the most important. The Frankfurt School's position can be distilled into three
main propositions: (1) The working class has
been bought off by the "safety net" introduced by
Keynesian welfare capitalism. (2) The media (or
"consciousness industry") have replaced the family as the main agent of socialization, leading to
a repressive desublimation of aggressive and erotic
instincts. (3) The only legitimate forms of communication are philosophy and high art. Philosophic discourse is critique, "negative thinking,"
which must be obscure in order to avoid capitulat-
ing to the established universe of discourse. High
art preserves memories of freedom and happiness
or else explicitly condemns the existing world. For
Marcuse (1978), Samuel Beckett emerges as the
greatest artist of the contemporary period, for he
brings a clear message to his audience: put an end
to things as they are.

Although Frankfurt Marxism remains the
most coherent and intellectually satisfying of all
varieties of critical Marxism to date, it too easily
lapses into political quietism and elitist rejection
of all forms of popular culture. Even Jürgen Habermas, of the Frankfurt School's second generation,
shares with Adorno, Horkheimer, and Marcuse
a tendency to reject strategic discourse (what we
would call "rhetoric") as inherently manipulative
(Habermas, 1979, p. 41).

A fourth and final variant of Marxism has
not been articulated fully as yet, but derives
from Antonio Gramsci's (1971) *Prison Notebooks*.
Gramsci has had tremendous influence on British cultural studies and on American media critics
such as Todd Gitlin (1982) and Douglas Kellner
(1982). The first steps toward the appropriation of
Gramsci for rhetorical theory have been made by
Michael McGee and Martha Martin (1983), and
by Frank Lentricchia (1983) in his book on Kenneth Burke. In contrast to Marx, Gramsci believed
that capitalism obtained consent (at least in Western societies) through persuasion, its ability to
make the status quo seem reasonable and necessary. Lentricchia points out the similarity between
Gramsci's idea of "hegemony" (the persuasive
domination of the masses by the ruling class) and
Kenneth Burke's analysis in *Attitudes Toward History*:

> [T]he various "priests" of the pulpit, schools, press,
> radio, and popular arts, (and we add television),
> educate the socially dispossessed person to feel
> "that he 'has a stake in' the authoritative structure
> that dispossesses him; for the influence exerted
> upon the policies of education by the authoritative
> structure encourages the dispossessed to feel that
> his only hope of repossession lies in his allegiance
> to the structure that dispossessed him." (Lentric-
> chia, 1983, pp. 76–77)

Gramsci's idea of hegemony, especially as interpreted by Gitlin and Kellner, leads to a more optimistic view of mass communication. The task of the
intellectual class at the present time is to help construct a counter-hegemony. A counter-hegemony
would be based on the following assumptions: (1)
Mass communication addresses real human needs
for happiness, diversion, and self-assertion but is
flawed because those needs are shown to be met
only through the purchase of commodities (Gitlin,
1982, p. 452; Kellner, 1982, p. 403). (2) Hegemony
is "leaky" in contemporary mass communication
because of the contradictory character of liberal
capitalism itself (Kellner, 1982, pp. 386–387). One
could interpret the television series M*A*S*H, for
example, as reinforcing traditional American values on one hand, while de-legitimating war on the

other. (3) The Left should learn how to use mass communication more effectively. As Douglas Kellner (1982) writes, "The left should learn how to produce, or how to participate in, the production of popular television, as well as documentaries, news commentaries, and programs, and political discussion suitable for broadcast media. . . . There must be a cultural/media politics to ensure public access and open new channels of communication" (p. 421).

The neo-Gramscians clearly possess an attitude toward communication that is more congenial to the traditional concerns of rhetorical studies. Most, however, have not addressed the problem of rhetoric and rational argument. They lack a theory of the production of discourse and of audience effects. They also lack a response to the charge of more traditional critics such as Wayne Booth (1974) that concepts such as "ideology" and "hegemony" undercut the possibility of rational argument because of their "motivism" (pp. 2–40). A similar charge is made by the Norwegian philosopher Jon Elster (1979), when he attacks the "functionalism" of the Marxist view of ideology in *Ulysses and the Sirens* (pp. 28–35).[4]

Terry Eagleton has begun a project for the reconstruction of traditional rhetorical theory along Marxist lines, although it largely is formulated as a critique of the field of English literature. In Eagleton's (1983) *Literary Theory: An Introduction* he argues that "literature" as a privileged concept in the academy is of recent invention. In his view, the rise of departments of English in the nineteenth century was tied to an ideological quest to legitimate the existing class society. The study of literature was seen as a "humanizing" force, one that could replace religion as a prop for the existing order (pp. 17–53). In contrast, he says that the earlier study of rhetoric in British and American universities made clear the political thrust of humanistic knowledge. In what is perhaps the most useful definition of rhetoric I have read, Eagleton (1981) writes that rhetoric "is the process of analyzing the material effects of particular uses of language in particular social conjunctures" and that traditional rhetoric was "the textual training of the ruling class in the techniques of political hegemony" (p. 101). He goes on to describe a brief program for the development of a Marxist rhetoric:

> As far as rhetoric is concerned, then, a Marxist must be in a certain sense a Platonist. Rhetorical effects are calculated in the light of a theory of the *polis* as a whole. . . . Since all art is rhetorical, the tasks of the revolutionary cultural worker are essentially threefold: First, to participate in the production of works and events which, within transformed "cultural" media, so fictionalize the "real" as to intend those effects conducive to the victory of socialism. Second, as "critic" to expose the rhetorical structures by which non-socialist works produce political undesirable effects, as a way of combatting what is now unfashionable to call false consciousness. Third, to interpret such works where possible against the grain, so as to appropriate whatever is valuable for socialism. (Eagleton, 1981, p. 113)

It should be clear that I am in basic sympathy with Eagleton's ideas, although they need to be extended and made more relevant to the American experience. One major problem with Eagleton's formulation is that, like most leftist intellectuals, he privileges critique over the teaching of advocacy skills. He also still privileges art and literature over the more humble modes of communication such as public speaking and debate. It is not enough to do Marxist analyses of Richardson and Emily Brontë. Nor is it enough to say, for instance, that Ronald Reagan abuses the ideograph of "family" in order to reinforce existing patterns of economic and sexual oppression. One would need to go on to understand the lived experience of American audiences that predisposes them, often in ways that have nothing at all to do with "false consciousness," to accept family-based arguments. One would also need to show students and politicians how to "steal the symbol" of the family and use it for liberatory purposes (Burke, 1984, p. 328).

If it is the case that Marxism has effaced the role of communication in mediating between social structure and human action and that students of communication have ignored capitalism as a determining force in society, how might we combine both fields' virtues while eliminating some of their vices? It may be that the *aporia* which Gouldner and others find in classical Marxism may be the result more of confusion over levels of abstraction in social analysis than failure of Marxism itself. Erik Olin Wright (suggests, in his recent book *Classes*, that Marxist social analysis operates at three levels of abstraction: mode of production, social formation, and conjuncture (p. 9). Further, within each of these three levels, Marx himself moved back and forth between describing an abstract structure of class relations (as in the first part of *Capital*, as he develops a "pure" model of capitalism) and describing concrete conjunctural moments

n the chapter of *Capital* where he
battles over the length of the work-
, or as in the historical writings such as the
__ghteenth Brumaire). Marx's conjunctural maps
are much less "reductive" than his other writings,
and it is important to note that neither the critical
nor scientific Marxists have given as much weight
to them as to the *1844 Manuscripts* or to the first
part of *Capital*.

In fitting together Marxism and argumentation,
it is necessary to clarify the levels of abstraction at
which one is working. In focusing on the mode of
production, one wants to isolate the way in which
dominant forms of argument relate to forces and
relations of production *in the most abstract way*.
One can avoid both Booth's critique of Marxian
motivism and Elster's refutation of Marxian functionalism if the focus is on argumentative forms.
This sort of periodization is no different from
that which intellectual historians of rhetoric have
already done, except that it provides for greater
parsimony of explanation. In focusing on social
formation, one traces patterns of argument as they
relate to a specific nation or region (as revealed,
for instance, in Eugene Debs's appropriation of the
images of the American Revolution in his arguments for socialism). In focusing on conjuncture,
one evaluates the relationship between text and
audience in a concrete rhetorical situation, much
as traditional neo-Aristotelian criticism did.

Capitalism, in my view, is ultimately determining only in the sense of establishing general patterns and rules for argument. Not all discourse in a
given social formation is conducted in class terms,
although it certainly is important to study the
·ays in which public languages of class are created
inhibited. The rhetorical construction and/
·ression of class consciousness in American
the rhetorical representation of work rela-
·he mass media, not to mention the very
·f American workers to develop rhe-
·to combat the deindustrialization of
· deskilling of work—all these are
·nics for the critic of American
·ursue.
·ommunication studies in
·r and of the often heroic
·kers against capitalist
·ch more productive
·ison-house of ide-
·from the Frank-
·lid or as more
·hat we are all
·ciety of spec-

tacle ignores the reality of resistance to capitalism
that we have seen in the British miners, American
farmers, and Local P-9 in Austin, Minnesota. By
maintaining Marx's original dialectical tension
between structure and struggle we may be able to
avoid the passivity that both scientific Marxism
and critical Marxism seem to encourage at their
worst moments.

Cultures of Discourse: Rhetoric, Criticism, and Poststructuralism

If the map of the research program implied by classical Marxism makes sense, how can we use it to
direct research in the study of communication?
The rest of this essay attempts to describe what an
analysis of the history of rhetorical theory would
look like in mode-of-production terms.

The recent resurgence of rhetorical studies,
inside and outside of departments of communication, is simultaneously encouraging and depressing.
Arguably, rhetoric shares with Marxism the distinction of being the only research tradition capable of uniting the various disciplines in the university and of combatting the specialization that
prevents academic discourse from affecting the
public world. (Positivism once served such a function, but at last count even social scientists were
hastening to arrange its funeral rites.) Rhetoric,
however, in its privileging of symbol-use over labor
as the constitutive activity of human beings, risks
being coopted by larger forces of domination in our
culture. Please note that I am neither impugning
the motives of many contemporary rhetoricians
(as if they were all covertly in the employ of the
National Association of Manufacturers), nor am
I arguing that the revival of rhetoric is somehow
functional in the reproduction of late capitalist
economic relations. I am suggesting, rather, that
particular stages in the development of a mode of
production—in this case capitalism—will create
certain social dislocations or class tensions with
which given discourses will attempt to cope.

The resurgence of rhetorical studies, whether in
its wholesome American form or in its rather sleazy
French version, is tied to a common conviction
among intellectual elites that the transcendental
signifiers of God, Truth, and the Classless Society
have failed us. What remains is rhetoric itself, the
free play of signifiers, which the belatedly canonized Kenneth Burke (1965) tells us to contemplate
with dismay and delight as we "huddle, nervously
loquacious, at the edge of the abyss" (p. 272). The

heroic impulse at the heart of rhetorical studies, however, is too easily subverted into the glorification of power. If, following Gramsci, we can conclude that capitalist hegemony is a persuasive process, it may be possible to read dominant theories of rhetoric as attempts to describe, explain, and occasionally criticize hegemonic techniques. Even when not explicitly or self-consciously "rhetorical," intellectuals and other wielders of power in society always develop cultures of discourse or argumentative grammars. These cultures of discourse exist in an occasionally uneven relationship with economic forces and relations of production, but reciprocally influence and are influenced by them. Cultures of discourse, then, are conventions for the production of discourse and are as historically material as a factory or a Hitler speech.

I will argue that three cultures of discourse are currently competing for the allegiance of rhetorical scholars. The first, which can simply be called "rhetoric," is largely dead in its classical and humanistic forms, especially as it existed in American colleges prior to 1850. The second, the culture of critical discourse (Alvin Gouldner's CCD), has been dominant for many years but is now collapsing under the weight of its own internal contradictions. The third, which lacks an appropriate name, although "the new rhetoric" or even "poststructuralism" may do, while it lacks the political and social influence of the other two cultures of discourse, reflects a society of "spectacle," in which nothing is experienced directly except as a sign.

Traditional rhetoricians can be characterized above all by their nostalgia. S. M. Halloran's important article, "Rhetoric in the American College Curriculum," draws an inspiring picture of American education before the decline of rhetoric. He concludes his essay by contrasting the miserable character of the public debate over AWACS with the intense involvement of the American public in Webster's debates with Hayne and Calhoun (Halloran, 1982, pp. 244–262). Halloran is right, of course, that the decline of rhetoric in American universities did parallel the decline of public involvement in politics (although the 1930s certainly come to mind as a counterexample). Nonetheless, he obscures the class character of the decline of traditional rhetoric. Rhetoric declined because it ceased to be an efficient means of education once the university shifted to a larger, more egalitarian constituency. Rhetoric was a useful tool for a propertied elite, but seemingly less necessary when public discourse became controlled by technical experts.

The culture of discourse or argumentative grammar associated with traditional rhetoric seems to have been based on the following communicative rules. (I rewrite here Gadamer's great synthesis of the rhetorical tradition in the first part of *Truth and Method* [1975, pp. 10–39].) First, speak in such a way that one embodies the values of one's culture in one's own character. Second, always adapt one's discourse to the common sense of one's listeners. Third, study past rhetorical situations in order to develop a sense of judgment, the virtue of prudence that will generalize to future rhetorical situations. Finally, study great speeches and history and literature in order to develop a sense of timing and taste.

This culture of discourse at its best sacrificed individual ambition to the needs of the community and at its worst, as Eagleton says, was simply a form of training the ruling class in the techniques of textual domination. And yet, rhetoric in its traditional form had to die. It had to be replaced by a new standard of discourse, one more tied to print and to the initially egalitarian drive of capitalism to find new markets. The culture of critical discourse arose to meet technological and economic needs—and it also served as a site of class struggle, since Marxism itself arose within the culture of critical discourse.

Gouldner (1979), in his account of the culture of critical discourse, ties it to the potential rise to power of the new class of humanistic intellectuals and technical intelligentsia (p. 28). I believe that his prediction that this new class will come to power eventually in both the East and the West is invalidated largely by the return of capitalism to earlier and more primitive forms of domination because of the world recession. I also believe that the culture of critical discourse is more a set of formal assumptions about the conduct of public communication than a set of propositions about the public world (despite the notorious difficulties, familiar to every rhetorician, of separating form and content). My point here, however, is less to criticize Gouldner's theory than to use it to characterize the type of speech about speech that replaced rhetoric in intellectual circles.

The rules of the culture of critical discourse as an argumentative grammar can be summarized as follows: (1) Make one's own speech problematic and try to account for its origins. Be reflexive and self-monitoring. (2) Justify claims without reference to the speaker's societal position or authority; in other words, eliminate the classical f_ of *ethos*. (3) Stand apart from th_

which the speech is occurring,
mmon sense of a culture is ultimately
malization for that culture's power relations.
(+) Thus, privilege theoretical discourse, speech
that is relatively context-free (Gouldner, 1979,
p. 29). This culture of discourse, which perhaps
has its finest expression in Habermas's notion of
the ideal speech situation, has been dominant in
universities for a long time. The culture of critical discourse is inherently hostile to traditional
rhetoric (as the tortured career of rhetorical studies in America's elite universities in the last fifty
years or so indicates), even though the culture of
critical discourse has become the main standard
of speech among theorists of argumentation. The
culture of critical discourse helped break down traditional class and race prejudices, the patriarchal
family, and religion, but rather than being tied to
the needs of Gouldner's new class, it was simply
the rhetorical justification for that process which
Marx and Engels (1972) so cogently described in
The Communist Manifesto:

> Constant revolutionizing of production, uninter-
> rupted disturbance of all social conditions, ever-
> lasting uncertainty and agitation distinguish the
> bourgeois epoch from all earlier ones. All fixed,
> fast-frozen relations, with their train of ancient
> and venerable prejudices and opinions are swept
> away, all new-formed ones become antiquated
> before they can ossify. All that is solid melts into
> air, all that is holy is profaned, and man is at last
> compelled to face with sober senses, his real con-
> ditions of life, and his relations with his kind.
> (p. 338)

The culture of critical discourse was and is the
argumentative grammar that justifies technological revolution, the expansion of markets by giving
workers a larger share of profits, and also managerial control over the workplace and over society
in general—but not, I must add, at the level of
propositional argument, but at the level of form.
By translating questions of political practice and
class struggle into questions of technical expertise,
the culture of critical discourse consolidated the
transition of capitalism from anarchic competition
to corporate liberalism.

The culture of critical discourse, however, and
corporate liberalism itself cannot survive the
worldwide crisis of capitalism. It has been replaced
ideo political realm by the politics of pure image
rented by Ronald Reagan. It has been
being slowly replaced—by a new
nication that denies the exis-

tence of objective reality, proclaims that everything is constructed rhetorically and that there is
nothing outside the text. Ironically enough, it is
the lapsed Marxist Kenneth Burke and the avowed
Marxist Jacques Derrida who seem to provide the
best ideological justification for the new rhetorical
world of late capitalism.

A grossly enlarged conception of rhetoric plays
directly into the hands of corporate capitalism,
which would just as soon have us believe that
mass persuasion is the solution to our collective
problems. To assume that all social problems are
problems of communication glosses over the presence of real problems that might, at some point,
require direct action, even violence. When our
most radical rhetoric-as-epistemicists (what we
might call left-Burkeians) tell us that even trees
are created rhetorically we are offered what Fredric Jameson (1972) described in another context
as "the spectacle of a world from which nature as
such has been eliminated, a world saturated with
messages and information, whose intricate commodity network may be seen as the very prototype
of a system of signs" (pp. viii–ix). The new orthodoxy that there is nothing outside the text, nothing outside of rhetoric itself, is the perfect ideological representation of life under late capitalism, in
which nothing, it seems, is experienced outside of
its media images.

It seems silly, however, to claim that poststructuralism is somehow "functional" in preserving
capitalist domination. It makes more sense to
indict poststructuralism's current influence in the
academy as a distraction from more productive
uses of rhetorical theory. It is silly, too, to claim
that late capitalism has created a seamless web of
ideological images—Marx himself wrote books
and participated in the labor movement in order
to dispel the myth that capitalism is an eternal
and natural type of social order. My contention in
this essay has been that a revitalized conception
of traditional rhetoric, one informed by Marxist
theory and practice, may be of some use in advancing, if not the Revolution, at least a more humane
practice of public argument. I want to conclude by
summarizing the main themes of my overall argument in the context of some theses toward a Marxist rhetorical theory:

1. The Marxist representative anecdote of
   human beings as producers rather than simply
   as symbol-users may help correct the "trained
   incapacity" or "occupational psychosis" of
   rhetorical theory. By foregrounding the role

of labor in constructing our human world, a Marxist approach to communication may help revitalize the criticism of public discourse.

2. By foregrounding class struggle rather than public consensus, a Marxist rhetorical theory may be better able to explain broad historical shifts in rhetorical practice and pedagogy than do existing theoretical alternatives.

3. Traditional rhetoric, in privileging common sense as a starting point for the construction of enthymemes, may provide a needed corrective to Marxism's tendency to view the common sense of a culture merely as a rationalization of that culture's relations of domination.

4. Uniting Marxism's traditional concern for economic democracy with rhetoric's traditional (if at times ambiguous) concern for political democracy may provide a narrative structure for a new politics, one that views revolution as a struggle against racial, sexual, and economic oppression and against the specialized languages of expertise, which have characterized "liberal" reform in this century. Marxism needs to correct rhetoric's avoidance of the category of labor in the construction of the social world, while rhetoric needs to correct Marxism's one-sided focus on labor at the expense of other forms of domination.

The preceding four points are perhaps too facile a sketch of a theory that needs further justification, revision, and empirical validation. I have tried to make a case, at a rather high level of abstraction, for the connection of developments in rhetorical theory with developments in modes of production. The next step is to develop longitudinal analyses of public discourse within a given social formation, using Marxist categories. As I suggested earlier, even traditional public address study has largely ignored the rhetoric of the American labor movement. Given what might be called "American exceptionalism," it still remains to be proved empirically that Marxist categories can illuminate the development of languages of labor and class in the United States. But the attempt must be made.

What Marxism has taught us, in admittedly flawed ways, is that human beings have the potential to build a heroic society. What students of rhetoric and communication can give Marxism is a more humane way of bridging the critique of ideology with political action. The ultimate point is that audiences, when presented with the contradictions inherent in their social systems, have a choice about the ideological narratives to which they will subscribe or which they will create. That these narratives may not be limited to the banal yet frightening ones of the White House or the Kremlin depends on our ability to extend our imaginative range. As Marx (1975) himself wrote, "Every emancipation is a restoration of the human world and of human relationships to man himself" (p. 240).

I am grateful to Joli Jensen, John Rodden, M. S. Piccirillo, and the members of my seminar on Marxism and Communication Studies at the University of Virginia (Spring 1986) and the University of Iowa (Summer 1986) for conversations that helped me clarify the ideas presented in this chapter.

NOTES

1. Marx, of course, cites Smith's economic and ethical writings in *Kapital*; he also cites De Quincey's *The Logic of Political Economy*; Whately was professor of political economy at Oxford from 1829 to 1831. One sign of the remarkably insular character of much scholarship in the history of rhetorical theory is that rhetoricians write about Smith, De Quincey, and Whately as if rhetoric were the only interest of these theorists.

2. By "rhetoric" here I mean a comprehensive rhetorical theory; for a more limited, practical rhetoric, see the work of Angelica Balabanoff and Willkie (1974).

3. See Ryan (1982) for a useful explication of the metaphor of "articulation," a term from metallurgy referring to the joining of two distinct metals. The nightmare side of my current project is that rhetoric and Marxism may be related more like two magnets opposing one another.

4. I first started reading Elster at the beginning of the final revision of this essay; were I to redraft the project from the bottom up I would make Elster's work central, including also his *Making Sense of Marx* (1985). Elster opens up the prospect of a Marxism without functionalist explanation, a prospect, alas, that most Marxist students of communication, whether in political economy or cultural studies, have yet to consider.

REFERENCES

Albert, M., and R. Hahnel. 1978. *Unorthodox Marxism.* Boston: South End Press.

Booth, Wayne. 1974. *Modern Dogma and the Rhetoric of Assent.* South Bend, IN: University of Notre Dame Press; paperback edition, Chicago: University of Chicago Press.

Burke, Kenneth. 1935. "Revolutionary Symbolism in America." In Henry Hart, ed., *American Writer's Congress* (New York: International Publishers), pp. 87–93.

Burke, Kenneth. [1950] 1969. *A Rhetoric of Motives*. Englewood Cliffs, NJ: Prentice-Hall; rpt., Berkeley and Los Angeles: University of California Press.

Burke, Kenneth. 1965. *Permanence and Change*. 2d ed. Indianapolis: Library of the Liberal Arts.

Burke, Kenneth. 1984. *Attitudes Toward History*. Berkeley and Los Angeles: University of California Press.

Condit, Celeste M. 1987. "Democracy and Civil Rights: The Universalizing Influence of Public Argumentation." *Communication Monographs* 54: 1–18.

Elster, Jon. 1979. *Ulysses and the Sirens*. Cambridge, UK: Cambridge University Press.

Elster, Jon. 1985. *Making Sense of Marx*. Cambridge, UK: Cambridge University Press.

Gadamer, H. 1975. *Truth and Method*. Translated by Garrett Barden and John Cumming. New York: Seabury Press.

Gitlin, Todd. 1982. "Prime Time Ideology: The Hegemonic Process in Television Entertainment." In Horace Newcomb, ed., *Television: The Critical View*, 3rd ed. (New York: Oxford University Press), pp. 507–532.

Gouldner, Alvin. 1979. *The Future of Intellectuals and the Rise of the New Class*. New York: Seabury Press.

Gouldner, Alvin. 1980. *The Two Marxisms*. New York: Oxford University Press.

Gramsci, Antonio. 1971. *The Prison Notebooks: Selections*. Translated by Quintin Hoard and Geoffrey Nowell Smith. New York: International Publishers.

Grossberg, Lawrence. 1979. "Marxist Dialectics and Rhetorical Criticism." *Quarterly Journal of Speech* 65: 235–249.

Habermas, Jürgen. 1979. *Communication and the Evolution of Society*. Translated by Thomas McCarthy. Boston: Beacon Press.

Halloran, S. M. 1982. "Rhetoric in the American College Curriculum." *PRE/TEXT* 3: 244–269.

Heilbroner, R. 1985. *Marxism For and Against*. New York: Norton.

Horkheimer, M., and T. W. Adorno. 1972. *The Dialectic of Enlightenment*. Translated by John Cumming. New York: Herder and Herder.

Jameson, Fredric. 1972. *The Prison-House of Language: A Critical Account of Structuralism and Russian Formalism*. Princeton, NJ: Princeton University Press.

Kellner, Douglas. 1982. "TV, Ideology, and Emancipatory Popular Culture." In Horace Newcomb, ed., *Television: The Critical View*, 3rd ed. (New York: Oxford University Press), pp. 386–421.

Lasch, Christopher. 1977. *The Culture of Narcissism*. New York: Norton.

Lenin, V. I. 1961. *What Is to Be Done?* Translated by Joe Fineberg and George Hanna. New York: International Publishers.

Lentricchia, Frank. 1983. *Criticism and Social Change*. Chicago and London: University of Chicago Press.

Lukács, Georg. 1971. *History and Class Consciousness*. Translated by Rodney Livingstone. Cambridge, MA: M.I.T. Press.

Marcuse, Herbert. 1964. *One-Dimensional Man: Studies in the Ideology of Advanced Industrial Society*. Boston: Beacon Press.

Marcuse, Herbert. 1978. *The Aesthetic Dimension: Toward a Critique of Marxist Aesthetics*. Boston: Beacon Press.

Marx, Karl. 1963. *The Eighteenth Brumaire of Louis Bonaparte*. New York: International Publishers.

Marx, Karl. 1972. "Theses on Feuerbach." In Robert C. Tucker, ed., *The Marx–Engels Reader* (New York: Norton).

Marx, Karl. 1975. "On the Jewish Question." In *Early Writings*, trans Rodney Livingston and Gregor Benton (New York: Vintage Books).

Marx, Karl, and Frederick Engels. 1972. *The Communist Manifesto*. In Robert C. Tucker, ed., *The Marx–Engels Reader* (New York: Norton).

McGee, Michael Calvin. 1982. "A Materialist's Conception of Rhetoric." In Raymie E. McKerrow, ed., *Explorations in Rhetoric: Studies in Honor of Douglas Ehninger* (Glenview, IL: Scott, Foresman).

McGee, Michael Calvin, and Martha A. Martin. 1983. "Public Knowledge and Ideological Argumentation." *Communication Monographs* 50: 47–65.

Mead, George Herbert. [1934] 1962. *Works of George Herbert Mead, Vol. 1: Mind, Self, and Society from the Standpoint of a Social Behaviorist*. Edited by C. W. Morris. Chicago: University of Chicago Press.

Mills, C. Wright. 1969. "The Politics of Responsibility." In Carl Oglesby, ed., *The New Left Reader* (New York: Grove Press).

Ryan, M. 1982. *Marxism and Deconstruction: A Critical Articulation*. Baltimore: Johns Hopkins University Press.

Wander, Philip. 1983. "The Ideological Turn in Modern Criticism." *Central States Speech Journal* 34: 1–18.

Willkie, R. W. 1974. "The Marxian Rhetoric of Angelica Balabanoff." *Quarterly Journal of Speech* 60: 450–458.

Wright, Michael. 1985, March 3. "National Security's New Insiders." *New York Times Magazine*.

Disciplining the Feminine

Carole Blair
Julie R. Brown
Leslie A. Baxter

I am reminded of a male colleague, a communication scholar, who has been trying to convince me that I and other feminists lack an internal grace or beauty of character that, once adopted, would allow us to move graciously through the world without anger and confrontation. I have responded that the admonition to "be nice" is precisely what is used to keep us in our places. We will be called crazy. We may be thought churlish and petty. We may be thought unscholarly and unintellectual. If so, we will be joining a long line of honorable women.
—RAKOW, 211

The ministers of knowledge have always assumed that the whole universe was threatened by the very changes that affected their ideologies and their positions. They transmute the misfortune of their theories into theories of misfortune.
—DE CERTEAU, 95–96

Academic writing of the kind published in this or any other professional journal is regulated by clear norms, usually among them the demand for a refined, ahistorical, smoothly finished univocality. That is, works published in most of our academic journals display as little as possible the circumstances and activities of their production. Notably missing, or at least reduced to virtual silence, is the passion that obviously drives our choices to write about particular topics in particular ways. Our writings suppress our convictions, our enthusiasm, our anger, in the interest of achieving an impersonal, "expert" distance and tone. Similarly, journal articles rarely reveal their own histories. The formative history of an essay is reduced to a notation of an "earlier version," or its history is constituted as a "disciplinary past" by situating the essay in the context of a literature review. Masked also are the mistakes we inevitably make

in the process of research and writing. These cannot remain, for we seek a coherent, authoritative, cleanly argued, singular, and defensible position, devoid of "extraneous" or "tangential" details. And gone are any overt signs, except perhaps in a note crediting them, of the "extra" voices of those who provided suggestions or sanctions for revision, in particular the voices of journal editors and referees. These voices are accommodated in such a way as to subsume them, to make them inaudible, to render them part and parcel of the unitary, uncomplicated speech of the author. Finally, the scholarly essay that addresses the working conditions or institutional apparatuses situating the professional scholar is rare indeed. "Scholarship," we would prefer to think, is vouchsafed by academic freedom and intellectual ethics. As a result, issues of institutional or professional power are deemed superfluous to the substance and character of our scholarly efforts.[1] These are but a few of the norms that govern our academic writing, but they surely are recognizable as vital rules to most of us who write in the professional academic milieu of speech communication.

Our approach in this essay is to misunderstand purposefully these norms in the interest of our goal: to point to and critique a constellation of practices in our discipline that some of us would prefer to believe were the relics of a time long past. We refer to the particular themes and enabling mechanisms of a masculinist disciplinary ideology, whose professionalized and seemingly liberal thematic motifs serve as a benign cover for a selectively hostile and exclusionary disciplinary practice.

Our belief that we must break the sacrosanct rules of scholarly writing in order to display these practices is worth examining. In fact, such a move would not be wholly necessary if we were to limit our objective to the one with which we began this project; our goal had been to urge our disciplinary colleagues to eschew any professional/institutional/authoritative use of the findings or rationale of Hickson, Stacks, and Amsbary's 1992 report, "Active Prolific Female Scholars in Communication." However, our project took on added dimension as we attempted to pursue that goal along the ordinary paths toward publication. We wrote an essay responding to the Hickson et al. report and submitted our essay to another prominent speech communication journal for editorial consideration. The anonymous reviews we received (attached to a rejection letter) themselves seemed sufficiently important as ideological fragments that we decided to "up the critical ante," to do more than comment on the Hickson et al. report. Those reviews constitute a rare find, tangible and unusually explicit fragments of what is almost certainly a larger, intolerant disciplinary text that typically remains implicit, unreadable, and deniable.[2] Thus, in addition to arguing against use of the Hickson et al. report, which we attempted to do before, we will suggest also that their report is a thematic marker of a masculinist ideology and that the anonymous reviews of our original essay are unusually explicit manifestations of the apparatuses that sustain and enable those ideological themes. We will begin in the next section with a description of our critical stance and with a narrative that chronicles the construction of this manuscript. The sections following are critical readings, in turn, of the Hickson et al. report and of the anonymous referees' reviews of our original

response essay. We will conclude by discussing the implications for feminist scholarship of the ideological themes and mechanisms represented by Hickson et al. and by the reviews of our original essay.

Following *and* Breaking Rules: Professional Precedents and Unprofessional Writing

If the professional disciplinary rules that we have specified were to find absolute adherence, this essay would have been derailed by now, for it already has revealed something of the history of its production, hinted of a motivation grounded in anger, and staked for itself an explicitly politicized position. Worse, perhaps, we have claimed that it is our *own* disciplinary apparatus that is under indictment. That claim entails two unpleasant possibilities, first, that we *all* have helped to perpetuate the undesirable practices of our discipline by reinforcing and accommodating ourselves to its rules, and second, that the rules themselves are in need of scrutiny and possibly of change. We suspect that a great many journal article submissions have been rejected for far less serious breaches of disciplinary etiquette than these.[3] However, there are precedents for breaking the rules, and this essay takes its particular stance at a nexus among several of them: a specific iteration of the rhetoric of inquiry project, as well as the general positions of the ideological turn, critical rhetoric, feminist theory, and the recent revelatory narrative project on sexual harassment in the *Journal of Applied Communication Research*.

The rhetoric of inquiry project is committed to understand the specific rhetorical constructions of various academic disciplines.[4] While most self-described adherents of POROI attend to the rhetorics of other fields, the aim of the project can and should be reflexive. That is, it can be turned back to examine its own professional instantiation.[5] As Hariman argues, "If rhetorical studies are read into a disciplinary scheme they are read poorly; if they are read sympathetically they subvert the disciplinary reading" (212). He suggests that "the rhetoric of inquiry can itself be aggressively rhetorical—which means more than recognizing that one's own text is as fabricated as any other. The full-blown rhetorical perspective replaces disinterestedness with advocacy, balances specialization with generality, and confronts expertise with an assertion of voice" (213). Hariman's point stands as a precedent, for it suggests that we confront rhetorically the professionalization of university culture, which "has become more a repressive power than a productive power" (212), and it implies that we consider our own field of inquiry in light of that power.

Such an extension of POROI toward a reflection on the professional codes and practices of speech communication is consistent with another set of precedents found in the literature of the "ideological turn," advocated first by Wander and Jenkins, elaborated by Wander ("Ideological Turn"; "Third Persona") and Crowley, and supplemented by discussions of a "critical rhetoric" (McGee, "Text"; McKerrow; Ono and Sloop). The "ideological" project clearly names our discipline's assumptions and apparatuses as targets of critical analysis. What the ideological turn and critical rhetoric literatures highlight and share with Hariman's construction of POROI is the element of the political. All three are explicitly attuned to issues of power as they are inscribed and exercised in all varieties of rhetorical practice, including academic work. They also are committed to understanding the repressive nature of power as it is constructed and acted in discourse. Wander suggests that we attend to the "third persona," a rhetorical excision of the "unacceptable, undesirable, insignificant" elements ("Third Persona," 209), the "audience/s ignored or denounced through the speech, the discourse, the text" ("Politics," 288). And McKerrow specifies a "critique of domination" as a component part of critical rhetoric. Both the ideological turn and critical rhetoric, also like Hariman's position, are animated by poststructuralist thinking, which frequently demands a grounding in practice (rather than in grand theory) and which counts the most "local," everyday life events as legitimate objects of critique (de Certeau; Foucault). The critical writings within the poststructuralist stance often assume extraordinary forms, because the orthodox and prescribed modes of academic writing are unfit or unable to accommodate their positions. Thus, this group of writings also serves as a precedent; it understands the professional as political and academic norms as, in part, repressive. Moreover, it points us to the "local"; it is our position that our own disciplinary practices can and should be counted among the localities we engage critically. Finally, this literature is willing to count as possibly legitimate those writings that would be delegitimized and/or silenced when held to the traditional strictures of professional academic work.

The same is frequently true of feminist theory. Writing is often differentially inscribed and valued in feminist theory; it legitimizes experiential and narrative "evidence," redirection and misappropriation of language, and celebration of *pathos*.[6] In addition, like ideological critique of the type advocated by Wander, feminist theory works at the focal point of power relations, but it understands them principally (sometimes exclusively) as sexually em-bodied or gender-normed. Virtually every iteration of feminist theory, from its most moderate to its most radical construction, claims a transformative or interventionist political stance. That entails changes in academic politics no less than it does alterations in the politics of the public sphere.[7] We see feminist theory as a precedent, for some of the same reasons that we have named the others, but feminist theory specifies our project further; it situates us within a resistant political stance, but one that recognizes the particularity of repressive academic politics with regard to gender-normed practices.

That gender politics are played out in material ways with material effects is starkly clear in the recent special issue of JACR, "'Telling our Stories': Sexual Harassment in the Communication Discipline." The vivid and poignant narratives about personal experiences of sexual harassment in the discipline must lead, as Taylor and Conrad suggest, away from the comforting but inaccurate characterization of gender politics as "someone else's problem" (402, note). They also point out that the university structure is "conditioned by popular images of its pastoral innocence, and of its highly cognitive and theoretical workers—seemingly 'disinterested' intellectuals" (405). Strine recognizes essentially the same image, and she links the disembodied, cognitive realm to material practices in her suggestion that those who engage "their academic work as dispassionate, tough minded 'objectivity' and methodological rigor" may fear "feminine sensibilities and supposedly softer, more experimental and participatory approaches to knowledge" as "contaminants to the rationalistic male-centered academic workplace" (399).

The narrative accounts of sexual harassment ("Our Stories") and the attendant critical analyses by Strine and Taylor and Conrad thus serve notice in two ways that our position takes as precedent. First, they confront our discipline's unique twist on the NIMBY (Not In My Back Yard) syndrome. While acknowledging that increasing numbers of women have populated the discipline, they display the manner in which some of them have been mistreated, not somewhere else, but here—in our midst. Second, they display the effects of gender politics concretely; they set the supposedly disembodied neutrality of academic professionals off against the em-bodied materiality of their persons.

Certainly the story we have to tell is *far* less frightening and grotesque than those told by the survivors of these sexual harassment events. However, in a sense, our story is of a piece with those events. "How things work," the "norms governing the rational operation of the academic sphere," constitute the ideological background (Strine, 391). This ideology enables both the episodic sexual harassment described in the narratives as well as the incidents of erasure and devaluation of women represented by the Hickson et al. report and enforced by the journal referees' reviews of our initial response essay.

The Hickson et al. report rank orders women in the field according to the number of articles they have published in journals indexed by Matlon and Ortiz. According to Hickson and his colleagues, the purpose of this ranking project is to "determine a yardstick for active, female researchers in communication" (351). They suggest that such a guideline is important for three reasons: (1) its use in tenure and promotion decisions; (2) its value in the sociology of knowledge, to determine where influence has been located in the discipline; and (3) its value to persons in other disciplines who want to know the comparative status of one individual's scholarly record (351). The report is one of several studies undertaken in recent years by Hickson and his colleagues to assess scholarly productivity in the discipline.[8] The research program by Hickson et al. represents but a portion of what Erickson, Fleuriet, and Hosman have recently described as the discipline's growing "cottage industry of counting articles authored by prolific researchers" (329).[9] However, the Hickson et al. study of active, prolific female researchers is unique in its exclusive focus on a specific demographic/cultural group.

Soon after the report was published, we found ourselves locked in conversations about it. Although the three of us are in most respects professionally dissimilar (in rank, in research and teaching interests, in intellectual assumptions, etc.), we found each other to be equally dismayed by the *idea* of the report and in agreement that we should write an essay responding to it. Our dismay was grounded in both general and particular concerns. At a general level, the Hickson et al. report represented evidence of our discipline's continuing fascination with identifying the most prolific scholars in our midst, a fascination we find misguided. However, because others have recently argued that this fascination is problematic, we will not elaborate here on these general concerns.[10] At a more particular level, we were fearful that Hickson et al.'s analysis of prolific female scholars would be embraced as a positive statement about women and for women in the discipline and that the masculinist ideology that ironically undergirds the analysis might be disregarded. This ideology is pervasive in the academy, including speech communication, and thus may not be immediately apparent to most readers in the absence of explicit discussion. The Hickson et al. report thus constitutes a fruitful "local" target for critique; it is, on one level, a seemingly benign if not positive statement about and for women but which, upon closer scrutiny, functions in precisely the opposite manner. By examining ways in which the masculinist ideology is apparent in the Hickson et al. report, we hoped to enter into the ongoing conversation about speech communication scholarship as gendered.[11]

Our response essay was, from our point of view, rather modest. In fact, we worried that it might be too moderate, an irony in light of what our referees' reviews would suggest about it and about us. Nonetheless, we submitted the essay and, within a few weeks, received those reviews. After the initial shock of reading the reviews wore off, we realized that what we had received was a gift of sorts—two institutionally sanctioned documents that displayed the enabling mechanisms that support the kinds of ideological themes Hickson et al. advance.

In the next section, we have reproduced almost the entirety of our original essay that responded to Hickson et al. We have eliminated one set of arguments and incidental markers thereof from the original version. This set of arguments addressed the factual accuracy, stylistic competence, and logical coherence of the Hickson et al. report.[12] Our decision to excise that component of the manuscript here is based on our realization that it probably served as a diversion from the principal point of our essay. We had attempted to link this set of arguments to our general ideological point by suggesting the possibility that such concerns as accuracy, style, and coherence simply might have been too easily disregarded in the case of an essay "merely" about women. However, ultimately the issues of accuracy and logical coherence seemed the only explicit substantive concerns of the initial referees; we had essentially provided them with an alibi for their refusal to address the primary arguments of our response. In the interest of providing the reader with an accurate rendering of our ideologically-based objections to the Hickson et al. report, we have refrained from revising our original argument, despite the fact that any number of minor changes have occurred to us with the passage of time. However, none of these changes would alter the substance of our reaction to the report. The next section, thus, contains the remainder of our original essay.

Subject of or Subject to Research?: A Response to Hickson, Stacks, and Amsbary's "Active Prolific Female Scholars in Communication"

A number of scholars have described the "chilly climate" that confronts female faculty members in higher education.[13] We believe that the temperature has dropped even further for females in the speech communication discipline with the publication of Hickson, Stacks, and Amsbary's report of "research productivity" among "active prolific" female scholars. The Hickson et al. article constitutes an overt, if unintended, display of insensitivity toward and aggression against women in the discipline. In writing this response, we hope to persuade our female and male colleagues in the field to resist any use of its results.

Our desire to resist the Hickson et al. report is based in one simple observation: Although it is a report about women, it neglects or implicitly denies the fact that it is about women in virtually all of its constituent features—rationale, assumptions, method, and language. That is, Hickson et al. have named "female" as a category and then failed to consider the gendered specificity of the category. Their omission of any hint of the female gender among their "Key Concepts" list is a telling marker of a discourse that *effaces* women even as it specifies them as a group for observation. We submit that a discourse about women must not forget or erase women. But that is, paradoxically, what the Hickson et al. report accomplishes. And it does so by means much more significant and consequential than neglecting to name as a key concept the gendered group it purports to study.

Before exploring our specific concerns with the Hickson et al. article, however, let us be clear about our own stance. First, we do not wish to detract from the many scholarly accomplishments of the particular women listed in Table I ("Most Prolific Active Female Scholars in Communication, 1915–1990") of the Hickson et al. report. These women and many more not listed in Table I merit our respect for their scholarly contributions. Second, we do not believe or assume that the three *individuals* named Hickson, Stacks, and Amsbary are themselves aggressors against women. Neither do we believe or assume that the "aggressor" label is appropriate to describe the *persons* who reviewed or approved publication of this article. But it is not necessary to assume or make such individual attributions in order to conclude that the Hickson et al. *discourse* functions as an act of aggression against women in the field. We adhere to the general positions taken by a number of contemporary thinkers that entire groups, institutions, or other power networks are speaking when individuals speak.[14] To put it most simply, a discourse of right, power, and privilege is approved within our (or any) discipline, and that discourse is spoken by individual members of the discipline. In this case, it is being spoken by Hickson, Stacks, and Amsbary. "Their" discourse indicts us all to the degree that we allow it to stand without resistance, because it is also *our* disciplinary discourse. So, when we refer to "Hickson et al.," "the authors," "they," "them," etc., we do not point to the individuals Hickson, Stacks, and Amsbary alone, but also to the entire institutional/discursive structure that legitimates their report.

Disciplinary discourses enable and ratify certain lines of argument and certain actions. In this case, "our" disciplinary discourse has authorized a ranking project grounded in an agenetic perspective of impersonal abstraction, disciplinary territoriality, individuation, and hierarchy. A number of scholars have identified this perspective with the "male paradigm" that dominates higher education.[15] These scholars, of course, are highlighting the themes of agency and communion that have been associated with males and females, respectively, in much social scientific research.[16] The fact that female scholars were subjects of, and arguably subject *to*, the Hickson et al. agenetic project is particularly distressing to us, because it is precisely this paradigm, and all that it represents, which constitutes the central obstacle to female achievement in academia. . . . A consideration of what/whose interests are likely to be served by their report [intensifies our distress]. We turn . . . [now] to the assumptions and ideological difficulties we find most disturbing in the Hickson et al. report. . . .

The Imposition of the "Male Paradigm"

The "male paradigm" is characterized, first, by *impersonal abstraction*. Initially, we wish to challenge the legitimacy of a project whose purpose is to develop context-free, universalistic "yardsticks" that can be applied in particular cases, in this instance, to female researchers in the field. Such a project, according to many scholars, is anchored by a male-centered system of logic and morality, in contrast to the personalized and contextualized ways of knowing that are more typical of female socialization.[17] The male-centered model of agency fundamentally is predicated on the separation of the person from contextual particulars. Thus, from the perspective of the "male paradigm," judgment should be based on universal principles and abstract laws that are characterized by "objectivity." The imposition of this male-centered model on females is offensive on its face, because it essentially forgets that they are female. Moreover, the resulting "yardsticks" ignore important contextual factors that distinguish female and male career patterns of research performance.

One of the most important of these contextual factors is the differing temporal rhythms that characterize the scholarly performances of female and male academics. Graphic representations of scholarly activity over the entire life of a career tend to be saddle-shaped for men and to be of a linear progression pattern for women. That is, male research activity tends to be high for the first five to ten years after the doctorate, then levels off at the associate level before picking up again at a later point in the career.[18] By contrast, female research activity tends to be less than male research activity prior to tenure, but greater than male activity after the point of tenure (Task Force on Women in Higher Education). We recognize that the possibility of different temporal rhythms in the research activities of female and male scholars in speech communication has not been systematically researched, but we note with interest that the descriptions of gender-linked patterns "ring true" for the three of us, based on our own career paths to date. Hickson et al. display insensitivity to the possibility of gender-linked trajectories of scholarly activity in electing to measure productivity "outputs" at a single point in time. Further, in emphasizing the importance of females publishing early in their careers (355), Hickson et al. promulgate the male career trajectory as the universal standard against which female scholars should be assessed. Obviously, females whose careers are better characterized by the linear progression pattern as opposed to the saddle-shaped pattern are ill-served early in their professional careers by evaluation grounded in the male career model. The issue of who is served (or not) by the Hickson et al. "yardsticks" is one we return to later in this response.

Also obscured in the Hickson et al. abstraction is the *character* of the publications they enumerate. While Hickson et al. claim that their report is "valuable in the sociology of knowledge to determine where influence has been in the discipline" (351), nowhere do they make even cursory mention of what is said in any of the articles they list. Their failure to do so suggests a cynically reductionistic view of scholarship and its purpose: *That* writing occurs is somehow more significant or influential than *what* is written or *how* that writing is read. This unidimensional portrait of scholarly activity insults both writers and readers by rendering their labors invisible and irrelevant.

Moreover, the authors' preoccupation with tabulating individual output evidences a naïve conception of "influence," a narrow conception of "knowledge," and a rather thorough misunderstanding of the sociology of knowledge project. Based on their operational definitions, Hickson et al. appear to believe that influence is strictly a function of output rate and that "output" can be unproblematically equated with "knowledge." Accepting these beliefs seems to require that we ignore an entire range of *institutional* routines that enable production, that set the priorities used to assess the significance of that production, and that condition the acceptance or rejection of something *as* "knowledge." In other words, Hickson et al. assume that "influence" and "knowledge" inhere in the fact of production. They fail to consider how these latter characteristics are indeed *interpretations* made possible by the social, historical, and ideological context surrounding scholarly production/consumption. What, for instance, leads the authors to focus on journal publications as an index of influence? Why choose the narrow range of publications indexed by Matlon and Ortiz? These questions cannot be answered at the level of product/output alone. The answers reside in the context surrounding product/output, that is, in the history and politics of this discipline and the disciplinary system generally. And it is these systemic, contextual factors—the ones that lead us to "produce" in certain ways and to define the relative influence of that production—that Hickson et al. leave unexamined.

In light of the authors' silence concerning the institutional dimensions of scholarly production and the assessment thereof, we find it difficult to accept their report as "valuable in the sociology of knowledge" (351). Simply put, their report lacks a clear *sociological* dimension. Rather, their report displays and attempts to aggregate *individual* profiles. This approach displaces the social by construing it as essentially epiphenomenal (i.e., as the by-product of aggregated individual activity). In so doing, Hickson et al. place themselves at conceptual odds with much existing work in the sociology of knowledge. From the vantage point of Berger and Luckmann, Bourdieu, Toulmin, and others, social systems prefigure individual actors and provide the logics in and against which individuals may justify and give meaning to activity. Individual activity, while not necessarily determined by extant social systems, occurs in continual *relationship* to these systems. This view of the individual–social relationship is fundamentally dissimilar to the one suggested by Hickson et al. Insofar as the authors attempt to justify their project by aligning it with a literature obviously not amenable to the perspective they advance, we find their justification considerably less than compelling.

The "male paradigm" is characterized, second, by *disciplinary territoriality*. Concern with strict disciplinary boundaries certainly varies among scholars in the field.[19] Our point is that concern with clearly demarcated disciplinary boundaries displays a kind of territoriality that is likely to be gender-linked. Female scholars in the humanities and social sciences, in fact, tend to be more interdisciplinary than their male counterparts (Ward and Grant). A number of scholars have argued that female academics may be attracted more than their male colleagues to scholarly projects that bridge several disciplines because of differing gender socialization experiences.[20] Females are socialized to construct social reality by connecting the multiple perspectives that constitute their relationship-oriented worlds.[21] An interdisciplinary perspective, in turn, could result in high rates of publication in interdisciplinary outlets or in the journals of other disciplines. In developing statistical "yardsticks" cast narrowly along disciplinary lines, Hickson and his colleagues render a portrait of scholarship by females in speech communication that may be seriously distorted in both quantity and profile. Although the three of us hardly constitute an adequate sample of female scholars in speech communication, we nonetheless note with interest that our own career experiences are captured much better by an interdisciplinary model of knowledge as opposed to a male-centered model of narrow disciplinarity; of our total of 66 scholarly publications, only 36 percent are included in the journals indexed by Matlon and Ortiz. Hickson et al. attempt to pre-empt this concern about interdisciplinary work by acknowledging that people, including those females listed as the "most active and prolific," may publish elsewhere (354–355). What Hickson et al. ignore is that females in the discipline may display disproportionately less disciplinary territoriality than males in their publication habits; if that is the case, Hickson et al.'s use of the Matlon and Ortiz index is inappropriate for establishing anything like a "yardstick" to measure scholarly activity among females in the field. Yet Hickson et al. *assert* that, "Certainly the journals in this study constitute where the vast majority of professors in the field of communication consider that they strive [*sic*] to publish" (355). This claim is open to serious question, and the confidence with which it is advanced itself reveals a territorial presumption.

Also revealing of the presumptiveness of disciplinary territoriality in the Hickson et al. report is their question: "Why are such yardsticks important to the discipline?" (351). If women are less territorial with respect to disciplines than their male colleagues, then Hickson et al. fail in their attempt to warrant the legitimacy of their project by answering this question. More pertinently, their question betrays the very territoriality that they presume to be characteristic of female scholars. The question manifests concern for a bloodless, abstract construct—"the discipline"—and not the material individuals and groups that constitute it. In fact, the three authors seem interested in "the discipline" at the *expense* of individuals and groups. They understand the results of previous studies of research activity as an "indictment" of individuals' publication records (351). Thus, this report and others like it are taken to be important on the grounds that they enable "the discipline" (or those who speak for it) to survey the "territory" of disciplinary publication records and render judgments on them. If publication records within the disciplinary territory are deemed inadequate, then indictment of individuals seems the only conclusion; on this logic, the possibility that individuals simply have crossed the disciplinary borders apparently is unthinkable.

Individuation is the third characteristic of the "male paradigm." By "individuation," we refer to a set of beliefs that revolve around the presumed autonomy or independence of the individual agent, in contrast to a communal view of the individual as embedded in a web of connections with others.[22] One of the beliefs implicated in the male model of individuation is a monadic conception of "influence." Hickson and his colleagues claim that their purpose is to "determine where influence has been in the discipline" (351). However, their understanding of "influence" is a male-centered, individualistic one in contrast to a more relationally-centered conception. Certainly, a person is positioned to be influential by publishing in scholarly outlets, but we would argue that "influence" is inherently a relational phenomenon; that is, whether or not an individual is "influential" can be determined only by what happens *between* people. If Hickson et al. were interested in the "influence" of published authors, perhaps their project would have been better advanced by studying citation patterns, that is, determination of the frequency with which a given author's work has been cited by others in the ongoing scholarly dialogue. Such an alternative approach would have the added benefit of broadening the domain of potentially influential publications to include articles published in other disciplines' journals, as well as books and articles published in interdisciplinary journals. And if citation patterns were studied across several disciplines, we might gain insight into the "influence" of given authors as their ideas and research gain currency outside the parameter of the journals indexed in Matlon and Ortiz.

A second belief implicated in the male model of individuation is the presumption of individual volition. Hickson et al. treat issues of female employment, publication, etc., as if they were entirely volitional. The authors remind readers of the importance of publishing early in one's career and of the correlation between research productivity and working in a doctoral-granting institution. But such advice presupposes that individual female academics are in sole control of their own scholarly activity, making choices without constraint concerning where to work and when to publish. Unfortunately, such advice, however well intended, ignores the structural constraints that still face female academics with respect to problems of sponsorship and mentorship, access to scholarly informal networks, burdens of institutional committee service, and so forth, all of which affect female research activity in ways unrelated to matters of individual volition.[23]

Last and perhaps most important, the "male paradigm" is characterized by *hierarchy*. By "hierarchy," we refer to the acceptance of asymmetrical relations between people, with some groups or individuals gaining dominance or empowerment through the subordination and disempowerment of others. "Hierarchy" is a simple and relatively straightforward concept in the abstract but one which surfaces in a myriad of insidious ways in the Hickson et al. report. It is in its hierarchical assumptions that we believe the Hickson et al. report most clearly moves from "mere" insensitivity and inappropriateness to aggression. The ranking offered by Hickson et al. discursively positions women against one another. The women ranked among the most "prolific" are transformed into evidence for a negative commentary about those not ranked. The hierarchical nature of the list also discursively casts the women on the list against one another; being ranked as #1, according to the obvious hierarchical logic of ranking, is "better than" being ranked as #2. In addition, "active" female scholars are discursively privileged over "inactive" female scholars. Thus, women are cast not merely in the role of objectified, scrutinized subjects; they are cast also in a hierarchically competitive position vis-à-vis one another. Such individually-based competition seems particularly inappropriate when applied to women who are socialized to work more relationally and collaboratively than are men.[24] And to play female scholars off against one another, when they have been playing against a stacked deck in any case, is nothing short of offensive.

Equally offensive is Hickson et al.'s description of their report as an attempt to establish a "yardstick for active, female researchers in communication" (351). Hickson et al.'s report-as-yardstick hearkens to the vulgar (and frequently brutal) political arrangements characterizing dominant/non-dominant group relations in times we have come to believe were "less enlightened." The yardstick (along with its metonymic associates, such as "the ruler" and "the rod") often functioned as the instrument used to "articulate" and reinforce the punitive politics of domination and oppression. The teacher took the ruler to the unruly or obstreperous child; the paternalistic master took the rod to the wayward or disobedient slave; the male authors of this report take the yardstick to female scholars—such is the associational chain summoned in their choice of language. In each case the yardstick (or its equivalent) is used by one individual to *discipline* another. In so doing, *discipline* and those traditionally charged with its preservation are maintained.

Yet, Hickson et al. explicitly link the yardstick with its most literal use—measurement. On its face, measurement seems to be a neutral enough activity. When we consider the myriad choices and assumptions made in even the most routine acts of measurement, however, even this seeming "neutrality" quickly disappears. Measurement necessitates division, categorization, and (more or less explicitly) comparison. Given that persons can be divided, categorized, and compared according to a variety of logics, and that choosing one logic over another changes the shape, orientation, or sense of value associated with the persons measured, acts of measurement, like language choices, are never free of tendency.

Equally significant is the fact that measurements are performed *on* (as opposed to, say, *with*) persons. In this sense, then, measurements function *to order, to contain*, and in these senses, *to discipline*. These functions certainly argue for the sociopolitical dimensions of measurement. Consequently, the "yardstick-that-measures" functions similarly to the "yardstick-that-punishes." While not as obviously brutal, the "yardstick-that-measures" functions as a show of strength by the institutionally powerful to those whose "unchecked" activities threaten order and discipline.

The fact that Hickson et al. have used the term "yardstick" in other studies ("Active Prolific Scholars") not segregated by gender fails to serve as an alibi for its use in a study about women. They are *communication* scholars, as are those who approved their manuscript for publication. It is no secret to any of us in this discipline that language comes laced with connotative history and unavoidable tendentiousness. These connotations and tendencies change with the context of utterance. The "yardstick" metaphor, when used by male authors to describe their examination of women, has a more sinister ring than it does when used inside a less lopsided set of power relations. Language choices are rarely innocent, even if motives are.

Hierarchy seems to be implicated as well in the authors' apparent lack of rationale for this research undertaking. It is important to note that they make no explicit case for the value of ranking *female* scholarly activity. They do include a paragraph that, we presume, is supposed to count as a rationale; in it, they note the number of women who have acted as president of the Speech Communication Association or as editors of three SCA journals.[25] That observation is the *only* initial remark Hickson et al. make about *women's* roles in the discipline. However, it is problematic on two counts. First, it implies that contributions to the field are or should be measured according to people's occupancy of positions at the "top" of organizational hierarchies. Second, it provides utterly no justification for the measurement of active scholarship. The suggestion that women have been journal editors and SCA presidents and that, *therefore*, an enumeration and ranking of women's publication records is legitimate, is a non sequitur.

Hickson and his colleagues also claim that, given prior research, "it is now possible" (351) to conduct their research project. Possibilities aside, the question of the *desirability* of this project still remains. It evidently *is* possible, but we are left with the issue of what licenses three men to single out women as a group for scrutiny. There is no obvious reason that presents itself in the literature for segregating research production by gender; no corresponding ranking of active *male* prolific scholars, for example, has presented itself. Rather, one must assume for purposes of warranting the Hickson et al. study that active female researchers have published systematically less than their active male colleagues in the field, in order to see any need at all for this research.[26] It may even be true that women have published less than men, but that is an unsupported hypothesis, not a documented claim. So, how can this unsupported hypothesis serve as an assumptive premise of this report? How, in fact, can it be assumptive when it is, itself a testable hypothesis? Its status as an assumption marks the ease with which women can be seen as inherently less accomplished than their male counterparts. The very taken-for-grantedness of the premise is itself the problem. To be less accomplished is one thing; to always be assumed to be less accomplished is another. Unfortunately, the assumption may well contribute to the condition. Whether or not it does, the assumption itself, and the apparent ease with which it is accepted, are offensive and inherently damaging to women.

The fact that Hickson et al. articulate no clear rationale for this study is disturbing not only because of what it forces the reader to accept as a premise; the lack of persuasive rationale is also troubling, given what the study *does*. Without any clear warrant, three men have conducted surveillance on women's research records (the bodies of their research?) and proceeded to rank order the most prolific among them (those whose bodies of research have the best measurements?). Our parenthetical questions suggest that we take this to be the academic equivalent of a beauty pageant. Indeed, it does seem an appropriate analog. It has all of the necessary trappings: line up the women, gaze on the parts you believe most pertinent, total up the points, and rank order them. That *this* pageant should be conducted strictly by men even does "real" beauty contests one better; the latter frequently have female judges or administrators. Of course, the analog breaks down on another profoundly telling point as well—women in beauty contests presumably choose to participate in such displays.[27]

The authors' consistent use of the term "prolific" to describe the women they display reinforces this sense of woman-as-object-of-male-surveillance. The reader comes away from the report knowing little more than which female bodies produced more than which other female bodies. This, coupled with the "prolific" language, summons an age-old way of construing female identity: Women are what their bodies can produce. And men monitor and regulate female production/reproduction as a means of asserting control over both the products and the power such products might afford the women who produce them.

It is neither fair nor convincing to assume that a woman's choice to publish in scholarly journals entitles three men, in essence, to reduce her activities to the fact of her physiology, to display her as a "better breeder" than other women, or to pit her "academic measurements" against other women's. These uses of women's labor are unfair, regardless of the interests such exhibitions may purport to serve and regardless of the voyeuristic pleasures such exhibitions offer. Just what purposes, and whose, might be served are issues to which we turn in the next section.

What/Whose Interests Are Served?

Hickson et al. conclude their "rationale" with the assertion that their report ought to provide colleagues in other disciplines with information useful in evaluating an individual female from the field "in a comparative sense" (351). But if the intended use of the "yardsticks" developed in the Hickson et al. piece is for tenure and promotion decisions, to whom would it be useful in the process of rendering such decisions? The majority of women named in Table I are full professors. The overwhelming majority are tenured. We have no wish or right to speak for these female colleagues or to comment on the personnel procedures at their respective institutions, but we suspect that the "yardsticks" would be of marginal utility, at least in terms of tenure and promotion issues, for

most of those listed. What of the women in the discipline *not* named to the list? Does this ranking have value for them? That seems even more doubtful. We find it exceptionally difficult to believe that anyone would volunteer to a personnel committee that she was not ranked among the most active female scholars of her field. So, if the ranking is of use to someone in personnel decisions, it seems unlikely that someone is the female candidate for promotion or tenure. Instead, the ranking seems more likely to be useful as an *impediment* to a woman's advancement. It requires little imagination to summon a scenario in which a female scholar is taken to task by her colleagues for not having accomplished "enough" or in the "right places" to be considered among the field's most active female scholars. Thus, this ranking serves the interests of those who would obstruct a woman's progress, for it makes acts of professional aggression against women even less difficult than they otherwise might be.

The Hickson et al. report threatens to work against the interests of women at a more "intimate" level as well. That is, what sorts of responses does the report most likely provoke in female readers? What do these likely responses "do" in terms of constructing, reinforcing, or modifying a sense of personal or professional identity? What do these likely responses suggest about how a given female reader sees herself in relation to both male and female colleagues?

As we see it, three types of response seem most likely given how the report was compiled and presented. First, someone who does not appear on the list is likely to feel anxious about her own rate of scholarly activity and thus about her professional future. This response also leads to nervousness about being shown up by "one's own." Second, what if one does appear on the list? Shouldn't this provide some measure of security and gratification? Perhaps. Yet, given the hierarchical nature of the list and the competitiveness that hierarchy almost inevitably promotes, we can imagine that women ranked lower than first might feel less than gratified. Even the number one spot could be an awkward one to occupy. Such a position may create the alienation that comes from being raised—presumably without being offered a choice—above one's peers.

A third response is to be disheartened, as we are, by the fact that such a list exists at all. We are disheartened to see women set against each other in this fashion. We are disheartened to see some of our male colleagues' apparent obliviousness to how this may harm and discourage us. We are disheartened by the fact that "our" discipline would, however tacitly, condone and encourage this sort of activity. We are disheartened when we consider what this says about the state of our collective consciousness regarding gender issues. And we are disheartened when we consider the kind of precedent this report threatens to set. Are "we" entitling the already secure to wield the "yardstick" against a host of marginalized groups? Does the publication of this report give the green light to future rankings of "prolific" African-American scholars? Hispanic scholars? Gay or Lesbian scholars? Are "we" authorizing the institutionally powerful to continue speaking *about* the less powerful, rather than encouraging the powerful to speak *with* us, or, more importantly, to let us speak?

Each of these reactions potentially invoked by the Hickson et al. report is painful in its own right. These reactions taken as a group are even more so. We find it difficult to imagine how any woman could be encouraged, gratified, or take any pleasure when she considers herself in relation to the report. Certainly it would be difficult to do so without simultaneously experiencing some sense of alienation from what could be a sustaining community—other women.

Finally, Hickson et al.'s report functions to reinscribe a disempowering form of subjectivity "offered" to women all too frequently in this culture. As John Berger describes it:

To be born a woman has been to be born, within an allotted and confined space, into the keeping of men. The social presence of women has developed as a result of their ingenuity in living under such tutelage within such a limited space. But this has been at the cost of a woman's self being split in two. A woman must continually watch herself. . . . From earliest childhood she has been taught and persuaded to survey herself continually.

And so she comes to consider the *surveyor* and the *surveyed* within her as the two constituent yet always distinct elements of her identity as a woman. (46)

The Hickson et al. report, then, serves to demarcate the space of female productivity and to remind us that we are under surveillance by male "colleagues."

More insidiously, however, reports such as this encourage us, quite literally, to split ourselves from ourselves. They do so at two levels. Most obviously, such reports isolate individual women from each other. And such reports isolate us from an integrated sense of self by handing us "the yardstick" so that we might survey and (often negatively) evaluate ourselves. We are hard pressed to think of a way that any community could more effectively control any group of members. We are equally hard pressed to imagine how reinforcing such an isolated and self-limiting form of identity could possibly be in the best interests of those to whom it is offered. Finally, we are hard pressed to see how splitting scholars from themselves and from each other serves "the discipline" in any meaningful way. How could encouraging isolation and self-alienation possibly lead to greater intellectual growth and creativity? How can any community flourish when more and more of its members are limited, made fearful, absorbed in self-surveillance, and, quite literally, broken? This is in no one's best interest, not even those with the most invested in maintaining traditional disciplinary boundaries and relations of power.

Approved Identities, Readings, and Politics: The Anonymous Reviews and the Denouement

Within a few weeks of submitting "Subject Of or Subject To Research?" we received a rejection letter, accompanied by two reviews that recommended against publication of our essay. In general we found the reviews to be overt displays of ideological mechanisms that not only approve the themes of the masculinist paradigm, but which seek to ensure that the masculinist paradigm represents the exclusive thematic directive for professional work in the discipline. The two reviews do more than reproduce the themes of the masculinist paradigm; they buttress its privilege by advancing what can count as approved (and disapproved) identities, readings, and politics within the discipline. In using these two reviews as explicit objects of analysis, we bring them into the public conversation of scholarly discourse. As Myers observes, a scholarly community's review of a text can be viewed as "a negotiation of the status that the . . . community will assign to the text's knowledge claim" (328).[28]

Before we turn to a discussion of the approved (and disapproved) identities, readings, and politics that are embedded in these two reviews, we think it is important to emphasize that the mechanisms of the masculinist paradigm, like those of any ideology, perform enabling functions for a scholarly community. The masculinist paradigm, like other paradigms, provides a scholarly community with what Foucault calls "apparatuses of knowledge" (*Power/Knowledge*, 106); these apparatuses enable the production of research by invoking shared motivations, vocabularies, assumptions, and methods. At the same time, however, these knowledge apparatuses constitute systems of control that exclude alternative intellectual practices.[29]

The focal work of both these reviews is the designation of approved and disapproved identities; that is, articulation of the range of what one is able to say and how, as well as who one can be as an acceptable member of a group, in this case the discipline. The related issues of approved readings and approved politics emerge in connection with the identity prescriptions. By approved readings, we mean prescriptions for "correct" ways of reading. By implication, "incorrect" ways of reading can be identified, rendered unacceptable, and, preferably, silenced. As Crowley observes, "[S]ince there are correct readings, misreading must occur through some fault in the reader who produces it. If two readers disagree, one of them has failed somehow" (459).[30] An approved politics refers to the roles particular individuals and groups are allowed to play vis-à-vis one another or the moves they are allowed to make—especially in cases of conflict or competition for scarce resources. In the case of an academic discipline, these supposedly "scarce resources" might be prestige, designations of "expertise," or even career survival.[31]

The overarching identity approved in the reviews of our essay is that of the professional intellectual or scholar.[32] Referee #1 questions our status as scholars by rejecting our manuscript's status as a "scholarly article," indicating, in part, that "there are too many feline, petty attacks in this manuscript and too much ball-bashing to be a scholarly article." Referee #2 marks us immediately as "unprofessional" and "anti-intellectual," indicating that he or she is "embarrassed" for the academic field for producing persons who have written "the single worst piece of 'scholarship'" that he or she has ever reviewed. Both reviews further specify the stances and attitudes that "professionals," "intellectuals," or "scholars" must demonstrate in order for these roles to be designated as approved identities within the discipline. Appropriately "professional" scholars should be: (1) politically neutral, (2) respectful toward science, (3) mainstream, and (4) politely deferential.[33]

Disciplinary professionals, first, must be *politically neutral*. Referee #2 opines that our manuscript was not a "critique of the published article" but a "political harangue against so-called 'male paradigm,' which is nothing more than the typical male-bashing brought forth by Marxist writers." This reviewer differentiates sharply between "critique" and "political harangue" but does not specify the boundary between them, apparently believing that it should be apparent to anyone wearing an approved identity. Certainly not all "political" discourse is "harangue," nor would most of us wish to be seen as engaging in the latter. But critique is always political and that seems to be the real problem for referee #2. That becomes clearer in an examination of the next identity characteristic and its attendant prescriptions for approved modes of reading.

The second identity characteristic, *respectfulness toward science*, is invoked in the second referee's claim that our manuscript was "laced with extreme anti-science orientations with the mask of the 'male' paradigm doing the front work." We understand the reproach of "anti-science" to define negatively a range of approved behaviors by which professionals either subscribe to the supposed value-neutrality of scientific work or at least agree not to expose the tendentious and valued character of so-called objective work.

The approved respect for the value-neutrality of science links naturally with a related directive for producing an approved reading. According to this view, published texts are transparent, easily and "correctly" readable; to read for or infer assumptions is unnecessary and apparently even unacceptable. This stance promulgates the naïve understanding of scholarly languages (prose, tabulations, calculations, and the like) as neutrally privileged and magically exempt from tendency. Both reviewers find our reading of the Hickson et al. report to be "wrong" because we challenged its value-neutrality. Referee #1 "find[s] it insulting," in her capacity as one of the original reviewers of the Hickson et al. report, that we were "incapable of seeing" that its goal was straightforwardly "to identify and recognize women in the field who have sustained records of scholarship." The second referee also concludes that our analysis of the Hickson et al. report was in error because we failed to read the piece as a celebratory documentation of the discipline's "advancement" of women in the field.

Ironically, however, these referees appear to speculate freely about the objectives of the Hickson et al. report. According to the referees' approved mode of reading, some readers (e.g., these referees) apparently may draw inferences about a text, provided that their inferences are consistent with other attributes of an approved reading. So, delegitimized readers "erroneously" "read into the piece" false inferences; they are deemed "criminal," "Marxist," and so forth. How can the referees' inferences be approved while our own cannot? The answer, of course, has to do in part with their institutional roles as referees and ours as mere authors of a manuscript. But that explanation, by itself, is too simple.

The answer is linked as well to a third element of approved identity—*occupancy of the mainstream.* Referee #2 suggests that our manuscript "represents the extremist fringe of the so-called feminist movement" and that it "does not represent the views of mainstream females in the field, or even that of most of us who see ourselves as feminists." As we will suggest further on, anyone who could characterize our response essay as "extremist" feminism cannot be very familiar with much contemporary feminist scholarship in this field or others. For now, it is enough to observe that referee #2 appears to define the "mainstream" of feminism as the ground occupied by most individual females in the field, not a ground of substantive views or reasoned stances. Feminism, thus, seems to be defined epiphenomenally.

Characterization of the mainstream as a population center provides an excellent opportunity for dismissing those who disagree. This practice makes it possible for an approved reader to draw inferences and to dismiss the inferences of disapproved readers, for example. Because the second referee reads our work as out of step with that of most other women or feminists, only one small move remains to reach the inevitable—dismissal or silencing. Precisely this move appeared in this referee's concluding remarks to us. S/he suggested the formation of "a whole new field that was off limits to males and heterosexual females. That field would appear to be more to the liking of these authors." By casting us as lesbians, a minority supposedly outside the mainstream female population center, this reviewer invokes the approved politics of exclusion and silencing accomplished via segregation. To be different, especially to be vocal about one's differences, is simply unacceptable, and action must be taken to silence those who would express their differences so openly. This stance is consistent with the remaining identity characteristic, which points also to the approved politics of exclusion/silencing.

Polite deference is the fourth and final characteristic, and its most important role seems to be

to vouchsafe hierarchy. Referee #1 demonstrates the linkage in her claim that the Hickson et al. rank order list serves "to identify and recognize women in the field who have sustained records of scholarship and point them out as role models for others to follow." The notions of role models and their followers, of course, reference a hierarchy. And everyone, apparently, should be arranged according to it. Referee #1 concludes that our response was "puffy and arrogant" and infers that we "didn't make the list (or weren't as high as [we'd] like to be)." This reviewer immediately proceeds to discuss her own ranking, noting that the Hickson et al. list "reflected a little over half of my journal articles (and, of course, none of my books)" and even claims that "this was the case for most of the women on the list." It apparently is difficult for this referee to believe that anyone would not *want* to be ranked, that anyone actually on the list could *object* to it, or that there could be any *discomfort* with the ranking except not being as high as one would like. This referee then concludes her comments with the hint that we should have "counted to ten" before sending off our response essay in order to avoid looking like "an immature ass." Clearly, this referee invokes a politics of exclusion in this comment. She equates anti-hierarchical positions with "immaturity," and this label functions to legitimate the silencing of unauthorized stances.

Referee #2 is no less clear about reinvesting hierarchy. S/he claims that "In the past 20 years this field has made giant strides toward empowering females to rise to the highest levels of our profession, both scholarly and otherwise. I read the Hickson et al. article as a celebration of that advancement." Again, the approved identity is to rise, to occupy the "highest levels." And the appropriate reaction for others is to honor those who have risen. What Referee #2 also honors is the hierarchical arrangement itself and particularly that which Hickson, Stacks, and Amsbary themselves have since referred to as the "numbers game" ("Active Prolific Scholars," 231). Referee #2 argues that it is "this field" that has "made giant strides toward empowering women." Apparently women have not been responsible for their own successes or in charge of their own careers; the field has been. As with the other prescriptions, if we are unable or unwilling to recognize the sanctity of hierarchical arrangements, the approved, exclusionary politics is put into play. Referee #2 goes so far as to advise that "since these authors publish two-thirds of their work outside the field, might I suggest that they raise that percentage to 100%?"

Rarely are the mechanisms of approval and enforcement so explicitly espoused as in these reviews, but then most referees probably do not expect that their reviews will appear in print. This kind of discourse is allowed to function to control and censor what is said in this discipline; it is absolutely privileged discourse, typically exempt from public scrutiny and always protected by anonymity. Certainly we believe, in fact we know, that all referees do not subscribe to the ideological prescriptions of these two referees. That attempts of this sort to censor and silence occur at all, however, should give us cause for consternation.[34]

Conclusions/Continuations

No conclusions offer themselves easily, for it is not up to the three of us alone to resolve the issues raised here. "Conclusions" will come only from the collective actions of the group we call our "discipline," a term which itself warns us against the seductive powers and dangers of our shared intellectual orthodoxies. We do wish to make three final points, however, that are more about continuing than with concluding.[35]

First, the Hickson et al. report must not be invoked or used in any of our workplaces. It misrepresents the accomplishments of women in the field, refuses to understand their experiences in context, and subordinates their interests to the abstraction called "the discipline." Women *not* included in the Hickson et al. ranking will be those most profoundly affected by it if we sanction its use. The effect will be institutional punishment. That is not to suggest that those women who *are* ranked have been or will be unaffected. This report domesticates them and their work, disciplining them with the "yardstick," ignoring *what* they have had to say, and refusing to acknowledge that their work (as well as that of other female scholars) often has been accomplished against great odds and at serious personal cost. Certainly they *and other women* of academic stripe should be recognized, even lauded, for their work. Ensnaring them within a hierarchical ranking, however, cannot be construed as a "celebration"; this hierarchy exploits women and their work, pressing them into service as unconsenting tokens and thereby perpetuating the ideology that diminishes women. Female tokenism is in play when "the power withheld from the vast majority of women is offered to

a few, so that it may appear that any truly qualified woman can gain access to leadership, recognition, and reward" (Adrienne Rich, quoted by Biesecker, 43).

The men and women who identify themselves as members of this discipline must not comply with such an arrangement. All of us—women and men alike—have been "trained" to speak in the assumptive argot of the masculinist paradigm. The issues are whether we are able or willing to retrain ourselves to think and speak outside of its impersonal abstractions, disciplinary territoriality, individuation, and hierarchy. One way to begin could be to acknowledge that everyone in the field—men as well as women—might be better served by different arrangements. We believe that competitive, hierarchical rankings projects of individuals' publication rates peculiarly damage women in the ways we discuss above. But we are not convinced that they serve the men in this discipline either. Perhaps we need to locate and sanction new ways of judging our scholarly efforts and effects besides simply counting them up and arranging them by rank. No one denies that judgment is a component of our working lives, but we *all* might benefit if the discipline's sanctioned grounds for judgment were reconfigured.

Second, the ideological apparatuses that approve a very narrow range of identities and readings and that force a politics of exclusion must not be allowed to silence other voices. The ideological mechanisms of professionalism as they are expressed in the initial referees' reviews would silence virtually any feminist voice.

Feminist stances of any ilk simply *are* political. As Campbell argues, "Feminist scholarship is distinguished by the systematic inclusion of women, by an absence of language and/or perspective that degrades women or minorities, by rigorous testing of assumptions that hark back to stereotypes and social mythology, and by a concern to rectify the omissions, the degradation, and the errors of the past" ("What Really Distinguishes," 4). To suggest that feminist critique must not be political is to suggest that it should not exist at all.[36]

Moreover, feminist stances cannot necessarily respect traditional science. As Gregg acknowledges, "Feminists have been concerned with the equation of the findings of science with truth and knowledge, the designation of scientists as experts, the distance between scientific concepts and research and everyday life: in short, the power of science to predict, control, define, and restrict reality by virtue of its privileged position among other social activities" (8). Such concerns are not "anti-scientific." They are sites of critique. Feminist critique of intellectual practice is neither unusual enough to be "radical," nor limited to challenging the tenets of traditional science. Within our own field, feminists have targeted intellectual practices of rhetorical theory, ethnography, histories of rhetoric, and postmodernism, as well as those of conservative science.[37] Feminist positions must not be silenced on the grounds of their "opposition" to science. Such an accusation is inaccurate, and it misses the transformative point of feminist critique, which is to change any academic stance that devalues, excludes, or effaces women's experience.

Feminism, similarly, does not respect "mainstream" or unitary stances. If the ideology of academic professionalism is allowed to accomplish such a reduction, feminism's virtues will be essentially obliterated. As Schwichtenberg suggests, "Feminism itself is a highly diverse terrain, which challenges monolithic assumptions deriving from a single feminist approach or style" (291). To silence any feminism, whether Marxist, African, Hispanic, Lacanian, or lesbian, is to diminish the extraordinary power of its diversity. Moreover, if arguments for the "mainstream" are allowed to prevail, it is very likely that we will return to the era (if, in fact, we ever left it) that witnessed feminist study of *any* kind declared to be outside the mainstream. Johnson describes it rather pointedly: "It is also not uncommon to hear one's colleagues describe a woman who does such research [gender studies] as 'a one-issue person,' 'narrowly focused,' 'politically motivated,' and 'not in touch with the mainstream of the field.' These comments are seldom heard about individuals who devote themselves to the study of, say, family communication, war rhetoric, communication theory, or small group communication; such individuals are, of course, 'specialists'" (320). If the "mainstream" is to serve as the arbiter, feminism will not pass muster.

Nor can feminist stances be held to the strictures of polite deference and survive. The demand for deference forces women's submission or surrender to masculinist conceptions. Deference simply reinforces a masculine hierarchy as if it characterized *human* ways of thinking, being, and acting. Women have no deference option except to submit and be counted against the measures created to characterize men. The result, as Tavris argues, is to be "mismeasured," to always be found inadequate.

Every ideological apparatus wielded by the initial referees would silence virtually any feminist statement. The silences would not be limited to those the referees would consider extremist, Marxist, lesbian, and so forth—those they clearly do wish to squelch. All of feminism would be quarantined at the disciplinary border and ultimately deported. Such an ideology cannot be allowed to govern an academic field that so proudly espouses pluralism, diversity, and communication. Disagreement is to be valued and kept in play in the dialogue of such a field, not silenced or kept cloistered behind the secretive curtain of blind reviewing.

Third, the writing practices that mark what counts as scholarly discourses in this field must not be maintained without scrutiny. It surely is incumbent upon the adherents of any academic field to scrutinize and evaluate their own rules of engagement and practice. It is the more so for scholars of rhetoric and communication; our written work reveals the assumptions and rules to which we hold vis-à-vis communicative practice and expression. If we have identified correctly the rules for writing the field's scholarship at the beginning of this essay, then we are obliged to acknowledge that these rules demand personae of singular, neutral, authoritative, observers who are detached from or ambivalent about their own histories and contexts. We are also bound to observe the coherence of these rules with the apparatuses that police the professional academic's approved identity and modes of reading by means of an exclusionary politics.

We began this essay by identifying several potent, yet rarely discussed, assumptions and practices characteristic of scholarly activity in the speech communication discipline. Our purpose in doing so goes well beyond the desire to vindicate our original manuscript or to settle scores with referees. We see this essay as the beginning of a process as well as the end of another, and as an invitation to invest in one conversation as well as an argument against investing in another.

We could include an additional entry on the list of troubling norms governing academic writing: the production and consumption of individual journal articles as if they were (or should be) free standing and finalized utterances on the topic at hand. Our talk about "scholarly dialogue" and "scholarly communities" notwithstanding, we tend to construe our work in monologic terms. We think in terms of single articles; rarely do articles past enter future discussions except as citations. In our estimation, this tendency to focus on single, isolated "scholarly turns" rather than on extended, interactive "scholarly conversations" reduces the chances for the kind of reflexive examination we suggest in this essay. The examination of ourselves as a community requires that we look at patterns in our writing and speaking and at the ideological positions such patterns depend on, reproduce, or refuse. Moreover, insofar as such examination focuses on ourselves as a community, it needs to be done as a community.

We hope, then, that our essay will evoke additional discussion of the issues we have raised. We hope that this discussion will be honest and passionate. We also hope that it will help to reinvest our scholarly activities with a sense of what is (or could be) at stake in them.

NOTES

1. For further comment on these and other such academic writing practices, see Bazerman; Brodkey; Wander and Jenkins; Wander, "Politics"; and Nothstine, Blair, and Copeland. Disciplinary practices—among them writing practices—seem to be at least a subtext of most of the essays in the Spring 1993 special issue of the *Western Journal of Communication* on "Ideology and Communication." See especially Wander's editorial introduction, as well as the essays by Rodden, Owen and Ehrenhaus, Condit, Rigsby, West, Lee, and Wood and Cox.

2. We are using the terms "text" and "fragment" in a fashion almost, but perhaps not entirely, consonant with their uses by McGee, in "Text," and Barthes. One understanding of "text" in their works is that of a combinatory fabric of multiple textual fragments constructed by a critic. Our use of the term here suggests that it may be constructed from material discursive fragments *and* the silences that surround those fragments. These silences might be the unarticulated "rules" of cultural or discursive codes or the silences of strategically unarticulated positions. In that sense, our use of the term links it to notions like Althusser's ideological apparatus, Foucault's discursive practice (*Archaeology*), or Lyotard's phrase regimen (*régime de phrase*) that link phrases or discursive fragments to one another (*The Differend*). In any case, Barthes' injunctions are ones we accept, that "the Text is a process of demonstration," and that it is "experienced only in an activity of production" (157).

3. For example, as Condit describes, the referees for Wander's "The Politics of Despair" expressed "a general rejection-reaction" to the essay ("Introduction," 249). It probably is no coincidence that Wander committed a number of disciplinary "violations" in that essay, one of which was a description of some of the negative consequences of academic writing norms. For example, he suggested that "as the system works to quash surprise, improvisation, and controversy, criticism begins to echo an established order" (278).

4. See Nelson, Megill, and McCloskey, eds.; and Simons, ed.

5. This seems to be consistent with Conquergood's point, when he argues that "it is ironic that the discipline of communication has been relatively unreflective about the rhetorical construction of its disciplinary authority. It would be illuminating to critique the rhetorical expectations and constraints on articles published in the *Quarterly Journal of Speech*, or *Communication Monographs*. What kinds of knowledge, and their attendant discursive styles, get privileged, legitimated, or displaced? How does knowledge about communication get constructed? What counts as an interesting question about human communication? What are the tacitly observed boundaries—the range of appropriateness—regarding the substance, methods, and discursive styles of communication scholarship? And, most importantly for critical theorists, what configuration of socio-political interests does communication scholarship serve?" (195). We find Conquergood's questions to be vital to the discipline at large, necessary for those who are concerned with the rhetoric of inquiry, and formative for our own critique in this essay.

6. For an elaboration, see Johnson's review of books on women's language, particularly her discussion of Mary Daly's book, *Pure Lust*.

7. This is the case, almost regardless of the particular feminist stance assumed or of the particular disciplinary specialty of the advocate. See, for example, Balsamo; Biesecker; Campbell, "Sound"; Cirksena; Dervin; Fine; Foss and Foss; Foss and Griffin; Gallagher; Gregg; Jarratt, "Performing"; Jarratt, "Speaking"; Kauffman; Muto; Press; Rakow; Rushing; Schwichtenberg; Self; Spitzack and Carter, "Women"; Steeves; Wood, "Feminist Scholarship"; and Wood and Phillips.

8. Other studies in the Hickson et al. research program include: Hickson ("Profiling the Chairs"); Hickson, Stacks, and Amsbary ("An Analysis of Prolific Scholarship"); Hickson, Stacks, and Amsbary ("Administrator-Scholars"); Hickson, Stacks, and Amsbary ("Active Prolific Scholars"); Hickson, Scott, Stacks, and Amsbary ("Scholarship in Mass Communication"). For convenience, we will refer to the report "Active Prolific Female Scholars" simply as the Hickson et al. report without further designation. Other articles by these three authors will be differentiated from this one—the object of our response—by parenthetical designation of title.

9. Other research in the bibliometric tradition of Hickson et al. includes Barker, Roach, and Underberg ("An Investigation of Articles . . . 1970 through 1978"); Barker, Roach, and Underberg ("An Investigation of Articles . . . Journal-by-Journal"); Burroughs, Christophel, Ady, and McGreal; Watson, Barker, Rav, and Hall.

10. See Erickson et al. for a discussion of general concern about studies that rank prolific scholars.

11. In the interest of fair reporting, we should note that none of our names appears on the Hickson, Stacks, and Amsbary list. As noted later in this essay, one of our initial referees accused us of list envy. The accusation is, of course, quite insulting. However, there are two very narrow senses in which it is quasi-accurate. First, one of our number would have been on the Hickson, Stacks, and Amsbary list but for an error in the Matlon and Ortiz index. Second, we were relatively concerned that our colleagues might raise the question about our non-presence on the list in the context of merit or promotion meetings. Our concerns were not ill-founded. One of our colleagues "casually" observed in a conversation that he had noticed that we were not included on the Hickson list. In those senses, and those only, we had self-interested reactions to our own non-inclusion. Principally, we were disgusted by the ideology of the report and worried about its likely uses.

12. We should note that the journal that published the Hickson, Stacks, and Amsbary report did later print corrections to the mistakes in the report, errors that had resulted in some women being mistakenly excluded from the ranking and in others being misranked. However, the tone of the correction should also be noted. Unlike the other item on the erratum page, which was listed as a "correction" and carried with it an apology, the Hickson et al. item was listed as an "update" and bore no traces of apologetic language. That women's careers had been placed potentially at risk apparently was not sufficient cause for regret.

13. For a review, see Sandler.

14. See, for example, Deetz and Mumby; Foucault, *Power/Knowledge*; Taylor; and Volosinov.

15. See, for example, Ward and Grant. Throughout our response to the Hickson et al. article, we refer to the "male paradigm." Elsewhere in this essay, we use the term "masculinist paradigm." We regard these terms as synonymous; neither is essentialist in nature.

16. For a general review of the agency–communion distinction, see McAdams.

17. See, for example, Belenky, Clinchy, Goldberger, and Tarule; Gilligan; and Lyons.

18. See, for example, Baldwin and Blackburn.

19. See, for example, the related essays by Charles R. Berger and by Redding.

20. See, for example, Renharz.

21. See Belenky et al.; Gilligan; and Lyons.

22. See Gilligan; and Lyons.

23. See, for example, Clark and Corcoran; Menges and Exum; Sandler; and the Task Force on Women in Higher Education.

24. See Belenky et al.; and Ward and Grant.

25. Why they would not acknowledge female editors of other SCA journals is unclear. They name only *QJS*, CM, and CE. What of CSMC? One of its most recent editors is Sari Thomas. And what of the current editor of *TPQ*, Kristin M. Langellier?

26. We suppose one could also justify the segregation on the assumption that women publish systematically more than men, but that seems inconsistent with the general tenor of the essay.

27. In respect to the issue of choice, the better analogs might be livestock shows or slave auctions.

28. We are not the first to conduct an analysis of the reviewing process as a lens through which to analyze the functioning of a scholarly community. See, for example, Cohen; Myers; Peters and Ceci. For an example within the speech communication discipline, see Medhurst.

29. The dual capacity of any social convention or practice to both enable and constrain is a theme addressed by a number of scholars, including Giddens and Foucault, among others.

30. For a further discussion of the implications of approved or correct readings, see Crowley's critique of Wander's respondents in the ideological turn discussion (Campbell, "Response"; Corcoran; Francesconi; Hill; McGee, "Another Philippic"; Megill; and Rosenfield). Crowley's discussion particularly turns on the responses of Megill, Hill, and Rosenfield. She argues that their responses to Wander turn on two warrants: (1) "that correct readings are possible," and (2) "that some critics cannot give correct readings of some texts" (456). These warrants, she argues, are conditioned by an ideology that appears under various names: "Kantian idealism, Enlightenment epistemology, liberal humanism, modernism" (457). Crowley's discussion points to the consequences of subscription to these warrants, in her argument that traditional critics "must perforce denigrate the work of critics whose readings . . . do not fall within the range of approved readings. More seriously, they must denigrate the work of critics who for some reason cannot become the readers they need to be in order to read the texts 'properly'" (459). Here Crowley notes not only the issue of approved readings but approved identities as well. Moreover, the notion of "denigration" points us to the political, for in the hands of sanctioned judges like journal manuscript reviewers, denigration is all too easily transformed into silencing and exclusion.

31. For a discussion of these issues, see Lyotard, *The Postmodern Condition*; Wilshire; and Nothstine, Blair, and Copeland. Also see Spitzack and Carter, "Feminist Communication," who argue that "The third lie concerns the cultural portrayal of power as a scarce resource. Attempting to get power is charged by the belief that power exists in limited quantities. There is only enough for a few, and those who struggle to get power must override the competition. This lie endorses a hierarchy in which few are winners and many are losers. In order to 'win,' the competitors must show them-

selves to be superior to others. . . . When feminists compete with each other, striving to 'win' . . . we run the risk of perpetuating the very hierarchy we criticize. The three lies about power serve to fragment communities of women and assure that none of us will generate fundamental changes either for ourselves or for women in general" (34).

32. In quoting from the two manuscript reviews in what follows, we will come close to exhausting their content. That is, they contain very little besides what is represented below. Both *do* also address issues of accuracy in the Hickson et al. report, as we have noted earlier. Beyond that, they are almost completely contained in our quotations. As a means of insuring that our quotations represent the reviews fairly, we have provided the editor of this journal with copies of the reviews. We should note also that we refer to the first referee as a woman and the second in gender-neutral ways. Referee #1 identifies herself as female in her review; referee #2 does not so specify.

33. At least *female* professionals must fit this profile. That the three of us identified ourselves as female in our response essay complicates the ideological profile to some degree, particularly in these referees' prescriptions of disapproved identities. Disapproved identity characteristics cited in the two reviews include being "vehement," "egotistical," "feline," "petty," "ball-bashing," "extremist," "puffy," "arrogant," "political," and "male-bashing." It hardly seems worth asking if it is acceptable for male professionals to be vehement or egotistical or political. But we are compelled to ask if the more stereotypical female descriptors here might have been transformed to read "assertive," "argumentative," "emphatic," "forthright," "direct," or "confident," if we had cloaked our gender under third-person references. In fact, we wonder if either of the referees would have been as likely to recite for us their professionalism lessons at all had we written in an androgynous tongue. Regardless, the uncertainty about whether male professionals would be required to assume the identities, read in these ways, and be subject to the politics that are all specified here, remains.

34. It is *not* sufficient, in our judgment, to dismiss these reviews as merely aberrant and thus insignificant. We cannot prove that there have been other cases just like these, but it is unnecessary to do so. For one thing, they represent privileged discourse, both because of the shielding provided by referee anonymity and because they were the sanctioned discourse of a journal in this field. In addition, we agree with the point made so clearly by Foucault, that statements actually uttered are those legitimized by the rules of a discursive practice. Such statements, even if rare, are indicators of the forces of power within a discursive field. See *Archaeology* 28, 120.

35. We are interested in continuations more than conclusions, because, despite Referee #2's invitation to us to leave the field, we have decided to stay.

36. Of course, it is equally absurd to suggest that any academic discourse be politically neutral, from our point of view. Feminist scholarship, though, is particularly vulnerable to this kind of demand, for it cannot effectively disguise itself as apolitical as many forms of academic discourse can.

37. See, for example, Balsamo; Biesecker; Foss; and Griffin and Kauffmann.

REFERENCES

Althusser, Louis. (1971). "Ideology and Ideological State Apparatuses (Notes Towards an Investigation)." In *Lenin and Philosophy and Other Essays*, trans. Ben Brewster (London: New Left Books), 121–173.

Baldwin, Roger G., and Robert T. Blackburn. (1981). "The Academic Career as a Developmental Process." *Journal of Higher Education* 52: 598–614.

Balsamo, Anne. (1987). "Un-Wrapping the Postmodern: A Feminist Glance." *Journal of Communication Inquiry* 11: 64–72.

Barker, Larry, Robert Hall, Deborah Roach, and Larry Underberg. (1979). "An Investigation of Quantity of Articles Produced in the Communication Discipline by Institutions: 1970 through 1978, Part 1." *Association for Communication Administration Bulletin* 30: 18–22.

Barker, Larry, Robert Hall, Deborah Roach, and Larry Underberg. (1980). "An Investigation of Articles Produced in the Communication Discipline by Institution: A Journal by Journal, Year by Year Analysis, Part 2." *Association for Communication Administration Bulletin* 34: 37–48.

Barthes, Roland. (1977). "From Work to Text." In *Image, Music, Text*, trans. Stephen Heath (New York: Hill and Wang), 155–164.

Bazerman, Charles. (1988). *Shaping Written Knowledge: The Genre and Activity of the Experimental Article in Science*. Madison: University of Wisconsin Press.

Belenky, Mary Field, Blythe McVicker Clinchy, Nancy Rule Goldberger, and Jill Mattuck Tarule. (1986). *Women's Ways of Knowing: The Development of Self, Voice, and Mind*. New York: Basic Books.

Berger, Charles R. (1991). "Communication Theories and Other Curios." *Communication Monographs* 58: 101–113.

Berger, John. (1977). *Ways of Seeing*. New York: Penguin Books.

Berger, Peter L., and Thomas Luckmann. (1967). *The Social Construction of Reality: A Treatise in the Sociology of Knowledge*. New York: Doubleday.

Biesecker, Barbara. (1992). "Coming to Terms with Recent Attempts to Write Women into the History of Rhetoric." *Philosophy and Rhetoric* 25: 140–161.

Bourdieu, Pierre. (1988). *Homo Academicus*. Translated by Peter Collier. Cambridge, UK: Polity Press.

Brodkey, Linda. (1987). *Academic Writing as Social Practice*. Philadelphia: Temple University Press.

Burroughs, Nancy F., Diane Christophel, J. Cole Ady, and Elizabeth A. McGreal. (1989). "Top Published Authors in Communication Studies." *Association for Communication Administration Bulletin* 67: 37–45.

Campbell, Karlyn Kohrs. (1983). "Response to Forbes Hill." *Central States Speech Journal* 34: 126–127.

Campbell, Karlyn Kohrs. (1986). "What Really Distinguishes and/or Ought to Distinguish Feminist Scholarship in Communication Studies?" *Women's Studies in Communication* 11: 4–5.

Campbell, Karlyn Kohrs. (1989). "The Sound of Women's Voices" [Review essay]. *Quarterly Journal of Speech* 75: 212–220.

Cirksena, Kathryn. (1987). "Politics and Difference: Radical Feminist Epistemological Premises for Communication Studies." *Journal of Communication Inquiry* 11: 19–28.

Clark, Shirley M., and Mary Corcoran. (1986). "Perspectives on the Professional Socialization of Women Faculty." *Journal of Higher Education* 57: 20–43.

Cohen, Ed. (1993). "Are We (Not) What We Are Becoming?: "Gay Identity," "Gay Studies," and the Disciplining of Knowledge." In Ellen Messer-Davidow, David R. Shumway, and David J. Sylvan, eds., *Knowledges: Historical and Critical Studies in Disciplinarity* (Charlottesville: University Press of Virginia), 397–421.

Condit, Celeste Michelle. (1993). "The Critic as Empath: Moving Away from Totalizing Theory." *Western Journal of Communication* 57: 178–190.

Conquergood, Dwight. (1991). "Rethinking Ethnography: Towards a Critical Cultural Politics." *Communication Monographs* 58: 179–194.

Corcoran, Farrel. (1984)."The Widening Gyre: Another Look at Ideology in Wander and His Critics." *Central States Speech Journal* 35: 54–56.

Crowley, Sharon. (1992). "Reflections on an Argument That Won't Go Away; or, A Turn of the Ideological Screw." *Quarterly Journal of Speech* 78: 450–465.

Daly, Mary. (1984). *Pure Lust*. Boston: Beacon Press.

de Certeau, Michel. (1984). *The Practice of Everyday Life*. Translated by Steven Rendall. Berkeley and Los Angeles: University of California Press.

Deetz, Stanley, and Dennis K. Mumby. (1990). "Power, Discourse, and the Workplace: Reclaiming the Critical Tradition." In James A. Anderson, ed., *Communication Yearbook 13* (Newbury Park, CA: Sage), 18–47.

Dervin, Brenda. (1987). "The Potential Contribution of Feminist Scholarship to the Field of Communication." *Journal of Communication* 37: 107–120.

Dervin, Brenda, Lawrence Grossberg, Barbara J. O'Keefe, and Ellen Wartella, eds. (1989). *Rethinking Communication, Vol. 2: Paradigm Exemplars*. Newbury Park, CA: Sage.

Erickson, Keith V., Cathy A. Fleuriet, and Lawrence A. Elosman. (1993). "Prolific Publishing: Professional and Administrative Concerns." *Southern Communication Journal* 58: 328–338.

Fine, Marlene G. (1986). "What Makes It Feminist?" *Women's Studies in Communication* 11: 18–19.

Foss, Sonja K., and Karen A. Foss. (1986). "What Distinguishes Feminist Scholarship in Communication Studies?" *Women's Studies in Communication* 11: 9–11.

Foss, Sonja K., and Cindy L. Griffin. (1992). "A Feminist Perspective on Rhetorical Theory: Toward a Clarification of Boundaries." *Western Journal of Communication* 56: 330–349.

Foucault, Michel. (1972). *The Archaeology of Knowledge and The Discourse on Language*. Translated by A. M. Sheridan Smith. New York: Pantheon Books.

Foucault, Michel. (1980). *Power/Knowledge: Selected Interviews and Other Writings, 1972–1977*. Edited by Colin Gordon. Translated by Colin Gordon, Leo Marshall, John Mepham, and Kate Soper. New York: Pantheon Books.

Francesconi, Robert. (1984). "Heidegger and Ideology: Reflections of an Innocent Bystander." *Central States Speech Journal* 35: 51–53.

Gallagher, Margaret. (1989). "A Feminist Perspective for Communication Research." In Brenda Dervin, Lawrence Grossberg, Barbara J. O'Keefe, and Ellen Wartella, eds., *Rethinking Communication, Vol. 2: Paradigm Exemplars* (Newbury Park, CA: Sage), 75–87.

Giddens, Anthony. (1984). *The Constitution of Society: Outline of the Theory of Structuration*. Berkeley and Los Angeles: University of California Press.

Gilligan, Carol. (1982). *In a Different Voice: Psychological Theory and Women's Development*. Cambridge, MA: Harvard University Press.

Gregg, Nina. (1987). "Reflections on the Feminist Critique of Objectivity." *Journal of Communication Inquiry* 11: 8–18.

Hariman, Robert. (1989). "The Rhetoric of Inquiry and the Professional Scholar." In Herbert W. Simons, ed., *Rhetoric in the Human Sciences* (Newbury Park, CA: Sage), 211–232.

Hickson, Mark, III. (1990). "Profiling the Chairs of Prolific Speech Communication Departments." *Association for Communication Administration Bulletin* 73: 4–14.

Hickson, Mark, III, Randall K. Scott, Don W. Stacks, and Jonathan H. Amsbary. (1992). "Scholarship in Mass Communication, 1915–1990: An Analysis of Active Researchers' Productivity." *Association for Communication Administration Bulletin* 82: 13–17.

Hickson, Mark, III, Don W. Stacks, and Jonathan H. Amsbary. (1989). "An Analysis of Prolific Scholarship in Speech Communication, 1915–1985: Toward a Yardstick for Measuring Research Productivity." *Communication Education* 38: 230–236.

Hickson, Mark, III, Don W. Stacks, and Jonathan H. Amsbary. (1992a). "Active Prolific Female Scholars in Communication: An Analysis of Research Productivity, II." *Communication Quarterly* 40: 350–356.

Hickson, Mark, III, Don W. Stacks, and Jonathan H. Amsbary. (1992b). "Administrator-Scholars in

Speech Communication: An Analysis of Research Productivity, II." *Association for Communication Administration Bulletin* 79: 66–74.

Hickson, Mark, III, Don W. Stacks, and Jonathan H. Amsbary. (1993). "Active Prolific Scholars in Communication Studies: An Analysis of Research Productivity, II." *Communication Education* 42: 224–233.

Hill, Forbes. (1983). "A Turn against Ideology: Reply to Professor Wander." *Central States Speech Journal* 34: 121–126.

Jarratt, Susan C. (1990). "Speaking to the Past: Feminist Historiography in Rhetoric." *Pre/Text* 11: 189–209.

Jarratt, Susan C. (1992). "Performing Feminisms, Histories, Rhetorics." *Rhetoric Society Quarterly* 22: 1–5.

Johnson, Fern L. (1986). "Coming to Terms with Women's Language" [Review essay]. *Quarterly Journal of Speech* 72: 318–330.

Kauffman, Bette J. (1992). "Feminist Facts: Interview Strategies and Political Subjects in Ethnography." *Communication Theory* 2: 187–206.

Lee, Wen-Shu. (1993). "Social Scientists as Ideological Critics." *Western Journal of Communication* 57: 221–232.

Lyons, Nona P. (1983). "Two Perspectives on Self, Relationships, and Morality." *Harvard Educational Review* 53: 125–145.

Lyotard, Jean-François. (1984). *The Postmodern Condition: A Report on Knowledge*. Translated by Geoff Bennington and Brian Massumi. Minneapolis: University of Minnesota Press.

Lyotard, Jean-François. (1988). *The Differend: Phrases in Dispute*. Translated by Georges van den Abbeele. Minneapolis: University of Minnesota Press.

Matlon, Ronald J., and Sylvia P. Ortiz. (1992). *Index to Journals in Communication Studies through 1990*. Annandale, VA: Speech Communication Association.

McAdams, Dan P. (1988). "Personal Needs and Personal Relationships." In Steve Duck, ed., *Handbook of Personal Relationships: Theory, Research and Interventions*. New York: Wiley, 7–22.

McGee, Michael Calvin. (1984). "Another Philippic: Notes on the Ideological Turn in Criticism." *Central States Speech Journal* 35: 43–50.

McGee, Michael Calvin. (1990). "Text, Context, and the Fragmentation of Contemporary Culture." *Western Journal of Speech Communication* 54: 274–289 [reprinted in this volume].

McKerrow, Raymie E. (1989). "Critical Rhetoric: Theory and *Praxis*." *Communication Monographs* 56: 91–111 [reprinted in this volume].

Medhurst, Martin J. (1989). "Public Address and Significant Scholarship: Four Challenges to the Rhetorical Renaissance." In Michael C. Leff and Fred J. Kauffeld, eds., *Texts in Context: Critical Dialogues on Significant Episodes in American Political Rhetoric* (Davis, CA: Hermagoras Press), 29–42.

Megill, Allan. (1983). "Heidegger, Wander, and Ideology." *Central States Speech Journal* 34: 114–119.

Menges, Robert J., and William H. Exum. (1983). "Barriers to the Progress of Women and Minority Faculty." *Journal of Higher Education* 54: 123–144.

Messer-Davidow, Ellen, David R. Shumway, and David J. Sylvan, eds. (1993). *Knowledges: Historical and Critical Studies in Disciplinarity*. Charlottesville: University Press of Virginia.

Muto, Jan. (1986). "If I'm Reading This, I Must Not Be by the Pool." *Women's Studies in Communication* 11: 20–21.

Myers, Greg. (1993). "The Social Construction of Two Biologists' Articles." In Ellen Messer-Davidow, David R. Shumway, and David J. Sylvan, eds., *Knowledges: Historical and Critical Studies in Disciplinarity* (Charlottesville: University Press of Virginia), 327–367.

Nelson, John S., Allan Megill, and Donald N. McCloskey, eds. (1987). *The Rhetoric of the Human Sciences: Language and Argument in Scholarship and Public Affairs*. Madison: University of Wisconsin Press, 1987.

Nothstine, William L., Carole Blair, and Gary A. Copeland. (1994). "Professionalization and the Eclipse of Critical Invention." In William L. Nothstine, Carole Blair, and Gary A. Copeland, eds., *Critical Questions: Invention, Creativity, and the Criticism of Discourse and Media*. (New York: St. Martin's Press), 15–70.

Ono, Kent A., and John M. Sloop. (1992). "Commitment to *Telos*—A Sustained Critical Rhetoric." *Communication Monographs* 59: 48–60.

"'Our Stories': Communication Professionals' Narratives of Sexual Harassment." (1992). *Journal of Applied Communication Research* 20: 363–390.

Owen, Susan A., and Peter C. Ehrenhaus. (1993). "Critical Rhetoric." *Western Journal of Communication* 57: 169–177.

Peters, Douglas P., and Stephen J. Ceci. (1982). "Peer Review Practices of Psychological Journals: The Fate of Published Articles, Submitted Again." *Behavioral and Brain Sciences* 5: 187–255.

Press, Andrea. (1989). "The Ongoing Feminist Revolution." *Critical Studies in Mass Communication* 6: 196–202.

Rakow, Lana F. (1989). "Feminist Studies: The Next Stage." *Critical Studies in Mass Communication* 6: 209–215.

Redding, W. Charles. (1992). "Response to Professor Berger's Essay: Its Meaning for Organizational Communication." *Communication Monographs* 59: 87–93.

Reinharz, Shulamit. (1992). *Feminist Methods in Social Research*. New York: Oxford University Press.

Rigsby, Enrique D. (1993). "African American Rhetoric and the 'Profession.'" *Western Journal of Communication* 57: 191–199.

Rodden, John. (1993). "Field of Dreams." *Western Journal of Communication* 57: 111–138.

Rosenfield, Lawrence W. (1983). "Ideological Miasma." *Central States Speech Journal* 34: 119–121.

Rushing, Janice Hocker. (1992). "Introduction to 'Feminist Criticism.'" *Southern Communication Journal* 57: 83–85.

Sandler, Bernice R. (1986). *The Campus Climate Revisited: Chilly for Women Faculty, Administrators, and Graduate Students.* Washington, DC: Project on the Status and Education of Women, Association of American Colleges.

Schwichtenberg, Cathy. (1989). "The 'Mother Lode' of Feminist Research: Congruent Paradigms in the Analysis of Beauty Culture." In Brenda Dervin, Lawrence Grossberg, Barbara J. O'Keefe, and Ellen Wartella, eds., *Rethinking Communication, Vol. 2: Paradigm Exemplars* (Newbury Park, CA: Sage), 291–306.

Self, Lois S. (1986). "What Distinguishes/Ought to Distinguish Feminist Scholarship in Communication Studies?: Progress Toward Engendering a Feminist Academic Practice." *Women's Studies in Communication* 11: 1–3.

Simons, Herbert W., ed. (1989). *Rhetoric in the Human Sciences.* Newbury Park, CA: Sage.

Spitzack, Carole, and Kathryn Carter. (1986). "Feminist Communication: Rethinking the Politics of Exclusion." *Women's Studies in Communication* 11: 32–36.

Spitzack, Carole, and Kathryn Carter. (1987). "Women in Communication Studies: A Typology for Revision." *Quarterly Journal of Speech* 73: 401–423.

Steeves, Leslie. (1986). "What Distinguishes Feminist Scholarship in Communication Studies?" *Women's Studies in Communication* 11: 12–17.

Strine, Mary S. (1992). "Understanding 'How Things Work': Sexual Harassment and Academic Culture." *Journal of Applied Communication Research* 20: 391–400.

Task Force on Women in Higher Education. (1988). *Women in Academe: Progress and Prospects.* New York: Russell Sage Foundation.

Tavris, Carol. (1992). *The Mismeasure of Woman.* New York: Simon & Schuster.

Taylor, Bryan C. (1992). "The Politics of the Nuclear Text: Reading Robert Oppenheimer's Letters and Recollections." *Quarterly Journal of Speech* 78: 429–449.

Taylor, Bryan, and Charles Conrad. (1992). "Narratives of Sexual Harassment: Organizational Dimensions." *Journal of Applied Communication Research* 20: 401–418.

Toulmin, Stephen. (1972). *Human Understanding: The Collective Use and Evolution of Concepts.* Princeton, NJ: Princeton University Press.

Volosinov, V. N. (1973). *Marxism and the Philosophy of Language.* Translated by Ladislav Mateejka and I. R. Titunik. Cambridge, MA: Harvard University Press.

Wander, Philip. (1983). "The Ideological Turn in Modern Criticism." *Central States Speech Journal* 34: 1–18.

Wander, Philip. (1984). "The Third Persona: An Ideological Turn in Rhetorical Theory." *Central States Speech Journal* 35: 197–216 [reprinted in this volume].

Wander, Philip. (1990). "The Politics of Despair." *Communication* 11: 277–290.

Wander, Philip. (1993). "Introduction: Special Issue on Ideology." *Western Journal of Communication* 57: 105–110.

Wander, Philip, and Steven Jenkins. (1972). "Rhetoric, Society, and the Critical Response." *Quarterly Journal of Speech* 58: 441–450.

Ward, Kathryn B., and Linda Grant. (1991). "Coauthorship, Gender, and Publication among Sociologists." In Mary Margaret Fonow and Judith A. Cook, eds., *Beyond Methodology: Feminist Scholarship as Lived Research* (Bloomington: Indiana University Press), 248–264.

Watson, Kittie W., Larry L. Barker, Vernon O. Ray, and Robert N. Hall. (1988). "A Study of Quantity of Articles Produced in the Communication Discipline by Institution, 1980 through 1985, I." *Association for Communication Administration Bulletin* 63: 85–90.

West, James T. (1993). "Ethnography and Ideology: The Politics of Cultural Representation." *Western Journal of Communication* 57: 209–220.

Wilshire, Bruce. (1990). *The Moral Collapse of the University: Professionalism, Purity, and Alienation.* Albany: State University of New York Press.

Wood, Julia T. (1986). "Feminist Scholarship in Communication: Consensus, Diversity, and Conversation among Researchers." *Women's Studies in Communication* 11: 22–27.

Wood, Julia T., and Robert J. Cox. (1993). "Rethinking Critical Voice: Materiality and Situated Knowledges." *Western Journal of Communication* 57: 278–287.

Wood, Julia T., and Gerald M. Phillips. (1984). "Report on the 1984 Conference on Gender and Communication Research." *Communication Quarterly* 32: 175–177.

Postcolonial Interventions in the Rhetorical Canon

An "Other" View

Raka Shome

There are times in life when the question of knowing if one can think differently than one thinks, and perceive differently than one sees, is absolutely necessary if one is to go on looking and reflecting at all.
—MICHEL FOUCAULT, The Use of Pleasure

In recent times, the discipline of rhetorical studies—a discipline that for years has celebrated the public voices of white men in power, and has derived most of its theories from such foci—is being challenged in various ways. Perhaps two of the most significant challenges that rhetorical studies has had to deal with in recent years are those posed by critical rhetoricians (McGee, 1990; McKerrow, 1989, 1991; Ono and Sloop, 1992; Pollock and Cox, 1991) and feminist rhetorical scholars (Biesecker, 1992, 1994; Condit, 1988, 1993; Campbell, 1973, 1988, 1989; Dobris, 1989; Foss, 1989; Foss and Foss, 1988, 1989; Spitzack and Carter, 1987, 1988). Arguing that the aim of contemporary rhetorical studies should be to "escape from the trivializing influence of universalist approaches" (McKerrow, 1989, p. 91) and that the canons of rhetorical studies "[are] overwhelmingly biased towards men, especially towards white men of the Western tradition" (Condit, 1993, p. 214), these incursions into the field have begun to question and problematize some of the criteria, assumptions, and methods (such as a transcendental subject, universal audience, critical objectivity, the "right" standards of eloquence) on which rhe-

torical scholarship has rested. In so doing, critical and feminist scholarship [has] begun to push the discipline's traditional paradigms of criticism and theory in significant ways.

In this essay, my aim is to continue this task of pushing the paradigms of rhetorical scholarship even further by underscoring the necessity of a postcolonial perspective for rhetorical studies. I believe that while postmodern and feminist perspectives are challenging the paradigms of rhetoric in useful and much needed ways, there is still more to be done if rhetorical studies is to truly open itself up to alternative and marginalized voices and dialogues. That "still more" that I have in mind are issues of racism and neocolonialism about which both traditional and nontraditional scholarship in the discipline [has] expressed little concern.[1]

In the paper, I thus argue for the importance of a postcolonial perspective for rhetorical studies. Postcolonialism, which is a critical perspective that primarily seeks to expose the eurocentrism and imperialism of western discourses (both academic and public),[2] has significantly influenced a wide range of fields across the humanities such as sociology, anthropology, education, literature, cultural studies, and even some areas in communication such as mass communication and development communication. However, the field of rhetorical studies has not adequately recognized the critical importance of a postcolonial perspective. By working from a postcolonial perspective, I argue that as we engage in rhetorical understandings of texts, or produce rhetorical theories, it is important to place the texts that we critique or the theories that we produce against a larger backdrop of neocolonialism and racism, and interrogate to what extent these discourses and our own perspectives on them reflect the contemporary global politics of (neo)imperialism. I believe that in today's world, when people are constantly discriminated against by virtue of their skin color, or by virtue of their belonging to "other worlds," to avoid the issues of racism and neocolonialism in our critical politics is to "avoid questions concerning ways in which we see the world; it is to remain imprisoned . . . by conditioned ways of seeing . . . without the self-consciousness that must be the point of departure for all critical understanding" (Dirlik, 1990, p. 395).

In order to highlight the importance of a postcolonial critical perspective for rhetorical studies, I provide in the first section of this essay a theoretical overview of postcolonialism and discuss how it calls for a self-reflexive perspective on academic work. In the second section, I delineate the implications of postcolonial theory and criticism for rhetorical studies and discuss how they point to a need for a reorientation of our field to the present historical and social exigencies of racism and neocolonialism.

Postcolonialism: An Overview

The interpretation of our reality through patterns not our own serves only to make us ever more unknown, ever less free, ever more solitary.
　　　—GABRIEL GARCÍA MÁRQUEZ,
　　　　"The Solitude of Latin America"

My aim here is not to provide an exhaustive survey of postcolonialism (for which I do not have space) but rather to introduce those themes/issues of postcolonialism that I perceive as having important implications for rhetorical studies. Specifically, I discuss three broad perspectives of postcolonialism, and the theoretical and critical issues they raise for the critical scholar: discursive

imperialism, hybrid and diasporic cultural identities, and postcolonial academic self-reflexivity.

Discursive Imperialism

Articulated mainly within the intersectional critical space of cultural studies, postcolonialism primarily challenges the colonizing and imperialistic tendencies manifest in discursive practices of "first world" countries in their constructions and representations of the subjects of "third world" countries and/or racially oppressed peoples of the world. Although most postcolonial critics writing today are from nations that were or are (in the case of Ireland or Hong Kong) historically under european imperial powers such as England and France, their critical focus is not restricted to the discursive practices of these nations during the time they were empires, and several other terms normally capitalized, lowercase.] Rather, many postcolonial critics now also focus on the neocolonialism of nations such as the United States and the United Kingdom, in their representations of subjects of developing countries and racially oppressed groups (whether in popular media or in academia), as an "other"—racially inferior and hence open to subjection by (white) western discursive practices. As Edward Said (1976) suggests, a postcolonial critic investigates those "system[s] of discourse by which the 'world' is divided, administered, plundered, by which humanity is thrust into pigeonholes, by which 'we' are 'human' and 'they' are not" (p. 41).

Among others, two questions that are central to the postcolonial project are: how do western discursive practices, in their representations of the world and of themselves, legitimize the contemporary global power structures? To what extent do cultural texts of nations such as the United States and England reinforce the neoimperial political practices of these nations? These are very important questions to investigate, for they illustrate how, in the present times, discourses have become one of the primary means of imperialism. Whereas in the past, imperialism was about controlling the "native" by colonizing her/him territorially, now imperialism is more about subjugating the "native" by colonizing her or him discursively.

There are a number of reasons, some of course very obvious, why the focus on western discursive imperialism—especially that of the United States and England—has been a relatively major preoccupation of postcolonial criticism. Here I will mention two. The first has to do with the historical relation of colonialism between the

East and the west. While discursive imperialism is and was surely in operation in countries such as Japan and the former U.S.S.R, countries that have wielded considerable influence in world politics, these countries do not have the same history of centuries of global colonialism and expansion behind them as England and France, for example. The historically colonized lands of the East such as India, Africa, parts of Southeast Asia, and Latin America, do not have the same relation of subjection and subordination with them as they do with western empires.

The second reason, which today is even more important, has to do with the tremendous global media presence of western nations, and it is here that the United States's role as a neoimperial power gets established. U.S. communication products (both print and tele/visual, popular and academic) penetrate most parts of the world. As Said (1993) notes, "Rarely before in human history has there been so massive an intervention of force and ideas from one culture to another as there is today from America to the rest of the world" (p. 319). The issue is not merely one of technological or cultural power, but also one of linguistic power. The universality of English makes communication products produced in the United States and England accessible to most parts of the world. In the case of the United States, such accessibility is even more significant because it is backed by financial and technological resources which are able to transport its culture to almost every part of the world. It is this tremendous global American presence that invites examination of U.S. discourses as neocolonial texts; for texts, after all, are sites of power that reflect the politics of their surroundings.

The construction of the people of non-western cultures as an insignificant "other"—an object of "study" and "interest" in "first world" discourses—is defined by Said (1978) as "Orientalism." Although in using the term *Orientalism*, Said had in mind specifically the construction of Eastern subjects by western discourses, this phenomenon that stereotypes and dehumanizes subjects of "underdeveloped" countries is also applicable to those countries and racial groups that are not regarded as "Oriental," but yet subject to the same processes of misrepresentation and colonization in eurocentric western discourses. Countries of Latin America and Africa, and racial groups in the U.S. such as Hispanics and African-Americans, to name a few, can surely fall in this category.

For Said (1978), "Orientalism" is a function of "intellectual power" (p. 41) that frames and stud-

ies the racial "other" in classrooms, in illustrated manuals, in the media, in scholarship, for scrutiny, judgement, discipline, and governing. To do so is to have "knowledge" of such subjects—who in the process become objects—and such "knowledge" then provides the intellectual power "to dominate it, to have authority over it," and in the process "deny autonomy to 'it'" (p. 32). Thus the study of the Orient and marginalized groups becomes "a learned field" (p. 63)—and because it is a learned "field," the subjects who are "learned about" are confined to a narrow and discursive space created by the west.

Such discursive confinement is not merely a scholarly confinement, but is ultimately a reflection of the ideological and political practices of "developed" nations; for it is only when two-thirds of the world can be so confined into such a manageable discursive field, which erases and neutralizes their differences and individualities, that it becomes possible for "first world" subjects to devise and adopt a generalized attitude toward natives of "third world" countries or "third world" origins. Abdul JanMohamed (1985) refers to this strategy of generalization as the "commodifi[cation]" of the native, "so that he is now perceived as a generic being that can be exchanged for any other native (they all look alike, act alike, and so on)" (p. 64). Said (1978) further observes that such generalizing strategies also depend on a "flexible *positional* superiority, which puts the westerner in a whole series of possible relationships with the Orient without ever losing him the relative upper hand" (p. 7).

Such a strategy of generalization that effaces cultural differences between peoples of various non-white cultures has, for instance, been a significant feature of much of western feminist discourse on the "third world." In such discourse, cultural differences between women of various "third world" cultures are often effaced in order to construct a monolithic image of a "third world" woman as passive, powerless, backwards, uneducated, victimized, and more (Mohanty, 1991)—categories that are easily interchangeable for the "other" must always be a generic "other" if the task of discursive colonization is to be made manageable.

Cultural Hybridity and Diasporic Identity

Although critique of western discursive imperialism is one of the central aims of postcolonial criticism, the postcolonial project is more than that. Postcolonialism is about borderlands and hybridity. It is about cultural indeterminacy and spaces in between. Resisting attempts at any totalizing forms of cultural understanding (whether imperialistic or nationalistic), the postcolonial perspective argues for a recognition of the "hybrid location of cultural value[s]" (Bhabha, 1992, p. 439). Just as postcolonial critics challenge the hegemonic operations of western discourses, many of them also rightly recognize that the answer to western hegemony does not reside in closing off boundaries and resorting to high nationalism (as has often been the case in some third world nations such as Iran). As Arif Dirlik (1990) points out, taking refuge in a pre-western past and indigenous traditions as a source for articulating identities is a "native chauvinism" (p. 401) that reproduces a kind of "internal orientalism" (Breckenridge and Van der Veer, 1993, p. 11) and rearticulates the binary of "us" versus "them" on which much of modernist understandings of identities rest. Instead of holding on to some notion of an indigenous cultural or national identity as a means to reject and resist western hegemony, the point is to recognize that today, with increasing globalization of the world, it is not possible to conceive of cultures and nations monolithically (Appadurai, 1990; Dirlik, 1990; Giddens, 1990; Hall, 1994; Said, 1993). As Said (1993) points out, everyone is at cultural intersections today. We cannot think of culture as an enclosed system of practices.

> [N]ew alignments made across borders, types, nations, and essences are rapidly coming into view, and it is those new alignments that now provoke and challenge the fundamentally static notion of *identity* that has been the core of cultural thought during the era of imperialism. (Said, 1993, pp. xxiv–xxv)

These perceptions of the postcolonial critic typically emerge from the experiential ambivalence that marks the position of the critic. Living between two (or more) cultures or between two nations, and yet not being of either one, the postcolonial "subject" is forced into a nomadic, diasporic position that is marked by what Gloria Anzaldua (1987) calls a "mestiza" consciousness—a consciousness of the borderlands. This mestiza consciousness shuttles between two or more cultures but is unable to situate itself in either one.

> But every place she went
> they pushed her to the other side
> and that other side pushed her to the other side
> of the other side of the other side. . . .

> Pushed to the edge of the world
> there she made her home on the edge. . . .
> Always pushed toward the other side
> In all lands alien, nowhere citizen. (Anzaldua, 1994, p. 3)

The postcolonial individual is thus cultureless (as we normally perceive culture), and yet cultured because she or he exists in a culture of borderlands (Anzaldua, 1987). It is this that bestows on the postcolonial subject's position an unique ambivalence. I emphasize this ambivalence not to delineate it as a weakness. Rather, this ambivalence is what makes the postcolonial perspective so significant in deconstructing grand cultural master narratives. Being a part of two or more cultures, and yet not belonging to either one, the postcolonial subject is equipped to see that national and cultural identities cannot be essentialized, that they are protean, that they cross borders, and that they are transnational.

Postcolonialism and Academic Self-Reflexivity

The importance of a postcolonial position to any scholarly practice is that it urges us to analyze our academic discourses and connect them to the larger political practices of our nations. This means that in examining our academic discourses, the postcolonial question to ask is: To what extent do our scholarly practices—whether they be the kind of issues we explore in our research, the themes around which we organize our teaching syllabi, or the way that we structure our conferences and decide who speaks (and does not speak), about what, in the name of intellectual practices—legitimize the hegemony of western power structures?

In posing this question, the postcolonial perspective does not suggest that, as scholars writing in the west, all that we do is legitimize the imperial political practices of western nations. Rather, the argument is that we need to examine our academic discourses against a larger backdrop of western hegemony, neocolonial, and racial politics. We need to engage in "contrapuntal lines of a global analysis" where we see "texts and worldly institutions . . . working together" (Said, 1993, p. 318). In the pursuit of our scholarly goals, we often do not stop to think or ask questions about why research agenda A seems more important to us than research agenda B? What is the ideology that operates in us that makes research agenda A seem more significant than research agenda B? How are we always already "interpellated" into examining A but not B? What does that interpellation say about our role in reproducing and participating in the hegemonic global domination of the Rest by the west? What does it mean, for instance, when I am told that there is a market for research agenda A but none for research agenda B? Or that if I did pursue research agenda B, I would have to do it in a way that would make it marketable? And what way would that be? Whose way would that be? Who decides what is marketable? What does that decision have to do with the political practices of our nations? How does this market serve the capitalistic and racist hegemony of western nations? And what is my position, as an intellectual, in reproducing this hegemony?

The point in asking such questions is to recognize the latent ideological structures that inform our scholarship and practices. As Van Dijk (1993) puts it, often "under the surface of sometimes sophisticated scholarly analysis and description of other races, peoples, or groups . . . we find a powerful ideological layer of self-interest, in-group favoritism, and ethnocentrism" (p. 160).

In fact, even when we do sometimes try to break out of the eurocentric canons informing contemporary academic scholarship by including alternate cultural and racial perspectives in our syllabi, we often do not realize that instead of really breaking free of the canon, all that we do is stretch it. Add things to it. But the canon remains the same and unchallenged. Our subject positions in relation to the canon remain the same and unchallenged.[3] Instead of examining how the canon itself is rooted in a larger discourse of colonialism and western hegemony, we frequently use the canon to appropriate "other" voices.[4]

The question then arises, "So what is to be done?" Perhaps the first step here is to do what Gayatri Spivak (1990) suggests: to unlearn our privilege (p. 9). And the first step towards that unlearning requires self-reflexivity, it requires seeing ourselves not sequestered in an academic institution, but connecting things that we think or not think, say or not say, teach or not teach, to the larger political and ideological practices of our nations in their interactions with the rest of the world.

A second aspect of postcolonial self-reflexivity is the problem of essentialism that a postcolonial critic is often faced with when she or he challenges the discursive constructions of nonwhite cultures

and racially oppressed peoples of the world in hegemonic western discourses. The problem of essentialism that this critical task brings about is that of having to challenge the misrepresentations of racial "others" in western discourses, while at the same time avoiding the suggestion that there *is* an authentic racial identity that the critic knows is being misrepresented. So for instance, when a postcolonial critic argues that a particular western feminist discourse on a third world culture, say India, is a misrepresentation of the lives of the women of that culture, the critic implicitly falls prey to a problem of essentializing because one has to know what it means to be an "Indian woman" to argue that a subaltern Indian woman is being misrepresented. This, then, raises the ensuing question about essentialism: "Is there anything such as an 'Indian woman'?" And if, to engage in her or his critical practice, the critic has to assert that there is, then does that not lead to a kind of colonization all over again, where the critic becomes the voice of authority that determines what constitutes or does not constitute a particular cultural or racial identity? The question then is: How can the critic engage in such postcolonial criticism without being once again the totalizing voice of authority that determines an "authentic" racial or cultural identity?

A way out of this critical dilemma is provided by Gayatri Spivak's (1988, 1990) notion of strategic essentialism. Spivak suggests that while it is true that to engage in a postcolonial criticism that challenges the misrepresentations of racial "others" in hegemonic discourses, one does to a certain extent end up essentializing, nonetheless that essentializing is only a necessary "strategic" essentializing—a risk that the critic *must* take "in a scrupulously visible political interest" (1988, p. 205): "In deconstructive critical practice, you have to be aware that you are going to essentialize anyway. So then strategically you can look at essentialisms, not as descriptions of the way things are, but as something one must adopt to *produce a critique of anything*" (1990, p. 51; italics added). Strategic essentialism, then, is only a political tool that the postcolonial critic often has to adopt to resist any kind of hegemony. The important point about strategic essentialism is that the critic always remains *aware* that she or he is essentializing only in order to realize certain political goals.

In suggesting that the essentialism that a postcolonial critic engages in has to be a *strategic* political essentialism, Spivak thus warns us against the temptation of really essentializing and carving a fixed and "authentic" identity for a particular racial group that we, as critics, claim is being misrepresented. Such a temptation is problematic because it has the potential to reproduce the colonizing power relations that postcolonialism is out to challenge in the first place. If, in strategically essentializing, the critic lapses into really essentializing and believing in the cultural essence that she/he creates (say of an Indian woman), then the critic ends up being the hegemonic voice that has already predetermined an indigenous cultural/racial identity.

The self-reflexivity that the term *strategic essentialism* then asks us to engage in has to do with constantly examining our subject positions as postcolonial critics when we challenge the misrepresentations of racial "others" in western texts. In Foucauldian terms, this means that instead of engaging only in a juridical/hierarchical examination of power in western discourses, the postcolonial critic also needs to conduct an "ascending analysis of power" (Foucault, 1980, p. 99) by seeing how she or he might be inscribed in the power relations that she or he is attempting to resist. That is, instead of merely uncovering hegemony in western discourses, the critic also needs to examine the power relations that structure her or his own discourses. This is especially important, because having been primarily schooled in western academic mode (even those of us who write from the "margins" or who write from metropolis institutions of non-western countries), the postcolonial critic's intellectual perspectives cannot wholly be free of the power relations that she or he is out to displace.

For me, as a person from the third world writing in western academia, such a postcolonial self-reflexive examination entails asking questions such as: What does it mean when I, as a postcolonial/"third world" critic, am able to be heard in the west? How much of a compromise do I make to be recognized and established as a postcolonial critic? What does the particular "postcolonial position" that I articulate in the western academy have to do with the institutional operations of power in western educational institutions? And if that power contributes to the capitalist hegemony of western nations, then what is my participation in that power that I am out to critique in the first place? These are important questions to ask because it is by asking such questions and engaging in such constant autocritiques that post-

colonial critics will be able to recognize and resist the possible operation of the very same colonial power in their critical endeavor that they are out to challenge in the first place.

Rethinking Our Paradigms: Implications of Postcolonial Theory and Criticism for Rhetorical Studies

As superpowers realign and markets diversify, many of the conventional boundaries of earlier eras have been dismantled. Yet our critical languages and our methodologies continue to refer to these older constructs.
—CAREN KAPLAN, "The Politics of Location as Transnational Feminist Critical Practice"

So far, I have presented a theoretical overview of postcolonialism and discussed the kind of theoretical issues that it raises for the critic and critical practice. Now I want to draw out some of the implications of postcolonial theory and criticism for rhetorical studies. First, one of the most significant implications of postcolonial theory and criticism for rhetorical studies is the notion of a postcolonial self-reflexivity. As I have already suggested, a postcolonial self-reflexivity entails that as scholars practicing in the west, we be aware of how our scholarly practices are often engaged in reproducing neocolonial patterns of intellectual domination (Breckenridge and Van der Veer, 1993). This has important implications for rhetoric. Rhetoric as a discipline that is largely based on humanist theories and speeches of white men in power has not been adequately self-reflexive about its scholarship in relation to issues of race and neocolonialism. In fact, as Dwight Conquergood (1991) recently and quite directly suggested, the limitation of rhetorical and communication scholarship is that it has ironically been "unreflexive about the rhetorical construction of its own disciplinary authority" (p. 193). Although calls for other kinds of self-reflexivity (feminist, postmodern, ideological) have been made, albeit all too briefly, the discipline on the whole has been disturbingly silent about its own disciplinary position in relation to issues of race and neocolonialism. The silence that I am talking of is not about the lack of studies on nonwhite people. (In fact there have been some rhetorical studies, although few, on nonwhite issues and cultures. Condit and Lucaites' [1993] valuable work on "equality" which, among other things, examines African American public rhetoric is a recent example.) The silence that I have in mind has to do with not rereading (and problematizing) our dominant rhetorical paradigms, our theories, our critical tools, and our research agendas, against a larger backdrop of racial and neocolonial politics. It has to do with not interrogating the extent to which our white universalistic rhetorical paradigms (whether of Aristotle, Plato or of Burke, Perelman, Toulmin, Bitzer) that we keep drawing on, as well as passing down to students without problematizing their eurocentric limits, inhibits alternative racial and cultural perspectives on rhetoric from emerging, and continues a pattern of eurocentric intellectual domination.[5]

Even the recent postmodern incursions in the field seem to be somewhat problematic in this regard. Scholars (McGee, 1990, 1975; McKerrow, 1989) operating from such a perspective have problematized the modernist subject on which the rhetorical tradition is largely based; however, they have not extended this problematizing to also identify this modernist subject (as well as the modernist canon) as being the subject of colonialism. For as Homi Bhabha (1990) reminds us, the advent of modernism in the west was also the moment of colonialism.[6]

The solution, however, is not merely to do more rhetorical studies on nonwhite people (e.g., Campbell's [1986] study on African American women speakers), for that only becomes a matter of extending, instead of displacing or challenging, the canon by adding "others." Rather, the solution is to critically examine and challenge the very value system on which the rhetorical canon and our scholarship [are] based. For instance, Rhetoric as a discipline has been traditionally built on public address. But historically public address has been a realm where imperial voices were primarily heard and imperial policies were articulated. The colonized did not always have access to a public realm, or if they did, their speeches were not always recorded in mainstream documents, since the means of production rested with the imperial subject. All this perhaps means that we have built a lot of our understanding of rhetoric, and the canon of rhetoric, by focusing on (and often celebrating) imperial voices. This calls for a reexamination of our paradigms. The move here is parallel to that made by feminists in their challenges of the masculinist biases of the discipline.

If rhetorical scholars are to reexamine the discipline in relation to issues such as imperialism, neocolonialism, and race, then they need to perhaps do what Spivak suggests, "unlearn" a lot of the rhetorical tradition and evaluate critically what kinds of knowledge have been (and continue to be) "privileged, legitimated, [and] displaced" in our texts and theories (Conquergood, 1991, p. 193). And "what configuration of socio-political [and racial] interests" this privileging, displacing, and legitimizing has served (and continues to serve) (p. 193). For one thing, this means engaging in some serious "soul searching" to uncover why scholarship in our discipline has been and continues to be so white (Rakow, 1989, p. 212).[7] It is through such postcolonial self-reflexivity of our discipline, as well as our individual scholarship, that we will be able to continue the task of pushing the traditional paradigms of rhetoric further in order to create spaces for racially and culturally marginalized voices and perspectives on rhetoric to emerge—voices and perspectives that would be comprised of sensitive postcolonial responses to the neocolonial and racist circumstances of our present time.

Second, the postcolonial critique of western discursive imperialism that constructs racial "others" and that legitimizes the contemporary global power structures has important implications for rhetorical criticism, in that it beckons us to recognize postcolonialism as a timely and important critical and political perspective. As Williams and Chrisman (1994) emphasize with great urgency in their introduction to Colonial Discourse and Post-Colonial Theory, it is alarming "how many of the attitudes, the strategies, and even how much of the room for manoeuvre of the colonial period [still] remain in place" (p. 3) in contemporary social, cultural, and I would add, academic practices. Given this, it is unfortunate that in our literature we hardly find articles, especially in our mainstream journals, that examine neocolonial representations of racial "others" or that analyze, for instance, the discursive processes through which the (white) "west" gets constantly legitimized in political, cultural, and social discourses.

For instance, it is significant that while other kinds of analyses were done on George Bush's Gulf War rhetoric,[8] there were hardly any analyses of how the U.S. rhetoric on the Gulf War constructed the Middle Eastern people (and different Muslim cultures) as uncivilized and immoral, and always already inclined towards barbaric terrorist activities. (The recent depictions of Muslims and Middle Eastern people in the media during the World Trade Center bombing [are] also an example of this kind of rhetoric.) Nor has there been any rhetorical study, that I am aware of, that examines how the U.S. political and media discourse always constructs the countries with whom U.S. foreign relations reach an impasse, as devilish "others" bent on destroying the world order envisioned by U.S. imperialism. (The media coverage of North Korea as "The headless *beast*" [my emphasis], a caption that *Newsweek* ran on its cover after the death of Kim Il Sung, North Korea's former Head of State, is a recent example.)[9] My point here is not necessarily to condone the activities of any of these groups or countries but rather to suggest that when the rhetoric of cultural "othering" is manifest in almost every aspect of public discourse, it is unfortunate that rhetorical scholars have not done much to expose and decry the neocolonial strategies through which such discourse operates. At a time when every form of bigotry (racial, cultural, and sexual) prevails, our discipline, by not adequately focusing on issues of neocolonialism and racism, seems to be imprisoning itself in an ivory tower from which it seems more and more unable to hear the many oppressed who are struggling to be heard.

The implications of all this for our discipline are simple. We simply *need* to engage in postcolonial analyses of texts. We *need* to develop critical perspectives that now seek to examine and expose to what extent neocolonial forces, whether they be representations of "others" or representations of Self, underwrite cultural, political, and academic discursive practices, for as I have already suggested, if texts are sites of power that are reproduced by their social conditions, then neocolonial and racial forces are, to some extent, always already written into our texts. It is when we embrace postcolonialism as a significant critical perspective that rhetorical studies will be able to adequately engage in the present historical and social conditions.

A promising collusion between rhetoric and postcolonialism is also possible given that neocolonialism operates more discursively, in contrast to colonialism, which was more territorial and that neocolonialism operates subtly. On the point of subtlety, Spivak (1991) states that "neocolonialism is like radiation—you feel it less like you don't feel it" (p. 221). Both of these aspects of neocolonialism, its discursivity and its subtlety, suggest that rhetorics constitute neocolonial discourses in their attempts to obscure power and their interpellating capacity.[10] Given this, it seems to me that rhetorical scholars could make significant contributions to the present historical moment if they took upon themselves the task of revealing and examining the various subtle rhetorical strategies through which neocolonialism establishes its hegemony. As I already mentioned earlier, one such strategy is the strategy of generalization whereby "others" are generically constructed, which makes the task of affirmation of the (white) western self that much easier. We need similar and more detailed insights into the various other rhetorical tropes through which discursive imperialism operates. While scholars (Spurr, 1993; Suleri, 1992) in other fields such as literature have done some work in this area, I believe that this is a critical terrain that rhetorical scholars, given their orientation, are best suited to engage in as well as contribute to.

Third, the postcolonial argument about diasporic cultural identities has important implications for the way identity has traditionally been conceptualized in rhetorical studies. Our mainstream rhetorical theories have generally presumed the "reality of the speaker and listener as transcendental subjects engaged in a mutual process of coming together" (Grossberg, 1979, p. 249). Although this position has been problematized by scholars in various ways (Biesecker, 1989; Grossberg, 1979; McKerrow, 1989, 1991), I believe that the postcolonial notion of diaspora and hybridity still has much to offer in this dialogue. As I have already discussed, the postcolonial notion of diasporic identity suggests that with increased globalization of the world, whereby people, technology, ideas, cultures and ethnic groups constantly cross borders (although not often physically) everyone is at cultural intersections. With the softening of national boundaries and the growth of a global economy, we are all in some way cultural hybrids (although some of us more than others) influenced by various transglobal movements of media, of ideas, of peoples, of cultures. In fact, as Tololyan (1991) points out, "diasporas *are* the exemplary communities of the transnational moment" (p. 5; emphasis added). Given this, it is no longer possible to conceive of cultures and cultural identities homogeneously, for each of us in some way occupies borderland territories.

This is slightly different from, or rather an extension of, the position articulated by postmodernism. In postmodernism, what is in question is the individual subject; in postcolonialism what is in question, among other things, is a homogeneous conception of culture. While this position overlaps with postmodernism, much of postmodern theory often itself (albeit implicitly) tends to view cultures homogeneously, since it works from a homogeneous notion of the western world as having reached the last stage of capitalism, which tends to efface cultural differences between countries.

The postcolonial notion of diasporic cultural identity calls for rhetorical theories that are able to address the rhetorical situations and experiences of disjunctured diasporic cultural identities. We now need insights into how rhetoric functions in hybrid borderlands and cultural spaces, as well as how rhetoric aids in the creation of diasporic disjunctured identities. For instance, a pertinent question here would be: How do cultural diasporas use rhetoric to negotiate through their different culturally disjunctured or pastiched states to enable some kind of shared meaning with people in their daily existence? In this connection, the concept of *shared* meaning and understanding, which has traditionally been regarded as one of the goals of rhetoric, also perhaps needs to be reexamined. How much meaning is shared when fractured and pastiched cultural states engage in rhetorical interactions? Furthermore, in dealing with issues of cultural diasporas, we also need to rethink many of our tools and methods of rhetorical criticism, most of which are laden with universalist implications, and examine to what extent, if any, they allow us to deal with and understand identity formation in a postcolonial world.

Fourth, the postcolonial notion of discursive imperialism, and its attendant rhetoric of generalization that tends to appropriate and efface differences between cultural groups, has important implications for feminist scholarship in rhetorical studies. Much of feminist scholarship in rhetorical studies has been carried out from a relatively liberal and generalized perspective. As feminist rhetorical scholars have begun arguing for the need to include and recognize women's rhetorical and communicative perspectives, they have not adequately addressed the important point (although it sometimes gets mentioned in passing, usually at conferences, and then forgotten) that a white woman's rhetorical and communicative perspectives, practices, and experiences are not the same as nonwhite women's, and cannot be universalized therein. Much of feminist rhetorical scholarship, by ignoring issues of race, implicitly tends towards a discursive colonization, whereby the discourses, more often than not, express and speak to the perspectives and voices of white women. Adrienne Rich has called such a phenomenon "white solipsism" which is a tendency "to think . . . and speak as if whiteness described the world" (cited in Spelman, 1988, p. 116).

Especially problematic in this regard is the generalized notion of a "woman's/feminist rhetorical or communication perspective" that often gets articulated by feminists in the discipline.[11] I believe that this notion needs to be problematized. As Stanback (1988) suggests, the rhetorical goals and experiences of women of different races are different. For instance, a white woman might use rhetoric to negotiate with a patriarchal structure, but a nonwhite woman may use rhetoric to negotiate simultaneously with a patriarchal and a racial structure, and perhaps more with the latter than the former. In other words, the experience, functions, and goals of rhetoric differ in the different cultural spaces of women, and hence the generic concept "feminist or woman's rhetorical/communication perspective" tends to erase the element of race (and other kinds of differences that are beyond the category of sexual difference). Such a perspective also falls prey to a concept of rhetoric that McKerrow (1991) terms (and critiques) as "unidimensional" instead of "multidimensional" (p. 76)—a perspective that once again secures, instead of displaces, the traditional rhetorical canon that feminist scholarship is out to challenge in the first place. Thus, feminist rhetorical scholarship, even though it is pushing the paradigms of the discipline in a laudable manner, still needs culturally localized perspectives, critical or theoretical, that address how race and gender work together to influence and often inhibit women's communicative experiences. Much of what I am saying here might seem obvious to some, but despite its obviousness, I believe that the point still begs to be made again. It is perhaps by recognizing and embracing postcolonialism as a significant critical practice that feminist scholarship in our discipline will be able to move into its next stage—where, in devising feminist interventions into the traditional rhetorical paradigm, it is also simultaneously able to examine, how and in what ways, it might be using gender as a signifier that covers up issues of race and neocolonialism (Spivak, 1990).

Having said this, I recognize that as feminist rhetorical scholars are engaged in the task of pushing the (white) male oriented paradigms of the discipline, it may not always be possible to fracture the term *woman* or splinter the politics around it. It may sometimes be necessary to engage in feminist interventions in a somewhat monolithic way. And it is perhaps here that the postcolonial notion of strategic essentialism provides us with a helpful political strategy for intervening in the discipline, whereby in strategically essentializing the term "woman," or mobilizing as a group, we are also simultaneously engaged in a vigilant self-reflexivity where we remain *aware* of the politics and power of race and neocolonialism that might be operating through us. It is hopefully through such postcolonial self-reflexivity that our feminist scholarship will become characterized by what Spivak (1994) defines as "an impossible risk" of a lasting essence (p. 3).

A postcolonial rhetorical intervention, as I have laid it out, has much in common with the theory of critical rhetoric developed by McKerrow (1989). McKerrow's call for "a critique of domination" (p. 92), critical self-reflexivity, a move towards heterogeneity, and a focus on the "absences" (p. 107) in texts also underlies a postcolonial rhetorical perspective. The important difference, however, is that McKerrow's postmodern rhetorical perspective does not extend the notion of critical rhetoric to issues of imperialism and neocolonialism. Although such a perspective might be implicit in McKerrow's postmodern perspective, I believe that the postcolonial move still needs to be explicitly made; for as Appiah (1991) rightly suggests, the "post-" in postmodernism is not necessarily the "post-" in postcolonialism. That is, engaging in a postmodern critical practice does not necessarily mean that one is also engaging in a critique of neocolonialism or imperialism. In fact, a postmodern perspective itself may be eurocentric and hegemonizing (Fredric Jameson's [1986] article "Third-World Literature in the Era of Multinational Capitalism" is a case in point).[12] Mishra and Hodge (1994) provide us with an important distinction here. They state: "If for postmodernism the object of analysis is the subject as defined by humanism, with its essentialism and mistaken historical verities, its unities and its transcendental presence, then for post-colonialism the object is the imperialist subject, . . . [and] the processes of imperialism" (p. 281). There are thus significant intersections between the two, but they are not the same.

Given this, I think that a postcolonial rhetorical perspective needs to be recognized as a challenge that productively adds to that posed by critical rhetoric (as well as feminist rhetoric, since it also has points of intersections with the latter). It is perhaps when all these critical forces come together, as well as draw resources from each other, that Rhetoric as a discipline will undergo its next paradigmatic shift where it is able to sensitively listen to all those diverse groups of people who, because of the stark historical reality of the late

twentieth century, have been relegated to places "out there." For as Janice Radway (1992) reminds us:

> [T]here are people "out there" who have voices. They speak in languages and practices that we don't ordinarily try to hear. The problem is our ability to hear different speech. The issue is that they're already speaking—with actions, with fury, with anger, and we don't know how to hear them yet. (p. 668)

NOTES

1. I am referring here to the rhetoric of racism/neocolonialism of the dominant culture, as opposed to examinations of the rhetoric of marginalized racial groups. Examining the rhetorical aspects of marginalized and nonwhite cultures, although important, is not the same as examining the rhetoric of racism and neocolonialism. While there surely have been studies (although few) in our discipline that have examined the rhetoric of nonwhite groups or rhetors, there are only very few studies that have examined racist rhetoric/discourse. Some examples of the latter are Celeste Condit and John Lucaites (1991), Cal M. Logue (1976, 1981), James Klumpp and Thomas Hollihan (1979), and Gordon Nakagawa (1990). A recent study that can also be included here (although it does not explicitly address racist rhetoric) is Nakayama and Krizek's (1995) exploration of the discursive space of whiteness.

I should also mention here that when I refer to the dearth of studies in our discipline/literature on the issues of racism and neocolonialism, I do not include the journal *Critical Studies in Mass Communication* (CSMC) as a part of this literature. Although CSMC is sponsored by the Speech Communication Association (SCA) and some rhetorical scholars have published in this journal, it is not oriented towards rhetorical studies in ways that *Quarterly Journal of Speech*, *Communication Monographs*, or some of the regional journals of SCA are. CSMC is primarily oriented towards mass communication theory and criticism, cultural studies and popular culture, and political economy—areas that have historically (and even now to a large extent) not been a focus of rhetorical scholarship.

2. Critique of eurocentric discourse and western imperialism is one of the primary thrusts of postcolonial criticism. However, it is not the only thrust. For instance, various critiques of indigenous nationalisms engaged in by scholars from many postcolonial and "third world" countries, who demonstrate the often hegemonizing and the elitist, colonialist, and eurocentric inflections of these nationalist discourses are also a part of the expanding literature on postcolonial criticism. See, for example, the subaltern project of South Asian scholars, specifically the different volumes of

Guha's (1982) *Subaltern Studies: Writings on South Asian History and Society*; various essays in Sangari and Vaid's (1990) *Recasting Women: Essays in Indian Colonial History*, especially Chatterjee's chapter, "The Nationalist Resolution of the Women's Question"; Radhakrishnan's (1992) "Nationalism, Gender, and the Narrative of Identity"; Natarajan's (1994) "Woman, Nation, and Narration in *Midnight's Children*"; and Spivak's (1994) "Woman in Difference" in her *Outside in the Teaching Machine*.

Some other works in postcolonial literature have examined the hegemonic cultural productions of postcolonial female subjects in many contemporary cultural discourses of some postcolonial countries. See, for example, Rajan's (1993) insightful book, *Real and Imagined Women: Gender, Culture, and Postcolonialism*.

Given the objective of my paper (and my own subject position in the United States), I will, however, limit my discussion of postcolonialism to what I perceive to be its most dominant impulse—the critique of eurocentrism, and (neo)colonialism and imperialism. This understanding should guide the reader's reading of my essay.

3. The argument here is similar to JanMohamed and Lloyd's (1990) caution that we must be wary of a particular kind of liberal "pluralism" in multiculturalism which "along with assimilation, continues to be the Great White Hope of conservatives and liberals alike" (p. 8). The authors note that "Such pluralism tolerates the existence of salsa, it even enjoys Mexican restaurants, but it bans Spanish as a medium of instruction in American schools" (p. 8).

4. See also, in this connection, essays by Giroux (1992), McCarthy (1993), McLaren (1994), and Mohanty (1989–1990).

5. Although I recognize that there are a few scholars such as Asante (1987) who have pointed out the eurocentric limits of some of our rhetorical conceptions, it is still a fact that such works are very few. It is also a fact that such reflexibility has not permeated most sections of our discipline. A dominant silence still prevails about the eurocentric limits of much of our scholarship.

6. Bhabha's (1990) argument here is worth quoting:

I think we need to draw attention to the fact that the advent of Western modernity, located as it generally is in the 18th and 19th centuries, was the moment when certain master narratives of the state, the citizen, cultural value, art, science, the novel, when these major cultural discourses and identities came to define the "Enlightenment" of Western society and the critical rationality of Western personhood. The time at which these things were happening was the same time at which the west was producing another history of itself through its colonial possessions and relations. That ideological tension, visible in the history of the West as a despotic power, at the very moment of the birth of democracy and modernity, has not been adequately written in a contradictory and contrapuntal discourse of tradition. (p. 8)

7. Although Lana Rakow (1989) makes this point specifically in relation to feminist scholarship in Com-

munication, I find it valid to extend it to the discipline of Rhetoric as well.

8. See, for example, Stuckey's (1992) "Remembering the Future: Rhetorical Echoes of World War II and Vietnam in George Bush's Public Speech on the Gulf War."

9. This particular issue of *Newsweek* is dated July 18, 1994.

10. For an excellent analysis of the tropes of imperialism, see Spurr's (1993) *The Rhetoric of Empire: Colonial Discourse in Journalism, Travel Writing, and Imperial Administration*.

11. For instance, Foss and Foss (1989) in their essay "Incorporating the Feminist Perspective in Communication Scholarship: A Research Commentary" discuss in a significantly generalized manner some of the "essential features" (p. 65, n. 1) of "the feminist perspective." Although the authors briefly mention in a footnote that such a perspective may include many approaches, yet their elaboration of "the essential features" of "the feminist perspective," without adequately factoring in issues of difference, especially racial difference, remains problematic. (Race is only cursorily addressed in a later section of the essay when the authors survey the "use of the feminist perspective in communication research" [p. 74]).

See also Dobris (1989), which provides a "rhetorical theory accounting for gender." Once again, race is not adequately addressed in the author's discussion of "a gender perspective on rhetorical theory and criticism" (p. 148) (and the author herself seems to acknowledge this when she indicates in her conclusion the need for research that addresses race, class, and culture).

See also Campbell's (1973) essay "The Rhetoric of Women's Liberation: An Oxymoron" [reprinted in this volume]. In this essay, Campbell's discussion of what she perceives to be some of the "distinctive" rhetorical features of women's liberation such as leaderlessness—"There is no leader, rhetor, or expert" (p. 79)—and participatory dialogue, tends to, I believe, express an egalitarian and privileged view of the feminist movement that elides the other issues of power, privilege, and silencing, which underwrite feminist rhetoric.

While these are only some examples, much of what passes in our discipline under notions such as "feminist rhetoric" or "women's communication" is usually a white perspective where race is not adequately factored in—a factoring that might very well problematize some of the perspectives that are articulated. My aim here is not to devalue the political impulses informing feminist work in our discipline. The efforts that have been made by feminists to intervene in the male oriented structures of our discipline are truly commendable. I am only arguing for a greater attention to issues of race and marginalization (and, by extension, power and privilege) as we begin to develop feminist rhetorical and communication perspectives. Whose (and what) perspective is ultimately being articulated in the notion of a feminist rhetorical and communication perspective is something that we need to address and examine more carefully than we have.

12. This essay by Jameson has generated various debate and critiques. See specifically Ahmad's (1987) critique of Jameson's totalizing perspectives on "third world literature." See also Young's (1990) essay "The Jameson Raid" in his *White Mythologies*.

For another cogent critique of Jameson's postmodern perspectives on the third world, see Colas's (1992) discussion of the role of the third world in Jameson's (1991) *Postmodernism or the Cultural Logic of Late Capitalism*.

REFERENCES

Ahmad, A. (1987). "Jameson's Rhetoric of Otherness and the National Allegory." *Social Text* 17: 3–25.

Anzaldua, G. (1987). *Borderlands/La Frontera: The New Mestiza.* San Francisco: Spinsters/Aunt Lute.

Anzaldua, G. (1994). "Del otro lado." In J. Ramos, ed., *Companeras: Latina Lesbians* (New York: Routledge), pp. 2–3.

Appadurai, A. (1990). "Disjuncture and Difference in the Global Cultural Economy." *Public Culture* 2(2): 1–24.

Appiah, K. A. (1991). "Is the 'Post-' in 'Postmodernism' the 'Post-' in 'Postcolonial'?" *Critical Inquiry* 17(2): 336–357.

Asante, M. K. (1987). *The Afrocentric Idea.* Philadelphia: Temple University Press.

Bhabha, H. (1990). "Interview with Homi Bhabha: The Third Space." In J. Rutherford, ed., *Identity: Community, Culture, Difference* (London: Lawrence & Wishart), pp. 207–221.

Bhabha, H. (1992). "Postcolonial Criticism." In S. Greenblatt and G. Gunn, eds., *Redrawing the Boundaries: The Transformation of English and American Literary Studies* (New York: MLA), pp. 437–465.

Biesecker, B. (1989). "Rethinking the Rhetorical Situation from within the Thematic of *Différance*." *Philosophy and Rhetoric* 22(2): 110–130 [reprinted in this volume].

Biesecker, B. (1992). "Coming to Terms with Recent Attempts to Write Women into the History of Rhetoric." *Philosophy and Rhetoric* 25(2): 140–161.

Biesecker, B. (1994, April). "Shifting Scenes: Rhetoric/Feminism/Postmodernism." Paper presented at the 64th annual meeting of the Southern States Communication Association, Norfolk, VA.

Breckenridge, C., and P. Van der Veer. (1993). "Orientalism and the Postcolonial Predicament." In C. Breckenridge and P. Van der Veer, eds., *Orientalism and the Postcolonial Predicament* (Philadelphia: University of Pennsylvania Press), pp. 1–19.

Campbell, K. (1973). "The Rhetoric of Woman's Liberation: An Oxymoron." *Quarterly Journal of Speech* 59: 74–86 [reprinted in this volume].

Campbell, K. (1986). "Style and Content in the Rhetoric of Early Afro-American Feminists." *Quarterly Journal of Speech* 72(4): 434–445.

Campbell, K. (1988). "What Really Distinguishes and/or Ought to Distinguish Feminist Scholarship in Communication Studies?" *Women's Studies in Communication* 11: 4–5.

Campbell, K. (1989). *Man Cannot Speak for Her.* 2 vols. New York: Praeger.

Colas, S. (1992). "The Third World in Jameson's *Postmodernism or the Cultural Logic of Late Capitalism*." *Social Text* 31–32: 258–270.

Condit, C. (1988). "What Makes Our Scholarship Feminist?: A Radical/Liberal View." *Women's Studies in Communication* 11: 6–8.

Condit, C. (1993). "Rhetorical Criticism and Feminism." In S. P. Bowen and N. Wyatt, eds., *Transforming Visions: Feminist Critiques in Communication Studies* (Cresskill, NJ: Hampton Press), pp. 205–230.

Condit, C., and J. Lucaites. (1991). "The Rhetoric of Equality and the Expatriation of African-Americans, 1776–1826." *Communication Studies* 42(1): 1–21.

Condit, C., and J. Lucaites. (1993). *Crafting Equality: America's Anglo-African Word.* Chicago: University of Chicago Press.

Conquergood, D. (1991). "Rethinking Ethnography: Towards a Critical Cultural Politics." *Communication Monographs* 58(2): 179–194.

Dirlik, A. (1990). "Culturalism as Hegemonic Ideology and Liberating Practice." In A. JanMohamed and D. Lloyd, eds., *The Nature and Context of Minority Discourse* (New York: Oxford University Press), pp. 394–431.

Dobris, C. A. (1989). "In the Year of Big Sister: Toward a Rhetorical Theory Accounting for Gender." In K. Carter and C. Spitzack, eds., *Doing Research on Women's Communication: Perspectives on Theory and Method* (Norwood, NJ: Ablex), pp. 137–160.

Foss, K. (1989). "Feminist Scholarship in Speech Communication: Contributions and Obstacles." *Women's Studies in Communication* 12: 1–10.

Foss, K., and S. Foss. (1988). "What Distinguishes Feminist Scholarship in Communication Studies?" *Women's Studies in Communication* 11: 9–11.

Foss, K., and S. Foss. (1989). "Incorporating the Feminist Perspective in Communication Scholarship: A Research Commentary." In K. Carter and C. Spitzack, eds., *Doing Research on Women's Communication: Perspectives on Theory and Method* (Norwood, NJ: Ablex), pp. 65–91.

Foucault, M. (1980). *Power/Knowledge: Selected Interviews and Other Writings by Michel Foucault.* Edited by C. Gordon. Translated by C. Gordon, L. Marshall, J. Mepham, and K. Soper. New York: Pantheon Books.

Foucault, M. (1990). *The History of Sexuality, Vol. 2: The Uses of Pleasure.* Translated by R. Hurley. New York: Vintage Books.

Giddens, A. (1990). *The Consequences of Modernity.* Cambridge, UK: Polity Press.

Giroux, H. A. (1992). "Postcolonial Ruptures and Democratic Possibilities: Multiculturalism as Anti-Racist Pedagogy." *Cultural Critique* 21: 5–39.

Grossberg, L. (1979). "Marxist Dialectics and Rhetorical Criticism." *Quarterly Journal of Speech* 65(3): 235–249.

Guha, R., ed. (1982–1987). *Subaltern Studies: Writings on South Asian History and Society.* 5 vols. Delhi, India: Oxford University Press.

Hall, S. (1994). "Cultural Identity and Diaspora." In P. Williams and L. Chrisman, eds., *Colonial Discourse and Postcolonial Theory: A Reader* (New York: Columbia University Press), pp. 392–403.

Jameson, F. (1986). "Third-World Literature in the Era of Multinational Capitalism." *Social Text* 15: 65–88.

Jameson, F. (1991). *Postmodernism or the Cultural Logic of Late Capitalism.* Durham, NC: Duke University Press.

JanMohamed, A. (1985). "The Economy of Manichean Allegory: The Function of Racial Difference in Colonialist Literature." *Critical Inquiry* 12: 59–87.

JanMohamed, A., and D. Lloyd. (1990). "Introduction: Toward a Theory of Minority Discourse: What Is to Be Done?" In A. JanMohamed and D. Lloyd, eds., *The Nature and Context of Minority Discourse* (New York: Oxford University Press), pp. 1–16.

Kaplan, C. (1994). "The Politics of Location as Transnational Feminist Practice." In I. Grewal and C. Kaplan, eds., *Scattered Hegemonies: Postmodernity and Transnational Feminist Practices* (Minneapolis: University of Minnesota Press), pp. 137–152.

Klumpp, J. F., and T. A. Hollihan. (1979). "Debunking the Resignation of Earl Butz: Sacrificing an Official Racist." *Quarterly Journal of Speech* 65: 1–11.

Logue, C. (1976). "Rhetorical Ridicule of Reconstruction Blacks." *Quarterly Journal of Speech* 62(4): 400–409.

Logue, C. (1981). "Transcending Coercion: The Communicative Strategies of Black Slaves on Antebellum Plantations." *Quarterly Journal of Speech* 67(1): 31–46.

Marquez, G. G. (1988). "The Solitude of Latin America" [Nobel Lecture, 1982]. In J. Ortega, ed., *Gabriel García Marquez and the Powers of Fiction* (Austin: University of Texas Press), pp. 87–91.

McCarthy, C. (1993). "After the Canon: Knowledge and Ideological Representation in the Multicultural Discourse on Curriculum Reform." In C. McCarthy and W. Crichlow, eds., *Race, Identity, and Representation in Education* (New York: Routledge), pp. 289–305.

McGee, M. (1975). "In Search of 'the People': A Rhetorical Alternative." *Quarterly Journal of Speech* 61(3): 235–249.

McGee, M. (1990). "Text, Context, and the Fragmentation of Contemporary Culture." *Western Journal of Communication* 54: 274–289 [reprinted in this volume].

McKerrow, R. (1989). "Critical Rhetoric: Theory and Praxis." *Communication Monographs* 56: 91–110 [reprinted in this volume].

McKerrow, R. (1991). "Critical Rhetoric in a Postmodern World." *Quarterly Journal of Speech* 77: 75–78.

McLaren, P. (1994). "Multiculturalism and the Postmodern Critique: Toward a Pedagogy of Resistance and Transformation." In H. A. Giroux and P. McLaren, eds., *Between Borders: Pedagogy and Politics of Cultural Studies* (New York: Routledge).

Mishra, V., and B. Hodge. (1994). "What Is Post(-) Colonialism?" In P. Williams and L. Chrisman, eds., *Colonial Discourse and Postcolonial Theory: A Reader* (New York: Columbia University Press), pp. 276–290.

Mohanty, C. (1989–1990). "On Race and Voice: Challenges for Liberal Education in the 1990s." *Cultural Critique* 14: 179–208.

Mohanty, C. (1991). "Under Western Eyes: Feminist Scholarship and Colonial Discourses." In C. Mohanty, A. Russo, and L. Torres, eds., *Third World Women and the Politics of Feminism* (Bloomington: Indiana University Press), pp. 51–80.

Nakagawa, G. (1990). "'What are we doing here with all these Japanese?': Subject-Constitution and Strategies of Discursive Closure Represented in Stories of Japanese American Internment." *Communication Quarterly* 38(4): 388–402.

Nakayama, T. K., and R. L. Krizek. (1995). "White: A Strategic Rhetoric." *Quarterly Journal of Speech* 81(3): 291–309.

Natarajan, N. (1994). "Woman, Nation, and Narration in *Midnight's Children*." In I. Grewal and C. Kaplan, eds., *Scattered Hegemonies: Postmodernity and Transnational Feminist Practices* (Minneapolis: University of Minnesota), pp. 76–89.

Ono, K., and J. Sloop. (1992). "Commitment to *Telos*: A Sustained Critical Rhetoric." *Communication Monographs* 59(1): 48–60.

Pollock, D., and R. Cox. (1991). "Historicizing 'Reason': Critical Theory, Practice, and Postmodernity." *Communication Monographs* 58(2): 170–178.

Radhakrishnan, R. (1992). "Nationalism, Gender, and the Narrative of Identity." In A. Parker, M. Russo, D. Sommer, and P. Yaeger, eds., *Nationalisms and Sexualities* (New York: Routledge), pp. 77–95.

Radway, J. (1992). "In the Discussion Section of M. Wallace's *Towards a Black Feminist Cultural Criticism*." In L. Grossberg, P. Treichler, and C. Nelson, eds., *Cultural Studies* (New York: Routledge), pp. 664–671.

Rajan, R. (1993). *Real and Imagined Women: Gender, Culture, and Postcolonialism.* New York: Routledge.

Rakow, L. (1989). "Feminist Studies: The Next Stage." *Critical Studies in Mass Communication* 6(2): 209–215.

Said, E. (1976). "Interview." *Diacritics* 6: 30–47.

Said, E. (1978). *Orientalism.* New York: Random House.

Said, E. (1993). *Culture and Imperialism.* New York: Alfred Knopf.

Sangari, K., and S. Vaid, eds. (1990). *Recasting Women: Essays in Indian Colonial History.* New Brunswick, NJ: Rutgers University Press.

Spelman, E. (1988). *Inessential Woman: Problems of Exclusion in Feminist Thought*. Boston: Beacon Press.

Spitzack, C., and K. Carter. (1987). "Women in Communication Studies: A Typology for Revision." *Quarterly Journal of Speech* 73: 401–423.

Spitzack, C., and K. Carter. (1988). "Feminist Communication: Rethinking the Politics of Exclusion." *Women's Studies in Communication* 11: 32–36.

Spivak, G. (1988). *In Other Worlds: Essays in Cultural Politics*. New York: Routledge.

Spivak, G. (1990). *The Postcolonial Critic: Interviews Strategies, Dialogues*. Edited by S. Harasym. New York: Routledge.

Spivak, G. (1991). "Neocolonialism and the Secret Agent of Knowledge." *Oxford Literary Review* 13: 220–251.

Spivak, G. (1994). *Outside in the Teaching Machine*. New York: Routledge.

Spurr, D. (1993). *The Rhetoric of Empire: Colonial Discourse in Journalism, Travel Writing, and Imperial Administration*. Durham, NC: Duke University Press.

Stanback, M. H. (1988). "What Makes Scholarship about Black Women and Communication Feminist Communication Scholarship?" *Women's Studies in Communication* 11: 28–31.

Stuckey, M. (1992). "Remembering the Future: Rhetorical Echoes of World War II and Vietnam in George Bush's Public Speech on the Gulf War." *Communication Studies* 43: 246–256.

Suleri, S. (1992). *The Rhetoric of English India*. Chicago: University of Chicago Press.

Tololyan, K. (1991). "The Nation-State and Its Others: In Lieu of a Preface." *Diaspora* 1(1): 3–7.

Van Dijk, T. A. (1993). *Elite Discourse and Racism*. Newbury Park, CA: Sage.

Williams, P., and L. Chrisman. (1994). "Colonial Discourse and Postcolonial Theory: An Introduction." In P. Williams and L. Chrisman, eds., *Colonial Discourse and Postcolonial Theory: A Reader* (New York: Columbia University Press), pp. 1–20.

Young, R. (1990). *White Mythologies: Writing History and the West*. New York: Routledge.

Refiguring Fantasy

Imagination and Its Decline in U.S. Rhetorical Studies

Joshua Gunn

Why could we not start by positing a dream, a poem, a symphony as paradigmatic
of the fullness of being and by seeing in the physical world a deficient mode of being,
instead of looking at things the other way around, instead of seeing in the imaginary—
that is, human—mode of existence, a deficient or secondary mode of being?

—CORNELIUS CASTORIADIS[1]

Despite a commonly recognized and longstanding relationship between rhetoric and imagination, little attention has been given to conceptualizing the imagination from a rhetorical perspective. This is because positing the primacy of the imaginary is troublesome for many scholars. For some, beginning with the imagination seems to deny the Real, a world beyond signification,[2] in favor of human thought and "the ideal."[3] For others, starting with imagination is essentialist, akin to claiming it as *the* defining characteristic of human being (as opposed to moral sentiment, reasoning, symbol using). In this essay, however, I address a problem more pressing than the difficulties of solipsism or essentialism: just as dreams connote an arbitrary, free association of image and symbol, the imagination connotes a lack of control or the absence of individual agency, which has been a fundamental concept in U.S. rhetorical theory.

Anxiety about agency is famously illustrated by the French rationalist René Descartes in *The Meditations Concerning First Philosophy*, in which he lamented that he might not be in control of his perceptions, that "the air, the earth, colors, shapes, sounds, and all other objective things that we see are nothing but illusions and dreams."[4] Descartes's project attempted to control the "befogging"

phantasms of the imagination with the clarity and distinctness of indubitable ideas, determined with the aid of Reason and guaranteed by the covenant of God.[5]

The primary goal of this essay is to outline a disciplinary genealogy of anxiety concerning the rhetorical agent within the psychoanalytic idiom or paradigm of the imaginary. Because the imagination has tended to provoke anxiety among modern thinkers, in this essay I argue that reading the evolution of rhetorical theory through the imaginary helps to highlight a general unwillingness to let go of the Cartesian ego, the autonomous, humanist subject who claims mastery over the material world in *conscious* thought, in favor of a more contingent and fragmented understanding of individual subjectivity, community, and world. Further, this reading indicates that attempts to move toward a more contingent understanding of subjectivity have tended to succumb to a transfigured humanism.[6] Finally, this reading suggests that one of these attempts, symbolic convergence theory, was the first to advance a more contingent understanding of rhetorical agency, suggesting fruitful directions for ideological criticism that unfortunately were derailed by misjudgments concerning the role of the unconscious in rhetorical invention. In addition to providing a corrective to recent disciplinary history, this essay urges a reconsideration of the role of the imagination and the imaginary in invention as a theoretical project that may reconcile or at least manage the tension between criticism that relies on a traditional, self-directed rhetorical agent and that which assumes a "decentered," posthumanist subject.

To these ends this essay is organized into two major sections. In the first I summarize Richard Kearney's understanding of the imagination as moving through three paradigms in the history of thought. In the second section, I illustrate the transformation of the imagination from the individual to the collective in rhetorical theory, particularly in relation to that "office" or "art" of rhetoric known as invention. In light of this imaginative re-narration, I conclude by suggesting that a current impasse regarding the rhetorical agent or subject may be overcome by reconciling materialist and psychoanalytic perspectives with the concept of a "social" or "popular imaginary."

Whose Imagination? Which Imaginary?

Throughout the Western intellectual tradition, the meaning of imagination has shifted to accommodate the interests and values of those who have written about it. In *The Wake of Imagination*, Irish philosopher Richard Kearney identifies three paradigms that helpfully organize thousands of years of intellectual history.

The Mimetic and Creative Imagination

The first "mimetic" paradigm is characteristically Aristotelian.[7] Its principal trope is the mirror because the imagination is understood as a mental faculty that reproduces images in the mind. This Aristotelian concept of the imagination as a mirror (*phantasia*) remained dominant until the twentieth century.[8]

In the "modern" age, roughly from the Renaissance to the death of humanism, the imagination is "productive" or "creative," and its corresponding figure is the lamp. Rather than a faculty of perception, the imagination became the generative origin of human existence, especially in magic and art.[9] After Copernicus, Galileo, and the explosion of Renaissance humanism, the creative imagination found intellectual legitimation in the work of Kant and the German idealists,[10] finally reaching its apogee in the aesthetic theories of the nineteenth-century Romantics, who treated the individual as the master of the universe and the origin of all meaningful things.[11]

The third "postmodern" and "parodic" paradigm of the imagination adopts the figure of a "labyrinth of looking-glasses."[12] The human imagination dissolves into the concept of "the imaginary," which is a complex concept informed by insights from sociology, psychoanalysis, and Althusserian Marxism. Moreover, the concept of the imaginary is part of the critique of humanism in the sense that it is juxtaposed against the notion of a discrete, autonomous, sovereign subject connoted by the imagination.

From Imagination to the Imaginary

The concept of the imagination does not escape the critique of the Enlightenment, particularly the attacks on the concept of reason and cosmopolitan humanism that evolved from the writings of those whom Louis Althusser describes as modernity's "three unexpected children": Nietzsche, Marx, and Freud.[13] While Nietzsche attacked the notion of truth,[14] Marx and Freud de-centered the sovereign, "rational" individual or subject.[15] Together, psychoanalysis and Marxian theory formulate a critique of the idealistic notion that the individual is a coherent whole, free to create a Self on the basis of existential choices. Freud suggests that individuals are motivated by inchoate desires that spring from the unconscious. Marxian and post-Marxian theory suggests that many unconscious forces are ideological, particularly in respect to a society's given mode of production, i.e., late capitalism.

Fundamentally, Freud's so-called "discovery" of the *reality* of the unconscious was the undoing of the creative imagination in the contemporary intellectual tradition. Positing an unconscious admits that the individual is motivated or moved by forces beyond immediate, conscious control. When analyzing the most accessible forms springing from the unconscious, the "rebus" language of dreams, Freud said that one eventually realizes that "there is at least one spot in every dream at which it is unplumbable—a navel, as it were, that [is] its point of contact with the unknown," the horizon of the unconscious.[16]

In his extension of Freud, Jacques Lacan brings rhetoric into psychoanalysis.[17] Lacan insists that the underlying structures of the psyche resemble language; thus, we learn as social creatures in our coming to be adults.[18] In the postmodern era of

Lacan, the humanistic notion of the imagination as the origin of creation and meaning is replaced by "a depersonalized consumer system of pseudo-images," commonly labeled the "imaginary."[19]

In Lacanian psychoanalysis the imaginary is both a stage of development and an order of the psyche that is shared socially. As a stage of development, the imaginary refers to a moment in childhood maturation that Lacan calls the "mirror stage." In this stage the child, who experiences herself as a fragmented, incoherent collection of desires and memories, happens upon an image of herself in a "looking glass" or reflective surface. This image stimulates the idea of an entity entirely independent of others: the *imago*.[20] As the child grows older, the *imago*, in turn, becomes invested with all sorts of expectations from without (e.g., from the Other of mother). This primary identification with the mirror image and the consequent *imago* is a mistake, however pragmatic it is as a necessity, because for Lacan the subject is necessarily divided, split between the familiar *Ego*, which posits independence, and the *Id*, the locus of unconscious desire. Lacan understands the primacy of the Ego as a destructive and delusional narcissism, the product of a frustration borne of the failure to assimilate an object of desire (especially the ideal self or *imago*). Because we are fundamentally divided, the task of psychoanalysis is to "subvert" identity and to remind the subject that she is "split."[21] Such reminders work politically to bring the subject into the proximity of the "Other," encouraging community and collectivity over the narcissism of individualism.

For Lacan, the imaginary is also a social field of deceptions, principally ideas of "wholeness, synthesis, autonomy, duality, and above all, similarity," any conception that connotes completion, perfection, or symmetry.[22] Paradoxically, it is always already structured by the symbolic (or linguistic) order because no image or representation can be expressed absent its symbolization as a signifier. The imaginary appears as a domain of the psyche, the principal object of which is the *imago*. The imaginary also contains a host of other mental images that necessarily *alienate* the divided subject because appearances, qua appearances, promise an impossible unity. Kearney suggests that "the *imaginary* thus serves as a repository of the falsehoods of the 'self' at both a psychological and social level. And this is why Lacan maintains that 'to disrupt the *imaginary* is to undermine the modern apotheosis of 'humanist [or autonomous] man,'" particularly as expressed in the fantasy of a creative, productive imagination.[23] Once the subject has discovered the illusory status of those social forms and individual fantasies that reside in the imaginary, she will experience a profound "lack" that is typical of the "otherness of self": In pursuit of the *imago* or other kinds of perfections, she realizes she is pursing the not-I, the Other. The illusion of the imaginary is that one exists for oneself, when in actuality one is always in need of the Other, the social and, hence, the symbolic for any notion of self, divided or complete. Thus, Lacan demolished the imagination in favor of a larger, structuring logic that robs the human subject of the ability to ask questions about origins. Although individuals develop within an "imaginary" stage, the imaginary is not the province of a given individual, but is shared socially as an order of the developing psyche in which every human participates.

Two responses to the Lacanian imaginary are important to this genealogy. First, Castoriadis's strident critique of Marxism in his magnum opus, *The Imaginary Institution of Society*, attempts to counter the Hegelian, historical determinism of orthodox Marxism with what he terms the progressive "autonomy" of social forms and the "instituting power" of society, the "social imaginary." In ways that are similar to Sartre's rehabilitation of the imagination as the distinctive mode of human being,[24] Castoriadis argues that the social imaginary is what is most distinct about humanity, and on its basis humans can realize their freedom and autonomy. The key feature of Castoriadis's social imaginary is that it is the creative, instituting capacity of individuals to collectively make the world, a notion in direct conflict with Lacan's distrust of notions of origin, creativity, and individual autonomy.

The second response to the Lacanian imaginary is that of Louis Althusser, who elevates the imaginary to a level that is completely autonomous in a manner similar to Castoriadis's "social imaginary." Yet unlike that of Castoriadis, Althusser's imaginary is somewhat deterministic insofar as it acts on or through the individual unconsciously. Admiring Lacan's attempts to rescue Freudianism from a mechanical ego psychology on the one hand and U.S. behaviorism on the other, Althusser established the imaginary as a larger social category by abstracting its locus from the human psyche to the field of discourse and, in the end, to ideology. In Althusser's work the imaginary became synonymous with false consciousness, and ideology took on a new, iconic formulation. Ideology was defined as "the representation of the subject's *imaginary* relationship to his or her *real* conditions of existence" (my emphasis).[25]

Althusser's move is innovative and significant for three reasons. First, he was developing a theory of ideology that Marx had failed to provide. Orthodox readings of Marx, particularly of *The German Ideology*, tend to treat ideology as conspiratorial, a deliberate attempt by those in power to impose their beliefs, attitudes, and values on the subclasses.[26] By casting ideology as the social imaginary, Althusser alters the simplistic, top-down notion of orthodox Marxism by making it—as in Lacan and Castoriadis—autonomous. Thus, those on "top" can be and are articulated by ideology as much as those on the "bottom" of the social hierarchy.[27] Althusser's notion of ideology as the articulation of an imaginary subjectivity of coherence, creativity, and freedom places the reigning class within the hegemonic field—the social totality itself.

In addition, Althusser's Lacanian understanding of ideology as establishing imaginary or delusional relationships to the world implicates a collective *unconscious*. False consciousness is born of the unconscious work of ideology; hence, Althusser suggests that ideology articulates the subject. The imaginary relationships that oppressive ideology forges are precisely those that are so vigorously defended by Castoriadis, central among them that human beings are ontologically "free" in the world to act creatively, institute society, and locate origins. For Althusser such notions of creativity, origin, and freedom are the kinds of delusions that keep the subaltern and the oppressed in their place.[28]

Althusser's concept of ideology is important because it places rhetoric as the suasive movement of images and discourse at the center of analysis. The Althusserian imaginary is a field of discourse that works to articulate or "interpellate" subjects into particular social roles that reinforce the notion of creative autonomy, fostering the illusion that one's social rank in life is natural and "freely" chosen. Modern understandings of the imagination and of the sovereign individual are rhetorical constructions, fantasies that perpetuate an illusion of freedom and thereby maintain the status quo. In this light, rhetorical criticism becomes a movement to demystify discourses that presume freedom and autonomy.

Euphantasiotos: Rhetoric, Imagination, and the Imaginary

In the Western rhetorical tradition, the imagination has been discussed in ways that generally resemble movement through the three paradigms described above. Since the time of Aristotle's *Rhetoric*, classical rhetoric has been seen as an art of oratory that consisted of invention (*heuresis*), arrangement (*taxis*), style (*lexis*), memory (*mneme*), and delivery (*hypocrisis*).[29] Not surprisingly, the mimetic imagination appears prominently in texts concerning the role of memory in oratory. In Cicero, for example, the imagination is said to play a role in "artificial memory" or mnemonics, which concerns the development of mental representations of a speech for handy recall during performance.

In discussions of style and word choice the mimetic imagination plays a different role. In his *Institutes of Oratory*, Quintilian argues that the imagination is a "power" that should be cultivated for eloquence:

> There are certain experiences which the Greeks call *phantasiai*, and the Romans *visiones*, whereby things absent are presented to our imagination with such extreme vividness that they seem actually to be before our very eyes. . . . Some writers describe the possessor of this power of vivid imagination whereby things, words and actions are presented in the most realistic manner, by the Greek word *euphantasiotos* ["people blessed with the imagination"]; and it is a power which all may readily acquire if they will.[31]

The role of the imagination here is predominately one of style or expression, whereby words are selected to create vivid images (*phantasma*) in the minds of audiences.[32] This role for the imagination persists into the modern era, as illustrated in the rhetorical theory of Francis Bacon, who held that "the duty and office of Rhetoric is *to apply Reason to Imagination* for the better moving of the will" (his emphasis).[33] In Bacon's formulation, the Platonic and Aristotelian distinction between the mind's rational faculties, or *nous*, and the imagination as a mimetic faculty, *phantasia*, is preserved. Bacon insists that reasoned arguments are, in themselves, dreadfully boring, and that outside of mere reportage (as in the communication of scientific discovery), arguments are always in need of "lively representations" to move audiences to moral behavior.

Bacon's theory reflects the widely known division between reason and the imagination popularized in rhetorical circles by Peter Ramus, a contentious, sixteenth-century thinker who argued that the discovery of arguments and their arrangement belonged to the discipline of philosophy, and that rhetoric should concern itself only with style and delivery, arts that are cultivated for the lowly task of addressing the stupid and ignorant.[34] Further, this longstanding and ubiquitous division, popularized by the Ramists, partakes in the centuries-old quarrel between the disciplines of philosophy and rhetoric begun in the dialogues of Plato. Throughout the history of rhetorical theory this binary relation develops in a number of ways, usually in regard to the art of invention: as the foregoing attests, traditionally the rhetor's rational capacities are said to be responsible for discovering the materials for arguments, while imagination dresses these arguments in poetic metaphors and emotive figures of speech. With the advent of the concept of the productive and creative imagination in the Renaissance, invention became the province of the imagination, and the distinction began to dissolve.

Imagination and Invention

The shift to a rhetoric of imaginative invention is first marked in the rhetorical theory and philosophical ideas of Giambattista Vico, an Italian thinker who is best known for countering Cartesian thought with a "philosophy of the imagination" and a social theory of history.[35] Vico incorporates the creative imagination into rhetoric via the concept of *sensus communis,* which he expanded to mean a collective consciousness structured by language. John Schaeffer explains:

> [Vico] develops *sensus communis* as an epistemological principle which united imagination, language, and social institutions in a dynamic, holistic relationship analogous to the simultaneity of invention, figurality, and organization that occurs in oral performance. *Sensus communis* becomes for Vico the affective, pre-reflective and somatic quality of language, created when both language and human institutions were formed. It is what makes eloquence possible.[36]

Thus, in Vico rhetorical invention became the process of retrieving arguments (wisdom) *and* their ornamentation (eloquence) from a larger culture reservoir, relegating the faculty of reason, as it were, to the canon of arrangement. The *topoi* or "places of argument" used by the rhetor to invent arguments were, for Vico, intersubjective forms that inhered in the *sensus communis,* a seemingly autonomous field of discourse, structured by language, that appears remarkably similar to the social imaginary of Castoriadis or the ideological imaginary of Althusser.

In the history of rhetorical theory, ideas similar to those of Vico would not reappear until the twentieth century. Notions of a creative imagination and an intersubjective "imaginary" realm began to take shape in the more general movement away from studying rhetors to studying audiences, first initiated in what came to be known as "reader response" criticism in literary circles, and simply "the turn to audience" in U.S. rhetorical studies in the 1950s and 1960s.[37] Among the most widely read rhetoricians who demonstrates the move away from the invention of the individual rhetor was Kenneth Burke, who argued for substituting identification for persuasion as the central concept of rhetoric. A person is persuaded, Burke says, "only insofar as you can talk his language by speech, gesture, tonality, order, image, attitude, idea, *identifying* your ways with his."[38] Burke even claimed that Plato's characterization of rhetoric as mere flattery can be embraced "if we systematically widen its meaning, to see behind it the conditions of identification."[39] To wit: Rhetoric concerns the convergence of social forms or symbols—"image, attitude, idea"—in the minds of individuals involved in a persuasive encounter. Importantly, however, Burke's theory helped to move the rhetorical understanding of audience away from an Aristotelian instrumentalism (how the individual rhetor "adapts" to an audience) toward a more encompassing focus on "symbolic action" within larger discursive fields, in effect shifting "the locus of the rhetorical influence from arguments to symbols as the means of evoking shared meaning."[40] Invention thus becomes a general suasive process, both consciously intended and unconsciously apprehended, which deals in material that is intersubjectively shared or "consubstantial."

The general trajectory of rhetorical theory toward the creative imagination, aptly demonstrated in the work of Burke, eventually led to a reconsideration of the canon of invention. Although theorizing about the convergence of the mimetic and imaginative, the rational and the poetic, had been occurring for some time in literary circles, e.g., in the work of figures like I. A. Richards, rhetoricians did not embrace the move until the turn to invention in the early 1970s. In

1971 the authors of a report commissioned by the Speech Communication Association called for an expansion of the rather limited classical notion of invention, a reconsideration of the "modes of discovery in all areas," and a "vigorous investigation of the relationship between 'rhetorical invention' and 'creativity.'"[41] One scholar to answer this call was Karl Wallace, who issued a widely read essay outlining a "modern" theory of invention and a new system of *topoi* based on Chaïm Perelman and Lucie Olbrechts-Tyteca's *The New Rhetoric*, which he suggested better reflected the current realities of the day and could more easily be taught to students than older theories of argument.[42]

Following Wallace's lead, a number of essays were published on the relationship between invention and creativity, one of which was Michael Leff's "Topical Invention and Metaphoric Interaction."[43] There Leff uses the interaction theory of metaphor to effect a thoughtful demolition of the binary opposition between style and invention in the creative imagination. "In classical rhetoric, of course, images belong to the office of style and function to ornament the language of oratory," and "topics . . . refer to matters of thought and to the office of invention." Yet Leff argues that a close analysis of the functions of metaphor and topical argument reveal that the latter is not "entirely removed from the imaginative inferences that operate in metaphor," the presumed province of style.[44] Because the interaction theory of metaphor holds that the ostensive subject ("tenor") and resignification with a different word-image (the representation or "vehicle") necessarily cues both meanings within a field of intersubjectively shared "social knowledge," the hard and fast distinctions between rational argument and poetic style, between reason and the imagination, cannot be maintained. "Metaphorical communication," says Leff, "depends on social knowledge and the intersubjective connections that exist within a speech community." Topical or reasoned and "warranted" arguments "effect a partial structuring of attitudes in the unstable domain of everyday thinking" as well, and "do not seem entirely removed from the imaginative inferences that operate in metaphor."[45] Leff's stress on an imaginative, intersubjective realm of "social knowledge" seems to push beyond the individual, creative imagination toward a kind of Vichean *sensus communis*, an imaginary realm within which arguments and images exist as autonomous social forms.

The clearest articulation of the imaginary as a rhetorical field of autonomous social forms, however, is found in the work of two scholars, Karen LeFevre in composition studies and Ernest Bormann in rhetorical studies.[46]

In *Invention as a Social Act*, LeFevre argues that invention is best understood as a dialogic or collective process in which "an individual who is at the same time a social being interacts in a distinctive way with society and culture to create something."[47] Invention is not solitary, but

> social in that the self that invents is, according to many modern theorists, not merely socially influenced but even socially constituted. Furthermore, one invents largely by means of language and other symbol systems, which are socially created and shared.[48]

Significantly, LeFevre suggests that invention always occurs as "an internal dialogue with an imagined other," thus necessarily involving social collectivity in a manner that Lacan would argue is intimately related to the divided nature of subjectivity, of "self-as-other." Although LeFevre asserts that invention is structured by language and that language *is* thought, she is hesitant to abandon the notion of the creative individual and the concept of origins. In her view, invention is a "dialectic" (or, in my terms, a dialogic) encounter between the individual subject and the collective other, internalized in the mind of the composing imagination as an audience. To be fair, LeFevre's project is to find new ways to teach composition, and this prevents her from dispensing entirely with the notion of an autonomous, creative individual (students can engage in collaborative drafting, but individual creative composition predominates). Invention as a "social act" thus becomes primarily an interiorized dialogue between the individual subject and the social in order to produce texts.

Among those theorizing rhetoric in the twentieth century, Ernest Bormann was the first scholar to come close to abandoning the category of the originating individual. Later the so-called "ideological turn" and the arrival of a "critical rhetoric" would pose serious challenges to the notion of individual autonomy, yet in the work of Bormann one finds both the imagination as a central concept and the genesis of "postmodern" modes of criticism. Bormann's symbolic convergence theory and its corresponding method of fantasy theme analysis posit the existence of a social imaginary by stressing the relative autonomy of social forms or "rhetorical visions," "fantasy types," and "fantasy themes." In Bormann's theory and in criticisms of it, there is a tension between the originating imagination and an intersubjective imaginary that is a helpful diagnostic for the principal problem of rhetorical theory: the social constitution of subjectivity and the limits of individual agency.

The Fruits and Failures of the Force of Fantasy

According to Bormann, symbolic convergence theory was inspired by the pioneering work of a Freudian scholar, Robert Bales, whose studies of group behavior led him to the notion that groups collectively dream. Just as the individual dreams during the day and night about events that do not presently exist, so groups create fantasies that help them cope with their social realities. Inspired by Bales's research, Bormann developed a rhetorical theory that concerned group or collective fantasies, which he defines as "dramatizations of events not in the here-and-now experience of speaker and listeners." Fantasies are intersubjectively created stories featuring characters, scenes, and plots that are used by members of a group to make sense of a common experience.[49] Fantasies are first articulated as "themes," and come in three basic types: "character themes," which focus on absent or mythical agents; "action themes," which deal with the plot of the drama; and "setting themes," which concern the place of action. When a theme becomes so popular that it forms a genre, it becomes a "fantasy type." When groups assemble types and themes into a larger narrative, they become a "rhetorical vision." In each case, the fantasy is the product of group catharsis, which Bormann described in the introduction of the theory in 1972:

> [Themes] would chain out through the group. The tempo of the conversation would pick up. People would grow excited, interrupt one another, blush, laugh, forget their self-consciousness. The tone of the meeting, often quiet and tense immediately prior to the dramatizing, would become lively, animated, and boisterous, the chaining process, involving both verbal and nonverbal communication, indicating participation in the drama.[50]

On the basis of small group interactions, Bormann was led to the idea that group- or community-centered rhetoric inevitably contains fantasy themes, types, and visions. Further, Bormann argued "that there is a connection between rhetorical visions and community consciousness."[51] This move is striking because it implies that rhetoric occurs within a field of a collective consciousness that is not reducible to any individual. Bormann concludes that "sharing fantasies is closely connected with motivation, and is an important means for people to create their social realities."[52] In other words, by identifying the rhetorical themes, types, and visions of a group, one can divine rhetorical purpose, intended or unintended, "rational or irrational."[53] Just what Bormann means by motivation is unclear, and as I shall detail, this ambiguity is a partial reason for the theory's undoing.

Shortly after Bormann advanced his theory, a number of publications appeared that used the prescribed method toward productive ends.[54] Canonized in textbooks of rhetorical criticism, "fantasy theme analysis" developed into a relatively straightforward method or critical approach that placed the imagination at center,[55] fundamentally because fantasies are defined as narratives or "dramatizations of events" absent from the perceiving subject. Further, in introducing the concept of symbolic convergence, Bormann featured the longstanding distinction between "rhetoric and poetic" and, by implication, reason and the imagination, as what was under investigation.[56] After the method of fantasy theme analysis had been used for ten years, Bormann argued that "research results have not supported a strong dichotomy between discursive logic and the creative imagination."[57] Bormann and his followers subsequently placed symbolic convergence theory within "a general movement in communication studies to recover and stress the importance of imaginative language (and the imagination) in nonverbal and verbal transactions," thus within the critical trajectory begun with renewed interest in invention in the early 1970s.[58]

Bormann emphasizes this claim about the primacy of the imaginary time and time again in elaborations of his theory: "Present evidence leads me now [1982] to the conclusion that the force of fantasy accounts not only for the irrational and nonrational aspects of persuasion but that it provides the ground for the relational elements in communication as well."[59] Ultimately, symbolic convergence is a theory of invention that posits the collective imaginary as the principal and primary locus of suasive movement. Although individual imaginations are responsible for "chaining" fantasies, they are not the *origin* of them; rather, "community consciousness" is the primary locus of fantasy, and no one theme, type, or vision originates in the solitary individual. Bormann's theory appears to rest on a concept of the "imaginary" that is similar to the social imaginary of Castoriadis or the ideological imaginary of Althusser.

Bormann and his followers, however, refused to relinquish the romantic, creative, productive imagination, which led to a number of internal contradictions that commentators and detractors were quick to recognize. An outspoken critic was G. P. Mohrmann, whose barbed criticisms betokened the diminished popularity of the theory. His criticisms reduce to three: (1) symbolic convergence theory reinvents the wheel; (2) the theory lacks rigor, and its method promotes "cookie-cutter" or formulaic criticism; and (3) the theory is based on Freud and, thus, is internally contradictory. The first two are easily dismissed, but the third is, in the end, inescapable.

First, Mohrmann charged Bormann and his followers with providing a new and confusing language for doing rhetorical criticism. "[T]he dramatistic hierarchy extending from fantasy themes to fantasy types of rhetorical visions is far from inviting," he argued.[60] Others seconded Mohrmann's charge by implying that there was nothing achieved in the idiom of fantasy that could not be achieved with Kenneth Burke's dramatistic vocabulary (in particular, the "pentad") or the semiotic analysis of myth advanced by Roland Barthes. This criticism is related to Mohrmann's second charge, that "basic definitions lack precision" and that symbolic convergence theory consequently "lacks sophistication and invites mechanical application." All that fantasy theme analysis seems to achieve, claims Mohrmann, is "the discovery of themes, types, and visions" as a "self-contained exercise, not signaling that life is drama, only that it can be described in dramatic terms."[61]

These two charges are premised, however, on a much deeper problem: Because the method is ultimately based on Freudian psychoanalysis, knowing and being able to describe a fantasy does not mean that one can predict behavior or divine motive.[62] For Freud, individual dreams were misleading distortions of wishes and unconscious desires; hence, the motive or source of group fantasy, likewise, could not be discerned on the basis of surface texts and apparent fantasies. Thus, Mohrmann concluded that the theory marked a disciplinary "instance when the baby has to be thrown out with the bath water because interpretation is so dependent on Freud."[63] For Mohrmann, in the idiom of fantasy, criticism became a descriptive enterprise that went nowhere, akin to an excited and "reckless" cowhand riding a "hobby-horse."[64]

Bormann and his followers' many responses to these and similar charges have met all criticisms but the last. They argued that a specialized vocabulary provided "a set of clear and heuristic terms," and that the proof of their clarity and utility was in the research studies that the theory generated. They embraced the "cookie cutter" charge insofar as symbolic convergence is "a general theory" akin to Marxism: "We would caution that to live in a symbolic reality that grants no room for replicative method is by definition to preclude both general theory-building and theory-testing and, by implication, the application of theory to specific communication problems."[65] What their reply amounts to is an indictment of the virtuoso performance that many take to be the best "method" of rhetorical criticism, which proceeds from the text in question and attempts to apply the method that the text seems to suggest, an approach some describe as the eclectic approach to rhetorical criticism.[66] In this mode, the power of criticism is entirely in the critic. Bormann and his followers argue that, at its worst, the virtuoso or eclectic critic "poses the danger of begging the question by changing [her or his key theoretical] terms in ways that confuse both the scholar producing the work and those reading it."[67] Rather than selecting theoretical terms willy-nilly from thinkers as diverse as Weaver, Burke, Freud, and Derrida, Bormann and his followers argue that their theory offers a self-referential and stable perspective that provides a "common ground."[68] They argue that with fantasy theme analysis, beginning students of rhetorical criticism are not left wondering what to do with a given text because the critical procedure is demystified by the clarity and cohesion of a "general theory" and approach.

Where the theory falters is in responding to the charge that the Freudian roots of the theory preclude its predictive value. Bormann and his followers summarize the charge against them erroneously, missing Mohrmann's crucial insight:

> The Freudian argument is that because Bales . . . who first discovered the sharing of group fantasies in his work at Harvard, was a Freudian the subsequent work also ought to have been Freudian. The practical ramifications of this need, according to critics, is that a Freudian would not generalize the sharing of fantasies beyond the group context.[69]

They then argue that a Freudian perspective would require cumbersome vocabulary and that there is ample evidence to support the existence and perpetuation of fantasies from small groups to larger social groups and environments.

Mohrmann's point, which is repeatedly elided, is not that there is no proof that fantasies *exist*, but rather that fantasies are always deceptive and, thus, cannot reveal *motive*. In Freud's work, fantasies and dreams are always deceptive, concealing actual motives in the language of myth and symbol. For Freud, the task of psychoanalysis is one of suspicion and eventually "transposition." As he says in *The Interpretation of Dreams*,

> The dream-thoughts and the dream-content are presented to us like two versions of the same subject-matter in two different languages. Or, more properly, the dream-content seems like a [translation] of the dream-thoughts into another mode of expression. . . . The dream-thoughts are immediately comprehensible, as soon as we have learnt them. The dream-content, on the other hand, is expressed as it were in a pictographic script, the characters of which have to be transposed individually into the language of the dream-thoughts. If we attempted to read these characters according to their pictorial value instead of according to their symbolic relation, we should clearly be led into error.[70]

Thus, the charge is not so much one of being faithful to one's theoretical forbears as it is the idea that there are no simplistic homologies, no transparent correspondences, between the substratum or motive and the superstratum or fantasy. Mohrmann reiterates that "the manifest content of a dream is intriguing not for what it is but for the way it functions as 'a distorted substitute.'" Analogously, group fantasies mean different things to different individuals; thus, by "knowing only fantasy we cannot predict behavior" or motive.[71] Forging analogues between a fantasy theme, type, or vision and "any 'corresponding phenomenon' appearing in 'society at large'" is for Mohrmann "hardly justified": "There is no necessary connection among fantasies and no reason to expect that the dramatistic content of one will share features with another."[72] In other words, one can identify fantasies that, as Freud says, "are immediately comprehensible," but if one understands the deceptive quality of the imaginary, one would realize that fantasies obscure motives and desires.

Bormann's apparent disdain for the unconscious and his fear of being labeled a closet Freudian made it difficult for him to address the homology problem directly. Instead of addressing the charge that fantasies are at best highly opaque, misleading

significations of motive, Bormann and his followers set about to undermine the argument by rejecting psychoanalytic perspectives wholesale. They correctly suggested that if they were to accept Freud's understanding of fantasy and dreams, then they would have to agree with "the Freudian principle of hidden forces pushing people to act in ways they do not understand."[73] The true source of the dispute thus emerges as Bormann's unwillingness to acknowledge the unconscious. He complained that if he acknowledged the unconscious, "rhetorical criticism . . . would become therapeutic and the critic would have to be able to read the messages and interpret their deeper symbolic meaning." He said that he found this perspective "unsatisfactory" because his commitment was "rhetorical," and, therefore, in the words of Max Weber, concerned "the self-conscious actions of individual persons."[74] Bormann defiantly concluded, "I am not now, nor have I ever been, a Freudian."[75]

In the end Mohrmann's charge about the unsound basis of symbolic convergence theory was correct, but for reasons different than those he suggested. Bormann's reluctance to admit that collective fantasies were motivated by unconscious, structuring logics in the process of group invention and, therefore, not the product of the creative, rational individual led to an uneasy theoretical oscillation between the autonomous, originating subject and a disembodied imaginary that worked to constitute subjects. What started as a push toward the imaginary ended up as a retreat into the humanistic imagination. What Bormann and his supporters needed was a concept that would free symbolic convergence of conscious control and resolve the problem of homology by suggesting that fantasy and symbol were indirect signifiers of larger social structures, not individual motives. That concept, of course, is ideology.

Concluding Remarks: The Ideological Turn

In this essay I have sketched three conceptions of the imagination—the mimetic imagination, the creative or productive imagination, and the imaginary—and identified moments when each conception appears in the rhetorical tradition. I suggested that in the 1970s rhetorical theory was in a moment of stasis, moving toward a disembodied imaginary but mired in humanistic notions of creativity and originality. Fantasy theme analysis is the most vivid example of this tension.

As I have suggested, the key limitation of fantasy theme analysis was that symbolic convergence was defended as an entirely conscious endeavor, although Bormann described a process that invited people to "grow excited, interrupt one another, blush, laugh, [and] *forget their self-consciousness*" (my emphasis).[76] Such observations suggest that fantasy may be in more control of the participants than they supposed. How different fantasy theme analyses might have been were fantasies presumed to be motivated by social structures or desires that were unknown to those who experienced catharsis—a loss of self-consciousness—in a given rhetorical vision. Nevertheless, it is important to underscore that Bormann's ground-breaking project arrived before the so-called "ideological turn" in U.S. rhetorical studies. The iconoclastic renovations effected by the work of Nietzsche, Marx, and Freud had yet to inform in any serious way (other than as distilled through Burke) the conduct of rhetorical criticism. In this light, Bormann's work can be read as the beginning of a theoretical move toward a notion of ideology that ends in rhetorical perspectives variously described as "critical" or "materialist."

After Bormann, the turn toward ideology became most pronounced in the work of Michael McGee, a scholar whose major contributions to a rhetorical theory of ideology consistently invoke Bormann as a starting point. McGee sensed in Bormann's work a thread needing an extension, particularly in terms of the concept of "the people," which was later woven into a call for a materialist rhetoric:

> Bormann believes that such concepts as "The People" may be strictly *linguistic* phenomena introduced into public argument as a means of "legitimizing" a collective fantasy. . . . "The people," therefore, are not objectively real in the sense that they exist as a collective entity in nature; rather, they are a fiction dreamed by an advocate. . . . [which a given audience agrees to enact]. [We may] conceive "people" as an essential rhetorical fiction with both a "social" and "objective" reality. This notion of dual realities is specifically "nonrational" in traditional terms.

McGee expanded the notion of the fantasy type and eventually argued that "the people" is a "mass illusion" because, in "purely objective terms, the only human reality is that of the individual."[77] The illusory aspect of "the people" speaks directly to Althusser's imaginary, as McGee turns to Marx's notion of "false consciousness" and argues that "the concept of people" is a rhetorical construction that participates in a "fantastic world of political myths" that keep the oppressed and subaltern in their place.[78] After this vindication of the propagandistic and ideological work of rhetoric, new research was published that secured a place for ideological criticism. Prominent in it was McGee's continued emphasis on ideology as a kind of collective consciousness that is synonymous with "false consciousness." "Such consciousness," says McGee, "is always false" because it is collective; although it has an empirical existence, collective consciousness is never the reality of one, solitary individual.[79]

Since McGee dared to utter the words "Marx" and "ideology," there has been a shift in rhetorical theory, dubbed by some the "ideological turn" and by others the "project of a materialist rhetoric."[80] Although the projects collected under these labels differ considerably, central to each is the notion that subjectivity is constituted by social structures and forces from without; hence, one desirable end for rhetorical criticism is the "demystification" and/or "cartography" of discourses that animate and constrain individuals as social actors. The aim of the "critical rhetoric" introduced by Raymie McKerrow in the late 1980s, for example, was to "demystify the discourse of power," understood as a simultaneous critique of "domination" and "freedom," the former consisting of an analysis of oppressive ideologies (e.g., patriarchal misogyny) and the latter consisting of a kind of critical reflexivity (premised on the realization that the critic, as a socially constituted subject, is always already party to the forces of domination that she critiques).[81] Analogously, in the "material rhetoric" advanced by Ronald Walter Greene, the aim of criticism is a cartography of those discursive elements that "articulate" subjects within a larger "governing apparatus." In either case, rhetoric is usefully recast as a form of mediation on the one hand, or as a practice on the other, that forges what Althusser described as "imaginary relations" between individuals and their material conditions of existence.[82]

Despite the now well-established "critical," Foucauldian, and Marxian perspectives in U.S. rhetorical studies, little of this work addresses the role of the imaginary and, by extension, the unconscious.[83] Instead of interrogating the autonomy of the imaginary as a repository of social and ideological forms located in the collective unconscious, these newer materialist or critical theories tend to eliminate any concern with interiors (i.e., the subject, the psyche, the individual imaginary, and so on).[84] As Greene notes, more recent materialisms are characterized by a radical exteriority and a tendency to elide the interior in favor of analyses that strive to operate within what Deleuze and Guattari describe as "the plane of immanence."[85] The plane of immanence refers to a distinctly *philosophical* understanding of reality that comprises "a structure of effects, . . . a multiplicity of planes of effects and the ways they intersect, transverse and disrupt each other."[86] Within this critical space, Lawrence Grossberg suggests, the critic should begin

> by describing events within human reality in their singularity and positivity; events are both themselves practices and the results of practices. A practice is a mode by which effects are produced and reality transformed. Its origin, whether biographical (in the intentions of the actor) or social (in the economic relations of its existence) is, to a large extent, irrelevant.[87]

The advantage of this kind of critical approach is that it makes room for possibility and optimism; absent a notion of transcendence, e.g., the notion that individuals need to be freed or liberated, nothing is determined or guaranteed. Further, "if there is nothing essential about any practice, then it is only defined by its effects," which liberates concrete, material practices from the problematic question of origins and a deterministic, progressive understanding of history. The upshot of this perspective on criticism, however, is that rhetoric, understood as suasive communication, as the interplay and contest among representations, or as the mediation of Self and Other, ceases to exist.

Grossberg suggests that newer modes of materialism obviate the critical need for interiors or understandings of mediation, representation, and communicative suasion,[88] but recent work by Dilip Gaonkar and others associated with the Chicago-based Center for Transcultural Studies confirms that both exteriors and interiors can find common ground in the concept of the imaginary. As Gaonkar notes in a recent issue of *Public Culture* devoted to the concept of the social imaginary,

> social imaginaries are ways of understanding the social that become social entities themselves, mediating collective life. Often, social scientists and historians have tried to understand these entities in terms of ideas, theories, philosophies— what might be called "third-person" or "objective" points of view. But some crucial self understandings are not formulated in explicit or theoretical

molds. They are first-person subjectivities that build upon *implicit understandings that underlie and make possible common practices.* They are embedded in the habitus of a population or are carried in modes of address, stories, symbols and the like. They are imaginary in a double sense: they exist by virtue of representation or implicit understandings, even when they acquire immense institutional force; and they are the means by which individuals understand their identities and their place in the world (my emphasis).[89]

A rhetoric of interiors concerns the critical examination of "modes of address, stories, symbols," and I would add, fantasies, that create and perpetuate "implicit understandings" and ideologies in the field of an imaginary. A rhetoric of exteriors could be said to concern the material cartography of practices, institutions, and technologies governing an imaginary and its population. Common to both is the critique of the humanistic subject.

There is no space here to detail what an "imaginary paradigm" of rhetorical theory might look like. I have attempted to lay the groundwork for such a project by arguing that ideological criticism and its extensions are rooted in scholarship that investigated creativity and the imagination. Somewhere along the way the movement toward a disembodied collective imagination or imaginary and the possibilities that this concept harbored were abandoned in favor of structures or principles of organization, e.g., McGee's "ideograph," that inhere in the linguistic order.

There are two possible explanations. First, if the plight of fantasy theme analysis tells us anything about disciplinarity, it is that there is a general stigma to using psychoanalytic theory for rhetorical criticism. For example, in an insightful review of works of criticism that utilize the insights of Lacanian psychoanalysis, Barbara Biesecker persuasively argued that a number of psychoanalytic concepts could be used productively in rhetorical criticism (particularly in terms of the category of the real).[90] Surprisingly few studies, however, have answered Biesecker's call.[91] As Bormann's work highlights, the reason is that a consideration of the language of the unconscious implies a secondary status for rational, deliberate argument, which is and likely will remain a favored object of rhetorical studies. The absence of the imaginary and related psychoanalytic concepts in rhetorical theory has more to do with political baggage and less to do with the intellectual or philosophical difficulties of psychoanalytic theory.

Second, materialist modes of criticism old and new tend to emphasize the analysis of structural and institutional objects, especially classes, populations, and social formations, bracketing issues that require a discussion of subjectivity as such (with the exception of those that concern alienation and class consciousness). As Althusser notes, "*there is nothing in Marx that can ground a theory of the psyche*," and many materialist theories have tended to replicate this lack.[92] Structural Marxism, materialism, and psychoanalysis can overlap, but they exist as different modes of inquiry. After Lacan and Althusser, psychoanalysis presumes ideology, yet its objects of concern (the psyche and the desiring subject) are different than those of the many materialisms (traditionally, the mode of production, and later, disciplinary apparatuses, governmental rationality or "governmentality," and so on); consequently, each approach necessarily operates on different critical levels. Although ideology is, by definition, unconscious, one cannot maintain that the unconscious is structured by ideology.[93] Hence, what is needed is a theoretical reconceptualization that admits and incorporates determining social structures and psychical structures simultaneously, a theoretical perspective that fashions ideology and lesser social forms as having both a mass or political and an individual, psychical existence. This is the central challenge of rhetorical theory. How we elect to negotiate it will determine how our successors retell the story of U.S. rhetorical studies.

This essay is derived from a chapter of [Joshua Gunn's] dissertation, titled Rhetorics of Darkness: Modern Occultism and the Popular Imaginary. *An alternate version was presented at the annual meeting of the Central States Communication Association in 2002. The author would like to thank Karlyn Kohrs Campbell, Edward Schiappa, Robert Lee Scott, and the reviewers for their kind patience and invaluable feedback.*

NOTES

1. Cornelius Castoriadis, *World in Fragments: Writings on Politics, Society, Psychoanalysis, and the Imagination*, ed. and trans. David Ames Curtis (Stanford, CA: Stanford University Press, 1997), 5.

2. Or as Žižek puts it, the Real is what resists "symbolic integration." See Slavoj Žižek, *The Sublime Object of Ideology* (New York: Verso, 1991), 3.

3. See W. T. Jones, *A History of Western Philosophy: Hobbes to Hume*, 2d ed. (Fort Worth, TX: Harcourt Brace Jovanovich, 1980), 154–190, 238–279.

4. René Descartes, *Philosophical Essays*, trans. Laurence J. Lafleur (New York: Macmillan, 1964), 80.

5. On Descartes's hostility to the imagination, see Jean-Paul Sartre, *Imagination: A Psychological Critique*, trans. Forrest Williams (Ann Arbor: University of Michigan Press, 1962), 7–36; and Richard Kearney, *The Wake of Imagination* (New York: Routledge, 1998), 161–63.

6. By humanism I refer to a mode of thought that is principally concerned with, as Foucault put it, "the majestically unfolding manifestation of a thinking, knowing, speaking subject" who is completely self-directed and autonomous. Michel Foucault, *The Archaeology of Knowledge and the Discourse on Language*, trans. A. M. Sheridan Smith (New York: Pantheon Books, 1972), 55. I do not mean to indict *humanist values*, to which I subscribe.

7. In most scholarly origin narratives of the concept of the imagination, Aristotle's writings on *phantasia*, often translated as "imagination" but best translated as "a state of being appeared to," is the starting point. On the problems of translation, see Alan R. White, *The Language of Imagination* (Cambridge, MA: Basil Blackwell, 1990), 7. On its role in the history of classical philosophy, see Martha Craven Nussbaum, "The Role of *Phantasia* in Aristotle's Explanation of Action," in her *Aristotle's De Motu Animalium* (Princeton, NJ: Princeton University Press, 1978), 221–69. Aristotle described the *phantasia* as a cognitive mediator that performed a number of necessary functions, all of which involved the act of thinking (and some action, as the *phantasia* is said to play a role in the creation of desire that leads to movement). In *De Anima* he remarked that the imagination is a mode, a kind of movement, state, or "process by which we say that an image is presented to us," and that "the soul never thinks without a mental image [*phantasma*]." Aristotle, *On the Soul, Parva Naturalia, On Breath*, trans. W. S. Hett (Cambridge, MA: Harvard University Press, 1935), secs. 428, 431.

8. Aristotle's functional understanding of the imagination as the capacity to represent the world mentally continues to thrive with some modification in a number of fields today. The key differences between Aristotle's *phantasia* and contemporary cognitive philosophy and science, for instance, is the notion that an image or mental representation is necessarily a picture. Many thinkers have challenged that view. Gilbert Ryle and Jean-Paul Sartre, for example, claim that the imagination is not limited to iconic or visual representations (Sartre, in fact, insisted that the imagination is a mode of being, not a faculty), while others, such as those associated with the analytic school of philosophy, argued that language, not pictures, was the fundamental mode of mental representation. See Gilbert Ryle, *The Concept of Mind* (London: Hutchinson, 1949); Jean-Paul Sartre, *Imagination: A Psychological Critique;* and Jean-Paul Sartre, *The Psychology of Imagination*, translator unlisted (Secaucus, NJ: The Citadel Press, n.d.).

9. Evidence in rhetorical texts around the beginning of the common era suggest, however, that the creative imagination was part of a Stoic tradition. See Flory, "Stoic Psychology." For discussion of important occult figures vis-à-vis the concept of the imagination, see Frances A. Yates, *Giordano Bruno and the Hermetic Tradition* (Chicago: University of Chicago Press, 1964). J. M. Cocking discusses this movement in the work of Ficino in *Imagination: A Study in the History of Ideas* (New York: Routledge, 1991), 168–94.

10. Immanuel Kant's *Critique of Pure Reason* effected a profound shift in epistemological thought by placing the individual subject at the center of the universe, what he called his "Copernican revolution." In place of the Aristotelian and empiricist tradition of describing the human mind as a passive receptor of external sensation, a role that he assigned to the "intuition," Kant argued that the conditions of subjective experience guarantee the objectivity of the outside world. Human beings actively stamp the world, as it were, with "categories" of experience that make it sensible. Significantly, the part of the mind that does most of the work is the imagination: "Imagination is the faculty for representing an object even without its presence in intuition. Because all of our intuition is sensible, the imagination, on account of the subjective condition under which alone it can give a corresponding intuition to the concepts of understanding, belongs to sensibility; . . . Now insofar as the imagination is spontaneity, I also occasionally call it the productive imagination . . ." Immanuel Kant, *Critique of Pure Reason*, trans. Paul Guyer and Allen W. Wood [New York: Cambridge University Press, 1998], 256). Also see Kearney, *Wake*, 167–81; Brann, *World of the Imagination*, 89–99; and Mary Warnock, *Imagination* (Berkeley: University of California Press, 1976), 13–71.

11. F. W. J. Schelling, *System of Transcendental Idealism (1800)*, trans. Peter Heath (Charlottesville: University Press of Virginia, 1997) offers an overview of the Romantics' conceptual groundwork. See also Samuel Taylor Coleridge, *Biographica Literaria*, ed. James Engell and Jackson Bate, Vol. 1 (Princeton, NJ: Princeton University Press, 1983), esp. 295–306.

12. Richard Kearney, *The Wake of Imagination*, 17.

13. Louis Althusser, *Writings on Psychoanalysis: Freud and Lacan*, ed. Olivier Corpet and Francois Matheron and trans. Jaffrey Mehlman (New York: Columbia University Press, 1993), 15.

14. See, for example, Friedrich Nietzsche, "On Truth and Lie in an Extra-Moral Sense," in *The Portable Nietzsche*, ed. and trans. Walter Kaufmann (New York: Penguin Books, 1982), 42–47. See also Douglas Thomas, *Reading Nietzsche Rhetorically* (New York: Guilford Press, 1999), esp. 15–50.

15. Althusser, *Lenin and Philosophy* (New York: Monthly Review Press, 1971), 31.

16. Sigmund Freud, *The Interpretation of Dreams*, trans. James Strachey (New York: Avon, 1998), n. 2, 143.

17. See Barbara A. Biesecker, "Rhetorical Studies and the 'New' Psychoanalysis: What's the Real Problem?: Or Framing the Problem of the Real," *Quarterly Journal of Speech* 84 (1998): 222–59.

18. The most famous articulation of this thesis is in Jacques Lacan, "The Function and Field of Speech and Language in Psychoanalysis," in *Ecrits: A Selection*, trans. Alan Sheridan (New York: W. W. Norton, 1977), 30–113.

19. Kearney, *Wake*, 252. "Imaginary" is used as a noun in another distinct body of literature, the "social imaginary" in sociological literature, which describes what Emile Durkheim called "collective consciousness," a result of a "*sui generis* synthesis of individual consciousnesses," whose product is "a whole world of feelings, ideas, and images that follow their own laws once born." See Emile Durkheim, *The Elementary Forms of Religious Life*, trans. Karen E. Fields (New York: Free Press, 1995), 426. See also Michel Maffesoli's guest edited issue of *Current Sociology* 41 (Autumn 1993) on "The Social Imaginary."

20. Jacques Lacan, "The Mirror Stage as Formative of the Function of the I as Revealed in Psychoanalytic Experience," in *Ecrits: A Selection*, trans. Alan Sheridan (New York: W. W. Norton, 1977), 1–7; also see "The Split Between the Eye and the Gaze," in *The Four Fundamental Concepts of Psychoanalysis*, ed. Jacques-Alain Miller, trans. Alan Sheridan (New York: W. W. Norton, 1998), 67–78.

21. Kearney, *Wake*, 272–3.

22. Dylan Evans, *An Introductory Dictionary of Lacanian Psychoanalysis*, 82.

23. Kearney, *Wake*, 259.

24. See Sartre, *Imagination: A Psychological Critique*; and Sartre, *The Psychology of Imagination*.

25. Louis Althusser, "Ideological State Apparatuses," in *Lenin and Philosophy*, 162.

26. Karl Marx, *The German Ideology*, translator unlisted (Amherst, NY: Prometheus Books, 1998), 41–44.

27. In this respect, Althusser was extending Gramsci's "post-Marxist" notion of hegemony, which was the ability of the reigning class to impose its ideology on the subclasses without coercion or force. See Antonio Gramsci, *Selections from the Prison Notebooks* (London: Lawrence and Wishart, 1971), 57–58.

28. Kearney notes that the imaginary works to "summon human individuals into existence by subjecting them to the fiction that they are freely creating their own world—whereas, in fact, they are merely responding to the 'false representations' of the established social order. 'There is no ideology,' claims Althusser, 'except by and for subjects.' The very purpose of ideology is to represent each individual as an imaginary *subject of* freedom in order that he [sic] remain *subject to* the prevailing socio-political system. . . . Only by abolishing the

imaginary order can we begin to construct a theory of the 'real object' of history." See Kearney, *Wake*, 262.

29. The exception, of course, is Isocrates, who argued that oratory is also the art of written texts. See Isocrates, *On the Peace; Areopagiticus; Against the Sophists; Antidosis; Panthenaicus* (Loeb Classics Collection), trans. George Norlin (Cambridge, MA: Harvard University Press, 1929). Also see Patricia Bizzell and Bruce Herzberg, "Isocrates," in *The Rhetorical Tradition*, 43–46.

30. Cicero, *On Oratory and Orators*, trans. J. S. Watson (Carbondale: Southern Illinois University Press, 1986), II: LXXXVIII (p. 188).

31. Quintilian, *The Institutio Oratoria of Quintilian*, Vol. 2, trans. H. E. Butler (Cambridge, MA: Harvard University Press, 1977), 432–435; as cited by Flory, "Stoic Psychology," 156.

32. Arguably, this role is first mentioned in the rhetorical tradition by Gorgias, who suggests that "through sight the soul receives an impression even in its inner features [mental existence]." Gorgias is more concerned with the persuasion of sight than with mental imagery, yet one still finds hints of the imagination. See "Encomium of Helen," trans. George Kennedy, in *The Older Sophists*, ed. Rosamond Kent Sprague (Columbia: University of South Carolina Press, 1972), 50–54.

33. Francis Bacon, *The Advancement of Learning*, 5th ed., ed. William Aldis Wright (Oxford, UK: Oxford University Press, 1926), 177.

34. Peter Ramus, *Arguments in Rhetoric Against Quintilian*, trans. Carol Newlands (DeKalb: Northern Illinois University Press, 1986).

35. Giambattista Vico, *The New Science of Giambattista Vico*, 3d ed., trans. Thomas Goddard Bergin and Max Harold Fisch (Ithaca, NY: Cornell University Press, 1994). See also Michael Mooney, *Vico in the Rhetorical Tradition* (Davis, CA: Hermagoras Press, 1994; and Vico, *On the Study Methods of Our Time*, trans. by Elio Gianturco (Ithaca, NY: Cornell University Press, 1990).

36. Schaeffer, *Sensus Communis: Vico, Rhetoric, and the Limits of Relativism* (Durham, NC: Duke University Press, 1990), 151.

37. In her discussion of "modern rhetoric" in the recently published *Encyclopedia of Rhetoric*, ed. Thomas O. Sloane (New York: Oxford University Press, 2001), 498–509, Karlyn Kohrs Campbell notes that a general shift from "the invention of the speaker to the interpretations of the consumer of discourse" is one of the distinctive features of rhetorical theory in the twentieth century.

38. Kenneth Burke, *A Rhetoric of Motives* (Berkeley: University of California Press, 1969), 55.

39. Burke, *A Rhetoric of Motives*, 55.

40. Campbell, "Modern Rhetoric," 504. The transformations of the concept of the "audience" in rhetorical theory are discussed in James Jasinski, *Sourcebook on Rhetoric: Key Concepts in Contemporary Rhetorical Studies* (Thousand Oaks, CA: Sage, 2001), 68–73.

41. Robert Scott, James R. Andrews, Howard H. Martin, J. Richard McNally, William F. Nelson, Michael M. Osborn, Arthur L. Smith, and Harold Zyskind, "Report of the Committee on the Nature of Rhetorical Invention," in *The Prospect of Rhetoric: Report of the National Development Project*, ed. Lloyd F. Bitzer and Edwin Black (Englewood Cliffs, NJ: Prentice-Hall, 1971), 236.

42. Karl R. Wallace, "*Topoi* and the Problem of Invention," *Quarterly Journal of Speech* 58 (December 1972): 387–395.

43. For examples, see Richard L. Larsen, "Some Techniques for Teaching Rhetorical Invention," *Speech Teacher* 21 (November 1972): 303–309; Bruce E. Gronbeck, "Rhetorical Invention in the Regency Crisis Pamphlets," *Quarterly Journal of Speech* 58 (December 1972): 418–430; Charles W. Kneupper and Floyd D. Anderson, "United Wisdom and Eloquence: The Need for Rhetorical Invention," *Quarterly Journal of Speech* 66 (1980): 313–216; James A. Berlin, "The Transformation of Invention in Nineteenth Century American Rhetoric," *Southern Speech Communication Journal* 46 (Spring 1981): 292–304; and Thomas B. Farrell, "Practicing the Arts of Rhetoric: Tradition and Invention," *Philosophy and Rhetoric* 24 (1991): 183–212 [reprinted in this volume].

44. Michael Leff, "Topical Invention and Metaphoric Interaction," *Southern Speech Communication Journal* 48 (Spring 1983): 214–29.

45. Leff, "Topical Invention," 219, 228.

46. For representatives in literary studies, see Clayton Koelb, *Inventions of Reading: Rhetoric and the Literary Imagination* (Ithaca, NY: Cornell University Press, 1988); and Eric Charles White, *Kaironomia: On the Will-to-Invent* (Ithaca, NY: Cornell University Press, 1987). The closest concept in rhetorical studies is "collective memory." See Barbie Zelizer, "Reading the Past Against the Grain: The Shape of Memory Studies," *Critical Studies in Mass Communication* 12 (1995): 214–39; and James P. McDaniel, "Fantasm: The Triumph of Form (An Essay on the Democratic Sublime)," *Quarterly Journal of Speech* 86 (2000): 48–66.

47. Karen Burke LeFevre, *Invention as a Social Act* (Carbondale: Southern Illinois University Press, 1987), 1.

48. LeFevre, *Invention*, 2.

49. Ernest G. Bormann, "A Fantasy Theme Analysis of the Television Coverage of Hostage Release and the Reagan Inaugural," *Quarterly Journal of Speech* 68 (1982): 134.

50. Ernest G. Bormann, "Fantasy and Rhetorical Vision: The Rhetorical Criticism of Social Reality," *Quarterly Journal of Speech* 58 (December 1972): 396–407. See also Ernest G. Bormann, "Symbolic Conver-

gence Theory: A Communication Formulation," *Journal of Communication* 35 (Autumn 1985); Ernest G. Bormann, *The Force of Fantasy: Restoring the American Dream* (Carbondale: Southern Illinois University Press, 1985); and Ernest G. Bormann, John F. Cragan, and Donald C. Shields, "In Defense of Symbolic Convergence Theory: A Look at the Theory and Its Criticisms After Two Decades," *Communication Theory* 4 (November 1994): 259–294.

51. Bormann, "Fantasy and Rhetorical Vision: Ten Years Later," *Quarterly Journal of Speech* 68 (1982): 289.

52. Bormann, "Fantasy and Rhetorical Vision," 289.

53. Bormann et al., "In Defense of Symbolic Convergence Theory," 264.

54. See, for example, James W. Chesebro, "Paradoxical Views of 'Homosexuality' in the Rhetoric of Social Scientists: A Fantasy Theme Analysis," *Quarterly Journal of Speech* 66 (1980): 127–39; and Marsha Vanderford Doyle, "The Rhetoric of Romance: A Fantasy Theme Analysis of Barbara Cartland Novels," *Southern Speech Communication Journal* 51 (Fall 1985): 24–48.

55. Sonja K. Foss, *Rhetorical Criticism: Exploration and Practice* (Prospect Heights, IL: Waveland Press, 1989), 293–94.

56. "Rhetorical critics have long known that rhetoric and poetic have much in common yet, still, are different. Many have viewed persuasive discourse in dramatistic terms. Now Bales provides the critic with an account of how dramatizing communication creates social reality for groups of people," presumably in ways that challenge the traditional distinction. Bormann, "Fantasy and Rhetorical Vision," 396.

57. Bormann, "Fantasy and Rhetorical Vision: Ten Years Later," 289.

58. Bormann et al., "In Defense of Symbolic Convergence Theory," 265.

59. Bormann, "Fantasy and Rhetorical Vision: Ten Years Later," 292.

60. G. P. Mohrmann, "An Essay on Fantasy Theme Criticism," *Quarterly Journal of Speech* 68 (May 1982): 119.

61. Mohrmann, "An Essay on Fantasy Theme Criticism," 119–20.

62. Mohrmann, "An Essay on Fantasy Theme Criticism," 113.

63. Mohrmann, "An Essay on Fantasy Theme Criticism," 116.

64. Mohrmann, "Fantasy Theme Criticism: A Peroration," *Quarterly Journal of Speech* 68 (1982): 306.

65. Bormann et al., "In Defense of Symbolic Convergence Theory," 282.

66. Bernard L. Brock, Robert L. Scott, and James W. Chesebro, *Methods of Rhetorical Criticism: A Twentieth-*Century Perspective, 3d ed. (Detroit, MI: Wayne State University Press, 1990), 90–91.

67. Bormann et al., "In Defense of Symbolic Convergence Theory," 277.

68. Bormann et al., "In Defense of Symbolic Convergence Theory," 276–277.

69. Bormann et al., "In Defense of Symbolic Convergence Theory," 269.

70. Freud, *The Interpretation of Dreams*, 312.

71. Mohrmann, "An Essay on Fantasy Theme Criticism," 113.

72. Mohrmann, "An Essay on Fantasy Theme Criticism," 115.

73. Bormann et al., "In Defense of Symbolic Convergence Theory," 270.

74. Bormann, "Fantasy and Rhetorical Vision," 292–293.

75. Bormann, "Fantasy and Rhetorical Vision," n. 22, 293.

76. Bormann, "Fantasy and Rhetorical Vision," 396.

77. Michael Calvin McGee, "In Search of 'the People': A Rhetorical Alternative," in *Contemporary Rhetorical Theory: A Reader*, ed. John Louis Lucaites, Celeste Michelle Condit, and Sally Caudill (New York: Guilford Press, 1999), 345. Originally published in *Quarterly Journal of Speech* 61 (October 1975): 235–249.

78. McGee, "In Search of 'the People,' " 347.

79. Michael Calvin McGee, "The 'Ideograph': A Link Between Rhetoric and Ideology," in *Contemporary Rhetorical Theory: A Reader*, 427. This essay was first published in 1982 [and is also reprinted in this volume].

80. See Philip Wander, "The Ideological Turn in Modern Criticism," *Central States Speech Journal* 34 (1983): 1–18; and Ronald Walter Greene, "Another Materialist Rhetoric," *Critical Studies in Mass Communication* 15 (1988): 21–41.

81. Raymie E. McKerrow, "Critical Rhetoric: Theory and *Praxis*," *Communication Monographs* 56 (June 1989): 91–111 [reprinted in this volume].

82. The notion of rhetoric-as-mediation is forcefully challenged by Lawrence Grossberg, who urges that we understand discourse as the cartography of the effects of "everyday life practices." See Lawrence Grossberg, *We Gotta Get Out of This Place: Popular Conservatism and Postmodern Culture* (New York: Routledge, 1992), esp. 37–67.

83. There are a few exceptions. Henry Krips's exemplary *Fetish: An Erotics of Culture* (Ithaca, NY: Cornell University Press, 1999) is an application of the Althusserian imaginary to the criticism of scientific treatises, novels, films, and other cultural objects that emphasizes the importance of the language of the unconscious. The mythic criticism of Janice Hocker Rushing and Thomas

S. Frentz makes use of Jung's theories of the psyche and strongly emphasizes the centrality of the unconscious in rhetorical phenomena; see Janice Hocker Rushing and Thomas S. Frentz, "Integrating Ideology and Archetype in Rhetorical Criticism," *Quarterly Journal of Speech* 77 (November 1991): 385–406; and Janice Hocker Rushing and Thomas S. Frentz, *Projecting the Shadow: The Cyborg Hero in American Film* (Chicago: University of Chicago Press, 1995).

84. The discussion of interiority and exteriority is informed by the lectures of Ronald Walter Greene in his "Rhetorical Subjects of/After Modernity" doctoral seminar at the University of Minnesota, Spring 2002. For an overview of Greene's theoretical orientation and commitments, see Ronald Walter Greene, *Malthusian Worlds: U.S. Leadership and the Governing of the Population Crisis* (Boulder, CO: Westview, 1999), esp. 1–16.

85. Gilles Deleuze and Félix Guattari, *What Is Philosophy?* (New York: Columbia University Press, 1994), 35–60.

86. Lawrence Grossberg, *We Gotta*, 48.

87. Grossberg, *We Gotta*, 51.

88. This call is to abandon "the model of communication [that] assumes a relationship between two discrete and independently existing entities: whether between individuals, or between audiences and texts, or between signifieds and signifiers. The result is that any cultural relation takes on the form of an unspecified and unspecifiable exchange—a mediation—between encoding and decoding." Grossberg, *We Gotta*, 38.

89. Gaonkar, "Toward New Imaginaries," 4.

90. Biesecker, "Rhetorical Studies and the 'New' Psychoanalysis," 222–59.

91. A notable exception is James P. McDaniel's critical work on social forms, tropes, and images, in which he stresses the importance of moving away from the autonomous, sovereign subject; see James P. McDaniel, "Fantasm: The Triumph of Form"; "Figures for New Frontiers, From Davy Crockett to Cyberspace Gurus," *Quarterly Journal of Speech* 88 (Feb. 2002): 91–111; and "Patriotic Paranoia and the Fantasmic Body: Unpacking the Tacit Dimension of 1940s Visual Culture," *Mythosphere* 2 (2000): 183–208.

92. Althusser, *Lenin*, 116.

93. Althusser, *Lenin*, 77.

Pure Persuasion

A Case Study of *Nüshu* or "Women's Script" Discourses

Lin-Lee Lee

Aspects of the work of Kenneth Burke often are ambiguous and apparently contradictory. Among the most puzzling and confusing parts of his work is the section in A *Rhetoric of Motives* entitled "Pure Persuasion." Burke refers to pure persuasion as the "ultimate form of persuasion,"[1] commenting that "pure persuasion in the absolute sense exists nowhere,"[2] suggesting that it is an abstraction, an ideal that cannot be realized in actual discourses. Nonetheless, he begins his discussion by saying that to understand this concept, "we should try as much as possible to keep particular examples in mind."[3] In what follows, I shall follow his advice. I begin by teasing out the clues that Burke provides about the characteristics of pure persuasion; then I turn to an unusual body of discourse, *Nüshu*,[4] a phonetic transcription of the Jiangyong dialect created and performed by women in a remote area of China, as a case study that may help to explain what pure persuasion might be in practice.

Pure Persuasion: Helpful Hints

Burke provides a number of clues about what pure persuasion might look like. Four concepts emerge out of his discussion: (1) pure persuasion is not acquisitive or instrumental as such—rather, it is primarily consummatory in purpose; (2) pure persuasion is a near relation of dramatic performance, ritual, and prayer; (3) one purpose or effect of pure persuasion may be the creation and affirmation of identity; and (4) pure persuasion relies on form— formal elements are essential to its enactment. These concepts emerge out of the discussion in A *Rhetoric of Motives*, but they are buttressed by comments in other works.

In the essay "'Pure Persuasion' and Verbal Irony," Peter L. Hagen notes these characteristics and acknowledges how perplexing this concept can be.[5] He explores the sense in which pure persuasion may arise out of the tension created by dialectical opposition or the aporia of incompleteness and suggests that it has an affinity to ambiguity and paradox. As noted below, these may emerge in situations in which the possibilities for any form of social change are minimal, despite oppressive conditions. Finally, in a highly creative move, he links pure persuasion to verbal irony, suggesting that elements of pure persuasion may lurk in ordinary discourse. In spite of Burke's recourse to a number of examples and the interpretative possibilities suggested by Hagen, pure persuasion remains a puzzling concept. I believe that an unusual body of discourse, *Nüshu*, can shed additional light on what pure persuasion might mean.

Burke's notion of pure persuasion is related to four concepts. First, pure persuasion is fundamentally distinctive in being primarily consummatory rather than instrumental in the usual sense, which is linked to its relatively impersonal, altruistic qualities. Burke writes:

> [T]he indication of pure persuasion in any activity is an element of "standoffishness," or perhaps better, *self-interference*, as judged by the tests of acquisition. . . . Pure persuasion involves the saying of something, not for an extra-verbal advantage to be got by the saying, but because of a satisfaction intrinsic to the saying.[6]

Those comments suggest that, as described in *A Grammar of Motives*, pure persuasion would feature the pentadic element of purpose and ideologically would be related to mysticism.[7] Consummatory discourse can be self-centered and egotistical, but that is not the case here, although Burke acknowledges the complications arising from its relationship to the concept of an "ideal" audience:

> Symbolically, the "pure exercise" of art for art's sake can become furtively and suicidally allied with motives ranging anywhere from castration to impotence, masturbation perhaps being the golden mean between them. . . . A particular audience may be but a pretext, itself the symbol of a transcendence within himself [the artist] (or, more accurately, a transcendence deriving from the nature of symbols as such).[8]

Even in pure persuasion, then, there is personal or symbolic transcendence that complicates or adds instrumental nuances to its consummatory character. Burke suggests that what "Malinowski called 'phatic communication' might seem close to 'pure persuasion,'"[9] suggesting that its function is social bonding. Consummatory discourse is not without purpose; rather, it has intrinsic purposes with potentially extrinsic effects, which may include personal or symbolic transcendence, expressing or reaffirming community, or maintaining social bonds.

This view of pure persuasion is echoed in *Language as Symbolic Action* in the essay on poetics. There Burke writes: "As for poetics pure and simple: I would take this motivational dimension to involve the sheer exercise of 'symbolicity' (or 'symbolic action') for its own sake, purely for love of the art."[10] He notes that sheer symbolicity is not really possible; complications inevitably arise:

> Even if you would write a drama, for instance, simply for the satisfaction of writing a drama, you must write your drama about *something*. . . . And even though your drama is still motivated poetically by the love of the exercising for its own sake, it becomes so interwoven with the problems you symbolically resolve, people tend to see these problems as the motivating source of your activity.[11]

These comments imply a close relationship between poetics and pure persuasion, and they heighten an awareness of how complex consummatory purposes can be.

The second concept is intertwined with the third. Consistent with his own advice to emphasize examples, Burke links pure persuasion to the dramatic performance of the actor. He writes, "Perhaps as near an instance of 'pure persuasion' as one could find is in the actor's relation to his audience."[12] The example is intriguing. An actor exists apart from any role, an example of "standoffishness." Performance is an enactment of an action, but ordinarily the response desired is not instrumental but consummatory—a moment of insight, a cathartic release, a sense of vicarious participation, a moment of identification; although these are transitory, they can be transformative. Subsequently, Burke comments that the actor's relation to the audience might become homosexual in its implications as "an appeal to socially 'superior' persons of the same sex. An audience, technically a sexless function, can stand in furtively for a kind of *alter ego* that is the narcissistic, socially idealized version of the beloved self."[13] These remarks hint at a performance that is a courtship of auditors as an idealized version of oneself, suggesting that a function of pure persuasion might be the creation and maintenance of an identity, a bonding with like others, a moment of intense sharing or joint expression. Likewise, the rhetorical appeal of identity creation is reiterated by Richard B. Gregg in the essay "The Ego-Function of the Rhetoric of Protest." One aspect of the protest rhetoric he describes verges on the intrinsic and consummatory, that is, "the act of communication wherein one's self is his [*sic*] primary audience and where others identify with the rhetoric insofar as they share similar ego concerns."[14] A second related aspect is that of "constituting self-hood through expression, that is, with establishing, defining, and affirming one's self-hood as one engages in a rhetorical act."[15] I shall argue that selfhood can also be constituted through expression in what are primarily consummatory acts. These comments conceptualize a rhetoric that embraces act and appeal. As such, rhetoric is part of performance, which simultaneously enhances the self-creation or the self-affirmation of the actor.

Still another example Burke offers, a performance by a Chinese ritual dancer, introduces ritual as another kind of practice, what Burke calls "a symbolic getting, not a real one" related to "'pure purpose' (Kant's purposiveness without purpose),"[16] emphasizing its intrinsic character, its link to performance, and introducing the role of form in its enactment. Ritual is a highly stylized, repeated, and repeatable action in which the form and quality of performance are vital. The relationship between repeatability and purpose is elaborated. Burke writes:

> Since the ultimate form of persuasion is composed of three elements (speaker, speech, and spoken-to), as regards the act of persuasion alone obviously you could not maintain this form except insofar as the plea remained unanswered. When the plea is answered, you have gone from persuasion to something else.[17]

In other words, judged in terms of ordinary persuasion, pure persuasion is always unsuccessful, that is, whatever its purpose, it does not alter the conditions that call it into being. That is, the plea implicit in such discourse may be answered, but the answer fails to change the circumstances that evoked the discourse and will evoke it anew. Put differently, pure persuasion, like ritual, is perpetual. In that regard, it resembles the ritualistic performances that Mircea Eliade described as existing "in *illud tempus*," time out of time, which suggests an affinity to epideictic discourse. Burke underscores this dimension when he writes, "For a persuasion that succeeds, dies. To go on eternally (as a form does) it could not be directed merely towards attainable advantages."[18] Like ritual, then, its effects are symbolic and ephemeral, and must endlessly be performed anew. Moreover, its repeatability and perpetuity are a function of its form, another link to the dramatic and poetic. Later Burke speaks of the "dialectical transcending of reality through symbols" that "culminates in pure persuasion, absolute communication, beseechment for itself alone,"[19] which he links to "prayer, as pure beseechment."[20] He refers to sexual fetishes and similar kinds of symbolic displacements as "remote variants of pure persuasion,"[21] suggesting that pure persuasion may be an indirect, even displaced form of social courtship.

Finally, in a note in *The Rhetoric of Religion*, Burke underscores the formal character of pure persuasion in an aside to his discussion of ordinary persuasion and expressiveness:

By "pure persuasion" is meant the sheerly formal use of such expressiveness, as were one to write a piece of invective not for the specific purpose of shifting people's attitude toward some policy or person, but through sheer "love of the art" (as, for instance, the voluble word-play that delights us in the case of a character like Falstaff). "Pure persuasion" would take delight in the sheer *forms* of courtship for their own sakes. Hence it could *remain* "pure" only insofar as a practically "successful" outcome were precluded. Protestations of love addressed to some ideal "unattainable" mistress such as Dante's Beatrice would represent a personalized variant on such formality.[22]

These comments underscore its idealized character, illustrated by the sheer pleasure of the creative use of form as in the poetic address of Dante to his all but divine and unapproachable beloved. Through its formal character pure persuasion once again is linked to poetics, and the example of Dante's address to Beatrice reinforces its aesthetic, romantic, and idealized character.

Based on these comments and illustrations, pure persuasion relies on form; it has close affinities to drama, ritual, and poetics. It is realized in enactment or performance, a public version of consummatory discourse that, at most, has as its purpose symbolic transcendence or beseechment or, perhaps, an affirmation of identity or of a social bond. Like ritual, it is perpetual and repeatable, like the communion ritual, never exhausted in its enactment. Whatever its function, it is intrinsic to the moment of performance, but the conditions that prompt it persist and recur. As a relative of phatic communication, it expresses and maintains social bonds, and like the performance of the actor, in its appeal to like others, it gives voice and body to an identity that finds an echo in others and with which they can identify.

The discovery of *Nüshu*, 女書 ("women's scripts"),[23] by Chinese scholars, an allegedly thousand-year-old female discourse articulated in a variety of texts sung and chanted by rural women over their needlework on pieces of red fabric, handkerchiefs, and fans, attracted the interest of other scholars in the 1980s and 1990s who attempted to decipher its cultural significance. Most considered *Nüshu* from sociological and anthropological perspectives; some investigated *Nüshu*'s distinctive linguistic characteristics; others analyzed its literary qualities.[24] This essay argues that *Nüshu* may be an exemplar of discourse with many characteristics of Burke's pure persuasion.

In what follows, I first describe the cultural context in which *Nüshu* developed, including the differences between *Nüshu* and *Hanzi*, 漢字 (standard Chinese/Mandarin scripts). I then analyze representative *Nüshu* scripts. Ultimately, I argue that, as a distinctive kind of rhetorical action, *Nüshu* might help us to understand what pure persuasion might mean.

Cultural Context of *Nüshu*

Scholars conclude that *Nüshu* was widely practiced in Shangjiangxu Township, Jiangyong County, in the southern Hunan Province of China, for more than one thousand years. Both William Wei Chiang and Cathy Silber note that the combination of Han and Yao cultures generated distinctive ethnic norms for the people of Shangjiangxu.[25] Zhao Liming writes that the area in which *Nüshu* developed is

> an important strategic spot and military passage fought over by successive armies. As a result, the cultures of Chu, Yue, and the Central Plains have been transplanted, merged, diffused, and settled here. . . . This place became a mingling place of nationalities, especially the Han and the Yao.[26]

In the home area of *Nüshu*, the worship of dogs, a Yao custom, was still practiced; some cultural ways of life were Han in origin: siblings carved beams and painted pillars on their houses; women bound their feet; young girls stayed in secluded quarters; husbands engaged in farming, and wives weaved.[27] Prior to the breakup of the Chinese government in 1949, the dominant religion in Shangjiangxu was Taoism, and Taoist festivals were associated with goddesses who were believed to protect women and children and to bring fertility in many Chinese communities.[28] In *Nüshu* prayers, women addressed female goddesses to whom they turned for comfort and help. Consequently, holidays designed and celebrated exclusively by women for women were settings that encouraged the performance of *Nüshu*.[29]

Despite the celebratory elements of women's festivals, the culture of Shangjiangxu was a Confucian patriarchal system in which men dominated women, whose low status was reflected in their omission from the genealogies of their natal families and their peripheral status in their husbands' lineages.[30] Shinobu Suzuki notes:

Women were one of the groups that suffered most because the Confucian ethic imposed all sorts of constraints on them (e.g., obedience, subservience, and devotion to their parents before marriage, to their husbands and in-laws after marriage, and to sons in widowhood, and a general suppression of the self and strict self-restraint). Generally, education for women was considered useless.[31]

In a similar vein, Mary G. Garrett explains that women of the elite class or the entry class were more likely to receive literary training in light of the early education of their children than their counterparts of the peasant family.[32] Culturally, men were in charge of the farm work, hunting, and fishing, whereas women performed the domestic chores of cooking, washing, doing needlework, and feeding the livestock. Foot-binding physically limited most of the women of Shangjiangxu who could not work in the fields but wove at home or managed the household chores.[33] Accordingly, women could not contribute economically to their marital homes, which left them wholly dependent on their husbands. Foot-binding combined with the domestic confinement embedded in Confucian principles limited their mobility, restricted them to household chores and embroidery, and excluded them from contacts with the outside world.

No one trained in ordinary Chinese can read or understand the original *Nüshu* scripts. *Hanzi*, 漢字 (standard Chinese/Mandarin script), is the official Chinese language that was created by men for use by men. As Garrett writes:

Most of the surviving written materials are records of, by, and for the elite of Chinese society, the 5 to 10 percent of the population that was literate and could afford books. These materials concentrate on issues of concern to this well-off, educated, male elite: statecraft, ethics, ritual, and history, all filtered through the perspective of enacting and maintaining a Confucian society.[34]

In the past, most Chinese women were excluded from formal education in *Hanzi* writing or literature. Only a few women of the gentry gained access to *Hanzi* literacy through reading and writing with their fathers, brothers, husbands, or lovers. In conformity to the Confucian saying that women without talents were virtuous, most women of peasant families remained uneducated and illiterate because education had no relevance to their lives and jeopardized their marriageability.[35] The naming practices of the different social levels in premodern China identify their different status levels, which Garrett describes:

> A peasant farmer had only a surname (*xing*) and a personal name (*ming*), and his wife took his surname, being referred to simply as 'Wife of X.' Women of the educated classes were referred to by their natal surname, as well as their personal names, and they also took or were accorded the same range of courtesy names (*zi*) and sobriquets or literary names (*hao*) as were their male literati counterparts.[36]

As one sign of this contrast, Wen Shu Lee notes that during the dynastic periods a man had multiple names as part of a dynamic process of acquiring more and more rights and identities through birth, marriage, schooling, and career. By comparison, most Chinese women of the uneducated classes remained nameless.[37] As such, *Nüshu* scripts revealed that women often were addressed generically as "flower," or in kin terms—as a wife of X family or a daughter of the Y family rather than by their given names. In the culture in which *Nüshu* developed, a woman's status could be improved only by bearing sons to her husband's family.

Nüshu is similar to *Hanzi* in regard to grammar, sentence structure, and other semantic functions but varies significantly from *Hanzi* in both its written and oral forms.[38] *Nüshu* is a phonetic writing system in a mosquito or diamond-shaped pattern from upper right to lower left, using character symbols to represent individual symbols. Conversely, *Hanzi*, in square graphs, is a logographic script. Zhao distinguishes between the two:

> A Chinese character may be pronounced differently in different times or places, but the meaning is consistent, because the square Chinese characters are basically logographic, with each character simultaneously representing a syllable and a semantic unit, be it a word or a morpheme. Usually the sound of a character is determined by its meaning. However, in Nüshu, there is no direct relationship between the form of a character and its meaning. Even the users of Nüshu cannot tell the meaning of a single character when it is taken out of context. The women read aloud to turn written symbols into spoken language and distinguish the homophones by meaning and context.[39]

Unlike *Hanzi*, *Nüshu* is an oral phonetic transcription passed from generation to generation by women. Chiang suggests that the practice of *Nüshu* "not only retained the Yao oral tradition, but also absorbed the Han oral tradition."[40] Simi-lar to the Yao people's oral folk tradition, *Nüshu* as a symbolic medium is realized in oral performance.

Although it was created and practiced exclusively by women for women, *Nüshu* was not inaccessible to men; that is, due to phonetic similarities between *Hanzi* and *Nüshu*, men who heard it could understand it when performed, but they could not perform it, read it, or speak it themselves.[41] Most men showed little interest in *Nüshu* or in its oral performances.[42] Some ignored it in the belief that *Nüshu* had no significance; all important matters were recorded in *Hanzi*, and men regarded *Nüshu* as a trivial feminine activity, rather like embroidery.[43] Others felt that the intense emotional expression intrinsic to the reading and chanting of *Nüshu* violated masculine norms of behavior.[44] In general, men did not prevent women from writing or participating in *Nüshu*, nor did they regard its practice as a threat to their power or status. Just as *Hanzi* was the writing and literature of the world of men, *Nüshu* was the writing and literature of the world of women. *Hanzi* symbolized men's control over public life and reinforced the socially accepted conditions that oppressed women; *Nüshu*, as an outlet for these rural women, reflected and responded to these constraints.

Nüshu's Resemblance to Pure Persuasion

As a distinctive body of discourse, *Nüshu* evinces many characteristics of Burke's pure persuasion. Pure persuasion has an intrinsic purpose, and dramatic performance, although addressed, is an end in itself. The following discussion attempts to demonstrate to what extent the elements of pure persuasion are evident in *Nüshu*.

Consummatory Purpose

Of all 210 *Nüshu* scripts I examined, none has an ostensibly instrumental purpose. Put differently, no text seeks to alter the material conditions of the speaker or of her sister; all aim at transcendence, to transform the world of the participants symbolically. That *Nüshu* scripts were chanted and performed jointly and repeatedly, particularly on ritual occasions, such as ceremonies in honor of a goddess or on the occasion of marriage, are strong indicators that their primary purposes were consummatory.

Nüshu scripts allowed women to have a voice, to create an individual and collective subjectivity that enabled them to confer value on and give importance to their lives. The Confucian three obediences put women under the control of the men in their lives—first fathers, then husbands, and finally sons. Before marriage, gender determined a woman's fate; being born female presupposed a woman's powerless and useless future. Consequently, women were expected to be silent. Yet *Nüshu* scripts made available a symbolic outlet to voice the feelings of these women. The text of *Marriage Congratulation*, for example, expressed a woman's true feelings about her wedding and its aftermath. On the one hand, it projected future happiness: "Forget your troubles at home. Look forward to happiness after marriage. You will have a good marriage like the star accompanying the moon."[45] On the other hand, it also described her future misery: "You pass your days meaninglessly there [in your husband's home], I am worried for you."[46] Likewise, *Folktales and Folksongs* offered detailed descriptions of the oppressive marriage system that dominated the lives of women. *Folksong before the Marriage* described the life of a daughter at her natal home; *Folksong after the Marriage* portrayed the life of a wife as a domestic servant who performed the household chores under the critical eyes of her mother-in- law and sisters-in-law.[47]

Nüshu scripts transformed the hardships of women into tales that validated their lives and experiences. Some texts described the details of a woman's life: "At ten I am skillful at needlework. . . . At eighteen I bear a golden Buddha [a son]."[48] In an *Admonitory Text*, we learn:

> Your grandmother had a good method in teaching children. She taught me needlework in the morning and reading in the evening. My memory was not good. I would often read and forget. My mother did not mind. She asked only that I recognize the words. . . . The purpose of reading is to understand things.[49]

The biography, "Book on the Hardships of Yi Nianhua's Niece [Yi Xixi]"[50] recorded women's suffering after the deaths of male heads of families but also joyfully reaffirmed the value of a woman's life: "Today is July the first. I wrote a book for the world to see."[51] Similarly, the *Narratives of Local Events* told the stories of individual women. *An Event during the Guangxü Era* began, "I write in sadness about a poor girl."[52] It reiterated the recurrent *Nüshu* theme that the lives of women were important and valuable. It rejoiced in the story of an individual who was distinct from all oth-

ers by detailing her misery-filled life from birth to death. The development of self-affirmation in performance of the *Nüshu* scripts is analogous to the ego-function for the speaker of expressive discourse described by Gregg. The women performing *Nüshu* experience psychological affirmation as they participate collectively.

In addition, some statements in these texts illustrate the intrinsic power of expressing one's feelings. For instance, some writings portrayed marriage as degrading, particularly on the occasion of bearing a daughter and the death of a husband. An unknown *Nüshu* writer stated, "I have no brothers. We five daughters are useless. . . . I am angry for being a useless woman."[53] Tang Baozhen wrote, "Women are useless people who leave their homes."[54] Likewise, in her *Autobiography*, Zhou Shuoqi described her powerless status: "I have neither elder nor younger brother. This makes mother and me sad all year long. . . . It's useless to raise daughters. They grow up and marry out."[55] Correspondingly, *Nüshu* texts protested the low status of women and their lack of control over their lives. For instance, wrote one author: "If I were a son, I could carry on my father's name. It was a mistake to be born a woman who would go to a man's house when grown up."[56] Another said, "I am angry for being a useless woman. We should not abandon our mother's home. If it were up to us, we would not leave home."[57] These texts in which the *Nüshu* women portrayed themselves as useless, and angry for being useless, and feeling resentment, are akin to Burke's framing of pure persuasion as "gloomy groveling," in which a person says things to the self that even an enemy might not say.[58] Furthermore, these images of negative selfhood, which prevailed in many of the *Nüshu* scripts, echo Burke's description of pure persuasion: "Its utterance may become the vehicle for all sorts of private ambitions, guilts, and vengeances."[59] Accordingly, *Nüshu* becomes an outlet through which women from Shangjiangxu were able to voice their feelings about sexual inequality, low social status, and bad treatment.

Dramatic Performance

Pure persuasion is associated with an actor's dramatic performance, which is an enactment of an action; ordinarily the response desired is consummatory—a moment of insight, a cathartic release, a sense of vicarious participation, and a moment of identification, although these experiences may be transformative. *Nüshu* scripts come into being as joint chanting by participants, including such emotional interjections as weeping and laughing. *Nüshu* is enacted through reading, chanting, or singing as a social event. Chanting *Nüshu* is never silent or solitary; it always requires responses from readers and audiences, dissolving the usual divisions between speakers and auditors. The flow of a group performance of *Nüshu* is interrupted by laughter, sobbing, or other emotional outbursts from the performers and participating audience members. Shouhua Liu and Xiaoshen Hu emphasize *Nüshu*'s oral character: "Literary works in *Nüshu* are totally versified, as they are actually scripts intended for singing. It would therefore not be incorrect to regard them as a form of folk oral literature."[60] Likewise, Silber comments: "Text [*Nüshu*] is more than words on a page, more even than words off the page. Literature 'happens' in relationships between text and audience and, just as important, between readers and each other."[61] *Nüshu* is powerful and distinctive precisely because it is a participatory rhetorical practice that challenges the rhetor/audience models of conventional Western and traditional Chinese practice. Revising and expanding the oral tradition from a fixed text to a flexible, vivid, and responsive discourse, *Nüshu* scripts redefine roles for "speakers" and audiences. Accordingly, the relationship among participants is transformed from a fixed text addressed to a passive audience, into a dramatic performance, in which all equally share in creating the symbolic act together.

That *Nüshu* practice is linked to prayers and women's festivals shows its resemblance to pure persuasion. Burke remarks, "And considered dialectically, prayer, as pure beseechment, would be addressed not to an *object*, but to the *hierarchic principle itself*, where the answer is implicit in the address."[62] *Prayer to Goddess Gupo* is a tale of a woman's life after she and her children were abandoned by her husband. She then turned to the Goddess Gupo for help.[63] She described her situation this way:

> He left me alone with one son and two daughters. There is no one to till the land. I have to do everything myself. . . . When will such a life end? I have sacrificed everything for his family. I can think of no way out. I stay awake all night and worry. That's why I am writing this prayer. I ask you to show your powers.[64]

In this script, the prayer is addressed to the hierarchic principle (Goddess Gupo) for comfort and consolation. Furthermore, Burke suggests that one might find the elements of pure persuasion in religious expression and writes, "And likewise a prayer might be pure courtship, homage in general, the ultimate idea of an audience, without thought of advantage, but sheerly through the love of the exercise."[65]

Nüshu is used to create and maintain identity, which is enacted in a dramatic performance, often linked to specific ritual occasions, prayers, and women's festivals. Although some of these activities were found elsewhere in China, what is distinctive is that *Nüshu* scripts were used by otherwise uneducated and illiterate women who sought the sheer joy derived from integrating *Nüshu* scripts into prayers and women's festivals.

Creation and Affirmation of Identity

Of most significance is that *Nüshu* scripts effect the creation of equality in a ritual or sworn sisterhood. *Nüshu* scripts are the means through which sisterhood and social bonds are created and maintained. In Jiangyong area, women's dependence on men, separation from their mothers and sisters when they married, and their inferior status were offset to some extent by formalized, non-kin relationships of sisterhood linking women of similar socioeconomic status. These included *tongnian*, 同年 (same year), and *laotong*, 老同 (old same), relationships among girls/women of the same age, and *jiebai zimei*, 结拜姊妹 (sworn or ritual sisters), relationships among girls/women of different ages. Sworn or ritual sisterhood, usually initiated when girls were very young, was a substitute or replacement for biological sisterhood, and the only nonhierarchical relationship in Confucian social ideology, in contrast to the hierarchical relations of husband/wife, father/son, elder/younger brother, ruler/minister, master/servant, and teacher/student.[66]

Nüshu scripts attest to the importance and strength of these relationships, and it is likely that ritual sisterhood and the creation and performance of *Nüshu* were interdependent. The intrinsic satisfaction of being understood and supported by equals sharply contrasts to their harsh treatment by men and by some other women. As women in similar circumstances, these are the sisters who could understand what others are enduring. In addition, these scripts reflect a willingness to express one's deepest feelings and intimate thoughts and the assumption that these would be accepted and understood. A strong sense of sisterhood permeates *Nüshu*: "When I feel troubled, I go to your house. I depend on my ritual sisters, the young girls. . . . I can vent my grief at your home. That's why we are ritual sisters."[67] Appeals for consolation and understanding reflect ritual sisterhood. A *Nüshu* script said:

> I was troubled when you came. The gods made our match. That's why I wanted to have you as a ritual sister. We three ritual sisters can console one another. . . . We console one another when we are troubled. We are ritual sisters. After three years we will become like natural sisters. I rely on you to cheer me up. We occasionally get together to chat. I tell you my woes and you pity me.[68]

> We speak of the same mind. We depend on each other. . . . Our becoming ritual sisters was destined in our former lives. We speak of one mind. I am happy. . . . I write you on this handkerchief. It is a humble gift. We two are the same. We are born under bad elements. You must visit me often so we can console each other.[69]

The opportunity for communication created through writing and performing *Nüshu* helps to alleviate their despair. Hu said, "I have no way to vent my anger. No parents and no brothers."[70] In *Prayer to a Dead Cousin*, ritual sisterhood continued even after death: "Although you are dead, it is as if you are still alive. It was hard to part from you. Several times I wanted to kill myself."[71] A ritual relationship based on equality and sameness transforms these women into a supportive sisterhood in which their inner feelings are voiced, exchanged, and heard through the performance of *Nüshu*.

Amazingly, *Nüshu* creates identities for women participants who become authors of autobiographies, biographies, folktales, and histories in defiance of their erasure in marriage, such as the *Autobiography* of Zhou Shuoqi. *Autobiographies* relate the ordinary life events of women. They are particularly vital evidences of identity creation or self-affirmation; they are valuable examples of women creating identities under conditions that denied their value or individuality. Similarly, Silber argues that *Nüshu* participants rewrote folktales, and some *Nüshu* tales were derived from classical tales, which were rewritten for female audiences. For instance, the famous *Nüshu* script of *The Carp Spirit* was derived from a vernacular *Hanzi* story called *Goldfish*. The *Nüshu* version treated Miss Jin as the central character, emphasizing her story throughout, whereas the original version concerned Mr. Liu Zhen, who was the central character, and whose story was told.[72] In *Narratives*

of Historical Events, these writers and performers became historians; for example one text began, "I will not sing of other dynasties but of the Qing Dynasty at war."[73] In these experiences women become central, as in the script of *The Heavenly Kingdom of Great Peace*:

> As we traveled by night, the women found it hard to walk in the dark. . . . Some couldn't keep up, like the young women. . . . Women with bound feet could hardly walk. They were like flowers in a gale. Do you pity us? We regret our lives deeply.[74]

These *Nüshu* rhetors are good story tellers who describe historical events in vivid, clear language. They present arguments, provide specific examples, and even level accusations about how slowly they receive aid from the soldiers. Recording the impact of the events on women reinforces the idea that women suffer most in the midst of any tragedy; as one wrote, "The women are most pitiable."[75] The authors of *Folktales*, *Autobiographies*, *Biographies*, and *Narratives of Historical and Local Events* write their own histories in *Nüshu*. By so doing, they are creators of their own identities and historians of their times.

The equality of ritual sisterhood is evident in many *Nüshu* scripts. In *Nüshu* scripts, the women of Shangjiangxu take on new personae, which have value and speak on equal terms. This symbolic equality is reflected in the forms with which they address each other, forms that incorporate rationality and understanding, gendered terms typically associated with men and seldom with women. Women frequently are addressed as *zhili jieniang*, 知理姐娘 (rational sisters), in *Nüshu* discourses. In *Invitation to Become Ritual Sisters*, Yi wrote: "You pity me, *zhili jieniang*, 知理姐娘 (rational sisters). I did many bad deeds in my former life. . . . We are like natural sisters born of the same mother. I want to console you. Listen to me, *zhili jieniang*, 知理姐娘 (rational sisters)."[76] *Nüshu* scripts confute female stereotypes when women address other women as "rational sisters." Interestingly, ritual sisters address each other as *zhili jieniang*, 知理姐娘 (rational sisters), which literally means "sisters with *zhi*, 知 (understanding), and *li*, 理 (rationality)," a surprising and unusual usage in Chinese.

Form

The final element of pure persuasion concerns its outcome. Burke concludes: "It could remain 'pure' only insofar as a practically 'successful' outcome were precluded."[77] The purpose of *Nüshu* discourse is neither the search for advantage, nor a revolution in the social conditions of women. In the face of enforced illiteracy and denial of education, the village women of Jiangyong pioneered in creating their own literacy through scripts in many genres. Denied education in standard *Hanzi*, these rural women jointly acted to create an alternative in which they could record their lives and express their feelings. *Nüshu*, as symbolic action, enabled these rural women temporarily to escape into a place where they expressed and shared their ideas freely, engaged with one another openly, and listened to each other.

The process of chanting *Nüshu* over women's needlework is tenuously linked to Karlyn Kohrs Campbell's descriptions of the rhetorical practices of early U.S. feminists as imitating the form of craft-learning that dominated the teaching of women's traditional skills of housekeeping, childrearing, and cooking, for example. Such rhetoric shares certain characteristics—use of personal experience, inductive structure, audience participation, and identification creation. Campbell concludes that such rhetoric empowers women to use familiar skills to address others.[78] Like such use of feminine style, *Nüshu* discourse draws on the common values and shared experiences of women to create identification among those who join in its creation and performance. Yet the goals of early U.S woman's rights activists differ from those who participate in *Nüshu* discourse. The former aimed to empower participants to become agents of change to work to alter their social conditions; the latter has the cathartic function of expressing women's true feelings joined with the sheer pleasure of creating a discourse of their own. As should now be evident, however, *Nüshu*, although primarily consummatory, also has instrumental effects. The assertion of value, identity, and importance and the shared experience of describing the conditions of life for women and expressing the miseries of their common lot were, by the testimony of the texts, transformative.

As Burke indicates, phatic communication is close to pure persuasion, done purely for the "satisfaction of talking together, the use of speech as such for the establishing of a social bond between speaker and the spoken-to."[79] The enactment of *Nüshu* scripts establishes a separate female culture, results in the social bonding of an egalitarian sisterhood that ties the village women together, allows them to support each other through the hardships of their lives, and gives them a symbolic escape from the oppression of a marriage system that separates them from their original families. As such, through the development and performance of *Nüshu*, these rural women become literate in *Nüshu* rather than illiterate in *Hanzi*, and transform themselves from persons incapable of reading and writing into authors capable of recording their history. More important, the satisfaction derived from the joint enactment of *Nüshu* symbolically brings to these rural women the sheer pleasure and joy of exercising their symbolic creativity.

Conclusion

Deprived of traditional education and confined by the principles of Confucianism, women of Jiangyong in China were situated in an inferior position in relation to their male counterparts. *Nüshu* came into being to meet the psychological exigencies that women faced. Creating and performing *Nüshu* discourse relieved the hardships of their lives with the help of their ritual sisterhood. *Nüshu* scripts are one of the most valuable writing codes that has survived to testify against the Confucian hierarchy that fettered and degraded women.[80] *Nüshu* scripts also illuminate what the concept of "pure persuasion" might mean. *Nüshu*, enacted in dramatic performance, accompanied by sewing, prayers, chanting, and women's festivals, has as its sole purpose the transformation of the symbolic world of participants.

In assessing the consciousness-raising groups of U.S. second-wave feminism, Campbell argues that unless such groups move beyond the "therapeutic" function of shared personal experience, they cannot raise consciousness about systemic wrongs or move toward group efforts to alter the social conditions of women. Similarly, Burke seems to indicate that pure persuasion is more ideal than actual, saying that no material world could run on such a motive, terming it "unfeasible" and a "state of intolerable indecision just preceding conversion to a new doctrine."[81] Furthermore, Burke writes that pure persuasion is "always to be on the verge of being lost, even as it is on the verge of being found. And so, to talk about it by citing particular examples of rhetoric is always to find it embodied in the 'impurities' of advantage-seeking."[82] Put differently, Burke seems to argue that pure persuasion is transient and rarely untainted by other motives.

As the social environment of Chinese women became less oppressive, the exigency for practicing *Nüshu* abated. Several social factors led to the demise of *Nüshu*: (1) The implementation of the New Marriage Law in 1950 terminated footbinding and altered other oppressive conditions that fostered *Nüshu*; (2) The institution of communes in 1958 and women's entry into the workforce allowed women to move out of the domestic realm and enabled them to have contact with many other people—this in turn encouraged women to abandon embroidery and needlework and, consequently, diminished the occasions for practicing *Nüshu*; and (3) In 1988, modern entertainment television entered the villages and replaced the traditional forms of folk dancing, storytelling, chanting, and so on.

In addition, two other traditional beliefs contributed to its decline. One concerns Taoist religious belief in the afterlife. *Nüshu* practitioners treasured their scripts so much that they were buried or burned at their deaths, [at] the deaths of their sworn sisters, or at the deaths of their husbands so they could continue practicing *Nüshu* in the afterlife. Hence, many texts died with the women who created them. The other was the "Destroying the Four Olds" campaign during the Cultural Revolution, which attacked old culture, old ideas, old habits, and old customs and banned the religious festivals and the temple of *Gupo*, which included the practice of *Nüshu*. In the 1990s, the Chinese government sponsored some scholarly *Nüshu* conferences to stimulate academic interest in these texts; many sessions to learn *Nüshu* also became available in the Jiangyong area. Yet all *Nüshu* writers are dead, and its ability to survive changing social forces and technology is slim.[83] Given the cultural circumstances of these women, instrumental changes in their conditions as women were impossible. The emergence of *Nüshu* helped to empower the marginalized women in a remote area of China, and it served as symbolic transcendence of an oppressive reality in order to celebrate and recognize their own existence and experiences. Hence, *Nüshu* persisted until those conditions changed.

In effect, *Nüshu* is an alternative, female form of literacy. *Nüshu* discourses are melancholic in nature but transcendent or therapeutic in function, articulating anger at the conditions of women's lives, lamenting their tribulations, but creating a place and a society of sworn sisters in which women's lives are valued and celebrated. As enacted, they create a community of equals, of sisters, who compassionately share each other's experiences in the joint performance of *Nüshu* scripts. At such moments they become authors, rational sisters, historians, autobiographers, and biographers whose lives have meaning and worth. The purpose of their rhetoric is not to produce social change but to relish the ability to speak and the satisfaction of jointly created meaning. Put differently, pure persuasion as evidenced in the case of *Nüshu* has the potential to produce extra-textual effects, as is the case in some other rhetorical artifacts, but it does not aim for instrumental changes in the material conditions of the women who create and perform these texts. Their astonishing creativity suggests the transcendent and transformative power of symbols, and their jointly performed texts are real world examples that suggest that, although an ideal, pure persuasion is a concept that attempts to describe the most fundamental, the most basic, perhaps the most human dimensions of symbolic action.

Hagen's study opens the door to decipher the notion that pure persuasion cannot be realized in actual discourse by using verbal irony as an example to explain that pure persuasion might derive from dialectical tension, and, consequently, some form of minimal social change might emerge as a result. *Nüshu*, on the other hand, offers a different reading of Burke's complicated but intriguing concept by taking a unique approach to argue that pure persuasion, as evidenced in ordinary discourse, includes some extra-textual effects, such as community creation, identity affirmation, and the like. *Nüshu*'s ultimate or sole purpose, however, is not to produce material changes in the condition of its creators and participants, which reflects the constraints on these women, who do not have the political or economic means to effect change. Creating and performing *Nüshu* is symbolic transcendence, a moment of sheer delight, a cathartic release, self-validation, an affirmation of identification, and a celebration of the experiences of the participants, and illustrates the ways in which the consummatory might become instrumental. The study of *Nüshu* is part of research that identifies rhetorical creativity and symbolic transcendence among even the most oppressed and marginalized groups. Of most importance, these remarkable texts become a means to tease out the possibilities in Burke's rich and intriguing concept of pure persuasion. This analysis also suggests that Western rhetorical theories can have critical relevance across gender, social, and cultural boundaries. The rhetorical artifacts of *Nüshu* also demonstrate that the sophisticated nuances of pure persuasion can be illuminated by the practices of uneducated but highly creative women in a remote area of the East.

This paper originated in Karlyn Kohrs Campbell's seminar on writing women into the history of rhetoric. The author thanks Karlyn Kohrs Campbell, Angela G. Ray, and Joshua Gunn for their valuable comments on earlier versions of this paper, and the anonymous reviewers for insightful suggestions.

NOTES

1. Kenneth Burke, *A Rhetoric of Motives* (Berkeley, CA: University of California Press, 1969), 274.

2. Burke, *A Rhetoric of Motives*, 269.

3. Burke, *A Rhetoric of Motives*, 267.

4. *Nüshu* scripts, which I examined, were produced by rural women in a small village, Shangjiangxu, Jiangyong, in the southern Hunan Province of China.

5. Peter L. Hagen, "'Pure Persuasion' and Verbal Irony," *Southern Communication Journal* 61 (1995): 46–58.

6. Burke, *A Rhetoric of Motives*, 269.

7. Kenneth Burke, *A Grammar of Motives* (Berkeley, CA: University of California Press, 1969), 123.

8. Burke, *A Grammar of Motives*, 286.

9. Burke, *A Rhetoric of Motives*, 269–70.

10. Kenneth Burke, *Language as Symbolic Action: Essays on Life, Literature, and Method* (Berkeley, CA: University of California Press, 1966), 29.

11. Burke, *Language*, 29.

12. Burke, *A Rhetoric of Motives*, 270.

13. Burke, *A Rhetoric of Motives*, 270.

14. Richard B. Gregg, "The Ego-Function of the Rhetoric of Protest," *Philosophy and Rhetoric* 4 (1971): 74.

15. Gregg, 74.

16. Burke, *A Rhetoric of Motives*, 273.

17. Burke, *A Rhetoric of Motives*, 274.

18. Burke, *A Rhetoric of Motives*, 274.

19. Burke, *A Rhetoric of Motives*, 275.

20. Burke, *A Rhetoric of Motives*, 276.

21. Burke, *A Rhetoric of Motives*, 284.

22. Kenneth Burke, *The Rhetoric of Religion: Studies in Logology* (Berkeley, CA: University of California Press, 1970), 34–5.

23. In 1958, a village woman from Jiangyong, Hunan Province of China, visited a relative in Beijing and spoke in a language unintelligible to others, which led to the discovery of *Nüshu*.

24. For sociological and anthropological perspectives, see Zhebing Gong, ed., *Nüshu: Shijie Wei Yi de Nuxing Wenzi* [The Only Women's Script in the World] (Taipei: Funu Xinzhi Jijinhui, 1991); Xuefei Huang, "Shangjiangxu Xiang Yaoli de Funu" [The Women of Yaoli Village in Shangjiangxu Township], in *Funu Wenzi He Yaozu Qianjiadong* [The Woman's Script and Qianjiadong of the Yao People], ed. Zhebing Gong (Beijing: Zhanwang, 1986), 124–8; Shihui Xiao, "Daoshien Tianguangdong de *Nüshu*" [*Nüshu* in Tianguangdong Village of Dao County], in *Funu Wenzi He Yaozu Qianjiadong* [The Woman's Script and Qianjiadong of the Yao People], ed. Zhebing Gong (Beijing: Zhanwang, 1986), 142–4; Zhiming Xie, *Jiangyong "Nüshu" Zhi Mi* [The Puzzle of *Nüshu* in Jiangyong] (Henan: Henan Renmin, 1991); Liming Zhao, ed., *Zhongguo Nüshu Jicheng* [Collections of Chinese *Nüshu*] (Beijing: Qignha Up, 1992); and Zhao Liming and Gong Zhebing, *Nüshu: Yige Jingrende Faxian* [*Nüshu*: A Surprising Discovery] (Wuchang: Huazhong Shifan Daxue, 1990). For linguistic characteristics, please see: Wei William Chiang, "We Two Know the Script: We Have Become Good Friends: Linguistic and Social Aspects of the Women's Script Literacy in Southern Hunan, China" (Ph.D. diss., Yale University, 1991); and Liming Zhao, "*Nüshu*: Chinese Women's Character," *International Journal of Social Languages* 129 (1998): 127–37. For literary qualities, please see: Qing Chen, "Shihhsi Nuzi Hsing Yin Yi De Tetien" [Tentative Analysis to the Characteristics of the Form, Sound, and Meaning of *Nüshu*], in *Funu Wenzi He Yaozu Qianjiadong* [The Woman's Script and Qianjiadong of the Yao People], ed. Zhebing Gong (Beijing: Zhanwang, 1986), 42–60; Shouhua Liu and Xiaoshen Hu, "Folk Narrative Literature in Chinese *Nüshu*: An Amazing New Discovery," *Asian Folklore Studies* 53 (1994): 307–318; Cathy Silber, "From Daughter to Daughter-in-Law in the Women's Script of Southern Hunan," in *Engendering China: Women, Culture, and the State*, ed. Christina K. Gilmartin, Gail Hershatter, Lisa Rofel, and Tyrene White (Cambridge, MA: Harvard University Press, 1994), 47–68; Cathy Silber, "*Nüshu* (Chinese Women's Script) Literacy and Literature" (Ph.D. diss., University of Michigan, 1995); Cathy Silber, "A 1,000-year-old Secret," Ms., Sept.–Oct. 1992, 58–61; and Shu-hui Tsai, "Women and Their Complaints in Women's Script" (M.A. thesis, University of Colorado, 1993). Gong Zhebing's two-month field trip in 1985 was mainly focused on editing the women's scripts with three living *Nüshu* writers who were able to chant, recite, write, and read *Nüshu*. The scripts cited in the text are taken from Chiang's dissertation for the comparison of English and Chinese translation, pp. 82–3, 85, 87, and 345–431. Chiang translated from *Nüshu* to *Hanzi* and from *Hanzi* to English.

25. Chiang, 35–7; Silber, "*Nüshu*," 42.

26. Zhao, "*Nüshu*," 128. According to Zhao, "Chu, Yue, and the Central Plains are traditional names. Chu includes Hunan and Hubei; Yue includes Zhejiang, Jiangsu, and Shandong; and the Central Plains refers to the middle and lower reaches of the Yellow River, which includes Henan, Shandong, Hebei, and Shanxi." See Zhao, "*Nüshu*," 137.

27. Zhao, "*Nüshu*," 128.

28. See Chiang, 50–2, 208. The Yao Goddesses include *Panhu, Gupo, Flower Old Woman, Guanyin, Mazu, Qixinggu,* and *Furenma.* A *Panhu* temple exists in most villages. The festivals of goddess *Gupo* take place annually on May 10. Goddess *Flower Old Woman* originates from the Zhuang and Miao ethnic groups who pray for children to the goddess who is believed to have control over the souls of children.

29. Huang, 126; Zhao, "Collections," 81. *Nüer Jie* or "women's day," *Douniu Jie* or "woman's bullfighting day," *Chuiliang Jie* or "cooling day," and "the ghost holiday" are all female festivals.

30. Chiang, 51–2.

31. Shinobu Suzuki, "Hiratsuka's 'Editor's Introduction to the First Issue of *Seito*': Where 'Feminine Style' Intersects High-Context Communication," *Women's Studies in Communication* 23 (2000): 185.

32. Mary Garrett, "Women and the Rhetorical Tradition in Premodern China: A Preliminary Sketch," in *Chinese Communication Studies,* ed. Xing Lu, Wenshan Jia, and D. Ray Heisey (Westport, CT: Ablex, 2002), 91.

33. Hu and Liu, 316–7. Foot-binding started in the Song Dynasty (960–1278 B.C.E.) and was widely practiced among women of the gentry as one criterion for marriageability in the Qing Dynasty. Traditionally, the smaller a girl's feet, the greater her marriageability. Women of the lower classes escaped this torture to meet the demands of helping with farming.

34. Mary Garrett, "Some Elementary Methodological Reflections on the Study of the Chinese Rhetorical Tradition," in *Rhetoric in Intercultural Context,* ed. Alberto Gonzalez and Dolores V. Tanno (Thousand Oaks, CA: Sage, 1999), 60.

35. The Chinese saying "**女子无才便是德**" is literally translated into "A woman without talents is virtuous," suggesting that women without knowledge should be praised as virtuous.

36. Mary Garrett, "Women and the Rhetorical Tradition," 91.

37. Wen Shu Lee, "In the Names of Chinese Women," *Quarterly Journal of Speech* 84 (1998): 283.

38. Chiang, 113–4; Zhao, "Nüshu," 129. Chiang comes up with 719 graphs after his close analysis of 24 *Nüshu* texts. Zhao sorts out about 1200 single characters; he concludes that more than 80 percent of the *Nüshu* characters derive from square Chinese characters, and less than 20 percent are of unknown origin.

39. Zhao, "Nüshu," 134–5. *Nüshu* graphs are so different from *Hanzi* and from any local dialect spoken in Jiangyong County that they would not be easily recognizable or readable to anyone schooled in the *Hanzi* system without special training.

40. Chiang, 180.

41. Silber argues that men could understand *Nüshu* because its phonetic aspect allowed them to understand while hearing it; Chiang discovered that a local male teacher was said to have been able to write it (Silber, *Engendering China,* 45; Chiang, 108–9). Zhao and Gong, during their field trips, learned of an elderly man who could read *Nüshu* with his spouse's help (Zhao and Gong, 9). Scholars assert that like men with high literacy skills in the Hanzi society, women with literacy in *Nüshu* in the Shangjiangxu area won the admiration and respect of both women and men. For more information, see: Qing Zan, "*Nüshu*: Chinese Women's Characters" (M.A. thesis, University of Florida, 1994), 35; Ann McLaren, "Women's Voices and Textuality: Chastity and Abduction in Chinese/Nüshu Writing," *Modern China* 22 (1996): 394.

42. McLaren, 394; Xie, 1859; Chiang, 1–2.

43. Silber, "Secret," 58.

44. *Nüshu* resembles the emergence of the Korean language. Although the phonetic Korean language was first introduced to Koreans in 1392, it was regarded as a female language suitable only for noble ladies by those learned in ideographic Chinese.

45. Chiang, 351.

46. Chiang, 348.

47. Chiang, 82–3.

48. Chiang, 83.

49. Chiang, 414–5.

50. This piece was written by Yi between 1988 and 1989.

51. Chiang, 422.

52. Chiang, 362. Emperor Dezong of the Qing Dynasty (1875–1908 A.D.) used the name Guangxü for the period title.

53. Chiang, 347, 352.

54. Chiang, 393.

55. Chiang, 357, 359.

56. Chiang, 347.

57. Chiang, 352.

58. Burke, *A Rhetoric of Motives,* 284.

59. Burke, *A Rhetoric of Motives,* 270.

60. Liu and Hu, 312.

61. Silber, "Nüshu," 192.

62. Burke, *A Rhetoric of Motives,* 276.

63. It is the only surviving text of this kind memorized by Hu.

64. Chiang, 89–91.

65. Burke, *A Rhetoric of Motives,* 293–4.

66. Silber, "Nüshu," 88.

67. Chiang, 383, 392.

68. Chiang, 395, 396–7.

69. Chiang, 403, 406–7, 408–9.

70. Chiang, 382.

71. Chiang, 430–1.

72. Silber, "Nüshu," 163–75.

73. Chiang, 367–8.

74. Chiang, 371–2.

75. Chiang, 374.

76. Chiang, 402.

77. Burke, Religion, 34–5.

78. For more information, see Karlyn Kohrs Campbell, Man Cannot Speak for Her (Westport, CT: Praeger, 1989), 13; Campbell, "The Rhetoric of Radical Black Nationalism: A Case Study in Self-Conscious Criticism," Central States Speech Journal (1971): 155.

79. Burke, A Rhetoric of Motives, 270.

80. Zhao also investigated another female writing script called Ban Niang Wu, or "inviting people from the parental family." He suggested that Ban Niang Wu had been used by married Yao women to elicit help from their parental family at times when they could not tolerate the misery of their marriages. Unfortunately, this script became extinct owing to the constraints of time, money, and the natural deaths of its users.

81. Burke, A Rhetoric of Motives, 294.

82. Burke, A Rhetoric of Motives, 285.

83. For more information, see Carol C. Fan, "Language, Gender, and Chinese Culture," International Journal of Politics, Culture, and Society 10 (1996): 109; Gong, 33; McLaren, 396; Silber, "Secret," 58; Tsai, 18; and Zan, 35–6. Just who the creators of Nüshu were remains unknown. Six possible legends have been discussed by scholars. (1) Some women invented Nüshu in the form of embroidery patterns on cloth and used it to write to their friends. (2) A woman named Hu Yuxiu from Jingtian village in Shangjiangxu was a royal concubine of the emperor of the Song Dynasty. After she experienced the oppressive and lonely court life, her brother, a learned court official, created and taught her the women's script to express her complaints to her family. Yuxiu later returned home and taught all her female relatives how to use this language. (3) This one resembles number 2. Before being a Song concubine, a beauty and her sworn sisters learned the women's script. After losing favor with the emperor, she used this secretive language to share her misery with female relatives and sworn sisters. She told her relatives that the characters were italicized and should be read with the local pronunciation, from left to right. (4) A local woman was born with a birth weight of approximately 5.4 kg or 11.9 pounds. Intelligent and talented, she created Nüshu to communicate with her sworn sisters. Chiang argues that this legend derives from "Nine-catty Woman," a Yew vernacular drama. (5) It is linked to Yao embroidery. In the past, women gathered for needlework and embroidery. With limited access to education, most women were illiterate. Accordingly, they created Nüshu over the needlework on cloth, fans, and handkerchiefs to record their memorable hardships. (6) It derives from prayers. While taking prayers from the shrine and singing them, some women wrote down their wishes and dedicated them to the goddesses. For more information, see Chiang, 109–11; Gong, 21–2; Tsai, 20–1; Xie, 5; Zhao, "Nüshu," 135.

Epilogue

Contributions from Rhetorical Theory

Mark Porrovecchio
Celeste Michelle Condit

The essays in this volume all exist within the discourse community identified as "contemporary rhetorical theory." Contemporary rhetorical theory, however, exists as just one set of voices within a large and varied academic community. The contributions that rhetorical studies have to make to this larger academic conversation arise from the unique situation and history of rhetorical studies in the discipline of communication.[1] As we have indicated in the Introduction to this volume, throughout its long history the field of rhetorical studies has been sensitive to the discursive qualities of context, of persuasiveness, and of the public space in which social and political interaction so frequently takes place. These contributions are no less important in an era where more and more of our interactions are conducted in digital places and spaces. For, while the rise of Internet and mobile devices has changed many of the ways in which we communicate, the aforementioned qualities retain the nuances that have made them the subject of rhetorical inquiry. Consequently, we continue to offer up what we humbly call the "rhetorical perspective," a view of the world that opens the possibilities for constituting a distinctive alternative to the projects of modernism and postmodernism.

Modernism places its faith in the possibility of certainty, absolute truth, and universal objectivity. Modernist communities thus rely upon the efforts of elite experts—priests, philosophers, scientists, urban planners, and so on—to obtain the knowledge of certain and universal truths, with the goal of translating these truths into normative social and political practices. In such a world, rhetoric is little more than the medium for disseminating these truths to nonexperts (i.e., "the masses") through various forms of "education." In a world governed by such views, social media and even political blogs do not open minds to new perspectives, but instead encourage them to seek out only those sources that confirm their existing dispositions, which it is easiest to assume to be objectively true. On screens large and increasingly small, modernists would see themselves as constructing a permanent edifice of truth and goodness.

By contrast, postmodernism eschews the faith in certainty and absolute or universal knowledge as woefully mistaken or a deceit.[2] Public statements that are claimed as true in any absolute or universal sense are characterized as the efforts of elites to deceive the less powerful into serving the interests of those with the power and capacity to speak the public will. Whereas modernism focuses on truth seeking, postmodernism excels at unmasking false truths, revealing that the so-called certainties of science, philosophy, and religion are inherently mutable—a mutability that is a function of both their history and their future. News about the public events of the day is delivered cocooned with critique by satirical entertainment programs such as *The Daily Show with Jon Stewart* (now *The Daily*

Show with Trevor Noah). Among many communities, the circulation dynamics of Tweets and blogs increase a tendency to slip into an ironic stance, to question everything, and to challenge the assumptions of those others, often gathered anonymously, in an assemblage of online communities. In contrast to modernism, postmodernism characterizes itself as "deconstructive," destroying the false monuments of modernism.

Each of these views has its comforts. Modernism offers a supremely powerful feeling of security—the presumption that one's beliefs extend everywhere and are representative of what others believe. Postmodernism offers the joy of unmasking authoritative pieties and the possibility of escaping otherwise inexorable, oppressive traps. Each view, however, also has important flaws. Modernism fails because societies do change, and their knowledge eventually changes with them. Plato's *Republic* does not specify appropriate applications of *in vitro* fertilization or proper governing systems for the colonization of Mars (colonization of Mars requires both local governance and international economic alliances, and the communication difficulties in such a transaction are not addressed in the Platonic dialogues). Moreover, what counts as the ideal "public good" varies across time and space, depending on one's role or position in the society.

Postmodernism's critique of modernism is thus well taken; unfortunately, postmodernism does not offer a viable independent alternative to modernism. As a perspective founded primarily in critique and opposition, postmodernism is always parasitic on that which it critiques. In presenting a world where public discourse is nothing but deceit, postmodernism precludes the possibility of any community whatsoever. The postmodern alternative to life as a citizen in a community is life as a "nomadic subject," an anomic body that wanders globally from place to place through time. Such a way of life may be necessary to those inhabiting the marginal positions of an oppressive society, and it may even be appealing to those who are young, who are single, and who have significant material resources. However, the life of the nomad is not inherently desirable for everyone; it offers little comfort and many problems for those concerned with raising children, the serenity of old age, and the construction and maintenance of a social order that can provide for the safety, comfort, and care of its people. Just as contemporary nomads are parasitic on the existence of the modern society, so too is the postmodern value of

"fragmentation" dependent on the existence of something to fragment. In the context of a unified global totality, fragmentation is a worthy instrumental value. However, "fragmentation" as a basic social goal leads to an undifferentiated mass of no particular characteristics whatsoever.

Rhetoric provides a third alternative to being-in-the-world. Instead of living inside the absolute totality of modernism, or living outside modernism in perpetual critique, the rhetorical perspective describes a *relatively* stable and *relatively* fluid community that eschews any permanent or clear distinctions between inside and outside. The rhetorical perspective enables such a worldview because it encourages us to employ the experience and understanding of a highly diverse citizenry as the most important component of communal decision making, not the presumed knowledge of timeless truths. The truth produced by rhetoric is always provisional, good enough for daily use, but also open to challenge when necessary. We describe such knowledge as "substantive," having a material consistency somewhere between the bedrock certainty of absolute and timeless truths and the total fluidity of permanent critique. In the rhetorical community that adopts such a perspective, it is the people (gathered in physical spaces and/or congregating in digital places), and not the members of an exclusive and powerful elite, who judge the substance of such social knowledge.

Of course, when we talk of "the people," we are not focusing on isolated individuals or anomic groups, but rather on persons who play the role of "citizen." Such people certainly strive for their own interests and their own good, but their "own good" is interpreted through their particular identity as members of a community. They are neither mere individuals, nor mere undifferentiated pawns in the community, but specific role players within the rhetorical vision that constitutes the community. These roles play out in the work that activists do both online and offline. Thus the rhetorical perspective won't exclude those who assert the right to challenge dominant paradigms via methods like Change.org, in favor of the advocates who arrive at our doors, pamphlets in hand. What this perspective will do, however, is examine the impact of these differences in role playing on the rhetorical messages that are disseminated. Neither role is excluded; both are subject to rhetorical theorizing.

The rhetorical perspective thus opens the possibility of a middle-ground orientation between modernism and postmodernism, no less between traditional and newer modes of discourse formation and dissemination. Oriented as such, the people are concerned to "get things right," but this does not mean that they can wait for certain truths to be delivered to them by the sacred keepers of truth and knowledge. Instead, they act on their shared and compromised visions of the most probable course of action, based on what they believe they know, here and now. This more fluid, process-oriented perspective is made possible by replacing the idealist, philosophical notion of "foundations" as universal and permanent truths, with a rhetorical conception of foundations as constituted by and within communities that publicly contest their principles and priorities in free and open debate and discussion. Such rhetorical communities legitimize specific rights, norms, and entitlements. To what end? So that the history of the community's experience and knowledge forms substantive anchors against tendencies that threaten to erode global citizens' capacities to pick and choose among alternatives, while also respecting other's rights to do the same. On a small scale, digital culture can create pop culture cul-de-sacs of confirmation bias, places where any idea is free to reign unencumbered by critical reflection. On a larger level, there remain the risks of totalitarianism—whether fueled by monarchical will, the tyranny of the majority, or solipsistic individualism—where individual choice is subordinated to the need for deified authority.

The rhetorical perspective is thus essentially "pragmatic" (in William James's and John Dewey's senses of the term). It is always open to reflection and revision, since the malleability and mutability of such anchors are self-evident from the fact that the community itself was the source of their substance. The rhetorical community's authority is thus never permanent or unquestionable. It exists in a context of contingency and situatedness, and exists for audiences and publics that are often differentially empowered and that must work to create coalitions in order to negotiate for their desired ends. On a rhetorical view, then, social and political arrangements are seldom rooted on firm and unmovable bedrock; nevertheless, even though significant social and political change can be expected, it never comes easily, and it requires substantial justification and rationale when it does occur.

Because it makes possible this third fundamental alternative, the rhetorical perspective offers distinctive approaches to particular questions in social theory. One of the primary criticisms of many postmodernist approaches to discourse

theory is that they favor a negative or deconstructive attitude that shows little or no concern for the affirmative, reconstructive potential in any given sociopolitical situation.[3] Rhetorical theorists who engage the problems and possibilities of discourse in the contemporary world tend to push the deconstructive critiques of postmodernism forward, but they do so with an eye toward the emancipatory possibilities in any given situation. Concepts such as "identity formation," "strategic liberation," and "counterpublics" illustrate this possibility. From a rhetorical perspective, identity formation suggests the use of rhetoric to develop a new or better sense of self. In complement, strategic liberation is the possibility of improving life within one's community in temporary and incomplete, but nonetheless meaningful, ways. Counterpublics suggest the options that exist beyond our personal rhetorical vistas. This perspective and these concepts stand in marked contrast to philosophical or religious conceptions of social change that presume the perfection of human organization based on universal truths and moral precepts. By employing such concepts, we mean to draw upon classical rhetoric's understanding of contingency to describe the manner in which individuals and groups seek to improve their local situations without presuming that such improvements are permanent, universal, or ideal solutions to particular problems.

The rhetorical theories represented in this volume similarly provide useful insights into the debate over the concept and phenomenon of "agency." In this debate, postmodernists have tended to discount the agency of individuals as message constructors or decoders by pointing to the ways in which an actor's beliefs and attitudes are prestructured by his or her placement in society as a function of gender, race, class, and the like. Modernists and those with a more traditional humanistic focus respond by pointing out the empirical experience of agency—there is at least the appearance that individuals and groups can affect the world in which they live—and its importance in theorizing the possibility of acting to make meaningful social and personal change. Contemporary rhetorical theories can help to resolve the disparity between social structure and lived experience by reconstituting our understanding of agency as a function of complex speaker–audience interactions, as a result of both inter- and intrapersonal dynamics that have often gone underexamined. Such a view denies neither the materiality nor the significance of the agency of speaker or audience. It does contextualize the agency of all parties to a social interaction as bound in relationship, rather than as the solitary product of some sort of determinism (be it economic or biological) or autonomous free will.

We hope these examples indicate that the rhetorical construction and reconstruction of human social action have broad implications. By emphasizing both individual agency and human collectivities as the products of material performances of discourse, rather than as abstract ideals, we can begin to open possibilities for resolving the *aporia*—the apparent unknowability or undecidability—raised in the debates between classical philosophy and rhetoric. The field of contemporary rhetorical studies thus harbors exciting possibilities for the affirmative reconstruction of collective life in an increasingly multicultural, mediated, and interactive world such as our own. It is to forward this agenda that we offer the essays in this volume and the general possibilities posed by the development of a critical and productive rhetorical theory for your use and consideration.

NOTES

1. In indicating that rhetoric has a "distinctive" contribution to make, we do not mean to say that this is a unique contribution made by no one else in any other field. The study of rhetoric is so pervasive in the modern academy that any position we might outline has undoubtedly been taken by someone somewhere. The rhetorical perspective, unlike the scientific or philosophical perspective, does not give priority to "origins" (i.e., the initial discovery and who made it). The best

rhetorician is not the one who espouses an idea first, but rather one who articulates it most effectively at a particular moment in time. To say that rhetorical study constitutes the possibility for distinctive contributions, then, is not to say that these contributions cannot be developed elsewhere. Rather, it is to say that rhetorical theory offers a productive site at which contributions can be effectively mined and elaborated because of a broad and sustained interest in the power of language-in-use.

2. As we have noted in the Introduction, there are many different postmodernisms. Our use of the singular "postmodernism" is not intended to suggest a totalizing philosophical or conceptual framework. Rather, our use of the word "postmodern" refers to the range of conceptual and philosophical oppositions to "modernist" thinking that have emerged in the wake of the cultural, social, political, and economic conditions of modernity. Put somewhat differently, "postmodernism" refers to the many and numerous attempts to break out of the demands of philosophical modernism as means of understanding the conditions of postmodernity (i.e., that which has come *after* modernity). As we have claimed earlier, no coherent alternative to the postmodern project (though some have been suggested) has come along since the first edition of this book. If anything, the rise of the Internet has only increased discussions in different camps about the divide between modernism *before* and postmodernism *after*.

3. For an earlier view of these issues, see, e.g., James Arnt Aune, "Rhetoric after Deconstruction," in Richard A. Cherwitz, ed., *Rhetoric and Philosophy* (Hillsdale, NJ: Erlbaum, 1990), 253–74. For a more recent and concise summary of the trends Aune pointed to, see Gary E. Aylesworth, "Rhetoric, Postmodern," in Wolfgang Donsbach, ed., *The International Encyclopedia of Communication* (Malden, MA: Blackwell, 2008), 4318–323.

▲ Index